New American World

A Documentary History of North America to 1612

NEW AMERICAN WORLD

A Documentary History of North America to 1612

IN FIVE VOLUMES

Volume I
America from Concept to Discovery. Early Exploration
of North America.

Volume II
Major Spanish Searches in Eastern North America.
The Franco-Spanish Clash in Florida. The Beginnings
of Spanish Florida.

Volume III
English Plans for North America. The Roanoke Voyages.
New England Ventures.

Volume IV
Newfoundland from Fishery to Colony. Northwest Passage Searches.

Volume V
The Extension of Settlement in Florida, Virginia, and the
Spanish Southwest.

VOLUME II

Major Spanish Searches in Eastern North America. Franco-Spanish Clash in Florida. The Beginnings of Spanish Florida.

Edited, with a Commentary by

DAVID B. QUINN

With the Assistance of
Alison M. Quinn and Susan Hillier

ARNO PRESS
A New York Times Company
and
HECTOR BYE, INC.
New York, 1979

Library of Congress Cataloging in Publication Data
Main entry under title:

Major Spanish searches in eastern North America.

(New American world ; v. 2)
1. America—Discovery and exploration—Spanish—
Sources. 2. Florida—History—Huguenot colony,
1562-1565—Sources. 3. Florida—History—Spanish
colony, 1565-1763—Sources. I. Quinn, David Beers.
II. Quinn, Alison M. III. Hillier, Susan.
E101.N47 vol. 2 [E123] 970.01s [970.01'6] 78-23463
ISBN 0-405-10761-7

Library of Congress Cataloging in Publication Data
Main entry under title:

New American world.

Includes bibliographies and indexes.
1. America—Discovery and exploration—Sources.
2. America—History—To 1810—Sources. I. Quinn,
David Beers. II. Quinn, Alison M. III. Hillier,
Susan.
E101.N47   970.01   77-20483
ISBN 0-405-10759-5

Printed in the United States of America

Contents

Maps
List of Plates

(Notes on the Maps will precede the plate section in each volume.)

VOLUME II

xi

Preface

OVER A considerable part of Volume I, the material which survives, however essential to our understanding of what happened, is largely secondhand or peripheral to the events with which it is concerned. With Cartier, Roberval, and, above all, the major interventions of Coronado and the west coast explorers, another world, a new dimension of North America, appeared. This new dimension—the impression of North America in detail and in depth—is enlarged in the present volume as we can follow Narváez, Cabeza de Vaca, Soto (above all), Cáncer, and Luna through their discoveries, successes, or, more often, failure and doom. Moreover, in the appearance of the French for the first time in the Southeast and the subsequent clash with Spain which it produced, we have for the first time the translation of the rivalries and hatreds of the Old World, of Reformation and Counter-Reformation Europe, to the New World of North America.

For most of these episodes we have credible narratives, sometimes contrasting and contradictory. They are full and detailed. The historian might well expect all of them to be given here, but, while everything of importance has, we believe, been presented, there have been inevitable omissions. Otherwise, the data would have grown out of scale for the work as a whole. The same problem will present itself when we come to deal with the earliest years of the seventeenth century. We believe, however, that by selecting judiciously where the evidence is thick and varied, and concentrating on proportionately fuller coverage where the material is sparse or novel, we are providing a service to the student who wishes to balance out materials and developments that could be obscured by concentration on the major episodes alone and documenting them, to the exclusion of others, *in extenso*.

Introduction

i

Between the years 1528 and 1565 soldiers, sailors, adventurers, and missionaries representing the Spanish crown explored the southern part of the present United States from Florida to California and coasted the Atlantic and Pacific shores—to the latter of which we have, in Volume I, already followed them. On their travels they encountered many contrasting types of terrain, flora, fauna, and human communities. In the east they first penetrated the interior through the swampy lowlands of the Gulf and Atlantic coasts and the Florida Peninsula, an area which was at the time heavily wooded. Having negotiated the swamps, they were then faced by the Appalachian Mountains, which attain an average altitude of 2,000 feet in modern North Carolina but which gradually give way to rolling country in the south. From the west, after crossing the present Mexican border, the Spaniards encountered the deserts of Arizona and the narrowing southern strip of the Rocky Mountains. Here and there they saw evidence of earlier volcanic activity and subsequent erosion, which had hewn the rock into isolated table mountains and canyons producing spectacular scenery. To the west of the mountains, the plateau descends in ridges into the low, fertile valley of California. Further inland, to the east of the Rockies, are extensive rolling plains that gradually level out into the Mississippi-Missouri Basin. There were at that time forests to the west of the great river, giving way to prairies that became more barren further west, supporting only sagebrush and cactus. The changing landscape was reflected in the varying types of fauna of the area. The Spaniards found alligators and water moccasins in the swamps; wolves, deer, black bears, mountain lions, lynx, and turkeys in the forests. To the west were grizzly bears, mountain sheep, and elk.

Similarly the explorers encountered many groups of Indian tribes, speaking different languages and belonging to very varied cultural groupings. Spanish practice, so far as possible, was to obtain Indian captives from each language group as early as they could, who were then taught Spanish and in turn taught sufficient of their language to selected Spaniards. Thence the informed Spaniard, with his *lengua*, his native interpreter, could carry on effective communication with successive groups. The southeastern coastal tribes, Timucua and the rest, spoke variants of the Muskogean group of languages, and the genius of one Spaniard, Juan Ortiz, prisoner with the Timucua for some years, opened up a working knowledge of the Indian languages to the Soto expedition. But even outside this linguistic area, in the tribes of the Mississippian culture complex, his magic worked. We may guess that there was some *lingua franca* that carried a basic trading vocabulary across formal linguistic divides. Soto was far from the homeland where Juan Ortiz learnt his first Indian language when the interpreter died, and yet to the end he continued to be able to communicate or arrange communication.

The Indians almost invariably had settled places where they lived, but they were to puzzle the French and others after them with their custom of disappearing in winter in search of game and roots. Colonists, like the French in Florida who had relied on Indians for surplus corn, were left with their own meager supplies when they most needed to supplement them. The tribes of the eastern coastlands shaded into the strong and well-organized tribes of the Mississippian culture that covered so much of the territory from the Appalachians westward beyond the Mississippi itself. There, great tribes like the Creeks and Choctaw could give hope of an approach to a civilized region, but as the expeditions went westward they encountered not culturally richer but poorer peoples. The Prairie Indians were reached from both sides, by Coronado from the west and by Soto from the east, but their transient agriculture and their bison-hunting shaded off westward into the purely hunting society of the Great Plains. Coronado's eastward limit was among the Prairie Indians in modern Arkansas and Kansas, the Wichitas. But after Soto's death Moscoso led his men down to the primitive, half-starved Texas tribes before retracing his steps to the richer Mississippian culture. Coronado was the first to encounter not only the Plains Indians, Apaches and Sioux, but also the settled groups of western and eastern Pueblos—the western typified by his "Seven Cities of Cíbola," the Zuñi homeland, and the eastern by the multiple villages of the Rio Grande Basin. Farther west, Alarcón encountered the tall people of Yuma stock and the Pima Indians along the borders of later Arizona and New Mexico. Although the range of Indian cultures was very considerable, they had common features when seen by the explorers: a generous impulse to share with the smaller groups of men who came in peace; the brave and sometimes foolhardy warfare against the larger groups that came, or were thought to come, in war; but no real wealth in terms of silver, gold, or jewels. Even their proudest Pueblo towns were relatively small settlements of adobe brick.

For some time these varied and extensive lands to the north of the areas first explored and conquered by Spain in the Americas were largely ignored by the Conquistadores. They naturally concentrated on the richer prizes they found in the Caribbean and, later, above all, in Mexico. Sooner or later, however, expansion outward from the islands and northward from Mexico was bound to bring them up against the prospects and problems of the American lands that lay to the north. They had no hesitation in principle to going there. The papal bulls and the Treaty of Tordesillas covered their legal progress, as they thought; if they did not, then their own firm limbs would carry them forward and who could stop them? But for the time being they concentrated on exploiting what they found in the West Indies and in Mexico. Such exploration as was undertaken north of the Caribbean was marginal to Spanish imperial activity. The attempts of Ponce de León and Ayllón between 1513 and 1526 to explore and settle Florida had proved disastrous. None of its explorers found anything to recommend in the country. There was no fountain of youth at Bimini or any gold, but there were hostile Indians and an unpleasant, swampy terrain. However, there were other men prepared to face these difficulties and dangers, explorers who, acting under varied impulses, succeeded in discovering large portions of the interior of the present United States. They were encouraged, if not extensively financed, by the Spanish monarchs which saw the exploration and conquest of the area as an extension of earlier efforts in the West Indies and in Central America.

Possession of the regions to the north would give additional security to Spain and her new lands in America. In particular, a presence on the Florida Peninsula would protect the route along the Florida Channel. This route taken by the treasure ships from the West Indies to Spain was notoriously dangerous, especially during the hurricane season, and many valuable vessels had been lost. Spanish settlers, it was argued, would be able to rescue the valuable cargoes of any ships driven aground. Additional weight was added to this argument when the French began to show an active interest in Florida and settled there in the 1560s. The French had, it was argued, to be removed from the peninsula since they posed a threat to trade and treasure fleets. The quarrels of Habsburgs and Valois at home provided a good excuse, and the war in Europe was extended across the Atlantic, an unhappy precedent for the following centuries. It was no coincidence that the first viable Spanish colony in North America was established in Florida as soon as the French had been driven out.

Despite the reports of the first explorers, the Spanish continued to hope that the discovery of gold and precious metals that had been made in the West Indies would be repeated to the north. The prospect of personal enrichment certainly was attractive to the individual explorer. The members of Hernando de Soto's expedition of 1539–1543 blindly followed every report of precious metals, rumors that were deliberately fostered by the Indians to get rid of the unwelcome white intruders. Any passing reference to such riches was seized upon and quickly exaggerated. There was no lack of willing volunteers to go with Coronado when Fray Marcos returned from his 1539 expedition to New Mexico with tales of the possibilities of riches to the north. Similarly, men were attracted to the area by rumors of fabulous lands. These fables were a mixture of old European legend and New World myth brought together and kept alive by the exaggerated stories of the Indians. It was hoped that Bimini, the fountain of eternal youth, would be found in Florida, and the Seven Cities of Cíbola, with their untold riches, would be located to the north of Mexico. Several expeditions set out in search of the latter, culminating in the realization by Coronado that the cities were in fact the fortified Zuñi pueblos of New Mexico. Other myths grew from the tales of the earliest explorers. The survivors of Soto's expedition told of Cofitachequi's Coosa, the land of milk and honey to the north of Florida. Subsequent expeditions, notably that led by Tristán de Luna in 1559–1561, spent much time and effort trying to find Coosa and were very disappointed when they eventually did locate the wrong one. Members of Coronado's expedition were led across the prairies by stories of the fabulous land of Quivira, which turned out to be the rather mundane lands of the Quivira (Wichita) Indians along the Arkansas River in Kansas. The search for gold and fabulous lands would, it was believed, ensure for the explorers not only wealth but also personal glory, a commodity much sought after by the sixteenth-century Spaniard.

Religion was a factor further influencing both the Spanish crown and the individual explorers.

From the time of the earliest discoveries in the West Indies, attempts were made to convert the heathen Indian. This attitude was strengthened after the Reformation had divided the Christian Church in Europe. The natives were now, in the Spanish view, in danger not only from their own heresies, but also from those preached by the Protestant churches. It is easy to be cynical about the role played by religion in the earliest discoveries. It was certainly a convenient excuse for exterminating or enslaving large numbers of American Indians. In the eyes of the secular officials, the conversion of the natives was secondary to the exploitation of mineral resources. However, the motives of the individual friars—Dominican, Franciscan, and Augustinian alike—who accompanied almost every early expedition were in many cases genuinely altruistic. Although small in number—often only two or three friars were present with each expedition because of pressure of work to the south—they were determined to preach the word of God to the natives and suffered great deprivations and often death in the pursuit of their goal. Fray Juan Padilla accompanied Pedro de Tovar to the Moqui villages in Arizona and traveled north to Quivira with Coronado. After the Spaniards left Arizona, he went north again with only Indians as guides but was killed by hostile natives. A similar fate was suffered by Fray Luis Cáncer and another friar who accompanied him to Florida in 1549. The task of such men was made even more difficult by the behavior of their secular companions whose life-styles bore little resemblance to the morality preached by the men of God.

Such were the motives that prompted men to undertake the discovery of the Southeast and Southwest. The Spanish expeditions in the area had a two-fold character. They were launched either from the Caribbean Islands or the Mexican Gulf ports (to Florida and the Atlantic Coast) or from central and western Mexico (north to New Mexico, the Great Plains, and the Pacific Coast). In the east the enterprise and the dogged endurance of Cabeza de Vaca, Hernando de Soto, Tristán de Luna, and Menéndez de Avilés led to the exploration from the Florida Keys north to the Appalachian Mountains of North Carolina and west to the Mississippi and beyond. Their topographical coverage is vital to our understanding of the historical geography of the region. In the west the exploration was seen as a continuation of discoveries to the north of Mexico City. The quality and scope of the narratives covering this scene have already been demonstrated in Volume I. Fray Marcos and Coronado traveled overland through modern Arizona and New Mexico and as far north as Kansas, some of Coronado's men discovering the Grand Canyon. At the same time, several coastal journeys were made by men like Francisco de Ulloa, who established the fact that Lower California was a peninsula, and Hernando de Alarcón who sailed up the Colorado River as far as Yuma, and Juan Cabrillo who coasted the Pacific shore as far north as the present border between California and Oregon. The eastern and western achievements may be observed separately, but they must be considered together to be fully understood.

Spanish dominance in this period was interrupted only once. In 1562 and 1564 France established colonies on the Atlantic coast of Florida. When the Spaniards had forcibly removed the French, they set up their own settlements in the region. Up until 1565 the lack of firm objectives (in the absence of the discovery of gold and silver) of these early explorers had ensured that the idea of settlement would be submerged in the chase after precious metals and exciting novelties. The members of the early expeditions had no intention of settling down and cultivating corn and good relations with the Indians. However, the threat posed by the French made Spanish officials realize that the only way of securing the land that had been explored in the previous decades was by the establishment of armed colonies. Thus the explorations of men like Hernando de Soto and Coronado gradually gave way to a firm, continued—if not uniformally successful—attempt at the colonization of the Southeast and later of the Southwest, although Spain never expended as much in manpower and money in the North American region as she was to do and did in the financially more lucrative colonies to the south.

ii

For the great land expeditions, 1539–1561, our choice of narrative materials is good. Marcos de Niza and Cabeza de Vaca were their own chroniclers, the latter in many ways an outstanding one. Castañeda, as has been seen in Volume I, left a memorable record of the Coronado expedition, although Coronado himself was by no means inarticulate or incapable of effective description. The fullest chronicle of the expedition of Hernando de Soto is that by the anonymous Portuguese member of the expedition we know as the Gentleman of Elvas, but Soto's secretary Rangel left a businesslike narrative, preserved for us by Oviedo, and Biedma, a shorter but often vivid one. Toward the end of the century, Garcilaso de la Vega, the Inca, wrote a dramatic narrative in which tradition, documents, and imagination created a fine, though not necessarily reliable, moving picture of a great, tragic enterprise. Strangely enough we do not have reports of any major official inquiries, with their invaluable but often boring and repetitious examinations of witnesses, made after the failure of these expeditions. For the Luna expedition we have no continuous narrative except that of the friar Agustín Davila Padilla, who was primarily interested in the missionary aspects of the expedition—a relative minor part of its history—so that most of the material is that collected for an official inquiry after Luna retired from the venture. This, collected and translated by Herbert I. Priestley, forms the greater part of the accessible documentation. It is, fortunately, enlivened by letters and complaints made during the course of the expedition, as well as by ex-parte statements made after its return. It has, therefore, narrative snatches, but most of the material is that of controversy, not exploration.

When we come to Florida in the 1560s, we have a clash of narrative materials. Jean Ribault, it is true, stands alone with his brief propagandist report compiled after his return from his 1562 voyage. But when we come to the major enterprise of 1564–1565, we have the significant history, Laudonnière's *Histoire notable*, covering the whole period from a partisan but reasonably objective French angle. This is supplemented by briefer narratives by Nicolas le Challeux and Jacques le Moyne de Morgues, as well as by a vivid and inflammatory pamphlet on the Gourgues revenge raid in 1568.

On the other side there are from the Spanish commander, Pedro Menéndez de Avilés, sharp on-the-spot reports in his letters that give a clear, although not unbiased or complete, report of what he was doing to the French and the Indians as he defeated and massacred the one and subjugated the other. His secretary Solís de Méras built the experience of the conquest into a fine piece of largely rhetorical but effective writing in honor of his leader, which is still our most complete picture of the nature and spirit of the Spanish conquest. Barrientos wrote its more sober counterpart only a little later. The counterpoint between the French and Spanish narratives gives the material a dramatic quality which, if it has not been wholly absent hitherto from the documents which survive, is here most effectively illustrated. The Spanish narratives spice the routine stream of orders, appointments, reports, and letters that signalize the continuing occupation of the first permanent, if scarcely stable, Spanish colony in North America. Back in Europe the diplomatic struggle between France and Spain over what occurred in Florida is brought to life in the letters of Fourquevaux, the French ambassador at the Spanish court.

The primary choice in selecting materials over the subjects covered in this volume must be narrative; narrative, indeed, which is mainly well known, but not so well known as to be merely stereotyped; material which is often tedious, always informative (though its unravelling has taken and will take great care and ingenuity), but often vivid too, revealing the men who explored and the country they began to unfold to the European world as they wandered, struggled, or fought their way into and across North America.

Besides narrative, there is in this volume the record of the first attempt to create a permanent Spanish colony in North America, that of Florida. Pedro Menéndez de Avilés was not only a ruthless antagonist of the French but a man of great ambition and energy. He hoped, within a year after the conquest of the French, to have at least 1,500 Spaniards in Florida, not only as soldiers but as settlers also. He also expected to spread out his influence from the peninsula northward to Port Royal Sound (Santa Elena), and far beyond, to the Bay of St. Mary's (or the Bay of the Mother of God) where he had been in 1561. He sponsored inland exploration that brought Spanish posts for a very short time into the Alabama River Valley. He did manage to create a string of three main posts, San Agustín, the capital, although one in which he found it hard to implant a substantial civilian element, San Mateo, the rebuilt French fort on the St. Johns which was, in its turn, to prove vulnerable to a French raiding party in 1568, and Santa Elena where a firm garrison failed to encourage a civilian settlement to flourish or even to take effective root. The years from 1565 to his death in 1574 are exciting ones, wildly fluctuating, as money and men came and went. But the inland explorations of Pardo and Boyano came to nothing, the annexation of the Carolina Outer Banks was not followed up; the Jesuit mission on Chesapeake Bay was a tragic failure. Pedro Menéndez de Avilés himself was involved in too many other things besides Florida to take stock fully of his assets and debits there, even though he continued to try to inspire, if he did not stay long enough to lead. At his death many of his early projects and experiments had been lost sight of, but as a garrison Florida was moderately sound. If she had not yet in her the seeds of growth, she had many of the signs of permanence. With the year 1565 North America had at last become the seat of at least one continuing European colony.

Note on Presentation
of Materials

SOME INDICATIONS of editorial methods must necessarily be given. We have modernized, except in a very few cases (where explanations are given), usages of "u," "v," "i," and "j." We have kept "y^e" although we are well aware that the bastardized thorn it contains annoys linguistic purists. Since we have retained "yt" or "y^t" meaning "it," we have expanded on grounds of possible confusion "y^t" meaning "that."

From 1582 onward continental dating was ten days ahead of English dating. For French and Spanish documents this must be kept in mind and, also, when relating English documents to continental. Where confusion is likely to arise, double dating has been given.

We have not been afraid to expand contracted words, without indication, in either printed or manuscript sources, except where there is a genuine ambiguity. We have capitalized proper names where we have thought fit to do so. We have added full points to complete sentences and occasionally used either the comma or full point for the slash (/) (where ambiguity might arise from its retention).

Sidenotes are frequent in sixteenth-century published works and less frequently in manuscripts. Usually, they simply form a running index to the contents of the document. Where they do so they have been omitted. But from time to time they either convey additional information or express the point of view of the contemporary editor. In such cases they have been added as footnotes.

Square brackets have been used to fill lacunae conjecturally, although usually with a question mark. They also comprise words or phrases in non-English languages that may not be conveyed clearly in the translation or where the exact words of the document appear important. Occasionally, but only occasionally, they are included to explain a word, or a place name, which otherwise might be wholly unintelligible.

Almost all documents have been printed in full, although where omissions have been made they are indicated in the headnotes. In a few cases where the text was not suitable for transcription in full, abstracts have been made.

For each document or closely associated group of documents bibliographical references have been given. In the case of major sources, of which there have been many editions, this has been expanded in the introduction to the appropriate section. The editors have been generous with their own writing. The introductions to each volume attempt to point to the major characteristics of the selection in that volume and to bring out major comparative points of relationship. Longish introductory passages have been given for main sections where it was felt that headnotes alone might not be sufficient. Subsections have been knit together by brief introductory summaries. Finally, individual headnotes have tried to throw light on the nature of the particular document without trying, however, to summarize its contents in detail. Precise consistency in producing introductory matter of these kinds has not been aimed at or achieved. What assistance appeared to be required for each group of documents was given, rather than attempt to follow a completely consistent plan. Over such a wide range of materials it would be surprising if some discrepancies in treatment, which were not intended, will be observed. A broad measure of uniformity has, it is hoped, been maintained. We believe that, within the terms of our brief, this is the best selection on this scale that we could make. We see many ways in which it could have been improved, but we profoundly believe it will be useful, although it cannot within its scale be definitive. Another generation of editors may perhaps put together on film, after spending unlimited time and money, the complete documentary record of earliest European contacts with America. We hope they do so, but we also wish the users of this present set many interesting and productive hours, reading from a well-printed set of books much of what remains on an endlessly stimulating and engrossing topic.

Abbreviations
Used in the Text

A.G.I., Seville. Archivo General de Indias, Seville

A.G. Simancas. Archivo General de Simancas

B.L. British Library, Reference Division (formerly British Museum Library)

Biggar, H.P. *Precursors of Jacques Cartier*. H.P. Biggar, *The Precursors of Jacques Cartier, 1497–1534*. Publications of the Public Archives of Canada, no. 5. Ottawa, 1911.

Calendar of State Papers, Spanish. (a) *Letters, Despatches and State Papers Relating to the Negotiations Between England and Spain, 1485–1558*. 14 vols., London, 1862–1954; (b) *Letters and State Papers Relating to English Affairs, Preserved Principally in the Archives of Simancas, 1558–1603*. 4 vols. London, 1892–1899.

Colección de documentos inéditos de Indias. *Colección de documentos inéditos relativos al descubrimiento, conquista y colonización de las posesiones Española en América y Oceanía*, edited by Joaquin F. Pacheco, Francisco de Cárdenas, and Luís Torres de Mendoza. 1st series. 42 vols. Madrid, 1864–1889.

Hist. MSS Comm. Historical Manuscripts Commission, *Reports*, London, 1868–.

N.Y.P.L. New York Public Library.

P.R.O. Public Record Office, London.

Quinn, D.B., *Gilbert*. D.B. Quinn, *The Voyages and Colonising Enterprises of Sir Humphrey Gilbert*. 2 vols. London, Hakluyt Society, 1940.

Quinn, D.B., *North American Discovery*. D.B. Quinn, *North American Discovery, c. 1000–1612*. New York, 1971.

Quinn, D.B., *Roanoke Voyages*. D.B. Quinn, *The Roanoke Voyages, 1584–1590*. 2 vols. Cambridge, Eng., Hakluyt Society, 1955.

Taylor, E.G.R., *Hakluyts*. Eva G.R. Taylor, *The Original Writings and Correspondence of the two Richard Hakluyts*. 2 vols. London, Hakluyt Society, 1935.

T.L.S. The Times Literary Supplement. London.

Williamson, J.A., *The Cabot Voyages* (1962). James A. Williamson, *The Cabot Voyages and Bristol Discovery under Henry VII*. Cambridge, Eng., Hakluyt Society, 1962.

Williamson, J.A., *The Voyages of the Cabots* (1929). James A. Williamson, *The Voyages of the Cabots and the English Discovery of North America in the Reigns of Henry VII and Henry VIII*. London, 1929.

Major Spanish Searches in Eastern North America. Franco-Spanish Clash in Florida. The Beginnings of Spanish Florida.

VII

Spain Invades the Interior from the Southeast, 1526–1561

The Spanish invasion of the interior of North America from the Southeast was prefaced by the abortive attempt of Pánfilo de Narváez to establish himself on or near the Gulf coast. His venture is important not for its achievements (for it was a disastrous failure) but because he is the first of the *conquistadores*, unsuccessful in one of the richer areas of Spanish penetration, in this case Mexico, to attempt to find in North America an alternative to the Aztec dominion. In the long run, the arrival of Cabeza de Vaca in western Mexico in 1536 did reveal the riches of possibilities as well as the limitations of the North American interior and led to the first official expedition to the interior of the Southwest, that of Coronado which has already been chronicled. In the Southeast, however, the second *conquistador*, fresh from ventures in Peru, found North America attractive as an alternative to the Inca realm which he had helped to conquer but where he did not wish to stay in association with the savage Pizarro clan. Hernando de Soto gave North America more than a fair trial as an alternative Peru but everywhere this continent proved inimical or barren. Consequently, it became clear after the return of the survivors under Moscoso in 1543, Hernando de Soto now being dead, that there were neither Mexicos nor Perus to be found in the interior. The final attempt, that of Tristán de Luna, had a more limited and specific objective, namely to use part of Hernando de Soto's route as a line of approach to an East coast colony of settlement whose objective was wholly strategic. The commander of this expedition, too, developed wider and grander ideas than originally had been intended and aimed to emulate and surpass his precursors, but he, too, fell victim to lack of realism and incompetence, failing even to achieve his original, limited objective. Before 1561 Spain's attempts to penetrate the Southeast were painful experiences indeed. They had led to great losses and few gains (except in the records of exploration which derived from them). They, however, had a lasting effect. Thereafter, Spain was aware that North America was no Peru, no Mexico, but a land from which it might be necessary to exclude other intruding followers, even at the cost of losing money and, perhaps, also further prestige.

Chapter Twenty-seven
The Expedition of Pánfilo de Narváez
to the Gulf Coast, 1526–1528

THE AMBITIONS of Pánfilo de Narváez to found a new Mexico northward and eastward from Cortés's conquest, from which he had been effectively excluded, led him to obtain a grant from the crown of the Gulf Coast between the Río de las Palmas (whose precise location at some little distance from Pánuco does not appear simple to define) and Florida. The expedition was, like that of Ayllón in 1526, mounted in Spain early in 1527 and was of formidable dimensions. His 600 men were mainly soldiers and had with them a few women and Negroes, but a permanent settlement was envisaged. He was hampered by bad weather and was unable to assemble his fleet in American waters so went on to Cuba to do so, sailing from there on June 17, 1528, with a reduced complement. It would appear that about 400 persons were set ashore near Tampa Bay in April, 1528. To provide immediate supplies, he raided local Indian villages and so assured himself of native antagonism. He moved northward up the Florida Peninsula, as Soto was to do after him, but his objective was to move westward from the head of the peninsula, while his ships would continue to patrol the coast as he went, and some would go back for supplies to be delivered to him farther to the west when he found a coastal base there. He anticipated Soto, too, in making his first resting place in the territory of the Apalachee Indians in the vicinity of modern Tallahassee, finding them difficult neighbors (not surprisingly as he had stolen their corn).

He moved westward to a site called Aute (apparently on a branch of the Apalachicola River but well inland) and sent his associate Alvar Núñez Cabeza de Vaca to find a coastal location where he could pick up supplies. Such a site being found farther down Apalachicola Bay, he moved there with some difficulty. Food was running short, discipline was becoming poor under harrying Indian attacks, and sickness was rife. After a considerable wait, it appeared evident that no supplies were going to reach him after all—the patrolling supply vessels found no trace of the expedition. By the time independent transport had been constructed, four large boats, the force had been reduced to some 200 men. Leaving the Bahía de los Caballos, where they had used the last of their horses for food, the expedition began its tragic course along the Gulf Coast, in an unavailing attempt to reach Mexico. Wherever they landed, both eastward and westward of the Great River (the Mississippi), the Indians took toll of their diminishing force. After several boats were grounded and Narváez himself had done his best to rescue their occupants, he set out to sea to cross the Gulf of Mexico, but never succeeded. Several times vessels went to look for him, the last early in 1529 when it was reported he had disappeared without trace.

The capitulations he signed on December 11, 1526, with Charles V show on what basis his expedition was constituted (232). An extract on the disintegration of his expedition is given from Antonio de Herrera, *Historia general*, published early in the next century (233), while a report of a vessel sent to find any trace of him in 1529 (234) indicates how his whole expedition was thought to have disappeared. The rest of our information on his disastrous failure comes from the narrative of Cabeza de Vaca (235) who, after all, survived him, and reappeared in 1536.

232. December 11, 1526. Capitulations between Charles V and Pánfilo de Narváez for the conquest of the land between the Río de las Palmas and Florida.

The capitulations of December 11, 1526, are distinguished by the inclusion in them of the royal decrees of November 17, 1526, laying down a detailed code for dealing with, and Christianizing, Indians in newly conquered territories. This code of conduct was of general application and was later applied to Hernando de Soto (however ignored by him in practice). It represents an advance in the "protective" character of Spanish policy under the influence of Bartolomé de las Casas, although it proved almost impossible to make the code effective in practice.

The capitulaciones *are printed in* Colección de documentos inéditos de Indias, *XXII (1874), 224-245, translated.*

[a] The King.

Whereas you, Pánfilo de Narváez, of the island of Fernandina [Cuba], have informed me that you, from the great goodwill that you feel to the service of the Catholic Queen my Lady and Myself, and for the expansion of Our Royal Realms, wished to explore, discover and settle the lands that lie between Río de las Palmas and the island of Florida, exclusive, and that you will also explore and settle the same Florida and all this coast from one sea to the other, and you will discover everything that there may be to discover in these areas; all at your own cost and expense, without our at any time being obliged to pay or reimburse you for the expenses incurred thereon, apart from what is granted to you in this commission; and you entreated and begged as a favour from me that I should grant you the right to explore these lands,

and should give and grant you the favours under the conditions mentioned below: concerning which I ordered the agreement and commission to be drawn up with you as follows:

Firstly, I grant you permission and authority that you may discover, explore and settle the said lands, which lie between Río de las Palmas and the cape known as Cape Florida, exclusive; on the condition that you are obliged to take and that you do take from these our Realms, people who are not prohibited to go to those parts, to carry out the said settlement, and to establish in these lands two settlements or more, as you think best, and in the places that you think to be most convenient, and that for each one of these settlements you should take at least a hundred men, and make on that land three fortresses: all this is at your own cost and expense; and that you should be obliged to leave Spain with at least these two hundred men on the first voyage, within one year from the date of this commission, and that for this purpose you give the sufficient security as will be indicated to you.

Also, respecting your person and the services which you have done for Us and we hope that you will do for Us, it is my wish and will to grant you the favour, which I hereby grant you, that for all the days of your life you should be Our Governor and Captain General of these lands which you should discover and settle in this way, with a salary as Our Governor of one hundred and fifty thousand maravedís each year, and I shall instruct that you be given Our orders concerning that.

Also, I shall grant you, as hereby I grant you, the office of Our Chief Magistrate on these lands, for yourself and for your heirs and successors for ever and always.

Also, I shall grant you, as I hereby grant you, the said three fortresses which you are obliged to make at your own cost and that you should make in these lands, for all the days of your life and of two of your heirs and successors as you indicate and wish, with a salary of seventy thousand maravedís each year for each fortress, and I shall instruct that they be given letters patent concerning this, provided that these fortresses are made if it seems to you and to Our officers in this land that they are needed, and that they are of the most suitable kind, in the view of these officers.

Also, respecting your person and the services that you have done for Us and which I hope you will do for Me, and in view of the necessary expenses to be incurred in this settlement, it is my wish and will to grant you, and I hereby grant you, the office of Our Adelantado of the said lands that you may settle in this way, to you and your heirs and successors, for ever and always: and I shall instruct that you be given our orders and title concerning that.

Also, respecting the goodwill with which you have acted to serve us in the above-mentioned, and the expense that you are likely to incur therein, it is my wish and will that in all these lands that you should discover and settle at your own expense in this way, as has been said, according to the manner and the way previously mentioned, you should have and take four per cent of all the profit that should accrue to Us in any way, for yourself and your heirs and successors for ever and always, after the payment of all the accounts and expenses that should have been made and be made on Our behalf in the care and settlement of the lands, however incurred, and the said salaries which we shall order to be paid, both to you and to any other people and Our officials that may be sent to this land under any circumstances.

Item, to grant you this wish and favour, that on all the clothing and provisions, arms, horses, and other things that you should take to those lands from these Realms, you should not pay customs duty nor any other tax, for all the days of your life, provided that you do not sell, trade or traffic in them.

Also, I grant you ten square leagues of the land that you should discover in this way, so that you should have land to farm and work, provided that it is neither the best nor the worst, in the views of yourself and of Our officers that we should order to be sent to this land, so that it can belong to

yourself and to your heirs and successors for ever and always, without having civil or criminal jurisdiction, nor anything else that is our prerogative and belongs to us as Kings and Lords.

Also, that I shall grant you permission, as I hereby grant you, that from Our islands of Hispaniola, or San Juan [de Puerto Rico], or Cuba, or Santiago, or from any of them you may take to these lands the horses, mares and other animals that you may wish and think suitable, without any hindrance or impediment being placed in your way.

And since it is our main desire and intention that this land should be settled by Christians, so that there should be sown and grow Our Holy Catholic Faith, and that the people of those parts should be attracted and converted to it, I order that, in order that this be carried out most completely and quickly, to those men who go with you on this first voyage or later to settle in these lands it is my wish to grant the following favours.

That for the first three years of this settlement there should not be paid to Us in this land more than just a tenth of the gold mined, and a ninth the fourth year, and to go on increasing in this way until it reaches the fifth, and of the rest that there should be, whether it is from trade or anything else, We should be paid Our fifth whole: and it is understood that of the trade and services and other profits from the land, we shall of course take Our fifth as everywhere else.

Also, that the first settlers and explorers should be given their own lands, two of the usual grants to knights and two houses, and that they should spend four years living there, and then after that they can sell it and dispose of it as their own property.

Also, that these men who go on this first voyage to this land for the five years immediately following should not pay customs duties on anything that they may take to this land for their houses, provided that they do not sell, trade or traffic in them.

Also, to show favour to you and to the people that should go to these lands, I order that for the period of these five years they should not be obliged to pay to Us any part of the salt that they eat and use, of the salt that there may be in these lands.

Also, I grant permission and authority to you

and to these settlers that those Indians that may be rebellious, even after being advised and warned, you may take as slaves: but you should observe in this matter that which is included below in this commission and agreement and Our other instructions and orders that we shall order to be given in this matter: and in this way, and respecting this order, those Indians which the chiefs and other people of the land have held as slaves you may take and buy, if they really are slaves already, paying them what they ask in the full view of the magistrates and officials and friars that will be going with you.

Also, I order that so that this land should be settled best and most quickly I shall instruct to be granted to these lands the favours that we have granted and are now held by the other lands and islands that are now settled, provided they are relevant to this land and not otherwise, which you would then be obliged to declare in order to decide in the matter what is most suitable and serves Us best.

And since we have been informed of the evils and disorders that have occurred and are occurring in discoveries and new settlements: and so that We can with a clear conscience grant permission for making them, to set this matter right, with the agreement of the members of Our council and advisers, a general instruction has been ordered and sent containing provisions in this matter which you are to observe in this settlement and discovery; we order this to be included here; it runs as follows:—

[b] "Don Carlos, etc. Whereas we have been informed and are aware that the unrestrained greed of some of Our subjects who went to Our islands and the Mainland of the Ocean Sea, and the bad way they treated the native Indians of these Indies, Islands and Mainland, in the great and excessive work that they gave them, keeping them in the mines to extract gold, and in the pearl fisheries, and others, and the farms, making them work excessively and immoderately, not giving them the clothing and food that was necessary to sustain their lives, treating them with cruelty and callousness worse than if they had been slaves, that these have been the cause of the death of a large number of these Indians: so much so that many of the islands and part of the Mainland were left barren and quite unpopulated by the native Indians: and that they caused many to flee and leave their lands and homes and go into the forests and elsewhere to save their lives and escape from this oppression and harsh treatment: which was also a great impediment to the conversion of these Indians to Our Holy Catholic Faith, and the cause of the fact that not all of them have come into whole and general understanding of it: which has been and is a great disservice to the Lord Our God: and we have also been informed that the captains and other people that went under Our instructions and with Our permission to discover and settle some of these Islands and Mainland—even though it was and is Our main desire and intention to bring these Indians to the true knowledge of the Lord Our God and His Holy Faith, by preaching to them and with the example of learnèd men and good monks, by treating them well and as fellow-men, without their receiving any force or pressure, damage or harm of any kind to their persons or possessions: and this has all been ordered and instructed by Us in this way— these captains and other officers and people on these fleets, despite taking these as their specific orders and instructions, were affected by this same greed to forget the service of Our Lord God and Myself: they wounded and killed many of these Indians in their discoveries and explorations, and took their possessions, without these Indians having given them just cause for that, and without their first having given them the advice and warning they were supposed to give them, and without the Indians having offered the Christians any resistance or harm to the preaching of Our Holy Faith: which, as well as being a great offence to the Lord Our God, gave rise and led not only to those Indians that had suffered this force, damage, and harm, but also many others from the same area who had news and warning of it, rebelling and joining forces against the Christians our subjects, killing many of them, even the friars and priests who were not to blame and died as martyrs, preaching them the Christian faith: for all these reasons we suspended for some time and gave up giving permission for these explorations and discoveries, wishing first to discuss and decide both how to punish what has happened and to set it right for the future, to relieve these Indians of damage and hardship, and to give orders for the

discoveries and settlements that are to be made from now on, that they should be carried out without offending God and without death or robbery of these Indians and without enslaving them injustly, so that the desire that we have had and have to spread Our Holy Faith, and that these Indians and heathens should come into the knowledge of it, should be fulfilled without a burden on Our conscience, and that Our purpose, and the intentions and works of the Catholic Kings, Our grandparents and Lords, should be achieved in all those parts of the Islands and of the Mainland of the Ocean Sea which we have in our area of exploration and remain to be discovered and settled: this was discussed at great length by the members of Our Council of the Indies and in consultations with Myself, and it was agreed that this letter of Ours ought to be ordered to be sent to you to this effect: in which We order and instruct that now and henceforth, both to repair the past and in the discoveries and settlements which should be made at Our orders and in Our name in these Islands and in the Mainland of the Ocean Sea, discovered and to be discovered within Our limits and boundaries, should be observed and fulfilled the provisions contained below, in this manner.

Firstly, We order and instruct Our letters and orders should be given at once to Our Judges of the High Court that live in the city of Santo Domingo on the Island of Hispaniola, and to the governors and other judges that are now and may be on this island and the areas of San Juan and Cuba to Jamaica, and to the Governors, mayors and other judges, both on the Mainland and in New Spain and the provinces of Panuco and Higueras and Florida and Tierra Nueva, and to the other people to whom it might be our wish to commit and entrust it: that at once, with great care and diligence, each one in his own place and area of jurisdiction, they should find out which of our subjects, captains, officers or anyone else, were responsible for these deaths and robberies and excesses and outrages, and enslaved Indians without reason or justice: and of those that they should find guilty in their jurisdiction, they are to send to Us in Our Council of the Indies, an account of the offence, with their views concerning the punishment that ought to be dealt out for it, so that when the members of Our Council have

considered it a decision can be made and orders sent to do what is in the best service of Our Lord God and Ourselves, and is most appropriate for the carrying out of Our justice.

Also, We order and instruct that if these Our justices should find from the information of these reports that any of Our subjects, of any quality or condition, or anyone else has kept any Indians as slaves, taken and carried them from their lands and homes unjustly and wrongly, they should take them out of their power, and if these Indians should so wish it, they should have them sent back to their lands and homes, if this can be done properly and conveniently; if this cannot be done properly and conveniently, they should place them under that freedom and protection that should fit them in reason and justice, according to the capability, ability and quality of their persons: always keeping in mind and under consideration what is best and advantageous for these Indians, so that they be treated as free men and not as slaves, and that they should be well kept and looked after, and that they should not be given excessive work, and that they should not be taken into the mines against their will: this is all to be done with the approval of the Prelate and his officer, if there is one in the place, and if he is not there, with the assent and approval of the priest or curate of the Church that might be there: concerning which we are placing a great charge on the consciences of all: and if these Indians should be Christians, they are not to be sent back to their lands, even if they wish it, unless they have been converted to Our Holy Catholic Faith, on account of the danger that might be affecting their souls.

Also, We order and instruct that now and henceforth all captains and officers and any other of Our subjects or from outside Our Kingdoms who with Our permission and orders may go, and go to discover and settle or trade in some of the Islands or the Mainland of the Ocean Sea, within Our limits and boundaries, should be held and obliged before they leave these Our Kingdoms, when they go on board to make their journey, to take at least two monks or qualified priests in their company, which they should appoint before the members of Our Council of the Indies: information should be sought about their lives, doctrines and example, and then they should be approved as being of a suitable nature for the service of the Lord Our God, and for the education and instruction of these Indians, and preaching to them, and converting them, according to the Papal Bull conceding these Indies to the Royal Crown of these Kingdoms.

Also, We order and instruct that these monks or priests should take great care and diligence in seeing that these Indians are well treated, as fellow-men, shown consideration and favour: that they should not permit them to suffer force nor robbery, harm or outrages, nor any kind of ill-treatment: and if anyone of any quality or condition should do otherwise, he should take care and concern to inform Us at once, if he can, in detail about it, so that We and the members of Our Council should order it to be seen to and full punishment to be carried out.

Also, We order and instruct that these captains and others that may go with Our permission to discover, settle or trade, when they should be about to set out onto some Island or Mainland that they may find during their voyage, within Our limits or the boundaries of what was specifically allotted to them in the orders, that they should do it and do do it with the agreement and assent of Our officers that shall have been appointed by Us for that purpose, and of these monks and priests that may go with them, and in no other manner, under penalty of losing half all their possessions for anyone who does otherwise, to Our Chamber and Treasury.

Also, We order that the first and main thing that these captains and other officers and anyone else should do after coming to land should be to make an attempt through interpreters that the Indians and inhabitants of the land or island should understand, saying and telling them now We have sent them to teach the Indians in good ways, and lead them from sin and cannibalism, and educate them in Our Holy Faith, and preach it to them so that they may be saved, and bring them into Our Realms, so that they should be better treated than they are, and with consideration and favour, as Our other Christian subjects: and they should say to them everything else that the Catholic Kings ordered to be said to them, explained and required of them, and we order that this edict, signed by Francisco de los Cobos, Our Secretary, and Our Council, should be taken, and that they should tell them of it, and make them know and understand, specifically through

these interpreters, once, twice, or more times, as many as seem justified to these monks or priests, discovers or settlers.

Also, We order that after this warning and announcement has been made, and the Indians have understood it, in the manner expounded in the foregoing paragraph, if you should see that it is necessary and suitable to the Service of God and Ourselves, and your safety, and that of those who henceforth should be living and staying in these lands and islands, to make some fortresses and strongholds and unfortified houses to live in, they should try with great care and diligence to make them in the places and parts where they are best and can be looked after and maintained, trying to do this with as little damage and grievance caused as possible, and without wounding or killing Indians for this reason, and without taking by force their possessions and homes: rather We order that they should be shown good treatment and good works, that they should be encouraged and brought together and treated as fellow-men, so that in this way and through the example of the lives of these friars and priests, and through their preaching, teaching and knowledge, they should come into an understanding of Our Faith, and in the love and desire of becoming Our subjects, and to be and remain in Our service, like Our other subjects.

Also, We order that the same procedure be observed and fulfilled in trading, and in all the treaties that are to be made and are made with these Indians, for what the Indians have and the Spaniards would like to have, a satisfactory equivalent so that they should be left content.

Also, We order that nobody can nor should take as a slave any of these Indians, under penalty of losing their goods, offices and favours, and themselves to Our mercy: except in a case where these Indians are not prepared to allow these monks or priests to come among them and teach them good ways and habits, and preach to them Our Holy Catholic Faith: if they should not wish to give us obedience, or should not acquiesce, resisting and defending themselves with weapons, in that they look for mines or take gold out of them, or the other metals that may be found in such cases, We permit that, for this reason, and in defence of their lives and property, these settlers should be able, with the agreement and consent of these monks and priests, supporting it and signing their names to it, to make war, and to do in it whatever the laws of Our Holy Faith and Religion permit and order should be done and can be done, and in no other way, and in no other circumstances, under the same penalty.

Also, We order that neither these captains nor anyone else should be able to force and compel these Indians to go into the mines of gold or other metals, nor into the pearl fisheries, nor any other farms of their own, under the penalty of losing their offices and goods to Our Chamber: but if these Indians should be willing to go and work of their own will, We also permit that they can be employed and used as free men, that they should be treated as such and not be given excessive work: special care should be taken to teach them in good ways and habits and lead them from sins and from eating human flesh and worshipping idols and sin and offences against nature, and to attract them into converting to Our Faith and living in it, caring for the lives and wellbeing of these Indians as they do for their own, giving them in payment for their work and service whatever they deserve and is reasonable, taking into consideration the quality of their persons and the condition of the land and their work, following in all these matters the opinions of these monks or priests: all of this, and in particular the good treatment of these Indians, we order should be undertaken with particular care so that nothing should be done which might be a burden and danger to Our consciences: and concerning this we lay a charge on theirs: so that if it is against the decision and opinion of these monks and priests there can and should be done none of the things mentioned in this section and in the others that set out the manner and way in which these Indians are to be treated.

Also, We order that if in view of the quality, condition and aptitude of these Indians it should seem to these monks or priests that it would be in the service of God and the best interests of the Indians that, in order to lead them from their sins and in particular from sodomy and cannibalism, and in order that they should be educated and taught good ways and habits and Our Faith and Christian Doctrine, and so that they live in an orderly way, it is necessary and fitting for them to be entrusted to Christians to treat them as free men, that these monks and priests should be able to entrust them, if they both agree, in the manner and way that they may decide, always bearing in mind the best service of God, the good, utility and good treatment of these Indians, and that in no matter should a burden be put on Our consciences as a result of what they do and decide, concerning which we trust in their consciences and We order that nobody should go nor act against the decision of these monks and priests concerning such cases of entrusting Indians to Christians, under the same penalty; and that on the first ship that should be coming to these Our kingdoms these monks or priests should send to us a true report concerning the qualities and abilities of these Indians, and an account of what they have ordered to be done in this matter, so that We can order it to be discussed in Our Council of the Indies, so that there can be approved and confirmed whatever is just and in the service of God and of these Indians, without harm or burden to Our consciences, and that what should not be so can be repaired and set right as best suits the service of God and Ourselves, without harm to these Indians or their freedom and lives, and that they be relieved of the former harm and oppression.

Item, We order and instruct that the settlers and explorers that with Our permission now and henceforth go to trade, settle and discover, within the limits of Our boundaries, should be held and obliged to take the people that are to go with them for any of these purposes from these Our Kingdoms of Castille and the other parts that are not expressly forbidden, without their being permitted to take with them any of those who now live or are staying on these Islands and the Mainland of the Ocean Sea, from any of them, except one or two people, no more, on each voyage of discovery, for interpreters, and other matters necessary to these voyages, under a penalty of losing half his goods to Our Chamber, for the settler, explorer or seaman who carries him without Our express permission.

And if they observe and comply, these captains and officers and others who now and henceforth should go with Our permission to these settlements, trade and discoveries, they are to take and should take and enjoy the salaries and rents, profits, graces and favours that should be arranged and settled by Us and in Our name: these, by this letter of Ours, We promise to observe and comply with, if they observe and comply with what is entrusted and instructed to them by Us and in this letter of Ours: and if they do not observe and comply, acting and going against it or against any part of it, as well as incurring the penalties detailed above, We declare and order that they shall have lost and shall lose all the offices and favours which by the agreements and commissions they were to enjoy.

Given in Granada, 17th November 1526.
      [signed:] I the King.

I, Francisco de los Cobos, Secretary to His Imperial Catholic Majesty, had this written at his orders. Mercur, Chancellor, Doctor Carvajal, Doctor Beltrán. Recorded by Juan de Samano. Urbina for the Chancellor.

[c]   So now, if you carry out the aforementioned at your own expense and according to the favours previously mentioned, and observe and comply with what is contained in this order included above, and all the other instructions that we shall in the future order you to observe and keep for this land and the good treatment of the natives there, and their conversion to Our Holy Catholic Faith: I hereby declare and promise that all this agreement will be observed for you in every manner, respect and detail as enumerated therein: and if you do not act in compliance with this, we shall not be obliged to order the above to be observed for you in any respect: rather we shall order that you be punished and proceeded against as someone who does not observe and comply, and disobeys the orders of his King and natural Lord: and concerning this I shall order that you be given this letter, signed by My name and authorized by my undersigned Secretary.

Given in Granada, 11th December 1526.
      [signed:] I the King.

At the orders of His Majesty. Francisco de los Cobos. Signed by the Bishop of Osma, the Bishop of the Canaries, Doctor Beltrán, and the Bishop of Ciudad Rodrigo.

233. 1528. Herrera's account of the breakup of the Narváez expedition.

Pánfilo de Narváez mounted a large expedition in Spain in 1527, which included some 600 men with a few women and Negro slaves, and a number of friars to convert the Indians. He reached Cuba after losses at sea and was unable to proceed until the spring of 1528. Landing near Tampa Bay, he moved, with his remaining men, up the Florida Peninsula and eventually settled in the middle of the Apalachee territory, near modern Tallahassee. When he used up all the supplies he had or could get there, he moved eastward to a village named Aute on the Apalachicola River. Lack of food, illness, and Indian attacks played havoc with the expedition. In the hope of making contact with supply ships coming along the coast, the expedition moved down to an arm of Apalachicola Bay. Narváez soon lost his initiative and control. Herrera vividly conveys from the outside the process of disintegration that took place. The earlier part of the narrative is more effectively conveyed from the inside by Cabeza de Vaca (235).

Antonio de Herrera, Historia general de los hechos de los Castellanos, 10 vols. (1944–1947), V, 230–236, translated.

The Unfortunate Outcome of the Expedition of Pánfilo de Narváez

These men left Aute along a very difficult road, and very exhausting, because there were not enough horses to carry the ill: for there were now so many of these that they could neither go on ahead nor turn back: and in such great need and so bad condition, and in land where no possible help could be expected, some of the horsemen began to show signs of wanting to leave the company; news of this was conveyed to the Governor, and he spoke to all of them, telling them not to do anything so disgraceful, but that what belonged to one belonged to all. Wondering what they could do to help themselves, and unable to imagine any way out of such a desperate position, in land they did not know, and with nothing to eat, they agreed to make ships to travel in. This would be extremely difficult, not having mainmasts, nor tools, nor rigging, nor any of the necessary materials. They stopped discussing it then, but next day one of them said that he would make some bellows with hides of deer, with tubes made out of wood: and then they decided to put the idea into effect, making saws, axes and nails, out of the stirrups, spurs and crossbows, and other things there were of iron: they decided that while work was going ahead on this, four expeditions to Aute should be made to look for food, and that on every third day they would kill a horse. They made the expeditions and got hold of up to four hundred fanegas of maize, with many fights against Indians: they took the tops of palmtrees, so that the fiber could serve as tow for the boats, which were beginning to be put together by the one carpenter there was among them all. Their need was pressing them so hard that from the 4th of August, when they began, to the 20th of September, five boats were finished, twenty cubits long each, caulked with tow made of the bark from the tops of palm trees and with tar pitch, made by a Greek called Teodoro, from pinetrees, and from the same stuff of the palm tops: and from the hair and tails of the horses they made ropes and rigging: from the palm bark, sails: and from savin trees, oars: and the land was such that they had difficulty in finding stones for ballast and anchors. They skinned the horses legs whole, and tanned the skins, to make water containers. Some of them went collecting shellfish along the coves and inlets of the sea, and twice the Indians attacked them, killing ten men; the others could not help them, and found them transfixed with arrows; and from the bay, which they called the Bay of the Cross, where they had set out from, to the place they now were, they had travelled more or less 280 leagues, without seeing any mountain or mountain range in all that.

On the 22nd of September they ate the last horse, and on this day they set to sea. They found that, apart from the men killed by the Indians, more than forty men had died of illness; they went into the five boats with their clothes and provisions, so tightly packed that there was no more than about six inches of the side of the boat above water: and like this they set off onto such a troublesome stretch of sea without carrying anyone who knew about the art of navigation. They went for seven days along these inlets, the water up to the topmost outer plank of the boats, without seeing a sign from the coast. Eventually they found an island close to the mainland, and saw five canoes; the Indians fled and left them. They went into a house on the island and found many dried mullets, which relieved their hunger. They went through a strait that separated the island from the mainland, and called it San Miguel, since they passed through it on St Michael's Day, and with the canoes they relieved the boats a bit, for they took them too, which meant the sides were two

palms width above the level of the water, and they went along the coast, towards the River of Las Palmas, because the water containers made of horse skin had rotted; they had no water and suffered great thirst. They went up inlets, which went a long way inland, low, and dangerous; all they found were a few Indians fishing, very poor people. In their great need of water they were travelling by night very close to the coast when they heard a canoe, which they hailed but did not want to come back to them: since it was night they did not follow it, and at daybreak they went to an island, but they found no water there, and there they had to stay because of bad weather, not daring to set out to sea; and, eventually, having spent so many days without drinking, their need became so pressing that they drank salt water, and some of them so immoderately that five men died at once. Seeing the damage done by this water and that their need was increasing, even though the sea was no calmer they commended themselves to God and went towards where they had seen the canoe; this was so dangerous that many times they expected to be drowned, but they rounded a point where the land sticks out and found it was well sheltered. Several canoes came out to them, and although the Indians spoke to them, they turned back, unwilling to wait. They were large and well built, but carried no weapons; they followed them and came to land, and in their houses, which were nearby, they found pitchers of good water and cooked fish: the chief offered everything to the Governor, and took him to his house: he gave some of the fish to the Spaniards: they gave the Indians some of the maize, and they ate it in their presence: but half an hour after nightfall the Indians attacked the Spaniards, and the Governor was wounded in the face by a stone. They grabbed the Chief, but as his men were near he slipped away from them, leaving in their hands a cloak of sable fur, smelling so strongly of musk that it could be noticed far off. The Governor ordered the men to gather together at the boats, except for fifty to defend against the Indians. They were attacked three times, with such force that each time they caught them with a barrage of stones, and there was not anyone who escaped unhurt. Captains Orantes, Téllez and Peñalosa set up an ambush, with fifteen Spaniards, and caught the Indians from behind, with the result that they all fled. The next day the Spaniards broke more than thirty of their canoes, with which they helped ward off the cold; and when the weather was calmer they set out to sea again. They sailed for three days, and as the water vessels were few, they returned to the same necessity. They found a canoe, and hailed it. The Indians waited, and the Governor, who was the first person they came to, asked them for water; they said they should give them something to bring it in. Teodoro, the Greek, insisted on going with them, although they did their best to stop him, and he took a negro with him, and the Indians left two of their number behind captive. The Indians came back at night, with the vessels, but without water or the Christians, and as the Indians spoke to the two who had remained as hostages, they wanted to jump into the water, but they were held back, and the Indians in the canoes fled; and the Spaniards were left very upset at the loss of their two companions.

Of the Unfortunate End of the Expedition of Pánfilo de Narváez

Next morning, many people came out in canoes asking for the two Indians who had stayed as hostages, and were told in reply to give back the Christians. These were Indians of a better size than they had seen up till then, and among them there were five or six Lords, with sable fur cloaks, and long loose hair. They asked the Spaniards to go with them, saying they would give them water, and other things, and the two Christians. And since it was dangerous to stay there, the boats put out to sea, and the Indians threw stones with slings, and sticks, and only a few arrows, because there were only about four or five bows to be seen among them. The sea got rough, and the canoes went back, and the Spaniards continued their way until they found a river, where they took on water, and since the North winds were increasing, for two days they were unable to land: and while they were in this difficulty, the boats got separated at night; but next morning three could be seen, and Cabeza de Vaca asked the Governor, since he wanted to get to land, and was carrying the healthiest men, to help him by giving him a tow; but he was unwilling to do that, saying that in that weather each boat should be responsible for itself. Cabeza de Vaca caught up with the other one, which was that of Captains Téllez and Pantoja, and for four days they sailed together, with each man eating at his

ration a handful of raw maize. A storm came on them, and separated these two boats, with the men being so weak that in the Treasurer's boat there were not four men able to stand. Next day they found themselves so close to land that a wave threw the boat out of the water, and the blow shook them all awake: and since they found themselves on land, they made a fire, and found rainwater, and with the heat of the fire the men began to feel a bit better. One of them was ordered to climb a few trees and spy out the land; he said that it looked as though they were on an island; he went along a path until he bumped into some Indians' houses, where he took a cooking pot, a small dog, a few fish and came back, pursued by some Indians. Up to a hundred came then, armed with their bows and arrows; the Treasurer managed to calm them down with beads and bells, and they said they would be back in the morning and bring something to eat; and they fulfilled their promise, because they brought a lot of fish and some roots, which they eat like nuts, and take out, with difficulty, under water. They came back in the afternoon with their women and the same gifts; and the next day were equally generous. And when the Spaniards saw they had some food, they decided to set to sea. They launched the boat into the water, but a great wave capsized it, and three of the company were drowned. The others, half-drowned, and very upset at what had happened in the midst of so many misfortunes, came out to land as naked as when they were born and desperate at the disappointment. Because now it was late November, and the weather very cold, and apart from being naked they had also lost their weapons and everything they had. They made a fire, which cheered them a bit. The Indians came back with food for them, but when they saw them in such a strange state, they went back; but Cabeza de Vaca called to them, and explained their position. And as they could see the three men dead, they came up and joined the Spaniards, commiserating with their troubles with weeping and tears, so much so, that it made the Spaniards all the more conscious of their plight. Cabeza de Vaca, although some of them did not think it a good idea, asked the Indians to take them into their houses: they were glad to do so, and sent thirty men to collect firewood, and the others helped them walk there, and to stop them dying of cold they had fires lit from time to time to warm themselves by. They put them in a house with large fires, and an hour later they began to dance, and have such a party that it lasted all night, with the Spaniards continually afraid that all the festivities were in order to make a sacrifice of them; but since in the morning they fed them well, their fears subsided.

Cabeza de Vaca recognized some beads which one of the Indians was wearing, and asked him where he had got them from. He said, from some Christians, who were staying further back. He sent two men to look for them, and they found them looking for Cabeza de Vaca, because they had had news of him: these were Captain Andrés Dorantes and Captain Alonso del Castillo, with the men from their boat. They were very upset to see the two Spaniards so thin and naked, because they had escaped without losing anything, even though their boat had run aground a league and a half away. When they had all met, they decided that those who were well enough should go off to the boats, and that the ill men should stay with the Indians until God should do what he wished. They struggled hard to recover the boat and repair it; and when they launched it on the water the boat sank, and a horseman called Tabera died. This was another appalling disappointment to those poor men, because they were without clothes in very cold and harsh weather; they commended themselves to God and decided they would spend the winter in that land, and that four of them, the best swimmers, should go along the coast to Panuco. Thinking it was close, they set off, with an Indian from Cuba; these were Álvaro Fernández Portuguese: Méndez Figueroa from Toledo: Estudillo from Zafra. The cold and storms were now so intense that the Indians could not gather their roots nor fish: and with food short, and the houses giving little shelter, people were dying. Five Christians, who were supporting themselves in a hut on the coast, reached such an extreme state that they ate each other, until just one was left, with no one to eat him. These were Sierra, Corral, Palacio, Diego López, and Gonzalo Ruiz, who would have preferred death to living in such misery. The Indians, despite being heathen, were much scandalized by this: and eventually, out of eighty men, soon there were only fifteen left alive. The Indians were affected by a fearsome stomach ache, which killed half of them, and they came to think that the Spaniards were caus-

ing it, so they wanted to kill them: but one of the Indians, in whose power was Cabeza de Vaca, told them not to believe this, because if those men had the power to give them this disease, they would also have the power to avoid so many of their own number dying; and since they were doing no harm, it was not right to kill them—and in this way God did not wish to abandon them, and saved them. And they named that island *Mal Hado*, bad fate.

These Indians had large bodies; they had no weapons other than bows, with which they were very skilful; the men had one nipple pierced and a piece of cane inserted through the hole; and the lower lip was also pierced, with another cane there. They stayed on that island from October to the end of February, and ate the roots previously mentioned. In November and December they had fish traps made of canes, in which there were no fish until this time. At the end of February they go off to look for food elsewhere, for the roots are not yet ready. They love their children very much, and treat them very kindly. If one dies the parents and relations weep for him for a year, and so do all the tribe; the relations start in the morning, and the tribe at midday. After a year, they hold the funeral rites, and then they wash themselves in the black dye which they use as mourning. They do not weep for the old who die, because they say that their time is gone and they take food out of the mouths of the children. They bury all their dead except for the *shamans* [literally "doctors"], which they burn, and while the fire burns they dance, and they keep the ashes of the bones to give them in water to the relations to drink after the year, after the funeral rites. Each man has his own wife: the *shamans* have two or three, and they get on well together: and when one of them marries off his daughter, the bridegroom gives her everything he has hunted or fished, and takes it to her father's house, and from the father-in-law's house they take food for the son-in-law. And for one year after he is married he does not go into the house of his parents-in-law or brothers-in-law; if they encounter him, they lower their eyes, because they think it is wrong to look at or talk to each other in this time. The wives talk to the parents-in-law and relations.

These are customs of the island of Mal Hado, and of all the province, fifty leages inland. In the house where a son or brother dies, they do not look for food for three months; instead they would let themselves die of hunger, except that relations and neighbours usually supply them with food. And for this reason there was great hunger in many houses while these Spaniards were there, because many of them died, and they observed there ceremonies well; and those who did go out looking for food did not find much, since the weather was so harsh, so many of them left the island and went to the mainland in canoes, and lived for three months on large oysters and drinking bad water, without firewood, and seriously troubled by mosquitoes. The houses where they gathered were made of matting, over many oyster shells—they slept on hides over them. And in this way they stayed there, and Cabeza de Vaca with them, until the month of April.

The Indians of the province of Tegesta, which goes from the Mártires to Cañaveral, are more skilful at maintaining themselves than the Indians here described, because they are such good fishermen that two of them go out in a canoe to sea and go where they already know whales are. One of them steers the canoe, and the other has two or three stakes and a mallet in his belt, and when he sees a whale he jumps into the sea and tries to climb on top of it behind its ears [eyes]. And once he is on it, he sinks a stake into its airhole, and then the whale sinks to the bottom, but as it cannot breathe there it comes back up again, and then the Indian drives in the stake with the mallet, and in this way covers its mouth in such a way that it cannot breathe—he ties a liana rope round its neck, and the other end to the canoe, and then they tow it back. And they reckon this is good food, and it lasts them a good while.

Cabeza de Vaca stayed with these Indians until

the time stated; and nothing was ever known of Pánfilo de Narváez, although it was rumoured that he turned up with six companions in the Southern Sea.

234. May 20, 1529. The disappearance of Narváez and his men is confirmed.

Searches made along the Gulf Coast after the disappearance of the Narváez expedition proved fruitless. Even where Indians were brought from the region he was believed to have penetrated, nothing intelligible could be obtained from them. The expedition had, it appeared, sunk without trace.

Lope Hurtado to Charles, May 20, 1529. A.G.I., Seville, Patronato 2-1-2 /26; copy in Library of Congress, A.G.I. Transcripts, General Series. Extract, translated.

Holy Imperial Catholic Majesty. . . .

A caravel arrived here that had just been looking for Narváez, carrying eight Indians taken from that coast where Narváez landed: and those Indians say by signs that Narváez is inland and that they do nothing but eat drink and sleep. I don't know what we should think of this. May Our Lord keep the Holy Catholic Person of Your Majesty in life for a long time, and that of the Empress Our Lady: from Santiago de Cuba, 20th May 1529. Your humble servant kisses the royal hands and feet of Your Majesty,

[signed:] Lope Hurtado.

Chapter Twenty-eight
The First Crossing of North America
by the Europeans

Aᴌᴠᴀʀ Núñᴇᴢ Cᴀʙᴇᴢᴀ ᴅᴇ Vᴀᴄᴀ is the first man (with his three companions, Estevánico, Andrés Dorantes de Carranca, and Alonzo del Castillo Maldonado, who tend to get less than their due) to cross the long land bridge between the eastern coastlands and the interior and western shores of North America. When he relates the fate of the Narváez expedition, he does so with the knowledge of the long years of slavery and the relatively short burst of effective action that lay ahead of him as he walked from Texas to western Mexico, the longest way around. His story is a historical document of the greatest interest and importance, but it is not only that; it is a personal record of an exceptional individual, as well as of a quite exceptional experience.

235. 1527–1536. The *Relation* of Alvar Núñez Cabeza de Vaca.

The two stages of the Narváez expedition are wholly distinct. The first is the collective one of the expedition as a whole from June 17, 1527, when Pánfilo de Narváez sailed from San Lúcar to cross the Atlantic until the final breakup of his expedition and his disappearance and death off the coast of modern Texas in November, 1528. The second begins when, on November 8, 1528, some of his men were thrown ashore on Galveston Island and disappeared for nearly eight years, after which time four persons, eventually identified as Alvar Núñez Cabeza de Vaca, with three companions, one black and two white, reached western Mexico and declared themselves to be the survivors of the expedition.

The collective recollections of these men form the basis of most of what we know about both stages: the hopeless attempt to form a colony on or near the Gulf Coast; the dispersal and loss of the expedition; and also the slavery and ultimate westward wandering of the little group of sur-

vivors. The three white men involved in this extraordinary episode were required to tell in Mexico and in Spain, 1536–1537, what they recollected of their experiences. This collective report was partly preserved for us by Oviedo (236), but the full story, with its personal nuances and vivid detail, was the work of Alvar Núñez Cabeza de Vaca alone, and it is from his recollections in his Relación, *published in 1542, that most of our information on both stages of the expedition is to be gathered. The* Relation *is a work of history blended by imagination and, no doubt, at times distorted memory, but it is a remarkable record, which stands out from all others in its period, a record of exploration, of human endurance, and of man's adaptability to a variety of wholly unexpected circumstances.*

Sources: Alvar Núñez Cabeza de Vaca published La relación que dio Alvar Núñez Cabeza de Vaca *(Zamora, Augustín de Paz and Juan Picardo for Juan Pedro Musetti) in 1542. It was incorporated in his* Commentarios *(Valladolid, 1555), which contained an account of his South American activities as well. The* Relación *found its way to Italy and appeared in Italian in G. B. Ramusio,* Navigationi et viaggi, *III (Venice, 1556), though Samuel Purchas's abbreviated version in his* Pilgrimes, *IV (London, 1625) was its first appearance in English. T. Buckingham Smith translated it from the 1555 edition as* The Journey of Cabeza de Vaca *(Washington, 1851). His version forms the foundation for the account in F. W. Hodge and T. H. Lewis,* Spanish Explorers in the Southern United States, 1528–1543 *(New York, 1906), pp. 12–126, from which the version given here is taken.The new edition,* The Narrative of Alvar Núñez Cabeza de Vaca, *with an introduction by J. F. Bannon (Barre, Mass., 1972) is an improved text. The standard Spanish edition of the* Relación *is by Manuel Serrano y Sanz, 2 vols. (Madrid, 1906).*

Relation that Alvar Nuñez Cabeça de Vaca gave of what befell the armament in the Indies whither Pánfilo de Narváez went for Governor from the year 1527 to the year 1536 [1537] when with three comrades he returned and came to Sevilla.

Proem

Sacred Caesarian Catholic Majesty:

Among the many who have held sway, I think no prince can be found whose service has been attended with the ardor and emulation shown for that of your Highness at this time. The inducement is evident and powerful: men do not pursue together the same career without motive, and strangers are observed to strive with those who are equally impelled by religion and loyalty.

Although ambition and love of action are common to all, as to the advantages that each may gain, there are great inequalities of fortune, the result not of conduct, but only accident, nor caused by the fault of any one, but coming in the providence of God and solely by His will. Hence to one arises deeds more signal than he thought to achieve; to another the opposite in every way occurs, so that he can show no higher proof of purpose than his effort, and at times even this is so concealed that it cannot of itself appear.

As for me, I can say in undertaking the march I made on the main by the royal authority, I firmly trusted that my conduct and services would be as evident and distinguished as were those of my ancestors and that I should not have to speak in order to be reckoned among those who for dili-

gence and fidelity in affairs your Majesty honors. Yet, as neither my counsel nor my constancy availed to gain aught for which we set out, agreeably to your interests, for our sins, no one of the many armaments that have gone into those parts has been permitted to find itself in straits great like ours, or come to an end alike forlorn and fatal. To me, one only duty remains, to present a relation of what was seen and heard in the ten years I wandered lost and in privation through many and remote lands. Not merely a statement of positions and distances, animals and vegetation, but of the diverse customs of the many and very barbarous people with whom I talked and dwelt, as well as all other matters I could hear of and discern, that in some way I may avail your Highness. My hope of going out from among those nations was always small, still my care and diligence were none the less to keep in particular remembrance everything, that if at any time God our Lord should will to bring me where I now am, it might testify to my exertion in the royal behalf.

As the narrative is in my opinion of no trivial value to those who in your name go to subdue those countries and bring them to a knowledge of the true faith and true Lord, and under the imperial dominion, I have written this with much exactness; and although in it may be read things very novel and for some persons difficult to believe, nevertheless they may without hesitation credit me as strictly faithful. Better than to exaggerate, I have lessened in all things, and it is sufficient to say the relation is offered to your Majesty for truth. I beg it may be received in the name of homage, since it is the most that one could bring who returned thence naked.

1.

In which is told when the Armada sailed, and of the officers and persons who went in it.

On the seventeenth day of June, in the year fifteen hundred and twenty-seven, the Governor Pánphilo de Narváez left the port of San Lúcar de Barrameda, authorized and commanded by your Majesty to conquer and govern the provinces of the main, extending from the River Palmas to the cape of Florida. The fleet he took was five ships, in which went six hundred men, a few more or less; the officers (for we shall have to speak of them), were these, with their rank: Cabeça de

Vaca, treasurer and high-sheriff; Alonso Enrriquez, comptroller; Alonso de Solis, distributor to your Majesty and assessor; Juan Xuarez, a friar of Saint Francis, commissary, and four more friars of the same order.

We arrived at the island of Santo Domingo, where we tarried near forty-five days, engaged in procuring for ourselves some necessary material, particularly horses. Here we lost from our fleet more than one hundred and forty men, who wished to remain, seduced by the partidos, and advantages held out to them by the people of that country.

We sailed from the island and arrived at Santiago, a port of Cuba, where, during some days that we remained, the Governor supplied himself further with men, also with arms and horses. It happened there that a gentleman, Vasco Porcallo of Trinidad, which is also on the island, offered to give the Governor some provisions which he had in the town, a hundred leagues from the port of Santiago. Accordingly the Governor set out with all the fleet for Trinidad; but coming to a port half way, called Cabo de Santa Cruz, he thought it well to wait there, and send a vessel to bring the stores. To this end he ordered that a Captain Pantoja should go for them with his ship, and for greater security, that I should accompany him with another. The Governor remained with four ships, having bought one at the island of Santo Domingo.

We having arrived with the two vessels at the port of Trinidad, Captain Pantoja went with Vasco Porcalle to the town, a league off, to receive the provisions, while I remained at sea with the pilots, who said we ought to go thence with the greatest despatch possible, for it was a very bad port in which many vessels were lost. As what there occurred to us was very remarkable, it appears to me not foreign to the purpose with which I write this, to relate it here.

The next morning began to give signs of bad weather; rain commenced falling, and the sea ran so high, that, although I gave the men permission to go on shore, many of them returned to the ship to avoid exposure to the wet and cold, and because the town was a league away. In this time a canoe came off, bringing me a letter from a resident of the place, asking me to come for the needed provisions that were there; from which request I excused myself, saying that I could not leave the ships. At noon the canoe returned with another letter, in which I was solicited again with much urging, and a horse was brought for me to ride. I gave the same answer as before, that I could not leave the ships; but the pilots and the people entreated me to go, so that I might hasten the provisions as fast as possible, and we might join the fleet where it lay, for they had great fear lest remaining long in this port, the ships should be lost. For these reasons, I determined to go to the town; but first I left orders with the pilots, that if the south wind, which often wrecks vessels there, came on to blow, and they should find themselves in much danger, to put the ships on shore at some place where the men and horses could be saved. I wished to take some of the men with me for company; but they said the weather was too rainy and cold, and the town too far off; that to-morrow, which was Sunday, they would come, with God's help, and hear Mass.

An hour after I left, the sea began to rise very high, and the north wind was so violent that neither the boats dared come to land, nor could the vessels be let drive on shore, because of the head wind, so that the people remained severely laboring against the adverse weather, and under a heavy fall of water all that day and Sunday until dark. At this time, the rain and the tempest had increased to such a degree, there was no less agitation in the town than on the sea; for all the houses and churches fell, and it was necessary in order to move upright, that we should go seven or eight holding on to each other that the wind might not blow us away; and walking in the groves, we had no less fear of the trees than of the houses, as they too were falling and might kill us under them. In this tempest and danger we wandered all night, without finding place or spot where we could remain a half-hour in safety. During the time, particularly from midnight forward, we heard much tumult and great clamor of voices, the sound of timbrels, flutes, and tambourines, as well as other instruments, which lasted until the morning, when the tempest ceased. Nothing so terrible as this storm had been seen in those parts before. I drew up an authenticated account of it, and sent the testimony to your Majesty.

On Monday morning we went down to the harbor, but did not find the ships. The buoys belonging to them were floating on the water; whence we knew the ships were lost, and we walked along the shore to see if any thing could be found of them. As nothing was discovered, we struck into the woods, and, having travelled about a quarter of a league in water, we found the little boat of a ship lodged upon some trees. Ten leagues thence, along the coast, two bodies were found, belonging to my ship, and some lids of boxes; but the persons were so disfigured by beating against the rocks that they could not be recognized. A cloak too was seen, also a coverlet rent in pieces, and nothing more. Sixty persons were lost in the ships, and twenty horses. Those who had gone on shore the day of our arrival, who may have been as many as thirty, were all the survivors of both ships. During some days we were struggling with much hardship and hunger; for the provisions and subsistence were destroyed, and some herds. The country was left in a condition piteous to behold; the trees prostrate, the woods parched, there being neither grass nor leaf.

Thus we lived until the fifth of November, when the Governor arrived with four ships, which had lived through the great storm, having run into a place of safety in good time. The people who came in them, as well as those on shore, were so intimidated by what had passed, that they feared to go on board in the winter, and they besought the Governor to spend it there. Seeing their desire and that it was also the wish of the townspeople, he staid through the season. He gave the ships and people into my charge, that I might go with them to pass the winter at the port of Xagua, twelve leagues thence, where I remained until the twentieth day of February.

2.
The coming of the Governor to the Port of Xagua and with a pilot.

At this time, the Governor arrived with a brigantine bought in Trinidad, and brought with him a pilot named Miruelo, who was employed because he said he knew the position of the River Palmas, and had been there, and was a thorough pilot for all the coast of the North. The Governor had also purchased and left on the shore of Havana another vessel, of which Alvaro de la Cerda remained in charge, with forty infantry and twelve cavalry.

The second day after arrival the Governor set sail with four hundred men and eighty horses, in four ships and a brigantine. The pilot being again on board, put the vessels among the shoals they call Canarreo, and on the day following we struck: thus we were situated fifteen days, the keels of our vessels frequently touching bottom. At the end of this time, a tempest from the south threw so much water upon the shoals that we could get off, although not without danger. We left this place and arrived at Guaniguanico, where another storm overtook us, in which we were at one time near being lost. At Cape Corrientes we had still another, which detained us three days. These places being passed, we doubled Cape Sant Anton, and sailed with head winds until we were within twelve leagues of Havana. Standing in the next day to enter the harbor, a wind came from the south which drove us from the land towards the coast of Florida. We came in sight on Tuesday, the twelfth day of April, and sailed along the coast. On Holy Thursday we anchored near the shore in the mouth of a bay at the head of which we saw some houses or habitations of Indians.

3.
Our arrival in Florida.

On the same day the comptroller, Alonzo Enrriquez, landed on an island in the bay. He called to the Indians, who came and remained with him some time; and in barter gave him fish and several pieces of venison. The day following, which was Good Friday, the governor debarked with as many of the people as the boats he brought could contain. When we came to the *buhíos*, or houses that we had seen, we found them vacant and abandoned, the inhabitants having fled at night in their canoes. One of the buhíos was very large; it could hold more than three hundred persons. The others were smaller. We found a tinklet of gold among some fish nets.

The next day the Governor raised ensigns for your Majesty, and took possession of the country in your royal name. He made known his authority, and was obeyed as governor, as your Majesty had commanded. At the same time we laid our commissions before him, and he acknowledged them according to their tenor. Then he ordered that the rest of the people and the horses should land. Of the beasts there were only forty-two; by reason of the great storms and the length of time passed at sea, the rest were dead. These few remaining were so lean and fatigued that for the time we could have little service from them. The following day the Indians of the town came and spoke to us; but as we had no interpreter we could not understand what they meant. They made many signs and menaces, and appeared to say we must go away from the country. With this they left us and went off, offering no interruption.

4.
Our entrance into the country.

The day following, the Governor resolved to make an incursion to explore the land, and see what it might contain. With him went the commissary, the assessor, and myself, with forty men, among them six cavalry, of which we could make little use. We took our way towards the north, until the hour of vespers, when we arrived at a very large bay that appeared to stretch far inland. We remained there that night, and the next day we returned to the place where were our ships and people. The Governor ordered that the brigantine should sail along the coast of Florida and search for the harbor that Miruelo, the pilot, said he knew (though as yet he had failed to find it, and could not tell in what place we were, or where was the port), and that if it were not found, she should steer for Havana and seek the ship of which Alvaro de la Cerda was in command, and, taking provisions, together, they should come to look for us.

After the brigantine left, the same party, with some persons more, returned to enter the land. We kept along the shores of the bay we had found, and, having gone four leagues, we captured four Indians. We showed them maize, to see if they had knowledge of it, for up to that time we had seen no indication of any. They said they could take us where there was some; so they brought us to their town near by, at the head of the bay, and showed us a little corn not yet fit for gathering.

There we saw many cases, such as are used to contain the merchandise of Castile, in each of them a dead man, and the bodies were covered with painted deer-skins. This appeared to the commissary to be a kind of idolatry, and he burned the cases with the bodies. We also found pieces of linen and of woollen cloth, and bunches of feathers which appeared like those of New Spain. There were likewise traces of gold. Having by signs asked the Indians whence these things came, they motioned to us that very far from

there, was a province called Apalachen, where was much gold, and so the same abundance in Palachen of everything that we at all cared for.

Taking these Indians for guides, we departed, and travelling ten or twelve leagues we came to a town of fifteen houses. Here a large piece of ground was cultivated in maize then ripe, and we likewise found some already dry. After staying there two days, we returned to where the comptroller tarried with the men and ships, and related to him and the pilots what we had seen, and the information the natives had given.

The next day, the first of May, the Governor called aside the commissary, the comptroller, the assessor, myself, a sailor named Bartolomé Fernandez, and a notary, Hieronymo Alaniz. Being together he said that he desired to penetrate the interior, and that the ships ought to go along the coast until they should come to the port which the pilots believed was very near on the way to the River Palmas. He asked us for our views.

I said it appeared to me that under no circumstances ought we to leave the vessels until they were in a secure and peopled harbor; that he should observe the pilots were not confident, and did not agree in any particular, neither did they know where we were; that, more than this, the horses were in no condition to serve us in such exigencies as might occur. Above all, that we were going without being able to communicate with the Indians by use of speech and without an interpreter, and we could but poorly understand ourselves with them, or learn what we desired to know of the land; that we were about entering a country of which we had no account, and had no knowledge of its character, of what there was in it, or by what people inhabited, neither did we know in what part of it we were; and besides all this, we had not food to sustain us in wandering we knew not whither; that with regard to the stores in the ships, rations could not be given to each man for such a journey, more than a pound of biscuit and another of bacon; that my opinion was, we should embark and seek a harbor and a soil better than this to occupy, since what we had seen of it was desert and poor, such as had never before been discovered in those parts.

To the commissary every thing appeared otherwise. He thought we ought not to embark; but that, always keeping the coast, we should go in search of the harbor, which the pilots stated was only ten or fifteen leagues from there, on the way to Pánuco; and that it was not possible, marching ever by the shore, we should fail to come upon it, because they said it stretched up into the land a dozen leagues; that whichever might first find it should wait for the other; that to embark would be to brave the Almighty after so many adversities encountered since leaving Spain, so many storms, and so great losses of men and ships sustained before reaching there; that for these reasons we should march along the coast until we reached the harbor, and those in the ships should take a like direction until they arrived at the same place.

This plan seemed the best to adopt, to the rest who were present, except the notary, who said that when the ships should be abandoned they ought to be in a known, safe haven, a place with inhabitants; that this done the Governor might advance inland and do what might seem to him proper.

The Governor followed his own judgment and the counsel of others. Seeing his determination, I required him in behalf of your Majesty, not to quit the ships before putting them in port and making them secure; and accordingly I asked a certificate of this under the hand of the notary. The Governor responded that he did but abide by the judgment of the commissary, and of the majority of the officers, and that I had no right to make these requirements of him. He then asked the notary to give him a certificate, that inasmuch as there was no subsistence in that country for the maintenance of a colony, nor haven for the ships, he broke up the settlement he had placed there, taking its inhabitants in quest of a port and land that should be better. He then ordered the people who were to go with him to be mustered, that they might be victualled with what was needed for the journey. After they had been provided for, he said to me, in the hearing of those present, that since I so much discouraged and feared entering the land, I should sail in charge of the ships and people in them, and form a settlement, should I arrive at the port before him; but from this proposal I excused myself.

After we had separated, the same evening, having said that it did not appear to him that he could entrust the command to any one else, he sent to me to say that he begged I would take it; but finding, notwithstanding he so greatly importuned me, that I still refused, he asked me the cause of my reluctance. I answered that I rejected the responsibility, as I felt certain and knew that he was never more to find the ships, nor the ships him, which might be foreseen in the slender outfit we had for entering the country; that I desired rather to expose myself to the danger which he and the others adventured, and to pass with them what he and they might go through, than to take charge of the ships and give occasion for it to be said I had opposed the invasion and remained behind from timidity, and thus my courage be called in question. I chose rather to risk my life than put my honor in such position. Seeing that what he said to me availed nothing, he begged many persons to reason with me on the subject and entreat me. I answered them in the same way I had him; so he appointed for his lieutenant of the ships an alcalde he had brought with him, whose name was Caravallo.

5.
The Governor leaves the ships.

On Saturday, first of May, the date of this occurrence, the Governor ordered to each man going with him, two pounds of biscuit and half a pound of bacon; and thus victualled we took up our march into the country. The whole number of men was three hundred: among them went the commissary, Friar Juan Xuarez, and another friar, Juan de Palos, three clergymen and the officers. We of the mounted men consisted of forty. We travelled on the allowance we had received fifteen days, without finding any other thing to eat than palmitos, which are like those of Andalusia. In all that time we saw not an Indian, and found neither village nor house. Finally we came to a river, which we passed with great difficulty, by swimming and on rafts. It detained us a day to cross because of the very strong current. Arrived on the other side, there appeared as many as two hundred natives, more or less. The Governor met them, and conversing by signs, they so insulted us with their gestures, that we were forced to break with them. We seized upon five or six, and they took us to their houses half a league off. Near by we found a large quantity of maize in a fit state to be gathered. We gave infinite thanks to our Lord for having succored us in this great extremity, for we were yet young in trials, and besides the weariness in which we came, we were exhausted from hunger.

On the third day after our arrival, the comptroller, the assessor, the commissary and I met, and together besought the Governor to send to look for the sea, that if possible we might find a port, as the Indians stated there was one not a very great way off. He said that we should cease to speak of the sea, for it was remote; but as I chiefly importuned him, he told me to go and look for it, and seek a harbor, to take forty men and to travel on foot. So the next day I left with Captain Alonzo de Castello and forty men of his company. We marched until noon, when we arrived at some sea sands that appeared to lie a good ways inland. Along this sand we walked for a league and a half, with the water half way up the leg, treading on oysters, which cut our feet badly and made us much trouble, until we reached the river we had before crossed, emptying into this bay. As we could not cross it by reason of our slim outfit for such purpose, we returned to camp and reported what we had discovered. To find out if there was a port and examine the outlet well, it was necessary to repass the river at the place where we had first gone over; so the next day the Governor ordered a captain, Valençuela by name, with sixty men and six cavalry, to cross, and following the river down to the sea, ascertain if there was a harbor. He returned after an absence of two days, and said he had explored the bay, that it was not deeper any where than to the knee, and that he found no harbor. He had seen five or six canoes of Indians passing from one shore to the other, wearing many plumes.

With this information, we left the next day, going ever in quest of Apalache, the country of which the Indians told us, having for our guides those we had taken. We travelled without seeing any natives who would venture to await our coming up with them until the seventeenth day of June, when a chief approached, borne on the back of another Indian, and covered with a painted deer-skin. A great many people attended him, some walking in advance, playing on flutes of reed. In this manner he came to where the Governor stood, and spent an hour with him. By signs we gave him to understand that we were going to Apalachen, and it appeared to us by those he made that he was an enemy to the people of Apalachen, and would go to assist us against them. We gave him beads and hawk-bells, with other articles of barter; and he having presented the Governor with the skin he wore, went back, when we followed in the road he took.

That night we came to a wide and deep river with a very rapid current. As we would not venture to cross on rafts, we made a canoe for the purpose, and spent a day in getting over. Had the Indians desired to oppose us, they could well have disputed our passage; for even with their help we had great difficulty in making it. One of the mounted men, Juan Velazquez by name, a native of Cuellar, impatient of detention, entered the river, when the violence of the current casting him from his horse, he grasped the reins of his bridle, and both were drowned. The people of that chief, whose name was Dulchanchellin, found the body of the beast; and having told us about where in the stream below we should find the corpse, it was sought for. This death caused us much regret, for until now not a man had been lost. The horse afforded supper to many that night.

Leaving that spot, the next day we arrived at the town of the chief, where he sent us maize. During the night one of our men was shot at in a place where we got water, but it pleased God that he should not be hit. The next day we departed, not one of the natives making his appearance, as all had fled. While going on our way a number came in sight, prepared for battle; and though we called to them, they would not return nor await our arrival, but retired following us on the road. The Governor left some cavalry in ambush, which sallying as the natives were about to pass, seized three or four, who thenceforth served as guides. They conducted us through a country very difficult to travel and wonderful to look upon. In it are vast forests, the trees being astonishingly high. So many were fallen on the ground as to obstruct our way in such a manner that we could not advance without much going about and a considerable increase of toil. Many of the standing trees were riven from top to bottom by bolts of lightning which fall in that country of frequent storms and tempests.

We labored on through these impediments until the day after Saint John's, when we came in view of Apalachen, without the inhabitants being aware of our approach. We gave many thanks to God, at seeing ourselves so near, believing true what had been told us of the land, and that there would be an end to our great hardships, caused as much by the length and badness of the way as by our excessive hunger; for although we sometimes found maize, we oftener travelled seven and eight leagues without seeing any; and besides this and the great fatigue, many had galled shoulders from carrying armor on the back; and even more than these we endured. Yet, having come to the place desired, and where we had been informed were much food and gold, it appeared to us that we had already recovered in part from our sufferings and fatigue.

6.
Our arrival at Apalache.

When we came in view of Apalachen, the Governor ordered that I should take nine cavalry with fifty infantry and enter the town. Accordingly the assessor and I assailed it; and having got in, we found only women and boys there, the men being absent; however these returned to its support, after a little time, while we were walking about, and began discharging arrows at us. They killed the horse of the assessor, and at last taking to flight, they left us.

We found a large quantity of maize fit for plucking, and much dry that was housed; also many deer-skins, and among them some mantelets of thread, small and poor, with which the women partially cover their persons. There were numerous mortars for cracking maize. The town consisted of forty small houses, made low, and set up in sheltered places because of the frequent storms. The material was thatch. They were surrounded by very dense woods, large groves and many bodies of fresh water, in which so many and so large trees are fallen, that they form obstructions rendering travel difficult and dangerous.

7.
The character of the country.

The country where we came on shore to this town and region of Apalachen is for the most part level, the ground of sand and stiff earth. Throughout are immense trees and open woods, in which are walnut, laurel, and another tree called liquid-amber, cedars, savins, evergreen oaks, pines, red-oaks, and palmitos like those of Spain. There are many lakes, great and small, over every part of it; some troublesome of fording, on account of depth and the great number of trees lying throughout them. Their beds are sand. The lakes in the country of Apalachen are much larger than those we found before coming here.

In this province are many maize fields; and the houses are scattered as are those of the Gelves. There are deer of three kinds, rabbits, hares, bears, lions, and other wild beasts. Among them we saw an animal with a pocket on its belly, in which it carries its young until they know how to seek food, and if it happen that they should be out feeding and any one come near, the mother will not run until she has gathered them in together. The country is very cold. It has fine pastures for herds. Birds are of various kinds. Geese in great numbers. Ducks, mallards, royal-ducks, fly-catchers, night-herons and partridges abound. We saw many falcons, gerfalcons, sparrow-hawks, merlins, and numerous other fowl.

Two hours after our arrival at Apalachen, the Indians who had fled from there came in peace to us, asking for their women and children, whom we released; but the detention of a cacique by the Governor produced great excitement, in consequence of which they returned for battle early the next day, and attacked us with such promptness and alacrity that they succeeded in setting fire to the houses in which we were. As we sallied they fled to the lakes near by, because of which and the large maize fields we could do them no injury, save in the single instance of one Indian, whom we killed. The day following, others came against us from a town on the opposite side of the lake, and attacked us as the first had done, escaping in the same way, except one who was also slain.

We were in the town twenty-five days, in which time we made three incursions, and found the country very thinly peopled and difficult to travel for the bad passages, the woods and lakes. We inquired of the cacique we kept and the natives we brought with us, who were the neighbors and enemies of these Indians, as to the nature of the country, the character and condition of the inhabitants, of the food and all other matters concerning it. Each answered apart from the rest, that the largest town in all that region was Apalachen; the people beyond were less numerous and poorer, the land little occupied, and the inhabitants much scattered; that thenceforward were great lakes, dense forests, immense deserts and solitudes. We then asked touching the region towards the south, as to the towns and subsistence in it. They said that in keeping such a direction, journeying nine days, there was a town called Aute, the inhabitants whereof had much maize, beans, and pumpkins, and being near the sea they had fish, and that those people were their friends.

In view of the poverty of the land, the unfavorable accounts of the population and of everything else we heard, the Indians making continual war upon us, wounding our people and horses at the places where they went to drink, shooting from the lakes with such safety to themselves that we could not retaliate, killing a lord of Tescuco, named Don Pedro, whom the commissary brought with him, we determined to leave that place and go in quest of the sea, and the town of Aute of which we were told.

At the termination of the twenty-five days after our arrival we departed, and on the first day got through those lakes and passages without seeing any one, and on the second day we came to a lake difficult of crossing, the water reaching to the paps, and in it were numerous logs. On reaching the middle of it we were attacked by many Indians from behind trees, who thus covered themselves that we might not get sight of them, and others were on the fallen timbers. They drove their arrows with such effect that they wounded many men and horses, and before we got through the lake they took our guide. They now followed, endeavoring to contest the passage; but our coming out afforded no relief, nor gave us any better position; for when we wished to fight them they retired immediately into the lake, whence they continued to wound our men and beasts. The Governor, seeing this, commanded the cavalry to dismount and charge the Indians on foot. Accordingly the comptroller alighting with the rest, attacked them, when they all turned and ran into the lake at hand, and thus the passage was gained.

Some of our men were wounded in this conflict, for whom the good armor they wore did not avail. There were those this day who swore that they had seen two red oaks, each the thickness of the lower part of the leg, pierced through from side to side by arrows; and this is not so much to be wondered at, considering the power and skill with

which the Indians are able to project them. I myself saw an arrow that had entered the butt of an elm to the depth of a span.

The Indians we had so far seen in Florida are all archers. They go naked, are large of body, and appear at a distance like giants. They are of admirable proportions, very spare and of great activity and strength. The bows they use are as thick as the arm, of eleven or twelve palms in length, which they will discharge at two hundred paces with so great precision that they miss nothing.

Having got through this passage, at the end of a league we arrived at another of the same character, but worse, as it was longer, being half a league in extent. This we crossed freely, without interruption from the Indians, who, as they had spent on the former occasion their store of arrows, had nought with which they dared venture to engage us. Going through a similar passage the next day, I discovered the trail of persons ahead, of which I gave notice to the Governor, who was in the rear-guard, so that though the Indians came upon us, as we were prepared they did no harm. After emerging upon the plain they followed us, and we went back on them in two directions. Two we killed, and they wounded me and two or three others. Coming to woods we could do them no more injury, nor make them further trouble.

In this manner we travelled eight days. After that occurrence we were not again beset until within a league of the place to which I have said we were going. There, while on our way, the Indians came about us without our suspicion, and fell upon the rear-guard. A hidalgo, named Avellaneda, hearing the cries of his serving boy, went back to give assistance, when he was struck by an arrow near the edge of his cuirass; and so severe was the wound, the shaft having passed almost entirely through his neck, that he presently died. The corpse was carried to Aute, where we arrived at the end of nine days travel from Apalache. We found all the inhabitants gone and the houses burned. Maize, beans, and pumpkins were in great plenty, all beginning to be fit for gathering. Having rested two days, the Governor begged me to go and look for the sea, as the Indians said it was near; and we had before discovered it, while on the way, from a very large stream, to which we had given the name of River of the Magdalena.

Accordingly, I set out the next day after, in

company with the commissary, Captain Castillo, Andrés Dorantes, seven more on horseback, and fifty on foot. We travelled until the hour of vespers, when we arrived at a road or entrance of the sea. Oysters were abundant, over which the men rejoiced, and we gave thanks to God that he had brought us there. The following morning I sent twenty men to explore the coast and ascertain its direction. They returned the night after, reporting that those creeks and bays were large, and lay so far inland as made it difficult to examine them agreeably to our desires, and that the sea shore was very distant.

These tidings obtained, seeing our slender means, and condition for exploring the coast, I went back to the Governor. On our arrival we found him and many others sick. The Indians had assaulted them the night before, and because of the malady that had come upon them, they had been pushed to extremity. One of the horses had been killed. I gave a report of what I had done, and of the embarrassing nature of the country. We remained there that day.

8.

We go from Aute.

The next morning we left Aute, and travelled all day before coming to the place I had visited. The journey was extremely arduous. There were not horses enough to carry the sick, who went on increasing in numbers day by day, and we knew of no cure. It was piteous and painful to witness our perplexity and distress. We saw on our arrival how small were the means for advancing farther. There was not anywhere to go; and if there had been, the people were unable to move forward, the greater part being ill, and those were few who could be on duty. I cease here to relate more of this, because any one may suppose what would occur in a country so remote and malign, so destitute of all resource, whereby either to live in it or go out of it; but most certain assistance is in God, our Lord, on whom we never failed to place reliance. One thing occurred, more afflicting to us than all the rest, which was, that of the persons mounted, the greater part commenced secretly to plot, hoping to secure a better fate for themselves by abandoning the Governor and the sick, who were in a state of weakness and prostration. But, as among them were many hidalgos and persons of gentle condition, they would not permit this to

go on, without informing the Governor and the officers of your Majesty; and as we showed them the deformity of their purpose, and placed before them the moment when they should desert their captain, and those who were ill and feeble, and above all the disobedience to the orders of your Majesty, they determined to remain, and that whatever might happen to one should be the lot of all, without any forsaking the rest.

After the accomplishment of this, the Governor called them all to him, and of each apart he asked advice as to what he should do to get out of a country so miserable, and seek that assistance elsewhere which could not here be found, a third part of the people being very sick, and the number increasing every hour; for we regarded it as certain that we should all become so, and could pass out of it only through death, which from its coming in such a place was to us all the more terrible. These, with many other embarrassments being considered, and entertaining many plans, we coincided in one great project extremely difficult to put in operation, and that was to build vessels in which we might go away. This appeared impossible to every one; we knew not how to construct, nor were there tools, nor iron, nor forge, nor tow, nor resin, nor rigging; finally, no one thing of so many that are necessary, nor any man who had a knowledge of their manufacture; and, above all, there was nothing to eat, while building, for those who should labor. Reflecting on all this, we agreed to think of the subject with more deliberation, and the conversation dropped from that day, each going his way, commending our course to God, our Lord, that he would direct it as should best serve Him.

The next day it was His will that one of the company should come saying that he could make some pipes out of wood, which with deer-skins might be made into bellows; and, as we lived in a time when anything that had the semblance of relief appeared well, we told him to set himself to work. We assented to the making of nails, saws, axes, and other tools of which there was such need, from the stirrups, spurs, crossbows, and the other things of iron there were; and we laid out for support, while the work was going on, that we would make four entries into Aute, with all the horses and men that were able to go, and that on every third day a horse should be killed to be divided among those who labored in the work of the boats and the sick. The incursions were made with the people and horses that were available, and in them were brought back as many as four hundred fanegas of maize; but these were not got without quarrels and contentions with the Indians. We caused many palmitos to be collected for the woof or covering, twisting and preparing it for use in the place of tow for the boats.

We commenced to build on the fourth, with the only carpenter in the company, and we proceeded with so great diligence that on the twentieth day of September five boats were finished, twenty-two cubits in length, each caulked with the fibre of the palmito. We pitched them with a certain resin, made from pine trees by a Greek, named Don Theodoro; from the same husk of the palmito, and from the tails and manes of the horses we made ropes and rigging, from our shirts, sails, and from the savins growing there we made oars that appeared to us requisite. Such was the country into which our sins had cast us, that only by very great search could we find stone for ballast and anchors, since in it all we had not seen one. We flayed the horses, taking the skin from their legs entire, and tanning them to make bottles wherein to carry water.

During this time some went gathering shell-fish in the coves and creeks of the sea, at which employment the Indians twice attacked them and killed ten men in sight of the camp, without our being able to afford succor. We found their corpses traversed from side to side with arrows; and for all some had on good armor, it did not give adequate protection or security against the nice and powerful archery of which I have spoken. According to the declaration of our pilots under oath, from the entrance to which we had given the name Bahía de la Cruz to this place, we had travelled two hundred and eighty leagues or therabout. Over all that region we had not seen a single mountain, and had no information of any whatsoever.

Before we embarked there died more than forty men of disease and hunger, without enumerating those destroyed by the Indians. By the twenty-second of the month of September, the horses had been consumed, one only remaining; and on that day we embarked in the following order: In the boat of the Governor went forty-nine men; in another, which he gave to the comptroller and the commissary, went as many others; the

third, he gave to Captain Alonzo del Castillo and Andrés Dorantes, with forty-eight men; and another he gave to two captains, Tellez and Peñalosa, with forty-seven men. The last was given to the assessor and myself, with forty-nine men. After the provisions and clothes had been taken in, not over a span of the gunwales remained above water; and more than this, the boats were so crowded that we could not move: so much can necessity do, which drove us to hazard our lives in this manner, running into a turbulent sea, not a single one who went having a knowledge of navigation.

9.
We leave the Bay of Horses.

The haven we left bears the name of Bahía de Caballos. We passed waist deep in water through sounds without seeing any sign of the coast, and at the close of the seventh day, we came to an island near the main. My boat went first, and from her we saw Indians approaching in five canoes, which they abandoned and left in our hands, finding that we were coming after them. The other boats passed ahead, and stopped at some houses on the island, where we found many dried mullet and roes, which were a great relief in our distress. After taking these we went on, and two leagues thence, we discovered a strait the island makes with the land, which we named Sant Miguel, for having passed through it on his day. Coming out we went to the coast, where with the canoes I had taken, we somewhat improved the boats, making waist-boards and securing them, so that the sides rose two palms above the water. This done we returned to move along the coast in the direction of the River Palmas, our hunger and thirst continually increasing; for our scant subsistence was getting near the end, the water was out, and the bottles made from the legs of the horses having soon rotted, were useless. Sometimes we entered coves and creeks that lay far in, and found them all shallow and dangerous. Thus we journeyed along them thirty days, finding occasionally Indian fishermen, a poor and miserable lot.

At the end of this time, while the want of water was great, going near the coast at night we heard the approach of a canoe, for which, so soon as it was in sight, we paused; but it would not meet us, and, although we called, it would neither come nor wait for us. As the night was dark, we did not follow, and kept on our way. When the sun rose we saw a small island, and went to it to find water; but our labor was vain, as it had none. Lying there at anchor, a heavy storm came on, that detained us six days, we not daring to go to sea; and as it was now five days since we had drunk, our thirst was so excessive that it put us to the extremity of swallowing salt water, by which some of the men became so crazed that three or four suddenly died. I state this so briefly, because I do not believe there is any necessity for particularly relating the sufferings and toils amidst which we found ourselves; since, considering the place where we were, and the little hope we had of relief, every one may conceive much of what must have passed.

Although the storm had not ceased, as our thirst increased and the water killed us, we resolved to commend ourselves to God our Lord, and adventure the peril of the sea rather than await the end which thirst made certain. Accordingly we went out by the way we had observed the canoe go the night we came. On this day we were ourselves many times overwhelmed by the waves, and in such jeopardy that there was not one who did not suppose his death inevitable. Thanks be to Him, that in the greatest dangers, He was wont to show us his favor; for at sunset doubling a point made by land, we found shelter with much calm.

Many canoes came off with Indians who spoke with us and returned, not being disposed to await our arrival. They were of large stature and well formed: they had no bows and arrows. We followed them to their houses near by, at the edge of the water, and jumped on shore. Before their dwellings were many clay pitchers with water, and a large quantity of cooked fish, which the chief of these territories offered to the Governor and then took him to his house. Their dwellings were made of mats, and so far as we observed, were not movable. On entering the house the cacique gave us fish, and we gave him of the maize we brought, which the people ate in our presence. They asked for more and received it, and the Governor presented the cacique with many trinkets. While in the house with him, at the middle hour of night, the Indians fell suddenly upon us, and on those who were very sick, scattered along the shore. They also beset the house in which the

Governor was, and with a stone struck him in the face. Those of our comrades present seized the cacique; but his people being near liberated him, leaving in our hands a robe of civet-marten.

These skins are the best, I think, that can be found; they have a fragrance that can be equalled by amber and musk alone, and even at a distance is strongly perceptible. We saw there other skins, but none comparable to these.

Those of us around, finding the Governor wounded, put him into his boat; and we caused others of our people to betake themselves likewise to their boats, some fifty remaining to withstand the natives. They attacked us thrice that night, and with so great impetuosity, that on each occasion they made us retire more than a stone's cast. Not one among us escaped injury: I was wounded in the face. They had not many arrows, but had they been further provided, doubtless they would have done us much harm. In the last onset, the Captains Dorantes, Peñalosa, and Tellez put themselves in ambuscade with fifteen men, and fell upon the rear in such manner that the Indians desisted and fled.

The next morning I broke up more than thirty canoes, which were serviceable for fuel in a north wind in which we were kept all day suffering severe cold, without daring to go to sea, because of the rough weather upon it. This having subsided, we again embarked, and navigated three days. As we brought little water and the vessels were few, we were reduced to the last extremity. Following our course, we entered an estuary, and being there we saw Indians approaching in a canoe. We called to them and they came. The Governor, at whose boat they first arrived, asked for water, which they assented to give, asking for something in which they might bring it, when Dorotheo Theodoro, a Greek spoken of before, said that he wished to go with them. The Governor tried to dissuade him, and so did others, but were unable; he was determined to go whatever might betide. Accordingly he went, taking with him a negro, the natives leaving two of their number as hostages. At night the Indians returned with the vessels empty and without the Christians; and when those we held were spoken to by them, they tried to plunge into the sea. Being detained by the men, the Indians in the canoe thereupon fled, leaving us sorrowful and much dejected for our loss.

10.
The assault from the Indians.

The morning having come, many natives arrived in canoes who asked us for the two that had remained in the boat. The Governor replied that he would give up the hostages when they should bring the Christians they had taken. With the Indians had come five or six chiefs, who appeared to us to be the most comely persons, and of more authority and condition than any we had hitherto seen, although not so large as some others of whom we have spoken. They wore the hair loose and very long, and were covered with robes of marten such as we had before taken. Some of the robes were made up after a strange fashion, with wrought ties of lion skin, making a brave show. They entreated us to go with them, and said they would give us the Christians, water, and many other things. They continued to collect about us in canoes, attempting in them to take possession of the mouth of that entrance; in consequence, and because it was hazardous to stay near the land, we went to sea, where they remained by us until about mid-day. As they would not deliver our people, we would not give up theirs; so they began to hurl clubs at us and to throw stones with slings, making threats of shooting arrows, although we had not seen among them all more than three or four bows. While thus engaged, the wind beginning to freshen, they left us and went back.

We sailed that day until the middle of the afternoon, when my boat, which was the first, discovered a point made by the land, and against a cape opposite, passed a broad river. I cast anchor near a little island forming the point, to await the arrival of the other boats. The Governor did not choose to come up, and entered a bay near by in which were a great many islets. We came together there, and took fresh water from the sea, the stream entering it in freshet. To parch some of the maize we brought with us, since we had eaten it raw for two days, we went on an island; but finding no wood we agreed to go to the river beyond the point, one league off. By no effort could we get there, so violent was the current on the way, which drove us out, while we contended and strove to gain the land. The north wind, which came from the shore, began to blow so strongly that it forced us to sea without our being able to overcome it. We sounded half a league out,

and found with thirty fathoms we could not get bottom; but we were unable to satisfy ourselves that the current was not the cause of failure. Toiling in this manner to fetch the land, we navigated three days, and at the end of this time, a little before the sun rose, we saw smoke in several places along the shore. Attempting to reach them, we found ourselves in three fathoms of water, and in the darkness we dared not come to land; for as we had seen so many smokes, some surprise might lie in wait, and the obscurity leave us at a loss how to act. We determined therefore to stop until morning.

When day came, the boats had lost sight of each other. I found myself in thirty fathoms. Keeping my course until the hour of vespers, I observed two boats, and drawing near I found that the first I approached was that of the Governor. He asked me what I thought we should do. I told him we ought to join the boat which went in advance, and by no means to leave her; and, the three being together, we must keep on our way to where God should be pleased to lead. He answered saying that could not be done, because the boat was far to sea and he wished to reach the shore; that if I wished to follow him, I should order the persons of my boat to take the oars and work, as it was only by strength of arm that the land could be gained. He was advised to this course by a captain with him named Pantoja, who said that if he did not fetch land that day, in six days more they would not reach it, and in that time they must inevitably famish. Discovering his will I took my oar, and so did every one his, in my boat, to obey it. We rowed until near sunset; but the Governor having in his boat the healthiest of all the men, we could not by any means hold with or follow her. Seeing this, I asked him to give me a rope from his boat, that I might be enabled to keep up with him; but he answered me that he would do much, if they, as they were, should be able to reach the land that night. I said to him, that since he saw the feeble strength we had to follow him, and do what he ordered, he must tell me how he would that I should act. He answered that it was no longer a time in which one should command another; but that each should do what he thought best to save his own life; that he so intended to act; and saying this, he departed with his boat.

As I could not follow him, I steered to the other boat at sea, which waited for me, and having come up, I found her to be the one commanded by the Captains Peñalosa and Tellez.

Thus we continued in company, eating a daily allowance of half a handful of raw maize, until the end of four days, when we lost sight of each other in a storm; and such was the weather that only by God's favor we did not all go down. Because of winter and its inclemency, the many days we had suffered hunger, and the heavy beating of the waves, the people began next day to despair in such a manner that when the sun sank, all who were in my boat were fallen on another, so near to death that there were few among them in a state of sensibility. Of the whole number at this time not five men were on their feet; and when night came, only the master and myself were left, who could work the boat. Two hours after dark, he said to me that I must take charge of her as he was in such condition he believed he should die that night. So I took the paddle, and going after midnight to see if the master was alive he said to me he was rather better, and would take the charge until day. I declare in that hour I would more willingly have died than seen so many people before me in such condition. After the master took the direction of the boat, I lay down a little while; but without repose, for nothing at that time was farther from me than sleep.

Near the dawn of day, it seemed to me I heard the tumbling of the sea; for as the coast was low, it roared loudly. Surprised at this, I called to the master, who answered me that he believed we were near the land. We sounded and found our- selves in seven fathoms. He advised that we should keep to sea until sunrise; accordingly I took an oar and pulled on the land side, until we were a league distant, when we gave her stern to the sea. Near the shore a wave took us, that knocked the boat out of water the distance of the throw of a crowbar, and from the violence with which she struck, nearly all the people who were in her like dead, were roused to consciousness. Finding themselves near the shore, they began to move on hands and feet, crawling to land into some ravines. There we made fire, parched some of the maize we brought, and found rainwater. From the warmth of the fire the people recovered their faculties, and began somewhat to exert themselves. The day on which we arrived was the sixth of November [1528].

11.
Of what befell Lope de Oviedo with the Indians.

After the people had eaten, I ordered Lope de Oviedo, who had more strength and was stouter than any of the rest, to go to some trees that were near by, and climbing into one of them to look about and try to gain knowledge of the country. He did as I bade, and made out that we were on an island. He saw that the land was pawed up in the manner that ground is wont to be where cattle range, whence it appeared to him that this should be a country of Christians; and thus he reported to us. I ordered him to return and examine much more particularly, and see if there were any roads that were worn, but without going far, because there might be danger.

He went, and coming to a path, took it for the distance of half a league, and found some huts, without tenants, they having gone into the field. He took from these an earthen pot, a little dog, some few mullets, and returned. As it appeared to us he was gone a long time, we sent two men that they should look to see what might have hap- pened. They met him near by, and saw that three Indians with bows and arrows followed and were calling to him, while he, in the same way, was beckoning them on. Thus he arrived where we were, the natives remaining a little way back, seated on the shore. Half an hour after, they were supported by one hundred other Indian bowmen, who if they were not large, our fears made giants of them. They stopped near us with the first three. It were idle to think that any among us could make defence, for it would have been dif- ficult to find six that could rise from the ground. The assessor and I went out and called to them, and they came to us. We endeavored the best we could to encourage them and secure their favor. We gave them beads and hawk-bells, and each of them gave me an arrow, which is a pledge of friendship. They told us by signs that they would return in the morning and bring us something to eat, as at that time they had nothing.

12.
The Indians bring us food.

At sunrise the next day, the time the Indians appointed, they came according to their promise, and brought us a large quantity of fish with certain roots, some a little larger than walnuts, others a trifle smaller, the greater part got from under the water and with much labor. In the evening they returned and brought us more fish and roots. They sent their women and children to look at us, who went back rich with the hawk-bells and beads given them, and they came afterwards on other days, returning as before. Finding that we had provision, fish, roots, water, and other things we asked for, we determined to embark again and pursue our course. Having dug out our boat from the sand in which it was buried, it became necessary that we should strip, and go through great exertion to launch her, we being in such a state that things very much lighter sufficed to make us great labor.

Thus embarked, at the distance of two crossbow shots in the sea we shipped a wave that entirely wet us. As we were naked, and the cold was very great, the oars loosened in our hands, and the next blow the sea struck us, capsized the boat. The assessor and two others held fast to her for preservation, but it happened to be far otherwise; the boat carried them over, and they were drowned under her. As the surf near the shore was very high, a single roll of the sea threw the rest into the waves and half drowned upon the shore of the island, without our losing any more than those the boat took down. The survivors escaped naked as they were born, with the loss of all they had; and although the whole was of little value, at that time it was worth much, as we were then in November, the cold was severe, and our bodies were so emaciated the bones might be counted with little difficulty, having become the perfect figures of death. For myself I can say that from the month of May passsed, I had eaten no other thing than maize, and sometimes I found myself obliged to eat it unparched; for although the beasts were slaughtered while the boats were building, I could never eat their flesh, and I did not eat fish ten times. I state this to avoid giving excuses, and that every one may judge in what condition we were. Besides all these misfortunes, came a north wind upon us, from which we were nearer to death than life. Thanks be to our Lord that, looking among the brands we had used there, we found sparks from which we made great fires. And thus were we asking mercy of Him and pardon for our transgressions, shedding many tears, and each regretting not his own fate alone, but that of his comrades about him.

At sunset, the Indians thinking that we had not gone, came to seek us and bring us food; but when they saw us thus, in a plight so different from what it was before, and so extraordinary, they were alarmed and turned back. I went toward them and called, when they returned much frightened. I gave them to understand by signs that our boat had sunk and three of our number had been drowned. There, before them, they saw two of the departed, and we who remained were near joining them. The Indians, at sight of what had befallen us, and our state of suffering and melancholy destitution, sat down among us, and from the sorrow and pity they felt, they all began to lament so earnestly that they might have been heard at a distance, and continued so doing more than half an hour. It was strange to see these men, wild and untaught, howling like brutes over our misfortunes. It caused in me as in others, an increase of feeling and a livelier sense of our calamity.

The cries having ceased, I talked with the Christians, and said that if it appeared well to them, I would beg these Indians to take us to their houses. Some, who had been in New Spain, replied that we ought not to think of it; for if they should do so they would sacrifice us to their idols. But seeing no better course, and that any other led to a nearer and more certain death, I disregarded what was said, and besought the Indians to take us to their dwellings. They signified that it would give them delight, and that we should tarry a little, that they might do what we asked. Presently thirty men loaded themselves with wood and started for their houses, which were far off, and we remained with the others until near night, when, holding us up, they carried us with all haste. Because of the extreme coldness of the weather, lest any one should die or fail by the way, they caused four or five very large fires to be placed at intervals, and at each they warmed us; and when they saw that we had regained some heat and strength, they took us to the next so swiftly that they hardly let us touch our feet to the ground. In this manner we went as far as their habitations, where we found that they had made a house for us with many fires in it. An hour after our arrival, they began to dance and hold great rejoicing, which lasted all night, although for us there was no joy, festivity nor sleep, awaiting the hour they should make us victims. In the morning they again gave us fish and roots, showing us such hospitality that we were reassured, and lost somewhat the fear of sacrifice.

13.
We hear of other Christians.

This day I saw a native with an article of traffic I knew was not one we had bestowed; and asking whence it came, I was told by signs that it had been given by men like ourselves who were behind. Hearing this I sent two Indians, and with them two Christians to be shown those persons. They met near by, as the men were coming to look after us; for the Indians of the place where they were, gave them information concerning us. They were Captains Andrés Dorantes and Alonzo del Castillo, with all the persons of their boat. Having come up they were surprised at seeing us in the condition we were, and very much pained at having nothing to give us, as they had brought no other clothes than what they had on.

Thus together again, they related that on the fifth day of that month, their boat had capsized a league and a half from there, and they escaped without losing any thing. We all agreed to refit their [our] boat, that those of us might go in her who had vigor sufficient and disposition to do so, and the rest should remain until they became well enough to go, as they best might, along the coast until God our Lord should be pleased to conduct us alike to a land of Christians. Directly as we arranged this, we set ourselves to work. Before we threw the boat out into the water, Tavera, a gentleman of our company, died; and the boat, which we thought to use, came to its end, sinking from unfitness to float.

As we were in the condition I have mentioned, the greater number of us naked, and the weather boisterous for travel, and to cross rivers and bays by swimming, and we being entirely without provisions or the means of carrying any, we yielded obedience to what necessity required, to pass the winter in the place where we were. We also agreed that four men of the most robust should go on to Panunco, which we believed to be near, and if, by Divine favor, they should reach there, they could give information of our remaining on that island, and of our sorrows and destitution. These men were excellent swimmers. One of them was Alvaro Fernandez, a Portuguese sailor and carpenter, the second was named Mendez, the third Figueroa, who was a native of Toledo, and the fourth Astudillo, a native of Çafra. They took with them an Indian of the island of Auia.

14.
The departure of four Christians.

The four Christians being gone, after a few days such cold and tempestuous weather succeeded that the Indians could not pull up roots, the cane weirs in which they took fish no longer yielded any thing, and the houses being very open, our people began to die. Five Christians, of a mess [quartered] on the coast, came to such extremity that they ate their dead; the body of the last one only was found unconsumed. Their names were Sierra, Diego Lopez, Corral, Palacios and Gonçalo Ruiz. This produced great commotion among the Indians giving rise to so much censure that had they known it in season to have done so, doubtless they would have destroyed any survivor, and we should have found ourselves in the utmost perplexity. Finally, of eighty men who arrived in the two instances, fifteen only remained alive.

After this, the natives were visited by a disease of the bowels, of which half their number died. They conceived that we had destroyed them, and believing it firmly, they concerted among themselves to dispatch those of us who survived. When they were about to execute their purpose, an Indian who had charge of me, told them not to believe we were the cause of those deaths, since if we had such power we should also have averted the fatality from so many of our people, whom they had seen die without our being able to minister relief, already very few of us remaining, and none doing hurt or wrong, and that it would be better to leave us unharmed. God our Lord willed that the others should heed this opinion and counsel, and be hindered in their design.

To this island we gave the name Malhado. The people we found there are large and well formed; they have no other arms than bows and arrows, in the use of which they are very dexterous. The men have one of their nipples bored from side to side, and some have both, wearing a cane in each, the length of two palms and a half, and the thickness of two fingers. They have the under lip also bored, and wear in it a piece of cane the breadth of half a finger. Their women are accustomed to great toil. The stay they make on the island is from October to the end of February. Their subsistence then is the root I have spoken of, got from under the water in November and December. They have weirs of cane and take fish only in this season; afterwards they live on the roots. At the end of February, they go into other parts to seek food; for then the root is beginning to grow and is not food.

Those people love their offspring the most of any in the world, and treat them with the greatest mildness. When it occurs that a son dies, the parents and kindred weep as does everybody; the wailing continuing for him a whole year. They begin before dawn every day, the parents first and after them the whole town. They do the same at noon and at sunset. After a year of mourning has passed, the rites of the dead are performed; then they wash and purify themselves from the stain of smoke. They lament all the deceased in this manner, except the aged, for whom they show no regret, as they say that their season has passed, they having no enjoyment, and that living they would occupy the earth and take aliment from the young. Their custom is to bury the dead, unless it be those among them who have been physicians. These they burn. While the fire kindles they are all dancing and making high festivity, until the bones become powder. After the lapse of a year the funeral honors are celebrated, every one taking part in them, when that dust is presented in water for the relatives to drink.

Every man has an acknowledged wife. The physicians are allowed more freedom: they may have two or three wives, among whom exist the greatest friendship and harmony. From the time a daughter marries, all that he who takes her to wife kills in hunting or catches in fishing, the woman brings to the house of her father, without daring to eat or take any part of it, and thence victuals are taken to the husband. From that time neither her father nor mother enters his house, nor can he enter theirs, nor the houses of their children; and if by chance they are in the direction of meeting, they turn aside, and pass the distance of a crossbow shot from each other, carrying the head low the while, the eyes cast on the ground; for they hold it improper to see or to speak to each other. But the woman has liberty to converse and communicate with the parents and relatives of her husband. The custom exists from this island the distance of more than fifty leagues inland.

There is another custom, which is, when a son or brother dies, at the house where the death takes place they do not go after food for three months, but sooner famish, their relatives and neighbors providing what they eat. As in the time we were there a great hunger, because of the keeping of this their custom and observance; for although they who sought after food worked hard, yet from the severity of the season they could get but little; in consequence, the Indians who kept me, left the island, and passed over in canoes to the main, into some bays where are many oysters. For three months in the year they eat nothing besides these, and drink very bad water. There is great want of wood: mosquitos are in great plenty. The houses are of mats, set up on masses of oyster shells, which they sleep upon, and in skins, should they accidentally possess them. In this way we lived until April [1529], when we went to the seashore, where we ate blackberries all the month, during which time the Indians did not omit to observe their *areitos* and festivities.

15.
What befell us among the people of Malhado.

On an island of which I have spoken, they wished to make us physicians without examination or inquiring for diplomas. They cure by blowing upon the sick, and with that breath and the imposing of hands they cast out infirmity. They ordered that we also should do this, and be of use to them in some way. We laughed at what they did, telling them it was folly, that we knew not how to heal. In consequence, they withheld food from us until we should practise what they required. Seeing our persistence, an Indian told me I knew not what I uttered, in saying that what he knew availed nothing; for stones and other matters growing about in the fields have virtue, and that passing a pebble along the stomach would take away pain and restore health, and certainly then we who were extraordinary men must possess power and efficacy over all other things. At last, finding ourselves in great want we were constrained to obey; but without fear lest we should be blamed for any failure or success.

Their custom is, on finding themselves sick to send for a physician, and after he has applied the cure, they give him not only all they have, but seek among their relatives for more to give. The practitioner scarifies over the seat of pain, and then sucks about the wound. The make cauteries with fire, a remedy among them in high repute, which I have tried on myself and found benefit from it. They afterwards blow on the spot, and having finished, the patient considers that he is relieved.

Our method was to bless the sick, breathing upon them, and recite a Pater-noster and an Ave-Maria, praying with all earnestness to God our Lord that he would give health and influence them to make us some good return. In his clemency he willed that all those for whom we supplicated, should tell the others that they were sound and in health, directly after we made the sign of the blessed cross over them. For this the Indians treated us kindly; they deprived themselves of food that they might give to us, and presented us with skins and some trifles.

So protracted was the hunger we there experienced, that many times I was three days without eating. The natives also endured as much; and it appeared to me a thing impossible that life could be so prolonged, although afterwards I found myself in great hunger and necessity, which I shall speak of farther on.

The Indians who had Alonzo del Castillo, Andrés Dorantes, and the others that remained alive, were of a different tongue and ancestry from these, and went to the opposite shore of the main to eat oysters, where they staid until the first day of April, when they returned. The distance is two leagues in the widest part. The island is half a league in breadth and five leagues in length.

The inhabitants of all this region go naked. The women alone have any part of their persons covered, and it is with a wool that grows on trees. The damsels dress themselves in deer-skin. The people are generous to each other of what they possess. They have no chief. All that are of a lineage keep together. They speak two languages; those of one are called Capoques, those of the other, Han. They have a custom when they meet, or from time to time when they visit, of remaining half an hour before they speak, weeping; and, this over, he that is visited first rises and gives the other all he has, which is received, and after a little while he carries it away, and often goes without saying a word. They have other strange customs; but I have told the principal of them, and the most remarkable, that I may pass on and further relate what befell us.

16.
The Christians leave the island of Malhado.

After Dorantes and Castillo returned to the island, they brought together the Christians, who were somewhat separated, and found them in all to be fourteen. As I have said, I was opposite on the main, where my Indians had taken me, and where so great sickness had come upon me, that if anything before had given me hopes of life, this were enough to have entirely bereft me of them.

When the Christians heard of my condition, they gave an Indian the cloak of marten skins we had taken from the cacique, as before related, to pass them over to where I was that they might visit me. Twelve of them crossed; for two were so feeble that their comrades could not venture to bring them. The names of those who came were Alonzo del Castillo, Andrés Dorantes, Diego Dorantes, Valdevieso, Estrada, Tostado, Chaves, Gutierrez, Asturiano a clergyman, Diego de Huelva, Estevanico the black, and Benitez; and when they reached the main land, they found another, who was one of our company, named Francisco de Leon. The thirteen together followed along the coast. So soon as they had come over, my Indians informed me of it, and that Hieronymo de Alvaniz and Lope de Oviedo remained on the island. But sickness prevented me from going with my companions or even seeing them.

I was obliged to remain with the people belonging to the island more than a year, and because of the hard work they put upon me and the harsh treatment, I resolved to flee from them and go to those of Charruco, who inhabit the forests and country of the main, the life I led being insupportable. Besides much other labor, I had to get out roots from below the water, and from among the cane where they grew in the ground. From this employment I had my fingers so worn that did a straw but touch them they would bleed. Many of the canes are broken, so they often tore my flesh, and I had to go in the midst of them with only the clothing on I have mentioned.

Accordingly, I put myself to contriving how I might get over to the other Indians, among whom matters turned somewhat more favorably for me. I set to trafficking, and strove to make my employment profitable in the ways I could best contrive, and by that means I got food and good treatment. The Indians would beg me to go from one quarter to another for things of which they have need; for in consequence of incessant hostilities, they cannot traverse the country, nor make many exchanges. With my merchandise and trade I went into the interior as far as I pleased, and travelled along the coast forty or fifty leagues. The principal wares were cones and other pieces of sea-snail, conchs used for cutting, and fruit like a bean of the highest value among them, which they use as a medicine and employ in their dances and festivities. Among other matters were sea-beads. Such were what I carried into the interior; and in barter I got and brought back skins, ochre with which they rub and color the face, hard canes of which to make arrows, sinews, cement and flint for the heads, and tassels of the hair of deer that by dyeing they make red. This occupation suited me well; for the travel allowed me liberty to go where I wished, I was not obliged to work, and was not a slave. Wherever I went I received fair treatment, and the Indians gave me to eat out of regard to my commodities. My leading object, while journeying in this business, was to find out the way by which I should go forward, and I became well known. The inhabitants were pleased when they saw me, and I had brought them what they wanted; and those who did not know me sought and desired the acquaintance, for my reputation. The hardships that I underwent in this were long to tell, as well of peril and privation as of storms and cold. Oftentimes they overtook me alone and in the wilderness; but I came forth from them all by the great mercy of God our Lord. Because of them I avoided pursuing the business in winter, a season in which the natives themselves retire to their huts and ranches, torpid and incapable of exertion.

I was in this country nearly six years, alone among the Indians, and naked like them. The reason why I remained so long, was that I might take with me the Christian, Lope de Oviedo, from the island; Alaniz, his companion, who had been left with him by Alonzo del Castillo, and by Andrés Dorantes, and the rest, died soon after their departure; and to get the survivor out from there, I went over to the island every year, and entreated him that we should go, in the best way we could contrive, in quest of Christians. He put me off every year, saying in the next coming we would start. At last I got him off, crossing him over the bay, and over four rivers in the coast, as he could not swim. In this way we went on with some Indians, until coming to a bay a league in width, and everywhere deep. From the appearance we supposed it to be that which is called Espiritu Sancto. We met some Indians on the other side of it, coming to visit ours, who told us that beyond them were three men like us, and gave their names. We asked for the others, and were told that they were all dead of cold and hunger; that the Indians farther on, of whom they were, for their diversion had killed Diego Dorantes, Valdevieso, and Diego de Huelva, because they left one house for another; and that other Indians, their neighbors with whom Captain Dorantes now was, had in consequence of a dream, killed Esquivel and Mendez. We asked how the living were situated, and they answered that they were very ill used, the boys and some of the Indian men being very idle, out of cruelty gave them many kicks, cuffs, and blows with sticks; that such was the life they led.

We desired to be informed of the country ahead, and of the subsistence: they said there was nothing to eat, and that it was thin of people, who suffered of cold, having no skins or other things to cover them. They told us also if we wished to see those three Christians, two days from that time the Indians who had them would come to eat walnuts a league from there on the margin of that river; and that we might know what they told us of the ill usage to be true, they slapped my companion and beat him with a stick, and I was not left without my portion. Many times they threw lumps of mud at us, and every day they put their arrows to our hearts, saying that they were inclined to kill us in the way that they had destroyed our friends. Lope Oviedo, my comrade, in fear said that he wished to go back with the women of those who had crossed the bay with us, the men having remained some distance behind. I contended strongly against his returning, and urged my objections; but in no way could I keep him. So he went back, and I remained alone with those savages. They are called Quevenes, and those with whom he returned, Deaguanes.

17.
The coming of Indians with Andrés Dorantes, Castillo, and Estevanico.

Two days after Lope de Oviedo left, the Indians who had Alonzo del Castillo and Andrés Dorantes, came to the place of which we had been told, to eat walnuts. These are gound with a kind of small grain, and this is the subsistence of the people two months in the year without any other thing; but even the nuts they do not have every season, as the tree produces in alternate years. The fruit is the size of that in Galicia; the trees are very large and numerous.

An Indian told me of the arrival of the Christians, and that if I wished to see them I must steal away and flee to the point of a wood to which he directed me, and that as he and others, kindred of his, should pass by there to visit those Indians, they would take me with them to the spot where the Christians were. I determined to attempt this and trust to them, as they spoke a language distinct from that of the others. I did so, and the next day they left, and found me in the place that had been pointed out, and accordingly took me with them.

When I arrived near their abode, Andrés Dorantes came out to scc who it could be, for the Indians had told him that a Christian was coming. His astonishment was great when he saw me, as they had for many a day considered me dead, and the natives had said that I was. We gave many thanks at seeing ourselves together, and this was a day to us of the greatest pleasure we had enjoyed in life. Having come to where Castillo was, they inquired of me where I was going. I told them my purpose was to reach the land of Christians, I being then in search and pursuit of it. Andrés Dorantes said that for a long time he had entreated Castillo and Estevanico to go forward; but that they dared not venture, because they knew not how to swim, and greatly dreaded the rivers and bays they should have to cross, there being many in that country. Thus the Almighty had been pleased to preserve me through many

trials and diseases, conducting me in the end to the fellowship of those who had abandoned me, that I might lead them over the bays and rivers that obstructed our progress. They advised me on no account to let the natives know or have a suspicion of my desire to go on, else they would destroy me; and that for success it would be necessary for me to remain quiet until the end of six months, when comes the season in which these Indians go to another part of the country to eat prickly pears. People would arrive from parts farther on, bringing bows to barter and for exchange, with whom, after making our escape, we should be able to go on their return. Having consented to this course, I remained. The prickly pear is the size of a hen's egg, vermillion and black in color, and of agreeable flavor. The natives live on it three months in the year, having nothing beside.

I was given as a slave to an Indian, with whom was Dorantes. He was blind of one eye, as were also his wife and sons, and likewise another who was with him; so that of a fashion they were all blind. These are called Marians; Castillo was with another neighboring people, called Yguases.

While here the Christians related to me how they had left the island of Malhado, and found the boat in which the comptroller and the friars had sailed, bottom up on the seashore; and that going along crossing the rivers, which are four, very large and of rapid current, their boats were swept away and carried to sea, where four of their number were drowned; that thus they proceeded until they crossed the bay, getting over it with great difficulty, and fifteen leagues thence they came to another. By the time they reached this, they had lost two companions in the sixty leagues they travelled, and those remaining were nearly dead, in all the while having eaten nothing but crabs and rockweed. Arrived at this bay, they found Indians eating mulberries, who, when they saw them, went to a cape opposite. While contriving and seeking for some means to cross the bay, there came over to them an Indian, and a Christian whom they recognized to be Figueroa, one of the four we had sent forward from the island of Malhado. He there recounted how he and his companions had got as far as that place, when two of them and an Indian died of cold and hunger, being exposed in the most inclement of seasons. He and Mendez were taken by the Indians, and while with them his associate fled, going as well as he could in the direction of Pánuco, and the natives pursuing, put him to death.

While living with these Indians, Figueroa learned from them that there was a Christian among the Mariames, who had come over from the opposite side, and he found him among the Quevenes. This was Hernando de Esquivel, a native of Badajoz, who had come in company with the commissary. From him Figueroa learned the end to which the Governor, the comptroller, and the others had come. Esquivel told him that the comptroller and the friars had upset their boat at the confluence of the rivers, and that the boat of the Governor, moving along the coast, came with its people to land. Narváez went in the boat until arriving at that great bay, where he took in the people, and, crossing them to the opposite point, returned for the comptroller, the friars, and the rest. And he related that being disembarked, the Governor had recalled the commission the comptroller held as his lieutenant, assigning the duties to a captain with him named Pantoja: that Narváez stayed the night in his boat, not wishing to come on shore, having a cockswain with him and a page who was unwell, there being no water nor anything to eat on board; that at midnight, the boat having only a stone for anchor, the north wind blowing strongly took her unobserved to sea, and they never knew more of their commander.

The others then went along the coast, and as they were arrested by a wide extent of water, they made rafts with much labor, on which they crossed to the opposite shore. Going on, they arrived at a point of woods on the banks of the water where were Indians, who, as they saw them coming, put their houses into their canoes and went over to the opposite side. The Christians, in consideration of the season, for it was now the month of November, stopped at this wood, where they found water and fuel, some crabs and shell-fish. They began, one by one, to die of cold and hunger; and, more than this, Pantoja, who was Lieutenant-Governor, used them severely, which Soto-Mayor (the brother of Vasco Porcallo, of the island of Cuba), who had come with the armament as camp-master, not being able to bear, had a struggle with him, and, giving him a blow with a club, Pantoja was instantly killed.

Thus did the number go on diminishing. The living dried the flesh of them that died; and the last that died was Soto-Mayor, when Esquivel preserved his flesh, and, feeding on it, sustained existence until the first of March, when an Indian of those that had fled, coming to see if they were alive, took Esquivel with him. While he was in the possession of the native, Figueroa saw him, and learned all that had been related. He besought Esquivel to come with him, that together they might pursue the way to Pánuco; to which Esquivel would not consent, saying that he had understood from the friars that Pánuco had been left behind: so he remained there and Figueroa went to the coast where he was accustomed to live.

18.
The story Figueroa recounted from Esquivel.

This account was all given by Figueroa, according to the relation he received from Esquivel, and from him through the others it came to me; whence may be seen and understood the fate of the armament, and the individual fortunes of the greater part of the people. Figueroa said, moreover, that if the Christians should at any time go in that direction, it were possible they might see Esquivel, for he knew that he had fled from the Indian with whom he was, to the Mariames, who were neighbors. After Figueroa had finished telling the story, he and the Asturian made an attempt to go to other Indians farther on; but as soon as they who had the Christians discovered it, they followed, and beating them severely, stripped the Asturian and shot an arrow through his arm. They finally escaped by flight.

The other Christians remained, and prevailed on the Indians to receive them as slaves. In their service they were abused as slaves never were, nor men in any condition have ever been. Not content with frequently buffeting them, striking them with sticks, and pulling out their beard for amusement, they killed three of the six for only going from one house to another. These were the persons I have named before: Diego Dorantes, Valdivieso, and Diego de Huelva: and the three that remained looked forward to the same fate. Not to endure this life, Andrés Dorantes fled, and passed to the Mariames, the people among whom Esquivel tarried. They told him that having had

Esquivel there, he wished to run away because a woman dreamed that a son of hers would kill him; and that they followed after, and slew him. They showed Dorantes his sword, beads, and book, with other things that had been his.

Thus in obedience to their custom they take life, destroying even their male children on account of dreams. They cast away their daughters at birth, and cause them to be eaten by dogs. The reason of their doing this, as they state, is because all the nations of the country are their foes; and as they have unceasing war with them, if they were to marry away their daughters, they would so greatly multiply their enemies that they must be overcome and made slaves; thus they prefer to destroy all, rather than that from them should come a single enemy. We asked why they did not themselves marry them; and they said it would be a disgustful thing to marry among relatives, and far better to kill than to give them either to their kindred or to their foes.

This is likewise the practice of their neighbors the Yguazes, but of no other people of that country. When the men would marry, they buy the women of their enemies: the price paid for a wife is a bow, the best that can be got, with two arrows: if it happens that the suitor should have no bow, then a net a fathom in length and another in breadth. They kill their male children, and buy those of strangers. The marriage state continues no longer than while the parties are satisfied, and they separate for the slightest cause. Dorantes was among this people, and after a few days escaped.

Castillo and Estevanico went inland to the Yguazes. This people are universally good archers and of a fine symmetry, although not so large as those we left. They have a nipple and a lip bored. Their support is principally roots, of two or three kinds, and they look for them over the face of all the country. The food is poor and gripes the persons who eat it. The roots require roasting two days: many are very bitter, and withal difficult to be dug. They are sought the distance of two or three leagues, and so great is the want these people experience, that they cannot get through the year without them. Occasionally they kill deer, and at times take fish; but the quantity is so small and the famine so great, that they eat spiders and the eggs of ants, worms, lizards, salamanders, snakes, and vipers that kill whom they strike; and they eat earth and wood, and all that there is, the dung of deer, and other things that I omit to mention; and I honestly believe that were there stones in that land they would eat them. They save the bones of the fishes they consume, of snakes and other animals, that they may afterwards beat them together and eat the powder. The men bear no burthens, nor carry anything of weight; such are borne by women and old men who are of the least esteem. They have not so great love for their children as those we have before spoken of. Some among them are accustomed to sin against nature. The women work very hard, and do a great deal; of the twenty-four hours they have only six of repose; the rest of the night they pass in heating the ovens to bake those roots they eat. At daybreak they begin to dig them, to bring wood and water to their houses and get in readiness other things that may be necessary. The majority of the people are great thieves; for though they are free to divide with each other, on turning the head, even a son or a father will take what he can. They are great liars, and also great drunkards, which they became from the use of a certain liquor.

These Indians are so accustomed to running, that without rest or fatigue they follow a deer from morning to night. In this way they kill many. They pursue them until tired down, and sometimes overtake them in the race. Their houses are of matting, placed upon four hoops. They carry them on the back, and remove every two or three days in search of food. Nothing is planted for support. They are a merry people, considering the hunger they suffer; for they never cease, notwithstanding, to observe their festivities and *areytos*. To them the happiest part of the year is the season of eating prickly pears; they have hunger then no longer, pass all the time in dancing, and eat day and night. While these last, they squeeze out the juice, open and set them to dry, and when dry they are put in hampers like figs. These they keep to eat on their way back. The peel is beaten to powder.

It occurred to us many times while we were among this people, and there was no food, to be three or four days without eating, when they, to revive our spirits, would tell us not to be sad, that soon there would be prickly pears when we should eat a plenty and drink of the juice, when our bellies would be very big and we should be content and joyful, having no hunger. From the time they first told us this, to that at which the earliest were ripe enough to be eaten, was an interval of five or six months; so having tarried until the lapse of this period, and the seasons had come, we went to eat the fruit.

We found mosquitos of three sorts, and all of them abundant in every part of the country. They poison and inflame, and during the greater part of the summer gave us great annoyance. As a protection we made fires, encircling the people with them, burning rotten and wet wood to produce smoke without flame. The remedy brought another trouble, and the night long we did little else than shed tears from the smoke that came into our eyes, besides feeling intense heat from the many fires, and if at any time we went out for repose to the seaside and fell asleep, we were reminded with blows to make up the fires. The Indians of the interior have a different method, as intolerable, and worse even than the one I have spoken of, which is to go with brands in the hand firing the plains and forests within their reach, that the mosquitos may fly away, and at the same time to drive out lizards and other like things from the earth for them to eat.

They are accustomed also to kill deer by encircling them with fires. The pasturage is taken from the cattle by burning, that necessity may drive them to seek it in places where it is desired they should go. They encamp only where there are wood and water; and sometimes all carry loads of these when they go to hunt deer, which are usually found where neither is to be got. On the day of their arrival, they kill the deer and other animals which they can, and consume all the water and all the wood in cooking and on the fires they make to relieve them of mosquitos. They remain the next day to get something to sustain them on their return; and when they go, such is their state from those insects that they appear to have the affliction of holy Lazarus. In this way do they appease their hunger, two or three times in the year, at the cost I have mentioned. From my own experience, I can state there is no torment known in this world that can equal it.

Inland are many deer, birds, and beasts other than those I have spoken of. Cattle come as far as here. Three times I have seen them and eaten of their meat. I think they are about the size of those in Spain. They have small horns like the cows of Morocco; the hair is very long and flocky like the merino's. Some are tawny, others black. To my judgment the flesh is finer and fatter than that of this country. Of the skins of those not full grown the Indians make blankets, and of the larger they make shoes and bucklers. They come as far as the sea-coast of Florida, from a northerly direction, ranging through a tract of more than four hundred leagues; and throughout the whole region over which they run, the people who inhabit near, descend and live upon them, distributing a vast many hides into the interior country.

19.
Our separation by the Indians.

When the six months were over, I had to spend with the Christians to put in execution the plan we had concerted, the Indians went after prickly pears, the place at which they grew being thirty leagues off; and when we approached the point of flight, those among whom we were, quarrelled about a woman. After striking with fists, beating with sticks and bruising heads in great anger, each took his lodge and went his way, whence it became necessary that the Christians should also separate, and in no way could we come together until another year.

In this time I passed a hard life, caused as much by hunger as ill usage. Three times I was obliged to run from my masters, and each time they went in pursuit and endeavored to slay me; but God our Lord in his mercy chose to protect and preserve me; and when the season of prickly pears returned, we again came together in the same place. After we had arranged our escape, and appointed a time, that very day the Indians separated and all went back. I told my comrades I would wait for them among the prickly-pear plants until the moon should be full. This day was the first of September, and the first of the moon; and I said that if in this time they did not come as we had agreed, I would leave and go alone. So we parted, each going with his Indians. I remained with mine until the thirteenth day of the moon, having determined to flee to others when it should be full.

At this time Andrés Dorantes arrived with Estevanico and informed me that they had left Castillo with other Indians near by, called Lanegados; that they had encountered great obstacles and wandered about lost; that the next day the Indians, among whom we were, would move to where Castillo was, and were going to unite with those who held him and become friends, having been at war until then, and that in this way we should recover Castillo.

We had thirst all the time we ate the pears, which we quenched with their juice. We caught it in a hole made in the earth, and when it was full we drank until satisfied. It is sweet, and the color of must. In this manner they collect it for lack of vessels. There are many kinds of prickly pears, among them some very good, although they all appeared to me to be so, hunger never having given me leisure to choose, nor to reflect upon which were the best.

Nearly all these people drink rain-water, which lies about in spots. Although there are rivers, as the Indians never have fixed habitations, there are no familiar or known places for getting water. Throughout the country are extensive and beautiful plains with good pasturage; and I think it would be a very fruitful region were it worked and inhabited by civilized men. We nowhere saw mountains.

These Indians told us that there was another people next in advance of us, called Camones, living towards the coast, and that they had killed the people who came in the boat of Peñalosa and Tellez, who arrived so feeble that even while being slain they could offer no resistance, and were all destroyed. We were shown their clothes and arms, and were told that the boat lay there stranded. This, the fifth boat, had remained till then unaccounted for. We have already stated how the boat of the Governor had been carried out to sea, and that of the comptroller and the friars had been cast away on the coast, of which Esquevel narrated the fate of the men. We have once told how the two boats in which Castillo, I, and Dorantes came, foundered near the Island of Malhado.

20.
Of our escape.

The second day after we had moved, we commended ourselves to God and set forth with speed, trusting, for all the lateness of the season and that the prickly pears were about ending, with the mast which remained in the woods [field], we might still be enabled to travel over a large territory. Hurrying on that day in great dread lest the Indians should overtake us, we saw some smokes, and going in the direction of them we arrived there after vespers, and found an Indian. He ran as he discovered us coming, not being willing to wait for us. We sent the negro after him, when he stopped, seeing him alone. The negro told him we were seeking the people who made those fires. He answered that their houses were near by, and he would guide us to them. So we followed him. He ran to make known our approach, and at sunset we saw the houses. Before our arrival, at the distance of two crossbow shots from them, we found four Indians, who waited for us and received us well. We said in the language of the Mariames, that we were coming to look for them. They were evidently pleased with our company, and took us to their dwellings. Dorantes and the negro were lodged in the house of a physician, Castillo and myself in that of another.

These people speak a different language, and are called Avavares. They are the same that carried bows to those with whom we formerly lived, going to traffic with them, and although they are of a different nation and tongue, they understand the other language. They arrived that day with their lodges, at the place where we found them. The community directly brought us a great many prickly pears, having heard of us before, of our cures, and of the wonders our Lord worked by us, which, although there had been no others, were adequate to open ways for us through a country poor like this, to afford us people where oftentimes there are none, and to lead us through immediate dangers, not permitting us to be killed, sustaining us under great want, and putting into those nations the heart of kindness, as we shall relate hereafter.

21.
Our cure of some of the afflicted.

That same night of our arrival, some Indians came to Castillo and told him that they had great pain in the head, begging him to cure them. After he made over them the sign of the cross, and commended them to God, they instantly said that all the pain had left, and went to their houses bringing us prickly pears, with a piece of venison, a thing to us little known. As the report of Castillo's performances spread, many came to us that night sick, that we should heal them, each bringing a piece of venison, until the quantity became so great we knew not where to dispose of it. We gave many thanks to God, for every day went on increasing his compassion and his gifts. After the sick were attended to, they began to dance and sing, making themselves festive, until sunrise; and because of our arrival, the rejoicing was continued for three days.

When these were ended, we asked the Indians about the country farther on, the people we should find in it, and of the subsistence there. They answered us, that throughout all the region prickly-pear plants abounded; but the fruit was now gathered and all the people had gone back to their houses. They said the country was very cold, and there were few skins. Reflecting on this, and that it was already winter, we resolved to pass the season with these Indians.

Five days after our arrival, all the Indians went off, taking us with them to gather more prickly pears, where there were other peoples speaking different tongues. After walking five days in great hunger, since on the way was no manner of fruit, we came to a river and put up our houses. We then went to seek the product of certain trees, which is like peas. As there are no paths in the country, I was detained some time. The others returned, and coming to look for them in the dark I got lost. Thank God I found a burning tree, and in the warmth of it I passed the cold of that night. In the morning, loading myself with sticks, and taking two brands with me, I returned to seek them. In this manner I wandered five days, ever with my fire and load; for if the wood had failed me where none could be found, as many parts are without any, though I might have sought sticks elsewhere, there would have been no fire to kindle them. This was all the protection I had against cold, while walking naked as I was born. Going to the low woods near the rivers, I prepared myself for the night, stopping in them before sunset. I made a hole in the ground and threw in fuel which the trees abundantly afforded, collected in good quantity from those that were fallen and dry. About the whole I made four fires, in the form of a cross, which I watched and made up from time to time. I also gathered some bundles of the coarse straw that there abounds, with which I covered myself in the hole. In this way I was sheltered at night from cold. On one occasion while I slept, the fire fell upon the straw, when it began to blaze so rapidly that notwithstanding the haste I made to

get out of it, I carried some marks on my hair of the danger to which I was exposed. All this while I tasted not a mouthful, nor did I find anything I could eat. My feet were bare and bled a good deal. Through the mercy of God, the wind did not blow from the north in all this time, otherwise I should have died.

At the end of the fifth day I arrived on the margin of a river, where I found the Indians, who with the Christians, had considered me dead, supposing that I had been stung by a viper. All were rejoiced to see me, and most so were my companions. They said that up to that time they had struggled with great hunger, which was the cause of their not having sought me. At night, all gave me of their prickly pears, and the next morning we set out for a place where they were in large quantity, with which we satisfied our great craving, the Christians rendering thanks to our Lord that He had ever given us His aid.

22.
The coming of other sick to us the next day.

The next day morning, many Indians came, and brought five persons who had cramps and were very unwell. They came that Castillo might cure them. Each offered his bow and arrows, which Castillo received. At sunset he blessed them, commending them to God our Lord, and we all prayed to Him the best we could to send health; for that He knew there was no other means, than through Him, by which this people would aid us, so we could come forth from this unhappy existence. He bestowed it so mercifully, that, the morning having come, all got up well and sound, and were as strong as though they never had a disorder. It caused great admiration, and inclined us to render many thanks to God our Lord, whose goodness we now clearly beheld, giving us firm hopes that He would liberate and bring us to where we might serve Him. For myself I can say that I ever had trust in His providence that He would lead me out from that captivity, and thus I always spoke of it to my companions.

The Indians having gone and taken their friends with them in health, we departed for a place at which others were eating prickly pears. These people are called Cuthalchuches and Malicones, who speak different tongues. Adjoining them were others called Coayos and Susolas, who were on the opposite side, others called Atayos, who were at war with the Susolas, exchanging arrow shots daily. As through all the country they talked only of the wonders which God our Lord worked through us, persons came from many parts to seek us that we might cure them. At the end of the second day after our arrival, some of the Susolas came to us and besought Castillo that he would go to cure one wounded and others sick, and they said that among them was one very near his end. Castillo was a timid practitioner, most so in serious and dangerous cases, believing that his sins would weigh, and some day hinder him in performing cures. The Indians told me to go and heal them, as they liked me; they remembered that I had ministered to them in the walnut grove when they gave us nuts and skins, which occurred when I first joined the Christians. So I had to go with them, and Dorantes accompanied me with Estevanico. Coming near their huts, I perceived that the sick man we went to heal was dead. Many persons were around him weeping, and his house was prostrate, a sign that the one who dwelt in it is no more. When I arrived I found his eyes rolled up, and the pulse gone, he having all the appearances of death, as they seemed to me and as Dorantes said. I removed a mat with which he was covered, and supplicated our Lord as fervently as I could, that He would be pleased to give health to him, and to the rest that might have need of it. After he had been blessed and breathed upon many times, they brought me his bow, and gave me a basket of pounded prickly pears.

The natives took me to cure many others who were sick of a stupor, and presented me two more baskets of prickly pears, which I gave to the Indians who accompanied us. We then went back to our lodgings. Those to whom we gave the fruit tarried, and returned at night to their houses, reporting that he who had been dead and for whom I wrought before them, had got up whole and walked, had eaten and spoken with them and that all to whom I had ministered were well and much pleased. This caused great wonder and fear, and throughout the land the people talked of nothing else. All to whom the fame of it reached, came to seek us that we should cure them and bless their children.

When the Cuthalchuches, who were in company with our Indians, were about to return to their own country, they left us all the prickly pears they had, without keeping one: they gave us

flints of very high value there, a palm and a half in length, with which they cut. The begged that we would remember them and pray to God that they might always be well, and we promised to do so. They left, the most satisfied beings in the world, having given us the best of all they had.

We remained with the Avavares eight months, reckoned by the number of moons. In all this time people came to seek us from many parts, and they said that most truly we were children of the sun. Dorantes and the negro to this time had not attempted to practise; but because of the great solicitation made by those coming from different parts to find us, we all became physicians, although in being venturous and bold to attempt the performance of any cure, I was the most remarkable. No one whom we treated, but told us he was left well; and so great was the confidence that they would become healed if we administered to them, they even believed that whilst we remained none of them could die. These and the rest of the people behind, related an extraordinary circumstance, and by the way they counted, there appeared to be fifteen or sixteen years since it occurred.

They said that a man wandered through the country whom they called Badthing; he was small of body and wore a beard, and they never distinctly saw his features. When he came to the house where they lived, their hair stood up and they trembled. Presently a blazing torch shone at the door, when he entered and seized whom he chose, and giving him three great gashes in the side with a very sharp flint, the width of the hand and two palms in length, he put his hand through them, drawing forth the entrails, from one of which he would cut off a portion more or less, the length of a palm, and throw it on the embers. Then he would give three gashes to an arm, the second cut on the inside of an elbow, and would sever the limb. A little after this, he would begin to unite it, and putting his hands on the wounds, these would instantly become healed. They said that frequently in the dance he appeared among them, sometimes in the dress of a woman, at others in that of a man; that when it pleased him he would take a buhío, or house, and lifting it high, after a little he would come down with it in a heavy fall. They also stated that many times they offered them victuals, but that he never ate: they asked him whence he came and where was his abiding place, and he showed them a fissure in the earth and said that his house was there below. These things they told us of, we much laughed at and ridiculed; and they seeing our incredulity, brought to us many of those they said he had seized; and we saw the marks of the gashes made in the places according to the manner they had described. We told them he was an evil one, and in the best way we could, gave them to understand, that if they would believe in God our Lord, and become Christians like us, they need have no fear of him, nor would he dare to come and inflict those injuries, and they might be certain he would not venture to appear while we remained in the land. At this they were delighted and lost much of their dread. They told us that they had seen the Asturian and Figueroa with people farther along the coast, whom we had called those of the figs.

They are all ignorant of time, either by the sun or moon, nor do they reckon by the month or year; they better know and understand the differences of the seasons, when the fruits come to ripen, where the fish resort, and the position of the stars, at which they are ready and practised. By these we were ever well treated. We dug our own food and brought our loads of wood and water. Their houses and also the things we ate, are like those of the nation from which we came, but they suffer far greater want, having neither maize, acorns, nor nuts. We always went naked like them, and covered ourselves at night with deer-skins.

Of the eight months we were among this people, six we supported in great want, for fish are not to be found where they are. At the expiration of the time, the prickly pears began to ripen, and I and the negro went, without these Indians knowing it, to others farther on, a day's journey distant, called Maliacones. At the end of three days, I sent him to bring Castillo and Dorantes, and they having arrived, we all set out with the Indians who were going to get the small fruit of certain trees on which they support themselves ten or twelve days whilst the prickly pears are maturing. They joined others called Arbadaos, whom we found to be very weak, lank, and swollen, so much so as to cause us great astonishment. We told those with whom we came, that we wished to stop with these people, at which they showed regret and went back by the way they came; so we remained in the field near the houses

of the Indians, which when they observed, after talking among themselves they came up together, and each of them taking one of us by the hand, led us to their dwellings. Among them we underwent greater hunger than with the others; we ate daily not more than two handfuls of the prickly pears, which were green and so milky they burned our mouths. As there was lack of water, those who ate suffered great thirst. In our extreme want we bought two dogs, giving in exchange some nets, with other things, and a skin I used to cover myself.

I have already stated that throughout all this country we went naked, and as we were unaccustomed to being so, twice a year we cast our skins like serpents. The sun and air produced great sores on our breasts and shoulders, giving us sharp pain; and the large loads we had, being very heavy, caused the cords to cut into our arms. The country is so broken and thickset, that often after getting our wood in the forests, the blood flowed from us in many places, caused by the obstruction of thorns and shrubs that tore our flesh wherever we went. At times, when my turn came to get wood, after it had cost me much blood, I could not bring it out either on my back or by dragging. In these labors my only solace and relief were in thinking of the sufferings of our Redeemer, Jesus Christ, and in the blood He shed for me, in considering how much greater must have been the torment He sustained from the thorns, than that I there received.

I bartered with these Indians in combs that I made for them and in bows, arrows, and nets. We made mats, which are their houses, that they have great necessity for; and although they know how to make them, they wish to give their full time to getting food, since when otherwise employed they are pinched with hunger. Sometimes the Indians would set me to scraping and softening skins; and the days of my greatest prosperity there, were those in which they gave me skins to dress. I would scrape them a very great deal and eat the scraps, which would sustain me two or three days. When it happened among these people, as it had likewise among others whom we left behind, that a piece of meat was given us, we ate it raw; for if we had put it to roast, the first native that should come along would have taken it off and devoured it; and it appeared to us not well to expose it to this risk; besides we were in such condition it would have given us pain to eat it roasted, and we could not have digested it so well as raw. Such was the life we spent there; and the meagre subsistence we earned by the matters of traffic which were the work of our hands.

23.
Of our departure after having eaten the dogs.

After eating the dogs, it seemed to us we had some strength to go forward; and so commending ourselves to God our Lord, that He would guide us, we took our leave of the Indians. They showed us the way to others, near by, who spoke their language. While on our journey, rain fell, and we travelled the day in wet. We lost our way and went to stop in an extensive wood. We pulled many leaves of the prickly pear, which we put at night in an oven we made, and giving them much heat, by the morning they were in readiness. After eating, we put ourselves under the care of the Almighty and started. We discovered the way we had lost. Having passed the wood, we found other houses, and coming up to them, we saw two women with some boys walking in the forest, who were frightened at the sight of us and fled, running into the woods to call the men. These arriving, stopped behind trees to look at us. We called to them, and they came up with much timidity. After some conversation they told us that food was very scarce with them; that near by were many houses of their people to which they would guide us. We came at night where were fifty dwellings. The inhabitants were astonished at our appearance, showing much fear. After becoming somewhat accustomed to us, they reached their hands to our faces and bodies, and passed them in like manner over their own.

We stayed there that night, and in the morning the Indians brought us their sick, beseeching us that we would bless them. They gave us of what they had to eat, the leaves of the prickly pear and the green fruit roasted. As they did this with kindness and good will, and were happy to be without anything to eat, that they might have food to give us, we tarried some days. While there, others came from beyond, and when they were about to depart, we told our entertainers that we wished to go with those people. They felt much uneasiness at this, and pressed us warmly to stay: however, we took our leave in the midst of their weeping, for our departure weighed heavily upon them.

24.
Customs of the Indians of that country.

From the Island of Malhado to this land, all the Indians whom we saw have the custom from the time in which their wives find themselves pregnant, of not sleeping with them until two years after they have given birth. The children are suckled until the age of twelve years, when they are old enough to get support for themselves. We asked why they reared them in this manner; and they said because of the great poverty of the land, it happened many times, as we witnessed, that they were two or three days without eating, sometimes four, and consequently, in seasons of scarcity, the children were allowed to suckle, that they might not famish; otherwise those who lived would be delicate, having little strength.

If any one chance to fall sick in the desert, and cannot keep up with the rest, the Indians leave him to perish, unless it be a son or a brother; him they will assist, even to carrying on their back. It is common among them all to leave their wives when there is no conformity, and directly they connect themselves with whom they please. This is the course of the men who are childless; those who have children remain with their wives and never abandon them. When they dispute and quarrel in their towns, they strike each other with the fists, fighting until exhausted, and then separate. Sometimes they are parted by the women going between them; the men never interfere. For no disaffection that arises do they resort to bows and arrows. After they have fought, or had out their dispute, they take their dwellings and go into the woods, living apart from each other until their heat has subsided. When no longer offended and their anger is gone, they return. From that time they are friends as if nothing had happened; nor is it necessary that any one should mend their friendships, as they in this way again unite them. If those that quarrel are single, they go to some neighboring people, and although these should be enemies, they receive them well and welcome them warmly, giving them so largely of what they have, that when their animosity cools, and they return to their town, they go rich.

They are all warlike, and have as much strategy for protecting themselves against enemies as they could have were they reared in Italy in continual feuds. When they are in a part of the country where their enemies may attack them, they place their houses on the skirt of a wood, the thickest and most tangled they can find, and near it make a ditch in which they sleep. The warriors are covered by small pieces of stick through which are loop-holes; these hide them and present so false an appearance, that if come upon they are not discovered. They open a very narrow way, entering into the midst of the wood, where a spot is prepared on which the women and children sleep. When night comes they kindle fires in their lodges, that should spies be about, they may think to find them there; and before daybreak they again light those fires. If the enemy comes to assault the houses, they who are in the ditch make a sally; and from their trenches do much injury without those who are outside seeing or being able to find them. When there is no wood in which they can take shelter in this way, and make their ambuscades, they settle on open ground at a place they select, which they invest with trenches covered with broken sticks, having apertures whence to discharge arrows. These arrangements are made for night.

While I was among the Aguenes, their enemies coming suddenly at midnight, fell upon them, killed three and wounded many, so that they ran from their houses to the fields before them. As soon as these ascertained that their assailants had withdrawn, they returned to pick up all the arrows the others had shot, and following after them in the most stealthy manner possible, came that night to their dwellings without their presence being suspected. At four o'clock in the morning the Aguenes attacked them, killed five, and wounded numerous others, and made them flee from their houses, leaving their bows with all they possessed. In a little while came the wives of the Quevenes to them and formed a treaty whereby the parties became friends. The women, however, are sometimes the cause of war. All these nations, when they have personal enmities, and are not of one family, assassinate at night, waylay, and inflict gross barbarities on each other.

25.
Vigilance of the Indians in war.

They are the most watchful in danger of any people I ever knew. If they fear an enemy they are awake the night long, each with a bow at his side and a dozen arrows. He that would sleep tries his bow, and if it is not strung, he gives the turn necessary to the cord. They often come out from their houses, bending to the ground in such manner that they cannot be seen, looking and watching on all sides to catch every object. If they perceive anything about, they are at once in the bushes with their bows and arrows, and there remain until day, running from place to place where it is needful to be, or where they think their enemies are. When the light has come, they unbend their bows until they go out to hunt. The strings are the sinews of deer.

The method they have of fighting, is bending low to the earth, and whilst shot at they move about, speaking and leaping from one point to another, thus avoiding the shafts of their enemies. So effectual is their manœuvring that they can receive very little injury from crossbow or arquebus; they rather scoff at them; for these arms are of little value employed in open field, where the Indians move nimbly about. They are proper for defiles and in water; everywhere else the horse will best subdue, being what the natives universally dread. Whosoever would fight them must be cautious to show no fear, or desire to have anything that is theirs; while war exists they must be treated with the utmost rigor; for if they discover any timidity or covetousness, they are a race that well discern the opportunities for vengeance, and gather strength from any weakness of their adversaries. When they use arrows in battle and exhaust their store, each returns his own way, without the one party following the other, although the one be many and the other few, such being their custom. Oftentimes the body of an Indian is traversed by the arrow; yet unless the entrails or the heart be struck, he does not die but recovers from the wound.

I believe these people see and hear better, and have keener senses than any other in the world. They are great in hunger, thirst, and cold, as if they were made for the endurance of these more than other men, by habit and nature.

Thus much I have wished to say, beyond the gratificiation of that desire men have to learn the customs and manners of each other, that those who hereafter at some time find themselves amongst these people, may have knowledge of their usages and artifices, the value of which they will not find inconsiderable in such event.

26.
Of the nations and tongues.

I desire to enumerate the natives and tongues that exist from those of Malhado to the farthest Cuchendados there are. Two languages are found in the island; the people of one are called Cahoques, of the other, Han. On the tierra-firme, over against the island, is another people, called Chorruco, who take their names from the forests where they live. Advancing by the shores of the sea, others inhabit who are called the Doguenes, and opposite them others by the name of Mendica. Farther along the coast are the Quevenes, and in front of them on the main, the Mariames; and continuing by the coast are other called Guaycones; and in front of them, within on the main, the Yguazes. At the close of these are the Atayos; and in their rear others, the Acubadaos, and beyond them are many in the same direction. By the coast live those called Quitoks, and in front inward on the main are the Chavavares, to whom adjoin the Maliacones, the Cultalchulches and others called Susolas, and the Comos; and by the coast farther on are the Camoles; and on the same coast in advance are those whom we called People of the Figs.

They all differ in their habitations, towns and tongues. There is a language in which calling to a person for "look here" they say "Arre aca," and to a dog "Xo." Everywhere they produce stupefaction with a smoke, and for that they will give whatever they possess. They drink a tea made from leaves of a tree like those of the oak, which they toast in a pot; and after these are parched, the vessel, still remaining on the fire, is filled with water. When the liquor has twice boiled, they pour it into a jar, and in cooling it use the half of a gourd. So soon as it is covered thickly with froth, it is drunk as warm as can be supported; and from the time it is taken out of the pot until it is used they are crying aloud: "Who wishes to drink?" When the women hear these cries, they instantly stop, fearing to move; and although they may be heavily laden, they dare do nothing further. Should one of them move, they dishonor her, beating her with sticks, and greatly vexed, throw away the liquor they have prepared; while they who have drunk eject it, which they do readily and without pain. The reason they give for this usage is, that when they are about to drink, if the women move from where they hear the cry, something pernicious enters the body in that liquid, shortly producing death. At the time of boiling, the vessel must be covered; and if it should happen to be open when a woman passes, they use no more of that liquid, but throw it out. The color is yellow. They are three days taking it, eating nothing in the time, and daily each one drinks an arroba and a half.

When the women have their indisposition, they seek food only for themselves, as no one else will eat of what they bring. In the time I was thus among these people, I witnessed a diabolical practice; a man living with another, one of those who are emasculate and impotent. These go habited like women, and perform their duties, use the bow, and carry heavy loads. Among them we saw many mutilated in the way I describe. They are more muscular than other men, and taller: they bear very weighty burthens.

27.
We moved away and were well received.

After parting with those we left weeping, we went with the others to their houses and were hospitably received by the people in them. They brought their children to us that we might touch their hands, and gave us a great quantity of the flour of mezquiquez. The fruit while hanging on the tree, is very bitter and like unto the carob; when eaten with earth it is sweet and wholesome. The method they have of preparing it is this: they make a hole of requisite depth in the ground, and throwing in the fruit, pound it with a club the size of the leg, a fathom and a half in length, until it is well mashed. Besides the earth that comes from the hole, they bring and add some handfuls, then returning to beat it a little while longer. Afterward it is thrown into a jar, like a basket, upon which water is poured until it rises above and covers the mixture. He that beats it tastes it, and if it appears to him not sweet, he asks for earth to stir in, which is added until he finds it sweet. Then all sit round, and each putting in a hand, takes out as much as he can. The pits and hulls are thrown upon a skin, whence they are taken by him who does the pounding, and put into the jar whereon water is poured as at first, whence having expressed the froth and juice, again the pits and husks are thrown upon the skin. This they do three or four times to each pounding. Those present, for whom this is a great banquet, have their stomachs greatly distended by the earth and water they swallow. The Indians made a protracted festival of this sort on our account, and great *areitos* during the time we remained.

When we proposed to leave them, some women of another people came there who lived farther along. They informed us whereabout were their dwellings, and we set out for them, although the inhabitants entreated us to remain for that day, because the houses whither we were going were distant, there was no path to them, the women had come tired, and would the next day go with us refreshed and show us the way. Soon after we had taken our leave, some of the women, who had come on together from the same town, followed behind us. As there are no paths in the country we presently got lost, and thus travelled four leagues, when, stopping to drink, we found the women in pursuit of us at the water, who told us of the great exertion they had made to overtake us. We went on taking them for guides, and passed over a river towards evening, the water reaching to the breast. It might be as wide as that at Seville; its current was very rapid.

At sunset we reached a hundred Indian habitations. Before we arrived, all the people who were in them came out to receive us, with such yells as were terrific, striking the palms of their hands violently against their thighs. They brought us gourds bored with holes and having pebbles in them, an instrument for the most important occasions, produced only at the dance or to effect cures, and which none dare touch but those who own them. They say there is virtue in them, and because they do not grow in that country, they come from heaven; nor do they know where they are to be found, only that the rivers bring them in their floods. So great were the fear and distraction of these people, some to reach us sooner than others that they might touch us, they pressed us so closely that they lacked little of killing us; and without letting us put our feet to the ground, carried us to their dwellings. We were so crowded upon by numbers, that we went into the houses they had made for us. On no account would we consent that they should rejoice over us any more that night. The night long they passed in singing and dancing among themselves;

and the next day they brought us all the people of the town, that we should touch and bless them in the way we had done to others among whom we had been. After this performance they presented many arrows to some women of the other town who had accompanied theirs.

The next day we left, and all the people of the place went with us; and when we came to the other Indians we were as well received as we had been by the last. They gave us of what they had to eat, and the deer they had killed that day. Among them we witnessed another custom, which is this: they who were with us took from him who came to be cured, his bow and arrows, shoes and beads if he wore any, and then brought him before us, that we should heal him. After being attended to, he would go away highly pleased, saying that he was well. So we parted from these Indians, and went to others by whom we were welcomed. They brought us their sick, which, we having blessed, they declared were sound; he who was healed, believed we could cure him; and with what the others to whom we had administered would relate, they made great rejoicing and dancing, so that they left us no sleep.

28.
Of another strange custom.

Leaving these Indians, we went to the dwellings of numerous others. From this place began another novel custom, which is, that while the people received us very well, those who accompanied us began to use them so ill as to take their goods and ransack their houses, without leaving anything. To witness this unjust procedure gave us great concern, inflicted too on those who received us hospitably; we feared also that it might provoke offence, and be the cause of some tumult between them; but, as we were in no condition to make it better, or to dare chastise such conduct, for the present we had to bear with it, until a time when we might have greater authority among them. They, also, who lost their effects, noticing our dejection, attempted to console us by saying that we should not be grieved on this account, as they were so gratified at having seen us, they held their properties to be well bestowed, and that farther on they would be repaid by others who were very rich.

On all the day's travel we received great inconvenience from the many persons following us.

Had we attempted to escape we could not have succeeded, such was their haste in pursuit, in order to touch us. So great was the importunity for this privilege, we consumed three hours in going through with them that they might depart. The next day all the inhabitants were brought before us. The greater part were clouded of an eye, and others in like manner were entirely blind, which caused in us great astonishment. They are a people of fine figure, agreeable features, and whiter than any of the many nations we had seen until then.

Here we began to see mountains; they appeared to come in succession from the North Sea, and, according to the information the Indians gave us, we believe they rise fifteen leagues from the sea. We set forth in a direction towards them with these Indians, and they guided us by the way of some kindred of theirs; for they wished to take us only where were their relations, and were not willing that their enemies should come to such great good, as they thought it was to see us. After we arrived they that went with us plundered the others; but as the people there knew the fashion, they had hidden some things before we came; and having welcomed us with great festivity and rejoicing, they brought out and presented to us what they had concealed. These were beads, ochre, and some little bags of silver. In pursuance of custom, we directly gave them to the Indians who came with us, which, when they had received, they began their dances and festivities, sending to call others from a town near by, that they also might see us.

In the afternoon they all came and brought us beads and bows, with trifles of other sort, which we also distributed. Desiring to leave the next day, the inhabitants all wished to take us to others, friends of theirs, who were at the point of the ridge, stating that many houses were there, and people who would give us various things. As it was out of our way, we did not wish to go to them, and took our course along the plain near the mountains, which we believed not to be distant from the coast where the people are all evil disposed, and we considered it preferable to travel inland; for those of the interior are of a better condition and treated us mildly, and we felt sure that we should find it more populous and better provisioned. Moreover, we chose this course because in traversing the country we should learn many particulars of it, so that should God our Lord be pleased to take any of us thence, and lead us to the land of Christians, we might carry that information and news of it. As the Indians saw that we were determined not to go where they would take us, they said that in the direction we would go, there were no inhabitants, nor any prickly pears nor other thing to eat, and begged us to tarry there that day; we accordingly did so. They directly sent two of their number to seek for people in the direction that we wished to go; and the next day we left, taking with us several of the Indians. The women went carrying water, and so great was our authority that no one dared drink of it without our permission.

Two leagues from there we met those who had gone out, and they said that they had found no one; at which the Indians seemed much disheartened, and began again to entreat us to go by way of the mountains. We did not wish to do so, and they, seeing our disposition, took their leave of us with much regret, and returned down the river to their houses, while we ascended along by it. After a little time we came upon two women with burthens, who put them down as they saw us, and brought to us, of what they carried. It was the flour of maize. They told us that farther up on the river we should find dwellings, a plenty of prickly pears and of that meal. We bade them farewell: they were going to those whom we had left.

We walked until sunset, and arrived at a town of some twenty houses, where we were received with weeping and in great sorrow; for they already knew that wheresoever we should come, all would be pillaged and spoiled by those who accompanied us. When they saw that we were alone, they lost their fear, and gave us prickly pears with nothing more. We remained there that night, and at dawn, the Indians who had left us the day before, broke upon their houses. As they came upon the occupants unprepared and in supposed safety, having no place in which to conceal anything, all they possessed was taken from them, for which they wept much. In consolation the plunderers told them that we were children of the sun and that we had power to heal the sick and to destroy; and other lies even greater than these, which none knew how to tell better than they when they find it convenient. They bade them conduct us with great respect, advised that they should be careful to offend us in nothing, give us all they might possess, and endeavor to take us where people were numerous; and that wheresoever they arrived with us, they should rob and pillage the people of what they have, since this was customary.

29.
The Indians plunder each other.

After the Indians had told and shown these natives well what to do, they left us together and went back. Remembering the instruction, they began to treat us with the same awe and reverence that the others had shown. We travelled with them three days, and they took us where were many inhabitants. Before we arrived, these were informed of our coming by the others, who told them respecting us all that the first had imparted, adding much more; for these people are all very fond of romance, and are great liars, particularly so where they have any interest. When we came near the houses all the inhabitants ran out with delight and great festivity to receive us. Among other things, two of their physicians gave us two gourds, and thenceforth we carried these with us, and added to our authority a token highly reverenced by Indians. Those who accompanied us rifled the houses; but as these were many and the others few, they could not carry off what they took, and abandoned more than the half.

From here we went along the base of the ridge, striking inland more than fifty leagues, and at the close we found upwards of forty houses. Among the articles given us, Andrés Dorantes received a hawk-bell of copper, thick and large, figured with a face, which the natives had shown, greatly prizing it. They told him that they had received it from others, their neighbors; we asked them whence the others had obtained it, and they said it had been brought from the northern direction, where there was much copper, which was highly esteemed. We concluded that whencesoever it came there was a foundry, and that work was done in hollow form.

We departed the next day, and traversed a ridge seven leagues in extent. The stones on it are scoria of iron. At night we arrived at many houses seated on the banks of a very beautiful river. The owners of them came half way out on the road to meet us, bringing their children on their backs. They gave us many little bags of margarite and pulverized galena, with which they rub the face. They presented us many beads, and blankets of cowhide, loading all who accompanied us with some of everything they had. They eat prickly pears and the seed of pine. In that country are small pine trees, the cones like little eggs; but the seed is better than that of Castile, as its husk is very thin, and while green is beaten and made into balls, to be thus eaten. If the seed be dry, it is pounded in the husk, and consumed in the form of flour.

Those who there received us, after they had touched us went running to their houses and directly returned, and did not stop running, going and coming, to bring us in this manner many things for support on the way. They fetched a man to me and stated that a long time since he had been wounded by an arrow in the right shoulder, and that the point of the shaft was lodged above his heart, which, he said, gave him much pain, and in consequence, he was always sick. Probing the wound I felt the arrow-head, and found it had passed through the cartilage. With a knife I carried, I opened the breast to the place, and saw the point was aslant and troublesome to take out. I continued to cut, and, putting in the point of the knife, at last with great difficulty I drew the head forth. It was very large. With the bone of a deer, and by virtue of my calling, I made two stitches that threw the blood over me, and with hair from a skin I stanched the flow. They asked me for the arrow-head after I had taken it out, which I gave, when the whole town came to look at it. They sent it into the back country that the people there might view it. In consequence of this operation they had many of their customary dances and festivities. The next day I cut the two stitches and the Indian was well. The wound I made appeared only like a seam in the palm of the hand. He said he felt no pain or sensitiveness in it whatsoever. This cure gave us control throughout the country in all that the inhabitants had power, or deemed of any value, or cherished. We showed them the hawk-bell we brought, and they told us that in the place whence that had come, were buried many plates of the same material; it was a thing they greatly esteemed, and where it came from were fixed habitations. The country we considered to be on the South Sea, which we had never understood to be richer than the one of the North.

We left there, and travelled through so many

sorts of people, of such diverse languages, the memory fails to recall them. They ever plundered each other, and those that lost, like those that gained, were fully content. We drew so many followers that we had not use for their services. While on our way through these vales, every Indian carried a club three palms in length, and kept on the alert. On raising a hare, which animals are abundant, they surrounded it directly and throw numerous clubs at it with astonishing precision. Thus they cause it to run from one to another; so that, according to my thinking, it is the most pleasing sport which can be imagined, as oftentimes the animal runs into the hand. So many did they give us that at night when we stopped we had eight or ten back-loads apiece. Those having bows were not with us; they dispersed about the ridge in pursuit of deer; and at dark came bringing five or six for each of us, besides quail, and other game. Indeed, whatever they either killed or found, was put before us, without themselves daring to take anything until we had blessed it, though they should be expiring of hunger, they having so established the rule, since marching with us.

The women carried many mats, of which the men made us houses, each of us having a separate one, with all his attendants. After these were put up, we ordered the deer and hares to be roasted, with the rest that had been taken. This was done by means of certain ovens made for the purpose. Of each we took a little and the remainder we gave to the principal personage of the people coming with us, directing him to divide it among the rest. Every one brought his portion to us, that we might breathe upon and give it our benediction; for not until then did they dare eat any of it. Frequently we were accompanied by three or four thousand persons, and as we had to breathe upon and sanctify the food and drink for each, and grant permission to do the many things they would come to ask, it may be seen how great was the annoyance. The women first brought us prickly pears, spiders, worms, and whatever else they could gather; for even were they famishing, they would eat nothing unless we gave it them.

In company with these, we crossed a great river coming from the north, and passing over some plains thirty leagues in extent, we found many persons coming a long distance to receive us, who met us on the road over which we were to travel, and welcomed us in the manner of those we had left.

30.
The fashion of receiving us changes.

From this place was another method of receiving us, as respects the pillage. Those who came out in the ways to bring us presents were not plundered; but on our coming into their houses, themselves offered us all they had, as well as the houses. We gave the things to the chief personages who accompanied us, that they should divide them; those who were despoiled always followed us until coming to a populous country, where they might repair their loss. They would tell those among whom we came, to retain everything and make no concealment, as nothing could be done without our knowledge, and we might cause them to die, as the sun revealed everything to us. So great was their fear that during the first days they were with us, they continually trembled, without daring even to speak, or raise their eyes to the heavens. They guided us through more than fifty leagues of desert, over rough mountains, which being dry were without game, and in consequence we suffered much from hunger.

At the termination we forded a very large river, the water coming up to our breasts. From this place, many of the people began to sicken from the great privation and labor they had undergone in the passage of those ridges, which are sterile and difficult in the extreme. They conducted us to certain plains at the base of the mountains, where people came to meet us from a great distance, and received us as the last had done, and gave so many goods to those who came with us, that the half were left because they could not be carried. I told those who gave, to resume the goods that they might not lie there and be lost; but they answered they could in no wise do so, as it was not their custom after they had bestowed a thing to take it back; so considering the articles no longer of value, they were left to perish.

We told these people that we desired to go where the sun sets; and they said inhabitants in that direction were remote. We commanded them to send and make known our coming; but they strove to excuse themselves the best they could, the people being their enemies, and they did not wish to go to them. Not daring to disobey, however, they sent two women, one of their own, the other a captive from that people; for the women can negotiate even though there be war. We followed them, and stopped at a place where we agreed to wait. They tarried five days; and the Indians said they could not have found anybody.

We told them to conduct us towards the north; and they answered, as before, that except afar off there were no people in that direction, and nothing to eat, nor could water be found. Notwithstanding all this, we persisted, and said we desired to go in that course. They still tried to excuse themselves in the best manner possible. At this we became offended, and one night I went out to sleep in the woods apart from them; but directly they came to where I was, and remained all night without sleep, talking to me in great fear, telling me how terrified they were, beseeching us to be no longer angry, and said that they would lead us in the direction it was our wish to go, though they knew they should die on the way.

Whilst we still feigned to be displeased lest their fright should leave them, a remarkable circumstance happened, which was that on the same day many of the Indians became ill, and the next day eight men died. Abroad in the country, wheresoever this became known, there was such dread that it seemed as if the inhabitants would die of fear at sight of us. They besought us not to remain angered, nor require that more of them should die. They believed we caused their death by only willing it, when in truth it gave us so much pain that it could not be greater; for, beyond their loss, we feared they might all die, or abandon us of fright, and that other people thenceforward would do the same, seeing what had come to these. We prayed to God, our Lord, to relieve them; and from that time the sick began to get better.

We witnessed one thing with great admiration, that the parents, brothers, and wives of those who died had great sympathy for them in their suffering; but, when dead, they showed no feeling, neither did they weep nor speak among themselves, make any signs, nor dare approach the bodies until we commanded these to be taken to burial.

While we were among these people, which was more than fifteen days, we saw no one speak to another, nor did we see an infant smile: the only one that cried they took off to a distance, and with the sharp teeth of a rat they scratched it from the shoulders down nearly to the end of the legs. Seeing this cruelty, and offended at it, I asked why they did so: they said for chastisement, because the child had wept in my presence. These terrors they imparted to all those who had lately come to know us, that they might give us whatever they had; for they knew we kept nothing, and would relinquish all to them. This people were the most obedient we had found in all the land, the best conditioned, and, in general, comely.

The sick having recovered, and three days having passed since we came to the place, the women whom we sent away returned, and said they had found very few people; nearly all had gone for cattle, being then in the season. We ordered the convalescent to remain and the well to go with us, and that at the end of two days' journey those women should go with two of our number to fetch up the people, and bring them on the road to receive us. Consequently, the next morning the most robust started with us. At the end of three days' travel we stopped, and the next day Alonzo del Castillo set out with Estevanico the negro, taking the two women as guides. She that was the captive led them to the river which ran between some ridges, where was a town at which her father lived; and these habitations were the first seen, having the appearance and structure of houses.

Here Castillo and Estevanico arrived, and, after talking with the Indians, Castillo returned at the end of three days to the spot where he had left us, and brought five or six of the people. He told us he had found fixed dwellings of civilization, that the inhabitants lived on beans and pumpkins, and that he had seen maize. This news the most of anything delighted us, and for it we gave infinite thanks to our Lord. Castillo told us the negro was coming with all the population to wait for us in the road not far off. Accordingly we left, and, having travelled a league and a half, we met the negro and the people coming to receive us. They gave us beans, many pumpkins, calabashes, blankets of cowhide and other things. As this people and those who came with us were enemies, and spoke not each other's language, we discharged the latter, giving them what we received, and we departed with the others. Six leagues from there, as the night set in we arrived at the houses, where great festivities were made over us. We remained one day, and the next set out with these Indians. They took us to the settled habitations of others, who lived upon the same food.

From that place onward was another usage. Those who knew of our approach did not come out to receive us on the road as the others had done, but we found them in their houses, and they had made others for our reception. They were all seated with their faces turned to the wall, their heads down, the hair brought before their eyes, and their property placed in a heap in the middle of the house. From this place they began to give us many blankets of skin; and they had nothing they did not bestow. They have the finest persons of any people we saw, of the greatest activity and strength, who best understood us and intelligently answered our inquiries. We called them the Cow nation, because most of the cattle killed are slaughtered in their neighborhood, and along up that river for over fifty leagues they destroy great numbers.

They go entirely naked after the manner of the first we saw. The women are dressed with deerskin, and some few men, mostly the aged, who are incapable of fighting. The country is very populous. We asked how it was they did not plant maize. They answered it was that they might not lose what they should put in the ground; that the rains had failed for two years in succession, and the seasons were so dry the seed had everywhere been taken by the moles, and they could not venture to plant again until after water had fallen copiously. They begged us to tell the sky to rain, and to pray for it, and we said we would do so. We also desired to know whence they got the maize, and they told us from where the sun goes down; there it grew throughout the region, and the nearest was by that path. Since they did not wish to go thither, we asked by what direction we might best proceed, and bade them inform us concerning the way; they said the path was along up by that river towards the north, for otherwise in a journey of seventeen days we should find nothing to eat, except a fruit they call *chacan*, that is ground between stones, and even then it could with difficulty be eaten for its dryness and pungency,—which was true. They showed it to us there, and we could not eat it. They informed us also that, whilst we travelled by the river upward, we should all the way pass through a people

that were their enemies, who spoke their tongue, and, though they had nothing to give us to eat, they would receive us with the best good will, and present us with mantles of cotton, hides, and other articles of their wealth. Still it appeared to them we ought by no means to take that course.

Doubting what it would be best to do, and which way we should choose for suitableness and support, we remained two days with these Indians, who gave us beans and pumpkins for our subsistence. Their method of cooking is so new that for its strangeness I desire to speak of it; thus it may be seen and remarked how curious and diversified are the contrivances and ingenuity of the human family. Not having discovered the use of pipkins, to boil what they would eat, they fill the half of a large calabash with water, and throw on the fire many stones of such as are most convenient and readily take the heat. When hot, they are taken up with tongs of sticks and dropped into the calabash until the water in it boils from the fervor of the stones. Then whatever is to be cooked is put in, and until it is done they continue taking out cooled stones and throwing in hot ones. Thus they boil their food.

31.
Of our taking the way to the maize.

Two days being spent while we tarried, we resolved to go in search of the maize. We did not wish to follow the path leading to where the cattle are, because it is towards the north, and for us very circuitous, since we ever held it certain that going towards the sunset we must find what we desired.

Thus we took our way, and traversed all the country until coming out at the South Sea. Nor was the dread we had of the sharp hunger through which we should have to pass (as in verity we did, throughout the seventeen days' journey of which the natives spoke) sufficient to hinder us. During all that time, in ascending by the river, they gave us many coverings of cowhide; but we did not eat of the fruit. Our sustenance each day was about a handful of deer-suet, which we had a long time been used to saving for such trials. Thus we passed the entire journey of seventeen days, and at the close we crossed the river and travelled other seventeen days.

As the sun went down, upon some plains that lie between chains of very great mountains, we found a people who for the third part of the year eat nothing but the powder of straw, and, that being the season when we passed, we also had to eat of it, until reaching permanent habitations, where was abundance of maize brought together. They gave us a large quantity in grain and flour, pumpkins, beans, and shawls of cotton. With all these we loaded our guides, who went back the happiest creatures on earth. We gave thanks to God, our Lord, for having brought us where we had found so much food.

Some houses are of earth, the rest all of cane mats. From this point we marched through more than a hundred leagues of country, and continually found settled domicils, with plenty of maize and beans. The people gave us many deer and cotton shawls better than those of New Spain, many beads and certain corals found on the South Sea, and fine turquoises that come from the north. Indeed they gave us every thing they had. To me they gave five emeralds made into arrowheads, which they use at their singing and dancing. They appeared to be very precious. I asked whence they got these; and they said the stones were brought from some lofty mountains that stand toward the north, where were populous towns and very large houses, and that they were purchased with plumes and the feathers of parrots.

Among this people the women are treated with more decorum than in any part of the Indias we had visited. They wear a shirt of cotton that falls as low as the knee, and over it half sleeves with skirts reaching to the ground, made of dressed deer-skin. It opens in front and is brought close with straps of leather. They soap this with a certain root that cleanses well, by which they are enabled to keep it becomingly. Shoes are worn. The people all came to us that we should touch and bless them, they being very urgent, which we could accomplish only with great labor, for sick and well all wished to go with a benediction. Many times it occurred that some of the women who accompanied us gave birth; and so soon as the child were born the mothers would bring them to us that we should touch and bless them.

These Indians ever accompanied us until they delivered us to others; and all held full faith in our coming from heaven. While travelling, we went without food all day until night, and we ate so little as to astonish them. We never felt exhaus-

tion, neither were we in fact at all weary, so inured were we to hardship. We possessed great influence and authority: to preserve both, we seldom talked with them. The negro was in constant conversation; he informed himself about the ways we wished to take, of the towns there were, and the matters we desired to know.

We passed through many and dissimilar tongues. Our Lord granted us favor with the people who spoke them, for they always understood us, and we them. We questioned them, and received their answers by signs, just as if they spoke our language and we theirs; for, although we knew six languages, we could not everywhere avail ourselves of them, there being a thousand differences.

Throughout all these countries the people who were at war immediately made friends, that they might come to meet us, and bring what they possessed. In this way we left all the land at peace, and we taught all the inhabitants by signs, which they understood, that in heaven was a Man we called God, who had created the sky and the earth; Him we worshipped and had for our master; that we did what He commanded and from His hand came all good; and would they do as we did, all would be well with them. So ready of apprehension we found them that, could we have had the use of language by which to make ourselves perfectly understood, we should have left them all Christians. Thus much we gave them to understand the best we could. And afterward, when the sun rose, they opened their hands together with loud shouting towards the heavens, and then drew them down all over their bodies. They did the same again when the sun went down. They are a people of good condition and substance, capable in any pursuit.

32.
The Indians give us the hearts of deer.

In the town where the emeralds were presented to us the people gave Dorantes over six hundred open hearts of deer. They ever keep a good supply of them for food, and we called the place Pueblo de los Corazones. It is the entrance into many provinces on the South Sea. They who go to look for them, and do not enter there, will be lost. On the coast is no maize: the inhabitants eat the powder of rush and of straw, and fish that is caught in the sea from rafts, not having canoes.

With grass and straw the women cover their nudity. They are a timid and dejected people.

We think that near the coast by way of those towns through which we came are more than a thousand leagues of inhabited country, plentiful of subsistence. Three times the year it is planted with maize and beans. Deer are of three kinds; one the size of the younger steer of Spain. There are innumerable houses, such as are called *bahíos*. They have poison from a certain tree the size of the apple. For effect no more is necessary than to pluck the fruit and moisten the arrow with it, or, if there be no fruit, to break a twig and with the milk do the like. The tree is abundant and so deadly that, if the leaves be bruised and steeped in some neighboring water, the deer and other animals drinking it soon burst.

We were in this town three days. A day's journey farther was another town, at which the rain fell heavily while we were there, and the river became so swollen we could not cross it, which detained us fifteen days. In this time Castillo saw the buckle of a sword-belt on the neck of an Indian and stitched to it the nail of a horseshoe. He took them, and we asked the native what they were: he answered that they came from heaven. We questioned him further, as to who had brought them thence: they all responded that certain men who wore beards like us had come from heaven and arrived at that river, bringing horses, lances, and swords, and that they had lanced two Indians. In a manner of the utmost indifference we could feign, we asked them what had become of those men. They answered us that they had gone to sea, putting their lances beneath the water, and going themselves also under the water; afterwards that they were seen on the surface going towards the sunset. For this we gave many thanks to God our Lord. We had before despaired of ever hearing more of Christians. Even yet we were left in great doubt and anxiety, thinking those people were merely persons who had come by sea on discoveries. However, as we had now such exact information, we made greater speed, and, as we advanced on our way, the news of the Christians continually grew. We told the natives that we were going in search of that people, to order them not to kill nor make slaves of them, nor take them from their lands, nor do other injustice. Of this the Indians were very glad.

We passed through many territories and found them all vacant: their inhabitants wandered fleeing among the mountains, without daring to have houses or till the earth for fear of Christians. The sight was one of infinite pain to us, a land very fertile and beautiful, abounding in springs and streams, the hamlets deserted and burned, the people thin and weak, all fleeing or in concealment. As they did not plant, they appeased their keen hunger by eating roots and the bark of trees. We bore a share in the famine along the whole way; for poorly could these unfortunates provide for us, themselves being so reduced they looked as though they would willingly die. They brought shawls of those they had concealed because of the Christians, presenting them to us; and they related how the Christians at other times had come through the land, destroying and burning the towns, carrying away half the men, and all the women and the boys, while those who had been able to escape were wandering about fugitives. We found them so alarmed they dared not remain anywhere. They would not nor could they till the earth, but preferred to die rather than live in dread of such cruel usage as they received. Although these showed themselves greatly delighted with us, we feared that on our arrival among those who held the frontier, and fought against the Christians, they would treat us badly, and revenge upon us the conduct of their enemies; but, when God our Lord was pleased to bring us there, they began to dread and respect us as the others had done, and even somewhat more, at which we no little wondered. Thence it may at once be seen that, to bring all these people to be Christians and to the obedience of the Imperial Majesty, they must be won by kindness, which is a way certain, and no other is.

They took us to a town on the edge of a range of mountains, to which the ascent is over difficult crags. We found many people there collected out of fear of the Christians. They received us well, and presented us all they had. They gave us more than two thousand back-loads of maize, which we gave to the distressed and hungered beings who guided us to that place. The next day we despatched four messengers through the country, as we were accustomed to do, that they should call together all the rest of the Indians at a town distant three days' march. We set out the day after with all the people. The tracks of the Chris-

THE FIRST CROSSING OF NORTH AMERICA BY THE EUROPEANS

tians and marks where they slept were continually seen. At mid-day we met our messengers, who told us they had found no Indians, that they were roving and hiding in the forests, fleeing that the Christians might not kill nor make them slaves; the night before they had observed the Christians from behind trees, and discovered what they were about, carrying away many people in chains.

Those who came with us were alarmed at this intelligence; some returned to spread the news over the land that the Christians were coming; and many more would have followed, had we not forbidden it and told them to cast aside their fear, when they reasssured themselves and were well content. At the time we had Indians with us belonging a hundred leagues behind, and we were in no condition to discharge them, that they might return to their homes. To encourage them, we stayed there that night; the day after we marched and slept on the road. The following day those whom we had sent forward as messengers guided us to the place where they had seen Christians. We arrived in the afternoon, and saw at once that they told the truth. We perceived that the persons were mounted, by the stakes to which the horses had been tied.

From this spot, called the river Petutan, to the river to which Diego de Guzmán came, where we heard of Christians, may be as many as eighty leagues; thence to the town where the rains overtook us, twelve leagues, and that is twelve leagues from the South Sea. Throughout this region, wheresoever the mountains extend, we saw clear traces of gold and lead, iron, copper, and other metals. Where the settled habitations are, the climate is hot; even in January the weather is very warm. Thence toward the meridian, the country unoccupied to the North Sea is unhappy and sterile. There we underwent great and incredible hunger. Those who inhabit and wander over it are a race of evil inclination and most cruel customs. The people of the fixed residences and those beyond regard silver and gold with indifference, nor can they conceive of any use for them.

33.
We see traces of Christians.

When we saw sure signs of Christians, and heard how near we were to them, we gave thanks to God our Lord for having chosen to bring us out of a captivity so melancholy and wretched. The delight we felt let each one conjecture, when he shall remember the length of time we were in that country, the suffering and perils we underwent. That night I entreated my companions that one of them should go back three days' journey after the Christians who were moving about over the country, where we had given assurance of protection. Neither of them received this proposal well, excusing themselves because of weariness and exhaustion; and although either might have done better than I, being more youthful and athletic, yet seeing their unwillingness, the next morning I took the negro with eleven Indians, and, following the Christians by their trail, I travelled ten leagues, passing three villages, at which they had slept.

The day after I overtook four of them on horseback, who were astonished at the sight of me, so strangely habited as I was, and in company with Indians. They stood staring at me a length of time, so confounded that they neither hailed me nor drew near to make an inquiry. I bade them take me to their chief: accordingly we went together half a league to the place where was Diego de Alcaraz, their captain.

After we had conversed, he stated to me that he was completely undone; he had not been able in a long time to take any Indians; he knew not which way to turn, and his men had well begun to experience hunger and fatigue. I told him of Castillo and Dorantes, who were behind, ten leagues off, with a multitude that conducted us. He thereupon sent three cavalry to them, with fifty of the Indians who accompanied him. The negro returned to guide them, while I remained. I asked the Christians to give me a certificate of the year, month, and day I arrived there, and of the manner of my coming, which they accordingly did. From this river to the town of the Christians, named San Miguel, within the government of the province called New Galicia, are thirty leagues.

34.
Of sending for the Christians.

Five days having elapsed, Andrés Dorantes and Alonzo del Castillo arrived with those who had been sent after them. They brought more than six hundred persons of that community, whom the Christians had driven into the forests, and who had wandered in concealment over the land. Those who accompanied us so far had drawn them out, and given them to the Christians, who thereupon dismissed all the others they had brought with them. Upon their coming to where I was, Alcaraz begged that we would summon the people of the towns on the margin of the river, who straggled about under cover of the woods, and order them to fetch us something to eat. This last was unnecessary, the Indians being ever diligent to bring us all they could. Directly we sent our messengers to call them, when there came six hundred souls, bringing us all the maize in their possession. They fetched it in certain pots, closed with clay, which they had concealed in the earth. They brought us whatever else they had; but we, wishing only to have the provision, gave the rest to the Christians, that they might divide among themselves. After this we had many high words with them; for they wished to make slaves of the Indians we brought.

In consequence of the dispute, we left at our departure many bows of Turkish shape we had along with us and many pouches. The five arrows with the points of emerald were forgotten among others, and we lost them. We gave the Christians a store of robes of cowhide and other things we brought. We found it difficult to induce the Indians to return to their dwellings, to feel no apprehension and plant maize. They were willing to do nothing until they had gone with us and delivered us into the hands of other Indians, as had been the custom; for, if they returned without doing so, they were afraid they should die, and, going with us, they feared neither Christians nor lances. Our countrymen became jealous at this, and caused their interpreter to tell the Indians that we were of them, and for a long time we had been lost; that they were the lords of the land who must be obeyed and served, while we were persons of mean condition and small force. The Indians cared little or nothing for what was told them; and conversing among themselves said the Christians lied: that we had come whence the sun rises, and they whence it goes down; we healed the sick, they killed the sound; that we had come naked and barefooted, while they had arrived in clothing and on horses with lances; that we were not covetous of anything, but all that was given to us we directly turned to give, remaining with nothing;

that the others had the only purpose to rob whomsoever they found, bestowing nothing on any one.

In this way they spoke of all matters respecting us, which they enhanced by contrast with matters concerning the others, delivering their response through the interpreter of the Spaniards. To other Indians they made this known by means of one among them through whom they understood us. Those who speak that tongue we discriminately call Primahaitu, which is like saying Vasconyados. We found it in use over more than four hundred leagues of our travel, without another over that whole extent. Even to the last, I could not convince the Indians that we were of the Christians; and only with great effort and solicitation we got them to go back to their residences. We ordered them to put away apprehension, establish their towns, plant and cultivate the soil.

From abandonment the country had already grown up thickly in trees. It is, no doubt, the best in all these Indias, the most prolific and plenteous in provisions. Three times in the year it is planted. It produces great variety of fruit, has beautiful rivers, with many other good waters. There are ores with clear traces of gold and silver. The people are well disposed: they serve such Christians as are their friends, with great good will. They are comely, much more so than the Mexicans. Indeed, the land needs no circumstance to make it blessed.

The Indians, at taking their leave, told us they would do what we commanded, and would build their towns, if the Christians would suffer them; and this I say and affirm most positively, that, if they have not done so, it is the fault of the Christians.

After we had dismissed the Indians in peace, and thanked them for the toil they had supported with us, the Christians with subtlety sent us on our way under charge of Zebreros, an alcalde, attended by two men. They took us through forests and solitudes, to hinder us from intercourse with the natives, that we might neither witness nor have knowledge of the act they would commit. It is but an instance of how frequently men are mistaken in their aims; we set about to preserve the liberty of the Indians and thought we had secured it, but the contrary appeared; for the Christians had arranged to go and spring upon those we had sent away in peace and confidence.

They executed their plan as they had designed, taking us through the woods, wherein for two days we were lost, without water and without way. Seven of our men died of thirst, and we all thought to have perished. Many friendly to the Christians in their company were unable to reach the place where we got water the second night, until the noon of next day. We travelled twenty-five leagues, little more or less, and reached a town of friendly Indians. The alcalde left us there, and went on three leagues farther to a town called Culiacan where was Melchior Diaz, principal alcalde and captain of the province.

35.
The chief alcalde receives us kindly the night we arrive.

The *alcalde mayor* knew of the expedition, and, hearing of our return, he immediately left that night and came to where we were. He wept with us, giving praises to God our Lord for having extended over us so great care. He comforted and entertained us hospitably. In behalf of the Governor, Nuño de Guzman and himself, he tendered all that he had, and the service in his power. He showed much regret for the seizure, and the injustice we had received from Alcaraz and others. We were sure, had he been present, what was done to the Indians and to us would never have occurred.

The night being passed, we set out the next day for Anhacan. The chief alcalde besought us to tarry there, since by so doing we could be of eminent service to God and your Majesty; the deserted land was without tillage and everywhere badly wasted, the Indians were fleeing and concealing themselves in the thickets, unwilling to occupy their towns; we were to send and call them, commanding them in behalf of God and the King, to return to live in the vales and cultivate the soil.

To us this appeared difficult to effect. We had brought no native of our own, nor of those who accompanied us according to custom, intelligent in these affairs. At last we made the attempt with two captives, brought from that country, who were with the Christians we first overtook. They had seen the people who conducted us, and learned from them the great authority and command we carried and exercised throughout those

parts, the wonders we had worked, the sick we had cured, and the many things besides we had done. We ordered that they, with others of the town, should go together to summon the hostile natives among the mountains and of the river Petachan, where we had found the Christians, and say to them they must come to us, that we wished to speak with them. For the protection of the messengers, and as a token to the others of our will, we gave them a gourd of those we were accustomed to bear in our hands, which had been our principal insignia and evidence of rank, and with this they went away.

The Indians were gone seven days, and returned with three chiefs of those revolted among the ridges, who brought with them fifteen men, and presented us beads, turquoises, and feathers. The messengers said they had not found the people of the river where we appeared, the Christians having again made them run away into the mountains. Melchior Diaz told the interpreter to speak to the natives for us; to say to them we came in the name of God, who is in heaven; that we had travelled about the world many years, telling all the people we found that they should believe in God and serve Him; for He was the Master of all things on the earth, benefiting and rewarding the virtuous, and to the bad giving perpetual punishment of fire; that, when the good die, He takes them to heaven, where none ever die, nor feel cold, nor hunger, nor thirst, nor any inconvenience whatsoever, but the greatest enjoyment possible to conceive; that those who will not believe in Him, nor obey His commands, He casts beneath the earth into the company of demons, and into a great fire which is never to go out, but always torment; that, over this, if they desired to be Christians and serve God in the way we required, the Christians would cherish them as brothers and behave towards them very kindly; that we would command they give no offence nor take them from their territories, but be their great friends. If the Indians did not do this, the Christians would treat them very hardly, carrying them away as slaves into other lands.

They answered through the interpreter that they would be true Christians and serve God. Being asked to whom they sacrifice and offer worship, from whom they ask rain for their cornfields and health for themselves, they answered of a man that is in heaven. We inquired of them his name, and they told us Aguar; and they believed he created the whole world, and the things in it. We returned to question them as to how they knew this; they answered their fathers and grandfathers had told them, that from distant time had come their knowledge, and they knew the rain and all good things were sent to them by him. We told them that the name of him of whom they spoke we called Dios; and if they would call him so, and would worship him as we directed, they would find their welfare. They responded that they well understood, and would do as we said. We ordered them to come down from the mountains in confidence and peace, inhabit the whole country and construct their houses: among these they should build one for God, at its entrance place a cross like that which we had there present; and, when Christians came among them, they should go out to receive them with crosses in their hands, without bows or any arms, and take them to their dwellings, giving of what they have to eat, and the Christians would do them no injury, but be their friends; and the Indians told us they would do as we had commanded.

The captain having given them shawls and entertained them, they returned, taking the two captives who had been used as emissaries. This occurrence took place before the notary, in the presence of many witnesses.

36.
Of building churches in that land.

As soon as these Indians went back, all those of that province who were friendly to the Christians, and had heard of us, came to visit us, bringing beads and feathers. We commanded them to build churches and put crosses in them: to that time none had been raised; and we made them bring their principal men to be baptized.

Then the captain made a covenant with God, not to invade nor consent to invasion, nor to enslave any of that country and people, to whom we had guaranteed safety; that this he would enforce and defend until your Majesty and the Governor Nuño de Guzman, or the Viceroy in your name, should direct what would be most for the service of God and your Highness.

When the children had been baptized, we departed for the town of San Miguel. So soon as we arrived, April 1, 1536, came Indians, who told us many people had come down from the mountains and were living in the vales; that they had made churches and crosses, doing all we had required. Each day we heard how these things were advancing to a full improvement.

Fifteen days of our residence having passed, Alcaraz got back with the Christians from the incursion, and they related to the captain the manner in which the Indians had come down and peopled the plain; that the towns were inhabited which had been tenantless and deserted, the residents, coming out to receive them with crosses in their hands, had taken them to their houses, giving of what they had, and the Christians had slept among them over night. They were surprised at a thing so novel; but, as the natives said they had been assured of safety, it was ordered that they should not be harmed, and the Christians took friendly leave of them.

God in His infinite mercy is pleased that in the days of your Majesty, under your might and dominion, these nations should come to be thorougly and voluntarily subject to the Lord, who has created and redeemed us. We regard this as certain, that your Majesty is he who is destined to do so much, not difficult to accomplish; for in the two thousand leagues we journeyed on land, and in boats on water, and in that we travelled unceasingly for ten months after coming out of captivity, we found neither sacrifices nor idolatry.

In the time, we traversed from sea to sea; and from information gathered with great diligence, there may be a distance from one to another at the widest part, of two thousand leagues; and we learned that on the coast of the South Sea there are pearls and great riches, and the best and all the most opulent countries are near there.

We were in the village of San Miguel until the fifteenth day of May. The cause of so long a detention was, that from thence to the city of Compostela, where the Governor Nuño de Guzman resided, are a hundred leagues of country, entirely devastated and filled with enemies, where it was necessary we should have protection. Twenty mounted men went with us for forty leagues, and after that six Christians accompanied us, who had with them five hundred slaves. Arrived at Compostela, the Governor entertained us graciously and gave us of his clothing for our use. I could not wear any for some time, nor could we sleep anywhere else but on the ground. After ten or twelve days we left for Mexico, and were all along on the way well entertained by Christians. Many came out on the roads to gaze at us, giving thanks to God for having saved us from so many calamities. We arrived at Mexico on Sunday, the day before the vespers of Saint Iago, where we were handsomely treated by the Viceroy and the Marquis del Valle, and welcomed with joy. They gave us clothing and proffered whatsoever they had. On the day of Saint Iago was a celebration, and a joust of reeds with bulls.

37.

Of what occurred when I wished to return.

When we had rested two months in Mexico, I desired to return to these kingdoms; and being about to embark in the month of October, a storm came on, capsizing the ship, and she was lost. In consequence I resolved to remain through the winter; because in those parts it is a boisterous season for navigation. After that had gone by, Dorantes and I left Mexico, about Lent, to take shipping at Vera Cruz. We remained waiting for a wind until Palm Sunday, when we went on board, and were detained fifteen days longer for a wind. The ship leaked so much that I quitted her, and went to one of two other vessels that were ready to sail, but Dorantes remained in her.

On the tenth day of April, the three ships left the port, and sailed one hundred and fifty leagues. Two of them leaked a great deal; and one night the vessel I was in lost their company. Their pilots and masters, as afterwards appeared, dared not proceed with the other vessels so, and without telling us of their intentions, or letting us know aught of them, put back to the port they had left. We pursued our voyage, and on the fourth day of May we entered the harbor of Havana, in the island of Cuba. We remained waiting for the other vessels, believing them to be on their way, until the second of June, when we sailed, in much fear of falling in with Frenchmen, as they had a few days before taken three Spanish vessels. Having arrived at the island of Bermuda, we were struck by one of those storms that overtake those who pass there, according to what they state who sail thither. All one night we considered ourselves lost; and we were thankful that when morning was come, the storm ceased, and we could go on our course.

At the end of twenty-nine days after our departure from Havana, we had sailed eleven hundred leagues, which are said to be thence to the town of the Azores. The next morning, passing by the island called Cuervo, we fell in with a French ship. At noon she began to follow, bringing with her a caravel captured from the Portuguese, and gave us chase. In the evening we saw nine other sail; but they were so distant we could not make out whether they were Portuguese or of those that pursued us. At night the Frenchman was within shot of a lombard from our ship, and we stole away from our course in the dark to evade him, and this we did three or four times. He approached so near that he saw us and fired. He might have taken us, or, at his option could leave us until the morning. I remember with gratitude to the Almighty when the sun rose, and we found ourselves close with the Frenchman, that near us were the nine sail we saw the evening before, which we now recognized to be of the fleet of Portugal. I gave thanks to our Lord for escape from the troubles of the land and perils of the sea. The Frenchman, so soon as he discovered their character, let go the caravel he had seized with a cargo of negroes and kept as a prize, to make us think he was Portuguese, that we might wait for him. When he cast her off, he told the pilot and the master of her, that we were French and under his convoy. This said, sixty oars were put out from his ship, and thus with these and sail he commenced to flee, moving so fast it was hardly credible. The caravel being let go, went to the galleon, and informed the commander that the other ship and ours were French. As we drew nigh the galleon, and the fleet saw we were coming down upon them, they made no doubt we were, and putting themselves in order of battle, bore up for us, and when near we hailed them. Discovering that we were friends, they found that they were mocked in permitting the corsair to escape, by being told that we were French and of his company.

Four caravels were sent in pursuit. The galleon drawing near, after the salutation from us, the commander, Diego de Silveira, asked whence we came and what merchandise we carried, when we answered that we came from New Spain, and were loaded with silver and gold. He asked us how much there might be; the captain told him we carried three thousand *castellanos*. The commander replied: "In honest truth you come very rich, although you bring a very sorry ship and a still poorer artillery. By Heaven, that renegade whoreson Frenchman has lost a good mouthful. Now that you have escaped, follow me, and do not leave me that I may, with God's help, deliver you in Spain."

After a little time, the caravels that pursued the Frenchman returned, for plainly he moved too fast for them; they did not like either, to leave the fleet, which was guarding three ships that came laden with spices. Thus we reached the island of Terceira, where we reposed fifteen days, taking refreshment and awaiting the arrival of another ship coming with a cargo from India, the companion of the three of which the armada was in charge. The time having run out, we left that place with the fleet, and arrived at the port of Lisbon on the ninth of August, on the vespers of the day of our master Saint Lawrence, in the year one thousand five hundred and thirty-seven.

That what I have stated in my foregoing narrative is true, I subscribe with my name.

Cabeza de Vaca

The narrative here ended is signed with his name and arms.

38.
Of what became of the others who went to Indias.

Since giving this circumstantial account of events attending the voyage to Florida, the invasion, and our going out thence until the arrival in these realms, I desire to state what became of the ships and of the people who remained with them. I have not before touched on this, as we were uninformed until coming to New Spain, where we found many of the persons, and others here in Castile, from whom we learned everything to the latest particular.

At the time we left, one of the ships had already been lost on the breakers, and the three others were in considerable danger, having nearly a hundred souls on board and few stores. Among the persons were ten married women, one of

whom had told the Governor many things that afterwards befell him on the voyage. She cautioned him before he went inland not to go, as she was confident that neither he nor any going with him could ever escape; but should any one come back from that country, the Almighty must work great wonders in his behalf, though she believed few or none would return. The Governor said that he and his followers were going to fight and conquer nations and countries wholly unknown, and in subduing them he knew that many would be slain; nevertheless, that those who survived would be fortunate, since from what he had understood of the opulence of that land, they must become very rich. And further he begged her to inform him whence she learned those things that had passed, as well as those she spoke of, that were to come; she replied that in Castile a Moorish woman of Hornachos had told them to her, which she had stated to us likewise before we left Spain, and while on the passage many things happened in the way she foretold.

After the Governor had made Caravallo, a native of Cuenca de Huete, his lieutenant and commander of the vessels and people, he departed, leaving orders that all diligence should be used to repair on board, and take the direct course to Pánuco, keeping along the shore closely examining for the harbor, and having found it, the vessels should enter there and await our arrival. And the people state, that when they had betaken themselves to the ships, all of them looking at that woman, they distinctly heard her say to the females, that well, since their husbands had gone inland, putting their persons in so great jeopardy, their wives should in no way take more account of them, but ought soon to be looking after whom they would marry, and that she should do so. She did accordingly: she and others married, or became the concubines of those who remained in the ships.

After we left, the vessels made sail, taking their course onward; but not finding the harbor, they returned. Five leagues below the place at which we debarked, they found the port, the same we discovered when we saw the Spanish cases containing dead bodies, which were of Christians. Into this haven and along this coast, the three ships passed with the other ship that came from Cuba, and the brigantine, looking for us nearly a year, and not finding us, they went to New Spain.

The port of which we speak is the best in the world. At the entrance are six fathoms of water and five near the shore. It runs up into the land seven or eight leagues. The bottom is fine white sand. No sea breaks upon it nor boisterous storm, and it can contain many vessels. Fish is in great plenty. There are a hundred leagues to Havana, a town of Christians in Cuba, with which it bears north and south. The north-east wind ever prevails and vessels go from one to the other, returning in a few days; for the reason that they sail either way with it on the quarter.

As I have given account of the vessels, it may be well that I state who are, and from what parts of these kingdoms come, the persons whom our Lord has been pleased to release from these troubles. The first is Alonzo del Castillo Maldonado, native of Salamanca, son of Doctor Castillo and Doña Aldonça Maldonado. The second is Andrés Dorantes, son of Pablo Dorantes, native of Béjar, and citizen of Gibraleon. The third is Alvar Nuñez Cabeça de Vaca, son of Francisco de Vera, and grandson of Pedro de Vera who conquered the Canaries, and his mother was Doña Tereça Cabeça de Vaca, native of Xeréz de la Frontera. The fourth, called Estevánico, is an Arabian black, native of Açamor.

236. 1528–1536. The joint report of Cabeza de Vaca and his companions.

The joint report made in 1537 by Alvar Núñez Cabeza de Vaca, Andrés Dorantes, and Alonzo del Castillo Maldonado, three of the first men who completed the epic journey across North America, survives only in the curtailed version preserved in Gonzalo Fernández de Oviedo, His-toria general y natural de las Indias, bk. xxxv, chaps. 1–6, written shortly after the events de-scribed in it, but published only in the first com-plete edition of the Historia, *4 vols. (Madrid, 1851). Oviedo uses rather than prints the report. He appears to have adhered closely to its outline, but provides an effective counterpart to Cabeza de Vaca's own story. His contents' summaries at the heads of the chapters have been omitted.*

A first translation was made by Herbert Davenport in The Southwestern History Quar-terly, *XXVII (1924), 120–139, 217–241, 276–304, XXVIII (1925), 56–74. It was retranslated by Gerald Theisen in* The Narrative of Alvar Núñez Cabeza de Vaca, *with an introduction by J. F. Bannon (The Imprint Society, Barre, Mass., 1972), pp. 161–271, from which it is reprinted.*

1.

From the account made by those who es-caped from the unfortunate fleet of Captain Pánfilo de Narváez and that which happened to them on the coast and northern lands.

Álvar Núñez Cabeza de Vaca, Alonso del Cas-tillo, Andrés Dorantes, and a black man named Estéban alone survived from the entire fleet of Governor Pánfilo de Narváez. This same Cabeza de Vaca was treasurer and official of His Majesty, and he said that from Xagua, which is a port or anchorage on the island of Cuba, he had written to His Majesty on the fifteenth of February, 1527 [1528]. He told that which had happened to them up until then, about the loss of two ships with sixty men and all that went on them. Having lost these people and ships, and more than twenty horses that went aboard them, they agreed to winter there in the port of Xagua. This same Cabeza de Vaca said that he stayed there from the sixth of November of the year, 1527, with four ships and all the people, until the twenty-second day of the month of February of the following year, 1528, when the Governor arrived there.

The Governor then embarked in order to con-tinue his journey with four hundred men and eighty horses in four ships and a brigantine. They sailed the seas until the twelfth day of April, the Tuesday of Holy Week, when they arrived at the mainland. They continued along the shore until Holy Thursday, when they entered into a shallow bay along the coast. At the end of this bay, they saw some Indian huts. On the next day, Good Friday, they went ashore with as many people as they could put into the launches. They disem-barked near the huts in which they found no people because the Indians had abandoned them. One of the huts was so large that three hundred people could fit inside, but the rest of them were small. They found many nets for fishing, and among these nets was found a timbrel of gold. On the next day, the Governor had His Majesty's flags raised, and he took possession of the land. He brought all His Majesty's officials together, along with the friars who were there, as well as the people who had gone ashore. The Governor then presented his royal orders which he carried, and they were recognized by all. He was accepted as Governor and Captain General. The officials also presented their orders, and likewise they were declared officials of His Majesty. Then, the order was given for the rest of the people to land, along with the horses which were very fatigued. It had been a long time that the horses had been aboard ship, and almost half of the number had been lost at sea.

The next Sunday, Easter, the Indians of that village came, and they talked to the Christians without being understood. However, it seemed as if they were threatening and were saying that the Christians should leave the land. The Indians also made gestures and grimaces, and, having done that, they left. On the next day, in order to see the land, and to probe what it was like, the Governor sent six men on horseback and forty men on foot to the northeast. They continued in that direction until they arrived that same day at a bay that cuts into the land, and from there they returned to the rest of the party. The Governor was among these men, as he was one of the six on horseback.

The next day, the Governor dispatched the brigantine that he had with him so that she might explore the coast of Florida. She could then look for a port, which the pilot Miruelo said he knew about, where he could take these people. He was mistaken about this, as he did not know where he was. The Governor sent the Brigantine so that looking in this manner she might return to the island of Cuba, and then she could go to the village and port of Havana. There they could search for another ship that they were waiting for, in which were to be forty men and twelve horses. If they could find this ship, both the ships would take on all the provisions they could in Havana. Then, they would take these provisions to where the Governor and the Christians were.

Having done this, the Christians left there. They pushed deeper into the bay, which is the one that they had discovered, and they sailed along its shoreline. When they had gone four leagues from where they started, they encountered some Indians. The Spaniards captured three of them and showed them a little maize, asking them if they

knew where there was some. They led the Christians to a village which was at the end of that bay. At this place, the Indians showed them a small amount of maize that they had sown there. This was the first which the Spaniards saw in that land. There they also found some large Castilian chests. In each one of them was a dead man, and the bodies were covered with some painted hides. It appeared to them, the *fray comisario* and the friars, that those objects were idolatrous, and the Governor had them burned. Likewise, the Christians found pieces of shoes and canvas, as well as pieces of cloth and some iron. Asking the Indians, they answered by signs that they had found them in a ship that had been lost on that coast and bay. The Governor showed them a little gold, and they said that there was not any in their land. However, far from there, in the province that they called Apalache, there was much gold in great quantity. As far as what the Christians could understand by their signs, all that was shown to the Indians which they thought the Christians valued, they said that there was much of it in Apalache.

With this simple information, the Christians departed from that place, taking with them those captive Indians. Ten or twelve leagues from that place, they found about twelve or fifteen houses in which there was maize. The Spaniards stayed there two days without seeing a single Indian. They then agreed to return to where they had left the purser and other people with the ships. After having arrived, they related to these people that which they had encountered inland, which was nothing more than what has already been stated.

The following day, the first of May, the Governor had all the officers of the King and the *fray comisario* gather together. By an official statement before a notary, he told them that he wanted to go inland while the ships continued along the coast. Then, the Governor asked them for their opinions about this. The treasurer, Cabeza de Vaca, replied that it seemed to him that the Governor should not depart from the ships without leaving them first in a harbor and a populated area. After having done this, the Governor could go inland along with those under his command. They would then have a place, at a specific point, to which they could return to look for the rest of the people when it suited them. For many reasons, it appeared to Cabeza de Vaca that the

Governor should not go inland. Based on the information of the Indians, besides that which the Christians had observed, the land which they had entered was a poor land and without people. Also, they were waiting for the brigantine and the other ship from Havana. As was mentioned, they were counting on these ships for provisions. Moreover, the pilots did not know, nor were they reaching an understanding of, where they were. Also, for other reasons that to the treasurer seemed correct, he said that that which the Governor was doing, he should not do.

The *fray comisario* said that his opinion was that they should go inland. They should travel staying near the coast until arriving at the harbor which the pilots said would be fifteen leagues from there, on the way to Pánuco. They would not be able to pass by without touching on this bay, because it went into the land for twelve leagues. There they would wait for the ships and the ships would wait for them. The *fray comisario* also said that they should not once again embark, because it would be to tempt God. They had already suffered so many misadventures and difficulties in order to arrive there.

The purser and the inspector agreed with the *fray comisario*, and the Governor resolved to do it in that manner. However, upon seeing his determination, the treasurer notified him many times that he should not go inland, for the reasons which the treasurer had already stated, as well as for others which mounted with his pleas. The treasurer maintained that the Governor should neither abandon the ships, nor the people that were on them, without first having them secure in a known and populated port. He added that afterwards the Governor might do that which seemed best to him. The treasurer then asked for a record of his statements from the notary who was present. The Governor replied further that he was moving the town which had been established. This was because there was neither a port nor a mandate to populate that area where they were, and also because of the sterility of the land. The Governor said that he was going in search of a port and land to settle, and he required that which he said to be recorded as an official statement. He then ordered that all the people should prepare themselves to go with him and that the ships should be provided with that which was necessary.

On the next day they left that place, taking with them forty men on horseback and two hundred and sixty men on foot. The previously mentioned officers, the *fray comisario*, and the other friars went with the Governor. They journeyed inland and went for fifteen days with a pound of bread and a half a pound of bacon for rations. They then arrived at a river which they swam across. After having crossed it, two hundred Indians came and confronted them. The Christians fought with these natives, and they captured five or six of them. These captured Indians took the Spaniards to their houses, which were near there. In the fields they found much maize which was ready for eating.

The next day both the officers and the friars entreated the Governor to send a group to search for the sea and for a port, if there was one. He sent the treasurer along with Alonso del Castillo. The Governor thought that they should go with forty men. It was thus that they left, on foot because they were not able to take horses. They went along the lowlands of the seacoast, through areas of oyster reefs. It had been a journey of two leagues when they arrived at a place where a river passed. It was the same river which they had crossed farther inland on the day before. Since it was deep, they could not cross it, and they returned to the base camp.

The following day the Governor sent a captain with six men on horseback and forty men on foot to follow the river from which the party had just returned. He was to explore that bay of the river so that he might see if there was a port. According to these instructions, he did it. The captain found that the bay was shallow, and ships would not be able to enter there. With this information, they left that place looking for the province called Apalache, taking with them as guides the Indians whom they had captured.

They travelled until a day after St. John's day in June, at which time they arrived at Apalache. This was the thing which they most desired in the world, since all during the long trip there was a great necessity for provisions. Even though in some places they found maize growing on the land, many times they walked four or five days' journey without finding any. Moreover, in addition to this reason, the Indians had said there was much gold in that province. When the Spaniards arrived at the town, they attacked with much force in order to enter it. However, they did not find anyone who could resist their attack, and they took women and the children captive. There were no men, as they had all gone. There were in that town forty small houses. These were built for protection because of the great cold and the storms that there are in that land. The Spaniards found many deerskins and some blankets of thick thread. There were numerous maize fields in the countryside, as well as much dry maize in the town.

The land, through which these Spaniards passed, is flat with crusty sand dunes. There are many pine forests, although they are sparse with some of the pines separated from the others. Also, there are many lagoons, as well as many deer, all over the land. Many groves of trees and single trees have fallen because of the great storms and hurricanes which occur very often in that region. Thus, they saw many trees scarred from top to base because of the lightening bolts which fall. During the entire journey since they crossed that river, they did not find any people who dared to show themselves.

At the end of the second day that the Christians had been in Apalache, the Indians came in peace. Their chief was among them. They asked for their women and children, and the Spaniards gave all of them to the Indians. Even though the Governor had their chief with him, they attacked on the next day. They managed to set fire to the huts where the Christians were. There were up to two hundred natives. However, since the Spaniards were vigilant, they went out quickly and daringly among the Indians, who took refuge by the mountain and in the hills. The Christians were not able to capture any, but they did kill two or three of them. Then, on the next day, two hundred more Indians came from another place and from other villages and peoples. Likewise, the Christians went out to them, and likewise, they withdrew and fled, as had the first Indians.

The Governor and the Spaniards stayed in this town for twenty-six days. During this time they made three journeys inland. They found all which they saw of this land very poor, and it was inhabited by few people. Moreover, the lagoons and the terrain were extremely hazardous with very dense groves of trees. The Christians asked the Indians about this land. They questioned the captured chief of this town, as well as the other natives whom the Spaniards had brought with them from the nearby land and villages. They replied that all areas of that land had fewer inhabitants and less food than the town where the Christians now were. They also stated that it was the most important town which there was in that land and that farther ahead there existed many unpopulated areas and swamps as well as lagoons and very large forests. The Spaniards then asked them if toward the sea there were villages and people. They said that eight days' journey from where they were was a village which was called Aute, which was inhabited by friends of theirs. The Indians also replied that those people had much maize and beans and that they lived near the sea.

The Spaniards agreed, at the end of twenty-six days, to leave this land for Aute. Besides that which the natives told them, there were other reason for departing from that land. During their forays, which they had made farther inland, the Christians saw that the land in which they were was not as had been described to them, and there was no hope of finding anything better up ahead. Also, in that place where they were, they had begun to harass the people and to make war upon them. The natives had killed a chief of those Indians who had accompanied the friars from New Spain. And besides, they wounded other companions when they went to drink. The Indians were at the lagoons and in the great denseness of those forests, and from those places they were shooting arrows at anyone who passed by there.

(Does it seem to you, reader, that these Christian sinners had a good pastime? I would like those friars, as well as Pánfilo de Narváez, to tell me what they preached to those Spaniards who so blindly went along with them. Misled by erroneous information, these men left their native lands, and in spite of the numbers that died, they never took heed. Who had assured them that they had seen that gold which they were looking for? What pilots did they take with them who were so experienced in navigation? These men did not even know the land, nor were they able to give an account of where they were. Moreover, what guides and what interpreters did they take with them? Oh, what a reckless blunder! What greater crime can a leader commit than to lead people into a land that neither he nor another from his group had ever been in before?

I certainly believe that Pánfilo remembered, and more than one time, that advice which I gave him in Toldeo. In truth, many times I am surprised and even angered by these captains. Often it seems that they are at the same time astute, clever, and valiant men. On the other hand, they do not know fear, nor do they take warning at any danger. This is even though they have seen many other people's heads broken, and they should have been taught a lesson. Thanks be to God that those who suffered this might have only paid with their lives, and not with any detriment to their souls! However, I am doubtful concerning the salvation of the rest. This is because I have lived in the Indies for many days, and I have seen that these men base their actions, for the most part, on this damned greediness. They set aside any scruple which their consciences might consider healthy and worthy of accepting, as well as find sensible.

Since I praised Pánfilo in the introduction as an able soldier, and afterward as captain, there is reason that I explain his actions in this case. I say that I have seen many who are valiant when they have the lance or the sword in hand. However, when deprived of weapons, they are very different individuals. I could easily point some of these men out. Fighting itself is the least important thing, because very rarely are there men of self-respect who do not fight when it is necessary for their honor. There are many captains who may know how to fight and how to command, but there are a few who can govern an army. Also, there are many captains who are good at taking orders, rather than knowing how to command. Pánfilo knew how to serve and how to do what was ordered of him, as long as Diego Velázquez commanded him on the island of Cuba. In book thirty-three of this history, one is able to see precisely what happened, when he left that place and went to New Spain. In this book thirty-five you will read how his last command ended.

Let us go on to the rest. It is something which cannot be changed or remedied. However, there is in it a warning, or rather this account will give one, for the future captains, governors, and governed. They will see it, if they do not wish to deceive themselves, closing their eyes to understanding. In this treatise they will discover what those who undertake new enterprises, like these, ought to be on their guard against and what they should fear. Every day I see that these enterprises are attempted. They bring men to destruction, without realizing where they are taking them. They know neither where they are going nor who they are following.

2.

Earlier, in the preceding chapter, it was related how these people determined to leave for Aute, and in what manner they accomplished this task. When they left Apalache, they went for eight or nine days until they arrived in Aute. In the rough terrain and the lagoons which they found, the Indians fought with them, and they killed a Spaniard. They also wounded five or six Christians and some horses. When they arrived in the village, they found that all the houses had been burned. Moreover, there were many maize fields, ready for harvest, which had also been burned. After two days the Governor ordered the treasurer, Cabeza de Vaca, as well as Andrés Dorantes and Alonzo del Castillo to go in search of the sea. They were accompanied by nine horsemen and fifty men on foot. The Governor remained with the others in that place, because a great number of the Christians were sick, and each day their conditions worsened. Thus, these gentlemen left in the company of those already mentioned, and they took the *fray comisario* with them.

(It is certainly to be believed that at this time the reverend father would have been content with the cell which he had left in Spain. These priests come to these parts looking for gremials or mitres of bishops, and thus these things cause them to lose their time, and some of them to lose their lives. Even though they are those who have served God, after they have obtained these dignified positions, which the least of them are granted, they forget their dedication. They should pray to God that their souls do not get harmed by this self-deception. Notwithstanding this, there are those priests who are neither motivated by self-interest, nor by desires and ambitions for prelacies, but strive only to serve God more in the conversion of the Indians. This is an honest, meritorious, and holy desire, and it is intentions such as these which are fruitful in these Indies. May God be merciful to the others.)

That day they left Aute, and they arrived at some lowlands by the sea, where they stayed that night. On the morning of the next day, they sent twenty men to reconnoiter the coast. They reported that they were not able to see it because it was too far away. When they returned to the base camp, they found the Governor, the purser, and the inspector fallen ill, as well as many others. After spending a day recovering in that place, they left on the following day to return to the point where they had earlier found the sea, or rather, had discovered it. They took with them as much maize as they could carry. They arrived at the coast with much difficulty, as they were not able to advance at a normal rate because of the sick men, of whom there were many.

They stayed there for two days, exploring and thinking about the ways there were to save their lives and for getting out of that land. When they thought about building ships in which they could leave, it seemed to them that it would be an impossible task. They had no nails, burlap, pitch, nor the other things which were necessary for this work. Since necessity had them in this extreme, they took the stirrups from the horses, as well as the bridles and the spurs, in order to have the materials to make tools. They also fashioned some pipes of wood, and with deerskins they made some bellows. Then, with these already mentioned materials, they made tools. Since the people were weak and were not able to work without sustenance, every third day they killed a horse. They then distributed it, both to those who worked and to those who were sick, and they ate it. In this manner, nourished by the eating of that meat, others began to work.

In the four or five forays which the horsemen and the stronger people made into Aute, these Spaniards returned with much corn. It was enough for all those who were there, and there was still some left to take along. It was four days into the month of August, and at this time they began to build the boats. They caulked them with palm leaves, and from these they also made cord. They greased them with resin that they made from pine trees, of which there were many. From their shirts they made sails, and from the skins taken from the legs of the horses, they fashioned containers for carrying water. While the boats were being made, the Indians killed ten Christians, who were fishing by those lowlands of the coast. From their base camp, the Spaniards saw these unfortunate men pierced from one side to the other with arrows, but they were not able to help them.

From the point at which they left the ships up to where they made these boats, the distance was as much as two hundred and eighty leagues, a little more or less. This was in the opinion of those who traversed it, and it included the entire area which these Christians had crosscrossed. In all that land they did not see mountains, nor did they receive information about them. In this place, the people are very large in size, with fine faces and gentle dispositions. They are all archers as well as very good marksmen. Their bows are of ten and twelve palms in length, and in the handles and near them, they are almost as thick as the wrist of an arm. They are fashioned from beautiful wood, and they are extremely strong. It is a terrifying thing to see what their arrows are able to pierce. It is difficult to believe without seeing it.

On the twentieth day of the month of September, they finished five boats, and each was twenty-two cubits in length. Forty men, a few more or less, died in that place from disease. The Governor took one of these boats for himself and for forty-eight men. He assigned another one with forty-seven men to the purser and the friars, and to the treasurer and inspector he gave another with forty-eight men. The Governor assigned the other two boats to captain Téllez, Peñalosa, Alonso del Castillo, and Andrés Dorantes. In each of these two boats there were another forty-eight men.

After they had eaten the last of the horses, they embarked on the twenty-second day of the month of September. The boats were crowded, as they were full due to the provisions, the clothes, and the weapons. They rose out of the water less than a foot. In that situation they travelled for seven days in those shallow waters. These unfortunate people then arrived at a small island which is close to the mainland. On that place they found a few huts, and they took five canoes. That same day they left for the mainland, which they had not as yet seen. On the shore they landed the boats, and with the canoes they made sideboards. The boats then rose up and were lifted two more palms out of the water. Having completed this task, they continued on their journey. As they went, they entered many anchorages along the coast. In those shallows which they found, they navigated by always keeping the land ahead of them, not knowing where they were going.

One night a canoe came toward the Christians, and it followed them for awhile. They turned to it, with the idea of speaking to those who were aboard. However, the natives did not desire to communicate, and they easily outdistanced the Spaniards, since their canoes are very light craft. The Christians then turned again and continued on their previous course. On the following day, in the morning, a storm overtook them, and they were washed up on an island. They stayed in that place for three days. During this time, they had great need for drinking water, but they did not find any on the island. When it was five days that they had not drunk fresh water, they drank some salt water, and quite a lot. Because of this, five or six men died suddenly, and it became evident that their thirst was unbearable. Therefore, even though the weather had not yet calmed, they decided to go toward that place where they had seen the canoe, which has already been mentioned. Thus, they were entrusting their fate to God and placing themselves in obvious danger of death.

It was thus that they sailed on. At the time when the sun was setting, they arrived at a point of land which created some shelter in that place and which was more protected from the sea. It was there that several canoes came up to them. The Indians talked to them, and the Christians continued, following the natives. It was a good league's distance to where they had their houses on a point of land at the water's edge. They had many jars and pots full of water, in front of these houses, as well as a lot of fish. As the Governor jumped ashore, the chief came out to meet him. This Indian took him to his house, and he offered the Governor the fish and the water which he had there. In return the Christians gave him beads and rattles, as well as some maize which they carried in their boats.

During that same night, the chief stayed with the Governor, and many Indians fell upon the Christians. They killed three men who were lying sick upon the shore, and they wounded the Governor in the head with a stone. Those who were there with him seized the chief. He broke away from the Spaniards, and in their hands he left a quilt which had covered him. It was made from very fine marten-sable pelts which had a musky oder. According to the treasurer, Cabeza de Vaca, they were of excellent quality, the best which he had seen. Moreover, the other Spaniards said the same thing. They took other quilts of marten, but they were not as fine as the first one. Since the Governor was injured and sick, they put him into one of the boats, with the other sick and weak that there were. During that night, the Indians attacked three times, but at last they ceased and left the Christians alone. Many of the natives were very badly slashed, and there were also many wounded among the Spaniards that night. In that place they remained two days longer, and during that time they were not able to locate even one Indian.

They departed that place in their boats, and after three or four days they arrived where some streams flowed into the sea. There they encountered a few Indians in a canoe, and the Spaniards asked them for some drinking water. They gave a container to the natives, so that they could carry the water, and two Christians went with them to get it. The Indians, who had remained in the boats as hostages, wanted to throw themselves into the water, but the Spaniards grabbed them. In the morning of the following day, canoes began to arrive, and the Christians went out of the estuaries and into the open sea. In a little more time than one hour, there were twenty canoes with three or four Indian chieftains in them. They wore around them some robes of those very fine marten skins, and their hair was long and hung loose. They asked for the Indians whom the Christians held, and the Christians asked them for the return of the two Spaniards. The Indians replied that they should go with them to their houses. The Christians did not want to do this, because the land was very flooded and there were many estuaries. The Spaniards did not want to give them the Indians, since they were not returning the Christians. The Indians then began to throw sticks and to shoot some arrows. In this way they entered into a fight with the natives, until they withdrew.

Our people went forward, and they continued on another two days. At the end of this time, the boat which carried the treasurer arrived at a point of land made by the line of the coast. On the other side of this promontory, there was a river that was flowing very swiftly, and it was large and swollen. A little farther behind, the boat of the Governor and the others went among some islands which were located nearby. The treasurer went to them and told them how he had discovered that river. They had been eating maize uncooked for two days, because in that place they had found no firewood to roast it. Therefore, they agreed to continue and to sail up that river from which they had collected sweet water in the sea. However, when the Christians went close to the mouth of the river, the strong current from it did not permit them to reach shore. As they strove to do this, a wind came up from the north. By this wind, as well as by the great current, the Spaniards were pushed farther out to sea. They sailed that night and the following day until nightfall, at which time they determined that they were in three fathoms of depth. As they had seen many columns of smoke on the coast that afternoon, they did not dare to go ashore at night. Therefore, they stayed at sea. Since the current was strong and the Christians did not have any anchors except for some fittings of stone, they were carried farther out to sea that night. When day began to break, they did not see land, nor was one boat visible to those in another.

It was in this manner that the treasurer, Álvar Núñez Cabeza de Vaca, who is the one who gave us this account, continued his journey. At the hour of noon he saw two boats of his companions. Arriving at the first one, he recognized that it was the one of the Governor, and they talked. The Governor asked the treasurer his opinion concerning what he ought to do. Cabeza de Vaca replied to him that they should join with the other boat which was approaching, and that all three boats together could then go where he would command. The Governor responded saying that he intended to reach land by force of rowing, and he added that the treasurer should attempt it in the same manner with his boat.

Although the treasurer and his boat followed along for a league and a half, they were not able to keep up with the boat of the Governor. This was because those in the boat of the treasurer were weak and tired. For three days they had been eating nothing but raw maize, and only a handful of that for a ration. Moreover, the Governor's boat was lighter, and it was less heavily loaded.

For these reasons, it was outdistancing the boat in which the treasurer and the others were riding. Then, Cabeza de Vaca pleaded with the Governor to order the towing of his boat. However, the Governor said that he was not able to do this. He maintained that the treasurer would have to do the best that he could alone. The Governor believed that there was not enough time to wait for anyone, and therefore he instructed each person to try to escape with his life. (This is not what that memorable Count of Niebla, don Enrique de Guzmán, said he did in similar circumstances. Picking up others in his own boat, it became so full from the many people that they drowned at Gibraltar.) However, the treasurer, and those who were with him, had not asked Narváez to take them aboard his boat. Rather, they requested that he give them a tow with a line. This was the only way in which they asked for assistance from those in the boat of the Governor. In the event that he would give them a tow, the line would be in the hand of the Governor. He could then let loose of it when it suited him.

Returning to the account, after hearing the unreasonable decision of the Governor, the treasurer followed his boat for awhile, until it was lost from sight. Then the treasurer came upon the other boat which was also at sea. It was the one which had Peñalosa and captain Téllez aboard, and they were waiting for the treasurer. Thus, the two boats sailed together for three hours until nightfall. Almost all the men had fallen ill, and there were not five healthy ones remaining. This was because they had gotten wet the night before from the waves of the sea, and it was also due to the fact that they all were in need of nourishment. Thus, they spent the night. At four that next morning, the pilot of the treasurer's boat took a sounding, and he determined that they were in seven fathoms of depth. Since the battering of the waves was great at this depth, they held their position in the sea until sunrise. They then found themselves a league from land. They landed, putting the prow of their boat on shore, and they gave thanks to God that they had arrived in safety.

The treasurer then sent a man to some trees that they saw, in order that from the top of them he could survey the land. He returned and reported that they were on an island. He then went back to see if he could locate either some path or a sail. The man returned again to the group in the afternoon, and he said he had found some fish, which he brought with him. Behind him there were three Indians, and behind those were another two hundred archers. They had their ears pierced, and they had placed pieces of cane in the middle of their ears. The treasurer and the inspector went out and called to them, and the Indians approached. The Christians gave them things from the trade goods which they carried. Each one of the Indians gave an arrow in a sign of friendship. They said by signs that on the next day, at the rising of the sun, they would bring things for the Christians to eat. They did do as they had said. On the morning of the next day, they returned, and they brought fish and some roots which were edible. On the following day, they did the same.

In that place, the Spaniards provided themselves with water, and they embarked in order to continue their journey. They took off their clothes, so that they could put the boat in the water. Thus, in this manner they put to sea. A wave hit the prow, and it splashed water onto that area where they were rowing. Because of the wetness and the cold, they let go of the oars which were lost as the boat passed over them. Then another wave hit them, and it turned over the boat. The inspector and two other men grabbed onto the boat, and they were swept underneath it and drowned. The rest of the Christians were naked, but they managed to save themselves. However, they did not save anything from among all those items which they had carried with them.

Following this incident, they remained on that shore, and it was very cold until the afternoon. At that time the same Indians returned to see the Christians, and they found them in this desperate condition. The natives began to weep with the Spaniards, as if they too were suffering from their hardship. The treasurer then pleaded with them to take the Christians to their houses, and they did it. They spent the night there, and on the morning of the next day, the Indians told them that there were others like the Christians near that place. For this reason, the treasurer sent two men to find out who these people were, and they determined that they were Alonso del Castillo and Andrés Dorantes, as well as the other people who had gone in their boat. They had likewise landed on that same island on the fifth of

November. However, the boat of the treasurer had arrived one day later on that shore. The other Spaniards shared the few clothes and the little food which they still had with the treasurer and his company.

3.

As was mentioned in the preceding chapter, the treasurer, Cabeza de Vaca, and those in his boat joined with those Christians of the other boat. Both had experienced misfortune, and they decided to patch up their boat and to embark in it. They went to work and repaired the boat the best they could. When they put to sea, these Spaniards were not able to keep themselves afloat, because of the wood worms and other problems. Thus, having experienced this misfortune in the boat, they decided to spend the winter on that island since they could not do anything else. As they believed that they were near Pánuco, they sent ahead a gentleman named Figueroa, so that he might reach that settlement. He was accompanied by another three Christians and an Indian. Upon arriving, these men were to report where the other Spaniards were and in what condition they had left them.

At the end of five or six days, the people began to die. Their hunger was so great that five men ate one another. At this same time, an ailment of the stomach struck among the natives of that land, and it killed one-half of their number. Upon experiencing this, the Indians considered killing those few Christians who remained alive, and they said that the Spaniards had brought that disease and pestilence to the land. God was willing, and a leader of those Indians said that it was not to be done in that manner. He explained that they should not think that those Christians had brought such a sickness, since the Indians saw that they had also died and but very few of them remained. This Indian reasoned that if the Christians had brought that disease, they would not have died. Thus, because of what that leader said, they stopped the planned killing of the Christians. In the condition in which the Spaniards were, it was more cruel to leave them alive, than to kill them. Thus, the Indians were allowing them to continue in this pitiful state. The Christians were experiencing such great punishment, hunger, and torture, as they were going two or three days without eating a morsel.

The Spaniards then decided to cross over to the mainland. They did this because they were all sick and dying, in the same manner which the natives were dying. They went to some swamps and lagoons to eat those same oysters which the Indians eat for three or four months of the year, without eating any other food. These natives experience great hunger, and they have great difficulty defending themselves, both in the day and in the night, from the mosquitos. There are so many of these insects that it is an unbearable thing to endure them. The Indians do not have firewood, and their only water is brackish. For four other months of the year, they eat herbs from the fields and blackberries. During another two months, they suck on some roots, and they eat some very large spiders, as well as lizards, snakes, and rodents. Then, sometimes they have deer. For the remaining two months, they eat fish which they kill from canoes. These Indians also eat roots, gathered from the water, which are like truffles. These people are very well disposed, and the women are extremely good workers.

The Indians took Alonso del Castillo and Andrés Dorantes with them to the mainland to eat those oysters already mentioned. There they remained until the end of the month of March, in the year 1529, at which time they returned to the same island. These men then assembled the Christians whom they found alive, and there numbered no more than fourteen. They left two of them in that place because they were very thin and without any strength. The treasurer, Cabeza de Vaca, was on the other part of the land. He was very sick and had no hope of living. These Spaniards crossed to the bay, and they continued along the coast. The treasurer remained in the place where he was for five and one-half years. He was digging from morning to night, collecting roots, with a sort of hoe, or stick. This was the tool which the Indians used for this digging into the land, as well as beneath the water. Each day he carried a load or two of firewood on his back. The wood rested directly upon his naked flesh, since, in the manner of a savage or an Indian, he did not wear any clothing. Thus it was that he served the Indians in the duties which have been mentioned, as well as in others as they ordered him. Cabeza de Vaca would carry the house or the belongings of these people on his back. They move every three or four days because it is their custom. This is necessary as they must look for roots in this manner, since throughout that land there is not one suitable place to support their great hunger. They neither eat corn nor are they able to obtain any. In fact, these Indians do not plant any crops whatsoever.

The land is very healthy and temperate, except when a north wind blows during the winter. This wind is such that even the fish within the sea freeze from the cold. Andrés Dorantes [Cabeza de Vaca?] said that on one particular day he saw both snowing and hailing at the same time. He also told of the great hunger which is suffered in that place. It is as serious as anyone can imagine, and further on the Christians found it even greater. He also said that these Indians feel death more than any other people he had ever seen and that they weep for those dead with great sorrow and much attention.

When he saw that their hardships were so great and excessive, this gentleman [Cabeza de Vaca] began to contract with these people to supply them with certain things. From other places, he brought them those items which they were not obtaining and of which they had need. Thus involved in this trade, he travelled several times into the interior. He also went farther up along the coast for a distance of forty leagues, and three times he passed what was a bay. By the landmarks of it, he believed it was the bay which the Spaniards called Espíritu Santo. Two times he returned those forty leagues in an attempt to bring back a Christian. This man, and another, had been left alive in that place by Castillo and Dorantes when they had departed that island. Both had been very weak, and the second man was now dead.

On his last trip, he took out this man, and he brought him to the other side of this previously mentioned bay of Espíritu Santo. They travelled ten leagues onward to where there were other Indians, and these were at war with those natives who had crossed the bay of Espíritu Santo with the Christians. The new Indians told them their names and that another three or four Christians had died. They also said that the other Spaniards near that place had all died of hunger and of cold and that those who were alive were in very bad condition. Along with this news, these natives also related much other bad news to these two Christians. (I am referring to this Dorantes

[Cabeza de Vaca] and the companion which he had recovered.) They put arrows at the hearts of the Spaniards, and they threatened them with death. From fear, the other Christians decided to return to where they had been. Thus he left Dorantes [Cabeza de Vaca], who was not able to stop him. After two or three days of staying in that place, he left there secretly. He encountered two Indians who took him to where Dorantes and Castillo were. Then, having arrived where these two Christians were, Andrés Dorantes [Cabeza de Vaca] waited there for an Indian of his.

On the first day of April [1529—at this point Oviedo has returned to a discussion of what had earlier happened to Andrés Dorantes and the other men] the already mentioned Andrés Dorantes as well as the others who will also be mentioned—Alonso del Castillo, Diego Dorantes, and Pedro Valdivieso—departed that place. There was also an Asturian cleric and a black man on an island behind where they had lost the boats. They had crossed to this place because of the great hunger they had there. The Indians took them another time in canoes across the bay where they had lost those boats. In that place were those few Christians who had escaped the hunger and cold of winter. Thus, they gathered another six people, and all together there were now twelve Christians. They had left two men on the island, who were not able to be taken because they were very weak. Cabeza de Vaca and another Christian were farther inland, and these two men could not be recovered to go with the group.

The Indians led them across another bay to get certain things which they gave the Spaniards. From there they went two leagues to a great river which was beginning to rise from floods and rains, and there they made rafts. In these they crossed the river with great difficulty, as they had few swimmers among them. Leaving that place, they went three leagues to another river which was swollen and flowing very powerfully. Its fury was such that sweet water poured for a great distance into the sea. There they made some rafts, and they crossed the river on them. The first one crossed well, because they helped each other. However, the second raft carried the people on it out to sea. They had been weak and tired due to the difficulties of the past winter, as well as from travelling. The Christians had been eating little except something which they called rock grass

[kelp], which is abundant on the coast. It is the same plant which they use in Spain to make glass. They also had been eating some shellfish which breed in caves along the coast, and these consist of little else but their shells. Thus, those Spaniards who went on the second raft did not have strength to proceed safely. Two men were drowned, and another two escaped by swimming. The raft was swept by the current more than a league out to sea, while one man clung to it. When he saw that he was out of the current, he raised himself onto the top of the raft. This Spaniard then made a sail of his own body, and as the wind was from the sea, it returned him. He was cast upon the land, and thus he escaped.

Of those twelve Christians who, as was mentioned, left together, only ten now remained. In that place they found another Christian, who also went with them. When they had walked three or four leagues, they came to another river. At that place they found another boat of their original five. They recognized that it was the one in which the purser, Alonso Enriquez, and the *fray comisario* had gone. However, they did not find out what had happened to the people who had been in that boat. They continued another five or six leagues to another great river. On the bank of this river were two small groups of Indian huts, and the inhabitants fled. From the other side of the river, Indians crossed to the Christians. These natives recognized the Spaniards, as they had already seen those in the boat of the Governor, as well as those in the boat of Alonso Enriquez. Being assisted, they crossed the river in a canoe. The Indians led them to their houses in which they did not have anything to eat. However, they did give the Christians a small amount of fish, and with this they made it through the night.

The following day they left that place, and on the fourth day they arrived at a bay. Two men had died during this journey from hunger and fatigue. For this reason now only nine people remained. This particular bay was wide, and it had a breadth of almost a league. In the direction of Pánuco, there was a point of land which went almost one-quarter of a league into the sea. On it are some very large knolls of white sand, and for this reason it should have been visible from far out at sea. Therefore, they suspected that it must be the river of Espíritu Santo. There they realized that they were very weary, as they were not able to find any way to cross. But at last they found a damaged canoe, and they repaired it the best they could. In the two days which they remained there, they crossed the bay. The Christians continued their journey weak from hunger, and most of them were bloated from the grasses which they were eating.

With much difficulty these Spaniards arrived at a small bay which was twelve leagues farther on. The bay was narrow in width, such that its breadth was no more than that of a river. In this place they stopped the day which they arrived. On the following day they saw an Indian on the other side of the river. Even though they called to him, he did not want to come to them. He then left, but he returned again that afternoon. He brought with him a Christian whose name was Figueroa. As has already been related, this Spaniard was one of the four who had been sent that previous winter to see if they could reach the land of the Christians. The Indian and the Christian then crossed to where the nine Spaniards were. There Figueroa told them how his other three companions had died. Two of them had been killed by hunger, and the other one by the Indians. He also related to them how he had come upon a Christian who was named Esquivel. This man was the only survivor from those two boats of the Governor and Alonso Enriquez. He had sustained himself by eating the flesh of those who had died. All the rest of the men had been killed by hunger. Some of these had even been eating one another. The Christians also learned that the boat of Alonso Enriquez had been wrecked where they had found it, as has been mentioned.

Figueroa also said that as survivors were coming up the coast they were located by the Governor, who was still travelling in his boat at sea. He decided to put all his people ashore, so that they all could be together on the coast. The Governor did this since then the boat would be lighter. Also, his people were weary of the sea, and they were not carrying anything to eat. He remained in the boat in sight of them. The Governor did this so that in case there was a bay or a river to cross, all could do so in the boat. In this manner, they reached a bay which, as already stated, they believed was that of Espíritu Santo. There the Governor transported all the people across to the other side of the bay, and he stayed in the boat, as he did not want to disembark. He remained there with only a pilot named Anton Pérez and a page of

his called Campo. Thus it was as night fell. Then a very strong north wind came up, and it carried these people out to sea. Nothing more was ever heard of them. The Governor was not only very weak and sick, but he was totally leprous. Moreover, those who were with him were not very strong either, and therefore one must conclude that the sea swallowed them up. All the Christians who remained in that place scattered among certain lagoons and swamps which were there and inland, like people without hope. In those places everyone died that winter from cold and hunger. Some of them even ate others, as has already been mentioned. Figueroa did not know anything else to tell them, except that Esquivel was still living around that area. Some Indians had him, and it might be that they would see him soon. However, within a month, more or less, they learned that Esquivel had been killed by the Indians he lived with. He had tried to escape, but they followed and killed him.

They stayed there with this Christian for a short time, listening to this bad news which was related. Because the Indian who came with him was not willing to let Esquivel go, he was forced to leave with this Indian. Because all but two of those other Christians did not know how to swim, they were all not able to go with them. One of those who did go was the cleric called Asturiano, and the other was a young boy who could swim. Because no one else knew how to swim, the rest remained. These two Christians went with the intention of getting some fish which the Indians said they had, and then they planned to return across the bay. However, once the natives had these two Spaniards in their houses, they did not want to return with them or to allow them return. First they moved their houses on their canoes, and they took these other two Christians with them. They said to them that they would return soon and that they were going nearby to gather a certain leaf which they had the custom of picking. From it they make a special beverage, which they drink as hot as they are able to stand. One of the two Christians returned the next morning to tell the seven Christians this, and he brought them a small amount of fish which the Indians had given him. They remained in that place that day due to the many needs which they had.

On the morning of the following day, the Spaniards saw two Indians from another place. They were from a small settlement, and they had come to begin the eating of blackberries, which grow in some areas along that coast. These natives go where these berries are during the season, and they remain as long as there are berries, since they know they are very good. This fruit gives them much nourishment, and it sustains these people while it lasts. The Christians called to them, and the Indians crossed to where they were. These natives did this as if they were coming to people they respected little. Even though they almost forcefully took part of what they had, they asked the Indians to help them across the water. They did this in a canoe, and they brought the Christians to their houses which were nearby. That night these natives gave them a bit of fish. On the next day they went fishing, and they returned that night with their catch. They gave part of this to the Spaniards. On the following day, these Indians moved, and they took the Christians with them. Because of this, they were never again able to see the two Christians whom the other Indians had taken away.

(Great God, what tribulations so excessive for such a short life as that of man! What torments so unheard of for a human body! What hunger so intolerable for a person so weak! What misadventures so extreme for such sensitive flesh! What deaths so unexpected for such rational minds! With what did the captains and ministers of these expeditions pay, that led so many pitiful men to die such deaths, so deceived and mocked! It can be answered that they paid them with that same greed which gave credit to their words.

Now we know that Pánfilo de Narváez was never in that land, where he planned to take these people. He was intending to be their lord and governor, but it seems to me that he, himself, did not know how to govern. Can there be greater frivolity than to listen and to follow such commanders? Moreover, see how skilled were his pilots. When they went to that place, they knew neither where they were going nor where they were! Thus, these men of the sea came to an end suffering difficult deaths, as did those of the land, with some not even knowing the others.

To die in battle, or to be struck by a terrible and sudden pestilence, is very terrifying, difficult, and unhappy to the many who suffer such a misfortune. This is also true of being drowned on a voyage, where many perish, because the ship is lost due to the weather, or on account of another unexpected event. However, even in these difficulties there is something good. If the man who goes to war, or dies in battle, is a Christian, he leaves to serve his prince, having made his will and having put his soul in order by confession. Thus, he is able to die in the state, and on the road, of salvation. As he was ordered by his king or lord, he should not disobey. Moreover, he cannot disobey without falling into disgrace and incurring the stigma of a bad vassal or servant.

As has been said, the man who is drowned, if he is a Catholic, has put his soul in order by confessing, and he has received communion, even before the voyage begins, or he enters upon the sea. He then continues on his way, and if he is under orders, he does this to fulfill his duty. He might also travel thus, because he is a merchant on business, or for other just and honest causes that suit him. Although death might cross his path, he would be seeking to make a living without harming any third party. If, in such cases as has been said, death comes to this man suddenly from disease, in his mercy God also gives time. This is in order for those who die thus to repair their souls. However, there are others not so fortunate, and these suffer so many and so diverse types of death. What can be equal to having their bad fortune and their sins be constantly opposing them, or to be killed while furiously hungry and thirsty? Such people also experience other difficulties and sicknesses never before suffered so continuously by men.

I tell you poor gentlemen—or for that matter, noble in need, artisan of bad standing, and poorly advised villager—that you, and all those of these qualities, found yourselves in this fleet. Moreover, there you received just payment for your bad decision. The poor gentleman was in a more secure position living as he had, serving others greater. The squire was acting in the manner that his own estate was not big enough for him, but let him be satisfied with it. Likewise, the artisan should not leave his trade, nor the villager his plow. These men left the digging and other acts of labor, as well as agriculture, in order to come to the Indies. There was more security and peace for the body and for the soul in these things than there was in following Pánfilo de Narváez. This choice represented a frivolity quite obvious and dangerous.

Narváez would have been very able to tell you men what there is in Cuba, and where he had been on that island. However, he did not know about that place where he took you. He did not even go where he had intended to go. Moreover, now that he has gone, he has not seen it either. It is still not known what place he was looking for. All that is known is that he wanted to leave his peaceful life in order to command. If he was the only one to be concerned about, the loss would not be so great. However, due to his inventions and bad advice, you had just as big a role as he did. This is because, while he did not escape death, neither did he stop death from overtaking all of you.

Make known to me now, those who have read, if you have heard of, or know, another people so unfortunate, so weary, or so poorly counseled. Compare this with the wanderings of Ulysses, the voyage of Jason, or the labors of Hercules. All these things are fiction and metaphor. Once this is understood, as it should be understood, you will not find anything at which to marvel. Their trials are not equal in comparison to the difficulties which these sinners experienced during their unhappy road and end. Moreover, which one of all those suffered more than the three captains already mentioned? Even if you place Perseus and his Medusa with them, they could not have walked the steps those Christians walked.

Oh, damned gold! Oh, such dangerous treasures and profits! Oh, marten-sable pelts! I certainly believe that the value which such furs have should be compared with that of others. I am here referring to those like that quilt which, as this account has related, remained with Narváez after the course of that stoning. Their value might reach that of those common linings which the lords and princes of Europe use in winter, and they might be held in more esteem. However, these European ones are bought with money, and the others are obtained with blood and with lives. Moreover, these Christians were not even able to bring these quilts out or to take them from among those savage people.

Let us return to the story, which had not yet come to an end. It continues even though there are now alive only a few men of all those people Narváez took with him. This has been mentioned before, and you will also read it in the next chapter. Thus, we proceed with the same relation of that gentleman Álvar Núñez Cabeza de Vaca and his companions.

4.

(When a captain, a man of reputation, or an important person from these parts of the Indies goes to Spain, he knows how to wag his tongue in order to recruit people. This is especially true of those who go to solicit governorships and new conquests. They go about spreading words among those who do not understand them. All the Spaniards who listen to these men think that everything here in these Indies is known, and very well understood. They are led to believe that without leaving out a single palm, every corner of the Indies, as well as the mainland, has been seen and explored. Such preachers as these do not hesitate to speak of everything. Those ignorant listeners imagine and believe that the Indies will be similar to the kingdom of Portugal or Navarre, or at least a small land with short distances. They figure that everyone who is here knows one another and is able to communicate with the same ease as from Cordova to Granada or to Seville, or when farther distant, as from Castile to Vizcaya.

From this misconception, some unusual addresses on letters result. They come here, to these Indies, from ignorant mothers and women who are looking for their sons and husbands, as well as for other relatives. These letters they write are addressed in this manner: "To my dear son Pero Rodríguez in the Indies." This is as if they might write, "To my son Mahomet in Africa," or "To Juan Martínez in Europe." It is the same thing as addressing the letter to another world. This is because all those who realize anything about the way the world is, and its geography, cannot help but suspect the size of this place here. It may be as large as the two parts of the world which I talk about, including Asia with them. It could be another new world, an *Orbe Novo*, as some call it. As I have stated other times in these histories, I call it that half of the one world not shared by Africa, Europe, and Asia.

Thus, I want to say that so many men come to these Indies as beclouded as those of the addresses that I have mentioned. They neither understand nor know where they are going, and it was men such as these that Narváez encountered. Other captains also find as many as they wish, or at least more than they have a need for. It is the poverty of some of these men, the greediness of others, and the insanity of the rest which will not allow them to understand what they are doing or whom they are following. The truth is that some other Spaniards, quite the opposite of these men, do come to these Indies. They have their purposes and plans established better because they are sent by a prince, or for other reasons more sensible and more excusable than those of the others.

It is possible that a prince might also be deceived, as is a poor volunteer. Therefore, I have taken notice of one thing which no one should forget. It is that Their Majesties almost never put their estate or their money into these new discoveries. They only give authorization and nice words. They say to these captains: "If you should do what you say, we will do this or that, or there will be privileges for you." They give him the title of *adelantado* or governor, with license and powers so that he may go where he offered in his agreement. This captain is confident of the ignorance of those who will follow him, and these men do come with their persons and belongings, enticed by his false honor.

After having been dispatched from the court, this man comes to Seville with less money than that amount which he might want. In the meantime, a drummer goes to one port, and a friar or two and some priests go to other places. They twist minds and promise riches from those places which they know nothing about. Afterwards it is these same clerics who arrive in the Indies under the pretext of the conversion of the Indians. The captain gets involved in making exchanges and in buying old and tired ships. These are such that they arrive over here by the mercy of God and by the force of doubled pumps. Moreover, they are in such a condition that they are not in any shape to return. They can take to Castile neither news nor an account of the cargo which they brought.

Furthermore, for another part, a young man acts as the secretary to this captain, and this man never knows which thing is a secret. There are also other crafty and flattering men who the captain sees will know best how to scheme. All these men become involved in talking to the poor volunteers to convince them to do two things. The first is that they lend money to the captain. These men give them as security only vain hopes and a document which he who receives it thinks is a legal certificate of exchange. Thus it is that the poor volunteer gives up what little money he has left. Moreover, if the trap is widened, he sells his cloak and coat. He then is left only in a jacket like a husbandman. He does this because he believes that besides coming to a hot land, he will arrive well dressed with the favor he expects, and which they have offered him.

The other thing they seek is that every ten, more or less, of the volunteers be obliged to pay jointly, at a certain time, ten or twelve ducats of gold each. This is for the freighting of their belongings to where they are going. It is also for the food, which they do not give to the volunteers, unless they can say they are returning to Spain. However, there are very few of these people cheated thus who are able to say this, because the voyage is long. Moreover, life is short and the occasions for losing it are innumerable. It is also true that almost all those who come over here are under contract to stay, and not to return to their native land. As you will now hear it, and as you have heard it, if you have read these histories from their beginning, these things are quite contrary to what is believed in Spain about these volunteers. You could also read that which is yet to be said, if you want to be further informed. Reading, even to the very end of my treatises, will serve as your warning and for the advisement of others.)[1]

The Christians remained in the company of those Indians, who have been mentioned in the earlier chapter, until the natives tired of giving them food. This is as happens everywhere when visitors stay longer than the host would like. It is especially the case when they are not wanted and contribute nothing of benefit. Therefore, they threw out the five Spaniards, telling them that they could go to some other Indians who they said were located on another bay six leagues ahead. The Christians did this, and three of them stayed there a long time. These men were Alonso del Castillo, Pedro de Valdivieso, who was a cousin of Andrés Dorantes, and another who was called Diego de Huelva. The other two Spaniards went farther down the coast, and there they died of hunger. This is known because Dorantes said that in that place he later found their bodies while he and his other Christian cousin, who was named Diego Dorantes, were walking around seeking to help them.

There remained in that other Indian village two gentlemen and a black man. It seemed to the Indians that those Christians would suffice for what they wanted, which was that they should cart firewood and water on their backs, serving

---

1. Oviedo's interpolation of his own views on the way expeditions were constituted is relevant to narratives other than those of the Narváez venture.

them as slaves. However, after three or four days, the natives threw them out in the same manner as those others. Then, for a few days they wandered lost without hope of help. These men were walking around those swamps stark naked, because other Indians had earlier robbed them and had left with their clothes at night. As has been said, they came upon the dead bodies of the other Christians who had been among those five the Indians had thrown out, or discarded. They left that place and encountered other Indians. Andrés Dorantes remained with them, and his cousin went ahead to that bay where the other three Christians had earlier come to a stop.

At that bay one of them, who was Valdivieso, came from where he was on the other side to see this Spaniard. Valdivieso told him how the two Christian swimmers, who had left them earlier, had passed by that place. The Indians had also stripped them and left them naked. They struck them many times with sticks, wounding them on their heads because the Christians did not want to stay with them. Thus, they departed both naked and bruised, even though they knew they might die. These Spaniards did this because they had made an oath not to stop until they reached land of the Christians. Andrés Dorantes said that in that settlement he saw the clothes of one of these men. They were those of the cleric, and with these clothes were a breviary and a diurnal.

Soon after this Valdivieso returned to the Indians. However, two days later they killed him because he wanted to leave. After a little while, they killed the other Spaniard, who was called Diego de Huelva, because he changed from one lodging to another. At this place the Indians took the Christians as slaves, using them more cruelly than a Moor might use them. On the other side along the coast, they had been walking on flesh to the quick, and at all times they had been naked and barefoot. This was in summer when that coast burned like a fire. Now, their function was nothing less than carrying loads of firewood close to their flesh, as well as everything else which the Indians needed. In that heat, they also dragged canoes through those floodlands.

During the entire year, these natives do not eat anything except for some fish, and very little of that. Nevertheless, with this food they experience much less hunger than do those Indians inland with whom these Spaniards later stayed.

However, among other things, these natives lack this fish much of the time, and for this reason, they move frequently. If they did not do this, they would not have anything to eat. Aside from this privation, these people suffer another very great one. There is very little fresh water in that land. As they travel in flooded lands and salt water, the water which they have to drink is very scarce and bad, as well as being far distant.

All this contributed to the greater fatigue of the Christians. They suffered that same thirst, when bringing water on their backs for the Indians, their masters, and even for their neighbors. Everyone ordered around the Spaniards, and they feared everyone. Moreover, all treated them poorly by deed and by words. The children cut away at their beards everyday, as a diversion. Moreover, when they saw that the Christians were not being careful, any child would give a jerk on their hair. This gave them the greatest laughter and pleasure in the world. They also scratched them in such a way that often these children drew blood, as they have such large fingernails. These are their principal weapons. They can also be used as ordinary knives among themselves, when it is not with these that they wage war.

The boys made many and great vexations against the Spaniards. When they encountered these Christians outside of their houses, they went after them with stones. They also used anything else which presented itself to them, or which they found more at hand. Pursuing in this manner, it was a game, or a new hunt and joy, for the young boys. Moreover, the Spaniards were worthy men and gentlemen, who were new at such a life. Therefore, it was necessary that their patience be strong and equal to the work and hardships which they had. Thus, they would be able to suffer so many and such intolerable torments.

This Dorantes attested to these things. He believed that God gave them the strength to be patient and to discount their sins, however much they might deserve their ordeal. Even though they did not desire to suffer such hardships, they could not do anything else, besides despairing. They were enclosed by water, as there were islands all around where they were. If it had been in their power, it would have been better to find death alone in the countryside, and not to live among such bestial and bad people. Thus, they would have been men without fortune, asking God for mercy to relieve their guilt.

The Spaniards were among these people for fourteen months. This was from the month of May until another month of May came in the next year. When this second month of May arrived, it was the year 1530. In the middle of the month of August, Andrés Dorantes was in a place which seemed to him most appropriate to seek escape. He commended himself to God, and he left. It was during the middle of the day in the midst of all the Indians, and God wished that they not see him. That day he passed a large body of water, and in great fear he walked as far as he could. On the next day he encountered some Indians who received him willingly, as they now knew that the Christians served well.

Castillo and the black man stayed at this time, because they could not go with Dorantes. After three months, the black man went after him, and they met, although they did not remain together. Castillo stayed, and he was in that place among those difficult people for another year and one-half. He then found an opportunity to leave in search of Dorantes. When he arrived, he did not find anyone except the black man. Dorantes had gone another twenty leagues behind, as he was not able to endure those Indians who were very unjust. He was now with some other natives, who were located at a river near the bay of Espíritu Santo.

As has been said, these Indians were those who had killed Esquivel. He was the only Christian who had escaped of those people who had been in the two boats of the Governor and of Alonzo Enriquez. According to what these same Indians told Dorantes, they had killed Esquivel, because a woman had dreamed I do not know what ridiculous thing. These people from this place believe in dreams, and they kill their own children because of them. This gentleman Dorantes said that in the course of four years he saw eleven or twelve children killed and (?) buried alive. These were the male children; they very seldom leave any females. These natives do not have any other form of idolatry. Moreover, they do not believe in idolatry, except for this misbelief, which has been mentioned.

Near that place, other Indians had killed Diego Dorantes, the cousin of Andés Dorantes. They did this at the end of two years during which he had

served and been among them. For this reason, none of the Christians had security of life from one day to the next. Thus it was that of all these Christians ultimately there did not remain alive anyone except Andrés Dorantes, Alonso del Castillo, the black man, and Cabeza de Vaca, about whom the others knew nothing.

Andrés Dorantes was alone for ten months among these people who have been mentioned. He suffered a good deal of hunger, and he labored continually. Moreover, he always had the fear that they would kill him some day. Dorantes had seen that because of crazy dreams they slew their own children, without pity or mercy. It was also true that they had killed Esquivel for this same reason. Thus, when he was walking or when he was working digging roots, he did not encounter an Indian that he did not think was coming to slay him because of some dream. Dorantes did not feel secure until he saw such an Indian continuing on. Moreover, when most of the Indians ran into this poor Christian, they showed themselves to him in a very fierce manner. Sometimes, even very often, they came running at him, and at the others who were in the same place. These Indians might also put arrows on their chests, and draw their bows to their ears. Afterwards, they would laugh and say to Dorantes: "Were you frightened?"

These natives eat roots which they take from under the ground during most of the winter. These are few, and they are dug out with much difficulty. These people pass most of the year in great hunger. From morning until night during every day of their lives, they have to work at staying alive. They also eat snakes, small lizards, mice, crickets, locusts, frogs, and all the other disgusting reptiles and insects which they are able to obtain. Sometimes, they also eat deer which they kill by setting fire to the land and to the savannahs. They hunt mice between those rivers, where there are great numbers of them. However, everything is scarce. This is because all winter they go along the river, from above to below, and from below to above and they never stop looking for food. Thus, they scare the game, and everything is lost. Sometimes, they eat fish which they kill in the river. However, these are very few, except when the river floods during the month of April. In some years it rises twice; the second time is in May. Then, the Indians kill great quantities of very good fish. They cut open much of it in order to save it, but most of it is lost. This is because they neither have salt, nor do they carry this catch to where they can put it in a place of safety. If they did this, the fish might be able to sustain them at a later time.

There are many walnuts along the banks of that river, and the Indians eat them in their season. These walnut trees in that place bear nuts one year, and they do not another. Sometimes, a year or two passes when there is no crop. However, when they are there, those nuts are many. At this time, the Indians gather from twenty or thirty leagues around that place, as they are extremely fond of eating them. These natives suffer great necessity, because there are so many people who come for these walnuts. In one day they scare away all the game, and they kill everything. The crop lasts for an entire month, and they eat nothing else during this time. These nuts are much smaller than those of Spain, and it is very difficult to get out what is inside, so that it can be eaten.

After the summer arrives at the end of May, these people eat some fish, if any is left of that which they collected from those flooded rivers. They begin to travel in order that they might eat prickly pears. These are fruits which exist in abundance over that land, and they journey more than forty leagues forward, towards Pánuco, to eat them. The Indians so enjoy these that they will not leave the harvest for anything in the world. This is the best food which they have all year, and it lasts for one and one-half or two months. During this period, they are eating the fruit, as they travel. Moreover, at times they kill some deer. It even happens that a few people might slay two or three hundred of these animals. This gentleman, Andrés Dorantes, said that in eight days he saw sixty Indians kill as many as the number that has been stated. It also happens that they could slay five hundred. However, many other times, or even most of the time, they do not kill any.

These people hunt in the following manner. As the deer walk along the coast, they run along the land in a wing. As this place is unpopulated, and without people all year long, these animals are plentiful. The natives drive them in a herd into the water. They then hold them in that place during the whole day, until the deer drown. The weather and the tide later cast them dead upon the shore. When the wind is not coming from the sea, the Indians do not pursue these animals. If they do, the deer will then come back because they only go against the wind.

It happens in this manner only once or twice, and they do not kill game the other times. However, if they do, it is little and not by chance, as I have described. After this activity, the Indians continue ahead on their journey. Thus, they travel away from the sea, and they go inland, consuming their prickly pears. They have now begun to eat this fruit. It continues ripe through August, thereby lasting fifty or sixty days. This the best time of the year for these people. Even though they eat nothing else except prickly pears, and some snails which they look for carefully, they are happy in this season. Only at this time do they gorge themselves day and night. During all the rest of the year, they long for this season, because of their hunger.

There among the prickly pears, Castillo, the black man, and Andrés Dorantes came together, and they decided to leave. However, since the Indians were never calm or together, these men then returned, each to his own area. Thus, from necessity these Christian sinners separated going with their masters. In such a condition, they could not effect their agreement and wish, at least at that time. Each one went his way with his master to eat those walnuts, and there were many of them that year. When they arrived at that place, Cabeza de Vaca came to join these others. It had been five years, since they had left him behind where they had lost the boats. Moreover, they had not seen him in that period. In that place, they made plans, after Cabeza de Vaca arrived. As had been stated, they were separated, and they could only come together during the season of the prickly pears. In this time, they joined to eat in the countryside, and many times, they were at the point of leaving. However, it seemed as if their sins hindered their departure, and they were separated, each one going to his own area.

At this point six years had passed, and in the seventh year the season of that prickly pear fruit was coming. Although each one of these Christians was separated from the others, they all left secretly. They arrived unexpectedly at a certain place inland where they used to eat prickly pears. The Indians did not go there then, because no longer was there fruit at that place. Dorantes was the first who arrived there. By chance, he encountered some Indian people who had come to that place the same day. They were great enemies of those other natives with whom the Christians had been, and they received him very well. At the end of three or four days that Dorantes had been there, the black man arrived on his trail. He was accompanied by Alonso del Castillo. All agreed to look for Cabeza de Vaca who was waiting for them farther ahead.

These Christians saw some columns of smoke at a good distance, and they agreed that Dorantes and the black man should travel to that smoke. Castillo was to remain in that place in order to assure the Indians, so that they would believe that the two were planning to return. They told these natives that they were going for another companion of theirs. They also made it clear that they believed he was at those smoke columns, and that they would bring him to that place to stay among them. The Indians were also told that Castillo would wait there until the others would return. They accepted this, and the two men left. They had to walk quite a lot, until night. At that time, they encountered a native who took them to where Cabeza de Vaca was, and they explained how they had come looking for him.

It pleased God that the Indians moved the next day, and they located themselves closer to where Castillo had stayed. At that place, these men joined together, and all three of them commended themselves to Our Lord. They had to do this, because they were obligated as Christians and as gentlemen, which they all were. This was for the best. They should not have lived such a savage life, so apart from the service of God and from all good reason. With this good resolution, they left, as determined men of good caste. Thus, Jesus Christ in His infinite mercy guided them and worked with them. Without there being any roads on the land, He opened them, as well as the hearts of such savage and uncontrollable men. God moved so that the natives humbled themselves to the Christians and obeyed them, as will be stated later.

Thus, these men left that day, without being detected and without knowing where they were going. However, they had confidence in divine mercy. They were looking for those prickly pears which might be on the land. This was even though it was through October, and therefore it was the time that their season would be ending. It pleased the Mother of God that they encountered some Indians that day at sunset. They wanted this, as these natives were very gentle. They had some knowledge of Christians, although little. They did not know how the other Indians had treated them, but this was very good for these sinners.

It was now the beginning of winter, and they were travelling without skins to cover themselves. Moreover, the prickly pears were growing scarce in the countryside through which they had to walk. Therefore, it was necessary for these men to stop there that year, in order to have some skins with which to cover themselves. The Indians told them that they would find these up ahead. Since they were travelling, these Christians thus would be better prepared for the next year. With the coming of the prickly pears, they would be able to proceed with their plan.

At that time, they rested from the first of October until the month of August came in the following year. These men suffered much hunger. It was not less, and rather more, than times in the past seven years. The cause for this was that these Indians were not near water, where they would be able to kill some fish. Therefore, they did not eat anything in that place except roots. These people have greater difficulty there than all the other natives who manage some fishing. Thus, in all that year they were never satisfied. The children in that place go about so skinny and swollen that they resemble toads. However, at least among these Indians, the Christians were well treated. These people let them live in liberty and do anything they pleased.

5.

By the time the month of August arrived, these gentlemen had collected some deerskins. Therefore, when they saw that the time was right, they fled cautiously and in secret, which was advisable, from that place and those Indians that have already been mentioned. On the same day which they departed, they walked for seven leagues until they encountered some other Indians. These people were friends of those natives they had left behind. They received the Christians well in that place, and they gave them from that which they had. On the next day these men moved on, and thus they arrived at a place where they joined with other Indians.

These people took the Christians with them, and they went to eat all of some seeds which were ripening at that time. In that place there are many large forests containing groves of trees which bear that fruit. There they joined with some other natives, and the Christians went over to them. This was because these people were from an area farther ahead, thus more to the purpose of their journey and intent. They remained in that place with these Indians for eight days. They were waiting for those seeds which still were not ready for harvesting, and they did not have anything to eat except some cooked prickly pear leaves. There the Christians gave them some deerskins in exchange for two dogs which they could eat. This was because they were so weak that they did not dare to walk a league. After they ate the dogs, they bid farewell to the Indians and departed.

These last Indians were very sorrowful because these men left, but they did not hinder them. That day they walked five or six leagues without finding anything to eat. Moreover, they did not encounter any Indians who could put them on the correct route. That night these Christians arrived at a forest where they slept. They buried many prickly pear leaves which they ate the next day in the morning. They did this because when buried from one day to the next, these leaves are less harsh, better fit to cook, and easier to digest. They continued on their route until midday, when they arrived at two or three groups of huts, where there were some Indians. These people told the Christians that they did not have anything to eat. They also told these men that they should continue farther on, and by night they would arrive at some houses, where the natives would give them food.

Thus, the Christians continued on from that place, and they arrived at the other place, where they found forty or fifty groups of huts. There it was where the Indians first began to fear and revere these few Christians. These natives held them in great esteem. They approached and rubbed them, and then they rubbed themselves in the same way. By signs, they explained to the Christians that should they rub and stroke them, they could cure them. They then brought some sick to these men so that they might heal them. The Christians did as they had been shown, even though they were more accustomed to hardship than to performing miracles. Yet, having faith in the goodness of God, they blessed them and blew upon them. This was in the same manner as those who are called healers do it in Castile. In a moment the Indians felt an improvement in their illnesses. They gave the Christians of those things which they had to eat. These were nothing except those buried prickly pear leaves and some prickly pears treated in the same manner, even though they were green.

These men stayed in that place with those Indians for fifteen days. They did this in order to rest somewhat, as they were so weak that they did not dare travel. They ate those leaves as well as some prickly pears which were beginning to ripen. They recovered their strength and convalesced, regaining some more strength. Thus, the Christians became themselves again. The Indians were very kind, and they gave them of all which they had. They did this with very good will, something which these men had never experienced until that time. In all the Indians they had seen and dealt with, they had found only wickedness and cruelty, as has been stated.

From that place, the Christians went to other Indians farther onward. These people gave them many things, so that they would cure them. They also had a great celebration for them, and they fed them very well with prickly pears and meat. Moreover, they went out to hunt solely for the Christians. At this place these men became somewhat more confident. Because of the uncomfortable and inconvenient aspects of such a trip, they had thought that they could not have travelled that distance, even though life might have continued for them eight years. However, God had watched over them so well that they had walked it in ten months. It was something of a very great miracle. Moreover, it happened that no one could believe it, except those who witnessed it.

When these men were in that place, some women who were from a place farther ahead came to carry their belongings. Then, the Christians left that settlement, and this caused great sadness to those Indians. They went after the Christians, begging them to return and to leave the next day with those women, who have been mentioned. Since they did not want to do this, the natives became very sad. The women left in pursuit of the Christians, so that they would not become lost. These men went along the route initially. However, in time they left it, and they were lost. It pleased God that after two or three leagues they all came together near some water, or a small river. The women were very languid and tired, as if their lives might leave them. From that place they continued on with the Christians. They walked eight or nine leagues that day, without stopping their travelling during all that time, as long as they were able to go on. Before the sun set, they arrived at a river, which in their opinion was wider than the Guadalquivir River in Seville. They crossed it, all in water up to their knees and thighs, and in approximately two lances in depth up to their chests. Nevertheless, there was no danger.

Continuing their journey, at nightfall these people arrived at a settlement of up to a hundred groups of huts, or more. There were many people, and there they came out to receive them with much shouting and noise. They had with them some large gourds full of pebbles, with which they make their rejoicing and music. Even though they believed that those Christians had much power for healing the sick, they experienced apprehension, as well as great alarm, as they approached to rub the Christians. Notwithstanding their fear, they continued to approach with much honor and devotion, in the manner of one who might touch a holy body. Thus, those Indians came, some before the others, and many not having regard for those there with them. They got in front of each other in such a way that they did not yield room. They were carried by their fear with such great urgency that they might have poked out their eyes with their fingers. Thus, these natives carried the Christians, with their feet in the air, to their houses. There they gave them of that which they had. They brought the sick to these men, so that they might cure them. These people gave many arrows and things to an Indian who had come with the Christians. This was because he had brought them and guided them there.

On the following day, these Indians took them a league and one-half from that place to another settlement of seventy or eighty groups of huts. At this place they ate prickly pears in great quantities. There, the natives received the Christians in the same manner as in the first settlement. They gave them twenty-eight loaves of bread made from flour. They call it *mesquite*, and it is

something which these people there eat. They also gave them other things, and they had a great celebration for the Christians, with dancing and rejoicing, as is their custom.

At that place they began a new form of travelling on their journey. This was when many people began to go with these Christians to accompany them. They also would bring to these men those Indians who came to be rubbed and to be cured by them, as they believed the Christians to be saints. These people stripped of their property those new natives who thus came to them, and they took from them what they had. They even went to the houses and stole what they found. It seemed that the owners who lost their belongings took satisfaction in this. They must have thought that this new sanctity was so ordained in heaven, where they thought the Christians came from.

They rested that day and the next with those people. From there the Indians took them another six leagues farther ahead to a settlement of as many groups of huts as the one before. Many men and women went with them, with the intention of stealing what they could, and they did it thus. Upon arriving at the settlement, the Christians were received, as they had been in the places which they had passed through, and even better. Their reception was such that the multitude of people annoyed them. They crowded around the Christians so that they might rub them and cure their diseases, and in fact, they did heal them. The Indians who had come with the Christians robbed those natives these men cured. They also stole from the rest of the people of the settlement to such a degree that they did not leave anything of this life. These robbers made the victims believe that the Christians wanted it this way.

Many among those Indians were blind, and there were great numbers of them who did not have the use of one eye, because of film on that eyeball. These people are well disposed, and the men and the women are of good appearance. At that settlement the Christians treated all the blind and one-eyed natives, as well as those with many other illnesses. At least, if the Christians did not heal all, the Indians believed that they were able to cure them.

Near that place there were mountains, and a range from those mountains looked like it crossed the land directly to the north. From there, the

Indians took the Christians another five leagues onward to a river, which was at the foot of the point where those mountains began. At that place were forty or fifty groups of huts, which they plundered like the others. These people who had been robbed then gave the Christians that little which they had left. Moreover, that entire night they had great celebrations, and rejoicings for them. Likewise, the Christians healed them, as was their custom.

Then, that night they sent down towards the sea to summon people. The next day many men and women came to see the Christians and their miracles, and to bring things which they gave to them. These people tried hard to take these men toward the sea, since there they intended to compensate themselves for that which had been taken from them by the other Indians. They said that there were many people there, and they would give many things to the Christians. However, these Christians did not want to go in any direction but inland to higher ground. This was because they had earlier experienced painful mistreatment at the hands of those people of the coast. Moreover, another reason was that they had always told them that they did not go out to the sea at sunset, and until that place, they had fear of coming out at the sea when they might not be thinking about it. For these reasons the Christians wanted to journey to higher ground. The Indians did not hinder them much, but they pointed out that there were neither people nor food, except very far from there. When the Indians realized that they could not change their intent, they sent some Indians to look for people.

On the next day following, the Christians left. Many people went with them, and among these there were many women who carried water for them on the trip. This was necessary as there was a lack of it, and moreover, it was very hot. These women also carried food to eat, as well as other things they had given them. After having walked two leagues, they encountered those Indians who had gone to look for people. They reported how they had not found any in a very long way from there. Because of this all were left sad, and they pleaded with the Christians to go with them where they wanted to take them. As they were not able to convince them, the Indians said farewell, crying. Thus, they returned toward their homes, and in that place they left them what they had carried. The Christians put these things

on their backs, and they travelled upstream along that river all the rest of that day.

At night they met some Indians who took them to eight or ten groups of huts, which were located in a thicket, or craggy spot. They found the Indians weeping from devotion. They received the Christians in the same manner in which they had been welcomed, as has been described in other places, and they gave them to eat from that which they had. In the morning of the next day, those Indians, who had left the Christians on the trail, arrived. They had received news concerning how the other Indians, who have been mentioned, were in that place. These people had come to rob them, in order to compensate themselves, or to be satisfied, for what the others had taken from them. Thus, they took as much as they were able, even though it was little. They also told these people the manner in which the Christians had to be treated.

The next day these Indians took the Christians from there, and they slept that night on the road. On the following day they arrived at many huts, where they were given the usual reception. The Indians with the Christians compensated themselves for what had been taken from them. However, they even took much more, as much as they could put on their backs. In this way they went along the skirt of the mountain for eighty leagues, a little more or less. They were entering inland directly to the north. There, at the foot of the mountain, they encountered four groups of huts of another nation and tongue. These people said that they were from farther inland and that they were travelling on their way to their land. They gave the Christians a rattle of brass, as well as certain quilts of cotton. They told them that it had come from an area toward the north, crossing the land in the direction of the South Sea.

The following day the Christians moved off for the mountains toward the west, or where the sun sets. And the people with them led them to some huts near a beautiful river. There the natives gave them much margarite and antimony. They told the Christians that those people who had given them the rattle had much of that, and they had not given it. From this it is surmised that from where it was brought, although it was not gold, there was a mining district and they forged. This is even though by reason these mines must have been on the South Sea.

By the time they had arrived at where they

gave them that rattle, they must have walked a hundred and fifty leagues, a little more or less, from where they had begun to travel. From this settlement where they had given them this, the Indians took the Christians to five different groups or congregations of huts. On this entire journey more than two thousand souls never left them. Along the way they killed many hares and deer, and they brought and gave to the Christians all this game which they killed. These people did not dare to take for themselves even a mouse. Moreover, they brought the worms and the crickets which the women and children found, and they also gave these to them. Even though they were dying of hunger, the Indians did this without daring to take anything for themselves, before having the Christians bless it and give it to them. This was because they believed that they would die if they would do any other thing. The Christians ordered them not to bury the game. Rather, after they secured it, they were first to place it in front of all. The Christians would then take what they wanted of it, and they would bless the rest. With this relationship, these people travelled all that way until they came to land of the Christians.

In those huts where the Indians took the Christians, there were many people who were well disposed. These natives gave them great quantities of piñon nuts. They were as good or better than those of Castile, since they have a shell which is such that they eat it with the rest. The nuts of these piñons are very small, and the trees in those mountains are full with great quantities of them. From that place the Indians took them forward for many days, and in this way they travelled without encountering any other people. As they saw that they were not finding anyone, they sent to all parts to look for people. They made settlements come more than fifteen or twenty leagues to wait for them on the road. This was the manner in which the Indians led the Christians.

From that place they took a new order in their travelling. It had been that those Indians who guided the Christians stole as much as there was, and as much as they found, in those new settlements which they entered. Now they took nothing, but like each one of the Christians, they made their own huts for themselves. Moreover, they had things put in order, and they gathered everything which these new Indians had. Thus, the

Christians could do with these things as they wished, and no one dared take anything of those belongings. The Christians took everything, or whatever they wanted from these goods. In this manner, they left their hosts stripped of all their possessions, so that they would have the necessity of leading these Christians forward. These Indians would then be able to compensate themselves in the same way.

These people took the Christians ahead through some hopelessly rugged mountains for more than fifty leagues. They experienced much hunger, because of the bad state of the land; there were neither prickly pears nor anything else. Almost at the end of the journey, they began to become ill. Thus, the Christians had great difficulty with the Indians, as they had to continually bless these people and blow upon them. This was because hardly anyone was left who had not taken sick. It was in this condition that they led the Christians to more than one hundred groups of huts, which were located on a plain. These natives had been ordered to come from afar to that place, and there were many people along that entire plain. Everyone among all these people gave them piñons in great quantity, and they received the Christians in the same manner as had those in the past. These Indians gave them what they had, without leaving anything of this life for themselves.

On the next day, these natives took the Christians onward. They discarded some things which they had that were old. Moreover, they left along the countryside those items which these Indians were not able to continue to carry. They also discarded those cases which they had used for boxes. These Indians told the Christians that there were not any other people, except very far from that place. They also mentioned that these people were their enemies. The Christians told them that they should send an Indian, who could tell those other people that they were coming. On the entire trip, this was their custom. When they were coming to some new settlements, four Indians would precede them. In this way, one Indian would represent each of these Christians. They did this so that the natives would get their houses ready for them. When they arrived, what these people had to give them would be near at hand.

Thus, these Indians agreed to send two women. One they had was a captive from those people from where they had come, and another woman went with her. They did not dare to send a man, because of the war which they had with those Indians ahead. Moreover, they did not understand each other. The Christians went along with all the people, after those two women. They were moving every day, in order to await the response they would bring to a certain place. As they began to travel, these people began to suffer pain. It was in such a manner that the Christians had much pity for them, as these were the best people they had encountered.

As they had determined to wait for the women, and for the reply which they were bringing, they stopped for three days. These people did not want to take the Christians to any other place, because of the war which existed. Then Andrés Dorantes said to an Indian of his that he should tell the others that they were probably going to die, because of this which they did not want to do. For this reason, the fear, which these Indians already held, grew in them. In the morning of the next day, the Indians went hunting. At noon they returned, and they were sick. Each day more natives fell ill. Within two days many had died, and more than three hundred people were suffering. They believed that the Christians were causing their suffering, out of anger. Thus, their fear so increased that they did not dare look the Christians in the face or raise their eyes from the ground when before them.

It was astonishing to observe these Indians. During the no more than fifteen days that the Christians were among them, they never saw one of these natives laugh, cry, or show any other emotional change. This was even though the parents of some died; others lost their women and children; and still others lost their husbands. In spite of all this, they concealed their real feelings. These people conducted themselves with such composure that it seemed as if no grief could be afflicting them. The nursing babies and children of a greater age were even more astonishing. They were never seen laughing or crying in all the time that the Christians were among these Indians. It was as if they were old people who had lived a hundred years. These people did not dare eat, drink, or do anything else of this life, without first asking permission from the Christians. They did this because they thought that these Christians had the power to kill them, or to give them life. For this reason, they believed that they were

dying because the Christians had been made angry.

After they had been in that place for two or three days, those women came back. They brought very ruinous news. Those people whom they had gone to look for had left after the cows. Therefore, throughout that entire region, there were no people. After the Indians learned this, they pointed out that they were all ill, as the Christians could see. They also mentioned that they were very far from their homes. They said that the Christians could go after the cows, which would be in a direction toward the north. Thus, they would find people. The Indians wanted to remain where they were and then to go away to some other place. This was because they were very hungry as the prickly pears had finished. The Christians told them that they could not do this. They reminded the Indians that they had to take them to that place which was toward the west, or where the sun sets, as this was their correct route. The Christians instructed that the sick should remain at that place and that twenty or thirty of those natives who were healthy should continue with them. They also decided that one of the Christians would go with those Indian women to look for those people and to bring them to the route of the Christians. It appeared that the Indians were pleased upon hearing this.

The next day following they left that place, and they walked for three days, one after the other. Alonso del Castillo, who was the most fit, also left. He went with the black man and the Indian women who took him to a river. There they found people and houses of permanence, as well as some beans and calabashes which they ate, although very little. At the end of three days, Castillo returned to the other Christians, and the black man remained in order to bring people to their route....

6.

Alonso del Castillo returned to where his companions, the treasurer Álvar Núñez Cabeza de Vaca and Andrés Dorantes, awaited him. On the next day following they left, and they met those people whom the black man was bringing. There these Indians gave them those things which they had brought. These included some robes of cowhides, or of the hides of tapirs—this distinction has already been discussed. They also carried deerskins for the Christians, and they gave them their bows and arrows, as well as many calabashes and some beans. The Christians then turned over all these things to those natives who had accompanied them to that place. Thus, these other people returned to their land content.

The Christians then left with new people, even though they had stripped them of their belongings. They continued the journey to the houses of these Indians. These were located on that river, five or six leagues from where they were. At this place these natives sowed crops. However, because of the great number of people who were there as well as the scarcity and harshness of the land, it was little that they realized for their efforts. They took the Christians upstream along that river to four groups of settlements which were there.

These people had little to eat. Their diet consisted of beans, calabashes, and a little maize. Moreover, they did not have anything in which to cook these foods. Nevertheless, they did manage to make a thick soup, which was like a pap or porridge. They cooked this in some large gourds in the following manner. They first built a fire, and then they would throw many small, clean stones into it. These stones would thus heat up, and these people would toss them into the gourds which they had filled with water. This would make the water become very hot, and it would boil. They would then add flour from the beans to the water. They would put more stones on top, until the porridge was good. At this time, they would eat it.

At this place these Indians told the Christians that farther ahead there were neither beans nor more flour. For that matter, there would be nothing to eat until after a journey of thirty or forty days, going onward in a northerly direction from that region where the sun sets. It was from this area that those Indians had procured, or had brought, that seed. These people also pointed out that all the Indians who lived on the way to that place suffered great hunger. They said that the Christians had to go along that river for a journey of another nine or ten days without anything to eat. At the end of this time, these Indians instructed them to cross the river at that place, which was where they must cross it. The Christians were then to continue all the rest of the time to the west, or where the sun sets, until they

arrived where there was maize, and very much of it. The natives mentioned that there was also maize toward the right hand to the north. Moreover, it must have existed lower down through all that land to the coast, as it appeared afterward. However, these people noted that the second region was located very much farther away than the first. This other maize area was the closer one, and all the people on the way to it were friends and of the same language. At this time, these Indians gave the Christians a great quantity of robes made from cowhide, and they said that they were from animals which they killed in the summer near that place. Moreover, they mentioned that there were many of these cows.

Thus, the Christians went upstream along this river for the nine-day journey. Each day they walked until nightfall, and they experienced very great hunger. At night they always slept in houses and with people who gave them many robes of cowhide, as well as other things. The Christians would have exchanged these willingly for those ring-shaped cakes made in Utrera, as they were not given anything to eat. This was because those people did not have any food, except for one item which those Indians called *masarrones*. It was something that they picked from some trees, and it was very bad. Although it was not even fit for animals, those people made use of it, after grinding it with some stones. In the end it was totally stringy, and thus it was eaten. The Christians ate some small pieces of deer fat which they carried on their backs.

On the road, they encountered a few people, and these told them that the other Indians had gone to eat cows at a distance of a three-day journey from that place. Moreover, these natives stated that they were also going to this same area, which was located on some plains between mountains which came from above, sloping toward the sea. Thus, the Christians travelled upstream along that river for a period of fifteen days. They did not rest, because of the great hunger which they had. At that point they crossed toward the west, or where the sun sets, and they travelled for a period of more than twenty days to that maize. During this time they encountered a people who were somewhat hungered. However, they were not so much so, because they ate some ground-up herbs and because they killed many wild hares. Thus, the

Christians always carried more of this game than they needed. On this road they rested sometimes, as they had the custom of doing.

When the Christians arrived at those first houses which had maize, they were probably more than two hundred leagues from Culua-cán—a place which was colonized by Nuño de Guzmán, and where there were peaceful Indians, as well as a town. At that native settlement, the Indians gave them great quantities of maize, toasted flour, beans, calabashes, and other seeds. They also presented more things to the Christians, as was their custom. These Indians had some small earthen houses made with adobe walls and with their roofs flat. The greatest number of the dwellings were constructed from covered hampers, or rather—it should be stated—from baskets. Thus, they would be like mud-walled houses, or something woven from palm leaves, vines, or another similar binding.

In this manner these Christians travelled more than eighty leagues. Every three days, or every two days, they would arrive at a settlement, and they would rest a day or two in each of these places. Beginning with these peoples, the Christians were given many quilts of cotton, and good ones. These natives offered everything which they had, so that nothing was kept by them. This included turquoise which was presented in the same manner. Just as they gave all these things to the Christians, they would turn them over to the other Indians. Moreover, there were many sick who afflicted them. This was because there were a great number of people, and they all had to be rubbed and greeted. He who was not greeted by the Christians thought that he would die. These natives would come from ten or twelve leagues around to bring them their sick. In whatever part these Christians went, a thousand or fifteen hundred people travelled with them. Sometimes, their number surpassed three thousand, until they came out to that plain near the coast. When they arrived at this place, it had been eight months that they had not left the mountains.

The Christians admonished and instructed all these people that they should dispose their thoughts to heaven and that they should raise their eyes toward it. They also told these Indians to put their hands together, while kneeling down whenever they had some necessity. Fur-thermore, they instructed them to commend themselves to God, the All-Powerful. The natives did as they had been told. They believed that the Christians came from heaven, and the Indians took much pleasure when they told them something about that place. However, the Christians did not know how to give them an understanding, as they wished, because of a lack of language. If they had had this facility, these Christians who escaped said that without a doubt they believed that these people might be good Christians. This was because of the faith and inclination with which they followed and listened to the Christians, and also it was considering the few mistaken beliefs and idolatries which these Indians had.

They had such love for the Christians that when they left, these people were weeping, as well as those natives who guided the Christians forward. Some women who were pregnant, and others who had recently given birth, came with children in their arms to say farewell to the Christians. They placed in the hands of each of these children three or four kernels of maize, in order that the Christians would take these and would give them leave. It meant to the Indians, if they took the maize from the children, that they would never have to suffer pain or to be sick.

When they passed through the mountains which have been mentioned, these four Christians arrived at three settlements. These men were the three Spaniards, who have been named, and the black man, who was a Christian called Estéban. These settlements were together and small, and there were as many as twenty houses in them. These were like the others they had seen. They were together and not spread out, one here and the other over there, as in the land of peace which they saw afterward. At this place the people of the coast came to the Christians. According to the signs which they made in order to be understood, at this place they were twelve or fifteen leagues from the coast. The Christians named this settlement, or better to say settlements as a group, the town of the hearts. This was because the natives there gave them more than six hundred deer hearts which had been cut open and dried.

Among all these people, since encountering those first houses with maize, the men walk around very immodestly without covering any part of their persons. However, the women are very modest. They wear outer skirts of deerskin to their feet. These garments have a train, which is something which drags behind them. In their front these are open to the ground and laced with some straps. These women use a cotton blanket underneath where the skirts are open. Moreover, they also use another such blanket on top, as well as some ruffs of cotton which cover their breasts completely.

Those Indians told them that along all that coast from the south to the north there were many people, much food, much cotton, and big houses. (Here it may be stated not "from the south" but rather "northerly." This is better, and it should be termed in this manner.) They also said that those other people had many turquoise stones which they brought from there for barter. However, these Indians did not have information to give them about any gold, nor did they have news concerning mines. Thus, these Christians believed that that rattle and those quilts of cotton which the natives had given them, as has been mentioned in this history, came from up above and from the other sea and coast, as was already stated. This was because of those things they had been told there, as well as by reason of what they had seen before entering into the mountains. The Indians stated to them that this other area was populated with many people and had much food. Moreover, it also seemed to the Christians that those small flat roofs and the way the women went about in such modest dress were things which the Indians learned and adopted from there. They concluded this because from there forward in this direction, a good three hundred leagues to a river which Nuño de Guzmán discovered, there existed that same manner of dressing and those types of houses. However, beyond that place forward in this direction, there was not anything but houses of that basket type and of straw. Moreover, in this area the women wore some blankets to their middle, and some more modest ones to the knee.

After that town they went for thirty leagues to this river now mentioned, and along the way the people gave receptions, as has been said, and accompanied the Christians. There it rained on them for fifteen days, and they were forced to stop. This was around Christmas. At that place the Christians always had many people with them, and they never left them, even though they were from far away.

There Castillo saw an Indian who had a small buckle, from either an ordinary belt or from a sword belt, hanging from his neck along with a shoeing nail, as if it were a small jewel. He took them, and the Christians asked this Indian what those things were. He responded that other men, like those Christians, had earlier arrived at that place with horses, lances, and swords. They showed how these men had speared and killed the Indians. These people maintained that for certain they had been Christians. The natives told them how, before these three Spaniards and the black man arrived there, an Indian had been at that place. He had come there from the direction of those men of the ships, and he had been going to take the natives to them. This they repeated to the Christians many times. Since they did not understand them, they were afraid. That Indian was one of two or three who had been left by Nuño de Guzmán when they arrived there, sick and tired. This was made known to them afterwards, from what the Spaniards later told them in Culuacán.

From there they began to travel with a very great desire and joy because of this news that these few Christians had of those Spaniards who were farther on. The Indians did nothing else but talk to the Christians concerning this, as if speaking about something which gave them pleasure. They did this to such an extent that even though they wanted to hide their real feelings, they could not. They feared that at the frontier of the Christians they would do something deceitful to them.

From where it had rained on them to where the other Christians were located, there were some hundred leagues or more. Since leaving the town of hearts, they had always travelled along the coast at a distance of ten or twelve leagues inland. For those hundred leagues, in some parts there was food. However, in other areas there existed much hunger, and they did not eat anything except the bark of trees and some roots. Because of these bad fortunes, they were so weak and mangy that it was pitiful to see them. It caused them to say that the Christians had made forays into that place three times. They had carried off the people and destroyed the settlements. These natives were so terrified and fearful that they did not dare to be visible in any place. One would be seen here and another there, like people beneath a small mat who had been driven away into the thickets. They were without peace, and they did not dare to sow crops.

Notwithstanding all their fear, everyone came together to receive these few Christians. This was because they considered them to be holy and divine, or men who came from heaven, and so they took them forward. These people even brought those small mats which they had to give to the Christians. These were their beds upon which they slept, and each one of the natives was accustomed to holding these mats rolled up over his shoulder or under his arm. Thus it was that where these Christians expected to receive more injury, the Indians respected them and received them with more honor. This was another thing which was marvellous.

Thus they went to a settlement which was in the mountains. It was situated on top of a high, craggy cliff, due to the fear of the Christians. This settlement was forty leagues from Culuacán, where the Spaniards were established. At this place the natives received them with much pleasure. Many people from all parts came together to see them. On the next day following, they sent their messengers ahead to other settlements which were three days on the route from there. This was so that these other natives might make houses or huts for them and also so that they might gather to receive them.

When these Indians went, they did not find the Spaniards there, as they were going about collecting people for slaves. One night they were nearby watching them. The following day these natives looked for people in those woods around that area. However, they did not find any, as they had gone very far away. Therefore, these natives returned and told the Christians what they had seen. They were so disturbed that they were almost not able to talk. Then, all the other people likewise became upset, and they were very afraid. Many bade farewell, and returned for their homes. These fortunate Christians told those who remained that they should not have fear. They assured these Indians that they would have those Christians, whom they feared, return to their own

area. Moreover, they stressed that those Spaniards would not do them harm and that they were their friends. These people took pleasure in hearing these words. They replied that they would go along with this as explained. They agreed because as it was they did not dare sow crops or be in their houses on account of those other Christians. Moreover, they were all dying of hunger. Being so assured, these people continued with the three Christians. Among them there were Indians who had come from more than eighty leagues back, and they said that they would never leave the Christians.

Thus, all these people continued on their journey. When they arrived at the settlement, they did not find the other Christians. However, they did locate their huts, and they determined that it had been two days since they had departed from that place. They decided to go after these Christians. They sent people to tell them that they would wait and that they should return to these others. Cabeza de Vaca assumed the responsibility of pursuing them, and he took with him the black man, as well as a dozen Indians. Those that remained, who were the other two Christians, sent to look for those people who had fled to the thickets and craggy places or to the woods. On the next day following, more than three hundred souls came, men as well as women. They said that the next day more people would come. These were those who had fled to a greater distance. Thus, they gathered others who were far away. More than four hundred of those individuals, who had gone away, came together. This was not counting those other Indians who had come with the Christians.

The treasurer Cabeza de Vaca travelled all that day until nightfall on the trail of those other Christians. The next day he arrived where these men had hastily lodged and settled near a river. They did not know where they should go next, as it had been fifteen days that they had not enslaved a native. Moreover, in this period they had not even been able to see an Indian. There were as many as twenty horsemen. When Cabeza de Vaca arrived at where these Christians were, they were astonished and afraid upon seeing him. However, they were much more amazed upon hearing him tell how he had passed through so many lands with different peoples and languages.

They gave many thanks to God, Our Lord, for such a new and very great mystery. Thus, these others asked them for a sworn statement concerning the manner in which they had come to that place and had brought those peaceful people of good will, who followed them. They gave this to them by faith and by an affidavit which was sent to Their Majesties. This document gave praise to Jesus Christ, Our Redeemer, who had seen fit to guard these few Christians from such innumerable difficulties. Thus, they were able to arrive to give a report for the Emperor King, our lord, about the fate of that unfortunate fleet, as well as about the state of the land which these men had seen. They remained with these other Christians for one day.

This group of Spaniards had experienced constant days when they had not been able to catch an Indian or person. As a result, they were in need of forage for their horses. Therefore, they implored these travellers to send a call for people from among those terrified natives who were concealed in the thickets. The messengers of these men did it for them, as they had been accustomed to do during the entire journey. Soon afterwards, on the next day, up to six hundred souls came. These included men and women, some with their nursing infants in their arms. They carried pots of maize with their openings smeared with mud. They had hidden these in the thickets out of fear of the Christians.

(Does it seem to you, Christian reader, that this passage, with the different actions of those Spaniards who were in that land, is worthy of contemplation? There were the four travellers who came curing the sick and performing miracles. As has been mentioned above, there were also some Spaniards who went about enslaving and assaulting people. From this you can surmise how great a part of these activities depends upon the good or bad intention, as well as the conduct, of these same Christians. By the number of those dead and those living you can conclude of which action you approve. Certainly, you may not believe that all those who travel, and have travelled, in these lands are Spaniards, although the majority of them are. There are also those from different nations who, calling themselves Christians, have come over here in search of this gold. Some find it to their detriment. Others do not encounter it, but they do experience such great anguish, as you are able to comprehend from this lesson.)

Let us return to the history and the relation of these gentlemen. It states that those people, who had gone around hidden, had gathered together by the order of those few Christians. Afterwards, that one who served as captain of the Spaniards they had encountered spoke to these travellers. He said that he [Cabeza de Vaca?] should speak with the Indians and tell them that they should return to their duties in their settlements and sow their crops, as they had been accustomed to do. He maintained that they should be assured that the Christians would do them neither any harm nor injury. Moreover, he instructed that the Indians be informed that these men did not want anything, except that when the Christians would pass by their houses, the Indians were to give food to them and to their horses. This was made known to the natives, and the Spaniards gave them leave so that they could go in safety to their settlements. However, they did not want to go, or to separate themselves from the Christians, saying that they had not served them well nor had they accompanied them, as should have been done.

At last, Cabeza de Vaca and his companions told them that they should leave without worry, because he and the others were going to where the lord of the Christians was. He also told these natives that he would talk to this lord, so that he would command his people not to persecute them or to become angry with them. Thus, these Indians went in peace, and these Christians went with three horsemen. They accompanied these travellers to the town of Culuacán, which had been established on the coast of the South Sea, to the west, by Nuño de Guzmán. It was located a good thirty-five leagues or more from there. Meanwhile, the leader, or captain of these Spaniards, went toward the mountains to find people to enslave.

When these Christians arrived at a peacefully settled valley eight leagues before reaching the town, Melchior Díaz, the chief official of the town, came out to them. He received them very well, giving thanks to God for the marvels which He had worked with these gentlemen. Near that place there were many settlements in rebellion, and their people had not [?] gone to the mountains. Because of this, they sent to these natives two or three Indians of those few who had been enslaved. They carried a sign which these travelling Christians gave them to call all the Indians who were hidden. They directed these two or three to say that the others should come safely and that no harm whatever would befall them. Thus, the messengers left with the sign, which was a gourd that each one of the travellers had been accustomed to carrying in his hand.

These Indians were gone from there for quite a while. At the end of five or six days they came back and brought three lords, or principal caciques, as well as fifteen or sixteen other natives of those in rebellion. These people carried beads and turquoise stones to offer. They also gave to these three travelling Christians very beautiful feathers. The Indians presented these gifts in front of the already mentioned Melchior Díaz, the chief official. It was he who made these natives converse. He gave them to understand how these Christians had come from heaven, and he pointed out that they had travelled through many places. He instructed the Indians to turn themselves to heaven, as this is where the Lord of all created things is. Díaz told them that when God wanted those who were good to die in this life, He gave glory to them. He also pointed out to these natives that those who did not love God fully, believe in Him, nor serve Him, as their only All-Powerful God, would be given the punishment of fire for evermore. Moreover, Melchior Díaz stated that those few Christians had come to that place in order to tell the others that they should not harm, injure, or kill the Indians.

Thus, the chief official of the town of Culuacán informed the Indians that they would not be molested so long as they would remain in their settlements, believe in God, and build churches where He might be served. Díaz also said to the natives that they should place crosses in their settlements and carry these with them. The Indians were also instructed that whenever some Christians might pass through their land, they should come out to receive them with a cross. Melchior Díaz concluded by making it clear to these people that in such an encounter all would humble themselves before this cross, and in this way the Spaniards would not do them harm, as they would take them as brothers.

The Indians understood these things very well. They said that they would act thusly, and they departed. Then, they began to come down from the mountains to settle and to build churches. These people put crosses, in the manner it had been ordered of them. Thus it was that all that land was populated in peace, because of our Christians.

([Note by Oviedo] Pray to Our Redeemer that these savage people, during the life and fortune of our Caesarean Catholic Majesty, may come to the knowledge and service of God, under obedience to the royal crown of Castile as good and faithful vassals of His Majesty. It was to this royal personage that these three gentlemen already mentioned, Álvar Núñez Cabeza de Vaca, Andrés Dorantes, and Alonso del Castillo, made a relation of that which this history has stated. They wrote this report, certifying that throughout all that land, where they had travelled, they did not see idolatry nor sacrifice of men. Moreover, they did not hear of such things until they arrived at the City of Compostela, which had been built and settled in those parts by Governor Nuño de Guzmán.

This chronicler took this relation from the letter these gentlemen sent to the Audiencia Real which resides in this city of Santo Domingo on this island of Española. It was dispatched to this body from the port of Havana where the travellers stopped last year, 1539 [1537]. They were going on their way to Castile to give an accounting of what has been said to the Emperor King, our lord, and his Royal Council of the Indies.

Thus, this was the fate of Captain Pánfilo de Narváez and of his fleet. In His infinite mercy, God may have pardoned him and the rest of those men, taking their inhuman difficulties and deaths in place of punishment for their faults. So, one ought to believe that the divine goodness saved their souls, as they were Christians. Moreover, one ought to conclude this because their desires must have been those which were reasonable. These men would have wanted to enlarge the Christian republic, to serve their Prince, and, each one in his honest fashion, to remedy their poverty or needs. Or, one may justly believe that they were saved because they might have deserved, in the last hour of their lives, that sigh spoken of by the prophet Ezekiel: "In whatever hour the sinner will sigh and will call, he will be pardoned."

If it should happen within my time, that which will come to pass in these territories has to be added in the prosecution of this history. I speak of those areas where Pánfilo de Narváez went to settle, or better to say, to get lost. Otherwise, he who will succeed me in the continuation of this *Historia general de estas Indias* has to write about the occurrences.)

Chapter Twenty-nine
The Expedition of Hernando de Soto and
His Successor, Luis de Moscoso, 1539–1543

THE EXPEDITION of Hernando de Soto was one of the greatest attempts to penetrate the interior of North America in the sixteenth century and one that brought to light more information than any other on the topography of southeastern and south-central parts of what is now the United States. Yet is is one that is peculiarly difficult to follow and to understand. It took a Spanish army into territories that are, in part, without identifiable landmarks and, even after intensive research, cannot always be located with precision. Moreover, the *rationale* of Soto's wanderings is itself obscure; his short-term objectives often seem little more than a wayward search for gold or precious stones, according to the latest rumors or guesses that reached him, or else were governed by news of possible food supplies in the hands of some Indian tribe, or some new natural food resources that might become accessible to him.

In its inception in 1537 the project was rational enough. Hernando de Soto, having taken part in the looting of Peru, proposed to do the same for the territory behind the Gulf Coast of North America, the object being to locate the new Peru, which he was confident must lie there. The early stage in his march, the landing at Tampa Bay on June 3, 1539, and his northward march to winter in the land of the Apalache Indians, 1539–1540, was a sensible venture. But his route-march up the Piedmont to the Savannah Valley and a little beyond was governed by no very coherent strategy beyond a search for gold on the strength of the slightest rumors. But by the time he turned westward to cross the Appalachians and enter the Tennessee Valley, his objective appears to have been even less specific. His army had taken on the character of a great caravan, soldiers and scouts in the lead, Indian bearers carrying the goods of the expedition, but the bulk of the men with their female slaves walking slowly behind, and a long trail of hogs slowly winding behind them. An Indian chief or two were carried with the leader's party until contact was made with the next tribe where men could be impressed to allow some of the existing bearers to return home. Then, the looting of the village of its corn (and mortars to grind it), and whatever skin mantles or furs that might be found was repeated. Then, on again to do likewise. His track up the Piedmont, across the mountains, down the Tennessee Valley, and over the watershed into the Alabama River Valley was straightforward enough, an extended piece of exploration, although without any very clear longer-term objectives. The casually looted mussel pearls of Cofitachequi appeared to him to justify diversions in search of gold or similar wealth at any point in his journey. He had refused to establish a settlement, as some of his men desired, in the Savannah Valley where traces of Ayllón's 1526 settlement were found. As he descended to the west of the Appalachians toward the Gulf, the increasing richness of the Indian tribes in agricultural wealth, in village size, and ceremonial structures, made him hope for a time he was reaching at last the borders of a higher civilization. His attempts to dominate the first really strong Indian group he met, the Choctaw tribe and their chief Tascalusa (as

90

Pizarro had done Atahualpa) failed, and it was he and his men who were surrounded and burned out of the Choctaw town of Mabila. After that he appeared to become the mere wanderer in a strange land. Pride fought down his rational arrangement to make contact with Maldonado's supply ships on the Gulf Coast. He marched his men away from and not toward safety, to the northwest, away from Indian plenty toward Indian poverty. The next two seasons, from October, 1540 to May, 1542, do not appear to have had any overall *rationale*. The expedition wandered from place to place, becoming more or less self-sustaining, although still battening on the Indians. Whenever acorn-rich country was reached, the opportunity was taken to enlarge the great herd of pigs that now followed him (his personal share in May 1542 was 700).

He achieved the remarkable feat not only of finding but of crossing the Mississippi successfully, but it was not clear for what purpose. He had skirmishes with Indian groups before and after the crossing, which weakened his men and depleted his stock of horses. He kept his men going for a time with a northwesterly march toward "the South Sea," which he considered lay not far from the Arkansas River. Eventually, pretenses fell away, and he turned round to make his way back to the Mississippi and, he hoped, Mexico. He died on May 21, 1542, a failure, a Don Quixote not a Cortés.

Luis de Moscoso, his successor, mistakenly tried to march directly southwestward to Mexico but before his men starved to death retraced his steps to the Mississippi. There at last they constructed the little fleet of boats that brought nearly half the original Spanish force (and some hundred slaves) to the Gulf Coast and eventually, in September, 1543, to Pánuco. The reports brought back (and we do not have Moscoso's) were of a land where the Indians were, if at all, rich only in food, not bullion or other precious products, and whose capacity to be effectively enslaved was, on account of their warlike nature, dubious. There was clearly no Peru to be discovered. Henceforth, the interior behind the Gulf Coast held few attractions for Spain. Soto had not only killed himself in his quest but had also killed the desire of other Spaniards to emulate him. The official memory retained only one favorable thing about the march, the easy access Soto had along the Piedmont in the spring of 1540 to the Savannah Valley and a possible approach from there to the Punta de Santa Elena, which lay not too far away on the Atlantic Coast. This alone was to inspire a later mission, that of Tristán de Luna.

Three members of the expedition wrote of their experiences. The first narrative to be published was by an unknown gentleman from Elvas in Portugal and appears to have been drawn from a capacious memory rather than a diary or notes (239). Hence the descriptions are necessarily vague and distances confused. But it does record the first description of the Mississippi River and is probably the best full account of the expedition. Another account was written by Rodrigo Rangel, Soto's private secretary, who kept a diary on which he based an official report of the expedition, although what we have is not complete (240). He gives a more accurate record of the tribes and towns visited than the Elvas narrative, but together they provide almost a daily record of events so far as they overlap (namely down to November, 1541). Help in locating places visited, especially to the west of the Mississippi, is found in the narrative of Luis Hernández de Biedma, the factor of the expedition (241). A later account was written at the end of the century by Garcilaso de la Vega, the Inca, who based his narrative largely on the experiences of one member of the expedition, Gonzalo Silvestre, and some others whom he names, but their recollections are heavily laced with his own romantic notions (242).

The capitulations and asiento were on traditional lines (237). Otherwise the documentary sources for the expedition of Hernando de Soto are rich and varied. Primary among them we must place *Relaçam verdadeira dos trabalhos que ho governador dom Fernando de souto & certos figalgos portugueses passarom no descobrimento da provincia da Frolida. Agora novamente feita per hum fidalgo Delvas*, Évora, André de Burgos, February 10, 1557. The narrative of the Gentleman of Elvas (no other name having been found for him) was reprinted in Lisbon in 1844, and 1875, and, as *Verdadeira relação*, edited by F. G. Pery Vidal, in facsimile, with a modern Portuguese version (Lisbon, 1940). Richard Hakluyt translated it as *Virginia richly valued, by the description of the maine land of Florida her next neighbour* (London, Felix Kingston for Matthew Lownes, 1609), and under a more realistic title as *The worthye and famous history of that great continent of Terra Florida, being lively paraleld, with that of our new inhabited Virginia* (1611), the standard modern edition being edited by W. B. Rye, *The Discovery and Conquest of Terra Florida by Don Fernando de Soto* (London, Hakluyt Society, 1851). Thomas Buckingham Smith made the first translation for American readers in his *Narratives of the Career of Hernando de Soto in the Conquest of Florida* (New York, 1866). This was reprinted in Edward Bourne, *Narratives of the Career of Hernando de Soto*, 2 vols. (New York, 1904), I, 3–223, with some corrections, and in F. W. Hodge and T. H. Lewis, *Spanish Explorers in the Southern United States, 1528–1543* (New York, 1907, and subsequently). The new translation by James A. Robertson, *True Relation of the Hardship Suffered by Governor Fernando de Soto and Certain Portuguese Gentlemen During the Discovery of the Province of Florida*, 2 vols. (Deland, Fla., 1933), is a superior version and has been used here.

The official report of Rodrigo Rangel is preserved only in Gonzalo Fernández de Oviedo, *Historia general y natural de las Indias* and was not published until the appearance of the complete *History* in 1851, 4 vols. (Madrid, 1851), reprinted, 5 vols. (Madrid, 1959), where it appears in Volume IV. The diary was abbreviated and lacks several chapters including those which described Soto's death and the subsequent expedition by Moscoso into Texas. A complete translation into English first appeared in Edward G. Bourne, *Narratives of the Career of Hernando de Soto*, 2 vols. (New York, 1904), II, 41–149.

Luis Hernández de Biedma's narrative was formerly extant among the Spanish records, but there is an eighteenth-century transcript by Juan Baptista Muños (represented in his own manuscripts in Academia Real de Historia, Madrid, and by copies in the Library of Congress and in the New York Public Library). Presented to the king and Council of the Indies in 1544, it was the version most widely current in Spanish official circles. Ternaux-Compans, *Voyages*, XX, *Receuil de pièces sur la Floride* (Paris, 1841), produced a French translation from which English versions were made by W. B. Rye (in the 1851 edition of the Gentleman of Elvas) and by B. F. French, *Historical Collections of Louisiana* (1857). T. Buckingham Smith's English version in his 1866 edition of the Gentleman of Elvas was the first to come directly from the Spanish, and it formed the basis for Edward G. Bourne, *Narratives of the Career of Hernando de Soto*, 2 vols. (New York, 1904), II, 1–40, which has remained the standard text.

Garcilaso de la Vega, the Inca, completed the first large book on Soto, *La Florida de la Inca* (Lisbon, 1605), on the basis of documents, memories of survivors or their descendants, and his own vivid historical imagination. J. G. and J. J. Varner's translation, *The Florida of the Inca* (Austin, Texas, 1951), provides an opportunity to sample its felicities and inventions.

237. April 20, 1537. Capitulations between Charles V and Hernando de Soto.

The capitulations transfer to Soto the rights and privileges, with some modifications, already granted to Narváez (232).

This was first translated from the Spanish by T. Buckingham Smith, Narratives of the Career of Hernando de Soto *(New York, 1866), and is reprinted with a few minor variations.*

The King

Inasmuch as you, Captain Hernando de Soto, set forth that you have served us in the conquest, pacification, and settlement of the Provinces of Nicaragua and Peru, and of other parts of our Indias; and that now, to serve us further, and to continue to enlarge our patrimony and the royal crown, you desire to return to those our Indias, to conquer and settle the Province of Rio de las Palmas to Florida, the government whereof was bestowed on Panfílo de Narváez, and the Provinces of Tierra-Nueva, the discovery and government of which was conferred on Lucas Vázquez de Ayllón; and that for the purpose you will take from these, our kingdoms and our said Indias, five hundred men, with the necessary arms, horses, munitions, and military stores; and that you will go hence, from these our kingdoms, to make the said conquest and settlement within a year first following, to be reckoned from the day of the date of these articles of authorization; and that when you shall leave the Island of Cuba to go upon that enterprise, you will take the necessary subsistence for all that people during eighteen months—rather over than under that time—entirely at your cost and charges, without our being obliged, or the kings who shall come after us, to pay you, nor satisfy the expenses incurred therefor, other than such as you in these articles may be authorized to make; and you pray that I bestow on you the conquest of those lands and provinces, and with it the government of the said Island of Cuba, that you may from there the better control and provide all the principal and important material for the conquest and settlement, whereupon I have ordered to be made with you the terms and contract following:

First, I give you, the said Captain Hernando de Soto, power and authority, for us and in our name, and in that of the royal crown of Castile, to conquer, pacify, and populate the lands that there are from the Province of the Rio de la Palmas to Florida, the government of which was bestowed on Panfílo de Narváez; and, further, the Provinces of the said Tierra-Nueva, the government whereof was in like manner conferred on the said Licentiate Ayllón.

Also, purposing to comply in this with the service of God our Lord, and to do you honour, we engage to confer on you the dignity of Governor and Captain-general of two hundred leagues of coast, such as you shall designate, of what you discover, so that within four years, to be reckoned from the time you arrive in any part of the lands and provinces before mentioned, you shall choose and declare whence you would have the two hundred leagues begin; that from where you designate they shall be measured along the coast, for all the days of your life, with the annual salary of fifteen hundred ducats, and five hundred ducats gratuity, in all two thousand, which you shall receive from the day you set sail in the port of San Lucar, to go upon your voyage, to be paid to you from the duties and profits to us appertaining in those said lands and provinces which you so offer to conquer and colonize; and in that time should there be neither duties nor profits, we shall not be obliged to order that you be paid any thing.

Also, we will confer on you the title of our Adelantado over the said two hundred leagues which you shall thus select and make known for your government in the said lands and provinces you so discover and colonize, and will likewise bestow on you the office of High-Constable [*alguazil mayor*] over those territories in perpetuity.

Also, we give permission, the judgment of our officers of said province being in accord, that you build there as many as three stone fortresses in the harbours and places most proper for them, they appearing to you and to our said officers to be necessary for the protection and pacification of that country; and we confer on you the Lieutenancy of them, and on one heir for life, or successor whom you shall name, with the annual salary to each of the fortresses of one hundred thousand maravedis, which you shall enjoy from the time they be severally built and finished and enclosed, in the opinion of our said officers; to be done at your own cost, without our being obliged, or any of the kings who shall come after us, to pay you what you may expend on those fortresses.

Again, inasmuch as you have petitioned us to bestow on you some portion of the land and vassals in said province you would conquer and populate, considering what you have served us, and the expenditure you will meet from this time in making said conquest and pacification, we receive the petitions favourably: hence we promise to bestow on you, and by these presents we do, twelve leagues of land in square in the said two hundred leagues you shall designate to hold in government in the said territories and provinces before declared, which we command your officers of the said province to assign after you have designated the said two hundred leagues, to include no sea-port, nor the principal town, and that with the jurisdiction and title we shall confer at the time we give you the deeds.

Again, as has been said, you have petitioned us, that for the better governing and providing of all the principal and important matters for the conquest and settlement of said territories and provinces, I should order that there be given to you with them the government of the said Island of Cuba, which, to that end, we deem well, and is our pleasure, for the time it shall be our will, that you hold the government of said island; and for thus much we will order to be given you our provision by which you will be obliged to have a Chief Justice, who shall be a lawyer to whom we shall require you to pay yearly on that Island the salary of two hundred *pesos* of gold; and we give to you five hundred ducats annual gratuity for the government of said Island, while you hold the same, to be paid from the duties and profits we may have from the provinces you have thus to conquer, pacify, and hold in government; and if there be none there, we shall not be obliged to pay you that, nor any other thing more than the two hundred *pesos* of the said Chief Justice.

Also, we give you liberty and right that you from these our kingdoms and lordships, or from the Kingdom of Portugal, or Islands of Cabo Verde, or Guinea, do and may pass, or whosoever may exercise your power, to the said Island of Cuba fifty negro slaves, not less than one-third of them to be females, free of the import duties that of right may belong to us at said island, upon paying the license of two ducats on each to Diego

de la Haya, which sum by our order he is charged to collect.

Again, also, we promise that upon your arrival in that country of your government, which you have thus to conquer and settle, we give liberty and right to whomsoever shall have your power, that you may take thither from these our said kingdoms, or from Portugal, or the Islands of Cabo Verde, other fifty negro slaves, the third part of them females, free from all duties.

Also, we concede to those who shall go to settle in that country within the six years first following, to be reckoned forward from the day of the date of these presents, that of the gold which may be taken from the mines shall be paid us the tenth, and the said six years being ended, shall pay us the ninth, and thus annually declining to the fifth part; but from the gold and other things which may be got by barter, or is spoil got by incursions, or in any other manner, shall be paid us thereupon one-fifth of all.

Also we give, free of all import duty, to the inhabitants of that country for the said six years, and as much longer as shall be our will, all they may take for the furnishing and provision of their houses, the same not being to sell; and whatsoever they or any other, merchants or traffickers, sell, shall go free of duty for two years, and not longer.

Likewise, we promise that for the term of ten years, and until we command otherwise, we will not impose on the inhabitants of those countries any excise duty, or other tribute whatsoever.

Likewise, we grant that to said inhabitants may be given through you the lots and grounds proper to their conditions, as has been done, and is doing, in the Island of Espanola; and we also give you license, in our name, during the time of your government, that you take the bestowal of the Indians of that land, observing therein the instructions and provisions that will be given to you.

Again, we bestow on the hospital that may be built in that country, to assist the relief of the poor who may go thither, the charity of one hundred thousand maravedis from the fines imposed by the tribunal of that country.

Again, also, according to your petition and consent, and of the settlers of that country, we promise to give to its hospital, and by these presents we do give, the duties of *escobilla* and *relabes*, existing in the foundries that may there be made; and, as respects that, we will order our provision to be issued to you in form.

Also, likewise we will order, and by the present command and defend, that from these our kingdoms do not pass into said country, nor go, any one of the persons prohibited from going into those parts, under the penalties contained in the laws and ordinances of our letters, upon which subject this by us and by the Catholic Kings are given, nor any counsellors nor attorneys to exercise their callings.

The which, all that is said, and each thing and part thereof, we concede to you, conditioned that you, the said Don Hernando de Soto, be held and obliged to go from these our realms in person to make the conquest within one year next following, to be reckoned from the day of the date of this charter.

Again, on condition that when you go out of these our said kingdoms, and arrive in said country, you will carry and have with you the officers of our exchequer, who may by us be named; and likewise also the persons, religious and ecclesiastical, who shall be appointed by us for the instruction of the natives of that Province in our Holy Catholic Faith, to whom you are to give and pay the passage, stores, and other necessary subsistence for them, according to their condition, all at your cost, receiving nothing from them during the said entire voyage; with which matter we gravely charge you, that you do and comply with, as a thing for the service of God and our own, and any thing otherwise we shall deem contrary to our service.

Again, whensoever, according to right and the laws of our kingdoms, the people and captains of our armaments take prisoner any prince or lord of the countries where, by our command, they make war, the ransom of such lord or cacique belongs to us, with all the other things movable found or belonging to him; but, considering the great toils and perils that our subjects undergo in the conquest of the Indias, as some recompense, and to favor them, we make known and command, that if in your said conquest and government any cacique or principal lord be captured or seized, all the treasures, gold, silver, stones, and pearls that may be got from him by way of redemption, or in

any other manner whatsoever, we award you the seventh part thereof, and the remainder shall be divided among the conquerors, first taking out our fifth; and in case the said cacique or lord should be slain in battle, or afterward by course of justice, or in any other manner whatsoever, in such case, of the treasures or goods aforesaid obtained of him justly we have the half, which, before any thing else, our officers shall take, after having first reserved our fifth.

Again, since our said officers of said province might have some doubt in making the collection of our duties, especially on gold and silver, stones and pearls, as well those that may be found in sepulchres, and other places where they may be hidden, as those got by ransom and incursion, or other way, our pleasure and will is, that, until some change, the following order be observed.

First, we order that of the gold and silver, stones and pearls that may be won in battle, or on entering towns, or by barter with the Indians, should and must be paid us one-fifth of all.

Likewise, that all the gold and silver, stones, pearls, and other things that may be found and taken, as well in the graves, sepulchres, *ocues*, or temples of the Indians, as in other places where they are accustomed to offer sacrifices to their idols, or in other concealed religious precincts, or buried in house, or patrimonial soil, or in the ground, or in some other public place, whether belonging to the community or an individual, be his state or dignity what it may, of the whole, and of all other, of the character that may be and is found, whether finding it by accident or discovering it by search, shall pay us the half, without dimunition of any sort, the other half remaining to the person who has found or made the discovery; and should any person or persons have gold, silver, stones, or pearls, taken or found, as well in the said graves, sepulchres, *ocues*, or Indian temples, as in the other places where they were accustomed to offer sacrifices, or other concealed religious places, or interred as before said, and do not make it known, that they may receive, in conformity with this chapter, what may belong to them, they have forfeited all the gold and silver, stones and pearls besides the half of their goods, to our tribunal and exchequer.

And we, having been informed of the evils and disorders which occur in making discoveries and new settlements, for the redress thereof, and that we may be enabled to give you license to make them, with the accord of the members of our Council and of our consultation, a general provision of chapters is ordained and dispatched, respecting what you will have to observe in the said settlement and conquest, and we command it here to be incorporated in tenor as follows:—

[A copy of the Decree of November 17, 1526, regarding the treatment of the Indians, was included in the capitulations with Narváez (232) where it is printed.]

Hence, by these presents, you, the said Captain Hernando de Soto, doing as aforesaid at your cost, according to and in the manner before contained, observing and complying with the said provision here incorporated, and all the other instructions we shall henceforth command you to obey, and to give with regard to that country, and for the good treatment and conversion to our Holy Catholic Faith of the natives of it, we promise and declare that to you will be kept these terms, and whatever therein is contained, in and through all; and you doing otherwise, and not complying therewith, we shall not be obliged to keep with you and comply with the aforesaid, nor any matter of it; on the contrary, we will order that you be punished, and proceed against you as against one who keeps not nor complies with, but acts counter to, the commands of his natural king and lord. In confirmation whereof we order that the present be given, signed by my name, and witnessed by my undersigned Secretary. Done at the town Valladolid, the twentieth day of the month of April, of the year one thousand five hundred and thirty-seven.

[signed:] I The King.

238. May 18, 1539. The officials of Hernando de Soto's army to Charles V.

This was first translated from the Spanish in T. Buckingham Smith, Narratives of the Career of Hernando de Soto *(New York, 1866), and is reprinted with a few variations.*

To the Sacred Caesarian Catholic Majesty of the Emperor and King our Lord, His High, Caesarian, Catholic Majesty:

We gave relation to Your Majesty from Saint Jago de Cuba of the favourable beginning of our expedition, which, it appears, the Adelantado Hernando de Soto brought with his good fortune, wherewith to serve in the manner of which he comes in control. Suffice it to say, that he has thought best to look both into the state of the Island and the population, as Your Majesty is informed; but with great toil and cost to himself, as he wished to travel throughout, visiting the towns, which had much need of attention. As well has he been detained, at great expense with his soldiers, longer than he wished, while providing himself, without loss of time, in every particular useful for his conquest, managing aptly in all matters, and setting everything in complete order.

We inform Your Majesty, that today, on the eve of departure, he has large vessels in port, two caravels and two brigantines, in all nine sail, having lost two since our arrival. He carries in them two hundred and thirty-seven horses, besides some of relief; three hundred and thirty foot, as well as those mounted; in all, five hundred and thirteen men, without the sailors. With these go more abundant subsistence than could have been gotten out of Spain for an armada. There are three thousand loads of [cacabi], twenty-five hundred shoulders of bacon, and twenty-five hundred *fanegas* of maize: moreover, there are beasts on hoof for the settlement, and for the butcher, to be in readiness on the return of the vessels, through which we are to receive large supplies. With this object, the Adelantado has bought many grazing farms, at the cost of much money, to be employed solely in affording us sustenance.

In order that Your Majesty may entertain good hopes of that country of Florida, we report, that directly upon our arrival here, in order that Juan de Añasco might go with fifty men to look for some port on the coast, he was elected to be the royal Comptroller; and although he passed through many hardships, because of the winter, he found the most convenient place that could be desired very near, only some seventy-five or eighty leagues from this land, inhabited and very secure. He brought four of the Indians, as interpreters, who are so intelligent that they already understand us, after a manner, and give grand expectations of that country, so much so, that all depart joyfully and contented.

The bearer of this letter is the Captain Hernan Ponce de León, companion of the Adelantado, who has been a witness to all this, and is a person of whom Your Majesty can be informed in whatsoever may most interest you.

We will say no more at present, save that on arriving in the land of Florida, we will, by Divine pleasure, take particular care to give a very long relation of all that shall hereafter occur.

Our Lord guard and increase the Sacred Caesarian Catholic life of Your Majesty with augmentation of more and greater kingdoms and lordships, as the servants of Your Majesty desire.

From the town of San Cristóbal de la Havana, the eighteenth day of May, in the year 1539.

From your Sacred Caesarian Catholic Majesty's servants, who kiss your imperial majesty's feet.

[signed:] Juan Gaytan
Jno. de Añasco
Luis Fernández de Biedma

239. *True relation of the hardships suffered by Governor Don Fernando de Soto and certain Portuguese Gentlemen in the Discovery of the Province of Florida. Now newly set forth by a Gentleman of Elvas.*

Many attempts have been made to translate and elucidate the text of the Fidalgo de Elvas's Relaçam verdadeira (1557), none of them more successful than that of James Alexander Robertson, who edited it under the above title, 2 vols. (Deland, Fla., 1933). It is reprinted here without the congratulatory poem by Fernando de Silveira and the epistle to the reader by its publisher André de Burgos. The notes to the book, which must be consulted in the original edition, and the United States De Soto Expedition Committee,

Final Report (Washington, D.C., 1939), are essential for a full understanding of the document.

Relation of what the adelantado of Florida, Don Fernando de Soto, suffered in conquering it: in which is set forth who he was, and some of those who went with him; some of the peculiarities and diversities of the country, and all they saw therein; and of what befell them.

Chapter I.
Which declares who Don Fernando de Soto was, and how he obtained the government of Florida.

Captain Soto was the son of an esquire of Feréz de Badajóz. He went to the Indies of Castile when Pedrárias Dávila was governor of the Indies of the Ocean Sea. There he found himself with nothing else his own except his sword and shield. Because of his good qualities and courage, Pedrárias made him captain of a troop of horse, and by his order he went with Fernando Pizarro to conquer Peru. There, according to the report of many creditable persons who were there, he distinguished himself over the other captains and principal persons, both at the seizure of Atabalipa, lord of Peru, and in making the entrance into the city of Cuzco, and in all other places where they encountered resistance, and where he happened to be. For that reason, aside from his part in the treasure of Atabalipa, he got a good repartimiento, from which in time he collected one hundred and eighty thousand cruzados, which he took to Spain, with what fell to him as his share. Of this, the emperor took a certain part which was repaid to him by six hundred thousand reales with interest in the silks of Granada, while all the rest was delivered to him at the casa de contratación in Seville. He employed servants, including a majordomo, grand master of ceremonies, pages, equerry, chamberlain, footmen, and all the other servants requisite for an establishment of a gentleman. From Seville, he went to court, and at court was accompanied by Juan de Añasco, of Seville, Luis Moscoso de Alvarado, Nuño de Tobar, and Juan Rodríguez Lobillo. With the exception of Juan de Añasco, all the others had come with him from Peru; and each brought fourteen or fifteen thousand cruzados. They all went well and expensively dressed; and Soto, although because of his cupidity he was not liberal, yet since that was the first time he had to appear at court, spent very liberally, and went about closely attended by those I have named and by his servants and many others who came to him at court. He married Doña Isabel de Bobadilla, daughter of Pedrárias Dávila, conde de Puñonrostro. The emperor rewarded him by making him governor of the island of Cuba and adelantado of Florida, with title of marquis to a certain part of the lands he might conquer.

Chapter II.
How Cabeza de Vaca came to court and gave account of the land of Florida; and of the men who were gathered together at Seville to go with Don Fernando de Soto.

After Don Fernando had obtained the government, a gentleman arrived at court from the Indies, Cabeza de Vaca by name, who had gone with Governor Narvaez who had perished in Florida. He told how Narvaez had perished at sea with all his men; and how he and four others had escaped and reached New Spain. He brought also a written relation of what he had seen in Florida. This stated in certain places, "In such a place I saw this. Most of what I saw there I leave for discussion between myself and his Majesty." He described in general the wretchedness of the land and the hardships he had suffered. To some of his kinsfolk, who were minded to go to the Indies and strongly urged him to tell them whether he had seen any rich land in Florida, he said that he could not tell this, because he and another (by name, Dorantes, who had remained in New Spain with the intention of returning to Florida—for which purpose he came to Spain to beg the government from the emperor) had sworn not to divulge certain things which they had seen, lest some person might beg for it beforehand. He gave them to understand that it was the richest land in the world. Don Fernando de Soto wished to take him with him and made him an advantageous proposal; but after they had come to an agreement, they fell out because Soto would not give him the money which he asked of him to buy a ship. Baltasar de Gallegos and Cristóbal de Espindola, his kinsmen, told him that since they had resolved to go to Florida with Soto because of what he had told them, he should advise them as to what they should do. Cabeza de Vaca told them that if he had given up going with Soto, it was because he expected to ask for another government and did not wish to go under the banner of another. Since Don Fernando de Soto already had the conquest of Florida, which he came to beg, he could not tell them, on account of his oath, what they wished to know. Nevertheless, he advised them to sell their estates and go with him, for in so doing they would act wisely. As soon as he had an opportunity, he spoke with the emperor and related to him all he had suffered and seen and the other things he had succeeded in learning. Of this relation, made orally to the emperor by Cabeza de Vaca, the marqués de Astorga was informed. He determined at once to send his brother, Don Antonio Osorio, with Don Fernando de Soto, and two of his kinsmen made ready to go with him, namely, Francisco Osorio and Garcia Osorio. Don Antonio disposed of an income of six hundred thousand reales which he received from the Church, and Francisco Osorio of a village of vassals he owned in the district of Campos. They joined the adelantado at Seville, as did also Nuño de Tobar, Luis de Moscoso, and Juan Rodríguez Lobillo, with the wealth, amounting to fourteen or fifteen thousand cruzados, which each one had brought from Peru. Luis de Moscoso took two brothers with him. Don Carlos, who had married the governor's niece, went also and took his wife. From Badajóz went Pedro Calderón and three kinsmen of the adelantado, namely, Arias Tinoco, Alonso Romo, and Diego Tinoco. As Luis de Moscoso passed through Elvas, André de Vasconcelos spoke with him, and requested him to speak to Don Fernando de Soto in his behalf, and gave him patents issued by the marqués de Vilareal, conferring on him the captaincy of Ceuta, so that he might exhibit them. The adelantado saw these and found out who he was and wrote him promising that he would favor him in every way and would give him men to command in Florida. From Elvas went André de Vasconcelos, Fernan Pegado, Antonio Martinez Segurado, Mem Royz Pereyra, Joam Cordeiro, Estevan Pegado, Bento Fernandez, and Alvaro Fernandez; and from Salamanca, Jaen, Valencia, Albuquerque, and other parts of Spain many persons of noble family gathered in Seville; so much so that many men of good condition, who had sold their estates, remained behind in San Lúcar because there was no ship for them; although for other known and rich countries it was usual to lack men. The cause of this was what Cabeza de Vaca had told the emperor and given persons who conversed with him to understand respecting that land. Soto made him fine proposals but Cabeza de Vaca, having agreed to go with him, as mentioned above, because Soto would not give him money to pay for a ship which he had bought, they disagreed, and Cabeza de Vaca went as governor to Rio de la Plata. His kinsmen, Cristóbal de Espindola and Baltasar de Gallegos went with Soto. Baltasar de Gallegos sold houses, vineyards, a rent of wheat, and ninety geiras of olive orchard in the district of Seville. He obtained the post of chief constable and took his wife with him. Many other persons of rank also went with the adelantado, and obtained the following posts aided by powerful influence, for they were posts which were desired by many, namely: Antonio de Biedma obtained the post of factor; Juan de Alñasco, that of contador; and Juan Gaytán, a nephew of Cardinal de Ciguenza, obtained the post of treasurer.

Chapter III.
How the Portuguese went to Seville and thence to San Lúcar; and how the captains were appointed over the ships, and the men who were to go in them distributed.

The Portuguese left Elvas on the 15th of January. They reached Seville on St. Sebastian's eve and went to the governor's lodging. They entered the patio upon which looked some balconies where he was. He looked down and went to meet them at the stairs where they went up to the balconies. When they were up, he ordered chairs to be given them so that they might be seated. André de Vasconcelos told him who he and the other Portuguese were and how they had all come to accompany him and to serve him on his voyage. He thanked him and appeared well pleased with their coming and proffer. The table being already laid, he invited them to eat; and while they were eating, he directed his majordomo to find lodgings for them near his inn. From Seville, the adelantado went to San Lúcar with all the men that were to go with him. He ordered a muster to be held, to which the Portuguese went armed with very splendid arms, and the Castilians very elegantly, in silk over silk, and many plaits and slashes. As

such finery was not pleasing to the governor on such an occasion, he ordered a muster to be held on the next day and for every man to appear with his armor. To this the Portuguese came as at first, armed with very excellent armor, and the governor set them in order near the standard borne by his alferez. Most of the Castilians wore poor and rusty coats of mail, and all helmets and carried worthless and poor lances. Some of them managed to get a place among the Portuguese. Thus they passed in review, and those who were to the liking of Soto and whom he wished were counted and enrolled and went with him to Florida. Those who went numbered in all six hundred men. He had already bought seven ships and had placed in them the provisions necessary, appointed captains, and assigned his ship to each captain, giving each one a list of the men he was to take.

Chapter IV.
How the adelantado and his men left Spain and arrived at the Canary Islands, and afterward at the Antilles.

In the month of April, of the year 1538, the adelantado delivered the ships over to the captains who were to go in them. He took a new and good sailing ship for himself and gave one to André de Vasconcelos, in which the Portuguese went. He left the bar of San Lúcar on Sunday morning, on the day of St. Lazarus in that month, and as was later written, amid great festivity, ordering the trumpets to be sounded and many rounds of artillery fired. For four days he sailed amid favoring weather and then the wind lulled. The calms with a rolling sea lasted for a week, during which no headway was made. On the fifteenth day after his departure from San Lúcar, he reached Gomera, one of the Canary Islands, on the morning of Easter Sunday. The count of that island was clad entirely in white—cloak jerkin, hose, shoes, and cap—and resembled a gypsy count. He received the governor very cordially. The latter was well provided with lodgings and all the men were lodged there without expense. For his money, he was provided with many provisions, bread, wine, and meat; and they took what was needful for the ships. On the following Sunday, a week after their arrival, they left the island of Gomera. The count gave Doña Isabel, the wife of the adelantado, a bastard daughter of his, as her maid. They reached the Antilles at the island of Cuba, at the port of the city of Santiago on Whitsuntide. As soon as they arrived there, a gentleman of the city sent a very beautiful and well caparisoned roan horse to the shore for the governor and a mule for Doña Isabel; and all the men of foot and horse who were in the town came to the shore to welcome them. The governor was lodged, visited, and served by all the citizens of that city, and all the men were lodged free of expense. Those who wished to go into the country were quartered among the dwelling and farm houses by fours and sixes, in accordance with the possibility of the owners of the dwellings, and were furnished by the latter with the provisions of which they had need.

Chapter V.
Of the citizens of the city of Santiago and the other towns of the island; and of the quality of the land and the fruits thereof.

The city of Santiago has about eighty large and well apportioned houses. Most of them have wooden walls and roofs of hay. A few are of stone and lime and are roofed with tiles. They have large farms on which are many trees differing from those of Spain—fig trees which produce figs as big as the fist, yellow inside and of little savor; and other trees which produce a fruit called "anona," of the shape and size of a small pineapple. It is a tasty fruit, and when the rind is removed, the pulp resembles a piece of curd. On the farms in the country are other large pineapples which grow on low trees that resemble the aloe. They are of excellent odor and of fine taste. Other trees yield a good fruit called "mamei," of the size of a peach, which the islanders consider the best of all the fruits of the land. There is another fruit called guava, resembling the hazel nut in form, the size of a fig. There are other trees as tall as a good lance, with a single stalk having no branches, with leaves broad and as long as a javelin, the fruit of the size and form of a cucumber (on one bunch twenty or thirty); and also as the fruit goes on ripening, the tree goes on bending lower with it. They are called plantains in that land and are of agreeable taste. They ripen after being gathered, although those that ripen on the tree itself are better. The tree produces fruit but once. When the tree is cut down, others grow at the root which yield fruit the next year. There is another fruit on which many people live, espe-

cially the slaves, which they call "batata". These now grow in the island of Terceira belonging to this kingdom of Portugal. They grow under ground and resemble the yam. They have almost the taste of chestnuts. The bread of that land is also made from roots which resemble potatoes. The bread made from those roots resembles the pith of the alder. The earth is heaped up and in each heap four or five stalks are planted; and after they have been planted for a year and a half, the roots are gathered. Should any person, thinking it to be a potato, eat any of it, he runs great risk of death, as was found by experience in the case of a soldier who, as soon as he ate a very little of a root, died immediately. They pare those roots and grate them, and crush them in a press. The juice that comes out has a bad smell. The bread has but little taste and less nourishment. Of the fruits of Spain, it has figs and oranges. They produce fruit all year long because the land is very hot and vigorous. In that land are many horses and cattle; and all through the year green grass. There are many wild cattle and hogs whereby the people of the island are well supplied with meat. In the country outside the town are many fruits; and it sometimes happens that some Christian gets lost and wanders about lost for fifteen or twenty days because of the many paths made by the cattle crisscrossing from one part to another through the dense forests. Thus wandering about lost, he keeps alive on fruits and palmetto cabbage, for there are many large palm trees throughout the island which yield no other fruit of any value. The island of Cuba is three hundred leagues in extent from east to southeast, and in some places thirty, and in others forty, leagues from north to south. There are six towns of Christians, namely, Santiago, Baracoa, the Bayamo, Puerto Principe, Sancti Spiritus, and the Havana. Each one has between thirty and forty citizens, except Santiago and the Havana, each of which has seventy or eighty houses. They all have churches and a chaplain who confesses the people and celebrates mass for them. In Santiago there is a Franciscan monastery. It has few friars, but is well provided with alms, because of the richness of the land. The church of Santiago has a suitable income, a parish priest, benefices, and many secular priests, it being the church of that city which is the capital of all the island. There is much gold in this land, but few slaves to get it out, for many hanged themselves because of the harsh treatment received in the mines from the Christians. An overseer of Vasco Porcallo, a resident of that island, having learned that his Indians were about to hang themselves, with a rope in his hands, went to await them in the place where they were to meet and told them that they could do nothing nor think of anything which he did not know beforehand; that he was going to hang himself with them, for if he had given them a hard life in this world, he would give them a worse in the other. This caused them to change their minds and return to do what he ordered them.

Chapter VI.
How the governor sent Doña Isabel with the ships to the Havana, and he with some of his men went overland.

From Santiago, the governor sent Don Carlos, his brother-in-law, in the ships together with Doña Isabel, with orders to await him at the Havana, which is a port at the eastern end of the island, one hundred and eighty leagues from the city of Santiago. The governor and those who remained with him bought horses and set out on their journey. The first town at which they arrived was the Bayamo, and they were lodged by fours and sixes just as they went in company. And there where they were lodged they were given their food without expense. Nothing else cost them money except maize for their horses, because from town to town, the governor went to visit each one and assessed it a tax on the tribute and service of the Indians. The Bayamo is twenty-five leagues from the city of Santiago. Near it runs a large river, larger than the Guadiana, called Tanto. In it are huge lizards which sometimes do harm to the Indians or animals crossing the river. In all the land there are no wolves, foxes, bears, lions, or tigers. There are wild dogs which have left the houses for the woods and live on the hogs. There are some snakes as thick as a man's thigh and more. They are very sluggish and do no harm. From Bayamo to Puerto Principe it is fifty leagues. Throughout the island, roads are made from town to town by means of the machete; and any year they neglect to do this, the thickets grow to such an extent that the road does not show. So many are the paths made by the cattle that no one can travel without an Indian of the country for a guide, for most of it is covered

with a very lofty and dense forest. From Puerto Principe, the governor went by sea in a canoe to the dwelling of Vasco Porcallo, which is near the sea, in order to get news there of Doña Isabel, who at that time (as was afterward learned) was in great distress—so much so that the ships were lost one from the other (two of them going within sight of the coast of Florida), and all suffered great need of water and food. After the storm ceased, and the ships were come together again, without knowing whither they had been driven, they came upon the cape of San Antón, an uninhabited district of the island of Cuba. There they got water, and forty days after they had left the city of Santiago they reached the Havana. The governor learned of this immediately and went to Doña Isabel. Those who came overland—in number one hundred and fifty of horse and divided into two divisions in order not to burden the islanders, made their way to Sancti Spiritus, sixty leagues from Puerto Principe. The food they took consisted of cassava bread, which is that I have mentioned above. It is of such quality that if water touches it, it immediately crumbles. On that account, it happened that some ate meat for many days without bread. They took dogs and a native of the country who hunted as they marched, or killed what hogs they needed at the place where they had to stop to sleep. They were well supplied with beef and pork on that journey. They suffered much annoyance from mosquitoes, especially in a swamp called the marsh of the watering trough, which gave them considerable trouble in crossing from midday to night. There was more than a half league of water and for the distance of a good crossbow-shot they had to swim it; and the rest of it reached to the waist. They were mired up to the knees; and on the bottom were clam shells which cut their feet badly, so that not a single sole of a boot or shoe lasted whole for half the way. Their clothes and saddles were taken over on bits of bark from the palm trees. While crossing that swamp without their clothes, many mosquitoes attacked them, which when they stung raised a lump and smarted badly. They would strike at them with the hand, and from the slaps given they killed so many that the blood ran over the arms and bodies of the men. That night they got very little rest because of them, and the same thing was experienced on other nights at like places and seasons. They reached Sancti

Spiritus, a town of thirty houses, near which flows a small river. It is very pleasant and luxuriant, with many fine orange and citron trees and fruits native to the land. Half the men were lodged there, while the others went on twenty-five leagues farther to another town called Trinidad, consisting of fifteen or twenty citizens. There is a hospital for the poor there, but no other in the whole island. They say that that town was once the largest of any in the island; and that before the Christians made an entrance into that land, while a ship was coasting along that shore, there came in it a very sick man who requested the captain to have him taken ashore. The captain did so and the ship proceeded on its way. The sick man remained on the shore in that land which so far had never been oppressed by Christians, where the Indians found him and took him and cared for him until he was well. The lord of that town gave him his daughter in marriage. He was at war with all his neighbors, and by means of the skill and courage of the Christian, he subdued and brought under his command all the people of that island. A long time afterward, Governor Diego Velázquez went to conquer it and discovered New Spain from that place. That Christian who was with the Indians, pacified them and brought them under the subjection and into the obedience of the governor. From that town of Trinidad to Havana, there is a stretch of eighty leagues without a town, which they traveled. They reached Havana at the end of March where they found the governor and all the rest of the men who had accompanied him from Spain. From Havana, the governor sent Juan de Añasco with a caravel and two brigantines with fifty men to explore the port of Florida. He brought two Indians from there whom he seized on the coast. Thereat (both because they would be needed as guides and interpreters, and because they said by signs that much gold existed in Florida), the governor and all the men were greatly pleased, and thought they would never see the hour of departure, for it seemed to them that that was the richest land which had yet been discovered.

Chapter VII.
How we left the Havana and reached Florida; and of what happened.

Before our departure, the governor deprived Nuño de Tobar of the post of captain general and gave it to Porcallo de Figueroa, a citizen of Cuba, who was to see that the ships should sail well provisioned, and who gave a number of large loads of cassava bread and many hogs. The governor took the post from Nuño Tobar because he had made love to the daughter of the conde of Gomera, the waiting maid of Doña Isabel. He, notwithstanding that the post was taken from him, took her to wife and went to Florida with Soto, in order to be restored to favor and because she was already pregnant by him. The governor left Doña Isabel in the Havana and with her the wives of Don Carlos, Baltasar de Gallegos, and Nuño de Tobar. As his lieutenant for the government of the island, he left a gentleman of the Havana, Juan de Rojas by name. On Sunday, May 18, of the year 1539, the adelantado left the Havana with his fleet consisting of nine ships—five vessels with topsails, two caravels, and two brigantines. For seven days, they sailed attended by good weather. On Whitsunday, May 25, they sighted the land of Florida, and for fear of shoals anchored a league from shore. On Friday, May 30, they disembarked on the land of Florida, two leagues from a town of an Indian chief called Ucita. They disembarked the two hundred and thirteen horses which they carried, in order to lighten the ships so that they would need less water. All the men landed and only the seamen stayed aboard, who in a week, by going up with the tide for a short distance daily, brought the vessels near to the town. As soon as the men landed the camp was established on the shore near the bay which went up to the town. The captain general, Vasco Porcallo, taking with him seven horse, immediately overran the land for a half league round about and found six Indians who tried to oppose him with their arrows—the weapons with which they are accustomed to fight. The horsemen killed two of them and the four escaped, for the land being obstructed by woods and swamps, the horses, because of weakness from voyaging on the sea, became mired there and fell with their masters. That night following, the governor with one hundred men in the brigantines came upon a town which he found without people, because the Christians were perceived as soon as they came within sight of land; and they saw many smokes along the whole coast, which the Indians make in order to give information to one another. On the following day, Luis de

Moscoso, maestre de campo, set the men in order, those on horse in three squadrons—the vanguard, the battle line, and the rear-guard—and in that way they marched that day and the next, going around great mud flats which come from the bay. They arrived at the town of Ucita, where the governor was, on Sunday, June first, the day of the Trinity. The town consisted of seven or eight houses. The chief's house stood near the beach on a very high hill which had been artificially built as a fortress. At the other side of the town was the temple and on top if it a wooden bird with its eyes gilded. Some pearls, spoiled by fire and of little value, were found there. The Indians bore them through in order to string them for beads, which are worn around the neck or arm, and they esteem them greatly. The houses were of wood and were covered with palm leaves. The governor was lodged in the houses of the chief and with him Vasco Porcallo and Luis de Moscoso; and in the other houses which were located in the middle of the town, the chief constable, Baltasar de Gallegos. And apart in the same houses were placed the provisions carried on the ships. The other houses and the temple were destroyed, and a mess of every three or four built a small house in which they were lodged. The land round about was greatly encumbered and choked with a vast and lofty forest. The governor ordered it to be cut down for the space of a crossbow-shot about the town, in order that the horses might run and the Christians have the advantage of the Indians if the latter should by chance try to attack them by night. They posted footsoldiers as sentinels, in couples at each position along the roads and at proper places, who stood watch for four hours. The horsemen visited them and were ready to aid them if there should be an alarm. The governor appointed four captains over the horsemen and two over the footsoldiers. Those over the horse were: one, André de Vasconcelos, and second, Pedro Calderón, of Badajóz, and the other two his kinsmen, the Cardeñosa (Arias Tinoco and Alfonso Romo), also natives of Badajóz. One of the captains over the footsoldiers was Francisco Maldonado of Salamanca, and the other Juan Rodríguez Lobillo. While they were in that town of Ucita, the Indians whom Juan de Añasco had captured along that coast and whom the governor brought along as guides and interpreters escaped one night through the carelessness of two men

who were guarding them. The governor and all were very sorry for this, for some forays had already been made, but no Indians could be captured, as the land was swampy and in many parts covered with very lofty and thick woods.

Chapter VIII.
How some forays were made and a Christian was found who had been in the power of an Indian Chief for a long time.

The governor sent the chief constable, Baltasar de Gallegos, from the town of Ucita with forty horse and eighty foot into the interior to see whether any Indian could be captured; and in another direction, Captain Juan Rodríguez Lobillo, with fifty foot, most of them armed with swords and shields. Others were arquebusiers and crossbowmen. They went over a swampy land where the horsemen could not go. A half league from camp they came upon some Indian huts near the river; the people who were inside them plunged into the river. They captured four Indian women, and twenty Indians came at us and attacked us so stoutly that we had to retreat to the camp, because of their being (as they are) so skilful with their weapons. Those people are so warlike and so quick that they make no account of footsoldiers; for if these go for them, they flee, and when their adversaries turn their backs they are immediately on them. The farthest they flee is the distance of an arrow shot. They are never quiet but always running and crossing from one side to another so that the crossbows or the arquebuses can not be aimed at them; and before a crossbowman can fire a shot, an Indian can shoot three or four arrows, and very seldom does he miss what he shoots at. If the arrow does not find armor, it penetrates as deeply as a crossbow. The bows are very long and the arrows are made of certain reeds like canes, very heavy and so tough that a sharpened cane passes through a shield. Some are pointed with a fishbone, as sharp as an awl, and others with a certain stone like a diamond point. Generally when these strike against the armor, they break off at the place where they are fastened on. Those of cane split and enter through the links of mail and are more hurtful. Juan Rodríguez Lobillo reached the camp with six men wounded, one of whom died. He brought the four Indian women whom he had captured in the quarters or huts. Baltasar de

Gallegos, on going into the level terrain two leagues from town, saw ten or eleven Indians, among whom was a Christian, naked and on that account burned by the sun. He had his arms tattooed after the manner of the Indians and in no wise did he differ from them. As soon as the horsemen saw them they ran at them. The Indians took to flight and hid from them in a forest. They overtook two or three of them who had been wounded. The Christian, as one of the horsemen was about to charge against him with his lance, began to cry out, "Sirs, I am a Christian; do not kill me. Do not kill these Indians, for they have given me my life." Thereupon, he called the latter and reassured them; whereupon, they came out of the woods. The horsemen took both the Christian and the Indians before them and entered the camp at nightfall very joyful. When this was learned by the governor, and those who had remained in camp, they were received with the same rejoicing.

Chapter IX.
How that Christian went to the land of Florida, who he was, and what took place with the governor.

That Christian was called Juan Ortiz and was a native of Seville, of a noble family. For twelve years he had been in the hands of the Indians. He had gone to that land with Governor Narvaez and had returned in the ships to the island of Cuba where the wife of Governor Pánfilo de Narvaez had remained. At her order, with twenty or thirty others he returned to Florida in a brigantine. Arriving at the port, within sight of the town, they saw on land a cane sticking in the ground with its top split and holding a letter. They believed that the governor had left it in order to give news of himself when he resolved to go inland. They asked four or five Indians who were walking on the beach for it, but the latter told them by signs to come ashore for it, which Juan Ortiz and another did contrary to the wish of the others. As soon as they reached land, many Indians came out of the houses of the town and surrounded them and seized them so that they could not escape. The other man who tried to defend himself, they killed immediately in that place, and Juan Ortiz they seized by the hands and led to their chief, Ucita. The men in the brigantine refused to land and made for the open sea and returned to the

island of Cuba. Ucita ordered Juan Ortiz to be bound hand and foot on a grill laid on top of four stakes. He ordered a fire to be kindled under him in order to burn him there. The chief's daughter asked him not to kill him, saying that a single Christian could not do him any ill or good, and that it would be more to his honor to hold him captive. Ucita granted this and ordered him taken care of; and as soon as he was well, gave him charge of the guarding of the temple, for at night wolves would carry off the corpses from inside it. He commended himself to God and watched over their temple. One night the wolves carried off from him the corpse of a child, the son of one of the principal Indians. Going after it, he threw a club which struck the wolf carrying the body, which finding itself wounded abandoned it and went off to die nearby. He, not knowing what he had done, as it was night, returned to the temple. At daybreak, when he found the body of the child gone, he became very sad. As soon as Ucita learned of it, he determined to have him killed. He sent along the trail where he said the wolves had gone and they found the boy's corpse and farther on the dead wolf. Whereupon, Ucita was greatly pleased with the Christian and at the watch he had kept in the temple, and thence forward showed him great honor. After being in captivity to him for three years, another chief named Mocoço who lived two days' journey from the port, came and burned the town. Ucita went in flight to another town he had in another seaport. Juan Ortiz lost his post and the favor he enjoyed from him. And since they are servants of the devil, they are accustomed to offer him souls and blood of their Indians or of any other people they can get. They say that when he desires that that sacrifice be made to him, he talks with them and tells them he is thirsty and that they should offer a sacrifice to him. Juan Ortiz learned from the girl who had saved him from the fire that her father had determined to sacrifice him the next day; and she told him that he should go to Mocoço, that she knew he would show him honor for she had heard him say that he would ask for him; and she said he would be glad to see him. At night, since he did not know the way, the Indian woman went a half league from the town and put him on it, and in order that this might not be perceived, returned. Juan Ortiz traveled that night and in the morning came to a river which was already within the boundary of Mocoço and there he saw two Indians fishing. And since they were hostile to those of Ucita and their languages were different, and he did not know that of Mocoço, he feared lest, inasmuch as he did not know how to say who he was and how he came nor how to give an explanation concerning himself, they would kill him thinking him to be an Indian of Ucita. Before they saw him, he came to where they had their weapons, and as soon as they saw him, they ran along the road to the town. And although he told them to wait, that he would do them no harm, they did not understand him and ran away as fast as they could. And when they reached the town, shouting, many Indians came out toward him and began to surround him in order to shoot him with arrows. Juan Ortiz, seeing himself in so great an emergency, hid behind some trees and began to call out very loudly and to cry out and to say that he was a Christian who was fleeing from Ucita and came to see and serve Mocoço, their chief. It was God's will that an Indian who knew the language came up at that time and understood him and made the other Indians keep still, telling them what he said to him. Three or four Indians were dispatched from there who went to report to their chief, who came out to welcome him a quarter league from the town and was very glad to see him. He immediately made him swear according to his custom as a Christian that he would not run off to any other chief, and promised him that he would show him much honor and that, if at any time, Christians should come to that land, he would release him freely and give him permission to go to them. And so he swore according to his custom as an Indian. Three years after that, some Indians who were fishing in the sea two leagues from the town came to inform Mocoço that they had seen some ships. He called Juan Ortiz and gave him permission to go, who having bade him farewell reached the sea as soon as he could. But not finding the ships, he thought he had been deceived and that the cacique had done that to ascertain his desire. So he remained with Mocoço for nine years, now with little expectation of seeing Christians. As soon as the governor reached Florida, it was known by Mocoço. He immediately told Juan Ortiz that Christians were lodging in the town of Ucita. It seemed to the latter that he was jesting with him as on the other occasion and told him that the Christians did not

come to his mind nor anything else than to serve him. He assured him of it and gave him permission to go to them, telling him that if he refused to do it, and the Christians returned, he must not hold him guilty, for he was accomplishing what he had promised him. So great was Juan Ortiz's joy that he could not believe it to be true. However, he thanked and took his leave of him. Mocoço gave him ten or twelve of the principal Indians to go in his company. On his way to the port where the governor was, he met Baltasar de Gallegos as I have said above. As soon as he reached the camp, the governor ordered some clothes to be given him and some good arms and a beautiful horse. He asked him if he had heard of any land where there was gold or silver. He said no, for he had never gone more than ten leagues round about from where he was, and that thirty leagues from there resided an Indian chief called Paracoxi, to whom Mocoço and Ucita and all those of that coast paid tribute; that perhaps he might have some information of any good land; and that his land was indeed better than that of the coast and more fertile and abounding in maize. At this the governor was greatly pleased and said that he wished only to find provisions in order that he might go inland; that the land of Florida was so vast that there could not but be rich land at one end or the other. The cacique of Mocoço came to the port to visit the governor and made him the following talk: "Very lofty and very mighty lord: In my own estimation, to obey you least of all those whom you hold under your command but greatest in my desire to perform greater services for you, I appear before your Lordship with as much confidence of receiving favor as if, in fact, this my good will were manifest to you by deeds (not for the small service which I did you of the Christian whom I held in my possession, by giving him his liberty freely, for I was obliged to do that in order to keep my honor and what I had promised him), but because it belongs to the great to exercise their office with great magnificence; and I hold that you precede all those of the land both in bodily perfections and in ruling good men, as well as in the perfections of the mind with which you can boast of the liberality of nature. The favor which I await from your Lordship is that you consider me as your own, and feel free to command me in whatever I may serve you." The governor answered him saying that, although in freeing and sending him the Christian, he had kept his honor and his promise, he thanked him and appreciated him so much that there was no comparison and that he would always consider him as a brother and that he would protect him in every way. He ordered a shirt and other clothing to be given him, with which the cacique very happy bade him farewell and went to his town.

Chapter X.
How the governor sent the ships to Cuba and left one hundred men in the port while he and the rest of the men marched inland.

From the port of Espiritu Santo, where the governor was, he sent the chief constable, Baltasar de Gallegos, with fifty horse and thirty or forty foot to the province of Paracoxi, in order to note the disposition of the land and gather information of the land that lay beyond and to send him word of what he found. He sent the ships to the island of Cuba with orders to return with provisions at a certain time. Since the principal intent of Vasco Porcallo de Figueroa, who came with the governor as captain general, was to send slaves from Florida to the island of Cuba where he had his lands and his mines, and since he had made some forays and found that he could not capture any Indians because of the dense thickets and vast swamps in that land, upon seeing the character of the land, he determined to return to Cuba. And although there was some difference between him and the governor so that they did not willingly hold any communication or conversation with each other he asked him courteously to leave and took his departure from him. Baltasar de Gallegos reached Paracoxi and thirty Indians came to him on the part of the cacique who was absent from his town, one of whom spoke as follows:

"King Paracoxi, lord of this province, whose vassals we are, sent us to your grace to learn what you seek in this his land and in what he can serve you." Baltasar de Gallegos answered them saying that he thanked him heartily for his offer and that they should tell their lord that he should come to his town and that there they could converse and make peace and friendship which he very greatly desired. The Indians went and returned next day saying that their lord was ill and on that account could not come; and that they came before him to see what he ordered. He asked them if they knew

or had information of any rich land where there was gold or silver. They said yes, that there was a province toward the west called Cale, and that the people of that land were hostile to others living in other lands where it was summer most of the year. That land had gold in abundance and when those people came to make war on the people of Cale, they wore hats of gold resembling helmets. When Baltasar de Gallegos perceived that the cacique did not come, as it seemed to him that all these messages were pretense, in order that he might meanwhile get away safely, and fearing lest if he allowed the thirty Indians to go, they would never return, he ordered them put in chains and had the governor informed by eight horse of what was happening. At this the governor and all those in the port with him received great joy, for they believed that what the Indians said might be true. The governor left Captain Calderón in the port with thirty horse and seventy foot with food for two years. He and all the rest of the men marched inland and reached Paracoxi where Baltasar de Gallegos was, and from there, with all the men of the latter, he took the road toward Cale. He passed through a small town, Acela by name, and reached another town called Tocaste. Thence, with thirty horse and fifty foot, he went on toward Cale. As they passed through a town which had been depopulated, they saw some Indians of that town in a shallow lake, to whom the interpreter spoke. They came and gave an Indian to act as guide. He came to a river with a swift current and on a tree in the middle of it, a foot bridge was made on which the men crossed. The horses crossed by swimming by means of a tackle which was drawn by those on the other side, for the first horse they drove in without it was drowned. From there, the governor sent two horsemen to the men who had stayed behind, ordering them to hurry for the road was long and provisions were lacking. He reached Cale and found the town without people. He seized three Indians who were spies. There he awaited the men who were coming behind, who were experiencing great hardship from hunger and bad roads as the land was very poor in maize, low, and very wet, swampy, and covered with dense forests, and the provisions brought from the port were finished. Wherever any village was found, there were some blites and he who came first gathered them and having stewed them with water and salt, ate them without anything else. Those who could not get any of them, gathered the stalks from the maize fields which being still young had no maize, and ate them. Having reached the river which the governor had crossed, they found palm cabbages in low palm trees like those of Andalusia. There came two horsemen whom the governor had sent, who told them that there was maize in abundance in Cale; at which all were rejoiced. As soon as they reached Cale, the governor ordered all the maize which was ripe in the fields to be taken, which was enough for three months. When they were gathering this, the Indians killed three Christians and one of two Indians who were captured told the governor that seven days' journey farther on was a very large province with maize in abundance, called Apalache. He immediately set out from Cale with fifty horse and sixty foot, leaving the maestre de campo, Luis de Moscoso, with all the rest of the men and ordering him not to move thence until getting word from him. Inasmuch as there was no one to serve them, the bread each one had to eat, he ground in a mortar cannon or mortar made of a log, with a pestle like a window bar. Some sifted the meal through their coats of mail. The bread was baked in some flat pieces of earthen vessels which they set on the fire, in the same way as I have already said was done in Cuba. It is so difficult to grind that many, who would not formerly eat it unless it was ground, ate the maize parched and sodden.

Chapter XI.
How the governor reached Caliquen, and thence, taking the cacique with him, went to Napetaca, where the Indians attempted to remove him from his power, and in turn many were killed and captured.

On the eleventh day of August, in the year 1540, the governor left Cale and went to sleep at a small town called Ytara, the next day at another called Potano, and the third at Utinama. He arrived at another town to which they gave the name of Mala Paz because an Indian came in peace saying that he was the cacique, that he wished to serve the governor with his people, that he should order twenty-eight Indian men and women, who had been seized from him the night before, to be set free; that he would order provisions taken to him and would give him a guide for the onward jour-

ney. The governor ordered the Indians freed and a guard put over him. On the morning of the next day many Indians came and took position about the town near the forest. The Indian asked to be taken near them as he wished to speak to them and assure them, and that they would do whatever he ordered them. As soon as he found himself near them, he attacked the Christians stoutly and escaped and no one was able to overtake him; and all the Indians went fleeing through the woods. The governor ordered loosed a hound which he brought along previously glutted on them, which passing by many other Indians went to seize the pretended cacique who had fled from the Christians and held him until the latter came to seize him. From there, the governor went to sleep at a town called Cholupaha; and as it had maize in abundance, they gave it the name Villafarta. In front was a river over which a bridge of wood was built, and he went for two days through an abandoned region. On August 17, he arrived at Caliquen and got information of the province of Apalache. They told him that Narvaez had arrived there and that he had taken to boats there because he found no road on beyond; that there was no other village, but that it was all water in every direction. All were saddened at this news and advised the governor to return to the port and leave the land of Florida; so that he might not get lost as had Narvaez; that, if he went on, when he might wish to return he could not; that the Indians would end by seizing the little maize that was to be found. To this the governor answered that he would not turn back until seeing with his own eyes what they said, which he could not believe, and that we should be ready saddled. He ordered Luis de Moscoso to set out immediately from Cale and that he was awaiting him there. It appeared to Luis de Moscoso and to many others that they must turn back from Apalache and they buried iron and other things in Cale. They reached Caliquen after great hardship for the land over which the governor had passed was destroyed and bare of maize. After all the men had gathered there, he ordered a bridge built over a river which flowed near the town. He left Caliquen on September ten, taking the cacique with him. After a march of three days, Indians came in peace saying that they came to see their lord; and every day they came to the road playing on flutes, which is their sign by which they make known that they come in peace. They said that farther on a cacique called Uzachil, a relative of the cacique of Caliquen, their lord, was waiting with great gifts. They asked the governor to free the cacique, but he refused to free him, for he feared lest they revolt and refuse to give him guides and from day to day he dismissed them with good words. He marched for five days, passing through several small towns, and reached a town, Napetuca by name, on September 15. There fourteen or fifteen Indians came and asked the governor to set the cacique of Caliquen, their lord, free. He answered them saying that he did not hold him captive, but that he wished to keep him with him as far as Uzachil. The governor learned from Juan Ortiz that an Indian had revealed to him that they had decided to assemble and to come against him in order to give him battle and to take from him the cacique whom he was holding. On the day agreed upon, the governor ordered his men to be ready, and the horsemen armed and mounted, each one to be within his lodging, so that the Indians might not see them and would accordingly come to the town without fear. Four hundred Indians came within sight of the camp with their bows and arrows and posted themselves in a wood. Then they sent two Indians to tell the governor to give up the cacique to them. The governor with six men of foot, taking the cacique by the hand and talking with him, in order to assure the Indians, went toward the place where they were and seeing the time ready ordered a blast of the trumpet to be given. Immediately those who were in the houses in the town, both foot and horse, attacked the Indians who were so surprised that their greatest thought was where they could escape. They killed two horses, one of which was that of the governor, who was immediately provided with another. Thirty or forty Indians were lanced. The rest fled toward two very large shallow lakes which were separated one from the other. There they went swimming about, while the Christians roundabout—arquebusiers and crossbowmen—shot at them from the outside. But as they were far away and they shot at them from a long distance they did no hurt to them. That night the governor ordered one of the two lakes to be surrounded; for, because of their large size, his men were insufficient to surround both of them. Being surrounded, the Indians, upon the approach of night, having made up their minds to

take to flight, would come swimming very softly to the edge, and so that they might not be seen, would place water-lily leaves on their heads. When the horsemen saw the leaves moving they would dash in until the water was up to the breasts of the horses and the Indians would return in flight within the lake. In that way they passed that night without the Indians or the Christians having any rest. Juan Ortiz told them that since they could not escape, they would better surrender to the governor, which forced by necessity and the coldness of the water, they did; and one by one as soon as the suffering from the cold conquered them, they would cry out to Juan Ortiz saying that they should not be killed for now they were going to put themselves into the hands of the governor. At day dawn they had all surrendered except twelve of the principal men who, being more honored and valiant, resolved to perish rather than come into his power. The Indians of Paracoxi who were now going about unchained, went in swimming after them and pulled them out by their hair. They were all put in chains and on the day following were allotted among the Christians for their service. While captive there they resolved to revolt and charged an Indian interpreter whom they held as a valiant man that as soon as the governor came to talk with him, he should seize him about the neck with his hands and choke him. As soon as he saw an opportunity he seized hold of the governor, and before he got his hands about his neck, struck him so hard on the nose that it was all covered with blood. Immediately they all rose in revolt. He who could get weapons in his hand or the pestle for crushing maize tried with all his might to kill his master or the first man he met. He who could get a lance or sword in his hand so handled himself with it as if he had used it all his life. An Indian with a sword surrounded by fifteen or twenty men on foot in the public place, uttered challenge like a bull, until some halberdiers of the governor came up, who killed him. Another one with a lance climbed up on a cane floor which they make to hold their maize (which they call barbacoa) and there he made a noise as if ten men were inside; and while defending the door, he was struck down by a javelin. In all, there were about two hundred Indians, all of whom were subdued. The governor gave some of the youngest boys to those who had good chains and cautioned them not to let them escape from them. All the rest he ordered to be punished by being fastened to a stake in the middle of the plaza and the Indians of Paracoxi shot them with arrows.

Chapter XII.
How the governor arrived at Palache and was informed that gold existed in abundance in the interior of the land.

On September the 23d, the governor left Napetaca and went to sleep at a river where two Indians brought him a stag on the part of the cacique of Uzachil. Next day he passed through a large town called Hapaluya and went to sleep at Uzachil. He found no people there, for because of the news which the Indians had of the massacre of Napetaca they dared not remain. In the town he found an abundance of maize, beans, and pumpkins, of which their food consists, and on which the Christians lived there. Maize is like coarse millet and the pumpkins are better and more savory than those of Spain. From there the governor sent two captains, each one in a different direction, in search of the Indians. They captured a hundred head, among Indian men and women. Of the latter, there, as well as in any other part where forays were made, the captain selected one or two for the governor and the others were divided among themselves and those who went with them. These Indians they took along in chains with collars about their necks and they were used for carrying the baggage and grinding the maize and for other services which so fastened in this manner they could perform. Sometimes it happened that when they went with them for firewood or maize they would kill the Christian who was leading them and would escape with the chain. Others at night would file the chain off with a bit of stone which they have in place of iron tools, and with which they cut it. Those who were caught at it paid for themselves and for those others, so that on another day they might not dare do likewise. As soon as the women and young children were a hundred leagues from their land, having become unmindful, they were taken along unbound, and served in that way, and in a very short time learned the language of the Christians. The governor left Uzachill for Apalache and in a march of two days, reached a town called Axille. And because the Indians had not heard of the Christians, they were careless, most of them escaped because the town was surrounded by a forest. On the morning of the next day, October first, the governor left there and ordered a bridge to be built over a river where he had to cross. It was necessary to swim for a stone's throw where the bridge was built, and beyond that a crossbow-shot's distance the water came up to the waist. And there was a very high, thick wood through which the Indians would come to see if they could prevent the passage and those who were building the bridge. The crossbowmen came to their aid and made the Indians take to flight. Some timbers were put in over which some men passed which assured the crossing. The governor crossed over on Wednesday, the day of St. Francis. He went to sleep at a town called Vitachuco which was subject to Palache. He found it burning for the Indians had set fire to it. Beyond that place, the land was very populous and maize abounded. He passed through many open districts like villages. On Sunday, October 25, he arrived at a town called Uzela, and on Monday, at Anhaica Apalache where the lord of all that land and province lived. In that town, the maestre de campo, whose office it is to allot and provide lodgings, lodged them all. Within a league and a half league about that town, were other towns where there was abundance of maize, pumpkins, beans, and dried plums native to the land, which are better than those of Spain and grow wild in the fields without being planted. Food which seemed sufficient to last over the winter was gathered together from those towns on into Anhaica Apalache. The governor was informed that the sea was ten leagues away from there. He immediately sent a captain and some horse and foot and after going six leagues the captain found a town called Ochete. He reached the sea and found a large tree which had been cut down and made into troughs fixed with some posts which were used as mangers and saw skulls of horses. With this message he came and what they said of Narvaez was considered true, namely, that he had there built the boats with which he left that land and in which he was lost at sea. The governor immediately sent Juan de Añasco with thirty horse to the port of Espiritu Santo, where Calderón was, ordering them to abandon that port and all to go to Apalache. He set out on Friday, November 17. In Uzachill and at other towns on the way, he found many people already careless.

He would not capture Indians in order not to be detained, for it did not suit him to give the Indians time to assemble. He passed through the towns at night and rested for three or four hours at a distance from habitation. In ten days he reached the port, brought twenty Indian women whom he captured in Ytara and Potano near Cale, sent them to Doña Isabel in two caravels which he sent from the port to Cuba, and brought all the men of foot in the brigantines, coasting along toward Palache. Calderón, with the men of horse and some foot crossbowmen went by land. In some places, the Indians attacked him and wounded some of his men. As soon as they reached Apalache, the governor immediately ordered planks hewn and spikes taken to the sea with which was built a piragua large enough to hold thirty well armed men who went by way of the bay to the sea and coasted about waiting for the brigantines. Several times they fought with Indians who were going along the keys in canoes. On Saturday, November 29, an Indian came through the sentinels without being seen and set fire to the town; and because of the high wind blowing two-thirds of it were quickly burned. On Sunday, the 28th of December, Juan de Añasco arrived with the brigantines. The governor sent Francisco Maldonado, captain of the foot soldiers, with fifty men to coast along toward the west and look for a port, for he had decided to go by land in order to explore in that direction. On that day, eight horse, by order of the governor, went out into the open country for two leagues about the town to look for Indians; for now the latter had become so daring that they would come within two crossbow-shots of the camp to kill the men. They found two Indians and one Indian woman gathering beans. Although the men could have escaped, in order not to abandon the Indian woman who was the wife of one of them, they resolved to die fighting. Before being killed they wounded three horses, one of which died a few days afterward. Calderón with his men marched along the sea-coast. From a wood close to the sea some Indians came out to attack him and forced him to leave the road, and many of those with him to abandon some necessary food they were carrying. Three or four days after the time limit set by the governor to Maldonado for going and coming (although he had planned and determined not to await him

longer if he did not come within a week from that time), he came and brought an Indian from a province called Ochua, sixty leagues from Apalache, where he had found a port of good depth and sheltered. And because he hoped to find farther on a good land, the governor was very happy and sent Maldonado to Havana for provisions with orders to wait at the port of Ochus which he had discovered; and that he would go overland in search of it; and that if he were delayed and should not go that summer he should return to the Havana, and the next summer return to wait at the port, for he would do nothing else than go in search of Ochus. Francisco Maldonado went and Juan de Guzmán remained in his stead as captain of the foot soldiers of his company. From among the Indians captured at Napetuca, the treasurer, Juan Gaytán brought along a youth who said that he was not of that land, but that he was from another very distant one lying in the direction of the sunrise, and that some time ago he had come in order to visit lands; that his land was called Yupaha and a woman ruled it; that the town where she lived was of wonderful size; and that that chieftainess collected tribute from many of her neighboring chiefs, some of whom gave her clothing and others gold in abundance. He told how it was taken from the mines, melted, and refined, just as if he had seen it done, or else the devil taught him; so that all who knew anything of this said it was impossible to give so good an account of it unless one had seen it; and all when they saw the signs he made believed whatever he said to be true.

Chapter XIII.
How the governor set out from Apalache to look for Yupaha and of what happened to him.

On Wednesday, the 3d of March, 1540, the governor left Anhaica Apalache in search of Yupaha. He ordered all his men to provide themselves with maize for a journey of sixty leagues through uninhabited land. Those of horse carried the maize on their horses, and those of foot on their backs; for most of the Indians whom they had to serve them, being naked and in chains, died because of the hard life they suffered during that winter. After a march of four days, they came to a deep river, where a piragua was made and, because of the strong current, a chain cable was made and fastened on each side of the river. The piragua crossed over alongside it and the horses crossed swimming by means of ropes and tackle which were pulled along by them. After crossing the river, in a day and a half they reached a town called Capachiqui. On Friday, March 11, they saw the Indians had risen. Next day, five Christians went to look for mortars which the Indians used for crushing their maize. They went to certain houses contiguous to the camp surrounded by a wood. Within the wood many Indians were walking about who came to spy on us. Five of them separated from the others and attacked our men. One of the Christians came running to the camp, shouting "To arms." Those who were most ready attended to the alarm. They found one Christian dead and three badly wounded. The Indians fled through a swamp with a very dense wood where the horses could not enter. The governor left Capachiqui and crossed over an abandoned region. On Wednesday, the 21st of the month, he came to a town called Toalli. Beyond that place, a difference was seen in the houses, for those behind were covered with hay and those of Toalli were covered with canes in the manner of tile. Those houses are very clean and some have their walls plastered and appear to be made of mud. Throughout the cold lands each of the Indians has his house for the winter plastered inside and out. They shut the very small door at night and build a fire inside the house so that it gets as hot as an oven, and stays so all night long so that there is no need of clothing. Besides those houses they have others for summer with kitchens nearby where they build their fires and bake their bread. They have barbacoas in which they keep their maize. This is a house raised up on four posts, timbered like a loft and the floor of canes. The difference which the houses of the lords or principal men have from those of the others is that besides being larger they have large balconies in front and below seats resembling benches made of canes; and round about many large barbacoas in which they gather together the tribute paid them by their Indians, which consists of maize and deerskins and native blankets resembling shawls, some being made of the inner bark of trees and some from a plant like daffodils which when pounded remains like flax. The Indian women

cover themselves with these blankets, draping one around themselves from the waist down and another over the shoulder with the right arm uncovered in the manner and custom of gypsies. The Indian men wear only one over the shoulders in the same way and have their privies covered with a truss of deerskin resembling the breech-clouts formerly worn in Spain. The skins are well tanned and are given the color that is desired; and so perfectly that if the color is vermillion, it seems to be very fine grained cloth, and that colored black is splendid. And of this same they make shoes. They give the same colors to the blankets. The governor left Toalli on March 24. At supper time on Thursday he came to a little stream where a footbridge was made on which the men crossed. Bento Fernandez, a Portuguese, fell off it and was drowned. As soon as the governor had crossed the stream, he found a village called Achese a short distance on. Although the Indians had never heard of Christians they plunged into a river. A few Indians, men and women, were seized, among whom was found one who understood the youth who was guiding the governor to Yupaha. On that account, the governor was more certain of what the latter said, for they had passed through lands having different languages, some of which he did not understand. The governor sent one of the Indians captured there to call the cacique who was on the other side of the river. He came and spoke as follows:

"Very exalted and very mighty and very excellent Lord: Things which seldom happen cause wonder. Therefore, what must the sight of your Lordship and your men, whom we have never seen, be to me and mine; and the entrance into my land with so great haste and fury, and on animals so fierce as are your horses, without me having known of your coming. It was a thing so new and caused such terror and fear in our minds that it was not in our power to await and welcome your Lordship with the ceremony due so exalted and distinguished a prince as is your Lordship. Confiding in your greatness and singular virtues, not only do I hope to be held free of guilt but to receive rewards. The first thing I beg of your Lordship is that with my person and land and vassals, you do as with a thing your own; and secondly, that you tell me who you are, whence you come, whither you go, and what you seek, so that I may better serve you." The governor answered him saying that he thanked him heartily for his offer and for his goodwill, as if he had welcomed him and offered him a great treasure; that he was a son of the sun and came from where it dwelt and that he was going through that land and seeking the greatest lord and the richest province in it. The cacique said that a great lord lived on ahead; that his domain was called Ocute. He gave him a guide and interpreter for that province. The governor ordered his Indians to be set free and departed from his town on the first day of April, marching through his land up along a river with many villages. He left a wooden cross raised very high in the middle of the public place. And as time did not allow more, he only declared that that cross was a memorial of that on which Christ suffered, who was God and man and created the heavens and the earth and suffered to save us and, therefore, they should reverence it. They signified that they would do so. On April 4, the governor passed through a town, by name, Altamaca; and on the tenth day of the month reached Ocute. The cacique sent him two thousand Indians bearing gifts, namely, many rabbits, partridges, maize bread, two hens, and many dogs, which are esteemed among the Christians as if they were fat sheep because there was a great lack of meat and salt. Of this there was so much need and lack in many places and on many occasions that if a man fell sick, there was nothing with which to make him well; and he would waste away of an illness which could have been easily cured in any other place, until nothing but his bones were left and he would die from pure weakness, some saying: "If I had a bit of meat or some lumps of salt, I should not die." The Indians do not lack meat; for they kill many deer, hens, rabbits, and other game with their arrows. In this they have great skill, which the Christians do not have; and even if they had it, they had no time for it, for most of the time they were on the march, and they did not dare to turn aside from the paths. And because they lacked meat so badly, when the six hundred men with Soto arrived at any town, and found twenty or thirty dogs, he who could get one and who killed it, thought he was not a little agile. And if he who killed one did not send his captain a quarter, the latter, if he learned of it, upbraided him and gave him to understand it in the watches or in any other matter of work that arose with which he

could annoy him. On Monday, April 12, the governor left Ocute, the cacique having given him four hundred tamemes, that is, Indians for carrying; He passed through a town, whose lord was called Cofaqui; and reached a province of an Indian lord called Patofa, who since he was at peace with the lord of Ocute and the other lords round about, had heard of the governor some days before and desired to see him. He came to visit him and spoke as follows:

"Powerful Lord: Now with reason I will beg fortune to pay me some slight adversity for so great happiness; and I call myself happy for I have obtained what I desired in this life—that of seeing your Lordship and being able to render you some service. Although speech is the image of what is in the heart and what my heart feels with this happiness it cannot conceal, yet my tongue is not sufficient to enable me to express that happiness entirely. From whence did this your land, which I am governing, merit the visit of so sovereign and so excellent a prince to whom all people in the world owe service and obedience? And from whence has come so great a good fortune to those who inhabit this land, they being so insignificant, unless to recall to their memory some great misfortune which might happen in accordance with the arrangement of fortune? Therefore, now and forever, if we are worthy of your Lordship holding us as yours, we can not cease to be favored and maintained in true justice and reason and called men; for those who lack reason and justice can be compared to brute beasts. In my heart with the respect due to such a prince as your Lordship, I offer myself, and beg you that in payment of this true goodwill, you may wish to be served by my person, land, and vassals." The governor answered him saying that his offers and goodwill exhibited by deeds would greatly please him; that he would always remember to honor and protect him as a brother. This land from that of the first peaceful cacique to the province of Patofa—a distance of fifty leagues—is a rich land, beautiful, fertile, well watered, and with fine fields along the rivers. From thence to the port of Espiritu Santo, where we first reached the land of Florida—a distance of about three hundred and fifty leagues or so—it is a lean land, and most of it covered with rough pine groves, low and very swampy, and in places having lofty dense forests, where the hostile Indians wandered so that no one could find them nor could the horses enter there—which was annoying to the Christians because of the provisions which had been carried off and the trouble experienced by them in looking for Indians to guide them.

Chapter XIV.
How the governor left the province of Patofa and came upon an uninhabited region, where he and all his men experienced great vicissitudes and extreme need.

In the town of Patofa, the youth whom the governor brought as interpreter and guide began to foam at the mouth and to throw himself to the ground as if possessed by the devil. They prayed the evangel over him and that fit left him. He said that four days' journey thence toward the rising sun was the province of which he spoke. The Indians of Patofa said that they knew of no settlement in that direction, but that toward the northwest they knew a province called Coça, a well provisioned land and of very large villages. The cacique told the governor that if he wished to go thither, he would furnish him service of a guide and Indians to carry; and if in the direction indicated by the youth he would also give him all those he needed; and with mutual words of affection and promises they said farewell to each other. He gave him seven hundred tamemes. He took maize for four days and marched for six days along a path which gradually grew narrower until it was all lost. He marched in the direction where the youth guided him and crossed two rivers by fording, each of which was two crossbow-shots wide. The water came to their stirrups and had a swift current, so that it was necessary for the men on horseback to form a line one in front of the other in order that those on foot might cross above them by virtue of their support. He came to another river with a more powerful current and wider which was crossed with greater difficulty for the horses swam as they got out for the length of a lance. That river being crossed, the governor came out to a pine grove and threatened the youth and made as if he would throw him to the dogs because he had deceived him, saying that it was a march of four days, and for nine days he had marched making seven or eight leagues on each day; and now the men and horses were become weak because of the great economy which had been practiced with regard to the maize. The

youth said that he did not know where he was. That there was no other whom Juan Ortiz understood availed in preventing him from being thrown to the dogs. The governor with them and with some horse and foot, leaving the camp established in a pine grove, marched five or six leagues that day looking for a road, and at night returned greatly disheartened without having found any signs of habitation. Next day different opinions were expressed as to whether he should turn back or what he should do. Inasmuch as the land behind through which they had come was left very desolate and lacking in maize, and the maize they brought was finished, and the men very weak, as well as the horses, they were in great doubt as to whether they could reach a place where they might be aided. Moreover, they considered that if they went on like defeated men, if any Indians dared to attack them, they could not escape either because of hunger or war. The governor determined to send horsemen thence in all directions to look for habitation. On the next day he sent four captains in different directions, each one with eight horsemen. They returned at night some leading their horses by the bridle and others driving them before them with a stick, for they could not carry them they were so tired out, and without finding any road or sign of habitation. Next day, the governor sent four others each with eight horse, men who could swim, in order to cross the mud and streams which they might come to, and chosen horses, the best in the camp. The captains were Baltasar de Gallegos who went upstream; Juan de Añasco who went down; Alonso Romo and Juan Rodríguez Lobillo who went inland. The governor had taken thirteen sows to Florida and was now driving three hundred pigs. He ordered half a pound of flesh to be given to each man daily, it having been three or four days since maize was lacking. With that small amount of meat and with some herbs boiled with considerable trouble, the men were sustained. The governor sent the Indians of Patofa back since he had nothing to give them to eat. They, upon ceasing to accompany and serve the Christians in their need, and manifesting great sorrow to him at returning without leaving them in a village returned to their own land. Juan de Añasco came on Sunday afternoon and gave news of finding a small town twelve or thirteen leagues away. He brought an Indian woman and a boy whom he captured. With his coming and with the news, the governor and all were so glad that it seemed to them that they had then come back from greedy death. On Monday, the 26th of April, the governor set out for the town which was called Aymay, to which the Christians gave the name of the town of Socorro. At the place where the camp was established he left a letter buried at the foot of a pine tree and on the pine some words cut on the bark with a machete, as follows: "Dig at the foot of this pine tree and you will find a letter," doing this so that when the captains came, who had gone to look for a village, they might see the letter and might learn what the governor had done and where he had gone. There was no other way to the town than marks left cut on the trees by Juan de Añasco. The governor, with some of those who had the best horses, reached the town on Monday; and all striving to reach it as soon as possible slept, some at a distance of two, and others at three or four, leagues from the town, each one according as he could march and his strength aided him. In the town was found a barbacoa full of parched maize meal and some maize which was given out by rationing. There four Indians were captured, and no one of them would say anything else than that they did not know of any other village. The governor ordered one of them to be burned. Thereupon, another said that two day's journey thence was a province called Cutitachiqui. On Wednesday, arrived the captains, Baltasar de Gallegos, Alonso Romo, and Juan Rodríguez Lobillo, who had found the letter and followed to the town whither the governor had gone. Two men belonging to the company of Juan Rodríguez were lost because of their tired horses. The governor chid him severely for having left them and sent him to look for them, and as soon as they came set out for Cutifachiqui. On the way three Indians were captured who declared that the chieftainess of that land had already heard of the Christians and was awaiting them in one of her towns. The governor sent to her by one of them an offer of his friendship and the information that he was coming thither. The governor arrived and immediately four canoes came to him in one of which was a sister of the cacica. Coming to the governor, she said these words:

"Excellent Lord: My sister orders me to kiss your Lordship's hands and say to you that the reason why she has not come in person is that she thought she could better serve you by remaining as she is doing to give orders that all her canoes should be made ready quickly so that your Lordship might cross and so that you might rest, for you will be served immediately." The governor thanked her and she returned to the other side of the river. Shortly thereafter, the cacica came from the town in a carrying chair in which certain principal Indians carried her to the river. She entered a canoe with an awning at the stern and on the bottom of which was already spread a mat for her and above it two cushions one on top of the other, on which she seated herself. With her principal men and other canoes filled with Indians who accompanied her, she went to the place where the governor was; and on her arrival spoke as follows:

"Excellent Lord: May your Lordship's coming to these your lands be of very good augury, although my possibility does not equal my wishes and my services are not equal to what I desire and to the merits of so powerful a prince as your Lordship; for goodwill is more worthy of acceptance than all the treasures of the world which may be offered without it. With very sincere and open goodwill I offer you my person, my lands, my vassals, and this poor service." And she presented him a quantity of clothing of the country which she brought in the other canoes, namely, blankets and skins. And from her neck she drew a long string of pearl beads and threw it about the neck of the governor, exchanging with him many gracious words of affection and courtesy. She ordered canoes to go thither in which the governor and his men crossed. As soon as he was lodged in the town, another gift of many hens was made him. That land was very pleasing and fertile, and had excellent fields along the rivers, the forest being clear and having many walnuts and mulberries. They said that the sea was two days' journey away. About the town within the compass of a league and a half league were large uninhabited towns, choked with vegetation, which looked as though no people had inhabited them for some time. The Indians said that two years ago there had been a plague in that land and they had moved to other towns. In the barbacoas of the towns there was a considerable amount of clothing— blankets made of thread from the bark of trees and feather mantles (white, gray, vermillion, and yellow), made according to their custom, elegant and suitable for winter. There were also many deerskins, well tanned and colored, with designs drawn on them and made into pantaloons, hose, and shoes. The cacica, observing that the Christians esteemed pearls, told the governor that he might order certain graves in that town to be examined, for he would find many, and that if he wished to send to the uninhabited towns, they could load all their horses. The graves of that town were examined and fourteen arrobas of pearls were found, babies and birds being made of them. The people were dark, well set up and proportioned, and more civilized than any who had been seen in all the land of Florida; and all were shod and clothed. The youth told the governor that he was now beginning to enter that land of which he had spoken to him. And since it was such a land and he understood the language of the Indians, some credence was given him. He requested that he be baptized for he wished to become a Christian. He was made a Christian and was called Pedro. The governor ordered him to be loosed from the chain in which he had gone until then. That land, according to the statement of the Indian, had been very populous and was reputed to be a good land. According to appearances, the youth whom the governor had taken as guide had heard of it, and what he learned from hearsay be asserted to have seen, and enlarged at will what he saw. In that town were found a dagger and some beads of Christians, whom the Indians said had been in the port two days' journey thence; and that it was now many years since Governor Licentiate Ayllón had arrived there in order to make a conquest of that land; that on arriving at the port, he died; and there ensued a division, quarrels, and deaths among several of the principal persons who had accompanied him as to who should have the command; and without learning anything of the land they returned to Spain from that port. All the men were of the opinion that they should settle in that land as it was in an excellent region; that if it were settled, all the ships from New Spain, and those from Peru, Santa Marta, and Tierra Firme, on their way to Spain, would come to take advantage of the stop there for their route passes by there; and as it is a good land and suitable for making profit. Since the governor's purpose was to seek another treasure like that of Atabalipa, the lord of Peru, he had no wish to content himself with good land or with pearls,

even though many of them were worth their weight in gold and, if the lamb were to be allotted in repartimiento, those pearls which the Indians would get afterward would be worth more; for those they have, inasmuch as they are bored by fire, lose their color thereby. The governor replied to those who urged him to settle that there was not food in that whole land for the support of his men for a single month; that it was necessary to hasten to the port of Ochus where Maldonado was to wait; that if another richer land were not found they could always return to that one whenever they wished; that meanwhile the Indians would plant their fields and it would be better provided with maize. He asked the Indians whether they had heard of any great lord farther on. They said that twelve days' journey thence was a province called Chiaha which was subject to the lord of Coça. Thereupon, the governor determined to go in search of that land; and as he was a man, hard and dry of word, and although he was glad to listen to and learn the opinion of all, after he had voiced his own opinion he did not like to be contradicted and always did what seemed best to him. Accordingly, all conformed to his will, and although it seemed a mistake to leave that land, for another land might have been found round about where the men might maintain themselves until the planting might be done there and the maize harvested, no one had anything to say to him after his determination was learned.

Chapter XV.
How the governor left Cutifachiqui to go in search of Coça; and of the things that happened to him on the way.

On May 3, the governor set out from Cutifachiqui, and because the Indians had already risen, and it was learned that the cacica was minded to go away if she could without giving guides or tamemes for carrying because of offenses committed against the Indians by the Christians—for among many men there is never lacking some person of little quality who for very little advantage to himself places the others in danger of losing their lives—the governor ordered a guard to be placed over her and took her along with him; not giving her such good treatment as she deserved for the goodwill she had shown him and the welcome she had given him. He made true the old proverb which says

"For well doing," etc. And so he took her along on foot with her slave women, so that they might show respect because of her. In all the towns through which the governor passed, the cacica ordered the Indians to come and carry the loads from one town to the other. We traversed her lands for a hundred leagues, in which, as we saw, she was very well obeyed, for all the Indians did with great efficiency and diligence what she ordered of them. Perico, the youth who was guiding us, said that she was not the ruler but that she was the ruler's niece and that she had come to that town to execute justice on certain of the principal men under command of the ruler who had rebelled against her and kept the tribute. No credit was given to him because of the lies in which he had been found; but everything was endured in him because of the need of him to tell what the Indians said. In seven days, the governor reached a province, by name Chalaque, the poorest land in maize seen in Florida. The Indians live on roots of herbs which they seek in the open field and on game killed with their arrows. The people are very domestic, go quite naked, and are very weak. There was a lord who brought the governor two deerskins as a great act of service. In that land are many wild hens. In one town they performed a service for him, presenting him seven hundred of them, and likewise in others they brought those they had and could get. It took five days to go from this province to another one called Jualla. They found little maize, and for that reason, although the men were tired and their horses very weak, the governor did not stop over two days. From Ocute to Cufitachiqui it was about one hundred and thirty leagues, eighty of which were without inhabitants. From Cutifa to Jualla it was two hundred and fifty leagues, over mountainous country. The governor set out from Jualla for Guaxule, crossing over very rough and lofty mountains. Along that way, the cacica of Cutifachiqui, whom the governor brought as abovesaid for the purpose of taking her to Guaxule—for her lands reached that far—going one day with her slave women who were carrying her, stepped aside from the road and went into a wood saying that she had to attend to her necessities. Thus she deceived them and hid herself in the woods; and although they sought her she could not be found. She took with her a box of canes made like a coffer which they call "petaca," filled with unbored pearls. Some who had most knowledge of them said they were very valuable. An Indian woman was carrying them for her whom she took with her. The governor, in order not to cause her unhappiness in everything, left them, intending to ask them from her at Guaxule, when he should give her leave to return. She took it and went to stop at Jualla with three slaves who had escaped from the camp and with a horseman who remained behind, for being sick with fever he wandered from the road and was lost. This man, named Alimamos, tried to have the slaves abandon their evil intention and go with him to the Christians—which two of them did. Alimamos and they overtook the governor fifty leagues from there in a province called Chiaha. They related how the cacica had remained in Jualla with a slave of André de Vasconcellos who refused to come with them; and it was very certain that they held communication as husband and wife, and that both had made up their minds to go to Cutifachiqui. In five days, the governor arrived at Guaxulle. The Indians there made him service of three hundred dogs, for they observed that the Christians liked them and sought them to eat; but they are not eaten among them. In Guaxulle and along all that road there was very little maize. The governor sent an Indian thence with a message to the cacique of Chiaha, asking him to order some maize brought them, so that they might rest several days in Chiaha. The governor left Guaxulle and after a march of two days reached a town called Canasagua. Twenty Indians came out to meet him each carrying his basket of mulberries which grow in abundance and good from Cutifachiqui thither and also on into other provinces, as well as walnuts and plums. The trees grow wild in the fields without being planted or manured and are as large and as vigorous as if they were cultivated and irrigated in gardens. After the governor left Canasagua, he marched five days through an uninhabited region. Two leagues before reaching Chiaha, fifteen Indians, bearing maize, whom the cacique sent, met him; and told him in behalf of the cacique that the latter was awaiting him with twenty barbacoas full, and he with all the rest, including his person, land, and vassals, were all at his service. On July 5, the governor entered Chiaha. The cacique moved out of his houses in which he was lodging and welcomed him very hospitably, with the following words:

"Powerful and excellent lord: I consider myself so fortunate in that your Lordship is pleased to use my services that no greater happiness could come to me nor any that I could esteem as much. Your Lordship ordered me from Guaxulle to have maize for you in this town for two months. I have here for you twenty barbacoas full of choice maize, and the best that can be found in all this land. If your Lordship was not received by me in accordance with what is due to so great a prince, have consideration for my few years which acquit me of guilt; and receive the goodwill which, with great, true, and sincere loyalty I shall always have for what concerns your service." The governor answered him saying that his service and offer pleased him greatly and that he would always consider him as a brother. In that town, there was an abundance of butter in gourds, in melted form like olive oil. They said it was bear's grease. There was also found considerable walnut oil which like the butter was clean and of a good taste, and a pot of bee's honey; which before or after was not seen in all the land—neither honey nor bees. The town was isolated between two arms of a river and was settled near one of them. At a distance of two crossbow-shots above the town, the river divided into those two arms which were reunited a league below. The field between the one arm and the other was in places about the width of one crossbow-shot, and in places of two. They were of great width and both were fordable. Very excellent fields lay along them and many maize fields. Inasmuch as the Indians were in their town, only the governor was lodged in the houses of the cacique, and his men in the open field. Wherever there were any trees each one took his own. In this way the camp was established with some widely separated from the others and without any order. The governor overlooked this since the Indians were peaceable and the weather was quiet and the men would have suffered great discomfort if they had not done this. The horses reached there so weak that they were unable to carry their owners through weakness, because of having come from Cutifachiqui all the way with but little maize. They had suffered hunger and fatigue all the way from the

unpopulated region of Ocute. Since most of the men were not fit to fight on them even if it should be necessary, they put the horses out to pasture at night a quarter of a league from the camp. The Christians were in great danger, for if at that time, the Indians had attacked them, they were in a poor position for defending themselves. There the governor rested for thirty days, during which time the horses grew fat because of the luxuriance of the land. At the time of his departure, because of the importunity of some who wished more than was proper, he asked the cacique for thirty Indian women as slaves. The cacique answered that he would talk with his principal men; but one night, before returning an answer, all the Indians left the town with their wives and children and went away. Next day, when the governor had made up his mind to go to look for them, the cacique came, and on arriving spoke as follows to the governor:

"Powerful Lord: I am ashamed and fearful of your Lordship, because my Indians, against my will, decided to go away. I fled without your permission; and having perceived the mistake I committed, I have come as a loyal vassal to deliver myself into your Lordship's power so that you may do what you please with my person, for my people do not obey me nor do anything except what an uncle of mine orders, who is governing these lands for me until I am of proper age. If your Lordship wishes to follow them and execute on them what they deserve for their disobedience, I will be your guide, for my fortune refuses at present to let me do more." The governor immediately went in search of the Indians with thirty horse and a like number of foot. Passing through some towns of the principal Indians who had gone off, he cut down and destroyed their large maize fields; and went to hold the river above where the Indians were on an islet, whither the men of horse could not go. He sent word to them there by an Indian that they should return to their town and should have no fear and that they should furnish him tamemes for carrying as had been done by all the Indians before; that he did not wish any Indian women since it cost them so dearly to give them to him. The Indians considered it well and came to the governor who made their excuses to him; and so they all returned to the town. A cacique from a province called Acoste came there to visit the governor. After offering himself to him and exchanging words of politeness and courtesy with him, the governor asked him whether he knew of any rich land. He said he did; that there was a province to the north called Chisca, and that there was a foundry for copper and other metal of that color except that it was finer and of much more perfect color and much better in appearance; and that they did not make so much use of it as it was softer. The same thing had been told the governor in Cutifachiqui where we saw some copper hatchets which they said had a mixture of gold. However, the land was thinly populated as far as that region and they said that there were mountain ridges which the horses could not cross. On that account, the governor did not wish to go thither by direct road from Cutifachiqui, and thought that if he went through a populated region while the men and horses were in better condition and he more certain of the truth of what there was, he could turn thither through ridges and better populated land where he could travel better. He sent two Christians from Chiaha with Indians who knew the land of Chisca and its language, in order that they might examine it, with orders that they should go to report what they found at the place where he said he would await them.

Chapter XVI.

How the governor set out from Chiaha and was in danger of being killed in Acoste at the hands of the Indians, and how he escaped through warning; and of what happened to him on this journey, and how he arrived at Coça.

So when the governor made up his mind to go from Chiaha to Acoste, he ordered the cacique to come to him, and took leave of him with courteous words, and gave him some pieces of cloth with which he was very happy. He reached Acoste in seven days. On the second of July, he ordered the camp made in the open field two crossbow-flights from the town and with eight men of his guard he went toward the town where he found the cacique, who apparently received him with great friendliness. While he was talking with him, some of the foot soldiers went to the town from the camp to look for maize, and not being satisfied with it, went rummaging around and searching the houses and seized what they found. Annoyed

at this the Indians began to get excited and to seize their arms. Some of them with clubs in their hands went to five or six Christians who angered them and with blows served them to their liking. The governor seeing them all excited and himself among them with so few Christians, in order to escape out of their hands, practiced a stratagem quite contrary to his usual disposition which was very direct and open; and although it grieved him greatly that any Indian should dare, either with or without reason, to show contempt for the Christians, he seized a club and went to their aid against his own men, which was done for the purpose of assuring them. Straightway he secretly sent a message to camp through a man for armed men to come to him. He took the cacique by the hand while conversing with him very courteously and with some of the principal Indians who were with him drew him from the town to a level road, and within sight of the camp whence the Christians begun gradually to come under an innocent guise and to take position round about. Thus the governor led the cacique and his principal men until he got into the camp with them. When near his tent, he ordered them to be placed under guard and told them that they could not go until giving him a guide and Indians for carrying and until some sick Christians should come from Chiaha whom he had ordered to come down the river in canoes, and those also whom he had sent to the province of Chisca, who had not yet come. He feared lest the Indians had killed both parties. Three days afterward they came. Those from Chisca said that the Indians had taken them through a land so poor in maize and so rough and with such lofty mountains that it was impossible for the camp to march through it; and seeing that the road was getting long and they were greatly delayed, they considered it advisable to return from a small, poor village where they saw nothing that might be of use. They brought a cowskin which the Indians gave them, as soft as the skin of a kid, with hair like that of the soft wool of sheep between that of the common and that of the merino. The cacique furnished a guide and tamemes, and with the governor's permission went away. The governor set forth from Coste on July 9 and went to sleep at a town called Cali. The cacique came out to meet him on the road and spoke as follows:

"Excellent lord Prince, worthy of being served and obeyed by all the princes of the world. Just as one can judge in greater part of the inner virtue by the face, and since who you are and your power have been known to me before now, I do not wish to bear the consequence of how small I am in your presence by expecting that my poor services will be pleasing and acceptable, for where the strength fails, it is not unbecoming for the good-will to be praised and received. On this account I dare to beg your Lordship only to consider and observe in this your land in which you command, how I may serve you." The governor answered him saying that he thanked him as much for his goodwill and tenders as if he had offered him all the riches of the world, and that he would always be protected and esteemed by him as a true brother. The cacique ordered brought thither the provisions needed for the two days the governor should be there; and at the time of his leaving he made him service of four Indian women and two Indian men who were needed as carriers. The governor marched for six days, passing through many towns subject to the cacique of Coça, and as he entered his lands, many Indians daily came to him on the way on the part of the cacique with messages, some going, others coming. He reached Coça on Friday, July 16. The cacique came out to welcome him two crossbow-flights from the town in a carrying chair borne on the shoulders of his principal men, seated on a cushion, and covered with a robe of marten skins of the form and size of a woman's shawl. He wore a crown of feathers on his head; and round about him were many Indians playing and singing. As soon as he came to the governor, he saluted him and addressed the following words to him:

"Excellent and powerful Lord, superior to all those of the earth: Although now I come to welcome you, long ago I have welcomed you in my heart, namely, from the day on which I heard of your Lordship. With so great a desire, joy, and happiness to serve you, what I show is nothing compared to what I feel, nor could it have any comparison. You may consider it as true that to receive dominion over the world would not gladden me so much as does the sight of you; nor should I consider it as great happiness. Do not expect me to offer you what is yours, namely, my person, lands and vassals. I wish only to occupy myself in commanding my people to welcome you with all diligence and due reverence from this place to the town with music and singing, where your Lordship will be lodged and served by me and by them; and you will do with all I possess as though it were your own for, if your Lordship so do, I shall be favored." The governor thanked him, and both talking together very joyfully, they went on to the town. He ordered his Indians to move out of their dwellings, in which the governor and his men were lodged. In the barbacoas and fields there was a great quantity of maize and beans. The land was very populous and had many large towns and planted fields which reached from one town to the other. It was a charming and fertile land, with good cultivated fields stretching along the rivers. In the open fields were many plums, both those of Spain and those of the land, and grapes along the rivers on vines climbing up into the trees. Beyond the streams were the low stocks of large, sweet grapes, but because they were not cultivated or well taken care of, they had large seeds. The governor was accustomed to place a guard over the caciques so that they might not go away, and took them along with him until leaving their land; for by taking them, the people would await in their towns and they would give a guide and Indians as carriers. Before departing from their lands, he would give them leave to return to their homes—as well as the tamemes— as soon as he reached another dominion where others were given to him. Those of Coça seeing their lord detained, thought ill of it and revolted and went away to hide themselves in the woods—both those of their lord's town and those of other chief towns, who were his vassals. The governor sent four captains, each in a different direction, to look for them. They seized many Indians, men and women, who were put in chains. Upon seeing the harm they received and how little they gained in absenting themselves, they came, saying that they wished to serve in whatever might be commanded them. Some of the principal men among those imprisoned were set free on petition of the cacique. Of the rest, each man took away as slaves those he had in chains, without allowing them to go to their lands. Nor did any of them return except some whose good fortune and assiduous industry aided them, who managed to file off their chains at night; or some, who were able, while on the march, to wander away from the road upon observing any lack of care in their guard, who went off with their chains and with their loads and the clothes they were carrying.

Chapter XVII.
How the governor went from Coça to Tastaluca.

The governor rested in Coça for twenty-five days. He set out on Friday, August 20, to look for a province, by name, Tascaluca, taking the cacique of Coça with him. That day he passed through a large town called Tallimuchase, which was without people. He went to sleep a half league beyond near a stream. Next day he reached a town called Ytaua, subject to Coça. He stayed there for six days because of a river which ran hard by the town, and was swollen at that time. As soon as the river allowed crossing, he set out, and went to sleep at a town called Ullibahali. Ten or twelve of the principal Indians, all with feather plumes, and with bows and arrows, came to him on the road bearing a message on the part of the cacique of that province, to offer themselves to him. The governor, on reaching the town with twelve horse and some foot belonging to his guard, for he had left his men a crossbow-flight from town, entered therein and found all the Indians under arms; and judging from their manner, he thought them evilly disposed. It was learned later that they had concerted to take the cacique of Coça out of the governor's possession, if he should request this of them. The governor ordered all his men to enter the town which was enclosed and near which flowed a small river. The enclosure, like that in other towns seen there afterward, was of thick logs, set solidly close together in the ground, and many long poles as thick as an arm placed crosswise. The height of the enclosure was that of a good lance, and it was plastered within and without and had loopholes. On the other side of the river was a town where the cacique was at the time. The governor ordered him to be summoned and he came immediately. After exchanging some verbal promises with the governor, he gave him the necessary tamemes and thirty Indian women as slaves. A Christian of noble parentage, named Manzano, a native of Salamanca, who wandered away to look for grapes which are abundant and excellent

there, was lost in that place. On the day the governor set out thence, he went to sleep at a town subject to the lord of Ullibahalli, and next day reached another called Toasi. The Indians gave the governor thirty Indian women and the necessary tamemes. He marched ordinarily five or six leagues daily when going through a peopled region, and as much as he could through a depopulated region, in order to avoid the necessity of a lack of maize. From Toasi, passing through some towns subject to a cacique, the lord of a province called Tallise, he marched for five days. He reached Talise on September 18. The town was large and was located near a deep river. On the other side of the river were other towns and many fields of maize. On both sides, it was a land very well supplied with maize in abundance. They had abandoned the town. The governor ordered the cacique summoned. He came and an exchange of words of courtesy and of promises took place between them. He gave him the service of forty Indians. At that town one of the principal Indians came to the governor in the name of the cacique of Tascaluca and spoke to him as follows:

"Very powerful, virtuous, and esteemed Lord: The great cacique of Tascaluca, my lord, orders me to kiss your Lordship's hands and to report to you that he is aware that you deservedly excel all those of the land, because of your perfections and power; that all, wherever your Lordship goes, serve and obey you, which he knows is your due. He desires as he does life to see and serve your Lordship. Therefore, he sends to offer with his person his land and his vassals, in order that whenever your Lordship should please to go through his lands, you may be received in all peace and love, and be served and obeyed; and that as payment of this desire which he has to serve you, you grant him the favor of informing him when you will come, for the earlier you come the greater favor and happiness will he receive." The governor received and dismissed him graciously, giving him some beads (which were not much regarded among them) and other pieces of cloth to take to his lord; and gave the cacique of Coça permission to return to his lands. The cacique of Tallise gave him the tamemes necessary; and after resting there for twenty days he set out for Tascaluca. The day he left Tallise, he went to sleep at a large town called Casiste, and next day he passed through another town and reached a small town of Tascaluca. The next day he slept in a wood two leagues from the town where the cacique lived and was at that time. He sent the maestre de campo, Luis de Moscoso, with fifteen horse to inform him that he was coming. The cacique was in his dwelling under a balcony. Outside, in front of his dwelling, on an elevated place, was spread a mat for him and on it two cushions, one above the other, where he came to seat himself. His Indians gathered about him, separated somewhat, so that they formed a court-yard and open space where he was—his most principal Indians being nearest him, and one holding a sort of fan of deerskin which kept the sun from him, round and the size of a shield, quartered with the black and white, and with a cross made in the middle. From a distance it looked like taffeta, for the colors were very perfect. It was set on a small and very long staff. This was the device he bore in his wars. He was a man, very tall of body, large limbed, lean, and well built. He was greatly feared by his neighbors and vassals. He was lord of many lands and many people. In his aspect he was very dignified. After the maestre de campo talked with him, he and his men came, galloped their horses in front of him, turning them from one side to the other, and at times toward the cacique. He with great gravity and unconcern from time to time raised his eyes and looked as if in disdain. The governor arrived but he made no movement to arise. The governor took him by the hand and both went to seat themselves on a seat below the balcony. The cacique spoke to him as follows:

"Powerful Lord: May the coming of your Lordship be very propitious. At sight of you, I receive as great pleasure and happiness as if you were one of my brothers whom I hold in great affection. Regarding this, it is unnecessary to discuss further, for it is not wise to utter in many words what can be said in few; for as it is one's desire that determines deeds, and deeds give testimony of truth, therefore you will perceive how determined and clear is my will to serve you, and how pure my motive. The favor which you showed me by reason of the pieces of cloth which you sent me, I esteem as much as it is proper to esteem them, and chiefly because they were yours. Now, see in what you may command me to serve you." The governor made him happy with pleasing and very brief words. When he set out thence, he determined, for several reasons, to take him with him. After a march of two days he reached a town called Piache. Near it flowed a large river. The governor asked the Indians for canoes. They said that they did not have any, but that they would make rafts of canes and dry wood on which he could cross. Diligently and quickly they made them and steered them; and since the water was quiet, the governor and his men crossed in great safety. From the port of Espiritu Santo to Palache—a distance of about one hundred leagues—from south to north; and from east to west; from Apalache to Cutifachiqui—a distance of about four hundred and thirty leagues—from southwest to northeast; from Cutifachiqui to Jualla—a distance of about two hundred and fifty leagues—from south to north; and from Jualla to Tascaluca—a distance of about two hundred and fifty leagues also—he marched one hundred and ninety from east to west, namely, to the province of Coça, and sixty from Coça to Tascaluca from north to south. After crossing the river of Piache, a Christian left the ranks there and went to look for an Indian woman who had escaped from him, and the Indians captured or killed him. The governor urged the cacique to inform him of the man and threatened him that if he did not appear, he would never let him go. The cacique sent an Indian from that place to Mavilla, whither they were marching—a town of one of the principal Indians, his vassal—saying that he was sending him to advise him to have provisions prepared and Indians for carrying; but as it afterward appeared he ordered him to assemble there all the warriors whom he had in his land. The governor marched for three days, the third day through a continuously peopled region. He reached Mavilla on Monday, the eighteenth of October, he going in the vanguard with fifteen horse and thirty foot. A Christian, whom he had sent with a message to the chief three or four days before, in order that the latter might not go away, and also in order to see the disposition of the Indians, came out of the town. He told him that it appeared to him that they were evilly disposed, because when he was there many men and many arms had entered the town and they had made great haste to strengthen the stockade. Luis de Moscoso told the governor that it would be well to camp in the open field since the Indians were so disposed. The governor answered that he would lodge in the town, and that he was tired out with sleeping in the open field. On his arrival near the town, the cacique came out to welcome him with many Indians playing music and singing, and after tendering his services to him, gave him three blankets of marten skin. The governor, with the caciques and with seven or eight men from his guard, and three or four horse, who dismounted in order to accompany him, entered the town and seated himself under a balcony. The cacique of Tascaluca asked him to let him stay in that town and not to give him more trouble of marching; and seeing by his talk that he did not grant him permission, changed his purpose and dissembling, pretended that he wished to talk with some of the principal Indians. He rose from the place where he was with the governor, and entered a house where were many Indians with their bows and arrows. When the governor saw that he did not come, he called him, but he said that he would not come out of there and that he would not leave that town and that if he wished to go in peace he should go immediately and should not insist on trying to take him out of his lands and dominion by force.

Chapter XVIII.
How the Indians rose against the governor and of what happened.

The governor, on seeing the determination and furious reply of the cacique, endeavored to soothe him with pleasant words. To them he made no reply but, on the contrary, he withdrew very haughtily and disdainfully to a place where the governor could not see or talk with him. As one of the principal Indians was passing that place, the governor called him to him in order to send him to tell him that he could stay and welcome in his land, but that he should consider it well to have a guide and Indians for carrying sent him, in order to see whether he could pacify him with soft words. The Indian with great haughtiness said that he would not do it. Baltasar de Gallegos, who was there, seized him roughly by a cloak of marten skin which he wore as a covering, but he slipped it off over his head and left it in his hands. And because all the Indians straightway rose in revolt, Baltasar de Gallegos gave him a slash which opened up his back. Immediately, all the Indians came out from the houses shouting loudly and discharging their arrows. The governor see-

ing that he could not escape if he stayed there, and that if he should order his men who were outside the town to enter, the Indians could kill the horses for him from inside the houses and do much damage, went out running; but before getting out of town, he fell two or three times and those who were with him helped him to rise. He and those with him were severely wounded. In the town five Christians were immediately slain. The governor went out from the town shouting for all his men to go outside, for they were doing him much damage from the stockade. The Indians seeing that the Christians were withdrawing but some or most of them nevertheless at a walk, with great boldness continued to shoot at them and to bring down those they could overtake. The Indians, whom the Christians were bringing in chains, had set down their loads near the stockade, and as soon as the governor and his men became separated, those of Mavilla put the loads on their backs and took them within the town and immediately freed them from their chains and gave them bows and arrows with which to fight. In this way they got possession of all the clothing and pearls, and everything the Christians had and which their Indians were carrying for them. And inasmuch as the Indians had been peaceful thitherto, some were bringing their weapons in the packs and were left without arms. From others of those who had entered with the governor, they took away their swords and halberds and fought therewith. When the governor found himself in the open field, he asked for a horse, and with some men who accompanied him, turned about and struck two or three Indians through with a lance. Most of the Indians withdrew into the town and continued to shoot their arrows from the stockade. Those who dared would insolently go out to fight for the distance of a stone's throw; and from there would again retire from time to time when the Christians turned on them. At the time when the return began, there were a friar and a secular priest in the town, as well as a servant of the governor with a slave woman, and they did not have time to go outside but shut themselves in their house. Thus they remained inside the town after the Indians got control of it. They closed the door with a grating; and they had one sword among them, which the governor's servant owned. He stationed himself behind the door with it, thrusting at the Indians who tried to effect an entrance; with the friar and the secular priest, on the other side, each with a club in his hands, to strike down whomever might first enter. The Indians, seeing that they could not enter through the door, began to uncover the house at the top. At this time, all the horse and foot who came marching behind, happened to reach Mavilla. They were of different opinions there as to whether they should attack the Indians in order to enter into the town or whether this should be avoided as the entrance was doubtful, but at last, it was decided to attack them.

Chapter XIX.
How the governor drew his men up in order and entered the town of Mavilla.

As soon as the battle line and rearguard reached Mavilla, the governor ordered all those who were best armed to dismount and made four companies of foot. The Indians, on seeing how the governor was drawing up his men, urged the cacique to leave, telling him, as was later learned from some Indian women who were captured there, that he was only one man and could fight for one only; that there were many principal men of the Indians there, very daring and skilful in matters of war, any of whom could direct all the other men; that since matters of war and victory were a hazard of fortune and there was no certainty as to which of the sides would be victorious, he should endeavor to place his person in safety, so that if they should end their lives there as they had resolved to do rather than allow themselves to be vanquished, he would be left to govern the land. However, he refused to go, but so much did they urge him that he went out of the town with twenty or thirty of his Indians. From the clothing of the Christians he took a scarlet cloak and some other pieces—all that he could carry and which pleased him most. The governor was advised that the Indians were going out of the town, and he ordered those who were mounted to surround it. In each foot company, he ordered a soldier with a firebrand to set fire to the houses so that the Indians would have no shelter. Having arranged all his men in order, he ordered an arquebus fired. At the signal, all four companies, each in its own position, attacked with great fury and doing great damage entered the town from one side and the other. The friar and the secular priest and those who were with them in the house, were rescued,

which cost the life of two men of ability and courage who went thither to help them. The Indians fought with so great spirit that they drove us outside again and again. It took them so long to get back that many of the Christians, tired out and suffering great thirst, went to get a drink at a pond located near the stockade, but it was tinged with the blood of the dead and they returned to the fight. The governor seeing this, with those who accompanied him, entered the town on horseback together with the returning foot. This gave an opportunity for the Christians to succeed in setting fire to the houses and overthrow and defeat the Indians. As the latter fled outside the town from those on foot, those on horse again drove them within the gates, where having lost hopes of escape, they fought courageously; and after the Christians had come among them cutting with the sword, seeing that they were assailed beyond repair, many fled into the burning houses where piled up one on top of the other they were suffocated and burned to death. In all, those who were killed there numbered two thousand five hundred or thereabout. Of the Christians eighteen were killed there, one of whom was Don Carlos, the governor's brother-in-law, another, his nephew, another, Juan Gamez, Mem Rodríguez, a Portuguese, and Juan Vázquez of Villanova de Barcarota—all men of honor and pride. The others were foot soldiers. Besides those killed, one hundred and fifty Christians were wounded, receiving seven hundred arrow wounds. It was God's will that they were healed shortly of very dangerous wounds. Twelve horses were also killed and seventy wounded. All the clothing carried by the Christians, the ornaments for saying mass, and the pearls were all burned there. The Christians set fire to them; for they considered as more annoying the hurt which the Indians could do them from within the houses where everything was gathered together. The governor learned there that Francisco Maldonado was awaiting him in the port of Ochuse and that it was six days' journey from there. He arranged with Juan Ortiz that he should keep still about it, so that the men might not oppose his determination, and because the pearls which he desired to send to Cuba as samples had been burned; for if the news were noised about the men might desire to go to that land. And fearing that if news were heard of him, unless they saw gold or silver, or anything of value, it would acquire such a reputation that no man would desire to go thither when people might be needed, consequently, he determined not to give news of himself so long as he did not find a rich land.

Chapter XX.
How the governor set out from Mavilla for Chicaça, and of what happened to him.

From the time the governor entered Florida until leaving Mavilla, one hundred and two Christians had died, some, of their illnesses and others being killed by the Indians. He remained in Mavilla for twenty-eight days because of the wounded, during which he was always in the open field. It was a very populous and fertile land. There were some large enclosed towns and a considerable population scattered about over the field, the houses being separated from one another one or two crossbow-flights. On Sunday, November 18, now that it was learned that our wounded men were getting well, the governor set out from Mavilla, all the men having provided themselves with maize for two days. They marched for five days through an unpeopled region, and arrived at a province called Pafallaya and a town called Taliepatava. Thence, they went to another town by name Cabusto, near which flowed a large river. The Indians on the other side of it gave loud cries, telling the Christians that if they crossed over the river to them they would have to kill them. The governor ordered a piragua built inside the town, so that the Indians might not perceive it. It was made in four days. When it was finished, he ordered it to be transported one night a half league up stream. In the morning, thirty well armed men entered it. The Indians perceived what was being planned and those who were nearest ran up to forbid the crossing. They resisted it as well as they could until the Christians were near them; and seeing that the piragua was about to land fled through some canebrakes. The Christians mounted their horses and went upstream to assure a crossing where the governor, with all those who remained with him, crossed over. Along the river, were some towns well provided with maize and beans. From that place to Chicaça, the governor marched for five days through an unpopulated region. He reached a river where some Indians on the other side tried to forbid him crossing. In two days another piragua was made. When it was finished, the governor ordered an Indian to announce to the cacique that he should desire his friendship and should await him peacefully. But the Indians on the other side of the river killed him in his sight, and immediately went away uttering loud cries. Having crossed the river next day, December 17, the governor reached Chicaça, a small town of twenty houses. After they were in Chicaça they suffered great hardships and cold, for it was already winter, and most of the men were lodged in the open field in the snow before having any place where they could build houses. This land was very well peopled, the population being spread out as was that of Mavilla. It was fertile and abounding in maize, most of this being still in the fields. The amount necessary for passing the winter was gathered. Certain Indians were captured, among whom was one who was greatly esteemed by the cacique. By means of an Indian the governor sent word to the cacique that he desired to see him and wished his friendship. The cacique came to offer himself to him, together with his person, land, and vassals. He said that he would cause two caciques to come in peace. A few days afterward they came with him accompanied by their Indians, one being named Alimamu and the other Nicalasa. They presented the governor with one hundred and fifty rabbits and some clothing of their land, namely blankets and skins. The cacique of Chicaça came to visit him frequently and sometimes the governor ordered him summoned and sent him a horse to go and come. He made complaint to him, that one of his vassals had risen against him withholding his tribute and asked that he protect him against him, saying that he was about to go to seek him in his land and punish him as he deserved—all pretense, for it was planned that while the governor went with him and the camp was divided into two parts, some would attack the governor and others those who remained in Chicaça. He went to the town where he lived and came with two hundred Indians with their bows and arrows. The governor took thirty horse and eighty foot and went to Saquechuma, as the province of the principal man was called, who he told him had rebelled against him. They found an enclosed town which had been abandoned by the Indians and those who were with the cacique set fire to the houses in order to conceal their treachery. But since the men taken by the governor were very watchful and prudent, as well as those who remained in Chicaça, on that occasion they did not dare attack us. The governor invited the cacique and certain of the principal Indians and gave them some pork to eat. And although they were not accustomed to it, they lusted after it so much that Indians would come nightly to certain houses a crossbow-shot away from the camp where the hogs were sleeping and kill and carry off as many as they could. Three Indians were seized in the act, two of whom the governor ordered to be shot with arrows and the hands of the other cut off. In that condition he sent him to the cacique, who expressed regret that they had troubled the governor and was glad that justice had been executed on them. He was in an open plain a half league from where the Christians were. Four of the horsemen went thither without orders, namely, Francisco Osorio, a servant of the marquis de Astorga, named Reynoso, and two servants of the governor, one his page, named Ribera, and the other his chamberlain, named Fuentes. They seized some skins and blankets from the Indians, at which the latter were greatly offended and abandoned their houses. The governor learned of it and ordered them seized. Francisco Osorio and the chamberlain, he sentenced to death, as being the principals, and all to the loss of their possessions. The friars and secular priests and other principal persons importuned him to leave Francisco Osorio alive, and to moderate the sentence, which he refused to do for any one. And while he was already giving the order to take them to the public place to behead them, certain Indians came who had been sent by the cacique to make complaint against them. Juan Ortiz, at the request of Baltasar de Gallegos and other persons, changed their words, telling the governor that the cacique said that he had learned that his Lordship had seized those Christians on his account; that they were not guilty, nor had they done any wrong to him; that if he would do him a favor, he should let them go free. To the Indians, he was to say that the governor said that he had seized them and would give them such punishment that it would be an example to others. The governor ordered the prisoners released. As soon as March was come, he determined to leave Chicaça and asked the cacique for two hundred tamemes. The latter

replied to him that he would talk it over with his principal men. On Tuesday, the eighth of March, the governor went to where the cacique was to ask him for the tamemes. He said he would send them next day. As soon as the governor came to Chicaça, he told Luis de Moscoso, the maestre de campo, that the Indians looked ill disposed to him, and that that night he should keep careful watch, which the latter heeded but slightly. The Indians came at the quarter of the modorra in four companies, each company coming from a different direction. As soon as they were perceived, they beat a drum, and with loud cries rushed forward, and so rapidly that they arrived at the same time as the spies who had carelessly gone out a distance from the camp; and when they were perceived by those who were within the town, half the houses were burning from the fire which they kindled. That night, three horsemen were by chance at watch, two of whom were of low degree, the most worthless of the camp, and the other was the governor's nephew, who until then had been considered a good man. There he proved himself as cowardly as each one of them, for they all fled and the Indians not finding any resistance came and set fire to the town and awaited the Christians outside behind the doors, who came out of the houses without having time to arm themselves; and as they rose, maddened by the noise and blinded by the smoke and flame of the fire they did not know where they were going nor did they succeed in getting their arms or in putting saddle on horse; neither did they see the Indians who were shooting at them. Many of the horses were burned in their stables, and those which could break their halters freed themselves. The confusion and rout were of such a nature that each one fled wherever it seemed safest, without any one resisting the Indians. But God who punishes His own as is His pleasure, and in the greatest needs and dangers holds them in His hand blinded the Indians so that they might not see what they had done, and they thought that the horses which were running about loose were the horsemen gathering together to assault them. The governor alone, and with him a soldier called Tapia, got mounted and attacked the Indians, and giving the first one he met a thrust with his lance, went down and his saddle with him; for in the haste he had badly fastened the girth and fell from his horse. All the men who were afoot and were in flight through a wood outside the town, sought protection there. And as it was night and the Indians thought the horses, as abovesaid, were mounted men who were attacking them, they fled away and only one remained there dead, namely, the one the governor had struck with his lance. The town was consumed by fire. A woman was burned there who had gone there with her husband. Both of them going outside the house, she returned for some pearls which they had forgotten; and when she tried to get out, already the fire was at the door and she could not, and her husband could not help her. Three other Christians got away from their houses so badly hurt by the fire that one of them died three days later and each of the other two was carried for many days in his bed upon some poles which the Indians carried on their shoulders, for they could not have journeyed in any other way. In that turn of fortune eleven Christians and fifty horses died. Of the swine, one hundred were left, and four hundred were burned. If, perchance, any one still had had any clothing left from the fire at Mavilla, it was now all burned up in that place; and many were naked, as they had no time to snatch their jerkins. There they endured great suffering from the cold, for which they got relief in large fires. The whole night was passed turning from one side to the other without sleeping, for if they were warmed on one side they froze on the other. They managed to make some mats out of dry grass, woven together, and placed one mat below and the other above. Many laughed at this contrivance, but afterward necessity forced them to do likewise. The Christians were become so demoralized, together with the lack of saddles and weapons, which had been burned, that if the Indians had returned the second night, they would have routed them with little trouble. They moved thence to the village where the cacique usually lived as it was a site in the open field. A week later they had made many saddles and lances. There were some ash trees there from which they were made as good as those of Vizcaya.

Chapter XXI.
How the Indians again attacked the Christians; and how the governor went to Alimamu, where they awaited him on the way to the fight.

On Wednesday, the 15th of March, 1541, after the governor had been for a week in a level field, a half league from the place where he had lodged during the winter, having already set up a forge and having tempered the swords which had been burned in Chicaça and having made many shields, saddles, and lances, on Tuesday night, at the hour of dawn, many Indians came to attack the camp, formed into three companies, each company coming from a different direction. Those who were on watch sounded the alarm. The governor, with great quickness, drew up his men in order in three other companies, with some men staying behind to guard the camp, and hastened to the attack. The Indians were thrown into confusion and took to flight. The land was flat and suitable for the Christians to profit thereby. Already the dawn had come bright and clear, but there was some confusion which was the reason why they did not kill thirty or forty more Indians, namely, a friar in the camp raised a loud cry "To the camp! To the camp!" without any reason for so crying out. On that account, the governor and all the men ran to the rescue, and the Indians had time to get away safely. Some Indians were captured, from whom the governor got information relative to the land beyond. On April 25, he left Chicaça and went to sleep at a small village called Alimamu. It had very little maize and it was necessary after leaving there to commit themselves to an unpopulated region for seven days' journey. Next day, the governor sent three captains with horse and foot—each one taking a different direction—to search out provisions in order to cross the unpopulated region. Juan de Añasco, the accountant, went with fifteen horse and forty foot along the road where the governor was to go, and found a strong stockade where the Indians were waiting. On top of it, were many armed men, daubed over with red ocher and with their bodies, legs, and arms painted black, white, yellow, and red, in the manner of stripes which made them look as though they were in breeches and doublet. Some had feather plumes on their heads and others horns, with their faces black and the eyes ringed round in red in order to look more ferocious. As soon as they saw the Christians approach, with loud cries and beating two drums, they came out in great fury to meet them. It seemed best to Juan de Añasco and those with him to keep away from them and to inform the governor. They withdrew over a level ground for the distance of a crossbow-flight from the stockade and in sight of it. The men of foot, the crossbowmen, and those having shields placed themselves before the horsemen so that the horses might not be wounded. The Indians came out by sevens and eights to shoot their arrows and then to retire. In sight of the Christians, they made a fire and seized an Indian—one by the feet and others by the head and pretended they were going to throw him into the fire, first giving him many blows on the head, signifying that so they would do to the Christians. Juan de Añasco sent three horse to inform the governor. The latter came immediately and since he thought he should drive them thence saying that if he did not do so, they would become emboldened to attack him at a time when they could do him more hurt, he ordered the horsemen to dismount and having divided them into four companies gave the signal and they attacked the Indians. The latter resisted until the Christians reached the stockade; and as soon as they saw that they could not defend themselves they fled along a way where a stream flowed near the stockade, and from the other shore shot some arrows. And inasmuch as no crossing was found for the horses for the time being, they had time to get away. Three Indians were killed there and many Christians were wounded, fifteen of whom died on the march a few days later. It seemed to all that the governor was much to blame in not having had an examination made of the disposition of the land which lay on the other side of the stream and of ascertaining the crossing before attacking them; for with their hope of escaping by flight in that direction whenever they might not be seen by his men, they fought until they were routed; and they were thus enabled to defend themselves until then and to offend the Christians with safety.

Chapter XXII.
How the governor went from Alimamu to Quizquiz and thence to a large river.

Three days having passed since they had looked for some maize (and it was little that was found in proportion to what was needed), and for this reason, even though rest was needed because of the wounded, on account of the great need of finding a place where there was maize, the governor was obliged to set out immediately for Quizquiz. He marched seven days through an unpopulated region of many swamps and thick woods, but all passable on horseback except several marshes or swamps which were crossed by

swimming. He reached the town of Quizquiz without being perceived. He seized all the people of the town before they got out of their houses. The cacique's mother was captured there, and then he sent to him one of the Indians who had been seized there, bidding him come to see him and that he would give him his mother and all the other people who had been taken there. For reply, he said that his Lordship should order them released and sent and that he would come to visit and serve him. Inasmuch as his men were ill and weary for lack of maize and the horses were also weak, he determined to pleasure him, in order to see whether he could have peace with him. So he ordered the mother and all the others released and dispatched them and sent them with words of kindness. Next day when the governor was awaiting the cacique, many Indians came with their bows and arrows with the intention of attacking the Christians. The governor ordered all the horsemen to be armed and mounted and all in readiness. When the Indians saw that they were on guard, they stopped a crossbow-flight from the spot where the governor was, near a stream, and after they had stayed there for a half hour, six of the principal Indians came to the camp and said that they were come to see what people they were and that they had learned from their ancestors that a white race would inevitably subdue them; and that they were about to return to the cacique to tell him to come immediately to render obedience and service to the governor. And after offering him six or seven skins and blankets which they brought they took leave of him and together with the others, who were waiting on the shore, returned. The cacique did not again come nor did he send another message. Inasmuch as there was little maize in the town where the governor was, he moved to another town located a half league from the large river where maize was found in abundance. He went to see the river and found there was an abundance of timber near it from which piraguas could be constructed and an excellently situated land for establishing the camp. He immediately moved thither, houses were built, and the camp was established on a level place, a crossbow-flight from the river. All the maize of all the towns behind was collected there and the men set to work immediately to cut timber and square the planks for canoes. Immediately the Indians came down the river, landed, and told the governor that they were vassals of a great lord called

Aquiro, who was lord of many towns and people on the other side of the river. On his behalf they informed him that he would come the next day with all his men to see what his Lordship would command him. Then next day, the cacique came with two hundred canoes full of Indians with their bows and arrows, painted with red ocher and having great plumes of white and many colored feathers on either side and holding shields in their hands with which they covered the paddlers, while the warriors were standing from prow to stern with their bows and arrows in their hands. The canoe in which the cacique came had an awning spread in the stern and he was seated under the canopy. Also other canoes came bearing other Indian notables. The chief from his position under the canopy, controlled and gave orders to the other men. All the canoes were together and came to within a stone's throw from the bluff. From there, the cacique told the governor, who was walking along the river with others whom he had brought with him, that he had come to visit him and to serve and obey him, for he had heard that he was the greatest and most powerful lord of all the earth and that he should bethink him in what to command him. The governor thanked him and asked him to land so that they might better be able to talk, but without answering this, he ordered three canoes to come up in which he brought a quantity of fish and loaves made of the pulp of plums in the shape of bricks. All having been received, he thanked him and again asked him to land. But since his intent was to see whether he might do some damage by means of that pretense, upon seeing that the governor and his men were on their guard, they began to withdraw from land. With loud cries, the crossbowmen who were ready, shot at them and struck five or six. They withdrew in splendid order; no one abandoned his paddle even though the one near him fell. Flaunting themselves, they retired. Afterward they came frequently and landed, and when they went toward them, they would return to their canoes. Those canoes were very pleasing to see, for they were very large and well built; and together with the awnings, the plumes of feathers, the shields, and banners, and the many men in them, they had the appearance of a beautiful fleet of galleys. During the thirty days the governor was there, they made four piraguas, in three of which, one early morning three hours before it

became light, he ordered a dozen horse to enter, four to each one—men whom he was confident would succeed in gaining the land in spite of the Indians and assure the crossing or die in doing it—and with them some of foot—crossbowmen and rowers—to place them on the other side. In the other piragua, he ordered Juan de Guzmán to cross with men of foot, he having become captain in place of Francisco Maldonado. And because the current was strong, they went up stream along the shore for a quarter of a league and in crossing they were carried down with the current of the river and went to land opposite the place where the camp was. At a distance of two stones' throw before reaching shore, the men of horse went from the piraguas on horseback to a sandy place of hard sand and clear ground where all the men landed without any accident. As soon as those who crossed first were on the other side, the piraguas returned immediately to where the governor was and, in two hours after the sun was up, all the men finished crossing. It was nearly a half league wide, and if a man stood still on the other side, one could not tell whether he were a man or something else. It was of great depth and of very strong current. Its water was always turgid and continually many trees and wood came down it borne along by the force of the water and current. It had abundance of fish of various kinds, and most of them different from those of the fresh waters of Spain as will be told hereafter.

Chapter XXIII.
How the governor went from Aquixo to Casqui and thence to Pacha; and how that land differs from that behind.

Having got across the great river, the governor marched a league and a half and reached a large town of Aquixo, which was abandoned before his arrival. Over a plain they saw thirty Indians coming whom the cacique had sent to learn what the Christians were intending to do, but as soon as the latter had sight of them they fled. Those of horse pursued them killing ten and capturing fifteen. And since the town whither the governor was marching, was near the river, he sent a captain with the men he deemed sufficient to take the piraguas up stream. And because by land they frequently turned away from the river in order to get around arms which thrust out of the river, the Indians had opportunity to attack those in the piraguas and put us in great danger. For, because of the strong current of the river, they did not dare to go any distance from land and they shot arrows at them from the bluff. As soon as the governor reached the town, he immediately sent some crossbowmen down stream who were to come as his rear-guard. When the piraguas reached the town, he ordered them taken apart and the nails kept for other piraguas when they might be needed. He slept there one night and next day marched in search of a province called Pacha, which he was informed lay near Chisca where the Indians said there was gold. He marched through large towns in Aquixo which had been abandoned for fear of the Christians. From some Indians who were captured, he learned that a great cacique lived three days' journey thence, called Casqui. He reached a small river where a bridge was made on which he crossed. On that day, they walked continually through water until sunset, which in places reached to the middle and in places to the knee. When they came to dry land, they were very glad, for it seemed to them that they would be walking about lost through the water all night. At noon they arrived at the first town of Casqui. They found the Indians off guard for they had not heard of them. Many Indians, both men and women, were seized, besides a quantity of clothing—blankets and skins—both in the first town and in another which was within sight of it in an open field a half league from it, whither the horsemen had galloped. That land is more high, dry, and level than the land of the river behind which they had thus far seen. In the open field were many walnut trees with soft nuts shaped like acorns; and in the houses were found many which the Indians had stored away. The walnut trees do not differ in any other way from those of Spain, nor from those seen before except only in having a smaller leaf. There were many mulberry trees and plum trees having red plums like those of Spain, and others gray, differing, but much better, and all the trees as verdant all year as if set out in gardens and in a clear grove. For two days the governor marched through the land of Casqui before arriving at the town where the cacique was, and most of the way continually through land of open field, very well peopled with large towns, two or three of which were to be seen from one town. He sent word to the cacique through an Indian that he was coming to where he was for the purpose of procuring his friendship and of considering him as a brother. To which he answered that he would be welcome, that he would receive him with special pleasure, and that he would do everything his Lordship ordered. He sent his offerings to him on the road, namely, skins and blankets and fish. After these gifts, the governor found all the towns through which he passed inhabited, in which the Indians were awaiting him peacefully and offered him blankets and skins and fish. The cacique, accompanied by many Indians came out from the town where he was living for a half league on the road to welcome the governor, and meeting him spoke as follows:

"Very lofty, powerful, and illustrious Lord: May the coming of Your Lordship be very propitious. As soon as I had notice of your Lordship, of your power and perfections, although you entered my land killing and making captive the inhabitants of it and my vassals, I resolved to conform my will to yours, and as yours to consider as good all that your Lordship might do; believing that it is proper that it might be so for some just consideration, in order to provide for some future event, revealed to your Lordship, but concealed from me; for, indeed, one evil may be permitted in order to avoid another greater evil, and therefrom good may result; which I believe will be so, for from so excellent a prince it is not right to presume that the nobility of your heart and the effect of your goodwill would allow you to permit an injustice. My capacity to serve you as your Lordship merits is so slight that if my goodwill should abundantly and humbly offer every kind of service, you would acquire no honor. In your Lordship's presence, I merit very little. But if it is proper that that capacity may be esteemed, may you receive it, and me and my land and vassals as your own, and of me and them make use according to your pleasure; for if I were lord of all the world, your Lordship would be received, served, and obeyed with the same goodwill." The governor replied to him fittingly and in few words made him happy. For a while after that, they both went on exchanging words generous in offers and of great courtesy, and he begging that he should lodge in his houses. The governor, in order to preserve peace better, excused himself, by saying that he preferred to lodge in the open field; and because the heat was very great, the camp was established a quarter league from the town among some trees. The cacique went to his town and returned with many Indians singing. As soon as they came to the governor, they all bowed themselves to the ground. Among them were two blind Indians. The cacique made a speech which, in order not to be prolix, I will relate in a few words only the substance of the matter. He said that since he was the son of the sun and a great lord, he begged him to do him the favor of giving health to those blind Indians. The blind men immediately rose and with great earnestness begged this of the governor. He replied saying that in the lofty heaven was He who had power to give them health and everything they might ask of Him; whose servant he was; and that that Lord made the heavens and the earth and man in His likeness; that He suffered on the tree of the true cross to save the human race, and rose again on the third day; that inasmuch as He was man He died, and inasmuch as He was divinity, He is immortal; that He ascended to heaven where He was with open arms in order to receive all those who wished to be converted to Him. He immediately ordered him to make a very high wooden cross which was set up in the highest part of the town, declaring to him that the Christians adored it in conformity to, and in memory of, that on which Christ suffered. The governor and his men knelt before it and the Indians did the same. The governor told him that thenceforth they should adore and beg the Lord, of whom he had told them and who was in the heaven, for everything of which they had need. He asked him how far it was from there to Pacaha. He said it was a day's journey and that on the edge of his lan was a marsh like an estuary which gave into the large river; that he would send men to build in advance a bridge by which he might cross. The day on which the governor left, he went to sleep at a town of Casqui; and the next day he passed in sight of the other towns and reached the swamp, which was half a crossbow-flight in width and very deep and flowing. When he reached it, the Indians had just finished building the bridge, which was constructed of wood in the manner of beams extending from tree to tree, and at one of the sides a line of wood higher than the bridge in order to support those who should cross. The cacique of Casqui went to the governor and took his men with him. The governor sent word by an Indian

to the cacique of Pacaha that although he was hostile to the cacique of Casqui and the latter should be there, he would make no quarrel with him or do him no harm if he waited peacefully and wished his friendship, but that he would treat him as a brother. The Indian whom the governor had sent came and said that the cacique gave no heed to what he had told him but that he had gone away in flight with all his people out of the other side of the town. The governor immediately entered and together with the men of horse charged ahead where the Indians were fleeing; and at another town situated a quarter of a league from that place captured many Indians. And as the horsemen captured them, they delivered them over to the Indians of Casqui, who being their enemies carefully and with great pleasure took them to the town where the Christians were; and the greatest sorrow they had was in not having permission to kill them. Many blankets, deer, lion, and bear skins, and many cat skins were found in town. Many were still poorly clad and there clothed themselves. From the blankets were made loose coats and cassocks; and some made gowns and lined them with the catskins, as well as the cassocks. From the deerskins were also made some jerkins, shirts, stockings, and shoes and from the bearskins very good cloaks, for water would not go through them. They found there shields made of raw cowhide with which the horses were provided with armor.

Chapter XXIV.
How the cacique of Pacaha came in peace, and he of Casqui went away and returned to excuse himself; and how the governor made him and the cacique of Pacaha friends.

On Wednesday, June 19, the governor entered Pacaha. He lodged in the town where the cacique lived, which was very large, enclosed, and furnished with towers; and in the towers and stockade many loopholes. In the town was abundance of old maize and new maize in the maize fields in great quantity. Located at a league and half a league were large towns, all enclosed. Where the governor was lodged, there was a large marsh which came near to the enclosure, and entered through a ditch round about the town so that but little of the town remained to enclose. A channel had been made from the marsh to the large river through which the fish entered the former. This the cacique had there for his recreation and pleasure. As many fish as they wished were caught with nets which were found in the town; and however many of them were drawn out, there was never lack of them found. In many other swamps thereabout, there were also many fish, but they were soft and not so good as those which came from the river, and most of them were different from those of the fresh water of Spain. There was a fish called "bagre," a third of which was head; and it had large spines like a sharp shoemaker's awl at either side of its throat and along the sides. Those of them which were in the water were as large as a "pico." In the river, there were some of one hundred and one hundred and fifty pounds. Many of them were caught with the hook. Another fish resembled the "barbel"; and others were like the "choupa," with a head like that of the "besugo" and between russet and brown. This was the one that was most relished. There was another fish called the "pexe palla." Its snout was a cubit in length and the tip of its upper lip was shaped like a shovel. There was another fish which resembled a shad. All had scales except the "bagres" and the "pexe palla." There was another fish which the Indians brought sometimes, of the size of a hog called "pexe perco". It had rows of teeth below and above. The cacique of Casqui frequently sent gifts of fish in abundance, and blankets, and skins. He told the governor that he would give the cacique of Pacaha into his hands. He went to Casqui, ordered many canoes brought up the river, while he went overland with many of his people. The governor, with forty of horse and sixty of foot took him with him up the river. His Indians who were in the canoes discovered where the cacique of Pacaha was on an islet between two arms of the river. Five Christians embarked in a canoe, among whom went Don Antonio Osorio, going ahead to see what people the cacique had with himself. There were five or six thousand souls on the islet. As soon as they saw them, thinking that the Indians in the canoes were Christians also, the cacique and those who belonged to three canoes they had there, fled in great haste to the other side of the river. The rest, in great fear and confusion, betook themselves hastily to the water swimming, where many people were drowned, principally women and children. Then the governor, who was on land, not knowing what was happening to Don Antonio

and those who went with him, ordered Christians and Indians to enter with great haste in the canoes of the Indians of Casqui; and they immediately went to Don Antonio on the islet where they captured many Indians—men and women—and a quantity of clothing, from the abundance of clothing which the Indians had in hurdles and on wooden rafts in order to take it across from the other side. It went floating down stream; and the Indians of Casqui filled their canoes with it. And fearing lest the Christians would seize it, the cacique and his men went down stream with them to his land without taking leave of the governor. On that account the governor was indignant at him. Immediately returning to Pacaha, two leagues away, along the road from Casqui, he made a raid, on which he seized twenty or thirty of his Indians. And because the horses were tired and there was no time to go farther that day, he returned to Pacaha, planning to attack Casqui from there three or four days later. He immediately released one of the Indians of Pacaha, and sent him to tell the cacique that if he wished for his friendship he should come to him and that they would go to make war on Casqui. Immediately many of the Indians of Pacaha came and brought an Indian under the name of cacique, which was revealed by a brother of the cacique who was a prisoner. The governor told the Indians that their lord should come, for he knew well that that one was not he, and that they could do nothing that he did not know before they thought of it. Next day came the cacique accompanied by many Indians bringing a gift of many fish, skins, and blankets. He made a talk which all were glad to hear and concluded by saying that even though his lordship had wrought damage to his land and vassals without him having deserved it, nevertheless he would not cease to be his, and would always be at his service. The governor ordered his brother and some others of the principal Indians whom he had captured to be released. That day came an Indian on the part of the cacique of Casqui and said that his lord would come immediately next day in order to beg pardon for the error he had committed in having gone away without the governor's permission. The governor told him to tell him that if he did not come in his own proper person he would go to get him and give him the punishment he deserved. Immediately next day came the cacique of Casqui, and made the governor a gift of many blankets, skins, and fish. He gave him one of his daughters, saying that his greatest desire was to unite his blood with that of so great a lord as he was. On that account he brought his daughter and begged him to take her as his wife. He made a long and discreet argument, praising him highly, and concluded by asking that he pardon him by the love of that cross which he had left him for having gone off without his permission; that he had gone away for shame of what his people had done without his consent. The governor answered him saying that he had taken a good protector and that if he had not come to beg pardon, he had planned to go to get him and burn his towns for him and kill him and his people and ravage his land for him. He replied to him saying: "Lord, I and mine are your Lordship's, and my land is yours. Therefore, if you should go, you would destroy your own land and kill your own people. All that comes to me from your hand, I shall receive as from my lord, both punishment and favor. Know that what you did for me in leaving me that cross, I consider a very notable thing and greater than I have ever deserved. For you will know that the maize fields of my lands were lost because of the great drouth; but as soon as I and my people knelt down before the cross and begged it for waters, our need was alleviated." The governor made him and the cacique of Pacaha friends and placed them at table with him so that they might eat with him. In regard to the seats, the caciques had a quarrel as to who was to sit at his right hand. The governor made peace between them by saying that among the Christians one side was accounted as the other, and that so they should consider it. Since they were his guests no one would pay any attention to them; and each should seat himself in the first seat he should find. Hence he sent thirty men of horse and fifty of foot to the province of Caluça to see whether they could bend back toward Chisca by that way where the Indians said there was a foundry for gold and copper. They went for seven days through an uninhabited region and returned after much hardship, eating green plums and maize stalks which they found in a poor town of six or seven houses. From there on toward the north, the Indians said that the land was very poorly inhabited because it was very cold, and that there were so many cattle that no field could be protected because of them, and that the Indians sustained themselves on their flesh. The governor, seeing that in that direction the land was so poor in maize that they could not sustain themselves, asked the Indians where the most populous district lay. They said that they had heard of a large province and of a very well provided land called Quiguate and it was toward the south.

Chapter XXV.
How the governor went from Pacaha to Quiguate and to Coligoa and arrived at Cayas.

The governor rested in Pacaha for forty days. During all that time, the two caciques gave him service of abundance of fish, blankets, and skins, and they tried to see which of them could perform the greater services. At the time of his departure, the cacique of Pacaha, gave two of his sisters to him, saying that if he would remember him he should take them as wives as a testimonial of love. The name of the one was Macanoche, and of the other Mochila. They were very well disposed, tall of body and plump in figure. Macanoche was of good appearance, and in her address and face appeared a lady; the other was robust. The cacique of Casqui ordered the bridge repaired, and the governor gave a turn through his land and lodged in the open field, near his town, whither he came with a quantity of fish and with two Indian women whom he exchanged with two Christians for two shirts. He gave a guide and tamemes. The governor went to sleep at one of his towns and next day at another near a river, where he ordered canoes brought for him in which to cross and with his permission returned. The governor took his way toward Aquiguate. On the fourth of August, he reached the town where the cacique was living. On the way, the latter sent him a service of many blankets and skins, but not daring to remain in the town went away. The town was the largest which had been seen in Florida. The governor and his men were lodged in the half of it; and a few days afterward seeing that the Indians were going about deceitfully, he ordered the other half burned, so that it might not afford them protection, if they came to attack him at night, and be an obstacle to his men of horse in resisting them. An Indian well attended by many Indians came, saying that he was the cacique. He delivered him to his guard that they might look after him. Many Indians went off and came bringing blankets and skins. Seeing poor opportunity for carrying out his evil thought, the pretended cacique going out of the house one day with the governor, started to run away so swiftly that there was no Christian who could overtake him; and plunged into the river which was a crossbow-shot's distance from the town. As soon as he had crossed to the other side, many Indians who were walking about there, uttering loud cries began to shoot arrows. The governor crossed over to them immediately with men of horse and of foot, but they did not dare await him. On going in pursuit of them, he arrived at a town which had been abandoned, and on beyond it a swamp where the horses could not cross. On the other side were many Indian women. Some men of foot crossed over and captured many of the women and a quantity of clothing. The governor returned to the camp; and soon after on that night a spy of the Indians was captured by those who were on watch. The governor asked him whether he would take them to the place where the cacique was. He said yes, and he went immediately to look for him with twenty men of horse and fifty of foot. After a march of a day and a half, he found him in a dense wood, and a soldier not knowing him, gave him a cutless stroke on the head. He cried out not to kill him, saying that he was the cacique. He was taken captive and with him one hundred and forty of his people. The governor went to Quiguate and told him that he should make his Indians come to serve the Christians; and after waiting for some days hoping for them to come, but they not coming, he sent two captains, each one on his own side of the river, with horse and foot. They captured many Indians, both men and women. Upon seeing the hurt they received because of their rebellion, they came to see what the governor might order them. Thus they came and went frequently and brought gifts of clothing and fish. The cacique and two of his wives were left unshackled in the governor's house, being guarded by the halberdiers of the governor's guard. The governor asked them in what direction the land was more densely populated. They said that on the lower part of the river toward the south were large settlements and caciques who were lords of wide lands and of many people, and that there was a province called Coligoa toward the northwest,

situated near some mountain ridges. It seemed advisable to the governor and to all the rest to go first to Coligoa, saying that perhaps the mountains would make a difference in the land and that gold or silver might exist on the other side of them. Both Aquiguate and Casqui and Pacaha were flat and fertile lands, with excellent meadow lands along the rivers where the Indians made large fields. From Tascaluca to the great river, the distance was about three hundred leagues, the land being very low and with many marshes. From Pacaha to Quiguate, the distance is about one hundred and ten leagues. The governor left the cacique of Quiguate in his town; and an Indian who guided him through large pathless forests conducted him for seven days through an uninhabited region where they lodged each night amid marshes and streamlets of very shallow water. So plentiful were the fish that they killed them by striking them with clubs; and the Indians whom they took along in chains roiled the water with the mud of the waters, and the fish, as if stupified would come to the surface, and they caught as many as they wished. The Indians of Coligoa had not heard of Christians and when they came within sight of the town so that they saw them, they took to flight up a river which flowed near the town. Some plunged into the river, but Christians who went along both banks captured them. Many Indians were captured there, both men and women, and among them, the cacique. At his command, many Indians came three days afterward bearing gifts of blankets and deerskins and two cowhides. They said that five or six leagues beyond toward the north were many cattle, but because the land was cold, it was poorly populated; that the best land they knew of, as being more plentifully supplied with food and better inhabited, was a province toward the south called Cayas. From Quiguate to Coligoa, the distance was about forty leagues. That town of Coligoa was situated at the foot of a mountain in a field of a river half the size of the Caya River which flows through Estremadura. It was a fertile land and so abundant in maize that the old was thrown out in order to store the new. There was also a great quantity of beans and pumpkins, the beans being larger and better than those of Spain; and the pumpkins likewise. When roasted, the latter have almost the taste of chestnuts. The cacique of Coligoa gave a guide to Cayas and remained in his town. We traveled for five days and reached the province of Palisema. The house of the cacique was found with coverings of colored deerskins drawn over with designs, and the floor of the house was covered with the same material in the manner of carpets. The cacique left it so, in order that the governor might lodge in it as a sign that he was desirous of peace and his friendship, but he did not dare remain. The governor, upon seeing that he had gone away, sent a captain with horse and foot to look for him. He found many people, but because of the roughness of the land they captured only some women and young persons. It was a small and scattered settlement and had very little maize. On that account, the governor left it immediately. He came upon another settlement called Tatalicoya, taking with him the cacique who guided him to Cayas. From Tatalicoya it is a distance of four days' journey to Cayas. When he reached Cayas and saw the scattered settlement, because of the information he had received, namely, that it was a well populated land, he believed that the cacique was lying to him and that that was not the province of Cayas. He threatened the cacique, bidding him to tell him where he was; and both the latter and the other Indians who had been captured near that place, asserted that that settlement was that of Cayas, and the best settlement of that province; and that although the houses were separated from one another, the populated land was considerable, and it had many people and many maize fields. The name of the settlement was Tanico. The camp was made in the best part of it near a river. The day on which the governor reached there with some men of horse, he went a league farther on and although he found no Indians, found on a road many skins which the cacique had left there for him to find as a sign of peace; for this is the custom of that land.

Chapter XXVI.
How the governor went to see the province of Tulla and what befell him there.

The governor abode in the province of Cayas for a month. During that interval, the horses grew fat and throve more than after a longer time in any other region because of the abundance of maize and the leaf thereof, which is, I think, the best that has been seen. They drank from a very warm and brackish marsh of water, and they drank so much that it was noticed in their bellies when they were brought back from the water. Thitherto the Christians had lacked salt, but there they made a good quantity of it in order to carry it along with them. The Indians carry it thence to other regions to exchange it for skins and blankets. They gather it along the river, which leaves it on top of the sand when the water falls. And since they can not gather it without more sand being mixed with it, they put it into certain baskets which they have for this purpose, wide at the top and narrow at the bottom. They hang the baskets to a pole in the air and put water in them, and they place a basin underneath into which the water falls. After being strained and set on the fire to boil, as the water becomes less, the salt is left on the bottom of the pot. On both sides of the river, the land had cultivated fields and there was an abundance of maize. The Indians did not dare to cross to the place where we were. When some appeared, some soldiers who saw them, called to them. The Indians crossed the river and came with them to the place where the governor was. He asked them for their cacique. They declared that he was friendly, but that he did not dare to appear. Thereupon, the governor ordered that he be told to come to see him and to bring a guide and interpreter for the region ahead, if he wished to be his friend; and that if he did not do this, he would go to fetch him and his hurt would be greater. He waited three days, and seeing that he did not come, went to look for him, and brought him back a prisoner with one hundred and fifty of his Indians. He asked him whether he had knowledge of any great cacique and where the most populated land was. He said that the best populated land thereabout was a province situated to the south, a day and a half away, called Tulla, that he could give him a guide, but that he did not have an interpreter, for the speech of Tulla was different from his; and because he and his forebears had always been at war with the lords of that province, they had no converse, nor did they understand each other. Thereupon, the governor set out for Tulla with men of horse and fifty foot in order to see whether it was a land through which he might pass with all his men. As soon as he arrived and was perceived by the Indians, the land was summoned. When fifteen or twenty Indians had gathered together, they came to attack the Christians. On seeing that they handled them roughly, and that when they took to flight the horses overtook them, they climbed on top of the houses, where they tried to defend themselves with their arrows; and when driven from some would climb on top of others; and while they were pursuing some, others would attack them from another direction. In this way, the running lasted so long that the horses became tired and could no longer run. The Indians killed one horse there and wounded several. Fifteen Indians were killed there and captives were made of forty women and young persons; for they did not leave any Indian alive who was shooting arrows if they could overtake him. The governor determined to return to Cayas before the Indians should have time to gather themselves together. Thereupon, that evening, after having marched part of the night, in order to get some distance from Tulla, he went to sleep on the road, and reached Cayas next day. Three days after that he set out with all his men for Tulla, taking the cacique with him. Among all the Indians of the latter, he did not find a single one who understood the speech of Tulla. He was three days on the way, and the day he reached the town, he found it abandoned, for the Indians did not dare await him. But as soon as they knew he was in Tulla, at the hour of dawn of the first night, they came in two bands from two different directions with their bows and arrows and long poles resembling pikes. As soon as they were perceived, both those of horse and those of foot sallied out against them and there many Indians were killed, and some Christians and horses wounded. Some Indians were captured, six of whom the governor sent to the cacique with their right hands and their noses cut off. He ordered them to tell him that if he did not come to make his excuses and obey him, he would go to get him; and that he would do to him and to as many of his men as he found what he had done to those whom he sent to him. He gave him the space of three days in which to come. This he gave them to understand the best he could by signs as he had no interpreter. After three days came an Indian whom the cacique sent laden with cowhides. He came weeping bitterly, and coming to the governor cast himself at his feet. He raised him up, and he made him a talk, but no one could understand him. The governor told him by signs that he should return and tell the cacique to send him an interpreter whom the people of Cayas

could understand. Next day, three Indians came laden with cowhides and three days after that twenty Indians came. Among them was one who understood those of Cayas. After a long discourse of excuses from the cacique and praises of the governor, he concluded by saying that he and the others were come thither on behalf of the cacique to see what his lordship ordered; and that he was ready to serve him. The governor and all the men were very glad, for they could in no wise travel without an interpreter. The governor ordered him under guard and told him to tell the Indians who had come with him to return to the cacique and tell him that he pardoned him for the past and that he thanked him greatly for his gifts and for the interpreter whom he had sent him and that he would be glad to see him and for him to come next day to see him. The cacique came after three days and eighty Indians with him. Both he and his men entered the camp weeping in token of obedience and repentance for the past mistake, after the manner of that land. He brought many cowhides as a gift, which were useful because it was a cold land, and were serviceable for coverlets as they were very soft and the wool like that of sheep. Nearby to the north were many cattle. The Christians did not see them nor enter their land, for the land was poorly settled where they were, and had little maize. The cacique of Tulla made his address to the governor in which he excused himself and offered him his land and vassals and person. No orator could more elegantly express the message or address both of that cacique and of the other caciques and of all those who came to the governor in their behalf.

Chapter XXVII.
How the governor went from Tulla to Autiamque where he wintered.

The governor informed himself of the land in all directions and learned that there was a scattering population toward the west and large towns toward the southeast, especially in a province called Autiamque, ten days' journey from Tulla—a distance of about eighty leagues;—and that it was a land abounding in maize. Since winter had already come and on account of the cold, rains and snows, they could not travel during two or three months of the year; fearing lest they could not feed themselves for so long a time because of its scattered population; also because the Indians said there was a large body of water near Autiamque—and according to what they said, the governor believed it to be an arm of the sea;—and because he now wished to give information of himself in Cuba, for it was three years and over since Doña Isabel, who was in the Havana, or any other person in a Christian land, had heard of him, and now two hundred and fifty men and one hundred and fifty horses were wanting: he determined to go to winter at Autiamque, and in the following summer to reach the sea and build two brigantines and send one of them to Cuba and the other to New Spain, so that the one which should go safely might give news of him; hoping from his property in Cuba to refit, take up his expedition again, and explore and conquer farther west than he had yet reached, whither Cabeza de Vaca had gone. He dismissed the two caciques of Tulla and Cayas, and set out toward Autiamque. For five days he proceeded through very rough ridges and reached a village called Quipana, where he was unable to capture any Indian because of the roughness of the land and because the town was located among ridges. At night he set an ambush in which two Indians were captured. They said that Autiamque was six days' journey away and that another province called Guahate lay a week's journey southward—a land plentifully abounding in maize and of much population. But since Autiamque was nearer and more of the Indians mentioned it to him, the governor proceeded on his journey in search of it. He reached a town called Anoixi in three days and sent a captain with thirty horse and fifty foot on ahead. The latter surprised the Indians unawares and captured many Indian men and women. Two days later, the governor arrived in another town called Catamaya and made camp in the open field of the town. Two Indians came with a false message from the cacique in order to ascertain what he was going to do. The governor told them to tell their lord that he should come to talk with him. The Indians went away but did not return, nor was there any other message from the cacique. Next day the Christians went to the town, which was without people, and took what maize they needed. They went to sleep on that day in a forest and next day reached Autiamque. They found considerable maize hidden away, as well as beans, nuts, and dried plums, all in great quantity. They seized some Indians who were collecting their

clothing, and who had already placed their women in safety. That land was cultivated and well peopled. The governor lodged in the best part of the village and immediately ordered a wooden stockade to be built about the place where the camp was established at some distance from the houses, so that the Indians without might not harm it with fire. Having measured off the land by paces, he allotted to each one the amount that was proper for him to build, in proportion to the number of Indians he had. Thereupon, the wood was brought in by them and within three days the stockade was built of very high timbers set close together in the ground and with many boards placed crosswise. Near this village flowed a river of Cayas and above and below it was densely populated. Indians came there on behalf of the cacique with gifts of blankets and skins, and a lame cacique subject to the cacique of Autiamque, lord of a town called Tietiquaquo, came frequently to visit the governor and brought him gifts of what he had. The cacique of Autiamque sent to ask the governor how long he intended to remain in his land. Upon seeing that he was a guest for more than three days, he sent no more Indians to him, nor any further message; but on the contrary, he conspired with the lame cacique to revolt. Forays were made in which many Indians, both men and women, were seized, and the lame cacique was captured. The governor, in consideration of the gifts he had received from him, rebuked and warned him, and gave him back his liberty, giving him two Indians to carry him on their shoulders. The cacique of Autiamque, desirous of driving the governor from his land, set spies on him. An Indian coming during the night to the gate of the stockade, a soldier who was on guard saw him and taking position behind the gate, thrust at him as he entered it and knocked him down; and in that condition brought him to the governor. On asking him why he had come, he fell down dead without being able to answer. Next night, the governor ordered a soldier to sound to arms and to say that he had seen Indians, in order to ascertain how soon they would hasten to the alarm. And both there and in other places, he did the same at various times when he thought his men were growing careless. Those who were slow in standing by, he reproved. And both on this account and because of what was his duty toward him, each one strove to be the first to respond when the alarm was given. They stayed three months in Autiamque, and had great abundance of maize, beans, walnuts, dried plums, and rabbits which until then they had no skill in killing. In Autiamque, the Indians showed them how they snared them, namely, by means of stout springs which lift the feet off the ground and a noose of strong cord fastened to which is a joint of cane which runs to the neck of the rabbit, so that it can not gnaw the cord. Many were taken in the maize fields, especially when it froze or snowed. The Christians were there a month amid snow during which they never left the town. When firewood was needed, the governor with those of horse going frequently to and from the woods, a distance of two crossbow-flights from the town, made a road by which those of foot went in a line. During that time, some Indians whom they were now taking along unshackled, killed many rabbits with their snares and arrows. The rabbits were of two kinds—some like those of Spain and others of the same color, form, and size as large hares, but larger and with larger loins.

Chapter XXVIII.
How the governor went from Autiamque to Nilco and thence to Guachoya.

On Monday, March six, of the year 1542, the governor set out from Autianque to go in search of Nilco, which the Indians said was near the great river, with the intention of reaching the sea and obtaining aid of men and horses; for he now had only three hundred fighting men and forty horses, and some of them lame and useful only for making a body of horse. For a year, because of lack of iron they brought them along all unshod; but because they were now accustomed to going in a flat country, this did not make their need felt much. In Autiamque died Juan Ortiz, which the governor felt deeply, for without an interpreter, not knowing where he was going, he feared lest he enter a region where he might get lost. After that, a youth who had been seized in Cutifachiqui, and who now knew something of the language of the Christians, served as interpreter. So great a misfortune was the death of Juan Ortiz, with regard to the exploring or trying to leave the land, that to learn from the Indians what he stated in four words, with the youth the whole day was needed; and most of the time he understood just the opposite of what was asked, so that

many times it came about that the road they took one day, and at times, two or three days, they would return on, and they would wander about lost from one side of those woods to the other. From Autiamque, it took the governor ten days to reach a province called Ayays. He reached a town near the river which flowed through Cayas and Autiamque. There he ordered a piragua to be constructed, by which he crossed the river. After crossing, such weather occurred, that he could not march for four days because of the snow. As soon as it stopped snowing, he marched for three days through an unpopulated region and a land so low and with so many swamps and such hard going that one day he marched all day through water that in some places reached to the knees and in others to the stirrups, and some passages were swum over. He came to a deserted village, without maize called Tutelpinco. Near it was a lake which emptied into the river and had a strong current and force of water. As five Christians, accompanied by a captain whom the governor had sent, were crossing it in a canoe, the canoe overturned. Some caught hold of it and others of trees which were in the lake. One Francisco Bastian, an honorable person, a native of Vilanueva de Barcarota, was drowned there. The governor went for a day along the lake looking for a crossing place, but he did not find it all that day nor any road leading from any other direction. Returning at night to the town, he found two peaceful Indians who showed him the crossing and the road he must take. Reed frames and rafts were made there from reeds and wood from the houses, on which they crossed the lake. They marched for three days and reached a town of the district of Nilco, called Tianto. Thirty Indians were captured there, among them being two of the principal men of that town. The governor sent a captain on ahead to Nilco with horse and foot, so that the Indians might not have any opportunity to carry off the food. They went through three or four large towns, and in the town where the cacique lived—located two leagues from where the governor remained—they found many Indians with their bows and arrows, and in appearance as if they wished to give battle, and who were surrounding the town. As soon as they saw that the Christians were coming toward them without any hesitation, they set fire to the cacique's house and escaped over a swamp that lay near the town, where the horses could not cross. Next day, Wednesday, March 29, the governor reached Nilco. He lodged with all his men in the cacique's town which was located on a level field, and which was all populated for a quarter of a league; while a league and a half-league distant were other very large towns where there was a quantity of maize, beans, walnuts, and dried plums. This was the most populous region which had been seen in Florida and more abounding in maize, with the exception of Coça and Apalache. An Indian came to the camp, accompanied by others, and in the cacique's name presented the governor with a blanket of marten skins and a string of pearl beads. The governor gave him some "margaridetas"—a kind of bead much esteemed in Peru—and some other trifles with which he was much pleased. He promised to return two days later, but he never did return. On the other hand, Indians came in canoes at night and carried off all the maize they could and set up their huts on the other side of the river in the thickest part of the forest, so that if they should go in search of them, they might escape. The governor, on seeing that he did not come at the promised time, ordered an ambush to be made at some barbacoas near the swamp where the Indians came for maize. Two Indians were captured there, who told the governor that the one who came to visit them was not the cacique, but one sent at the latter's command under pretense that it was he, in order to ascertain whether the Christians were off their guard, and whether they planned to settle in that region or go on farther. Thereupon, the governor sent a captain across the river with men of horse and foot, but on crossing they were perceived by the Indians, and for that reason, he could not capture more than ten or twelve Indians, men and women, with whom he returned to camp. That river which flowed through Anilco was the same that flowed through Cayas and Autianique and emptied into the large river which flowed through Pacaha and Aquixo hard by the province of Guachoya. The lord of the upper part came in canoes to make war on the lord of Nilco. Sent by him, an Indian came to the governor and told him that he was his servant and as such he should consider him and that two days later he would come to kiss the hands of his Lordship. He came at that time with some of his principal Indians who accompanied him. With words of great promise and courtesy, he presented many blankets and deerskins to the governor. The governor gave him some trifles and showed him great honor. He questioned him about the settlement down the river. He said that he knew of none other except his own; and that on the other side was a province of a cacique called Quigaltam. He took his leave of the governor and returned to his town. A few days later, the governor made up his mind to go to Guaçhoya, in order to ascertain there whether the sea were nearby, or whether there were any settlement nearby where he might subsist himself while brigantines were being built which he intended to send to the land of Christians. As he was crossing the river of Nilco, Indians came up it in canoes from Guachoya, and when they saw him, thinking that he was going after them to do them some hurt, they turned back down the river and went to warn the cacique. The latter, abandoning the town with all his people, with all they could carry off, on that night crossed over to the other side of the great river. The governor sent a captain and fifty men in six canoes down the river, while he, with the rest of his men, went overland. He reached Guachoya on Sunday, April 17, and lodged himself in the cacique's town, which was surrounded by a stockade, a crossbow-flight from the river. There, the river was called Tamalisen, at Nilco, Tapatu, at Coça, Mico, and at the port, Ri.

Chapter XXIX.
Of the message sent by the governor to Quigaltam and of the answer given by the latter; and of what happened during this time.

As soon as the governor reached Gauchoya, he sent Juan de Añasco up the river with as many men as could get into the canoes; for when they were coming from Anilco, they saw newly made huts on the other side. Juan de Añasco went and brought back the canoes laden with maize, beans, dried plums, and many loaves made from the pulp of the plums. On that day, an Indian came to the governor in the name of the cacique of Guachoya and said that his lord would come next day. On the following day, they saw many canoes coming from downstream. They assembled together for the space of an hour on the other side of the great river, debating as to whether they should come or not. At last, they made up their minds and crossed the river. The cacique of Guachoya came in them, bringing with him many Indians bearing a considerable quantity of fish, dogs, skins, and blankets. As soon as they landed at the town, they went immediately to the town to the governor's lodging and presented the gifts to him; and the cacique spoke as follows:

"Powerful and excellent lord: May your Lordship pardon me for the mistake I made in going away and not waiting in this town to receive you and serve you; for the obtaining of this opportune occasion was, and is, a great victory for me. But I feared what I shoud not have feared and on that account did what it was not proper to do. However, since hasty actions cause unfavorable results, and I had acted without deliberation, as soon as I reflected on this, I made up my mind not to follow the advice of the foolish, which is to persist in their error, but to imitate the wise and prudent ones in changing one's opinion; and I am come to see what your Lordship might command me in order to serve you in so far as my possibility suffices." The governor welcomed him with much hospitality and gave him thanks for his gifts and promises. He asked him whether he had any knowledge of the sea. He said he did not, nor of any settlement down the river from that place, except that there was a town of one of his principal Indians subject to him two leagues away, and on the other side three days' journey downstream the province of Quigaltam, who was the greatest lord of that region. It seemed to the governor that the cacique was lying to him in order to turn him aside from his towns, and he sent Juan de Añasco downstream with eight horse to see what population there was and to ascertain whether there were any knowledge of the sea. He was gone for a week and on his coming said that during that whole time he could not proceed more than fourteen or fifteen leagues because of the great arms leading out of the river, and the canebrakes and thick woods lying along it; and that he found no settlement. The governor's grief was intense on seeing the small prospect he had for reaching the sea; and worse, according to the way in which his men and horses were diminishing, they could not be maintained in the land without succor. With that thought, he fell sick, but before he took to his bed, he sent an Indian to tell the cacique of Quigaltam that he was the son of the sun and that wherever he went all obeyed him and did him

service. He requested him to choose his friendship and come there where he was, for he would be very glad to see him; and in token of love and obedience that he should bring him something of what was most esteemed in that land. By the same Indian, he answered him saying that with respect to what he said about being the son of the sun, let him dry up the great river and he would believe him. With respect to the rest, he was not accustomed to visit any one. On the contrary, all of whom he had knowledge visited and served him and obeyed him and paid him tribute, either by force or of their own volition. Consequently, if he wished to see him, let him cross there. If he came in peace, he would welcome him with special goodwill; if he came in war, he would await him in the town where he was, for not for him or any other would he move one foot backward. When the Indian came with this reply, the governor was already in bed, badly racked by fever. He was very angry that he was not in condition to cross the river forthwith and go in quest of him to see whether he could not lessen that arrogant demeanor. However, the river was now very powerful there, being about half a league wide and sixteen brazas deep, and very furious because of its strong current. On both sides of it were many Indians; and his strength was now no longer so great that he did not need to take advantage of cunning rather than force. The Indians of Guachoya came daily with fish, so many that the town was filled with them. The cacique said that the cacique of Quigaltam was going to come on a certain night to do battle with the governor. The governor, believing that he was planning thereby to drive him out of his land, ordered him placed under guard. That night and every other night a very strict watch was kept. Asking him why Quigaltam did not come, he said that he had come, but saw that he was on the watch and he did not dare to attack him. He importuned him frequently, to order his captains to cross to the other side of the river and that he would give him many men to attack Quigaltam. The governor told him that as soon as he got well, he would go to look for him. Noting how many Indians came to the town daily, and how many people were in that land, and fearing lest some of them conspire with others and plan some treason against him; and because the town, having no gates by which advantage could be taken, had some openings which had not been completely closed: he left them in that condition without repairing the stockade in order that the Indians might not think he feared them. He ordered that men of horse be stationed at them and at the gates. All night long the horses were left bridled and from each company mounted men rode by couples and went to visit the sentinels who were stationed on the roads at their posts outside the town, and the crossbowmen who were guarding the canoes on the river. In order that the Indians might fear him, the governor determined to send a captain to Nilco, which those of Guachoya had told him was inhabited, in order that by treating them cruelly, neither the one town nor the other should dare attack him. He sent Nuño de Tobar with fifteen horse and Juan de Guzmán, captain of men of foot, with his men upstream in the canoes. The cacique of Guachoya sent for canoes and for many Indian warriors who went with the Christians. A captain of the Christians, Nuño de Tobar, by name, with the men of horse went overland. At a distance of two leagues before reaching Nilco, he awaited Juan de Guzmán and at night they crossed the river at that place. Those of horse arrived first. At daybreak next morning, in sight of the town they came upon a spy, who, on seeing the Christians, ran away uttering loud cries in order to give the alarm to those of the town. Nuño de Tobar and those who accompanied him set such a pace that before the Indians of the town had all come out, they were on them. The land was open, that part which was peopled being about a quarter of a league. There were about five or six thousand souls in that settlement. And since many of the people came out of the houses and went fleeing from one house to the other, and many Indians were gathering together in all directions, there was not a single one of the horse who did not find himself along among many. The captain had ordered that no male Indian's life should be spared. So great was their confusion that not an Indian shot at a Christian. The cries of the women and little children were so loud that they deafened the ears of those who pursued them. A hundred or so Indians were killed there and many were badly wounded with the lances, who were let go in order that they might strike terror into those who did not happen to be there. There were men there so cruel and such butchers that they killed old men and young men and all they came upon without any one

offering them little or much resistance. Those who trusted in themselves, who went to prove themselves wherever there was any resistance, and who were considered as such men, broke through the Indians, overthrowing many with the stirrup and breasts of their horses; and some they lanced and let them go in that condition; but on seeing a child or a woman, they would capture and deliver such a person to those of foot. Those who were cruel, because they showed themselves inhuman, God permitted their sin to confront them, very great cowardice assailing them in the sight of all at a time when there was greater need of fighting, and when at last they came to die. Of the Indians at Nilco, eighty women and children were seized, and much clothing. The Indians of Guachoya stopped before reaching the town and stayed outside, beholding how the Christians dealt with the people of Nilco; and seeing them defeated and those of horse going about lancing them, they went to the houses to loot, and from the booty loaded their canoes with clothing and went to Guachoya before the Christians came. And full of wonder at what they had seen done to the Indians of Anilco, they told their cacique with great fear everything as it had happened.

Chapter XXX.
How the adelantado, Don Fernando de Soto, died and how Luis Moscoso de Alvarado was chosen governor.

The governor realized within himself that the hour had come in which he must leave this present life. He had the royal officials summoned, and the captains and principal persons. To them he gave a talk, saying that he was about to go to give an accounting before the throne of God of all his past life; and that since He was pleased to take him at such a time, and to arrive at a time when he could perceive his death, he a very unworthy servant gave Him many thanks; and to all those present and absent, to whom he confessed his great obligation for their singular virtues, love, and loyalty toward himself, which he had well proven in the hardships they had suffered. This he had always had in mind and had hoped to recompense and to reward when God should be pleased to give leisure to his life with greater prosperity of his estate. He asked them to pray God for him and in His mercy to pardon him his sins, and place his soul in glory. He asked them to give him release and remission from the obligation in which he stood to them and of what he was owing to them all; and to pardon any feelings of offense they might have received from him. In order to avoid any disunion that might arise at his death, with regard to the one who was to act as governor, he asked them to consider it fitting to elect one of the principal and capable persons to govern, in whom they all might be satisfied, and before whom having been elected they should take oath to obey him. For this, he would be very grateful, for it would soften somewhat his grief and the sorrow he felt at leaving them in so great confusion as he was doing in a land in which they did not know where they were. Baltasar de Gallegos answered him in the name of all, and first consoling him, spoke to him of how brief was the life of this world and of how many hardships and sufferings; that he who earliest left it, to him God showed signal mercy; saying to him many other things proper at such a time; and lastly that since God was pleased to take him to Himself, although his death, with much reason they greatly grieved over, it was necessary and proper for him as it was for all to conform to the will of God. And as to the governor whom he ordered them to choose, let his Lordship appoint him whom he might delegate and they would obey him. Therefore, he appointed Luis de Moscoso de Alvarado as their captain general, and by all those who were present he was immediately sworn and elected as governor. Next day, May 21, died the magnanimous, virtuous, and courageous captain, Don Fernando de Soto, governor of Cuba and adelantado of Florida, whom fortune exalted as she is wont to do with others, so that he might fall from a greater height. He died in a land and at a time when his illness had very little solace. The danger of being lost in that land, which stared all of them in the face, was the reason why each one himself had need of consolation and why they did not visit him and wait upon him, as was fitting. Luis de Moscoso determined to conceal his death from the Indians, for Fernando de Soto had given them to understand that the Christians were immortal. Also because they knew him to be bold, wise, and courageous, if they should learn of his death, they would be emboldened to attack them even though they were at peace, because of their nature and their entire lack of constancy. They believe everything told them. The adelantado had made them believe that certain things which had happened among them in secret, which he had succeeded in discovering without their knowing how or in what manner, and that the face which appeared within the mirror (which he showed them) told him whatever they were planning and thinking about. Consequently, they did not dare by word or deed to attempt anything which might be to his hurt. As soon as he died, Luis de Moscoso ordered him to be placed secretly in a house where he was kept for three days; and from thence he ordered him to be buried at night inside at a gate of the town. And since the Indians had seen that he was sick and found him missing, they suspected what might have happened; and passing by where he was buried and seeing the earth had been disturbed, looked and talked among themselves. Luis de Moscoso having learned this, ordered him disinterred at night and a considerable quantity of sand was placed within the blankets in which he was shrouded, and he was taken in a canoe and cast into the middle of the river. The cacique of Guachoya asked for him, inquiring what had been done with his brother and lord, the governor. Luis de Moscoso told him that he had gone to the sky as he had often done before; and since he was to stay there for some days, he had left him in his stead. The cacique believed that he was dead, and ordered two young and well built Indians to be taken there. He said it was the custom in that land when any lord died to kill Indians to accompany him and serve him on the way; and on this account, those had come thither at his order; and he told Luis de Moscoso to have them beheaded so that they might accompany and serve his brother and lord. Luis de Moscoso told him that the governor was not dead but that he had gone to the sky and that he had taken from among his soldiers Christians who were sufficient for his service; and that he requested him to order those Indians freed and from thenceforth not to follow so evil a custom. Thereupon, he ordered them set free and commanded them to go to their homes. One of them refused to go saying that he did not wish to remain under the power of any one who had sentenced him to death undeservedly, and that he desired to serve while life lasted him who had freed him. Luis de Moscoso ordered the property of the governor to be sold at auction, namely, two men slaves, two women slaves, three horses, and seven hundred hogs. For each horse or slave, two or three thousand cruzados were given, which were to be paid at the first melting of gold or silver, or from their repartimientos. They pledged themselves that, even though there might be nothing in the land, they would make payment within a year, and for that purpose, those who had no property in Spain, gave bonds. For a hog, two hundred cruzados, pledged in the same way. Those who had property in Spain bought more timidly and bought less. Thenceforward, most of the men had hogs and reared and ate them. They observed Fridays and Saturdays and the vespers of holidays, which they had not done before; for two or three months would pass without their eating meat, and they had eaten it on any day they could get it.

Chapter XXXI.
How Governor Luis de Moscoso departed from Guachoya and went to Chaguate and thence to Aguacay.

There were some who rejoiced at the death of Don Fernando de Soto, considering it as certain that Luis de Moscoso (who was fond of leading a gay life) would rather prefer to be at ease in a land of Christians than to continue the hardships of the war of conquest and discovery, of which they had long ago become awearied because of the little profit obtained. The governor ordered the captains and principal men to assemble in order to consult them and plan what should be done. Having obtained information of the population all thereabout, he learned that there was a more populous land toward the west and that the river below Quigaltam was uninhabited and had little food. He asked each to express his opinion in writing and to sign his opinion with his name, so that having the opinions of them all, he might make up his mind whether to descend the river or to penetrate inland. It seemed advisable to all to take the road overland toward the west, for New Spain lay in that direction; and they considered as more dangerous and of greater risk the voyage by sea; for no ship could be built strong enough to weather a storm, and they had no master or pilot, and no compass or sailing chart, and they did not know how far away the sea was, nor had they any information of it; nor whether the river made some great bend through the land or whether it fell over any rocks where they would perish. Some men who had seen the sailing chart, found

that the distance to New Spain along the coast in the region where they were, was about five hundred leagues or so. They declared that even although they might have to make some detours by land, because of looking for a settlement, they would not be prevented from going ahead that summer except by some great uninhabited district which they could not cross. If they found food to pass the winter in some settlement, the following summer they would reach the land of Christians. It might be also that by going by land, they would find some rich land from which they might get profit. Although the governor's desire was to leave the land of Florida in the shortest time possible, on seeing the difficulties which lay before him in making the voyage by sea, he resolved to follow what seemed best to all. On Monday, June 5, he left Guachoya. The cacique gave him a guide to Chaguate and remained in his village. They passed through a province called Catalte and after passing through an uninhabited region for six days, they reached Chaguete on the twentieth of the month. The cacique of that province had gone to visit the governor, Don Fernando de Soto, at Autiamque where he brought him gifts of skins, blankets, and salt. A day before Luis de Moscoso arrived at his village, a sick Christian got lost, and he suspected that the Indians had killed him. He sent word to the cacique to have him looked for and sent to him, and said that he would consider him a friend as formerly; but that if he did not do so, there was no place of escape for him or his people, and that his land would be burned. The cacique came forthwith and brought a rich gift of blankets and skins and the Christian, and made the following speech:

"Excellent Lord: For all the treasure in the world, I would not desire the opinion you have of me. Who forced me to go to visit the excellent lord governor, your father, at Autiamque (which you should have remembered) where I offered myself with all loyalty, fidelity, and love to serve and obey him as long as I lived? Therefore, what could be the reason, after I had received favors from him and without you or he having done me any injury that I could be induced to do what I ought not do? Believe me, neither injury nor human interest were enough to make me act so, nor would it have blinded me. But since it is a natural thing in this life for many griefs to happen after one pleasure, fortune has pleased by your indignation to moderate the gladness which my heart felt at your coming, and that I should err wherein I thought to succeed, in sheltering that Christian who had become lost and in treating him in such manner as he can tell; for it seemed to me that by so doing I was rendering a service and I planned to go to deliver him to you at Chaguete, and to serve you in everything for which my strength sufficed. If I merit punishment from your hand on this account, I shall receive it as from a lord, as if it were a reward; for the love I bore to the excellent governor and that which I have for you has no limit. Thereafter, whatever punishment you give me, you will do me a favor. And what I now ask of you is that you declare your will to me and those things in which I can best serve you." The governor answered him saying that because he did not find him in that town he was angry at him, as it appeared to him that he had gone away as others had done; but since he now understood his loyalty and love, he would always consider him as a brother, and would favor him in all his affairs. The cacique accompanied him to the town where he was living, which was a day's journey thence. They passed through a small town where there was a lake where the Indians made salt. The Christians made some on a day they rested there from some briny water which rose near the town in pools like springs. The governor stayed six days in Chaguete. There he got information of the people to the west. They told him that three days' journey from there was a province called Aguacay. The day he left Chaguete, a Christian named Francisco de Guzmán, bastard son of a gentleman of Seville, remained behind. He went away to the Indians in fear lest they seize from him as a gaming obligation an Indian woman whom he had as a mistress and whom he took away with him. The governor marched for two days before he found he was not with them. He sent word to the cacique to look for him and to send him to Aguacay, whither he was going, which he never did. On behalf of the cacique of Aguacay, before reaching that province, fifteen Indians came to meet him on the way with a present of skins and fish and roasted venison. The governor reached his town on Wednesday, July 4. He found the town abandoned and lodged therein. He stayed there for some time, during which he made several inroads, in which many Indians, both men and women, were captured. There they heard of the south sea. There a considerable quantity of salt was made from the sand which they gathered in a vein of earth like slate and which was made as it was made in Cayas.

Chapter XXXII.
How the governor went from Aguacay to Naguatex and what happened to him.

On the day the governor left Aguacay, he went to sleep near a small town subject to the lord of that province. The camp was pitched quite near to a salt marsh, and on that evening some salt was made there. Next day he went to sleep between two ridges in a forest of open trees. Next day he reached a small town called Pato. The fourth day after he left Aguacay, he reached the first settlement of a province called Amaye. An Indian was captured there who said that it was a day and a half journey thence to Naguatex, all of which lay through an inhabited region. Having left the village of Amaye, on Saturday, July 20, camp was made at midday beside a brook in a luxuriant grove between Amaye and Naguatex. Indians were seen there who came to spy on them. Those of horse rushed at them, killing six and capturing two. On being asked by the governor why they had come, they said it was to ascertain what people he had and of what manner they were, and that they had been sent by their lord, the cacique of Naguatex; that the latter, with other caciques, who were in his company and under his protection, had made up their minds to give him battle that day. While this questioning and answering was going on, many Indians came in two bands from two directions. As soon as they saw they had been perceived, uttering loud cries they rushed upon the Christians with great fury, each band in its own part. But on seeing the resistance they met with from the Christians, they turned and fled, and in their flight many of them lost their lives. While most of the horse were going in pursuit of them, quite forgetful of the camp, two other bands of Indians who had been concealed, attacked them. They were also resisted and had their pay as the first had. After the Indians had fled and the Christians had gathered together, they heard a loud cry at the distance of a crossbow-flight from where they were. The governor sent twelve horse to see what it was. They found six Christians, two of horse and four of foot, among many Indians, those on horse with great difficulty defending those on foot. These had got lost from those who pursued the first two bands of Indians, and while returning to camp, met those with whom they were fighting. Both they and those who went to their aid killed many of the Indians. They brought one Indian to camp alive, whom the governor asked who those were who had come to do battle with him. He said that they were the cacique of Naguatex and he of Maye and another of a province called Hacanac, lord of vast lands and many vassals; and that he of Naguatex came as captain and head of all. The governor ordered his right arm and his nostrils cut off and sent him to the cacique of Naguatex, ordering him to say that on the morrow he would be in his land to destroy him and that if he wished to forbid him entrance, he should await him. That night he slept there and next day reached the village of Naguatex which was very extensive. He asked where the town of the cacique was and they told him it was on the other side of a river which ran through that district. He marched toward it and on reaching it saw many Indians on the other side waiting for him, so posted as to forbid his passage. Since he did not know whether it was fordable, nor where it could be crossed; and since several Christians and horses were wounded: in order that they might have time to recover in the town where he was, he made up his mind to rest for a few days. Because of the great heat, he made camp near the village, a quarter of a league from the river, in an open forest of luxuriant and lofty trees near a brook. Several Indians were captured there. He asked them whether the river was fordable. They said it was at times in certain places. Ten days later he sent two captains, each with fifteen horse up and down the river with Indians to show them where they could cross, to see what population lay on the other side of the river. The Indians opposed the crossing of them both as strongly as possible, but they crossed in spite of them. On the other side they saw a large village and many provisions; and returned to camp with this news.

Chapter XXXIII.
How the Cacique of Naguatex came to visit the governor; and how the governor left Naguatex and went to Nondacao.

From the town of Naguatex, where the governor was, he sent word by an Indian to the cacique to come to serve and obey him and said that he would pardon him for the past; and that if he did not come he would go to look for him and give him the punishment he merited for what he had done

against him. Two days later the Indian came and said that the cacique would come next day. The very day before he came, he sent many Indians ahead, among whom were some of the principal men. He sent them to see in what mood they found the governor, in order to make up his mind with himself whether to go or not. The Indians reported he was coming and immediately returned. The cacique came two hours later well attended by his men. They all came after his manner, one ahead of the other in double file, leaving a lane in the middle through which the cacique came. They reached the place where the governor was, all weeping after the manner of Tula which lay to the east not very far from that place. The cacique paid his respects fittingly and spoke as follows:

"Very exalted, very mighty Lord, to whom the whole world owes service and obedience: I venture to appear before your Lordship after having committed so enormous and vile an act, for which even because it passed through my mind I merit punishment, trusting in your greatness, that although I have not even deserved pardon, but because it is your custom, you will observe clemency toward me, considering how insignificant I am in comparison with your Lordship, so that you will not be mindful of my weaknesses, which, because of my evil, I have come to know for my greater good. I believe that you and your men must be immortal and that your Lordship is Lord of the realm of nature, since everything submits to and obeys you, even the hearts of men. For, seeing the death and destruction of my men in the battle, which I fought with your Lordship through my ignorance and the counsel of a brother of mine, who was killed in the action, I immediately repented me in my heart of the mistake I had committed and desired to serve and obey you. I come, therefore, so that your Lordship may punish me and order me as your own." The governor answered him saying that he pardoned him for the past, that thenceforth and in the future he should act as he ought and that he would consider him his friend and protect him in all his affairs. Four days later he departed thence, but on reaching the river could not cross, as it had swollen greatly. This appeared a wonderful phenomenon to him because of the season then and because it had not rained for more than a month. The Indians declared that it swelled often in that way without it having rained anywhere in the land. It was conjectured that it might be the sea which came up through the river. It was learned that the increase always came from above, and that the Indians of all that land had no knowledge of the sea. The governor returned to the place where he had been during the preceding days. A week later, hearing that the river could be crossed, he passed to the other side and found a village without any people. He lodged in the open field and sent word to the cacique to come where he was and give him a guide for the forward journey. A few days later, seeing that the cacique did not come or send, he sent two captains, each in a different direction, to burn the towns and capture any Indians they might find. They burned many provisions and captured many Indians. The cacique, on beholding the damage that his land was receiving, sent six of his principal men and three Indians with them as guides who knew the language of the region ahead where the governor was about to go. He immediately left Naguatex and after marching three days reached a town of four or five houses, belonging to the cacique of that miserable province, called Nisohone. It was a poorly populated region and had little maize. Two days later, the guides who were guiding the governor, if they had to go toward the west, guided them toward the east, and sometimes they went through dense forests, wandering off the road. The governor ordered them hanged from a tree and an Indian woman, who had been captured at Nisohone, guided him, and he went back to look for the road. Two days later, he reached another wretched land called Lacane. There he captured an Indian who said that the land of Nondacao was a very populous region and the houses scattered about one from another as is customary in mountains, and that there was abundance of maize. The cacique and his Indians came weeping like those of Naguatex, that being their custom in token of obedience. He made him a gift of a great quantity of fish and offered to do as he should order. He took his leave of him and gave him a guide to the province of Soacatino.

Chapter XXXIV.

How the governor went from Nondacao to Soacatino and Guasco, and crossed through an unpeopled region, whence for lack of a guide and interpreter, he returned to Nilco.

The governor departed from Nondacao for Soacatino and after he had marched for five days arrived at the province called Aays. The Indians who lived there had not heard of Christians, and as soon as they perceived that they had entered their lands, the country was aroused. As soon as fifty or a hundred had gathered together, they would go out on the road to fight. While some were fighting, others came and attacked them on another side, and when some pursued, the Indians pursued them. The affair lasted the greater part of the day before they reached their village. Some horses and Christians were wounded, but not so badly that it presented any obstacle to their march, for no one had a dangerous wound. Great damage was done the Indians. The day the governor departed thence, the Indian who was guiding him said that he had heard Nondacao say that the Indians of Soacatino had seen other Christians. At this all were very glad, as they thought it might be true and that they might have entered by way of New Spain; and that, if it were so, they would have it in their power to get out of Florida, since they had found nothing of profit, for they feared lest they get lost in some unpeopled region. That Indian led him off the road for two days. The governor ordered him to be tortured. He said that the cacique of Nondacao, his lord, had ordered him to lead him in that way, because they were his enemies; and that he had to do so, since his lord so ordered. The governor ordered him thrown to the dogs, and another one guided him to Soacatino, whither he arrived next day. It was a very poor land and there was great lack of maize there. He asked the Indians whether they knew of other Christians. They said they had heard it said that they were traveling about near there to the southward. He marched for twenty days through a very poorly populated region where they endured great need and suffering; for the little maize the Indians had they hid in the forests and buried it where, after being well tired out with marching, the Christians went about trailing it, at the end of the day's journey looking for what they must eat. On reaching a province called Guasco, they found maize with which they loaded the horses and the Indians whom they were taking. Thence they went to another village called Naquiscoça. The Indians said they had never heard of other Christians. The governor ordered them put to the torture and they said that they had reached another domain ahead called Naçacahoz and had returned thence toward the west whence they had come. The governor reached Naçacahoz in two days and some Indian women were captured there. Among them was one who said that she had seen Christians and that she had been in their hands but had escaped. The governor sent a captain and fifteen horse to the place where the Indian woman said she had seen them, in order to ascertain whether there were any trace of horses or any token of their having reached there. After having gone three or four leagues, the Indian woman who was guiding them said that all she had said was a lie; and so they considered what the other Indians had said about having seen Christians in the land of Florida. And inasmuch as the land thereabout was very poor in maize, and there was no tidings of any village westward, they returned to Guasco. There the Indians told them that ten days' journey thence toward the west was a river called Daycao where they sometimes went to hunt in the mountains and to kill deer; and that on the other side of it they had seen people, but did not know what village it was. There the Christians took what maize they found and could carry and after marching for ten days through an unpeopled region reached the river of which the Indians had spoken. Ten of horse, whom the governor had sent on ahead, crossed over to the other side, and went along the road leading to the river. They came upon an encampment of Indians who were living in very small huts. As soon as they saw them, they took to flight, abandoning their possessions, all of which were wretchedness and poverty. The land was so poor, that among them all, they did not find half an "alqueire" of maize. Those of horse captured two Indians and returned with them to the river where the governor was awaiting them. They continued to question them in order to learn from them the population to the westward, but there was no Indian in the camp who understood their language. The governor ordered the captains and principal persons summoned, in order to plan what he should do after hearing their opinions. Most of them said that in their opinion they should return to the great river of Guachoya, for there was plenty of maize at Anilco and thereabout. They said that during the winter they would make brigantines and the following summer they would descend the river in them to look for the sea, and once having reached the sea, they would coast along it to New Spain which, although it seemed a difficult thing, be-

cause of what they had already said, yet it was their last resort because they could not travel by land for lack of an interpreter. They maintained that that land beyond the river of Daycao, where they were, was the land which Cabeza de Vaca said in his relation he had traversed, and was of Indians who wandered about like Arabs without having a settled abode anywhere, subsisting on prickly pears, the roots of plants, and the game they killed. And if that were so, if they entered it and found no food in order to pass the winter, they could not help but perish, for it was already the beginning of October; and if they stayed longer, they could not turn back because of the waters and snows, nor could they feed themselves in such a poor land. The governor, who was desirous now of being in a place where he could sleep out his full sleep, rather than to govern and conquer a land where so many hardships presented themselves to him, at once turned back to the place whence they had come.

Chapter XXXV.
How they returned to Nilco and went to Milnoya, where they set about making ships in order to get out of the land of Florida.

When the plan determined on was published in the camp, there were many who regretted it keenly, for they considered the journey by sea as doubtful on account of their lack of equipment, and as risky as the journey overland; and they hoped to find a rich land before reaching the land of Christians, because of what Cabeza de Vaca had told the emperor. This was that, while he had found cotton cloth, he had seen gold and silver and precious gems of much value. They had not yet reached the place where he had gone, for he had gone continually along the coast up to that point and they had gone inland. If they traveled toward the west, they would of necessity have to come out whither he had gone. For he said that he had traveled many days in a certain direction and had penetrated inland toward the north. Already at Guasco, they had found some turquoises and cotton blankets which the Indians gave them to understand by signs were brought from the west; and if they took that way, they would reach the land of Christians. But in addition to this they were greatly discontented, and it grieved many of them to turn back, for they would rather have risked death in the land of Florida than to leave it poor. They were unable to prevent what had been determined upon, because the principal men were of the governor's mind. But afterward there was one who said he would willingly put out one of his own eyes if he could put out one of Luis de Moscoso, for it grieved him greatly to see him prosperous; for which he would have maltreated both him and others, his friends, but he did not dare do it, seeing that two days later, he was to leave the command. From Daycao, where they were, it was one hundred and fifty leagues to the great river—a distance they had marched continually to the westward. On the backward journey, they found maize to eat with great difficulty, for where they had already passed the land was left devastated, and any maize which the Indians had, they had hidden. The towns which they had burned in Naguatex, which was now regretted by them, had now been rebuilt and the houses were full of maize. This region is very well populated and well supplied with food. Pottery is made there of refined clay, which differs but little from that of Estremoz or Montemor. At Chaguete, the Indians, by order of the cacique, came in peace and said that the Christian who had remained there refused to come. The governor wrote to him and sent him ink and paper so that he could reply. The substance of the words of the letter was to declare to him his determination, namely, to leave the land of Florida, and to remind him that he was a Christian and should not desire to stay in the power of infidels; that he pardoned him the error he had committed in going to the Indians, and that he should come; and if they tried to detain him, he should so inform him in writing. The Indian went with the letter and came without other reply than on its back his name and rubric so that they might know he was alive. The governor sent twelve men of horse to look for him, but having his spies, he hid himself so that they could not find him. For lack of maize the governor could not stop longer to look for him. He left Chaguete and crossed the river before Aays, and going down it came to a town called Chilano, which they had not seen until then. Reaching Nilco, they found so little maize, that it did not suffice for the building of ships. The cause of this was that when the Christians were at Guachoya at seed time, the Indians had not dared sow the lands of Anilco for fear of them; and they knew no other land thereabout where there was any maize. That was the most fertile land there-

about and where they had most hope of finding maize. They were all thrown into confusion; and most of them thought it had been a bad plan to have turned back from Daycao and not to have followed their fortune by going ahead by land in the way they had taken, for it seemed impossible that they could escape by sea unless a miracle were performed for them; for there was neither pilot nor chart, they did not know where the river entered the sea, they had no information concerning the latter; they had nothing with which to make sails nor enough "henequen" (a plant like tow which grew there) and what they found they were keeping to calk the brigantines; nor was there anything with which to pitch them; nor could they build ships strong enough so that they would not be placed in great danger at any untoward happening. They feared greatly the fate that had befallen Narvaez who had perished on that coast; and especially the disadvantage in not finding maize, for without it they could not sustain themselves; nor could they do anything of the things they had to accomplish. All were thrown into great confusion. For their relief they commended themselves to God and besought Him to show them how to save themselves. By His goodness it was pleasing to Him that the Indians of Anilco should come in peace and say that at a distance of two days' journey thence, near the great river were two towns of which the Christians had never heard, called Aminoya, and that the region was fertile. They did not know whether there was any maize there now or not, because there was war between them. But they would be very glad to go to destroy them with the help of the Christians. The governor sent a captain thither with men of horse and foot and the Indians of Anilco with him. He reached Aminoya and found two large towns which were in an open and level region, at a half league's distance apart; and in them he captured many Indians and found a great quantity of maize. He immediately took up his lodging in one of them and sent word to the governor of what he had found, whereat all were very joyful. They left Anilco at the beginning of December. On that journey, as on that before from Chilano, they suffered great hardship, for they had to cross many waters, and often it rained with a north wind and it became very cold; added to which they found themselves in the open fields with water below and above. While on the way, if they found any dry land to rest on at night, they gave many thanks to God. Almost all the Indians of service died from these sufferings, and after they had reached Aminoya, many Christians, and most of them were ill with severe and dangerous diseases which were akin to lethargy. There died André de Vasconcelos and two Portuguese of Elvas, who were of kin to him, who were brothers and called by the nickname of the Sotis. The Christians lodged in one of the towns, the one which appeared to them to be the better. It was surrounded with a stockade and was a quarter of a league from the great river. The maize of the other town was withdrawn thither—in all estimated at six thousand "fanegas." For building ships there was there the best wood they had seen in all the land of Florida. Thereupon, all gave hearty thanks to God for so notable a mercy and took hope of their desire being realized, namely, that they would come into a Christian land.

Chapter XXXVI.
How seven brigantines were constructed and how they departed from Aminoya.

As soon as they were come to Aminoya, the governor ordered the chains which each one had brought for his Indians to be taken and all the iron shot and all the iron in the camp to be collected together. He ordered a forge set up, nails made, and timber cut for the brigantines. A Portuguese of Ceuta who had been taught to saw with saws while a captive at Fez—and they brought him for that reason—taught others who were aiding him to saw timber; and a man from Genoa whom it was God's will to preserve (for without him they could not have left that land, as there was no other who knew how to build ships), together with four or five other Basque carpenters who hewed the planks and knees for him, built the brigantines. Two calkers, one a Genoese, and the other from Sardinia, calked them with tow from a plant like daffodils (of which I have previously spoken and which is there called "henequen"). But because there was not enough of it, they calked them with flax of the country and blankets which were unraveled for that purpose. A cooper among them fell sick and was at the point of death and there was no other man who could do that work. It pleased God to give him health; and though he was very weak and could not work, two weeks ere they departed, he made for each brigantine two hogsheads called quarter casks by sailors because

four of them make a water cask. The Indians of a province located two days' journey up the river, by name Tagoanate, as well as those of Anilco and Guachoya and others roundabout seeing that the brigantines were being built and thinking that since their harvests lay along the water, it was for the purpose of going to look for them; and because the governor asked them for blankets which were needed for use as sails, they came frequently and brought many and an abundance of fish. It surely seems that it was God's will to protect them in so great need, disposing the Indians to bring them; for there would have been no remedy except to go to take them; for, in the town where they were, as soon as winter set in, they became isolated and surrounded by water, so that it was impossible to go more than a league or a league and a half by land; and they could not take their horses to get away from there, and without them there was no place where they could attack them because there were many of them; and opposed on foot, one to the other, on water or land, they had the advantage, because they were more cunning and agile; and because of the lay of the land which suited their wishes in the manner of their warfare. They also brought some ropes and what was lacking for the cables were made from the bark of mulberry trees. They made stirrups out of wood and made anchors out of the stirrups. In the month of March, although it had not rained in that land for over a month, the river rose in such manner that it stretched clear to Nilco, nine leagues away; and the Indians said that it spread over another nine leagues of land on the other side. In the town where they were—which was higher land where one could go about better—the water rose to the stirrups. Wood was piled up in heaps, and many branches laid on top, and there they fastened the horses; and in the houses they did likewise. Finding that nothing was sufficient, they climbed up above. And if they left the house they used canoes or went horseback in places where the land was higher. Thus they lived for two months, during which the river did not fall and during which no work was done. The Indians did not cease to come to the brigantines, for they came and went in their canoes. The governor feared lest they attack him during that time, and ordered one of those who came to the town to be seized secretly and kept until the others should be gone. One was seized and the governor ordered him tortured in order to get him to tell whether the Indians were preparing any act of treachery. He stated that the caciques of Anilco, Guachoya, Taguanate, and others—in all about twenty caciques—had planned to attack him with a great number of men, and that three days before doing so they were to send a gift of fish in order to conceal their great treason and ill will; and on the very day they were to send some Indians on ahead with another gift. These latter, with those who served and who had conspired with them, were to set fire to the houses, but were first to possess themselves of the lances which were leaning against the doors of the houses. The caciques, with all their men, were to be placed in ambush in the woods near the town, and when they saw the fire lit, they were to hasten and rout the horsemen. The governor ordered the Indians to be chained; and on the day of which he spoke, thirty Indians came with fish. He ordered their right hands cut off, and in that condition sent them to the cacique of Guachoya to whom they belonged. He ordered them to tell him that he and the others could come whenever they wished, for he desired nothing better; but that he should know that they could think of nothing which he did not know before they had thought of it. Thereupon, they were all greatly terrified. The caciques of Anilco and Taguanate came to excuse themselves; and a few days later the cacique of Guachoya came, accompanied by one of his principal Indians and vassals. He said that by trustworthy information which he had, the caciques of Anilco and Taguanete had made an agreement to come to make war on the Christians. As soon as Indians came from Anilco, the governor questioned them and they confessed that this was true. He immediately handed them over to the principal man of Guachoya who led them outside the town and killed them. On the morrow, others came from Taguanete and they also confessed. The governor ordered their right hands and nostrils cut off and sent them to the cacique. Thereupon, those of Guachoya were very happy and came frequently bearing gifts of blankets, fish, and hogs which had been bred from some sows which had got lost there the year before. As soon as the waters fell, they agreed with the governor that he should send men to Taguanate. They came with canoes in which men of foot went down the river and a captain with men of horse and the Indians of Guachoya who guided him went overland until reaching Taguanete. They assaulted the town, capturing Indian

men and women and blankets, which with those they had, were sufficient for their needs. The building of the brigantines having been completed in the month of June, although the Indians had declared that the river rose only once during the year, namely, when the snows melted—at the time I have already mentioned it as having risen—it now being summer and a long time having passed since it had rained, it was God's will that the water rising came up to the town until it reached the brigantines, whence they were taken by water to the river; for had they been taken over by land, there would have been danger of their breaking and their bottoms opening up and being altogether disjointed, because for lack of iron the spikes were short and the planks and timbers thin. During their stay there, the Indians of Aminoya, forced by necessity, came to serve them, so that they might give them some of the ears of maize they had taken from them. And since the land was fertile and they were accustomed to eat maize, and they had taken from them all they had, and the people were many in number, they could not sustain themselves. Those who came to the town were so weak and enfeebled that they had no flesh on their bones; and many near the town died of pure hunger and weakness. The governor ordered, under grievous penalties, that no maize should be given them. However, seeing that they had no lack of hogs and that they were submitting themselves to serve them; and seeing their wretchedness and pitiful condition, having shared with them their maize out of pity for them: when they came to the time of embarking, there was not as much as was necessary. What there was they loaded into the brigantines and into large canoes fastened together in pairs. They put twenty-two horses aboard—the best ones in camp—and the rest were made into salt meat; and they did the same with the hogs they had. They left Aminoya on the second day of July, 1543.

Chapter XXXVII.
How the Indians of Quigaltam attacked the Christians on the river while going on their voyage and of what happened.

One day before they left Aminoya, they made up their minds to dismiss the Indians of service whom they had—both men and women—with the exception of some hundred or so whom the governor embarked or let those whom he wished embark. And because there were many persons of quality to whom he could not refuse what he granted to others, he made use of a trick saying that while they were on the river, they might serve them, but that as soon as they reached the sea, they would have to abandon them because of the need of water, there being but few casks. To his friends he said in secret that they should take them, that they could take them to New Spain; and all those for whom he did not have a good countenance—who were in the majority—ignorant of what was concealed from them (which time later made known) thought it inhuman for so short a time of service, in payment of the great service they had performed, to take them away in order to abandon them outside their lands to become captives of others. They abandoned five hundred head of Indians, male and female, among whom were many boys and girls who spoke and understood Spanish. Most of them were overcome with weeping, which was a great pity seeing that they had all readily become Christians and were now lost. Three hundred and twenty-two Spaniards left Aminoya in seven brigantines, of good construction except that the planks were thin because of the shortness of the spikes and they were not pitched. They had no decks by which to keep the water from coming in. In place of decks, they laid planks so that the sailors could go above to fasten the sails and the men might be sheltered below and above. The governor appointed captains of them and gave each one his brigantine, taking from each one his oath and word that he would be obedient to him until reaching the land of Christians. The governor took one of the brigantines for himself—the one he considered best. The day they left Aminoya, they passed Guachoya where the Indians were awaiting them in canoes on the river. They had built a large arbor on land and besought them to disembark. But he excused himself and passed by at a distance. The Indians accompanied him in their canoes. Coming to where an arm of the river led off to the right, they said that the province of Quigualtam lay nearby. They importuned the governor to go to make war on them, and said that they would aid him. But since they had said that it lay three days' journey below, it seemed to the governor that they had planned some treachery against him. There he took his leave of them and proceeded on his voyage where the force of the

water was greater. The current was very powerful and, aided by their oars, they journeyed at a good rate. The first day they landed in a wood on the left side of the river and at night they collected in the brigantines. Next day they came to a town where they landed, but the people there did not dare await them. An Indian woman whom they captured there, on being questioned, said that that town belonged to a cacique called Huhasene, a vassal of Quigaltam, and that Quigaltan was awaiting them with many men. Men of horse went down the river and found some houses in which was considerable maize. They immediately went there and stopped for a day, during which they threshed out and gathered what maize they needed. While they were there many Indians came down the river in canoes and placed themselves somewhat carelessly in form of battle in front on the other side. The governor sent in two canoes what crossbowmen he had and what men could get into them. They took to flight, but seeing that the Spaniards could not overtake them, gaining courage they turned back and coming nearer and shouting menaced them. As soon as they left there, they followed after them, some in canoes and others on land along the river. Going ahead of them, when they reached a town near the bluff, they all united, as if to show that they were of a mind to wait there. Each brigantine had a canoe fastened astern for its use. Men immediately entered them all and put the Indians to flight. He burned the town. Then on that day they landed at a large open field where the Indians did not dare await them. Next day, they got together one hundred canoes, some of which held sixty or seventy Indians, and those of the principal men with their awnings, and they with white and colored plumes of feathers as a device. They came within two crossbow-flights of the brigantines, and sent three Indians in one small canoe with a false message so that they might see the nature of the brigantines and the weapons they had. On coming up to the governor's brigantine, one of the Indians went in and told the governor that the cacique of Quigaltam, his lord, sent him to implore his protection, and to inform him that whatever the Indians of Guachoya had told him was false, namely, that they had revolted because they were his enemies; that he was his servitor and considered himself as such. The governor answered him saying that he believed all he said to be true and that he appreciated his friendship highly. Thereupon, they went to the place where the others were awaiting them in their canoes; and from that place, they all came down and came upon the Spaniards yelling and threatening them. The governor sent Juan de Guzmán, who had been captain of foot in Florida, in the canoes with twenty-five armed men to get them out of the way. As soon as the Indians saw them coming, they divided into two bands and remained still until the Spaniards reached them, when putting out from each side, they came together, taking between them Juan de Guzmán and those who came ahead with him and closed with them with great fury. Since their canoes were larger and since many of them jumped into the water in order to keep them upright, the others to seize the canoes of the Spaniards, and cause them to overturn, they immediately overturned them. The Christians fell into the water and because of the weight of their armor sank to the bottom. And if any, by swimming or laying hold of a canoe, were able to keep afloat, they struck them over the head with their paddles and the clubs they were carrying and made them sink. When the men in the brigantine beheld their defeat, although they desired to aid them, they were unable to turn back because of the current of the river. Four Spaniards escaped to that brigantine which was nearest the canoes; and these only of all who had gone to the Indians escaped. Eleven men were killed there, among them being Juan de Guzmán and a son of Don Carlos called Juan de Vargas. Most, also, were persons of honor and men of much bearing. Those who escaped by swimming said they saw the Indians enter one of their canoes by the stern with Juan de Guzmán, but whether they bore him away dead or alive, they could not determine.

Chapter XXXVIII.
Which relates how they were pursued by the Indians.

The Indians, on seeing that they had gained the victory, were so greatly encouraged that they went out to engage the brigantines which they had not dared to do before. First they went to that in which Calderón was captain. It was going in the rear guard. At the first flight of arrows twenty-five men were wounded. In the brigantine were only four men with armor. These were stationed at the side in order to defend it. Those who had no armor, seeing that they were being wounded, abandoned the oars and hid away below the covering. The brigantine began to run crosswise and to go whither the current of the water might bear it. On seeing this, one of the men in armor, without awaiting the captain's approval for his action, forced a foot soldier to take the oar and steer the brigantine, placing himself before him and covering him with his shield. The Indians did not come up nearer than an arrow's flight, where they took the offensive without being attacked and without receiving any injury, for there was not above one crossbow in each brigantine, and those that there were, were now in very bad condition; so that the Christians did nothing else except to stand as a mark waiting for their arrows. Having left that brigantine, they went to another and fought against it for half an hour. And in this way they circulated from one to another of them all. The Christians had brought mats to put under themselves which were doubled and very close and strong so that the arrows did not pierce them. As soon as the Indians gave them time, the brigantines were hung with them. The Indians, seeing that they could not shoot direct, shot their arrows haphazardly into the air which fell down into the brigantines and wounded some of the men. Not satisfied with this, they tried to get at those who were coming in the canoes with the horses. Those of the brigantines came about in order to protect them and convoyed them in their midst. And now, finding themselves so closely pursued by them and so tired out that they could not endure it they resolved to travel all that night following, thinking that they would pass by the land of Quigualtam and that they would leave them. But when they were going along more freely, thinking that they had already left them, they heard very loud cries hard by, which stunned them. In this manner, they followed us that night and the next day, until noon, when we had now reached the land of others whom they advised to treat us in the same way; and so they did. Those of Quigualtam returned to their own lands and the others in fifty canoes, continued to fight us for a whole day and night. They boarded one of the brigantines which was coming as a rearguard by means of the canoe which it bore astern, and they took away an Indian woman whom they found in it. And from there they wounded some of those in the brigantine. Those who came in the canoes with the horses, wearied out with paddling night and day, sometimes allowed themselves to rest. Then the Indians were on them at once, and the men in the brigantines would wait for them. The governor made up his mind to land and kill the horses, because of the slowness with which they sailed on account of them. As soon as they saw a place suitable for this, they went thither and killed the horses there, and loaded the meat into the brigantines after salting it. They left four or five of the horses alive on the shore and the Indians went up to them after the Spaniards had embarked. The horses were unused to them and began to neigh and to run about in various directions, whereat the Indians jumped into the water for fear of them. Entering their canoes behind the brigantines, they continued to shoot at them without any pity and followed us that afternoon and the night following until ten o'clock next morning, and then went back up stream. Soon seven canoes came out from a small town located near the river and followed them for a short distance down the river shooting at them. But seeing that because of their small number they were doing them little injury, they went back to their town. After that they had no trouble, until they came almost to the sea. They went for seventeen days along the river, a distance of about two hundred and fifty leagues or so. Near the sea, it divided into two branches each of which was about a league and a half wide.

Chapter XXXIX.
How they reached the sea; and what happened to them before and after they started their voyage.

A half league before they came to the sea, they anchored there for a day to rest, for they were very tired from rowing and greatly disheartened because of the many days during which they had eaten nothing but parched and boiled maize, which was doled out in a ration of a leveled-off helmet to each mess of three. While they were there, seven canoes of Indians came to attack those in the canoes they brought. The governor ordered armed men to enter and go out against them and put them to flight. They also came to attack them by land through a thicket and a swamp. They had clubs set with very sharp

fishbones, and with these they fought courageously with those of us who sallied out to oppose them. The others who came in their canoes were awaiting with their arrows those who went out to them; and as soon as we came up, both those on land and those in canoes wounded some of us. When they saw that they were approaching, they would turn about face, and like swift horses before foot soldiers, would make off, and after turning hither and thither, and again gathering together without ever getting farther away than an arrow's flight, for thus gathering they would come on shooting without receiving any injury from the Christians. For, although they had some bows, they did not know how to shoot with them, and came on rowing, breaking their arms to come up. The Indians kept circling tirelessly around them in their canoes, waiting and turning about as if in a skirmish. Those who went after them seeing that they could do them no harm; and that the closer they obstinately tried to approach them, the more injury they received: as soon as they managed to drive them off, they returned to the brigantines. They stayed there two days. From thence they went to the place where that branch of the river flowed into the sea. They took soundings in the river near the sea and found a depth of forty fathoms. They stopped there and the governor ordered all and every one of them to state his opinion regarding their voyage—whether, committing themselves to the sea, they should cross direct to New Spain, or whether they should go coasting along. There were various opinions about this. In this matter, Juan de Añasco, who had great self-conceit and set high value on his understanding of navigation and sea matters, but who really had small experience in its practice, influenced the governor. His opinion accorded with that of some others who said that it was much better to take to the open sea and cross the gulf—a voyage one-fourth as long—for if they coasted along, they would make many windings, because of the bends in the land: Juan de Añasco saying that he had seen the sailing chart and that where they were, the coast ran east and west to the river Las Palmas, and from the river Las Palmas to New Spain, it ran north and south, and for that reason, if they went continuously within sight of land, they would make a great circuit and their course would be very slow. They would also run greater danger of winter overtaking them ere they could reach a Christian land. They could arrive within ten or twelve days by crossing, if they had good weather. The majority opposed this opinion and said it would be safer to coast along even if it did take longer, for their ships had little strength, had no decks, and a slight storm would be enough to wreck them, and if calm or contrary weather should come upon them because of the small space they had for water, they would also run great risk. Even were the ships such that they could venture in them, since they had no pilot or sailing chart by which to steer, to cross over was not a good counsel. This opinion of the majority was confirmed, and they agreed to coast along. When they were about to depart, the cable by which the anchor of the governor's brigantine was cast, broke, and the anchor was lost in the river; and although they were near land, so great was the depth of water that however much swimmers looked for it, it could not be found. This was the cause of great distress to the governor and to all in his brigantine. With a stone for grinding maize which they had brought along, and the bridles still remaining to some of those hidalgos and gentlemen who had horses, they made a weight which passed by way of remedy for an anchor. On July 18, they put out to sea and undertook their voyage amid calm and fair weather. The governor, accompanied by Juan de Añasco, put out to sea in their brigantines, and all followed them. On seeing that they had got two or three leagues offshore, the captains of the other brigantines overtook them and asked the governor why he was holding offshore, that if he intended to leave the coast, he ought to say so, but that he should not do so without getting the opinion of all, and that if he tried to act in any other manner, they would not follow him, but each one would do what seemed best to him. The governor answered saying that he would do nothing without their advice, but that he desired to leave the land in order to be able to sail better and safer by night, and that next day when it was time he would return within sight of land. They sailed that day with a fine wind, the night following and the next day until vespers always in fresh water, at which they were greatly surprised, for they were very far offshore. But so great is the force of the current of the river, and the coast there so

shallow and gentle that fresh water runs out very far into the sea. That night, they saw some keys on the right, whither they went. They rested there that night. There Juan de Añasco, by means of his arguments, finished by getting all to consent and consider it proper to take to the open sea, saying, as he had said already, that it would be a great advantage and would shorten their voyage greatly. They sailed for two days and when they tried to return within sight of land, they could not, because the wind was blowing offshore. On the fourth day, seeing that the water was giving out, and fearing want and danger, they all cursed Juan de Añasco and the governor who had taken his advice. Each one of the captains declared that he would never again get away from the land, although the governor could go wherever he wished. It was God's will that the wind should shift, although only a bit, and four days after having taken to the open sea, and now in need of water, they came within sight of land by dint of rowing and, after great labor, reached it along an unsheltered beach. That afternoon, the wind veered to the south, which is a cross wind along that coast and drove the brigantines ashore, for it was a very stiff wind; and the anchors straightened out because they had little iron and went dragging. The governor ordered them all into the water, and by placing themselves on the land side and by forcing the brigantines seaward when the wave passed by, they kept them up until the wind softened.

Chapter XL.
How some got lost from others because of the storm and afterward came together on a key.

After the storm had ceased, they landed on the beach where they were and by means of some hoes they had brought along they dug some holes which filled with fresh water with which they filled their water casks. Next day they left that place and sailed for two days; and entered a small creek like an estuary sheltered from a south wind which was then blowing and which was contrary to them. Four days passed before they could leave there; and as soon as the sea became quiet, they went out by rowing. They went along that day and about eventide the wind strengthened so that it drove them ashore and they regretted having left there, for as soon as night fell the storm began to rage on sea and the wind to strengthen more and more because of the storm. The brigantines got lost one from the other. The two farthest out to sea went two leagues beyond the place where the others were that night and entered an arm of the sea which ran up into the land. The five which were behind, separated one from the other by a distance of a league or a half league found themselves without knowing anything of one another on a very unsheltered beach where the wind and wave drove them ashore, for the anchors straightened out and went dragging and the oars could not keep them upright, although seven or eight men laid hold of one oar and rowed seaward. All the other men leaped into the water and as the wave which was driving the brigantine ashore passed by, they pushed it seaward with as much force as possible. Before another wave came, other men bailed out with bowls the water they had shipped. While suffering this hazard of fortune, in great fear of being lost there, from midnight on they had to endure an insufferable torment from myriads of mosquitoes which came upon them and which caused an irritation whenever they stung as if they were poisonous. In the morning the sea calmed and the wind softened, but not the mosquitoes; and although the sails were white, in the morning, they appeared black with them. The men who were at the oars, could not row unless other men drove them away. The terror and danger of the storm having subsided, upon beholding the disfigurement of their faces and the slaps which they had given one another to drive them away, they laughed. They came together in the estuary where were the two brigantines which had gone on ahead. There a scum was found called "copee" which the sea cast up and which resembles pitch (with which they pitch their ships in certain regions where pitch is lacking). There they pitched their brigantines. They stayed two days and then resumed their voyage. They sailed another two days and anchored at a bay or arm of the sea where they stayed two days. The day they left, six men went up the bay in a canoe but did not come to its head. They left there with a south wind which was against them, but since it was light and their desire to shorten their voyage great, they went out by rowing into the sea, and journeyed for two days in that way and with great toil, a very little

distance, and entered behind an islet by means of a branch of the sea which surrounded it. While they were there, such weather ensued that they gave fervent thanks to God that they had reached such a shelter. There was an abundance of fish there which they caught with nets and a hook. A man threw out a hook with a line, tying the end of it about his arm. A fish seized it and drew him into the water until he was up to his neck. It was God's will that he remembered his knife which he drew out and cut the line therewith. They stayed there fourteen days, at the end of which God was pleased to send them good weather. Because of that, they very devoutly arranged a procession and walked along the beach praying God to take them to a land where they might serve Him better.

Chapter XLI.
How they came to the River of Panico.

All along the seacoast wherever they dug, they found water. There they filled their casks and after the procession was ended, they embarked, and always keeping within sight of land, sailed for six days. Juan de Añasco said that they would do well to put out to sea, for he had seen the sailing chart and remembered that the coast ran north and south from the river of Palmas on, and that so far it had run east and west. According to his opinion, judging by his reckonings, the river of Palmas ought not to be far from where they were. That night they put out to sea and in the morning, over the rim of the water, beheld palm trees and the coast running north and south; and from noon on great mountains which they had not seen thitherto; for from that point to the port of Espiritu Santo where they had entered Florida, it was a very level and low land, and for that reason it could not be seen except when they were very close to it. From what they saw, they believed that that night they had passed the river of Palmas, which is sixty leagues from that of Panico, which is in New Spain. All gathered together. Some said that they would do well not to sail by night, in order not to pass the river of Panico; and others, that it was not advisable to lose time during favoring weather, and that it could not be so near that they would pass it that night. They agreed to set the sails half reefed and sail in that way. Two brigantines which sailed that night with all sails set passed the river of Panico at dawn without seeing it. The first to arrive of the five which were behind was that of which Calderón was captain. For a quarter of a league before they reached it, and before they saw it, they saw the water was muddy and perceived that it was fresh. Coming opposite the river, they saw that water was breaking over a shoal where it flowed into the sea. Because there was no one there who knew it, they were in doubt as to whether they should enter or pass by at a distance. They made up their minds to enter, and they put in to land before reaching the current, and entered the port. As soon as they were inside, they saw Indians, both men and women, on the shore, clad according to the Spanish custom, whom they asked in what land they were. They replied in the Spanish language that that was the river of Panico and that the town of the Christians was fifteen leagues inland. The joy received by all at this news could not be wholly told. For it seemed to them that then they had received birth. Many leaped ashore and kissed the ground and kneeling down with hands and eyes raised to heaven, one and all ceased not to give thanks to God. As soon as those who were coming behind saw Calderón with his brigantine anchored in the river, they immediately set out thither and entered the port. The two other brigantines which had passed beyond, put out to sea in order to turn back to look for the others, but they could not because the wind was against them and the sea was choppy. Fearing lest they be lost, they ran toward the land and anchored. While there, a storm came up, and seeing that they could not hold themselves there, nor less in the sea, they determined to run up on the land. And as the brigantines were small, they drew but little water, and as there was a sandy beach there, the force of their sails drove them to dry land without harm coming to the men in them. At that time, if those in port were very joyful, these felt a double sadness in their hearts, for they knew nothing of the others, nor in what land they were, and feared lest it be one of hostile Indians. They came out two leagues below the port, and as soon as they found themselves free of the sea, each one took as much of his clothing as he could carry on his back. They went inland and found Indians who told them where they were, whereat their sorrow was turned into joy. They gave many thanks to God for having delivered them from so many dangers.

Chapter XLII.
How they reached Panico and how they were received by the inhabitants.

From the time they went out from the great river of Florida into the sea until they reached the river of Panico, they took fifty-two days. They entered the river of Panico on the tenth of September of the year 1543. They went upstream with their brigantines for four days; and as the wind was light and frequently useless to them because of the many windings of the river; and in towing them up because of the powerful current in many places they could for this reason make but little headway, and with heavy toil; and seeing that the accomplishment of their desire—namely, to see themselves among Christians and to see the divine offices celebrated which they had not seen for so long—was delayed; they left the brigantines to the sailors and went overland to Panico. All were clad in deerskins, tanned and dyed black—namely, cassocks, breeches, and shoes. Upon entering Panico, they went immediately to the church to pray and give thanks to God for having so miraculously saved them. The inhabitants, whom the Indians had already advised and who knew of their coming, took them to their homes and entertained them—some among them whom they knew and with whom they had had contact, or because they had come from their districts. The alcalde mayor took the governor to his home, and all the others, as soon as they arrived, he sent to lodgings in groups of six and ten, according to the capacity of each of the inhabitants; and all were supplied by their hosts with many hens, maize bread, and fruits of the land, which are identical with those of Cuba of which I have spoken above. The town of Panico has about seventy householders. Most of them have houses of cut stone; some are of wood and all are thatched with hay. The land is poor and there is no gold or silver in it. People there are very well supplied with food and service. The richest do not have an income of five hundred cruzados at the outside, which they get in cotton clothing, fowls, and maize, paid to them as tribute by the Indians, their vassals. Of those who left Florida, three hundred and eleven Christians entered that port. The alcalde mayor immediately sent one of the citizens by post to inform the viceroy, Don Antonio de Mendoza (who was living in Mexico) that of the men who had gone with Fernando de Soto to conquer and explore Florida, there had ported there three hundred men, for whom he had determined to provide since they came in the service of his Majesty. At this, the viceroy and all those of Mexico were surprised, for they considered them lost because they had plunged into the land of Florida, and they had had no news of them for a long time. It seemed to them a marvel that they could sustain themselves for so long a time among heathen being without a fortress where they might build strongholds and without any other relief. The viceroy immediately issued an order in which he decreed that, wherever they should be ordered, the necessary food and Indian porters should be given them; and wherever any refused to make provision, they could take by force what they needed without incurring any penalty. That order was so well obeyed that on the way before they reached the towns the people went out to meet them with fowls and food.

Chapter XLIII.
Of the favor they found with the viceroy and inhabitants of Mexico.

From Panico to the great city of Mestitam Mexico is a distance of sixty leagues. There are another sixty leagues, both from Panico and from Mexico to the port of Vera Cruz where one embarks for Spain and where those on their way to New Spain land. Those three towns, which were settled by Spaniards, form a triangle, to wit, with Vera Cruz at the south, Panico at the east, and Mexico at the west, with a distance of sixty leagues one from the other. The land is so thickly populated with Indians that from town to town those which are farthest apart are separated only by a league or half a league. Some of those who came from Florida remained in Panico for a month resting and others for a fortnight—each as long as he wished, for no one showed a long face toward his guests, but gave them everything they had, and showed they were sorry when they bade them goodbye. This can be believed, for the food which the Indians gave as tribute was more than enough for them, and there was nothing to buy or sell in that town. Few Spaniards were there and rejoiced to talk with them. The alcalde mayor divided among all who wished to go to get it, all the clothing there belonging to the emperor (which is paid there as taxes). Those who still had

coats of mail rejoiced, for each one found a horse there for it. Some got mounts, and those who could not (the majority of them) set out on their journey afoot. On their way they were well received by the Indians who abode in their towns, and better served than they could have been in their own homes, even though they lived decently as to food. For, if they asked an Indian for a hen, he would bring four; and if they asked for some fruit, they would go off running for it, even if it were a league away. And if any Christian were ill, they would carry him from one town to the next in a chair. To whatever town they came, the cacique, through the agency of an Indian who carried a rod of justice in his hand (whom they call "tapile," signifying magistrate), ordered them to be supplied with provisions and Indians as bearers of any clothing they had and for carrying those who were ill, as many as were needed. The viceroy sent a Portuguese to a distance of twenty leagues from Mexico with a quantity of sugar, raisins, pomegranates, and other things given to sick people, for those who might have need of them. He had determined to clothe them all at the emperor's cost. And the inhabitants of Mexico having heard that they were coming, went out to meet them; and with great courtesy requesting it as a favor, each one took to his home those whom he could and gave them clothing—each the best he could—so that he who was least well clad had clothing worth thirty cruzados and upward. To all who cared to go to the lodging of the viceroy, the latter ordered clothing to be given, and those who were persons of quality ate at his table. For men of lesser sort, he had a table in his house for all who cared to eat at it. He was immediately informed who each one was, in order to show him the honor he merited. Some of the conquistadors placed them all, both gentlemen and peasants, at the same table with themselves and frequently made the servant sit shoulder to shoulder beside his master. This was mainly done by artisans and men of low sort. However, those of better breeding, asked who each one was and differentiated among persons. But all did what they could with great goodwill, each telling those he had in his house not to be vexed or hesitate to take what was given them, for they had formerly beheld themselves in like circumstances and others had helped them and that such was the custom in that land. May God reward them; and those whom He was pleased to let escape from Florida and come to the land of Christians, may it please Him that this be for His service; and to those who died there and all those who believe in Him and confess His holy faith, may He grant them through His mercy the glory of paradise. Amen.

Chapter XLIV.
Which declares certain diversities and peculiarities of the land of Florida; and the products and birds and animals of that land.

From the port of Espiritu Santo, where they landed when they entered Florida, to the province of Ocute, a distance of about four hundred leagues or so, the land is very level and has many lakes and thick woods. In places there are wild pine groves and the soil is lean, and without a mountain or hill in it. The land of Ocute is the most fertile and vigorous and has the most open forest and very excellent fields along the rivers. From Ocute to Cutifachiqui is a distance of about one hundred and thirty leagues, eighty of which are without inhabitants and covered with many wild pine groves. Large rivers flow through the uninhabited part. From Cutifachiqui to Juala is a distance of about two hundred and fifty leagues, all the land being mountainous. Cutifachiqui and Juala are loacted on level ground, high, and with excellent river meadows. Thence, as far as Chiaha, Coça, and Talise, the land is level, dry, and fertile, and greatly abounding in maize. From Juala to Tascaluça is a distance of about two hundred and fifty leagues. From Tascaluça to the great river it is about three hundred leagues, the land being low and having many swamps. From the great river onward, the land is higher and open and the most densely populated of all the land of Florida. And along this river, from Aquixo to Pacaha and Coligoa, a distance of one hundred and fifty leagues, the land is level and covered with open forest, and in places has very fertile and pleasant fields. From Coligoa to Autiamque is a distance of about two hundred and fifty leagues of mountainous country. From Autiamque to Guacay is a distance of about two hundred and thirty leagues of level land. From Aguacay to Daycao, a distance of one hundred and twenty leagues, is all a mountainous country. From the port of Espiritu Santo to Apalache, they marched from east to west and northeast; from Cutifachiqui to Juala, from south to north; from

Juala to Coça, from east to west, from Coça to Tascaluça, and to the great river as far as the provinces of Quizquiz and Aquixo, from east to west; from Alquixo to Pacaha, northward; from Pacaha to Tula, from east to west; and from Tula to Antiamque, from north to south, as far as the province of Guachoya and Daycao. The bread which is eaten in all the land of Florida is of maize which resembles coarse millet. This maize is found in all the islands and Indies of Castile from the Antilles on. In Florida, there are also many walnuts, plums, mulberries, and grapes. They sow and harvest the maize, each one cultivating his own. The fruits are common to all, for they grow very abundantly in the open fields, without it being necessary to plant or cultivate them. Wherever there are mountains, there are chestnuts. They are somewhat smaller than those of Spain. From the great river westward, the walnuts differ from the others, for they are easier to crush and shaped like acorns. From the great river to the port, they are, for the most part, hard and the trees and walnuts seem similar to those of Spain. In all parts of the country is a fruit which comes from a plant like "ligoacam," which the Indians sow. The fruit resembles the royal pear, and has an excellent smell and a delicious taste. Another plant grows in the open field, which produces a fruit near the ground like the strawberry, which is very tasty. The plums are of two kinds, red and gray, of the form and size of walnuts. They have three or four stones. They are better than all those of Spain and they make much better dried ones of them. Only in the grapes can one perceive the lack of cultivation, which, although they are large have large seeds. All the other fruits are very perfect and less harmful than those of Spain. In Florida, are many bears and lions, wolves, deer, jackals, cats, and rabbits. There are many wild fowl there, as large as peafowls, small partridges like those of Africa, cranes, ducks, turtle doves, thrushes, and sparrows. There are certain black birds which are larger than sparrows and smaller than starlings. There are goshawks, falcons, sparrowhawks, and all the birds of prey found in Spain. The Indians are well proportioned. Those of the flat lands are of taller stature and better built than those of the mountains. Those of the interior are better supplied with maize and clothing native to the country than those of the coast. The land along the coast is lean and poor; and the more warlike people are along the coast. From the port of Espiritu Santo to Apalache, and from Apalache to the river of Palmas from east to west; from the river of Palmas to New Spain, from north to south, with a gentle coast, but with many shoals and high sand hills.

Deo Gratias.

This relation of the discovery of Florida was printed in the house of André de Burgos, printer and gentleman of the house of the Lord Cardinal Infante. It was finished on the tenth day of February of the year one thousand five hundred and fifty-seven in the noble and ever loyal city of Evora.

240. 1539–1541. The official narrative of the expedition of Hernando de Soto, by Rodrigo Rangel, his secretary, as rendered by Gonzalo Fernández de Oviedo.

The Rangel narrative follows most closely the progress of the expedition, although it has lacunae and it is incomplete. Oviedo notes that Rangel gave an account of his experiences to the Audiencia of Santo Domingo and was instructed by it, before Oviedo left Santo Domingo in 1546, to give him (Oviedo) a full account in writing of the expedition. It may be that Rangel never completed his report before Oviedo departed. The version printed by Oviedo in Historia general y natural de las Indias, *bk. XVII, section i, chaps. i–viii, contains also the elisions and interpolations of the historian; it carries the story only to November, 1541. The original manuscript has not been found. The translation is taken from E. G. Bourne,* Narratives of the Career of Hernando de Soto, *II, 49–149.*

1.

The Emperor, our lord, appointed as his Governor and Captain-General of the Island of Cuba and of the Province of Florida and the adjacent regions in the northern mainland, which had been discovered by the commander Johan Ponce de Leon, Hernando de Soto, who was one of the soldiers of the Governor Pedrarias de Ávila, of whom in the history of Terra-Firma there has been frequent mention, since he was one of the pioneers in those parts and was in the lead in the capture of Atabaliba when he was one of those who obtained a large share of the spoils. He brought so much to Spain that it was reported that he found himself in Castile with over one hundred thousand pesos de oro, where, for his services and merits, he was very well received by the Emperor, our lord; and he made him Knight of the Order of St. James and bestowed other honours and made him Governor and Captain-General, as has been related.

And while he was in Castile he married one of the daughters of the Governor Pedrarias Dávila, whose name was Doña Isabel de Bovadilla, and, who, like her mother, was a woman both good and great and truly noble in mind and bearing. With her De Soto went to the island of Cuba where he arrived in the month of [June] in the year 1539. And after he had viewed the island and its settlements, and made the provision needful for its well being and for the preservation of the land, he gave orders to arm and to pass over to the mainland to conquer and settle and reduce to peaceful life those provinces which his Majesty had bestowed upon him; and in this enterprise the events took place which will be narrated in the following chapters.

2.

On Sunday, May 18, 1539, the Governor Hernando de Soto departed from the City of Havana with a noble fleet of nine vessels, five ships, two caravels and two brigantines; and on May 25, which was Whitsuntide, land was seen on the northern coast of Florida; and the fleet came to anchor two leagues from shore in four fathoms of water or less; and the Governor went on board a brigantine to view the land, and with him a gentleman named Johan de Añasco and the chief pilot of the fleet whose name was Alonso Martin, to discover what land it was, for they were in doubt as to the port and where to find it; and not recognizing it, seeing that night was approaching, they wished to return to the ships, but the wind did not suffer them for it was contrary; therefore they cast anchor near the land and went on shore, where they came upon traces of many Indians and one of the large cabins that are seen in the Indies and other small ones. Later they were told that it was the village of Oçita.

The Governor and those with him were in no small peril, since they were few and without arms; and no less was the distress of those left in ships to see their General in such an evil case, for they could neither succour nor assist him if there were need. In fact, to take such great care, was really heedlessness and excessive zeal, or a lack of prudence on the part of the Governor; for such work belongs to other persons and not to him who has to govern and rule the army, and it is enough to send a captain of lower rank for such a reconnoissance and the protection of the pilot who has to go to examine the coast. And the ships there were in sore travail and the whole fleet too, in which there were 570 men, not counting the sailors; including them the number was fully 700. The next morning, Monday, the brigantine was far to the leeward of the ships and labouring to come up to them and was no wise able to. Seeing this, Baltasar de Gallegos shouted to the Admiral's ship that the Lieutenant-General, who was a knight named Vasco Porcallo, should go and see what had best be done, and, when he heard him not, to bring aid to the Governor he ordered a large caravel to weigh anchor in which that gentleman went as captain, and which put out in the direction where the brigantine appeared; and although the Governor regretted it, yet it was well done since it was in his service and to succour his person. Finally the caravel came up to the brigantine, much to the satisfaction of the Governor.

In the meantime the harbour was recognized and the other brigantine stationed in the channel as sign for the ships, and the Governor's brigantine approached to station the caravel also in the channel of the harbour; and he ordered that it should take a position on one side of the channel and the brigantine on the other so that the ships might pass between them. This they now began to do under sail, for they were four or five leagues off. The Governor had to be there to show them the way, because the chief pilot was in the brigantine and because there were many shallows. In spite of all their pains two of the ships scraped bottom, but, as it was sandy, they received no damage. This day there were hard words between the Governor and Johan de Añasco, who

came as the King's auditor, but the Governor restrained his feelings and was patient.

The ships entered the harbour constantly sounding the lead, and sometimes they scraped bottom, but, as it was mud, they passed on. This took up five days, during which they did not land except that some men went ashore and brought water and forage for the horses. Finally, since the ships with their loads could not, on account of the shoals, proceed to where the village lay, they anchored about four leagues farther back.

On Friday, May 30, they began to put the horses ashore. The place where they disembarked was due north of the Island of Tortuga, which is in the mouth of the Bahama channel. The chief of this land was named Oçita, and it is ten leagues west of the Bay of Johan Ponce.

As soon as some of the horses were on shore, General Vasco Porcallo de Figueroa and Johan de Añasco and Francisco Osorio rode off to see something of the country; and they lighted upon ten Indians with bows and arrows who, in their turn, were coming as warriors to get a look at these Christian guests and to learn what manner of folk they were, and they shot two horses and the Spaniards slew two Indians and put the rest to flight.

There were in that expedition two hundred and forty-three horses. Of these nineteen or twenty died on the sea, but all the rest were put ashore. The General and some foot soldiers went in the brigantines to see the village; and a gentleman named Gomez Arias returned in one of them and gave a good report of the country and likewise told us how the people had gone away.

On Trinity Sunday, June 1, 1539, this army marched by land toward the village, taking as guides four Indians that Johan de Añasco had captured when in search of the harbour; and they lost their bearings somewhat, either because the Christians failed to understand the Indians or because the latter did not tell the truth. Thereupon the Governor went ahead with some horsemen, but since they were unfamiliar with the land they wearied the horses following deer and floundering in the streams and swamps for twelve leagues till they found themselves opposite the village on the other side of the roadstead of the harbour, which they could not pass around. And that night worn out they slept scattered about and not at all in order for war. During all that week the ships gradually approached the village, being unloaded little by little with boats, and in that way they took ashore all the clothes and provisions which they carried.

Some paths were found, but no one knew or was able to guess which to take to find the natives of the country. The four Indians understood very little, and then only by signs, and it was not easy to guard them as they had no fetters. Tuesday, June 3, the Governor took possession of the country in the name of their Majesties, with all the formalities that are required, and despatched one of the Indians to persuade and allure the neighbouring chiefs with peace. That same night two of the three Indians that remained ran away, and it was only by great good luck that all three did not get away, which gave the Christians much concern.

On Wednesday the Governor sent Captain Baltasar de Gallegos with the Indian that was left to look for some people or a village or a house. Toward sunset, being off their road, because the Indian, who was the guide, led them wandering and confused, it pleased God that they descried at a distance some twenty Indians painted with a kind of red ointment that the Indians put on when they go to war or wish to make a fine appearance. They wore many feathers and had their bows and arrows. And when the Christians ran at them the Indians fled to a hill, and one of them came forth into the path lifting up his voice and saying, "Sirs, for the love of God and of Holy Mary, slay not me; I am a Christian like yourselves and was born in Seville, and my name is Johan Ortiz."

The delight of the Christians was very great in God's having given them a tongue and a guide, of which, at that time, they were in great need; and, with every one very much elated, Baltasar de Gallegos and all the Indians who came with him, returned that night very late to the camp; and the Spaniards of the army were greatly wrought up, believing it was something else, and seized their arms; but seeing what it was, great was the joy that they felt, for they believed that by means of that interpreter they could accomplish much more. Without loss of time, on the Saturday following, the Governor resolved to go with that Johan Ortiz, interpreter, to the chief that had held him who was called Mococo, to make peace and to induce him to make friends with the Christians. And he awaited them in his village with his

Indians, his wives and his sons, not one missing, and he made complaint to the Governor of the chiefs Orriygua, Neguarete, Capaloey, and Eçita, all four of whom are chiefs of this coast, saying that they threatened him because he accepted our friendship and saw fit to give up this Christian as an interpreter to the Christians. The Governor made this same interpreter to say that he should have no fear of these chiefs or of others, since he would protect him; and that all the Christians and many more that were to come soon would be his friends and help him and show him favour against his enemies.

That same day Captain Johan Ruiz Lobillo went up into the country with about forty foot soldiers and came upon some huts, but were able to take only two Indian women. To rescue them, nine Indians followed him, shooting at him for three leagues; and they slew one Christian and wounded three or four, yet without his being able to do them any harm, although he had arquebusiers and crossbow-men, because these Indians are as agile and as good fighters as can be found among all the nations of the world.

3.

This Governor [Hernando de Soto] was much given to the sport of slaying Indians, from the time that he went on military expeditions with the Governor Pedrarias Dávila in the provinces of Castilla del Oro and of Nicaragua; and likewise he was in Peru and present at the capture of that great Prince Atabalipa, where he was enriched. He was one of the richest that returned to Spain because he brought to Seville, and put in safe keeping there, upwards of one hundred thousand pesos of gold; and he decided to return to the Indies to lose them with his life and to continue the employment, blood-stained in the past, which he had followed in the countries I mention.

So then, continuing his conquest, he ordered General Vasco Porcallo de Figueroa to go to Oçita because it was reported that people had come together there; and this captain having gone there, he found the people departed and he burned the village and threw an Indian, which he had for a guide, to the dogs. The reader is to understand that *aperrear* [to throw to the dogs], is to have the dogs eat him, or kill him, tearing the Indian in pieces, since the Conquistadores in the Indies have always used to carry Irish greyhounds and very bold, savage dogs. It is for this reason that reference was made above to the chase of Indians. In this way this Indian guide was killed because he lied and guided badly.

While Vasco Porcallo was doing what has been related, the Governor despatched another Indian as a messenger to the chief Orriparacogi, and he did not return because an Indian woman told him not to, and for this reason she was thrown to the dogs. There were among those in this army divers opinions whether it would be well to settle there or not, because the soil seemed to be barren, and such in fact is its repute. For this reason the Governor resolved to send Captain Baltasar de Gallegos to Orriparagi with eighty horse and one hundred foot, and he set out on Friday, June 20.

And the Governor likewise sent Johan de Añasco in the ship's boats along the shore with some foot soldiers to disperse a gathering of the Indians, or to see and hear what was up. He found them on an island, where he had a fray with them and killed with the small cannons that he carried nine of ten Indians and, they in turn, shot or cut down as many or more Christians. And since he could not dislodge them from the island he sent for help, and the messenger was a hidalgo named Johan de Vega, and he asked for horsemen to take possession of the mainland at the place where they were likely to come away; since with the force that he had and with the increase he expected to land and fight the Indians.

The Governor sent Vasco Porcallo with forty horse and some foot, but when this reinforcement arrived the Indians had gone; and the Spaniards, not to have come in vain, raided the land and captured some women whom they took to the camp. Vasco Porcallo, upon his return from this raid, had something of a clash with the Governor (which is concealed in this narrative) nor was the historian able, on account of certain considerations, to find any one who could inform him what he said to him. And it was accepted as a good settlement that Vasco Porcallo should return to Cuba to look after the affairs of the government there, and to provide the Governor and his army when it should be necessary with what they might have need of. The departure of this cavalier was regretted by many since he was a friend of good men and did much for them.

The Governor had ordered Baltasar de Gallegos even though he found no good land, that he should write good news to encourage the men; and, although it was not his nature to lie since he was a man of truth, yet to obey the order of his superior and not to dismay the men, he always wrote two letters of different tenor, one truthful, and the other of falsehoods, yet falsehoods so skilfully framed with equivocal words that they could be understood one way or the other because they required it; and in regard to this, he said that the true letter would have more force to exculpate himself than the false one evil to harm him. And so the Governor did not show the true letters, but announced beforehand that what he did not show was very secret information which later on would be made clear for the great advantage of all. The ambiguous and deceptive letters he showed and made such declarations as seemed best to him.

Those letters, although they promised no particular thing, gave hopes and hints that stirred their desires to go forward and emerge from doubts to certainty; wherefore as the sins of mankind are the reason that falsehood sometimes finds reception and credit, all became united and of one mind and requested the invasion of the land, which was just what the Governor was contriving; and those that were ordered to stay behind with Captain Calderon were heavy in spirit, and there were of them forty horse and sixty foot left in guard of the village and the stuff and the harbour and of the brigantines and boats that were left, for all the ships had been despatched to Havana.

The Governor, gratified at this agreement, set out from the village and harbour of Spiritu Sancto (so called from the day when the Governor and his fleet arrived). This departure took place on Tuesday, July 15, 1539, and that night they bivouacked on the river of Mocoço, and they took with them a large drove of pigs which had been brought over in the fleet to meet any emergency. They made two bridges where the army crossed the river. The next day they were at the lake of the Rabbit, and they gave it this name because a rabbit suddenly started up in the camp and frightened all the horses, which ran back over a league, not one remaining; and all the Christians scattered to recover the loose horses; and if there had been any Indians around, even a few, they would have had the Spaniards at their mercy and, in return for their lack of caution, a shameful ending of the war would have been prepared for them.

The horses having been recovered, the next day they reached St. John's Lake, and the next day under a grievous sun they came to a plain, and the soldiers arrived much exhausted and a steward of the Governor's, who was named Prado, died of thirst; and many of the foot soldiers were hard pressed, and others must needs have followed the steward if they had not been helped with the horses. The next day they came to the plain of Guaçoco, and the soldiers went into the corn fields and gathered the green corn [*mahiz*] with which they cheered themselves not a little, for it was the first they had seen in that country.

The next day, early, they came to Luca, a little village, and there Baltasar de Gallegos came to meet the Governor. The Monday following, July 21, they were joined by the soldiers that Baltasar de Gallegos had, and the Governor sent a messenger to Urriparacoxi, but no reply was received; and on Wednesday, July 23, the Governor set out with his army and came to Vicela and went beyond it to sleep. On Thursday they slept at another village called Tocaste which was on a large lake. And this same day the Governor went on with some horsemen along the road to Ocale because he had great reports of the riches he expected to find there. And when he saw the roads broad he thought he had his hands already on the spoil and ordered one of his knights, named Rodrigo Ranjel, because, besides being a good soldier and a man of worth, he had a good horse, to return to the camp for more soldiers to accompany him; and this esquire did so, although not without misgiving of what might happen, since for the Governor to stay with only ten horsemen seemed to him too few; and he sent that gentleman alone and through a land of enemies and bad trails and where, if any found him, he must die or rush through, if he was not to return without response; and since he felt ashamed to ask for company he bowed his head and obeyed. But I do not praise him for that determination since, indeed, in matters that are necessary and obvious, it is allowable that with reason one should submit to the prince who provides in order that he may be well served and his orders best carried into effect. What befell this messenger horseman on that day he did not wish to say, because what he said would be about himself. Suffice it to say that he well proved his resolution to be a brave man, and that

he fell upon Indians enough that were on the trail of the Governor and got through. When he arrived at headquarters the *Maestre de Campo* gave him fourteen horse with which the number with the Governor was increased to twenty-six.

The next day, Friday, they moved the headquarters along the trail of the Governor, and on the road they came up with two horsemen whom the Governor had sent to the master of the camp, who was a knight named Luis de Moscoso, to order him not to move, and they returned to where they started from to sleep, because they had a brush, which is the same as a skirmish, with the Indians who killed a horse belonging to Carlos Enriquez, the husband of the Governor's niece, a native of Xerez de Badajoz, and wounded some Christians. And there was much suffering from hunger so that they ate the ears of corn with the cobs or wood (which is *cassi*) on which the grains grow.

The next day, Saturday, the Governor found the roads broader and the aspect of the country fine, and he sent back two horsemen for thirty others and gave orders for the camp to follow him. And the Master of the Camp sent Nuño de Tovar with thirty horse and moved the headquarters as the Governor had ordered. The Governor, with the twenty-six horse that were with him, on St. Anne's day reached the river or swamp of Cale. The current was strong and broad and they crossed it with great difficulty, and where there was no need of a bridge they waded through the water up to their necks, with clothes and saddles on their heads, a distance of more than three cross-bow shots. The thirty horsemen that Nuño de Tovar took had crossed the following Sunday and the current carried off one horse which was drowned. Seeing that, the rest crossed with ropes just as those had done who were with the Governor.

These soldiers and the Governor came to the first village of Ocale, which was called Uqueten, where they took two Indians. Next the Governor sent back some of the horsemen with mules, that had been brought from Cuba, loaded with corn and other provisions for those that were behind, since he had come upon an abundance. This succour came in good time for they found them in that swamp eating herbs and roots roasted and others boiled without salt, and what was worse, without knowing what they were. They were cheered by the arrival of the food and their hunger and need gave it a relish and flavour most acceptable. From this refreshment their energies revived and strength took the place of weakness, and on the following Tuesday, the last of those lagging behind arrived at the Governor's camp. But some soldiers who had strayed had been wounded, and a crossbow-man named Mendoça had been slain. The camp was now at Ocale, a village in a good region for corn, and there, while they were sent to Acuera for provisions, the Indians, on two occasions, killed three soldiers of the Governor's guard and wounded others, and killed a horse; and all that through bad arrangements, since these Indians, although they are archers and have strong bows and are skilful and sure marksmen, yet their arrows have no poison, nor do they know what it is.

4.

On August 11, the Governor set forth from Ocale with fifty horse and one hundred foot in search of Apalache, since it was reputed to be populous; and Luis de Moscoso remained behind with the remainder of the camp until it should appear how the advance section got on. That night they slept at Itaraholata, a fine village with plenty of corn. There an Indian crowded up to Captain Maldonado and badly wounded his horse and he would have snatched his lance from his hands, had not the Governor by chance come up, although Maldonado was a good knight and one of the most valiant in that army; but the Indians of that land are very warlike and wild and strong.

The next day they were at Potano, and the next, Wednesday, they reached Utinamocharra, and from there they went to the village of Bad Peace. This name was given to it because when Johan de Añasco had captured on the way thirty persons belonging to that chief, he, in order that they might be surrendered, sent to say that he wished to make peace, and sent in his stead to treat, a vagabond, who was believed to be the chief himself, and his people were given to him. The sequel was that this Indian, escaping from the Christians another day, took refuge among the mass of Indians which were in a dense wood; and a blooded Irish greyhound which came up at the call, went in among the Indians, and, although

he passed by many, he seized no one in the crowd except that fugitive; him he took by the fleshy part of the arm in such a way that the Indian was thrown and they took him.

The next day the Christians arrived at a fair-sized village where they found much food and many small chestnuts dried and very delicious, wild chestnuts; but the trees that bear them are only two palms high and they grow in prickly burrs. There are other chestnuts in the land which the Spaniards saw and ate, which are like those of Spain, and grow on as tall chestnut trees; and the trees themselves are big and with the same leaf and burrs or pods, and the nuts are rich and of very good flavour. This army went from there to a stream which they named Discords, and the reason therefore he desired to conceal who prepared this narrative, because as a man of worth, he did not purpose to relate the faults or weaknesses of his friends.

On that day they built a bridge of pines which abound there, and the next, Sunday, they crossed that stream with as much or more toil than was the case with the Ocale. The next day, Monday, they arrived at Aguacaleyquen, and Rodrigo Ranjel and Villalobos, two gentlemen, equestrians, yet gentlemen (I say equestrians because there were cavalry in that army) captured an Indian man and an Indian woman in a corn field; and she showed where the corn was hidden, and the Indian man took Captain Baltasar de Gallegos where he captured seventeen persons, among them the daughter of the chief, in order that it might impel her father to make peace; but he would have liked to free her without it, if his deceptions and shrewdness had not been less than those of these conquerors.

On August 22, a great multitude of Indians appeared, and the Governor, seeing the land proved to be more populous and better supplied with provisions, sent eight horse in all haste to summon the Master of the Camp, Luis de Moscoso, to join him with all the force; and the Master of the Camp, took no small pains to comply with this order and arrived where the Governor was on September 4, and all rejoiced to be united once more, because, as they held the chief captive, there was alarm lest the Indians should make haste to get together, which was not far wrong, as presently appeared.

On September 9 they all departed in a body from Aguacaleyquen, taking with them the chief and his daughter, and an Indian of rank named Guatutima as guide, because he professed to know much of the country beyond and gave abundant information. And they made a bridge of pines to cross the river of Aguacaleyquen, and reached a small village for the night. The next day, Friday, they were at Uriutina, a village of pleasant aspect and abundant food, and there was in it a very large cabin with a large open court in the middle. The population there was considerable. When they left Aguacaleyquen messengers were coming and going from Uçachile, a great chief, playing upon a flute for ceremony. On Friday, September 12, these Christians came to a village which they named Many Waters, because it rained so much that they could not go on either Saturday or Sunday; the Monday following, the 15th, they proceeded and came upon a very bad swamp and all the way was very toilsome, and they slept at Napituca, which is a very pleasant village, in a pretty spot, with plenty of food.

There the Indians employed all their deceptions and devices to recover the chief of Aguacaleyquen, and the affair reached a point that put the Governor in great peril; but their deceptions and tricks were seen through, and he played them a greater one in this fashion. Seven chiefs from the vicinity came together, and sent to say to the Governor that they were subjects of Uçachile, and that by his order and of their own will, they wished to be friends of the Christians and to help them against Apalache, a mighty province hostile to Uçachile and to themselves, and that they had come to him persuaded and requested by Aguacaleyquen (the chief that the Christians had in captivity), and that they were afraid to enter the camp and to be detained; therefore, let the Governor bring Aguacaleyquen with him and go with them to a large plain that was there to negotiate this business. Their dealings were understood, and the message accepted and the Governor went forth to speak with them; but he gave command to the Christians to arm and to mount their horses and at the sound of the trumpet to rush upon the Indians. And having gone to the plain with only his guard and a saddle to sit upon, and accompanied by the chief of Aguacaleyquen, hardly was the Governor seated and the discourse begun, than he saw himself suddenly surrounded with Indians with bows and arrows. From many directions countless others were coming, and immediately the peril was obvious, which the Governor anticipated; and before the trumpet sounded the Master of the Camp, Luis de Moscoso, struck the legs of his horse, shouting "Come on, Knights, Santiago, Santiago, at them!" And so in a jiffy the cavalry were thrusting many Indians with their lances and their stratagem was of no use to them and enabled our men to get the start of them in the fighting; yet notwithstanding that they fought like men of great spirit and they killed the Governor's horse and also that of a gentleman named Sagredo, and they wounded others. And after the fighting had lasted a considerable time, the Indians took flight and sought refuge in two ponds; and the Spaniards surrounded one, but the other they could not, and they held that enclosure, watching all the night and until morning, when the Indians surrendered, and they took out from there three hundred and five or six chiefs among them.

Uriutina remained to the last and would not go out until some Indians of Uçachile swam in to him and pulled him out, and as he came out he asked for a messenger for his country. When the messenger was brought before him, he said: "Look you, go to my people and tell them that they take no thought of me; that I have done as a brave man and lord what there was to do, and struggled and fought like a man until I was left alone; and if I took refuge in this pond, it was not to escape death, or to avoid dying as befits me, but to encourage those that were there and had not surrendered; and that, when they surrendered, I did not give myself up until these Indians of Uçachile, which are of our nation, asked me to, saying that it would be best for all. Wherefore, what I enjoin upon them and ask is, that they do not, out of regard for me or for any one else, have anything to do with these Christians who are devils and will prove mightier than they; and that they may be assured that as for me, if I have to die, it will be as a brave man."

All of this was immediately reported and declared to the Governor by Johan Ortiz, the interpreter, that Christian who was found in the land, as the history has related. The Indians that were taken in the manner described were carried and put in a wigwam with their hands tied behind their backs; and the Governor went among them to recognize the chiefs, encouraging them in order to induce them to peace and harmony; and he had them released that they might be treated better than the common Indians. One of those chiefs, as they untied him, while the Governor was standing by, threw back his arm and gave the Governor such a tremendous blow that he bathed his teeth in blood and made him spit up much. For this reason they bound him and the others to stakes and shot them with arrows. Other Indians did many other deeds which cannot be fully described, as the historian said, who was present. Wherefore, the Governor seeing that the Christians with so few Indians and without arms were so hard pressed, not being less so himself, spoke as follows: "Would to God that those lords of the Council were here to see what it is to serve his majesty in this country!" And it is because they do know it, says the Chronicler, that they have ordered the tyrannies and cruelties to cease, and that the pacification of the Indians shall be carried on in a better way, in order that God our Lord and his Imperial Majesty may be better served, and the consciences of the conquerors be more at peace, and the natives of the country no longer maltreated.

Tuesday, September 23, the Governor and his army departed from Napituca and came to the river of the Deer. This name was given to it because there the messengers from Uçachile brought thither some deer, of which there are many fine ones in that land; and across this river they made a bridge of three great pine-trees in length and four in breadth. These pines are well proportioned and as tall as the tallest in Spain. After the whole army had finished crossing this river, which was on the 25th of this month, they passed through on the same day two small villages and one very large one, which was called Apalu, and they came by nightfall to Uçachile. In all these villages they found the people gone, and some captains went out to forage and brought in many Indians. They left Uçachile on the following Monday, the 29th, and having passed by a high mountain, they came at nightfall to a pine wood. And a young fellow named Cadena went back without permission for a sword, and the Governor was going to have him hanged for both offences; and by the intervention of kind persons he escaped. Another day, on Tuesday, the 30th of September, they came to Agile, subject to Apalache and some women were captured; and

they are of such stuff that one woman took a young fellow named Herrera, who staid alone with her and behind his companions, and seized him by his private parts and had him worn out and at her mercy; and perhaps, if other Christians had not come by who rescued him the Indian woman would have killed him. He had not wanted to have to do with her in a carnal way, but she wanted to get free and run away.

On Wednesday, the first of October, the Governor Hernando de Soto, started from Agile and came with his soldiers to the river or swamp of Ivitachuco and they made a bridge; and in the high swamp grass on the other side there was an ambuscade of Indians, and they shot three Christians with arrows. They finished crossing this swamp on the Friday following at noon and a horse was drowned there. At nightfall they reached Ivitachuco and found the village in flames, for the Indians had set fire to it. Sunday, October 5, they came to Calahuchi, and two Indians and one Indian woman were taken and a large amount of dried venison. There the guide whom they had ran away. The next day they went on, taking for a guide an old Indian who led them at random, and an Indian woman took them to Iviahica, and they found all the people gone. And the next day two captains went on further and found all the people gone.

Johan de Añasco started out from that village and eight leagues from it he found the port where Pamphilo de Narváez had set sail in the vessels which he made. He recognized it by the head-pieces of the horses and the place where the forge was set up and the mangers and the mortars that they used to grind corn and by the crosses cut in the trees.

They spent the winter there, and remained until the 4th of March, 1540, in which time many notable things befell them with the Indians, who are the bravest of men and whose great courage and boldness the discerning reader may imagine from what follows. For example, two Indians once rushed out against eight men on horseback; twice they set the village on fire; and with ambuscades they repeatedly killed many Christians, and although the Spaniards pursued them and burned them they were never willing to make peace. If their hands and noses were cut off they made no more account of it than if each one of them had been a Mucius Scaevola of Rome. Not one of them, for fear of death, denied that he belonged to Apalache; and when they were taken and were asked from whence they were they replied proudly: "From whence am I? I am an Indian of Apalache." And they gave one to understand that they would be insulted if they were thought to be of any other tribe than the Apalaches.

The Governor decided to go further inland, because an Indian lad gave great reports of what there was in the interior; and he sent Johan de Añasco with thirty horse for Captain Calderon and the soldiers left in the harbour; and they burned the supplies which they left and the village; and Captain Calderon came by land with all the soldiers, and Johan de Añasco came by sea with the brigantines and boats to the harbour of Apalache.

On Saturday [rede Wednesday], November 19, Johan de Añasco arrived at the harbour and immediately Maldonado was despatched along shore with the brigantines to discover a harbour to the west. At the same time Captain Calderon arrived with all his force, less two men and seven horses, that the Indians killed on the way. Maldonado discovered an excellent harbour and brought an Indian from the province adjacent to this coast which was called Achuse, and he brought a good blanket of sable fur. They had seen others in Apalache but none like that. Captain Maldonado was sent to Havana and left Apalache the 26th of February, 1540, with the instructions and command of the Governor that he should return to the port that he had discovered and to that coast where the Governor expected to arrive. The Province of Apalache is very fertile and abundantly provided with supplies with much corn, kidney beans, pumpkins, various fruits, much venison, many varieties of birds and excellent fishing near the sea; and it is a pleasant country, though there are swamps, but these have a hard sandy bottom.

5.

The departure from Iviahica in search of Capachequi began on Wednesday, March 3, 1540, and by night the Governor came to the river Guacuca; and departing from there they came to the river Capachequi, where they arrived early the following Friday; and they made a canoe or barge to cross it. And the river was so broad that Christopher Mosquera, who was the best thrower, was not able to throw across it with a stone. And they took the chains in which they were bringing the Indians, and with some "S" hooks of iron, fastened them together and made one chain of them all. They fastened one end of the chain to one bank and the other to another in order to take over the barge, and the current was so strong that the chain broke twice. Seeing this, they fastened many ropes together and made of them two, and they fastened one to the stern and the other to the bow and drawing the barge first one way and then the other, they got the people and the baggage across. To get the horses over they made long ropes and tied them about their necks and although the current carried them down, by pulling on the ropes they drew them over, yet with toil and some were half drowned.

On Wednesday, March 9, the whole force finished crossing the river Capachequi and went on to sleep in a pine wood. The next day, Thursday, they came to the first village of Capachequi, which contained an abundance of supplies. They passed through much undergrowth or land closely covered with bushes, and then came by nightfall to another village further along where they struck a bad swamp close to the village with a strong current, before they arrived. And they crossed a great stretch of water up to the girths and saddlepads of the horses; and it was not possible for all the force to get across that day, on account of the hard passage. And there a hundred [five?] soldiers with swords and bucklers strayed off, and as many Indians beset them and killed one of them and would have killed all if they had not been rescued.

On the 17th of March they left Capachequi and at nightfall came to White Spring. This was a very beautiful spring with a large flow of good water and containing fish. The next day they came at nightfall to the river Toa where they made two bridges; and the horse belonging to Lorenzo Suarez, son of Vasco Porcallo, was drowned. On the following Sunday, March 21, they came to cross the river Toa, and they twice made a bridge of pines and the strong current broke them.

Another bridge was made with timbers crisscrossed in a way suggested to them by a gentleman named Nuño de Tovar, at which everybody laughed; but it was true what he said, and after it was made they passed over very well by that means; and Monday all the force got across and came by nightfall to a pine wood, although separated into many sections and in bad order. On Tuesday morning they arrived early at Toa, a large village, and the Governor wanted to go on further, but they would not suffer him. On Wednesday, the 24th, the Governor went off at midnight in secret with about forty horse, knights and gentlemen and some others, who for various reasons had not wished to be under another captain. And they went on all that day until night, when they came to a bad passage of water quite deep. Although it was night, they got over it, and that day they went twelve leagues. And the next day, in the morning, which was Holy Thursday, they arrived at the settlement of Chisi and they crossed a branch of a big river, very broad, wading and a good part of it swimming. And they came to a village, which was on an island in this river, where they captured some people and found some provisions; and, as it was a perilous place, before canoes should appear, they turned to go back the way they came; but first they breakfasted on some fowl of the country, which are called *guanaxas* and some strips of venison which they found placed upon a framework of sticks [*en barbacoa*] as for roasting on a gridiron. And though it was Holy Thursday there was no one so strict a Christian that he scrupled to eat flesh; and there the lad Perico, whom they brought from Apalache as a guide, took them, and they passed on to other villages and to a bad passage through a swamp where some horses nearly got drowned. The horses swam with their saddles, while their masters crossed on a beam stretched over the channel, and in so crossing, one Benito Fernandez, a Portuguese, fell off the log and was drowned. This day they came to a village where some principal Indians appeared as messengers from Ichisi; and one of them addressed the Governor and said three words, one after the other, in this manner: "Who are you, what do you want, where are you going?" And they brought presents of skins, the blankets of the country, which were the first gifts as a sign of peace. All of this took place on Holy Thursday and on the Day of the Incarnation. To the questions of the Indian the Governor replied that he was a captain of the great King of Spain; that in his name he had come to make known to them the holy faith of Christ; that they should acknowledge

him and be saved and yield obedience to the Apostolic Church of Rome and to the Supreme Pontiff and Vicar of God, who lived there; and that in temporal affairs they should acknowledge for king and lord the Emperor, King of Castile, our Lord, as his vassals; and that they would treat them well in every thing and that he would maintain toward them peace and justice just the same as towards all his Christian vassals.

Monday, March 29, they went from there to Ichisi; and it rained very hard and a small stream rose so much that if they had not made great haste in crossing all the army would have been in danger. This day Indian men and women came forth to receive them, and the women were clothed in white and made a fine appearance; and they gave the Christians corn cakes and some bunches of young onions just like those of Castile, as big as the end of the thumb and larger. And from now on, this food was of great assistance to them and they ate the onions with the cakes roasted and boiled and raw, and they were a great refreshment, for they are very good. The white clothing, with which the Indian women were clothed, were mantles, apparently of homespun linen and some of them were very thin. They make the thread of them from the bark of the mulberry tree, not the outside, but the intermediate layers; and they know how to make use of it and to spin it, and to dress it as well and to weave it. They make very fine mantles, and they wear one from the girdle down and another fastened on one side with the end over the shoulders like those Bohemians, or gypsies, who wander sometimes through Spain; and the thread is of such a quality that one who was there assured me that he saw the women spin it from that mulberry bark and make it as good as the best thread from Portugal that women can get in Spain for their work, and finer and somewhat like it and stronger. The mulberry trees are quite like those of Spain, just as tall and larger, but the leaf is softer and better for silk, and the mulberries are better eating and larger than those of Spain, and they were very frequently of great advantage to the Spaniards for food.

That day they came to a village of a chief, a subject of Ichisi, a small village with abundant food; and he gave of what he had with good will. They rested there Tuesday and on Wednesday the last of March the Governor set out with his army and came to Great River, where they took many canoes, in which they crossed easily and came to the village of the lord, who was one-eyed and he gave them much food and fifteen Indians as porters. As he was the first that came to them in peace they did not wish to burden him overmuch. They were there Thursday, the first of April, and they set up in the mound of the village a cross and interpreted to them the holiness of the cross, and they received it and worshipped it devoutly to all appearance. On Friday, April 2, the army departed from that place and slept in the open country. On the next day they came to a considerable stream and found deserted cabins, and there messengers came from Altamaha and took them to a village where they found an abundance of food; and a messenger came from Altamaha with a present and the next day they brought many canoes and the army crossed very comfortably. And from there the Governor sent to call the chief Camumo, and they told him that he always ate and slept and went about armed; that he never laid aside his arms because he was on the borders of another chief named Cofitachequi, his enemy; and that he would not come without them; and the Governor replied and said: that he might come as he pleased; and he came, and the Governor gave him a large plume adorned with silver. And the chief took it very gladly and said to the Governor: "You are from Heaven, and this plume of yours which you have given me, I can eat with it; I shall go to war with it; I shall sleep with my wife with it;" and the Governor said, yes, he could do all that. And this Camumo and the others were subjects of a great chief whose name was Ocute. And the chief with the plume asked the Governor to whom he should give tribute in the future, whether to the Governor or to Ocute; and the Governor suspected that this question was put with cunning; and he replied that he regarded Ocute as a brother and that he should pay his tribute to Ocute until the Governor ordered otherwise.

From there he sent messengers to summon Ocute, and he came thither; and the Governor gave him a cap of yellow satin and a shirt and a plume; and he set up a cross there in Altamaha and it was well received. The next day, Thursday, April 8, the Governor departed from that place with his army and took with him Ocute, and they passed the night in some cabins; and Friday he came to the village of Ocute; and the Governor was angry with him and he trembled with fear. Soon a large number of Indians came with supplies and offered as many Indians as porters as the Christians needed; and a cross was set up and they received it very devoutly to all appearances and worshipped it on their knees as they saw the Christians do. Monday, April 12, they departed from Ocute and reached Cofaqui and the leading men came with gifts. This chief Cofaqui was an old man, with a full beard, and his nephew governed for him. Hither came the chief Tatofa and another principal Indian; and they gave their present, both food and tamemes, all that they had need of. And in that language tameme means the same as carrier. Thursday, the 15th of this month, Perico, who was the Indian lad whom they took for a guide from Apalache, began to lose his bearings because he no longer knew anything of the country. And he made believe that he was possessed of the devil, and he knew how to act the part so well that the Christians believed it was real, and a priest whom they brought with them named Friar John, the Evangelist, said it was so. The upshot of it was that they had to take guides that Tatofa gave them to go to Cofitachequi through a desert country some nine or ten days' march.

I have wondered many times at the venturesomeness, stubbornness, and persistency or firmness, to use a better word for the way these baffled conquerors kept on from one toil to another, and then to another still greater; from one danger to many others, here losing one companion, there three and again still more, going from bad to worse without learning by experience. Oh, wonderful God! that they should have been so blinded and dazed by a greed so uncertain and by such vain discourses as Hernando de Soto was able to utter to those deluded soldiers, whom he brought to a land where he had never been, nor put foot into, and where three other leaders, more experienced than he, had ruined themselves: Johan Ponce, Garay, and Pamphílo de Narváez, any one of whom had more experience than he in the affairs of the Indies, and inspired more confidence than he; for he neither in the islands nor in the mainland of the north had knowledge except of the government of Pedrarias, in Castilla del Oro and Nicaragua, and in Peru, which was quite another sort of embroilment with Indians. He thought that that experience in the South was sufficient to show him what to do in the North, and he was deceived as the history will tell. Let us return now to the narrative and the march of this captain or Governor, whom I knew very well, and with whom I talked and associated, as well as with the other three mentioned above, and with the Lawyer Ayllón.

On Friday, the 16th of the month, this Governor and his army spent the night by a small stream on the way to Cofitachequi; and the next day they crossed a very large river, divided into two branches, wider than a long shot from an arquebuse. And the fords were very bad, with many flat stones, and the water came up to the stirrups and in places to the saddlepads. The current was very strong and none of the horsemen dared to take a foot soldier on the croup. The foot soldiers crossed the river further up where it was deeper in this way. They made a line of thirty or forty men tied together and so they crossed over supporting each other; and although some were in much danger, it pleased God that none was drowned, for the horsemen helped them with their horses and gave them the butt of the lance or the tail of the horse, and in that way they all got out and passed the night on a hill. That day they lost many pigs of those which they had brought tame from Cuba, as they were carried down by the current.

The next day, Sunday, they came to another hill or grove to stop, and the next day, Monday, they marched without any trial and crossed another very large river. Tuesday they passed the night beside a small stream and Wednesday reached another very large river and hard to cross which was divided into two streams which were very difficult to enter and worse to get out of. The Christians now were without provisions and with great labour they crossed this river and reached some huts of fishermen or hunters. And the Indians whom they carried had now lost their bearings and no longer knew the way; nor did the Spaniards know it, or in what direction they should go; and among them were divers opinions. Some said they should turn back; others said they ought to go on in a different direction; and the Governor proposed, as he always had done, that it was best to go on, without knowing, either himself or they, what they were aiming at or whither they were wandering. And being at a loss in this labyrinth, on Friday, the 23d of April, the Gover-

nor sent to look for roads or villages in the following manner: Baltasar de Gallegos was to go up the river northwest, and Johan de Añasco was to go along the river southeast, each with ten horsemen and rations of ten days. And on that day other captains returned from searching and they had found nothing. And on Saturday the Governor sent Johan Ruiz Lobillo with four horsemen to the north, with ten days' rations, and he ordered that some of the grown pigs in the army should be slaughtered, and they gave as rations to each man a scant pound of flesh and with it herbs and blite [*bleda*] that they gathered. And so as best they could they supplied their needs, not without great struggle and toil, the horses without any food; they and their masters dying of hunger; with no trail, drenched with continual rain, the rivers always rising and narrowing the land, and without hope of villages or knowledge where to find them, lamenting and calling on God for mercy. And our Lord did bring the succour in the following manner. That Sunday, April 25, Johan de Añasco came with news that he had found a village and food, and he greatly cheered the soldiers, and he brought an interpreter and guide. And so they stopped the rations of flesh and each one helped himself out as he could with unknown herbs and blite that the flesh might be left for a reserve.

And the Governor decided immediately to set out, and writing some letters and putting them in some pumpkins he buried them in a secret place and wrote on a tall tree some directions where to find them. And so they set out with Johan de Añasco on Monday, April 26. That day the Governor, with some of the horse, although a few, reached the village which was called Hymahi; and the army remained two leagues behind, the horses exhausted. There was found in the village a barbacoa covered with corn and more than thirty bushels of *pinol* prepared, which is parched corn. And the next day the main force arrived and rations of corn and *pinol* were distributed. And there was no end of mulberries, because there were many trees and it was their season; and this was a great help. And likewise there were found in the plains some berries such as in Italy grow on vines close to the ground and are like *madroños*, [strawberries] very savoury, palatable, and fragrant and they also grow abundantly in Galicia. In the Kingdom of the Naples this fruit is called *fraoles* [strawberries] and it is a finer delicate fruit and highly thought of. And besides those, they found there along the trails countless roses growing wild like those in Spain; and although they have not so many leaves since they are in the woods they are none the less fragrant and finer and sweeter. This village they named Succour.

The next day Captain Alonso Romo came who likewise had been out reconnoitering, and he brought four or five Indians, and not one would show any knowledge of his lord's village or discover it, although they burnt one of them alive before the others, and all suffered that martyrdom for not revealing it. The next day Wednesday, Baltasar de Gallegos came with an Indian woman and news of a populated region. The next day Lobillo returned with news of trails, and he had left behind two companions lost; and the Governor rated him soundly and without suffering him to rest or to eat made him go back to look for them under pain of death, if he brought them not back. And that was a better order and a better deed and judgment than burning alive the Indian that Alonso Romo brought for not consenting to reveal his lord; for to such a one as him the Romans set up a memorable statue in the Forum; and to Christians no such cruelty is allowable toward any one and especially toward an Indian who was ready to die to be loyal to his country and to his lord. But later on the account was squared.

6.

Let us return to the sequel and continuation of what we have in hand and are here narrating. Friday the last day of April the Governor took some horse, those that were most refreshed, and the Indian woman that Baltasar de Gallegos brought for a guide, and went along the road to Cofitachequi, and spent the night near a large, deep river; and he sent on Johan de Añasco with some horsemen to secure some interpreters and canoes for crossing the river, and he got some. The next day the Governor came to the crossing opposite the village, and the chief Indians came with gifts and the woman chief, lady of that land whom Indians of rank bore on their shoulders with much respect, in a litter covered with delicate white linen. And she crossed in the canoes and spoke to the Governor quite gracefully and at her ease. She was a young girl of fine bearing; and

she took off a string of pearls which she wore on her neck, and put it on the Governor as a necklace to show her favour and to gain his good will. And all the army crossed over in canoes and they received many presents of skins well tanned and blankets, all very good; and countless trips of venison and dry wafers, and an abundance of very good salt. All the Indians went clothed down to their feet with very fine skins well dressed, and blankets of the country, and blankets of sable fur and others of the skin of wild cats which gave out a strong smell. The people are very clean and polite and naturally well conditioned.

Monday, May 3, all the rest of the force came up; but all were not able to get across until the next day, Tuesday, nor then without the cost and loss of seven horses that were drowned, from among the fattest and strongest ones which struggled against the current. The thin ones that let themselves go with the stream got across better. On Friday, May 7, Baltasar de Gallegos, with the most of the soldiers of the army, arrived at Ilapi to eat seven barbacoas of corn, that they said were there stored for the woman chief. That same day the Governor and Rodrigo Ranjel entered the mosque and oratory of this heathen people, and opening some burying places they found some bodies of men fastened on a barbacoa. The breasts, belly, necks and arms and legs full of pearls; and as they were taking them off Ranjel saw something green like an emerald of good quality and he showed it to the Governor and was rejoiced and he ordered him to look out of the enclosure and to have Johan de Añasco called, the treasurer of their majesties; and Ranjel said to him: "My lord, let us not call any one. It may be that there is a precious stone or jewel?" The Governor replied, somewhat angry, and said: "Even if there should be one, are we to steal it?" When Johan de Añasco came they took out this emerald and it was glass, and after it many beads of glass and rosaries with their crosses. They also found Biscayan axes of iron from which they recognized that they were in the government or territory where the lawyer Lucas Vazquez de Ayllón came to his ruin. They took away from there some two hundred pounds of pearls; and when the woman chief saw that the Christians set much store by them, she said: "Do you hold that of much account? Go to Talimeco, my village, and you will find so many that your horses cannot carry them." The Governor replied: "Let them stay there; to whom God gives a gift, may St. Peter bless it." And there the matter dropped. It was believed that he planned to take that place for himself, since it was the best that they saw and with the land in the best condition, although there did not appear to be much people or corn, nor did they delay to look for it there. Some things were done there as in Spain, which the Indians must have been taught by the followers of the lawyer Lucas Vazquez de Ayllón; since they make hose and moccasins and leggings with ties of white leather, although the leggings are black, and with fringes or edging of coloured leather as they would have done in Spain. In the mosque, or house of worship, of Talimeco there were breastplates like corselets and head-pieces made of rawhide, the hair stripped off; and also very good shields. This Talimeco was a village holding extensive sway; and this house of worship was on a high mound and much revered. The *caney*, or house of the chief, was very large, high and broad, all decorated above and below with very fine handsome mats, arranged so skilfully that all these mats appeared to be a single one; and, marvellous as it seems, there was not a cabin that was not covered with mats. This people has many very fine fields and a pretty stream and a hill covered with walnuts, oak-trees, pines, live oaks, and groves of liquidamber, and many cedars. In this river, Alaminos, a native of Cuba (although a Spaniard), was said to have found a trace of gold, and rumour of this spread abroad among the Spaniards in the army, and from this it was believed that it was a land of gold and that good mines would be found there.

Wednesday, May 13, the Governor went on from Cofitachequi, and in two days came to the territory of Chalaque; but they were not able to come upon the village of the chief, nor was there an Indian that would reveal it. And they bivouacked in a pine wood, whither many Indian men and women began to come in peace with presents and gifts; and they were there on Whitsuntide, and from there the Governor sent a letter to Baltasar de Gallegos with some Indians to the barbacoas where, as has been said above, they had gone to eat the corn, requesting him to come on behind the Governor. On Monday, the 17th of this month, they departed thence, and spent the night at a mountain; and on Tuesday they came to

Guaquili, and Indians came forth in peace and gave them corn, although little, and many fowls roasted on a barbacoa, and a few little dogs which were good eating. These are dogs of a small size that do not bark; and they breed them in their homes for food. Likewise they gave them tamemes, which are Indians to carry their burdens. On Wednesday, the next day, they came to a region full of reeds, and Thursday to a small plain where one of the horses died, and some of the foot soldiers who had been with Baltasar de Gallegos came up to inform the Governor that he would come soon. The next day, Friday, they were at Xuala, which is a village in a plain between two rivers, and the chief was so prosperous that he gave the Christians whatever they asked—tamemes, corn, dogs, *petacas*, and as much as he had. *Petacas* are baskets covered with leather and likewise ready to be so covered with their lids, for carrying clothes or whatever they want to. And on Saturday Baltasar de Gallegos came there with many sick and lame who must needs be restored whole, particularly in view of the mountain ranges before them. In that Xuala region it seemed that there were more indications that there were gold mines than in all the country they had traversed and viewed in that northern region.

Tuesday, May 25, they left Xuala, and on that day went over a very high range and at nightfall they encamped at a little mountain; and the next day, Wednesday, in a plain where they suffered from severe cold, although it was the 26th of May. There they crossed the river, wading up to their shins, by which later they were to depart in the brigantines they had made. This, when it reaches the sea, the chart indicates to be the Rio del Spiritu Santo, which, according to the maps of the geographer Alonso de Chaves, empties into a great bay; and the mouth of this river, where the water is salt, is in 31 degrees north of the equator.

Returning to my narrative, from this place where, as was said, they waded across the river, the woman chief of Cofitachequi, whom they carried with them in return for the good treatment which they had received from her, escaped; and that day there remained behind, it was supposed intentionally, Mendoça de Montanjes and Alaminos of Cuba. And since Alonso Romo kept that day the rearguard and left them, the Governor made him return for them, and they waited for them one day. When they arrived, the Governor wished to hang them. In that region of Xalaque was left a comrade whose name was Rodriquez, a native of Peñafiel; and also an Indian slave boy from Cuba, who knew Spanish, and belonged to a gentleman named Villegas; and there was also left a slave belonging to Don Carlos, a Berber, well versed in Spanish; and also Gomez, a negro belonging to Vasco Gonçalez who spoke good Spanish. That Rodriquez was the first, and the rest deserted further on from Xalaque. The next day they passed the night in an oak grove, and the day following along a large stream, which they crossed many times. The next day messengers of peace appeared and they arrived early at Guasili, and they gave them many tamemes, many little dogs and corn; and since this was a fine stopping place, the soldiers afterwards in throwing dice called out "the house of Guasuli," or, a good throw.

Monday, which was the last day of May, the Governor left Guasili and came with his army to an oak wood along the river; and the next day they crossed by Canasoga, and at night they slept in the open country. Wednesday they slept near a swamp, and that day they ate an enormous amount of mulberries. The next day, Thursday, they went along a large stream near the river which they had crossed in the plain where the woman chief went off. It was now very large. The next day, Friday, they came to a pine wood on the stream, where appeared peaceful Indians from Chiaha and brought corn. The next day, Saturday, in the morning the Spaniards crossed one arm of the river, which was very broad, and went into Chiaha, which is on an island in the same river.

It was Saturday, the 5th of June, that they entered Chiaha, and since all the way from Xuala had been mountainous and the horses were tired and thin, and the Christians were also themselves worn out, it seemed best to tarry there and rest themselves; and they were given an abundance of corn, of which there was plenty of good quality, and they were also given an abundance of corn cakes [maçamorras], and no end of oil from walnuts and acorns, which they knew how to extract very well, which was very good and contributed much to their diet. Yet some say that the oil from nuts produces flatulence. However, it is very delicious. The Indians spent fifteen days with the

Christians in peace, and they played with them, and likewise among themselves. They swam with the Christians and helped them very much in every way. They ran away afterwards on Saturday, the 19th of the month, for something that the Governor asked of them; and, in short, it was because he asked for women. The next day in the morning the Governor sent to call the chief and he came immediately; and the next day the Governor took him off with him to make his people come back, and the result was they came back. In the land of this Chiaha was where the Spaniards first found fenced villages. Chiaha gave them five hundred carriers, and they consented to leave off collars and chains.

Monday, June 28, the Governor and his soldiers departed from Chiaha, and, passing through five or six villages, they spent the night in a pine grove near a village. There they had much labour in crossing a river which flowed with a strong current, and they made a bridge or support of the horses in the following manner, so that the foot soldiers should not be endangered, and it was this way: They put the horses in the river in line, head and tail, and they were as steady as they could be, and on each one his master, and they received the force of the stream, and on the lower side, where the water was not so violent, the foot soldiers forded, holding on to the tails and stirrups, breast-pieces, and manes, one after the other. And in this way the whole army got across very well.

The next day, Tuesday, they passed through a village and took corn and went beyond to sleep in the open country. Wednesday they passed over a river and through a village and again over the river and slept in the open country. On Thursday the chief of Coste came out to receive them in peace, and took the Christians to sleep in a village of his; and he was offended because some soldiers provisioned themselves from, or, rather, robbed him of, some barbacoas of corn against his will. The next day, Thursday, on the road leading toward the principal village of Coste, he stole away and gave the Spaniards the slip and armed his people. Friday, the 2d of July, the Governor arrived at Coste. This village was on an island in the river, which there flows large, swift, and hard to enter.

And the Christians crossed the first branch with no danger to any of the soldiers, yet it was no small venture, and the Governor entered into the village careless and unarmed, with some followers unarmed. And when the soldiers, as they were used to do, began to climb upon the barbacoas, in an instant the Indians began to take up clubs and seize their bows and arrows and to go to the open square.

The Governor commanded that all should be patient and endure for the evident peril in which they were, and that no one should put his hand on his arms; and he began to rate his soldiers and, dissembling, to give them some blows with a cudgel; and he cajoled the chief, and said to him that he did not wish the Christians to make him any trouble; and they would like to go out to the open part of the island to encamp. And the chief and his men went with him; and when they were at some distance from the village in an open place, the Governor ordered his soldiers to lay hands on the chief and ten or twelve of the principal Indians, and to put them in chains and collars; and he threatened them, and said that he would burn them all because they had laid hands on the Christians. From this place, Coste, the Governor sent two soldiers to view the province of Chisca, which was reputed very rich, toward the north, and they brought good news. There in Coste they found in the trunk of a tree as good honey and even better than could be had in Spain. In the river were found some mussels that they gathered to eat, and some pearls. And they were the first these Christians saw in fresh water, although they are to be found in many parts of this land.

Friday, July 9, the commander and his army departed from Coste and crossed the other branch of the river and passed the night on its banks. And on the other side was Tali, and since the river flows near it and is large, they were not able to cross it. And the Indians, believing that they would cross, sent canoes and in them their wives and sons and clothes from the other side, away from the Christians; but they were all taken suddenly, and as they were going with the current, the Governor forced them all to turn back, which was the reason that this chief came in peace and took them across to the other side in his canoes, and gave the Christians what they had need of. And he did this also in his own land as they passed through it afterwards, and they were there Saturday and were given carriers and they

set out Sunday and passed the night in the open country.

Monday they crossed a river and slept in the open country. Tuesday they crossed another river and Wednesday another large river and slept at Tasqui. During all the days of their march from Tali the chief of Tali had corn and mazamorras and cooked beans and every thing that could be brought from his villages bordering the way. Thursday they passed another small village, and then other villages, and Friday the Governor entered Coça.

This chief is a powerful one and a ruler of a wide territory, one of the best and most abundant that they found in Florida. And the chief came out to receive the Governor in a litter covered with the white mantles of the country, and the litter was borne on the shoulders of sixty or seventy of his principal subjects, with no plebeian or common Indian among them; and those that bore him took turns by relays with great ceremonies after their manner.

There were in Coça many plums like the early ones of Seville, very good; both they and the trees were like those of Spain. There were also some wild apples like those called canavales in Extremadura, small in size. They remained there in Coça some days, in which the Indians went off and left their chief in the power of the Christians with some principal men, and the Spaniards went out to round them up, and they took many, and they put them in iron collars and chains. And verily, according to the testimony of eye-witnesses, it was a grievous thing to see. But God failed not to remember every evil deed, nor were they left unpunished, as this history will tell.

On Friday, August 20, the Governor and his people left Coça, and there stayed behind a Christian named Feryada, a Levantine; and they slept the next night beyond Talimachusy, and the next day in a heavy rain they went to Itaba, a large village along a fine river, and there they bought some Indian women, which were given them in exchange for looking-glasses and knives.

Monday, August 30, the Governor left Itaba, and came by nightfall to an oak wood; and the next day they were at Ulibahali, a very fine village close to a large river. And there were many Indians lying in wait for them planning to rescue the chief of Coça from the Christians because they were his subjects, and in order that the land should not rise in revolt nor refuse them supplies they took him with them, and they entered the village very cautiously.

And the chief of Coça ordered the Indians to lay aside their arms, and it was done; and they gave them carriers and twenty Indian women and were peaceful. A gentleman of Salamanca named Mancano left them there, and it was not known whether he did so of his own will or whether he lost his way, as he kept by himself walking alone and melancholy. He had asked the other soldiers to leave him to himself before they missed him. This was not known for certain, but it was reported in the camp after he was gone. A negro, who spoke Spanish and who belonged to Captain Johan Ruiz Lobillo, was also missing. His name was Johan Biscayan. The day that they left this village they ate many grapes as good as those grown in the vineyards of Spain. In Coça and further back they had eaten very good ones, but these of Ulibahali were the best. From this village of Ulibahali the Spaniards and their Governor departed on Thursday, September 2, and they passed the night at a small village near the river, and there they waited a day for Lobillo, who had gone back without permission to look for his negro. On his return the Governor rated him soundly. Sunday, they went on and spent the night in the open country, and the next day, Monday, they came to Tuasi, where they were given carriers and thirty-two Indian women. Monday, the 13th of September, the Governor departed thence, and they slept in the open country. Tuesday they made another day's march and again spent the night in open country, but Wednesday they came to an old village that had two fences and good towers, and these walls are after this fashion: They drive many thick stakes tall and straight close to one another. These are then interlaced with long withes, and then overlaid with clay within and without. They make loopholes at intervals and they make their towers and turrets separated by the curtain and parts of the wall as seems best. And at a distance it looks like a fine wall or rampart and such stockades are very strong.

The next day, Thursday, they slept at a new village close by a river, where the Spaniards rested the following day. On the next day, Saturday, they were at Talisi and they found the chief and his people gone. This village is extensive and abounding in corn and near a large river. And there a messenger came to them from Tascaluça, a powerful lord and one much feared in that land. And soon one of his sons appeared and the Governor ordered his men to mount and the horsemen to charge and the trumpets to be blown (more to inspire fear than to make merry at their reception). And when those Indians returned the Commander sent two Christians with them instructed as to what they were to observe and to spy out so that they might take counsel and be forewarned.

September 25, came the chief of Talisi, and he gave what they asked, such as carriers, women, and supplies; and from that place they sent and released the chief of Coça, so that he might return to his land; and he went in anger and in tears because the Governor would not give up a sister of his that they took, and because they had taken him so far from his country.

Tuesday, October 5, they went on from Talisi and came to Casiste for the night. This was a small village by the river. The next day, Wednesday, they came to Caxa, a wretched village on the river banks on the direct line from Talisi to Tascaluça. And the next day, Thursday, they slept by the river; and on the other side of the stream was a village called Humati; and the next day, Friday, they came to another settlement, a new one named Uxapita; and the next day, Saturday, the force encamped in the open country, a league this side of the village of Tascaluça. And the Governor despatched a messenger, and he returned with the reply that he would be welcome whenever he wished to come.

The historian asked a very intelligent gentleman who was with this Governor, and who went with him through his whole expedition in this northern country, why, at every place they came to, this Governor and his army asked for those tamemes or Indian carriers, and why they took so many women and these not old nor the most ugly; and why, after having given them what they had, they held the chiefs and principal men; and why they never tarried nor settled in any region they came to, adding that such a course was not settlement or conquest, but rather disturbing and ravaging the land and depriving the natives of their liberty without converting or making a single Indian either a Christian or a friend. He replied and said: That they took these carriers or tamemes to keep them as slaves or servants to carry the loads of supplies which they secured by plunder or gift, and that some died, and others ran away or were tired out, so that it was necessary to replenish their numbers and to make more; and the women they desired both as servants and for their foul uses and lewdness, and that they had them baptized more on account of carnal intercourse with them than to teach them the faith; and that if they held the chiefs and principal men captive, it was because it would keep their subjects quiet, so that they would not molest them when foraging or doing what they wished in their country; and that whither they were going neither the Governor nor the others knew, but that his purpose was to find some land rich enough to satiate his greed and to get knowledge of the great secrets this Governor said he had heard in regard to those regions according to much information he had received; and as for stirring up the country and not settling it, nothing else could be done until they found a site that was satisfactory.

Oh, wicked men! Oh, devilish greed! Oh, bad consciences! Oh, unfortunate soldiers! that ye should not have understood the perils ye were to encounter, and how wasted would be your lives, and without rest your souls! That ye were not mindful of that truth which the blessed St. Augustine uttered in lamenting the miseries of this life, saying, this life is a life of misery, frail, and uncertain, full of toil and strain; a life, Lord, of ills, a kingdom of pride, full of miseries and terror, since it is not really life, nor can be called so, but rather death, for in a moment it is ended by various changes of fortune and divers kinds of deaths! Give ear, then, Catholic reader, and do not lament the conquered Indians less than their Christian conquerors or slayers of themselves, as well as others, and follow the adventures of this Governor, ill governed, taught in the School of Pedrarias de Avila, in the scattering and wasting of the Indians of Castilla del Oro; a graduate in the killing of the natives of Nicaragua and canonized in Peru as a member of the order of the Pizarros; and then, after being delivered from all those paths of Hell and having come to Spain loaded with gold, neither a bachelor nor married, knew not how nor was able to rest without returning to the Indies to shed human blood, not content with what he had spilled; and to leave life as shall be

narrated, and providing the opportunity for so many sinners deluded with his vain words to perish after him. See what he wanted most of what that queen or woman chief of Cofitachequi, lady of Talimeco, offered him when she told him that in that place of hers he would find so many pearls that all the horses in the army could not carry them off; and, when she received him so courteously, see how he treated her. Let us proceed, and forget not this truth which you have read, how as a proof of the number of pearls which were offered him, this Governor and his people took over two hundred pounds, and you will know what enjoyment they got out of them in the sequel.

7.

Sunday, October 10, the Governor entered the village of Tascaluça, which is called Atahachi, a recent village. And the chief was on a kind of balcony on a mound at one side of the square, his head covered by a kind of coif like the almaizal, so that his headdress was like a Moor's which gave him an aspect of authority; he also wore a *pelote* or mantle of feathers down to his feet, very imposing; he was seated on some high cushions, and many of the principal men among his Indians were with him. He was as tall as that Tony of the Emperor, our lord's guard, and well proportioned, a fine and comely figure of a man. He had a son, a young man as tall as himself but more slender. Before this chief there stood always an Indian of graceful mien holding a parasol on a handle something like a round and very large fly fan, with a cross similar to that of the Knights of the Order of St. John of Rhodes, in the middle of a black field, and the cross was white. And although the Governor entered the plaza and alighted from his horse and went up to him, he did not rise, but remained passive in perfect composure and as if he had been a king.

The Governor remained seated with him a short time, and after a little he arose and said that they should come to eat, and he took him with him and the Indians came to dance; and they danced very well in the fashion of rustics in Spain, so that it was pleasant to see them. At night he desired to go, and the commander told him that he must sleep there. He understood it and showed that he scoffed at such an intention for him, being the lord, to receive so suddenly restraints upon his liberty, and dissembling, he immediately despatched his principal men each by himself, and he slept there notwithstanding his reluctance. The next day the Governor asked him for carriers and a hundred Indian women; and the chief gave him four hundred carriers and the rest of them and the women he said he would give at Mabila, the province of one of his principal vassals. And the Governor acquiesced in having the rest of that unjust request of his fulfilled in Mabila; and he ordered him to be given a horse and some buskins and a scarlet cloak for him to ride off happy. And now that the chief had given him four hundred carriers, or rather slaves, and was to give him in Mabila a hundred women, and what they were most in need of, see how happy he could be made with those buskins and the cloak and with riding on a horse when he felt as if he were mounted on a tiger or a most savage lion, since this people held horses in the greatest terror!

At last, Tuesday, October 12, they departed from that village of Atahachi, taking along the chief as has been said and with him many principal men and always the Indian with the sunshade attending his lord, and another with a cushion. And that night they slept in the open country. The next day, Wednesday, they came to Piachi, which is a village high above the gorge of a mountain stream; and the chief of this place was evil intentioned, and attempted to resist their passage; and as a result, they crossed the stream with effort, and two Christians were slain, and also the principal Indians who accompanied the chief. In this village, Piachi, it was learned that they had killed Don Teodoro and a black, who came from the ships of Pamphilo de Narvaez.

Saturday, October 16, they departed thence into a mountain where they met one of the two Christians whom the Governor had sent to Mabila, and he said that in Mabila there had gathered together much people in arms. The next day they came to a fenced village, and there came messengers from Mabila bringing to the chief much bread made from chestnuts, which are abundant and excellent in that region.

Monday, October 18, St. Luke's day, the Governor came to Mabila, having passed that day by several villages, which was the reason that the soldiers stayed behind to forage and to scatter themselves, for the region appeared populous. And there went on with the Governor only forty

horsemen as an advance guard, and after they had tarried a little, that the Governor might not show weakness, he entered into the village with the chief, and all his guard went in with him. Here the Indians immediately began an areyto, which is their fashion for a ball with dancing and song. While this was going on some soldiers saw them putting bundles of bows and arrows slyly among some palm leaves, and other Christians saw that above and below the cabins were full of people concealed. The Governor was informed of it and he put his helmet on his head and ordered all to go and mount their horses and warn all the soldiers that had come up. Hardly had they gone out when the Indians took the entrances of stockade, and there were left with the Governor, Luis de Moscoso and Baltasar de Gallegos, and Espindola, the Captain of the Guard, and seven or eight soldiers. And the chief went into a cabin and refused to come out of it. Then they began to shoot arrows at the Governor. Baltasar de Gallegos went in for the chief, he not being willing to come out. He disabled the arm of a principal Indian with the slash of a knife. Luis de Moscoso waited at the door, so as not to leave him alone, and he was fighting like a knight and did all that was possible until, not being able to endure any more, he cried: "Señor Baltasar de Gallegos, come out, or I will leave you, for I cannot wait any longer for you." During this, Solis, a resident of Triana of Seville, had ridden up, and Rodrigo Ranjel, who were the first, and for his sins Solis was immediately stricken down dead; but Rodrigo Ranjel got to the gate of the town at the time when the Governor went out, and two soldiers of his guard with him, and after him came more than seventy Indians who were held back for fear of Rodrigo Ranjel's horse, and the Governor, desiring to charge them, a negro brought up his horse; and he told Rodrigo Ranjel to give aid to the Captain of the Guard, who was left behind, for he had come out quite used up, and a soldier of the Guard with him; and he with a horse faced the enemy until he got out of danger, and Rodrigo Ranjel returned to the Governor and had him draw out more than twenty arrows which he bore fastened in his armour, which was a loose coat quilted with coarse cotton. And he ordered Ranjel to watch for Solis, to rescue him from the enemy that they should not carry him inside. And the Governor went to collect the soldiers. There was great valour and shame that day among all those that found themselves in this first attack and beginning of this unhappy day; for they fought to admiration and each Christian did his duty as a most valiant soldier. Luis de Moscoso and Baltasar de Gallegos came out with the rest of the soldiers by another gate.

As a result, the Indians were left with the village and all the property of the Christians, and with the horses that were left tied inside, which they killed immediately. The Governor collected all of the forty horse that were there and advanced to a large open place before the principal gate of Mabila. There the Indians rushed out without venturing very far from the stockade, and to draw them on the horsemen made a feint of taking flight at a gallop, withdrawing far from the walls. And the Indians believing it to be real, came away from the village and the stockade in pursuit, greedy to make use of their arrows. And when it was time the horsemen wheeled about on the enemy, and before they could recover themselves, killed many with their lances. Don Carlos wanted to go with his horse as far as the gate, and they gave the horse an arrow shot in the breast. And not being able to turn, he dismounted to draw out the arrow, and then another came which hit him in the neck above the shoulder, at which, seeking confession, he fell dead. The Indians no longer dared to withdraw from the stockade. Then the Commander invested them on every side until the whole force had come up; and they went up on three sides to set fire to it, first cutting the stockade with axes. And the fire in its course burned the two hundred odd pounds of pearls that they had, and all their clothes and ornaments, and the sacramental cups, and the moulds for making the wafers, and the wine for saying the mass; and they were left like Arabs, completely stripped, after all their hard toil. They had left in a cabin the Christian women, which were some slaves belonging to the Governor; and some pages, a friar, a priest, a cook, and some soldiers defended themselves very well against the Indians, who were not able to force an entrance before the Christians came with the fire and rescued them. And all the Spaniards fought like men of great courage, and twenty-two died, and one hundred and forty-eight others received six hundred and eighty-eight arrow wounds, and seven horses were killed and twenty-nine others wounded.

Women and even boys of four years of age fought with the Christians; and Indian boys hanged themselves not to fall into their hands, and others jumped into the fire of their own accord. See with what good will those carriers acted. The arrow shots were tremendous, and sent with such a will and force that the lance of one gentleman named Nuño de Tovar, made of two pieces of ash and very good, was pierced by an arrow in the middle, as by an auger, without being split, and the arrow made a cross with the lance.

On that day there died Don Carlos, and Francis de Soto, the nephew of the Governor, and Johan de Gamez de Jaen, and Men Rodriguez, a fine Portuguese gentleman, and Espinosa, a fine gentleman, and another named Velez, and one Blasco de Barcarrota, and many other honoured soldiers; and the wounded comprised all the men of most worth and honour in the army. They killed three thousand of the vagabonds without counting many others who were wounded and whom they afterwards found dead in the cabins and along the roads. Whether the chief was dead or alive was never known. The son they found thrust through with a lance.

After the end of the battle as described, they rested there until the 14th of November, caring for their wounds and their horses, and they burned over much of the country. And up to the time when they left there, the total deaths from the time the Governor and his forces entered the land of Florida, were one hundred and two Christians, and not all, to my thinking, in true repentance.

Sunday, November 14, of the year already mentioned, the Governor left Mabila, and the Wednesday following came to a fine river. Thursday, the 28th [18th], their way lay over bad places and through swamps, and they found a village with corn which was named Talicpacana. The Christians had discovered on the other side of the river a village which appeared to them from a distance to be finely situated.

On Sunday, the 21st of November, Vasco Gonçalez found a village half a league distant from this named Moçulixa, from which they had transported all the corn to the other side of the river and had piled it in heaps covered with mats; and the Indians were across the river, and were making threats. A barge was constructed which was finished the 29th of the month, and they made a large truck to carry it to Moçulixa; and when it was launched in the water sixty soldiers embarked in it. The Indians shot countless darts, or rather arrows. But when this great canoe reached the shore they took flight, and not more than three or four Christians were wounded. The country was easily secured, and they found an abundance of corn.

The next day, Wednesday, the whole force came to a village which was called Zabusta, and there they crossed the river in the boat and with some canoes that they had found in that place; and they tarried for the night in another village on the other side, because up above they found a fine one, and took the chief, whose name was Apafalaya, and carried him along as guide and interpreter; and this stream was called the river Apafalaya. From this river and town the Governor and his army set out in search of Chicaça on Thursday, December 9. The following Tuesday they arrived at the river of Chicaça, having traversed many bad passages and swamps and cold rivers.

And that you may know, reader, what sort of a life these Spaniards led, Rodrigo Ranjel, an eye-witness, says that among many other great hardships that men endured in this undertaking he saw a knight named Don Antonio Osorio, brother of the Lord Marquis of Astorga, wearing a short garment of the blankets of that country, torn on the sides, his flesh showing, no hat, bareheaded, bare-footed, without hose or shoes, a buckler on his back, a sword without a shield, amidst heavy frosts and cold. And the stuff of which he was made and his illustrious lineage made him endure his toil without laments such as many others made, for there was no one who could help him, although he was the man he was, and had in Spain two thousand ducats of income through the Church. And the day that this gentleman saw him he did not believe that he had eaten a mouthful, and he had to dig for it with his nails to get something to eat.

I could hardly help laughing when I heard that this knight had left the Church and the income above mentioned to go in search of such a life as this, at the sound of the words of De Soto; because I knew Soto very well, and, although he was a man of worth, I did not suppose that he was so winning a talker or so clever, as to be able to delude such persons. What was it that a man like

him wanted of a land unexplored and unknown? Nor did the Captain that took him know anything more than that in this land had perished Johan Ponce de León and the lawyer Lucas Vazquez de Ayllón and Pamphílo de Narváez and others abler than Hernando de Soto. And those that follow such guides have to go in that manner, since they found regions where they were able to make a settlement and rest and gradually push in and make their inferences and learn the country. But let us proceed, for the toil of this knight is little compared with those that are dying and escape.

The river of Chicaça they found overflowing its bed, and the Indians on the other side in arms with many white flags. Orders were given to make a barge, and the Governor sent Baltasar de Gallegos with thirty horsemen, swimmers, to search the river up above for a good crossing place, and to fall suddenly upon the Indians; and it was perceived, and they forsook the passage and they crossed over very comfortably in the barge on Thursday, the 16th of the month. And the Governor went on ahead with some horsemen, and they arrived late at night at a village of the lord which had been deserted by all the people. The next day Baltasar de Gallegos appeared with the thirty that went with him, and they spent that Christmas in Chicaça, and there was a snowstorm with a heavy fall of snow, just as if they had been in Burgos, and the cold was as severe, or more so. On Monday, January 3, 1541, the chief of Chicaça came proffering peace, and promptly gave the Christians guides and interpreters to go to Caluça, a place of much repute among the Indians. Caluça is a province of more than ninety villages not subject to any one, with a savage population, very warlike and much dreaded, and the soil is fertile in that section. In Chicaça the Governor ordered that half of his army make war on Sacchuma; and on their return the Chief Miculasa made peace, and messengers came from Talapatica. In the meantime, while this war was going on, the time came to march, and they asked the chief for carriers; and the Indians raised such a tumult among themselves that the Christians understood it; and the settlement was that they would give them on the 4th of March, when they had to start, and that on that day they would come with them. On the evening of that day the Governor mounted his horse and found the Indians evilly disposed, and realizing their dangerous intentions he returned to the camp and said in public: "To-night is an Indian night. I shall sleep armed and my horse saddled." And they all said that they would do the same, and he called the Master of the Camp, who was Luis de Moscoso, and told him that they should take extra precautions that night in regard to the sentinels, since it was the last. The Governor as he went away from where he left those soldiers to whom he had given these warnings, lay down undressed on his couch, and neither was his horse saddled nor any other, and all those in the camp lay down to sleep without precautions and unarmed. The Master of the Camp put on the morning watch three horsemen, the most useless and with the poorest horses in the army. And on the day before mentioned, the 4th of March, when the Indian carriers had been promised them, at dawn, the Indians, fulfilling their word, entered the camp in many detachments, beating drums as if it had been in Italy, and setting fire to the camp, they burned and captured fifty-nine horses, and three of them they shot through both shoulders with arrows.

And the Christians were like heedless people on this occasion; and few arms, coats-of-mail, lances and saddles remained after the fire; and all the horses had run off, escaping the fire and the noise. Only the commander was able to mount his horse, and they did not fasten the horse's girth, nor did he buckle his coat of arms, and Tapia de Valladolid was with him; and he fell over the first Indian that he thrust at who had thrust at him, saddle and all, and if the Indians had known how to follow up their victory, this would have been the last day of the lives of all the Christians of that army, and made an end of the demand for carriers.

Next the Spaniards went to a plain, a league from that village where they were; and they had cabins and supplies, and they set up the camp on a sloping hillside. And they made haste to set up a forge, and they made bellows of bear skins, and they retempered their arms, and made new frames for their saddles, and they provided themselves with lances for there were in that place very good ash-trees. And within a week they had everything repaired. There were slain in Chicaça and burned alive twelve Christians.

Tuesday, March 15, the morning watch, the Indians returned upon the Christians, determined to finish them up, and attacked them on three sides; and as necessity had made them cautious, and, as they were informed and on the watch, they fought with them bravely and put the Indians to flight. And it pleased God that the Christians should not suffer much loss, and few Indians perished. Some Spaniards displayed great valour that day, and no one failed to do his duty. And unfortunate was he on that occasion who did not well defend his life and who failed to prove to the enemy the quality and arms of the Christians.

8.

Tuesday, April 26, in the year aforesaid, 1541, the Governor Hernando de Soto set out from the plain of Chicaça, and arrived at Limamu for the night; and there they searched for corn, because the Indians had hidden it, and they had to pass over a desert. And Thursday they came to another plain where the Indians had taken the position, having made a very strong barricade, and within it there were many Indian braves, painted red and decorated with other colours which appeared very fine (or rather, very bad, at least it meant harm to the Christians). And they entered the barricade by force, and with some loss by death and wounds on the part of the Commander and his army, and with a loss greater beyond comparison on the part of the conquered; and it would have been still more if the Indians had not taken flight.

Saturday, the last of April, the army set out from the place of the barricade and marched nine days through a deserted country and by a rough way, mountainous and swampy, until May 8, when they came to the first village of Quizqui, which they took by assault and captured much people and clothes; but the Governor promptly restored them to liberty and had everything restored to them for fear of war, although that was not enough to make friends of these Indians. A league beyond this village they came upon another with abundance of corn, and soon again after another league, upon another likewise amply provisioned. There they saw the Great River. Saturday, May 21, the force went along to a plain between the river and a small village, and set up quarters and began to build four barges to cross over to the other side. Many of those conquerors said this river was larger than the Danube.

On the other side of the river, about seven thousand Indians had got together, with about two hundred canoes, to defend the passage. All of them had shields made of canes joined, so strong and so closely interwoven with such thread that a cross-bow could hardly pierce them. The arrows came raining down so that the air was full of them, and their yells were something fearful. But when they saw that the work on the barges did not relax on their account, they said that Pacaha, whose men they were, ordered them to withdraw, and so they left the passage free. And on Saturday, June 8 [June 18?], the whole force crossed this great river in the four barges and gave thanks to God because in His good pleasure nothing more difficult could confront them. Soon, on Sunday, they came to a village of Aquixo.

Tuesday, June 21, they went from there and passed by the settlement of Aquixo, which is very beautiful, or beautifully situated. The next day, Wednesday, they passed through the worst tract for swamps and water that they had found in all Florida, and on that day the toil of the soldiers was very heavy.

The next day following, Thursday, they entered the land of Quarqui, and passed through small villages; and the next day, Friday, St. John's day, they came to the village of the Lord of Casqui, who gave food and clothing to the army. It was Saturday when they entered his village, and it had very good cabins, and, in the principal one, over the door, were many heads of very fierce bulls, just as in Spain, noblemen who are sportsmen mount the heads of wild boars or bears. There the Christians planted the cross on a mound, and they received it and adored it with much devotion, and the blind and lame came to seek to be healed. Their faith, says Rodrigo Ranjel, would have surpassed that of the conquerors if they had been taught, and would have brought forth more fruit than those conquerors did.

Sunday, June 26, they departed thence to go to Pacaha, an enemy of Casqui; and after passing several villages, they spent the night in one. And the following day they crossed a swamp over which the Indians had thrown a well-constructed bridge, broad and very cleverly built. On Wednesday they came to the village of Pacaha, a village and lord of wide repute and highly thought of in that country.

This town was a very good one, thoroughly well stockaded; and the walls were furnished with towers and a ditch round about, for the most part full of water which flows in by a canal from the river; and this ditch was full of excellent fish of divers kinds. The chief of Casqui came to the Christians when they were entering the village and they entertained him bravely. In Aquixo, and Casqui, and Pacaha, they saw the best villages seen up to that time, better stockaded and fortified, and the people were of finer quality, excepting those of Cofitachequi. The Commander and his soldiers remaining some days in Pacaha, they made some incursions further up country.

And the chief of Casqui, on one occasion, when he saw a chance for it, went off without seeking permission, on account of which the Governor tried to secure peace with Pacaha; and he came to the camp to recover a brother of his whom the Christians had taken when they entered the village; and an agreement was made with Pacaha that they should war against Casqui, which was very gratifying to Pacaha. But Casqui got wind of this resolve and came with fifty Indians of his in fine array, and he brought a clown for display, who said and did much that was amusing, making those who saw him laugh a good deal. The Governor assumed an air of irritation and sternness to please Pacaha, and sent word that Casqui should not come into the village. Casqui replied that he would not refrain from coming even if they cut off his head. Pacaha asked the Governor to allow him to give Casqui a slash in the face with a knife that he had in his hand, which the Christians had given him. But the Governor told Pacaha that he should do no such thing, nor do him any harm, for he would be angry at him; and he ordered Casqui to come so as to see what he wanted, and because he wished to ask him the reason why he had gone without his permission. Casqui came and spoke to the Governor as follows:—as it was reported by the interpreter Johan Ortiz and the other Indian interpreters that the Governor and the Christians had—"How is it, my Lord, possible, that after having given me the pledge of friendship, and without my having done any harm to you, or given any occasion, you desire to destroy me, your friend and brother? You gave me the cross for a defence against my enemies, and with it you seek to destroy me." (This he said because the Indians of Pacaha, his enemy, that went with the Christians, against him, wore crosses on their heads, high up, that they might be seen.) "Now, my Lord," said Casqui, "when God has heard us by means of the cross; when the women and boys and all those of my country threw themselves on their knees before it to pray for water to the God who you said suffered on it; and He heard us and gave us water in great abundance and refreshed our corn-fields and plantations; now, when we had the most faith in it and in your friendship, you desired to destroy these boys and women that are so devoted to you and your God. Why did you desire to use us with such cruelty without our deserving it from you? Why did you desire to destroy the faith and confidence which we had in you? Why did you desire to offend your God and us, when for Him, and in His name, you gave us assurances and received us for friends, and we gave you entire confidence and trust in the same God and His cross, and have it for our safeguard and protection, and hold it in the reverence and veneration which is proper? With what object or purpose were you actuated to do, or even to think of a thing so grievous against a people without blame, and friends of the cross and of yours?"

This said, he held his peace. The Governor, his eyes melting and not without trace of tears, considering the faith and words of this chief, replied to him, through the interpreters, in the presence of many of the Christian soldiers, who, attentively, and not without tears, overcome by such goodness and faith, had heard what was said, and spoke as follows: "Look you, Casqui, we are not come to destroy you, but to do for you what you know and understand is the work of the cross and our God, as you tell me. And these favours, which it has bestowed upon you, are a small thing in comparison with many others and very great ones, which it will secure you if you love it and believe in it. Be assured of this, and you will find it so and realize it better every day. And when you ran off without my permission I thought that you held the teaching we had given you of little account, and for that contempt that you had for it I wanted to destroy you; supposing that in pride you had gone off, for that is the thing which our God most abhors, and for which He punishes us the most. Now that you have come in humility, be assured that I wish you more good than you think;

and if you have need of anything from me, tell me of it and you will see, since we do what our God commands us, which is not to lie; and, therefore, believe that I tell you the truth, since to speak a lie is a very great sin amongst us. For this good-will be not grateful to me or mine, since if you hold what you say, God, our Lord, commands that we love you as a brother, and that we treat you as such because you and yours are our brethren, and such is the injunction of our God."

The Indians, as much as the Christians, had heard with wonder what Casqui had said. It was now the hour for dinner and the commander sat down and ordered both chiefs to be seated. And between them there was much contention, as to which of them should sit on the right hand of the Governor. Pacaha said to Casqui: "You know well that I am a greater lord than you, and of more honourable parents and grandparents, and that to me belongs a higher place." Casqui replied as follows: "True it is that you are a greater lord than I, and that your forbears were greater than mine. And since this great lord here tells us that we must not lie, I will not deny the truth. But you know well that I am older and mightier than you, and that I confine you in your walls whenever I wish, and you never have seen my country." Finally this was left to the Governor to settle and he ordered that Pacaha should be seated on his right hand because he was a greater lord and more ancient in rank, and he showed in his good customs more of the manners of the courtier after their fashion.

Casqui had brought a daughter, a fine young girl, to the Governor. Pacaha gave him one of his wives, blooming, and very worthy; and he gave him a sister and another Indian woman of rank. The Governor made them friends and embraced them and ordered that there should be merchandising and business between one country and the other, and they agreed to it. And after this the Governor departed thence the 29th of July.

But I could wish that along with the excellencies of the cross and of the faith that this Governor explained to these chiefs, he had told them that he was married, and that the Christians ought not to have more than one wife, or to have intercourse with another, or to commit adultery; that he had not taken the daughter whom Casqui gave him, nor the wife and sister and the other woman of rank whom Pacaha gave him; and that they had not got the idea that the Christians, like the Indians, could have as many wives and concubines as they desired, and thus, like the Indians, live as adulterers.

Let us pass on. To my thinking it would have been better after baptizing a chief of so much intelligence as Casqui, and making him and his people Christians, to have remained there, than to go on to what the history will relate. Nor do I approve of their having gone further than to Cofitachequi, for the same reason, and on account of what was said of that land. However, this army and its Governor having departed, they came by nightfall to a village of Casqui. And the next day to the principal village of the same lord of Casqui, which they had already passed. And they departed from there Sunday, the last day of that month and came to a village of that province. And Monday, August 1, they came to another village, which is on the river of Casqui, which is a branch of the great river of Pacaha, and this branch is as large as the Guadalquivir. Thither came Casqui and assisted them across the river in canoes, August 2.

On Wednesday, they slept in a burned village. The next day, Thursday, in another near the river, where there were many pumpkins and an abundance of corn, and beans. And the next day, Friday, they came to Quiguate, which is the largest village which they saw in that country, situated on the river of Casqui; and it was later known that the banks of this river were thickly populated further down (although they did not find it out there) and along it they took the trail of Coligua which was not peopled in the intervening country.

Friday, August 26, they left Quiguate in search of Coligua and passed the night by a swamp, and from swamp to swamp they made a journey over four swamps and days' marches; and in these swamps, or pools, there was no end of fish, because all that country is flooded by the great river when it overflows its banks. And, Tuesday, they came to the river of Coligua, and, Wednesday, likewise, to the same river. And the next day, Thursday, September 1, to the town of Coligua; and they found it populated, and from it they took much people and clothes, and a vast amount of provisions and much salt. It was a pretty village, between some ridges along the gorge of a great

river. And from there, at midday, they were to kill some cows, of which there are very many wild ones.

Tuesday, the 6th of September, they left Coligua and crossed the river again, and Wednesday they passed some mountains and came to Calpista, where there was an excellent salt spring which distilled very good salt in deposits. The Thursday following they came to Palisma, and on Saturday, September 10, they went on to encamp by a water; and Sunday they came to Quixila, where they rested over Monday. Tuesday they went on to Tutilcoya, and Wednesday, to a village along a large river. And Thursday they encamped near a swamp. And the Governor went on ahead with some horsemen, and came to Tanico, and the next day they came to the same settlement of Tanico, which was built in a somewhat scattered fashion, but was very abundantly provided with supplies. Some would have it that it was Cayase, of which they had heard much, a large stockaded town, but they were never able to see that place or discover it; and subsequently they were told that they had left it near the river.

From there the Governor, with thirteen horsemen and fifty foot, went on to see Tula, and he returned from there in a hurry, and the Indians killed one horse and wounded four or five, and he resolved to go there with the army. One ought not to omit and leave in forgetfulness that in Cayase our Spaniards gathered baskets of dry sand from the river and strained water through it, and there came out a brine, and they boiled it down, and let it harden, and in that way made excellent salt, very white and of very good flavour.

Wednesday, October 5, they departed from the station of Tanico, and came, Friday, to Tula, and found the inhabitants gone, but abundant provisions. On Saturday, in the morning, the Indians came to give them a brush, or a battle, and they had large, long poles, like lances, the ends hardened by fire, and they were the best fighting people that the Christians met with, and they fought like desperate men, with the greatest valour in the world. That day they wounded Hernandarias, the grandson of the marshal of Seville, and, thank God, the Christians defended themselves so valiantly that they did not receive much damage, although the Indians tried to round up the whole force.

Wednesday, October 19, the army and the

Governor departed from Tula, and passed the night at two cabins. And the next day, Thursday, at another cabin, and Friday, at another, where Hernandarias de Saavedra, who had been wounded at Tula, died in convulsions; and he died like a Catholic knight, commending his soul to God. The next day they came to Guipana, which is between ridges of mountains near a river; and from there they went for the night to a place where they could cross over, and all the country was mountainous from Tula. The next day they left the mountain and came on to the plains and Monday the last day of the month, they came to a village called Quitamaya, and Tuesday, the 1st of November, they went through a small village; and Wednesday, the 2d of November, they came to Utiangüe, which was a plain well peopled and of attractive appearance. [Unfinished in MS].

241. Extract from the narrative of Luis Hernández de Biedma.

Biedma's is the shortest of the three main narratives and the least easy to follow chronologically: it would appear that he composed it after returning to Spain. It seemed worthwhile picking up its story from late in 1541, a little time before that of Rangel ends, since Biedma provides an alternative version to what the Gentleman of Elvas offers for that period. The translation is taken from E. G. Bourne, Narratives of the Career of Hernando de Soto, *2 vols. (New York, 1904), II, 26–40.*

... on the way to that Province of Pacaha, we came first to the province of another lord, called Iscasqui.... The Cacique came out peacefully to meet us, saying that he had heard of us for a long time, and that he knew we were men from heaven, whom their arrows could not harm; wherefore, he desired to have no strife and wished only to serve us. The Governor received him very kindly, and permitting no one to enter the town, to avoid doing mischief, we encamped in sight, on a plain, where we lay two days.

On the day of our arrival, the Cacique said that inasmuch as he knew the Governor to be a man from the sky, who must necessarily have to go away, he besought him to leave a sign, of which he might ask support in his wars, and his people call upon for rain, of which their fields had great need, as their children were dying of hunger. The Governor commanded that a very tall cross be made of two pines, and told him to return the next day, when he would give him the sign from heaven for which he asked; but that the Chief must believe nothing could be needed if he had a true faith in the cross. He returned the next day, complaining much because we so long delayed giving him the sign he asked, and he had good-will to serve and follow us. Thereupon he set up a loud wailing because the compliance was not immediate, which caused us all to weep, witnessing such devotion and earnestness in his entreaties. The Governor told him to bring all his people back in the evening, and that we would go with them to his town and take thither the sign he had asked. He came in the afternoon with them, and we went in procession to the town, while they followed us. Arriving there, as it is the custom of the Caciques to have near their houses a high hill, made by hand, some having the houses placed thereon, we set up the cross on the summit of a mount, and we all went on bended knees, with great humility, to kiss the foot of that cross. The Indians did the same as they saw us do, nor more nor less; then directly they brought a great quantity of cane, making a fence about it; and we returned that night to our camp.

In the morning, we took up our course for Pacaha, which was by the river upward. We travelled two days, and then discovered the town on a plain, well fenced about, and surrounded by a water-ditch made by hand. Hastening on as fast as possible, we came near and halted, not daring to enter there; but going about on one side and the other, and discovering that many people were escaping, we assailed and entered the town, meeting no opposition. We took only a few people, for nearly all had fled, without, however, being able to carry off the little they possessed. While we yet halted in sight of the town, before venturing to enter it, we saw coming behind us a large body of Indians, whom we supposed to be advancing to the assistance of the place; but going to meet them, we found they were those we had left behind, among whom we had raised the cross, and were following to lend us their succour, should we need any. We took the Cacique to the town, where he gave the Governor many thanks for the sign we had left him, telling us the rain had fallen heavily in his country the day before, and his people were so glad of it that they wished to follow and not leave us. The Governor put him into the town, and gave him every thing found there, which was great riches for those people—some beads made of sea-snails, the skins of cats and of deer, and a little maize. He returned home with them, much gratified. We remained in his town twenty-seven or twenty-eight days, to discover if we could take a path to the northward, whereby to come out on the South Sea.

Some incursions were made to capture Indians who might give us the information; particularly was one undertaken to the northwest, where we were told there were large settlements, through which we might go. We went in that direction eight days, through a wilderness which had large pondy swamps, where we did not find even trees, and only some wide plains, on which grew a plant so rank and high, that even on horseback we could not break our way through. Finally, we came to some collections of huts, covered with rush and sewed together. When the owner of one moves away, he will roll up the entire covering, and carry it, the wife taking the frame of poles over which it is stretched; these they take down and put up so readily, that though they should move anew every hour, they conveniently enough carry their house on their backs. We learned from this people that there were some hamlets of the sort about the country, the inhabitants of which employed themselves in finding places for their dwellings wherever many deer were accustomed to range, and a swamp where were many fish; and that when they had frightened the game and the fish from one place, so that they took them there not so easily as at first, they would all move off with their dwellings for some other part, where the animals were not yet shy. This Province, called Caluç, had a people who care little to plant, finding support in meat and fish.

We returned to Pacaha, where the Governor had remained, and found that the Cacique had come in peacefully, living with him in the town. In this time arrived the Cacique from the place behind, at which he had put up the cross. The efforts of these two chiefs, who were enemies, each to place himself on the right hand when the Governor commanded that they should sit at his sides, was a sight worth witnessing.

Finding that there was no way by which to march to the other sea, we returned towards the south, and went with the Cacique to where was the cross, and thence took the direction to the southwest, to another Province called Quiquate. This was the largest town we found in Florida, and was on an arm of the Rio Grande. We remained there eight or nine days, to find guides and interpreters, still with the intention of coming out, if possible, on the other sea; for the Indians told us that eleven days' travel thence was a province where they subsisted on certain cattle, and there we could find interpreters for the whole distance to that sea.

We departed with guides for the Province called Coligua, without any road, going at night to the swamps, where we drank from the hand and found abundance of fish. We went over much even country and other of broken hills, coming straight upon the town, as much so as if we had been taken thither by a royal highway, instead of which not a man in all time had passed there before. The land is very plentiful of subsistence, and we found a large quantity of dressed cows' tails, and others already cured. We inquired of the inhabitants for a path in the direction we held, or a town on it, near or far. They could give us no sort of information, only that if we wished to go in the direction where there were people, we should have to return upon a west-southwestern course.

We continued to pursue the course chosen by our guides, and went to some scattered settlements called Tatil Coya. Here we found a copious river, which we afterwards discovered empties into the Rio Grande, and we were told that up the stream was a great Province, called Cayas. We went thither, and found it to be a population that, though large, was entirely scattered. It is a very rough country of hills. Several incursions were made; in one of which the Cacique and a large number of people were taken. On asking him about the particulars of the country, he told us that in following up the river we should come upon a fertile Province, called Tula. The Governor, desiring to visit there, to see if it were a place in which he could winter the people, set off with twenty men on horseback, leaving the remainder in the Province at Cayas.

Before coming to the Province of Tula, we passed over some rough hills, and arrived at the town before the inhabitants had any notice of us. In attempting to seize some Indians, they began to yell and show us battle. They wounded of ours that day seven or eight men, and nine or ten horses; and such was their courage, that they came upon us in packs, by eights and tens, like worried dogs. We killed some thirty or forty of them. The Governor thought it not well to stay there that night with his small force, and returned on the way we had come, going through a bad passage of the ridge, where it was feared the natives would beset us, to a plain in a vale made by the river. The next day we got back to where the people lay; but there were no Indians of ours, nor could any in the province be found, to speak the language of these we brought.

Orders were given that all should make ready to go to that province. We marched thither at once. The next morning after our arrival, at daybreak, three very large squadrons of Indians came upon us by as many directions: we met them and beat them, doing some injury, so much that they returned upon us no more. In two or three days they sent us messengers of peace, although we did not understand a thing they said, for want of an interpreter. By signs we told them to bring persons in there who could understand the people living back of us; and they brought five or six Indians who understood the interpreters we had. They asked who we were, and of what we were in search. We asked them for some great provinces where there should be much provision (for the cold of winter had begun to threaten us sharply), and they said that on the route we were taking they knew of no great town; but they pointed, that if we wished to return to the east and southeast, or go northwest, we should find large towns.

Discovering that we could not prevail against the difficulty, we returned to the southeast, and went to a Province that is called Quipana, at the base of some very steep ridges; whence we journeyed in a direction to the east, and having crossed those mountains, went down upon some plains, where we found a population suited to our purpose, for there was a town nigh in which was much food, seated by a copious river emptying into the Rio Grande, from whence we came. The Province was called Viranque. We stopped in it to pass the winter. There was so much snow and cold, we thought to have perished. At this town the Christian died whom we had found in the country belonging to the people of Narvaez, and who was our interpreter. We went out thence in the beginning of March, when it appeared to us that the severity of the winter had passed; and we followed down the course of this river, whereon we found other provinces well peopled, having a quantity of food, to a Province called Anicoyanque, which appeared to us to be one of the best we had found in all the country. Here another Cacique, called Guachoyanque, came to us in peace. His town is upon the River Grande, and he is in continual war with the other chief with whom we were.

The Governor directly set out for the town of Guachoyanque, and took its Cacique with him. The town was good, well and strongly fenced. It contained little provision, the Indians having carried that off. Here the Governor, having before determined, if he should find the sea, to build brigantines by which to make it known in Cuba that we were alive, whence we might be supplied with some horses and things of which we stood in need, sent a Captain in the direction south, to see if some road could be discovered by which we might go to look for the sea; because, from the account given by the Indians, nothing could be learned of it; and he got back, reporting that he found no road, nor any way by which to pass the great bogs that extend out from the Rio Grande. The Governor, at seeing himself thus surrounded, and nothing coming about according to his expectations, sickened and died. He left us recommending Luis de Moscoso be our Governor.

Since we could find no way to the sea, we agreed to take our course to the west, on which we might come out by land to Mexico, should we be unable to find any thing, or a place whereon to settle. We travelled seventeen days, until we came to the Province of Chavite, where the Indians made much salt; but we could learn nothing of them concerning the west: thence we went to another province, called Aguacay, and were three days on the way, still going directly westward. After leaving this place, the Indians told us we should see no more settlements unless we went down in a southwest-and-by-south direction, where we should find large towns and food; that in the course we asked about, there were some large sandy wastes, without any people or subsistence whatsoever.

We were obliged to go where the Indians directed us, and went to a Province called Nisione, and to another called Nondacao, and another, Came; and at each remove we went through lands that become more sterile and afforded less subsistence. We continually asked for a province which they told us was large, called Xuacatino. The Cacique of Nondacao gave us an Indian purposely to put us somewhere whence we could never come out: the guide took us over a rough country, and off the road, until he told us at last he did not know where he was leading us; that his master had ordered him to take us where we should die of hunger. We took another guide, who led us to a Province called Hais, where, in seasons, some cattle are wont to herd; and as the Indians saw us entering their country, they began to cry out: "Kill the cows—they are coming;" when they sallied and shot their arrows at us, doing us some injury.

We went from this place and came to the Province of Xacatin, which was among some close forests, and was scant of food. Hence the Indians guided us eastward to other small towns, poorly off for food, having said that they would take us where there were other Christians like us, which afterwards proved false; for they could have had no knowledge of any others than ourselves, although, as we made so many turns, it might be in some of them they had observed our passing. We turned to go southward, with the resolution of either reaching New Spain, or dying. We travelled about six days in a direction south and southwest, when we stopped.

Thence we sent ten men, on swift horses, to travel in eight or nine days as far as possible, and see if any town could be found where we might re-supply ourselves with maize, to enable us to pursue our journey. They went as far as they could go, and came upon some poor people without houses, having wretched huts, into which they withdrew; and they neither planted nor gathered any thing, but lived entirely upon flesh and fish. Three or four of them, whose tongue no one we could find understood, were brought back. Reflecting that we had lost our interpreter, that we found nothing to eat, that the maize we

brought upon our backs was failing, and it seemed impossible that so many people should be able to cross a country so poor, we determined to return to the town where the Governor Soto died, as it appeared to us there was convenience for building vessels with which we might leave the country.

We returned by the same road we had taken, until we came to the town; but we did not discover so good outfit as we had thought to find. There were no provisions in the town, the Indians having taken them away, so we had to seek another town, where we might pass the winter and build the vessels. I thank God that we found two towns very much to our purpose, standing upon the Rio Grande, and which were fenced around, having also a large quantity of maize. Here we stopped, and with great labour built seven brigantines, which were finished at about the end of six months. We threw them out into the water, and it was a mystery that, calked as they were with the bark of mulberry-trees, and without any pitch, we should find them stanch and very safe. Going down the river, we took with us also some canoes, into which were put twenty-six horses, for the event of finding any large town on the shore of the sea that could sustain us with food, while we might send thence a couple of brigantines to the Viceroy of New Spain, with a message to provide us with vessels in which we could get away from the country.

The second day, descending the stream, there came out against us about forty or fifty very large and swift canoes, in some of which were as many as eighty warriors, who assailed us with their arrows, following and shooting at us. Some who were in the vessels thought it trifling not to attack them; so, taking four or five of the small canoes we brought along, they went after them. The Indians, seeing this, surrounded them, so that they could not get away, and upset the canoes, whereby twelve very worthy men were drowned, beyond the reach of our succour, because of the great power of the stream, and the oars in the vessels being few.

The Indians were encouraged by this success to follow us to the sea, which we were nineteen days in reaching, doing us much damage and wounding many people; for, as they found we had no arms that could reach them from a distance, not an arquebuse nor a crossbow having remained, but only some swords and targets, they lost their fears, and would draw very nigh to let drive at us with their arrows.

We came out by the mouth of the river, and entering into a very large bay made by it, which was so extensive that we passed along it three days and three nights, with fair weather, in all the time not seeing land, so that it appeared to us we were at sea, although we found the water still so fresh that it could well be drunk, like that of the river. Some small islets were seen westward, to which we went: thenceforward we kept close along the coast, where we took shell-fish, and looked for other things to eat, until we entered the River of Pánuco, where we came and were well received by the Christians.

[signed:] Luys Hernandez de Biedma

242. June 20–27, 1542. The death of Hernando de Soto.

Garcilaso de la Vega, the Inca, certainly deserves representation, if only by a nominal sample, in any compilation on Hernando de Soto. His treatment of Soto's illness and death provides a specimen of his eloquent rhetoric and the intimate detail with which he invested so many aspects of the expedition.

Gascilaso de la Vega, the Inca, The Florida of the Inca, *translated and edited by John G. Varner and J. J. Varner (Austin, Texas, 1951).*

An account is given of the
Governor's death and of the
successor whom he appointed.

Desiring as a good father that the many hardships he and his men had experienced and that the expenditures they had incurred in the exploration should not be wasted and without fruit for them, this heroic cavalier was absorbed day and night in the cares and aspirations we have described, when on the twentieth of June of the year 1542 he felt a slight fever. On the first day this fever was slow, but on the third very severe; and, observing its inordinate increase, the Governor realized that his illness was mortal. So he prepared himself at once for dissolution, and as a good Catholic Christian, arranged his will, almost in cipher, however, because of his not possessing an adequate supply of paper. Then in sorrow and repentance at having offended God, he confessed his sins.

As his successor in the position of governor and captain general of the kingdom and provinces of Florida, he selected Luis de Moscoso de Alvarado, the gentleman whom in the province of Chicaza he had deprived of the office of campmaster. For the ceremony of appointment, he summoned before him his cavaliers, captains, and soldiers of higher rank, and then on the part of His Imperial Majesty, he begged and charged these men that out of respect for the virtue, rank and merits of Luis de Moscoso, they look upon him as their governor and captain general until such time as His Majesty should send another decree. Afterward he took their solemn vow that they would thus comply. This task completed, he called before him the noblest of his army in groups of two and three; and later he instructed the remainder of his people to come to him in groups of twenty and thirty. To these men he bade farewell with much sorrow on his part and copious tears on theirs, and he charged them with the conversion of the natives to the Catholic Faith and with the augmentation of the Spanish Crown, declaring that death was depriving him of fulfilling these ambitions. Then he very earnestly besought them to keep peace and affection among themselves.

Five days Hernando de Soto consumed in this matter, during which time his raging fever was increasing; and then on the seventh day, the fever deprived him of this present life. He died as a Christian Catholic, beseeching mercy of the most Holy Trinity, invoking in his favor and protection the blood of Jesus Christ Our Lord, and calling for the intercession of the Virgin and all the Celestial Court as well as the Faith of the Roman Church. With such words, which he repeated numerous times, this magnanimous and never conquered cavalier who was worthy of great titles and estates and undeserving that his history be written by an Indian, thus rendered his soul to God. He died at the age of forty-two.

The Adelantado Hernando de Soto was, as we stated in the beginning, a native of Villanueva de

Barcarrota and an hidalgo in all four successions of his ancestry. When His Caesarean Majesty was informed of this fact, he sent him the order of Santiago, but this honor he never enjoyed, for by the time the decree reached the island of Cuba, he had already entered upon the discovery and conquest of Florida. More than medium in stature, and graceful, he appeared well both on foot and mounted. He had a dark but merry face and was skillful in both saddles, more so however with the short stirrups than the long. In hardships and want, he was very patient, indeed so patient that the greatest comfort of his soldiers at such times was to behold the suffering and forbearance of their captain general.

Hernando de Soto was fortunate in those particular expeditions which he undertook personally, although not in the principal one since he lost his life at the moment of his greatest opportunity. He was the first Spaniard to see and speak with Atahuallpa, a tyrant king who was the last of the Incas to rule Peru, as I shall disclose in my history of the discovery and conquest of that empire if Our Lord God vouchsafe to lengthen my life, which already grows feeble and tired. Severe in punishing transgressions of military science, he pardoned others freely. He esteemed highly those of his soldiers who were strong and brave, and he personally was most courageous, in fact so courageous that wherever he entered a battlefield fighting, he cut a path through which ten of his men could pass. Thus all confessed that ten lances from his entire army were not of such worth as his own.

This valorous captain possessed one very notable and memorable characteristic, which was that in the unexpected attacks made on his camp day by day, he was always the first or the second to rush forth at the alarm, and never the third. But in those assaults which the enemy made by night, he was the first and never the second. So it appears that it was only after having prepared himself to go out to a battle that he gave his men the alarm. With such promptness and vigilance as this, he always conducted himself in war. In sum he was one of the best lancers who have gone to the New World; and there were few as good and none better, unless it were Gonzalo Pizarro, to whom by common consent was invariably given the honor of first place.

In this exploration, Hernando de Soto spent the more than one hundred thousand ducats which he had obtained in the first conquest of Peru from the division of that rich ransom the Spaniards had collected at Cajamarca. Moreover, he paid with his life, and, as we have seen, died in action.

Chapter Thirty
The Tragic Mission of Fray Luis Cáncer,
1549

THE INFLUENCE of Bartolomé de las Casas on Spanish policy towards the Christianizing of the Amerindian peoples was bound at some time or another to find expression in North America. The Dominican Order was especially susceptible to his teaching that the Indians should be introduced to Christianity in an indigenous setting and not under the aegis of Spanish adventurers, soldiers, and officials. Luis Cáncer de Barbastro and his Dominican associates bravely decided to make the attempt and set out to do so in 1549. Unfortunately, the friars knew nothing of the earlier experiences of the Indians of the western part of the Florida Peninsula at the hands of the Spaniards. The result was that when the unarmed ship *Santa María de la Ençina* put into Tampa Bay the local Indians, exploited much earlier by Hernando de Soto and others, lured the Spaniards ashore and eventually set on them and killed Cáncer and one of his companions when they courageously exposed themselves to Indian attack. The ship and the remaining missionaries left hurriedly. Fray Gregorio de Beteta, who survived the trip, left a vivid account of the episode, not minimizing its potential as hagiographical material, since the Catholic Church now, for the first time, had a North American martyr.

The sources are introduced by a brief note from Gómera, *Historia general de las Indias* (243). The Beteta account (244) was printed by T. Buckingham Smith in *Colección de varios documentos para la historia de la Florida* (London, 1857), I, 190–202, from a copy he found in the Muñoz Collection, Academia Real de Historia, Madrid, LXXXV; it has not been previously translated in full. A brief account (245) shows that as late as 1553 attempts were being made to discover the whereabouts of the vessel that returned from the venture. This letter is from the John Carter Brown Library, Reales Cédulas, *Codex Sp* 8, fols. 86—96v.

243. Gómera on the abortive mission of Fray Luis de Cáncer in Florida, 1549.

Francisco López de Gómera, Historia general de las Indias *(Madrid, 1932), I, 98, translated.*

Nevertheless they sent Fray Luis Cancel Balvastro [Luis Cáncer de Barbastro], with other Dominican friars who offered to pacify that land and to convert the people and bring them to serve and obey the emperor by their words alone. The friar then set out at the king's cost in 1549. He went on shore with four friars whom he had brought with him and with certain laymen— unarmed sailors—for this was the way they had to begin preaching. There came down to the shore many of the Floridians, who, without listening, clubbed him, with another, or two other, companions, and ate them and so they died, martyred for preaching the faith of Christ. May He keep them in His Glory. The others took refuge on board ship, preserving themselves to hear confessions as some say. Many who favoured the purpose of these friars now recognised that by such means it is difficult to bring the Indians to friendship with us or to our holy faith, although if it could be done it would be better thus.

244. 1549. The mission of Fray Luis Cáncer to Florida as told by Beteta.

A copy of the account of Fray Gregorio de Beteta was found in the Muñoz Collection of the Academia Real de Historia, Madrid, LXXXV and printed by Thomas Buckingham Smith in Colección de varios documentos para la historia de la Florida (London, 1857), I, 190–202, translated.

A Report from Florida for
the Most Illustrious Viceroy
of New Spain, brought
by Friar Gregorio de Beteta.

With more time and leisure than I have available at present I began to note down and write about what was happening every day on this trip to Florida, so that unintentional forgetfulness should not lead me to write more nor less than was appropriate. For since this matter is and has been taken to be of importance, good if we should succeed or very bad if we should fail, I always believed and expected that there would occur events of joy and sorrow well worth recording, and indeed that is how it has turned out; and I also considered that there would happen even more than we have seen so far. I refer to the task of staying alone in such a large deserted area, although well accompanied by my firm and certain hope and the expectation that Our Lord, *qui est potens de lapidibus istis suscitare filios habrahae,*[1] should enlighten them and protect me so

that this work can be carried out in the best service of Our Lord where those who have no eyes shall see. And those who have not ears shall hear, how Our Lord, when he wishes to carry out a most holy and marvellous work, he places it in such a state and circumstances that it seems so hopeless in the eyes of men that no success can be foreseen. And then at the best time God raises and exalts his work, choosing for it not the richest nor the wisest nor the most powerful in his eyes, but *contemptibilia mundi ut confundat queque fortia,*[2] so that from this the result should be that the praise and glory that was going to be given to the great power, wealth or riches of men should be given and ascribed to the great power and goodwill which is the wisdom of God Our Lord: Who I beg to give me this grace and divine and supreme assistance. And to those who shall read this brief report I ask them to beg His Divine Majesty that in everything and through everything he should give me light and guidance that I should not offend him and convert these people to know him, serve him and love him.

Leaving apart[3] the time and manner in which we set out, and what has happened from Vera Cruz and from Havana until we arrived within sight of this land, which was the day before the Glorious Ascension of Our Lord, I shall say briefly whatever time allows me to, because I am in the launch at the place where they are taking me to land and where I am to remain alone; and although I realize that it would be better for me to be considering and regretting my sins as a man far from home, that only God knows what will become of me, even so I am happy to take this trouble to give an account to whoever may be concerned of a task as important as this.

Once we had arrived in sight of this land, which as I said was the day before the Glorious Ascension of Our Lord, we anchored in less than ten fathoms at approximately 28 degrees north. Then the next day, Ascension Day, the launch left for the land with five or six seamen. Although the pilot told them not to jump over nor go to land, but to reconnoitre it and see if there was a port for the

---

1. Gospel of St Matthew, Chap. III, verse 9.

2. St Paul's 1st Epistle to the Corinthians, Chap. I, vv. 27-28.
3. Except that Friar Gregorio, when in Havana, wanted to go to the river they call Santa Elena, beyond the Bahama Channel, in a caravel that was going to Castille, since he did not want to go to a place where Spaniards had already been. He dropped this plan because the caravel was not prepared to take him.

ship to anchor in, they did the opposite, for when they saw such beautiful groves of trees they decided to jump onto the land. And at the time they were wanting to do this one of them saw three Indians and began to shout "Indians, Indians," and the others, without thinking to see where they were or how they were coming, set to some of them to the "trica" [sail?] and the others to the oars, and one of them, thinking the Indians had already caught them, said "I swear they're breaching the bottom of our boat"; eventually they got away, but before they could reach the ship they were involved in such a great skirmish that they became separated quite a way from the ship, and since they were in danger the Pilot ordered the anchors to be raised and sail to be set so we could go and protect them, because some of them would certainly have preferred to be among the Indians than in that skirmish.

And as the wind and the weather were getting calmer, the Pilot ordered that the sails should stay up: and the seamen gradually came closer to the ship, and once on board they all began to talk about the part they had played in the encounter. I asked the Pilot to reprimand them, so that they would act better another day.[4] And since on that coast there was no sign of the port we were searching for, which was in fact very close to there, we went away from the shore thinking that it was further up, towards the bay of Miruelo or Apalache: we reached 28 and a half degrees north,[5] and then the launch set out to land. Father Friar Juan and I went in it, and after going three leagues[6] we saw land, another three leagues away; we went through water of four, three and two fathoms until we reached a small bay, where we all jumped out: not where I wanted to, because had there been half a dozen Indians in the forest we would all have been shot with their arrows, and it was quite daft not to have landed on the flat open ground where we could have had the advantage over an enemy, and go into the trees ourselves. We slept that night on a little island slightly off shore, and there there was another oversight, since the launch was left grounded on

the sand and we had to wait for the high tide next morning. There too just a couple of canoes with Indians in could have done us considerable damage. That morning we went on another three leagues in search of a port, and since we saw nothing worthwhile we went back to the ship, now nine leagues distant, although they had come three leagues towards us trying to find us, which was so distant that had we not happened to find them close, a large fight could have separated us a long way from them, whereas we and they had arrived together at the same time and we went on board. And many times I warned and asked the Pilot that we should not leave so much to chance, because men find themselves deceived when they least expect it. I did not dare speak out loud, because someone told me that I was frightening the seamen with my fears.[7] We left there and retraced our steps, so that we anchored near the place where we had reconnoitred the land. The Pilot with the seamen and the launch landed to find a port or signs of Indians. I went with him, and Father Friar Diego de Tolosa, and we were going into a bay, without thinking of seeing Indians, and when we were not looking one of them shouted "huts, huts"; we saw them and looked more closely and they were some three or four fishermen's huts. Father Friar Diego and Fuentes, who was a good Christian man in our company, asked me to let them jump out to land, and since there seemed to be nobody there and the Pilot had left, it seemed to me better to leave and see if anyone was there than to go back to the ship with no news, because by now some of the monks were thinking of landing and advancing into the forests, since they saw that the Pilot could not find the Bay of the Holy Spirit[8]: when I saw this I thought I ought to leave them, and I could not stop them for another was moving them more than I.

The Friar and the other good man were wanting to go two leagues inland, and to stop them doing it I told them that just one was to go on land, and if they were not willing I would jump out myself. They begged me to let them jump over together, but it did not seem a good idea to me for the reasons mentioned. Eventually the Monk

---

4. At this point Father Friar Gregorio wanted to land, with the aim of staying there, although there seemed to be no Indians; fearing what did, in fact, happen afterwards, they did not let him go.

5. 29.

6. Because the ship could not approach closer to the coast than 6 leagues.

7. Friar Gregorio said this because the seamen were so scared that they mutinied every day in the ship about going and none of them dared approach land in the launch, nor go within arquebus-range.

8. Not having gone before to the Bay of the Holy Spirit.

jumped over and I told him that unless he saw Indians he was to climb up a tree and from there see what there was without going inland at all. He climbed up it, and as he was there looking in all directions, there appeared an Indian, and then another from the trees and approached the monk: some fifteen or twenty other Indians came out. We were all pleased to have found what we were looking for; although I was also very upset because I would have preferred, since this was how I had always planned it and thought it out, to stay in the launch for three or four hours waiting to see if we could see anyone, but I saw that it could not be done like this because the Pilot and the seamen were already tired. When I saw the Indians I sent ashore the interpreter, who was an Indian girl we had brought from Havana and came from those parts, and the good man Fuentes went with her. The Pilot would not let me go, but I was sure that with the interpreter and giving them something they would do no harm to the monk, so I lifted up my habit without telling the Pilot and plunged into the sea waist-deep, and the Lord knows the speed at which I went to stop them dealing with the monk before they heard the reason for our voyage. When I reached the shore I fell to my knees and begged for God's grace and help, then I went up to the flat bit where I found them all together; before I reached them I did again what I had done on the beach, and then got up and began to take out from my sleeve some things from Flanders, which may not seem very important or valuable to Christians, but which they regarded as valuable and great gifts.

Then they came to me, and I gave them part of what I was carrying, then I went to the monk, who came to me, and I embraced him with great pleasure, and we both knelt down, with Fuentes and the Indian girl, took out the book and recited the litanies, commending ourselves to the Lord and His Saints. The Indians knelt, some of them squatting, which pleased me very much, and once they had got up I left the litanies in the middle and sat down with them on a log and soon found out where the port and the bay we were looking for were, about a day and a half's journey by land from where we were; we told them of our aims and wishes.

When the Indian girl saw it was all so peaceful she was very pleased and said to me "Father, didn't I tell you that if I spoke to them they would not kill you? These people are from my land and this one speaks my language." Our Lord knows how pleased we were to see them as peaceful as they were being then; I was getting covered in their red dye from all the embracing that was going on, although I managed to get the worst of it on my habit to leave the skin untouched. To see if I was free to do so, if they would let me go to the launch, I was careful to tell them that I had more to give them and I was going back to get it, although in fact I had it already in my sleeve, but I had not wanted to give them all of it since I had intended to do this: I went, and came back, and found so many who wanted to embrace me that I could not get away from them. This friendship and affection was obviously based on what they thought they could get from us than on ourselves, but since this world is the route to the other, and as we all know from experience and say that love is good deeds and that gifts can break rocks, I was pleased that they should receive us so well for these material matters: the spiritual and true would come bit by bit, like the fear of being bad is considered a good thing because afterwards there enters the true and good. I was very surprised that as they were all asking for beads, knives and axes which we had not brought, they did not dare to take anything of what I had in front of me, but instead I gave it to the brother of the Chief for him to share it out, but he told me to share it out and count them. He told me this via the interpreter.

The Pilot was urging me to come back on board quickly, for which reason I did not stay as long as I should have. The monk said that he wanted to stay there with Fuentes and the interpreter and go off by land. I could not stop him doing this, for as I said, someone else was moving him more than I. He stayed behind very content. Such was the harmony that a seaman jumped twice to land and returned, and an Indian climbed into the launch and told them to take him to the ship, wanting them to give him something, and when he was given it he went back to land. We saw many other signs of concord there, which made us very happy. I told the monk to wait there while I went to the ship and came back with some food for them and for the Chief. When I went to get on board an Indian got on board with me in the boat and we all went to the ship in good spirits, and we were similarly received by those who were on board[9]; Then I gave the Indian something to eat and wear, and we came back to where we left the monk. At three stonesthrows distance I said to the captain of the launch, "It's a bad sign that our friend is not coming out to land." At two stonesthrows I said: "This is worse": at one, since he did not come out, I said: "stop the launch and arrange everything as is best to escape or defend ourselves from arrows." During all this there were four or occasionally six Indians on the shore, waiting for us with fish in their hands. When we had arrived, they shouted to us several times that we should come out and get it, and that the Chief was in the huts with the Christians. We stayed like this for quite a while, the Indians waiting for us to come out to the land, and ourselves waiting for the Indians to come to the launch. One seaman, without saying anything, went over to get the fish, and thinking that it was all as safe as it had been in the morning, he went on up to the huts; an Indian came up to him kindly and openly and slowly walked him by the arm from side to side. The poor man man must have smelt a rat, for he shouted out to me with great urgency to land with the Cross. I told him to go and call for the monk for me, but he went I don't know where and came back with the Indian at his side and said that he was there nearby with the Chief, that I should come out with the Cross. The poor man wanted to grab me, thinking that through me we would both of us be freed, but I was upset and afraid and did not do so, to preserve myself for when some occasion of greater need should arise (such as the one I am in at the moment). Eventually I told him "You come here and then I'll go there," and he replied "They won't let me leave," and this made it obvious to us that the monk and his companion were in the same plight. We waited until after sunset to see if there was any way of seeing them before they were taken prisoner and taken away, and so we left too, very much saddened, and quite unlike the way we had felt that morning. Next day I went out with Father Friar Gregorio, and not seeing any Indians around, he went on land. And since he did not see anyone, he returned to the launch and we all went back to the ship, and the ship set sail with everyone hoping to see the monk and the interpreter in the port, or find out about them there.

We took more than eight days getting to the entrance, and as many more in getting into the bay, which was of about six or seven leagues in length. We came in short of water, which we had trouble in finding. On Corpus Christi day Father Friar Juan and I went ashore, and seeing a safe place to say Mass we said it between us, and then we collected the water we were looking for.[10] Next day we were in considerable doubt as to whether it was the port or not, because the ship was unable to go in, and was in two fathoms of water without being within three leagues of the huts; Father Friar Gregorio and I went to look for them or see if there seemed to be any people around, and we saw a small hill, and on top of it a good hut and at the door one Indian alone. Although we made many signs to him that he should come and get a shirt, he did not budge from where he was. We left it for him hanging on a piece of wood in the sea, and went to some other huts that were to our left, along the coast a league from the hill, and seeing that there seemed to be nobody about we decided to stop and have something to eat, and we even slept for quite a while, and all this time no man turned up; and as soon as we set sail. . . . [lacuna] an Indian came out, carrying a stick and on top of it a bunch of white palm leaves, and behind him another Indian running and shouting loud "Friends, friends, good, good." These and other words in Spanish they told us that they had had to learn them from the Christians who had passed this way.

When they reached the beach they waved to us and shouted "come here, come here," "no sword, no sword," as much as to say that they were peaceful people, for they had no swords. I said to them in their own language "he oza ulvata," which means "we are men of goodwill," and they all shouted aloud the same. We tried our best to get some of them to come out to the launch by showing them shirts, and as they did not come out, we decided to set off and left with the water at waist level, Father Friar Gregorio with one shirt and I with another, going very slowly, and with some fear they came towards us. When we had arrived the one who was carrying the sign of peace gave it

9. Not by all of them.

10. In the vessels of some Xorguayes.

to the Father in return for the shirt, and the other one took the one I gave him, and after we had told them through signals for a time that they should bring us the monk and the Christians and the interpreter as they had promised us they would, they went off to their huts and we went back to the ship feeling fairly pleased. I forgot to say that after those two had come out from the pine trees there appeared thirty well built men without arrows, making signs of peace and saying "no sword, give me an axe, come here, give me a shirt.... [lacuna] and when we arrived at the ship, thinking we were carrying great news, we found others waiting both much better and much worse: they told us that there had come there one of the Spaniards that Soto had taken, who had fled from his master in a canoe. I was very pleased with such good news, and it would have been a great help to our purpose if he had not added other sadder and more terrible information, saying that the Indians who had taken the monk and his companion had killed them as soon as I left them, and that they were holding the seaman alive. When he was asked how he had found this out, he said "I have often heard it from other Indians who saw them being killed, and I also saw the skin from the head of the monk, which an Indian showed me who was taking it about as an exhibit, and he said that they were doing and saying many things when they killed them." All this is a most terrible thing and very distressing for us all, but even so it could be endured, and is the kind of event involved in these affairs of the faith, and I always used to think, whenever I considered the importance of this matter, that, as it was with the Apostles, it would be with our own blood that we would plant and establish the law and the faith of the one who even to give it and preach it to us suffered and died; and since this is the way it is, and is only to be expected in the preaching of so great a law, there is no reason to despair of future success because of something like this happening. Even after this there is no cause to see, as I saw and heard, people saying that this immensely important task should be abandoned and we should go back, for certainly it would be no progress to sail back to Mexico. With such news this was one of the most terrible things that I could have seen and heard in the world. And this was not the worst of it, because if Our Lord was not pleased that the task should succeed now,

there was still time for it, but if we were to go back with this news, as almost all of them thought and suggested, they would conclude, and it would be the wrong conclusion, that all these pagans deserved death, and deserved having people conquer them and take their lands, although I am absolutely sure that Our King and his Councillors, being sensible and wary of offending Our Lord, would never order such a thing just because of what happened here.

As regards the Viceroy of New Spain, I know that his feelings are the same as mine in this matter, for it is in accordance with the law of Christ, because he told me once that if this enterprise were successful it would be one of the best things ever done in the Indies, but if it failed it would be the worst thing ever done in the Indies, and when I asked him why it would be the worst, he answered that they would destroy all those that did not accept us and killed us. In reply I expounded the view that if they killed us at once at the start they should deal with them through their law, and that was not sufficient reason for making war on them: and His Lordship replied as a Catholic and Christian that that was true, but he had meant if they were to kill us after they had taken us in, welcomed us and listened to us in their lands for some time, because in such a case it would seem that they did not act out of immediate passion but knew what they were doing and what the monks were after; this was his reply, and even in a case like this we ought first to look very carefully and see if the monks gave sufficient cause for this: but as the devil is clever, he never lacks the strong arms of men who seem to be holy and wise in the world, with whom he sometimes does and achieves more with the aid of one of them than the King with many good and holy men to defend himself.

I was afraid of this, and did not want such an evil thing to happen to this land on my account, since I was wanting to do them good, so I thought it was my duty (and even if it was not I have reason and legitimate excuse enough) to risk my life to save such a large number of people, trusting in Our Lord and in His great power to give me special support, and to give light and knowledge to the Indians, so that I should preach to them and they should listen to me and receive me in peace, and apart from this great hope I have, it seems to me to be very likely, I have good reasons to believe, that not only will they not kill me but that they will receive me in peace and be completely willing to hear about our holy catholic faith, and if I was not sure of this, nothing in the world would be enough to keep me here, since my companions are worried that they will kill them or enslave them, and for this reason they are going back to Mexico and I am staying here in this land alone,[11] and time and events will show that in the very hard work of Our Lord there is more to see and feel than some people think.

I forgot to mention above what happened another time we jumped ashore before we heard from the Christian who came to the ship [lacuna] it was that as they had promised us the day before[12] to bring the interpreter and the monk, we landed very cheerfully. And the treacherous Indians had gone to the other side from where we first met, which was towards the Eastern side, and even before anyone emerged they kept us waiting a long time, thinking that we would jump out; and after a while they shouted to us, and eight or ten Indians set off into the water to bring us there, looking as if they were coming for us. We did not want to go straight to the pine-trees where they were because it looked like a trap to us, but we went further on to the flat part, and to judge from the reluctant way they came out of there, it is likely that they had an ambush, or at the least they had their bows and arrows at their feet out of our sight.

When we came close to the shore, without our making a sign to them that they should come to us, one of them dashed headlong into the sea as if his life depended on it; and when he arrived he gave me the fish he was carrying. I was going to give him a shirt then, but since I could not get it out quickly enough, one of my companions was upset and going to give him a tunic or sash of his own, which showed that it was a good idea to keep and take things to give them, although many people complained at me bringing them these things. And when he had received the shirt another one came out with more fish. I did not want to take it and gave him something or other I had to hand, and when he had taken it he asked me for a cross of wood, two spans wide, that I was holding in my hand, and I thought that he wanted

it to throw it in the water, or something like that, so I did not give it to him, and he asked for it many times, so I asked my companions "Should I give it him?" and they said that I should, so I did, and he kissed it very sincerely, and went back to the land and gave it to the Indian girl who had been our interpreter to kiss, which we still had not recognized, because she was naked, and then he went from Indian to Indian giving it to them to kiss, and after they had gone he went in front of all of them with it as the happiest man in the world. I took great heart and comfort from this as regards the purpose of what I am doing now.

The Indian girl shouted to us that we should come to land, saying "Come here, these are not carrying bows." One of the men in the launch said "It's Madelena, the interpreter." No one could believe this, and however much we told her to come out into the water so that we could hear and recognize her, she was not prepared to for the Indians did not let her. Eventually, to find out if it was her or not, I went into the sea up to my waist and went halfway there, and she came down to the edge, so I could see her, talk to her and recognize that she was the interpreter, which pleased me greatly. I told this to the men in the launch, and at once Father Friar Juan jumped into the water and came up to me and together we found out many things from the Indian girl. In particular she told us that the monk and the two Christians were together in the house of their chief, and if this was a lie then the Chiefs must certainly have threatened to kill her if she said the truth. She also said the whole area had been in turmoil thinking we were a navy, and she had told them that all we were were four friars come to preach them important things, and that that was why those fifty or sixty men had gathered together there: at this point Father Friar Gregorio, who was wanting to look for a chance to go to land,[13] jumped from the boat and came up to me, the water not quite up to his waist, as Father Friar Juan and I were talking to the interpreter, and said to me "You stay here with God: I am going, and tomorrow send me such and such." Father Friar Juan García went with him to the land with the intention of staying there, and I went back to the launch without ever reaching dry land, for all through I was afraid of the tricks

---

11. For they had no ship to go on in.
12. Sunday 23rd June.

13. To find out about his companions.

of the Indians. Soon afterwards I asked Father Friar Juan to come back to the launch to see if they would let him. And certainly, according to what he said to me, they would not let him. Eventually he came to the launch and Friar Gregorio stayed behind, and I went to speak to him and arrange to meet each other the next day and that he should order the Christians to be brought there: after that I had a present brought out for the Chief, of many things, and others which were all given out to the others there, so that they all had one: Father Friar Juan, who was in the launch at this time, I saw surrounded by Indians, and I was taken aback that they went so far out into the sea, and the seamen had let them reach the launch. I found out afterwards that he was stripping the seamen, he took the shirt off one of them, the jacket off another, and the hat off another, to give to those Indians, and afterwards I found myself in great difficulty calming down these seamen, and paying them for what they had given out of what we brought. For this reason also the Fathers thought how good it was to have something to give them, and I saw to it and brought it, and I have never regretted it, least of all now, and what I saw then with my own eyes I had first intuited with understanding and read in the Doctors, particularly St. Thomas, Vitoria and Gaetano, and the Decretos approve and reckon to be a very good idea the attraction of the heathen with good example and gifts of "monusculos," which means little presents like these. Anyway, the Indians let me go back to the boat. Although Father Friar Gregorio wanted to stay on land with them, they did not let him, and more or less led him by the hand and with a little force[14] told him to go back to the launch. So we all went away, they to their houses with the intention of bringing back the Christians, and we to the ship with the intention of seeing them next day and giving them the axes they wanted. And then, when we got back to the ship, we found out the news mentioned before, of their sad death. This made the Fathers and the Pilot want to go straight back to Mexico. I said I wanted to stay, for the reasons mentioned.

Before we got to this point, seeing how badly organized that port was to our purpose, and suspecting that our companions were dead, as they were, we had been trying to go somewhere else; and seeing that the ship was unsuitable for that coast, since it could not come within five or six leagues of land, that we had no water and nowhere to get it from enough to start a new journey, that all the meat and fish had gone bad and been thrown into the sea, and the seamen were mutinying every day, so that there was no-one prepared to go to land in the launch, and most of them were suffering from such a temperature that there was hardly anyone to man the pump, so that every four hours on the hourglass saw one glassful of water coming into the ship, we had taken a decision to go back to Havana or to New Spain, and take a boat and go somewhere else. Father Friar Luis was not to happy about this, and so he wanted to expose himself to the final danger. As the Sunday, the day before Midsummer Day, we came back to the ship very unhappy from not having seen any of our companions, although we had seen the Indian girl, and Friar Gregorio had his doubts since the Indians had thrown him out in that way. When we reached the ship we found there a Spaniard called Juan Muñoz, who had stayed behind from the naval expedition of Soto, and then come to the ship by canoe, and was now almost unable to speak, and then having come to the ship he said as best he could that two of the Christians had died and one was being held alive, and that he had held the skin of the head of the monk in his hands. He said the same again when we arrived, making the death of our companions quite certain. Father Friar Juan García and Friar Gregorio de Beteta said to Friar Luis, since things had turned out like this, that they should go the next day as they had agreed with the Indians to find out more, and that if none of our companions should turn up we should give the order to go back or to go somewhere else. He said that he was sure that this business could not be done without bloodshed, and since his companions had died there he wanted to stay there, because he thought he could do more good there and hoped to quieten them by giving them what he took there. Having decided this, he did not want to go on Midsummer's Day, to write some letters and arrange the things he was going to take. We tried to talk him out of it all day in every way we could, but our persuasion and entreaties had little effect on him, because he always thought us over-suspicious, and particularly in this matter.

So on the morning of Tuesday the 25th of June we went in in the launch to land on shore, and

---

14. With rather a lot of force.

after we had gone two leagues we met such a fierce storm head on, of wind and rain, that we thought we were done for, and many of the things he was taking to the land were damaged, for they all got wet. We could not reach land, and only got back to the ship with some difficulty. Juan Muñoz, the one who had come out from the land, and was with us, kept on saying that this was a sign that God did not want him to go out there, because then they would kill him, because now they knew that he had fled, and that the death of the others had been found out, so they would not wait for him at all, and other such things that everyone was telling him. But when we got back to the ship, that night he again got ready things to take. And on Wednesday the 26th of June we had just as much trouble going back towards land in the launch from rainstorms that day as the day before, and we never thought we would be able to get to land; but he stayed as firm as ever in his desire to go into that land. So as not to have to turn back next day we waited for the weather to get calmer, and with the seamen rowing in some difficulty we reached land. There were some Indians up trees at intervals, which we did not take to be a good sign. As soon as they saw us they came down, and went running to a small wood where the people were. When we got close we shouted to them and they answered, but none of them came from the wood to the flat ground. We asked for the interpreter, and they said she was in a house far away from there. Some of them were running from one side to another with their bows and arrows, clubs and darts, that could be clearly seen; Father Friar Luis was getting ready to go, and Friar Gregorio was begging and trying to persuade him not to go. They shouted from the shore asking "Is Yague there?" that is, the slave. And Juan Muñoz stood up and said "It's me, what do you want, are you thinking of killing us as you killed the others? Well you won't, because we know all about it." This seemed to alarm them, and Father Friar Luis said to him "Quiet, brother, don't get them all worked up for me." Father Friar Gregorio said to him "There can't be anyone in the world more worked up than this lot, so for the love of God hold on a bit, don't land." But he did not listen, but dived in and aimed for the land; we must have been about an arrow's distance from the little wood. Once he reached land he asked us for a small cross that he had forgotten, and although there was no danger in

taking it to him I said "Father, please come for it yourself, for there is noone here who can take it for you, for it is obvious that those people are up to some evil trickery." He went along the shore, and we went in the launch, towards the little wood where the Indians were; when they saw that we were going towards them they began to withdraw. Father Friar Luis told us to stop and not alarm the Indians; he came close to them and must have begun to realize the danger, for he knelt down and stayed there for a little time and then went off to the wood. When he got close an Indian came out and embraced him, then took him by the arm and pulled him quickly along, then another came out and others, pushing and pulling him along to the way into the wood; one of them hit his hat with his hand and knocked it off his head; another came up and knocked him down with a club to the head; we were close enough to see and hear clearly what they were saying. He gave a shout "Oh help . . ." but they did not let him finish, so many came onto him that they finished him there; then they gave a loud shout and came out to shoot their arrows at us; I told the seamen to take us a little way out to sea, and we stopped at a bow's distance. They took out their bows there, fired a volley of arrows at us and then went. We returned to the ship, fearing that some canoes were going to come out after us.

When we reached the ship we decided at once to leave there, but we had no water. The same day we went to the beach to look for it and collected a little. I asked the pilot to take us to another part of Florida, as he was supposed to do, and he replied that he was prepared to do so but that he did not have enough water and the ship was in no state to undertake a new voyage, and that we should go to Havana, which was not far away, and when he had taken on water and provisions he would do so, and so we left that Port of the Holiest on Friday the 28th of June 1549, to go to Havana.

245. December 18, 1553. Philip, Prince of Spain, to the Treasury Officials of New Spain.

The Spanish imperial administration almost never forgot anything, but it often took a long time for it to remember. Four years after Fray

Luis Cáncer died, the accounts of his mission were still incomplete, and his ship and its remaining contents had not been accounted for; so in December, 1553 orders were sent to find the ship, inventory her, and lock up the surviving materials securely. What had happened to her by that time is wholly unknown.

Copy in John Carter Brown Library, Reales Cédulas, *Codex Sp 8, fols. 86–96v., translated.*

On the brigantine that went to Florida.

By the Prince To our [Treasury] officials for New Spain.

You are already aware that in the past year of [1]548, by our command, Fray Luis Cáncer was despatched to sail to Florida with other religious in a brigantine, in which he carried certain things which by our command were delivered to him for the voyage and for the stay he was to make in the said province, [and] because the said Fray Luis and the other religious who disembarked with him died at the hand of the Indians the said brigantine returned to the province of New Spain with some men who remained in it, and with the said things that were in it, as and according to what we have been informed, wherefore I order you, if the said brigantine reached this province [i.e., New Spain] and if you received what was in her, to inform us of it, and if you did not receive it, to cause enquiry to be made in that province whether it did reach it, and into the hands of which persons it came, and what its condition is. You are furthermore to recover it from them and arrange for its sale, and whatever price it fetches you are to put in the chest with three keys, and you are to inform us of everything as has been said, and to proceed no further.

Signed in the town of Valladolid on the 18th day of the month of December, 1553.

I the Prince

By command of His Highness, Juan de Sámano

Chapter Thirty-one
The Expeditions of Tristán de Luna and
Ángel de Villafañe, 1559-1561

THE UNFAVORABLE REPORTS brought back by the remnants of Soto's expedition were widely circulated in Spain, and her American colonies and the Southwest became quickly known as a country "full of bogs and poisonous fruits, barren, and the very worst country that is warmed by the sun." This prevented any major interest in the area for almost two decades. In 1544 Julian de Samano and Pedro de Alurnada applied for the right of conquest in the region but were refused by Philip II. Later ventures by friars also failed. Most notable of these was Fray Luis Cáncer, who was supported by Luis de Velasco, viceroy of Mexico, in his scheme to convert the Indians of Florida. As has been shown, he landed in the vicinity of Tampa Bay in 1549, but he and another friar were killed by the Indians. However, Velasco was still optimistic and, along with other kindred spirits, believed that riches could indeed be found to the north of the Caribbean and that both the Florida Peninsula and Indian souls should be conquered by Spain. Their persistence eventually obtained results, and well before the end of 1557, a decision to send out another expedition had been made (245–247).

In 1558 Guido de las Bazares set out on a preliminary reconnaissance of the Atlantic Coast but found himself exploring instead the Gulf Coast in the Mississippi Delta area. In contrast to the earlier expeditions, he brought back favorable reports of the country that emphasized the easy availability of supplies (249). As a result of his findings and the length of time—seventeen years—which had elapsed since the return of Soto's party, another major expedition was authorized and sent out to Florida under Don Tristán de Luna, who had served the king in New Spain for some thirty years and who had been second in command to Coronado in the west (250–252). In 1559 he landed at Pensacola Bay with a party of soldiers and civilians. The expedition was ill-prepared and its purpose confused (253–256). Was it basically for exploration or for settlement? The confusion was compounded by a total ignorance of distances. It was thought that only a short distance separated the Gulf and Atlantic coasts from those parts where Ayllón had been. Hence, the party landed on the Gulf Coast with the intention of marching overland to Santa Elena and there forming a settlement, rather than by risking a hazardous journey around the Florida Cape. However, the main party stayed to the west of the Florida Peninsula, moving from one unfavorable site to another, while reconnaissance parties were sent out to choose a suitable site for a permanent colony (257–259).

The Luna expedition depended for its knowledge of Soto's expedition on the narrative of Luis de Moscoso, which has not been found. In it he evidently stressed the easy passage Soto had had between Apalachee and Cofitachequi, with the information that in or near the south of the Savannah River was the site of Ayllón's colony of 1526 and also the Punta de Santa Elena. Moreover, the people of this area were, he gathered, Coosa or Cusabo. The 1559 plan was to follow this part of Soto's journey and so reach and occupy the Punta de Santa Elena and the country behind it, famed in the Soto narratives for its fertility (258). The difficulty was that there was another Coosa, one on the Coosa River, which Soto had reached when he crossed the watershed between the Tennessee and Alabama rivers. Moreover, Luna had interpreters with him who must have come from one or the other area: the languages were close since the northern group represented a branch of the Lower Creeks and the southern the Upper Creeks. However the confusion arose, Mateo de Sauz and his reconnaissance force found their way to the inland, southern Coosa, and, hence, Luna's persistent attempt to carry the main force forward to there had no relevance to his primary task of securing the Punta de Santa Elena against the French.

The southern Coosa proved fertile and the Indians cooperative, although they rationed the intruders carefully with corn, but it was clear there was no place there for a larger contingent. The attempt of Luna to force his main body to advance to southern Coosa brought to a head the revolt that had long been simmering among his men (260-274). A long debate took place, and when Luna at length tried to enforce his authority (275), his men took matters into their own hands; his staff officers, the royal officials, and the friars supporting the rank and file refused to advance as he ordered (278-288).

Eventually, in January, 1561, when the authorities in Mexico at last came to understand what was happening, Luna was licensed to return to Spain and, after some controversy, his place was taken by Ángel de Villafañe in April, 1561. Luna cannot take all the blame for his failure on himself (291). Certainly a firmer line with his subordinates and a willingness to consult with them would have enhanced his authority and perhaps kept the friars who accompanied the party on his side, but there is evidence that his health was not good. His poor administration of the expedition virtually ensured its failure. The party was overburdened with men and women who could have made adequate colonists, but who were not explorers—the expedition turned out to be essentially an exercise in discovery rather than settlement. Additionally, the supply line between New Spain became overstretched and often broke down, causing delay in the receipt of goods and resulting of shortages or even starvation. After Villafañe had explored the Atlantic Coast and found no suitable harbor or site for a colony (292-293), Philip II decided that Florida was not an ideal area for settlement and on September 23, 1561, he declared that no further attempt should be made to colonize the eastern coast.

The quarrels between Luna and his followers resulted in a law suit in Spain, and therefore many papers relating to the expedition have survived. From these a composite picture of the attempted colony can be created using the views of both sides in the dispute. Of great interest are the letters between Luna and Velasco in which the latter outlined the colonial aims and policies of Spain with regard to Florida (276-277, 289-290).

The practical value of the expedition, except in its illustration of Spanish policies, is minimal. However, it proved valuable in another respect. The reports of the exploring party that settled at Coosa, and in particular the reports of the friars who accompanied the party, throw considerable light, which would not have been available otherwise, on the Indians of the Alabama Valley (266-270).

The principal early source was material on the activities of the Dominican friars during the expedition included in Fray Agustín Dávila Padilla, *Historia de la fundación y discurso de la provincia de Santiago de Mexico de la orden de predicatores* (Madrid, 1596). An extract from the 1625 edition, pp. 189-229, translated, appeared in J. R. Swanton, "Early History of the Creek Indians," Bureau of American Ethnology, *Bulletin* 73 (Washington, D.C.), pp. 231-217, translated by Fanny Bandelier, and this is given below (270). John Gilmary Shea referred to some other ecclesiastical material in Justin Winsor, *Narrative and Critical History of America*, 8 vols. (Cambridge, Mass., 1886–1889), II, 256. The report of Guido de Bazares on his preliminary reconnaissance of the Gulf Coast appeared in translation in B. F. French, *Historical Collections of Louisiana and Florida*, second series (New York, 1875), p. 236, and is given from a later translation below (249). The letter from Luis de Velasco to Philip II, on the setting out of Luna, appeared in Spanish first in T. Buckingham Smith, *Colección de varios documentos* (London, 1857), I, 10–13, and is given in a later translation (250). *The Luna Papers, 1559–1651*, edited and translated by Herbert I. Priestley, 2 vols. (Deland, Fla., 1928; Freeport, N.Y., 1971), constitute the only full collection of sources. Assembled from the inquiries held after the failure of the expedition, preserved in the A.G.I., Seville, they follow an archival rather than a chronological order, but are held together by a good introduction and notes. The selections made are intended to indicate the main stages in the expedition (a preliminary document on the early organization is interpolated from a copy in the John Carter Brown Library, 246) and the character of the country and peoples encountered by Luna and his exploring parties.

246. December 29, 1557. Arrangements for the expedition to be made to the Punta de Santa Elena.

The decision to establish a Spanish post at the Punta de Santa Elena was taken during 1557. The royal order of December 29, 1557, authorized the viceroy to expend money on the preparation of the expedition and on the workmen who were to establish permanent stone buildings there, as well as reminding him to send missionaries to convert the Indians. John Carter Brown Library, Reales Cédulas, Codex Sp 8, fol. 98, copy (translation by Lawrence C. Wroth, November, 1941, John Carter Brown Library, Wroth Papers, 1958, file Yonge, published by permission).

Concerning the expeditions
for Florida.

The King.

Know ye, our officials of New Spain who reside in the city of Mexico, that we are sending orders to Don Luis de Velasco, our viceroy of that country, that he is to provide for making a settlement on the point of Santa Elena, which is in Florida, and that he is to send the people who it seems to

him should be sent and with them some religious who understand how to bring peace and to bring to the knowledge of our holy Catholic faith the natives of that country. In order that the people may be taken in ships to the said point of Santa Elena, as well as the provisions which it is advisable that they carry for use until they may sow and reap enough to sustain themselves, he is to spend from our treasury that which is necessary. And he is to send such workmen and master-masons as seem necessary in order that they, with the aid which they may have from those who are going to settle and from the negroes whom they take with them, may build the required buildings, and he is to choose the workmen and the people whom he shall send. Let the salary which it seems should be given them for the time they foresee they must be engaged be paid by you, as at greater length is contained in the [letter] concerning this which we are sending to our viceroy. And because our will is that he go ahead with the said colony I command you that by warrants of the said viceroy you spend and pay for the abovesaid from our treasury what he may order and command you, that with this our edict and the warrant of the said viceroy, signed with his name, and receipts from the persons concerned, you are to pay whatever he may give you a warrant for paying. And I command that what you thus give and pay may be received and passed into account.

Dated in Valladolid on the twenty-ninth of December of fifteen hundred fifty-seven. The princess, by command of his majesty, her highness in his name.

[signed:] Francisco de Ledesma.

247. December 29, 1557. Philip II to Luis de Velasco about the Luna expedition.

These are recited in a set of instructions to Luna issued by the viceroy and audiencia of Mexico on March 30, 1559, translated in Priestley, Luna Papers, *I, 43–47. Priestley's documents, except where otherwise stated, are all copied from a single dossier compiled during legal proceedings subsequent to the expedition. This is from A.G.I., Seville, Mexico 51/6/10, 27, no. 2, ramo 1, foliated (formerly Patronato 44).*

This is a transcript, well and faithfully made, of a royal provision of the Majesty of the king, Don Felipe, our lord, sealed with his royal seal, signed by the most illustrious viceroy of New Spain, Don Luis de Velasco, and countersigned by Antonio de Turcios, notary of the royal audiencia and government thereof for his Majesty. Registered by Cristóbal Pérez de Luzana and sealed by Pedro Ordóñez. For Don Tristán de Luna y Arellano. The tenor of the said royal provision is as follows:

Don Felipe, by the grace of God, king of Castile, of León, of Aragon, of England, of France, of the two Sicilies, of Jerusalem, of Navarre, of Granada, of Toledo, of Valencia, of Galicia, of Majorca, of Seville, of Sardinia, of Corsica, of Murcia, of Jaen, of the Algarves, of Algeciras, of Gibraltar, of the Canary Islands, of the Indies, of the islands and the firm land of the ocean sea, count of Barcelona, lord of Vizcaya and of Molina, duke of Athens and of Neopatria, count of Roussillon and of Sardinia, marquis of Oristan and of Gociano, archduke of Austria, duke of Burgundy, of Brabant, and Milan, count of Flanders and of Tyrol, *et cetera*. Since we, by a letter of ours and

royal provision given in Valladolid on December 29 of the year '57, have given license and faculty to Don Luis de Velasco, our viceroy and captain-general of New Spain and president of the royal audiencia which resides therein, that he may, in spite of the prohibition which has been issued ordering that he shall make no new discoveries or settlements, if he should see it to be conducive to the service of God our Lord and to ours, send out to make them, especially in the provinces subject to our said audiencia and [in] La Florida, which shall be settled and placed under orderly government, both to the end that the natives thereof, who are without the light of faith, may be illuminated and taught, and that the Spaniards may be benefited and may become established in them, as is expressed at greater length in our aforesaid letter and royal provision, the tenor of which is as follows: Don Felipe, by the grace of God, king of Castile, of León, of Aragon, of England, of France, of the two Sicilies, of Jerusalem, of Navarre, of Granada, of Toledo, of Valencia, of Galicia, of Majorca, of Seville, of Sardinia, of Córdova, of Corsica, of Murcia, of Jaen, of the Algarves, of Algeciras, of Gibraltar, of the Canary Islands, of the Indies, and of the islands and firm land of the ocean sea, count of Barcelona, lord of Vizcaya and of Molina, duke of Athens and of Neopatria, count of Roussillon and of Sardinia, marquis of Oristan and Gociano, archduke of Austria, duke of Burgundy, Brabant, and Milan, count of Flanders and of Tyrol, *et cetera*. To you, Don Luis de Velasco, our viceroy and captain-general of New Spain and president of the royal audiencia which resides therein: Since you may not, in accordance with what we have ordered and commanded, send to make new discoveries and settlements nor provide governors for them without our license and special command, and since we [now] desire very much that that land and the provinces thereof which are subject to that audiencia [of New Spain] and [also the land] of La Florida, may be settled and placed under orderly government, both to the end that the natives thereof who are without the light of the faith may be illuminated and instructed in it, and that they and the Spaniards who reside in those lands and go out to them may be benefited and may become established in them and may have homes and means of living, it has seemed wise to give orders that such settlements may be made. And because of the great confidence which we have in you, we have decided to defer to you in this, in order that you, as a person who has the matter before you and can see what is fitting to be done for the service of God our Lord and of ourself and also for the welfare of the land, may order what may seem good to you in the situation. By these presents then, we give your license and faculty, in case it seems to you good, that you may and shall send to make such discoveries and settlements in conformity with the instructions which we ordered sent to you concerning this matter. These instructions you shall observe and cause to be observed in and for all things as expressed therein; to the persons whom you may send to these settlements and new discoveries, you and the judges of that audiencia shall give the necessary commission, in conformity with the said instructions, in order that the injuries and disorders may be avoided which up to this time have occurred in new discoveries. You shall always take care to find out how the orders and instructions which are given to you are complied with, and how the natives of the land to which they may go are treated. Given at Valladolid, December 29, 1557.

[signed:] The Princess.

I, Francisco de Ledesma, secretary of his Catholic Majesty, had [the foregoing] written by his command.

> Her Highness, in his name.
> Licenciate Briviesca.
> Licenciate Don Juan Sarmiento.
> Doctor Vázquez.
> Licenciate Villagómez.

> > Registered, Ochoa de Loyando.
> > By the chancellor, Juan de Anguciano.

248. December 29, 1557. Philip II to Luis de Velasco on the Luna expedition.

This elaborates the cédula *of the same date to the royal officials (246) above, and was communicated in this form to Tristán de Luna by the viceroy and audiencia of Mexico on March 30,* *1559. Translated in Priestley,* Luna Papers, *I, 47–53.*

Besides what is contained in our foregoing provision, by another *cédula* of ours, dated at Valladolid on the same day month and year aforesaid [December 29, 1557], we have charged and ordered you to give orders that the provinces of La Florida and the Punta de Santa Elena shall be settled, and that a strong settlement shall be made at the Punta de Santa Elena, so that from it the attempt shall be made by preaching and kind treatment to bring the people of that land and those provinces to the knowledge of our holy Catholic faith, and that with the people who go thither may be sent a few religious, in order that through them and their preaching [the natives] may come into the knowledge of God our Lord and may live under Christian government; and in order that the said settlement may be the better made, and that all which is ordered may be observed, you shall name as governor of the people who shall go a person who shall seem suitable to you, one fearful of God our Lord and zealous in our service, who shall govern them. In fulfilment of that which has thus been ordered and commanded by us, we having discussed it and communicated concerning it with the judges of our royal audiencia and with other persons of experience, the resolution was taken that there should be sent a certain number of people, both of infantry and of cavalry, to settle the said province of La Florida and the Punta de Santa Elena, and with them the said religious. And since recently by the grace of God a certain number of people have been recruited, and the said expedition has been and is being brought about, and since by virtue of the said faculty [the viceroy] has named officials of the royal treasury, and as governor of the people who are going to settle the said provinces, yourself, Don Tristán de Luna y Arellano, because of the good account which he has had and has of your person, your fidelity and Christianity and zeal in our service, in attention thereto by these presents we approve and confirm this nomination made by the viceroy of you the said Don Tristán; and it is our grant that *for the time during which it may be our pleasure you shall be our governor* of the people who are sent to settle the said provinces of La Florida and the Punta de Santa Elena. That which you are thus to hold under your government shall be [these people] and those who may go later and the natives of the said provinces from fifty leagues to the westward from the mouth of the Río Grande de Espíritu Santo, which is in 29 degrees latitude. A straight line being drawn from the seacoast toward the north, [you shall govern] from the said line all the provinces which may be and lie to the eastward thereof, both that which is already discovered therein and the remainder which you may discover and settle within the confines of this district without exceeding it. As such our governor you shall have charge and care of the good government of the said provinces, and you shall see to all that touches the service of God our Lord and our own, and the perpetuation and conservation of the natives of the said provinces, observing in all things the instruction or instructions which may be given you either by us or by our viceroy, president, and the judges of our royal audiencia, without exceeding what is therein contained. And we command all the captains, both of infantry and of cavalry, and all the persons who may go with you on the expedition, and who may be in the said provinces, in whatsoever state or condition they may be, to have and to hold you, Don Tristán de Luna y Arellano, as our governor and general of the said people; and they shall obey you and comply with your orders, both written and oral, and appear at your summons, for the time and under the penalties which in our name you may impose upon them and command them to submit to. [All these your orders] we now by these presents impose upon them, and we give you power and faculty to execute them upon the persons and goods of all rebels and disobedient ones. Furthermore, we give you power, in case of the end and death of the captains who have been appointed, to put others in their places, and you may remove those who have been nominated, as has been said, if there is just reason therefor. You may also have, and you shall take, cognizance of all cases civil and criminal which may arise and happen among your people and among the natives of the lands and towns of your government. For the purpose of hearing and deciding such cases, you may appoint a lieutenant, or two or more as you may consider desirable, and you may remove them and put others in their places. In regard to the good

treatment of the natives of those provinces, you shall also observe the instructions which have been given by us to those persons who go to discover, pacify, and settle new lands, without exceeding what is contained in these instructions. And we command that in the exercise of your duty as governor and general of the said lands, no embargo or other impediment whatsoever shall be placed upon you, but that everyone shall [act] in agreement with you, give you the help and show you the favor which you may have need of and ask of them, offering no excuse or delay whatever; and, under the penalties already stated, you may cause these instructions to be enforced against rebels and disobedient ones. For the exercise of this office and all the rest herein specified we give you full power as may be required in such case, with all its concomitant, dependent, annexed, and connected implications, as in such case required. And we charge you that the lands and provinces which you shall thus colonize and which shall be brought and some into peace and obedience to ourself as their king and natural lord, you shall protect and defend in our royal name; and you shall defend the natives thereof, that no injuries may be done to them nor any other evil by any persons. They shall not enter [your provinces] nor take nor occupy any dwelling place, claiming that the government belongs to them or under any other pretext whatever. And inasmuch as you, Don Tristán de Luna y Arellano, have in our royal name been granted as *encomiendas* certain towns of Indians in New Spain, and considering that you are making this expedition in our service, and that you have accepted this duty, it is our will and we do order that these Indians shall not be removed or taken from you, but that you shall keep them until such times as we may be pleased to order otherwise. Given in the City of Mexico on March 30, 1559.

[signed:] Don Luis de Velasco.

I, Antonio de Turcios, chief secretary of the royal audiencia and chancellery of New Spain and the government thereof for his Majesty, caused [the foregoing] to be written at his command and that of his governor and viceroy.

[signed:] Antonio de Turcios.

Registered, Cristóbal Pérez de Luzana.
Chancellor, Pedro Ordóñez.

249. September to December, 1558. Expedition of Guido de la Bazares along the Gulf Coast from Pánuco to Florida.

This report was received by Velasco on February 1, 1559, and formed part of the documentation that Luna took with him on his expedition.

The original has not been located. It is taken from a copy in the T. Buckingham Smith Papers, in the Library of the New York Historical Society, translated in Priestley, Luna Papers, *II, 333–337.*

Declaration of Guido de las Bazares concerning the voyage he made to explore the ports and bays on the coast of La Florida for the safeguard of the people who are to be sent in his Majesty's name to colonize La Florida and the Punta de Santa Elena. It was received from him by order of the viceroy Don Luis de Velasco in Mexico, February 1, 1559, and is as follows:

The viceroy of this New Spain charged and commanded him something like four or five months ago to go in his Majesty's name with certain mariners and other people to explore the coast of La Florida and make a study of its ports for the safeguard of the people who are to go in his Majesty's name to colonize La Florida and the Punta de Santa Elena. For this purpose the viceroy gave him a certain commission and instruction, in compliance wherewith he set sail from the port of San Juan de Ulúa of this New Spain on September 3 of last year, 1558, to explore the coast of La Florida and search therein for some good and secure port where the people who go to settle the said La Florida may disembark. He took a large bark, a foist, and a shallop, with sixty soldiers and mariners. He reached the Río de Pánuco on September 5, setting sail from there on the fourteenth. He made land on the said coast in 27° 30′ latitude, and, going along the coast, discovered a bay in 28° 30′ latitude, to which he gave the name San Francisco. In it he took possession in the name of his Majesty and of the viceroy in the former's name. Thence he went toward Los Alacranes in order that he might course from that point and reach the coast of La Florida, which runs from northwest to southeast and which he could not make at the part he desired because of the contrary winds which pre-

vailed. They made land in 29° 30′ on a coast running east and west where they found an island which lies something like four leagues from the mainland. They sailed between the mainland and this island and others which are in its vicinity toward the mainland; and when he had explored the entire coast he found it all shallows, and country unadapted for making settlements, for it was all subject to overflow. Nevertheless he took possession there in the name of his Majesty and for the viceroy in his royal name, and called the place La Bahía de Bajos. Thence he sailed east a matter of ten leagues and discovered a bay to which he gave the name Filipina. This was the largest and most commodious bay he found in that region for the purpose which his Majesty orders. The mouth of its entrance is in 29° 30′ latitude at its southern part; it goes in between the point of an island seven leagues long running east and west and, on the other side of the entrance, the point of the mainland. The opening, from the one point to the other, was about half a league wide. In all that they saw and explored, either on the eastern side or the western, they found no bay or port so suitable or so good and commodious as this bay called Filipina. The special characteristics which this bay has are as follows: From the entrance to the place they reached was twelve leagues, and it extends three or four leagues farther, making a length of fifteen leagues in all; its width is four leagues. It has a good mud anchorage, and on the inside its depth is fourteen to fifteen fathoms more or less. The bar at the entrance of this bay has at low tide three and a half fathoms, and almost a fathom more at high tide. The bay is very healthful and has the climate of Spain both in respect to rain and in occurrence of cold. The country to the east of the bay is higher than that on the west side. In the bay and its vicinity are many fish and shellfish; there are many pine trees suitable for making masts and yards; there are oaks, live oaks, nut trees, cedars, junipers, laurels, and certain small trees which bear a fruit like chestnuts. All this forest from which ships can be made begins at the water's edge and runs inland. There are many palmettos and grape-vines. There are many small streams of fresh water which flow into the bay besides a large mouth at the end of the bay which seems to be a copious river, for where they were in the bay, near the northern part where this mouth is, they obtained fresh water when they took their supply. The forest is open, not thick with underbrush, and underneath it the cavalry might skirmish. Under these trees there is grass for horses and cattle. Around the bay itself there are also high red broken lands on the east side where bricks can be made, and near them are building-stones; on the west side there is yellow and grayish clay for making jars and other things. There are many birds, such as eagles, geese, ducks, partridges, doves, and many others. There are deer in great numbers. On that bay were seen Indians and large canoes which they bring for their service; there are also fish-traps. Corn, beans, and pumpkins were found in their villages. He also took possession in this bay in the name of his Majesty and for the viceroy in his royal name, and called it the Bahía Filipina. From the port of San Juan de Ulúa to this Bahía Filipina it is two hundred and seventy leagues, a little more or less. From that bay he tried twice to explore the coast which continues toward the east; and he did traverse it for more than twenty leagues. He found it to run to the east, at the end turning southeast, but because of the contrary winds which allowed them no opportunity to navigate farther they turned back both times, returning to the Bahía Filipina. On that [eastward] coast he also took possession in the name of his Majesty and for the viceroy in his royal name, and he gave to it the name Ancón de Velasco. Then because the winter was very severe and he was running great risk, and because it seemed to the pilots and seamen that the weather was unsuited for further navigation along that coast, it seemed to him wise for them to return to this New Spain to report on what they had discovered in order that the people and the fleet which were being equipped to make the journey to La Florida and the Punta de Santa Elena might be made ready and leave port in suitable time to make certain of their navigation. So they left the coast of La Florida on December 3, and entered the port of San Juan de Ulúa on the fourteenth of the same month. This is the truth and what he knows, under the oath he took; and when [the foregoing] had been read to him he ratified it and signed it with his name.

[signed:] Guido de Lavazares. [=las Basares]

Done before me, Antonio de Turcios.

250. September 30, 1558. Luis de Velasco, Viceroy of Mexico, to Philip II.

Velasco describes the preparations for the expedition of Luna. Translated in Priestley, Luna Papers, *II, 257–261, extract.*

The ships and people which are to go to colonize on the coast of the land of La Florida and the Punta de Santa Elena are being prepared; I think they will be ready to set sail sometime in May of '59. Five hundred Spaniards will go, four hundred of them soldiers, two hundred being mounted, and two hundred on foot armed with arquebuses and crossbows for the defense of the religious and ecclesiastics who are to go to preach our holy faith to the natives, and one hundred artisans to engage in building the towns and the fort which your Majesty commands to be built. Also the instructions are being drawn up which are to be given to the governor, religious, and officials of the royal treasury, and other persons who are to have positions of authority. They will conform with those your Majesty ordered sent to me, and, without exceeding those, a few important points will be added for their better observance. Before the religious and settlers set out I will inform you in full detail how they are going and what orders they were given. I will also inform you whether the French are in La Havana, and if they are, the fleet will be reinforced and will sail by that port, for the voyage is not long, and I believe they can be captured with little risk. I am having six large barks of one hundred tons each made for one hundred men and four pieces of artillery each. They will be of such build that when laden they will navigate in four palms of water. This is necessary to enter and come out of the rivers and bays which are on the coast of La Florida and for defense from the canoes of the Indians, for I am told that they gather in great numbers to defend the rivers and ports.

In the interval while the ships are being built and the people prepared, I have sent a foist and a bark to examine, sound, and mark the rivers and ports which are on the coast of La Florida from here to the district opposite La Havana, to choose the most secure and convenient one where the people may disembark and make the first town and fort. From there they are to go overland to the Punta de Santa Elena where your Majesty commands that a settlement be made. For I have understood from sailors who have experience of the coast and from soldiers who were with Soto and traversed the country, that the surest way is to go by land the eighty leagues which lie between the district opposite La Havana and Santa Elena, rather than by sea; both because the voyage is long, since the land projects a great deal there, as well as because there are shoals on that coast and the ships run risk of being lost if they go close to land seeking port. There is no certainty in what location Santa Elena is, other than what the people say who were with Soto, [namely] that they came upon a river which the Indians told them was the River of Pearls, and that they were three days' journey from the sea. This river is the one which flows into the sea near the Punta de Santa Elena. There is no certainty that there is a good port at this Punta; the one that is set down on the sailing charts mariners say is not correct. If no such port is found at the Punta the settlement will have to be made at the one nearest to it which has the qualities your Majesty commands in this expedition to La Florida. Of necessity a quantity of pesos de oro will have to be spent to bring it about and get it done with the safety, Christianity, and reputation suitable to an enterprise so important and which has failed every time it has been attempted. I trust in our Lord that this one which your Majesty orders will succeed, and redound to the augmentation of our holy faith and of the kingdoms and seigniories of your Majesty.

I gathered together the provincials of the orders of St. Dominic, St. Francis, and St. Augustine, in the presence of this royal audiencia, and asked their opinion as to whether it would be fitting at the beginning for the religious of all three orders to go or only of one, and if they agreed that only one should be represented, which it should be. They all were agreed that religious of but one order should go, and that they should be those of St. Dominic, as your Majesty will order observed by the contract drawn between the provincials which goes herewith. Six religious have been named, men of chosen life, letters, doctrine, and of age to be able to work among the Indians and learn their languages. It seems that for the present these will suffice. They will have to be provided with ornaments, crosses, chalices, bells, and other things necessary for the

service of the divine cult, with clothing and shoes for the religious, and these cost four times as much in this country as in Spain. . . .

Mexico, the last day of September, 1558.

Your Catholic Royal Majesty's faithful servant who kisses your Majesty's royal feet.

[signed:] Don Luis de Velasco.

251. November 1, 1558. Oath and Covenant of Luna.

Translated in Priestley, Luna Papers, I, 35–43.

This is a transcript well and faithfully made of the covenant of homage which, in fulfilment of his Majesty's command, the most excellent viceroy of New Spain, Don Luis de Velasco, took and received from Don Tristán de Luna y Arellano, governor-elect of the provinces of La Florida, in the principal church of the City of Mexico in the presence of the archbishop, Fray Alonso de Montúfar, the officials of his Majesty, and the religious of the orders of St. Dominic, St. Francis, and St. Augustine. Signed by the most illustrious viceroy of New Spain and by the said Don Tristán de Luna y Arellano, and countersigned by Antonio de Turcios, chief notary of the government thereof, and having the following tenor:

In the notable, very noble, very loyal, and great City of Mexico of New Spain, on the day of All Saints, the first day of the month of November, in the year of the birth of our Savior Jesus Christ, 1558, there being present in the principal church of the city, on the steps of the high altar thereof, the most illustrious Don Luis de Velasco, viceroy, governor, and captain-general for his Majesty in the said New Spain, and president of the royal audiencia thereof, the judges of the royal audiencia, the most reverend Don Alonso de Montúfar, archbishop of the church and member of the council of his Majesty, certain religious of the three orders of St. Dominic, St. Francis, and St. Augustine, the officials of the royal treasury, of justice, and of the government of the city, many other gentlemen and principal persons and residents thereof, and a great concourse of people, before me, Antonio de

Turcios, chief notary of the royal audiencia and government of this New Spain, after the royal standard had been blessed by the archbishop with the ceremonies and solemnities in such cases required, the said viceroy made to Don Tristán de Luna y Arellano, who was present, being the person who in the name of his Majesty he had nominated and appointed as governor of the provinces of La Florida, before turning over to him the royal standard, the following discourse:

In compliance with that which the royal Majesty of the king, Don Felipe our lord, has sent to me as a commandment, that I should send [an expedition] in his royal name to settle the land of La Florida and the Punta de Santa Elena and to preach our holy Catholic faith to the natives, in order that they may come into the knowledge thereof, and for other purposes important to the service of God our Lord and of his Majesty, I have, after communing with the most reverend archbishop and with the provincials of the orders of St. Dominic, St. Francis, and St. Augustine, and with other prudent and experienced persons, selected the religious who are to go; the number of Spanish people who are to be sent for its defense and the settlements which are to be made have been agreed upon, and it is now fitting to appoint a person to govern them, as his Majesty commands. Wherefore, considering that you, Don Tristán de Luna y Arellano, are a Christian gentleman, prudent, with much experience, fearful of God our Lord and zealous in His service, and a person in whom are found the other necessary qualities, I have appointed you, sir, as you know, as governor and captain-general of the Spanish people and Indians who are to go in your company and fleet and of those who may henceforth go, and of the settlements and fortifications which you may make and settle in conformity with the commission and instruction which will be given to you. As such governor and captain-general you are to have delivered to you this royal standard with the insignia and the sign of the holy cross (†) upon which God our Lord redeemed mankind, in order that with these arms and with the evangelical preaching of the religious you may labor to bring those people into peace and into obedience to our holy mother church and into the dominion and overlordship of his Majesty, without subjecting them to war, force, or bad treatment. What I charge and command you in his royal name is that

you should have principally before your eyes the service of God and of his Majesty, the welfare, conversion, and good treatment of the natives, and of the religious and the Spaniards who go in your company, keeping them in peace and in justice. Especially by your good example, your works, and your Christian life, will you endeavor to attract the natives to imitate and obey you, rather than by use of arms, whereof you shall not make use save in case of force and necessity for the defense of our holy faith and the preachers thereof. The expedition is of great importance and it will be much to your honor and benefit, sir, both for you and for the gentlemen, hidalgos, and other persons who may go upon it; for the land is large, good, healthful, and fertile, and in it you shall be free and with good conscience, honored and benefited. In addition to what is faithfully provided and will be provided from the royal treasury in the way of necessaries for the expedition, as his Majesty commands me in the matter of ships and supplies in order that God may be served by the voyage, I promise you that upon notice I will aid and succor you with men, horses, and flocks and in all that may be necessary. And I will beseech his Majesty with great insistence to make to you such grants as are fitting, as being owed to such loyal vassals, and defenders and amplifiers of our holy faith. All these things being provided, [if] I understand the spirit and goodness of the Spanish people of this New Spain, all those who are of sufficient age and capacity and have no serious impediment which prevents them will endeavor to go on the journey, since it is of so great honor and importance. I assure you that if I had license from his Majesty to do so I myself would go on this expedition in person. Since you, sir, have accepted [this duty] it is fitting that you should, in the presence of the judges of this royal audiencia, of the most reverend archbishop, the religious, the gentlemen, and the officials of his Majesty who are present, take the oath and covenant of homage which must be taken in such cases.

When this discourse by the viceroy was ended, Don Tristán de Luna y Arellano replied and said that in order to serve God our Lord and the royal Majesty of the king, Don Felipe, as his loyal servant he had accepted this grant and that he now accepted it more fully and anew, and that he was ready to take the oath and covenant of homage required of him. Thereupon, immediately, in the presence of myself, Antonio de Turcios, chief notary of the government of this New Spain for his Majesty, Don Tristán de Luna y Arellano took the oath and covenant of homage in the hands of the most illustrious Don Luis de Velasco, viceroy, governor, and captain-general of this New Spain for his Majesty, a cavalier of the order of Santiago, and an hidalgo, with his hands folded together between those of the said viceroy, who administered the oath to him in the following form and manner: You, Don Tristán de Luna y Arellano, do swear and take oath of homage as a cavalier and hidalgo, one, two, and three times—one, two, and three times—one, two, and three times, in accordance with the custom of Spain, to hold the lands, towns, and fortifications which may be settled in the land of La Florida, its confines and its ports, for the royal Majesty of the king, Don Felipe, our lord, and for his service; and as such you will defend them both in war and in peace as a good and loyal vassal of his, keeping in all things the service of his Majesty; and you will surrender, with the said land, provinces, towns, fortified places and ports thereof, the people, artillery, ships, and munitions, and the tributes and revenues which his Majesty may have, to whomever his Majesty may send to take command by his order, letter, or royal cedula, without opposing thereto any excuse, impediment, or any other delay whatsoever; and you will obey and comply with whatever you may be ordered by his Majesty, by me, or by the royal audiencia of this New Spain, under penalty of [being declared] treacherous and of falling into evil state and of incurring the other penalties established by law which are incurred by gentlemen and persons who break the oath and covenant of homage made to their king and natural lord. To this Don Tristán de Luna y Arellano replied and said, having his hands folded between those of the viceroy: that he swore and took covenant of homage as a gentleman and hidalgo one, two, and three times, according to the custom of Spain, that he would hold the lands, towns, and fortified places which might be settled in the land of La Florida, its confines and ports, for the royal Majesty of the king, Don Felipe, our lord, and for his service; and as such he would defend them and protect them both in war and in peace as a faithful and loyal vassal of his, and that in all things he would keep his loyal

service, and that he would surrender the said land, provinces, towns, fortresses, and forts thereof, with the people, artillery, ships, and munitions, and with the tributes and revenues which his Majesty might have, to whomever his Majesty might send to take command by his order, letter, or royal cedula, without opposing thereto any excuse, impediment, or other delay whatsoever; and that he would obey and comply with that which his Majesty might command him, or his Lordship the viceroy, or the royal audiencia of this New Spain, under penalty of [being declared] treacherous, and of falling into evil state, and under the other penalties established by law which are incurred by gentlemen and persons who break the oath and covenant of homage made to their king and natural lord. And he promised to guard it and keep it and not to oppose it by any method or for any cause or reason whatsoever. Thereupon they signed with their names.

[signed:] Don Luis de Velasco.
Don Tristán de Luna y Arellano.

Done before me, Antonio de Turcios.

When the oath and covenant of homage was made, the viceroy in the name of his Majesty gave and delivered to Don Tristán de Luna y Arellano the royal standard, who received from his Lordship's hand in the name of his royal Majesty all the rights [thereto appertaining]. In witness whereof I affixed here this my signature as appears below, in testimony of the truth.

Antonio de Turcios.

252. April 3, 1559. Instructions of Luis de Velasco, Viceroy of Mexico, to Luna.

Translated in Priestley, Luna Papers, I, 19–33, extract.

This is a transcript, well and faithfully made, of certain instructions and ordinances which the most illustrious viceroy of New Spain and the judges of the royal audiencia who reside therein for his Majesty, Licenciate de Zurita, Doctor Bravo, and Doctor Villalobos, issued to be kept and complied with by Don Tristán de Luna y Arellano, governor-elect of the provinces of La Florida. The tenor of the said instructions and ordinances is as follows:

We the viceroy-president and the judges of the royal audiencia of New Spain make known to you, the municipal judges and councilmen, the other officers of the councils, the ministers of justice, and the settlers and inhabitants of all and whatever towns which may be settled in La Florida and the provinces thereof and in the Punta de Santa Elena, that in a cedula by his Majesty the king, Don Felipe our lord, dated at Valladolid, December 29, 1557, directed to me, the viceroy, there is a chapter the tenor of which is as follows:

There shall be appointed officers of justice, councilmen, clerics, and religious; and to each of them you shall give instructions concerning the preëminences and duties they are to have, so that they shall know what they will have to do, and that those who have such offices in charge shall know that they have the obligation to give account of any excesses which the people may commit, either against the Indians or against each other. . . .

For Ordinary Justices

Whenever the staffs of office are delivered to the ordinary justices their oaths shall be taken in such necessary cases, and shall be set down in the form of an auto in the book of the council, and they shall keep and comply with that which has been already set forth for the councilmen. The staffs are to be delivered and the oaths received by the governor or his lieutenant and in the absence of these by the ranking councilman.

They shall hold public audiences in the place which may be set aside for the purpose on every day except feast days, both in the morning and in the afternoon, executing justice equitably to all parties without affection or hatred or enmity, and they shall not be partisans of any of the parties. They shall swear to do this in the oath which shall be received from them.

If there are prisoners they shall visit the jails every day and transact their business therein promptly.

They shall take especial care to punish public sins such as blasphemy, prohibited games, concubinage, witchery, soothsaying, usury, and other similar sins, and all of those which may set a bad example. Of these they shall take great care, lending all diligence thereto without dissimulating with any person whomsoever.

They shall take especial care of orphans and minors; for this purpose they shall name a person to defend them and demand what is necessary for them, and place them to learn a trade and perform service in the homes of virtuous persons.

They shall name another person who shall have supervision of vagabonds. He shall punish them and urge and compel them to take masters and follow trades.

They shall not carry their staffs outside the boundaries of the town, nor enter with them into the towns of the Indians, in order to avoid difficulties.

They shall take care to keep the schedule of fees of his Majesty, charging threefold; they shall not consent to charging nor shall they charge excessive fees and they shall punish him who does to the contrary and does not keep what is here ordered.

From the Indians they shall receive fees in conformity with the cedula of his Majesty according to the schedule of the kingdom, without levying them threefold upon those who are poor; nor shall they levy nor consent to the levying of any fees upon the Indians as upon others.

They shall see to it that there is a tablet publicly situated in the place where they hold audience on which the schedule of fees shall be exhibited so that all may know what fees the [judges] may collect, and litigants what sums they have to pay.

They may not, nor shall they, make any concert with the [treasury] officers to the end that they may be given or paid any part of the fees.

They may not be, nor shall they be, lawyers, procurators, nor solicitors. In business affairs and suits they may give neither counsel, favor, nor aid to the parties thereto.

They shall not receive, nor may they receive bribes, gifts, or presents, in large quantity or small, not even things to eat.

They may not impose, nor shall they impose, the death penalty save in cases of murder or in which the culprit merits death.

They may not, nor shall they, take anything for themselves from auctions of the estates of deceased persons, either through their own action or by the interposition or aid of another person. One of them shall be present at such auctions to preserve order and see that the ordinances by his Majesty in the matter are observed. The executors of deceased persons shall observe this regulation also.

They shall not permit the constables to receive fees for the execution [of orders] before they are paid with the consent of the litigant.

They shall not collect fines [setenas, sevenfold penalties] nor any part of them nor any fine whatsoever, prior to passage of sentence.

They shall take care to inspect weights and measures, and to set prices and tariffs for foodstuffs and wages.

They shall personally take testimony in criminal and civil cases of importance, and also the confessions of litigants, without confiding them to the clerks.

The notaries shall keep a book in which they shall set down fines imposed for the chamber and public and pious works. They shall cause them to be collected and turned over to the receiver thereof, and within one day after the passage of such sentence they shall give him notice of it.

There shall be and they shall name a receiver for said fines; where there are officials of his Majesty he shall be the treasurer.

The jailer shall keep a book of entries and departures; he shall treat the prisoners well, and keep the women by themselves in a dwelling separate and apart from that of the men. He shall not reduce or augment sentences of imprisonment without license, nor shall he receive gifts or bribes.

The constables shall not make arrests without orders except in cases of criminals taken in the act. They shall treat all [prisoners] well, and they shall make oath as to whether they have given or are giving any payments for the offices they hold.

They shall all observe what they should and are obliged to observe in their offices, as the laws of the kingdom provide, and they shall keep them unsullied without receiving bribes.

The justices shall take especial care to defend the royal jurisdiction and not allow the ecclesiastical judges to serve writs upon them to inhibit their actions.

They shall not permit nor give opportunity for the building of towers or strongholds without license from his Majesty.

All of the foregoing herein contained you shall keep and comply with as it may concern each of you, according to what is contained herein, keeping both the laws, the pragmatics, and the capitulations of *corregidores* and judges of *residencias* and the laws and ordinances made for these parts and the cedulas, letters, and orders of his Majesty under the penalties therein and in each of them contained. For each of the towns which may be settled the governor must and shall give a transcript of this instruction signed with his name and countersigned by a notary, and we command that it shall be obeyed as if it were given by myself the viceroy and his royal audiencia, and as though it had been spoken to each and every one of you particularly and expressly, under the penalties indicated. Dated in Mexico, April 3, 1559.

Don Luis de Velasco.
Licentiate de Zurita.
Doctor Bravo.
Doctor Villalobos.

253. May 1, 1559. Tristán de Luna to Philip II.

Luna describes the voyage to Florida and the landing on the Gulf Coast.

Translated in Priestley, Luna Papers, *II, 211–213.*

I wrote your Majesty from the city of Tlaxcala that I was going to embark from the port of San Juan de Ulúa. I did embark there with five hundred soldiers, one thousand serving people, and two hundred and forty horses, but of the latter there were landed only one hundred and thirty. The fleet being well provided with supplies, I set sail on June 11, and until the day of our Lady of August, when it pleased God that the entire fleet should enter this port of Ochuse, there was nothing done but sail in search of it as we did, both because it is a very good [port] and because it is in a locality of good land. As we entered on the day I say, and to give it the name of your Majesty, it was named the Bahía Filipina del Puerto de Santa María. Seamen say that it is the best port in the Indies, and the site which has been selected for founding the town is no less good, for it is a high point of land which slopes down to the bay where the ships come to anchor. Concerning the country I have up to now learned no secret. It seems to be healthy. It is somewhat sandy, from which I judge that it will not yield much bread. There are pine trees, live-oaks, and many other kinds of trees. Until now there have appeared in this bay a few Indian fishermen only. The viceroy, Don Luis de Velasco, gave me instructions to erect a town here as your Majesty ordered. Work is to be begun on it, and when it is built and organized, so that the eighty or one hundred persons who will remain here may be safe, it will be necessary to go inland with the rest of the people. For at present there is no means of supporting so many people here, and if your Majesty has to sustain them a long time as you are now doing it will be very expensive, as I am writing to the viceroy. I supplicate your Majesty to send orders to him to supply us with provisions, for we have food left for only eighty days, and to provide ships in which to bring us horses and beasts of burden; for without your Majesty [having done so], we who are here have written asking to be provided with more animals from our estates, for, if we lack them we shall have nothing with which to transport the food and baggage, and if we cannot do this your Majesty's intention may fare badly. Hence, it is necessary for your Majesty to command that those who may remain here shall be well looked after to see that they are provided with necessaries, as must we ourselves be until we depart from here. After that, I consider that it will be difficult to provision us except at great effort until the port of Santa Elena is colonized and a road overland to New Spain is discovered by means of which I understand that we are to be supplied with all manner of herds in abundance. When I have acquired any clear knowledge or account of the condition of this country and of the success which God may give us in it, I will write concerning it to your Majesty through the viceroy, Don Luis de Velasco. I supplicate your Majesty to remember what I have besought in other letters concerning myself. May our Lord guard the sacred catholic royal person of your Majesty, and increase you with the increase of greater kingdoms and seigniories as we your servants and vassals desire. From the city of Tlaxcala, May 1, 1559.

Your sacred Catholic Majesty's Humble servant and vassal, who kisses your hands and feet,

[signed:] Don Tristán de Luna y Arellano.

254. May 12, 1559. Luis de Velasco to Luna.
Translated in Priestley, Luna Papers, *I, 55–57.*

I wrote to you from here that it seemed to me desirable to send some person to Jalapa to take the muster-roll of the men and horses, and that after he had done so, he should stay there to provision the people and take charge of them until you should order them to embark. Confident that Ángel de Villafañe will do this better than any of those who remain here [I have sent him], and if you are in Jalapa when he arrives, you will order the people to give him the muster-roll and in your absence obey him and comply with his orders upon going to embark and in everything else which may occur there. It also seems to me that when Villafañe arrives it will be well for you to go to the port to give orders concerning the embarkation in order that it may be properly done with all possible promptness; for you can see how important it is not to lose any time. They tell me that the *canaille* of halfbreeds, mulattoes, and Indians whom the people are taking with them is very numerous; you will note that the greater part of these will serve no purpose save to put the camp in confusion and eat up the supplies. It seems to me that it would be sufficient to take only as many serving people as there are soldiers who go, and that no more of the people should go down from Jalapa than are to embark. And I charge you for the service of his Majesty not to permit an unmarried woman of suspicious character to embark, for you know how much she will offend, and that one public mortal sin is enough to cause an army to be lost. They have informed me that the ensign of Don Alonso de Castilla took a young woman from the town, and they tell me that she is a singer, and that the captain does not object to her going in the company. This you will remedy. They also tell me that the woman of

Porras whom they call La Lechera and her daughter have been in Tepeaca. She is the one who importuned us in Mexico, and went in the company of Don Alonso. Please find out whether they intend to go [on the expedition], and make them come back. The old woman may be given a waist for the return journey.

The officials [of the treasury] for La Florida, the treasurer and the accountant, arrived here yesterday; they tell me that the entire herd of animals will reach Puebla today and tomorrow, that they will set out from there on Monday, and that the cinches and rings for embarking the horses will be sent on with all possible diligence.

As I said to you here, it appears that if the ships cannot carry all the cargo of supplies, arms, and clothing which is here, it would be least inconvenient to leave here the clothing to be taken on the second voyage rather than the supplies. This you should order done, endeavoring to take all the soldiers possible but not overcrowding the ships.

The officials [of the treasury] are taking a well stocked supply of drugs, and for the physician I have sent a successor. I will have him go, and if he will not, another will be sent. Please inform me as to how you reached Jalapa and how you found the people. Diego Téllez came here yesterday and was to go to Puebla and will set out from there on Monday. Don Carlos is well and seems happy in my company. Do not worry about him, for I will take as good care of him as if he were my own son. May our Lord protect your illustrious person. Tlaxcala, Friday, May 12, [1559].

Your servant,

[signed:] Don Luis de Velasco.

255. May 25, 1559. Luis de Velasco to Philip II.

Translated in Priestley, Luna Papers, II, 221–231, extract.

After I had provided the supplies for the cavalry and infantry which by your Majesty's command are being sent for the settlement and pacification of the land of La Florida, and after I had provided the food, arms, and artillery necessary for the expedition, I left Mexico on April 24, sending the people on in advance so that they should move along the road to the port in order and not commit disorders. I came to this city of Tlaxcala, which is twenty leagues from Mexico on the way to the port. Here the people have just been collected and set upon the way, and it has been labor enough. It seemed best to me not to give them arms until they were embarked, so as to avoid any difficulties which might arise if they should have them in their hands, especially some who feel injured at what they consider the unreasonable treatment they have received at the hands of the ordinary justices of the City of Mexico and the ministers of the royal audiencia. In truth, if I had not made haste to get the men out of Mexico, trouble hard to remedy might have arisen. Who gave the occasion for it your Majesty shall be informed, and of the little blame which attaches to the captains and people in authority for a certain disturbance which happened on March 8 in the city while I was absent. I had gone away to recuperate from a severe illness I had. If at the time it happened the oidores had suspended the punishment which was inflicted upon a soldier, and had sent word to me one league from the city, where I was, I would, although weak, have come, and with my coming the men who were excited would have been quieted, and justice would have been done to the guilty with fitting authority and rigor without its having been necessary for the oidores to place the city under arms as they did. I am sure, because I know the people of our nation, that if the affair had come to a break, those who took up arms in defense of justice would have turned those arms against it, and from the account I send you of what happened, which is true, you will learn how few soldiers there were in the city, and how they had no arms other than their swords, how their captains were absent from the city, and the governor Don Tristán and some of the captains were with me one league from the city. The people and horses will be embarked, and I believe they will set sail.

During all this present month of May it has been necessary to have them provided with food [on the march] from Mexico to the port at the cost of the tributes given by the towns which are in the vicinity of the road in order that it should not be taken from the Indians. As is well known to me, the assistance which was given to the men they spent before leaving Mexico, for horses and for coats of mail to wear beneath their cotton armor. For the one arm without the other is easily penetrated by the arrows of the Indians. One horse and a reasonably good coat of armor cost little less than two hundred pesos; on linen, clothes, shoes, and other things which are necessary, and objects to barter which they carry to exchange with the Indians for what they may have, the captains and men who go have spent, aside from the assistance that has been given them from the royal treasury, more than 300,000 pesos. . . .

The sketch I have ordered made of how the towns of Spaniards that are to be settled are to be formed I send you in order that your Majesty may order it examined. If it seems that they should have a different arrangement your Majesty will order it sent to me. I have intended that the first town to be built and settled in the port shall have no more than one hundred and forty houselots, and that the forty shall be utilized for the plaza, a monastery, a church, and a royal house in which the governor shall dwell and where shall be stored the arms, artillery, munitions, and food supplies. This house is to be large enough for everything and is to be separate and have its defenses and the form of a stronghold. The four gates the town is to have are to be visible from the plaza; it is to be large enough to contain all the people. The hundred houses are to be for one hundred heads of families, which seem enough for the defense of the town.

The religious who go at present number six; as vicar-provincial goes Fray Pedro de Feria, a religious of good life, example, and doctrine; [there are also] Fray Domingo de la Anunciación, he who wrote the letter to the bishop of Chiapas, the copy of which your Majesty ordered me to send, Fray Domingo de Salazar, Fray Juan Mazuelas, Fray Diego de Santo Domingo, and Fray Bartolomé Mateos. They are select religious and such as they ought to be for such an expedition.

[One of] the good effects which, God helping, this expedition will have will be this: if a port is colonized on the coast of La Florida, which is from one hundred to one hundred and thirty leagues from the port of La Havana and lies midway of the Bahama Channel, where all the ships are forced to go which come to Tierra Firme, Nombre de Dios, and New Spain, I believe that when it is known by the corsairs who are accustomed to pass these parts that there are Spanish ships and people on both sides of the Bahama Channel to impede their passing and assist each other from La Florida to La Havana and from La Havana thither, they will not go by here, and the route will be assured as far as the Azores Islands, which is of much importance.

Don Tristán de Luna y Arellano, who goes as governor, leaves his elder child in company and care of myself as representative of the officials of the royal treasury, to collect the tributes from the towns he has in encomienda in this New Spain, so that from them may be collected what has been lent him from the royal treasury. He asked me to assign him a salary, and it seemed to me his request was reasonable, so I assigned him 8,000 Castilian ducats to be drawn on the officials of La Florida from the revenues which may be derived from that country, with the proviso that they were to be paid to him if your Majesty should be pleased to have it so. It seemed to him little, and not very sure pay. He is writing to your Majesty asking that you grant him the favor of ordering him given more salary, and that it be drawn on and paid from the revenues of this New Spain until there are revenues in La Florida. He deserves any favor which your Majesty may order granted him, for he is a good gentleman, and goes to serve with Christian spirit and great good will. It is necessary that he shall have enough to maintain himself and to aid the people who go with him, so as to keep them contented. With him go gentlemen and people of quality, as your Majesty may order verified by the copies of the muster-rolls and the assistance given to the people whom I am sending. . . .

256. September 24, 1559. Tristán de Luna to Philip II.

Translated in Priestley, Luna Papers, II, 245–247.

After I had written to your Majesty at length everything concerning this expedition to the provinces of La Florida, with everything that had happened on the voyage and afterwards until that day, and I had referred you in part to Juan Rodríguez, who was pilot major of this fleet, there has since happened here an event of which I must make a report to your Majesty, in order that you may be pleased to order a suitable remedy promptly provided. It is that on Monday, during the night of the nineteenth of this month of September, there came up from the north a fierce tempest, which, blowing for twenty-four hours from all directions until the same hour as it began, without stopping but increasing continuously, did irreparable damage to the ships of the fleet. [There was] great loss by many seamen and passengers, both of their lives as well as of their property. All the ships which were in this port went aground (although it is one of the best ports there are in these Indies), save only one caravel and two barks, which escaped. This has reduced us to such extremity that unless I provide soon for the need in which it left us—for we lost, on one of the ships which went aground, a great part of the supplies which were collected in it for the maintenance of this army, and what we had on land was damaged by the heavy rains—I do not know how I can maintain the people, unless it is by the means of which I am herein telling your Majesty. For this purpose as soon as some four captains whom I expect shortly—for I ordered them to go inland—return and give me information of the character of the country and the towns they may find, I shall be forced lest we all perish to go into the interior with all these people to some place where there are facilities making it possible to maintain them. I shall leave the few supplies which I have at present for the people who will remain settled in the city which is left at this port, so that they may have something to eat during the interval before Don Luis de Velasco provisions them from New Spain. However, if I am able, and have anything to do it with, I shall not fail to send them help down a river which flows into this Bahía Filipina and up which I shall have to go. For I consider that it will be difficult to provision the entire camp by sea from New Spain as safely and completely as may be done if I go away from this port into the interior. All that I have written to

your Majesty in that other letter I wrote shall be done, that your Majesty's purpose may be attained and that a thing which has cost your Majesty so much may not be lost, with the end and death of your vassals who are here in your royal service, and whom I have under my command. I shall always send to the viceroy of New Spain, asking him to provide for them until they can all be maintained by means of the grants which your Majesty may be pleased to make us in the country. As I shall, whenever there is opportunity, always give your Majesty information, through the viceroy, Don Luis de Velasco, of the events which occur in this land, I beg your Majesty that, in order that grants may be made to those whom I have in my company in your royal service, you will represent to him the many hardships they must pass through before the most Christian purpose of your Majesty is achieved. May our Lord God guard your sovereign life, with the exaltation of your royal crown for many and very happy years so that by means thereof your Majesty may see diffused in these parts the doctrine of the holy evangel as your Majesty desires and strives. Amen. From this Bahía Filipina and Puerto de Santa María, September 24, 1559.

Your Sacred Catholic Majesty's humble servant and vassal, who kisses your hands and feet,

[signed:] Don Tristán de Luna y Arellano.

257. October 25, 1559. Luis de Velasco to Luna.

In this letter Velasco gives encouragement and advice to Luna after studying the early reports he has received. Translated in Priestley, Luna Papers, I, 57–79, extract.

The letters which you wrote me by Luis Daza on August 24 from the port of Santa María de Ochuse I received on September 7, and on the twelfth I had the news of your arrival at the port. It gave me as much contentment as the pain I felt on seeing what you wrote me by Felipe Boquín on September 28. The bark in which he and the other masters and pilots came arrived after six days between that port [and] San Juan de Ulúa. Yesterday, the thirteenth instant, I received the letter you wrote me, and before I express my sorrow I will reply to the first ones and say: that having seen the account which you give me of the voyage which the fleet made, it seems that our Lord was pleased to guide the ships to that port. If you had not gone out toward the open sea as you did, you would have reached it some days sooner; if the pilots had been able to do so they would have saved time and labor and the loss of some of the horses, and possibly the loss of the ships. But since our Lord ordained it thus there is nothing to be said except to give Him many thanks, and pray Him that in what remains for you to do He will guide, enlighten, and assist you. That, I could wish to do myself in person, and you must believe that I grieve for your troubles as much as though I were passing through them myself. I trust in our Lord that He will give you your reward for them in this life and the next.

I have seen what you and the maestre de campo and the captains write me concerning the good order and diligence which you have and are maintaining, and the great satisfaction they have in your prudence and valor. Fray Pedro de Feria and the other religious write me the same thing.

At the hour when Luis Daza arrived I ordered that the galleon in which he came should be repaired in conformity with the opinion of Gonzalo Gayón the pilot. He at once returned to the port to undertake the work, and another medium-sized ship was also taken so that the two might with all possible speed carry the supplies for which you ask. The roads from this city to Vera Cruz have been and are so bad that it has not been possible to carry [supplies] with the promptness I should like. All diligence is and has been observed. The memoir of what I have ordered to be taken will be with this letter, and as I do not know of a certainty what the ships may be able to carry, I refer you to the memoir which will be sent by the Bachiller Martínez, *alcalde mayor* of the city and port of La Vera Cruz. He is at the port engaged in dispatching these two ships. I believe that, if it pleases our Lord, they will leave the port, if the weather is favorable, between the fourth and the tenth of November. They are commanded by Gonzalo Gayón because he is a good pilot and knows the route well. The other ship will, I believe, be commanded by a brother of his who they say is a good pilot. I fear that some mishap may befall them, going at the time they do, and after conversing with skilful pilots and mariners, it has seemed to me that the route which they should take is the same as that which the ships take between here and La Havana. If the weather compels them they may make the latter port or that of Matanzas, where they may remain until the weather becomes favorable for them to set sail and make your port. If the weather is not very contrary they may make their voyage without changing their course. Having seen what you write of your necessity for supplies it seemed wise to me to hazard these two ships; it will be fitting, if our Lord brings them safe to port, that they return as soon as they are unloaded, so that they may make another voyage in the month of February or March with part of the horses and other things which have to be taken. If in the meantime any ships come from Spain I shall take one of them to help carry some of the horses and supplies which do not go now. Luis Daza is in good humor to return with the succor [but] he will not set out until these two ships have returned.

They tell me that the hundred horses which belong to the soldiers and were left behind are well and are being well treated. They tell me that among them are eight or ten so old and lame that they are not fit to make the journey. Others are to be sent in their places, and the residents of this city who have sons, brothers, relatives, and friends there want to send them horses; a memoir has been made of more than fifty; if there are ships in which they can go they will all be sent. If not, they will wait until, God willing, cattle are to be sent by land, although this seems a great undertaking, with much delay, which cannot be performed save at great cost. It would seem that by taking them from Los Zacatecas or the mines of San Martín and about there, it might be done most quickly and safely by going along the coast from here to the Río del Espíritu Santo if there are any means of being able to reach the shore from this side, and from the opposite one. It remains to be found out—since the river cannot be crossed because of its size and fury—whether the horses and cattle can be taken in barks from one bank to the other at the coast. Please look into this and discuss it with the persons of prudence and experience who are there, and advise me by these ships as to what you think, for there will be time.

From the letter which you wrote me on September 28 it seems that the ships with main topsails, the galleon of Andonaguín, and one of the three barks were lost. The hurricane must have been terrible to have worked such destruction in such a good port.

You say that in view of your need of supplies you have changed your mind, since necessity compels you, and that, leaving some sixty soldiers with Captain Juan Xaramillo in that port, you are thinking of going inland with the rest of the army to search for a town where the people can be sustained and [from which] you may be able to succor those left at the port. This has seemed well to me, for necessity compels you to do it. I hope that these two ships may arrive before you go, that they may, with the supplies which they carry, assist you in your forward movement as well as [those you] leave at the port. But as it may be that you will have already set out, I am writing to Juan Xaramillo that as soon as the ships arrive he shall send you word if possible. I am also writing him that, in addition to the service which he has rendered his Majesty, his remaining there in your place has made me confident that there will be no failure and the port will be secure. It seems to me that (if this arrives in time for you to discuss it) if you find a land where the people may be sustained until the winter passes and until the horses, shields, helmets, and the other things which are set down in the memoir but cannot be made for lack of time, go [forward to you], that you ought not to go farther from the port than may be necessary to sustain the people. For by God's help if these two ships come back in January they will return [to you] in March or April at the latest, and they will carry as many as fifty horses, some live cattle, and part of the things for which you ask that are not going now. When they have made this voyage it seems to me that it would be well for them to go from your port to La Havana to take you what cattle they can and some horses or mares. I have written to the governor there to have them ready by that time, and that he who goes will take the money to pay for them. And I have arranged with Luis Daza that he shall go

from the port as soon as he is provided with what he should take to La Havana with the ships for the purpose; and by God's help if the weather permits, in the year [15]60 these two ships and one of those expected from Spain will make three voyages to your port with large and small cattle, and with the greater part of the things which you ask to have sent by sea.

I see clearly that if that land is to be promptly supplied with an abundance of cattle and horses it would be desirable that most of them should be taken overland, but the road is so long, so difficult to travel, and so lacking in water in some parts and with such great rivers and swamps in others, that I am in doubt whether they can be so taken. For the purpose of finding out whether there be a road and what route to follow, God willing, [I shall send out] in the month of December or January twenty-four or thirty horsemen with rations necessary for three or four months, to explore the land for two hundred leagues above Los Zacatecas; returning from that land by crossing the rivers on the heights of the mountain slopes, after investigating the country well, they will come out again below, between the valleys of Pánuco and Ogitipa, in order to find out which route will be the best to take. In the interval while these men are going and returning, the horses and mares and large cattle which are to be sent will be collected and placed in Querétaro and San Miguel in time so that a year from now, God willing, they may begin to travel provided a route be found over which it is possible to go until they strike the Río del Espíritu Santo at a place where they can cross it. I think that for the purpose of finding the route Juan de Busto and Muñoz the partner of Antonio de Luna in the matter of the *plas* will go, for up to now neither one has made very much money in the business. The others who will go will be suitable persons. In the meantime, while this is being arranged and provided for here, you will give me information as to where you are, what the distance is from the Río del Espíritu Santo, and whether or not the people who go with the cattle and horses should go [across] to where you are or return from there. This it seems to me should depend upon what kind of people may be needed. For if they are to be people who are to remain in the land, they ought to be soldiers and persons who have nothing here except what they carry with them. But if they are to return, there should be [among them] some corregidores and persons who have some employment here. I believe that the leader will be Juan de Busto or Lope de Arellano. If those who go to discover the road find that it cannot be traveled for lack of water or other notable impediments, I will notify you, and I will double the number [of animals] to be sent by sea.

I saw what you wrote me about what happened to the maestre de campo and to Captain Álvaro Nieto on the expedition which they made up the river, and how the father vicar, Fray Pedro de Feria, was so merciful with the Indian men and women who were captured that he opposed their being brought to you, and that this was the reason why no provisions were found in that town. Inasmuch as it was intended to do them no harm by bringing them, but good, and for the purposes of making them understand this and to acquire the language of the country, it was a mistake to set them free. It will be necessary as you say to use a moderate and temperate rigor, without excesses, above all things giving the natives the admonitions which his Majesty commands and which you took with you as instructions. For your army must not perish from hunger because the Indians do not want to give it food. Thus in case of necessity, such as exists, you may take it from them, leaving them what is necessary for their sustenance. Moreover you may act on the defensive and offensive against those who take up arms against the army and impede the preaching of the holy gospel; this the father vicar knows very well. Since you went, there has come to this city a book by Fray Domingo de Soto which treats of this matter. If one can be had I will send you a copy by these ships, and if not the factor Luis Daza will take you one. They tell me that a few arquebuses have been fired in the air in reply to the arrows of the Indians; it seems to me that you ought to avoid shooting at them as much as possible, but when it is necessary and fitting, it is right that they be fired upon in such a way that they will fear more than the noise. You will act in this and in all other things with your well-known temperance, prudence, and spirit, and as you see will conduce to the service of God our Lord and of his Majesty and to the preservation of your army and people.

You say that, in view of the necessity in which you are, especially of cattle and horses, Captain Baltazar Sotelo offered to leave his command there and come to solicit aid. It was wise that he did not come, as no petition is necessary with me, for I have no purpose in view so important as giving aid to you and your people with all I have and in every way I can. It is true that in all the losses and all the troubles which have befallen me, which have not been few, I have regretted nothing so much as the loss of the ships and supplies. I wish I could remedy that with my life and blood, and I believe that I have felt it more keenly than you can have done. But considering that our Lord permitted it for our sins, it is fitting to give Him thanks for what He has done and keep a good spirit in the future. And since it was not only the marquis del Valle who sank his vessels when he entered this land, our Lord permitted that another such event should occur there in order that we should trust in Him alone. And so I hope that by His divine will things will turn out in that land as they have in this; and while his Majesty keeps me in this position and I have life you may be sure that the principal thing in which I shall busy myself will be in succoring you and your army in all that I can and with all that I possess, as I have said. Of this you may assure all those gentlemen and hidalgos; and in order that you may understand and cause them to understand what I have arranged for with his Majesty in their favor, I am sending you a transcript of the letter which his Majesty ordered sent in answer to one of mine. In it he makes a grant to them of a part of the tributes which are to be levied upon the Indians in conformity with the *repartimiento* which I am to make in perpetuity for them and their heirs, or, they having no heirs, they may leave [the repartimientos] for one or two lives to whomever they wish and consider proper. Although his Majesty has confided this repartimiento to me, it is to be made in whatever way you may order and as may seem good to you, preferring the principal persons and those in command whom you took in company with you. Especially [deserving is] Jorge Cerón Carvajal, to whom it is only right that the greater share should be given after yourself. The other captains and persons in command should, I think, have equal shares. I well realize that I am dealing with this matter early, but I am writing this to inform you of what his Majesty has ordered, and also that you may proceed to draw up whatever plan may seem suitable to you, in order that you may advise me in time what should be done.

His Majesty also commands, as you will see in his letter, that you place alcaldes mayores and corregidores in the provinces and towns which give their allegiance, in order that they, together with the religious, may preserve the natives in justice and teach them spiritual and temporal things, and that the Indians may give these persons that which is necessary for their maintenance; and for this you may issue orders. His Majesty promises, as you will see in his letter, that whatever I may order concerning the repartimiento shall be observed. Until now, in the discoveries and conquests which have been made in the Indies, his Majesty has never made such liberal grants as he makes to you and to that army. May it please our Lord that the land be pacified and populated and the natives come into knowledge of our holy faith; for if this end which we hope for [is realized] I believe that in this life and in the next the labors which now present themselves will be remunerated. When Luis Daza goes he will take you the original of his Majesty's letter. I replied to it, kissing his royal feet and hands for you, that army, and myself, for the grant which he made to them. I also asked him to order the period of ten years reduced, that being the time during which he thought that the Indians should pay no tribute. For that time is so long that the people could not maintain themselves without having some support in general for them all. So I asked him to have an order issued promptly, and I believe that he will remove the time limit entirely or the greater part of it.

I saw what you write to his Majesty in the two letters which you sent to me; what you say in them is very good. They will be sent in my parcel of letters on the first ship.

It was well that the mariners who escaped from the ships which were sunk should remain there, for they are artisans, and it was just that they should be assigned salaries, for they will have to perform service. For them, and for the others who are without arms I am sending on these two ships thirty-nine counterpanes and one hundred blankets of three breadths which were found among the stock of this royal house. It is a fact

that not another one is left in it; if there were it would be sent to you. I am also sending you for your arquebuses and for those of the members of your guard two barrels, half a quintal each, of the good powder which I brought from Flanders for my own arquebuses. A quantity is now being made, and when Luis Daza goes it will be sent with the other things.

Some gentlemen resident in this city are sending a few things for their sons, brothers, and relatives. You will see that these are given to them. Whenever ships go they will be provided with all the comforts and presents possible and whatever may be asked for from there. Everything that is being taken goes consigned to Juan Xaramillo, or to the person whom you may have left in the port, and I am writing to him to open one of the packets of letters which is addressed to you, in order that he may see and understand what his Majesty has ordered done and what is being and will be done here. I am ordering him not to leave the port, but to hold it with the courage for which he is reputed, in attention to the fact that it is to be and is the principal defense of those kingdoms, and the one which it is most important to keep well secured; and I am ordering him to observe great vigilance that the ships and barks which are in it or may go to it shall be well protected, in order that the Indians of the vicinity may not come and burn them or injure them, as well as that neither mariners nor other persons may have an opportunity to go away in them. For this purpose it will be well to have the sails, oars, masts, and rudder in the munition-house under good guard. I am also writing him that if it is possible to recover the anchors of the ships which were lost, he is to recover them and put them where they will serve to anchor the ships to them as [is done] with those which are at the port of San Juan de Ulúa; this will be of some aid in preventing another disaster like the past one. The memoir of what the ships are taking goes with this letter, and another also goes in the one to Juan Xaramillo. I am writing to him that if you are not there when they arrive he shall send the ships back as soon as they are discharged, for I desire, as I have said, that by March or April, God willing, they might return with some horses and cattle.

It is true, as the head bailiff has said, that I sent

you an order to send back as prisoners two soldiers for the murder of a man. You say that they are among the best ones in that camp, but that you will send them if it seems good to me. Since they are such and are serving well, and since no one here demands them or is prosecuting them, they are better there than here.

You say that because it is winter and because there is no vessel in that port except the new bark, it will not be possible to send a messenger until some bark or small ship goes from here; for you think that large ships should not be sent because it is very costly and dangerous to make port on the coast in them [and that] for the future they should be built here. The two which are now going are of medium size. If it is possible to build a frigate like the one which went, between now and the end of March, it shall be done, for I think one will be needed to explore and sound the rivers which lie between the Río del Espíritu Santo and that port, and to be used there for whatever purpose may be convenient.

The mariners fear to go on this voyage, suspecting that you will detail them in that port. You will order that all who go may freely return, and some of those who were saved from the ships which were lost and who have wives in Spain you will send back in order that they may collect the wages which are due them and go home from here. . . .

It seems to me very important that there should be two barks in the port, so that one could be on regular and ordinary duty in it for whatever might occur, and the other for sending me word whenever it might suit. If we were not just now in the middle of winter, I would send one with these two ships. It will go when they return, but before that time it will not be proper to risk it. They sent me from Spain a few stones of quicksilver metal with which to search for mines in this country, and because it might be that some might be found there I am sending you one of the stones which they sent me from Spain, and the nugget or pellet which is [found] near it. The one containing the metal is the red stone which has some spots, and the pellet which is near it is the other one, which goes with it. The memoir of how they are submitted to metallurgical process in Spain also goes herewith. I commend to you Ortizico and Velázquez y Romero. It appears to me that both of them are yet on foot, and horses will have to be

sent to them on the first ships. In order that those who are now going with these letters may not be detained, this one is not any longer. I know that the Señora Doña Juana is very well, and very happy. Of the Señora Doña Juana, and of Don Luis I am taking and shall take care, in order to serve your Lordship, as is right and as I owe to you, whose illustrious person may our Lord preserve.

It is true, my lord, that I have been almost ready to lose my senses and my life for grief over what happened in the loss of the ships and [your] need of provisions. May our Lord, who permitted it, be praised that it came when you and the army were on shore. The two ships are being sent with all the diligence possible with all the supplies they can carry; they are not more heavily laden because they go at a stormy time. As soon as they are discharged you will order them to return so that they can make another voyage in March or April with horses and cattle and some supplies of whatever may be most needed. It seems to me that until the horses go and some more people, if necessary, that you should not go farther away from the port than may be required in order to maintain the people. But if the province of Coosa is not more than fifty leagues from the port and is the best part of the land to settle, send [a colony] to settle there as you write me, notwithstanding what I say. You will do whatever you consider most proper as one who has the matter before him. In order that we here may know what is happening, it will be convenient to build in the port a frigate and a small foist from the wood and nails of the ships which sank. This may serve to bring and take dispatches. Another one will be constructed with diligence in the port of San Juan de Ulúa between now and May for the same purpose, but do not fail to do there as I say because of this. If there are any persons ill with contagious diseases and who are of no service to you, please return them and others will go in their places. I shall send from here to discover the road in January, and [the animals] which are to go by land will soon be collected and set on the road. In everything which I can provide here there will be no lack, and you need not worry about Don Carlos. May God guard and prosper your illustrious person. Do not detain any of the mariners who are going [to you] now, and if it should be possible to grant license to return to some of those who are now there it would be well, for it makes them discontented to go suspecting that they are to be detained. Mexico, October 25, [1559].

[signed:] Don Luis de Velasco.

258. December 18, 1559. Philip II to Tristán de Luna.

Translated in Priestley, Luna Papers, II, 15–17.

Don Tristán: As you know from having been told, it was fitting and very necessary to make a strong settlement at the Punta de Santa Elena, which is in that land of La Florida, in order to make an effort from there by means of preaching and good treatment to bring the people of that land to our holy Catholic faith, and in order that the ships which come from New Spain and other parts of the Indies to these kingdoms and make port there may find shelter instead of being lost on account of there being no settlement at all at the Punta; and also in order to prevent people from France or any other foreign kingdom from entering there to settle or take possession in our lands. We [therefore] sent to command Don Luis de Velasco, our viceroy of New Spain, to issue the order to send people and necessary equipment to make such a settlement, and religious to undertake to bring the Indians of that land into peace and into the knowledge of our Lord. He in compliance therewith sent [an expedition] to make that settlement and made you captain and leader of the people he sent. He gave you orders as to what you were to do [in effecting] the settlement, and I am very well pleased at the nomination which was made of yourself for this enterprise, for I am confident that with prudence and good government you will do it in a Christian manner conducive to the service of God our Lord and of ourself and to the welfare of the natives of that country. But though it may be by order which the viceroy gave you that you have made first another town than that which is to be placed at that Punta de Santa Elena, this appears here not to be suitable, but that first of all the settlement we have ordered must be made at the Punta before any other town whatsoever. For notwithstanding that we

are at peace with France, we have learned that Frenchmen, under pretext of going to Los Bacallaos, may possibly be desirous of going to that land of La Florida to settle in it and take possession of our lands. This it is necessary to prevent them from doing, and I therefore command you, notwithstanding whatever other order you may have to the contrary from our viceroy, to make first a town at the Punta de Santa Elena rather than at any other place. You will do this in the form and manner for which you already have orders, and in so doing you will see to it that all possible haste is made; and you are to inform us how it is being done and in what time it can be completed. For this reason alone I am ordering this letter sent to you by several ways, so that it may come quickly to your hands. You are not to understand that because of this you should abandon what you may have already settled, but, leaving it in proper condition, you are to go forward to make a settlement at the Punta de Santa Elena. Toledo, December 18, 1559.

[signed:] I the King

By command of his Majesty, Francisco de Eraso.

259. May 6, 1560. Luis de Velasco to Luna.

Velasco gives further orders and suggestions on the basis of the reports he has received.

Translated in Priestley, Luna Papers, I, 93–129, extract.

The galleon *San Juan* and the French ship which I sent with succor in the month of November returned at the end of January, and anchored at the mouth of the Río de Pánuco because they did not have time to go to La Vera Cruz. At the beginning of February I received here by land the news of their arrival, and you may believe that it gave me great contentment and joy to know that they arrived safely and in good season, and that you and all those captains and gentlemen were in good health.

It is true, as you say, that I was deeply concerned over the ill fortune of losing the ships, but since our Lord willed it there is nothing to say but give Him thanks that nothing worse happened. I saw what you say about having decided to go inland with the greater part of the camp, and that which was later decided upon. All of this seems to me to have been done as was expected of your valor and prudence; and although Don Cristóbal de Arellano and Álvaro Nieto endured hardships on the journey which they made, it appears that it was successful, for they came upon towns, a moderate number of people, and some provisions, and they nearly reached the river which is understood to flow into the Bahía Filipina. God our Lord led them better than the guides, for, according to the account and from what you write me, it seems that [the Indians] wanted to make an end of our people. This must have been their purpose, as also it was when the people of the towns gathered up their provisions and went across the river. It was wisely decided that the captains and men should go into the town, seeing that the weather compelled them, and the natives were not returning to it. It seems to me a good sign that they came without bows or arrows to treat with the Spaniards, although one must not have confidence in them on account of this. You say that you suspected that they would not give the provisions by barter, and that if they did not, and you had need of them, it would be necessary to fight for them; [you also say] that I am to believe that if it cannot be avoided you will see to it that the action is made as justifiable as possible. It is to be hoped that you will do this wherever you and such honorable captains and gentlemen are. It is also understood that when there is necessity, and the measures have been taken which his Majesty commands, they are to search for food where they can find it, and that in taking it fitting order and limitation will be observed, so that it will be done properly and in a Christian manner. It seemed well to me that you deferred until the middle of February going to the place where the sargento mayor and Captain Don Cristóbal remained, in order not to consume the provisions of the Indians. It was also wise to send the treasurer Alonso Velázquez and Gamboa to La Havana. The persons who have come here to be paid the money which was taken from them have been paid, and those who bring authorization will be paid.

You say that inasmuch as there is plenty of very good timber on that coast you decided to build two brigantines, and that one of them was to be launched within eight or ten days, that it is a good piece of workmanship, will be very substantial, and that it has the necessary deck; that it is for use in navigating the rivers, in learning what is on them, and in taking from the port to the towns the supplies and food they may need, and in bringing down to the port maize and whatever else there may be in the land. When these things have been reasonably attended to, you may be able to send one of the brigantines to the Río del Espíritu Santo, and the other one along the other coast to Las Tortugas; thus little by little, God willing, all the ports will be discovered which are on that coast in each direction. I have had a frigate made which will go in company with the two ships. It is somewhat larger than the one which you took; those who have seen it say that it is a very good piece of workmanship. I should like it to serve for coming and going, that I may know promptly how you and that army are, what you are doing, and what it is suitable to consult about and order, to bring back any of the people who are especially ill and cannot serve, and to take from here others in their place, and [to attend to] other details. And if anything comes up there in which it can be used, this may be done provided it is detained for only a few days.

You say that you were thinking of sending a brigantine, a bateau, and a small shallop to the bay where you were anchored, namely, La Filipina, to go up the river in search of Upiachi. They were to take a part of the supplies which I sent, but not any maize. They were to take clothing and cattle to the people who had gone inland. You are sure, from what you understand, that this can be none other than the river which comes from La Filipina. This would be an important thing if it were true, as you say, for to be able to provision the inland towns and those above the port by [using] the rivers would both for the present and in the future be of as great importance as would navigation from Mexico to San Juan de Ulúa. By this time the expedition made by captains Don Alonso de Castilla and Sotelo up the river which comes to the port of Santa María de Ochuse at which you have made a settlement, must have been studied and understood. It seems that it could not have been of importance, as the river makes many turns and flows so swiftly, and the land is not well populated. In view of what you say about how unhealthy the site of that port is, and how advantageous the Bahía Filipina seems to you, as well on account of the navigable rivers which flow into it as because it is more fertile and might be healthier, it would be well to move the town to that bay, or farther inland on the Río de Piachi as close to the bay and port as possible. Apparently the land is black and good, and if a site be found where a settlement can be made it would be wiser to place one there rather than in any other place. What you say seems good to me, although I consider it unwise to leave the ports unprotected unless the settlement be made near enough so that in one day they may be succored, and unless some kind of defense is left at one of them, where some of the people might stay to load and unload the ships and guard those which are to be made in the future, and make repairs; and since you have the situation before you and will have seen and understood what is most fitting, I have no other opinion in the matter but to leave it to your judgment, provided, as I say, the first settlement be at a place from which the ports can be protected; for, aside from its being of great importance, this is what his Majesty commands in the instructions which he sent to me and I gave to you.

It was wisely decided to send Carbajal of Michoacán with the twelve soldiers to the place where the sargento mayor and Don Cristóbal are, with notice of the succor and of the grant which his Majesty makes and which I will make in his royal name. Luis Daza takes the original of the letter which his Majesty wrote me, in order that it may be more fully credited than the transcript. I wrote to his Majesty at once as soon as I received it, asking him to order the time shortened from the ten years before the encomiendas should be begun, and I think it certain that he will be pleased to do so. Meantime, in the provinces and towns which you pacify, and which give their allegiance to his Majesty, you will place the persons who seem suitable, and indicate their compensation according to the quality of the land and the capacity of the natives. You will proceed to make a memoir of the provinces and towns, indicating what should be placed under the direct control of his Majesty and what should be intrusted to private persons and to which persons. For in the meantime and while I have the command, everything is to be done as seems good to you.

Luis Daza has not been able to set out before on account of waiting until the galleon *San Juan* could be repaired, and until it should be possible to provide the necessary things which he takes, and also because at the time when they were beginning to receive the cargo of clothing and provisions the occasion came for dispatching the fleet to Spain. Ten ships are going, and in them many people and much treasure, so, in order not to cause confusion between the two in the despatch, we have waited until the vessels which go to Spain have sailed before dispatching those which go to your land. I think, God willing, that the two ships and the tender will set sail at the end of this month of the first of May. They will take only sixty horses, for there is not room for more in the two ships. Among them are four for you, and eight packmules, which I think will be quite necessary. A memoir of the cattle, supplies, clothing, and powder which the ships are taking will be signed with my name and goes herewith. In view of the fact that the other horses which you have here belonging to the soldiers cannot be taken now, it has seemed best to me to sell them so that others can be taken from La Havana with the money. As soon as Luis Daza arrives through the help of God, and his ships are discharged, let them go to La Havana and he in them, so that two voyages may be made this year with horses and cattle. While they are making the first voyage, Luis Daza is to stay in La Havana and go inland to the Savanna de Vasco Porcallo and bring from there to the port the horses and cattle, for they tell me that in that place they are good, and cheap. If our Lord preserves the ships, they may be able to introduce this year at least two hundred horses besides those which go from here, and a reasonable number of cattle, for I believe they are the two most essential things of which at present you and your army have most need.

As to sending horses and cattle by land at present, it appears that this will be very difficult until you have examined the land thoroughly as far as the Río del Espíritu Santo [and know] where it is. Meantime two things will be ordered done here; first, to collect as many as three thousand cows on the road which runs to Zacatecas, near San Martín, and fifteen hundred or two thousand mares, so that when it pleases God that the road be known and safe they may be taken by way of Santiago de los Valles. I have had the road examined for seventy or ninety leagues from here. The country is rough and bad and unoccupied. It is not to be thought that the journey can be made this way; it is in part that which was followed by the Portuguese, through the cactus country said to belong to the savage Chichimecs. This is thirty leagues farther along, on the road to Los Zacatecas. In the month of May twenty horsemen and three hundred friendly Indians will go in, keeping a little to the right hand, and see what kind of land there is on the road northward toward the Río del Espíritu Santo. When the frigate comes back I will advise you of what may have been learned concerning this road.

I saw that you say that what I wrote you seemed good, about not going far inland until a settlement had been made in some good place and you had the horses and cattle necessary to be able to extend farther out. I suppose you will have done this and I desire very much to know about it, and how it has gone with you and all those gentlemen and captains, and in what places the people are distributed; [you will write me about this] before Luis Daza leaves. And in order that I may reply to what you may write, and provide what is needful, if the bark does not come in the meantime, as soon as Luis Daza arrives you are to dispatch the shallop, giving me an account of everything. Neither mares nor mules will be sent at this time, and will not be until they are asked for. As I have already stated, since the ships now leaving are to make two voyages to La Havana, they will be able to carry horses [from there] for all or for most of the people. As many cattle as I can arrange for will be continuously sent both from here and from there. The fleet which is to come from Spain is expected at any time during the present month of April or the beginning of May. If any ship which can be taken comes [then] I have already effected an agreement that it shall be sent to Campeche to take [to you] Hernando de Bracamonte and the other soldiers who have been collected there, who number, according to what they have written me, at least fifty men. They write me that these men will go well equipped with horses and arms, that they are people accustomed to the fatigues of the Indies, and that they will know well how to be of service to God. I have written to the audiencia of Guatemala asking license for Bracamonte and the others to leave, and am now awaiting their reply. As soon as I have

it, and when the fleet comes, as I say, I will send a ship to Campeche as I am asked to do. In order that they may serve in the place of [your] dead and sick, there are being collected in this city some thirty or forty soldiers. As captain goes Diego de Biedma, who is an honest hidalgo and an old soldier. You will receive him as especially commended to you, honor him, and favor him; and do not commit the excess of depriving him of his position as a captain, for he goes under that condition. I have given him my word that he shall not be relieved of that rank if he does as he should, and that he shall be considered as among the first ones in the distribution of the land. As yet I do not know the exact number of men he will take, but I will write when the enlistment is completed, the provisions ready, and he is prepared to set out.

It seems well to me that you have decided to make a settlement in the province of Coosa, for it is understood to be in the most fertile part of the land, and is so situated that from it the route from the Río del Espíritu Santo to Santa Elena may be protected. But it seems to me that this should not be done until you have [more] people and horses and the country is sufficiently quieted that you may explore in each direction with safety. It is well considered for you to try to utilize the rivers as much as possible, and until you have a greater force of men, as I say, and horses and cattle, it seems to me that the people ought not to be distributed in more than two or three places, and that these should be able to render assistance to each other, it being necessary.

I have written to his Majesty what happened on the voyage, and with my letters went yours and the account which came lately. I begged him to order sent with all possible promptness two ships with five or six hundred Spaniards, who should all be people from rural districts and bring the tools needed to cultivate the soil. I am sending to ask for other things which have seemed to me necessary and convenient. I am sure that his Majesty will order it done. I am begging him as earnestly as I can that he be pleased to make you the grant for which you asked. The duty of bearing the request is confided to Hortuño de Ibarra, who goes as general of the fleet. It seemed to me wise to send him to give an account to his Majesty of the state in which things are in this land and in yours and he carries a special account of everything and a message of mine for his Majesty. He goes in good season, as he will find the latter in Spain, for he returned there in safety last September as you will learn from the account of the news I have from there and which goes herewith....

You say that you learn that the natives who are near the coast will likely be of little use because they are lazy, and that if they are treated with rigor, this and the scantiness of the possessions and roots which they have will cause them to go into exile from their native territory into other parts, and that it therefore seems that the principal pacification to be effected in that land should be for the purpose of conserving its people, and that this will have to be done by establishing towns of Spaniards in all the provinces and parts where there are people and the facilities for so doing. This is what I always told you I thought ought to be done, and that thereafter new towns might be gradually pacified, the Indians being attracted thus rather by good works and gifts than by force, but that this ought to be done without placing much confidence in them. In order that this may be done, it is necessary that people be provided, for one of the things which will quiet the natives and make them gentle will be to see the Spaniards sow and reap and support themselves without their help. In order that this may be done it is fitting to supply from here and from Spain what is necessary. I have said that on my part all will be done that is possible, and it is understood that it is as you say, and since I shall discuss this farther on in treating of what his Majesty commands, I will not do so in this chapter....

The letter which goes with this one is a copy of another that his Majesty wrote me. In it he commands me, as you will understand therefrom, to send you with all despatch the one which he writes to you. It goes herewith; in it he orders that a settlement be made with all haste at the Punta de Santa Elena. For it is suspected, notwithstanding there is peace with France, that either the French or the Scotch may enter there to take possession in the lands of his Majesty and occupy them. I am replying to his Majesty that I am sending his letter by these ships and telling him what is being done in the matter, and that it is somewhat difficult to make a settlement at the Punta de Santa Elena as promptly as he commands, both because it is not fitting to depopulate

or abandon what has already been settled, and because the people cannot go overland without having a number of horses. But when you have them, and can leave in safety that which remains behind, you will go or send to see what there is in the matter of settling at Santa Elena. If you see that it can be done without much hazard it seems to me that his Majesty's command ought to be complied with, for he is so insistent about it that he must have indications that foreigners desire to enter there. If you do not make the journey in person, it seems to me it should be intrusted to Don Pedro de Acuña or Captain Sotelo, for I think it is not fitting to remove the maestre de campo from your side. Although I could wish that the new brigantine which goes with the ships might return as soon as it arrives to give me an account of your health and of what has been going on, it seems to me since I wrote that it will be more useful for it to go to explore the coast as far as Santa Elena and return with a report of what may be found. If you decide to send at once by land, I think it would be proper that this brigantine, and a bark, if there be one, should go to carry some artillery, powder, munitions, and weapons. You will make provision for all this according to your ability and the condition of your affairs, and you will inform his Majesty of your receipt of his letter and make him a detailed report of the state of things in that land. You may send one despatch to La Havana in one of the ships which is to go there, and send me the other one here so that it may go in my parcel of letters from here....

Captain Biedma is taking from this city twenty-two or twenty-three soldiers and bears a commission to enlist up to fifty in the City of Los Ángeles and in La Vera Cruz, with [authority to collect] provisions for their maintenance. He is an honest hidalgo, a very good soldier, and well-controlled, as you will see. I have promised him that his company will not be taken from him as long as he does his duty; and since I have pledged my word in this, you will comply with it. It seems to me that you ought to obey the order to establish a settlement at Santa Elena with all possible promptness, as his Majesty commands, and omit for the present sending men on the journey to the Río del Espíritu Santo, for there are not enough of them for everything. In order to encourage people to go from this country and from Spain it would be well to send some specimens of metals, pearls, and other things to be found in that land which may be of utility. In order that I may be informed as to what has happened and what you are thinking of doing, it would be well, if the brigantine does not come, that some bark should come as far as Pánuco to bring your despatch and return from there with salt and fowls and whatever else may be there. Don Carlos and Doña Juana continue well, and Don Carlos has grown; he is strong and robust and a good horseman; and is the instructor of Don Luis. They have their room together, and make each other good company. If there is anything else to write, I shall do it before the ships sail. May our Lord guard your illustrious person. Mexico, May 6, 1560.

Your servant,

[signed:] Don Luis de Velasco.

260. June 17, 1560. Petition of the married soldiers of the expedition to Luna.

They express their dissatisfaction with the uncertainties of the expedition and ask Luna to be more careful of their safety. Translated in Priestley, Luna Papers, I, 139–143.

We married soldiers who are in the service of the king our lord in this town of Nanipacana appear before you in a body and say: that in a petition of ours we asked and supplicated you for the relief befitting the service of God and of his royal Highness, that our wives and children and we ourselves should not perish from hunger without relief, as is set forth at greater length in the petition. To the said petition you replied that we should keep silence under penalty of [being declared] traitors, and in addition to this of being punished as is more fully [set forth] in the reply, to which we refer. But if we do not address our petition for proper relief to you, as the person who represents the king our lord, Don Felipe, to whom would it be proper to address it? Speaking with due respect we say that you ought not to give such an order, for many causes and reasons: first, because we asked for this relief for [the sake of] the lives of our wives, our children, and our-

selves, for we are so near to losing them that it is not just that we should be charged with treason for it and punished; another reason why we ask it is because we see that we have no prospect of food from any quarter, either from up the river or from down it, or much less from the interior, for the Indians have the whole [country] in revolt and burned over, as is notorious among all the captains and men who have gone out for the purpose [of finding food]; another reason is that we see that the fleet from New Spain does not come, has not come, and even in case it should come now we would not have relief so near but that more than fifty days would pass before any food might reach this camp, and during that interval the army might die, as is evident to you; another reason is that if we have sustained ourselves until now on the ordinary ration which is given us, this was because it has been intermixed with a small amount of maize or acorns, of which there is nothing left, or even with some herbs which there used to be but which are no longer to be found within a circuit of three leagues from this camp; and a half pound of meat for two or three days, the ration given us, is a very small quantity, for by no means can men maintain themselves having no other food than that described. Not only do we ourselves suffer, but so also do our servants suffer in great degree; moreover, we have no hope from whatever fields the Indians might possess, for there are none nor have they any, and if there were any they have destroyed them and pulled them up, for which reason no relief is to be expected from them. Furthermore, the territory inland is quite as swampy and overgrown with forests and brambles as it is here, and is so uninhabitable that no men who are human can possibly live in it. Besides this, the Indians who are there are in revolt, and cannot be brought by any means to the service of the king nor to the knowledge of our holy faith, as is notorious to everyone in common. And if you compel us under such dire penalties to keep our mouths shut, to whom shall we appeal, for it is notorious that thereby God our Lord is not served, nor his Majesty as a Catholic.

Furthermore, it has come to our notice that you desire to send the brigantine to La Havana, for what purpose we know not, [but] we say that it is to the prejudice of the whole camp for many causes and reasons. The principal ones are that the affairs of the sea have no end, because the voyage from this town and back again will take more than three months, in which time God knows what will become of us all because of the extremity in which we are. Another reason is that if it goes it may be lost, from which much damage would result because of waiting for it. For these and other reasons set forth, it is expedient for our liberty that you do not permit the voyage, nor allow the brigantine to depart from where the camp is situated, for all hope of saving our lives is in it and in the other ships which are now here.

Wherefore, we beg and request you, one, two, and three times, and as many more as in legal form we may, that for the service of God our Lord you grant the remedy which is necessary, as the most Christian gentleman which you are; that you take compassion on so many infants, women, and Christian men who here repeat in the same manner and in conformity therewith what we asked in our [former] petition. This is the last recourse we have here, for finally it will come to have to be done, and with fewer losses from deaths of men. If you do not do so we protest all the deaths, injuries, calamities, and losses of men which may after all come upon the army. And if it be necessary we ask those present to be our witnesses hereto, and above all things we ask that justice be done.

[twenty-one signatures]

261. June 19, 1560. Declaration of Tristán de Luna.

Luna encourages the men with hopeful reports of the land of plenty being discovered by the expedition to Coosa.

Translated in Priestley, Luna Papers, I, 147–151.

On the nineteenth day of the month of June in the year one thousand five hundred and sixty, being at the site of Santa Cruz (✠) de Nanipacana of these provinces of La Florida of the Indies of the Ocean-Sea, the very illustrious Don Tristán de Luna y Arellano, governor and captain-general of the pacification and settlement of these said provinces and the Punta de Santa Elena, et

cetera, for his Majesty, his Lordship, the said governor, having been importuned, required, and threatened many and divers times by many petitions both from the married men who are in these provinces with their wives, and by the unmarried soldiers who reside in them, he, understanding that they asked license from him to depart from the land because of the want and sterility which existed in it, and because of the general hunger which was being suffered, did not wish to hear nor admit their requests and petitions. Wherefore the master of the camp, the captains, and the officials of his Majesty, asked and supplicated him to hear them and grant them in the best manner he could. In view of this his Lordship convoked an *ayuntamiento, junta,* and council of his gentlemen advisers who are in the said provinces in the service of his Majesty, namely: Jorge Cerón Saavedra, maestre de campo and chief justice for his Majesty, Don Martín Doz, ensign-general and warder of the royal standard, in which position he had been placed by his Lordship because of the absence of Don Carlos de Zúñiga, the treasurer, Alonso Velázquez Rodríguez, the accountant, Alonso Pérez, Captain Baltazar de Sotelo, Captain Don Pedro de Acuña, Captain Diego Téllez, Captain Juan de Porras, Captain Antonio Ortíz de Matienzo, Captain Julián de Acuña, the alcalde mayor Alonso Fajardo, and Pedro López de Nava. All these being convened in the said council, his Lordship spoke to them. He represented and indicated the want and the difficulty in which the army was on account of the hunger from which it was suffering, the clamors which the women and children made, and above all, the requests which the other people of the camp presented in their petitions. This want was evident and notorious to them, but [he said] he could give no relief to satisfy their requests and alleviate such general hunger. For he had, in accord with the above named men, sent in all directions both by land and by water to search for food with captains and men of discretion for the sustention of the camp; but they did not nor could they find any, for which reason the clamor of the army was almost continuous and daily grew worse. His Lordship had sent the sargento mayor and four captains with one hundred and fifty fighting men to pacify the province of Coosa, from whom he had news that they were in a well-populated land with abundant food, according to what they wrote him. It was already well known to them, [he said] that he had sent to acquaint himself better with the land in order to make decision in the matters touching the service of God and of his Majesty and the welfare of all. But since the necessity was so extreme and so notorious that he could not await a reply from the interior, his Lordship had decided to go to where the aforesaid captains were with the people who would follow him, for he would not presume to use force with anyone, nor compel them to do more than they were able. He therefore commanded the captains of horse and foot soldiers to prepare their people within two days for the said purpose. And [he said] that it seemed well to him that the maestre de campo should stay there with the married men and take them away a little distance and put them in a place where they might in some degree be sustained until he could provide relief; and if any of the married men were free and desired to follow him, he protested that he would aid them in everything else; and that as to all the rest which they asked for, it should be discussed and an agreement reached as to what would be most suitable to make it possible to save their lives, all of which were at risk, for they were dying of hunger, and there was scarcely anyone who could keep on his feet; that he expected shortly to set out as has been said; and he asked of them, in my presence, Martín de Aguirre, chief notary named by the governor in this army and camp, that those who wished to follow him would declare themselves and sign their names.

[signed:] Don Tristán de Luna y Arellano.

By command of his Lordship,
Martín de Aguirre, Notary appointed.

262. June 19, 1560. Reply of Jorge Cerón, *Maestre de Campo*, to Luna.

This and the following documents illustrate the growing hostility of the members of the expedition to Luna's leadership.
Translated in Priestley, Luna Papers, I, 153–159.

Replying to your Lordship's command imparted to the officials and captains, and to me together with them as maestre de campo, and given on June 19, 1560, to which I refer, I say: that in other meetings which your lordship has ordered held, composed of the officials of his Majesty, captains, and other persons who have voice in these matters, the dearth of food and provisions which this camp and people suffers and have suffered for the past four months has been discussed; and for the purpose of obtaining provisions all the efforts possible have been made by sending captains with brigantines and barks to obtain them and to search for them on the rivers, the inlets, and in the swamps, with great sufferings on the part of the captains and soldiers, as is public and notorious. But with all these exertions and the diligence which has been shown, it has not been possible to provision the camp or the people. Rather, during the period mentioned, the soldiers and the people have become so weak and have grown so thin that for a month past there has not been a man who has spirit or strength for anything. For these reasons and others which I have mentioned or which might be mentioned, relief has been discussed and attempted as I have said; but the last hope of relief which the people had, that of the coming of the ships from New Spain and the succor which they expected with them at the end of April and throughout all of May, the months just passed, has not yet materialized on the nineteenth of this month of June.

Moreover, there remained another hope of relief which the people had, that of the cornfields and grainfields and certain wild vegetables which were found on the banks of this river of Nanipacana and the Tome. Captains Baltazar de Sotelo, Juan de Porras, and Diego Téllez went to these rivers, but returned with all their people dying of hunger, not having found one grain of corn; the cornfields had been pulled up, and all the fields burned and pulled up by the natives, [as had] even the wild herbs, which they had learned that we could make use of and which we eat. For this reason the camp has fallen into the want described, and some deaths have occurred from the same cause.

For the remedy of this situation your Lordship has on many occasions held numerous consultations, due to which it was decided that a brigantine should go to La Havana for aid and provisions. This recourse I was the one to urge most, for certain reasons and causes which were given; but when the brigantine was about to sail, with your Lordship's money, clothing, and jewels to the value of over three thousand pesos, it was alleged and claimed by the captains and officials of his Majesty that the voyage was not necessary nor a suitable recourse, for reasons and causes which they gave, saying that the provisions which might be brought from there would not suffice for the many people which this camp contains. To this I replied that the voyage was necessary, and the most prompt and effective remedy which at the time could be obtained; for, God willing, the round trip voyage could be made in a month and a half. As a matter of fact this recourse was given up, a more effective remedy was discussed, and both because of the opinions of the officials and captains and of the petitions and protestations which all the camp and the soldiers made, it was concluded that the best solution would be for all the people and the camp to go down this river to the Bahía Filipina.

Your Lordship had an opinion concerning all these necessities and argument, and you proposed [an expedition] to move inland to where the maestre de campo and the captains are, as appears from the aforesaid notice, to which I refer [you]. Replying to this I say: that in knowledge and view of the bad road, through marshes, swamps, canebrakes, and forests, and of the great privations through which the camp and the people have passed, and in the fear that the ill will of the natives has been spread throughout all the land, so that they may have hidden the food and destroyed the houses which they had, as has been done in this district for twelve or fifteen leagues around about, for they have even burned their towns, it is evident that you and all the people would pass through much danger, especially since they are so debilitated; the horses are not able to go a league in an entire day, and it is not possible to take from this settlement or camp any supply of food, nor is it to be hoped that any can be obtained on all the road, of which more than forty leagues are through unpopulated territory. Therefore it is my opinion and that of everyone that the decision to make the journey ought for the present to be given up, for the causes and reasons given and for the following ones:

First, because of the hope and certainty which is felt as to the coming of the fleet and the aid which is expected from New Spain wherewith this camp will be succored and restored. There will then be provisions wherewith the people who are to go inland may have enough to make the journey and traverse the road without the difficulties and the danger through which they would at present have to pass.

Moreover, it is necessary to wait for twenty-two soldiers who have been sent to the port where Captain Xaramillo stayed, to obtain information concerning him and the people who are with him, and to learn whether the fleet has come, it being expected every day that it will arrive.

Another [reason] is that there has also been sent out a bateau which left this site and camp six days ago with forty men to obtain information concerning the people and the camp in the interior and to obtain some maize or other food for this camp.

Moreover we are also awaiting the reply of the illustrious viceroy to the report which was sent to New Spain on the bark, telling of the necessity in which this camp is. It is believed that this reply will soon come, because it is now forty days since the bark left. Therefore on account of all that I have said it appears to me that the departure which your Lordship and the people have thought of should be deferred until in the pleasure of our Lord some succor is obtained, and some solution found for what I have recounted. In the meantime, while this is being awaited the relief which this camp and people shall have from the necessities of the present, has been and must be considered, for by twelve or fifteen days more the entire camp may perish or come to eating all the horses, which is the [only] recourse we have. And this is my reply and opinion touching what has been conferred about and discussed.

[signed:] Jorge Cerón.

263. June 19, 1560. Representation of the six captains to Luna.

Translated in Priestley, Luna Papers, *I, 159–165.*

We captains, Don Pedro de Acuña, Baltazar de Sotelo, Diego Téllez, Juan de Porras, Antonio Ortíz de Matienzo, and Pedro López de Nava, having been called by your Lordship on Wednesday morning, the nineteenth day of the month of June, 1560, there being present also Jorge Cerón

Saavedra, maestre de campo, the officials Alonso Velázquez, the treasurer and Alonso Pérez, the accountant, Licenciate Barandalla, [and the father] vicar, were ordered to give our opinions concerning the extreme suffering from hunger which all the camp and the people in it are enduring, from which it is notorious that nothing is expected but the death of everyone in general, and as to whether it would be better to go inland with the people who are in this camp to search for the sargento mayor, Mateo del Sauz, and the other captains who are there, or to go down to the Bahía Filipina, so as to maintain ourselves while we await the relief we are hoping for from the viceroy of New Spain. Having examined the situation we all join unanimously in the following opinion.

As to that which concerns going inland with your Lordship, there is very great difficulty and notorious risk to our lives, and danger that we perish and all the army be broken up; for at present those of us who are here, it is notorious, have no maize or acorns or any other kind of food to enable us to go up and travel inland. And as is known to your Lordship from the captains and the religious who are there, and from the expeditions and the efforts which we have made, we know for certain that for sixty or seventy leagues up the river there is no food which can be found by marching the army inland. Besides this, your Lordship knows from the letters from those captains who are in the interior what great trouble they have passed and are passing through from hunger because the whole land is in revolt and without any manner of food whatever. And there being, as there are, few natives, and the land so disposed that they cannot be taken, especially with the mildness which his Majesty in his royal instruction commands that they be treated, it would be necessary, in order to get to where the said sargento mayor and captains must be, to carry food for more than forty days; and even if we could reach there, which is impossible, it would only be to place in greater need and detriment those who are there. For since they, though few, as they are, are experiencing the necessity which they do, there would be so much the less wherewith to sustain them and us, for of course we should have need of more food, being a greater number of people, and we should all perish. And if your Lordship leaves any people here, as it ap-

pears you desire to do, with the maestre de campo, in order that they may go down to La Filipina, it must be remembered that they are so bold and unruly that unless there are many to prevent it, and especially unless you and your captains are present, it is certain from their disrespectful attitudes and the things which have happened, that those who could do so would revolt with the brigantines and barks which the army has at present, and they would go away in them and leave the rest, if they lived, lost and with no recourse other than to wait for death.

Moreover, if you were to go up into the interior in this way, supposing there were enough provisions for you to do so, it seems an unwise thing to divide into so many parts the few fighting men who are now in the army. It would cause the Indians, they being hostile, as they are, to destroy us by availing themselves, as they have hitherto done, of the opportunity to lie in wait for us at certain places where they could attack us while we, not knowing the country or the roads, could not oppose them.

More than this, there is no opportunity at present for you to go up into the interior, for it is not known where the sargento mayor and the other captains are nor the road by which to go and find them, since the land is so swampy, so full of canebrakes and brambles, and so full of obstructions. Also, not knowing the road, we might [not] strike it, and go through some desert which would delay us a long time; the rains might come and the winter set in, so that we should all die. Hence it appears to us that by no means can we remain where we are at present, for the reasons stated above, because of the lack of food which we actually suffer and because all the country downstream is deserted, the natives have gone from their houses, and have cut down and burned and pulled up all the fields, as we who have passed through them have seen. If by chance on this very day the fleet and the succor were right in the port of Polonza, we should not be able to help our condition, for it would take the first barks to come up from there to here with food at least twenty-five or thirty days, and here are no men who could or who would do the rowing or have enough strength to do it even though they might be well fed on what the fleet might bring, on account of being, as they are, so weak and debilitated from the hunger they have been and are enduring. And even if they could and would, they would eat up all the food they might carry while bringing it up, and this town would never be relieved of the need of food. More than this, in such a crisis we should not be wise to let the barks and brigantines go down to the port, for the soldiers who might go in them would revolt with them and would go away without having concern for anything else.

As to the desirability of our going to La Filipina, this seems to us a more fitting and congruous idea; for it might take at most four or five days to go down there from here, and in this time the people might go with little hardship, for the barks would be going downstream and they might without other food whatever sustain themselves with what few herbs they might gather on the banks of the river until they should arrive. After reaching the bay and establishing themselves there, they could sustain themselves on the many shellfish such as oysters, crawfishes, and the many fish which there are in the bay, and on the great quantity of palmettos which are there; and besides these there are a great many deer, all of which we are without in this country, as you know. In addition, we should be closer at hand while awaiting the succor which the most illustrious viceroy of New Spain might send us or which we might attempt to bring from La Havana or from any other place at the expense of our own private estates, which each and every one of us offers to give according to the amount of wealth he possesses. For this enterprise, which has cost his Majesty, and the most illustrious viceroy in his name, so much money, we would aid with all our powers to sustain and move forward. After the succor shall have reached there in one way or another, Juan Xaramillo could remain settled there with all the married people who are not disposed to go inland with women and children. Then your lordship and we will take whatever of provisions we may easily carry and go inland in light marching order. In the meantime you will find out where the sargento mayor and the other captains are, and more definitely what the character of the country is, for Captain Sotelo is going for this purpose, and when he brings you guides you will be bound to succeed on your expedition, and thus what is most fitting to his Majesty's service will be done. This is the opinion of us who hereto subscribe, and we offer it as a response to that which was asked us by your

lordship. If these arguments do not satisfy you nor seem sufficient to induce you to give up your decision to go inland, all of us as loyal vassals of his Majesty and good captains under your Lordship as our general and governor placed over us by his Majesty, will follow you until death in the service of God and his Majesty. But we protest that if a blind expedition to a place unknown under the difficulties which we have named and declared is followed, as we believe it will be, by deaths and excessive injuries, and if the land comes to be depopulated as in matter of fact it will be, and the army lost as in truth it will be lost, then let it be charged against you, and not against us nor our successors or descendants. This is what we all give as our reply, and we sign it with our names.

[signed:] Don Pedro de Acuña.
Baltazar de Sotelo.
Antonio Ortíz de Matienzo.
Diego Téllez.
Juan de Porras.
Pedro López de Nava.

264. June 22, 1560. Decision of Tristán de Luna to move to the coast.

Translated in Priestley, Luna Papers, *I, 177–179.*

After the foregoing in the said town of Nanipacana on the twenty-second [*i.e.,* fourth] day of the month of June of the said year, when the illustrious Don Tristán de Luna y Arellano, governor and captain-general for his Majesty in these provinces, had seen the opinions of the maestre de campo, the captains, and the other gentlemen of his council, and the demand made by the officials of the royal treasury, he decided to go down with the people and camp to the Bahía Filipina where they may be supported on shellfish, such as crawfishes and oysters, and fish, until such time as God our Lord may provide them with some relief in the way of supplies, so that he may therewith do that which will more amply satisfy the service of his Majesty. In compliance with this determination he ordered all the captains to have their people equipped and ready in two days to go down to the said Bahía Filipina. And he signed it with his name.

Don Tristán de Luna y Arellano.

265. June 23, 1560. Mexican Indians request that they might go home.

A feature of the Luna expedition is that a number of Mexican Indians were included among the intending colonists. When divisions in the ranks of the expedition's members developed, they proved willing to assert themselves. They were eventually repatriated.

Translated in Priestley, Luna Papers, I, 143–145.

All the principal Indians, natives of the City of Mexico and of El Tatebula, appear before you and say: that on account of the great necessity which exists in this army from hunger, we are suffering very greatly. Until now we have been sustaining ourselves with a few herbs which used to be found here, but now there are no more, nor can any be found within more than four leagues around about here nor can we obtain any corn or acorns in large or small quantity. So, in order that we may not perish here in greater number than those who have died and perished, will you not, in the name of his royal Highness, be pleased to give us a ship so that we may go to New Spain that we may preserve our lives, in conformity with the cedulas whereby the most illustrious viceroy of New Spain made to us certain grants inasmuch as we did not want to take any money in payment, as is evident to you from the said cedulas, which we present to you.

Wherefore, we ask and beseech you for the service of God our Lord to order these cedulas complied with to the letter as the viceroy in the name of his Highness made the grants to us. In so doing you will act as a most Christian gentleman, for the service of God and his Highness. If you do to the contrary it will be to the end that we all perish. If it be necessary we swear to this; and we ask for a copy hereof in legal form; and above all may justice to us be done.

Don Miguel.
Francisco Vizcaíno.
Martín Moyle [?].
Francisco García.
Antón de Santiago.
Cristóbal Daniel.
Francisco Sánchez.
Miguel Mendoza.
Papia.
Pedro Yizomo [?].
Arti [?].
Horti Vilosdos [?].
Pedro Antón de la Cruz.
Pedro de Paloxi.
Todu Seqba [?].
Pedro Díaz.
Agustín Francisco.
Juan García.
Pedro Gerónimo.
Francisco Senilio [?].
Juan Pélez.

When this petition was presented to the governor, he said that he heard it, and that he would do justice. Witnesses, Captain Julián de Acuña and Juan de Paz. Done before me,

Martín de Aguirre,
Chief notary.

THE SEARCH FOR AND THE DESCRIPTION OF COOSA

MATEO DE SAUZ, *sargento mayor* of the expedition, Fray Domingo de la Anunciación, and other members of the party that explored inland found the site on the Coosa River that Soto had occupied when he crossed the watershed from the Tennessee Valley to the Alabama River Valley. They provide some of the more interesting glimpses of the Upper Creek country in the period that links with the explorations of Pardo and Boyano later in the 1560s.

On July 6, 1560, Mateo de Sauz, military leader of the party, reports on his progress inland (266); at the end of July, Fray Domingo Salazar gives his first reactions to his arrival at Coosa (267); on August 1, Fray Domingo de la Anunciación, leader of the Dominican missionary party, Mateo de Sauz, and others report on their approach to and impressions of Coosa (268–269); Padilla, long afterwards, provides a synthetic account of the Coosa (Upper Creek) Indians, based on the reports of the Dominican friars (270). Orders to return reached them by the end of September, 1560.

266. July 6, 1560. Mateo de Sauz to Tristán de Luna.

Translated in Priestley, Luna Papers, I, 419–423.

Very Illustrious Sir:

It is due to the warm friendship and favor of your Lordship that these gentlemen, captains, and I are writing [to describe] everything in the country so far as it has been seen up to this time. Although the country has not pleased us it is populated, and it is understood that from now on there will be plenty of food judging by the cornfields which have been seen. It may be that after arriving at the settlement of Coosa we shall find something that will please us better or prove more nearly adapted to [making possible] what you command us by your instruction to do. If this proves true it shall be done, and whether or not it be so notice will be given you when [your] people reach Atache, for the trading business of these Indians extends to that place, and it would be possible to send word to you by them. We people who are here have no more shoes, salt, or certain other things, as shirts for instance. For this reason, and because the people are worn out, so few in number, and somewhat discouraged, I would not dare to divide them at all, since we are in such a thickly populated country, if it were not for the grave necessity of getting into touch with Juan de Porras, believing that he is bringing the things we lack. [For this purpose] Captain Don Cristóbal is setting out with ten soldiers on horseback and six on mules, in the belief that Juan de Porras must now be in Atache where he stayed with me. For this reason we are forced to detach this party, especially as we know that all the natives we left behind are of good disposition and friendly. They even make us happy with the things they want to

give us, and if your Lordship perchance has not obtained supplies, it would be very desirable to have some men go out very promptly and provide us with the things we lack; I should consider it more fitting that you yourself should go. See to it that you are not deceived into being detained there, for at least if you do not find land suitable for settling you comply with the duty of your position and close the mouths of base criticism. And now is the time, for now the dearth of food experienced hitherto will not have to be endured, the green corn and the beans being ready to gather. I consider the best land for settling to be that of Talpa, Ynicula, and Atache, because the country is suitable for cattle and there are some small tracts of grass lands there. Do not marvel that the country does not please the friars, for they are inclined to have their own way and not to do anything else; they are the ones who are the most discontented. I do not think that this is because of lack of natives, but because the soil in this country is poor, and they do not share in the assistance which may come from New Spain. This camp is in good health, thanks to our Lord; it has lost only two horses, one of which was drowned, and the other died of colic. We are in dire need of supplies, and I am fearful the people here may rise against us when they harvest their crops; for now, thinking we are only passing through, they give us burden-bearers and all we ask for in order to get us out of the country. The chief whom Cossa sent to go with us and be a messenger goes with us without any change. We are all going thither, as he says that there is plenty of food and that the chief is there awaiting us. I do not know what will happen; we shall get on as best we may until Don Cristóbal returns from Atache; and even though we may suffer for lack of food, and have not as much provender for the horses as is necessary, we shall have to endure it, for it does not seem to us wise to break with these people. I have need that your Lordship be so kind as to remember me in case horses have come, and send me some. This camp lacks shoes; if this can be remedied there by bringing us some, they are very necessary. At least there are some soles, which can be mended with deerskin. We also need some things to trade, for we have none, and I owe more than the king possesses. As Don Cristóbal will write you what you should in our opinion do in this situation, I will say no more. May our Lord guard the very illustrious person of your Lordship with the increase and condition which your servants desire for you.

Apica, July 6, 1560. We must be twenty leagues from Coosa, according to what we have understood from the interpreters.

Very illustrious, I kiss your feet, Your servant,
[signed:] Mateo del Saz.

267. End of July, 1560. Fray Domingo Salazar to Francisco Navarro.

Translated in Priestley, Luna Papers, *I, 245.*

To the very gentle Franciso Navarro in Nanipacana.

Most Amiable Sir: Jesus Christ our Lord be always with you. I set about writing this to forefend the complaints you would make against me if I should not, rather than because of any necessity which might exist; for all that I can say by way of an account you will learn from those who are going, and other things they will not tell there is no reason for me to tell.

There must be, as we now think, one hundred and twenty or one hundred and thirty leagues between here and Nanipacana. All the country we have seen is like that seen there, in some parts worse in a few places better. There has not been found in all that we have seen any place where Spaniards could settle even though we should take the Indians' own lands away from them. These Indians of Coosa are of very good disposition; they give us what we need and do what we command them very willingly and with joy. It gives me great pain to see that people of such good will are not in a place where they might be taught, although the secrets of God are so great that

affairs are directed whither man least expects. The language is another one, very different and more difficult, although they have some words from there. They all go as naked as they were born except the women, who dress according to the custom of those there. Our people are in good health but broken and worn by the journey. Besides, they are very discontented with the country, and it kills them to tell them they will have to stay in it. May the Lord remedy it as he may. These gentlemen are writing together there to the governor, who will see what is his duty. I am hoping for a letter from you as long as this one is short, although it would be better if we could see each other; but if we do not meet, write me at length how the governor is and the rest of the gentlemen and captains; how it has gone with them there; who went to New Spain; who have died; how the fathers are, and what news there is of the father vicar; and if it is possible do not fail to come to see us, for there is little danger. Give Juan Muñoz de Zayas our salutations, and do you and he receive those of Father Fray Domingo. I do not write to him because this letter seems to me enough, for he already knows how few gifts I possess, and in this I do nothing but fulfil my duty. Father Fray Domingo and I are well, though very worn and fatigued. There is no more [to say] except that the Lord, whose we are, may do with us as with a thing of his own, Amen. Dated at Coosa, the end of July, 1560. The characteristic or climate of the country is that every week it rains, or nearly every week.

Your servant,

[signed:] Fray Domingo.

268. August 1, 1560. Fray Domingo de la Anunciación and others to Tristán de Luna.

Translated in Priestley, Luna Papers, *I, 223–233.*

Inasmuch as accounts given by each one in particular, although very true, cannot fail to disagree in something because ordinarily the judgments and opinions which many persons have of one and the same thing are diverse, and inasmuch as all of us who came on this expedition at your Lordship's command are equally your servants and as such desire the good success of affairs, especially of this one which is so important, we have agreed to relieve your Lordship of the confusion which many accounts might produce and become the reason whereby orders might not be given as appropriately as is desirable, and all to unite as we have hitherto done in all cases which have occurred, giving with one opinion and will an account of all that has happened until now, together with this our opinion, so that when you have seen all that concerns this place, your Lordship may command and order what will be most pleasing.

The country which we have seen thus far, which must be one hundred and twenty leagues a little more or less between Nanipacana and here, is all of one character and appearance. It has the same trees and herbs, so that one who has seen it there has seen it all, save that the country about here is in some parts more densely forested, and has more brambles and undergrowth. High rugged mountains like those of Spain or New Spain we have not seen, although we have passed many hills and rough stony broken ground which this land was said to lack.

The people of this land are more numerous than in that land, for the towns from fifteen or sixteen leagues back of where we now are and from here to Coosa are, according to what the Indians say, near to each other, although we have seen no large towns, not even as large as Nanipacana. Neither have we seen many people together in the towns, but these are close together, and by the fields which are found and the roads which cross them, we judge that the land is [well] populated. In character these people appear more domestic and probably more easily subjugated, but not to be of the high culture of those down below, for here the men go entirely as naked as when they were born, and in no town have we seen a temple such as those to be found there.

The great fatigue which we endured from the time we took leave of you until we reached Caxiti, whence we sent Juan de Porras with the people and the food, you will have heard of already. It continued with us for ten days' march farther because we could not until then find a place to rest. After those ten days we reached a town called Onachiqui. It is, we believe, the first town of Coosa. Here, finding the Indians very different from the preceding ones, for these did not flee from their houses, we remained in this town seven days, where they brought us food to our lodging without our going to search for it, and the towns we have found from there on have done the same thing. Although they do not give us maize in as great abundance as our necessity requires, yet we think it better to conserve the peace by suffering some lack rather than cause war to break out by searching for an abundance.

As it is the end of the year the maize is beginning to become exhausted, therefore we cannot stay in each town as long as we should like. But we stay in each of them as long as possible, and we travel as slowly as we can, first in order not to get too far away from your Lordship until we hear from Juan de Porras, in search of whom Captain Don Cristóbal Ramírez de Arellano sets out to-day with ten men on horseback and six who go on the king's mules. They are to bring back the salt and peppers and the horseshoes which are to come in the shallop, of all of which we are in dire necessity. The other reason why we move slowly is to rest the people and the horses from the fatigue of the road, for however much haste we may make with ourselves and with them, we cannot [stay] in this town or in others farther on until we reach Ulibaali, the town mentioned so often by Soto's followers, which must be, as the Indians indicate, five or six leagues from here. There we expect that Captain Don Cristóbal will find us when he returns with the supplies we are expecting from below.

Regarding how the land to which we have come appears to us and how we like it, not only those of us who are writing the present letter but all who are in the camp are agreed in one opinion. This is that, aside from the land of Talpa—the forest of which is more open and the soil of better quality, and some other pieces of ground which are between this province and Atache, where there are some savannas for cattle and good river valleys for planting, which continued along the road we traveled for some six leagues, not all savannas nor good land, but in these six leagues only did we see savannas—all that we have seen is densely forested damp land in which no cattle of any kind at all can be raised, nor can anything be sown without first clearing it, which appears impossible. Hence it seems to us all that no settlement can be made in any of the country which we have, as has been said, left behind us. These gentlemen who came with Soto and are now in this camp say that all of Coosa is just like what we have already seen. We do not swear to this however, but only to what we know from what we have actually seen.

What your Lordship should do at present is that you yourself, or some of those gentlemen and captains, if any great and legitimate reason prevents your Lordship coming, should at once set out with all the people possible and follow our route for three very urgent reasons. The first is in order that the people who set out may give way to those who stay, and the supplies not become so quickly exhausted; for those who set out at this time cannot experience any want.

The second is in order that you may with your own eyes see this land of Talpa and Atache and if it is at all suitable to colonize, it would be fitting to make a settlement there. For if that part does not please you, from there to where we are now there is no part at all where any settlement can be made. The third is in order that the people who come may serve as protection to us who are here; for we are so few and so poorly equipped that if [the Indians] attack us we shall run great risk, or it may be that they will cease to have respect for us, seeing us so few and with no support. Another result would be obtained by your coming to Atache, for up to there everything necessary for the camp can be brought up in the barks, though this is impossible by land. From there on to here each man can gradually bring up his provisions by means of the pack animals you may have; especially as with the peace we have with these people, they may be kept from town to town and aid us to bring up the clothing which may be brought on the barks, for they are [serving as carriers] now for us of their own free will, and without reluctance they give us people to carry the supplies of those who march on foot. This has been a great relief to the camp, for those on foot were no longer able to take a step forward. When the Indians go back we give them some trifle, with which they go away well content.

While you are coming to Atache we will examine all that remains to be seen of Coosa, and if there is any part which is suitable for a settlement, you [will be] in a very good place for us to give you very prompt information about it by means of the Indians, who will go that far very willingly; then we can very quickly join each other, be it by your coming up to where we are and where there may be opportunity to settle, or be it by our going down to where you are if there is none. Although the people of this land are very peaceable, they do not keep their women and clothing in their houses, wherefore we fear that when they have gathered their corn they will also themselves go into hiding. Hence it is needful that you make haste to come, so that before they reap their crops we may be in a place where we can provision ourselves for next year. Especially is it necessary [for us] to know at once about the people whom you may bring with you, so that they may find provisions in the camp; for if you delay a long time they might find themselves in the extremity of hunger as all we people of this camp now find ourselves in extreme need of shoes—which we are all now without—and of salt, peppers, horseshoes, and other things without which one passes this life badly. Your Lordship will be pleased to order that these necessities be provided as soon as possible in the manner already indicated, for the winter is very cruel in this country, there is very bad equipment with which to venture to await it, and the hardships which these gentlemen and soldiers have endured in the service of his Majesty and your Lordship very well deserve that you should keep this obligation to them in mind.

After this letter had been written and the departure of Captain Don Cristóbal decided upon, it seemed right to us to send you a complete account and to defer his departure until we should reach Coosa. Between Apica and Coosa there is some improvement in the land over that up to here, also the country is more thickly settled and the forest in some parts less dense; the natives are of better disposition, for they have always given us carriers and food apparently with little reluctance. We reached this settlement of Coosa in sixteen days. Here we found the chief and all his people in their houses, and they made no move to take away their food or women, as if they had talked and had dealings with us before this. We took up our lodging in a small savanna one or two arquebus shots' distance from the town. Here they provide us with necessities—I mean corn, beans, and other little things for which we barter. They are apparently such good Indians that they are at ease with all the Spaniards, and show good will. The ration which they give us for each day is a *casyco* of corn for each Spaniard and horse. The servants are given no ration because they are few, except in the cases of some who have a double number of servants. With these there is an arrangement to give them a ration now and then for the servants. There are also roasting ears and pumpkins, which have their place; so that, blessed be our Lord, there is no lack of food, nor do we even expect to lack it. As to making a settlement, it appears to us that the country is not as well suited for it as we thought. It seems very densely forested, and inasmuch as the Indians have the good part of it occupied, if a settlement were to be made it would be imperative to take their lands from them. So for this reason and for others it is desirable that you come or send orders as to what is to be done. For even though the natives have been observed to be so disposed that they can be utilized profitably, the country is so poor and with such scant opportunities for gainful pursuits that we think it would be difficult to maintain ourselves in it. Also in deciding the matter care should be taken to search and inquire whether there is anything useful for the service of God and his Majesty; and it must be sought in such a way as to fulfil what your Lordship commands. We are really deeply indebted to these Indians as far as we have seen up to the present; for if twenty or thirty or ten Indians are needed to build a camp or a house they give them, showing good will in the matter. It seems that certain [other] Indians have entered their lands, demanded them and usurped them, and in so doing have caused them injuries and vexations. They have occupied the roads of these natives and cut off their communications with their own related groups, preventing trade and communication between them; moreover, they have attacked them on the roads and given them many other troubles. [These Indians] asked us, as they were our friends, had given us of whatever they had, and had placed themselves under the protection of the king, Don Felipe our lord, that we would show them favor and aid so that those other Indians should not prevent their communication, trade, and intercourse thus with their own natural lord. For precisely these reasons had they come to serve us and trade with us,

so that we might preserve to them the use of the roads and passes. In this connection they wanted to know whether we were going to deal with them in friendship and truth. So for this reason and for the others we decided to join together to give your Lordship a report of everything. It has appeared to us right to give them favor and help, in which we are influenced by many causes which move us thereto, which your Lordship will realize better. We also understand that this land is in a good district for towns, and if Captain Don Cristóbal arrives where you are you may inform yourself from him concerning whatever you may desire, for he can give you an account as an eyewitness. The people and the horses are well, although both are unshod. Will you not provide [shoes] for they are indeed essential?

May our Lord guard and give greater increase to the very illustrious person of your Lordship, as we your servants desire. Coosa, August 1, 1560. Illustrious sir, your servants kiss your Lordship's hands.

> [signed:] Fray Domingo de la Anunciación.
> Mateo del Sauz.
> Don Cristóbal Ramírez de Arellano.
> Don Alonso de Castilla.
> Gonzalo Sánchez de Aguilar.
> Álvaro Nieto.
> Rodrigo Vázquez.

269. August 1, 1560. Fray Domingo de la Anunciación and others to Tristán de Luna.

Translated in Priestley, Luna Papers, I, 235–243.

We do not think that we can in any way comply with our duty to your Lordship, all we who are in this land, better than by giving a summary and true relation of all that we have seen in it together with what we think of it. But since accounts given by each one in detail, however true they may be, cannot help disagreeing in something, since the opinions and judgments of many persons about one and the same thing are so divergent, we have agreed, in order to avoid this divergence, that we who are writing the present letter shall unite [in this account] thus serving your Lordship, for there is nothing else we can do.

From the letters your Lordship received by the bark sent from this country you will have learned how by command of the governor we set out from Nanipacana on this journey to Coosa, first, to provide the camp with some food, of which there was already great necessity and greater want was anticipated, and second, to find some place where a settlement could be made, for in the territory until then seen there was none such.

We set out for this purpose on the second day of the feast of Easter, which was April 15 of this present year. We thought to find food, with which we set out very scantily supplied as there was little in the camp, within three or four days' march; but we went for forty-three days without being able to find any corn to give the horses, and there were many days on which we ate none ourselves. We sustained ourselves on some herbs and blackberries which were beginning to ripen, some nuts and oak acorns which, if not prepared as the Indians know how to do, are too bitter to eat.

Forty days after we had set out from there we received a letter from the governor through some friendly Indians, from which we learned of the great straits from hunger in which all the camp was placed, without any hope of relief except from God and your Lordship. As this would have to come by sea, we were afraid it might be delayed in coming for a time longer than those below could hold out. It pleased our Lord that at the time the letter came we had chanced upon a little corn which the Indians were keeping hidden away, and although we felt the need of it which our past hunger had given us, we decided to use it to aid those we thought to be in greater need. And so, with two or three canoes which we found in the river, and some rafts which we made of canes and wood, we sent about thirty-five or forty fanegas of corn with six men to take it; but we have heard nothing of the result.

After saying goodbye to those who went on the rafts, we went on for another ten or twelve days' journey with somewhat less trouble than we had had up to that point. At the end of that time we came upon the first towns of Coosa. There the Indians received us with good will, and gave us food without our having to go and forage for it as we had done up to that time at great trouble and danger to our persons, for all the towns behind us had been deserted and the food had been hidden. We rested from our hardships endured, and the men and the horses were recuperated. We were fifty-seven days in reaching this first town of Coosa, which is called Onachiqui, and according to the days' marches which we made in this time we believe the road to be from ninety to one hundred leagues long. The roads are traveled with more difficulty in this country than in others previously discovered, for, besides the dearth of food which we have experienced until now in all the expeditions which have been made, the thing which has been most keenly felt is that the men have had to travel on foot loaded with their equipment and rations, and arms.

The hardships we have all endured on this and other expeditions, being the natural expectation in a new country, neither terrify us nor is there any point in setting them down here, for we are very happy to have passed through them in the service of God and the king our lord and at your Lordship's command, and are determined to suffer greater ones in the same cause.

The people of this land of Coosa seem to us to be more peaceful and to confide in us more than all those we have left behind, though they are not so confident as to neglect to put their property and women in safety, while they wait for us in their towns with a few serving women and bring us food to our quarters. Ordinarily we camp somewhat apart from the towns, lest the horses or any uncontrolled persons injure the cornfields or raise a commotion among the inhabitants. They do not give us food in as great abundance as our need requires, but we think best to preserve the peace by suffering a little want rather than to bring on war by seeking abundance.

Temporizing thus with all the towns which came out to meet us in peace, and leaving them very good friends of ours, three months after we had left Nanipacana we arrived at the town of Coosa, where the lord of the country resides. This Indian received us with apparent great good will, and gave us to understand that he was delighted at our arrival; and when we declared, through interpreters whom we had brought, the purpose for which we had come, he announced himself our friend and submitted himself to the protection of the king our lord.

The character and quality of this country, at least of that part over which we have traveled, which taking in all the area traversed must be something over two hundred leagues, may be described very briefly.

The country is generally flat though it is not without a few not very high hills, on which there are plenty of stones and gravel, which we were told were not to be found here. It is very densely forested, with many creeks and many copious rivers, from which it comes to have numerous swamps and to be very humid. The trees of this country are mostly pines, oaks, walnuts, and chestnuts; of these the land is full, although there are some different ones along the banks of the rivers. We have seen very few fruits, but there are walnuts in great quantity although with very hard shells. There are a few chestnuts which though small and few are not inferior to those of Spain. On this road to Coosa we have found great quantities of blackberries, though not so many as they told us down there. We have also seen plums and hazel-nuts, but as they are not yet ripe we do not know how good they are. The climate of this country is unequal, with extremes of heat and cold. The rains do not come at fixed times, for it rains now as well as in winter.

The people in this country have good constitutions and appearance; although they live in a cool country they have as brown a color as those down there. Their dress is what nature gave them, except that the women wear kirtles made of thread from mulberry roots; they are about two palms wide and with them they cover their privy parts. They all live together in little towns, for so far we have seen none which contains as many as one hundred and fifty houses, and very few which number above forty or fifty. They have winter and summer houses. The winter houses are all covered with earth, and they sow whatever they like over them. All the towns have a good-sized plaza outside the town, in which there is a pole like the *rollo* of Spain; they are very tall, and they have them for their sports. There are some towns inclosed by a pair of walls as high as a man's stature, and although there must be something between them yet it is of no value [for defense]. There are temples in some of the towns, but they are as rudely constructed and as little frequented as is uncouth the religion which they practice in them.

All the towns that there are in this country are on the banks of the rivers, for all the rest is so densely wooded that it can by no means be inhabited; this, we think, is the reason there are so few people in this country, for even those who are here have very limited tracts of land; except that which is cleared around the towns, all the rest is claimed by the forest. The principal reason why we left Nanipacana was, as said above, to search for a site possessing the conditions which his Majesty and you in his royal name command. There must be from Coosa where we now are, to Nanipacana where we started, one hundred and twenty or one hundred and thirty leagues, and in all of this we have seen no location where a settlement of Spaniards could be made, even though we might be willing to turn the natives out of their houses, for the reason that the cleared land is so scant that it does not even suffice for the natives themselves. So that no cattle of any kind can be raised here to the owner's profit, without which and other sources of gain that this country lacks, your Lordship may readily see how the Spanish people could [not] live.

This province of Coosa is somewhat better as regards the land and the forest, and much more densely populated than any we have left behind. There is a mountain range to the north of the town, which runs east and west. It is fairly high and well-wooded, but up to this time we do not know where it begins or ends. This town is situated on the banks of two small rivers which unite within it. Around the town there are some good savannas, and a valley well peopled with Indians where they plant all that they raise to eat. After one leaves here all the rest is forest.

As we have had no news from the governor since we left Nanipacana, and as we know not whether the rafts and canoes which we sent laden with corn arrived safely or not, we are in some uncertainty; we have therefore agreed to send Captain Don Cristóbal with twelve men on horses to the place where we took leave of the canoes, and if he obtains there no news of how it fared with those who went [in them], it has been concerted that he shall go as far as Nanipacana and give the governor an account of all we have so far seen.

Captain Don Cristóbal is not taking more

people with him—although for such a long road through enemy country they are very few—because we are altogether so few that if the need were not so urgent we would not allow ourselves to be divided; for when we set out from the camp we were not more than forty men on horseback and one hundred on foot, and of these we now lack thirteen who left the road and went to the main camp, and two or three horses that have died.

We are writing to the governor another letter signed with our names, in which we give account of everything up to this time, and ask him to send to command what he wishes us to do. We believe that, because the distance is so great and the roads as bad as they are between here and where the governor is, when we are reunited it will no longer be the season in which we can march until the winter passes. During this interval your Lordship will receive notice of everything there is here, and may send to command us what you wish us to do. For although we have on this march worn out all the shoes we brought, we have not outworn the good will we have to serve your most illustrious Lordship.

What we think of doing until we receive news from below is to find a good place in which to pass the winter and provide ourselves there with food in order not to see ourselves in the same want as last year. May our Lord guard the most illustrious person of your Lordship, and give you increase in your condition. Dated at Coosa, August 1, 1560. We kiss your most illustrious Lordship's hands.

[signed:] Fray Domingo de la Anunciación.
Mateo del Saz.
Don Cristóbal Ramírez de Arellano.
Don Alonso de Castilla.
Gonzalo Sánchez de Aguilar.
Álvaro Nieto.
Rodrigo Vázquez.

270. Circa 1560. Padilla's account of Coosa.

Apart from The Luna Papers, *the principal authority (who writes very much from the standpoint of the Dominican Order) is Fray Augustín Davíla Padilla,* Historia de la fundación y discurso de la provincia de Santiago de Mexico de la Orden de Predicadores *(Brussels, 1625); a translation by Fanny Bandelier of his important account of the Coosa Indians (pp. 205–217), first published in Madrid, 1596, was given in John R. Swanton, "Early history of the Greek Indians and their neighbours," Smithsonian Institution, Bureau of American Ethnology, Bulletin, no. 73 (1922), pp. 231–239, from which it is reprinted here.*

The whole province was called Coza, taking its name from the most famous city within its boundaries. It was God's will that they should soon get within sight of that place which had been so far famed and so much thought about and, yet, it did not have above thirty houses, or a few more. There were seven little hamlets in its district, five of them smaller and two larger than Coza itself, which name prevailed for the fame it had enjoyed in its antiquity. It looked so much worse to the Spaniards for having been depicted so grandly, and they had thought it to be so much better. Its inhabitants had been said to be innumerable, the site itself as being wider and more level than Mexico, the springs had been said to be many and of very clear water, food plentiful and gold and silver in abundance, which, without judging rashly, was that which the Spaniards desired most. Truly the land was fertile, but it lacked cultivation. There was much forest, but little fruit, because as it was not cultivated the land was all unimproved and full of thistles and weeds. Those they had brought along as guides, being people who had been there before, declared that they must have been bewitched when this country seemed to them so rich and populated as they had stated. The arrival of the Spaniards in former years had driven the Indians up into the forests, where they preferred to live among the wild beasts who did no harm to them, but whom they could master, than among the Spaniards at whose hands they received injuries, although they were good to them. Those from Coza received the guests well, liberally, and with kindness, and the Spaniards appreciated this, the more so as the actions of their predecessors did not call for it. They gave them each day four fanegas of corn for their men and their horses, of which latter they had fifty and none of which, even during their worst sufferings from hunger, they had wanted to kill and eat, well knowing that the Indians were more afraid of horses, and that one horse gave them a more warlike appearance, than the fists of two men together. But the soldiers did not look for maize; they asked most diligently where the gold could be found and where the silver, because only for the hopes of this as a dessert had they endured the fasts of the painful journey. Every day little groups of them went searching through the country and they found it all deserted and without news of gold. From only two tribes were there news about gold—one was the Oliuahali which they had just left; the others were the Napochies, who lived farther on. Those were enemies to those of Coza, and they had very stubborn warfare with each other, the Napochies avenging some offense they had received at the hands of the people of Coza. The latter Indians showed themselves such good friends of the Spaniards that our men did not know what recompense to give them nor what favor to do them. The wish to favor those who humiliate themselves goes hand in hand with ambition. The Spaniards have the fame of not being very humble and the people of Coza who had surrendered themselves experienced now their favors. Not only were they careful not to cause them any damage or injury, but gave them many things they had brought along, outside of what they gave in the regular exchange for maize. Their gratitude went even so far that the sergeant major, who accompanied the expedition as captain of the 200 men, told the Indians that if they wanted his favor and the strength of his men to make war on their enemies, they could have them readily, just as they had been ready to receive him and his men and favor them with food. Those of Coza thought very highly of this offer, and in the hope of its fulfillment kept the Spaniards such a long time with them, giving them as much maize each day as was possible, the land being so poor and the villages few and small. The Spaniards were nearly 300 men between small and big [young and old] ones, masters and servants, and the time they all ate there was three months, the Indians making great efforts to sustain such a heavy expense for the sake of their companionship as well as for the favors they expected from them later. All the deeds in this life are done for some interested reason and, just as the Spaniards showed friend-

ship for them that they might not shorten their provisions and perhaps escape to the forests, so the Indians showed their friendship, hoping that with their aid they could take full vengeance of their enemies. And the friars were watching, hoping that a greater population might be discovered to convert and maintain in the Christian creed. Those small hamlets had until then neither seen friars nor did they have any commodities to allow monks to live and preach among them; neither could they embrace and maintain the Christian faith without their assistance. . . .

Very bitter battles did the Napochies have with those from Coza, but justice was greatly at variance with success. Those from Coza were in the right, but the Napochies were victorious. In ancient times the Napochies were tributaries of the Coza people, because this place (Coza) was always recognized as head of the kingdom and its lord was considered to stand above the one of the Napochies. Then the people from Coza began to decrease while the Napochies were increasing until they refused to be their vassals, finding themselves strong enough to maintain their liberty which they abused. Then those of Coza took to arms to reduce the rebels to their former servitude, but the most victories were on the side of the Napochies. Those from Coza remained greatly affronted as well from seeing their ancient tribute broken off, as because they found themselves without strength to restore it. On that account they had lately stopped their fights, although their sentiments remained the same and for several months they had not gone into the battlefield, for fear lest they return vanquished, as before. When the Spaniards, grateful for good treatment, offered their assistance against their enemies, they accepted immediately, in view of their rabid thirst for vengeance. All the love they showed to the Spaniards was in the interest that they should not forget their promise. Fifteen days had passed, when, after a consultation among themselves, the principal men went before the captain and thus spoke:

"Sir, we are ashamed not to be able to serve you better, and as we would wish, but this is only because we are afflicted with wars and trouble with some Indians who are our neighbors and are called Napochies. Those have always been our tributaries acknowledging the nobility of our superiors, but a few years ago they rebelled and stopped their tribute and they killed our relatives and friends. And when they can not insult us with their deeds, they do so with words. Now, it seems only reasonable, that you, who have so much knowledge, should favor and increase ours. Thou, Señor, hast given us thy word when thou knowest our wish to help us if we should need thy assistance against our enemies. This promise we, thy servants, beg of thee humbly now to fulfill and we promise to gather the greatest army of our men [people], and with thy good order and efforts helping us, we can assure our victory. And when once reinstated in our former rights, we can serve thee ever so much better."

When the captain had listened to the well concerted reasoning of those of Coza, he replied to them with a glad countenance, that, aside from the fact that it has always been his wish to help and assist them, it was a common cause now, and he considered it convenient or even necessary to communicate with all the men, especially with the friars, who were the ministers of God, and the spiritual fathers of the army; that he would treat the matter with eagerness, procuring that their wishes to be attended to and that the following day he would give them the answer, according to the resolutions taken in the matter.

He [the captain] called to council the friars, the captains, and all the others, who, according to custom had a right to be there, and, the case being proposed and explained, it was agreed that only two captains with their men should go, one of cavalry, the other of infantry, and the other four bodies of their little army remain in camp with the rest of the people. Then they likewise divided the monks, Fray Domingo de la Anunciación going with the new army and Fray Domingo de Salazar remaining with the others in Coza. The next day, those who wished so very dearly that it be in their favor, came for the answer. The captain gave them an account of what had been decided, ordering them to get ready, because he in person desired to accompany them with the two Spanish regiments and would take along, if necessary, the rest of the Spanish army, which would readily come to their assistance. The people from Coza were very glad and thanked the captain very much, offering to dispose everything quickly for the expedition. Within six days they were all ready. The Spaniards did not want to take more than fifty men, twenty-five horsemen and

twenty-five on foot. The Indians got together almost three hundred archers, very skillful and certain in the use of that arm, in which, the fact that it is the only one they have has afforded them remarkable training. Every Indian uses a bow as tall as his body; the string is not made of hemp but of animal nerve sinew well twisted and tanned. They all use a quiver full of arrows made of long, thin, and very straight rods, the points of which are of flint, curiously cut in triangular form, the wings very sharp and mostly dipped in some very poisonous and deadly substance. They also use three or four feathers tied on their arrows to insure straight flying, and they are so skilled in shooting them that they can hit a flying bird. The force of the flint arrowheads is such that at a moderate distance they can pierce a coat of mail.

The Indians set forward, and it was beautiful to see them divided up in eight different groups, two of which marched together in the four directions of the earth (north, south, east, and west), which is the style in which the children of Israel used to march, three tribes together in the four directions of the world to signify that they would occupy it all. They were well disposed, and in order to fight their enemies, the Napochies, better, they lifted their bows, arranged the arrows gracefully and shifted the band of the quiver as if they wanted to beseech it to give up new shafts quickly; others examined the necklace [collar] to which the arrow points were fastened and which hung down upon their shoulders, and they all brandished their arms and stamped with their feet on the ground, all showing how great was their wish to fight and how badly they felt about the delay. Each group had its captain, whose emblem was a long stave of two brazas in height and which the Indians call Otatl and which has at its upper end several white feathers. These were used like banners, which everyone had to respect and obey. This was also the custom among the heathens who affixed on such a stave the head of some wild animal they had killed on a hunt, or the one of some prominent enemy whom they had killed in battle. To carry the white feathers was a mystery, for they insisted that they did not wish war with the Napochies, but to reduce them to the former condition of tributaries to them, the Coza people, and pay all since the time they had refused obedience. In order to give the Indian army more power and importance the captain had ordered a horse to be fixed with all its trappings for the lord or caçique of the Indians, and as the poor Indian had never seen much less used one, he ordered a negro to guide the animal. The Indians in those parts had seen horses very rarely, or only at a great distance and to their sorrow, nor were there any in New Spain before the arrival of the Spaniards. The caçique went or rather rode in the rear guard, not less flattered by the obsequiousness of the captain than afraid of his riding feat. Our Spaniards also left Coza, always being careful to put up their tents or lodgings apart from the Indians so that the latter could not commit any treachery if they so intended. One day, after they had all left Coza at a distance of about eight leagues, eight Indians, who appeared to be chiefs, entered the camp of the Spaniards, running and without uttering a word; they also passed the Indian camp and, arriving at the rear guard where their caçique was, took him down from his horse, and the one who seemed to be the highest in rank among the eight, put him on his shoulders, and the others caught him, both by his feet and arms, and they ran with great impetuosity back the same way they had come. These runners emitted very loud howlings, continuing them as long as their breath lasted, and when their wind gave out they barked like big dogs until they had recovered it in order to continue the howls and prolonged shouts. The Spaniards, though tired from the sun and hungry, observing the ceremonious superstitions of the Indians, upon seeing and hearing the mad music with which they honored their lord, could not contain their laughter in spite of their sufferings. The Indians continued their run to a distance of about half a league from where the camp was, until they arrived on a little plain near the road which had been carefully swept and cleaned for the purpose. There had been constructed in the center of that plain a shed or theatre nine cubits in height with a few rough steps to mount. Upon arriving near the theatre the Indians first carried their lord around the plain once on their shoulders, then they lowered him at the foot of the steps, which he mounted alone. He remained standing while all the Indians were seated on the plain, waiting to see what their master would do. The Spaniards were on their guard about these wonderful and quite new ceremonies and desirous to know their mysteries and understand their object and meaning. The caçique began to promenade with great majesty on the theatre, looking with severity over the world. Then they gave him a most beautiful fly flap which they had ready, made of showy birds' plumes of great value. As soon as he held it in his hand he pointed it towards the land of the Napochies in the same fashion as would the astrologer the alidade [cross-staff], or the pilot the sextant in order to take the altitude at sea. After having done this three or four times they gave him some little seeds like fern seeds, and he put them into his mouth and began to grind and pulverize them with his teeth and molars, pointing again three or four times towards the land of the Napochies as he had done before. When the seeds were all ground he began to throw them from his mouth around the plain in very small pieces. Then he turned towards his captains with a glad countenance and he said to them: "Console yourselves, my friends; our journey will have a prosperous outcome; our enemies will be conquered and their strength broken, like those seeds which I ground between my teeth." After pronouncing these few words, he descended from the scaffold and mounted his horse, continuing his way, as he had done hitherto. The Spaniards were discussing what they had seen, and laughing about this grotesque ceremony, but the blessed father, Fray Domingo de la Anunciación, mourned over it, for it seemed sacrilege to him and a pact with the demon, those ceremonials which those poor people used in their blind idolatry. They all arrived, already late, at the banks of a river, and they decided to rest there in order to enjoy the coolness of the water to relieve the heat of the earth. When the Spaniards wanted to prepare something to eat they did not find anything. There had been a mistake, greatly to the detriment of all. The Indians had understood that the Spaniards carried food for being so much more dainty and delicate people, and the Spaniards thought the Indians had provided it, since they (the Spaniards) had gone along for their benefit. Both were to blame, and they all suffered the penalty. They remained without eating a mouthful that night and until the following one, putting down that privation more on the list of those of the past. They put up the two camps at a stone's throw, being thus always on guard by this division, for, although the Indians were at present very much their friends, they are people who make the laws of friendship doubtful and they had once been greatly offended with the Spaniards, and were now their reconciled friends.

With more precaution than satiety the Spaniards procured repose that night, when, at the tenth hour, our camp being at rest, a great noise was heard from that of the Indians, with much singing, and dances after their fashion, in the luxury of big fires which they had started in abundance, there being much firewood in that place. Our men were on their guard until briefly told by the interpreter, whom they had taken along, that there was no occasion for fear on the part of the Spaniards, but a feasting and occasion of rejoicing on that of the Indians. They felt more assured yet when they saw that the Indians did not move from their place and they now watched most attentively to enjoy their ceremonials as they had done in the past, asking the interpreter what they were saying to one another. After they had sung and danced for a long while the cacique seated himself on an elevated place, the six captains drawing near him, and he began to speak to them admonishing the whole army to be brave, restore the glory of their ancestors, and avenge the injuries they had received. "Not one of you," he said, "can help considering as particularly his this enterprise, besides being that of all in common. Remember your relatives and you will see that not one among you has been exempt from mourning those who have been killed at the hands of the Napochies. Renew the dominion of your ancestors and detest the audacity of the tributaries who have tried to violate it. If we came alone, we might be obliged to see the loss of life, but not of our honor; how much more now, that we have in our company the brave and vigorous Spaniards, sons of the sun and relatives of the gods." The captains had been listening very attentively and humbly to the reasoning of their lord, and as he finished they approached him one by one in order, repeating to him in more or fewer words this sentence: "Señor, the more than sufficient reason for what thou hast told us is known to us all; many are the damages the Napochies have done us, who besides having denied us the obedience they have inherited from their ancestors, have shed the blood of those of our kin and country. For many a day have we wished for this occasion to show our courage and serve thee, especially now, that thy great prudence has won

us the favor and endeavor of the brave Spaniards. I swear to thee, Señor, before our gods, to serve thee with all my men in this battle and not turn our backs on these enemies the Napochies, until we have taken revenge." These words the captain accompanied by threats and warlike gestures, desirous (and as if calling for the occasion) to show by actions the truth of his words. All this was repeated by the second captain and the others in their order, and this homage finished, they retired for the rest of the night. The Spaniards were greatly surprised to find such obeisance used to their princes by people of such retired regions, usages which the Romans and other republics of considerable civilization practiced before they entered a war. Besides the oath the Romans made every first of January before their Emperor, the soldiers made another one to the captain under whose orders they served, promising never to desert his banner, nor evade the meeting of the enemy, but to injure him in every way. Many such examples are repeated since the time of Herodianus, Cornelius Tacitus, and Suetonius Tranquilus, with a particular reminiscence in the life of Galba. And it is well worth consideration that the power of nature should have created a similarity in the ceremonials among Indians and Romans in cases of war where good reasoning rules so that all be under the orders of the superiors and personal grievances be set aside for the common welfare. This oath the captains swore on the hands of their lord on that night because they expected to see their enemies on the following day very near by, or even be with them, and the same oath remained to be made by the soldiers to their captains. At daybreak hunger made them rise early, hoping to reach the first village of the Napochies in order to get something to eat, for they needed it very much. They traveled all that day, making their night's rest near a big river which was at a distance of two leagues from the first village of the enemy. There it seemed most convenient for the army to rest, in order to fall upon the village by surprise in the dead of night and kill them all, this being the intention of those from Coza. In order to attain better their intentions, they begged of the captain not to have the trumpet sounded that evening, which was the signal to all for prayer, greeting the queen of the Angels with the Ave Maria, which is the custom in all Christendom at nightfall. "The Napochies" said the people of Coza, "are ensnarers and always have their spies around those fields, and upon hearing the trumpet they would retire into the woods and we would remain without the victory we desire; and therefore the trumpet should not be sounded." Thus the signal remained unsounded for that one night, but the blessed father Fray Domingo de la Anunciación, with his pious devotion, went around to all the soldiers telling them to say the Ave Maria, and he who was bugler of the evangile now had become bugler of war in the service of the Holy Virgin Mary. That night those of Coza sent their spies into the village of the Napochies to see what they were doing and if they were careless on account of their ignorance of the coming of the enemy; or, if knowing it, they were on the warpath. At midnight the spies came back, well content, for they had noticed great silence and lack of watchfulness in that village, where, not only was there no sound of arms, but even the ordinary noises of inhabited places were not heard. "They all sleep," they said, "and are entirely ignorant of our coming, and as a testimonial that we have made our investigation of the enemies' village carefully and faithfully, we bring these ears of green corn, these beans, and calabashes, taken from the gardens which the Napochies have near their own houses." With those news the Coza people recovered new life and animation, and on that night all the soldiers made their oath to their captains, just as the captains had done on the previous one to their cacique. And our Spaniards enjoyed those ceremonies at closer quarters, since they had seen from the first ceremony that this was really war against Indians which was intended, and not craft against themselves. The Indians were now very ferocious, with a great desire to come in contact with their enemies. . . .

All of the Napochies had left their town, because without it being clear who had given them warning, they had received it, and the silence the spies had noticed in the village was not due to their carelessness but to their absence. The people of Coza went marching towards the village of the Napochies in good order, spreading over the country in small companies, each keeping to one road, thus covering all the exits from the village in order to kill all of their enemies, for they thought they were quiet and unprepared in their houses. When they entered the village they were astonished at the too great quiet and, finding the houses abandoned, they saw upon entering that their enemies had left them in a hurry, for they left even their food and in several houses they found it cooking on the fire, where now those poor men found it ready to season. They found in that village, which was quite complete, a quantity of maize, beans, and many pots filled with bear fat, bears abounding in that country and their fat being greatly prized. The highest priced riches which they could carry off as spoils were skins of deer and bear, which those Indians tanned in a diligent manner very nicely and with which they covered themselves or which they used as beds. The people of Coza were desirous of finding some Indians on whom to demonstrate the fury of their wrath and vengeance and they went looking for them very diligently, but soon they saw what increased their wrath. In a square situated in the center of the village they found a pole of about three estados in height which served as gallows or pillor where they affronted or insulted their enemies and also criminals. As in the past wars had been in favour of the Napochies, that pole was full of scalps of people from Coza. It was an Indian custom that the scalp of the fallen enemy was taken and hung on that pole. The dead had been numerous and the pole was quite peopled with scalps. It was a very great sorrow for the Coza people to see that testimonial of their ignominy which at once recalled the memory of past injuries. They all raised their voices in a furious wail, bemoaning the deaths of their relatives and friends. They shed many tears as well for the loss of their dead as for the affront to the living. Moved to compassion, the Spaniards tried to console them, but for a very long time the demonstrations of mourning did not give them a chance for a single word, nor could they do more than go around the square with extraordinary signs of compassion or sorrow for their friends or of wrath against their enemies. Then they [the Indians] got hold of one of the hatchets which the Spaniards had brought with them, and they cut down the dried out tree close to the ground, taking the scalps to bury them with the superstitious practices of their kind. With all this they became so furious and filled with vengeance, that everyone of them wished to have many hands and to be able to lay them all on the Napochies. They went from house to house looking for someone like enfuriated lions and they found only a poor strange Indian [from another tribe] who was ill and very innocent of those things, but as blind vengeance does not stop to consider, they tortured the poor Indian till they left him dying. Before he expired though, the good father Fray Domingo reached his side and told him, through the interpreter he had brought along, that if he wished to enjoy the eternal blessings of heaven, he should receive the blessed water of baptism and thereby become a Christian. He further gave him a few reasonings, the shortest possible as the occasion demanded, but the unfortunate Indian, with inherent idolatry and suffering from his fresh wounds, did not pay any attention to such good council, but delivered his soul to the demon as his ancestors before him had done. This greatly pained the blessed Father Domingo, because, as his greatest aim was to save souls, their loss was his greatest sorrow.

When the vindictive fury of the Coza people could not find any hostile Napochies on whom to vent itself, they wanted to burn the whole village and they started to do so. This cruelty caused much grief to the merciful Fray Domingo de la Anunciación, and upon his plea the captain told the people of Coza to put out the fires, and the same friar, through his interpreter, condemned their action, telling them that it was cowardice to take vengeance in the absence of the enemies whose flight, if it meant avowal of their deficiency, was so much more glory for the victors. All the courage which the Athenians and the Lacedemonians showed in their wars was nullified by the cruelty which they showed the vanquished. "How can we know," said the good father to the Spaniards, "whether the Indians of this village are not perhaps hidden in these forests, awaiting us in some narrow pass to strike us all down with their arrows? Don't allow, brethren, this cruel destruction by fire, so that God may not permit your own deaths at the hands of the inhabitants of this place [these houses]." The captain urged the cacique to have the fire stopped; and as he was tardy in ordering it, the captain told him in the name of Fray Domingo, that if the village was really to be burnt down, the Spaniards would all return because they considered this war of the fire as waged directly against them by burning down the houses, where was the food which they all needed so greatly at all times. Following this menace, the cacique ordered the

Indians to put out the fire which had already made great headway and to subdue which required the efforts of the whole army. When the Indians were all quieted, the cacique took possession of the village in company with his principal men and with much singing and dancing, accompanied by the music of badly tuned flutes, they celebrated their victories.

The abundance of maize in that village was greater than had been supposed and the cacique ordered much of it to be taken to Coza so that the Spaniards who had remained there should not lack food. His main intention was to reach or find the enemy, leaving enough people in that village [of the Napochies] to prove his possession and a garrison of Spanish soldiers, which the captain asked for greater security. He then left to pursue the fugitives. They left in great confusion, because they did not know where to find a trace of the flight which a whole village had taken and although the people of Coza endeavored diligently to find out whether they had hidden in the forests, they could not obtain any news more certain than their own conjectures. "It can not be otherwise," they said, "than that the enemy, knowing that we were coming with the Spaniards became suspicious of the security of their forests and went to hide on the great water." When the Spaniards heard the name of great water, they thought it might be the sea, but it was only a great river, which we call the River of the Holy Spirit, the source of which is in some big forests of the country called La Florida. It is very deep and of the width of two harquebuse-shots. In a certain place which the Indians knew, it became very wide, losing its depth, so that it could be forded and it is there where the Napochies of the first village had passed, and also those who lived on the bank of that river, who, upon hearing the news, also abandoned their village, passing the waters of the Oquechiton, which is the name the Indians give that river and which means in our language the great water (la grande agua). Before the Spaniards arrived at this little hamlet however, they saw on the flat roof (azotea) of an Indian house, two Indians who were on the look out to see whether the Spaniards were pursuing the people of the two villages who had fled across the river. The horsemen spurred their horses and, when the Indians on guard saw them, they were so surprised by their monstrosity [on horseback] that they threw themselves down the embankment towards the river, without the Spaniards being able to reach them, because the bank was very steep and the Indians very swift. One of them was in such a great hurry that he left a great number of arrows behind which he had tied up in a skin, in the fashion of a quiver.

All the Spaniards arrived at the village but found it deserted, containing a great amount of food, such as maize and beans. The inhabitants of both villages were on the riverbank on the other side, quite confident that the Spaniards would not be able to ford it. They ridiculed and made angry vociferations agianst the people from Coza. Their mirth was short lived, however, for, as the Coza people knew that country, they found the ford in the river and they started crossing it, the water reaching the chests of those on foot and the saddles of the riders. Fray Domingo de la Anunciación remained on this side of the water with the cacique, because as he was not of the war party it did not seem well that he should get wet. When our soldiers had reached about the middle of the river, one of them fired his flint lock which he had charged with two balls, and he felled one of the Napochies who was on the other side. When the others saw him on the ground dead, they were greatly astonished at the kind of Spanish weapon, which at such a distance could at one shot kill men. They put him on their shoulders and hurriedly carried him off, afraid that other shots might follow against their own persons. All the Napochies fled, and the people of Coza upon passing the river pursued them until the fugitives gathered on the other side of an arm of the same stream, and when those from Coza were about to pass that the Napochies called out to them and said that they would fight no longer, but that they would be friends, because they [the Coza people] brought with them the power of the Spaniards; that they were ready to return to their former tributes and acknowledgment of what they owed them [the Coza people]. Those from Coza were

glad and they called to them that they should come in peace and present themselves to their cacique. They all came to present their obedience, the captain of the Spaniards requesting that the vanquished be treated benignly. The cacique received them with severity, reproaching them harshly for their past rebellion and justifying any death he might choose to give them, as well for their refusal to pay their tributes as for the lives of so many Coza people which they had taken, but that the intervention of the Spaniards was so highly appreciated that he admitted them into his reconciliation and grace, restoring former conditions. The vanquished were very grateful, throwing the blame on bad counselors, as if it were not just as bad to listen to the bad which is advised as to advise it. They capitulated and peace was made.

The Napochies pledged themselves to pay as tributes, thrice a year, game, or fruits, chestnuts, and nuts, in confirmation of their [the Coza people's] superiority, which had been recognized by their forefathers. This done, the whole army returned to the first village of the Napochies, where they had left in garrison Spanish soldiers and Coza people. As this village was convenient they rested there three days, until it seemed time to return to Coza where the 150 Spanish soldiers were waiting for them. The journey was short and they arrived soon, and although they found them all in good health, including Father Fray Domingo de Salazar who had remained with them, all had suffered great hunger and want, because there were many people and they had been there a long time. They began to talk of returning to Nanipacna, where they had left their general, not having found in this land what had been claimed and hoped for. As it means valor in war sometimes to flee and temerity to attack, thus is it prudence on some occasions to retrace one's steps, when the going ahead does not bring any benefit.

THE BREAKUP OF THE LUNA EXPEDITION

WHILE THE VICEROY was writing from Mexico to speed up Luna's activities, a growingly acrimonious debate was developing over whether or not the main force should march inland. Soon it became clear that Luna was fighting almost a lone battle against the bulk of his subordinates. The royal officials, who represented the financial interests of the crown, were also a forceful voice in the debates. That such debates took place and were reported showed that the minor officials, officers, and even soldiers were by no means wholly bound, in any circumstances, to obey their commanding officer. Eventually, they were to prevail.

The first stage in the great debate is selected from the translation by Priestley, *Luna Papers*, I, 199–219. The translations comprise (271) August 27, 1560, the opinion of Tristán de Luna that the whole force should proceed inland; (272) August 27, 1560, the contrary opinion of Jorge Cerón, *maestre de campo* and chief justice; (273) the opinion, opposing Luna, of the royal officials, Alonzo Velázques Rodríguez and Alonso Pérez, and also that of the six captains (274).

271. August 27, 1560. The opinion of Tristán de Luna that they should go inland.

In this port of Santa María de Ochuse of these provinces of La Florida on the twenty-seventh day of the month of August of the year 1560, in the presence of me, Juan de Vargas, chief notary therein, there were gathered together in consultation the illustrious Don Tristán de Luna y Arellano, Jorge Cerón Saavedra the maestre de campo, the treasurer, Alonso Velázquez Rodríguez, the accountant, Alonso Pérez, Captain Baltazar de Sotelo, Captain Don Pedro de Acuña, Captain Don Cristóbal, Captain Diego Téllez, Captain Juan de Porras, and Captain Julián de Acuña, to see the letters that have been written from the interior to the viceroy and the governor concerning what has been seen of the land. When they had been seen and discussed, et cetera, the governor said that in view of what the sargento mayor and the captains of the province of Coosa write him, he desires to go inland with the captains and persons in command and the rest of the people, and to leave in this port people and a captain to guard it.

272. The opinion of Jorge Cerón, *Maestre de Campo*.

Immediately the maestre de campo [gave his opinion, after] having seen the letters which Cap-
tain Don Cristóbal brought from the province of Coosa from the sargento mayor, the captains, and the religious—who write to the most illustrious viceroy and the governor—with other letters from private persons who write to friends and soldiers in this camp; [and after hearing] the account which the said Don Cristóbal and those who returned with him give, all of which tend to conform and do conform in saying that the best territory they have seen in all the land in the two hundred leagues they have traveled is in Nanipacana and Talpa where this camp was. For at that place there was a little clear land, but all the rest they have seen is wooded and swampy, with few inhabitants and so wanting in food that it is held for certain that a large number of people could not live in it, there being no opportunity for cattle-raising or other activities necessary for existence, as is written at greater length by the reverend father, Fray Domingo de Salazar, a religious who desires that this country be settled. Understanding this, and the reasons there are against the governor's wishing to go inland as he says—reasons which would be too long to tell—[the maestre de campo] said: that it is not fitting that the journey contemplated be made because of the little food at present in this port, for from the reckoning of it which has been made it is believed and it is true that there will not be more than enough for this coming month of September. If from this supply rations were to be given to the one hundred men and horses which the governor might take, however it might be doled out, there would not be enough to give to those who might go and those who were to stay here. This would be to throw the entire camp into confusion, on the supposition that the governor's expedition as he

proposes is necessary, and the land of other quality and character than it is, whereas there can result from colonizing it thus very little of the profit which is expected for the service of our Lord and the conversion of the natives, which is what his Majesty desires, because this cannot be attempted from this port; and from any other place it is so difficult, and so scant is the food supply, as has been seen, that it is impossible for any kind of men to traverse the country or have communication in it unless they be of the same condition and manner of life as the natives. For every eight or ten days there are hard rains, cold, and great heat, in such intemperate succession that the clothing which the men wear does not last twenty days; that which the soldiers have at present is so scanty that they are nearly naked and barefoot. So also, it is thought certain, are those who remain there, for those who come, it appears, are in the same condition as all must be. Thus the most fitting thing is to make to the most illustrious viceroy a report of what the country is like, so that he may order and provide that which is suited to his Majesty's service; for it would not be right that his Majesty spend his royal treasury nor any part of it [only to produce] such great hardships and privations for his vassals as those who settle in the country are expected to experience, and with such scant profit, as has been said. In the interval, then, until the decision of the viceroy is learned, and while we are awaiting it, a captain should be sent with about twenty-five or thirty men, to go inland to where the sargento mayor and his camp are. These will be sufficient, for eight men have returned from there on horseback and the others on foot and on mules, meeting no opposition in the entire country to prevent their progress; yet they experienced such great dearth of food, so little being found, that they were always nearly dead of hunger, though marching every day six to eight or ten leagues; for if they marched less they encountered risk and hardship. So this is his opinion as to the expedition which the governor says he wants to make; and when it has been discussed pro and con, and the opinions of the officials and the captains have been seen, if these all agree that another captain should go with some soldiers we will decide what he should receive by way of instructions, so that whatever may be decided upon shall be done and fulfilled. And he signed it with his name,

273. The opinion of the royal officials.

We, the treasurer, Alonso Velázquez Rodríguez, and the accountant, Alonso Pérez, officials of the royal treasury of his Majesty for these provinces of La Florida, reply to the proposal made by the governor in his opinion given in this port of Polonza on the twenty-eighth of August of the year 1560. [The proposal was] to go inland to where the sargento mayor and the other captains are, if it be wise to do so. He gave, recapitulated, and clarified said opinion, and he commanded the notary, Juan de Vargas, whom he ordered called for the purpose, to set it down in writing. It was that he was ready and willing to go inland, without giving any cause or reason for so doing save that the sargento mayor had written him to that effect; the maestre de campo was to remain here in this port, and he and we and the other captains who were present were to give our opinions, for he would do nothing until first and above all things [this should be done]. He had previously ordered that we be shown a letter written to him by the religious, the sargento mayor, and the captains, and another written by the sargento mayor alone. So, having information that he had written to the viceroy concerning the matter, in order to know the business more completely and clearly, we asked him to show the letter which he had written so that it might be seen whether [it and the letters from the interior] were in accordance. The letter was publicly read on the day mentioned in the presence of the junta; and when all the letters had been seen and understood as has been said, and we had obtained complete information concerning the country both from them and from the account we had from Captain Don Cristóbal, who had come from the interior the day before and had seen it, as well as from many other soldiers and credible persons who also came from there, what it appeared to us should be done, after having commended the matter to God, having seen the letters, and resting our belief in God and in our consciences without reservation or passion but as Christians, is:

That, having seen and learned all that concerns the settlement and permanent occupation of this country by the Spaniards, [we believe that] they should not carry the plan into effect nor stay in the future, especially in this part where we now are. Nor should they enter the interior, this being an impossible thing, because it is understood, as is seen from the letters and what those say who have come from there, that it is a hundred and eighty leagues (rather more than less) from here to Coosa where [our people] are. In all that distance there is no place to settle nor plant a town of Spaniards, not even in Coosa itself; for that country is shut in by forests full of marshes and swamps, the greater part of it is unpopulated, and the populated part contains so few people that they are not enough to support any town of Spaniards which might be established. Nor could they do any farming, because there are no lands nor any place to keep their cattle where they could avail themselves of them for their needs and support.

Another reason is that they say the best of the land is that in the province of Talpa, Upiache, and Nanipacana, which is the part to which the governor went. But it is plain to see that even it is no country to settle in on account of the forests and swamps it contains. In view of this and of the account which was obtained of the interior, the vicar, Fray Pedro de Feria, went to New Spain to inform the viceroy that this country is not fit to settle in. For the best part that has been seen and which they say is suitable for settlement is now known not to be so; and as to what has been said about Coosa being the best part of the country, we now see from what they write and say that it is not fit to be settled by Spaniards because of the many forests and the few lands and people that it contains. All the rest of the country yet to be seen must be just like it, for what was called the best of the land is not fit to settle in, nor capable of sustaining one town of Spaniards.

Moreover, in the letter which the sargento mayor writes alone, he says to the governor that he ought to go there and now allow himself to be deceived into staying here even though no good land on which to settle be found, for by so doing he would act as his position required, and close the mouth of base criticism. It is thus clear that he writes with mental reserve and knows that he has not found country fit to settle in, but only advises that the journey be made and the country be penetrated because of what might be said of him and not for the service which might be rendered to God and his Majesty. Even so, as we are

informed, he thought that the camp and the governor were in Atache or Nanipacana with a strong force of cavalry and provisions which had come from New Spain.

Another reason is that there is no food to take, nor horses with which to go inland; for there are only about fifty or sixty horses, and these are in such condition that it happens when [our people] go out to hunt they come back on foot all tired out, the horses being unable to carry them because they have eaten no corn for a year. Also the people are nearly naked, and desperate at having found out what the country is like, as those describe it who have come from there.

Another reason is that in the one hundred eighty leagues or rather more which lie between this port and Coosa, for a great part of the road the country is unpopulated, and if the people who might be expected to do so were to go with the governor, many, marching loaded down with their arms and rations, would necessarily perish from hunger, let alone from the swamps and brambles in the road. And once arrived at the town of Coosa where at present they [i.e., the sargento mayor and his men] are, and declare they are fed by ration and eat by ration, moreover, a ration incommensurate with the service which it is understood they have to render, as we saw done in the towns of Nanipacana and Upiache so it will be done, and this must be until [the Indians] reap their crops and place their women in shelter as did those of Nanipacana and Upiache, from which places [our people] wrote that there were such abundant provisions, whereas we were forced to come down to the sea to keep from perishing there of hunger. The same thing will happen if all the people are taken to Coosa, for how can they be sustained while settling and establishing themselves there when even the natives have no lands on which to sow crops? Hence we know already what the idea of going inland will result in as far as Coosa is concerned, for they said it was the best part of the country. The sargento mayor writes also that it is to be feared that the natives may revolt when they collect their corn from the fields, and the Spaniards take it from them as they will have to do so as to maintain themselves. Even now the Indians think that they [i.e., the Spaniards] are only passing through, and give them carriers and everything they ask merely to get them out of the country.

Another reason is that neither the governor nor the captains will suffice to console or control the people, nor can his Majesty maintain them or give them lands to cultivate to maintain themselves, or any place to keep their cattle, or any clothes to wear, or anything that can profit them. So it is too much to try to make so long a march, especially without the hope of any gain. For these reasons and many others which might be recited, seeing and knowing that the foregoing arguments will turn out as we say, to what end will the governor go inland except to cause both those who are there now and those who go with him to perish? For the reasons given the settlement cannot be made, but if his Lordship still desires to go, we are ready to go with him and follow him, giving ourselves as best we may; but it seems to us that it would be better to send [someone] inland to the sargento mayor and the captains who are there, with thirty soldiers, the best horses there are, and ten mules to help them carry some provisions, that they may return to this port if they find nothing better than what has yet been seen and written about. This should be done with all promptness as winter is so near. And they should let the natives alone in all love and peace, without doing them any harm. Meantime, orders could be received from the viceroy, who would have been informed from what has been written him what the country is like, and he will command what is to be done. If it be necessary to send people to Santa Elena they may go; for in this part, even though the land were very good and great in possibilities, they could not be maintained for the reasons given. Particularly is this so, as there is nothing to be found in the entire country of which the Spaniards may avail themselves, even to provide food alone. Also there are very few Indians, and they live in such dense undergrowth, amid rivers and swamps, that it is very difficult to capture an Indian, or even see one if he does not wish to show himself. We know that if we become settled and remain permanently, they will do as did those of Nanipacana, Upiache, and Utchile; for whenever they wanted to, they appeared and shot a few arrows at us, but when we sought them not an Indian could be seen, nor could any be found because of the dense undergrowth of the country.

We ask that the originals of the letters which the captains wrote to the governor and the one the sargento mayor wrote be filed with this our reply together with a transcript of the one written to the viceroy; and because of the existing great scarcity of food, it seems to us that while a message is being sent to the people inland and they are coming, the tender which is in this port should be sent to the viceroy of New Spain to give him a report of what has happened; it should carry also the suggestions and opinions which have been presented in this case so that they may be seen by his very illustrious Lordship and he may then order what he sees to be most suitable. This is what appears to us to be called for unless something else seems to the governor, the maestre de campo, and the captains to be desirable. We sign it with our names:

Alonso Velázquez Rodríguez.
Alonso Pérez.

274. The opinion of the six captains.

In compliance with what the governor ordered, that each captain should give his opinion concerning going to Coosa where the captains and the sargento mayor are, it being the mind of his Lordship to go, [we captains say:]

That it seems to us that, above all things, his Lordship should order placed at the beginning of this our opinion the original letters of the captains and friars who are there, signed with their names, that of the sargento mayor, and the one which he is writing to the very illustrious viceroy of New Spain. And so we ask and supplicate his Lordship to order this opinion so placed, and if necessary, we do with due respect require and protest that he do so, in order that they and what is contained in them may be placed in evidence before his Majesty; for, in addition to the reasons contained in them concerning what the country is like, there are the following objections [to the governor's plans]:

First: For the hundred men with their servants whom his Lordship desires to take with him, there is not sufficient food which can be taken from here or carried the two hundred leagues between here and [their destination], and if perchance in over a hundred leagues from here any can be found, it will be very little, as is very well known from what we have traveled over and seen many other times. We consider it very certain that all of us who might go with his Lordship would perish and those who would remain here would run great risk from the failure of the supplies which would be left them.

Second: The horses and mules which are here, which must number about fifty, are so thin and weak from eating no corn for so long, that if any of us go hunting from this camp on them it always happens that within half a league from here they become exhausted, and those who go on them have to leave them behind and come back carrying the saddles on their shoulders.

> [signed:] Don Pedro de Acuña.
> Don Cristóbal Ramírez de Arellano.
> Baltazar de Sotelo.
> Diego Téllez.
> Juan de Porras.
> Julián de Acuña.

275. August 29, 1560. List of the men who were thought well enough to go on the inland expedition.

Luna tried to force the hands of his opponents by producing a list of those whom he considered fit enough to go on the proposed revival of the inland march. It is significant that only eighty-seven men were listed as fit. This produced the second stage in the great debate.

Translated in Priestley, Luna Papers, I, 246–249.

The People of his Lordship
Guillermo de Birues
Pedro de Barrios
Mezquita
Juan Muñoz de Zayas
Féliz Ponce
Juan de Carbajal
Luis Hernández
Alonso Ruiz
Pedro Romero
Barrientos
Pedro Bermúdez

Captain Sotelo
The Captain
Reynoso
Alonso de Vega
Juan de Porras
Verdugo
Gutiérrez
Aguilar
His Brother
Marmolejo
Gil González

Mestanza
Captain Don Cristóbal
The Captain
Antón Martín
Guirola
Pedro Hernández
Muñoz
Cristóbal Sánchez
Cáceres
The Sergeant's men:
Cristóbal Núñez
Hipólito Hernández
La Guardia
Resusta
Simón Rodríguez
Lianez
Sánchez
Pedro de Ecija
Pedro de Rivera
The Company of Téllez:
The Captain
The Ensign
Julián Téllez
Cuevas
Martín de Bilbao
Alonso González
Zubieta
Nuño Caravallo
Xaramillo's Company:
Francisco Molina
Acevedo
Domingo Alonso
Guillermo Vázquez
Arciniega
Hernán Rodríguez
Juan de Ávila
Francisco Rodríguez
Rocha
Antón Sánchez
Francisco Luis
The Company of Don Pedro:
The Captain
Ortiz

Velasco
Vasco Hernández
Rivera
Agurto
Juan Gutiérrez
The Company of Gonzalo Sánchez:
  Francisco Rodríguez
  Hernán Gómez
  Carrión
  Vellido
  Gabriel López
  Juan G[ue?]ra
The Company of the maestre de campo:
  Francisco Navarro
  Alonso Martín
  Guillermo López
  G[ue?]ra de León
  Felipe Hernández
  Juan de Vargas
  Beltrán
The Company of Álvaro Nieto:
  The Sergeant
  Belloso
  Francisco Martín
  Peñaranda
  Cobos
  Velasco
  Mexía
  The accountant, who just arrived
  Cristóbal Nieto
  Miguel de Campo
The Company of Porras:
  The Captain

Juan Quadrado
The Sergeant
Álvaro de la Cruz
Hernando de la Cruz
Pantoja
Magarino
Machín
Juan Vizcaíno
Ramírez
The Licentiate Arias
The Treasurer
The Accountant
Pedro López de Nava
Julián de Acuña
Two trumpeters
Diego de Zamora

Don Tristán de Luna y Arellano.

The foregoing having been communicated to the said captains, to the effect that the soldiers of the companies here named are found sound and fit for the expedition, therefore he informs them that they are to get ready. I, the notary, swear that after these men had been named, I notified the said captains and officials to equip themselves and the men here named. They replied that his Lordship should give them the order in writing and they would see what his Lordship would command. . . .

CONTINUING ORDERS FROM MEXICO TO PROCEED WITH THE EXPEDITION AS PLANNED, AUGUST—SEPTEMBER, 1560

LUIS DE VELASCO and his advisers in Mexico were quite unaware of the tensions arising in Luna's camp. On August 20 (276) he is sending them help (recognizing they had to move down to Polenza) but reiterating his orders to them to take up as soon as possible their original plans to go to Santa Elena. In letters of September 3 (277), 13 and 14 (289–290), he has become aware of some difficulties but regards them only as temporary setbacks and insists that the original plan he adhered to. This makes a curious counterpoint with the events in Luna's camp where, before Velasco's last letter was written, Luna's authority had been effectively overthrown by the recall of the advance party from Coosa on September 9.

276. August 20, 1560. Luis de Velasco to Luna.

Translated in Priestley, Luna Papers, I, 181–195.

The letter you wrote me by Don Carlos de Zúñiga and Father Fray Juan de Mázuelos from the town of Nanipacana I received at the end of July. They were delayed so long on their voyage because the weather drove them into La Havana, where they were detained two weeks. I saw what you wrote me about the illness you have had; I certainly have felt as sorry for this as one could, and no less sorry for the want which you write me the whole camp was suffering. Our Lord be praised Who gave you health to endure those troubles and provide your necessities. Anticipating that those who were left at the port would have these difficulties I provided the supplies which Luis Daza took; but I thought from what you wrote that you and the other people of the camp who went inland would not be likely to lack food; for unless those who were in that country with Soto lied, they never suffered want. But it seems that you have not reached the good country where Soto was and where the Indians are more sedentary and have greater intelligence and better government than those about you, besides possessing abundant supplies. I well believe that you used all due industry and diligence in searching for them and in everything else.

I am sorry for the return of Don Carlos, and no less for that of Juan Xaramillo, for they are of the kind of people by whom that land is to be maintained, but as I shall speak of this in more detail later, I shall proceed to [tell you] what has been ordered. Luis Daza set sail on June 23 with four ships, the galleon *San Juan*, the French vessel, a tender, and the new brigantine. He could not leave sooner because La Vera Cruz and the port were left bare of provisions on account of the quantity of them taken by the fleet which went to Spain. There were ten ships that went, and there was also a great deal to do in providing other things. It seems that [Daza's ships] were longer than we expected in reaching your port, for your last letter is dated July 19, by which time they should have arrived. God willing, they should not have been longer in arriving than four or five days after Xaramillo left, and with their arrival you will have some relief and refreshment.

In view of the fact that you decided to go down from Nanipacana to the port, impelled by necessity and because the people refused to go inland, it seemed wise to me to send the brigantine with news of how he [Xaramillo] arrived, and the bark, so that you might know what is here contemplated. I [decided also] to arrange to send Juan de Busto to visit you and all the captains, gentlemen, and principal persons of that camp, and to give you opportunity to advise me of the state of affairs and of what it is necessary to provide. I certainly feel very sorry for the troubles of each and all; for their remedy I am providing what has at present seemed necessary and is nearest at hand. This was to send a ship as soon as possible laden with supplies; it will take at least one thousand *fanegas* of corn, biscuit, meat, and other viands which can be sent, so that there may be no lack of food in the camp. This ship was being prepared to go to Campeche so that Bracamonte and other hidalgos and good soldiers might go in it to that land in search of you to serve his Majesty; but seeing the need there is to provide your camp with food, I decided to defer for the present sending the ship to Campeche and send it to that port of Polonza laden with supplies. I have also ordered the bark in which Don Carlos returned to be fitted out so that it may as shortly as possible be laden with corn and go to that port. Thus if it please our Lord the camp will have been refreshed and restored with what Luis Daza took in the four ships, and with the one now being sent there will be a moderate supply of food; later I will order everything that can be provided and sent, so that there may not be a similar dearth of provisions again. Inasmuch as it is not a new thing with armies that there should occur shortage of provisions, misfortunes, and failures, we need not marvel that such a thing has happened to that camp, nor need we despair because of it of achieving through the help of our Lord the desired end by which his divine Majesty will be greatly served as also will the king our lord; and you and all those captains and gentlemen, hidalgos, and good and honorable soldiers, will gain great honor by doing what good and honorable soldiers ought, besides the benefits which, our Lord willing, will accrue later on; for after rough and adverse weather usually come the mild and favoring winds. This is what I trust in our Lord will happen to that camp, for although the devil may prevent as best he may that the planting of our holy Catholic faith in that land of La Florida should have effect, our Lord will be pleased to take pity on those poor, wretched barbarians, and on that camp which in order to serve Him is undergoing so much hardship. For you did not go to that land in the expectation of [obtaining control] of what lies between the Miruelo country and here, but for the sake of Coosa, the other provinces in that part, and Santa Elena and beyond there; and your disembarking on this side of the Bahama Channel was for no other purpose than to lead the camp overland in search of Coosa and Santa Elena, leaving at the port at which you disembarked or in some other more convenient for that purpose a captain with the necessary people to settle a town whereby that camp might be succored and helped with whatever it might have need of from this New Spain and from La Havana, the navigation by way of the Bahama Channel being too difficult and dangerous. And since we are sure that Coosa, [blank in original], Sonora, and many other provinces in that part, have good fertile soil for [raising] foods, that there are people, pearls, and other good things, that the people are higher in organization, manner of life, and intelligence than those barbarians in your part, and that the French come quite near to Santa Elena nearly every year to buy from the Indians gold, pearls, marten-skins, and other things, it must not be said that it is not a suitable country to colonize or that no benefit is to be derived from it because the character of the land and the people is what it is; this is all the more true because we know from experience that the Spaniards themselves have begun to learn that the new lands which they settle will, through industry and labor, make them increasingly richer. Soto learned that not far from Coosa there was copper; he sent two Spaniards thither, and they learned that it was true. He also learned that north of [blank in original] there were many people and gold, and the land is such that it produces everything that grows in Spain. Great confidence must be felt that that land ought to be of great utility to the Spaniards. Just as they [were found to have] told the truth about the copper, so they will about the gold, particularly since there are Spaniards who say they have seen

it and bartered for it in the places mentioned. It is also to be imagined that there must be other minerals, such as silver. Therefore, inasmuch as you have seen that his Majesty sends to order you and writes to you to colonize in the direction of Santa Elena, and since you are in that land, whence you can enter Coosa and Santa Elena, it would by no means be proper to abandon that land or leave it unpopulated; on the other hand you ought to establish your hold upon it and thence enter Coosa. It being true that the sargento mayor has entered there and has opened a road by which entry may be made, it would be well and proper, if he has returned by spring, for you and the whole camp or the greater part of it, to go inland in search of Coosa or of the territory toward Santa Elena, whichever offers the best facilities, leaving at your port a captain with enough soldiers to face whatever Indians are in that district. After the winter passes, you will be provided from La Havana with horses and supplies. I will look out for what is necessary for this purpose. In case the sargento mayor shall not have returned, but winters there, you in person with the other captains ought to go in search of him, leaving as I have said one captain at the port with the people necessary. Luis Daza took a bountiful supply of arquebuses and powder for this enterprise, and money to buy horses in La Havana. I should be very much gratified if the sargento mayor should winter there, and if you have perhaps sent forward the horsemen and foot-soldiers of which you write me in your letter, that they may be more secure until you arrive with the rest of the camp. It is certainly true that in order to maintain the necessary precautions in that port it is wise to leave a cautious person there. Such a man is Juan Xaramillo, for you are well aware what a good soldier he is and what a fine account he has given of himself. If he recovers sufficiently to go back there I will send him again, for such persons are the ones who are needed in that country, and I am very sorry that you sent such a man and others like him away from your side and out of the country; I regret it because they are the persons who keep up a good front amid the dangers and troubles which occur. By such men those are to be animated who do not have the experience to do what they ought. I am not at all grieved at the return of the married men with their wives and children, for in that section there is very little assurance of having provisions, and they are not likely to be profitable at present, for they only eat up what is sent from here or found there, so that it is to be feared that they might be the cause of bringing the camp to want. I told you many times not to try to take so many married men with their wives and children, and since experience has shown that for the time being such people are of little use for what is needed, it is just as well that those who have done so have returned. But if it seems there that those who remain will be wanted and needed let them stay by all means. All whom you leave at the port we will provide from here with enough to eat and whatever else may be necessary. It may be that our Lord will shortly be pleased to let you have a goodly land to which the married men with their wives and children may go, so that by their good example they may aid and be of utility in the conversion of the natives. By no means should you grant leave to any captain or soldier to leave that country, especially to such as Don Cristóbal and Juan Xaramillo, for everything necessary which can be furnished will be provided from here and from La Havana in order to follow up what has been begun and achieve the purpose for which it was commenced. This winter you ought to take great pains to see that the soldiers are well clothed and lodged, and then advise me by Juan de Busto what it is necessary to provide from here, so that you may be sent with all diligence all that can be sent. I should think it wise to divide the camp between the two ports so that [the people] might the better sustain themselves; you will have ordered what was most fitting. This is understood to apply until summer comes and you return from Coosa, for as has been said, it is enough that only one port, whichever is best, be settled. If it seems better to you there that the camp should travel divided into two parties I would be agreeable to that decision, so that the soldiers might suffer less want and the Indians receive less vexation. It ought not to be very hard for Spanish soldiers to march overland from those ports to Coosa, for as we have learned, Spaniards have traveled a hundred leagues by land in other parts of the Indies through deserts without taking a single horse and carrying only what each man could. But you could take a good number of horses which you could import from La Havana in addition to those you may have and although the country is not very densely peopled yet it has

some population and there is food. Even in case troubles do occur, good soldiers in difficulties show their valor by both the spirit and industry which habitually cause them to be held in esteem and honored.

If it please our Lord, after you have settled in Coosa or in the place which offers best facilities for the purpose, and after the ports of Santa Elena and along that coast are known, that country will be colonized by all the people who are needed both from Spain and from here. Hence in order to become acquainted with those ports I will send two ships next summer to Santa Elena and up to the fortieth degree along that coast, so that when information as to what ports there are has been obtained you may be advised of it; we will also have it here and will give an account of it to his Majesty so that he may order a goodly number of people sent out with everything necessary to settle that country. He [will be asked] to send among those who come a goodly number of farmers to cultivate the land. If it appears that conditions are better in the region of Santa Elena for introducing horses and cattle from La Havana, it will be ordered done as you advise, so that all that can be taken may be sent from there. If you do not find suitable conditions near Santa Elena, and if it would be better to introduce the cattle and horses into the part nearest here, it shall be done. Also our Lord willing, when the camp is in the land of Coosa, if any way could be found to send to discover what point of land projects from La Florida toward La Havana, it would be an important thing to open that road, for if it is passable a number of cattle and horses might be taken to that point, for the distance to cross is short. For this purpose it would be well for the first brigantine or bark which you send to La Havana to go along that coast of La Florida to discover the ports which lie between that of Juan Ponce and the Bay of Juan Paz which is at the end of the point of La Florida. And now, since it is very important to his Majesty that the land of Santa Elena and the rest of La Florida be peopled, and that to all those captains, gentlemen, good soldiers, and you more than anyone, go the honor and profit, it is desirable that you all do your duty with that fidelity and courage with which Spaniards always set resolute face toward troubles and dangers. Since you have there captains and other such persons who not only have courage to spare but also can offer good opinions and counsel, tell such persons what the plans are whereby the entry into Coosa will be made, and impose silence on the thought of deserting the country, for this is necessary for the service of God and of the king our lord and for the honor of all who are in that camp. On my part, I will provide from his Majesty's treasury everything that may be necessary and can be provided. And even though all the soldiers who are in that camp are not experienced in the affairs of war and its toilsome incidents, nevertheless it is by experience that men are made expert, and since they will go forth from there with ample experience it is to be believed that they will not, being Spaniards, lack the courage which makes of raw recruits the expert and spirited veterans Spanish soldiers are wont to become. I recommend to your Lordship that, since at present it is [not?] found possible to reward them for their work and services, at least so far as may be, both by deed and word, you favor and honor them.

On the ships which I shall order sent next spring I shall send a Frenchman who has been there several times to trade for gold, marten-skins, and pearls, for which the French trade in the country northward from Santa Elena. He is to reconnoiter the country and the port where this business is carried on. I am expecting him from day to day to come in a bark from Campeche. Some of his companions who came in another bark have reached this city. The man whom I called a Frenchman is an Englishman, but is married in France. If he should come in time, it may be that he will go in the brigantine with Juan de Busto to give you an account of what he has seen. But it would be better for him to go with the ships which are to go toward Santa Elena and along that coast, for if he goes by land he will do no reconnoitering, but if by sea he will be of much benefit.

I think I wrote you by Luis Daza saying I had written by the accountant Hortuño de Ibarra, who went as general of the fleet which set sail on April 8 of this year, to his Majesty telling him the state of affairs of that country. I also sent the letters you wrote to his Majesty in which you informed him how you had taken that port and how misfortune had damaged the ships and supplies. I wrote to him that you would be forced to go inland to search for supplies, and that it was to be feared that you would undergo hardships before finding them, but that you would exert yourself to maintain the people at the port and at

another place or two others, until his Majesty might order more people, arms, horses, and food provided, so that the country could be penetrated and pacified and settled at the Punta de Santa Elena. For this is what his Majesty chiefly desires as you will have learned from his letters, to which you will reply as your opportunity and health permit, unless you have already done so before receiving this.

There are suspicions and some indications that the French who have settled at Los Bacallaos, which is not very far from the Punta de Santa Elena, are trying to come and take the port or ports which may be there, and settle them so as to impede the passage of the Bahama Channel. They will be able to do this easily if they find a port. If there is none the Channel will be secure if his Majesty has La Havana and your port fortified; the other ports along that coast I do not believe will serve for ships to stay in for many days. For the purpose of finding out whether there is a port at the Punta de Santa Elena or within a hundred leagues of coast from there on, we have decided that Pedro Menéndez de Valdés, who is here and is to go as general of the fleet which will sail for Spain in January, God willing, shall take with him two light vessels; these are to sail from La Havana to search for the ports or bays which may exist at the Punta de Santa Elena or up the coast a hundred leagues. Whether they find one or not, one ship is to go to Spain to inform his Majesty of what has been found, and the other is to return to La Havana by sailing through the Lucayos, thence to inform you, and me here, so that if there is a port, expeditions by land and sea to take it and settle it shall be sent as has been planned. May our Lord direct it so as to serve Him best, and guard and prosper your illustrious person. Mexico, August 20, 1560.

Your servant,

[signed:] Don Luis de Velasco.

277. September 3, 1560. Luis de Velasco to Luna.

Translated by Priestley, Luna Papers, *II, 195–197.*

After I had written the foregoing [the letter of August 20, above] Juan Xaramillo arrived in this city. When I had seen the report he brought and [had heard] the account by word of mouth which he told, I called together the audiencia, prelates, provincials, fathers, officials of his Majesty, and gentlemen of age and experience who were here, and they joined in a memorial which you will find herewith. In the presence of them all the report which Juan Xaramillo brought was read and the account which he told was heard. After the difficulties which the business presents had been discussed, it seemed to everyone that that country should not be abandoned until his Majesty can be informed of what has happened, what is known about the country, and what kind of territory was found by the sargento mayor and the captains whom you sent on the expedition to the province of Coosa; after that, his Majesty may provide and order as he sees fit as to whether the country and the ports shall be maintained or abandoned. In the meantime [it was agreed] that food, clothing, cattle, and whatever else seems most necessary shall be provided from here, La Havana, and Yucatan in the best manner possible, as will be done. And so, sir, this is how it appears to everyone here. Besides the report which has already been made to his Majesty, everything that has happened will be reported to him in detail by General Pedro Menéndez, with information as to what ought to be done, so that he may promptly order it; and I will not fail in providing whatever may be furnished here. In view of the fact that the brigantine in which Juan Xaramillo came is a very small ship and can carry no more food than is needed for the sailors, and also in view of the sea hazard for it, I decided that it should not go, but that haste should be made in dispatching the caravel. So it is going; it takes the food, clothing, shirts, and shoes which it has been possible to collect hastily. When it is unladen please have it sent back so that it may come in time for General Pedro Menéndez to carry letters from you to his Majesty and an account of what has happened. He will leave about January, or earlier, if possible; therefore the caravel can make another voyage with supplies in company with the fleet which is to go to Spain. . . . Sealed September 3 [1560], Mexico.

Your Servant,
    [signed:] Don Luis de Velasco.

THE SECOND STAGE IN THE DEBATE IN WHICH TRISTÁN DE LUNA'S AUTHORITY IS CHALLENGED AND OVERTHROWN, AUGUST 30–SEPTEMBER 9, 1560

THE CAPTAINS and men refused to accept the order of August 29 to get ready to march inland. Luna reiterated it, and on August 30 they appealed to Jorge Cerón, who was chief justice as well as second in command (*maestre de campo*), to take over authority as Luna was no longer able to govern on account of loss of reason. At a meeting it was resolved that for the time being Cerón would assume authority. Luna ignored these actions, while Cerón sent full reports to Mexico but avoided openly usurping Luna's place. He did try to restore, at least, the authority of the captains. Luna emerged to request Cerón not to receive further petitions from the soldiers. Meantime, Luna ordered a food-gathering expedition inland that Cerón resisted, until orders should come from Mexico. The two royal officials, Alonso Velázquez Rodríguez and Alonso Pérez, representing the interests of the crown, supported Cerón. The breaking point came when Luna was refused rations for his household from the storehouse on September 2. He finally lost his self-control and issued an order condemning all his captains to death; he also ordered that his officials should lose their Indians. Ignoring him, the men in a general meeting decided to send Captain Juan de Porras, with a small party, inland to Coosa to evacuate the men still there. Later, backed by the support of another meeting, Cerón resisted Luna's order to him, on September 9, to refuse petitions and cease to usurp his authority as governor. On September 9, after a tussle with Luna, who wanted to send the available ship to Mexico with only his own dispatches, Luna finally agreed that the ship should go with full reports from all sides and carry with it 100 incapacitated persons as well. These events can only be briefly illustrated.

The documents are translated by Priestley, *Luna Papers*, II, 3–135. The following extracts are given. (278) August 30, petition of the five captains to Jorge Cerón; (279) reply by Jorge Cerón; (280) August 30, the reply of Tristán de Luna; (281) August 30, the answer of Jorge Cerón; (282) August 30, Luna closes the debate; (283) September 2, confrontation over the governor's rations; (284) September 2, Luna condemns his captains to death; (285) September 2, Cerón insists that a meeting be called; (287) September 9, Luna refuses to have any part in recalling the Coosa party; (288) September 9, report on the situation at Polonza sent by Cerón and others to the Coosa party advising them to return.

278 August 30, 1560. Petition of five captains to Jorge Cerón, *Maestre de Campo.*

On the thirtieth day of the month of August of the year aforesaid the captains appeared before the very magnificent Jorge Cerón Saavedra, maestre de campo, and presented this petition, the tenor of which is as follows:

Very Magnificent Sir: We captains who here sign our names say: that yesterday the twenty-ninth instant, the illustrious Don Tristán de Luna y Arellano, governor of these provinces, ordered us to join in a meeting with yourself and the officials of his Majesty to consider and determine whether it was desirable to go inland to Coosa where the sargento mayor and the captains are. But the governor himself decided to go inland, giving no other reason than to say that the sargento mayor wrote him to do so. To this were directed opinions on the part of yourself, the officials of the king, and ourselves; these the governor has not been willing to have discussed although he has been asked to do so, and there have been several replies made, in which he has in effect not been willing to accept anyone's opinion, being determined to follow only his own. . . . In all this we have been very loyal servants of his Majesty, and so we will be in everything that

comes up in these provinces; and because we brought him as our governor and have held him as such, we have in all that has concerned ourselves obeyed and held and do hold him as such notwithstanding that since he was ill he has not been nor is he fit to govern; for he has lacked and still lacks the balance of judgment required therefor, as is public and notorious. But we have overlooked this and sustained him, and we have not spoken plainly about it because there were no important matters which we could not endure to pass through, especially as you have been in the camp, for you with your authority could remedy them, as you have done. But the business we have at present does not permit of being left to his opinion alone, for he has not formed it so deliberately that it suffices for an affair like this, which he decides upon without taking any opinions whatever, he being as has been said, under such an indisposition as he is, which is evident and appears from a report made to you at the Bahía Filipina on request of the officials of his Majesty. This document is in the possession of the notary. Nevertheless we ask you to order it received. And if it is not sufficiently proved that he is not fit to govern, as he is not at present, we are ready to give more ample information if it be necessary. [Now therefore] since it is evident that he is not fit to govern or undertake affairs, as he is not, we ask you, and if necessary we demand of you, that you take it upon yourself to govern us and attend to whatever befits the service of God and of his Majesty. For we are ready to serve his Majesty very loyally, as we have always done. In so doing you will perform a service for God and his Majesty, and do what you ought and is incumbent upon the office you hold. If because you do not there may occur any disturbance or scandal, let it be at your charge and blame and not ours. And we ask the present notary to give us a certified statement of the fact that we ask, say, and demand this, so that it may bear witness in protecting our rights.

[signed:] Don Pedro de Acuña.
Baltazar de Sotelo.
Diego Téllez.
Juan de Porras.
Julián de Acuña.

279. Reply by Jorge Cerón.

The above petition having been seen by the maestre de campo, he said: that as to what the captains asked and requested in their petitions, to which he refers, where they say that they have held and do hold Don Tristán de Arellano as their governor and as such have obeyed him notwithstanding he was indisposed as they say, it was then and at that time that there was the greater need to take action concerning his ill health so that the affairs of the camp could have been managed more calmly and effectively than they were. And in order that the maestre de campo might assume the responsibility, he asked the governor, all the captains, and the officials of his Majesty who were present in the town of Nanipacana to come before his Lordship because he the maestre de campo wanted to discuss the need then existing of appointing some person to serve in the governor's place. So it was done, the opinions of all being taken, and they unanimously voted and said that the maestre de campo should take charge of all matters that might come up in the camp, and that because of the illness which the governor had he should stay in his quarters, and everything would be done for his health in every way possible, and that they would keep him

in the position they had always held him, save that he should be given no part in affairs nor be allowed to concern himself with them. This arrangement the maestre de campo accepted, and took charge of the dispatch of business which might offer, under a certain protestation which he made stating that he did not yield to the request because of desire to govern in his own name, as was set forth at great length and discussed at the meeting alluded to. . . .

To say now that he is, at a time so critical in the face of all the charges which all the soldiers and the camp are publishing and making, even though they are well-founded, is out of time and season; nor is there occasion for what is asked and demanded in the protestation made by the captains [nor reason why] the maestre de campo should assume the indicated responsibility or do any of the things asked or demanded, lest he receive injury thereby for the reasons mentioned and for others which he might set forth at greater length. But what he will do [will be] to fulfil his obligation to his office and that of chief justice, for in this he is ready and prepared to serve with his person and position as he has been doing, but in nothing further.

Moreover, a lengthy account of everything that has happened up to date has been sent both by the captains and the maestre de campo to the royal audiencia and the very illustrious viceroy in the bark which was dispatched from Nanipacana. Another was sent by Captain Xaramillo, and [still another] later by the French ship, on which the reverend father vicar went taking long reports and accounts which were sent to his most illustrious Lordship. Answer to all these is expected every day, and so, just as it has been up to now, by ordering whatever it has been possible to do, will it continue to be done for the present and for whatever may come up in the future until we learn what has been provided and ordered by the viceroy. In this interval the maestre de campo will do and aid and serve with his person and office in all that arises whatever is for the best service of his Majesty. But he will not take charge of affairs or of the camp as the captains with protestations ask him to do, as has been said, lest in some delicate way or by some method or manner something might happen which might be charged against him. For as he has said, he has always been [and will be] ready and prepared every time any business may come up, to join with the officials of his Majesty and the captains, and he will give his opinion, and sign it with his name, as he has done in matters of importance which have occurred, but not in any other manner. He then asked that the foregoing reply be communicated to the said captains present, and that it be given to them in a sworn statement; and he signed it with his name.

[signed:] Jorge Céron.

280. August 30, 1560. The reply of Tristán de Luna.

I, Don Tristán de Luna y Arellano, governor and captain-general of these provinces of La Florida and the Punta de Santa Elena for his Majesty, say: that it has come to my notice that after I ordered the captains and soldiers of this army and the officials of his Majesty to prepare to set out from here next Monday, the second of September, and after I indicated for them the rations which would be necessary by a memoir [showing] that these would be sufficient to make our journey as far as Coosa, and when the order was published this morning that they should go for their rations, notwithstanding what has been said, all the foregoing presented to-day to you as my maestre de campo whom I have appointed a certain petition or petitions asking you to govern in this port of Polonza in my place. Inasmuch as you and all who are in this camp know that I was elected as governor and captain-general of this army by the very illustrious viceroy and the royal audiencia which resides in the City of Mexico, and as such they have always written to me and I have replied; and inasmuch as I have letters from his Majesty in which he approves my election as good, and me as one obedient to what I am ordered, I have always issued orders for what has seemed appropriate both as regards this country and the Punta de Santa Elena.... Wherefore, I ask and require you not to receive the petition which the captains and men of this army may have presented to you. And since I have made no relinquishment of my office, and since no such thing can be surmised from the least to the greatest part thereof, if you will do thus you will

do as you ought, and I shall not have to make complaint against you to his Majesty or his viceroy and audiencia. And I ask that this petition be placed with the other [papers].

[signed:] Don Tristán de Luna y Arellano.

281. August 30, 1560. Reply of Jorge Cerón.

The foregoing petition having been presented and read as above expressed, and it having been seen by the maestre de campo, he said: that he held and holds the governor in the position in which his Majesty, his royal audiencia, and his most illustrious viceroy hold him; that he has had for him all respect and obedience as such governor in everything that has occurred in this army and camp; and that if any petition or legal processes have been presented to him either by the officials of his Majesty or by the captains, he has replied to them as he thought he ought to do. Inasmuch as everything that has happened in this country up to the state in which affairs were when the French ship left this port has been reported to the most illustrious viceroy by his Lordship as well as by everyone in this camp, and as the reply and decision is shortly expected and might arrive to find his Lordship not in this port, [as a result of which] that might not be ordered done which would befit the service of his Majesty and the welfare of this people and army, he supplicated his Lordship to defer his determination to set out from this camp and go inland.

282. August 30, 1560. Tristán de Luna closes the debate.

The reply of the maestre de campo to what his Lordship has asked having been seen by the governor, he said that he had already discussed with him and the captains all that there was to do in the case, which is to set out inland on Monday.

That he has nothing else to say or reply, and that he was giving and gave this as his answer.

[signed:] Don Tristán de Luna y Arellano.

283. September 2, 1560. Confrontation over the governor's rations.

In this port of Santa María de Ochuse, September 2, 1560, I, Juan de Vargas, notary of this government appointed by the illustrious governor, Don Tristán de Luna y Arellano, captain-general of these provinces of La Florida and the Punta de Santa Elena, attest and certify to all persons who may see these presents: that on Monday, September 2, of the aforesaid year [15]60, the illustrious Don Tristán de Luna y Arellano, governor and captain-general of these provinces of La Florida and the Punta de Santa Elena, after having heard mass, said in the presence of the maestre de campo, the captains, the officials of his Majesty, and other persons that he [the maestre de campo] knew, from a memoir signed with his [the governor's] name, what provisions those persons whom he had indicated in a memoir (to which he referred him) were to take; but as he saw that no one went to get rations, he begged the maestre de campo to order provisions issued to him for himself and the members of his household. The maestre de campo replied that he was ready and prepared to give the provisions for the governor and the people of his house if there were enough captains and soldiers who [also] wished to take some; but if there were not, he could not give them for his Lordship alone, for it was not right that he should go alone.

284. September 2, 1560. Tristán de Luna condemns his captains to death.

On September 2, 1560, the illustrious Don Tristán de Luna y Arellano, governor and captain-general of these provinces of La Florida and the Punta de Santa Elena said: seeing that none of the captains or soldiers of the camp have gone to get rations as they were commanded by his Lordship, and that the petition which the captains had made to him had awaited the day of his departure [for an answer], he said: that he was condemning and did condemn all the said captains to death; and inasmuch as Captain Diego Téllez has Indians and has been sentenced to lose them, he said that he condemned him to the loss of the said Indians; and that as to the petition which they all had made, he authorized Diego Téllez and the other captains to bring it before the most illustrious viceroy of New Spain and the royal audiencia which resides in the City of Mexico, so that they might do justice in the case and determine from what has occurred in this suit, what persons have been to blame in not being willing to accede to his requests nor to anything that they have been commanded.

[signed:] Don Tristán de Luna y Arellano.

285. September 2, 1560. Cerón obtains authority from a meeting of officers and officials to send Porras to evacuate Coosa.

In this port of Santa María de Ochuse of these provinces of La Florida, on September 2, 1560, I, Juan de Vargas, chief notary of this government appointed by the illustrious Don Tristán de Luna y Arellano, governor and captain-general of these provinces of La Florida and the Punta de Santa Elena, attest and bear true witness to all gentlemen who may see these presents: that on Monday, which was the second day of the month and year aforesaid, the very magnificent Jorge Cerón Saavedra, maestre de campo and chief justice of this army, joined in a meeting with the very magnificent gentlemen, [namely], the treasurer, Alonso Velázquez Rodríguez, the accountant, Alonso Pérez, Captain Baltazar de Sotelo, Captain Don Pedro de Acuña, Captain Diego Téllez, Captain Don Cristóbal, Captain Juan de Porras, and Captain Julián de Acuña, to discuss and consider the things which befitted the service of his Majesty and the good of this camp. It was agreed and decided in this consultation that Captain Juan de Porras should go with a number of soldiers to Coosa where the sargento mayor and the other captains are. Of this it was ordered that a public announcement be made. . . .

286. September 9, 1560. Cerón insists that a meeting shall be called.

In the port of Santa María de Ochuse, September 9, 1560, the very magnificent Jorge Cerón Saavedra, maestre de campo and chief justice of these provinces of La Florida for his Majesty, in the presence of me the notary and the undersigned witnesses, appeared before the illustrious Don Tristán de Luna y Arellano, governor and captain-general of these said provinces for his Majesty, and before his Lordship caused to be summoned the officials of his Majesty, [namely] the treasurer, Alonso Velázquez Rodríguez, and the accountant, Alonso Pérez, captains Don Pedro de Acuña, Baltazar de Sotelo, Don Cristóbal Ramírez de Arellano, Diego Téllez, Juan de Porras, and Julián de Acuña, captain of the artillery. They all being in the presence of the governor, [the maestre de campo] said that it was well known and apparent to them all how Captain Don Cristóbal had come to give an account and news of the people and the camp under command of the sargento mayor and the other captains, Don Alonso de Castilla, Álvaro Nieto, and Gonzalo Sánchez. For this reason, having seen the letters and accounts which the aforesaid Don Cristóbal brought, they had tried to determine what reply should be sent to the letters mentioned; and because there has been dissension and litigation concerning certain opinions and arguments which have passed between the governor and the captains of his Majesty (to which he referred them) he, as maestre de campo and chief justice, had arranged to avoid delays for the officials and captains by ordering Captain Juan de Porras to make the journey to the province of Coosa, where the said sargento mayor and captains are, with twenty-four soldiers, horses, arms, and necessary supplies. [This it was] proper to do for the considerations and reasons which have been given in the presence of the governor, by the captains and the officials of his Majesty, to which he also referred them. And because Captain Juan de Porras and the men who are to go with him are about to start, and since he is going to-day it is fitting that he bear instructions from the governor as to what he will have to do; for which purpose, and in order that the aforementioned captains and men who are in the province of Coosa may know that what they have to do is fitting to his Majesty's service, in order to avoid debates and differences, Captain Juan de Porras should carry instructions from the governor. [The maestre de campo therefore] was asking and supplicating, and did so ask and supplicate, and with due respect required legally as many times as the law permits, that his Lordship would hold and consider it proper to issue the said instructions for the said purpose, for which purpose he should assemble with the said officials and captains, in the manner and way in which affairs have been managed and effected in this camp. Also, as such maestre de campo and chief justice he had commanded and did command the officials of his Majesty and captains aforementioned to meet with the governor as they have done hitherto, so that the aforesaid business might be settled and that the despatch of the tender which is anchored in this port [might be arranged]. For it is an important matter to give a report to the royal audiencia which resides in the City of Mexico and to the very illustrious viceroy concerning what has happened, with an account and report on the land and province of Coosa and of everything else that has been seen and learned in this land. For it befits the service of God and of his Majesty as an important matter to be talked over, discussed, determined and agreed upon in the despatch of the tender, some persons being chosen to go as captain if necessary, that some people be sent away in it because of the scantiness of food in the royal house and because of the small quantity which is expected, and the long time which must pass before we receive the command and decision of the royal audiencia and of the most illustrious viceroy. Because at present there are in this camp and port three hundred and sixty-two persons to be fed, but among them there are not fifty useful and available soldiers, for the rest are sick, women, children, Indian men and women, and other incapable people who do nothing but eat. Besides these, there are those in the interior, who number two hundred persons, without counting those on the patache and on the ship *San Juan* which is expected from La Havana, who will make another thirty—altogether five hundred souls. So, because it is essential to consider the foregoing in the manner most fitting and appropriate for the service of his Majesty and the welfare of this camp with all promptness,—because of all this, I ask and supplicate the governor again and yet again, and I command and require the captains and officials of his Majesty to meet together as I have said. If they refuse, [he said] he asked for such refusal in a sworn statement with whatever they might say and reply, so that he might give notice and report thereof to the viceroy. For the aforesaid maestre de campo is ready, disposed, and prepared to meet as such with them to give his opinion signed with his name as are the aforesaid officials and captains. Them he commands to give [their opinions], and he as chief justice will order, in the case or cases which may come up from this time forward, as most befits the service of God our Lord and his Majesty, and the benefit and profit of this camp. [He makes also] protestation that this demand, petition, and protestation shall be understood to be applicable in all affairs which may from this day forth arise until his Majesty shall command as he sees fit.

[signed:] Jorge Cerón.

Done before me, Juan de Vargas.

287. September 9, 1560. Luna refuses to send instructions by Porras to Coosa as petitioned by Cerón and the rest.

The said petition and request having been presented by the maestre de campo in the presence of the officials of his Majesty and the captains, and in the presence of me the said notary, and it having been seen by the governor, he said: that in the meeting which was held with the maestre de campo, the officials, and the captains, he was asked to give in writing what he desired to do. This he did, and he referred them to said writing. But after the maestre de campo, the officials, and the captains had left the meeting, they convened in his dwelling and ordered that Juan de Porras, captain of infantry, should go as captain with twenty-five or thirty men. Pursuant thereto they immediately announced publicly before his dwelling with attendance of a bailiff and notary, that they were sending the said Juan de Porras as has been said, without his [the governor's] knowing anything about it nor any notice thereof having been given him, the said announcement being now placed in the process which he was sending to the viceroy. As to the rest, the governor has not desired to intervene; for, he says, since he is governor of these provinces of La Florida and the captains take action without advising him thereof, therefore he has not wanted to have anything to do with the affair. He was writing to the captains and the sargento mayor how he had wanted to make the expedition, but that since he was not allowed to have either supplies or men he was not going. They might do whatever seemed good to them, for in the matter of the coming [of the party in Coosa] he had not known or done anything whatever....

[signed:] Don Tristán de Luna y Arellano.

288. September 9, 1560. Report on the situation at Polonza sent by Cerón and others to the Coosa party.

Very Magnificent Sirs: The letter from you which, on the first of July of this present year, was written in Coosa and given to the governor by Captain Don Cristóbal de Arellano, was shown to us on August 28 by the governor in this port of Polonza where we at present are. By this letter, signed with all of your names, we learned about the state of [that] camp what all of us here desired so much to know, and we surely gave many thanks to our Lord God for the known mercy which he showed us in letting us hear from you, so that our pain and care should not be so great as it was until that day; for we did not know where you could be nor what convenient means or method you might have for hearing from us, because on our part we had had so many misfortunes and for many other reasons, we could get no word from you. And even though every possible diligence was exercised here to bring about communications, we found no possible way for the entire fulfilment of our desire which would satisfy us. This was the principal reason why we who are here considered our own hardships, which have been notably severe, as less than your own, which were always represented to us as being as great as we have this day learned that they were. Thus it would appear that you have passed through hardships like ours more satisfactorily, judging from what [you] have said, than could be believed in view of what you have had to contend with, no matter what kind and how many they may have been.

You must be informed that we have continued in the same want of supplies as we were suffering when you left us in the province of Upiache, although we worked as hard as possible with all necessary diligence [to get more]; the supplies kept on growing fewer, the men kept getting weaker, and the natives continued to keep away from us. All this put us in worse straits than we might have expected, as we were hoping momentarily for relief and help from the fleet and the news which we expected to come from you; finally, although after long delay, [your letters] brought to an end the solicitude which we mentioned above. Meantime, our need grew to such extremity after a thousand difficult and laborious efforts to sustain ourselves, that horse-meat was publicly weighed out to give rations to the people, but not until for many days the most of us had had, not a handful of corn, which would have been like an abundance, but not even a few bitter acorns.

In view of the very bad way in which things were going, and of the great want from which the people of the camp were suffering, after we had besought and supplicated the governor to remedy our condition, the measure considered suitable was that of coming to the [Bahía] Filipina to maintain ourselves upon the shellfish there until the fleet should come. This determination being put into effect, many of us had a very difficult time; some lost their lives, for the hunger grew so great, and we were so long in getting down the river, that those who escaped from this disaster

consider themselves well off to find themselves wherever they may be.

After many ups and downs we reached this port of Polonza. Eight days later came the fleet, in which there came from the king scant supplies indeed; for it had been understood in New Spain from letters which had been written from here that there were supplies in plenty in the country and that [the fleet] would not find us here. It was necessary therefore to send some of the children, the sick, and the unfit to New Spain so that they should not eat from us the scant supplies which were brought. Luis Daza, the factor, was sent with the galleon *San Juan* to La Havana to be laden with more supplies, the better to sustain us while we should be here awaiting news from you, and until an account of everything that had happened should be given to the very illustrious viceroy of New Spain and his reply sent to us as to what ought to be done in the case. God, who is a great Lord, has given us relief, for it is surely good fortune for us to have heard from all of you.

The characteristics of the country and its possibilities, the traits of the natives, and everything connected with each of these having been ascertained after all these gentlemen had given and taken [information] concerning the situation, without the intervention therein of the governor because of his notable indisposition and lack of health (in which we have been no less unfortunate than in everything else) it was decided, during all that has been negotiated upon to-day—and you who are acquainted with the business in hand will understand, since the country is just as you have described it in your letter, and in fact the profit cannot be obtained in it which is desired in conformity with the royal intention of the king our lord—that you shall come to this port after having first satisfied yourselves of the insufficiency of the country, discussing it first with the very reverend fathers who are with you, with the opinion of whom as Christians and religious you should conform for the fulfilment of what we say in this letter. For since we are to leave the country it will be well for us all to await here together the will of the viceroy who in his Majesty's name sent us to these provinces, both for the sake of that which concerns this [withdrawal] and for the solution of other matters no less important than this. For if his Lordship [the viceroy] orders more people sent to Santa Elena than have been, this must be done with the required energy to which we are all obliged, and which is expected of your fidelity and ours.

The governor, on August 10, sent Don Martín Doz to the Punta de Santa Elena with fifty or sixty men to make a temporary settlement, for it appears from a royal cedula which was brought to him in these ships that the king, Don Felipe our lord, prefers the settlement of that district to that of all the rest of the provinces of La Florida. This he especially commended to the governor, and it appears from what his Majesty commands him in his cedula that he will consider himself best served by us if that point be colonized even though to do so most efficiently everything here should be abandoned. If you will bear this in mind, with respect to what we have already said, we consider that it will be the most acceptable thing for you to do as we are herewith writing to you. . . .

We only ask and beseech you that your return through any inhabited territory between there and here be made with all the just dealing which has always been ordered by the governor, and that you will observe his instructions as you have done. For by so doing, [we] have been protected and sustained, even though laboriously, as neither in our goings or comings have we fallen short in any point from that which is the will of the king our lord. The same we hope for from you, whose magnificent persons may God protect.

[signed:] Jorge Cerón Saavedra.
Alonso Velázquez Rodríguez.
Alonso Pérez.
Baltazar de Sotelo.
Diego Téllez.
Juan de Porras.
Don Pedro de Acuña.
Julián de Acuña.

289. September 13, 1560. Luis de Velasco to Luna.

Translated in Priestley, Luna Papers, II, 137–151, extracts.

[September 13] I have seen what you write me you have done as to what his Majesty sent to command you to do by the letters which Luis Daza carried, [in which he said] that notwithstanding what I might have ordered, you should go or send to make a settlement at the Punta de Santa Elena for the reasons which his Majesty indicates in his letter. This is that you have in compliance therewith sent Don Martín, your nephew, and Captain Biedma with about fifty-five soldiers; that Don Martín goes as senior in rank, and that if our Lord should dispose of him, the chief in command will be Captain Biedma; that they carry a quantity of goods for barter; that they took appointed [treasury] officials, and that they have two frigates, one small bark, eight pieces of the artillery taken from here, and the supply of powder and balls necessary, good arquebuses, and a forge. [You say that] you think they ought to be contented, and that with them goes Father Fray Gregorio de Beteta, who went from here with that purpose; and you think that he will harvest much fruit in the preservation of both the Spaniards and the Indians. For these latter are more domestic in that part than are those in yours. What you have done in this matter has seemed wise to me, because it is in fulfilment of that which the king our lord sent to command you, although I fear that the weather when they went was not favorable on that coast, and if they have not left La Havana at the time when this letter arrives, I think it would be wise to send orders to them not to set sail until the end of February or the beginning of March; for that coast is, they say, rough in winter, and they do not have complete information of what ports there are at the Punta de Santa Elena and the near-by territory, and it is to be believed that if no foreigners have come to those ports they will not do so during the stress of winter. On the other hand I have in mind the haste his Majesty feels to have that country taken possession of and a settlement made there; I also think that your port should not be abandoned until we know that possession has been taken of the other. For this taking possession of new lands is a matter of much importance between kings, especially during the time when there is peace between the king our lord and the king of France. You will keep each of these considerations in mind, and order that which appears to you most fitting to his Majesty's service.

I think I wrote by Luis Daza that General Pedro Menéndez was still here but was to set out to return to Spain about the middle or the last of

February, and would take with him two light ships so that they might go from La Havana to discover what ports there are at the Punta de Santa Elena and the coast for eighty or one hundred leagues from there on toward Los Bacallaos. One of these ships, it seemed best, ought to go to give information to his Majesty of what had occurred there, and the other was to come to report to you and to me on what it might find. This measure will not be taken if Don Martín and Biedma have gone to discover the port and have made a settlement in it; but if they have not left La Havana at the time when the general arrives, these ships I speak of may go with those which Don Martín has; they will help carry the people and supplies, and they will be able to take food for one year so that there shall be no lack in the interval before his Majesty orders it provided, and [the colonists] are provisioned from this country and from the islands with food and cattle, and more people are sent. If Don Martín shall have gone, and there is any information as to where they [he and his men] are, these two ships are to take them more supplies, and one of them is to go to give notice to his Majesty as I have said. This, as I say, is how it appears here with reference to the settlement of the Punta de Santa Elena. If there is found any facility near the port to plant any fields of corn and of other vegetables, let it not be neglected.

As to the matter of abandoning your port, it seems to me that it ought not to be done until we know that possession has been taken of that of Santa Elena for his Majesty, a settlement made, and news had from the captains and men who are in the interior with the sargento mayor. If it is ascertained that they are in a country where they can maintain themselves and whence there is a route by land over which to reach them, you should send from among the people whom you have there say about twenty or thirty soldiers with some horses, if any of the pack animals are left, so that these may carry clothing, munitions, and arquebuses. [This party] should advise [the men in the interior] that his Majesty has sent a command to go and colonize at the Punta de Santa Elena, and that you have sent people there, so that if they are, as is thought, in the province of Coosa, which is not far from Santa Elena, as appears from the painting and description which we have of it, they may in the month of March or April send some people to try the road from there

to the Punta de Santa Elena and to learn how much distance and what kind of country and road may lie between the province of Coosa and there, and whether, as time passes, supplies may be taken from that province or any other one, to the port.

I am in great anxiety and sorrow because you have had no word since the beginning of April until August 10 from the captains and people who are in the interior. May it please our Lord to conserve them in his service, and that no great misfortune may have happened to them. It seems to me you ought not to abandon that port until you hear from them or they rejoin you; if they return to you and bring a report that they have not found land in which it is possible to make a settlement, you may in that case leave at that port some thirty or forty soldiers with a person in whom you have confidence to govern them, so that the possession of the country may not be lost, as I have said, and they may receive what may be sent from here, and yourself proceed to La Havana in order to go from there, God willing, to the Punta de Santa Elena or such port as may there be settled, to reinforce it and order what has to be done there during the interval before his Majesty is given an account of what has happened and shall order provision of supplies and whatever most befits his service. The letter which you wrote to him will be sent on the first ships, and I will write to his Majesty asking him to give you the government of the island of Cuba; I will indicate to him how important this will be for the colonization and preservation of the ports of La Florida. You will make this more certain of success by not returning to Mexico nor leaving that country, except to go to La Havana when the time comes, until his Majesty sends to command what it pleases him that you should do. . . .

Regarding what you say has occurred between you and the maestre de campo and officials concerning courteous treatment and other matters, what I have to reply is that it grieves me much that they do not have the proper respect and love for your person and office. I am writing to them about this. It seems to me you should treat them with all love, and honor and favor them according to their rank and services, and take counsel with persons of authority and experience and accept their opinions rather than those of young men; especially [should you take] that of the maestre de campo, for he is a person of much age and prudence, and I know that he is a friend and servant of yours. . . .

In another letter which I had written before this one I believe I told how repairs are being made on the large bark *La Imposición* on which came Don Carlos and Father Fray Juan de Mazuelas, and how it will go in the month of January or the first of February to be laden at Campeche with corn and clothing to take to your port in the interval before Luis Daza goes with what he may have brought or may have sent from La Havana. [With that] and with what his caravel takes, I think the people can be sustained if good care is taken of the supplies. By the time the bark goes we shall know what is to be done about maintaining that port or moving you to La Havana or the Punta de Santa Elena. I have already said that that port ought not to be abandoned until you are rejoined by the people who are in the interior, or until you hear from them and and furnish them with arquebuses, munitions, and clothing if this can be done. Inasmuch as it may be that affairs have turned out in such a way that this ship will not find you at the port of Polonza, which may God our Lord forbid, it carries orders to go in search of you to La Havana. If it does so, the people are to be provided for with the supplies it takes, and the clothing apportioned among those who need it; it is then to be sent separately to the Punta de Santa Elena in case those who are to go there have already embarked. If they have not, they are to be provided with whatever is needed at the time they set out. . . .

I send a copy of the description of the country Soto traveled over. It is copied from the one which Luis de Moscoso gave to the viceroy and was sent to the emperor our lord [apparently not now extant]. It is considered trustworthy, from what those say who were in the country and have seen it. They assert that in the more than five years during which Soto traversed it they never lacked food, and that in some of the towns where they wintered, staying four or five months, they left food to spare when they went away. [Hence] I am surprised at the great scarcity of it which you have encountered. I think it has been because you have not reached the country which Soto traveled through, and the Indians had time to gather and hide the food. Everything has combined with my bad luck so that the expedition has not been as successful as was expected. May our Lord rem-

edy this in that which remains to be done, for He knows that it is fitting that the natives of that land shall come into the knowledge of his holy faith. . . .

290. September 14, 1560. Luis de Velasco to Luna.

Repeats his order that Coosa is to be occupied.
Translated in Priestley, Luna Papers, II, 155–157.

[September 14] Although I know that you have there the description of the road Soto followed when he went into that country, it seemed wise to me to send the one which goes herewith, to the end that, as it seems here, if you take the road which he did you will not want for food, nor will you fail to find settled and provisioned country all the way to the province of Coosa, where it was intended to colonize. Now that the mistake has been made, may our Lord grant that it may be corrected. The remedy which it here appears might be taken is that if the sargento mayor and the captains and men who went inland came upon the province of Coosa and have remained there, you should join them if you can do so advantageously, and effect a settlement in the province of Coosa or in its vicinity as being territory of the Punta de Santa Elena, where his Majesty orders a town planted. If the people [in the interior] took the road toward the Río del Espíritu Santo, whither Soto came out, it does not seem to me that you should go where they are, but report to them if possible what determination you will make, so that if it can be done the end which his Majesty commands may be attained, namely, that of going to settle at the Punta de Santa Elena. I find one difficulty in your going to La Havana. It is that once there the men cannot be well commanded or governed or made to return to La Florida, though only to the Punta de Santa Elena. I fear they will get into the interior of the island of Cuba without the possibility of preventing it, even though you and the governor exercise all possible diligence. I am writing asking him to be pleased to exercise great precaution that no soldier shall absent himself from the port. . . .

291. January 30, 1561. Luis de Velasco to Luna.

License for Luna to leave for Spain. Velasco is sending Ángel de Villafañe to replace him.
Translated in Priestley, Luna Papers, I, 9–15, extract.

In view of what you and the religious, the maestre de campo, and the captains write me, and understanding the dissensions, passions, and lack of conformity which have existed and still prevail between you and them, the little accomplishment effected by the expedition or to be expected from it, and the great amount which his Majesty has spent upon it; considering all this, and also the lack of health which you have experienced, and the desire which you express in one of your letters to get out of that country, it has seemed wise to me, after laying the case before this royal *audiencia*, the archbishop, the officials of his Majesty, and certain other gentlemen and principal persons, to send you license to make the journey to Spain to give account to his Majesty of what has happened, or to come to this country to choose whatever may seem best to you. In your place I am sending Ángel de Villafañe, that he may order whatever may seem to him most conducive to the service of God Our Lord and of his Majesty. [He is to] leave as many people at that port as he sees fit, to guard it and to serve as companions for the religious who are to remain there, and to keep the port from being closed in order that it may be possible to keep it supplied with food and cattle; he is to take the remainder of the people away to La Havana, where they are to join the others who go from this New Spain; and with the ships and supplies which are being sent he is to go to the Punta de Santa Elena, occupy it, and make a settlement at the port there or near there, as his Majesty commands. You will deliver to him the royal standard and enjoin the people to obey him and do what he orders them to do.

292. March 8, 1561. An account of events in the church at Ochuse (Polonza).

The demands of the captains and the friars to meet with Luna.

Translated in Priestley, Luna Papers, I, 87–91.

I, Gonzalo Suárez, a notary appointed by the very illustrious Don Tristán de Luna y Arellano, governor and captain-general in these provinces of La Florida and the Punta de Santa Elena for his Majesty, bear testimony and true witness to those persons by whom this writing may be seen: that upon a certain day, that is, on the seventh day of the present month of March, of this year of our Savior Jesus Christ one thousand five hundred and sixty-one, when the governor of this port, the maestre de campo, the officials of the king, the captains, and many other persons were in the church, the very reverend father, Fray Domingo de la Anunciación, began to preach. Among other things contained in his sermon, he said that the governor ought to call a meeting with the maestre de campo, the [treasury] officials of the king, and the captains, to order the things necessary for this port. When the sermon and the mass were ended, the said Fray Domingo de la Anunciación and Fray Domingo de Salazar came to where his Lordship was, and spoke to him, again using the same words as those of the sermon. He replied that they should come with him to his house and that they would there discuss the matter, as he did not wish to accede [there] to what the friars asked. When the maestre de campo saw this, he cried in a loud voice, "Ho, soldiers, my brothers and companions, follow me, for this thing cannot be endured." At these words all the others present became very much excited, and, following the maestre de campo, they went out behind the governor and the friars, who were walking beside his Lordship and trying to induce him to agree to call the meeting and be the friend of the maestre de campo, the officials of the king, and the captains. When they all arrived together at the doors of the governor's house, his Lordship, replying to what the friars had been saying as they walked along, said: "I have already spoken these words to you before this, and I again repeat, that if the maestre de campo, or the king's officials, or the captains were to come to my house I would receive them with all the affection in the world, and listen to the opinions which they might give me concerning the affairs of this camp, if it should be to the service of God and of his Majesty, whether in writing or orally, and if it is not concerning past affairs. And this I will do, as I have already said. But as to entering into a formal council with them, that I will not do, because of the way the maestre de campo, the king's officials, and the captains, have treated me. I have made a report to the viceroy concerning the whole affair, and until his Lordship appoints a person to hear us all and to do justice in the case, I have nothing further to do than what I here say." To these words the maestre de campo again said, speaking very rapidly and angrily and in loud tones: "Ho, captains, soldiers, brothers and companions of mine, if you are with me, I will ask in the name of all of you what I have to ask." At these words a great part of the people present again became excited. The friars, seeing this, took with them the maestre de campo, some of the captains, and a great part of the soldiers, and, without giving opportunity for anything else, went toward the church, leaving the governor there. With him remained captains Mateo del Sauz, Álvaro Nieto, Don Cristóbal, and Don Alonso de Castilla, the head bailiff Rodrigo Vázquez, ensigns Álvaro Muñoz and Cristóbal Asnal de Luna, and other persons. After this had happened on the day, month, and year above named, the governor in the presence of me the present notary, went to the church at the hour when the friars were accustomed to say the *Salve*. While he was kneeling Fray Domingo de la Anunciación came to him and said these words: "Your Lordship will please leave the church, for while you are here we cannot say the *Salve*." To this his Lordship replied that he would finish praying, and would then go, which he did. When he had finished he went out of the church, and although the captains Mateo del Sauz and Álvaro Nieto, the head bailiff, and other persons tried to go out with him, he would not permit them to do so, but asked and persuaded them to remain and hear the *Salve*. Thereupon, the governor went alone to his house. When we had come out from the *Salve*, we, the said captains Álvaro Nieto and Mateo del Sauz, the head bailiff, Don Cristóbal and other persons, went to where the governor was. Then, in the presence of them and of me the present notary, he commanded Juan de Vargas to go to the church and ask Father Fray Domingo de la Anunciación whether, since he had not permitted the governor to be present at the *Salve*, he would be allowed to attend the mass on the following

day. If he were not to be allowed to do so, the friar was to tell him the reason. This Juan de Vargas asked in my presence of Fray Domingo de la Anunciación, who replied that we should tell his Lordship that they would not permit him to hear mass either, and the reason was because his Lordship would not hold the meeting nor talk with the maestre de campo, the king's officials, and the captains; and that until he did so, since it was a matter vital to this camp and republic, they would not admit him nor allow him to be present at divine offices. With this reply Juan de Vargas and I returned and told his Lordship, all of which the governor asked me, the present notary, to give him in a sworn statement. In accordance with this order I had it written, and I signed it with my name. Done in this port of Santa María de Ochuse on the eighth day of the month of March, in the year above mentioned, being present as witnesses to what is said the captains Álvaro Nieto, Mateo del Sauz, and Don Alonso de Castilla and Álvaro Muñoz, ensign. . . .

Gonzalo Suárez,
Notary appointed.

293. August, 1561. Report of Tristán de Luna to Philip II.

Translated in Priestley, Luna Papers, *I, 5–7.*

When I, Don Tristán de Luna y Arellano, a widower, was in New Spain, the viceroy, Don Luis de Velasco, having heard of a certain expedition which I had made to Cíbola, ordered me in the name of your Majesty to make the expedition to La Florida. I accepted, and took five hundred and fifty men and one hundred and eighty horses. I took your Majesty's officials, a maestre de campo, captains, and all the other officers necessary for such an enterprise. All these positions were filled by your viceroy, and, beside the great amount which we all spent, I believe that your Majesty must have expended over three hundred thousand pesos [on this expedition]. I disembarked my people from the eleven vessels which were given me, at a point some eighty or one hundred leagues farther down, toward New Spain, than where Soto landed. I took a good port, which they call Polonza. I then sent out the sargento mayor and my nephew Don Cristóbal with a few of the people. They informed me that they had come upon a town in which they had found some supplies. Inasmuch as these were what I lacked, I left a captain with fifty or sixty men at the port, and with the remainder of the force set out inland, penetrating forty or fifty leagues from the port to where they were awaiting me. Thence I again sent out the sargento mayor, my nephew, some other captains, and two Dominican friars; inasmuch as I have here a transcript of the instructions which I gave them I will not repeat them. Certain of the captains and the friars whom I mention availed themselves of such wiles with the people whom they took with them, that although the sargento mayor strove to establish a settlement as he had been ordered, they would not do so, but persisted in returning. Nor could I [reach them] although I attempted to do so at two different times; neither would the maestre de campo, the officials, nor the captains go with me, but persisted in leaving the country and would not remain in it. Now, therefore, inasmuch as I made a report of all this to the viceroy, and he wrote me certain letters, I beseech your Majesty

to review all these, and certain other writings which were made there, or else send them all to the Council of the Indies or to some one else who shall make a report, in order that your Majesty may order what is most fitting. For if I am to blame, I desire your Majesty to order me punished; but if others are to blame, may they be punished according to law. For I was only Don Tristán de Luna y Arellano, and those under my command were so placed by virtue of orders from your Majesty. And because the viceroy appointed another governor, ordering me to turn over to him all the instructions which I held, I had transcripts made of them all, and the secretary who gave them to me has come now in these ships to inform your Majesty of what the viceroy commanded him. From him it may be learned whether there may be any lacking among those which I am bringing, I can also give you information concerning the conquest or discovery which your Majesty ordered made in the South Sea, as one who has seen it all for over thirty-three or thirty-four years. Concerning all of this I will give information as a vassal and servant of your Majesty, and as one who has seen it throughout the period of time which I mention.

REPORTS ON THE EXPEDITION OF ÁNGEL DE VILLAFAÑE, 1561

DEPOSITIONS GIVEN at the port of Ocoa, Española, in August, 1561, by a number of soldiers who had served under Luna and Villafañe (294–295) contain important incidental information on Villafañe's expedition which is not otherwise well documented. Scrappy and incomplete as they are, they throw some clear light on the reasons why the expedition did not succeed in its attempt to establish a permanent Spanish post on the coastland between the mouth of the Savannah River and St. Helena Sound.

Copy from an unidentified source in T. Buckingham Smith Papers in the Library of the New York Historical Society. They are translated in Priestley, *Luna Papers*, II, 281–311, from which extracts are taken.

294. August 11, 1561. Testimony of Alonso de Montalván.

And inasmuch as it seemed that it would be fitting to the service of God our Lord and his

Majesty, the maestre de campo, the religious, and the captains met together with the assent of all the other soldiers and wrote to the viceroy beseeching him to send them someone to govern them because Don Tristán de Arellano was not fit to govern them and so he should send to command them what they should do. They sent these letters in a caravel which was commanded by Gonzalo Gayón a pilot, who had come with the supplies which the viceroy had sent to them three or four times in addition to the ship *San Juan*, which had come a third time loaded with supplies from New Spain. The said despatch having been sent to the viceroy, as has been told, all the people were waiting with the governor in the port until they could see what the viceroy would send to order them to do, for a period of three or four months more or less, during which time they suffered greatly from hunger because they had come down from the towns. They were reduced to eating the hides of the cattle which they had brought from New Spain and all the horses that they had, and while they were in this extreme necessity at the end of these three or four months, there came to the port Ángel de Villafañe with fifty men and many supplies which the viceroy had sent to them. This declarant does not know the commission or power which he [Villafañe] carried, because he saw that he respected and obeyed Don Tristán as governor and captain-general, calling him his Lordship, and that the governor, Don Tristán de Arellano, said that he wanted to go to Spain and asked Ángel de Villafañe in the presence of the entire camp to give him one of the frigates which he had brought. Villafañe gave it to him, and the governor set out in it for the port of La Havana, saying that he wished to overtake there the general, Pedro Menéndez de Valdés, and so he went away. Villafañe and all the captains and men stayed behind, at the port, for Don Tristán went away taking only two servants and a negro woman, and seeming very happy and content such as he never had been for the preceding eight or ten months, at which everyone was surprised. As soon as Don Tristán had gone, upon the following day Ángel de Villafañe caused all the captains and soldiers to be gathered together, and he made a speech to them, saying that he had come by command of his Majesty and the viceroy in his royal name to go to the Punta de Santa Elena, for this his Majesty our lord had commanded, and that he wished to designate those who were to go with him and that all whom he should designate must take oath to him as their captain. So everyone took oath upon a crucifix except the maestre de campo, Captain Diego Téllez, the accountant, Alonso Pérez, and the

treasurer, Alonso Velázquez, who did not take the oath. When this was done Ángel de Villafañe left at the port Captain Biedma and Antonio Velázquez with fifty men, commanding them not to desert the place because the viceroy had so commanded. With the rest of the people, who must have been one hundred and sixty in all, he set out for La Havana at the end of two or three days and on reaching the said port of La Havana he held a review of all the people and designated amongst them those who were to go with him, to the number of about ninety people, all of whom said that they would be happy to go with him. The maestre de campo remained behind in La Havana, and Ángel de Villafañe set out from there in perhaps three months and a half more or less, with the ship *San Juan* and a lateen caravel and two frigates, with something like seventy-five men of the ninety whom he had designated, because the others hid from him and fled in La Havana. They passed through the [Bahama] Channel with very good weather and went to the Punta de Santa Elena taking Gonzalo de Gayón as pilot-major in the flagship. In the other ships went Juan de Puerta and Hernán Pérez and other men. They anchored at the said point three leagues out to sea because of the shoals which are many. Being thus anchored Ángel de Villafañe set out in a frigate with twenty men. He went ashore, and traveled along the shore of the sea and back inland about half a league, looking for the river of the said Punta de Santa Elena until they hit upon it, and there on the bank of the river Ángel de Villafañe took possession of that land in the name of his Majesty, as is evident and appears in the autos of possession referring thereto which were drawn up before his Majesty's notary, and which are hereby cited. They went on, searching by sea and by land along that entire coast as far as the Río Jordán and the Río de Canoas up to 34° 30', but they did not find any port or river where ships could be anchored. While they went along performing these duties a hurricane came upon them which lasted an entire night and another day until noon, and on that night they lost the two frigates upon which were stationed as pilots Juan de Puerta and Hernán Pérez with twenty-two other men, soldiers and mariners. Although [those on the frigates] asked succour from [the land party] during the night and they saw them near at hand and heard them, they were not able to succour them because the storm was so severe. The ship *San Juan*, which was at anchor, broke loose, losing two anchors and two cables and the bateau, and they broke away so that they were not seen any more for the time being. The aforesaid Ángel de Villafañe, seeing how he was left alone, and realizing the loss which had come upon him, asked the pilot-major what was the nearest land which was peopled with Spaniards; and the pilot said to him that it was the island of La Española, which was four hundred leagues away. So Ángel de Villafañe told him that since we were left alone he should turn his prow thither and make for the nearest port. So they came to Monte Cristo, which is on the island of La Española, and while they were going there they met the *San Juan* on the seas. When they reached Monte Cristo, he repaired the ships, took on water and wood, and said that he wanted to return to La Havana, to find out what had become of the fifty men who had remained at the port of Ochuse with Captain Biedma and to advise the viceroy what a bad country the Punta de Santa Elena was, that there was no port there suitable for anchorage, and that he would await there whatever he might be commanded to do in order that the people might not perish. So he set sail with the ship *San Juan* and the caravel from the port of Monte Cristo after something like twenty-five days, taking with him the people whom he had brought with him in the two ships except this declarant and one Francisco Rodríguez; to these men Ángel de Villafañe gave license to remain upon that island on account of illness. He also gave license to another man, Miguel Sánchez Serrano, and to one Cristóbal Velázquez and another, Martín de Menchaca and to one Baracaldo, an arquebusier, and to another, Antón Núñez, to one Bermúdez and one Gutiérrez. Other soldiers to the number of eleven fled in the port of Monte Cristo from the ship *San Juan* in which they came, and although Ángel de Villafañe searched for them he could not capture them nor four mariners who also fled. This is the truth and all that he knows under the oath which he took, and this declaration being read to him he affirmed it and ratified it and signed it with his name.

Asked whether, before Ángel de Villafañe reached the Punta de Santa Elena, the governor, Don Tristán de Arellano, had sent any people to that port, the declarant said that while he was in the province of Coosa, as he has said, he learned that the governor, Don Tristán de Arellano, sent to the Punta de Santa Elena Don Martín de Hoz, his nephew, with the ship *San Juan*, two frigates, and one hundred men. They sailed beating against head winds; Don Martín with the ship *San Juan* in which he went made port in New Spain and the two frigates made the port of La Havana, and, as they did not find Don Martín de Hoz whom they had for their captain, after some days they also went to New Spain. From there the viceroy again sent out the said ship and the two frigates under Villafañe.

[signed:] Alonso de Montalván.

295. August 11, 1561. At Ocoa, Española. Deposition of Cristóbal Velázquez, foot soldier with Tristán de Luna, with Mateo del Sauz at Coosa, and at Puerta de Santa Elena with Ángel de Villafañe.

When they reached there [Ochuse] this declarant learned that the governor, Don Tristán, was on bad terms with the captains, the officials of his Majesty, the religious, and all the people because he had had a certain illness before he went to Nanipacana from which it was said that he had lost his senses and that he was not in fit condition to govern. For this reason they all with one accord wrote to the viceroy to send them a person to govern them. In this situation Ángel de Villafañe came from New Spain with forty or fifty soldiers, and certain supplies which the viceroy was sending to them in addition to others which he had first sent them three times under the pilot-major, Juan de Puerta, and Hernán Pérez, the maestre. Seven or eight days after Villafañe arrived, the declarant not knowing for what cause, Don Tristán departed from the port in a frigate saying that he was going to La Havana; he took as pilot Juan de Puerta, while Ángel de Villafañe, the maestre de campo, Jorge Cerón de Saavedra, and the other captains who were there remained behind. After Don Tristán set sail with only one or two servants and a negro woman, Ángel de Villafañe gathered all the people together, they numbering something like two hundred men more or less, with another forty or fifty men whom Ángel de Villafañe brought, and he made a certain speech to them saying that he had come there by the command of the viceroy to go to the Punta de Santa Elena, and that those who wanted to go with him to the said Punta de Santa Elena might go and welcome, but those who did not want to go would not be compelled to do so. So four or five days after Don Tristán set out for La Havana saying that he was going to Spain, Ángel de Villafañe set sail from the port of Ochuse with the ship *San Juan*, a lateen caravel, and a frigate with about two hundred men more or less, leaving at the port of Ochuse Captain Biedma with about fifty or sixty men so that he might keep the port occupied, that being the command of the viceroy. [Biedma was told] that if in the space of four or five months he should receive no word from his Lordship as to what they were to do he might go at the end of that time. And so Ángel de Villafañe arrived with these people in La Havana where he designated certain people, the witness does not remember the number of them, to go with him. In effect Ángel de Villafañe left the port of La Havana with about seventy soldiers in the ship *San Juan*, the lateen caravel, and two frigates. All the rest of the people stayed at the port of La Havana. He could not get any more soldiers because they all hid except the maestre de campo, Jorge Cerón de Saavedra, Captain Diego Téllez, Captain Don Cristóbal de Arellano, and Captain Gonzalo Sánchez de Aguilar; for these remained there publicly, not desiring to go to the Punta. It was perhaps four or five months, more or less, until Villafañe set out from La Havana, and this witness went with him among the other soldiers. They passed through the Bahama Channel with good weather, and having passed through it they went to the Punta de Santa Elena and went along the coast searching for the river of that Punta de Santa Elena; but being unable to find a port into which the ships could enter because of the many shoals, they anchored in the open sea two leagues more or less from land, and Ángel de Villafañe went ashore with about twenty soldiers. It was said that he had taken possession at the Punta de Santa Elena, the witness not being present thereat because he was on the ship *San Juan* and was not commanded to go ashore. After this they ran along the coast up to 32° 30′ or 33° and

reached the river called Jordán and the Río de Canoas. They went ashore and took water in some swamps, but they never could find a port where they could anchor a ship. While they were engaged in this a very severe storm struck them which lasted a day and a night and perhaps more. As a result of it they lost the two frigates with up to twenty-six soldiers and mariners. The lateen caravel which came as flagship and the ship *San Juan* separated. The latter escaped with the loss of two anchors, two cables, and the bateau. As they were going toward Porto Rico, at the end of a week of navigation, they came upon the lateen caravel flagship in which was Ángel de Villafañe; when they sighted each other they hailed each other and landed on this island of La Española at the port of Monte Cristo on the northern shore of the island. There they repaired the ships and took on water and wood during five or six days in which they remained at the port. After perhaps twenty-five or twenty-six days Ángel de Villafañe left with the two ships and the people he was taking in them, saying that he was going to La Havana to report to the viceroy what had happened and await what he might order him to do. Fifteen soldiers and four mariners remained on this island, some of them having license from Villafañe and others not, and so this declarant remained. This is the truth and what he knows under the oath which he has taken, etc.

Being asked to say and declare who are the soldiers who remained on this island from among those brought by Villafañe, and which of them had permission and which had not, he said that those who stayed are Alonso de Montalván, Miguel Sánchez, Machin de Menchaca, Baracaldo, Antón Núñez, this declarant, Antón Sánchez, one Yllescas, Tomás Rodríguez, Bermúdez, Juan López, one Montoya, Francisco Sánchez, Francisco Gutiérrez, and Francisco Rodríguez. These are soldiers but he does not remember the names of the mariners nor does he know which of the soldiers had permission, although he had understood that certain of them had been granted it by Villafañe.

Being asked if Don Tristán de Arellano sent any people to the Punta de Santa Elena before Ángel de Villafañe went, the declarant said that, while he was engaged on the expedition that he has spoken of, he learned and understood, although he was not present, that Don Tristán had sent

Don Martín de Hoz, his nephew, with certain men, to make a settlement at the Punta de Santa Elena by command of his Majesty. They encountered contrary winds after sighting La Havana, and made port in New Spain, not having been able to make the port of La Havana. For this reason, the viceroy had commanded that Ángel de Villafañe should be sent to settle at the Punta de Santa Elena, and this is what he knows and what happened. When his statement had again been read to him, he said that what is contained in it is the truth and he affirmed and ratified it and signed it with his name,

[signed:] Cristóbal Velázquez.

VIII

The French Colonies in Florida, 1562–1565, and Their Fatal Termination

BARELY FOUR MONTHS after the decision of Philip II that Spain was no longer interested in the southeast of North America as a place for settlement, in January, 1562 Chantône, his ambassador in Paris, reported that vessels under Jean Ribault were about to leave France for the west. For several decades France had expressed an interest in America. By the expeditions of Giovanni de Verrazzano, Jacques Cartier, and the Sieur de Roberval and the yearly visits of the fishermen, she had gained much knowledge of the northeast. Information on the area to the south had been gleaned by more unofficial means. French sailors managed to get themselves employed on Spanish ships going to the Indies, and French pirates attacked homecoming Spanish treasure fleets. The expedition of Ribault was the concrete manifestation of a dream of the Huguenot Admiral Coligny to undermine Spanish power in America by establishing a French presence on the Florida coast. In June, 1562 Ribault set out to return to France, leaving a small colony that he had established at Charlesfort on Port Royal Sound. However, he was unable to get in France the supplies and reinforcements he needed for the colony because of the outbreak of civil war. The French in Florida were thrown back on their own resources, which proved to be very meager. After several incidents, including the murder of their leader, they constructed a vessel and returned to France.

In May, 1564 a Spanish expedition under Hernando Manrique de Rojas was sent to find the French colony and expel the settlers. He found only the remnants of the fort and one Frenchman, Guillaume Rufin [Rouffin], who had been left behind (301). Rojas sailed back to the West Indies, confident that he had removed all trace of the French presence, but he made his search too early to discover the second French colony under René Goulaine de Laudonnière, established at La Caroline on the St. Johns River in June, 1564.

The members of this colony were as feckless and troublesome as those of the first settlement. Some exploration was undertaken inland, and Jacques Le Moyne de Morgues has left a fine pictorial record of the natives, but much of the settlers' time appears to have been taken up with attempts at mutiny and depredations against the Indians, resulting in their alienation. One diversion took the form of a piratical expedition against Spain in the West Indies and ended up with the capture of the whole party, thus confirming Spanish suspicions about the intentions of the French and the strengthening of the conviction that they had to be removed. However, by the spring of 1565 the French had experienced enough of the pioneering life and were determined to return of their own accord. Food supplies had dwindled and little planting had been done. In late August, just as they were on the point of departure, reinforcements and supplies arrived in a fleet under Jean Ribault. A few days later, Spanish ships commanded by Pedro Menéndez de Avilés, arrived at the St. Johns River. He had been ordered to remove the French, set up a Spanish colony, and reconnoiter the Atlantic Coast as far north as Newfoundland. Ribault, fully aware of the Spanish intentions, attempted to give chase to the Spaniards, but by taking the ablest men from the fort, he left it in a vulnerable position. The Spaniards, with the aid of the Indians, attacked by land and killed most of the French, although some, including Laudonnière, managed to escape (306). Later Menéndez de Avilés encountered and put to death the shipwrecked survivors of Ribault's expedition. Suddenly, Florida once more assumed a position of importance in the eyes of Philip II.

THE FIRST FRENCH EXPEDITION TO FLORIDA, 1562

IN THE SPRING of 1562 Jean Ribault and a small party of Frenchmen reconnoitered the coast of the Florida Peninsula northwards to what is now the area between the Savannah River and St. Helena Sound. They made careful notes of the coast they passed and named the rivers from those they knew in France. They made a map, a copy of which has survived and on which were notes of the river names (297). The entry finally chosen by the French for the foundation of an advance post was Port Royal Sound. There they built the first small post called Charlesfort, after Charles IX. Traditionally, its location is thought to have been Parris Island (the site of the later Spanish fort of San Marcos). It is now reasonably well established that it was on Battery Creek, near the modern small town of Port Royal, although the precise site has never been positively identified.

The twenty-six men left at Charlesfort expected to be relieved soon, but they were not. Captain Albert de la Pierria kept them well together for a time, until food ran out and the local Cusabo Indians could not (or would not) supply more. When the commander attempted to quell indiscipline by having one offender hanged and another exiled to a nearby island, the men rose in revolt and killed him, electing in his place Captain Nicolas Barré, the author of the map that has survived. Barré restored some degree of discipline and established satisfactory relations with the Indians, the latter coming about the fort when the plan for building a vessel took hold of the men, since this meant the French would soon move away and cease to be a burden on the Indians. Without any special skills, they built, rigged, and equipped a brigantine (with much aid from the Indians) and set out in her. After they had made some progress, the vessel was becalmed, provisions went short, and the men suffered great hardship, especially when they were almost overcome by waves and wind and damage (they thought) from a rock. To get strength to bail, they decided on a sacrifice and killed and ate one of their number. This enabled them to sight the coast of Brittany. At that point they encountered an English ship, which was, ironically, one of an English squadron Ribault had induced to prepare to go to Florida to their aid, but which had gone privateering instead. A few of the men who were in the best condition were taken to England, but their tale is not likely to have kindled any enthusiasm there for a further Anglo-French American venture to Florida.

The account of the French colony is prefaced by René de Laudonnière's general description of the Indians of Florida from *L'histoire notable de la Floride*.

The primary source is Jean Ribault, *The whole and true discoverye of Terra Florida* (London, Rowland Hall for Thomas Hacket, 1563). The best manuscript is B. L., Sloane MS 3644, fols. 111–121. The latter was printed by H. P. Biggar, "Jean Ribault's *Discoverye of Terra Florida*," *English Historical Review*, XXXII (1917), 263–270. Both were reprinted, the former in facsimile, in *The Whole & True Discoverye of Terra Florida* (Deland, Fla., 1928, reprinted Gainesville, Fla., 1966). The latter is given below (298).

Lancelot Voisin, Seigneur de la Popellinière, *Les trois mondes* (Paris, 1582), gave a somewhat inaccurate account of the events of 1562, which includes something about the return voyage (300).

René de Laudonnière included a full account of the venture in *L'histoire notable de la Floride* (Paris, 1586), which is extracted below (299).

Chapter Thirty-two
The Indians of Florida

296. René de Laudonnière's description of Florida and its Indians.

Laudonnière's description of Florida and its Indians first appeared in L'histoire notable de la Floride *(Paris, 1586), fols. 2v.–7v., and in translation in* A notable history containing foure voyages made by certaine French captaines unto Florida *(London, 1587), fols. 1–8; reprinted in* Richard Hakluyt, *Principal navigations, III (1600), 306–307 (VIII [1904], 450–456). It can now be used in close conjunction with the graphic material in Paul Hulton,* The Work of Jacques Le Moyne de Morgues *(London, 1977). It should be recognized that Laudonnière's descriptive material rests on information acquired both in 1562 and in 1564–1565.*

New France is almost as great as all our Europe. Howbeit the most known and inhabited part thereof is Florida, whither many Frenchmen have made divers voyage at sundry time, insomuch that nowe it is the best knowen Countrey which is in all this part of newe France. The Cape thereof is as it were a long head of lande stretching out into the Sea an hundred leagues, and runneth directly towarde the South: it hath right over against it five and twentie leagues distant the Isle of Cuba otherwise called Isabella, toward the East the Isles of Bahama and Lucaya, and toward the West the Bay of Mexico. The Countrey is flat, and divided with divers rivers, and therefore moyst, and is sandie towards the Sea shore. There groweth in those partes great quantitie of Pinetrees, which have no kernels in the apples which they beare. Their woods are full of Oakes, Walnuttrees, blacke Cherrietrees, Mulberry trees, Lentiskes, and Chestnut trees, which are more wilde then those in France. There is great store of Cedars, Cypresses, Bayes,

Palme trees, Hollies, and wilde Vines, which climbe up along the trees and beare good Grapes. There is there a kinde of Medlers, the fruite whereof is better then that of France, and bigger. There are also Plumtrees, which beare very faire fruite, but such as is not very good. There are Raspasses, and a little berrie which we call among us Blues, which are very good to eate. There growe in that Countrey a kinde of Rootes which they call in their language Hasez, whereof in necessitie they make bread. There is also there the tree called Esquine, which is very good against the Pockes and other contagious diseases. The Beastes best knowen in this Countrey are Stagges, Hindes, Goates, Deere, Leopards, Ounces, Luserns, divers sortes of Wolves, wilde Dogs, Hares, Cunnies, and a certaine kinde of beast that differeth little from the Lyon of Africa. The foules are Turkeycocks, Partridges, Parrots, Pigions, Ringdoves, Turtles, Blackbirdes, Crowes, Tarcels, Faulcons, Laynerds, Herons, Cranes, Storkes, wilde Geese, Malards, Cormorants, Hernshawes, white, red, blacke and gray, and an infinite sort of all wilde foule. There is such abundance of Crocodiles, that oftentimes in swimming men are assayled by them; of Serpents there are many sorts. There is found among the Savages good quantitie of Gold and Silver, which is gotten out of the shippes that are lost upon the coast, as I have understood by the Savages themselves. They use traffique thereof one with another. And that which maketh me the rather beleeve it, is, that on the coast towarde the Cape, where commonly the shippes are cast away, there is more store of Silver then toward the North. Neverthelesse they say, that in the Mountaines of Appalatcy there are Mines of Copper, which I thinke to be Golde. There is also in this Countrey great store of graynes and herbes, whereof might be made excellent good dyes and paintings of all kind of colours. And in trueth the

Indians which take pleasure in painting of their skins, know very well how to use the same. The men are of an Olive colour, of great stature, faire, without any deformitie, and well proportioned. They cover their privities with the skinne of a Stagge well dressed. The most part of them have their bodies, armes, and thighes painted with very faire devises: the painting whereof can never bee taken away, becase the same is pricked into their flesh. Their haire is very blacke and reacheth even downe to their hips, howbeit they trusse it up after a fashion that becommeth them very well. They are great dissemblers and traitours, valiant of their persons & fight very well. They have none other weapons but their bowes and arrowes. They make the string of their bow of a gut of a Stag, or of a Stags skin, which they know how to dresse as well as any man in France, and with as different sorts of colours. They head their arrowes with the teeth of fishes and stone, which they worke very finely and handsomly. They exercise their yong men to runne well, and they make a game among themselves, which he winneth that hath the longest breath. They also exercise themselves much in shooting. They play at the ball in this maner: they set up a tree in the middest of a place which is eight or nine fathom high, in the top whereof there is set a square mat made of reedes or Bulrushes, which whosoever hitteth in playing thereat, winneth the game. They take great pleasure in hunting and fishing. The kings of the Countrey make great warre one against the other, which is not executed but by surprise, and they kill all the men they can take: afterward they cut of their heads to have their haire, which returning home they carry away, to make thereof their triumph when they come to their houses. They save the women and children and nourish them and keepe them alwayes with them. Being returned home from the warre, they assemble all their subjects, and for joy three days and three nights they make good cheare, they daunce & sing, likewise they make the most ancient women of the Countrey to dance, holding the haires of their enemies in their hands: and in dauncing they sing praises to the Sunne, ascribing unto him the honour of the victory. They have no knowledge of God, nor of any religion, saving of that which they see, as the Sunne and the Moone. They have their Priests to whom they give great credit, because they are great magicians, great soothsayers, and

callers upon divels. These Priests serve them in stead of Physitions and Chirurgions. They carry alwayes about them a bag full of herbes and drugs to cure the sicke diseased which for the most part are sick of the pocks, for they love women & maidens exceedingly, which they call the daughters of the Sunne: and some of them are Sodomites. They marry, and every one hath his wife, and it is lawfull for the King to have two or three: yet none but the first is honoured and acknowledged for Queene: and none but the children of the first wife inherite the goods and authoritie of the father. The women doe all the businesse at home. They keepe not house with them after they know they be with child. And they eate not of that which they touch as long as they have their flowers. There are in all this Countrey many Hermaphrodites, which take all the greatest paine, and beare the victuals when they goe to warre. They paint their faces much, and sticke their haire full of feathers or downe, that they may seeme more terrible. The victuals which they carry with them, are of bread, of hony, and of meale made of Maiz parched in the fire, which they keepe without being marred a long while. They carry also sometimes fish, which they cause to be dressed in the smoke. In necessitie they eat a thousand rifraffes, even to the swallowing downe of coales, and putting sand into the pottage that they make with this meale. When they goe to warre, their King marcheth first, with a clubbe in the one hand, and his bowe in the other, with his quiver full of arrowes. All his men follow him, which have likewise their bowes and arrowes. While they fight, they make great cries and exclamations. They take no enterprise in hand, but first they assemble oftentimes their Councell together, and they take very good advisement before they growe to a resolution. They meete together every morning in a great common house, whither their King repaireth, and setteth him downe upon a seate which is higher then the seates of the other: where all of them one after another come and salute him: and the most ancient begin their salutations, lifting up both their handes twise as high as their face, saying, ha, he, ya, and the rest answer ha, ha. Assoone as they have done their salutation, every man sitteth him downe upon the seates which are round about in the house. If there be any thing to intreate of, the King calleth the Jawas, that is to say, their Priestes, and the most ancient men, and asketh them their advise. Afterward he commaundeth Cassine to be brewed, which is a drinke made of the leaves of a certaine tree: They drinke this Cassine very hotte: he drinketh first, then he causeth to be given thereof to all of them one after another in the same boule, which holdeth well a quart measure of Paris. They make so great account of this drinke, that no man may taste thereof in this assembly, unlesse hee hath made proofe of his valure in the warre. Moreover this drinke hath such a vertue, that assoone as they have drunke it, they become all in a sweate, which sweate being past, it taketh away hunger and thirst for foure and twenty houres after. When a King dyeth, they burie him very solemnly, and upon his grave they set the cuppe wherein he was woont to drinke: and round about the sayde grave they sticke many arrowes, and weepe and fast three dayes together without ceassing. All the kings which were his friends make the like mourning: and in token of the love which they bare him, they cut of more then the one halfe of their haire, as well men as women. During the space of sixe Moones (so they reckon their moneths) there are certaine women appoynted which bewaile the death of this King, crying with a loude voyce thrise a day, to wit, in the Morning, at Noone, and at Evening. All the goods of this King are put into his house, and afterward they set it on fire, so that nothing is ever more after to be seene. The like is done with the goods of the Priestes, and besides they burie the bodies of the Priests in their houses, and then they set them on fire. They sowe their Maiz twise a yere, to wit, in March and in June, and all in one and the same soyle. The sayd Maiz from the time that it is sowed untill the time that it be ready to be gathered, is but three moneths on the ground. The other 6. moneths they let the earth rest. They have also faire Pumpions, & very good Beanes. They never dung their land, onely when they would sowe, they set the weedes on fire, which grewe up the 6. moneths, and burne them all. They dig their ground with an instrument of wood which is fashioned like a broad mattocke, wherewith they digge their Vines in France, they put two graines of Maiz together. When the land is to be sowed, the King commaundeth one of his men to assemble his subjects every day to labour, during which labour the King causeth store of that drinke to be made for them, whereof we have spoken. At the time when the Maiz is gathered, it is all carried

into a common house, where it is distributed to every man according to his qualitie. They sowe no more but that which they thinke will serve their turnes for six moneths, & that very scarcely. For during the Winter they retire themselves for three or foure moneths in the yeere into the woods, where they make little cotages of Palme boughes for their retraite, and live there of Maste, of Fish which they take, of Oisters, of Stagges, of Turkeycockes, and other beasts which they take. They eate all their meate broyled on the coales, and dressed in the smoake, which in their language they call Boucaned. They eate willingly the flesh of the Crocodile: and in deede it is faire and white: and were it not that it savoureth too much like Muske we would oftentimes have eaten thereof. They have a custome among them, that when they finde themselves sicke, where they feele the paine, whereas we cause ourselves to be let blood, their Physitions sucke them untill they make the blood follow.

The women are likewise of good proportion and tall, and of the same colour that the men be of, painted as the men be: Howbeit when they are borne, they be not so much of an Olive colour, and are farre whiter. For the chiefe cause that maketh them to be of this colour proceedes of annointings of oyle which they use among them: and they doe it for a certaine ceremonie which I could not learne, and because of the Sunne which shineth hote upon their bodies. The agilitie of the women is so great, that they can swimme over the great Rivers bearing their children upon one of their armes. They climbe up also very nimbly upon the highest trees in the Countrey.

Beholde in briefe the description of the Countrey, with the nature and customes of the Inhabitants: which I was very willing to write, before I entred any further into the discourse of my historie, to the end that the Readers might be the better prepared to understand that, which I meane hereafter to entreate of.

297. Description of Florida
on a map by Nicolas Barré.

Nicolas Barré (Nicolaus Parreus, as the Spaniards knew him) was the cartographer of the first French Florida expedition of 1562 and the second commander of the unfortunate settlement at Charlesfort. Some time after his return to France, the Spaniards obtained a copy of his map and translated its nomenclature, etc. into Spanish. Now in the Museo Naval, Madrid, Navarrete, Colección, XIV, fol. 459 (a sixteenth-century version, although the rest of the material in the volume is composed of copies of a much later date), it was first published by W. P. Cumming, "The Parreus map (1562) of French Florida," Imago mundi, XVII (1963), 27–40, the translation of the notes being reprinted from there.

The description of Florida, which goes with this, begins from the said Cabo François, which is called Cape of Florida in the maps which have been made up to this time, which is the point from which Frenchmen appeared and began this discovery and placed upon it the said name Cabo François [French Cape] which goes along the coast to the River of May where there is an island which they call Island of May which is the first. Farther on there is another river which they call Seme and another island which has the same name which is the second. There follows another river the third, which is called Some and another island which has the same name. There is another river, the fourth, which is called Loyer and an island of the same name. Another river, the fifth, of Charont, and an island of the same name. The sixth, River Garone and an island of the same name. The seventh—Belle and an island of the same name. The ninth, River of Liborne Port Royal. The tenth River of Belleaus ut. On all those rivers and islands the French placed those said names, which are said to be the names which those ports have from Calais to Brittany.

The Cabo François is at 29 degrees.
Island of May at 30 degrees.
River of Loyer at 31 degrees.
Grande Isle at 32 degrees.
River of Belleaus ut at 33.

According to the calculations which they have here, this discovered coast, which goes from the Cabo François to the River of Belleaus ut, is held to be 72 or eighty leagues.

[Endorsed fol. 460 verso:] Year 15[6]2 Relation of the description of Florida.

Chapter Thirty-three
The French Reconnaissance, 1562–1563

298. 1563. Jean Ribault, "The true discoverie of Terra Florida."

This is an English translation of Ribault's report to Gaspard de Coligny, Admiral of France; the French version of the narrative has not been found. Both manuscript and printed versions were used to try to gain support for an English venture in 1563 under Thomas Stukely that was to relieve Charlesfort.

The proposed English intervention on Jean Ribault's behalf was frustrated by the exigencies of Anglo-French politics, which led to a breach between Ribault and the English authorities (and involved his imprisonment in London for a time). The Spanish ambassador in London, Alvaro de Quadra, sent reports to Spain indicating the nature and extent of the English preparations (Calendar of State Papers, Spanish, 1558–1567 [London, 1892], pp. 323, 333, 334–346), and suggesting that he had influenced the proposed English commander against intervening in what Quadra insisted was Spanish territory. Thomas Stukely, the English commander-designate, assembled five vessels, the Anne Stucley, *the* Thomas Stucley, *the* William Stucley, *the* Trenite Stucley, *and the* Fortune Stucley, *and claimed to have manned and equipped them and to have had 300 soldiers on board when he was granted a passport on March 26, 1563, to pass to "the Countrey called Terra Florida for the farther discovering of those partes which as yet be unknown" (P.R.O., High Court of Admiralty, Exemplifications, H.C.A. 14/5, nos. 32, 36, 37, 381; H.C.A. 14/6, no. 4). Although he set out shortly after, Stukely made no attempt to cross the Atlantic, but cruised in waters between Ireland and Spain, taking prizes and behaving simply as a pirate. He eventually landed in Ireland and after some time received an implied pardon for his delinquencies. He discredited Florida enterprises in England*

and, indeed, Ribault's report and a few ephemeral ballads were the sole results of the brief emergence of English interest in North American colonization.

Whereas in the yeare 1562 it pleased God to move your grace to chose and appoynt us to discover and vieu a certen long coste of the West Indea, from the hed of the lande called la Florida, drawing towardes the northe parte untill the hed of Britons, distant from the said hed of la Florida 900 leages, or therabout, to the ende that we might certifie you and make true reporte of the temperature, fertilitie, portes, havens, rivers, and generally of all the comodities that might be founde and seen in that lande, and also to learn what people were there dwelling, which thing long tyme agon ye have desiered, being stirred [thereunto] by this zeale, that France might one daye through newe discover[ie]s have knowledg of strange conteries, and also thereof to receave, by meanes of contynewall trafficque, riche and inestimable comodities, as other nations have don, by taking in hand suche farre navegacions, bothe to the honnour and praise of theire Kinges and prynces, and also to thincrease of great proffite and use of their common wealthes, counteris and domynions. And which is most of all, withowt comparison, to be considered and estemed, it semeth well that you have byn hereto stirred from God above, and led to yt by the hope and desire you have that a numbre of brutishe people and ignoraunt of Jesus Christ, may by his grace come to some knowledge of his holly lawes and ordynaunces, so as it semeth that it hathe pleased the lyving God by his godly providence to reserve the care he hathe had of there salvation until this tyme, and will bryng them to our faithe, at the tyme by himself alone foreseen and ordeyned. For if it were nedefull to shewe howe manye from tyme to tyme have gon about to fynd owt this great land, to inhabite there, who nevertheles have alwaies failed and byn put by of there intention and purpose, some through feare of shipwracke, and some by great wyndes and tempestes that drove them backe, to theire marvelous greif; of the which ther was one a verry famyous strainger [named] Sebastian Cabot, an excellent pilote, sent thither by the King of England, Henery the vii, anno 149[8] and many others, who never could attayne to any habytation or take posession there of one only fote of grownd, nor yet approche nor enter into those portes and faire rivers, into the which God hathe brought us, wherfore, my lorde, it may be well said that the living God hathe reserved this greate lande for the Kinges poore subiectes, aswell to the ende they might be made great over this pooer people and rude nation, as also tapprove the former affection which our Kinges have had to this discover[ie]: for the late King Francis [the first] of happie memorye, a prynce endued with excellent vertues, anno 1524, sent a famyous and notable man, a Florentyne, named Messire Jehan de Verrazane to searche and discover the west partes as farre as might be, who departyng from Depe with two vesselles, litle differing from the making and burden of these two pynnases of the Kinges, which your grace hath ordained for this present navegation, in the which lande he arrived where he founde the elevation of the pole of 38 degrees, the cuntery, as he writeth, goodly, frutefull, and of so good a temperaunce as is not possible to have better, being then as yet of no man seen, nor discovered. But he being not able at his first voiage to bring to passe that [whiche] he had intended, nor arrive in any porte, by reason of sondery inconvenyences, which happen comenlye, was constrayned to retourn into Fraunce, where after his arrivall he never ceased to make sute untill he was sent thither agayn, where at the last he died, which gave smale lust to send thither agayn and was cause that this laudable enterprise was leift of, untill the yeare 1534, at which tyme his Majestie, desiering allwaies thenlardging of his Kingdom, cuntries and domynions, and the advauntage and ease of his pooer subiectes, sent thither a pilote of St. Malos in Bryttayne, named Jaques Carter, well seen in the art and knowledg of navegation, and speceally for the northe partes, comonly called the Newland, led

by some hope to fynd passage that waies to the southe seeas, who being not able at this his ffirst going to bring any thing to pase of that he pretended to do, was sent thither agayn the yere ffollowing, and likewise le Sieur de Beuernall. And as it is well known, they did inhabite, builde [and] plant the Kinges armes in the northe partes a good way within the lande, as far as Cavadu and Ochelaga. Wherfore (my lorde) trusting that in a thinge so comendable and wortheye to be with good curradge attempted, that God would guyde and kepe us, desiering alwaies to fulfill your commaundementes, when we had don our bussines, and made our preparations, the 18 daye of February last past, through the favor of God, we departed with our two vesselles owt of the havon of Havor de Grace into the rode of Caux, and the next daye hoised up sailes, the wynd being at east, which lasted so fewe daies that we could scant passe the Manche, that is from the coast of Brytayne and England and the Isles of Surlynges and Wisan. So that the wynd blowing with great furye and tempest owt of the west and west southe west, althogether contrary to our waye and course, and that all that we could do was but to no effecte and to the [great] daunger of breaking of our mastes, or to be lett in our other labours. Therefore, as well to shon manye other inconveniences, which might followe to the preiudice and breache of our voiage, having regarde also to the likely daunger of deathe, that some of our gentilmen and souldiours trubled with fevers and hote sicknesses might have fallen into, as also for many other considerations, we thought good to fall into the rode of Brest in Britaine, to sett there our sicke folkes on lande, and suffer the tempest to passe. From whence, after we taryed there two dayes, [we] retourned agen to seward to followe our navegation, so that (my lorde) albeit the wynd was for a long tyme verye muche agenst us and trublesome, yet at the end, God geving us through his grace and accustomed goodnes a metelye favorable wynde. I determiend with all dilligence to prove a neue course which hathe not byn yet attempted, traversing the seas of the oction 1800 leagues at the least, which in dede is the true and shorte course that herafter must be kepte, to the honnour of our nation, rejecting thould conseaved oppynnion, which to longe tyme hathe byn holden for true, which is that it was thought a thinge impossible to have the wynde at east north east, and kepe the race and course we enterprised but that the shuld be dreven towardes the region of Affricque, the Isles of Canari[a], Medera and other landes therabowt. And the cause why we have byn [the] more spurred and provoked to take this newe race, hathe byn [because] that it seamed to every one that men might not pass nor go in this navegation without the sight and towching of the Antilles and Lucayes and there to soiourne and take freshe water and other necessaries, as the Spaniardes do in their voiag to newe Spayne, wherof, thanked be God, we have had no nede, nor entred the Chanell of Boham, which hath byn thought impossible, forseing also that it was not expedient for us to passe through their islandes, aswell to shon manny inconveniences that hapen in passing that waies, wherof there spring nothing but inumerable quarrelles, pleadinges, confusion, and breache of all worthie enterprises and goodly navegations, with infenite complaintes and odious questions betwen the subiectes of the Kinge and his frendes and allyes, as also to thende they myght understand that in tyme to come (God having shewed to us suche grace as theis his wonderfull benefites first knowen to the pooer people of this so goodly newe France, a people of so gentill a nature, and a cuntry so pleasant and frutfull, lacking nothing of all that maye seme necessarye for mans foode) we would not have to do with there ilandes and other landes, which for that they first discovered them, they kepe with muche jelozie, trusting that if God will suffer the Kinge, through your perswasion, to cause some partes of this incomparable cuntrye to be peopled and inhabited with suche a number of his pooer subiectes as you shall thinke good, there never hapened in the memorye of man so great good and comoditie to France as this. And, my lorde, for manny causes wherof a man is never hable to saye or wrytte to the full, as under the assured hope that we have allwaies had, that executing uprightly that which I had receaved in chardge of you, God would blesse our wayes and navegation, after we had constantlye and with dilligence, in tyme convenient, determioned upon the waye we would take (though noisome and longe to all our company, if it had byn bifore knowen unto them) withowt turning or wavering to or fro from our first intention, notwithstanding that Sathan did often what he could to sowe many obstacles,

trubles and lettes, according to his accustomed subtilities. So yt is come to passe, that God, by his onlye goodnes, hathe geven us grace to make the furthest cut and travers of the seaes that ever was made in our memorye or knoweledg in longitude from the east to the west, and therfore was it comonly said bothe in France and Spayne and also amonges us, that it was impossible [for us] to come and salfely arrive thither where the Lorde did conduct us, all which proceaded but of ignoran[ce] and lacke of attempting that which we have not byn afraied to give thadventure to prove, albeit that in all marryne cardes, they sett fourthe the coast with shippwrackes, withowt portes or rivers which we have found otherwise as yt ffollowithe.

Thursday the last of Aprill at the breke of the daye we discovered and clearly perceaved a faire cost, streching of a gret lenght, covered with an infenite number of highe and fayre trees, we being not past 7 or 8 leages from the shore, the countrye seming unto us playn, withowt any shewe of hilles, and approching nearer within 4 or 5 leages of the land, we cast ancre at ten fadom watter, the bottom of the sea being playn with muche osse and of fast hold. On the southe side as far as a certen poynt or cape, scituate under the latitude of 29 degrees and a half, which we have named the cap Francoys, we could espie nether river not baye, wherfore we sent our boates, furnished with men of experience, to sound and knowe the coast nere the shore, who retourning agen unto us abowt one of the clocke at after none, declared that they had found, amonges other thinges, viij fadom watter at the harde bancke of the sea. Wherupon, having dilligently wayed up our ancres and hoist up saile, with wynd at will we sailed and veewed the coast all along with an inspeakeable pleasure of thoderiferous smell and bewtye of the same. And bicause there apeared unto us no sine of any porte, abowt the setting of the sonne, we cast ancre agayn, which don, we did behold to and fro the goodly order of the woodes wherwith God hathe decked everywhere the said lande. Then perceiving towardes the northe a leaping and breking of the water, as a streme falling owt of the lande unto the sea, forthewith we sett agayn up saile to duble the same while it was yet daye. And as we had so don, and passed byonde yt, there apeared unto us a faire cnter[ye] of a great river, which caused us to cast ancre agen and tary there nere the lande, to thende that the next mornyng we myght see what it was. And though that the wynd blewe for a tyme vehemently to the shore warde, yet the hold and auncordge is so good there, that one cable and one ancre held us fast withowt driving or slyding.

The next daye in the morninge, being the ffirst of Maye, we assaied to enter this porte with two rowe barges and a boate well trymed, finding littell watter at the entrye and many surges and brekinges of the water which might have astuned and caused us to retourn backe to shippborde, if God had not speedely brought us in, where fynding fourthwith 5 or 6 fadom water, entered in to a goodly and great river, which as we went we found to incres still in depth and lardgnes, boylling and roring through the multytute of all sortes of fishes. Thus entered we perceved a good numbre of the Indians, inhabytantes there, coming alonge the sandes and seebanck somewhate nere unto us, withowt any taken of feare or dowbte, shewing unto us the easiest landing place, and thereupon we geving them also on our parte tokens of assuraunce and frendelynes, fourthewith one of the best of apparance amonges them, brother unto one of there kinges or governours, comaunded one of the Indians to enter into the water, and to approche our boates, to showe us the easiest landing place. We seeing this, withowt any more dowbting or difficulty, landed, and the messenger, after we had rewarded him with some loking glases and other prety thinges of smale value, ran incontenently towardes his lorde, who forthwith sent me his girdell in token of assurance and ffrendship, which girdell was made of red lether, aswell couried and coulored as is possible. And as I began to go towardes him, he sett fourthe and came and received me gentlye and rejosed after there mannour, all his men ffollowing him with great silence and modestie, yea, with more then our men did. And after we had awhile with gentill usage congratulated with him, we fell to the grownd a littell waye from them, to call upon the name of God, and to beseche him to contynewe still his goodnes towardes us, and to bring to the knoweledg of our Savior Jesus Christ this pooer people. While we were thus praying, they sitting upon the grownd, which was dressed and strewed with baye bowes, behelde and herkened unto us very attentively, withowt eyther speaking or

moving. And as I made a sygne unto there king, lifting up myne arme and streching owt one fynger, only to make them loke up to heavenward, he likewise lifting up his arme towardes heven, put fourthe two fynge[rs] wherby it semed that he would make us tunderstand that thay worshipped the sonne and mone for godes, as afterward we understode yt so. In this meane tyme there number increased and thither came the kinges brother that was ffirst with us, their mothers, wifes, sisters and childern, and being thus assembled, thaye caused a greate nombre of baye bowes to be cutt and therwith a place to be dressed for us, distant from theires abowt two ffadom; for yt is there mannour to parle and bargayn sitting, and the chef of them to be aparte from the meaner sorte, with a shewe of great obedyence to there kinges, superyours, and elders. They be all naked and of a goodly stature, mighty, faire and aswell shapen and proportioned of bodye as any people in all the worlde, very gentill, curtious and of a good nature.

The most parte of them cover their raynes and pryvie partes with faire hartes skins, paynted cunyngly with sondry collours, and the fore parte of there bodye and armes paynted with pretye devised workes of azure, redd, and black, so well and so properly don as the best paynter of Europe could not amend yt. The wemen have there bodies covered with a certen herbe like unto moste, wherof the cedertrees and all other trees be alwaies covered. The men for pleasure do allwayes tryme themselves therwith, after sundry fasshions. They be of tawny collour, hawke nosed and of a pleasaunt countenaunce. The women be well favored and modest and will not suffer that one approche them to nere, but we were not in theire howses, for we sawe none at that tyme.

After that we had tarried in this northe side of the river the most parte of the daye, which river we have called by the name of the river of Maye, for that we discovered the same the first day of that mounthe, congratulated and made alyance and entered into amytie with them, and presented theire kinge and his brethern with gownes of blewe clothe garnished with yellowe flowers de luce, yt semed they were sorry for our departure, so that the most parte of them entered into the watter up to the necke, to sett our barges on flote, putting into us soundry kindes of fishes, which with a marvelus speed they ran to take them in there parkes, made in the watter with great redes, so well and cunyngly sett together, after the fashion of a labirinthe or maze, with so manny tourns and crokes, as yt is impossible to do yt with more cunning or industrye.

But desiering to imploye the rest of the daye on the other side of this river, to veue and knowe those Indians we sawe there, we traversed thither and withowt any diffycutye landed amonges them, who receaved us verry gentelly with great humanytie, putting us of there fruites, even in our boates, as mulberies, respices and suche other frutes as thay found redely by the waye.

Sone after this there came thither there kynge with his brethern and others, with bowes and arrowes in there handes, using therewithall a good and grave ffashion and bihavior, right soulddier like with as warlike a bouldnes as might be. They were naked and paynted as thothers, there hear likewise long, and trussed up with a lace made of hearbes, to the top of there hedes, but they had neither there wives nor children in there company.

After we had a good while lovengly intretayned and presented them with littell giftes of haberdasherye wares, cutting hookes and hatchettes, and clothed the king and his brethern with like robes we had geven to them on the other side, [we] enterd and veued the cuntry therabowte, which is the fairest, frutefullest and plesantest of all the worlde, habonding in honney, veneson, wildfoule, forrestes, woodes of all sortes, palme trees, cipers, ceders, bayes, the hiest, greatest and fairest vynes in all the wourld with grapes accordingly, which naturally and withowt mans helpe and tryming growe to the top of okes and other trees that be of a wonderfull greatnes and height. And the sight of the faire medowes is a pleasure not able to be expressed with tonge, full of herons, corleux, bitters, mallardes, egertes, woodkockes, and of all other kinde of smale birdes, with hartes, hyndes, buckes, wild swyne, and sondery other wild beastes as we perceved well bothe then by there foteing there and also afterwardes in other places by ther crye and brayeng which we herde in the night tyme. Also there be cunys, hares, guynia cockes in mervelus numbre, a great dele fairer and better then be oures, silke wormes, and to be shorte it is a thinge inspeakable, the comodities that be sene there

and shalbe founde more and more in this incomperable lande, never as yet broken with plowe irons, bringing fourthe all thinges according to his first nature, wherof the eternall God endued yt.

About there howses they laboure and till there ground, sowing there fildes with a grayn called Mahis, wherof the[y] make there meale, and in there gardens the[y] plant beans, gourdes, cowekcumbers, citrons, peasen, and many other simples and rootes unknon unto us. There spades and mattockes be of wood, so well and fyttely made as ys possible, which they make with certen stones, oister shelles, and mustelles, wherwith the[y] make also ther bowes and smale lances, and cutt and pullishe all sortes of woodes that they employe abowt there buldinges and necessarye use. There grovith [also] many walnuttrees hazeltrees and smale cherytrees verry faire and great, and generally we have sene there of the same symples and herbes that we have in Fraunce and of like goodnes savour and tast. The people are verry good archers and of great strenght; there bowe strynges are made of lether and there arrowes of reades which the[y] do hedd with the teathe of certen ffishes.

As we [nowe] demaunded of them for a certen towne called Sevola, wherof some have wrytten not to be farr from thence, and to be scituate within the lande and towardes the southe sea, they shewed us by signes which we understode well enough, that they might go thither with there boates by rivers in xxiie dayes. Those that have wrytten of this kingdom and towne of Sevolla, and other towns and realmes therabowtes, say that ther is great aboundaunce of gould and silver, precious stouns and other great riches, and that the people hedd ther arrowes, instedd of iron, with [sharpe] poynted turqueses. Thus the night aproching, and that it was conveynient for us to retire by daye to ship bourd, we toke leve of them muche to their greif and more to oures withowt comparison, for that we had no meane to enter the river with our shippes. And albeyt it was not ther custome either to eate or drynke from sonne rising till his goyng down, yet there kyng openly would nedes drinke with us, praying us verry gentelly to give him the cupp wherowt he had dronke. And so makyng him understand that we would see him agen the next daye, we retired agayn to our shipps, which laye abowt vj leages from the haven to the sewarde.

The next day in the morning we retourned to land agayne, accompaned with the captayns, gentilmen, souldiers, and others of our smale troup, carring with us a piller or colume of hard stone, our kinges armes graven therin, to plaint and sett [the same] at the entrye of the porte in some high place wher yt might be easelly sene. And being come thither bifore the Indyans were assembled, we espied on the southe side of the river a place verry fyt for that purpose upon a littell hill compassed with cipers, bayes, palmes, and other trees, and swete pleasaunt smelling shrubbes, in the mydell wherof we planted the first bounde or lymete of his majestie. Thus don, perceving our first Indians assembled and loking for us we went first unto them according to our promisse, not withowt some mislyking of those on the southe parte, wher we had sett the said lymete, who tarried for us in the same place where they mete with us the day before, seming unto us that there ys some ennemytie bytwen them and the others. But when the[y] perceved our long tarring on this side, the[y] ran to se what we had don in that place where we landed ffirst and had sett our lymete, which they vewed a gret while withowt touching yt any waye, or abasshing, or ever speaking unto us therof at any tyme after. Howebeit we could scant departe but as yt were with greif of mynde from theis our first alies, they runyng unto us [all] along the river from all partes, presentyng us with some of there harte skins, paynted and unpaynted, meale, littell cakes, freshe watter, roottes like unto rubarbe, which they have in great estymation, and make therof a kinde of bevradg or potion of medyzen. Also they brought us littell bagges of redd coullours and some smale peces like unto oore, perceving also amonges them faire thinges paynted as yt had byn with grayn of scarlett, shewing unto us by signes that they had within the lande gould, silver, and copper wherof we have brought some muster; also leade like unto ours, which we shewed unto them, turqueses, and a great abundaunce of perlles, which, as they declared unto us, they toke owt of oysters, wherof there is taken every along the river side and amonges the reedes and in the marishes and in so mervelous aboundaunce as ys scant credeble. And we have perceved that ther be as many and as faire perles found there as in any contry in the worlde, for we sawe a man of theires, as we entered into our boates, that had a perle hanging at a collour of gould and silver about his necke as great as an acorn at the least. This man, as he had taken ffishe in one of there fishing parkes therby, brought the same to our boates, and our men perceving his great pearle and making a wonderinge at yt for the greatnes therof, one of them putting his fynger towardes yt, the man drewe backe and would no more come nere the boate, not for any feare he had that they would have taken his collour and perle from him; for he would have geven yt them for a lokingglasse or a knyfe, but that he dowbted least they would have pulled him into the boate and so by force have carried him awaye. He was one of the goodlyest men of all his company.

But for that we had no leysure to tarry any longer with them, the day being well passed, which greved us for the comodyties and great ryches which as we understode and sawe might be gotton there, desiering also to imploye the rest of the daye amonges our second allies, the Indians on the south side, as we had promissed them the day before, which still tarried loking for us, we passed the river to there shore where we founde them tarring for us quietly and in good order, trymed with newe pictures upon there faces, and fethers upon ther heddes, their king with his bowes and arrowes lieing by him, sett on the ground, strewed with baye bowes, bitwen his two brethern [whiche were] goodly men [&] well shapen and of wonderfull shewe of activetie, having about there heddes and heare, which was trussed up of a height, a kinde of heare of some wilde beast died redd, gatherd and wrought together with great cunyng, and wrethed and facioned after the forme of a diedeme. One of them had hanging at his necke a littell round plate of redd copper well pollished, with an other lesser of silver in the myddst of yt (as ye shall se) and at his eare a littell plate of copper wherwithe they use to scrape and take awaye the sweat from their bodies. They shewed unto us that there was grett store of this mettall within the cuntry, abowt five or six jurnaies from thence, bothe on the southe and nourthe side of the same river, and that they went thither in there boates, which boates they make but of one pece of a tree working yt hollowe so cunyngly and fyttely, that they put in one of these thus shapen boates or rather great troughes, xv or xxᵗⁱ persons, and go therwith verry swiftly. They that rowe stand upright having there owers short, made after the fashyon of a peele. Thus being amonges them they presented us with there meale, dreassed and baked, verry good and well tasting and of good nurishment, also beanes, fishe, as crabbes, lopsters, crevices and many other kindes of good fishes, shewing us by signes that there dwellinges were far of, and that if there provision had byn nere hande, they would have presented us with many other reffreshinges.

The night nowe approching we were fayne to retourn to our shippes, muche to our greef, for that we durst not hasarde to enter with our shippes by reason of a barr of sande that was at [the] entre of the porte, howebeyt at a full sea there is two fadom and a half of water at the most, and yt is but a leap or surge to passe this barr, not passing the lengthe of two cables, and thenfourth with every where within vj or vij fadom water, so that it makethe a verry faire haven and shippes of a meane burden from iiij^{xx} to c. tonnes may entre therein at all flodes, yea, of a farre greater burthen if there were Frenchemen dwelling there that myght scoure thentree as they do in Fraunce, and where nothing is lacking for the lief of man. The scituation is under the elevation of xxx degrees, a good clymate, helthfull, of good temperaunce, marvelous pleasaunt, the people gentill and of a good and amyable loving nature, which willingly will obaye, ye, be content to serve those that shall with gentilnes and humanytie go aboute to alure them as yt [is] nedefull for all those that shalbe sent thither hereafter so to do, and as I have chardged those of oures that be lefte there to do, to thende that by these meanes they may ask and learn of them where the[y] take there gould, copper, turquises, and other thinges yet unknown unto us, by reason of the shortnes of tyme we soiurned there; for if any rude and rigorious meanes shuldbe used towardes this people, they would flye hither and thither through the woodes and forestes and abandon there habitations and cuntrye.

The nexte day being the thirde day of Maye, desiering alwaies to fynd owt harborough to rest in, we sett up saile agayn, and after we had ranged the coast as nere the shore as we coulde, there appeared unto us abowt vij leages on this side the river of Maye, a great oppening or baye of some faire river, whither with one of our boates we rowed and there found an entre almost like unto that of the river of Maye, and within the

same as great a depthe and as large, dividing yt self into many sea armes, great and brood, streching towardes the highe lande, with many other lesse that devide the countrye into faire and greate landes and a great number of smale and faire medowes. Being entred into them abowt 3 leages we found in a place verry comodyous, strong and pleasaunt of scituation, certen Indians who receved us verry gentelly, howebeyt we being somewhat nere there howses yt semed yt was [somewhat] agenst there good willes that we went thither, for at theire cryes and noise they made, all there wiefes and childern and how-should stuf were fledd and carried furthewith into the woodes. Howebeyt they suffered us to go to there howses, but they themselves would not accompany us thither. There howses be fyttely made and close of woode, sett upright and covered with reed, the most parte of them after the fashion of a pavillion, but there was one [house] amonges the rest verry great, long and broode, with settelles round abowte made of reedes, tremly couched together, which serve them bothe for beddes and seates; they be of hight two fote from the ground, sett upon great round pillers paynted with redd, yellowe and blewe, well and [trimly] pullished. Some of this people, perceving that we had [in] no mannour of wise hurted there dwellinges nor gardens which the[y] dresse verry dilligently, they retourned all unto us byfore our imbarking, semyng verry well contented by there putting into us watter, frute[s] and hartes skynes.

It is a place wonderfull fertill, and of strong scituation, the ground fat so that it is lekely that it would bring fourthe wheate and all other corn twise a yeare, and the comodities there for livelode and the hope of more riches be like unto those we found and considered upon the ryver of May, and men may travell thither through a great arme of the sea in hoyes and barkes as great as ye maye do in the river of Maye withowt coming into the sea. This arme dothe devide and makethe the Isle of Maye, as many other rivers and armes of the see which we have discovered devide and make many other great islandes, by the which we maye travell from one island to an other bitwen land and lande. And yt semeth that men may goo and saile withowt daunger through all the contrye, and never enter in [to] the great seas, which were a wonderfull advauntag. This is the land of

Chicore wherof some have wrytten, and which many have gon abowt to fynd, for the great riches they perceved by some Indians to be found there. It is sett under so good a clymate, that none of all our men, though we were there in the hotest tyme of the yere, the sonne entering into Cancer, were troubled with any sicknes. The people there live long and in great helthe and strength, so that aged men go withowt staves, and are able to do and ron like the yongest of them, who only are known to be ould by the wrynkeles in ther face and decaye of sight.

We departed from them verry frendly and with there contentation, but the flood and the night overtaking us, we were constrayned to lie in our boates all [that] night, till yt was day, fliting upon this river which we have called Seyne, bycause at the entrye yt is as broade as from Havre de Grace unto Honefleu. At the breake of the daye we espied on the southe side one of the fairest, pleasantest and greatest medowe ground that might be sene, into the which we went, fynding at the verry entre a longe a faire and great lake [and] an innumerable numbre of fotestepes of hartes and hyndes of a wonderfull greatnes, the stepes [beynge] all freshe and newe. And yt semeth that the people do nurishe them like tame cattell, in great herdes; for we sawe the fotestepes of an Indian that followed them. The channell and depthe of this river of Seyne is on the side of the medowe that is on the isle of May.

Being retourned to our shippes, we sailed to knowe more and more of the coast, going as nere the shore as we could. And as we had sailed so all alonge abowt six or seven leages, there apered unto us another baye where we cast ancre twart of yt, tarring so all the night. In the morrowe we went thither, and fynding by our sounding at the entre many bankes and beatynges, we durst not venture to entre there with our great shippes, we having named this river Some, which within is a leage over and of viij, ix, x, and xj fadom deapthe, deviding yt self into many great rivers, that sever the cuntry into many faire and great ilandes and smale goodly medowe ground and pastures, and every where suche aboundaunce of fishe as is increadeble. And on the west northewest side there is a great river that comithe from the highe country, of a great leage over, and on the other on the northest side which retourn into the sea. So that (my lorde) yt is a country full of havens,

rivers and islandes of suche frutefullnes as cannot with tonge be expressed, and where in shorte tyme great and precyous comodyties might be founde. And besides theis, we discovered and founde also seven rivers more, as great and as good, cutting and deviding the land into faire and great ilandes, th'Indians inhabytantes therof like in manours, and the countrey in fertilitie apte and comodious throughowt to make suger and to beare and bring fourthe plentifully all that men would plant or sowe upon it. There be every where the highest, fayrerest and greatest firr trees that can be sene, verry well smelling and whereowt myght be gotton with cutting only the bark, as muche rosin, turpentyne and frankinsense as men would have; and to be shorte, there lackethe nothing. Wherfore being not able to entre and lye with our great vesselles there, where we would make no long abode, not entre so farr into the rivers and cuntres as we would fayne have don: for yt is well inough known howe many inconvenyences have hapened unto men, not only in attempting of newe discover[ie]s, but also in all places by leving there great vesselles in the sea, farr from the lande, unfurnished of there heddes and best men. As for thother rivers, we have given them suche names as followe, and unto the Indians joining to them, the same name that the next river unto yt hathe, as ye shall see by the protracture or carte I have made thereof, as to the fourth the name of Loire, to the vth Charent, to the vith Garone, to the vijth ryviere Belle, to the viijth Riviere Grande, to the ixth Porte Royall, to the xth Belle a Veoir.

Upon Whitsontide, Sondaye the xvij of Maye, after we had well perceved and considered that there was no remedye but to assaye to fynde the meanes to harborough our shippes, aswell for to amend and tryme them as to gett us fresshe water, wood and other necessaries wherof we had nede, being of opynion that there was no fayrer or fytter place for the purpose then porte Royall. [And] when we had sounded the entrey and the channell, (thanked be God) we entred salfely therin with our shippes agenst the opynyon of many, fynding the same one of the greatest and fayrest havens of the worlde. Howebeyt, it must be remembred, lest that men approching nere yt within vij leages of the lande, be abasshed and afrayed, fynding on the east side, drawing towardes the south est, the ground to be flatt, for neverthelesse at a full sea ther is every where foure fadom water keping the right channell.

In this porte are many armes of the sea depe and lardg, and here and there of all sides many rivers of a meane biggnes, where withowt danger all the shippes in the worlde myght be harbored. We founde no Indians inhabyting there abowt the porte and river side nerer than x or xij leages upward into the cuntryes, although yt be one of the goodlyest, best and frutfullest cunteres that ever was sene, and where nothing lacketh, and also where as good and like[ly] comodities be founde as in the other places therby; for we found there a great numbre of peper trees, the peper upon them yet grene and not redy to be gatherd; also the best watter of the worlde, and so many sortes of fishes that ye maye take them withowt nett or angle, as many as you will; also guinea foule and innumerable wildfoule of all sortes, and in a lyttell ilande at the entrye of this haven, on the est northerest side, there is so great numbre of egretes that the bushes be all white and covered with them, so that one may take of the yong ones with his hande as many as he will carry awaye. There be also a nombre of other foule, as herons, bytters, curleux, and to be shorte, so many smale birdes that yt is a straung thing to be sene. We found the Indians there more dowbtfull and fearfull then thothers byfore; yet after we had byn att there howses, and congratulated with them, and shewed curtysie to those that we founde to have abondoned their troughbotes, meale, vyctualles, and smale howshold stuf, as bothe in not taking awaye or touching any part therof, and in leaving in the place where the[y] dressed there meate, knyves, loking glasses and littell beades of glasse, which they love and esteme above gould and pearles for to hang them at there eares and necke, and [to] give them to there wives and childern, they were somewhate emboldened; for some of them came to our boate, of the which we carriede two goodly and strong abourd our shippes, clothing and using them as gentlly and lovingly as yt was possible; but they never ceassed day nor nyght to lament and at lengh they scaped awaye. Wherfore, albeyt I was willing, according to your comaundment and memoriall, to bring away withe us some of that people, yet by thadviz of those that were sent with us on the Princes behalf and youres, I forbare to do so for many considerations and reasons that they tould

me, and for that also we were in doubte that, leving some of our men to inhabyte there, all the country, man, woman, and childe would not have ceassed to have pursued them for to have theires agayn, seing they be not able to consider nor waye to what intent we shuld have carried them awaye. And this may be better don to theire contentation when they have better acquaintance of us, and knowe that there is no suche cruelltye in us as in other people and nations, of whom they have byn begilled under coulour of good faythe, which usage in the end tourned to the doers to no good.

This is the river of Jordayne in myne oppynion, wherof so muche hathe byn spoken, which is verry faire, and the cuntrye good and of grete consequence, both for theire easye habitation and also for many other thinges which shuld be to long to wrytt. The xxii of May we planted another colme graven with the Kinges armes, on the southe side, in a comodyous pleasaunt and high place, at the entrye of a faire great river, which we have called Lybourne where ther is a faire lake of freshe water verry good, and on the same side a lyttell lower towardes the entry of the haven, is one of the fairest and best fountaynes that a made may drynke of, which falleth with voyelence down to the river from a highe place owt of a redd and sandy ground, and yet for all that frutfull and of good aire, where yt shuld seme that the Indians have had some faire habytation.

Ther we sawe the fairest and the greatest vynes with grapes according, and yong trees, and smale woodes very well smelling, that ever were sene, wherby yt aperithe to be the pleasantest and most comodious dwelling of all the worlde.

Wherfore (my lorde) trusting you will not thinke yt amisse, considering the great good and comodyties that may be brought thence into France, if we leve a nombre of men there, that may fortifye and so provide themselves of thinges necessarye, for in all newe discovers yt is the chef and best thinge that may be don at the begining, to fortifye and people the country which is the true and chef possession. I had not so sonne sett fourthe this thinge to our company, but many of them offered to tarry there, yea with suche a good will and jolly curradg, that suche a nombre did thus offre themselves as we had muche ado to staye there importunytie, and namely of our shipmasters and principall pilottes, and of suche as we could not spare. Howebeyt, we have leift there but to the number of xxx in all, of gentil-men, souldiers, and merryners, and that at ther own suite and prayer, and of there one fre and good willes, and by the adviz and delyberation of the gentilmen sent on the behalf of the Prynces and youres, and have leift unto them for hed and ruler (following therin your goodwill) Capten Alberte della Pirie, a souldier of long experyence and the ffirst that from the beginning did offre to tarry; and furthere by there adviz, choise and will, installed and fortified them in an iland on the northe est side, a place of strong scytuation and comodyous, upon a river which we have called Chenonceau and the inhabytacion and fortresse Charle forte.

After we had instructed and duelye admonished them of that they shuld do aswell for there mannour of proceeding as for there good and loving behavior of themselves towardes this poore and simple Indians and there conversacon with them, the xi of the mounthe of June last past, we departed from Port Riall, mynding yett to range and veue the coast untill the xl degrees of the elevation: but forasmuche as there came upon us trublesome and cloudy whither and verry incomodyous for our purpose, and considering also amonges many other thinges that we had spent our cables and furiture therof, which is the most pryncipall and necessarye thinge that longeth to them that goo to discover cuntryes, where contynewally night and daye they must lye at ancre; also our victualles being perished and spilte, our lacke of botswayns to sett fourthe our row bardges and boates, and leve our vesselles furnished; the declaration made unto us of our master pilotes and some others that had bifore byn at some of those places where we purposed to saile, and have byn allready founde by [some of] the Kinges subiectes; the daunger also and inconvenyences that might therof hapen unto us, and that by reason of the great mistes and fogges wherof the seacen was allredy come, we percaved verry well whereas we were, that we could do no good and that yt was to late, and the good and fyttest season to undertake this thinge allredy past. All these thinges thus well considered and wayed, and for that also we thought yt mete and necessarye that your grace shuld with dilligence be advertised of that which we had don and discovered, which is of great consequence, we concluded through the helpe of God to retourn into France to make relation unto you of the effecte of our navegation. Praying to God that yt may please him to kepe you in long helthe and prossperytie and give unto you the grace to cause this faire discoverture of this Newe France to be cuntynewed and dylligently followed.

299. 1562–1563. René de Laudonnière's account of the first French settlement at Charlesfort.

René de Laudonnière accompanied Jean Ribault on his first voyage of exploration to Florida and assisted in the establishment of the small settlement at Charlesfort. It is certain, also, that he obtained accounts of what happened in the settlement after his own return with Ribault. It is not known precisely when he wrote this account (probably in the early 1570s).

This was first printed in L'histoire notable de la Floride *(Paris, 1586), fols. 7v.–32; and in translation in* A notable history containing foure voyages made by certaine French captaines unto Florida *(London, 1587), fol. 4v.–17v.), reprinted in R. Hakluyt,* Principal navigations, *III (1600), 308–319 (VIII [1904], 457–486).*

My Lord Admirall of Chastillon, a noble man more desirous of the publique then of his private benefite, understanding the pleasure of the King his prince, which was to discover new and strange Countreys, caused vessels fit for this purpose to be made ready with all diligence, and men to bee levied meete for such an enterprise: Among whom hee chose Captaine John Ribault, a man in trueth expert in sea causes: which having received his charge, set himselfe to Sea the yeere 1562, the eighteenth of Februarie, accompanied onely with two of the kings shippes, but so well furnished with Gentlemen, (of whose number I my selfe was one) and with olde Souldiers, that he had meanes to atchieve some notable thing and worthy of eternall memorie. Having therefore sayled two monethes, never holding the usuall course of the Spaniards, hee arrived in Florida, landing neere a Cape or Promontorie, which is no high lande, because the coast is all flatte, but onely rising by reason of the high woods, which at his arrivall he called Cape François in honour of our France. This Cape is distant from the Equator about thirtie degrees. Coasting from this place towards the North, he discovered a very faire and great River, which gave him occasion to cast anker that hee might search the same the next day very early in the morning: which being done by the breake of day, accompanied with Captaine Fiquinville and divers other souldiers of his shippe, he was no sooner arrived on the brinke of the shoare, but straight hee perceived many Indians men and women, which came of purpose to that place to receive the Frenchmen with all gentlenesse and amitie, as they well declared by the Oration which their king made, and the presents of Chamois skinnes wherewith he honoured our Captaine, which the day following caused a pillar of hard stone to be planted within the sayde River, and not farre from the mouth of the same upon a little sandie knappe, in which pillar the Armes of France were carved and engraved. This being done hee embarked himselfe againe, to the ende alwayes to discover the coast toward the North which was his chiefe desire. After he had sayled a certaine time he crossed over to the other side of the river, and then in the presence of certaine Indians, which of purpose did attend him, hee commaunded his men to make their prayers, to give thankes to GOD, for that of his grace hee had conducted the French nation unto these strange places without any danger at all. The prayers being ended, the Indians which were very attentive to hearken unto them, thinking in my judgement, that wee worshipped the Sunne, because wee alwayes had our eyes lifted up toward heaven, rose all up and came to salute the Captaine John Ribault, promising to shew him their King, which rose not up as they did, but remained still sitting upon greene leaves of Bayes and Palmetrees: toward whom the Captaine went and sate downe by him, and heard him make a long discourse, but with no great pleasure, because hee could not understand his language, and much lesse his meaning. The King gave our Captaine at his departure a plume or fanne of Hernshawes feathers died in red, and a basket made of Palmeboughes after the Indian fashion, and wrought very artificially, and a great skinne painted and drawen throughout with the pictures of divers wilde beasts so lively drawen and por-

trayed, that nothing lacked but life. The Captaine to shew himselfe not unthankfull, gave him pretie tinne bracelets, a cutting hooke, a looking glasse, and certaine knives: whereupon the King shewed himselfe to be very glad and fully contented. Having spent the most part of the day with these Indians, the Captaine imbarked himselfe to passe over to the north side of the River, whereat the king seemed to bee very sorie. Neverthelesse being not able to stay us, hee commaunded that with all diligence they should take fish for us: which they did with all speede. For being entred into their Weares or inclosures made of reedes and framed in the fashion of a Labirynth or Mase, they loaded us with Troutes, great Mullets, Plaise, Turbuts, and marveilous store of other sortes of fishes altogether different from ours.[1]

This done, we entred into our Boates and went toward the other shore. But before we came to the shore, we were saluted with a number of other Indians, which entring into the water to their armepits, brought us many litle baskets full of Maiz, and goodly Mulberries both red and white: Others offered themselves to beare us on shoare, where being landed we perceived their King sitting upon a place dressed with boughes, and under a little Arbour of Cedars and Bay trees somewhat distant from the waters side. He was accompanied with two of his sonnes which were exceeding faire and strong, and with a troope of Indians who had all their bowes and arrowes in marveilous good order. His two sonnes received our Captaine very graciously: but the king their father, representing I wot not what kinde of gravitie, did nothing but shake his head a little: then the Captaine went forward to salute him, and without any other moving of himselfe he reteined so constant a kind of gravitie, that hee made it seeme unto us that by good and lawfull right hee bare the title of a King. Our Captaine knowing not what to judge of this mans behaviour, though he was jelous because wee went first unto the other king, or else that he was not well pleased with the Pillar or Columne which he had planted. While thus he knew not what hereof to thinke, our Captaine shewed him by signes, that he was come from a farre Countrey to seeke him, to let him understand the amitie which he was desirous to have with him: for the better

1. Sidenote: "There fish are very like those of Virginia."

confirmation whereof, hee drewe out of a budget certaine trifles, as certaine bracelets covered as it were with silver and guilt, which hee presented him withall, and gave his sonnes certaine other trifles. Whereupon the King beganne very lovingly to intreate both our Captaine and us. And after these gentle intertainments, wee went our selves into the woods, hoping there to discover some singularities: where were great store of Mulberrie trees white and red, on the toppes whereof there was an infinite number of silke-wormes. Following our way wee discovered a faire and great medowe, divided notwithstanding with divers Marishes, which constrained us by reason of the water, which environed it about, to returne backe againe towarde the Rivers side. Finding not the King there, which by this time was gone home to his house, wee entred into our Boates and sayled towarde our shippes: where after we arrived, we called this River The River of May, because we discovered it the first day of the sayde moneth.

Soone after we returned to our shippes, wee weighed our ankers and hoysed our sailes to discover the coast farther forward, along the which wee discovered another faire River, which the Captaine himselfe was minded to search out, and having searched it out with the king and inhabitants thereof, hee named it Seine, because it is very like unto the River of Seine in France. From this River wee retired toward our shippes, where being arrived, we trimmed our sailes to saile further toward the North, and to descry the singularities of the coast. But wee had not sayled any great way before wee discovered another very faire River, which caused us to cast anker over against it, and to trimme out two Boates to goe to search it out. Wee found there an Ile and a king no lesse affable then the rest, afterwarde we named this River Somme. From thence wee sayled about six leagues, after wee discovered another River, which after wee had viewed was named by us by the name of Loyre. And consequently we there discovered five others: whereof the first was named Cherente, the second Garonne, the third Gironde, the fourth Belle, the fift Grande: which being very well discovered with such things as were in them, by this time in lesse then the space of threescore leagues wee had found out many singularities along nine Rivers. Neverthelesse not fully satisfied wee sayled yet further towarde the North, following the course that might bring us to the River of Jordan one of the fairest Rivers of the North, and holding our wonted course, great fogges and tempests came upon us, which constrained us to leave the coast to beare toward the maine Sea, which was the cause that we lost the sight of our Pinnesses a whole day and a night untill the next day in the morning, what time the weather waxing faire and the Sea calme, wee discovered a River which wee called Belle a veoir. After wee had sayled three or foure leagues, wee began to espie our Pinnesses which came straight toward us, and at their arrivall they reported to the Captaine, that while the foule weather and fogges endured, they harboured themselves in a mightie River which in bignesse and beautie exceeded the former: wherewithall the Captaine was exceeding joyfull, for his chiefe desire was to finde out an Haven to harbour his shippes, and there to refresh our selves for a while. Thus making thitherward wee arrived athwart the sayde River, (which because of the fairenesse and largenesse thereof wee named Port Royall) wee strooke our sailes and cast anker at ten fathom of water: for the depth is such, namely when the Sea beginneth to flowe, that the greatest shippes of France, yea, the Arguzes of Venice may enter in there. Having cast anker, the Captaine with his Souldiers went on shoare, and hee himselfe went first on land: where we found the place as pleasaunt as was possible, for it was all covered over with mightie high Oakes and infinite store of Cedars, and with Lentiskes growing underneath them, smelling so sweetly, that the very fragrant odor only made the place to seeme exceeding pleasant. As we passed thorow these woods we saw nothing but Turkeycocks flying in the Forrests, Partridges gray and red, little different from ours, but chiefly in bignesse. Wee heard also within the woods the voyces of Stagges, of Beares, of Lusernes, of Leopards, & divers other sortes of Beastes unknowen unto us. Being delighted with this place, we set our selves to fishing with nets, & we caught such a number of fish, that it was wonderfull. And amongst other wee tooke a certaine kind of fish which we call Sallicoques, which were no lesse then Crevises, so that two draughts of the net were sufficient to feede all the companie of our two ships for a whole day. The River at the mouth thereof from Cape to Cape is no lesse then

3. French leagues broad; it is divided into two great armes, whereof the one runneth toward the West, the other towards the North: and I beleeve in my judgement that the arme which stretcheth towarde the North runneth up into the Countrey as farre as the River Jordan, the other arme runneth into the Sea, as it was knowen and understoode by those of our company, which were left behind to dwell in this place. These two armes are two great leagues broad: and in the middest of them there is an Ile, which is poynted towardes the opening of the great River, in which Iland there are infinite numbers of all sortes of strange beasts. There are Simples growing there of so rare properties, and in so great quantitie, that it is an excellent thing to behold them. On every side there is nothing to be seene but Palmetrees, and other sorts of trees bearing blossoms and fruite of very rare shape and very good smell. But seeing the evening approch, and that the Captaine determined to returne unto the shippes, wee prayed him to suffer us to passe the night in this place. In our absence the Pilots and chiefe Mariners advertised the Captaine that it was needefull to bring the shippes further up within the River, to avoyde the dangers of the windes which might annoy us, by reason of our being so neere to the mouth of the River: and for this cause the Captaine sent for us. Being come to our shippes, wee sayled three leagues further up within the River, and there we cast anker. A little while after, John Ribault accompanied with a good number of souldiers imbarked himselfe, desirous to sayle further up into the arme that runneth toward the West, and to search the commodities of the place. Having sayled twelve leagues at the least, we perceived a troope of Indians, which assoone as ever they espied the Pinnesses, were so afrayd that they fled into the woods leaving behind them a yong Lucerne which they were a turning upon a spit: for which cause the place was called Cape Lucerne: proceeding foorth on our way, we found another arme of the River, which ranne toward the East, up which the Captaine determined to sayle and to leave the great current. A little while after they began to espie divers other Indians both men and women halfe hidden within the woods: who knowing not that wee were such as desired their friendship, were dismayed at the first, but soone after were emboldened, for the Captaine caused store of marchandise to bee shewed them openly whereby they knew that we meant nothing but well unto them: and then they made a signe that we should come on lande, which wee would not refuse. At our comming on shoare divers of them came to salute our Generall according to their barbarous fashion. Some of them gave him skins of Chamois, others little baskets made of Palme leaves, some presented him with Pearles, but no great number. Afterwards they went about to make an arbour to defend us in that place from the parching heate of the Sunne. But wee would not stay as then. Wherefore the Captaine thanked them much for their good will, and gave presents to each of them: wherewith hee pleased them so well before hee went thence, that his suddaine departure was nothing pleasant unto them. For knowing him to bee so liberall, they would have wished him to have stayed a little longer, seeking by all meanes to give him occasion to stay, shewing him by signes that he should stay but that day onely, and that they desired to advertise a great Indian Lorde which had Pearles in great abundance, and Silver also, all which things should bee given unto him at the Kings arrivall: saying further that in the meane time while that this great Lord came thither, they would lead him to their houses, and shewe him there a thousand pleasures in shooting, and seeing the Stagge killed, therefore they prayed him not to denie them their request. Notwithstanding wee returned to our shippes, where after wee had bene but one night, the Captaine in the morning commanded to put into the Pinnesse a pillar of hard stone fashioned like a columne, wherein the Armes of the king of France were graven, to plant the same in the fairest place that he could finde. This done, wee imbarked our selves, and sayled three leagues towards the West: where we discovered a little river, up which we sayled so long, that in the ende we found it returned into the great current, and in his returne to make a litle Iland separated from the firme land, where wee went on shore: and by commandement of the Captaine, because it was exceeding faire and pleasant, there wee planted the Pillar upon a hillock open round about to the view, and invironed with a lake halfe a fathom deepe of very good and sweete water. In which Iland wee sawe two Stagges of exceeding bignesse, in respect of those which we had seene before, which we might easily have killed with our

harguebuzes, if the Captaine had not forbidden us, mooved with the singular fairenesse and bignesse of them. But before our departure we named the little river which environed this Ile, The River of Liborne. Afterward we imbarked our selves to search another Ile not farre distant from the former: wherein after wee had gone a land, wee found nothing but tall Cedars, the fairest that were seene in this Countrey. For this cause wee called it The Ile of Cedars: so wee returned into our Pinnesse to go towards our shippes.

A few dayes afterward John Ribault determined to returne once againe toward the Indians which inhabited that arme of the River which runneth toward the West, and to carrie with him good store of souldiers. For his meaning was to take two Indians of this place to bring them into France, as the Queene had commaunded him. With this deliberation againe wee tooke our former course so farre foorth, that at the last wee came to the selfe same place where at the first we found the Indians, from thence we tooke two Indians by the permission of the king, which thinking that they were more favoured then the rest, thought themselves very happy to stay with us. But these two Indians seeing we made no shew at all that we would goe on land, but rather that wee followed the middest of the current, began to be somewhat offended, and would by force have lept into the water, for they are so good swimmers that immediatly they would have gotten into the forrestes. Neverthelesse being acquainted with their humour, wee watched them narrowly and sought by all meanes to appease them: which we could not by any meanes do for that time, though we offered them things which they much esteemed, which things they disdained to take, and gave backe againe whatsoever was given them, thinking that such giftes should have altogether bound them, and that in restoring them they should be restored unto their libertie. In fine, perceiving that all that they did avayled them nothing, they prayed us to give them those things which they had restored, which we did incontinent: then they approched one toward the other and began to sing, agreeing so sweetely together, that in hearing their song it seemed that they lamented the absence of their friendes. They continued their songs all night without ceasing: all

which time we were constrained to ly at anker by reason of the tyde that was against us, but we hoysed sayle the next day very earely in the morning, and returned to our ships. Assoone as we were come to our ships, every one sought to gratifie these 2 Indians, & to shew them the best countenance that was possible: to the intent that by such courtesies they might perceive the good desire and affection which we had to remaine their friends in time to come. Then we offered them meate to eate, but they refused it, and made us understand that they were accustomed to wash their face and to stay untill the Sunne were set before they did eate, which is a ceremonie common to all the Indians of Newe France. Neverthelesse in the end they were constrained to forget their superstitions, and to apply themselves to our nature, which was somewhat strange unto them at the first. They became therefore more jocunde, every houre made us a 1000 discourses, being merveilous sory that we could not understand them. A few daies after they began to beare so good wil towards mee, that, as I thinke, they would rather have perished with hunger & thirst, then have taken their refection at any mans hand but mine. Seeing this their good wil, I sought to learne some Indian words, & began to aske them questions, shewing them the thing wherof I desired to know the name, how they called it. They were very glad to tell it me, and knowing the desire that I had to learne their language, they encouraged me afterward to aske them every thing. So that putting downe in writing the words and phrases of the Indian speech, I was able to understand the greatest part of their discourses. Every day they did nothing but speak unto me of the desire that they had to use me wel, if we returned unto their houses, and cause me to receive all the pleasures that they could devise, aswell in hunting as in seeing their very strange and superstitious ceremonies at a certaine feast which they call Toya. Which feast they observe as straightly as we observe the Sunday. They gave me to understand, that they would bring me to see the greatest Lord of this countrey which they called Chiquola, which exceedeth them in height (as they tolde me) a good foote and a halfe. They said unto me that he dwelt within the land in a very large place and inclosed exceeding high, but I could not learne wherewith. And as farre as I can judge, this place whereof they spake unto me, was a very faire citie.[2] For they said unto me that within the inclosure there was great store of houses which were built very high, wherein there was an infinite number of men like unto themselves, which made none account of gold, of silver, nor of pearles, seeing they had thereof in abundance. I began then to shew them al the parts of heaven, to the intent to learne in which quarter they dwelt. And straightway one of them stretching out his hand shewed me that they dwelt toward the North, which makes me thinke that it was the river of Jordan. And now I remember, that in the raigne of the Emperour Charles the fift, certaine Spaniards inhabitants of S. Domingo (which made a voyage to get certaine slaves to work in their mines) stole away by subtilty the inhabitants of this river, to the number of 40, thinking to cary them into their new Spaine. But they lost their labour: for in despite they died al for hunger, saving one that was brought to the Emperor, which a litle while after he caused to be baptised, and gave him his own name & called him Charles of Chiquola, because he spake so much of this Lorde of Chiquola whose subject hee was. Also, he reported continually, that Chiquola made his abode within a very great inclosed citie. Besides this proof, those which were left in the first voyage have certified me, that the Indians shewed them by evident signes, that farther within the land toward the North, there was a great inclosure or city, where Chiquola dwelt. After they had staied a while in our ships, they began to be sory, and stil demanded of me when they should returne. I made them understand that the Captaines will was to send them home againe, but that first he would bestow apparell of them, which fewe dayes after was delivered unto them. But seeing he would not give them licence to depart, they resolved with themselves to steale away by night, and to get a litle boat which we had, and by the help of the tyde to saile home toward their dwellings, and by this meanes to save themselves. Which thing they failed not to doe, and put their enterprize in execution, yet leaving behinde them the apparel which the Captaine had given them, and carrying away nothing but that which was their owne, shewing well

2. Sidenote: "This seemeth to be La grand Copal."

hereby that they were not void of reason. The Captaine cared not greatly for their departure, considering they had not bene used otherwise then well: and that therefore they would not estrange themselves from the Frenchmen. Captaine Ribault therefore knowing the singular fairenes of this river, desired by all meanes to encourage some of his men to dwell there, well foreseeing that this thing might be of great importance for the Kings service, and the reliefe of the Common wealth of France. Therfore proceeding on with his intent, he commanded the ankers to bee weighed and to set things in order to returne unto the opening of the river, to the ende that if the winde came faire he might passe out to accomplish the rest of his meaning. When therefore we were come to the mouth of the river, he made them cast anker, whereupon we stayed without discovering any thing all the rest of the day. The next day he commanded that all the men of his ship should come up upon the decke, saying that he had somewhat to say unto them. They all came up, and immediatly the Captaine began to speake unto them in this manner.

I thinke there is none of you that is ignorant of how great consequence this our enterprize is, and also how acceptable it is unto our yong King. Therefore my friendes (as one desiring your honour and benefite) I would not faile to advertise you all of the exceeding good happe which should fall to them, which, as men of valure and worthy courage, would make tryall in this our first discoverie of the benefits and commodities of this new land: which should be, as I assure my selfe, the greatest occasion that ever could happen unto them, to arise unto the title and degree of honour. And for this cause I was desirous to propose unto you and set downe before your eyes the eternall memorie which of right they deserve, which forgetting both their parents and their countrey have had the courage to enterprize a thing of such importance, which even kings themselves understanding to be men aspiring to so high degree of magnanimitie and increase of their majesties, doe not disdaine so wel to regard, that afterwards imploying them in maters of weight & of high enterprize, they make their names immortall for ever. Howbeit, I would not have you perswade your selves, as many doe, that you shall never have such good fortune, as not being knowen neither to the king nor the Princes of the Realme, and besides descending of so poore a stocke, that few or none of your parents, having ever made profession of armes, have bene knowen unto the great estates. For albeit that from my tender yeeres I my selfe have applyed all my industry to follow them, and have hazarded my life in so many dangers for the service of my prince, yet could I never attaine therunto (not that I did not deserve this title and degree of government) as I have seene it happen to many others, onely because they descende of a noble race, since more regard is had of their birth then of their virtue. For wel I know that if vertue were regarded, ther would more be found worthy to deserve the title, & by good right to be named noble and valiant. I will therefore make sufficient answere to such propositions and such things as you may object against me, laying before you the infinite examples which we have of the Romans; which concerning the point of honour were the first that triumphed over the world. For how many finde we among them, which for their so valiant enterprizes, not for the greatnesse of their parentage, have obtained the honour to tryumph? If we have recourse unto their ancesters, wee shall finde that their parents were of so meane condition, that by labouring with their hands they lived very basely. As the father of Ælius Pertinax, which was a poore artisan, his Grandfather likewise was a bond man, as the historiographers do witnes: and neverthelesse, being moved with a valiant courage, he was nothing dismayed for all this, but rather desirous to aspire unto high things, he began with a brave stomacke to learne feates of armes, and profited so wel therein, that from step to step he became at length to be Emperour of the Romans. For all this dignitie he despised not his parents: but contrariwise, & in remembrance of them, he caused his fathers shop to be covered with a fine wrought marble, to serve for an example to men descended of base & poore linages, to give them occasion to aspire unto high things notwithstanding the meannesse of their ancesters. I wil not passe over in silence the excellencie & prowesse of the valiant and renowned Agathocles the sonne of a simple potter, and yet forgetting the contemptible estate of his father, he so applied himselfe to vertue in his tender yeeres, that by the favour of armes he came to be king of Sicilie: and

for all this title he refused not to be counted the sonne of a Potter. But the more to eternize the memorie of his parentes and to make his name renowned, he commanded that he should be served at the Table in vessels of gold and silver and others of earth: declaring thereby that the dignitie wherein hee was placed came not unto him by his parents, but by his owne vertue onely. If I shal speake of our time, I will lay before you onely Rusten Bassha, which may be a sufficient example to al men: which though he were the sonne of a poore heard-man, did so apply his youth in all vertue, that being brought up in the service of the great Turke, he seemed to aspire to great and high matters, in such sort that growing in yeres he increased also in courage, so far forth, that in fine for his excellent vertues he married the daughter of the great Turke his Prince. Howe much then ought so many worthy examples to move you to plant here? Considering also that hereby you shalbe registred for ever as the first that inhabited this strange countrey. I pray you therfore all to advise your selves thereof, and to declare your mindes freely unto mee, protesting that I will so well imprint your names in the kings eares, and the other princes, that your renowme shall hereafter shine unquenchable through our Realme of France. He had scarcely ended his Oration, but the greatest part of our souldiers replyed: that a greater pleasure could never betide them, perceiving well the acceptable service which by this meanes they shoulde doe unto their Prince: besides that this thing should be for the increase of their honours: therfore they besought the Captaine, before he departed out of the place, to begin to build them a Fort, which they hoped afterward to finish, and to leave them munition necessarie for their defence, shewing as it seemed that they were displeased, that it was so long in doing. Whereupon John Ribault being as glad as might be to see his men so well willing, determined the next day to search the most fit and convenient place to be inhabited. Wherefore he embarked himselfe very earely in the morning and commanded them to followe him that were desirous to inhabite there, to the intent that they might like the beter of the place. Having sayled up the great river on the North side, in coasting an Isle which ended with a sharpe point toward the mouth of the river, having sailed a while, he discovered a small river, which entred into the Islande, which hee would not faile to search out. Which done, & finding the same deep inough to harbour therein Gallies and Galliots in good number, proceeding further, he found a very open place, joyning upon the brinke thereof, where he went on land, and seeing the place fit to build a Fortresse in, and commodious for them that were willing to plant there, he resolved incontinent to cause the bignes of the fortification to be measured out. And considering that there stayed but sixe and twentie there, he caused the Fort to be made in length but sixteene fathome, and thirteene in breadth, with flankes according to the proportion thereof. The measure being taken by me and Captaine Salles, we sent unto the shippes for men, and to bring shovels, pickaxes and other instruments necessarie to make the fortification. We travailed so diligently, that in a short space the Fort was made in some sort defenciable. In which meane time John Ribault caused victuals and warrelike munition to be brought for the defence of the place. After he had furnished them with all such things as they had neede of, he determined to take his leave of them. But before his departure he used this speech unto Captaine Albert, which he left in this place.

Captaine Albert, I have to request you in the presence of al these men, that you would quit your selfe so wisely in your charge, and governe so modestly your small companie which I leave you, which with so good cheere remaineth under your obedience, that I never have occasion but to commend you, and to recount unto the king (as I am desirous) the faithfull service which before us all you undertake to doe him in his new France: And you companions, (quoth he to the Souldiers) I beseech you also to esteeme of Captaine Albert as if hee were my selfe that stayed here with you, yeelding him that obedience which a true souldier oweth unto his Generall and Captaine, living as brethren one with another, without all dissention: and in so doing God wil assist you and blesse your enterprises. Having ended his exhortation, we tooke our leaves of each of them, and sayled toward our shippes, calling the Forte by the name of Charles-fort, and the River by the name Chenonceau. The next day wee determined to depart from this place being as well contented as was possible that we had so happily ended our

busines, with good hope, if occasion would permitte, to discover perfectly the river of Jordan. For this cause we hoysed our sayles about ten of the clocke in the morning: after wee were ready to depart Captain Ribault commanded to shoote off our Ordinance to give a farewel unto our Frenchmen, which failed not to doe the like on their part. This being done wee sailed toward the North: and then we named this river Porte Royal, because of the largenes and excellent fairenes of the same. After that we had sailed about 15 leagues from thence, we espied a river, whereupon wee sent our pinnesse thither to discover it. At their return they brought us word that they found not past halfe a fathom water in the mouth thereof. Which when we understood, without doing any thing els, we continued our way, and called it the Base or Shallow river. As we stil went on sounding we found not past five or sixe fathome water, although we were sixe good leagues from the shoare: at length we found not past three fathomes, which gave us occasion greatly to muse. And without making any farther way we strook our sayles, partly because we wanted water, & partly because the night approched: during which time Captaine John Ribault bethought with himselfe whether it were best for him to passe any farther, because of the eminent dangers which every houre we saw before our eyes: or whither he should content himselfe with that which he had certainely discovered, & also left men to inhabite the countrey. Being not able for that time to resolve with himselfe, he referred it until the next day. The morning being come he proposed to all the company what was best to be done, to the end that with good advisement every man might deliver his opinion. Some made answere, that according to their judgement he had occasion fully to content himselfe, considering he could doe no more: laying before his eyes, that he had discovered more in sixe weekes, then the Spaniards had done in two yeres in the conquest of their New Spaine: and that he should do the king very great service, if he did bring him newes in so short a time of his happy discoverie. Other shewed unto him the losse and spoile of his victuals, and on the other side the inconvenience that might happen by the shallow water that they found continually along the coast. Which things being well and at large debated we resolved to leave the coast, forsaking the North, to take our way toward the East, which is the right way and course to our France, where we happily arrived the twentieth day of July, the year 1562.

The state and condition of those which were left behind in Charles-fort.

Our men after our departure never rested, but night and day did fortifie themselves, being in good hope that after their fort was finished, they would begin to discover farther up within the river. It happened one day, as certaine of them were in cutting of rootes in the groves, that they espied on the sudden an Indian that hunted the Deere, which finding himselfe so neere upon them, was much dismayed, but our men began to draw neere unto him and to use him so courteously, that he became assured and followed them to Charles-fort, where every man sought to doe him pleasure. Captaine Albert was very joyfull of his comming, which after he had given him a shirt and some other trifles, he asked him of his dwelling: the Indian answered him that it was farther up within the river, and that he was vassal of king Audusta: he also shewed him with his hand the limits of his habitation. After much other talke the Indian desired leave to depart, because it drew toward night, which Captaine Albert granted him very willingly. Certaine dayes after the Captaine determined to saile toward Audusta, where being arrived, by reason of the honest entertaynment which he had given to the Indian, he was so courteously received, that the king talked with him of nothing else but of the desire which he had to become his friend: giving him besides to understand that he being his friend and allie, he should have the amitie of foure other kings, which in might & authoritie were able to do much for his sake: Besides all this, in his necessitie they might be able to succour him with victuals. One of these kings was called Mayon, another Hoya, the third Touppo, and the fourth Stalame. He told him moreover, that they would be very glad, when they should understand the newes of his comming, and therefore he prayed him to vouchsafe to visit them. The Captaine willingly consented unto him, for the desire that he had to purchase friends in that place. Therefore they departed the next morning very earely,

and first arrived at the house of king Touppa, and afterward went into the other kings houses, except the house of king Stalame. He received of each of them all the amiable courtesies that might be: they shewed themselves to be as affectioned friends unto him as was possible, and offered unto him a thousand small presents. After that he had remained by the space of certaine daies with these strange kings, he determined to take his leave: and being come backe to the house of Audusta, he commanded al his men to goe aboord their Pinnesse: for he was minded to goe towardes the countrey of king Stalame, which dwelt toward the North the distance of 15 great leagues from Charles-fort. Therefore as they sailed up the river they entred into a great current, which they followed so farre till they came at the last to the house of Stalame: which brought him into his lodging, where he sought to make them the best cheere he could devise. He presented immediatly unto Captaine Albert his bow and arrowes, which is a signe and confirmation of alliance betweene them. He presented him with Chamoys skinnes. The Captaine seeing the best part of the day was now past, tooke his leave of king Stalame to return to Charles-fort, where hee arrived the day following. By this time the friendship was growne so great betweene our men and king Audusta, that in a manner all things were common betweene him and them: in such sort that this good Indian king did nothing of importance, but he called our men thereunto. For when the time drew neere of the celebrating their feasts of Toya, which are ceremonies most strange to recite, he sent Ambassadours to our men to request them on his behalfe to be there present. Whereunto they agreed most willingly for the desire that they had to understand what this might be. They imbarked themselves therefore and sailed towards the kings house, which was already come forth on the way towards them, to receive them courteously, to bid them welcome & bring them to his house, where he sought to intreat them the best he might. In the meane while the Indians prepared themselves to celebrate the feast the morrow after, and the king brought them to see the place, wherein the feast should be kept: where they saw many women round about, which laboured by al meanes to make the place cleane & neat. This place was a great circuit of ground with open prospect and round in figure. On the morrow therefore early in the morning, all they which were chosen to celebrate the feast, being painted and trimmed with rich feathers of divers colours, put themselves on the way to go from the kings house toward the place of Toya: whereunto when they were come they set themselves in order, & followed three Indians, which in painting and in gesture were differing from the rest: each of them bare a Tabret in their hand, dancing & singing in a lamentable tune, when they began to enter into the middest of the round circuit, being followed of others which answered them again. After that they had sung, danced, and turned 3 times, they fel on running like unbridled horses, through the middest of the thickest woods. And then the Indian women continued all the rest of the day in teares as sad & woful as was possible: & in such rage they cut the armes of the yong girles, which they lanced so cruelly with sharpe shels of Muskles that the blood followed which they flang into the ayre, crying out three times, He Toya. The king Audusta had gathered all our men into his house, while the feast was celebrated, and was exceedingly offended when he saw them laugh. This he did, because the Indians are very angry when they are seene in their ceremonies. Notwithstanding one of our men made such shift that by subtile meanes he gatte out of the house of Audusta, and secretly went and hid himselfe behinde a very thicke bush, where at his pleasure, he might easily discry the ceremonies of the feast. They three that began the feast are named Jawas: and they are as it were three Priestes of the Indian law: to whom they give credite and beliefe partly because that by kinred they are ordained to be over their Sacrifices, and partly also because they be so subtile magicians that any thing that is lost is straightway recovered by their meanes. Againe they are not onely reverenced for these things, but also because they heale diseases by I wotte not what kinde of knowledge and skill they have. Those that ran so through the woodes returned two dayes after: after their returne they began to dance with a cherefull courage in the middest of the faire place, and to cheere up their good olde Indian fathers, which either by reason of their too great age, or by reason of their naturall indisposition and feeblenesse were not called to the feast. When all these dances were

ended, they fell on eating with such a greedinesse, that they seemed rather to devoure their meate then to eate it, for they had neither eaten nor drunke the day of the feast, nor the two dayes following. Our men were not forgotten at this good cheere, for the Indians sent for them all thither, shewing themselves very glad of their presence. While they remained certaine time with the Indians, a man of ours got a yong boy for certaine trifles, and inquired of him, what the Indians did in the wood during their absence: which boy made him understand by signes, that the Jawas had made invocations to Toya, and that by Magicall Characters they had made him come that they might speake with him and demand divers strange things of him, which for feare of the Jawas he durst not utter. They have also many other ceremonies, which I will not here rehearse for feare of molesting the reader with a matter of so small importance.

When the feast therefore was finished our men returned unto Charles-fort: where having remained but a while their victualles beganne to waxe short, which forced them to have recourse unto their neighbours, and to pray them to succour them in their necessitie: which gave them part of all the victualles which they had, and kept no more unto themselves then would serve to sow their fieldes. They tolde them farther that for this cause it was needeful for them to retire themselves into the woods, to live of Mast and rootes untill the time of harvest, being as sory as might be that they were not able any farther to ayde them. They gave them also counsell to goe toward the countreys of King Covexis a man of might and renowme in this province, which maketh his aboad toward the South abounding at all seasons and replenished with such quantitie of mill, corne, and beanes that by his onely succour they might be able to live a very long time. But before they should come into his territories, they were to repayre unto a king called Ovade the brother of Covexis, which in mill, beanes, and corne was no lesse wealthy, and withall is very liberall, and which would be very joyfull if he might but once see them. Our men perceiving the good relation which the Indians made them of those two kings resolved to go thither; for they felt already the necessity which oppressed them. Therfore they made request unto king Maccou, that it would please him to give them one of his subjects to guide them the right way thither: wherupon he condescended very willingly, knowing that without his favour they should have much ado to bring their interprize to passe. Wherefore after they had given order for all things necessary for the voyage, they put themselves to Sea, and sayled so farre that in the end they came into the countrey of Ovade, which they found to be in the river Belle. Being there arrived they perceived a company of Indians, which assoone as they knew of their being there came before them. Assoone as they were come neere them, their guides shewed them by signes that Ovade was in this company, wherefore our men set forward to salute him. And then two of his sonnes which were with him, being goodly and strong men saluted them againe in very good sort, and used very friendly entertainment on their part. The king immediatly began to make an Oration in his Indian language of the great pleasure and contentment which he had to see them in that place, protesting that he would become so loyall a friend of theirs hereafter, that he would be their faithfull defendour against all them that would offer to be their enemies. After these speeches he led them toward his house, where he sought to entreate them very courteously. His house was hanged about with Tapistrie of feathers of divers colours the height of a pike. Moreover the place where the king tooke his rest was covered with white Coverlettes embroydered with devises of very wittie and fine workemanship, and fringed round about with a Fringe dyed in the colour of Skarlet. They advertised the king by one of the guides which they brought with them, how that (having heard of his great liberalitie) they had put to the Sea to come to beseech him to succour them with victuals in their great want and necessitie: and that in so doing, he should binde them all hereafter to remaine his faithfull friends and loyall defenders against all his enemies. This good Indian assoone ready to doe them pleasure, as they were to demand it, commanded his subjects that they should fill our Pinnesse with mil and beanes. Afterward he caused them to bring him six pieces of his Tapistry made like little coverlets, & gave them to our men with so liberal a minde, as they easily perceived the desire which he had to become their friend. In recompence of all these giftes our men

gave him two cutting hookes and certaine other trifles, wherewith he held himselfe greatly satisfied. This being done, our men tooke their leave of the king, which for their farewell, sayd nothing els but that they should returne if they wanted victuals, & that they might assure themselves of him, that they should never want any thing that was in his power. Wherefore they imbarked themselves, and sayled towards Charles-fort, which from this place might be some five and twenty leagues distant. But as soone as our men thought themselves at their ease, & free from the dangers whereunto they had exposed themselves night and day in gathering together of victuals here and there: Lo, even as they were asleepe, the fire caught in their lodgings with such furie, being increased by the winde, that the roome that was built for them before our mens departure, was consumed in an instant, without being able to save any thing, saving a little of their victualles. Whereupon our men being farre from all succours, found themselves in such extremitie, that without the ayd of Almighty God, the onely searcher of the hearts and thoughts of men, which never forsaketh those that seeke him in their afflictions, they had bene quite and cleane out of all hope. For the next day betimes in the morning the King Audusta and King Maccou came thither, accompanied with a very good companie of Indians, which knowing the misfortune, were very sory for it. And then they uttered unto their subjects the speedy diligence which they were to use in building another house, shewing unto them that the Frenchmen were their loving friends, & that they had made it evident unto them by the gifts and presents which they had received: protesting that whosoever put not his helping hand unto the worke with all his might, should be esteemed as unprofitable, and as one that had no good part in him, which the Savages feare above all things. This was the occasion that every man began to endevour himselfe in such sort, that in lesse then 12 houres, they had begun and finished a house which was very neere as great as the former. Which being ended, they returned home fully contented with a few cutting hookes, and hatchets, which they received of our men. Within a small while after this mischance, their victuals began to waxe short: and after our men had taken good deliberation, thought and bethought themselves againe, they found that there was no better way for them then to returne againe to the king Ovade and Covexis his brother. Wherefore they resolved to send thither some of their company the next day following: which with an Indian Canoa sayled up into the countrey about 10 leagues: afterward they found a very faire & great river of fresh water, which they failed not to search out: they found therein a great number of Crocodils, which in greatnes passe those of the river Nilus: moreover, al along the bankes thereof, there grow mighty high Cypresses. After they had stayed a smal while in this place, they purposed to follow their journey, helping themselves so wel with the tydes, that without putting themselves in danger of the continuall perill of the Sea, they came into the countrey of Ovade: of whom they were most courteously received. They advertised him of the occasion wherefore they came againe to visite him, and told him of the mischance, which happened unto them since their last voyages: how they had not onely lost their houshold stuffe by casualtie of fire, but also their victuals which he had given them so bountifully: that for this cause they were so bolde as to come once againe unto him, to beseech him to vouchsafe to succour them in such neede and necessitie.

After that the king had understood their case, he sent messengers unto his brother Covexis, to request him upon his behalfe to send him some of his mill and beanes, which thing he did: and the next morning, they were come againe with victuals, which the king caused to be borne into their Canoa. Our men would have taken their leave of him, finding themselves more then satisfied with this liberalitie. But for that day hee would not suffer them, but retained them, and sought to make them the best cheere hee could devise. The next day very earely in the morning, he tooke them with him to shewe them the place where his corne grewe, and saide unto them that they should not want as long as all that mil did last. Afterward he gave them a certaine number of exceeding faire pearles, & two stones of fine Christal, and certaine silver oare. Our men forgot not to give him certaine trifles in recompence of these presentes, and required of him the place whence the silver oare and the Christall came. He made them answere, that it came ten dayes jour-

ney from his habitation up within the countrey: and that the inhabitants of the countrey did dig the same at the foote of certaine high mountaines, where they found of it in very good quantitie. Being joyfull to understand so good newes, and to have come to the knowledge of that which they most desired, they tooke their leave of the king, and returned by the same saw, by which they came.

Behold therefore how our men behaved themselves very well hitherto, although they had endured many great mishaps. But misfortune or rather the just judgement of God would have it, that those which could not bee overcome by fire nor water, should be undone by their owne selves. This is the common fashion of men, which cannot continue in one state, and had rather to overthrow themselves, then not to attempt some new thing dayly. We have infinite examples in the ancient histories, especially of the Romanes, unto which number this little handfull of men, being farre from their countrey and absent from their countreymen, have also added this present example. They entred therefore into partialities and dissentions, which began about a souldier named Guernache, which was a drummer of the French bands: which, as it was told me, was very cruelly hanged by his owne captaine, and for a smal fault: which captaine also using to threathen the rest of his souldiers which staied behind under his obedience, and peradventure (as it is to be presumed) were not so obedient to him as they should have bene, was the cause that they fell into a mutinie, because that many times he put his threatnings in execution: wherupon they so chased him, that at the last they put him to death. And the principall occasion that moved them thereunto was, because he degraded another souldier named La Chere (which he had banished) and because he had not performed his promise: for hee had promised to send him victuals, from 8 dayes to 8 dayes, which thing he did not, but said on the contrary, that he would be glad to heare of his death. He said moreover, that he would chastise others also, & used so evil sounding speeches, that honestie forbiddeth me to repeat them. The souldiers seeing his madnes to increase from day to day, and fearing to fall into the dangers of the other, resolved to kil him. Having executed their purpose, they went to seeke the souldier that was banished, which was in a small Island distant from Charles-fort about 3 leagues, where they found him almost half dead for hunger. When they were come home againe, they assembled themselves together to choose one to be governour over them whose name was Nicolas Barre a man worthy of commendation, and one which knewe so well to quite himselfe of his charge, that all rancour and dissention ceased among them, and they lived peaceably one with another. During this time, they began to build a smal Pinnesse, with hope to return into France, if no succours came unto them, as they expected from day to day. And though there were no man among them that had any skill, notwithstanding necessitie, which is the maistresse of all sciences, taught them the way to build it. After that it was finished, they thought of nothing else saving how to furnish it with all things necessarie to undertake the voyage. But they wanted those things that of all other were most needefull, as cordage and sayles, without which the enterprise coulde not come to effect. Having no meanes to recover these things, they were in worse case then at the first, and almost ready to fall into despayre. But that good God, which never forsaketh the afflicted, did succour them in their necessitie.

As they were in these perplexities king Audusta and Maccou came to them, accompanied with two hundred Indians at the least, whom our Frenchmen went forth to meete withall, and shewed the king in what neede of cordage they stood: who promised them to returne within two dayes, and to bring so much as should suffice to furnish the Pinnesse with tackling. Our men being pleased with these good newes & promises, bestowed upon them certaine cutting hookes and shirtes. After their departure our men sought all meanes to recover rosen in the woodes, wherin they cut the Pine trees round about, out of which they drew sufficient reasonable quantitie to bray the vessell. Also they gathered a kind of mosse which groweth on the trees of this countrey, to serve to calke the same withall. There now wanted nothing but sayles, which they made of their owne shirtes and of their sheetes. Within few dayes after the Indian kings returned to Charles fort with so good store of cordage, that there was found sufficient for tackling of the small Pinnesse. Our men as glad as might be, used great

liberalitie towards them, and at their leaving of the countrey, left them all the marchandise that remained, leaving them thereby so fully satisfied, that they departed from them with all the contentation of the worlde. They went forward therefore to finish the Brigandine, & used so speedie diligence, that within a short time afterward they made it ready furnished with all things. In the meane season the winde came so fit for their purpose that it seemed to invite them to put to the Sea: which they did without delay, after they had set all their things in order. But before they departed they embarked their artillerie, their forge, and other munitions of warre which Captaine Ribault had left them, and then as much mill as they could gather together. But being drunken with the too excessive joy, which they had conceived for their returning into France, or rather deprived of all foresight & consideration, without regarding the inconstancie of the winds, which change in a moment, they put themselves to sea, and with so slender victuals, that the end of their interprise became unluckly and unfortunate.

For after they had sayled the third part of their way, they were surprized with calmes which did so much hinder them, that in three weekes they sailed not above five and twentie leagues. During this time their victuals consumed, and became so short, that every man was constrained to eate not past twelve graines of mill by the day, which may be in value as much as twelve peason. Yea, and this felicitie lasted not long: for their victuals failed them altogether at once: and they had nothing for their more assured refuge but their shooes and leather jerkins which they did eat. Touching their beverage, some of them dranke the sea water, others did drink their owne urine: and they remained in such desperate necessitie a very long space, during the which part of them died for hunger. Beside this extreme famine, which did so grievously oppresse them, they fell every minute of an houre out of all hope ever to see France againe, insomuch that they were constrained to cast the water continually out, that on al sides entred into their Barke. And every day they fared worse and worse: for after they had eaten up their shooes and their leather jerkins, there arose so boystrous a winde and so contrary to their course, that in the turning of a hande, the waves filled their vessel halfe full of water and brused it upon the one side. Being now more out of hope then ever to escape out of this extreme peril, they cared not for casting out of the water which now was almost ready to drowne them. And as men resolved to die, every one fell downe backewarde, and gave themselves over altogether unto the will of the waves. When as one of them a little having taken heart unto him declared unto them how litle way they had to sayle, assuring them, that if the winde held, they should see land within three dayes. This man did so encourage them, that after they had throwne the water out of the Pinnesse they remained three dayes without eating or drinking, except it were of the sea water. When the time of his promise was expired, they were more troubled then they were before, seeing they could not discry any land. Wherefore in this extreme despaire certaine among them made this motion that it was better that one man should dye, then that so many men should perish: they agreed therefore that one should die to sustaine the others. Which thing was executed in the person of La Chere, of whom we have spoken heretofore, whose flesh was devided equally among his fellowes: a thing so pitifull to recite, that my pen is loth to write it.

After so long time and tedious travels, God of his goodnesse using his accustomed favour, changed their sorow into joy, and shewed unto them the sight of land. Whereof they were so exceeding glad, that the pleasure caused them to remaine a long time as men without sence: whereby they let the Pinnesse flote this and that way without holding any right way or course. But a small English barke boarded the vessell, in the which there was a Frenchman which had bene in the first voyage into Florida, who easily knew them, and spake unto them, and afterward gave them meat and drinke. Incontinently they recovered their naturall courages, and declared unto him at large all their navigation. The Englishmen consulted a long while what were best to be done, and in fine they resolved to put on land those that were most feeble, and to cary the rest unto the Queene of England, which purposed at that time to send into Florida.[3] Thus you see in briefe that which happened to them which Captaine John

3. Sidenote: "It seemeth hee meaneth the voyage intended by Stukely."

Ribault had left in Florida. And now will I go forward with the discourse of mine owne voyage.

300. 1562. The fate of the first garrison at Charlesfort.

Lancelot Voisin, seigneur de La Popellinière, Les trois mondes (Paris, Olivier de Pierre l'Huillier, 1582), fols. 26–28v., extracts translated.

Thus certain Frenchmen basing themselves on such considerations [i.e. the monopoly of obtaining wealth from the New World by the Spanish and Portuguese] decided to make discoveries in the New World, some to the west on the fringes of America, others going to the north. A number took the route to Africa and Ethiopia, as I will show in another place in order not to confuse the order of time and place. I will speak here only of the Dieppe men, who under Jean Ribaud, a Norman, holding the favor and appointment of the king (by the law of the sea) in 1565 [=1562], following his first plan to people Florida in 1561.

Florida is a coast which takes the form of a long point of land in the continent of the West Indies, the which trends toward the north and which expands like a channel and extends about a hundred leagues towards the south—having about fifty leagues in breadth. It is more than six hundred leagues from Vera Cruz—the port of New Spain in the Gulf of Mexico. From the coast of the west [*Ponent*] towards the south it has a good hundred leagues to the island of Cuba. To the east it has the Island of Bahana [Bahama] and the Lucayes or Luçoises. The tip of this land is at twenty five degrees from the equinoctial toward the north and it extends northeastward, broadening out bit by bit toward the north. Near by the Cape on the east coast there are small, low islands called the Martirs.

It was there that Ribaud first landed, being well received by the savages—and here he raised a fort which he called Charlesfort. Then, leaving there twenty-six soldiers under the command of Captain Aubert [Albert de la Pierria], he returned, intending to raise in France as many men, women and workmen as he could to settle the whole province and form there a safe retreat for his nation against all those who would molest her.

Those who were left behind behaved themselves well enough for a time. But eventually divisions arose over the hanging of a soldier by the Captain, and the degradation of another, whom he had confined to an island three leagues distant from the fort. They put their commander to death, and then they recalled the banished soldier. This done, they elected Captain Nicolas [Barré] as their commander, who governed them well until, tired of having no news from France, and lacking supplies, they resolved to construct a brigantine in which to return if relief did not come soon, even though no one knew how to build one. The boat completed, they asked the savages to give them ropes, which they did, and in recompense they gave them their knives, bill-hooks, mirrors and such household goods. This done, and having searched for resin in the woods, tapping pine, fir and other gum-bearing trees, they took enough to staunch the ship. They also used a kind of moss to seal and caulk her. They then hoisted sails made from their shirts and bedclothes. Setting sail on the first good wind, they were soon in the doldrums and were becalmed and their fresh water and provisions failed them. Since they had made only twenty-five [= two hundred and twenty-five?] leagues in three weeks they were forced to eat as little as twelves grains of meal a man each day. But even this gave out and they were compelled to attempt to digest shoes, collars, hides and skins. Those who tried the sea water had burned throats and scalded intestines and endured harsh tortures, so much so that others preferred to swallow their own urine. Suddenly, thereafter, the vessel opened at the seams; it became impossible to get rid of the water. A tide of water and wind caught hold of them so fiercely that the boat was driven aground. Because the waves passed over them they were no longer able to get rid of the water, so that even the bravest of them was not able to encourage the others with assurances that they would see land. Then for three days they were all in the depths of despair, but even so strength was needed to bail out the water. They remained for three days without drinking or eating. Eventually, it was suggested that it would be expedient for one to die rather than all. The lot fell on him

who had been banished, Larcher, who was killed, and whose flesh was shared equally among all after they had drunk his blood warm. At last, having been tossed about on the sea, they sighted the coast of Brittany, whereupon they were so elated that they allowed the boat to drift at the mercy of the waves. An English vessel (*Taberge*) approached and some were grateful they had food and drink to spare. But the English left the weakest behind and brought the rest to England to present to the Queen, who was then considering sending men to New France to which many had sailed, Bretons, Normans and Basques.

301. May–June, 1564. Expedition of Hernando Manrique de Rojas to search for evidence of French occupation on the Florida coast.

News of French activities on the coast of Florida in 1562–1563 caused alarm among the Spanish authorities in Cuba when information on them came from Europe. This led to the frigate La Concepción, *under Hernando Manrique de Rojas, being employed in an effort to locate the places where the French had been and to eradicate all traces of their presence. This expedition was strikingly successful, in that the fort site (Charlesfort) was located on Port Royal Sound and its remnants destroyed (the column with the French arms placed there being brought back), while the capture of a French straggler, Guillaume Rufin, enabled the story of French activity to be pieced together. Armed with this information, the Spaniards were well able to estimate in 1565 where the French might be found and to take countermeasures, although by then they had further information. The efficiency of this expedition is in contrast with many of those which preceded it.*

A.G.I., Seville Santo Domingo, 99 (54/1/15), translated by Lucy L. Wenhold, "Manrique de Rojas's report on French settlement in Florida, 1564," Florida Historical Quarterly, XXXVIII (1959), 45–62. It was reprinted in C. W. Bennett, Laudonnière and Fort Caroline (1964), pp. 108–124, and is again reprinted.

[a] In the town of San Cristóbal, Havana, on the ninth of July, 1564, after midnight, there entered the harbor of this town the frigate called *La Concepción*, in which arrived Hernando Manrique, formerly captain in Florida. Later, on the tenth of July, before His Excellency Diego Mazariegos, Governor and Captain General by appointment of His Majesty, and in the presence of myself, Francisco Zapata, government scrivener by royal appointment, the said captain, Hernando Manrique de Rojas, appeared and declared that he went, by command of His Excellency, to Florida and Point St. Helena, with a certain expedition, with instructions from His Excellency and with a royal letter from His Majesty; that he went and fulfilled his commission and was accordingly reporting to His Excellency the Governor what he had done. He returned the royal letter he had received, and delivered a stone marker bearing the arms of France, the inscription R., and four Arabic numerals. These things the Governor received in the presence of witnesses.[1]

[b] The report made by Hernando Manrique is as follows:

Diego Mazariegos, Governor and Captain General by royal appointment in this Island of Cuba, to you, Hernando Manrique de Rojas, citizen of this town of San Cristóbal, Havana. Know that His Majesty has been pleased to state in a royal letter that certain Frenchmen have established themselves on the coast of Florida and taken possession there. He desires and commands that I obtain information concerning these persons and what settlement they have made, according as he directs me in the royal letter, the original of which you will carry with you. For the fulfillment of His Majesty's command I have decided to send to Point St. Helena a frigate with twenty-five men. As the royal service demands for this matter a qualified person who shall explore the territory and gain information as to what is happening there, I, believing you to be such a person, qualified and trustworthy, who will do in all things what is most advisable for the service of His Majesty, hereby name and appoint you captain of the said frigate, of the twenty-five men and of all others who may go in her or be required for the

needs of this affair. You will go as captain under the flag, commanding and controlling the men, ordering them in whatever may seem to you most to the service of His Majesty and the success of the expedition, and punishing the disobedient for whatever offenses they may commit, as is your right. When you shall have embarked in this port, for the ordering of this expedition and the carrying out of His Majesty's command you shall keep and follow instructions signed with my name and countersigned by this present scrivener. In all respects you will act as becomes a good and loyal captain, and I will give you full and complete power according as I have it from His Excellency, with all its incidents and accessories, appurtenances and rights. If you enter any port of call, whether in this island or in Hispaniola or elsewhere, I command all justices, knights, gentlemen, officials and good men of the place that they give you favor and aid and such supplies, men and ships, as you may need. If you enter ports in the island or Hispaniola or in other parts of these Indies, I beseech the judges of those towns and ports that of their grace and in my name, requiring it of them also in the name of His Majesty, it being a thing so important for the royal service, that they give you whatever needed assistance you may request. In case of such necessity you will formalize your request by means of the royal letter which you carry, leaving a copy of it and keeping with you your original which was made in the city of Havana on the twenty-ninth of April, 1564.

[signed:] Diego Mazariegos.
Francisco Zapata, scrivener,
By order of His Excellency the Governor.

[c] That which you, Captain Hernando Manrique, are to do on this expedition to Point St. Helena and the coast of Florida, of which expedition I place you in charge, is the following:

Having gone out of this harbor, with fortune favoring you you will enter the Bahama Channel and sail along the Florida coast until you arrive at the shore of La Cruz, which is in the twenty-ninth parallel of latitude. There you will land men to seek a stone column or marker bearing the arms of France, which is set up there. Having found it you will remove it and destroy it, or, if it proves to be a thing that can be transported in the frigate you will bring it with you. This is to be done in the

1. Names of witnesses omitted here and elsewhere by the translator.

presence of witnesses, and of a scrivener whom you will appoint for this and other necessary occasions.

Then you will continue along the shore of Las Corrientes which is on the thirtieth parallel and there you will find another of the same sort.

You will proceed thus along the coast until you reach the Saint Helena River which is in latitude thirty-two. You will enter the river and attempt to find a wooden fort which is there, and to learn whether there are any French in it, and if so, their number and quality, what artillery they have, where they are established, what are their relations with the Indians, what force they have, and what preparation will be necessary in order to expel them. If you find the circumstances such that you can drive them out of the fort you will do so, bringing to me as prisoners those of them whom you can capture. You will also bring all the artillery, arms and booty which you may take from them, razing the fort so completely that no trace of it shall remain.

If by chance you encounter in Florida some captain of His Majesty with Spanish soldiers who may have gone out for the same purpose, you will require of him in His Majesty's name and with the royal letter which you carry that he allow you and your men, without depriving you of any of the latter, to explore the Florida coast in order to report to His Majesty concerning it as is his command.

If you should hear that elsewhere there is some enterprise such as the aforementioned, or should discover a settlement of French or of any other people who are not vassals of His Majesty, you will endeavor to reach the place where they are and to acquaint yourself with all the facts, acting in the matter according to the above directions. In all respects you will act as a good and loyal captain, with due regard for the royal service and in conformity with the trust and confidence I place in you.

On board the frigate called *Nuestra Señora de la Concepción*, at present anchored in the river called Las Corrientes which is in latitude twenty-seven on this Florida coast, on May 24 of this year 1564, Captain Hernando Manrique de Rojas, commander of the frigate and its men, in the presence of me, Juan Guerra, scrivener of the frigate, and of other witnesses, declared:

[d]   That in accordance with the instructions given him by the Governor, after he left the harbor of Havana he came to explore the coast of Florida in latitude twenty-seven and a half, and proceeded from that point along the coast to this harbor which is in latitude twenty-nine, without going more than half a league away from land, going northward and sailing only by day in order to have a better view of the coast. The frigate being anchored in the mouth of the harbor, he ordered Gonzalo Gayon, her pilot, to calculate the latitude. This was done by Gayon and several other persons who had the necessary knowledge, on the night of last Monday, the twenty-second of this present month, and they found the latitude to be twenty-nine. As this is the latitude in which, according to the Governor's instructions, the shore of La Cruz is and where one of the columns bearing the arms of France should be found, the captain went ashore to seek it and remove it according to his orders. He explored the shores of the harbor on the side next to the sea and on the inner, river sides and went to an Indian village which is on the bank of one of the rivers. Nowhere did he find the column nor anything that would appear to have been placed there for that purpose by the hands of Christians. He communicated with the Indians, but as neither he nor any of his men could understand their speech he could not learn anything from them about the matter. As he had been two days in that harbor and wished to go out at high tide [translator's suggestion for *tiempo*] to continue the voyage, in order to put on record the fact that he had carried out the directions given him he commanded me, the scrivener, to make an affidavit concerning all the above, I being one of those who went ashore with him. Even so he commanded me to make a true report of all that might occur in the harbors into which he might enter, of what he might find there and what might be done, and to certify it as an eye-witness in order that His Majesty may be informed of everything. Witnesses being those aforementioned, he signed: Hernando Manrique de Rojas, before me, Juan Guerra, scrivener.

That same day the captain ordered the anchor weighed, set sail and anchored again somewhat further north. After this, on the twenty-fifth of May, he again ordered the frigate put under sail and ran along the coast until he found a river of some eight or nine leagues from the one mentioned before. He sailed the frigate in and when it was anchored he calculated the latitude and declared it to be twenty-nine and a half. Thereupon he went ashore to some Indians' huts which he saw close to the river mouth, on the arm which is on the north side. Neither in them nor anywhere on the coast thereabout, on river or seashore, did he find Indians or any other people, nor any trace of them, nor did he find any of the French columns. Crossing to the other bank of the river he explored it completely, going more than a league along the other arm which is on the south side, and neither there nor in the other directions in which he explored could he find the column nor anything that appeared made for such use by Christian hands.

The same day, having sailed a league further north, the frigate anchored overnight. Next day, the twenty-sixth, we sailed along the coast northward to a river which the captain and Gonzalo Gayon, the pilot of the frigate, said was in latitude thirty. The frigate having run in and anchored in the river, the captain went ashore to an Indian village which is on the arm that runs south. There he found about eighty Indians, and from their signs he learned that there had been on that river three ships of Christians and that these had gone northward to where the point and river of St. Helena are said to be. In one of the huts of the village he found a wooden box with a lid, made by the hands of Christians. The Indians gave it to be understood that this and other things found among them had been given them by bearded men who came in the ships. The captain searched the village and the river banks from one extreme to the other, as also the river mouth, for the French column, but did not find it anywhere.

On May twenty-ninth he ordered the frigate's anchor weighed. But as the weather conditions were not good for coastwise sailing he anchored again on the coast a league north of the river just mentioned. In the afternoon of that same day, as he believed the vessels to be in a dangerous position anchored on the coast in the shallows of the river mouth, he ordered her out to sea until the night of the next day, May thirtieth, when he again anchored on the coast in latitude which he and Gonzalo Gayon declared to be thirty-two.

On May thirty-first he again set sail and entered a river which was said to be the St. Helena. There he and Gonzalo Gayon again calculated the latitude and declared it to be thirty-two.

That same day the captain went ashore and found three Indians two of whom came willingly with him to the frigate. From their signs it was learned that ships of Christians had been in the harbor of St. Helena and had gone to an Indian village which, these Indians said, was called Guale, and which is situated on an arm of a river that flows out of another that is north of this harbor. This they indicated by signs and by speaking the name. Then the captain put them ashore and went to the place they indicated, which could be seen from the frigate. On June first, while in this harbor, he took the frigate's boat and went up the arm of the river. He landed near the aforementioned village and went to the *micoo* [*mico*, Timucua word for a leading chief], as he is called there. In the house of the *micoo* and in his possession were found two felt hats of the kind made in Spain, and in possession of other Indians were found other things also from Spain. Speaking by signs with the *micoo* he learned from him and from the other Indians that the aforementioned ships had been in the harbor and the Christians, whom he described by signs as bearded as we are, had been in the village and had gone away northward up the coast. The captain, with me, the scrivener, searched the entire village and its huts. Neither there nor on the shores of the rivers or the harbor did he find the fort which the Governor, in his instructions, says the French built. Nor did he find any structure at all which could have been built by the French or by any other Christians for that purpose.

On the second of June he ordered the frigate sailed out of the arm of the river and anchored at a point in the harbor, above an arm on the southern side, to look for the fort and the French. He landed and explored all the shore from the mouth of the river to the seashore, along the banks and inland, and found nothing.

On June third twelve Indians came by land, among them the *micoo* of their town which is called Yanahume and lies to the south. They gave it to be understood that they wished the captain and the other people to go to their village, and they pointed with their hands to show where it was. The captain made signs to the effect that he would go there at once. He ordered the frigate under way and anchored above their town, went ashore to it and found neither French nor fort, nor anything Spanish in the possession of the Indians. From the signs made by the *micoo* and the other Indians it was learned that the Christians had gone to the village of Guale and had not come to this one nor to any other of the seventeen which, according to the signs they made, are on this harbor. They pointed with their hands to show the directions in which these villages are located and spoke their names. Other Indians who came in canoes and by land to see the frigate confirmed by their signs what the first ones had said. For this reason, and because he could not find the French nor their fort, the captain declared himself convinced that there was no French settlement there.

On the sixth of June he went ashore and explored the coast northward for about two leagues, but found neither fort nor French nor trace of them nor of any other Christians. Then, aboard the frigate *Nuestra, Señora de la Concepción* anchored in the harbor, on the same day, month and year, in the presence of me, the scrivener, and of witnesses, the captain declared:

That as he had evidence, furnished both by the testimony of the Indians of the village called Guale and by the presence among them of things of Spanish make, that Christian vessels had been in that harbor and had gone out of it and sailed up the coast; that as he had obtained the same information from the Indians of the river which is in latitude thirty, these may be the ships of the French of whom the governor speaks in his instructions, in spite of the fact that they have not left the markers on the former harbors nor built on this one the fort and settlement which the instructions say is in latitude thirty; that it may be possible that the French left the markers on his harbor and the Indians have taken them away, or that the fort and settlement are in some place where it has not been possible to find them, or that they have been located on another harbor or other harbors further to the north, and that it is proper for the service of His Majesty to seek them well in order to report accurately to him concerning the matter. He therefore ordered Gonzalo Gayon, pilot, there present, to weigh anchor as soon as the weather should allow and set sail northward along the coast until he should find

another harbor, or harbors, where the French and the fort might be, or where he might obtain more exact information.

On the seventh of June Gonzalo Gayon, as ordered, weighed anchor, went out of the harbor and sailed up the coast to another harbor some three or four leagues further on. He entered it and sailed the frigate along its shores. The captain then ordered Gonzalo Gayon and me, the scrivener, and others, soldiers, to go ashore and look for the French, the fort and the marker. We explored but we found neither these nor any settlement, either of Christians or of Indians.

Smoke was seen inland, apparently at a distance and where the frigate could not sail because of the shallows and flooded land, and thus it was not possible to go there to make inquiries of the Indians.

That same day the captain ordered the frigate out of that harbor and sailing along the coast entered another harbor two leagues further on, where he found neither French nor fort nor Indians nor houses nor any sign of what he sought. Next day he had the anchor weighed and proceeded on his voyage to another harbor two leagues further up the coast. There he disembarked and found traces of Indians in a pine grove which is between two rivers that the harbor has. He found no huts nor Indians, though smoke appeared far inland, and neither fort nor French were found anywhere on the shores of the harbor.

On June the ninth he sailed a league further up the coast and came to two harbors joined in one. He entered with the frigate and went through one of them a distance of about two leagues. Nowhere thereabout did he find the French nor the fort nor Indians nor any settlement except two abandoned houses.

On June tenth he sailed a league further to where appeared two mouths of harbors which are close one to the other. Into these he did not enter as it was late and he wished to reach another harbor which was visible further on, and after sailing two or three leagues along the coast he entered harbor in which he anchored.

On June the eleventh he weighed anchor to go to a river which is on a point on the south side of the harbor. As they sailed along, those in the frigate saw a canoe anchored at the point, and immediately two Indians came out of the forest and got into the canoe to go away. The captain ordered Mateo Díaz, master of the frigate, to go to speak with them and to bring them to the frigate if they would come without being made captives or harmed. They came aboard willingly with Mateo Díaz and showed by signs where their village was, on the northwest side of the harbor. The captain took the frigate to that place, and at once other Indians came on board. The captain landed and went to the Indian village. There he found in the possession of the Indians two iron axes, a mirror, some pieces of cloth, small bells, knives and many other things made by the hands of Christians. The Indians explained by signs and some intelligible words that there had been at their village thirty-four men with a ship; that thirty-three of them had gone away and one had remained with them in that land and was now in a village they said was called Usta. They said that they would send for him and he would come the next day when the sun should be high. The captain, having understood, sent two of the Indians to the other village to summon this Christian and gave them a piece of wood with a cross made upon it which they were to give the Christian as proof that there were Christians in the land. The Indian messengers departed at once, and at noon on the twelfth of June there appeared before the captain, in the presence of me, the scrivener, and of witnesses, the said Christian, clothed like the Indians of that country, who declared himself to be a Frenchman.

Immediately the captain ordered Mateo Díaz, master of the frigate, to calculate the latitude in order to know the location of the harbor. Mateo Díaz calculated it by the sun, the captain being present, and found it to be thirty-two and a third. Then the captain said that inasmuch as it was desirable to find out some things from this Frenchman in order to know what was to be done in this matter he was giving command that the man be sworn and his deposition taken. He therefore summoned him and called Martín Pérez, one of the frigate's sailors who said he was French, who should translate into Castilian the things the Frenchman might say in his deposition which might not be understood. The two were then put under oath. The Frenchman swore to speak the truth in whatever he knew and might be asked concerning the matter in which they wished him to give evidence, and Martín Pérez swore to translate into Castilian whatever the Frenchman

might say that was not understood, without excepting or reserving anything. In absolution [or "acquittal"] of the oath they said: "Thus I swear" and "Amen!"

[e] The Frenchman was asked whether he is a Christian, what is his name and of what country he is a native. He replied that he is a Christian, that his name is Guillaume [Rouffin?], and that he is a native of Unfein in the kingdom of France. Asked who brought him to these parts he replied that Captain Ribaut did. Asked by the captain from where was this Captain Ribaut, with what ships he came to these parts, what force of men and what artillery he brought, he replied that Captain Jean Ribaut was a native of Dieppe, France, that he came to these parts with two armed galleasses, one of about 160 tons and the other of sixty, a shallop with three lateen sails, and two other, smaller shallops which, at sea, were carried on board the galleasses; that the large galleass carried a hundred men, twenty-five of whom were sailors and seventy-five were arquebusiers, fifteen large brass cannon and two of smaller size and eight brass falcons, besides other arms and ammunition; that the small galleass, captained by the Frenchman Finqueville, carried fifty men, three large guns, one smaller one and six falcons, all of brass, twenty-five arquebuses and other arms and ammunition.

He was asked in what season and from what port they left France, and he replied that they sailed from New Havre in the kingdom of France on the first day of Lent of the year 1561. Asked by whose command and at whose cost the expedition had been arranged and what had been its destination, he replied that he understood the expedition to have been made up and sent out at the command and cost of the Queen Mother of France, the Admiral [Gaspard de Coligny] and Monsieur de Vendôme, and that each of these gave one thousand ducats to equip the expedition; that it came directly to this coast of Florida to settle on the Point and River of St. Helena, and to discover whether it was a good location for going out into the Bahama Channel to capture the fleets from the Indies. This he knows because he heard it said by everyone and it was common knowledge.

He was questioned as to whether they explored any other territory or harbor of the Indies or any other parts before they arrived at this coast, and how long they were on the way. He said that after they left New Havre they neither entered any other harbor nor explored any other territory than this coast of Florida; that he had heard the pilot call the first land they saw Cape Florida near the Bahama Channel; that they were two and a half months on the way from France to this land. Asked whether they met on the ocean any other ship, he replied that he heard it said that the large galleass, having gotten separated from the small one in which he was, had met off Bermuda a Spanish vessel which was returning from the Indies, but that the French captain and his men did not wish to take the ship nor attack her; that they saw no other ship during the voyage.

He was asked whether any Spaniard came in the galleasses or whether the people were all French, also whether they were Protestants [luteranos]. He replied that the pilot they brought was a Spaniard called Bartolomé who had with him a son called Bartolomé, and that he heard it said that they were from Seville; that there was one Englishman and that all the rest were Frenchmen and almost all were Protestants; that there was one among them who preached the doctrines of Luther.

He was questioned as to whether the Frenchmen made a settlement or built a fort or set up anywhere any markers bearing the arms of France, and if so, in what places and on what harbors they placed them and where they are; whether there are other Frenchmen besides himself or what has become of the others. He answered that they set up a stone marker bearing the arms of France in the place on the coast where they first explored; that the galleasses entered a harbor three or four leagues south of this one and there set up another marker like the first one, that on a river a little nearer this way, on the same bay, they built an enclosed house of wood and earth covered with straw with a moat [cava] around it, with four bastions, and on them two brass falcons and six small iron culverins; that twenty-six men remained in this house and fort and the others returned to France; that Captain Ribaut commanded them to remain there and promised that within six months, for which length of time he left them supplies, he would return from France with more ships and many people, with cattle and other things, to settle that land. They did not set up any more markers, and of the five they

brought from France three were taken back in the galleasses.

Asked whether he would know how to go where the fort and the markers are and in what latitude they are, he replied that he would know quite well how to go to the fort and to one of the markers, that it was possible to go up the river to them without going out to sea; that he saw the Spanish pilot and two Frenchmen calculate the latitude in the harbor, that the Spaniard said it was thirty-two and a quarter and that the two Frenchmen said it was exactly thirty-two; that the other marker is where he has said, but that he does not know in what latitude it is nor whether he could find the spot unless he could see the river there which he would recognize.

Questioned as to whether the twenty-six Frenchmen whom the captain left there are still in the fort, or what has become of them, he said that two of them were drowned in crossing a river in a canoe; that the one who had been left as captain over the others one day struck a soldier with a club, that the soldier drew his sword and in struggling with him killed him; that he and the twenty-two others who remained, seeing that Captain Jean Ribaut did not come nor did any other Frenchmen, decided to go away to France and for that purpose built a twenty-ton boat near the fort; that when it was finished the Indians of the country gave them a number of ropes made of the strong bark of trees and they rigged the boat with these. The Indians also supplied them with native produce and fed them until they went away in the boat to the province of Guale which is just south of this place. There they were given some native blankets which they made into sails for the boat. Those Indians also gave them supplies. They then returned to this harbor, and the declarant, realizing that there would not be in the boat anyone who understood navigation, was not willing to go with them and remained among the Indians of this section where he has been until now. It is about fourteen months since they went away and no news of them has ever been received.

He was asked whether the two falcons and six culverins and the other arms they had were carried away in the ship or were left in the fort or in some other place. He answered that to his knowledge everything was taken away in the boat and nothing at all was left. Questioned with regard to the harbor where they built the fort and where the galleasses entered, whether it is a good harbor with a good entrance, he replied that he knows it to be a very good harbor with a good entrance and five fathoms or more of water in the channel, for he saw it sounded and is himself acquainted with it.

He was asked whether the galleasses entered any other harbor of this coast. He answered that they did not, for the shallops, used also for communication with the Indians, were used for sounding the mouths of the harbors further south to see whether there was enough depth for the galleasses which were anchored outside meanwhile; that a harbor with enough water in its channel was never found, or so said those who did the sounding.

Asked whether the French took away from this land any silver or pearls or other things, he replied that Captain Jean Ribaut took two or three small pieces of silver that a sailor had gotten in barter among the Indians of the province south of Guale, that he also took some pearls, deerskins, blankets and other native things; that the twenty-two soldiers who went away in the boat took a hatful of pearls which their captain said he had obtained in trade with the Indians.

Questioned as to whether since he had been in this country he had seen or heard it said that there had come any ship or ships, Spanish, French or of any other nation, he answered that he had not seen any ship in this country except those he has described and the one in which he now is. He said that some two months ago, as he was going out in a canoe with some Indians to hunt deer and bears, they went out to a seacoast a league from this harbor and found thick timbers of a ship and rotted fragments of sail and four kegs [*cestas de una potta cada una*] of the sort that they call *corbillon* in France and he believes that the vessel was French, both because the French are accustomed to carry in their ships these kegs to take out biscuit and because the arms of France were stamped on them and on one of them was traced with the point of a knife a name, Jean Marin; also because the Indians of the section have told him that some fifteen days before, in a province called Suye which lies some thirty leagues to the north near a large river, they saw two large ships and two small ones out at sea, that one of the small ones, which little vessels the declarant thinks must have been the ships' boats, came to the

shore and the Indians fled and would not communicate with those in the boat. That likewise he had heard the Indians say that something like two and half years ago a large ship came to a province on this coast called Amy, which is a little way beyond the province of Suye; that it entered the harbor and the ship's people killed most of the Indians who were there, that very few escaped and fled; that then the ship went away leaving there a fragment of iron cannon. He has not heard from these Indians that any Christians other than those mentioned have come to these parts. He swears to the truth of what he has said and declares himself to be about seventeen years of age. He did not sign the deposition as he says he does not know how to write, and the captain signed it. Some things in the deposition which he, Guillaume Rouffi, did not make clear in Castilian Martín Pérez explained. The latter did not sign as neither does he know how to write. The deposition was read and was certified by Hernando de Rojas before me, Juan Guerra, scrivener.

[e]   That same day, on board the frigate, the captain declared that as Guillaume Rouffi was shown to be French and had come with the other Frenchmen to take possession of this land of Florida, had built a fort and placed there markers bearing the arms of France, he should be held prisoner under close guard on board the frigate and taken to the town of San Cristóbal, Havana, and delivered to the governor to be dealt with as justice might demand. He then ordered that the fort and the markers which the French had built and placed be razed and demolished so that no vestige of them may remain. On June the thirteenth, in the presence of me, the scrivener, he declared that as it seems that the fort and the one marker bearing the arms of France are near this harbor and can be reached by going up the river, and as the weather [*tiempo*] is contrary and it is not possible to take the frigate there, and as it is proper for him to go in person to remove and destroy the fort and the marker in the presence of a recorder who shall certify the act according to the Governor's orders, he has decided to go up the river in the frigate's boat. He then commanded Gonzalo Gayon, the pilot, that during his absence he, Gonzalo Gayon, was not to allow ashore anyone of those who remained with the frigate, that he was to maintain the usual watches and take all

proper precautions for the safety of the frigate and the men in his charge. This command was formally pronounced in the presence of the said Gayon and duly witnessed.

That same day the captain embarked in the boat, taking with him me, the scrivener, and other persons from the frigate. Guillaume Rouffi, the Frenchman, led the captain to the place where was the fort [*casa*, rather than *fuerte*] the Frenchman built. The place is distant two leagues on an arm of a river on a large harbor, one of two which are close to the southern edge of it. On arrival the captain and the persons with him found a house and fort, which they entered, together with me, the scrivener, and witnesses. In it was found nothing at all. Then the captain commanded that the building be set on fire and burned, and he ordered me, the scrivener, to certify in writing that the house was burned and destroyed. I, the said scrivener, hereby certify and declare that it was burned and destroyed in my presence. Witnesses: Pedro de Torrea, Salinas, Martín Pérez and others.

Then the captain went in the boat to another harbor where the stone marker was said to be, to the place where Guillaume Rouffi said it was. It was found on an elevation above an arm of the river of the harbor, somewhat back in the forest. It is of white stone, about the size of a man, and on the upper part of it is inscribed a shield with a crown above it and on the shield three fleurs de lis, and below these the character *R*. which Guillaume Rouffi says is the name in cipher of the Queen Mother of France whose name, he says, is Catherine [de Médici]. Below this are four Arabic numerals which read 1561. By order of the captain this marker was taken down and thrown to the ground. Thereupon the captain in the presence of me, the scrivener, had the stone marker put into the boat to be taken to the frigate and carried to the Governor at Havana. This was done and witnessed.

On June the fourteenth, on board the frigate, the captain said that as it appeared evident that the French had not made any settlement beyond this harbor and had gone back to France, it was advisable to render to His Majesty prompt account of what has been found on this coast; that since time does not allow of re-exploration of the coast already passed in order to take away the other marker which Guillaume Rouffi says the French set up in the vicinity of the Bahama Channel, because Guillaume Rouffi says he does not know in what latitude it is, that therefore he is commanding Gonzalo Gayon, pilot of the frigate, present, to sail next day for Havana by the best and shortest route; that if before passing the other side of Bahama the wind should again become favorable for long enough to allow of running the Florida coast he should put into harbor to go in search of the marker and do with it as was done with the other one, this being to the royal service.

On June the fifteenth Gonzalo Gayon sailed the frigate out of the harbor and announced his course as via the Lucayas en route for Havana, as the conditions were not favorable for coasting Florida.

Having inspected these proceedings of Captain Hernando Manrique de Rojas, His Excellency the Governor commanded me, the notary, to make an authorized transcript of them, signed and sealed, to be sent to His Majesty in order that he may know what has been done on this expedition to Florida. Thus he commanded. Witnesses: Juan de Ynestrosa and Antonio de la Torre, residents of this town, before me, Francisco Zapata, notary.

This transcript was made from the submitted copy of these affidavits.

Nicolás López, secretary of the Royal Camara

Chapter Thirty-four
La Caroline, Its History and Its
Destruction, 1564–1565

THE STORY of Laudonnière's colony is fully told by him (302). It follows a course too often paralleled in early colonizing ventures in North America in the sixteenth century—the easy establishment of an advanced military post, and then the discovery that the country has relatively little of value to keep the men occupied. They concern themselves with a few limited explorations into the interior and also along the coast, but nothing very ambitious is attempted, since stores run short and the men depend on corn supplies obtained willingly or under pressure from the local Indians. Revolts, desertions, and the restoration of order at a lower level of subsistence characterize the later stages. The discovery of gold and silver in Indian hands provides some incentives to stay; the failure to find its source and the realization that some or all of it was looted from Spanish shipwrecks make the longer-term prospects less alluring. The greatest problem is the failure of reinforcements and supplies to arrive when they should. This leads to a slow determination to abandon the venture altogether.

Such a move is in preparation when John Hawkins, in July, 1565, provides shipping and enough help to enable evacuation to take place successfully. Delay in doing so costs the colonists their lives. The relieving fleet under Jean Ribault was very late in setting out; it ranged the coast of Florida for some time before bothering to come to the aid of the nearly desperate colonists. It also arrived too late to establish its men and deploy its ships before the pursuing Spanish fleet under Pedro Menéndez de Avilés came up.

Consideration of the narratives from both French and Spanish sides must lead to a decision on whether Ribault threw away his chances by his tactics or whether the storm that wrecked his ships was primarily responsible. Clearly, the French were themselves responsible for the indefensible condition in which La Caroline was left when Ribault sailed away and the fort fell an easy victim to the Spanish attack on September 20. The subsequent massacre at the fort and the gradual rounding up of the majority of the shipwrecked Frenchmen (except for those who got away by sea) is told here from the French point of view as it will be told later from that of the Spanish participants.

For the 1564–1565 colony and its destruction by the Spaniards the major source is still René de Laudonnière, *L'histoire notable de la Floride* (1586), given here (302) in Richard Hakluyt's translation, *Principal navigations*, III (1600), 319–356 (IX [1904], 1–100), and covering the second and third voyages, the second, that outward in 1564 and through the history of the colony, and the third, that of Jean Ribault, in 1565, which led to his own expulsion from La Caroline by the Spaniards and his fortunate survival to return to Europe. The earliest piece on the Florida colony to be published was the small pamphlet, *Coppie d'un lettre venant de la Floride, envoyée a Rouen et depuis au seigneur d'Everon* (Paris, V. Norment & Jeanne Bruneau, 1565), giving a glimpse of the establishment of the colony as it appeared at the time when a number of the ships left to go home after the fort (a cut of which is given) had been built. It records the optimism with which the colony was regarded by its members in its early days (304).

A short, unofficial report by Captain Bourdet, who visited the colony in September, 1564, throws some light on the colony in the period immediately after that covered in *Coppie d'un lettre*. The manuscript is at Fort Caroline National Memorial Site, Florida, and is translated in C. E. Bennett, *Settlement of Florida* (Gainesville, Fla., 1968), p. 129. It is not reprinted. A later glimpse of the colony in July, 1565, before disaster struck, is given in John Sparke's narrative on John Hawkins' second voyage to the West Indies. "The voyage made by the worshipful M. John Hawkins Esquire, now knight, . . . to the coast of Guinea, and the Indies of Nova Spania, being in Africa, and America: begunne in An. Dom. 1564," first printed in Richard Hakluyt, *Principall navigations* (London, 1589), pp. 537–543; reprinted in *Principal navigations*, III (1600), 501–521 (X [1904], 9–63), from which it is here reprinted (305).

Very different in tone and content from the earliest accounts was Nicolas Le Challeux, *Discours de l'histoire de la Floride, contenant le cruauté des Espanols contre les subjets du Roy, en l'an mil cinq cens soixante cinq* (Dieppe, 1566), giving an account of the overthrow of the colony by the forces of Pedro Menéndez de Avilés and the killing of almost all those Frenchmen whom the Spaniards could catch. An English translation came out in the same year, *A true and perfect description of the last voyage or navigation attempted by Captaine Rybaut . . . into Terra Florida this last year past 1565* (London, H. Denham for Thomas Hacket, 1566). A new translation (306) has been made.

A further item was picked up by the French ambassador in Madrid, M. de Fourquevaux, in October, 1566, when he was able to record and send back to France a narrative by one of the few male survivors to reach Spain and to be rescued there by the French representative. This was Jean Memyn, who went out with Jean Ribault in 1565, and who does not indicate why he was spared and eventually brought back to Spain. His narrative helps to round off the story. It was first printed by Paul Gaffarel, *La Floride française* (Paris, 1875), pp. 443–446, later in L'Abbé Douais, ed., *Dépêches de M. de Fourquevaux*, 3 vols. (Paris, 1896–1904), I, 131–133. It is newly translated (307).

The other major account from the French side is that by Jacques Le Moyne de Morgues, the artist of the expedition, which was published in Latin and German in Theodor de Bry, *America*, part ii (Frankfurt-am-Main, 1591), along with engravings of scenes from the colony of 1565–1566. A new English translation by Neil M. Cheshire will be found in Paul Hulton, *The Work of Jacques Le Moyne de Morgues* (London, 1977).

The Spaniards obtained vital information on the location and strength of the French colony by the capture of a number of mutineers who sailed from La Caroline in 1564 to attack Spanish vessels in the Caribbean and were themselves captured. The deposition of Stefano de Rojomonte (Étienne de Rougemont) is in A.G.I., Seville, Patronato 1/1/1, 19, ramo 4, and is translated from a copy in the Woodbury Lowery Manuscripts, Library of Congress, in C. E. Bennett, *Laudonnière and Fort Caroline* (1964), pp. 94–98. It is not reprinted.

302. 1564–1565. René de Laudonnière on "The second voyage unto Florida."

René de Laudonnière was commander of the French colony at La Caroline on the St. Johns River from June, 1564, to August, 1565. He was the most important of those who escaped from the attack on the fort by Pedro Menéndez de Avilés in September, 1565, and was in the best position to give an authoritative account of the achievements and defeat of this French experiment in colonization. Since he had no journal, he had to rely on his memory, although he may well have consulted other survivors before he wrote. He is, therefore, somewhat vague on chronology and the order of the incidents (and the content is at times at variance with that of other narrators). It is also important to regard the narrative as primarily an eloquent defense of his stewardship as the king's lieutenant in the colony before he was superseded by Jean Ribault in August, 1565.

The narrative constitutes the central section of L'histoire notable de la Floride (Paris, 1586), fols. 33–114, and in Hakluyt's translation, A notable historie (London, 1587), fols. 18–51v., reprinted in Hakluyt, Principal navigations, III (1600), 319–349 (IX [1904], 1–81).

The second voyage unto Florida, made and written by Captaine Laudonniere, which fortified and inhabited there two Summers and one whole Winter.

After our arrivall at Diepe, at our comming home, from our first voyage (which was the twentieth of July 1562) we found the civil warres begun, which was in part the cause why our men were not succoured, as Captaine John Ribault had promised them: whereof it followed that Captaine Albert was killed by his souldiers, and the country abandoned, as heretofore we have sufficiently discoursed, and as it may more at large be understood by those men which were there in person. After the peace was made in France, my Lord Admiral De Chastillon shewed unto the king, that he heard no newes at all of the men which Captaine John Ribault had left in Florida, & that it were pity to suffer them to perish. In which respect, the king was content he should cause 3 ships to be furnished, the one of sixe score tunnes,

the other of 100, and the third of 60, to seeke them out, and to succour them.

My Lord Admirall therefore being well informed of the faithfull service which I had done, aswell unto his Majestie as to his predecessors kings of France, advertised the king how able I was to doe him service in this voyage, which was the cause that he made me chiefe Captaine over these 3 shippes, and charged me to depart with diligence to performe his commandement, which for mine owne part I would not gainesay, but rather thinking my selfe happy to have bene chosen out among such an infinite number of others, which in my judgement were very well able to have quitted themselves in this charge, I embarked my selfe at New Haven the 22 of Aprill 1564, and sayled so, that we fell neere unto the coast of England: and then I turned towards the South, to sayle directly to the fortunate Islands, at this present called the Canaries, one of which called the Isle Salvage (because as I thinke it is altogether without inhabitants) was the first that our ships passed. Sayling therefore on forward, we landed the next day in the Isle of Teneriffa, otherwise called the Pike, because that in the middest thereof there is an exceeding high mountaine, neere as high as that of Etna, which riseth up like a pike, into the top whereof no man can go up but from the middest of May untill the middest of August, by reason of the over great colde which is there all the yere: which is a wonderfull strange thing, considering that it is not past 27 degrees and an half distant from the Equator. We saw it all covered over with snow, although it were then but the fift of May. The inhabitants in this Isle being heretofore pursued by the Spaniards, retired themselves into this mountaine, where for a space they made warre with them, and would not submit themselves to their obedience, neither by foule nor faire meanes, they disdained so much the losse of their Island. For those which went thither on the Spaniards behalfe, left their carkases there, so that not so much as one of them returned home to bring newes. Notwithstanding in the ende, the inhabitants not able to live in that place according to their nature, or for want of such things as were necessary for the commoditie of their livelyhood, did all die there. After I had furnished my selfe with some fresh water, very good and excellent, which sprang out of a rocke at the foote of this mountaine, I continued my course toward the West, wherein the windes favoured me so well, that 15 dayes after our ships arrived safe and sound at the Antilles: and going on land at the Isle of Martinino, one of the first of them, the next day we arrived at Dominica, twelve leagues distant from the former.

Dominica is one of the fayrest Islands of the West, full of hilles, and of very good smell. Whose singularities desiring to know as we passed, and seeking also to refresh our selves with fresh water, I made the Mariners cast anker, after wee had sayled about halfe along the coast thereof. As soone as we had cast anker, two Indians (inhabitants of that place) sayled toward us in two Canoas full of a fruite of great excellencie which they call Ananas. As they approched unto our Barke, there was one of them which being in some misdoubt of us, went backe againe on land, and fled his way with as much speede as he could possibly. Which our men perceived and entred with diligence into the other Canoa, wherein they caught the poore Indian, & brought him unto me. But the poore fellow became so astonied in beholding us, that he knew not which way to behave himselfe, because that (as afterward I understood) he feared that he was fallen into the Spaniards hands, of whom he had bene taken once before, and which, as he shewed us, had cut of his stones. At length this poore Indian was secure of us, and discoursed unto us of many things, wherof we received very small pleasure, because we understood not his minde but by his signes. Then he desired me to give him leave to depart, and promised me that he would bring me a thousand presents, whereunto I agreed on condition that he would have patience untill the next day, when I purposed to goe on land, where I suffered him to depart after I had given him a shirte, and certaine small trifles, wherewith he departed very well contented from us.

The place where we went on shore was hard by a very high Rocke, out of which there ran a litle river of sweet and excellent good water: by which river we stayed certaine dayes to discover the things which were worthy to be seene, and traffiqued dayly with the Indians: which above all things besought us that none of our men should come neere their lodgings nor their gardens, otherwise that we should give them great cause of jelousie, and that in so doing, wee should not want of their fruite which they call Ananas, whereof they offered us very liberally, receiving in recompence certaine things of small value. This notwithstanding, it happened on a day that certaine of our men desirous to see some new things in these strange countries, walked through the woods: and following still the litle rivers side, they spied two serpents of exceeding bignes, which went side by side overthwart the way. My souldiers went before them thinking to let them from going into the woods: but the serpents nothing at all astonied at these gestures glanced into the bushes with fearful hyssings: yet for all that, my men drew their swords and killed them, and found them afterward 9 great foote long, and as big as a mans leg. During this combate, certaine others more undiscreete went and gathered their Ananas in the Indians gardens, trampling through them without any discretion: and not therewithall contented they went toward their dwellings; whereat the Indians were so much offended, that without regarding any thing they rushed upon them and discharged their shot, so that they hit one of my men named Martine Chaveau, which remained behind. We could not know whether hee were killed on the place, or whether he were taken prisoner: for those of his company had inough to doe to save themselves without thinking of their companion. Whereof Monsieur de Ottigni my Lieuetenant being advertised, sent unto me to know whether I thought good that he should lay an ambush for the Indians which had either taken or killed our man, or whether hee should go directly to their dwellings to know the trueth. I sent unto him after good deliberation hereupon, that he should not attempt any thing, and that for divers occasions: but contrariwise that he should embarke himself with al diligence, & consequently al they that were on land: which he did with speed. But as he sayled towards our ships he perceived along the shore a great number of Indians which began to charge them with their arrowes: hee for his part discharged store of shot against them, yet was not able to hurt them, or by any meanes to surprise them: for which cause he quite forsooke them, and came unto our ship. Where staying untill the next day morning we set sayle following our wonted course, and keeping the same, we discovered diverse Isles conquered by the Spaniards, as the

Isles of S. Christopher, and of the Saintes, of Monserrate, and La Redonda: Afterward we passed between Anguilla and Anegada, sayling toward New France. Where we arrived 15 dayes after, to witte, on Thurseday the 22 of June about 3 of the clocke in the afternoone, and landed neere a litle river which is 30 degrees distant from the Equator, and 10 lagues above Cape François drawing toward the South, and about thirtie leagues above the River of May. After wee had strooken sayle and cast anker athwart the River, I determined to goe on shore to discover the same. Therefore being accompanied with Monsieur Ottigni, with Monsieur de Arlac mine Ensigne, & a certaine number of Gentlemen and souldiers, I embarked my selfe about 3 or 4 of the clocke in the evening. And being arrived at the mouth of the river, I caused the chanell to be sounded, which was found to be very shallow, although that farther within the same the water was there found reasonable deepe, which separateth it selfe into two great armes, whereof one runneth toward the South, and the other toward the North. Having thus searched the River, I went on land to speake with the Indians which waited for us upon the shore, which at our comming on land, came before us, crying with a loude voyce in their Indian language, Antipola Bonassou, which is as much to say, as brother, friend, or some such like thing. After they had made very much of us, they shewed us their Paracoussy, that is to say, their King and Governour, to whom I presented certaine toyes, wherewith he was well pleased. And for mine owne part, I prayse God continually, for the great love which I have found in these Savages, which were sory for nothing, but that the night approched, and made us retire unto our ships.

For though they endevoured by al meanes to make us tary with them, and shewed by signes the desire that they had to present us with some rare things, yet neverthelesse for many just and reasonable occasions I would not stay on shore all night: but excusing my selfe for all their offers, I embarked my selfe againe and returned toward my ships. Howbeit, before my departure, I named this River, the river of Dolphines, because that at mine arrivall, I saw there a great number of Dolphines, which were playing in the mouth thereof. The next day the 23 of this moneth (because that toward the South I had not found any

commodious place for us to inhabit, and to build a fort) I gave commandement to weigh anker, & to hoise our sailes to saile toward the river of May, where we arrived two dayes after, & cast anker. Afterward going on land, with some number of Gentlemen and Souldiers to know for a certaintie the singularities of this place, we espyed the Paracoussy of the countrey, which came towards us (this was the very same that we saw in the voyage of Captaine John Ribault) which having espied us, cryed very far off, Antipola, Antipola: and being so joyful that he could not containe himselfe, he came to meet us, accompanied then with two of his sonnes, as faire and mightie persons as might be found in al the world, which had nothing in their mouthes but this word, Amy, Amy: that is to say, friend, friend: yea, and knowing those which were there in the first voyage, they went principally to them to use this speech unto them. There was in their trayne a great number of men and women, which stil made very much of us, and by evident signes made us understand how glad they were of our arrivall. This good entertainment past, the Paracoussy prayed me to goe see the pillar which we had erected in the voyage of John Ribault (as we have declared heretofore) as a thing which they made great account of.

Having yeelded unto him and being come to the place where it was set up, wee found the same crowned with crownes of Bay, and at the foote thereof many little baskets full of Mill which they call in their language Tapaga Tapola. Then when they came thither they kissed the same with great reverence and besought us to do the like, which we would not denie them, to the ende we might drawe them to be more in friendship with us. This done, the Paracoussy tooke me by the hand, as if he had desire to make me understand some great secret, & by signes shewed me very well up within the river the limits of his dominion, and said that he was called Paracoussy Satourioua, which is as much as King Satourioua. His children have the selfe same title of Paracoussy: The eldest is named Athore, a man, I dare say, perfect in beautie, wisedome, and honest sobrietie, shewing by his modest gravitie that he deserveth the name which he beareth, besides that he is gentle and tractable. After we had sojourned a certaine space with them, the Paracoussy prayed one of his sonnes to present unto me a wedge of silver, which hee did & that with a good wil: in recompence whereof I gave him a cutting hooke and some other better present: wherewith he seemed to be very well pleased. Afterward we tooke our leave of them, because the night approched, & then returned to lodge in our shippes. Being allured with this good entertainment I failed not the next day to imbarke my selfe againe with my Lieutenant Ottigni and a number of souldiers to returne toward the Paracoussy of the river of May, which of purpose waited for us in the same place, where the day before we conferred with him. We found him under the shadow of an arbour accompanied with fourescore Indians at the least, and apparelled at that time after the Indian fashion, to wit, with a great Harts skinne dressed like Chamois, and painted with devices of strange and divers colours, but of so lively a portrature, and representing antiquity, with rules so justly compassed, that there is no Painter so exquisite that could finde fault therewith: the naturall disposition of this strange people is so perfect and well guided that without any ayd and favour of artes, they are able by the helpe of nature onely to content the eye of artizans, yea even of those which by their industry are able to aspire unto things most absolute.

Then I advertised Paracoussy Satourioua, that my desire was to discover farther up into the river, but that this should be with such diligence that I would come againe unto him very speedily: wherewith he was content, promising to stay for me in the place where he was: and for an earnest of his promise, he offered me his goodly skinne, which I refused then, and promised to receive it of him at my returne. For my part I gave him certaine small trifles, to the intent to retaine him in our friendship.

Departing from thence, I had not sayled three leagues up the river, still being followed by the Indians, which coasted me a long the river, crying still, Amy, Amy, that is to say friende, friende: but I discovered an hill of meane height, neere which I went on land, hard by the fieldes that were sowed with mil, at one corner whereof there was an house built for their lodging, which keepe and garde the mill: for there are such numbers of Cornish choughes in this Countrey, which continually devoure and spoyle the mill, that the Indians are constrained to keepe and watch it, otherwise they should be deceived of their har-

vest. I rested my selfe in this place for certaine houres, & commanded Monsieur de Ottigni, and my Sergeant to enter into the woodes to search out the dwellings of the Indians: where after they had gone awhile, they came unto a Marish of Reeds, where finding their way to be stopped, they rested under the shadow of a mightie Bay tree to refresh themselves a little and to resolve which way to take. Then they discovered, as it were on the suddaine, five Indians halfe hidden in the woodes, which seemed somewhat to distrust our men, untill they said unto them in the Indian language Antipola Bonassou, to the end that understanding their speech they might come unto us more boldely, which they did incontinently. But because they sawe, that the foure that went last, bare up the traine of the skinne wherewith he that went formost was apparrelled our men imagined that the foremost must needes bee some man of greater qualitie then the rest, seeing that withal they called him Paracoussy, Paracoussy, wherfore, some of our company went towards him, and using him courteously shewed him, Monsieur de Ottigni, their Lieutenant, for whom they had made an harbour with Bay and Palme boughes after the Indian fashion, to the ende that by such signes the Savages might thinke the Frenchmen had compained with such as they at other times.

The Indian Paracoussy drew neere to the French, and began to make him a long Oration, which tended to no other end, but that he besought the Frenchmen very earnestly to come and see his dwelling and his parents, which they granted him, and straight for pledge of better amitie, he gave unto my Lieuetenant Ottigni, the very skinne that he was clad with.

Then he tooke him by the hande, leading him right toward the Marishes, over which the Paracoussy, Monsieur Ottigni, and certaine other of our men were borne upon the Indians shouldiers: and the rest which could not passe because of the myre and reedes, went through the woodes, and followed a narrow path which led them foorth untill they came unto the Paracoussyes dwelling; out of which there came about fiftie Indians to receive our men gallantly, and to feast them after their manner. After which they brought at their entrance a great vessell of earth, made after a strange fashion full of fountaine water cleare and very excellent.

This vessell was borne by an Indian, and there was another younger which bare of this water in another little vessell of wood, and presented thereof to every one to drinke, observing in doing the same, a certaine order and reverence, which hee made to each of them, to whome hee gave drinke. Our thirst well quenched by this meanes, and our men beeing sufficiently refreshed, the Paracoussy brought them to his fathers lodging, one of the oldest men that lived upon the earth. Our men regarding his age, began to make much of him, using this speech, Amy, Amy, that is to say, friende, friende, whereat the olde sier shewed himselfe very glad.

Afterward they questioned with him concerning the course of his age: whereunto he made answere, shewing that he was the first living originall, from whence five generations were descended, as he shewed unto them by another olde man that sate directly over against him, which farre exceeded him in age. And this man was his father, which seemed to be rather a dead carkeis then a living body: for his sinewes, his veines, his artiers, his bones, and other parts, appeared so cleerely thorow his skinne, that a man might easily tell them, and discerne them one from another. Also his age was so great, that the good man had lost his sight, and could not speake one onely word but with exceeding great paine. Monsieur de Ottigni having seene so strange a thing, turned to the yoonger of these two olde men, praying him to vouchsafe to answere him to that which he demanded touching his age. Then the olde man called a company of Indians, and striking twise upon his thigh, and laying his hand upon two of them, he shewed him by signes, that these two were his sonnes: againe smiting upon their thighes, he shewed him others not so olde, which were the children of the two first, which he continued in the same maner untill the fift generation. But though this olde man had his father alive more olde then himselfe, and that both of them did weare their haire very long, and as white as was possible, yet it was tolde them, that they might yet live thirtie or fortie yeeres more by the course of nature: although the younger of them both was not lesse then two hundred and fiftie yeeres olde. After he had ended his communication, hee commaunded two young Egles to be given to our men, which he had bred up for his pleasure in his house. Hee caused also little Paniers made of Palme

leaves full of Gourds red and blew to bee delivered unto them. For recompence of which presents he was satisfied with French toyes.

These two olde men caused our men to bee guided backe againe to the place from whence they came, by the young Paracoussy which hath brought them thither. And having taken leave of the Paracoussy, they came and sought me out in the place where I stayed, and rehearsed unto mee all that they had seene, praying mee also that I would rewarde their guide, which so frankely and heartily had received them into his house, which I would not faile to doe by any meanes.

Nowe was I determined to search out the qualities of the hill. Therefore I went right to the toppe thereof, where we found nothing else but Cedars, Palme, and Baytrees of so sovereigne odour, that Baulme smelleth nothing like in comparison. The trees were environed rounde about with Vines bearing grapes in such quantitie, that the number would suffice to make the place habitable. Besides this fertilitie of the soyle for Vines, a man may see Esquine wreathed about the shrubs in great quantitie. Touching the pleasure of the place, the Sea may bee seene plaine and open from it, and more then six great leagues off, nere the River Belle, a man may beholde the medowes divided asunder into Iles and Islets enterlacing one another: Briefly the place is so pleasant, that those which are melancholicke would be inforced to change their humour.

After I had stayed there a while, I imbarked againe my people to sayle towards the mouth of the River, where wee found the Paracoussy, which according to his promise waited for us. Wherefore to content him, we went on shore, and did him that reverence that on our part was requisite. Then hee gave me the skinne so richly painted, and I recompensed him with somewhat of our marchandise. I forgat not to demaund of him the place whence the wedge of silver came which he had given me before: whereunto he made me a very sudden answere, which notwithstanding I understood not, which he well perceived. And then he shewed me by evident signes that all of it came from a place more within the River by certaine dayes journeyes from this place, and declared unto us that all that which they had thereof, they gat it by force of armes of the inhabitants of this place, named by them Thimogoa, their most ancient and naturall enemies, as hee largely declared. Whereupon when I sawe with what affection hee spake when hee pronounced Thimogoa, I understoode what he would say. And to bring my selfe more into his favour, I promised him to accompany him with all my force, if hee would fight against them: which thing pleased him in such sorte, that from thenceforth hee promised himselfe the victorie of them, and assured mee that hee would make a voyage thither within a short space, would cause store of Mill to be prepared, and would commaund his men to make ready their Bowes, and furnish themselves with such store of arrowes, that nothing should bee wanting to give battaile to Thimogoa. In fine hee prayed mee very earnestly not to faile of my promise, and in so doing, hee hoped to procure mee Golde and Silver in such good quantitie, that mine affaires shoulde take effect according to mine owne and his desire.

The matter thus fully resolved upon, I took my leave of him to returne unto my shippes, where after wee had rested our selves all the night following, wee hoysed sayles the next day very earely in the morning, and sayled towarde the River of Seine, distant from the River of May about foure leagues: and there continuing our course towarde the North, wee arrived at the mouth of Somme, which is not past six leagues distant from the River of Seine: where wee cast Anker, and went on shoare to discover that place as wee had done the rest. There wee were gratiously and courteously received of the Paracoussy of the Countrey, which is one of the tallest men and best proportioned that may bee founde. His wife sate by him, which besides her Indian beautie, wherewith shee was greatly endewed, had so vertuous a countenance and modest gravitie, that there was not one amongst us but did greatly commend her; shee had in her traine five of her daughters of so good grace and so well brought up, that I easily perswaded my selfe that their mother was their Mistresse, and had taught them well and straightly to preserve their honestie. After that the Paracoussy had received us as I have sayde, hee commaunded his wife to present mee with a certaine number of bullets of silver, for his owne part hee presented mee with his bowe and his arrowes, as hee had done unto Captaine John Ribault in our first voyage, which is a signe of a perpetuall amitie and alliance with those which they honour with such a

kinde of present. In our discoursing with one another, wee entred into speach as touching the exercise of armes. Then the Paracoussy caused a corselet to be set on end, and prayed me to make a proofe of our Harguebuzes and their bowes: but this proofe pleased him very little; for assoone as he knew that our Harguebuzes did easily pearce that which all the force of their bowes could not hurt, he seemed to be sorie, musing with himselfe how this thing might bee done. Neverthelesse going about to dissemble in his minde that which his countenance could not doe by any meanes, hee began to fall into another matter, and prayed us very earnestly to stay with him that night in his house or lodging, affirming that no greater happinesse could come unto him then our long abode, which he desired to recompence with a thousand presents.

Neverthelesse wee could not grant him this poynt, but tooke our leave of him to returne to our shippes: where soone after I caused all my companie to bee assembled, with the Masters and Pilots of my shippes, to consult together of the place whereof wee should make choise to plant our habitation. First I let them understand, howe none of them were ignorant, that the part which was towarde the Cape of Florida, was altogether a marish Countrey, and therefore unprofitable for our inhabitation: A thing which could yeelde neither profite to the King, nor any contentment or pleasure to us, if peradventure we would inhabite there. On the other side if wee passed further toward the North to seeke out Port Royall, it would be neither very profitable nor convenient: at the least if wee should give credit to the report of them which remained there a long time, although the Haven were one of the fairest of the West Indies: but that in this case the question was not so much of the beautie of the place, as of things necessary to sustaine life. And that for our inhabiting it was much more needefull for us to plant in places plentifull of victuall, then in goodly Havens, faire, deepe and pleasaunt to the view. In consideration whereof that I was of opinion, if it seemed good unto them, to seate our selves about the River of May: seeing also that in our first voyage wee found the same onely among all the rest to abounde in Maiz and corne, besides the Golde and Silver that was found there: a thing that put me in hope of some happie discoverie in time to come.

After I had proposed these things, every one gave his opinion thereof: and in fine all resolved, namely those which had beene with me in the first voyage, that it was expedient to seate themselves rather on the River of May then on any other, untill they might heare newes out of France. This poynt being thus agreed upon, wee sayled toward the River, and used such diligence, that with the favour of the windes wee arrived there the morrow after about the breake of day, which was on Thursday the 29 of the moneth of June. Having cast anker, I embarked all my stuffe and the souldiers of my companie, to sayle right toward the opening of the River: wherein we entred a good way up, and found a Creeke of a reasonable bignesse, which invited us to refresh our selves a little, while wee reposed our selves there. Afterward wee went on shoare to seeke out a place plaine without trees, which wee perceived from the Creeke.

But because wee found it not very commodious for us to inhabite there: wee determined to returne unto the place which wee had discovered before, when wee had sayled up the River. This place is joyning to a mountaine, and it seemed unto us more fit and commodious to build a fortresse, then that where we were last. Therefore we tooke our way towards the forrests being guided therein by the young Paracoussy which had ledde us before to his fathers lodging. Afterward we found a large plaine covered with high Pinetrees distant a little from the other: under which wee perceived an infinite number of Stagges which brayed amidst the plaine, athwart the which we passed: then wee discovered a little hill adjoyning unto a great vale very greene and in forme flat: wherein were the fairest medowes of the world, and grasse to feede cattel. Moreover it is invironed with a great number of brookes of fresh water, & high woods, which make the vale more delectable to the eye. After I had taken the viewe thereof at mine ease, I named it at the request of our souldiers, The Vale of Laudonniere. Thus we went forward. Anon having gone a little forward, we met an Indian woman of tall stature, which also was an Hermaphrodite, who came before us with a great vessell full of cleere fountaine water, wherwith she greatly refreshed us. For we were exceeding faint by reason of the ardent heate which molested us as we passed through those high woods. And I beleeve that

without the succour of that Indian Hermaphrodite, or rather, if it had not bene for the great desire which we had to make us resolute of our selves, we had taken up our lodging all night in the wood. Being therefore refreshed by this meane, wee gathered our spirits together, and marching with a cheerefull courage, wee came to the place which wee had chosen to make our habitation in: whereupon at that instant neere the rivers brinke we strowed a number of boughes and leaves, to take our rest on them the night following, which wee found exceeding sweete, because of the paine which before we had taken in our travell.

On the morrow about the breake of day, I commaunded a trumpet to be sounded, that being assembled we might give God thankes for our favourable and happie arrivall. There wee sang a Psalme of thankesgiving unto God, beseeching him that it would please him of his grace to continue his accustomed goodnesse toward us his poore servaunts, and ayde us in all our enterprises, that all might turne to his glory and the advancement of our King. The prayer ended, every man began to take courage.

Afterward having measured out a piece of ground in forme of a triangle, wee indevoured our selves of all sides, some to bring earth, some to cut fagots, and others to raise and make the rampire, for there was not a man that had not either a shovell, or cutting hooke, or hatchet, as well to make the ground plaine by cutting downe the trees, as for the building of the Fort, which we did hasten with such cheerfulnesse, that within few dayes the effect of our diligence was apparant: in which meane space the Paracoussy Satourioua our neerest neighbour, & on whose ground wee built our Fort, came usually accompanyed with his two sonnes and a great number of Indians to offer to doe us all courtesie. And I likewise for my part bestowed divers of our trifles frankely on him, to the end he might know the good will we bare him, and thereby make him more desirous of our friendship, in such sort, that as the dayes increased, so our amitie and friendship increased also.

After that our Fort was brought into forme, I began to build a Grange to retire my munition and things necessarie for the defence of our Fort: praying the Paracoussy to command his subjects to make us a covering of Palme leaves, and this to the ende that when that was done, I might un-fraight my shippes, and put under coverture those things that were in them. Suddenly the Paracoussy commaunded in my presence all the Indians of his companie to dresse the next day morning so good a number of Palme leaves, that the Grange was covered in lesse then two dayes: so that businesse was finished. For in the space of those two dayes, the Indians never ceassed from working, some in fetching Palme leaves, others in interlacing of them: in such sort that their Kings commandement was executed as he desired.

Our Fort was built in forme of a triangle. The side toward the West, which was toward the lande, was inclosed with a little trench and raised with turves made in forme of a Battlement of nine foote high: the other side which was toward the River, was inclosed with a Pallisado of plankes of timber after the maner that Gabions are made. On the South side there was a kinde of bastion within which I caused an house for the munition to be built: it was all builded with fagots and sand, saving about two or three foot high with turfes, whereof the battlements were made. In the mid-dest I caused a great Court to be made of eighteene paces long and broad, in the middest whereof on the one side drawing toward the South I builded a Corps de gard, and an house on the other side toward the North, which I caused to bee raised somewhat too high: for within a short while after the wind beat it down: and experience taught me, that we may not build with high stages in this Countrey, by reason of the windes whereunto it is subject. One of the sides that inclosed my Court, which I made very faire and large, reached unto the Grange of my muni-tions: and on the other side towardes the River was mine owne lodging, round about which were galleries all covered. The principall doore of my lodging was in the middest of the great place, and the other was towarde the River. A good distance from the Fort I built an Oven to avoyde the danger against fire, because the houses are of Palme leaves, which will soone be burnt after the fire catcheth holde of them, so that with much adoe a man shall have leasure to quench them. Loe here in briefe the description of our Four-tresse, which I named Caroline in the honour of our Prince King Charles.

After wee were furnished with that which was most necessarie, I would not lose a minute of an houre, without imploying of the same in some vertuous exercise: therefore I charged Monsieur de Ottigni my Lieutenant, a man in trueth worthy of all honour for his honestie and vertue, to search up within the River, what this Thimogoa might be, whereof the Paracoussy Satourioua had spo-ken to us so often at our comming on shoare. For execution hereof the Paracoussy gave him two Indians for his guides, which taking upon them to lead him in this voyage, seemed to goe unto a wedding, so desirous they were to fight with their enemies.

Being imbarked they hoised sayle, and having sayled about twentie leagues, the Indians which still looked on this side and that side to espie some of their enemies, discovered three Canoas. And immediatly they began to crie Thimogoa, Thimogoa, and spake nothing else but to hasten forward to goe fight with them: which the Cap-taine seemed to be willing to doe, to content them. When they came to boord them, one of the Indians gat holde of an Halbert, another of an Coutelas in such a rage, that hee would have leapt into the water to have fought with them alone. Never-thelesse Ottigni would not let them doe it, for while hee deferred to boord them, he gave the others respite to turne the prowes of their Canoas toward the shoare, and so to escape into the woods. Againe, the meaning of Ottigni was not to make warre upon them of Thimogoa, but rather to make them friendes, and to make them thence-forth to live in peace one with another if it were possible, hoping by this meane to discover dayly some new thing, & especially the certaine course of the River. For this purpose he caused the barke to retire, wherein were the two Indians his guides, and went with his men towarde the Canoas which were on the Rivers side. Being come unto them, he put certaine trifles into them, and then retired a good way from them, which thing caused the Indians which were fled away to returne to their boats, and to understand by this signe, that those of our Barke were none of their enemies, but rather come onely to traffique with them. Wherefore being thus assured of us, they called to our men to come neere unto them: which they did incontinently and set foote on lande, and spake freely unto them, with divers ceremonies over long to recount. In the ende Ottigni de-maunded of them by signes if they had any Golde or Silver among them. But they tolde him they had none as then: and that if he would send one of his men with them, they would bring him without danger into a place where they might have some. Ottigni seeing them so willing, delivered them one of his men which seemed very resolute, to undertake this voyage: this fellow stayed with them untill tenne of the clocke the next morning, so that Captaine Ottigny somewhat offended with his long stay, sayled ten great leagues further up the River: although he knew not which way he should goe, yet he went so farre up that hee espied the Boate wherein his souldier was: which reported unto him, that the Indians would have carried him three great dayes journey further, & told him that a King named Mayrra rich in Gold and Silver, dwelt in those quarters, and that for small quantitie of marchandise enough might be had of him: yet that hee would not hazard himselfe without his leave, and that he brought but a very little Golde. This being done, our men returned toward our Fort Caroline, after they had left the souldier with the Indians to enforme himselfe more and more of such things as he might discover more at leasure.

Fifteene dayes after this voyage to Thimogoa, I dispatched Captaine Vasseur and my Sergeant also to returne againe into this Countrey, and to seeke out the souldier which remained there in the former voyage. Being therefore imbarked, they sayled two whole dayes: and before they came to the dwelling of the Indians, they found two of them on the Rivers side, which were expresly sent unto that place to descry whether any of their enemies were come to that part, with intention to surprise them, as they did usually.

When they perceived Captaine Vasseur, they knew incontinently that he was none of their enemies, and therefore made no difficultie to come neere unto the Barke, and shewed him by signes that the Souldier which they sought was not in that place, but was at that present in the house of King Molloua which was vassall unto another great King named by them Olata Ouae Utina: and that if the Captaine would sayle thitherward, hee should come thither very quickly: wherwith he was content, and caused his men to rowe to that part which the Indians shewed him: whereat they were so glad, that they ranne quickly before by land to declare his arrivall, which was at the lodging of king Molloua, after he had rowed not past halfe a league. While

king Molloua had ended intertaining Captaine Vasseur and his men, the souldier came in with five or six pounds weight of silver which he had trucked and traffiqued with Indians.

This King caused bread to bee made, and fish to bee dressed after the Indian fashion to feast our men: to whom, while they were at meate, hee made a discourse of divers other Kings his friends & allies, reckoning up to the number of nine of them by name, to wit, Cadecha, Chilili, Eclauou, Enacappe, Calany, Anacharaqua, Omittaqua, Aequara, Moquoso: all which with him to the number of more then fortie, hee assured us to bee the vassals of the most renowmed Olata Ouae Utina.

This done, hee went about likewise to discover the enemies of Ouae Utina, in which number hee placed as the first the Paracoussy Satourioua Monarch of the confines of the river of May, which hath under his obeysance thirtie other Paracoussies, whereof there were ten which were all his brethren, and that therefore hee was greatly esteemed in those partes: then hee named three others no lesse puissant then Satourioua, whereof the first dwelt two dayes journey from his lord Olata Ouae Utina, and ordinarily made warre upon him, whose name was Potanou, a man cruell in warre, but pitifull in the execution of his furie. For hee tooke the prisoners to mercy, being content to marke them on the left arme with a great marke like unto a seale, and so imprinted as if it had bene touched with an hotte yron, then hee let them goe without any more hurt. The two others were named Onatheaqua, and Houstaqua, being great Lords, and abounding in riches, and principally Onatheaqua, which dwelt neere unto the high mountaines, wherein there was abundance of many rare things, & infinite quantitie of a kinde of slate stone, wherewith they made wedges to cleave their wood. The occasion which (as he sayd) mooved Potanou to wage warre against Olata Ouae Utina, was the feare that he had, lest he and his companions should get of that hard stone in his Countrey, wherewith they headed their arrowes, and could not get it in any neerer place.

Besides all this, Molloua recited to Captaine Vasseur, that the kings allies the vassals of the great Olata, armed their brests, armes, thighes, legs & foreheads with large plates of gold and silver: and that by this meanes the arrowes that were discharged upon them could do them no maner of hurt at all, but rather were broken against them. Hereupon Captaine Vasseur inquired whether the Kings Onatheaqua and Houstaqua were like unto us. For by the description that they made of them, he began to doubt whether they were Spaniards or no: but Molloua tolde him that they were not, but that they were Indians like the rest, saving that they painted their faces with blacke, and that the rest as Molloua, painted them with red. Then my Lieutenant Vasseur, and my Sergeant promised him, that one day I should march with my forces into those Countreys, and that joyning my selfe with his Lord Olata, I would subdue the inhabitants of the highest of those mountaines. Hee was very glad of this speach, and answered that the least of these Kings which hee had named, should present unto the Generall of these succours the height of two foot of gold and silver, which by force of armes they had already gotten of those two Kings, Onatheaqua, and Houstaqua.

The good cheere being done, and the discourses ended, my men imbarked themselves againe, with intention to bring mee those good newes unto the Fort Caroline. But after they had sayled a very long while downe the River, and were come within three leagues of us, the tyde was so strong against them, that they were constrained to goe on lande, and to retire themselves because of the night, unto the dwelling of a certaine Paracoussy named Molona, which shewed himselfe very glad of their arrivall: for hee desired to know some newes of Thimogoa, and thought that the Frenchmen went thither for none other occasion but for to invade them. Which Captaine Vasseur perceiving, dissembled so wel, that he made him beleeve that he went to Thimogoa with none other intention, but to subdue them, and to destroy them with the edge of the sworde without mercy, but that their purpose had not such successe as they desired, because that the people of Thimogoa being advertised of this enterprise, retired into the woods, and saved themselves by flight: that nevertheless they had taken some as they were fleeing away, which carried no newes thereof unto their fellowes.

The Paracoussy was so glad of this relation, that he interrupted him, and asked Vasseur of the beginning and maner of his execution, and prayed

him that hee would shew him by signes howe all things passed. Immediatly Francis la Caille the Sergeant of my band tooke his sword in his hand, saying, that with the point thereof he had thrust through two Indians which ranne into the woods, and that his companions had done no lesse for their partes. And that if fortune had so favoured them, that they had not beene discovered by the men of Thimogoa, they had had a victorie most glorious and worthie of eternall memorie. Hereupon the Paracoussy shewed himselfe so well satisfied, that he could not devise how to gratifie our men, which hee caused to come into his house to feast them more honourably: and having made Captaine Vasseur to sit next him, and in his owne chaire (which the Indians esteeme for the chiefest honour) and then underneath him two of his sonnes, goodly and mightie fellowes, hee commanded all the rest to place themselves as they thought good. This done, the Indians came according to their good custome, to present their drinke Cassine to the Paracoussy, and then to certaine of his chiefest friends, and the Frenchmen. Then hee which brought it set the cup aside, and drew out a little dagger stucke up in the roofe of the house, and like a mad man he lift his head aloft, and ranne apace, and went and smote an Indian which sate alone in one of the corners of the hall, crying with a loud voyce, Hyou, the poore Indian stirring not at all for the blowe, which he seemed to endure patiently. He which held the dagger went quickly to put the same in his former place, and began againe to give us drinke as hee did before: but he had not long continued, and had scarce given three or foure thereof, but he left his bowle againe, tooke the dagger in his hand, and quickly returned unto him which hee had strocken before, to whom he gave a very sore blow on the side, crying Hyou, as he had done before: and then hee went to put the dagger in his place, and set himselfe downe among the rest. A little while after he that had bene stricken fell downe backwards, stretching out his armes and legs, as if hee had bene ready to yeeld up the latter gaspe. And then the younger sonne of the Paracoussy apparelled in a long white skinne, fell downe at the feete of him that was fallen backward, weeping bitterly halfe a quarter of an houre: after, two other of his brethren clad in like apparell, came about him that was so stricken, and began to sigh pitifully. Their mother bearing a little infant in her armes came from another part, and going to the place where her sonnes were, at the first shee used infinite numbers of outcries, then one while lifting up her eyes to heaven, another while falling downe unto the ground, shee cryed so dolefully, that her lamentable mournings would have moved the most hard and stony heart in the world with pitie. Yet this sufficed not, for there came in a companie of young gyrles, which did never leave weeping for a long while in the place where the Indian was fallen downe, whom afterward they tooke, and with the saddest gestures they could devise, carried him away into another house a little way off from the great hall of the Paracoussy, and continued their weepings and mournings by the space of two long houres: in which meane while the Indians ceassed not to drinke Cassine, but with such silence that one word was not heard in the parlour.

Vasseur being grieved that he understood not these ceremonies, demanded of the Paracoussy what these things meant: which answered him slowly, Thimogoa, Thimogoa, without saying any more. Being more displeased then he was before with so sleight an answere, he turned unto another Indian the Paracoussyes brother, who was a Paracoussy as well as his brother, called Malica, which made him a like answere as hee did at the first, praying him to aske no more of these matters, and to have patience for that time. The subtill old Paracoussy prayed him within a while after, to shew him his sword, which he would not denie him, thinking that hee would have beheld the fashion of his weapons: but he soone perceived that it was to another ende: for the old man holding it in his hand, behelde it a long while on every place, to see if he could finde any blood upon it, which might shew that any of their enemies had bene killed: for the Indians are woont to bring their weapons wherewith their enemies have beene defeated, with some blood upon them, for a token of their victories. But seeing no signe thereof upon it, he was upon the point to say unto him, that he had killed none of the men of Thimogoa: when as Vasseur preventing that which hee might object, declared and shewed unto him by signes, the manner of his enterprise, adding, that by reason of the two Indians which he had slaine, his sword was so bloudy, that hee

was inforced to wash and make it cleane a long while in the River: which the olde man beleeved to be like to be true, and made no maner of replie thereunto.

Vasseur, La Caille, and their other companions went out of the hal to go into the roome whither they had carried the Indian: there they found the Paracoussy sitting upon tapistries made of small reedes, which was at meate after the Indian fashion, and the Indian that was smitten hard by him, lying upon the selfe same tapistry, about whom stoode the wife of the Paracoussy, with all the young damsels which before bewailed him in the hall; which did nothing else but warme a great deal of mosse instead of napkins to rub the Indians side. Hereupon our men asked the Paracoussy againe for what occasion the Indian was so persecuted in his presence: hee answered, that this was nothing else but a kinde of ceremonie, whereby they would call to minde the death and persecutions of the Paracoussies their ancestours executed by their enemie Thimogoa: alleaging moreover, that as often as he himselfe, or any of his friends and allies returned from the Countrey, without they brought the heads of their enemies, or without bringing home some prisoner, hee used for a perpetuall memorie of all his predecessors, to beate the best beloved of all his children with the selfe same weapons wherewith they had bene killed in times past: to the ende that by renewing of the wound their death should be lamented afresh. Now when they were thus informed of those ceremonies, they thanked the Paracoussy for their good intertainement which they had received, & so setting saile came to me unto the fort: where they declared all unto me as I have recited it heretofore. The eight and twentieth of July our shippes departed to returne into France. And within a while, about two moneths after our arrivall in Florida, the Paracoussy Satourioua sent certaine Indians unto mee to knowe whether I would stande to my promise which I had made him at my first arrivall in that Countrey, which was that I would shewe my selfe friend to his friendes, and enemie unto his enemies, and also to accompany him with a good number of Harquebuzes, when he should see it expedient, and should finde a fit occasion to goe to warre. Now seeing he rested upon this promise, he prayed mee not to deferre the same: seeing also that making accompt thereof, hee had taken such good order for the execution of his enterprise, that he was ready, and was furnished with all things that were necessary for the voyage: I made him answere, that for his amitie I would not purchase the enmitie of the other, and that albeit I would, yet notwithstanding I wanted meanes to doe it. For it behoved mee at that present to make provision of victuals and munition for the defence of my Fort. On the other side, that my Barkes were nothing ready, and that this enterprise would require time: Moreover, that the Paracoussy Satourioua might holde himselfe ready to depart within two moneths, and that then I would thinke of fulfilling my promise to him.

The Indians caried this answere to their Paracoussy, which was litle please with it, because hee could not deferre his execution or expedition, aswell because all his victuals were ready, as also because tenne other Paracoussies were assembled with him for the performance of this enterprise. The ceremonie which this Savage used before hee embarked his armie deserveth not to be forgotten. For when hee was set downe by the Rivers side, being compassed about with ten other Paracoussies, hee commaunded water to be brought him speedily. This done, looking up into heaven, he fell to discourse of divers things with gestures that shewed him to be in exceeding great choller, which made him one while shake his head hither and thither, and by and by with I wote not what furie to turne his face toward the Countrey of his enemies, and to threaten to kill them. Hee oftentimes looked upon the Sunne, praying him to graunt him a glorious victory of his enemies. Which when hee had done by the space of halfe an houre, hee sprinkled with his hand a little of the water which hee helde in a vessell upon the heads of the Paracoussies, and cast the rest as it were in a rage and despite into a fire which was there prepared for the purpose. This done, hee cried out thrise, He Thimogoa, and was followed with five hundreth Indians at the least, which were there assembled, which cried all with one voyce, He Thimogoa. This ceremonie, as a certaine Indian tolde mee familiarly, signified nothing else, but that Satourioua besought the Sunne to graunt unto him so happy a victory, that hee might shed his enemies blood, as he had shed that water at his pleasure. Moreover, that the Paracoussies which were sprinckled with a part of

that water, might returne with the heads of their enemies, which is the onely and chiefe triumph of their victories.

The Paracoussy Satourioua had no sooner ended his ceremonies and had taken a viewe of all his company, but he embarked himselfe, and used such diligence with his Almadies or boates, that the next day two houres before the Sunnes set, he arrived on the territories of his enemies about eight or tenne leagues from their villages. Afterward causing them all to goe on land, hee assembled his counsell, wherein it was agreed that five of the Paracoussies should saile up the River with halfe of the troupes, and by the breake of the day should approche unto the dwelling of their enemie: for his owne part, that hee would take his journey through the woods and forrests as secretly as hee coulde: that when they were come thither, as well they that went by water as hee which went by land should not faile by the breake of the day to enter into the village, and cut them all in pieces, except the women and little children.

These things which were thus agreed upon, were executed with as great fury as was possible: which when they had done, they tooke the heades of their enemies which they had slaine, and cut off their haire round about with a piece of their skulles: they tooke also foure and twentie prisoners, which they led away, and retired themselves immediatly unto their Boates which wayted for them. Being come thither, they beganne to singe praises unto the Sunne, to whom they attributed their victorie. And afterwards they put the skins of those heads on the end of their javelings, and went altogether toward the territories of Paracoussy Omoloa, one of them which was in the company. Being come thither, they devided their prisoners equally to each of the Paracoussies, and left thirteene of them to Satourioua, which straightway dispatched an Indian his subject, to carry newes before of the victory to them which stayed at home to guard their houses, which immediatly beganne to weepe. But assoone as night was come, they never left dancing and playing a thousand gambols in honour of the feast.

The next day the Paracoussy Satourioua came home, who before hee entred into his lodging caused all the hairie skuls of his enemies to bee set up before his doore, and crowned them with branches of Lawrell, shewing by this glorious spectacle the triumph of the victory which hee had obtained. Straightway beganne lamentation and mournings, which assoone as the night beganne were turned into pleasures and dances.

After that I was advertised of these things, I sent a Souldier unto Satourioua, praying him to sende mee two of his prisoners: which hee denied mee, saying that hee was nothing beholding unto mee, and that I had broken my promise, against the oath which I had sworne unto him at my arrivall. Which when I understoode by my Souldier, which was come backe with speede, I devised howe I might be revenged of this Savage, and to make him know how dearely this bolde bravado of his should cost him: therefore I commanded my Sergeant to provide mee twentie Souldiers to goe with mee to the house of Satourioua: Where after I was come and entered into the hall without any maner of salutation, I went and sate mee downe by him, and stayed a long while without speaking any woorde unto him, or shewing him any signe of friendship, which thing put him deeply in his dumpes: besides that certaine Souldiers remained at the gate, to whom I had given expresse commaundement to suffer no Indian to goe foorth: having stoode still about halfe an houre with this countenance, at length I demaunded where the prisoners were which hee had taken at Thimogoa, and commaunded them presently to be brought unto me.

Whereunto the Paracoussy angry at the heart, and astonied wonderfully, stoode a long while without making any answere, notwithstanding at last hee answered me very stoutly, that being afraide to see us comming thither in such warrelike manner they fled into the woods, and that not knowing which way they were gone, they were not able by any meanes to bring them againe; Then I seemed to make as though I understood not what he saide, and asked for his prisoners againe, and for some of his principall allies. Then Satourioua commaunded his sonne Athore to seeke out the prisoners, and to cause them to be brought into that place, which thing he did within an houre after.

After they were come to the lodging of the Paracoussy, they humbly saluted mee, and lifting up their hands before me, they would have fallen downe prostrate as it were at my feet: but I would not suffer them, and soone after ledde them away with me unto my owne Fort. The Paracoussy being wonderfully offended with this bravado, bethought himselfe by all meanes how hee might be revenged of us. But to give us no suspition thereof, and the better to cover his intention, hee sent his messengers oftentimes unto us bringing alwayes with them some kinde of presents. Among others one day hee sent three Indians, which brought us two baskets full of great Pumpions, much more excellent then those which we have in France, and promised me in their Kings behalfe, that during mine abode in that Countrey, I should never want victuals: I thanked them for their Kings good will, and signified unto them the great desire which I had, aswell for the benefit of Satourioua, as for the quiet of his Subjects, to make a peace betweene him and those of Thimogoa: which thing coulde not choose but turne to their great benefite, seeing that being allied with the Kings of those parts, hee had an open passage against Onatheaqua his ancient enemie, which otherwise he could not set upon. Moreover that Olata Ouae Utina was so mightie a Paracoussy, that Satourioua was not able to withstand his forces: but being agreed together they might easily overthrow all their enemies, and might passe the confines of the farthest Rivers that were towards the South. The messengers prayed mee to have patience untill the morrowe, at what time they would come againe unto me to certifie me of their Lords inclination: which they failed not to doe, advertising me that Paracoussy Satourioua was the gladdest man in the world to treate of this accord (although indeed hee was quite contrary) and that he besought mee to be diligent therein, promising to observe and performe whatsoever I should agree upon with those of Thimogoa: which things the messengers also rehearsed unto the prisoners which I had ledde away. After they were departed, I resolved within two dayes to sende backe againe the prisoners to Olata Ouae Utina, whose subjects they were: but before I embarked them, I gave them certaine small trifles, which were little knives or tablets of glasse, wherein the image of King Charles the ninth was drawen very lively, for which they gave me very great thankes, as also for the honest entertainment which was given them at the Fort Caroline. After this they embarked themselves, with Captaine Vasseur, and with Monsieur de Arlac mine Ensigne, which I had sent of purpose to remaine a certaine time with Ouae Utina, hoping that the favour of this great Paracoussy would serve my turne greatly to make my discoveries in time to come. I sent with him also one of my Sergeants, and six gallant Souldiers.

Thus things passed on this manner, and the hatred of Paracoussy Satourioua against mee did still continue, until that on the nine and twentieth of August a lightning from heaven fell within halfe a league of our Fort, more worthy I beleeve to be wondered at, and to bee put in writing, then all the strange signes which have bene seene in times past, and whereof the histories have never written. For although the medowes were at that season all greene, and halfe covered over with water, neverthelesse the lightning in one instant consumed above five hundred acres therewith, and burned with the ardent heate thereof all the foules which tooke their pastime in the medowes, which thing continued for three dayes space, which caused us not a little to muse, not being able to judge whereof this fire proceeded: for one while wee thought that the Indians had burnt their houses, and abandoned their places for feare of us: another while wee thought that they had discovered some shippes in the Sea, and that according to their custome they had kindled many fires here and there, to signifie that their Countrey was inhabited: neverthelesse being not assured, I determined to sende to Paracoussy Serrany to knowe the trueth thereof. But even as I was upon the point to sende one by boate to discover the matter, six Indians came unto mee from Paracoussy Allimacany, which at their first entrie made unto mee a long discourse, and a very large and ample oration (after they had presented mee with certaine baskets full of Maiz, of Pompions and of Grapes) of the loving amitie which Allimacany desired to continue with mee, and that hee looked from day to day when it would please mee to employ him in my service. Therefore considering the serviceable affection that hee bare unto mee, hee found it very strange, that I thus discharged mine Ordinance against his dwelling, which had burnt up an infinite sight of greene medowes, and consumed even downe unto the bottome of the water, and came so neere unto his mansion, that hee thought hee sawe the fire in his house: wherefore hee besought mee most humbly to commaund my men that they would not

shoote any more towards his lodging, otherwise that hereafter he should be constrained to abandon his countrey, and to retire himselfe into some place further off from us.

Having understood the foolish opinion of this man, which notwithstanding coulde not choose but bee very profitable for us, I dissembled what I thought thereof for that time, and answered the Indians with a cheerefull countenance, that the relation which they made unto mee of the obedience of their Paracoussy did please mee right well, because that before hee had not behaved himselfe in such sort towards mee, especially when I summoned him to sende mee the prisoners of great Olata Ouae Utina which he detained, where of notwithstanding he made no great accompt, which was the principall cause wherefore I had discharged mine Ordinance against him: not that I meant to reach unto his house (as I might have done easily, if it had pleased me) but that I was content to shoote the halfe way to make him knowe my force: assuring him furthermore, that on condition that he would continue in his good affection, no more ordinance should be discharged against him hereafter: and besides that I would become his faithfull protectour against his greatest enemies.

The Indians contented with mine answere returned to assure their Paracoussy, which notwithstanding the assurance withdrewe himselfe from his dwelling twentie or five and twentie leagues off and that for the space of more then two moneths. After that three dayes were expired, the fire was quite extinguished. But for two dayes after there followed such an excessive heate in the aire, that the River neere unto which we planted our habitation, became so hoat, that I thinke it was almost ready to seeth. For there died so great abundance of fish, and that of so many divers sorts, that in the mouth of the River onely there were founde dead ynough to have loaden fiftie Carts, whereof there issued a putrefaction in the aire, which bred many dangerous diseases amongst us, insomuch that most of my men fell sicke, and almost ready to ende their dayes. Yet notwithstanding it pleased our mercifull God so to provide by his providence, that all our men recovered their health without the losse of any one of them.

Monsieur de Arlac, Captaine Vasseur, and one of my Sergeants being embarked with their tenne

Souldiers about the tenth of September, to cary backe the prisoners unto Utina, sailed so farre up the River, that they discovered a place called Mayarqua distant from our Fort about fourescore leagues, where the Indians gave them good entertainement, and in many other villages which they found. From this place they rowed to the dwelling of Paracoussy Utina, which after hee had feasted them according to his abilitie and power, prayed Monsieur de Arlac and all his Souldiers to stay a while with him, to ayde and assist him in battaile against one of his enemies called Potanou, whereunto Monsieur de Arlac consented willingly. And because hee knew not how long he might have occasion to stay in these parts, hee sent mee Captaine Vasseur and the Barke backe againe, which brought home onely five Souldiers with him.

Now because the custome of the Indians is always to wage war by surprise, Utina resolved to take his enemie Potanou in the morning by the breake of the day: to bring this to passe, hee made his men to travaile all the night, which might be in number two hundred persons, so well advised, that they prayed our French-shot to be in the fore-front, to the ende (as they saide) that the noyse of their pieces might astonish their enemies: notwithstanding they coulde not march so secretly, but that those of the village of Potanou, distant from the dwelling of Utina about five and twentie leagues, were ware of them: which suddenly employed and bestowed all their endevour to defend their village enclosed all with trees, and issued out in great companies: but finding themselves charged with shotte, (a thing wherewith they never had bene acquainted) also beholding the Captaine of their bande fall downe dead in the beginning of their skirmish, with a shot of an Harquebuse which strooke him in the forehead, discharged by the hande of Monsieur de Arlac, they left the place: and the Indians of Utina gate into the village, taking men, women, and chiidren prisoners. Thus Paracoussy Utina obtained the victory by the ayde of our men, which slew many of his enemies, and lost in this conflict one of their companions, wherewith Utina was very much grieved. Eight or tenne dayes after, I sent Captaine Vasseur backe againe with a Barke to fetch home Monsieur de Arlac and his Souldiers, which at their returne brought mee certaine presents from Utina, as some silver, a small

quantitie of golde, painted skinnes, and other things, with a thousand thankes, which the Paracoussy gave me, which promised that if in any enterprise of importance I should have neede of his men, he would furnish mee with three hundreth and above.

While I thus travailed to purchase friends, & to practise one while with one here, an other while with another there, certaine Souldiers of my company were suborned under hand by one named la Roquette of the Countrey of Perigort, which put in their heads that hee was a great Magician, and that by the secrets of Art-magicke he had discovered a Mine of golde and silver farre up within the River, whereby (upon the losse of his life,) every Souldier should receive in ready Bullion the value of tenne thousand Crownes, beside and above fifteene hundred thousand which should be reserved for the Kings Majestie: wherefore they allied themselves with La Roquette and another of his confederates, whose name was Le Genre, in whom notwithstanding I had great affiance. This Genre exceeding desirous to enrich himselfe in those parts, and seeking to be revenged, because I would not give him the carriage of the Paquet into France, secretly enfourmed the Souldiers that were already suborned by La Roquette, that I would deprive them of this great gaine, in that I did set them dayly on worke, not sending them on every side to discover the Countreys: therefore that it were a good deede, after they had made mee understand so much, to seeke meanes to dispatch mee out of the way, and to choose another Captaine in my place, if I would not give them victuals according to their disordinate appetite. Hee also brought mee word hereof himselfe, making a large discourse unto mee of the good affection of the Souldiers, which all besought mee that I would conduct them to the Countreys where the Mine was: I made him answere that all could not goe thither, and that it was necessary before their departure to settle our Fortresse in such estate, that those which were to stay at home behind should remaine in securitie against the Indians which might surprise them. Furthermore, that their maner of proceeding seemed strange unto mee, for that they imagined, that the Kings Majestie was at the charges of our voyage for none other ende, but onely to enrich them at their first arrivall, in as much as they shewed themselves much more given unto covetousnesse, then unto the service of their Prince: But seeing mine answere tended unto none other ende but to make our Fortresse strong and defensible, they determined to travaile in the worke, and made an ensigne of olde linnen, which ordinarily they bare upon the rampart when they went to woorke, alwayes wearing their weapons, which I thought they had done to incourage themselves to worke the better. But as I perceived afterwards, and that by the confession of Genre sent mee in letters which he writ to mee of that matter, these gentle Souldiers did the same for none other ende, but to have killed mee, and my Lieutenants also, if by chance I had given them any hard speeches.

About the twentieth of September, as I came home from the woods and coppises to finish the building of my Fort, (and that according to my usuall maner, I marched first to give encouragement unto my Soldiers) I chafed my selfe in such sort, that I fell into a sore and grievous sicknesse, whereof I thought I should have died: During which sicknesse, I called Le Genre often unto mee, as one that I trusted above all others, and of whose conspiracies I doubted not any whit at all. In this meane while assembling his complices, sometime in his chamber and sometime in the woods to consult with them, hee spake unto them to choose another Captaine besides mee, to the intent to put mee to death: but being not able by open force to execute his mischievous intention, hee gate him unto mine Apothecarie praying him instantly to mingle in my medicine, which I was to receive one or two dayes after, some drugge that should make mee pitch over the pearch, or at the least that hee would give him a little Arsenike or quicke Silver, which hee himselfe would put into my drinke. But the Apothecary denied him, as did in like maner Master S. which was Master of the fire-workes. Thus wholly disappointed of both his meanes, hee with certaine others resolved to hide a little barrell of gunne-powder underneath my bed, and by a traine to set it on fire.

Upon these practises a Gentleman which I had dispatched to returne into France, being about to take his leave of me, advertised me, that Genre had given him a booke full of all kinde of lewde invectives and slanders against me, against Monsieur de Ottigny, and against the principal of my company: upon which occasion I assembled all my Souldiers together, and Captaine Bourdet with all his, which on the fourth of September arrived in the roade, and were come into our River. In their presence I caused the contents of the booke to bee read alowde, that they might beare record of the untruths that were written against mee. Genre, which had gotten him into the woods for feare of being taken, (where he lived for a while after with the Savages by my permission,) writ unto mee often, and in many of his letters confessed unto mee, that hee had deserved death, condemning himselfe so farre-foorth, that he referred all to my mercie and pitie.

The seventh or eighth day of November, after I had caused sufficient provision of such victuals as were needfull to bee made, I sent two of my men, to wit, La Roche Ferriere, and an other towarde King Utina, to discover every day more and more of the Countrey: where hee was the space of five or six moneths, during which hee discovered many small villages, and among others one named Hostaqua, the King whereof being desirous of my friendship, sent unto mee a quiver made of a Luserns skinne full of arrowes, a couple of bowes, foure or five skinnes painted after their maner, and a cheine of Silver weying about a pounde weight. In recompence of which presents I sent him two whole sutes of apparell, with certaine cutting hookes or hatchets.

After these things therefore in this sort passed, about the tenth of this moneth, Captaine Bourdet determined to leave mee and to returne into France. Then I requested him, yea rather was exceeding importunate with him, to carry home with him some sixe or seven Souldiers, whom I coulde not trust by any meanes: which hee did for my sake, and would not charge himselfe with Genre, which offered him a great summe of money, if it would please him to carry him into France: hee transported him onely to the other side of the River. Three dayes after his departure thirteene Mariners which I had brought out of France, suborned by certaine other Mariners which Captaine Bourdet had left me, stole away my Barkes in maner following. These Mariners of Captaine Bourdet put mine in the head, that if they had such Barkes as mine were, they might gaine very much in the Isles of the Antilles, and make an exceeding profitable voyage. Hereupon they beganne to devise howe they might steale away my Barkes, and consulted that when I should command them to goe unto the village of Sarauahi distant about a league and an halfe from our Fort, and situated upon an arme of the River, (whither according to my maner I sent them dayly to seeke clay, to make bricke and morter for our houses) they would returne no more, but would furnish themselves with victuals as well as they might possibly: and then would embarke themselves all in one vessell, and would goe their way: as indeede they did. And that which was worse, two Flemish Carpenters, which the saide Bourdet had left mee, stole away the other Barke, and before their departure cut the cables of the Barke, and of the shipboate, that it might goe away with the tyde, that I might not pursue them: so that I remained without either Barke or boate, which fell out as unluckily for mee as was possible. For I was ready to imbarke my selfe with all speede, to discover as farre up our River, as I might by any meanes. Nowe my Mariners, (as I understood afterwards) tooke a Barke that was a passenger of the Spaniards neere the Isle of Cuba, wherein they founde a certaine quantitie of golde and silver, which they seazed upon. And having this bootie they lay a while at Sea, untill their victuals beganne to faile them: which was the cause, that oppressed with famine they came unto Havana the principall Towne of the Isle of Cuba: whereupon proceeded that mischiefe which hereafter I will declare more at large.[1] When I saw my Barkes returned not at their wonted houre, and suspecting that which fell out in deed, I commanded my Carpenters with all diligence to make a little boat with a flat bottome, to search those Rivers for some newes of these Mariners. The boate dispatched within a day and a night, by reason that my Carpenters found planks and timber ready sawed to their hands, as commonly I caused my Sawyers to provide it, I sent men to seeke some newes of my thieves: but all was in vaine. Therefore I determined to cause two great Barkes to be built, eche of which might be thirtie five, or thirtie six foote long in the keele.

And now the worke was very well forwarde which I set my workemen about, when ambition and avarice, the mother of all mischiefe, tooke roote in the hearts of foure or five souldiers which could not away with the worke and paines taking: and which from hence forward (namely one Fourneaux, and one La Croix, and another called Steven le Geneuois, the three principall authors of the sedition) beganne to practise with the best of my troupe, shewing them that it was a vile thing for men of honest parentage, as they were, to moyle themselves thus with abject and base worke, seeing they had the best occasion of the worlde offered them to make themselves all riche: which was to arme the two Barkes which were in building, and to furnish them with good men: and then to saile unto Peru, and the other Isles of the Antilles[2], where every Souldier might easily enrich himselfe with tenne thousand Crownes. And if their enterprise should bee misliked withall in France, they should bee alwayes able, by reason of the great wealth that they should gaine, to retire themselves into Italy, untill the heate were overpassed, and that in the meane season, some warre would fall out, which would cause all this to be quite forgotten.

This word of riches sounded so well in the eares of my Souldiers, that in fine, after they had oftentimes consulted of their affaires, they grew to the number of threescore and sixe: which to colour their great desire which they had to goe on stealing, they caused a request to bee presented unto mee by Francis de la Caille Sergeant of my company, contayning in sum a declaration of the small store of victuals that was left to maintaine us, until the time that shippes might returne from France: for remedy whereof they thought it necessary to sende to New Spaine, Peru, and all the Isles adjoyning, which they besought mee to be content to graunt. But I made them answere, that when the Barkes were finished, I would take such good order in generall, that by meanes of the Kings marchandise, without sparing mine owne apparell, wee would get victuals of the inhabitants of the Countrey: seeing also that wee had ynough to serve us for foure moneths to come. For I feared greatly, that under pretence of searching victuals, they would enterprise somewhat against the King of Spaines Subjects, which in time to come might justly bee layde to my

---

1. Sidenote: "One of these Mariners named Francis Jean betrayed his own countrey men to the Spaniards, and brought them into Florida."

2. Sidenote: "By Peru the French meane the coast of Carthagena and Nombre de Dios."

charge, considering that at our departure out of France, the Queene had charged me very expresly, to doe no kinde of wrong to the King of Spaines Subjects, nor any thing whereof he might conceive any jelousie.

They made as though they were content with this answere. But eight dayes after, as I continued in working upon our Fort, and on my Barkes, I fell sicke. Then my seditious companions forgetting all honour and duetie, supposing that they had found good occasion to execute their rebellious enterprise, beganne to practise afresh their former designes, handling their businesse so well, during my sicknesse, that they openly vowed that they would seaze on the Corps de gard, and on the Fort, yea, and force mee also, if I woulde not consent unto their wicked desire. My Lieutenant being hereof advertised, came and tolde mee that he suspected some evill practise: and the next day in the morning I was saluted at my gate with men in complet harnesse, what time my Souldiers were about to play mee a shrewde tricke: then I sent to seeke a couple of Gentlemen whom I most trusted, which brought mee word that the Souldiers were determined to come to me to make a request unto me: But I tolde them that this was not the fashion to present a request unto a Captaine in this maner, and therefore they should send some few unto me to signifie unto mee what they would have. Hereupon the five chiefe authours of the sedition armed with Corslets, their Pistolles in their handes already bent, prest into my chamber, saying unto mee, that they would goe to New Spaine to seeke their adventure. Then I warned them to bee well advised what they meant to doe: but they foorthwith replyed, that they were fully advised already, and that I must graunt them this request. Seeing then (quoth I) that I am enforced to doe it, I will sende Captaine Vasseur and my Sergeant, which will make answere and give mee an accompt of every thing that shall be done in this voyage: And to content you, I thinke it good that you take one man out of every chamber, that they may accompany Captaine Vasseur and my Sergeant. Whereupon, blaspheming the Name of God, they answered that they must goe thither: and that there lacked nothing, but that I should deliver them the armour which I had in my custodie, for feare least I might use them to their disadvantage (being so villanously abused by them:) wherein

notwithstanding I would not yeeld unto them. But they tooke all by force, and caried it out of my house, yea and after they had hurt a Gentleman in my chamber, which spake against their doings, they layd hands on mee, and caried mee very sicke, as I was, prisoner into a shippe which rode at ancker in the middest of the River, wherein I was the space of fifteene dayes, attended upon with one man onely without permission for any of my servants to come to visite mee: from every one of whom, as also from the rest that tooke my part, they tooke away their armour. And they sent mee a passeport to signe, telling me plainely after I had denied them, that if I made any difficulty, they would all come and cut my throat in the shippe. Thus was I constrained to signe their Passe-port, and forthwith to grant them certaine mariners, with Trenchant an honest and skilfull Pilot. When the barks were finished, they armed them with the kings munition, with powder, with bullets, and artillery, asmuch as they needed, and chose one of my Sergeants for their Captain, named Bertrand Conferrent, and for their Ensigne one named La Croix. They compelled Captaine Vasseur to deliver them the flag of his ship. Then having determined to saile unto a place of the Antilles called Leauguave, belonging unto the king of Spaine, and there to goe on land on Christmasse night, with intention to enter into the Church while the Masse was sayd after midnight, and to murder all those that they found there, they set saile the eight of December. But because the greatest part of them by this time repented them of their enterprise, and that now they began to fall into mutinies among themselves, when they came foorth of the mouth of the river, the two barks divided themselves; the one kept along the coast unto Cuba, to double the Cape more easily, and the other went right foorth to passe athwart the Isles of Lucaya: by reason whereof they mette not untill six weeks after their departure. During which time the barke that tooke her way along the coast, wherein one of the chiefe conspiratours named De Orange was Captaine, and Trenchant his Pilot, neere unto a place called Archaha, tooke a Brigantine laden with a certaine quantity of Cassavi, which is a kinde of bread made of roots, and yet neverthelesse is very white, and good to eat, and some little Wine, which was not without some losse of their men: for in one assault that the inhabitants of Archaha made upon them, two of their men were taken, to wit, Steven Gondeau, and one named Grand Pré, besides two more that were slaine in the place, namely Nicolas Master and Doublet: yet neverthelesse they tooke the Brigantine, wherein they put all their stuffe that was in their owne Barke, because it was of greater burthen and better of saile then their owne. Afterward they sailed right unto the Cape of Santa Maria nere to Leauguave, where they went on land to calke and bray their ship which had a great leake. In this meane while they resolved to saile to Baracou, which is a village of the Isle of Jamaica: where at their arrivall they found a Caravel of fifty or threescore tunnes burden, which they tooke without any body in it: and after they had made good cheere in the village the space of five or six dayes, they embarked themselves in it, leaving their second ship: then they returned to the Cape of Tiburon, where they met with a Patach, which they tooke by force after a long conflict. In this Patach the governour of Jamaica was taken, with great store of riches, aswell of golde and silver as of merchandise and wine, and many other things; where with our seditious companions not content, determined to seeke more in their caravell, and their governour of Jamaica also. After they were come to Jamaica, they missed of another caravel which did save it selfe in the haven. The governour being fine and subtile, seeing himselfe brought unto the place which he desired and where he commanded, obtained so much by his faire words, that they which had taken him let him put two little boyes which were taken with him into a little cocke boat, and send them to his wife into the village, to advertise her that she should make provision of victuals to send unto him. But in stead of writing unto his wife, he spake unto the boyes secretly that with all diligence she should send the vessels that were in the havens neere that place to succour and rescue him. Which she did so cunningly, that on a morning about the breake of the day, as our seditious companions were at the havens mouth (which reacheth above two leagues up within the land) there came out of the haven a malgualire which maketh saile both forward and backward, and then two great shippes, which might be ech of them of fourescore or an hundred tunnes a piece, with good store of ordinance, and well furnished with men: at whose comming our mutinous fel-

lowes were surprised, being not able to see them when they came, aswell because of the darknesse of the weather, as also by reason of the length of the haven, considering also they mistrusted nothing. True it is that five or six & twenty that were in the brigantine discovered these ships when they were nere them, which seeing themselves pressed for want of leasure to weigh their anker, cut their cable, and the trumpeter which was in it advertised the rest: whereupon the Spanyards seeing themselves descried, discharged a volley of canon shot against the French men, which they followed by the space of three leagues, and recovered their own ships: the brigantine which escaped away, passed in the sight of the Cape des Aigrettes, and the Cape of S. Anthony situate in the Isle of Cuba, & from thence passed within the sight of Havana; but Trenchant their pilot, and the trumpeter, and certaine other mariners of this brigantine, which were led away by force in this voyage (as elsewhere we have declared) desired nothing more then to returne to me: wherefore these men agreed together (if peradventure the wind served them well) to passe the chanell of Bahama, while their seditious companions were asleepe: which they did accomplish with such good successe, that in the morning toward the breake of the day about the five and twentieth of March they arrived upon the coast of Florida: where knowing the fault which they had committed, in a kinde of mockery they counterfaited the Judges: but they played not this pranke untill they had tippled well of the Wine which remained yet in their prize. One counterfeited the Judge, another presented my person: one other after he had heard the matter pleaded, concluded thus: Make you your causes as good as it pleaseth you, but if when you come to the fort Caroline the Captaine cause you not to be hanged, I will never take him for an honest man: others thought that my choler being passed, I would easily forget this matter. Their saile was no sooner descried upon our coast, but the king of the place named Patica, dwelling eight leagues distant from our fort, and being one of our good friends, sent an Indian to advertise me that he had descried a shippe upon the coast, and that he thought it was one of our nation. Hereupon the brigantine oppressed with famine, came to an anker at the mouth of the river of May, when at the first blush we thought they had beene shippes come from France; which gave us occasion of great joy: but after I had caused her to be better viewed, I was advertised that they were our seditious companions that were returned. Therefore I sent them word by Captaine Vasseur and my Sergeant, that they should bring up their brigantine before the fortresse: which they promised to doe. Now there was not above two leagues distance from the mouth of the river where they cast anker unto the fortresse. The next day I sent the same Captaine and Sergeant with thirty souldiers, because I saw they much delayed their comming. Then they brought them: and because certaine of them had sworne at their departure, that they would never come againe within the fort, I was well pleased they should keepe their oth. For this purpose I waited for them at the rivers mouth, where I made my barks to be built, and commanded my Sergeant to bring the foure chiefe authours of the mutiny on shore; whom I caused immediatly to be put in fetters: for my meaning was not to punish the rest, considering that they were suborned, and because my councell expresly assembled for this purpose had concluded that these foure only should die, to serve for an example to the rest. In the same place I made an Oration unto them in this maner.

My friends, you know the cause why our king sent us unto this countrey; you know that he is our naturall Prince, whom we are bound to obey according to the commandement of God, in such sort, that we ought neither to spare our goods nor lives to do those things that concerne his service: ye know, or at least you cannot be ignorant, that besides this general and naturall obligation, you have this also joyned thereunto, that in receiving of him reasonable pay and wages, you are bound to follow those whom he hath established over you to be your governours, and to command you in his name, having for this purpose given him an oth of fidelitie, which you cannot by any meanes revoke for any faire apparance which you have to doe the contrary: for this is reason, that seeing you live upon his charges on this condition, (this is reason I say) that you should be faithfull unto him. Notwithstanding you have had more regard unto your unbridled affections then unto vertue, which invited you to the observance of your oth, in such sort that being become contemners of all honesty, you have passed your bonds, and thought that all things were lawfull for you. Whereupon it is fallen

out, that while you thought to escape the justice of men, you could not avoid the judgement of God, which as a thing by no meanes to be avoided hath led you, and in spight of you hath made you to arrive in this place, to make you confesse how true his judgements are, and that he never suffereth so foule a fault to escape unpunished.

After that I had used unto them these or the like speeches, following that which wee had agreed upon in councell, in respect of the crimes which they had committed, aswel against the kings Majesty as against mee which was their Captaine, I commanded that they should be hanged. Seeing therefore that there was no starting hole, nor meanes at all to save themselves from this arrest, they tooke themselves unto their prayers: yet one of the foure, thinking to raise a mutiny among my souldiers, sayd thus unto them: What, brethren and companions, will you suffer us to die so shamefully? And taking the word out of his mouth, I sayd unto him, that they were not companions of authours of sedition and rebels unto the kings service. Heereupon the souldiers besought me not to hang them, but rather let them be shot thorow, & then afterward, if I thought good, their bodies might be hanged upon certaine gibbets along the havens mouth: which I caused presently to be put in execution. Loe here what was the end of my mutinous souldiers, without which I had alwayes lived peaceably, and enjoyed the good desire which I had to make an happy and quiet voyage. But because I have spoken of nothing but their accidentes and adventures which happened unto them after their departure, without making any mention of our fort, I will returne to the matters from which I digressed, to declare that which fell out after their departure. First I began to consider to the end I might confirme and make my selfe more constant in mine affliction, that these murmurers could not ground their sedition upon want of victuals: for from the time of our arrivall, every souldier dayly unto this day, and besides untill the eight and twentieth of February, had a loafe of bread weighing two and twenty ounces. Againe I recounted with my selfe that all new conquests by sea or by land are ordinarily troubled with rebellions, which are easie to be raised, aswell in respect of the distance of place, as in respect of the hope that the souldiers have to make their profit, as we may be well informed both by ancient histories and also by the troubles which lately happened unto Christopher Columbus, after his first discovery, to Francis Pizarro, & Diego de Almagro in Peru, & to Fernando Cortes. An hundred thousand other things came unto my minde, to incourage and confirme me. My Lieutenant Ottigny, and my Sergeant of my band came to seeke me in the ship, where I was prisoner, and caried me from thence in a barke assoone as our rebels were departed. After I was come unto the fort, I caused all my company that remained, to be assembled in the midst of the place before the Corps de garde, and declared unto them the faults which they that had forsaken us had committed, praying them to beare them in memory, to beare witnesse thereof when need should require. Foorthwith I ordained new Captaines to command the troups; and prescribed them an order, according whereunto they were to governe themselves from thence forward, and to enter into their watch: for the greatest part of the souldiers, of whom I had the best opinion, were gone away with them. My declaration ended, they promised mee all with one accord to obey mee most humbly, and to doe whatsoever I should command them, though it were to die at my feet for the Kings service; wherein assuredly they never after failed: so that I dare say, after the departure of my mutinous companions I was as well obeyed as ever was Captaine in place where he commanded. The next day after my returne unto the fort, I assembled my men together againe, to declare unto them that our fort was not yet finished, and that it was needfull that all of us should put thereto our helping hands, to assure our selves against the Indians: wherein having willingly agreed unto mee, they raised it all with turfes from the gate unto the river which is on the West side. This done, I set my Carpenters on worke to make another barke of the same bignesse that the others were of: I commanded the Sawyers that they should prepare plancks, the Smithes to prepare yron and nailes, and certaine others to make coales: so that the barke was finished in eighteene dayes. Afterward I made another lesser then the first, the better to discover up the river. In this meane space the Indians visited me, and brought me dayly certaine presents, as Fish, Deere, Turki-cocks, Leopards, little Beares, and other things according to the place of their habitation. I recompensed them with certaine Hatchets, Knives, Beads of glasse, Combes, and Looking-glasses. Two Indians came unto me one day to salute me on the behalfe of their King, whose name was Marracou, dwelling from the place of our fort some forty leagues toward the South, and tolde mee that there was one in the house of King Onathaqua which was called Barbu or the bearded man, and in the house of King Mathiaca another man whose name they knew not, which was not of their nation: whereupon I conceived that these might be some Christians. Wherefore I sent to all the kings my neighbours to pray them, that if there were any Christian dwelling in their countreys, they would finde meanes that he might be brought unto mee, and that I would make them double recompense. They which love rewards, tooke so much paine, that the two men, whereof we have spoken, were brought unto the fort unto me. They were naked, wearing their haire long unto their hammes as the Savages use to do, and were Spanyards borne, yet so well accustomed to the fashion of the countrey that at the first sight they found our maner of apparell strange. After that I had questioned of certaine matters with them, I caused them to be apparelled, and to cut their haire; which they would not loose, but lapped it up in a linnen cloth, saying that they would cary it into their countrey to be a testimony of the misery that they had indured in the Indies. In the haire of one of them was found a little gold hidden, to the value of five and twenty crownes, which he gave unto me. And examining them of the places where they had bene, and how they came thither, they answered me that fifteene yeeres past, three shippes, in one of which they were, were cast away over against a place named Calos upon the Flats which are called The Martyres, and that the king of Calos recovered the greatest part of the riches which were in the sayd shippes, travelling in such sort that the greatest part of the people was saved, and many women; among which number there were three or foure women married, remaining there yet, and their children also, with this king of Calos. I desired to learne what this king was. They answered me, that he was the goodliest and the tallest Indian of the country, a mighty man, a warrier, and having many subjects under his obedience. They tolde me moreover, that he had great store of golde and silver, so farre foorth that in a certaine village he had a pit full thereof, which was at the least as high as a man, and as large as a tunne: all which wealth the Spanyards fully perswaded themselves that they could cause me to recover, if I were able to march thither with an hundred shot, besides that which I might get of the common people of the countrey, which had also great store thereof. They further also advertised me, that the women going to dance, did weare about their girdles plates of golde as broad as a saweer, and in such number; that the weight did hinder them to dance at their ease; and that the men ware the like also. The greatest part of these riches was had, as they sayd, out of the Spanish shippes, which commonly were cast away in this straight; and the rest by the traffique which this king of Calos had with the other kings of the countrey: Finally, that he was had in great reverence of his subjects; and that hee made them beleeve that his sorceries and charmes were the causes that made the earth bring foorth her fruit: and that hee might the easier perswade them that it was so, he retired himselfe once or twise a yeere to a certaine house, accompanied with two or three of his most familiar friends, where hee used certaine inchantments; and if any man intruded himselfe to goe to see what they did in this place, the king immediately caused him to be put to death. Moreover, they tolde me, that every yeere in the time of harvest, this Savage king sacrificed one man,[3] which was kept expresly for this purpose, and taken out of the number of the Spanyards which by tempest were cast away upon that coast. One of these two declared unto me, that hee had served him a long time for a messenger; and that often times by his commandement he had visited a king named Oathcaqua, distant from Calos foure or five dayes journey, which alwayes remained his faithfull friend: but that in the midway there was an Island situate in a great lake of fresh water, named Sarrope, about five leagues in bignesse, abounding with many sorts of fruits, specially in Dates, which growe on the Palme trees, whereof they make a woonderfull traffique; yet not so great as of a kinde of root, whereof they make a kinde of meale, so good to make bread of, that it is unpossible to eate better, and that for fifteene leagues about, all the countrey is fed therewith: which is the cause that the inhabitants of the Isle gaine of

their neighbours great wealth and profit: for they will not depart with this root without they be well payed for it. Besides that, they are taken for the most warlike men of all that countrey, as they made good proofe when the king of Calos, having made alliance with Oathcaqua, was deprived of Oathcaquaes daughter, which he had promised to him in mariage. He tolde me the whole matter in this sort: as Oathcaqua well accompanied with his people caried one of his daughters, exceeding beautifull, according to the colour of the countrey, unto king Calos, to give her unto him for his wife, the inhabitants of this Isle advertised of the matter, layed an ambush for him in a place where he should passe, and so behaved themselves, that Oathcaqua was discomfited, the betrothed yoong spouse taken, and all the damosels that accompanied her; which they caried unto their Isle; which thing in all the Indians countrey they esteeme to be the greatest victory: for afterward they marry these virgins, and love them above all measure. The Spanyard that made this relation, tolde mee that after this defeat he went to dwell with Oathcaqua, and had bene with him full eight yeeres, even untill the time that he was sent unto me. The place of Calos is situate upon a river which is beyond the Cape of Florida, forty or fifty leagues towards the Southwest: and the dwelling of Oathcaqua is on this side the Cape toward the North, in a place which we call in the Chart Cannaveral, which is in 28 degrees.

About the five and twentieth of January Paracoussy Satourioua my neighbour sent me certaine presents by two of his subjects, to perswade me to joyne with him, and to make warre upon Ouae Utina which was my friend: and further besought me to retire certaine of my men which were with Utina; for whom if it had not bene, he had often times set upon him, and defeited him. He besought me heerein by divers other kings his allies, which for three weekes or a moneths space sent messengers unto mee to this end and purpose: but I would not grant unto them that they should make warre upon him; yea rather contrariwise I endevoured to make them friends; wherein they condescended unto me, so farre foorth that they were content to allow of any thing that I would set downe: whereupon the two Spanyards which of long time knew well the nature of the Indians, warned me that in any case I should not trust unto them, because that when

---

3. Sidenote: "One of these Spanyards names was Martin Gomes."

they shewed good countenance and the best cheere unto men, then was the time that they would surprise and betray them; and that of their nature they were the greatest traitours and most deepe dissemblers of the world. Besides I never trusted them but upon good ground, as one that had discovered a thousand of their crafts and subtilties, aswell by experience as by reading of the histories of late yeres. Our two barks were not so soone finished, but I sent Captaine Vasseur to discover along the coast lying toward the North, and commanded him to saile unto a river, the king whereof was called Audusta, which was lord of that place, where those of the yere 1562 inhabited. I sent him two suites of apparell, with certaine hatchets, knives, and other small trifles, the better to insinuate my selfe into his friendship. And the better to win him, I sent in the barke with captaine Vasseur a souldier called Aimon, which was one of them which returned home in the first voyage, hoping that king Audusta might remember him. But before they were imbarked I commanded them to make inquiry what was become of another called Rouffi, which remained alone in those parts when Nicolas Masson[4] and those of the first voyage embarked themselves to returne into France. They understood at their arrivall there, that a barke passing that way had caried away the same souldier: and afterward I knew for a certainty that they were Spaniards which had caried him to Havana. The king Audusta sent me backe my barke full of mill, with a certaine quantity of beanes, two stags, some skinnes painted after their maner, and certaine pearles of small value, because they were burnt: and sent me word that if I would dwel in his quarters, he would give me a great countrey: and that after he had gathered his mill, he would spare me as much as I would have. In the meane while there came unto our fort a flocke of stocke-doves in so great number[5], and that for the space of seven weeks together, that every day wee killed with harquebush shot two hundred in the woods about our fort. After that Captaine Vasseur was returned, I caused the two barks to be furnished againe with souldiers & mariners, and sent them to cary a present from me unto the widow of king

Hiocaia, whose dwelling was distant from our fort about twelve legues Northward. She courteously received our men, sent me backe my barks full of mill and acornes with certaine baskets full of the leaves of Cassine, wherwith they make their drinke. And the place where this widow dwelleth is the most plentiful of mill that is in all the coast, and the most pleasant. It is thought that the queene is the most beautifull of all the Indians, and of whom they make most account: yea, and her subjects honour her so much, that almost continually they beare her on their shoulders, and will not suffer her to go on foot. Within a few dayes after the returne of my barks, she sent to visit me by her Hiatiqui, which is as much to say, as her interpreter. Now while I thought I was furnished with victuals untill the time that our ships might come out of France (for feare of keeping my people idle) I sent my two barks to discover along the river, and up toward the head thereof, which went so far up that they were thirty leagues good beyond a place named Mathiaqua, and there they discovered the entrance of a lake, upon the one side whereof no land can be seene, according to the report of the Indians, which had oftentimes climbed on the highest trees in the countrey to see land, and notwithstanding could not discerne any: which was the cause that my men went no further, but returned backe; and in comming home went to see the Island of Edelano situated in the midst of the river, as faire a place as any that may be seene thorow the world: for in the space of some three leagues, that it may conteine in length and bredth, a man may see an exceeding rich countrey, and marvellously peopled. At the comming out of the village of Edelano to go unto the rivers side a man must passe thorow an alley about three hundred paces long and fifty paces broad: on both sides whereof great tres are planted, the boughes whereof are tied together like an arch, and meet together so artificially that a man would thinke it were an arbour made of purpose, as faire I say, as any in all christendome, although it be altogether natural. Our men departing from this place rowed to Eneguape, then to Chilily, from thence to Patica, & lastly they came unto Coya: where leaving their barks in a litle creeke of the river with men to guard them, they went to visit Utina, which received them very courteously: and when they departed from his house, he intreated them

4. Sidenote: "Nicolas Masson otherwise called Nicolas Barre."
5. Sidenote: "Peter Martyr writeth cap. 1. decad. 7. that the like flocks of pigeons are in the Isles of the Lucayos."

so earnestly, that sixe of my men remained with him; of which number there was one gentleman, named Groutald, which after he had abode there about two moneths, and taken great paines to discover the countrey, with another which I had left a great while there to that intent, came unto me to the fort, and tolde me that he never saw a fairer countrey. Among other things, he reported unto me that he had seene a place named Hostaqua, and that the king thereof was so mighty, that he was able to bring three or foure thousand Savages to the field; with whom if I would joyne and enter into league, we might be able to reduce all the rest of the inhabitants unto our obedience: besides that this king knew the passages unto the mountaine of Apalatci, which the French men desired so greatly to atteine unto, and where the enemy of Hostaqua made his abode; which was easie to be subdued, if so be wee would enter into league together. This king sent me a plate of a minerall that came out of this mountaine, out of the foote whereof there runneth a streame of golde or copper, as the Savages thinke, out of which they dig up the sand with an hollow and drie cane of reed untill the cane be full; afterward they shake it, and finde that there are many small graines of copper and silver among this sand: which giveth them to understand, that some rich mine must needs be in the mountaine. And because the mountaine was not past five or sixe dayes journey from our fort, lying toward the Northwest, I determined assoone as our supply should come out of France, to remoove our habitation unto some river more toward the North, that I might be nerer thereunto. One of my souldiers whose name was Peter Gamby, which had remained a long space before in this countrey to learne the languages and traffique with the Indians, at the last came to the village of Edelano, where having gotten together a certaine quantity of golde and silver, and purposing to returne unto me, he prayed the king of the village to lend him a canoa (which is a vessell made of one whole piece of wood, which the Indians use to fish withal, and to row upon the rivers) which this lord of Edelano granted him. But being greedy of the riches which he had, he commanded two Indians, which he had charged to conduct him in the canoa, to murder him & bring him the merchandise and the gold which he had. Which the two traitours villanously executed: for they knockt him on the head with an hatchet, as he was blowing of the fire in the canoa to seethe fish. The Paracoussy Utina sent certeine dayes afterward, to pray me to lend him a dozen or fifteene of my shot, to invade his enemy Potanou, and sent me word, that this enemy once vanquished, he would make me passage, yea, and would conduct me unto the mountaines in such sort, that no man should be able to hinder me. Then I assembled my men to demand their advice, as I was woont to do in all mine enterprises. The greater part was of opinion, that I should do well to send succour unto this Paracoussy, because it would be hard for me to discover any further up into the country without his helpe: and that the Spanyards when they were imployed in their conquests, did alwayes enter into alliance with some one king to ruine another. Notwithstanding, because I did alwayes mistrust the Indians, and that the more after the last advertisement that the Spanyards had given me, I doubted lest the small number which Utina demanded might incurr some danger; wherefore I sent him thirty shot under the charge of my Lieutenant Ottigny, which stayed not above two dayes with Utina, while he prepared victuals for his voyage, which ordinarily and according to the custome of the countrey are caried by women and yoong boyes, and by hermaphrodites. Utina setting forward with three hundred of his subjects, having ech of them their bowe and quiver full of arrowes, caused our thirty shot to be placed in the foreward, and made them march all the day, until that the night approching, and having not gone past halfe the way, they were inforced to lie all night in the woods, nere a great lake, and there to incampe themselves: they separated themselves by sixe and sixe, making ech of them a fire about the place where their king lay, for whose guard they ordeined a certeine number of those archers, in whom he put most confidence. Assoone as day was come, the campe of the Indians marched within three leagues of Potanou: there king Utina requested my Lieutenant to grant him foure or five of his men to go and discover the countrey; which departed immediatly, and had not gone farre, but they perceived upon a lake, distant about three leagues from the village of Potanou, three Indians which fished in a canoa. Now the custome is that when they fish in this lake, they have alwayes a company of watchmen, armed with bowes and arrowes to guard the fishers. Our men being hereof advertised by those of the company, durst not passe any further, for feare of falling into some ambush: wherefore they returned towards Utina, which suddenly sent them backe with a greater company to surprise the fishers, before they might retire and advertise their king Potanou of the comming of his enemies. Which they could not execute so politikely, but that two of them escaped; the third also did the best he could to save himselfe by swimming, in which meane while he was stayed with shot of arrowes, and they drew him starke dead unto the banks side, where our Indians flayed off the skinne of his head, cut off both his armes in the high way, reserving his haire for the triumph, which their king hoped to make for the defeat of his enemy. Utina fearing least Potanou advertised by the fishers which were escaped, should put himselfe in armes to withstand him valiantly, asked counsell of his Jawa, which is as much to say in their language as his Magician, whether it were best to goe any further. Then his Magician made certeine signes, hidious and fearefull to beholde, and used certeine words; which being ended, he sayd unto his king, that it was not best to passe any further, and that Potanou accompanied with two thousand Indians at the least stayed in such and such a place for him, to bidde him battell: and besides this, that all the sayd Indians were furnished with cords to binde the prisoners which they made full account to take.

This relation caused Utina to be unwilling to passe any further: whereupon my Lieutenant being as angry as ever he might be, because hee had taken so great paines without doing of any thing of account, sayd unto him, that hee would never thinke well of him nor of his people, if hee would not hazzard himselfe: and that if he would not doe it, at the least, that he would give him a guide to conduct him and his small company to the place where the enemies were encamped. Heereupon Utina was ashamed, and seeing the good affection of Monsieur de Ottigny determined to go forward: and he failed not to finde his enemies in the very place which the Magician had named: where the skirmish beganne, which lasted three long houres: wherein without doubt Utina had beene defeated, unlesse our harquebusiers had not borne the burthen and brunt of all the battell, and slaine a great number of the souldiers of Potanou, upon which occasion they were put to

flight. Wherewithall Utina being content for the present, caused his people to retire and returne homeward to the great discontentment of Monsieur de Ottigny, which desired nothing more, then to pursue his victorie. After he was come home to his house he sent messengers to eighteene or twentie villages of other kings his vassals, and summoned them to be present at the feasts and dances which he purposed to celebrate because of his victorie. In the meane while Monsieur de Ottigny refreshed himselfe for two dayes: and then taking his leave of the Paracoussi, and leaving him twelve of his men to see that Potanou, bethinking himselfe of his late losse, should not come to burne the houses of Utina, he set forward on his way to come unto me unto our Fort, where he up and told me how every thing had passed: and withall that he had promised the twelve souldiers, that he would come backe againe to fetch them. Then the kings my neighbours all enemies to Utina, being advertised of the returne of my Lieutenant, came to visite me with presents and to enquire how things had passed, praying me all to receive them into my favour, and to become enemie to Utina, which notwithstanding I would not grant them for many reasons that mooved me.

The Indians are wont to leave their houses and to retire themselves into the woods the space of three moneths, to wit January, February, and March: during which time by no meanes a man can see one Indian. For when they goe on hunting, they make little cottages in the woods, whereunto they retire themselves, living upon that which they take in hunting. This was the cause that during this time, we could get no victuals by their meanes: and had it not beene that I had made good provision thereof, while my men had store, untill the end of Aprill (which was the time when at the uttermost, we hoped to have had succour out of France) I should have beene greatly amazed. This hope was the cause that the souldiers tooke no great care to looke well unto their victuals, although I devided equally among them that which I could get abroad in the countrey, without reserving unto my selfe any more then the least souldier of al the company. The moneth of May approching and no manner of succour come out of France, we fell into extreme want of victuals, constrained to eate the rootes of the earth and certaine sorrell which we found in the fields. For although the Savages were returned by this time unto their villages, yet they succoured us with nothing but certaine fish, without which assuredly wee had perished with famine. Besides they had given us before the greatest part of their maiz and of their beanes for our marchandise. This famine held us from the beginning of May untill the middest of June. During which time the poore souldiers and handicraftsmen became as feeble as might be, and being not able to worke did nothing but goe one after another in Centinel unto the clift of an hill, situate very neere unto the Fort, to see if they might discover any French ship. In fine being frustrated of their hope, they assembled altogether, & came to beseech me to take some order that they might returne into France, considering that if we let passe the season to embarke our selves, we were never like to see our contrey, where it could not be chosen but that some troubles were fallen out, seeing they had broken their promise made unto us, and that no succour was come from thence. Thereupon it was consulted and resolved by all the company, that the barke Breton should be trimmed up, whereof Captaine Vasseur had charge. But because the ship was not bigge enough to receive us all, some thought good to build the Brigandine two deckes higher, which our mutinous souldiers had brought backe, and that 25 men should hazard themselves to passe therein into France. The rest being better advised said that it should be farre better to build a faire shippe upon the keele of the Galiote which I had caused to be made, promising to labour couragiously therupon. Then I enquired of my shipwrights to knowe in what space they could make this shippe readie. They assured the whole company that being furnished with all things necessarie, they would make it readie by the 8. of August. Immediately I disposed of the time to worke upon it, I gave charge to Monsieur de Ottigny my Lieutenant to cause timber necessary for the finishing of both the vessels to be brought, and to Monsieur de Arlac my Standart-bearer to goe with a barke a league off from the Fort to cut downe trees fit to make plankes, and to cause the sawiers which he carried with him to saw them: and to my Sergeant of the company to cause fifteene or sixteene men to labour in making coales: and to Master Hance keeper of the Artillery, & to the gunner to gather store of rosen to bray the vessels: wherein he used such diligence,

that in lesse then 3 weekes he gathered 2 hoghsheads of the same together. There remained now but the principal, which was to recover victuals to sustaine us while our worke endured: which I undertooke to doe with ye rest of my company & the Mariners of the ship. To this end I embarked my selfe making up the thirtieth in my great barke, to make a voyage of forty or fifty leagues, having with us no provision at all of victuals: whereby it may easily be gathered how simply those of our Fort were provided. True it is that certaine souldiers being better husbandes then the rest, and having made some provision of mast, solde a little measure thereof for fifteene and twentie sous unto their companions. During our voyage we lived of nothing else but raspices, of a certaine round graine little and blacke, and of the rootes of palmitos which we got by the river sides: wherein after we had sayled a long time in vaine, I was constrained to returne to the Fort: where the souldiers beginning to be wearie of working, because of the extreme famine which did consume them, assembled themselves and declared unto me, that seeing we could get no victuals of the Indians, it was expedient for the saving of their lives, to seaze upon the person of one of the Kings of the Countrie: assuring themselves that one being taken, the subjects would not suffer our men to want victuals. I made them answere that this enterprise was not rashly to be attempted: But that wee ought to have good regarde unto the consequence that might insue thereof. Hereupon they replyed unto me, that seeing the time was past of our succour from France, & that we were resolved to abandon the Countrie, that there was no danger to constraine the Savages to furnish us with victuals: which for the present I would not grant unto them, but promised them assuredly that I would send to advertise the Indians that they should bring me victuals for exchange of marchandise and apparell: which they also did for the space of certaine daies, during which they brought of their mast and of their fish: which these Indians being traiterous, & mischievous of nature, and knowing our exceeding strange famine, sold us at so deere a price, that for lesse then nothing they had gotten from us al the rest of our marchandise which remained. And which was worse, fearing to be forced by us and seeing that they had gotten all from us, they came no neerer to our Fort then the shot of an Harquebuze. Thither they brought their fish in their little boats, to which our poore souldiers were constrained to goe, and oftentimes (as I have seene) to give away the very shirts from their backs to get one fish. If at any time they shewed unto the Savages the excessive price which they tooke, these villaines would answere them roughly & churlishly: if thou make so great account of thy marchandise, eat it, and we will eat our fish: then fell they out a laughing and mocked us with open throat. Whereupon our souldiers utterly impatient, were oftentimes ready to cut them in pieces, and to make them pay the price of their foolish arrogancie. Notwithstanding considering the importance hereof, I tooke paines to appease the impatient souldier: for I would not by any meanes enter into question with the Savages, & it suffised me to delay the time. Wherefore I devised to send unto Utina to pray him to deale so farre foorth with his subjects, as to succour me with mast and maiz: which he did very sparingly, sending me 12 or 15 baskets of mast, and two of pinocks, which are a kind of little greene fruits which grow among the weedes in the river, and are as big as cheries: yea, & this was not but by giving of them in exchange twise as much marchandise and apparell as they were worth. For the subjectes of Utina perceived evidently the necessitie wherein we were, & began to use the like speech unto us, as the others did: as it is commonly seene that neede altereth mens affections. While these things were in doing, a certain breathing space presented it selfe for Utina gave me to understand that there was a king his subject whose name was Astina, which he determined to take prisoner, and to chastise him for his disobedience: that for this cause, if I would give him aide with a certaine number of my souldiers, he would bring them to the village of Astina, where there was meanes to recover mast and maiz. In the meane season he excused himselfe unto me because he had sent me no more maiz, and sent me word that the little store that he had left, was scarsely sufficient for his seede-corne. Now being somewhat relieved, as I thought, by the hope which I had of this offer, I would not faile to send him the men which he desired of me, which neverthelesse were very evill intreated: for he deceived them, and in stead of leading them against Astina, he caused them to march against his other enemies. My Lieutenant which had the charge of this enterprise with Captaine Vasseur and my Sergeant was determined to be revenged of Utina and to cut him in pieces & his people: and had it not bene that they feared to do any thing against my wil, without all doubt they would have put their enterprise in execution. Therfore they would not passe any further without advertising me thereof. Wherefore being come backe againe unto the Fort, angry & pricked deepely to the quicke for being so mocked, they made their complaints unto me, declaring unto me that they were almost dead for hunger. They told the whole matter to the rest of the souldiers, which were very glad that they had not entred into that action, & resolved, assembling themselves againe together, to let me understand that they did persist in their first deliberation, which was, to punish the boldnesse and maliciousnes of the Savages, which they could no longer endure, & were determined to take one of their kings prisoner: which thing I was enforced to grant unto them, to ye end to avoid a greater mischiefe, and the sedition which I foresaw would ensue, if I had made refusall thereof. For, sayd they, what occasion have you to deny us, considering the necessitie wherein we are, and the small account that they make of us. Shall it not be lawfull for us to punish them for the wrongs which they doe unto us, besides that we know apparantly how little they respect us? Is not this sufficient although there were no necessitie at all, since they thus delude us, and have broken promise with us? After I had therefore resolved with them to seaze on the person of Utina, which besides that he had given us occasion hereof, was also most able to help us to recover victuals, I departed with fiftie of my best souldiers all embarked in two Barkes & we arrived in the dominions of Utina, distant from our Fort about 40 or 50 leagues: then going on shore we drew towards his village situated 6 great leagues from the river, where we tooke him prisoner, howbeit not without great cries and alarmes, and led him away in our barkes, having first signified unto his Father in law and his chiefe subjects, that in that I had taken him, it was not for any desire that I had to doe him any harme, but onely to relieve my necessitie and want of victuals which oppressed me, and that in case they would helpe me to some, I would find meanes to set him againe at libertie: that in the meane space I would retire my selfe into my Barkes (for I feared least they would there assemble themselves together, and that some mischiefe might thereof insue) where I would stay for him two dayes to receive his answere: notwithstanding that my meaning was not to have any thing without exchange of marchandise. This they promised they would doe. And in very deede the very same evening, his wife accompanied with all the women of the village came unto the Rivers brinke, and cryed unto me to enter into the barke, to see her husband and her sonne, which I held both prisoners. I discovered the next day five or sixe hundred Indian archers, which drew neere unto the river side, and came to me to signifie unto me how that during the absence of their king, their enemie Potanou, being thereof advertised, was entred into their village, and had set all on fire. They prayed me that I would succour them: neverthelesse in the meane while they had one part of their troope in ambush, with intent to set upon me if I had come on land, which was easie for mee to discerne. For seeing that I refused so to doe, they greatly doubted that they were discovered, and sought by all meanes to remoove out of my minde that evill opinion which I had conceived of them. They brought mee therefore fish in their little boates and of their meale of Mast, they made also of their drinke which they call cassine, which they sent to Utina and me.

Now albeit I had gotten this point of them that I held their king prisoner, yet neverthelesse I could not get any great quantitie of victuals for the present: the reason was, because they thought that after I had drawen victuals from them, I would put their king to death. For they measured my will according to their custome, whereby they put to death all the men prisoners that they take in warre. And thus being out of all hope of his libertie, they assembled themselves in the great house, and having called all the people together they proposed the election of a new King, at which time the Father in lawe of Utina set one of the kings young sonnes upon the Royall throne: and tooke such paynes that every man did him homage by the major part of the voyces. This election had like to have bene the cause of great troubles among them. For there was a kinsman of the kings neere adjoyning, which pretended a Title to the kingdome, and in deede he had gotten one part of the subjects: notwithstanding this enterprise could not take effect, forasmuch as by a common

consent of the chiefe, it was consulted and concluded, that the sonne was more meete to succeede the Father then any other. Now all this while I kept Utina with me, to whom I had given some of mine apparell to cloth him, as I had likewise done unto his sonne. But his subjects which before had an opinion that I would have killed him, being advertised of the good entertainment which I used towards him, sent two men which walked along the river, and came to visite him, and brought us some victuals. These two men at their comming were received by me with all courtesie, and entertained according to the victuals which I had. While these things thus passed, there arrived from all quarters many Savages of the countries adjoyning, which came to see Utina, and sought by all meanes to perswade me to put him to death, offering that if I would do so, they would take order that I should want no victuals. There was also a King my neighbour whose name was Saturioua, a subtill and craftie man, and one that shewed by proofe that he was greatly practised in affaires. The King sent ordinarily messengers unto me, to pray me to deliver Utina unto him: and to win me the more easily, he sent twise seven or eight baskets of Maiz or of Mast, thinking by this way to allure me, & to make me come to composition with him: in the end notwithstanding when he saw he lost his time, he ceased to visite me with ambassages & victuals: & in the meane while I was not able with ye same store of victuals which I had, so well to proportion out the travaile upon the ships which we built to returne into France, but that in the end we were constrained to indure extreme famine, which continued among us all the moneth of May: for in this latter season, neither Maiz nor Beanes, nor Mast was to be found in the villages, because they had employed all for to sowe their fields, insomuch that we were constrayned to eate rootes, which the most part of our men punned in the morters which I had brought with me to beate gunnepowder in, and the graine which came to us from other places: some tooke the wood of Esquine, beate it, and made meale thereof, which they boyled with water, and eate it: others went with their harquebusies to seeke to kill some foule. Yea this miserie was so great, that one was found that gathered up among the filth of my house, all the fish bones that he could finde, which he dried and beate into powder to make bread thereof. The effects of this hideous famine appeared incontinently among us, for our bones eftsoones beganne to cleave so neere unto the skinne, that the most part of the souldiers had their skinnes peirced thorow with them in many partes of their bodies: in such sort that my greatest feare was, least the Indians would rise up against us, considering that it would have bene very hard for us to have defended our selves in such extreme decay of all our forces, besides the scarsitie of all victuals, which fayled us all at once. For the very river had not such plentie of fish as it was wont, and it seemed that the land and water did fight against us. Now as we were thus upon termes of dispayre, about the end of the moneth of May, and the beginning of June, I was advertised by certaine Indians that were my neighbours, that in the high Countrey up above the river, there was new Maiz, and that that countrey was most forward of all. This caused me to take upon me to go thither with a certaine number of my men, and I went up the river to a place called Enecaque: where I met the sister of Utina in a village where she made us very good cheere and sent us fish. We found that which was tolde us to be true: for the maiz was now ripe: but by this good lucke one shrewde turne happened unto me. For the most part of my souldiers fell sicke with eating more of it then their weakened stomackes could digest. We had also beene the space of foure dayes since we departed from our Fort, without eating any thing, saving little pinockes, and a little fish, which we got of the fishers which wee met sometimes along the river. And yet this was so little that certaine souldiers eate privily little whelpes which were newly whelped. The next day I purposed to go into ye Ile of Edelano to take the king which had caused one of my men to be slaine, as I have mentioned before: but being advertised of my departing out of my Fort, and of the way which I tooke up the river, he feared that I went foorth with a purpose to be revenged of the evill turne which he played: so that when I came thither, I found the houses emptie, for he was retyred a little before with all his people: & I could not by any meanes keepe my souldiers, being angry because they had lost one of their companions, from setting the village on fire. At my departure from thence I passed backe againe by Enecaque, where I gathered as much maiz as I could possibly: which with great diligence I con-

veied to our Fort to succour my poore men, which I had left in great necessitie. They therefore seeing me a farre off comming, ranne to that side of the river where they thought I would come on land: for hunger so pinched them to the heart, that they could not stay untill the victuals were brought them to the Fort. And that they well shewed assoone as I was come, and that I had distributed that little maiz among them, which I had given to ech man, before I came out of the barke: for they eate it before they had taken it out of the huske. But seeing my selfe in this extreme neede, I tooke paines day by day to seeke some villages where there was some food. And as I travailed this way and that way, it happened that two of my Carpenters were killed by the two sonnes of king Emola, and by one whose name was Casti, as they went on walking to the village called Athore. The cause of this murder was, because they could not refraine themselves as they walked through the fields from gathering a little maiz, which as they were doing, they were taken in the manner: whereof I was presently advertised by an Indian which a little before had brought me a present from Nia Cubacani Queene of a village, and neighbour to our Fort. Upon receipt of this advertisement, I sent my Sergeant with a number of souldiers which found nothing else but the 2 dead corpses, which they buried and returned without doing any other exploit, because the inhabitants were fled away, fearing they should be punished for such a foule fact. As these things thus passed, & that by this time we had almost driven out the moneth of May, two subjects of king Utina came unto me with an Hermaphrodite, which shewed mee that by this time the maize was ripe in the greatest part of their quarters. Whereupon Utina signified unto me that in case I would carrie him home to his house, he would take such good order that I should have plentie of maiz & beanes: and withall, that the field which he had caused to be sowen for me, should be reserved to my use. I consulted with my men concerning this matter, and found by the advice of all my company, that it was best to grant him his request, saying, that he had meanes to succour us with food sufficient to serve our turnes for our embarkement, and that therefore I might do well to carry him home. Wherefore I caused the two barks forthwith to be made readie, wherin I sailed to Patica, a place distant from his village 8 or 9 leagues, where I found no bodie, for they were gotten into the woods, and would not shew themselves, albeit Utina shewed himselfe unto them, for as much as they imagined that I should be constrained to let him go. But seeing no body to shew themselves, I was constrained to hazard one of my men which had bene acquainted with the state of the countrie, to whom I delivered the young sonne of Utina, and commanded him to goe with diligence to the village of Utina, unto his father in law and his wife, to advertise them that if they would have their king againe, they should bring me victuals unto the side of the little river whither I was gone. At my mans comming every one made much of the little childe, neither was there a man that thought not himselfe well appaide to touch him. His father in law and his wife hearing of these newes came presently towards our barkes, and brought bread which they gave unto my souldiers, they held me there three dayes, and in the meane while did all that they could to take me: which presently I discovered, and therefore stood diligently upon my gard. Wherefore perceiving they could not have their purpose, and that they were already discovered, they sent to advertise me that as yet they could not helpe me to victuals, and that the corne was not yet ripe. Thus I was constrained to returne and to carry backe Utina home, where I had much adoe to save him from the rage of my souldiers: which perceiving the maliciousnes of the Indians, went about to have murdered him. Moreover it seemed they were content that they had gotten the sonne, & that they cared not greatly for the father. Now my hope fayling me on this side, I devised to send my men to the villages where I thought the maiz was by this time ripe; I went to divers places, and continued so doing 15 daies after, when as Utina besought me again to send him unto his village, assuring himselfe that his subjects would not sticke to give me victuals: and that in case they refused so to do, he was content that I should do what I thought good with him. I undertooke this voyage the second time with the two barkes furnished as before. At my comming unto the little river, we found his subjects there, which failed not to come thither with some quantitie of bread, beanes, and fish, to give my souldiers. Neverthelesse returning againe to their former practise they sought all meanes to entrap me, hoping to

cry quittance for the imprisonment of their king, if they might have gotten the victorie of me. But after that they sawe the small meanes, which they had to annoy me, they returned to intreaties, and offered that if I would give them their king with certaine of my souldiers, they would conduct them unto the village, and that the subjects seeing him, would be more willing to give us victuals. Which thing notwithstanding I would not grant unto them (mistrusting their subtilitie, which was not so covert, but that one might espie day at a little hole) untill they had first given me two men in pledge with charge that by the next day they should bring me victuals. Which thing they granted, and gave mee two men which I put in chaines for feare they should escape away, as I knew well they were instructed to doe. Foure dayes were spent in these conferences, at the end whereof they declared unto me, that they could not fully and wholly performe their promise: and that the uttermost that they could doe for the present, was to cause each subject to bring his burthen of mill. To conclude, they were content to doe so on condition that I would send them their two pledges within ten dayes. As my Lieutenant was ready to depart, I warned him above all things to take heede he fell not into the Indians hands: because I knew them to be very subtill and craftie to enterprize and execute any thing to our disadvantage. He departed therefore with his troope, and came to the small river whereinto we were accustomed to enter to approach as neere as we could unto the village of Utina, being six French leagues distance from thence. There he went on shore, put his men in good array, and drew streight towards the great house that was the kings, where the chief men of the countrey were assembled, which caused very great store of victuals to be brought now one and then another, in doing whereof they spent notwithstanding three or foure dayes: in which meane while they gathered men together, to set upon us in our retreit. They used therefore many meanes to holde us still in breath. For one while they demanded their pledges, another while (seeing my Lieutenant would not yield to them, untill such time as they had brought the victuals unto the boats; according to the agreement passed betwene us) they signified unto him that the women and young children were affraide out of all measure to see fire in their matches so neere their harquebuses: and that therefore they most earnestly besought them to put them out, that they might more easily get people ynough to carry the victuals, and that they for their partes would leave their bowes and arrowes, and would be contented that their servants should carrie them. This second request was as flatly denied them as the former: For it was an easie matter to smel out their intention. But while these things were thus in handling, Utina by no meanes was to be seene, but hid and kept himselfe secret in a little house apart, where certaine chosen men of mine went to see him shewing themselves agreeved with him for the long delayes of his subjects: whereunto he answered, that his subjects were so much incensed against us, that by no meanes possible he was able to keepe them in such obedience as he willingly would have done, and that he could not hold them from waging of warre against Monsieur de Ottigny. That he also called to minde, that even while he was prisoner, at what time our men ledde him into his Country to obtaine some victuals, he saw along the high wayes arrowes stucke up, at the endes whereof long haires were fastened, which was a certaine signe of open warre proclaimed, which arrowes the Captaine also carried with him to the fort. He said further that in respect of the good will he bare to the Captaine, he forewarned his Lieutenant that his subjects were determined to cut downe the trees, and cause them to fall a thwart the little river where the boates were, to keepe them from departing thence, that they might fight with them at their ease, and that if it thus fell out, he assured him for his part he would not be there to meddle in the matter. And that which much more augmented the suspition of warre was, that as my messengers departed from Utina, they heard the voyce of one of my men, which during the voyage had alwayes beene among the Indians, and whom as yet they would never render, untill they had gotten their pledges home. This poore fellow cryed out a maine because two Indians would have carried him into the woods to have cut his throat: whereupon he was succoured and delivered. These admonitions being well understoode, after ripe deliberation thereof Monsieur de Ottigny resolved to retire himselfe the seven and twentieth of July. Wherefore he set his souldiers in order, and delivered to ech of them a sacke full of mill: and afterward hee marched toward his

barkes, thinking to prevent the enterprise of the savages. There is at the comming foorth of the village a great alley about three or foure hundred paces long, which is covered on both sides with great trees. My Lieutenant disposed his men in this alley and set them in such order as they desired to march: for he was well assured that if there were any ambush, it would be at the comming out of the trees. Therefore he caused Monsieur de Arlac mine Ensigne to march somewhat before with 8 harquebusiers to discover whether there were any danger: besides he commanded one of my Sergeants & Corporals to march on the out side of the alley with foure harquebusiers while he himselfe conducted the rest of his company through it. Now as he suspected, so it fell out: for Monsieur de Arlac met with two or three hundred Indians at the end of the alley, which saluted him with an infinite number of their arrowes, & with such furie that it was easie to see with what desire they sought to charge us. Howbeit they were so well sustained in the first assault which mine Ensigne gave them, that they which fell downe dead, did somewhat abate the choler of those which remained alive. This done my Lieutenant hasted to gaine ground in such sort as I have already said. After he had marched about foure hundred paces, he was charged afresh with a newe troope of Savages which were in number about 300, which assayled him before, while the rest of the former set upon him behind. This second assault was so valiantly sustayned, that I may justly say that Monsieur de Ottigny so well discharged his dutie, as was possible for a good Captaine to doe. And so it stood them upon: for he had to deale with such kind of men, as knewe well how to fight and to obey their head which conducted them, and which knewe so well to behave themselves in this conflict, as if Ottigny had not prevented their practise, he had beene in danger to have bene defeated. Their maner in this fight was, that when two hundred had shot, they retyred themselves and gave place to the rest that were behind, and all the while had their eye and foot so quicke and readie, that assoone as ever they saw the harquebuze laide to the cheeke, so soone were they on the ground, and eftsoone up to answere with their bowes and to flie their way, if by chance they perceived we went about to take them: for there is nothing that they feare so much, because of our swords and daggers. This conflict continued and lasted from nine of the clocke in the morning, until the night departed them. And if Ottigny had not bethought himselfe to cause his men to breake the arrowes which they found in the way, & so to deprive the Savages of the means to beginne againe, without all doubt he should have had very much to do: for by this meane they lacked arrowes, and so were constrained to retire themselves. During the time of the conflict they cryed and made signes that they were the Captaines and Lieutenants friends: and that they fought for none other cause but to be revenged on the souldiers, which were their mortall enemies. My Lieutenant being come unto his boates tooke a review of his companie, and found two men wanting which were killed, of whom the one was called James Sale, and the others name was Mesureur. He found moreover 22 of them wounded, which with much adoe he caused to be brought unto the boates. All the mill that he found among his company came but to two mens burdens, which he devided equally among them. For assoone as the conflict began, every man was constrained to leave his sacke to put his hand to his weapon. In this meane while I remained at the Forte, and caused every man diligently to travell, hoping that my Lieutenant would bring us victuals. But seeing the time consume away, I began to suspect the truth of that which fell out, whereof I was assured immediately after at their returne. Seeing therefore mine hope frustrate on that side, I made my prayer unto God, and thanked him of his grace which hee had shewed unto my poore souldiers which were escaped: Afterward I thought upon new meanes to obtaine victuals, aswell for our returne into France, as to drive out the time untill our embarking. I was advertised by certaine of our company, which usually went on hunting into the woods and through the villages, that in the village Sarauahi situated on the other side of the river, and two leagues distant from the Forte, and in the village Emoloa there were fields wherein the mill was very forward, and that there was thereof in those partes in great abundance. Wherefore I caused my boates to be made ready, and sent my Sergeant thither with certaine souldiours, which used such diligence, that wee had good store of mill. I sent also to the river which the Savages call Iracana, named by Captaine Ribault the River of Somme, where Captaine

Vasseur and my Sergeant arrived with two boates and their ordinary furniture, and found there a great assembly of the Lords of the countrey, among whome was Athore the sonne of Satourioua, Apalou, and Tacadocorou, which were there assembled to make merrie: because that in this place are the fairest maids and women of all the countrey. Captaine Vasseur in my name gave certaine small trifles to all the Lords, to the Queene, to the maids and women of the villages. Whereupon the boates were foorthwith laden with mill, after they had made our men as good cheere as they could devise. The Queene sent me two small Mats so artificially wrought as it was unpossible to make better. Nowe finding our selves by this meane sufficiently furnished with victuals, we began each of us in his place, to travaile and use such diligence, as the desire to see our native countrey might moove us. But because two of our Carpenters were slaine by the Indians (as heretofore I mentioned) John de Hais, master Carpenter, a man very worthy of his vocation, repaired unto me, and tolde me that by reason of want of men hee was not able to make me up the ship against the time that he had promised me: which speech caused such a mutinie among the souldiers that very hardly he escaped killing: howbeit I appeased them aswell as I could, and determined to worke no more from thencefoorth upon the shippe, but to content our selves to repaire the Brigandine which I had. So we began to beate downe all the houses that were without the Fort, and caused coles to be made of the timber thereof: likewise the souldiers beate downe the pallisade which was toward the waters side, neither was I ever able to keepe them from doing it. I had also determined to beate downe the Fort before my departure and to set it on fire, for feare least some new-come guest should have enjoyed and possessed it. In the meane while there was none of us to whom it was not an extreme griefe to leave a countrey, wherein wee had endured so great travailes and necessities, to discover that which we must forsake through our owne countreymens default. For if wee had bene succoured in time & place, & according to the promise that was made unto us, the warre which was between us and Utina, had not fallen out, neither should wee have had occasion to offend the Indians, which with all paines in the world I entertained in good amitie, aswell with merchandise and apparel, as with promise of greater matters, and with whom I so behaved myself, that although sometimes I was constrained to take victuals in some few villages, yet I lost not the alliance of eight Kings and Lords my neighbours, which continually succoured and ayded me with whatsoever they were able to afford. Yea this was the principall scope of all my purposes, to winne and entertaine them, knowing how greatly their amitie might advance our enterprise, and principally while I discovered the commodities of the countrey, and sought to strengthen my selfe therein. I leave it to your cogitation to thinke how neere it went to our hearts, to leave a place abounding in riches (as we were throughly enformed thereof) in comming whereunto, and doing service unto our Prince, we left our owne countrey, wives, children, parents, and friends, and passed the perils of the sea, and were therein arrived, as in a plentifull treasure of all our hearts desire. As ech of us were much tormented in minde with these or such like cogitations, the third of August I descried foure sayles in the sea, as I walked upon a little hill, whereof I was exceeding well apaid: I sent immediately one of them which were with me to advertise those of the Fort thereof, which were so glad of those newes, that one would have thought them to bee out of their wittes to see them laugh and leape for joy. After these ships had cast anker, we descried that they sent one of their ship boates to land: whereupon I caused one of mine to be armed with diligence to send to meete them, and to know who they were. In the meane while, fearing lest they were Spaniards, I set my souldiers in order and in readinesse, attending the returne of Captaine Vasseur and my Lieutenant, which where gone to meete them, which brought me word that they were Englishmen: and in trueth they had in their company one whose name was Martine Atinas of Diepe, which at that time was in their service, which on the behalfe of Master John Hawkins their Generall came to request mee that I would suffer them to take fresh water, whereof they stood in great neede, signifying unto me that they had bene above fifteene dayes on the coast to get some. Hee brought unto mee from the Generall two flagons of wine, and bread made of wheate: which greatly refreshed me, forasmuch as for seven moneths space I never tasted a drop of wine: neverthelesse it was all divided among the

greatest part of my souldiers. This Martine Atinas had guided the Englishmen unto our coast, wherewith he was acquainted: for in the yeere 1562 he came thither with me, and therefore the Generall sent him to me. Therefore after I had granted his request, hee signified the same unto the Generall, which the next day following caused one of his small shippes to enter into the river, and came to see me in a great shipboate, accompanied with gentlemen honourably apparelled, yet unarmed. He sent for great store of bread and wine, to distribute thereof to every one: On my part I made him the best cheere I could possibly, and caused certaine sheepe and poultry to be killed, which untill this present I had carefully preserved hoping to store the countrey withall. For notwithstanding all the necessities and sicknesse that happened unto me, I would not suffer so much as one chicken to be killed: by which meanes in a short time I had gathered together above an hundred pullets. Nowe three dayes passed, while the English General remained with me, during which time the Indians came in from all parts to see him, and asked me whether he were my brother: I tolde them he was so, and signified unto them, that he was come to see me and ayde me with so great store of victuals, that from thence forward I should have no neede to take any thing of them. The bruite hereof incontinently was spread over all the countrey, in such sort as Ambassadours came unto me from all parts, which on the behalfe of the kings their masters desired to make alliance with me: and even they, which before sought to make warre against me, came to offer their friendship and service unto me: Whereupon I received them and gratified them with certaine presents. The General immediately understood the desire & urgent occasion which I had to returne into France: whereupon he offred to transport me and all my company home: whereunto notwithstanding I would not agree, being in doubt upon what occasion he made so large an offer. For I knewe not how the case stood betweene the French and the English: and although hee promised me on his faith to put mee on land in France, before hee would touch in England, yet I stood in doubt least he would attempt somewhat in Florida in the name of his mistresse. Wherfore I flatly refused his offer: whereupon there arose a great mutinie among my souldiers, which sayd that I sought to destroy them all, and that the Brigandine, wherof I spake before, was not sufficient to transport them, considering the season of the yeere wherein wee were. The bruite and mutiny increased more and more: for after that the Generall was returned to his ships, he told certaine gentlemen and souldiers which went to see him, partly to make good cheere with him, hee declared, I say unto them, that he greatly doubted that hardly we should be able to passe safely in those vessels which we had: and that in case we should enterprise the same, we should no doubt be in great jeopardy: notwithstanding, if I were so contented, he would transport part of my men in his ships, and that he would leave me a small ship to transport the rest. The souldiers were no sooner come home, but they signified the offer unto their companions, which incontinently consented together that in case I would not accept the same, they would embarke themselves with him and forsake mee, so that he would receive them according to his promise. They therefore assembled themselves all together and came to seeke me in my chamber, and signified unto me their intention, wherunto I promised to answere within one houre after. In which meane space I gathered together the principall members of my company, which after I had broken the matter with them, answered me all with one voyce, that I ought not to refuse this offer, nor contemne the occasion which presented it selfe, and that they could not thinke evill of it in France, if being forsaken, as we were, we aided our selves with such means as God had sent us. After sundry debatings of this matter, in conclusion I gave mine advise, that wee ought to deliver him the price of the ship which he was to leave us, and that for my part I was content to give him the best of my stuffe, and the silver which I had gathered in the countrey. Wherupon notwithstanding it was determined that I should keepe the silver, for feare lest the Queene of England seeing the same, should the rather bee encouraged to set footing there, as before she had desired: that it was far better to carie it into France to give encouragement unto our Princes not to leave off an enterprise of so great importance for our commonwealth, and that seeing wee were resolved to depart, it was farre better to give him our Artillerie, which otherwise we should be constrained to leave behind us, or to hide it in the ground by reason of the weakenesse

of our men, being not able to embarke the same. This point being thus concluded and resolved on, I went my selfe unto the English Generall, accompanied with my Lieutenant, and Captaine Vasseur, Captaine Verdier, and Trenchant the Pilot, and my Sergeant, all men of experience in such affaires and knowing sufficiently how to drive such a bargaine. We therefore tooke a view of the ship which the Generall would sell, whom we drew to such reason, that he was content to stand to mine owne mens judgement, who esteemed it to be worth seven hundreth crowns, whereof we agreed very friendly. Wherefore I delivered him in earnest of the summe, two bastards, two mynions, one thousand of iron, & one thousand of powder. This bargaine thus made, he considered the necessity wherin we were, having for all our sustenance but mill and water: wherupon being moved with pitie, he offred to relieve me with 20 barels of meale, six pipes of beanes, one hogshead of salt, and a hundred of waxe to make candels. Moreover forasmuch as he sawe my souldiers goe barefoote, hee offred me besides fifty paires of shoes, which I accepted and agreed of a price with him, and gave him a bill of mine hand for the same, for which untill this present I am indebted to him. He did more then this: for particularly he bestowed upon my selfe a great jarre of oyle, a jarre of vineger, a barell of Olives, and a great quantitie of Rice, and a barell of white Biscuit. Besides he gave divers presents to the principall Officers of my company according to their qualities: so that I may say that we received as many courtesies of the Generall, as it was possible to receive of any man living. Wherein doubtlesse he hath wonne the reputation of a good and charitable man, deserving to be esteemed asmuch of us all as if he had saved all our lives. Incontinent after his departure I spared no paine to hasten my men to make biscuits of the meale which he had left me, and to hoope my caske to take in water needfull for the voyage. A man may well thinke what diligence we used, in respect of the great desire we had to depart, wherein we continued so well, that the fifteenth day of August the biscuit, the greatest part of our water, & all the souldiers stuffe was brought aboord: so that from that day forward wee did nothing but stay for good windes to drive us into France: which had freed us from an infinite number of mischiefes which afterward wee suffred, if they had come as we desired: but it was not Gods good pleasure, as shall appeare hereafter. Being thus in a readinesse to set sayle, we bethought our selves that it would doe well to bring certaine men and women of the countrey into France, to the end that if this voyage should be taken in hand againe they might declare unto their Kings the greatnesse of our King, the excellencie of our Princes, the goodnesse of our Countrey, and the maner of living of the Frenchmen: and that they might also learne our language, to serve our turnes thereby in time to come. Wherein I tooke so good order, that I found meanes to bring away with me the goodliest persons of all the countrey, if our intentions had succeeded as I hoped they would have done. In the meane season the Kings my neighbours came often to see and visite me: which, after that they understood that I would returne into France, demanded of mee whether I meant to returne againe or no, and whether it should be in short time. I signified unto them that within tenne Moones (so they call their Moneths) I would visite them againe with such force, that I would be able to make them Conquerours over all their enemies. They prayed me that I would leave them my house, that I would forbid my souldiers to beate downe the Fort and their lodgings, and that I would leave them a boate to ayde them withall in their warre against their enemies. Which I made as though I would grant unto them, to the end I might alwaies remaine their friend until my last departure.

303. 1565. René de Laudonnière on "The third voyage of the Frenchmen made by Captain John Ribault unto Florida."

Laudonnière's account of the arrival of Jean Ribault to supersede him and the subsequent overthrow of the colony by the Spaniards is very much a case in his own defense against inevitable charges of having been surprised and routed in ignominious circumstances by Pedro Menéndez de Avilés. He makes a case for himself, if not a wholly convincing one, by blaming Jean Ribault for attempting with great rashness to destroy the Spaniards by a single blow at sea, while leaving Laudonnière in charge of a fort that was so ruined that it was indefensible. He must remain culpable for not pushing ahead with the reconstruction of the fort, at least on a temporary basis, and for laxity in maintaining his guard at night. His account of the Spanish attack, his own escape, and the rigors of his return to Europe are well told, but Ribault remains (with the Spaniards of course) the villain of the piece.

The narrative formed apparently the third and final part of his manuscript, to which a fourth was added by its editor, Martin Basanier in L'histoire notable de la Floride *(Paris, 1586), fols. 99-114; in R. Hakluyt's translation,* A notable historie *(London, 1587), fols. 18ff.; reprinted in* Principal navigations, *III (1600), 349-356 (IX [1904]), 82-100, which is reprinted here.*

The third voyage of the Frenchmen made by Captaine John Ribault unto Florida

As I was thus occupied in these conferences, the winde and the tide served well to set sayle, which was the eight and twentieth of August, at which instant Captaine Vasseur which commanded in one of my shippes, and Captaine Verdier which was chiefe in the other, now ready to goe foorth, began to descry certaine sayles at sea, whereof they advertised mee with diligence: whereupon I appointed to arme foorth a boate in good order to goe to discrie and know what they were. I sent also to the Centinels, which I caused to be kept on a little knappe, to cause certaine men to climbe up to the toppe of the highest trees the better to discover them. They descried the great boate of the shippes, which as yet they could not perfectly discerne, which as farre as they could judge, seemed to chase my boate, which by this time was passed the barre of the river: so that we could not possibly judge whether they were enemies which would have caried her away with them: for it was too great a ken to judge the trueth thereof. Upon this doubt I put my men in order and in such array as though they had beene enemies: and indeede I had great occasion to mistrust the same: for my boate came unto their ship about two of the clocke in the afternoone, and sent me no newes all that day long to put me out of doubt who they should be. The next day in the morning about eight or nine of the clocke I saw seven boates (among which mine owne was one) full of souldiers enter into the river, having every man his harquebuze and morion on his head, which marched all in battaile along the cliffes where my centinels were, to whom they would make no kind of answere, notwithstanding all the demandes that were made unto them, insomuch as one of my souldiers was constrained to bestowe a shot at them without doing hurt neverthelesse to any of them, by reason of the distance between him and the boates. The report hereof being made unto me, I placed each of my men in his quarter, with full deliberation to defend our selves, if they had bene enemies, as in trueth wee thought them to have bene: likewise I caused the two small field-pieces which I had left me, to be trimmed in such sort, as if in approching to the Fort they had not cryed that it was Captaine Ribault, I had not failed to have discharged the same upon them. Afterward I understood that the cause why they entred in this maner, proceeded of the false reports which had bene made unto my Lord Admirall by those which were returned into France in the first shippes. For they had put in his head, that I played the Lord and the King, and that I would hardly suffer that any other save my selfe should enter in thither to governe there. Thus we see how the good name of the most honest is oftentimes assayled by such, as having no meanes to win themselves credit by vertuous and laudable endevours, thinke by debasing of other mens vertues to augment the feeble force of their faint courage, which neverthelesse is one of the most notable dangers which may happen in a commonwealth, and chiefly among men of warre which are placed in government. For it is very hard, yea utterly unpossible, that in governing of a company of men gathered out of divers places and sundry Nations, and namely such as we know them to be in our warres, it is, I say, unpossible, but there will be always some of evill conditions and hard to be ruled, which easily conceive an hatred against him, which by admonitions and light corrections endevoureth to reduce them to the discipline of warre. For they seeke nothing else, but for a small occasion grounded upon a light pretext to sound into the eares of great Lords that which mischievously they have contrived against those, whose execution of justice is odious unto them. And albeit I will not place my selfe in the ranke of great and renowmed Captaines, such as lived in times passed, yet we may

judge by their examples, how hurtfull backbiters have beene unto commonwealths. I will onely take Alcibiades for witnesse in the commonwealth of the Athenians, which by this meane was cast into banishment, whereupon his citizens felt the smart of an infinite number of mischiefes: insomuch as in the end they were constrained to call him home againe, and acknowledge at length the fault they had committed in forgetting his good services, and rather beleeving a false report, then having had regard unto so many notable exploits which in former time hee had atchieved. But that I loose not my selfe in digressing so farre in this my justification, I will returne againe to my first course. Being therfore advertised that it was Captaine Ribault, I went foorth of the Fort to goe to meete him, and to do him all the honour I could by any meanes, I caused him to be welcommed with the artillery, and a gentle volley of my shot, whereunto he answered with his. Afterward being come on shore and received honourably with joy, I brought him to my lodging, rejoycing not a little because that in this company I knew a good number of my friends, which I intreated in the best sorte that I was able, with such victuals as I could get in the countrey, and that small store which I had left me, with that which I had of the English General. Howbeit I marveiled not a little when as all of them with one voice began to utter unto me these or the like speeches. My Captaine, we praise God that we have found you alive, and chiefly because we know, that the reports which have bene made of you, are false. These speeches mooved me in such sort, that I would needes out of hand know more, mistrusting some evill. Wherefore having accosted Captaine John Ribault, & going both of us aside together out of the Fort, he signified unto me the charge which he had, praying mee not to returne into France, but to stay with him my selfe and my company, and assured me that he would make it well thought of at home. Whereupon I replyed that out of this place I would do him all service: that for the present I could not nor ought not accept this offer, since he was come for no other intent then to occupie the place which I before possessed, that I could have no credite to be there commanded: that my friends would never like of it, and that he would hardly give me that counsaile, if in good earnest I should demand his advise therein. He made me answere, that he would not command me, that we should be companions, & that he would build another fortresse, & that he would leave mine owne unto me. This notwithstanding I fully advertised him that I could not receive a greater comfort then the newes which he brought me to returne into France: and farther that though I should stay there, yet it must needes be that one of us both was to command with title of the Kings Lieutenant, that this could not well agree together: that I had rather have it cast in my teeth to be the poorest begger in the world, then to be commanded in that place, where I had endured so much to inhabite and plant there, if it were not by some great Lord or Knight of the order: and that in these respects I prayed him very hartily to deliver me the letters which my Lord Admirall had written unto me, which he performed.

The contents of those letters were these

Captaine Laudonniere, because some of them which are returned from Florida speake indifferently of the Countrey, the King desireth your presence, to the end, that according to your tryall, he may resolve to bestow great cost thereon, or wholly to leave it: and therfore I send Captaine John Ribault to bee governour there, to whom you shall deliver whatsoever you have in charge, and informe him of all things you have discovered. And in a postscript of the letter was thus written. Thinke not, that whereas I send for you, it is for any evill opinion or mistrust that I have of you, but that it is for your good and for your credit, and assure your selfe that during my life you shall find me your good Master.
    [signed:] Chastillon.

Now after I had long discoursed with Captaine Ribault, Captaine la Grange accosted mee, and told me of an infinite number of false reports which had bene made of mee to my great hinderance: and among other things he informed me, that my Lord Admirall tooke it very evill that I had caried a woman with mee: likewise that some bodie had tolde him that I went about to counterfeit the King, and to play the tyrant: that I was too cruell unto the men that went with mee: that I sought to be advanced by other meanes then by my Lord Admirall: and that I had written to many Lords of the Court, which I ought not to have done. Whereunto I answered, that the woman

was a poore chambermayd, which I had taken up in an Inne, to oversee my houshold businesse, to looke to an infinite sort of divers beasts, as sheepe and poultrie which I caried over with me to store the countrey withall: that it was not meete to put a man to attend this businesse: likewise, considering the length of the time that I was to abide there, mee though it should not offend any body to take a woman with me, aswell to help my souldiers in their sickenesses, as in mine owne, whereinto I fell afterward. And how necessary her service was for us, ech one at that time might easily perceive: That all my men thought so well of her, that at one instant there were sixe or seven which did demand her of me in mariage; as in very deede one of them had her after our returne. Touching that which was sayd that I playd the King, these reports were made, because I would not beare with any thing which was against the duety of my charge, and the Kings service. Moreover, that in such enterprises it is necessary for a Governour to make himselfe knowen and obeyed, for feare least every body would become a master, perceiving themselves far from greater forces. And that if the tale-tellers called this rigour, it rather proceeded of their disobedience, then of my nature lesse subject to cruelty then they were to rebellion. For the two last points, that I had not written to any of the Lords of the Court but by the advice & commandement of my Lord Admirall, which willed me at my departure to send part of such things as I should find in the countrey unto the Lords of the Counsel: to the end that being mooved by this meane, they might deale with the Queene mother for the continuance of this enterprise: that having bene so small time in the countrey, continually hindred with building of fortresses, and unlading of my ships, I was not able to come by any newe or rare things to send them, whereupon I thought it best to content them in the meane while with letters, untill such time as I might have longer space to search out the Countrey, and might recover something to sende them: the distribution of which letters I meant not otherwise but to referre to my Lord Admirals good pleasure: that if the bearer had forgot himselfe so farre, as that he had broken the covering of the letters, and presented them himselfe for hope of gaine, it was not my commandment. And that I never honoured noble man so much, nor did to any man more willing and faithfull service then to my Lord Admirall, nor ever sought advancement but by his meanes. You see how things passed for this day. The next day the Indians came in from all parts, to know what people these were: to whom I signified that this was he which in the yeere 1562. arrived in this countrey, and erected the pillar which stood at the entrie of the river. Some of them knew him: for in trueth he was easie to be knowen by reason of the great bearde which he ware. He received many presents of them which were of the villages neere adjoyning, among whom there were some that he had not yet forgotten. The kings Homoloa, Serauahi, Alimacani, Malica, and Casti came to visit him and welcome him with divers gifts according to their manner. I advertised them that hee was sent thither by the king of France, to remaine there in my roome, and that I was sent for. Then they demanded and prayed him, if it might stand with his good pleasure, to cause the merchandise that hee had brought with him to be delivered them, and that in fewe daies they would bring him to the mountaines of Apalatcy, whither they had promised to conduct me, and that in case they performed not their promise, that they were content to be cut in pieces. In those mountaines, as they sayd, is found redde copper, which they call in their language Sieroa Pira, which is as much to say as red mettall, whereof I had a piece, which at the very instant I shewed to Captaine Ribault, which caused his gold-finer to make an assay thereof, which reported unto him that it was perfect golde. About the time of these conferences, commings and goings of the kings of the countrey, being weakened with my former travaile, and fallen into a melancholy upon the false reports that had bene made of mee, I fell into a great continuall fever, which held me eight or nine dayes: during which time Captaine Ribault caused his victuals to be brought on shore, and bestowed the most part thereof in the house which my Lieutenant had built about two hundred pases without the forte: which hee did to the ende they might bee the better defended from the weather, and likewise to the intent that the meale might bee neerer to the bake-house, which I had built of purpose in that place, the better to avoide the danger of the fire, as I sayd before. But loe howe oftentimes misfortune doth search and pursue us, even then when we thinke to be at rest! loe see what happened after that captaine Ribault

had brought up three of his small ships into the river, which was the fourth of September! Six great Spanish ships arrived in the rode, where four of our greatest ships remained, which cast anker, assuring our men of good amity. They asked how the chiefe captaine of the enterprise did, & called them all by their names and surnames. I report me to you if it could be otherwise but these men before they went out of Spaine must needs be informed of the enterprise & of those that were to execute the same. About the breake of day they began to make toward our men: but our men which trusted them never a deale, had hoysed their sailes by night, being ready to cut the strings that tyed them. Wherefore perceiving that this making toward our men of the Spaniards was not to doe them any pleasure, and knowing wel that their furniture was too smal to make head against them, because that the most part of their men were on shore, they cut their cables, left their ankers, and set saile. The Spaniards seeing themselves discovered, lent them certaine volleis of their great ordinance, made saile after them, and chased them all day long: but our men got way of them still toward the sea. And the Spaniards seeing they could not reach them, by reason that the French ships were better of saile then theirs, and also because they would not leave the coast, turned backe and went on shore in the river Seloy, which we cal the river of Dolphines 8 or 10 leagues distant from the place where we were. Our men therefore finding themselves better of saile then they, followed them to descry what they did, which after they had done, they returned unto the river of May, where captaine Ribault having descried them, embarked himselfe in a great boat to know what newes they had. Being at the entry of the river he met with the boat of captaine Cousets ship, wherin there was a good number of men which made relation unto him of all the Spaniards doings: and how the great ship named the Trinitie had kept the sea, and that she was not returned with them. They told him moreover that they had seen three Spanish ships enter into the river of Dolphins, & the other three remained in the rode; farther that they had put their souldiers, their victuals & munition on land. After he understood these newes hee returned to the fortresse, and came to my chamber where I was sick, and there in the presence of the captaines, La Grange, S. Marie,

Ottigny, Visty, Yonville, and other gentlemen, he propounded, that it was necessary for the kings service, to embarke himselfe with all his forces, and with the three ships that were in the rode to seeke the Spanish fleete, whereupon he asked our advise. I first replyed, and shewed unto him the consequence of such an enterprise, advertising him among other things of the perilous flawes of windes that rise on this coast, and that if it chanced that hee were driven from the shore, it would be very hard for him to recover it againe, that in the meane while they which should stay in the Forte should be in feare and danger. The Captaines, Saint Marie, and La Grange declared unto him farther, that they thought it not good to put any such enterprise in execution, that it was farre better to keepe the land, & do their best indevour to fortifie themselves: And that after that the Trinitie (which was the principall ship) were returned, there would be much more likelyhood to enterprise this voyage. This notwithstanding he resolved to undertake it, and that which more is, after he understoode by king Emola, one of our neighbours which arrived upon the handling of these matters, that the Spaniards in great numbers were gone on shore, which had taken possession of the houses of Seloy, in the most part whereof they had placed their Negros, which they had brought to labour, and also lodged themselves and had cast divers trenches about them. Thus for the considerations which he had, and doubting (as he might well doe) that the Spanyards would encampe themselves there to molest us, and in the ende to chase us out of the Countrey, he resolved and continued in his embarkment, caused a Proclamation to be made, that all souldiers that were under his charge should presently with their weapons embarke them, and that his two ensignes should march: which was put in execution. He came into my chamber, and prayed me to lend him my Lieutenant, mine ensigne, and my sergeant, and to let all my good souldiers, which I had, goe with him, which I denied him, because my selfe being sicke, there was no man to stay in the fort. Thereupon he answered me that I needed not to doubt at all, and that he would returne the morrow after, that in the meane space Monsieur de Lys should stay behind to looke to all things. Then I shewed unto him that he was chiefe in this Countrey, and that I for my part had no further authoritie: that there-

fore he would take good advisement what hee did, for feare least some inconvenience might ensue. Then he tolde me that he could doe no lesse, then to continue this enterprise, and that in the letter which he had received from my Lord Admirall, there was a postscript, which hee shewed mee written in these wordes: Captaine John Ribault, as I was enclosing up this letter, I received a certaine advice, that Don Pedro Melendes departeth from Spaine to goe to the coast of Newe France: see you that you suffer him not to encroch upon you, no more then he would that you should encroch upon him. You see (quoth he) the charge that I have, and I leave it unto your selfe to judge, if you could do any lesse in this case, considering the certaine advertisement that we have, that they are already on lande, and will invade us. This stopped my mouth. Thus therefore confirmed or rather obstinate in this enterprise, and having regard rather unto his particular opinion then unto the advertisements which I had given him, and the inconveniences of the time whereof I had forewarned him, he embarked himselfe the eight of September, and tooke mine ensigne and eight and thirtie of my men away with him. I report mee to those that know what warres meane, if when an ensigne marcheth, any souldier that hath any courage in him will stay behind, to forsake his ensigne: Thus no man of commandement stayed behind with mee, for ech one followed him as chiefe, in whose name straight after his arrivall, all cries and proclamations were made. Captaine Grange, which liked not very well of this enterprise, was unto the tenth of the moneth with mee, and would not have gone aborde, if it had not beene for the instant requestes that Captaine Ribault made unto him, which staid two dayes in the rode attending untill La Grange was come unto him: Who being come abord, they set sayle altogether, and from that time forward I never saw them more. The very day that he departed, which was the tenth of September, there rose so great a tempest accompanied with such stormes, that the Indians themselves assured me that it was the worst weather that ever was seene on the coast: whereupon two or three dayes after, fearing least our ships might be in some distresse, I sent for Monsieur du Luys unto mee, to take order to assemble the rest of our people to declare unto them what neede wee had to fortifie our selves: which was done accordingly: and then I gave them to understand the necessity and inconveniences whereinto we were like to fall, aswel by the absence of our ships, as by the neerenesse of the Spanyards, at whose hands we could looke for no lesse then an open and sufficient proclamed war, seeing they had taken land and fortified themselves so neere unto us. And if any misfortune were fallen unto our men which were at Sea, we ought to make a full account with our selves that wee were to endure many great miseries, being in so small number, and so many wayes afflicted as we were. Thus every one promised mee to take paines: and therefore considering that their proportion of victuals was small, and that so continuing, they would not bee able to doe any great worke, I augmented their allowance: although that after the arrivall of Captaine Ribault my portion of victuals was allotted unto mee as unto a common souldier, neither was I able to give so much as part of a bottell of wine to any man which deserved it: for I was so farre from having meanes to doe so, that the Captaine himselfe tooke two of my boates, wherein the rest of the meale was, which was left me of the biscuits which I caused to bee made to returne into France: so that if I shoulde say that I received more favour at the handes of the Englishmen beeing Strangers unto mee, I shoulde say but a trueth. Wee beganne therefore to fortifie our selves and to repaire that which was broken downe, principally toward the water side, where I caused three-score foote of trees to be planted, to repaire the Palissado with the plankes which I caused to bee taken of the Shippe which I had builded. Neverthelesse notwithstanding all our diligence and travaile, we were never able fully to repaire it by reason of the stormes, which commonly did us so great annoy, that wee could not finish our inclosure. Perceiving my selfe in such extremitie I tooke a muster of the men, which captaine Ribault had left me, to see if there were any that wanted weapon: I found nine or ten of them whereof not past two or three had ever drawen sword out of a scabbard, as I thinke. Let them which have bene bold to say, that I had men ynough left me, so that I had meanes to defend my selfe, give eare a little now unto mee, and if they have eyes in their heads, let them see what men I had. Of the nine there were foure but yong striplings, which served Captaine Ribault and kept his dogs, the fift was a cooke: among those that were

without the fort, and which were of the foresaid company of Captaine Ribault, there was a Carpenter of threescore yeeres olde, one a Beerebrewer, one olde Crosse-bow maker, two Shoomakers, and foure or five men that had their wives, a player on the Virginals, two servants of Monsieur du Luys, one of Monsieur de Beauhaire, one of Monsieur de la Grange, and about fourescore and five or sixe in all, counting aswel Lackeys as women and children. Behold the goodly troupe so sufficient to defend themselves, and so couragious as they have esteemed them to be: and for my part I leave it to others consideration to imagine whether Captaine Ribault woulde have left them with me to have borrowed my men, if they had bene such. Those that were left me of mine owne company were about sixteene or seventeene that coulde beare armes, and all of them poore and leane: the reste were sicke and maymed in the conflict which my Lieutenant had against Utina. This view being thus taken, wee set our watches, whereof wee made two Centinels, that the souldiers might have one night free. Then wee bethought our selves of those which might bee most sufficient, among whome wee chose two, one of whom was named Monsieur Saint Cler, and the other Monsieur de la Vigne, to whom we delivered candles and Lanterns to goe round about the fort to viewe the watch, because of the foule and foggie weather. I delivered them also a sandglasse or clocke, that the Centinels might not be troubled more one then another. In the meane while I ceased not, for all the foule weather nor my sicknesse which I had, to oversee the Corps de garde. The night betweene the nineteenth and twentieth of September La Vigne kept watch with his company, wherein he used all endevour, although it rayned without ceasing. When the day was therefore come, and that hee saw that it rayned still worse then it did before, hee pitied the Centinels so too moyled and wette: and thinking the Spanyardes woulde not have come in such a strange time, hee let them depart, and to say the trueth, hee went himselfe unto his lodging. In the meane while one which had something to doe without the fort, and my trumpet which went up unto the rampart perceived a troupe of Spanyards which came downe from a little knappe. Where incontinently they beganne to cry alarme, and the Trumpetter also: Which assoone as ever I understoode, foorthwith I issued out, with my target and sword in my hand, and gatte mee into the middest of the Court, where I beganne to crie upon my souldiers. Some of them which were of the forward sort went toward the breach, which was on the Southside, and where the munitions of the artillerie lay, where they were repulsed and slaine. By the selfe same place two ensignes entred, which immediately were planted on the wals. Two other ensignes also entred on the other side toward the West, where there was another breach: and those which were lodged in this quarter, & which shewed themselves, were likewise defeated. As I went to succour them which were defending the breach on the southwest side, I encountred by chance a great company of Spaniards, which had already repulsed our men and were now entred, which drave me backe unto the court of the fort: being there I espied with them one called Francis Jean, which was one of the Mariners which stole away my barks, and had guided and conducted the Spanyards thither. Assoone as he saw me, he began to say, This is the Captaine. This troupe was led by a captaine whose name, as I thinke, was Don Pedro Melendes: these made certain pushes at me with their pikes which lighted on my tarket. But perceiving that I was not able to withstand so great a company, and that the court was already wonne, and their ensignes planted on the ramparts, & that I had never a man about me, saving one only whose name was Bartholomew, I entred into the yard of my lodging, into which they followed me, and had it not bene for a tent that was set up, I had bin taken: but the Spanyards which followed me were occupied in cutting of the cordes of the tent, and in the meane while I saved my selfe by the breach which was on the West side neere unto my Lieutenants lodging, and gate away into the woods: where I found certain of my men which were escaped, of which number there were three or foure which were sore hurt. Then spake I thus unto them: Sirs, since it hath pleased God that this mischance is happened unto us, we must needs take the paines to get over the marshes unto the ships which are at the mouth of the river. Some would needs go to a little village which was in the woods, the rest followed me through the reedes in the water, where being able to go no farther by reason of my sicknesse which I had, I sent two of my men which were with me, which could swim well, unto the

ships, to advertise them of that which had happened, and to send them word to come and helpe me. They were not able that day to get unto the ships to certifie them thereof: so I was constrained to stand in the water up to the shoulders all that night long, with one of my men which would never forsake me. The next day morning, being scarcely able to draw my breath any more, I betooke me to my prayers with the souldier which was with mee, whose name was John du Chemin: for I felt my selfe so feeble, that I was afraid I should die suddenly: and in truth if he had not imbraced me in both his armes, and so held me up, it had not bene possible to save me. After we had made an ende of our prayers, I heard a voyce, which in my judgement was one of theirs which I had sent, which were over against the ships and called for the ship boat, which was so in deed: and because those of the ships had understanding of the taking of the fort by one called John de Hais, master Carpenter, which fled unto them in a shallop; they had set saile to run along the coast to see if they might save any: wherin doubtlesse they did very well their endevour. They went straight to the place where the two men were which I had sent, and which called them. Assoone as they had received them in and understood where I was, they came and found me in a pitifull case. Five or six of them tooke me and caried me into the shallop: for I was not able by any means to go one foot. After I was brought into the shallop some of the Mariners took their clothes from their backs to lend them me, and would have caried me presently to their ships to give me a little Aqua vitæ. Howbeit I would not goe thither, untill I had first gone with the boat along the reeds, to seeke out the poore soules which were scattered abroad, where we gathered up 18 or 20 of them. The last that I took in was the nephew of the Treasurer le Beau. After we were al come to the ships, I comforted them as well as I could, and sent back the boat againe with speed to see if they could fine yet any more. Upon her returne, the Mariners told mee how that captaine James Ribault which was in his ship about two muskets shot distant from the fort, had parled with the Spaniards, and that Francis Jean came unto his ship, where hee staied along space, whereat they greatly marveiled, considering hee was the cause of this enterprise, how hee would let him escape. After I was come into the ship called the

Greyhound, captaine James Ribault & captaine Valvot came to see me: and there we concluded to returne into France. Now forasmuch as I found the ship unfurnished of Captaine, Pilot, Master, and Masters-mate, I gave advice to choose out one of the most able men among al the mariners, & that by their owne voices. I tooke also sixe men out of another small ship, which we had sunke because it wanted ballast and could not be saved. Thus I increased the furnitue of the ship wherein I was my selfe embarked, and made one, which had bene Masters-mate in the foresaid small ship, Master of mine. And because I lacked a pilot, I prayed James Ribault that he would grant me one of the foure men that he had in his ship, which I should name unto him, to serve me for a Pilot: he promised to give me them, which neverthelesse he did not at the instant when wee were ready to depart, notwithstanding all the speech I used to him, in declaring that it was for the kings service. I was constrained to leave the ship behind me which I had bought of the English Captaine, because I wanted men to bring her away. For captaine James Ribault had taken away her furniture: I tooke away her ordinance onely, which was all dismounted, whereof I gave nine pieces to James Ribault to carrie into France, the other five I put into my ship. The 25 of September wee set sailes to returne into France, and Captaine James Ribault and I kept company all that day and the next untill three or foure a clock in the afternoone: but because his ship was better at bowline then ours, he kept him to the wind and left us the same day. Thus we continued our voyage, wherein we had marveilous flawes of wind. And about the eight and twentieth of October in the morning at the breake of the day we discried the Isle of Flores, one of the Açores, where immediatly upon our approching to the land we had a mightie gust of wind which came from the Northeast, which caused us to beare against it foure dayes: afterward the wind came South and Southeast, and was alwayes variable. In all the time of our passage we had none other foode saving biscuit and water. About the tenth or eleventh of November, after we had sailed a long time, and supposing we were not farre from land, I caused my men to sound, where they found threescore and fifteene fathoms water, whereat we all rejoyced, and praised God because we had sailed so prosperously. Immediatly after I caused

them to set saile again and so we continued our way: but forasmuch as we had borne too much toward the Northeast we entred into Saint Georges channell, a place much feared of all Sailers, and whereas many ships are cast away: But it was a faire gift of God that we entred in it when the weather was cleare. We sailed all the night, supposing wee had bene shot into the narrow Sea betweene England and France, and by the next day to reach Diepe, but we were deceived of our longing: for about two or three of the clocke after midnight as I walked upon the hatches, I discried land round about me, whereat wee were astonied. Immediatly I caused them to strike saile and sound: we found we had not under us past 8 fathoms of water, whereupon I commanded them to stay till breake of day: which being come, and seeing my Mariners told me that they knew not this land, I commanded them to approch unto it. Being neere thereunto I made them cast anker, & sent the boat on shore to understand in what Countrey we were. Word was brought me that we were in Wales a province of England. I went incontinently on land, where after I had taken the ayre, a sickenesse tooke mee whereof I thought I should have dyed. In the meane while I caused the ship to be brought into the bay of a small towne called Swansey, where I found merchants of S. Malo, which lent me money, wherewith I made certaine apparel for my selfe and part of my company that was with me: and because there were no victuals in the ship, I bought two Oxen, and salted them, and a tunne of Beere, which I delivered into his hands which had charge of the ship, praying him to cary it into France, which he promised me to doe: for mine owne part I purposed with my men to passe by land, and after I had taken leave of my Mariners, I departed from Swansey, and came that night with my company to a place called Morgan, where the Lord of the place, understanding what I was, stayed me with him for the space of 6 or 7 dayes, and at my departure mooved with pitie to see me goe on foot, especially being so weake as I was, gave me a litle Hackny. Thus I passed on my journey first to Bristoll, & then to London, where I went to doe my duty to Monsieur de Foix, which for the present was the kings Ambassador, and holpe me with mony in my necessitie. From thence I passed to Caleis, afterward to Paris, where I was informed that the king was gone to Molins to sojourne there: incontinently, & with all the hast I could possibly make, I gate me thither with part of my company. Thus briefly you see the discourse of all that happened in New France since the time it pleased the kings Majesty to send his subjects thither to discover those parts. The indifferent and unpassionate readers may easily weigh the truth of my doings, and be upright judges of the endevor which I there used. For mine owne part I wil not accuse nor excuse any: it sufficeth mee to have followed the trueth of the history, whereof many are able to beare witnesse, which were there present. I will plainly say one thing, That the long delay that Captaine John Ribault used in his embarking, and the 15. daies that he spent in roving along the coast of Florida, before he came to our fort Caroline, were the cause of the losse that we susteined. For he discovered the coast the 14 of August, and spent the time in going from river to river, which had bene sufficient for him to have discharged his ships in, and for me to have embarked my selfe to returne into France. I wote well that al that he did was upon a good intent: yet in mine opinion he should have had more regard unto his charge, then to the devises of his owne braine, which sometimes hee printed in his head so deeply, that it was very hard to put them out: which also turned to his utter undoing: for hee was no sooner departed from us, but a tempest tooke him, which in fine wrackt him upon the coast, where all his shippes were cast away, and he with much adoe escaped drowning, to fall into their hands which cruelly massacred him and all his company.

304. 1565. The first published report of the Laudonnière colony.

Coppie d'un lettre venant de la Florida, envoyée a Rouen, et depuis au seigneur d'Everon *(Paris, Vincent Norment et Jeanne Bruneau, 1565), a rare pamphlet, a copy of which is in the John Carter Brown Library, contained a rather sketchy engraving of La Caroline, the fort on the St. Johns River. Its author's name is not known. Henri Ternaux-Compans included it in his* Voyages, *XX (Paris, 1841), 233–245. It was translated in Charles E.* Bennett, Laudonnière and Fort Caroline *(Gainesville, Fla., 1964), pp. 65–70. It is here retranslated.*

Copy of a letter coming from Florida, sent to Rouen and then to Seigneur d'Everon, together with the plan and picture of the fort which the French built there

My very honored father, having arrived in this land of New France, in prosperity and good health (thanks be to God), which I pray may also be true of you, I could not fail to take pen in hand, and make it run over the paper in order to make you a short discourse of the isle of Florida, called New France, and of the manner and customs of the natives, the which I shall be pleased should be to your liking. I beg you humbly to forgive me if I do not write to you more fully, as I would wish. But the reason is that we work each day on our fort, which is now in a state of defence.

We left Havre on April 22, under the command of the Seigneur René de Laudonnière, a Poitevin gentleman, with three ships of war, of these the one on which he sailed was called the *Ysabeau* of Honfleur of which Jean Lucas is master, the same being the admiral; the other is the vice-admiral commanded by Captain Vasseur, of Dieppe, which is called the *Petit Breton*, on which I embarked and made my voyage. The other is called the *Faulcon* which was commanded by Captain Pierre Marchant. These (with the aid of our good God, who was ever present) sailed together for some time without being separated by more than three leagues, so much so that we can say (rendering thanks to God) that we had one of the happiest voyages ever made by sea, seeing the great blessings that the good Lord bestowed on us, poor sinners. We were led safely without running into any difficulty except that as we passed along the coast of England we encountered about eighteen to twenty hulks which were thought to be English, which were waiting to take us but soon they discovered that we had formed ourselves into battle order to resist them: for we had been told before leaving that the English were lying in wait in order to take us. And when these hulks perceived us and saw our ensigns displayed and our maintops manned ready for battle, the admiral and vice-admiral of these hulks lining up the others in formation came directly towards us and we towards them. At that point we saw that they were Flanders hulks, with whom we spoke, and they told us that they were going to Brouage to take on salt, on which account we let them proceed and we continued on our way until the 22nd day of June, when we arrived in sight of New France, otherwise known as Florida. There, because the wind came from the land, we sensed the sweet smell of many good things, seeing the land very flat without a single hill, all along the shore, and all replenished with fine trees with woods to the seaside. I leave it to you to imagine the joy we all felt. To the south we perceived a very beautiful river, which prompted the Seigneur de Laudonnière to disembark and reconnoiter, in doing which he was accompanied by only a dozen soldiers. As soon as he set foot on the land, three kings with more than 400 savages came to give the Seigneur de Laudonnière their own greeting, fawning over him as though they were worshipping an idol. This done, the kings led him a short distance away (about the length of an arrow-shot) where there was a beautiful arbor of bay trees and here all sat down and gave signs of their great joy at our arrival, and also made signs (pointing at the Seigneur de Laudonnière and at the Sun), saying that he was a brother of the Sun and that he should go with them to make war against their enemies which they called *Tymangoua* and they signified to us by bowing their heads three times that they were only three days away. The Seigneur de Laudonnière promised to go with them, then one after the other, according to their rank, they stood up and thanked him. A short time afterwards the said seigneur wished to go further up the river again and while looking towards a small sand dune, he became aware of the marker of white stone on which the arms of the King were engraved and which had been erected by Captain Jean Ribault [*Bibault*] of Dieppe on his first voyage. The Seigneur de Laudonnière was very happy about this and realized that this was the River of May, so called by Jean Ribault at his arrival there on the first day of May. And we stayed close to the said pillar for the space of half an hour, as the Indians brought us bay and their excellent beverage *mil du laurier* [maize?], and embracing the pillar, they all cried *Tymangoua*, as though by saying this they would gain a victory over their enemies whom they called *Tymangoua*, and that the Sun

had sent the Seigneur de Laudonnière, his brother, to avenge them. After giving them presents, the said Seigneur de Laudonnière ordered us to return on board, leaving these poor people wailing and weeping at our departure: so much so that one of them forced his way on board and slept there but was returned to land on the Friday.

Then after weighing anchor and ranging the coast until Sunday, we discovered a fine river into which the Seigneur de Laudonnière sent Captain Vasseur, accompanied by ten soldiers, of whom I was one. As soon as we landed we found another king with three of his sons and more than 200 savages, their wives and little children. This chief was very old, and signed to us that he had seen five generations, that is to say the children of his children up to the fifth generation. After he had made us sit down under the bay tree which was close to him, he made the sign of *Tymangouam* to us, just as the others had done. However they are the biggest thieves in the world, for they can steal with their feet as well as they can with their hands, notwithstanding they have only a skin covering their private parts. They are painted black all over, in beautiful designs. The women drape themselves in a certain long white moss, which covers their breasts and their private parts. They are very obedient to their husbands, not such thieves as the men, but they covet rings and necklets to put round their necks. One day having sounded the said river, it was found to be deep enough for the ships to enter, but not as deep as the River of May. Thus the Seigneur de Laudonnière returned on board the ship, and discussed with Captain Vasseur the possibility of returning to the River of May. The following Tuesday we weighed anchor to go back there, arriving the next Friday, and we landed at once, where we were honorably received by the savages just as before, and they led us to the same place where we are now building our fort which is called La Carreline, of which you can see the picture below.

This fort is on the said River of May, about six leagues upstream from the sea. Within this brief period we have it so well fortified that we shall be able to defend ourselves. It is very well appointed, with water coming into the moat. We have found an Esquine tree [sassafras], that has dietary value, which is the least of its virtues, for the sap which comes from it has such properties that if a thin man or woman drinks it regularly, he or she would become very big and plump. It has also other good uses. We have heard from the surgeons that it sells very well in France and that it is very well received. The said Seigneur de Laudonnière forbade the soldiers to send it by the ships that were ready to leave and that he alone would send some to be given to the King, to the other princes of France and to Monsieur l'Admiral [Coigny], together with the gold from a mine which we found hereabouts. But he gave his permission to have a supply of it put on the first ships that would return so that, with God's help, there would be a good supply, assuring me that it will be much in demand there and in other places. If there is a profit, the said Seigneur de Laudonnière wishes that his soldiers should have their share. We have also found a certain kind of cinammon, but not of the best quality, somewhat too red, and also some rhubarb, though very little. However we hope that in time we will be able to secure for ourselves all the things which can be had from here.

Twenty-five leagues from our fort there is a river which is called the Jordan [le lourdain], in which are found sables [fort belles peaux de martres sablines]. With God's help we hope to go to that place within about six weeks. Furthermore, there are some very beautiful blood-red cedar trees, and the woods are full of them, almost to the exclusion of other things, and there are also many pines and—another sort of timber which is quite yellow, and even the woods are so full of vines that one cannot walk two paces without finding an abundance of grapes which are beginning to ripen so that we hope to make plenty of wine, which will be very pleasant. Also a fortnight after the fort was fortified, the Seigneur de Laudonnière decided to send two barks to Tymangoua and they actually went there on Saturday the 15th day of this month. They were led by Monsieur d'Antigny [d'Ottigny] and Captain Vasseur and stayed there in some uncertainty until the 18th. On their return they brought very good news, saying they had discovered a mine of gold and silver, at a place about 60 leagues from our fort by way of our River of May. Arriving there, they traded with the savages who were very frightened of them, and were always on their guard because of their neighbours, who were constantly waging war against them as they

later demonstrated to the Seigneur d'Antigny and to Captain Vasseur. On their arrival they [the savages] left their offerings at the water's edge; there some merchandise was placed by order of the Seigneur d'Antigny who then withdrew the barks. Having thus withdrawn, the savages approached their own offerings and found the wares, and began to gain reassurance, making signs as they drew nearer, calling *Amy Thypola Panassoon* which means brother and friend like the fingers of the hand. Seeing this the said Seigneur d'Antigny and Captain Vasseur went to them and having received from them a ceremonious welcome, they led them to their village and treated them according to their custom, which is to give them maize [*mil*] and water boiled with a certain herb which they use, which is very good, so that if it pleases God to give us the grace to live another two years, we hope with the help the king will be pleased to send us, to secure the said mine for him. In the meantime I hope to attain an understanding of the ways these savages do things, who are a fine people. Trading with them is very easy. They make signs to the effect they will offer us gold and silver to the extent we would give them hatchets, bills and knives or cheap necklaces.

I did not want to forget to write to you that last Friday a large crocodile [*cocodrilla*] was captured, which was like a lizard, but it had arms with joints like a human and five fingers on its front feet and four on its back ones. Its hide is being sent to France by the ships that are presently returning. In that river one only sees crocodiles, and if one casts a net into the water to fish, one catches the most frightful fish that one has ever seen.
Farewell.

305. July, 1565. John Sparke's report on Florida.

Although English disillusionment at the failure of Stukely's plan for an English reinforcement to the French colony in Florida was considerable, it was important for the long-term trading and plundering plans of John Hawkins to know what the French were doing on the St. Johns River.

Cooperation, if possible, rivalry, if necessary, could be important to him. His close examination of the Florida coast on his return from his African and West Indian voyage in 1565 and his visit to Laudonnière are, therefore, of some significance. Hawkins found Laudonnière, deserted as he believed by Ribault, preparing to abandon the colony. Hawkins was able to spare a small amount of supplies and to sell a ship (largely on credit) to enable the French to return to Europe. The narrator, John Sparke the younger, showed a lively curiosity about Florida, which perhaps justified Laudonnière's suspicion that the English had come to spy as well as to assist.

Richard Hakluyt, Principall navigations (1589), pp. 537–543; reprinted in Principal navigations, III (1600), 516–521 (X [1904], 51–63).

In which coast ranging, we found no convenient watering place, whereby there was no remedy but to disemboque, and to water upon the coast of Florida: for, to go further to the Eastward, we could not for the shoalds, which are very dangerous; and because the current shooteth to the Northeast, we doubted by the force thereof to be set upon them, and therefore durst not approch them: so making but reasonable way the day aforesayd, and all the night, the twelfth day in the morning we fell with the Islands upon the cape of Florida, which we could scant double by the meanes that fearing the shoalds to the Eastwards, and doubting the current comming out of the West, which was not of that force we made account of; for we felt little or none till we fell with the cape, and then felt such a current, that bearing all sailes against the same, yet were driven backe againe a great pace: the experience whereof we had by the Jesus pinnesse, and the Salomons boat, which were sent the same day in the afternoone, whiles the ships were becalmed, to see if they could finde any water upon the Islands aforesaid; who spent a great part of the day in rowing thither, being further off then they deemed it to be, and in the meane time a faire gale of winde springing at sea, the ships departed, making a signe to them to come away, who although they saw them depart, because they were so neere the shore, would not lose all the labour they had taken, but determined to keepe their way, and see if there were any water to be had,

making no account but to finde the shippes well enough: but they spent so much time in filling the water which they had found, that the night was come before they could make an end. And having lost the sight of the ships, they rowed what they could, but were wholly ignorant which way they should seeke them againe; as indeed there was a more doubt then they knew of: for when they departed, the shippes were in no current; and sailing but a mile further, they found one so strong, that bearing all sailes, it could not prevaile against the same, but were driven backe: whereupon the captaine sent the Salomon, with the other two barks, to beare neere the shore all night, because the current was lesse there a great deale, and to beare light, with shooting off a piece now and then, to the intent the boats might better know how to come to them.

The Jesus also bare a light in her toppe gallant, and shot off a piece also now and then, but the night passed, no newes could be heard of them, but the ships and the morning was come, being the thirteenth day, and barkes ceased not to looke still for them, yet they thought it was all in vaine, by the meanes they heard not of them all the night past; and therefore determined to tary no longer, seeking for them till noone, and if they heard no newes, then they would depart to the Jesus, who perforce (by the vehemency of the current) was caried almost out of sight; but as God would have it, now time being come, and they having tacked about in the pinnesses top, had sight of them, and tooke them up: they in the boats, being to the number of one and twenty, having sight of the ships, and seeing them tacking about; whereas before at the first sight of them they did greatly rejoyce, were now in a greater perplexitie then ever they were: for by this they thought themselves utterly forsaken, whereas before they were in some hope to have found them. Truly God wrought marvellously for them, for they themselves having no victuals but water, and being sore oppressed with hunger, were not of opinion to bestow any further time in seeking the shippes then that present noone time; so that if they had not at that instant espied them, they had gone to the shore to have made provision for victuals, and with such things as they could have gotten, either to have gone for that part of Florida where the French men were planted (which would have bene very hard for them to have done, because they wanted victuals to bring them thither, being an hundred and twenty leagues off) or els to have remained amongst the Floridians; at whose hands they were put in comfort by a French man, who was with them, that had remained in Florida at the first finding thereof, a whole yeere together, to receive victuals sufficient, and gentle entertainment, if need were, for a yeere or two, untill which time God might have provided for them. But how contrary this would have fallen out to their expectations, it is hard to judge, seeing those people of the cape of Florida are of more savage and fierce nature, and more valiant then any of the rest; which the Spanyards well prooved, who being five hundred men, who intended there to land, returned few or none of them, but were inforced to forsake the same: and of their cruelty mention is made in the booke of the Decades, of a frier, who taking upon him to persuade the people to subjection, was by them taken, and his skin cruelly pulled over his eares, and his flesh eaten.

In these Islands they being a shore, found a dead man, dried in a maner whole, with other heads and bodies of men: so that these sorts of men are eaters of the flesh of men, aswel as the Canibals. But to returne to our purpose.

The fourteenth day the shippe and barks came to the Jesus, bringing them newes of the recovery of the men, which was not a little to the rejoycing of the captaine, and the whole company: and so then altogether they kept on their way along the coast of Florida, and the fifteenth day come to an anker, and so from six and twenty degrees to thirty degrees and a halfe, where the French men abode, ranging all the coast along, seeking for fresh water, ankering every night, because we would overshoot no place of fresh water, and in the day time the captaine in the ships pinnesse sailed along the shore, went into every creeke, speaking with divers of the Floridians, because hee would understand where the French men inhabited; and not finding them in eight and twenty degrees, as it was declared unto him, marvelled thereat, and never left sailing along the coast till he found them, who inhabited in a river, by them called the river of May, and standing in thirty degrees and better. In ranging this coast along, the captaine found it to be all an Island, and therefore it is all lowe land, and very scant of fresh water, but the countrey was marvellously

sweet, with both marish and medow ground, and goodly woods among. There they found sorell to grow as abundantly as grasse, and where their houses were, great store of maiz and mill, and grapes of great bignesse, but of taste much like our English grapes. Also Deere great plentie, which came upon the sands before them. Their houses are not many together, for in one house an hundred of them do lodge; they being made much like a great barne, and in strength not inferiour to ours, for they have stanchions and rafters of whole trees, and are covered with palmito-leaves, having no place divided, but one small roome for their king and queene. In the middest of this house is a hearth, where they make great fires all night, and they sleepe upon certeine pieces of wood hewen in for the bowing of their backs, and another place made high for their heads, which they put one by another all along the walles on both sides. In their houses they remaine onely in the nights, and in the day they desire the fields, where they dresse their meat, and make provision for victuals, which they provide onely for a meale from hand to mouth. There is one thing to be marvelled at, for the making of their fire, and not onely they but also the Negros doe the same, which is made onely by two stickes, rubbing them one against another: and this they may doe in any place they come, where they finde sticks sufficient for the purpose. In their apparell the men onely use deere skinnes, wherewith some onely cover their privy members, othersome use the same as garments to cover them before and behind; which skinnes are painted, some yellow and red, some blacke & russet, and every man according to his owne fancy. They do not omit to paint their bodies also with curious knots, or antike worke, as every man in his owne fancy deviseth, which painting, to make it continue the better, they use with a thorne to pricke their flesh, and dent in the same, whereby the painting may have better hold. In their warres they use a sleighter colour of painting their faces, thereby to make themselves shew the more fierce; which after their warres ended, they wash away againe. In their warres they use bowes and arrowes, whereof their bowes are made of a kind of Yew, but blacker then ours, and for the most part passing the strength of the Negros or Indians, for it is not greatly inferior to ours: their arrowes are also of a great length, but yet of reeds like other

Indians, but varying in two points, both in length and also for nocks and feathers, which the other lacke, whereby they shoot very stedy: the heads of the same are vipers teeth, bones of fishes, flint stones, piked points of knives, which they having gotten of the French men, broke the same, & put the points of them in their arrowes head: some of them have their heads of silver, othersome that have want of these, put in a kinde of hard wood, notched, which pierceth as farre as any of the rest. In their fight, being in the woods, they use a marvellous pollicie for their owne safegard, which is by clasping a tree in their armes, and yet shooting notwithstanding: this policy they used with the French men in their fight, whereby it appeareth that they are people of some policy: and although they are called by the Spanyards Gente triste, that is to say, Bad people, meaning thereby, that they are not men of capacity: yet have the French men found them so witty in their answeres, that by the captaines owne report, a counseller with us could not give a more profound reason.

The women also for their apparell use painted skinnes, but most of them gownes of mosse, somewhat longer then our mosse, which they sowe together artificially, and make the same surplesse wise, wearing their haire downe to their shoulders, like the Indians. In this river of May aforesayd, the captaine entring with his pinnesse, found a French ship of fourescore tun, and two pinnesses of fifteene tun a piece, by her, and speaking with the keepers thereof, they tolde him of a fort two leagues up, which they had built, in which their Captaine Monsieur Laudonnière was, with certeine souldiers therein. To whome our captaine sending to understand of a wateringplace, where he might conveniently take it in, and to have licence for the same, he straight, because there was no convenient place but up the river five leagues, where the water was fresh, did send him a pilot for the more expedition thereof, to bring in one of his barks, which going in with other boats provided for the same purpose, ankered before the fort, into the which our captaine went; where hee was by the Generall, with other captaines and souldiers, very gently enterteined, who declared unto him the time of their being there, which was fourteene moneths, with the extremity they were driven to for want of victuals, having brought very little with them; in

which place they being two hundred men at their first comming, had in short space eaten all the maiz they could buy of the inhabitants about them, and therefore were driven certeine of them to serve a king of the Floridians against other his enemies, for mill and other victuals: which having gotten, could not serve them, being so many, so long a time: but want came upon them in such sort, that they were faine to gather acorns, which being stamped small, and often washed, to take away the bitternesse of them, they did use for bread, eating withall sundry times, roots, whereof they found many good and holesome, and such as serve rather for medecines then for meates alone. But this hardnesse not contenting some of them, who would not take the paines so much as to fish in the river before their doores, but would have all things put in their mouthes, they did rebell against the captaine, taking away first his armour, and afterward imprisoning him: and so to the number of fourescore of them, departed with a barke and a pinnesse, spoiling their store of victuall, and taking away a great part thereof with them, and so went to the Islands of Hispaniola and Jamaica a roving, where they spoiled and pilled the Spanyards; and having taken two caravels laden with wine and casavi, which is a bread made of roots, and much other victuals and treasure, had not the grace to depart therewith, but were of such haughty stomacks, that they thought their force to be such that no man durst meddle with them, and so kept harborow in Jamaica, going dayly ashore at their pleasure. But God which would not suffer such evill doers unpunished, did indurate their hearts in such sort, that they lingered the time so long, that a ship and galliasse being made out of Santa Domingo came thither into the harborow, and tooke twenty of them, whereof the most part were hanged, and the rest caried into Spaine, and some (to the number of five and twenty) escaped in the pinnesse, and came to Florida; where at their landing they were put in prison, and incontinent foure of the chiefest being condemned, at the request of the souldiers, did passe the harquebuzers, and then were hanged upon a gibbet. This lacke of threescore men was a great discourage and weakening to the rest, for they were the best souldiers that they had: for they had now made the inhabitants weary of them by their dayly craving of maiz, having no wares left to content them withall, and therefore were inforced to rob them, and to take away their victual perforce, which was the occasion that the Floridians (not well contented therewith) did take certeine of their company in the woods, and slew them; wherby there grew great warres betwixt them and the Frenchmen: and therefore they being but a few in number durst not venture abroad, but at such times as they were inforced thereunto for want of food to do the same: and going twenty harquebuzers in a company, were set upon by eighteene kings, having seven or eight hundred men, which with one of their bowes slew one of their men, and hurt a dozen, & drove them all downe to their boats; whose pollicy in fight was to be marvelled at: for having shot at divers of their bodies which were armed, and perceiving that their arrowes did not prevaile against the same, they shot at their faces and legs, which were the places that the Frenchmen were hurt in. Thus the Frenchmen returned, being in ill case by the hurt of their men, having not above forty souldiers left unhurt, whereby they might ill make any more invasions upon the Floridians, and keepe their fort withall: which they must have beene driven unto, had not God sent us thither for their succour; for they had not above ten dayes victuall left before we came. In which perplexity our captaine seeing them, spared them out of his ship twenty barrels of meale, & foure pipes of beanes, with divers other victuals and necessaries which he might conveniently spare: and to helpe them the better homewards, whither they were bound before our comming, at their request we spared them one of our barks of fifty tun. Notwithstanding the great want that the Frenchmen had, the ground doth yeeld victuals sufficient, if they would have taken paines to get the same; but they being souldiers, desired to live by the sweat of other mens browes: for while they had peace with the Floridians, they had fish sufficient, by weares which they made to catch the same: but when they grew to warres, the Floridians tooke away the same againe, and then would not the Frenchmen take the paines to make any more. The ground yeeldeth naturally grapes in great store, for in the time that the Frenchmen were there, they made 20 hogsheads of wine. Also it yeeldeth roots passing good, Deere marvellous store, with divers other beasts, and fowle, serviceable to the use of man. These be things wherewith a man may live,

having corne or maiz wherewith to make bread: for maiz maketh good savory bread, and cakes as fine as flowre. Also it maketh good meale, beaten and sodden with water, and eateth like pap wherewith we feed children. It maketh also good beverage, sodden in water, and nourishable; which the Frenchmen did use to drinke of in the morning, and it assuageth their thirst, so that they had no need to drinke all the day after. And this maiz was the greatest lacke they had, because they had no labourers to sowe the same, and therfore to them that should inhabit the land it were requisit to have labourers to till and sowe the ground: for they having victuals of their owne, whereby they neither rob nor spoile the inhabitants, may live not onely quietly with them, who naturally are more desirous of peace then of warres, but also shall have abundance of victuals profered them for nothing: for it is with them as it is with one of us, when we see another man ever taking away from us, although we have enough besides, yet then we thinke all too little for our selves: for surely we have heard the Frenchmen report, and I know it by the Indians, that a very little contenteth them: for the Indians with the head of maiz rosted, will travell a whole day, and when they are at the Spanyards finding, they give them nothing but sodden herbs & maiz: and in this order I saw threescore of them feed, who were laden with wares, and came fifty leagues off. The Floridians when they travell, have a kinde of herbe dried, who with a cane and an earthen cup in the end, with fire, and the dried herbs put together, doe sucke thorow the cane the smoke thereof, which smoke satisfieth their hunger, and therwith they live foure or five dayes without meat or drinke, and this all the Frenchmen used for this purpose: yet do they holde opinion withall, that it causeth water & fleame to void from their stomacks. The commodities of this land are more then are yet knowen to any man: for besides the land it selfe, whereof there is more then any king Christian is able to inhabit, it flourisheth with medow, pasture ground, with woods of Cedar and Cypres, and other sorts, as better can not be in the world. They have for apothecary herbs, trees, roots and gummes great store, as Storax liquida, Turpintine, Gumme, Myrrhe, and Frankinsence, with many others, whereof I know not the names. Colours both red, blacke, yellow, & russet, very perfect, wherewith they so paint their bodies, and

Deere skinnes which they weare about them, that with water it neither fadeth away, nor altereth colour. Golde and silver they want not: for at the Frenchmens first comming thither they had the same offered them for little or nothing, for they received for a hatchet two pound weight of golde, because they knew not the estimation thereof: but the souldiers being greedy of the same, did take it from them, giving them nothing for it: the which they perceiving, that both the Frenchmen did greatly esteeme it, and also did rigorously deale with them, by taking the same away from them, at last would not be knowen they had any more, neither durst they weare the same for feare of being taken away: so that saving at their first comming, they could get none of them: and how they came by this golde and silver the French men know not as yet, but by gesse, who having travelled to the Southwest of the cape, having found the same dangerous, by meanes of sundry banks, as we also have found the same: and there finding masts which were wracks of Spanyards comming from Mexico, judged that they had gotten treasure by them. For it is most true that divers wracks have beene made of Spanyards, having much treasure: for the Frenchmen having travelled to the capeward an hundred and fiftie miles, did finde two Spanyards with the Floridians, which they brought afterward to their fort, whereof one was in a caravel comming from the Indies, which was cast away fourteene yeeres ago, & the other twelve yeeres; of whose fellowes some escaped, othersome were slain by the inhabitants. It seemeth they had estimation of their golde & silver, for it is wrought flat and graven, which they weare about their neckes; othersome made round like a pancake, with a hole in the midst, to boulster up their breasts withall, because they thinke it a deformity to have great breasts. As for mines either of gold or silver, the Frenchmen can heare of none they have upon the Island, but of copper, whereof as yet also they have not made the proofe, because they were but few men: but it is not unlike, but that in the maine where are high hilles, may be golde and silver aswell as in Mexico, because it is all one maine. The Frenchmen obtained pearles of them of great bignesse, but they were blacke, by meanes of rosting of them, for they do not fish for them as the Spanyards doe, but for their meat: for the Spanyards use to keepe dayly afishing some two or three hundred Indians, some of them that be of choise a thousand: and their order is to go in canoas, or rather great pinnesses, with thirty men in a piece, whereof the one halfe, or most part be divers, the rest doe open the same for the pearles: for it is not suffered that they should use dragging, for that would bring them out of estimation, and marre the beds of them. The oisters which have the smallest sort of pearles are found in seven or eight fadome water, but the greatest in eleven or twelve fadome.

The Floridians have pieces of unicornes hornes which they weare about their necks, whereof the Frenchmen obtained many pieces. Of those unicornes they have many; for that they doe affirme it to be a beast with one horne, which comming to the river to drinke, putteth the same into the water before he drinketh. Of this unicornes horne there are of our company, that having gotten the same of the Frenchmen, brought home thereof to shew. It is therfore to be presupposed that there are more commodities aswell as that, which for want of time, and people sufficient to inhabit the same, can not yet come to light: but I trust God will reveale the same before it be long, to the great profit of them that shal take it in hand. Of beasts in this countrey besides deere, foxes, hares, polcats, conies, ownces, & leopards, I am not able certeinly to say: but it is thought that there are lions and tygres as well as unicornes; lions especially; if it be true that is sayd, of the enmity betweene them and the unicornes: for there is no beast but hath his enemy, as the cony the polcat, a sheepe the woolfe, the elephant the rinoceros; and so of other beasts the like: insomuch, that whereas the one is, the other can not be missing. And seeing I have made mention of the beasts of this countrey, it shall not be from my purpose to speake also of the venimous beasts, as crocodiles, whereof there is great abundance, adders of great bignesse, whereof our men killed some of a yard and a halfe long. Also I heard a miracle of one of these adders, upon the which a faulcon seizing, the sayd adder did claspe her tail about her; which the French captaine seeing, came to the rescue of the faulcon, and tooke her slaying the adder; and this faulcon being wilde, he did reclaim her, and kept her for the space of two moneths, at which time for very want of meat he was faine to cast her off. On these adders the Frenchmen did feed, to no little admiration of us, and affirmed the same to be a delicate meat. And the captaine of the Frenchmen saw also a serpent with three heads and foure feet, of the bignesse of a great spaniell, which for want of a harquebuz he durst not attempt to slay. Of fish also they have in the river, pike, roch, salmon, trout, and divers other small fishes, and of great fish, some of the length of a man and longer, being of bignesse accordingly, having a snout much like a sword of a yard long. There be also of sea fishes, which we saw comming along the coast flying, which are of the bignesse of a smelt, the biggest sort whereof have foure wings, but the other have but two: of these wee sawe comming out of Guinea a hundred in a company, which being chased by the gilt-heads, otherwise called the bonitos, do to avoid them the better, take their flight out of the water, but yet are they not able to flie farre, because of the drying of their wings, which serve them not to flie but when they are moist, and therefore when they can flie no further they fall into the water, and having wet their wings, take a new flight againe. These bonitos be of bignesse like a carpe, and in colour like a makarell, but it is the swiftest fish in swimming that is, and followeth her prey very fiercely, not onely in the water, but also out of the water: for as the flying fish taketh her flight, so doeth this bonito leape after them, and taketh them sometimes above the water. There were some of those bonitos, which being galled by a fisgig, did follow our shippe comming out of Guinea 500. leagues. There is a sea-fowle also that chaseth this flying fish aswell as the bonito: for as the flying fish taketh her flight, so doth this fowle pursue to take her, which to beholde is a greater pleasure then hawking, for both the flights are as pleasant, and also more often then a hundred times: for the fowle can flie no way, but one or other lighteth in her pawes, the number of them are so abundant. There is an innumerable yoong frie of these flying fishes, which commonly keepe about the ship, and are not so big as butter-flies, and yet by flying do avoid the unsatiablenesse of the bonito. Of the bigger sort of these fishes wee tooke many, which both night and day flew into the sailes of our ship, and there was not one of them which was not woorth a bonito: for being put upon a hooke drabling in the water, the bonito would leap thereat, and so was taken. Also, we tooke many with a white cloth made fast to a hooke, which being tied so short in the water, that

it might leape out and in, the greedie bonito thinking it to be a flying fish leapeth thereat, and so is deceived. We tooke also dolphins which are of very goodly colour and proportion to behold, and no lesse delicate in taste. Fowles also there be many, both upon land and upon sea: but concerning them on the land I am not able to name them, because my abode was there so short. But for the fowle of the fresh rivers, these two I noted to be the chiefe, whereof the Flemengo is one, having all red feathers, and long red legs like a herne, a necke according to the bill, red, whereof the upper neb hangeth an inch over the nether; and an egript, which is all white as the swanne, with legs like to an hearnshaw, and of bignesse accordingly, but it hath in her taile feathers of so fine a plume, that it passeth the estridge his feather. Of the sea-fowle above all other not common in England, I noted the pellicane, which is fained to be the lovingst bird that is; which rather then her yong should want, wil spare her heart bloud out of her belly: but for all this lovingnesse she is very deformed to beholde; for she is of colour russet: notwithstanding in Guinea I have seene of them as white as a swan, having legs like the same, and a body like a hearne, with a long necke, and a thick long beake, from the nether jaw whereof downe to the breast passeth a skinne of such a bignesse, as is able to receive a fish as big as ones thigh, and this her big throat and long bill doeth make her seem so ougly.

Here I have declared the estate of Florida, and the commodities therein to this day knowen, which although it may seeme unto some, by the meanes that the plenty of golde and silver, is not so abundant as in other places, that the cost bestowed upon the same will not be able to quit the charges: yet am I of the opinion, that by that which I have seene in other Islands of the Indians, where such increase of cattell hath bene, that of twelve head of beasts in five & twenty yeeres, did in the hides of them raise a thousand pound profit yerely, that the increase of cattel onely would raise profit sufficient for the same: for wee may consider, if so small a portion did raise so much gaines in such short time, what would a greater do in many yeres? and surely I may this affirme, that the ground of the Indians for the breed of cattell, is not in any point to be compared to this of Florida, which all the yeere long is so greene, as any time in the Summer with us: which surely is not to be marvelled at, seeing the countrey standeth in so watery a climate: for once a day without faile they have a shower of raine; which by meanes of the countrey it selfe, which is drie, and more fervent hot then ours, doeth make all things to flourish therein. And because there is not the thing we all seeke for, being rather desirous of present gaines, I doe therefore affirme the attempt thereof to be more requisit for a prince, who is of power able to go thorow with the same, rather then for any subject.

From thence wee departed the 28 of July, upon our voyage homewards, having there all things as might be most convenient for our purpose: and tooke leave of the Frenchmen that there still remained, who with diligence determined to make as great speede after, as they could. Thus by meanes of contrary windes oftentimes, wee prolonged our voyage in such manner that victuals scanted with us, so that we were divers times (or rather the most part) in despaire of ever comming home, had not God of his goodnesse better provided for us, then our deserving. In which state of great miserie, wee were provoked to call upon him by fervent prayer, which mooved him to heare us, so that we had a prosperous winde, which did set us so farre shot, as to be upon the banke of Newfound land, on Saint Bartholomews eve, and we sounded therupon, finding ground at an hundred and thirty fadoms, being that day somewhat becalmed, and tooke a great number of fresh codde-fish, which greatly relieved us: and being very glad thereof, the next day we departed, and had lingring little gales for the space of foure or five dayes, at the ende of which we sawe a couple of French shippes, and had of them so much fish as would serve us plentifully for all the rest of the way, the Captaine paying for the same both golde and silver, to the just value thereof, unto the chiefe owners of the saide shippes, but they not looking for any thing at all, were glad in themselves to meete with such good intertainement at sea, as they had at our hands. After which departure from them, with a good large winde the twentieth of September we came to Padstow in Cornewall, God be thanked, in safetie, with the losse of twentie persons in all the voyage, and with great profit to the venturers of the said voyage, as also to the whole realme, in bringing home both golde, silver, Pearles and

other jewels great store. His name therefore be praised for evermore. Amen.

The names of certaine Gentlemen that were in this voyage.

M. John Hawkins.

M. John Chester, sir William Chesters sonne.

M. Anthony Parkhurst.

M. Fitzwilliam.

M. Thomas Woorley.

M. Edward Lacie, with divers others.

The Register and true accounts of all herein expressed hath beene approved by me John Sparke the younger, who went upon the same voyage, and wrote the same.

306. 1566. Nicolas Le Challeux, *Discours de l'histoire de la Floride*.

Nicolas Le Challeux's Discours de l'histoire de la Floride *(Dieppe, Sellier, 1566) was the first publication to reveal in print the circumstances of the extinction of the French Florida colony in 1565. This was the first of four editions in the same year, indicative of the public concern the affair aroused in France. They are listed in the facsimile edition of Laudonnière's* A Notable Historie *(Farnsworth, Surrey, 1964), in the preface by Thomas R. Adams. A simple, straightforward narrative by a carpenter (though containing in its second book material outside his personal experience), it was also an explosive attack on Spanish cruelty in killing off French captives in Florida and did something to lay foundations for the revenge raid in 1568. The English translation,* A true and perfect description of the last voyage or navigation attempted by Captaine Rybuat... into Terra Florida this last year past 1565 *(London, Henry Denham for Thomas Hacket, 1566), also stimulated anti-Spanish feeling in England. The best edition is in Suzanne Lussagnet, ed.,* Les Français en Amérique pendant la deuxième moitié de XVIe siècle, *part ii,* Les Français en Floride *(Paris, 1959). A new translation is given here.*

Florida, or a memorable history of events on the last voyage of Captain John Rybault, undertaken by command to the King, to the Island of the Indies commonly called Florida

i

Before the troubles and turmoils of the civil war arose in the kingdom, the King and several princes and Lords of his Council decided to send a good number of men with several ships to one of the lands of the Indies called Florida which had recently been discovered by the French. After the war had been concluded the proposal was revived, and to undertake the enterprise Jean Rybault, a man of courage and wisdom, and well versed in matters of the sea, was summoned to the court and received the King's commission to equip seven ships which would carry thither men, supplies and arms. He was honoured with the title of King's Lieutenant and made commander of all the soldiers which he found necessary to raise for such an undertaking. He was expressly forbidden to attempt any landing in another country or island in the area, especially one that was under the rule of the King of Spain. Similarly, crossing the Atlantic, he was to take a direct route to Florida. The news of the voyage spread at once and several men were persuaded to serve under the command of the Captain and under the authority of the King. They were guided by various motives; some were urged on by a praiseworthy and honest desire to increase their knowledge of the world which is a natural wish of a well established man, hoping that the expedition would profit them later. Others also came who wished with heart and soul to wage war, preferring to risk the stormy waters rather than to lay down their arms and retire to their former positions. Others were encouraged by the spread of a rumour that Florida was able to furnish all that a man could wish on earth, for that country had received a particular favour from heaven. There was neither the snow nor the frost of the raw, cold weather of the North, and it escaped the burning heat of the South. Without cultivation, the fields yielded sufficient to maintain the inhabitants. It appeared that this country could be made the most fertile in the world, only needing diligent and hard working men to reap the bounty and fat of the land for the use of mankind.

The land stretches in a northerly direction in almost the same longitude as Europe, and is in 23° of latitude. Sometimes when the sun is directly overhead, it is very hot; however the heat is moderated not only by the cool of the night and the dew but also by the soft rain which falls in such quantities that the ground is fertile and the crops grow strong and high. The country is rich in gold and in all species of animals for it has open and spacious fields. Nevertheless there are also quite high hills, exceedingly pleasant rivers, several kinds of trees emitting a sweet smelling sap. Considering all this, it was impossible that a man could not find there great pleasure and delight. Several men were attracted by such promises, others by the gold, having an avaricious wish to make money from the expedition and they came in legions to this town where the muster was taken to choose those who, in the opinion of the King's Lieutenant—were the most suitable for the enterprise. But this was not done as quickly as some, chiefly those who lodged the soldiers, wished, for they were angered by looking after such expensive men who did not pay their bills, despite the promise of the soldiers that their accounts would be soon settled. They spent over four months in the town before setting out, and in the end were bound by oath to behave themselves whilst in the service of the King and they received six months pay. This was not to the satisfaction of the Colonel for, about May, when a second muster of men was taken in order that embarkation could begin, some of those who had been paid, seized with anxiety at the prospect of such a long expedition and worried by the stormy appearance of the sea, changed their minds and deserted secretly without going any further. To prevent further desertions, another muster was taken at once, on May 10, and at the same time the men were ordered to embark.

We stayed in the harbour until May 22 waiting for animals and grain. About three hundred men were on board, including several craftsmen and their families. Whilst we awaited the orders of our lieutenant and a favourable wind, on Tuesday, [May] 22, we were caught in a great storm, the wind blowing from all directions with such force that the waves rose to a great height, frightening our sailors, whose only remedy was to cut the cables, raise the anchors and abandon us to the will of the wind. The most violent gust, coming from the north, drove us into Havre de

Grâce, where we remained three days, awaiting news from Dieppe by a brigantine which we had at once sent there. We prepared to leave this harbor on the 26 of the month [May]. As soon as we were on the right course we encountered a contrary wind which forced us into the Isle of Wight, an English possession, where the English asked us about our enterprise and, after we had told them about it, they offered us hospitality. We arrived there on May 28 and rode at anchor until June 14, when the wind changed to the north east, which is what we wanted, and we hoisted our sails to steer a straight course for Florida, which we longed to see. We were at sea for two whole months until we first sighted the land of Florida, except we did see one of the Isles of the Antilles, called by its natives Vocaiouques and by the French the Great Juçoise [Grand Lucaya, the largest of the Bahama Islands]. Some of our company wished to give it the name of Catherine, after the Queen Mother, and said it was situated at the latitude of 27°. We also encountered a ship 200 leagues seaward from there, but we did not come closer to it than three or four leagues.

When we reached Florida, which was on August 14, we saw the fire which the Indians had made for us. We sent out the brigantine which discovered a small river and, below its mouth, several Indians were found, who bartered silver for the goods we had brought to the country. They said that the silver had come from a ship which had been wrecked coming from the Antilles. We also discovered there a solitary Spaniard who had escaped a shipwreck twenty years before. We gave him hospitality and enquired whether he had heard anything of the French and the location of their settlement. To which he replied that he knew nothing but what he had heard from the natives; that they were located fifty leagues to the north of the place where we had landed. Accordingly we set sail and followed the coast, which was low and sandy, planted with fairly small trees and with narrow streams flowing south west, among which we found the River of May which our people had named previously. Even the rivers flowing from the north north east are not large, and because of the shallowness of the water, we could see the marks of anchors and we ascertained that there were not more than six or seven fathoms of water within three to four leagues of the land. I also recollect that between the River of

May and another called the Ay, we discovered another stream about two leagues to the north of the May. Here as night fell, we dropped anchor in eight or nine fathoms of water, finding the bottom either sandy or muddy. We also sounded the River of Dolphins and found it was two fathoms deep at the bar but at high tide the depth increased to two and three quarter fathoms.

After we had followed the coast looking for a landing place, on August 27 we came to anchor in seven fathoms, in the road of the River of May, about two leagues from the nearest land. On Wednesday August 29 we ascended the river in three small boats directly up to Fort Caroline, which our people had built for their protection in a convenient spot, bordered on one side by the river and on the other by woods, less than a quarter of a league away, with fields between the fort and the woods, a pleasant open space covered with various kinds of grasses and plants. There is no way into the woods except by means of a path which our men have made when going to the spring in the woods.

After we arrived, our lieutenant ordered the supplies and arms to be unloaded and carried to the fort to reinforce it. He also gave orders that the workmen, wives and children should go there. We were led by a gentleman of the house of Ully, by Beauchaire, and by others, who were also entrusted with the care of the most valuable part of his [Ribault's] baggage. Those who waited for us at the fort were delighted with our arrival for they had been distressed at being so long without any news from France, and to increase their worry, they had lived without supplies, saving those they could obtain by living like the natives, being unable to get anything from them except by resorting to force, as I shall relate in more detail later.

When we were settled there I studied the habits of the natives who seemed to me to be honest and gentle, for the men are upright and well proportioned, and have a somewhat ruddy complexion. I heard that each village had its own king, and for decoration they use leather, worked into strange patterns. Neither the men nor the women have any other clothing, except that the women girdle themselves with a small apron made of the skin of deer or other animals, tied on the left side in order to cover the most shameful part of their body. They are neither flat nosed nor thick lipped, having round, even faces, and good eye-sight. They wear their hair very long and they bind it neatly round their heads, this truss of hair serving as a quiver in which to carry their arrows when they go to war; it is remarkable how quickly they can get them into their hands ready for firing as straight as possible. They have loose morals; they never teach or correct their children; they steal unscrupulously and claim for themselves all they can secretly carry away. Each one has one wife and they strongly uphold the bond of marriage. They wage war against their neighbours, who have different languages, the most important arms being bows and arrows. Their houses are round, similar to dovecotes, built of weed and roofed with palm leaves. They never fear winds or storms but are often plagued by small flies which they call *Maringons*. To rid themselves of these vermin, they light fires in their houses, especially under the beds. They say that they sting very fiercely and the skin which has been stung looks like that of a leper. They consider nothing is as rich or as beautiful as the feathers of various coloured birds; they also highly prize small counters which they make from the bones of fish, and from green and red stones. They eat roots, fruits, plants and various kinds of fish, the largest fish they catch is called a *Bouquaué*, the fat of which they use instead of butter or another sauce. They have no wheat, but there is an abundance of corn which grows to the height of seven feet, the stalk is as thick as a cane, the seed as big as a pea, and the ear a foot long and the colour of natural wax. Firstly it is crushed and pounded into flour, then mixed and made into their *Migan* which looks like the rice which we have in this country. It must be eaten as soon as it is made for it deteriorates quickly and can never be kept. There are plenty of wild vines, entwined among the trees, as we see in several parts of this kingdom, but they are never used to make wine. Their drink called *Cassinnet* is made from a mixture of plants and is similar in colour to our beer. I have tasted it and it did not appear to be very unusual.

The country is hilly and thickly forested which may be the reason for the presence of wild animals which they say are a great danger to the unwary. I will not say much on these animals about which I only know by hearsay. I think it is sufficient to recount here what I have seen and that which I believe to be of interest to posterity. Especially we noted the crocodiles which are often seen coming across the sand in search of their prey. We have observed many, in particular a dead one whose flesh we ate. It was tender and white like veal and had a similar taste. It was killed by a shot between its scales which is the only way to kill one; their scales are strong enough to withstand all blows. The jaw opens up in a hideous way and it has a very large mouth in which the teeth are as straight as a comb and is able to open its mouth wide enough to swallow a cow. It is twelve or thirteen feet in length and has legs which are short in comparison with the body, unusual, vicious claws and a long, strong tail which is the chief means of defence. In the mouth I found no signs of a tongue, unless it was concealed in the palate (as I have said the lower jaw protrudes over the upper in a hideous manner the mere sight of which frightens all men). I have also seen, close to the weeds, a snake which had been killed by one of our group. It had wings which enabled it to leave the ground. The natives cut off its head and carried it away with painstaking care, I never found out the reason behind this. Some thought that the natives acted this way through some superstition and as far as I could see they were not without some idea of a divinity. I believe that under certain circumstances, if it is God's will, one could easily instruct them, not only in humanity and virtue, but also in holiness and religion, for as soon as the bell of the fort sounded for prayers, they would be there, and with us raise their hands to heaven with reverence and consideration.

During this time our colonel discharged his duties faithfully and gave orders that the settlement should be fortified and armed, so that it would be a safeguard if the natives should rise against us. On Monday September 3, five Spanish ships sailed close to our fleet. The flag ship appeared to be of 400 tons, the bark of 150 tons and there were also three pinnaces. About nine o'clock in the evening, they dropped anchor near our ships. They talked together that night and when our men asked why they had been looking for us,—they replied that they were our enemies since an all-out war had been declared. Then our men, realizing the strength of the Spaniards and their evil intentions, weighed anchor and hoisted their sails, The Spaniards gave chase but could not catch them. Hence they withdrew into the

River of Dolphins for they had decided to attack us. After plotting with the natives for our downfall, as the results of their enterprise would later reveal, they sent out their men from the river in numbers they thought sufficient to carry out their plan. We later heard from the Indians that they [the Spaniards] had about six hundred armed men. Not long afterwards three of our ships returned to the harbour (the *Trinity*, our flagship was carried down river), the Captain Jean Rybault discussed with the men on the ships the possibility of going to find the Spaniards.

It was decided that it was necessary to move against them by water, otherwise we would run the danger of losing our ships. Since our men were on land there was nothing to prevent them from boarding our ships and seizing them which seemed an unacceptable threat, for one reason in particular; we had no convenient way of sending to France to let the King know of the state of our undertaking. Accordingly on Monday September 10, at three in the afternoon, the Captain and Lieutenant of the King [Jean Ribault] reviewed his men and having exhorted them to do well for the service of the King, they all embarked; taking for defence not only those soldiers who have recently arrived but also the best of those who were already at the settlement, namely Captain Laudonnière's ensign, corporal and sergeant.

Laudonnière, a little before we arrived, worried at not hearing news from France and annoyed at being short of supplies, had thought of returning. He did not care if some of his men mistreated the Indians and he allowed them to bring prisoners into the fort, take their grain by force and other things required by necessity which knows no law. This caused the natives to turn from their good feelings towards the French and since the desire for vengeance is planted in men's hearts by nature, and as it is also the common instinct of all animals to defend life and limb, and to remove the source of trouble, it cannot be doubted that the natives conspired and intrigued with the Spaniards to free themselves from us since not only their bodies but also their goods had been interfered with. On Tuesday September 11 at around eight in the morning when our men were very near to the Spaniards, there arose a hurricane which continued for a long time, bringing heavy rain, thunder and lightning which at times made the sky appear to be on fire.

Fearing the threat from the heavens, both sides separated. Our three ships waited out the storm, and the Spanish flagship and bark took advantage of the wind. This bad weather lasted until September 23. Meanwhile the Spaniards having disembarked, had plenty of time in which to spy on us and to decide on the best means of surprising us, knowing that our men were still at sea, and that those left in the fort, comprised in part of those suffering from sea sickness and in part of workmen, women and children, in all 240 people under the care and protection of Captain Laudonnière, who in no way suspected that any force would come by land to injure them. Hence the guards left their posts a little before sunrise, on account of the bad weather which had lasted throughout the night.

Whilst the majority of people in the fort were in their beds sleeping, the Spaniards, guided by the Indians, having negotiated woods, ditches and rivers, arrived on Thursday, September 20 in rainy weather and, the gate being open, entered the fort with no resistance. They engaged in a terrible slaughter so great was the anger and hatred they had borne against our nation. They vied with each other as to who could best cut the throats of our men, ill and healthy alike, women and children, in such a way that it is impossible to conceive of a massacre which could be equal to this one in cruelty and barbarity. Some of our nimblest men, hurried from their beds and escaped into the ships which were in the river, left there by the colonel in the care of Jacques Rybault, the commander of the *Pearl* and of Loys Ballard, his lieutenant. Others, caught by surprise leapt over the pallisade, notably Laudonnière along with his chambermaid.

I was overtaken whilst on my way to work, carrying my tools. For as I was coming from my hut, I encountered the enemy and could think of no other means of escape except by turning round and running as quickly as possible and jumping over the pallisade, pursued every step by a pikeman. Nothing but the grace of God enabled me to double my effort, and old grey haired man that I am, nevertheless I jumped over the ramparts, which if I thought about it, I could not have done, for they were eight or nine feet in height. Once over I rushed towards the woods. When I was close to the edge of the trees, I looked back towards the fort and waited a little while, made braver because there was no one chasing me. From where I stood, I could see all of the fort, even the furthest courtyard, and I observed the horrible slaughter of our people and noted three of the standards of the enemy planted on the ramparts.

Having now lost all hope of seeing our people reunited, I put my trust in God and rushed into the wood, for it seemed to me that I could find no greater cruelty among wild animals than our enemies had wrought on our people. Misery and suffering encircled me, for I saw on earth no other hope except that God in His special grace, which overrides all thoughts of man, would deliver me. I sighed and wept, and in a voice of sorrow, prayed to God, saying "O God of our fathers, and Lord of Mercy, who has commanded us to call on Thee even from the depths of hell and the bottomless pit of death, promising at once Thine help and succour, show me by the hope which I have in Thee, which way I should take, to come to the end of my unhappy old age, plunged into a gulf of grief and bitterness. At least feeling the effect of Thy mercy, the confidence which Your promises bred in my heart, will not make me turn away for fear of the cruelty of wild, howling beasts on the one hand, and of Thine enemies and ours on the other, who bear ill will against us more because the memory of Your name is invoked amongst us than for any other reason. Help me my God, assist me, for I am so distressed that I can take no more!" Meanwhile whilst I was delivering this prayer, I was struggling through thick woodland interwoven with brambles and thorns, under high trees, in which there was neither roadway nor footpath.

I had been travelling this way for barely half an hour when I heard a noise near me which was like the weeping and moaning of men. Advancing in the name of God and with the assurance of His help, I discovered one of our men, the Seigneur de la Blondèrie, and a little behind him another, called master Robert, a man well known to all because he conducted prayers at the fort. Shortly afterwards we found the servant of Seigneur d'Ulli, the nephew of M. le Beau (the treasurer), Master Jacques Tousé, and several others. Having collected together, we commiserated with each other and considered what we had to do to save our lives. One member of the group, who was well thought of and well versed in the Scriptures put forward an idea: "Brothers, you see what

extreme misery we are in, in whichever direction we look, we are faced with nothing but cruelty. Heaven, earth, sea, woods, men, in short, nothing favours us. How do we know if we surrender ourselves to the mercy of the Spaniards, they will not show us compassion? Even if they kill us, we shall only suffer for a short time. For they are only human, and it might be that when their fury has been appeased, they will come to a compromise with us, otherwise what shall we do? Is it not better to fall into the hands of men than into the jaws of wild animals, or to allow oneself to die of hunger in this strange land?" After he had spoken in this way, the greater part of the group agreed with him, and applauded his plan. Despite this, I warned them of the overwhelming bloody cruelty of the enemy, and that it was not only for earthly reasons that they had carried out their mission with such passion, but chiefly because they had been told that we were among those who had turned to the teachings of the Gospel. That we would be cowards to attach more importance to men rather than God, who serves His own people in the midst of death, and usually gives His help even when men lose hope. I referred to some suitable passages from the scriptures, of Joseph, Daniel, Elijah and other prophets, even the Apostles, of St. Peter and of St. Paul. All of whom were saved from suffering by means which were unusual and strange to the sense and reason of mankind. His aim, I said, is not weakened nor ever enfeebled. Do you not remember, I went on, the flight of the Israelites from Pharoah? What hope had these people of escaping from the clutches of this powerful and cruel tyrant. He followed hard on their heels, before them was the sea, on two sides impenetrable mountains? What happened then? He who opened up the sea to make a way for His people, and afterwards swallowed up their enemies in the same waters, will He not lead us through the fields of this foreign land? But as I made these remarks, six of the company, following the first suggestion, left us to go to our enemies, hoping to receive mercy from them. But they should have known at once by experience what folly it is to trust more in men than in the promises of the Lord; for as soon as they emerged from the woods, as they were making their way to the fort, they were at once seized by the Spaniards and met the same fate as the others. They were killed and then dragged to the banks of the river, where the bodies of the others killed in the fort had been piled in heaps.

I must here relate an example of extreme cruelty. Jacques Rybault, Captain of the *Pearl*, rode his ships at anchor one hundred yards away from this massacre, where he took on board many of those who escaped from the butchery. The Spaniards, in good heart because of their victory, ruthlessly determined to kill the rest of the Frenchmen, trained the cannon of the fort on the ships and small boats, but no damage was done to our people because of the rainy weather and the fact that the cannon had been badly primed. But they sent a trumpeter to order them to surrender. When they realised that this would not intimidate them, they sent one of their men to our ships, showing the authority of Don Pedro de Menéndez, their commander, to make a compromise with our people; that they should leave their ships and withdraw, with their baggage, in the small boats to the other ships which were lower in the middle of the river, two leagues away from the fort. To which our people replied that there was no state of war between their two countries when six months ago, they had received orders from the King to make this voyage. We had done no wrong nor made any demands from anyone. The King and the Admiral had forbidden them expressly to make any landing in any part of the possessions of Spain, nor even approach it, for fear of giving offence. We have kept inviolate the King's command, and you cannot assert that we caused the massacre which you have carried out against our men; a massacre against all the rules of warfare for which our hearts bleed and for which, in another time and place, you may well be punished. As for the demands for our ships, you could sooner take our lives, and if you would restrain us, we shall employ the means which God and nature have given us to defend ourselves. The Spaniard returned and passed on the information which our men had given him; that they would not retreat and that they were determined to defend themselves. Then the angry company vented their wrath and bloody cruelty on the dead and showed them to the French who remained in the ships, endeavouring to touch their hearts, which was not possible, for they were forced to dismember the bodies, pulling out the eyes of the dead, fixing them on the points of their daggers and then, with shrieks of abuse and ribald laughter, hurled them at the French.

As for those of us who remained in the woods, we kept on moving, following what was in our opinion, the right course for the sea. And as it pleased God to direct our steps and mark out the paths, by and by we came to the brow of a hill, from where we could see the sea. But it was a good distance away, and, worse, the path we were to take appeared very difficult. To begin with the hill down which we had to climb was so high and steep that it was not possible for a man to descend on foot, and we would never have dared to begin to go down except that we helped steady ourselves by using the branches of the many bushes which grew on the hillside. In order to save our lives, we did not spare our hands, which, like our legs, were scratched and bleeding, and our bodies were almost torn to pieces. On climbing down the hill, we lost sight of the sea, since we were confronted by a copse situated on a small hill and to get to the wood, we had to cross a wide meadow of marshy ground, covered with reeds and other unusual plants which had branches and leaves as hard as wood which cut our legs and feet until they bled and we were constantly in water which came up to our thighs. Our misery was increased by the constant rain which was so heavy that it was like travelling between two seas. The further we went, the deeper the water became, and now, thinking we were at the end of our lives, we embraced each other, and with a shared love, we began to sigh and call to the Lord, professing our sins and acknowledging the severity of his judgement on us. "Alas, O Lord", we said, "what are we but wretched worms of the earth. Our souls, corrupted by grief, give themselves up into Your hands. O Father of mercy and God of love, deliver us from this death-like situation, or, if it is Your will, that we end our lives in this desert, help us so that when death, that most terrible of things, comes to us, we will not be daunted, but that we will remain steady and unshaken in the belief in your favour and good will, which we have experienced many times through Your son, Jesus Christ, and not give in to Satan, spirit of despair and suspicion. For if we are to die, we now proclaim in front of Your Majesty, that we wish to die for You, but if we are to live, it will be to tell of Your miracles amidst the Congregation of Thy Saints."

Having completed our prayers, we proceeded with difficulty directly towards the wood, as far as a swollen river which ran through the middle of the meadow. The channel was narrow, but quite deep and swift flowing, since the field sloped towards the sea. This increased our distress further, for no one dared to swim across. Whilst we were thinking of a way to cross over, I remembered the wood behind us. After urging my brothers to be patient and keep their trust in God, I returned to the wood and using a large axe which I was carrying when the fort was taken, I cut down a large branch and went back to the others who were waiting for me in great puzzlement. "Now", I said, "let us see if God will help us complete our journey, with the use of this staff." We laid the staff across the water, each of our men in turn holding onto the end, entered the water, supporting himself by means of the branch. In the middle of the channel, when he was out of sight, we pushed the staff with enough force to reach near to the opposite bank where he went ashore with the help of reeds and other plants found on the far shore. Using this method we crossed over one by one. But this was not without great danger, for we swallowed so much salt water that when we reached the other bank our hearts were beating fast and we were so weak as if we had been half drowned. When we had recovered and revived our spirits, heading towards the wood which we had noted was close to the sea, we were forced to use the branch again to negotiate another arm of water which gave us as much trouble as the first but, thanks to God, we crossed it, and in the evening entered the wood where we spent the night in great fear and trembling, standing upright against the trees. Despite the fact we had suffered so much, we did not have the will to sleep. For who could rest with their mind so full of fear. We also saw, about daybreak, within fifty yards of us, an animal as big as a deer, with a large head, blazing, staring eyes, hanging ears and prominent hindquarters. She appeared monstrous to us because of her large gleaming eyes which were a great wonder. But she never came near enough to us to do any harm.

At dawn, we emerged from the wood and saw the sea again which, after God, was the only hope of saving our lives but we were once more angered and upset for we saw before us marshland full of water and covered in reeds, the same as we had crossed the previous day. We were going across this field when we saw close to our path among the reeds a group of people which we thought, at first glance, were our enemies who

had come to cut off our escape-route, but when we came closer and saw that they were distressed, naked and frightened as us, we realised at once that they were our own people. There was Captain Laudonnière, his chambermaid, Jacques Morgues of Dieppe [Jacques de Moyne de Morgues, the painter], François de Val of Rouen, the son of the Count of Rouen, Nigaise de la Crotte, Nicholas the joiner, the trumpeter of M. Laudonnière, and others amounting to twenty-six men.

Whilst we were discussing what should be done, two men climbed to the top of one of the highest trees and spotted one of our small ships which was under the command of Captain Maillard to whom they signalled to make him aware that we needed his help. He sent us a small boat, but for us to reach the shore we had to cross more reeds and two other rivers similar to those we had traversed the previous day. For this purpose the staff which I had cut the other morning was of great use as well as two others provided by Captain Laudonnière. As we came close to the boat, our strength failed us because of the hunger and hardship we had undergone, and we would have remained there had not the sailors, proving themselves very able rescuers, given us a helping hand and carried us one by one into the boat where we were received with affection. They gave us bread and water and after eating we regained our strength little by little which was a sure sign of the grace of God, who had saved us against all hope, from the numerous dangers of death which surrounded and besieged us throughout, in order that we would always give thanks and praises to Him. We spent the whole night relating the miraculous works of God and we comforted each other in the remembrance of our safe delivery.

At daybreak Jacques Rybault, Captain of the *Pearl* came on board to discuss with us the best way to rescue the rest of our men and our ships. He told us of the shortage of supplies, the breakdown of our forces, the seizure of our weapons and means of defence and the uncertainty of the fate of our leader, not knowing if he had been carried off by the storm and stranded on some distant coast. We therefore concluded that the best thing we could do was to try and return to France. It was the view of the majority of the company that those who had escaped from the fort should be divided into two parties, one remained on the *Pearl* and the other went under the command of Captain

Maillard. Having decided to return to France, on Thursday September 25, taking advantage of a strong north wind, we left the coast. The ships became separated from the first day and we did not meet again at sea.

We sailed five hundred leagues without any mishap but one morning at sunrise we were attacked by a Spanish ship which we withstood as best we could so that we brought her under our control and hitting them in such a manner that one could see blood overflowing from the scupper holes, and all the men gave up and went below deck. There was no chance of boarding her because of the stormy weather for there was a danger that whilst holding onto her, the ships would hit each other and we would be overwhelmed and sink. The Spaniards were happy to see us go, and we left them, thanking God that no one, except the cook, had been killed or injured in the skirmish. We met with no enemies on the rest of the voyage but we were badly troubled by the winds which often threatened to cast us up on the Spanish coast which we feared most and which would have been the last straw. We also suffered from cold and hunger at sea, for it must be understood that we had escaped from Florida without any clothes or equipment for day or night except a shirt or some other rag of clothing which was little protection against the ravages of the weather. What is worse we had to ration the bread which was putrid and rotten and even the water which had become infected was, nevertheless, rationed to one small cup a day. This poor diet is the reason why after we landed we fell ill with various diseases from which several of our men died. At the end of this dangerous and unhappy voyage we landed on the coast of La Rochelle where we were welcomed and gently and kindly treated by the people living in the country and in the town, who gave us all we needed and, helped by their good will, we received sufficient to enable everyone to return home.

ii

You have heard how Jean Rybault set sail with the best of our sailors to look for the Spaniards and, after five days of searching, he did not find them, but did meet the *Trinité*, flagship of his fleet. Not knowing what had happened at the fort, he determined to protect the coast against a Spanish attack and went on board [the *Trinité*] which, following, the customary naval discipline,

enabled him to command his men better. The weather was very unfavourable. The wind blew hard and it rained continously. On the fifth day the storm increased and drove them with such force that no one was able to prevent the ship running aground on the coast about fifty leagues above the River of May. The ships were broken up and the weapons lost. However all the men managed to get on land, except Captain la Grangé who threw himself onto a mast and was drowned. His death was lamented by the others not only for the good advice and leadership which he gave but also for his friendly companionship for he had the ability to raise the spirits of the men and make them courageous and follow his example. Having been saved from the fury of the sea our men soon encountered another problem. There was no cure for their hunger except by eating what nature provided, that is to say weeds, roots and similar things which had to satisfy their empty stomachs. Nor was there anything with which to quench their thirst, except old pools of muddy water, and one look at the scum which floated on it was enough to make the fittest man sick. Nevertheless they were carried away with the frenzy of their hunger and consumed many things which seemed outlandish to them. They lived in this miserable way for eight days.

On the ninth day they found a small boat by chance. This was some comfort to them for it would enable them to get news of their shipwreck to the fort. They were twelve leagues from the fort by land and fifty by water. To get there they had to cross the River of Dolphins which was deep and a good quarter of a league wide. It was impossible to cross without some vessel. After they had retrieved the boat they caulked it using their shirts in place of oakum. After this Captain Jean Rybault with his usual courtesy and modesty called together several men for advice and spoke to them in this manner: "Companions and friends, we cannot continue to live with such miseries and disasters. It were better to wish for death than to live burdened down with such sorrows, unless our God gives us faith in His providence to wait for such help as He will be pleased to give us. However it is up to us to use all our wits if we are to put an end to our sufferings. I suggest that several of us, using this small boat, go to the fort to inform them of our extreme situation and tell they they must give us help." And he and the rest of the company threw themselves on the ground and began to cry in the name of God. Having finished their prayers, they looked for the most suitable man to undertake the journey and chose Thomas Le Vasseur of Dieppe to whom Jean Ribault gave orders that first he must inform the men of the distress into which they had fallen. With him went Vincent Simon, Michel Gover and others, making sixteen in all. As I have said before, our men were on the opposite bank of the river from the fort and on the same day they saw on the side near the fort a company of armed men displaying an ensign. Because they were so far away they could only guess that they were Spaniards. The French were plunged into such depths of despair, that as a last resort some of the company swam across and offered to surrender if their lives would be saved. They were, at first, received courteously. The Captain of the company of Spaniards, called Vallemande, declared by his honour as a gentlemen, knight and Christian, his good will towards the French. It was the common custom of the Spanish in warfare to be satisfied with victory against the French without carrying things to excess. He spoke by means of an interpreter in order, that they would be taken in by such fine promises, so that nothing would be done which would later be resented by their countries.

He immediately ordered a barge to be equipped and sent five Spaniards on board to take the ship across to our men. Which they did. When they had crossed and had made a speech on behalf of Vallemande, Jean Rybault went on board, one of the first group of thirty men, and was received courteously by Vallemande. But the others of his company were led away from him in pairs with their hands tied behind their backs. The rest of our men came across, thirty at a time, whilst Vallemande kept the attention of Captain Jean Rybault with false and flattering remarks. Rybault surrendered to Vallemande, trusting in his good will. When all our men had crossed and had been tied together, two by two, French and Spaniards together made their way to the fort. When Captain Rybault and others, notably the Sieur d'Ottigny, saw that the men were tied up, they began to see things in a different light and asked Vallemande for further assurances of good faith, which he gave, saying that the bonds were only used to get the men safely to the fort. Once there, he would adhere to the promises he had made. When they came close to the fort, he en-

quired who among them were sailors, ships' carpenters, gunners or men who had jobs connected with the sea. These amounted to thirty men. Soon afterwards a company came from the fort to meet our men who were made to march behind the Sieur de Vallemande and his company, like a herd of cattle being led to the slaughter. Then at the sound of fifes, drums and trumpets, these enraged Spaniards unleashed their wrath on the wretched Frenchmen who were still tied up. They vied with one another to see who could strike the most telling blow with pike, halberd and sword so that in half an hour they triumphed and achieved a "glorious" victory, cruelly killing those who, trusting in their word, had surrendered themselves into their protection.

During this massacre, Captain Jean Rybault pleaded several times with Vallemande to save his life. Similarly the Sieur d'Ottigny, on his knees, reminded him of his promise. But all to no avail, for he turned his back on them and one of his assassins struck Captain Rybault from behind with a dagger which caused him to fall to the ground where he was stabbed two or three more times until he was dead. This then was the treatment which our men (who had surrendered themselves in good faith) received from the Spaniards. To complete their cruelty and barbarity they cut off the beard of the King's lieutenant, and later sent it to Seville, as a proof of their actions, along with several of our sailors who had been spared and who were employed on the voyage. This was recounted by one of these sailors, Christopher le Breton from Havre de Grâce, who fled in secret from Seville to Bordeaux and thence by ship to Dieppe. And as a trophy of their victory, they dismembered the body of that good and faithful servant of the King and cut the head into quarters which they placed on four pikes planted in the four corners of the fort.

307. October 16, 1566. Deposition by Jean Memyn, survivor of the Spanish attack on Florida.

The French ambassador at Madrid was able to discover one survivor who had escaped being executed in Florida and obtained his story before managing to have him repatriated. His account of the fleet actions does not accord with those in other sources, French and Spanish.

First printed in Paul Gaffarel, La Floride française *(Paris, 1815), pp. 443–446; reprinted in* Dépêches de M. de Fourquevaux, *edited by Célestin Douais, 3 vols. (Paris, 1896–1904), I, 131–134. This was translated in C. E. Bennett,* Laudonnière and Fort Caroline *(Gainesville, Fla., 1964), pp. 99–102. It is here newly translated.*

On 16th day of October 1566, in the presence of Monseigneur de Fourquevaux, Knight of the King's Order, counsellor of His Majesty and his ambassador in Spain. Jean Memyn, aged between twenty-three and twenty-four years, native of La Rochelle, son of Guillaume Memyn, citizen of La Rochelle and Lord of Viart, upon his oath to tell the whole truth.

Questioned about his reasons for being in Spain, he replied that he came with the fleet of forty-two ships and two caravels from New Spain and other places in the West Indies to the harbor of Sanlúcar on 26th August last, having embarked at the harbor of Santo Domingo in Hispaniola as a prisoner of a Spanish soldier called Herrere, a native of Palagos near Seville. They left Santo Domingo a few days before the feast of St. John [December 27].

Questioned as to why he was a prisoner of this soldier, he replied that three years ago next May in the town of La Rochelle, Captain Jean Dubois was recruiting men-at-arms to sail to Florida with victuals and assistance for the French who had gone there one year previously. Memyn, being a young man curious to see the world, joined the captain as a private individual and embarked on a *reberge* [=*raborge*] which at Belle Île took its place in the fleet commanded by Captain Jean Ribbault. Their course took them to the Canaries and the island of Dominica, where they anchored for a fortnight to take on fresh water, and thence to the island of Mona, and finally to Florida, where they arrived towards the end of July of that year on a Friday. They were six vessels in all: the *Trinité* of Dieppe, the *Epaule de Mouton*, the *reberge* of La Rochelle, mentioned above, of which Jean Ribbault was captain, and three others whose names he does not remember. When they arrived in Florida they met captain Laudon-

nière and other Frenchmen at the fort they had built, and to them they had carried the supplies transported on the ships: corn, wine, biscuits, salted meat and other necessary provisions together with artillery and ammunition for the defence of the harbor.

Questioned about the number of men there might have been in the naval force and in the fort, and about the names of the captains, he replied that they had brought as well [as men] women and children and young men to work the land. Counting them, and all the soldiers of the fleet and the fort, there might have been in all six hundred souls or thereabouts under four ensigns. The captains were Jean Ribbault, Louis [Jacques?] Ribbault his son, Jean Dubois, Gros, Bellot, Martin, Pierre Rennat and others. There were also some gentlemen of Normandy, even one called the Seigneur de Grandpied who is still alive and a prisoner in Havana. There was with him a child from Paris by the name of Jacques, whose father is domestic servant to His Excellency the Cardinal de Bourbon.

Questioned about the taking of the fort and the defeat of the French, he replied that about a fortnight after their arrival on a Thursday morning, twenty-five ships were sighted making straight for the fort. Captain Jean Ribbault once he had spotted them, sent his son in a patrol boat to reconnoiter the ships and parley with them. As it came near, the ships, which were Spanish and Portuguese, fired, all twenty-five of them, six-pounders, at the patrol boat and had not the least desire to parley. Seeing this the patrol boat returned to harbor at the fort. Then captains Jean Ribbault and Laudonnière agreed to embark soldiers on their ships, to go and find out what exactly the twenty-five ships were, and in fact six French ships set sail towards them. The twenty-five ships, seeing the six French vessels making straight for them, fled and were lost to sight, since they slipped into a river mouth fifteen leagues from the fort. The French ships returned to harbor near their fort, whereupon a great storm arose. Captain Jean Ribbault, realising that the storm was intensifying, went ashore accompanied by a number of his men and proceeded to the fort in small boats. They arrived there about midnight, when the storm became so fierce that the cables of the ships left at anchor broke. Four of them capsized and were lost with all hands drowned except for three sailors and a boy, all four of Dieppe; they are still alive, prisoners of the Spanish in Havana. The other two ships with Captain Laudonnière and Captain Louis [Jacques] Ribbault, because of the violence of the storm, weighed anchor and put out to sea. The storm lasted for two days and two nights.

Meanwhile, the twenty-five ships which had retreated into the river mouth fifteen leagues from the fort disembarked their soldiers to take the fort by surprise, which they did on the second night of the storm. One of them who spoke French advanced to meet the sentry. He told him that he was a Frenchman and in the middle of their conversation he killed him. Immediately he returned to his friends and they all arrived together at the fort about midnight and entered it. They found the French asleep and, apart from a few, butchered them; among the few were the depository, three drummers, one from Dieppe and two from Rouen, and four trumpeters, three from Normandy and one from Bordeaux called Jacques Dulac. He does not know the names of the others, who are still in Florida or on the islands over there with Pedro Menéndez and who were all found sleeping fully clad on a bed. As for Jean Ribbault and about sixty others, they were kept till the next day and then put to the sword. They cut off the beard of Jean Ribbault, saying that they wanted to send it to the King of Spain. The number of those killed both in the fort and on an island nearby may have been about three hundred and fifty men.

Captain Laudonnière, when he saw the fort had been taken, fled to France with one ship and one patrol boat, whereas Captain Louis [Jacques] Ribbault retired into a river mouth thirty leagues from the fort with one ship and about thirty-six men, both soldiers and sailors.

Captains Jean Ribbault, Jean Dubois, Gros, Martin, Rennat, and many others, whose names he does not remember, all lost their lives at the defeat and shipwreck. The women and children were taken to the island of Porto Rico. He says also that the Seigneur de Grandpied and about seventeen or eighteen sailors are alive and prisoners in Havana.

At this defeat the Portuguese were as many as the Spanish in number, perhaps even more. It was the Portuguese who were more murderous and more cruel than the Spanish. The fort was fired the next day and all the victuals destroyed.

After the taking of the fort,—Menéndez sent two hundred men to a mountain thirty leagues away from the fort, the respondant being among them. There is a silver mine in the mountain. After two weeks the respondant was taken to Havana. There they are building a castle of hewn stone which will be very strong when it is finished, though at present it is only six to eight metres high. Havana has perhaps three hundred dwellings, but is merely an open village. He says that he saw eleven Frenchmen hanged in Havana, but cannot say why. Then he was taken to Porteriche [San Juan de Puerto Rico?], a fortified town; eight Frenchwomen and four little children were taken there from Florida. One of them was the wife of a Rouen goldsmith, but she has now married a Portuguese. Afterwards the respondant was taken to Santo Domingo which is a large fortified town, and there he was put aboard a ship of the fleet which a short time ago arrived in Spain. Two ships of the fleet that had sailed with Menéndez laden with sugar and copper carried fifteen or sixteen French sailors and letters to the King of Spain, but corsairs captured them near Sanlúcar.

Chapter Thirty-five
The Spanish Conquest of Florida, 1565

PHILIP II CONTINUED to be well informed by his ambassador in Paris of the departure of the French expedition of 1564 and of its probable objectives, while later in the year he had at his disposal the report of Manrique de Rojas (301) on where the French had been in 1562. Early in 1565 he determined to destroy the French settlement and to replace it by a Spanish one. The French were so placed as to be able to cut out vessels from the fleets coming through the Florida Strait and also to use their post or posts as bases from which to mount raids on the Caribbean islands and the Spanish shipping in the area. In the spring of 1565 he confided the command of his expedition to Pedro Menéndez de Avilés (308) and accelerated his departure as he received reports of the relief expedition, with its provisions for a fully fledged French colony that Jean Ribault was making in France. As it happened, Menéndez, on August 28, entered an inlet in the offshore island chain and founded San Agustín. The two fleets reached Florida at much the same time. On September 4, on a reconnaissance by sea, Menéndez de Avilés located the French fleet standing off the entrance to the St. Johns River and, after a preliminary skirmish with it, turned south again to San Agustín. Meanwhile, Jean Ribault had mobilized all his forces and moved down the coast on September 14 in an abortive attempt to intercept and bring Menéndez's ships to battle. In doing so he was caught in a hurricane and, eventually, had all of his vessels driven ashore well to the south of San Agustín. In the meantime, Menéndez, using a Frenchman captured in the West Indies and some Indian helpers as guides, marched by land on La Caroline, surprising the fort in the early hours of September 20. He killed almost every Frenchman he could find, although he rescued a few women and children from his men. Leaving a garrison at the site, he hurried south, to discover that Ribault had not, as he feared, destroyed San Agustín. Soon, receiving reports of parties of stranded Frenchmen along the coast to the south, by bluff, arrogance, and dubious offers of mercy, he succeeded in obtaining the surrender of successive groups of Frenchmen, including Jean Ribault himself. He had his men butcher them, without distinction of rank, after he had selected a handful of Catholics from among them.

The French disposed of, Menéndez proceeded to develop his garrison system. La Caroline, renamed San Mateo, burned down and had to be rebuilt. San Agustín was established as something more than a fortified Indian village. The territory of the Ays tribe in the south was visited and a military post placed at San Antonio on the St. Lucia River. He then sailed to Havana to plead, largely unsuccessfully, with the governor, García Osorio, for supplies for his men. By his efficiency, ruthlessness, and energy, he appeared to have achieved in a few months the basic objectives of his mission. The materials on the Spanish conquest of Florida are numerous and can be given only in selection. The two memoirs, by Gonzalo Solís de Merás and Bartolomé Barrientos, take precedence as coherent and literate narratives, written to expound and to justify the actions of Pedro Menéndez de Avilés and his associates. Sections from both, dealing with the period of conquest (316 and 317) are given below. Solís de Merás, writing as an eyewitness and probably completing his account in 1567, is the more authoritative; Barrientos, having the use of some of the former's materials, but collecting in the University of Salamanca, where he was a professor, materials from other observers is able to vary the story in detail, although samples only of his contribution can be given. Solís de Merás appeared in full (from the surviving defective manuscript) in E. Ruidíaz y Caravia, *La Florida*, 2 vols., (Madrid, 1893), I; and in translation by Jeanette T. Connor as *Pedro Menéndez de Avilés. Memorial by Gonzalo Solís de Merás* (Deland, Fla., 1923; reprinted, Gainesville, Fla., 1965); Barrientos first appeared in Genero García, ed., *Dos antigus relaciones de la Florida* (Mexico City, 1902), translated by Anthony Kerrigan, as *Pedro Menéndez de Avilés, Founder of Florida written by Bartolemé Barrientos* (Gainesville, Fla., 1965).

Administrative documents include the *Capitulación* and *Asiento* of March 20, 1565 (given below in Jeanette Connor's translation) (308), an order of September 8, 1565, by Philip II to Pedro Menéndez de Avilés, A.G.I., Seville, Patronato 1/1/19, translated in C. E. Bennett, *Laudonnière and Fort Caroline* (1964), pp. 126–127, not reprinted. An order by the king to the Casa de Contratación, dated August 15, 1565, to prepare further reinforcements for Florida is also translated (somewhat obscurely) in Bennett, pp. 125–126. Letters of Pedro Menéndez de Avilés of August 13, September 11, October 15, December 12, and December 15, 1565 provide an almost continuous account of the progress of the expedition from the crossing of the Atlantic until what can be regarded as the successful completion of the first two stages of its mission, the destruction of the French colony and the laying of the foundations of a Spanish settlement in Florida.

Originals of some but not all of them are extant in A.G.I., Seville, but they have become best known through the set of transcripts made for Martin Fernández de Navarrete and preserved in the Museo Naval, Madrid. They were first published from this source in Luis Cebreiro Blanco, ed., *Colección de diarios y relaciones para la historia de los viajes y descubrimientos*, 5 vols. (Madrid, 1943), II, 47–82. They were published in facsimile in M. Fernández de Navarrete, *Colección de documentos y manuscritos compilados para Fernández de Navarrete*, 38 vols. (Nendeln, Liechtenstein, 1971), XIV, fols. 281–318. A number of them were published from the originals by E. Ruidíaz y Caravia, *La Florida*, 2 vols. (1893), II; the first set of English translations was made by Henry Ware, "Letters of Pedro Menéndez de Avilés," *Massachusetts Historical Society Proceedings*, second series, VIII, 416–468. Translations from several sources are given below (309–315).

The "Memoria" of Francisco Lopez de Mendoza Grajales, a priest who was a member of the expedition, is a useful account by one who took part in the voyage and the attack on La Caroline. It is printed in *Colección de documentos inéditos de Indias*, III, 460ff. Translations appear in B. F. France, ed., *Historical Collections of Louisiana and Florida* (New York, 1875), pp. 191–234, and in C. E. Bennett, *Laudonnière* (1964), pp. 141–163. It is not included.

308. March 20, 1565. Capitulations and Asiento between Philip II and Pedro Menéndez de Avilés regarding the conquest of Florida.

The agreements concluded in March 1565 between Philip II and Pedro Menéndez de Avilés are based on those with earlier conquistadores, except that by this time the expansion of the Spanish empire had been slowed down and that which had been normal in the 1520s and 1530s was now exceptional. The adelantado was given wide responsibilities he must undertake in Florida, and to which he must contribute from his personal fortune, but, exceptionally, the crown promised substantial naval assistance in the conquest and thereafter. It is notable that the grant extended northward to include Newfoundland between 50° and 60° N.

Printed in Colección de documentos inéditos de Indias, *XXIII 242-258; Eugenio Ruidíaz y Caravia, La Florida, 2 vols. (Madrid, 1893), 415-427. There is a translation in J. T. Connor, Pedro Menéndez de Avilés. Memorial by Gonzalo Solís de Merás (Deland, Fla., 1923), pp. 259-270, which is reprinted.*

The King:—Whereas we have given *asientos* at various times for the discovery and settlement of the provinces of Florida, and likewise charged Don Luis de Velasco, who was our Viceroy of New Spain, to send a certain number of people and religious to settle that country, and an *asiento* was last made concerning this with Lucas Vasquez de Ayllon; and efforts have been made by the persons to whom we gave the said *asientos*, as well as by the Viceroy aforesaid; never up to now has that land been colonized; nor has what we desired, which was the aforesaid settlement, been accomplished; nor the teaching and conversion of the natives of those provinces, and the bringing them into our Holy Catholic Faith; and as we have in mind the good and the salvation of those souls, we have decided to give the order to send religious persons to instruct the said Indians, and those other people who are good Christians and our subjects, so that they may live among and talk to the natives there may be in those lands and provinces of Florida, and that [the Indians] by intercourse and conversion with them may more easily be taught our Holy Catholic

Faith and be brought to good usages and customs, and perfect polity. And to you, Pedro Menéndez de Avilés, Knight of the Order of Santiago, have I offered and do offer, because of the desire you have for the service of God Our Lord, and for the increase to the Royal Crown of these kingdoms, that during the coming month of May of this present year, you shall hold ready and prepared to sail, in San Lucar de Barrameda, in the port of Santa Maria or in the Bay of Cadiz, in order to depart with the first opportunity, six shallops of fifty *toneles* each, more or less; and four swift *zabras*, with their oars, arms and munitions, laden with supplies and fully prepared for war; and that you shall take five hundred men, one hundred of them farmers and one hundred sailors, and the rest of them naval and military men and officials, others professional stonecutters, carpenters, sawyers, smiths, barbers, locksmiths; all of them with their arms, arquebuses and crossbows, and helmets and bucklers, and the other offensive and defensive weapons which you may see fit and which may be suitable for the said voyage; and two priests; and that you shall do other things declared above, all of this at your cost and under your commission, without Our being obligated, or the Kings who may come after Us, to pay or indemnify you anything thereof other than what may be conceded to you by this Agreement, as you have entreated me to make it with you and to grant you certain favors; whereupon, because of the confidence and satisfaction we have in you; because the qualities required are found in you, and because you have served Us often and well; I commanded that with you, the said Pedro Menéndez de Avilés, the following agreement and *asiento* be made:

Firstly, you, the said Pedro Menéndez, bind and commit yourself to hold ready and prepare to sail, for the said month of May, in San Lucar, Cadiz or the port of Santa Maria, the said six shallops of the tonnage mentioned; and four swift *zabras* with their oars, arms, artillery and munitions, laden with supplies and fully prepared for war; and to take the five hundred men aforesaid, and among them seamen and soldiers, priests and tradesmen, as has been said.

Item: You shall offer and bind yourself to hold ready for the said time, the galleon you have, called *San Pelayo*, which has a capacity of more than six hundred *toneles* and is new, about to make her first voyage; and you shall load and sail her for whatever place in the Indies you may choose, laden to half or two thirds of what she can carry, and the remaining space you shall leave vacant to take over therein about three hundred men of the five hundred aforesaid whom you must carry thus, and any food and sustenance they may need, as far as Dominica or the Cape of Tiburon, or the Cape of San Antón, as you shall prefer, which is seventy leagues from Havana, more or less, and as many more from Florida; because the said shallops being small and open vessels, cannot carry the said people, and they would sicken and die with the great heat from the sun and the heavy showers there are in the said parts; nor could they take the supplies necessary for the men aforesaid, as the voyage is long. And on arriving at Dominica, or the place which may appear best to you, you shall transfer the men from the said galleon to the said shallops, and the said galleon shall continue her voyage, and you shall go with the said shallops and four *zabras*, and the said five hundred men, supplied and prepared for war as has been said, to the coast of Florida, where you pledge yourself to test and reconnoitre the best and most convenient places of the said coast, as it seems to you; coasting along by sea and searching and investigating on land where a harbor and place for a settlement can best be found; and you will try to obtain information as to whether there are on the said coast or [in the said] country, any settlers who are corsairs, or of any other nations not subject to Us, and you shall endeavor to cast them out by the best means that seem to you possible; you shall take the said land of Florida for Us and in our name, trying to attract the natives thereof to our obedience; and you shall explore from Los Ancones and the Bay of San Josepe, which is one league from Florida toward the west, as far as the Cape of Los Mártires, in twenty-five degrees; and thence as far as Terranova, which lies between fifty and sixty degrees [north latitude], east or west and north and south: the whole coast, in order to reconnoitre and test the harbors and currents, rocks and shoals and inlets there may be on the aforesaid coast; having them marked and indicated as accurately as you can by their latitudes and ships' courses, so that the secret of the said coast and the harbors which may be thereon, shall be known and understood; and you must do what you can within this year, and

the rest within three years, the period wherein by this *asiento* you obligate yourself to settle the aforesaid country.

Furthermore: You offer and pledge yourself to take over on the said voyage sufficient supplies for all the said five hundred men for one year, the time being counted from when the men shall be on the ships ready to depart.

Item: You pledge yourself that in the three years following the day you set sail, you will bring to the said land and coast of Florida about five hundred men to be settlers thereof, two hundred of whom shall be married, or one hundred at least; and the rest for the greater part must be farmers and workmen, in order that the land may be cultivated with more ease; and they shall be people of pure descent and not of those who are prohibited.

Item: You offer and pledge yourself that with the aforesaid people you will build and settle, within the said three years, two or three towns of at least one hundred inhabitants each, in the parts and places which shall seem best to you; and that in each of them there shall be a large house of stone, mud or wood, according to the nature and character of the land, with its moat and drawbridge; the most substantial that can be built according to weather and circumstances, so that in case of need the residents may gather therein and shelter themselves from the perils which may beset them from Indians, corsairs or other people.

Furthermore: You offer and pledge yourself that within the said time, and among the number of the said people whom you bind yourself to take, you will include at least ten or twelve religious, of the Order which may appear best to you: persons who are of a good life and example; likewise four others of the Society of Jesus, so that there may be religious instruction in the said land, and the Indians can be converted to our Holy Catholic Faith and to our obedience.

Furthermore: You pledge yourself to bring to the said country within the said time, one hundred horses and mares, two hundred calves, four hundred swine, four hundred sheep and some goats, and all the other cattle and live stock that shall seem proper to you.

Item: You offer that in all that is possible to you the said voyage for discovery and settlement shall be with all peace and amity, and in a Christian spirit; and you will carry on the government of the people under your charge with the greatest Christianity and best treatment that you can, so that in everything Our Lord and Ourselves may be served, in accordance with the instructions which shall be given you, and which it is customary to give to those who go to make similar settlements.

Furthermore: You pledge yourself to import to the aforesaid country, within the said three years, five hundred [negro] slaves for your service and that of the people you are to take over, and in order that the towns may be built and the land cultivated with greater ease; and for planting sugar cane for the sugar mills that may be built, and for building the said sugar mills.

Item: Inasmuch as there are shallops and *zabras* on the coasts of Biscay, Asturias and Galicia which are more suitable than [those] in Andalusia; likewise carpenters, smiths, stone-cutters and laborers; We declare and deem it well that the section of this armada and the people who may set out from those parts, shall go directly to the Canary Islands without proceeding to the said towns of San Lucar and Cadiz, being first examined before the magistrate, or person whom We shall appoint, of the port whence the people and vessels are going.

Furthermore: Under condition that the aforesaid armada which you have thus to assemble, as has been said, must first be inspected by one of our officials, according to the system which it is customary to follow, so that it may be ascertained that it goes by the order and in fulfilment of this *asiento*.

Item: You pledge yourself to give security which shall be *legas, llanas y abonadas*, that in case you shall not be ready to set sail in the first fair weather, in the coming month of May of this present year; and in case you should not have everything prepared which you are obligated to take over at the aforesaid time, in accordance with this *asiento*, you will return to us fifteen thousand ducats which we grant you and order to be given you, and you must give the said security at this court or in the city of Seville, and submit it to those [gentlemen] of our Royal Council of the Indies and to our other courts of Justice.

And as an aid to the great expenses, dangers and labors that you, the said Pedro Menéndez, must have in the said discovery and settlement,

that which on our part shall be fulfilled with you is the following:

And in order that you, the said Pedro Menéndez de Avilés, may the more willingly accomplish and fulfil all the aforesaid, it is our will and pleasure to appoint you our Governor and Captain-General of the said coast and country of Florida, and of all the settlements you may establish therein, for all the days of your life, and of that of a son or son-in-law of yours; and you shall receive from Us each year a salary of two thousand ducats, which are to be paid you from the products and rents which may belong to us in the said country; but if there be none, we shall not be obliged to give and pay you the said salary.

Furthermore: In order to grant you more favor, we promise to give you now fifteen thousand ducats, so that you can make yourself ready.

Furthermore: We shall give you license so that from these kingdoms and dominions, or the kingdom of Portugal, or the Islands of Cape Verde, or Guinea, you or whoever you may empower, may transport to the said coast and country of Florida five hundred negro slaves, at least one third of whom shall be females, free of any duty which may belong to us from them; whom you must take registered for the said coast and country, and not for any other parts, under penalty of your losing them if you should take them to other parts.

Item: I shall grant you the favor of bestowing on you the title of our Adelantado of the said coast and country, for you and your heirs and successors in perpetuity.

Furthermore: I shall give you authority so that to those who may go to settle in the said country, you can give *repartimientos* and lands and estates, for their establishments, farm lands and pastures, in accordance with the station of each one and what may appear best to you, [but] without prejudice to the Indians.

Furthermore: If we establish a Royal Audiencia in the aforesaid country of Florida, we shall grant you the favor of giving you the title of *alguacil mayor* of the said Audiencia, for you and for your heirs and successors, in perpetuity.

Item: Of what you shall thus discover and settle in the said country of Florida, we will grant you twenty-five square leagues, in one place or in two, as you may prefer; and it shall be good land and in a locality which shall be convenient to you, [but] without prejudice to the Indians; the which shall belong to you and your heirs and successors in perpetuity, forever and ever, [but] without your holding any jurisdiction therein, or owning any mines, because that must remain for Us. And inasmuch as you have begged Us to bestow on you the title of Marquis of those twenty-five square leagues, which we command to be given you, we say that when the expedition has come to an end, and you have fulfilled in all things what is contained in this *asiento*, we will grant you the favor that may be deserved in conformity with your services.

Furthermore: We grant you in perpetuity, free of costs, for you and your heirs and successors, one fifteenth part of all the income, mines of gold and silver, precious stones, pearls and products which We shall have from the said lands and provinces of Florida.

Item: We will grant you in the said lands of Florida, for you and your heirs and successors, in perpetuity, two fisheries which you shall choose, the one for pearls and the other for fish.

Item: We grant to you, the said Pedro Menéndez, and to the settlers and inhabitants of the country aforesaid, and to those who may go to it hereafter, that for the first ten years after the said country has been settled, you and they shall not pay any duties of *almoxarifazgo* on anything that you and they may bring over as supplies for your persons, wives, children and houses.

Furthermore: We grant to you, the said Pedro Menéndez, and to the residents and inhabitants who are settlers in the said country that from all the gold and silver, pearls and precious stones which may be discovered therein, you and they shall not pay us more than one tenth, for the period and space of ten years, which shall be counted from the day that the first smelting of metals shall take place.

Furthermore: We hold it to be well that in case you, the said Pedro Menéndez, should absent yourself from the said country and should wish to come to these kingdoms or navigate in the Indies, you shall be able to leave a lieutenant in your place, so that in everything he may have the same authority as yourself, providing that the lieutenant you appoint shall be a person possessing the qualities requisite therefor.

Furthermore: We think it well, and we so grant it to you, that during the whole of the three years wherein you must fulfil this *asiento*, you shall not pay to us or any other person, any duties of *almoxarifazgo*, or on galleys; nor any other charges or taxes, either on ships, or on supplies, arms and munitions, or on articles for barter with the Indians, or on any manner of food or beverages; for all the aforesaid nothing shall be paid, as has been said; it being understood from what is said that these things are to be taken to the said country of Florida.

Furthermore: We give you license and authority that in the first year following the day you shall depart from these kingdoms to go to the said land of Florida, you may have for the navigation of our Indies for the term of six years, two galleons of a capacity of from five to six hundred *toneles*, and two pataches of one hundred and fifty or two hundred *toneles*, armed and with mounted ordnance, either merchant vessels or armed, with the fleet or independently, as shall be and seem best for you; and that you may send them together or separately to any part or parts of our said Indies that you may desire, although they cannot go laden with any merchandise save supplies of food and drink; that for those that they may fetch and carry, and the freight charges and ship dues, you shall not be compelled to pay fleet duties for any armada or galleys, the which we give you as a help in the expenses and labors that you must have to encounter in the settlement and provisioning of the said land of Florida; and that on the return from the Indies you may bring the goods you choose, free from cost of port duties, as is said; but you cannot bring gold or silver, or pearls or precious stones; you may only bring the funds which may belong to you and be yours, and the proceeds from the freight charges of the galleons and pataches, upon which, as has been said, no port duty shall be paid.

Likewise, we give you license and authority that for a period of six years you may take from these our kingdoms, and from whatever part therof, to the islands of Puerto Rico, Santo Domingo and Cuba, and the said country of Florida, and from those parts to these, six shallops and four *zabras*, together or separately, with the fleet or independently, for the trade and commerce of the said country of Florida, and so as to fulfil the said *asiento*, and carry on board thereof what may seem best to you and be needful for the people who may be in the said country of Florida; wherefore if you should wish to unload in the aforesaid islands any provisions of food or drink that the said shallops and *zabras* may carry, you can do so, in order that in place thereof they may be laden with cattle and the things necessary for the said country of Florida; and that if any shallop or *zabra* of these should remain in those parts or be lost, you can take others in their place; which six years must be counted, and we so desire it, from the month of June of the coming year 1566; and we hold it well that if the masters and pilots who may go on those ships are natives of these our kingdoms, they may serve as such even though they have not been examined.

Item: We deem it well and we command that these shallops and *zabras* aforesaid, which must navigate during the said six years, as is said, shall not and must not pay any port duties on what they may bring the first time they sail on their voyage to the said country of Florida; but that if, during the period of the said six years, they should bring any goods to these kingdoms from the country of Florida, or the islands of Santo Domingo, or San Juan de Puerto Rico, or Cuba; or take over from these kingdoms supplies of food and drink, or other things needful for the aforesaid land of Florida; in such case they shall pay the fleet duties apportioned among the galleys that navigate along this western coast of Spain, whereof Don Alvaro de Bazan is Captain-General; and that if the said shallops and *zabras* go from our Indies under convoy of the armada which goes there, they must likewise pay the fleet duties on that; but that if the said shallops and *zabras* shall sail alone, and not under convoy of the said armada which goes to the Indies, they shall not have to pay the fleet duties of the said armada which goes there.

Furthermore: We think it well that in what concerns the ship's clerk to be taken over, the order we have given be observed in what relates to the two galleons and two pataches; but as to the six shallops and four *zabras*, we hold it well and we command that not more than one ship's clerk be appointed by Us, for all of them jointly, inasmuch as they are your ships, and the whole cost of the arms, artillery, munitions, supplies and all the rest they may or should take, must be yours and at your risk; and inasmuch as they are small vessels, of little tonnage, and it would be very expensive for you to carry a ship's clerk on each one.

Item: We grant you the favor, as we do by these presents, of giving you the commission of our Captain-General of all the said armada and the ships and people that may belong thereto, and we shall command that a formal commission be given you to that effect.

Furthermore: We wish and deem it well that everything you may capture from corsairs with the said galleons, *zabras* and pataches during the term of the said six years shall be your property and that of your heirs and successors; and the same shall apply to whatever prisoners you may take or seize from them without prejudice [to you arising] from the tithe collector, as we do hereby grant this to you.

Item: It is stipulated and agreed that in no manner during the period of the said six years, shall anyone place any embargo upon, or detain for our service, in these kingdoms or in any of our Indies aforesaid, any of the said galleons, pataches, shallops or *zabras;* but that if for any necessary or imperative reason, any of the said vessels should be requisitioned, you shall have the right to put others of a like tonnage in their place; and in case you should not do this, you shall have the right at the end of the said six years to use them in accordance with this said *asiento*, for the whole period of time they shall have been requisitioned or detained; and our Officials of Cadiz, or of the Casa de la Contratación at Seville, and any other courts of justice of these kingdoms and of the Indies where the said vessels may stop, shall give them every assistance for the safe and speedy dispatch thereof, and shall give them their clearance papers with all promptness, so that they may not be detained for the aforesaid; likewise that they shall give all aid and protection to the captains and officers who may come on board thereof; and we command that the persons and courts of justice whom the contents of this paragraph may concern, shall so observe and fulfil it.

Furthermore: If perchance God Our Lord should remove you, the said Pedro Menéndez, from this present life before the expiration of the said three years, in such wise that you shall not have been able to carry out your part of what is contained in this said agreement, we deem it well, and so desire, that it shall be done by the person whom you shall name and appoint; and if you should not have appointed anyone, the heir of your house and property can name the person who shall fulfil [these conditions], in order that he may enjoy all the concessions contained in this *asiento*.

Therefore by these presents, if you, the said Pedro Menéndez, do carry out the aforesaid at your cost, according to what is contained in the aforesaid, in the manner thereof; and if you fulfil all that is included in this agreement, in the instructions which shall be given you, and in those which shall be given you later on; likewise the provisions and ordinances we shall make, and order to be observed, for the said country and settlements, and for the good treatment and conversion to our Holy Catholic Faith of the natives there, and of the settlers who may go there; I say and promise, by my faith and my Royal word, that this Agreement shall be observed in your favor, and everything therein contained, wholly and absolutely, according as it is therein contained,

without your meeting any opposition thereto; but that if you should not so fulfil and accomplish that to which you obligate yourself, we shall not be compelled to keep with you and carry out the aforesaid [agreement], nor any part thereof; rather shall we order that you be punished, and we shall proceed against you as a person who does not observe and fulfil, but trespasses against, the commands of his King and natural Master.

And we order that these presents be given to that effect, signed by our hand, and by the members of our Council of the Indies, and countersigned by Francisco de Erasso, our Secretary.

[signed:] I the King.

By order of his Majesty,
Francisco de Erasso.

Done in Madrid, on the 20th of March, 1565.

THE LETTERS OF PEDRO MENÉNDEZ DE AVILÉS TO PHILIP II, AUGUST, 1565–JANUARY, 1566

THIS SERIES of letters gives us our best consecutive account of the progress of the Spanish conquest of 1565 and the gradual mopping up of French opposition, together with some indication of the new problems of maintaining Spanish forces in a country from which no revenues or local supplies could be obtained. During the course of five months, Menéndez turns from being the all-conquering soldier to the anxious administrator, struggling at Havana and Matanzas to collect and direct stores and men to maintain and expand his new conquest.

309. August 13, 1565. Pedro Menéndez de Avilés to Philip II.

This letter from San Juan de Puerto Rico gives an account of the crossing of the Spanish fleet from the Canaries to the West Indies. A storm scattered his ships, but with those he has he is making all speed for Florida in order, if possible, to outsail Jean Ribault's fleet.

E. Ruidíaz and Caravia, La Florida, 2 vols. (Madrid, 1892), II 70–73; Navarrete, Colección, XIV (1971), fols. 281–283, newly translated.

Catholic Royal Majesty: I left the calm waters of Grand Canary on the 8th of last month, and that

night, while I had a considerable wind two leagues offshore, the ships that were coming out were becalmed: so that although I stopped to wait for them, and did what I could, by daybreak, I was eight leagues offshore and unable to see the ships (except for one of them that came ahead with me): seeing that I was alone, and that I could not go back towards the land to look for them, I continued sailing with fair weather. 350 leagues from La Florida I was hit by a hurricane, and it was a miracle that we did not sink, for as we carried so much artillery and it was rolled out ready for action, since I was expecting to meet the French fleet, it was not advisable to bring it back inside and shut the gunports; and the wind was so strong and the sea so rough that we had to throw much of the artillery into the sea, although none of Your Majesty's was thrown in; and the strength of the storm and the wind was so great that it swept away all our masts and sails, except only the main mast, without the main topmast [mast-erero]. This lasted for two nights and a day: and as the ship was so watertight, and is so strong and seaworthy, Our Lord was pleased to spare us. When the weather improved, I turned round to make repairs as best I could with some spare topmasts we were carrying, and canvas, out of which we made masts and sails, and with the lightness of the ship it sailed moderately well: and we had to sail here to Puerto Rico, where I arrived on the 8th of this month without having seen any other land between the Canaries and here. I did not find here any store of masts or rigging, and because of the time that would have been wasted in waiting for it and sending elsewhere for it,—as a result of which considerable damage could have been done, since if the French have not already arrived in La Florida, they would have been able to arrive and fortify themselves without any trouble—for this reason I decided after three days to leave here and go to Havana or Matanzas; and I am advising the Audiencia of Santo Domingo as to the most accurate, short and safe voyage that we can make, because they assure me in this town that in Santo Domingo they are very nervous about sailing to La Florida in the hurricane season, and according to the orders which I shall give there is, with the help of Our Lord, little to fear: and I am sending them an expert pilot who, with the marine chart in his hands, can explain it to them, because I am sure that once they have understood the best and safest navigation route that we shall be able to make, the seamen and soldiers will pluck up the courage to make the voyage: and it is true that, with the help of Our Lord, it will be shorter and safer, and time will be gained, and there will not be as much expense incurred by the ships that go at Your Majesty's expense from this port and from Santo Domingo. With this arrangement, and with the help of Our Lord, I hope to be in La Florida, if they do send the ships shortly from Santo Domingo, during the rest of this month of August and until the 10th September, and I trust in the Lord that the voyage will be short and without danger.

I left Seville twenty-two days after Pedro de las Roelas had left with his *flota* and *armada:* and I arrived at the Canaries eight days after he had left Gomera: two of the ships in his *flota* were coming to this port, and neither of them has arrived. If the weather that hit me has hit him, his fleet will have been in trouble: may God bring him to safety. I am afraid that I will not be able to make use of his flagship, since it will arrive late at Havana: but I tell Your Majesty that if neither the people nor the horses should arrive in time from Santo Domingo, that will not stop me landing soon in La Florida with any men I may find, because if that happens before the French arrive, I think we shall be enough to hold the mouth of the Port against them and to fortify ourselves there, to prevent them receiving the help they are waiting for, for it seems to me that the most important means of stopping this war soon is for me to get to La Florida before the French do; for it stands to reason, given the speed at which I have come here, and will go from here to La Florida, that I shall arrive before they do, and even if to this purpose we should run risks and undergo difficulties, that seems to me to be no reason whatsoever for our failing to take the risk, because if the French get to La Florida first, then all the forces I command, even if they all went together, are not going to be sufficient to attack them.

About a month ago a French *zabra* passed by San Germán on the way to La Florida, and took a ship with the instructions that Your Majesty was sending here: I believe it took a message to those who were in La Florida advising them of the help that was coming to them, and that as I was coming after them they should fortify themselves and dig in until it arrived. This is unfortunate, but no reason at all for my failing to go and look for them as soon as possible with any forces there are at hand.

From this city I am taking a good ship with 50 men, soldiers and sailors, and 20 horses, and the Governor and Your Majesty's officers have given me all favour and assistance for quick arrangements and departure from here: they have sent this ship for me to take with me, and are giving me two very good boats: one of these is going with the news to Santo Domingo and Havana, and the other I am taking with me so that on the coast of La Florida I can unload the ship and send it in two or three days to this port, so that it should not be costing money and incurring expense, and because it runs a considerable risk at the mouth of the port since it needs deep water, and the boats will be enough to unload the people, artillery, provisions and equipment going in this Galleon.

Juan Ponce de León, accountant of Your Majesty in this island, and Commander of the Fortress, is an excellent gentleman. I have explained to him how important it is to the service of Your Majesty that I should go ahead with this enterprise, and that I intend to spend all my life and money on it, since in this way is served God, Our Lord: and I asked him to undertake my delegated authority and be my lieutenant in this city and Port, so that all the ships and men that are to go to La Florida should come to him, and they should come here to load with horses and cattle destined for there, since for this purpose we need a man of integrity who should be a local official. He has accepted this, to serve Your Majesty and please me, and to him Your Majesty can send any communication intended for me, for he will send it on to me in La Florida. I beg Your Majesty to favor me by writing to him acknowledging this service, since that will make him more cheerful and willing to do all the things that I need for La Florida, and these will be the things of most importance for the service of Your Majesty. May Our Lord watch over and cause to prosper the Catholic Royal Person of your Majesty with the growth of greater kingdoms and realms, as desire we the servants of Your Majesty, and as Christendom needs.

Written in Puerto Rico on August 13th 1565. The humble servant of Your Majesty, who kisses your Royal hands,

    [signed:] Pedro Menéndez

310. September 11, 1565. Pedro Menéndez de Avilés to Philip II.

Pedro Menéndez de Avilés reports how he made his first contact with the French fleet off the mouth of the St Johns River, but the engagement was broken off in stormy weather. He landed well to the south of the river on August 28 and called the place, which he decided to make his base, San Agustín. Throwing up a temporary fortification there, and so giving shelter to the non-combatants who were with him, he was making preparations for an overland march against the French fort to the north, on the location of which he had precise information.

A.G.I. Seville, Santo Domingo, 231 (formerly 54/5/16); Ruidíaz y Caravia, La Florida, II, 74–84; Navarrete, Colección, XIV (1971), fols. 283–288v; translated by Henry Ware, "Letters of Pedro Menéndez de Avilés," Massachusetts Historical Society Proceedings, second series, VIII (1894), 419–425, and reprinted.

Your Royal Catholic Majesty. I sailed from Puerto Rico on the 15th of August, for the Havana with the ship that I found with me, to join there the reinforcements from Santo Domingo, and proceed to this province of Florida, and continued to prosecute my voyage, the appearance of the sun and moon seeming to indicate fair weather. Thinking that, if I could succeed in reaching this harbor where the Frenchmen were, before the French fleet should arrive, I had sufficient force to take and hold it until the reinforcements from Santo Domingo and the troops that I required shall reach me, for the reason that they had built their fort five leagues up the river inland, and that there is an island at the mouth of the river of about a league long within, and alongside of the harbor, which they must necessarily enter, and which, whoever holds, is master of the sea, and can easily hold it, so that no ship can enter or go out of that harbor, without leave of the Alcayde who may command there. Hearing this secret from the two Frenchmen with me, (whom Your Majesty ordered to be handed over to me,) and who were the first who had been there, who also told me that, if the Frenchmen should arrive there before me, they would fortify this island so that they should be masters of the sea, it seemed to me the best plan, as I found myself with 800 persons, 500 of them soldiers, who could be landed, with 200 seamen, the other hundred being useless people, married men, women and children and officials, to sail for this port, and take and fortify this island. And having held a council concerning this with all the captains and officers, both naval and military, and they being unanimously of the same opinion, thinking that, if the French fleet should arrive first, the war was at an end, and that, when the cavalry from Santo Domingo should reach us, we should be masters of the campaign, both by land and by sea, and should have them surrounded, however strong they might be, and be able to destroy them, without their being able to receive help, either by land or sea; and so, being of this mind, we pursued our course to this place, and on the 25th of August, being Sunday at noon, we made this land at Cape Cañaveral, in latitude of 28 degrees, at the mouth of the Bahama Channel. We sailed along the coast, seeking this harbor, as far as the 29th degree, (for such was the account that I had, that the Frenchmen were between the 28th and 29th degrees.) Not finding it, we went on as far as twenty-nine and a half degrees, and then, seeing fires on the coast, on the second of September I sent ashore a Captain with 20 soldiers, to endeavor to get speech of the Indians, that they might give us news of this harbor; and so this Captain came up with them and spoke with them, and they told him, by signs, that the harbor was further on, in higher latitude, towards the North; and having returned the same day with this answer, I determined to go ashore myself the next day in the morning to see these Indians, who seemed to be a noble race, and I took some things for barter with them. They were well pleased with me, assuring me that the harbor was further on, and so we went on our way to seek it, sailing thence on our search on the 4th of September, and the same day at two in the afternoon we discovered it, and four ships anchored there, showing the flags of Captain and Admiral. Being thus certain that the succor had come to them, and that by falling suddenly on these four ships we should be able to take them, I decided to attack, and being yet half a league away from them, there came up great thunder and lightning and rain, and then the wind left us becalmed. But about ten at night, it came on to blow again, and, it appearing to me that, in the morning, the ships that might be in the harbor would come out with reinforcements for these four, I resolved to anchor alongside of them, with the intention of attacking them at daybreak. So, I anchored between the Captain and Admiral with my flag ship, and having spoken them, asking, what they were doing there? And who was their Captain? They answered that they had Juan Ribas [Jean Ribault] for Captain General, and that they had come to this country by command of the King of France, and asked what

ships were ours, and who was our General? I answered them, that I, Pero Menendez, by command of Your Majesty, had come to this coast to burn and hang the French Lutherans whom I should find there, and that, in the morning I should board their vessels to see if any of that people were on them, and that, if there were any, I should not fail to execute upon them the justice that Your Majesty commanded. They answered that it was no use, and that I might come on and not wait till morning. As it appeared to me that this opportunity was not to be lost, although it was night, turning my ship from stem to stern, I ordered cable to be paid out, so as to come alongside of her, but they cut their cables, and hoisted their sails, and all four of them took to flight. We were able to fire five heavy guns at the Admiral, and we suspect that we sank her, for many people abandoned her, getting into a large boat, a sort of pinnace, of twenty oars, and put themselves on board another ship, leaving the boat. I chased the three ships that night, but as my galleon was dismasted by the storm, they sailed faster than I, and so, at dawn finding them five or six leagues distant from me, I returned to the harbor to land 500 soldiers on the island. Being yet half a league off from it, we perecived three ships anchored there with flags and banners flying, and on shore two more flags, and it appearing to me that there was no reason for wasting time there, as my flag ship could not go in there, and the little ones could enter only with great risk, I decided to turn back to the Bahama Channel to look for a harbor where I could land near them, and eight leagues from that harbor by sea and six by land, I found one which I had reconnoitered before, on St. Augustine's Day, being in about twenty nine and a half degrees. There, on the sixth, I landed 200 soldiers, and on the 7th, three small vessels went in with the other 300, and the married men with their wives and children, and I discharged most of the artillery and ammunition, and, it being eight o'clock on Our Lady's Day, while we were engaged landing the other hundred persons who were to go on shore, with some guns and ammunition, and much store of provisions, the flag ship of the French Captain and Admiral came down within a half league of us, sailing round and round us; we anchored as we were, making signals to them to come alongside, and, at three in the afternoon, they made sail and went to their harbor, and I went ashore and took possession, in the name of Your Majesty, and took the oaths, before the captains and officers as Captain General and Admiral of this land and coast, in conformity with Your Majesty's instructions.

Many Indians were present, many of them chiefs, who showed themselves to be very friendly to us, and appear to us to be hostile to the French. They told us that, inside this harbor, and without going to sea, we could come to the river where the Frenchmen were, in front of their fort, by going up the river seven or eight leagues, which would be a very good thing, on account of being able to carry up the artillery and camp stores and cavalry, if we should wish to land near their fort, without being hindered by their island, although they have fortified it; moreover, we can go by land with horses and artillery. I decided to fortify myself as well as I can till reinforcements shall come, and within three days, I shall send to Havana, by a short route, and with God's help I hope they will be able to start within eight or ten days, and I shall send pilots so that the reinforcements can come with all despatch to this port, and when they arrive, I shall so manage, by the help of Our Lord, that I shall take from them the island of this harbor, and plant my guns upon their fort, so that with the cavalry, I shall hold it securely, and be master of the campaign. The Indians of this harbor, tell us that ten ships came to them here in one month and that many caciques are friendly to them, and so we are sure that they will come upon us with such Indians as are friendly, and also upon this galleon, which, as it is loaded with much stores, artillery and ammunition, it would be our total destruction if they should capture from us. If they attack her, having but a small crew, she is in great danger, as I have been sailing her for fifteen days along this coast, among shoals and currents, so as to get inside the harbor to reconnoitre them, and to discharge what I have discharged. She is on such a coast, that, if any side winds or bad weather should come, she will be lost. We need at least another fifteen days to finish unloading and to take in ballast, in which time it would be a mystery, in case of a storm, or attack from the enemy, if she could escape with all she contains, so that I have finished landing all the artillery and ammunition that was on board her, and I send her

to Hispaniola or Monte Cristo or Port Royal, that she may be laid up there with a quantity of biscuit and some wine which I cannot unload. I shall also send there the provisions that have come for the month of January, as we have biscuit on hand for the whole month of December, and with the prudent regulations that we shall establish we shall make it last through the whole of January; and, if it shall be advisable, the galleon may come out armed to this coast in the spring, so that I shall be master of the sea, while in the meantime I make myself stronger on land, and also so as to intercept the supplies that may come to the French, it should be arranged that the Audiencia of Santo Domingo shall pay the charges necessary for fitting her up, and pay the crew and provision her, for without this she cannot sail, as there will be no means otherwise of paying her.

It seems to me that what I have most need of is horses, for of those that sailed from Puerto Rico, only one came alive and every soldier should be mounted, to be master of the campaign, and to prevent the Indians from treating with the Frenchmen, and the Frenchmen from sallying out from their fort, for, when the Indians see this and that the Frenchmen fear us, and that we are stronger than they, they will all be our friends, which I shall endeavor to bring about with all possible diligence, on account of the great importance of gaining reputation with them, and that they should fear us, while, in order that they shall love us, I shall make them all the presents possible. I find myself with two shallops of between 70 and 80 tons each, good vessels, drawing very little water, which I am sending to Havana that each may bring back forty horses, and if orders should be given there to this effect it would be a great thing. I am writing about it to the Governor and I send him a bond, in case Your Majesty shall not give orders for these payments, that I will pay them myself, and when the vessels have come back with the horses, (or if they come without them,) I shall send them to Puerto de Plata, or Monte Christo, to load horses, and shall write to the Audiencia of Santo Domingo to pay for them and hold them in readiness; and, if they will not, I will send them a bond to pay for them myself. The chief cost of the horses will be for the vessels and crews, for, as each vessel can carry 40 horses, they will cost, one with another, one thousand ducats; for they must be good field horses, large boned and able to do work; also for drivers; and a vessel that is to carry them will need carpenter work to be done, the crews must be paid, there must be money and stores, and the vessels must be prepared and strengthened, so they can be careened, and fitted for this coast as they should be with cables, double anchors and tackle, so that each bark must cost in the whole, at least two thousand ducats. As to myself, Your Majesty can be assured, that if it were a million more or less, I would lay out and expend the whole in this enterprise so great in the service of God Our Lord, for the increase of our Holy Catholic Faith, and for the service and authority of Your Majesty, and thus have I offered to Our Lord all that he may give me in this world, all that I may acquire and possess, in order to plant the gospel in this land and enlighten the nations thereof, and so do I promise Your Majesty.

It will be well that Your Majesty should write immediately to the Governor of Puerto Rico, to the Audiencia of Santo Domingo, and to the Governor of the Havana, that, whenever my ships shall come into port there, they shall give them all aid and comfort. As to the horses that I shall send to look up there, with the food and water alone, there will not be a horse that will cost less than 25 or 30 ducats, and they shall be the best for the price that there are in the land. As to the saddles and bridles, which will cost more, I do not wish them to furnish them, for I will send to Spain for them, and in this way, even if it be at the cost of my whole substance, I will soon have a supply of horses in these parts, and Your Majesty will be pleased to do me the favor to direct that I shall be paid for the expenses that may be incurred, as may be required in Your Majesty's service. And inasmuch as I shall write to Your Majesty in a few days, I have no more to say in this letter, except that the people who have come with me are laboring with great zeal and good-will, and that it appears to me that Our Lord visibly strengthens and encourages them in their work, at which I am greatly contented.

I sent on shore with the first two hundred soldiers, two captains, Juan de San Vicente a brother of the Captain San Vicente, and Andres Lopez Patiño, both old soldiers, in order to throw up a trench in the place most fit to fortify themselves in, and to collect there the troops that were landed so as to protect them from the enemy, if he should come upon them. They did this so well, that when I landed on Our Lady's Day to take possession of the country in Your Majesty's name, it seemed as if they had had a month's time, and if they had had shovels and other iron tools, they could not have done it better; for we have none of these things, the ship laden with them not having yet arrived. I have smiths and iron so that I can make them with despatch, as I shall. When I shall go on shore, we shall look out a more suitable place to fortify ourselves in, as it is not fit where we now are. This we must do with all speed, before the enemy can attack us, and if they give us eight days more time, we think we shall do it.

I have appointed as my Lieutenant and Master of the Camp, Pedro Menéndez de Valdés (with whom I have contracted to marry my daughter) and on whom Your Majesty was pleased to confer the Order of Santiago, who embarked secretly and against my will at Cadiz. He is a soldier of Italy, of five or six years' service, experienced in vessels, a man of good understanding and of brains, with whom every body is well pleased. I have appointed as Sergeant Major Gonzalo de Villaroel, a good soldier, of good family and a man of brains. I have appointed ten Captains, all men of good family and trustworthy, most of them men of experience; to those who have not so much I have given for sergeants and ensigns, soldiers of Italy, skilled in war, and each company is of fifty soldiers and no more. When more troops arrive, I shall reform these companies of infantry and cavalry as it is expedient that there should be few men in each company, so as to have good discipline among the soldiers, and that they may be well drilled in arms in a short time; also that the Indians may be well treated, and that the Captains shall arm themselves with the strong armor of patience to endure labors, humility, and obedience to their General, and whoever does not do this, and understand how to bring it about, I shall take away his office, but shall not, for that reason cease to honor him, and so, not being adapted to these labors, he can henceforth eat and stretch out his legs and sleep at his ease; and so I think I shall manage while I am in these parts.

The Captains whom I have appointed, are the following, Bartolomé Menendez, my brother, one of Your Majesty's regular naval captains, Juan de San Vicente, Andres Lopez Patiño, Diego de

Alvarado, Alonso de Medrano, Francisco de Recaldi, Martin Ochoa, Francisco de Moxica. Diego Flores de Valdés I have brought as Admiral of this fleet, and I shall send him back to Havana within three days, with the two shallops, so that he may bring back the fleet that is there, and when he returns, if he brings the ships from Asturias, I shall have a reasonable supply of naval officers, especially, as among them will be Diego Flores de Valdés, Estevan de las Alas, and Pedro Menendez Marques, my cousin, either one of whom is able to command the fleet; while, in my company, I have Diego de Amaya, to whom I have given a company of infantry, being a most skilful man, a general in every respect, and a great seaman. I brought him out from Spain as Chief Pilot, and he has done good service. I shall always take him with me in the field with his company, for the crossing of the arms of rivers, and the navigation of the brigantines and boats that we must have in order to navigate the river, and take our artillery over, in which he will aid me greatly. There are also among these people, and those who are to come from Biscay many gentlemen who have not seen service with others, good soldiers, who come with great zeal and love to serve Your Majesty. It would be well if Your Majesty would write, thanking them for undertaking the voyage, and promising them every favor and reward, for this will animate them to endure with the more zeal all sorts of toils and dangers, and as this land is very great, it would be best, in time, to apportion it out among those who may deserve it, to the end that they may bring out here their kindred and relatives, and that the Gospel shall be planted upon the sure foundation of a noble race.

It will be well that Your Majesty shall order that, with every horse that I shall ship for these provinces, they send me a supply of maize for the first year, for although the whole supply cannot come with the horses, I shall send for it every four months, and for the future, after this year, I shall give orders for the planting of grain and maize, so that they shall have something to eat here, for in no manner, will it be well to take it from the Indians, that they shall not take up enmity against us. It will be better even that we shall give to eat to those who have not got it, to the end that they shall have love and firm friendship to us.

Seven or eight leagues from this place, when I went on shore on the 2ᵈ of September, to speak with those Indians who gave us information that the harbor of the French was farther north, we found great traces of gold, both ordinary and fine, which the Indians wore on them, on their ears, lips and arms. I did not allow any to be taken from them, that they should not suppose that we coveted it, although they did give to one soldier a small piece of more than 22 carets.

May Our Lord protect and increase the Royal Catholic Person of Your Majesty, giving increase of greater kingdoms and realms as Christendom demands and as we Your Majesty's servants desire.

In this Province of Florida, the 11th of September, in the year 1565, Your Majesty's faithful servant, who kisses your Royal hands.

[signed:] Pero Menendez.

311. October 15, 1565. Pedro Menéndez de Avilés to Philip II.

In the period of less than five weeks since his previous letter, Pedro Menéndez de Avilés was able to report the accomplishment of his principal objectives in Florida. He recorded his successful attack on La Caroline and the total destruction of its garrison. Leaving a garrison there to establish a Spanish fort, he returned to San Agustín, to learn very shortly that Jean Ribault's fleet, attempting to catch up with Spanish vessels going southward from San Agustín, had destroyed itself, its ships having been driven ashore by a hurricane. As news came of parties of stranded Frenchmen making their way north, he went out to meet them, and as each surrendered to him, he had them butchered. He was preparing to go farther south to deal with Ribault, if he found him, and others in the same way, when news came on October 10 that the French commander was in fact moving north. He went to meet his party of some 200 and induced them to surrender at mercy, when he again had them all butchered. He reserved only a handful of declared Catholics and a few musicians, and also some women and children. There now remained only mopping up operations for scattered groups of French to be completed. He set out also some information on the topographical problems involved in the future garrisoning of Florida.

A.G.I. Seville, Santo Domingo, 221 (formerly 54/5/6); Navarrete, Colección, XIV (1971), fols. 289v.–300; translated by Henry Ware, "Letters of Pedro Menéndez de Avilés," Massachusetts Historical Society Proceedings, *second series, VIII (1894), 425–439.*

Royal Catholic Majesty, I wrote to Your Majesty, by the Galleon San Salvador, on the 10th of September, being the day she left this harbor, a duplicate of the letter which accompanies this; and immediately, within that very hour, I being on the bar, in a shallop, with two boats loaded with artillery and ammunition, the four French galleons which we had put to flight, came down on us, together with two or three pinnaces astern, in order to prevent us from landing here, and to capture our artillery and stores. Although the weather was bad for the bar, I was obliged to attempt it, even at the risk of being lost myself and the 150 who were with me, with the brass pieces and the demi-culverins, rather than see myself in their power, or see them fortify themselves. Our Lord was pleased to deliver us miraculously at this low tide, for there was only a scant fathom and a half of water on the bar, and the ship required a full fathom and a half. They, seeing that I had escaped them, for that reason came to speech with me, wishing me to surrender and not be afraid, and kept away some distance so as to look for the galleon which I have heard they supposed could not escape them; and, within two days, a hurricane and terrible storm came upon them, and as it appeared to me that they could not have returned to their fort, and ran risk of being lost, and that in order for them to come and attack me, as they had done, they must bring a larger and better force than they did, that their fort must have been left weak and that now was the time to go and attack it, I conferred with the captains as to the splendid enterprise we might engage in, and they were of the same opinion. I immediately ordered 500 men to be got ready, 300 of them arquebusiers, and the remainder armed with pikes and bucklers (although few of these,) and we packed our knapsacks so that every man carried six pounds of biscuit on his back, with his canteen of a measure and a half or two of wine, together with his arms, which every captain and soldier and I myself among the first for example's

sake, carried with this provision and drink, on my shoulder. As we did not know the way, we thought that we should arrive in two days and that it was only six or eight leagues distant, for so the Indians who went with us had indicated to us. So we left this fort of St. Augustine in this manner and with this intention. On the 18th of September we found the rivers greatly swollen with the much rain that had fallen, so that we advanced but little until the 19th at night, when we came to sleep a league more or less from the Fort; then for more than 15 leagues, through morasses and desert paths never yet trod, so as to be able to get round the streams, and on the 20th on the eve of the day of the Blessed Apostle and Evangelist St. Matthew, in the morning when it began to dawn, having prayed to God Our Lord and to his Blessed Mother that they would give us the victory over these Lutherans, for we had already determined to attack it openly with twenty scaling ladders that we had brought with us, and the Divine Majesty showed us such favor and so directed us that, without losing a man killed, nor wounded, save one, who is well already, we gained the fort and all that it contained. One hundred and thirty men were put to death, and the next day, ten more, who were taken in the mountain, among them many gentlemen; and he who had been Governor and Chief Magistrate, who called himself Monsieur Ludunier [Laudonnière] a relative of the Admiral of France, who had been his major domo, fled to the woods, and a soldier pursuing him gave him a blow with a pike. We could not see what became of him. About 50 or 60 persons escaped by swimming to the mountain, and also in two boats from the three ships that they had in front of the fort. I immediately sent a trumpet to the ships to demand that they should surrender, and give up their arms and their ships, but they refused. We sent one ship to the bottom with the guns that were in the Fort, and the other took in her crew, and went down the river where, a league distant were two other ships with much provisions, being some of the seven that had come from France, and had not yet been unloaded. As it seemed to me that I ought not to lose this prize, I forthwith left this fort to get ready three barges there were there, in order to go and seek them, but they were warned by the Indians, and because their force was small they took the two best of the three ships that they had, and sunk the other, and within three days they took to flight, and I, being advised of this gave up going there. They wrote to me from the Fort that after these ships had gone, about twenty Frenchmen in their shirts, appeared in the mountain, many of whom were wounded, among them, it is believed was Monsieur Ludunier. I gave orders that they should use all diligence to take them and execute justice upon them. There were, between women, infants, and boys of 15 years and under, some 50 persons, whom it gives me the greater pain to see in the company of my men, by reason of their wicked sect, and I have feared that Our Lord would chastise me if I shall deal cruelly with them, for the eight or ten children were born here. These Frenchmen had many Indians for friends who have shown much feeling for their loss; and especially for two or three Masters of their bad sect, who were teaching the caciques and Indians, who followed round after them as the Apostles followed Our Lord, so that it is a wonderful thing to see how these Lutherans have bewitched this poor savage people. I shall do everything possible to gain the good will of these Indians who were friendly to these Frenchmen, and to see that there is no occasion given for my breaking with them for if they are not effectually resisted they are such traitors thieves and such malignants that it is impossible to live well with them. The caciques and Indians who are their enemies all show me friendship, which I shall preserve and maintain with them, even though it be not agreeable to them, and it shall be only from their own evil dispositions if I do otherwise.

On the 28th of September, two Indians came to inform me that there were many Frenchmen about six leagues from here, at the sea-shore, who had lost their ships, and had escaped by swimming; so I took 50 soldiers in a barge and we reached them the next day and keeping my men concealed, I went, with one companion down to the shore of a river where they were on the opposite bank, and I, being on this side, spoke to them and told them I was a Spaniard; and they answered me that they were Frenchmen. They asked that, either with or without my companion, I should swim across the stream where they were, for it was narrow. I told them that we did not know how to swim, but that one of them should come over confidently. They determined to do this, and to send over a man of good under-standing, the master of a ship. He related to me particularly that they sailed from the fort with four galleons and eight pinnaces each of 24 oars, with 400 picked soldiers and 200 seamen, with Juan de Rivao [Ribault] for General and Monsieur Lagrange, who was General of Infantry, and other good captains, soldiers and gentlemen, with the intention of seeking for and engaging me at sea; and, if I had already landed, to land their troops in the pinnaces and attack me, and that, if they had decided to land, they might well have done so, but that they did not venture to; that intending to return to their fort, a storm and hurricane had struck them so that, about 20 or 25 leagues from here, three of them had gone to the bottom, which had on board upwards of 400 persons, of whom only 140 had reached this place alive; as for the rest, some of them were drowned, others had been killed by the Indians, and about 50 of them had been taken by the Indians and carried away; that Juan de Rivao, whith his flagship was five leagues away from them, anchored in three fathoms, near some shoals, dismasted, for he had cut away his masts and that the ship had about 200 persons more or less on board, and they think she is lost; that all the brass guns, of which there were many and very good ones, with the ammunition, were lost in these three ships, part of them being in the ship of Juan Rivao, which they thought was certainly lost. He also told me that his companions, the officers and soldiers who had been saved, prayed me to allow them safe passage to their fort, as they were not at war with the Spaniards. I replied that we held their fort, having taken and put to death those who were in it, for having erected it there without the leave of Your Majesty, and because they were planting their wicked Lutheran sect in these, Your Majesty's provinces, and that I made war with fire and blood as Governor and Captain General of these Provinces upon all who might have come to these parts to settle and to plant this evil Lutheran sect, seeing that I had come by Your Majesty's command to bring the gospel into these parts, to enlighten the natives thereof with that which is told and believed by the Holy Mother Church of Rome, for the salvation of their souls; that, therefore I should not give them passage, but on the contrary should pursue them by sea and by land, until I had their lives. He begged me that he might go back with this message, and said that he would return at night, by swimming, and prayed that I would grant him his life. Which I did, seeing that he was dealing truly with me, and that he was able to inform me concerning many things. And, as soon as he was returned to his companions, there came across to this side, a gentleman, the Lieutenant of Monsieur Ludunier, very crafty, to tempt me; who having discussed some time with me, offered that they would lay down their arms and give themselves up if I would spare their lives. I asnwered that they might give up their arms and place themselves at my mercy; that I should deal with them as Our Lord should command me, and that he had not moved me from this nor could move me, unless God Our Lord should inspire in me something different. And so he departed with this reply, and they came over and laid down their arms, and I caused their hands to be tied behind them, and put them to the knife. Only 16 were left, of whom 12 were Breton seamen whom they had kidnapped, the other 4 being carpenters and caulkers of whom I had great need. It seemed to me that to chastise them in this way would serve God Our Lord, as well as Your Majesty, and that we should thus be left more free from this wicked sect to plant the Gospel in these parts and to enlighten the natives, and bring them to allegiance to Your Majesty; and forasmuch as this land is very great, it may well take 50 years to do this, but a good beginning gives hope of a good ending, and so, I hope in Our Lord, that he will in everything give me good success, that I and my descendants may give these kingdoms over to Your Majesty cleared of them, and that their people may become Christians; this is what particularly interests me, as I have written Your Majesty. We shall gain much reputation with the Indians, and shall be feared by them, although we also make them gifts.

Considering that Juan de Rivao had made a halt, that within ten leagues of where he was anchored with his ship, the three other ships of his company had been lost and that, if he should be lost and abandon his ship, he would land his forces and entrench himself, landing what provisions he could from his ship, and would occupy himself in getting out what brass guns he might be able to from the three ships, and also, if he was not lost, from the masts and rigging of the other three ships, he would repair damages as he best could,

and would come back to the fort, thinking it still his. If the ship were lost, getting all the force he could, he would march along the shore, and, if he does this I am waiting for him, so that, with God's help, he will be destroyed; yet he may go inland to a cacique who is friendly to him and very powerful, who is about 30 leagues distant. If this is the case I shall go there to seek him, for it must not be that he or his companions remain alive, and if he comes with his ship to the fort, I have ordered that two cannon and two demi-culverins shall be planted at the entrance of the bar, to sink him after he shall have entered, and have a brigantine in readiness to take his crew there and I shall do everything possible that he may not escape me.

The articles that were found in the fort [La Caroline] were only the four brass pieces, of from 10 to 15 quintals; for the rest of the cannon that they brought from France, they carried dismounted, and were in the ballast in the galleons when they went to look for me, with all the rest of the ammunition. They also found 25 brass muskets, of about two quintals, with about twenty quintals of powder and all the ammunition for these pieces; also 170 pipes of flour, of three to a ton. They found also about 20 pipes of wine, and the rest of the stores had not been landed, they being in doubt whether they should fortify themselves so strongly in this harbor, on account of their fear that I might disembark there. They might have done it, but they spent all the days after they came here in carousing for joy at their arrival, and because they had news that, a hundred leagues North north east of Santa Elena they possess the mountain chain that comes down from Zacatecas and that there is much silver there, and Indians have come to them with many pieces, and they found of these pieces of silver (which the Indians of those parts had brought to them) a quantity of some five or six thousand ducats in value. There was found a quantity of three thousand ducats worth, more or less, of cloth and all kinds of goods for barter; hogs male and female; also sheep and asses. All this the soldiers sacked, nothing escaping save the artillery, the ammunition and the flour. There were also in the harbor, not reckoning the two ships that were there and the two near the bar, two others that they had captured near Yaguana, laden with hides and sugar; the crews they had thrown overboard, and the cargoes they had given to some English vessels [John Hawkins' ships], that they might take them to France or England to be sold. There remained with them two Englishmen as hostages, for the French had no seamen to send these ships with. Those two Englishmen were killed at the taking of the fort. The English vessels to which they gave this cargo, had arrived at the harbor where they were, which is where they held this fort that we took from them, in the beginning of August in this year, and were, a galleon of a thousand tons, which belonged to the Queen of England, with three tiers of guns, very heavy [the *Jesus*]; certainly those who saw them say they never saw a ship so armed, yet it drew very little water. The other three vessels were smaller. It had been agreed between these English and the French, as the French were looking for succor from France, that Monsieur Ludunier, (who was Governor) should wait here through September, and, if it did not come, that he should go to France to look for it; and that, in the next April, they would come and bring a great fleet to await and capture the convoy for New Spain or Nombre de Dios, which must of necessity pass this way; and if the succor should arrive, he would have abundant force for this, for so he had already written to France. That the English vessels would come, as has been said, in April to this coast; that they had for this purpose therefore, at the fort, a great galliot and seven ships, five of their own and two captured ones. The four galleons they were to send out to France, to be laden with troops and provisions, and if these should come back so as to unite with those that remained in April, together with the English who would also be there by that time, Juan Rivao with the 800 men who remained with him, intended to go in January to Martires, over against Havana, about 25 leagues off, and build a fort there, for which they say he had surveyed a very fine harbor, and thence in the spring when he would have his whole fleet there together watching for the convoys, he intended to take Havana. Your Majesty may be certain that this matter was discussed, treated of and agreed upon between them; and before Juan Rivao left France he received orders to fortify at Martires over against Havana and about 25 or 30 leagues distant, so that no vessel could sail out of the Channel nor could come out without being seen by him, and to keep their six gallies, (for it is the best sea

in the world for them) and from that point to take Havana and to set at liberty all the negroes, and to send thence to offer the same to all those at Hispaniola, Porto Rico and all Terra Firma, for I have informed myself of this very sufficiently from the intelligent Frenchman whose life I spared. They brought with them six Portuguese for pilots, of whom two were put to death, two were killed by the Indians, and Juan Rivao has the other two with him.

The river which is near the Fort San Matteo which we took from the French, runs sixty leagues through the country, and does not extend quite to the turning at the Southeast, so that it comes out almost into the Bay of Juan Ponce, and thence one can go to New Spain, and to the harbor of San Juan de Lua there is not above 200 leagues. There they intended in the coming year to build a fort in that Bay of Juan Ponce, on account of its being so near to New Spain, and about 150 leagues from Honduras, and the same from Yucatan, and from which point the six gallies that they had could sail easily. On this river are large settlements of Indians, all very friendly to the French, for the Frenchmen had been there three times to seek maize; for they landed here very short of provisions, so that, within eight days they had nothing to eat. There is very little maize on this coast and they took it by force from the Indians, being greatly disposed to take without giving being very poor but very valiant. All these Indians did not have so perfect friendship with them but that they may have it even more firmly with us, for I shall not consent that one kernel of maize shall be taken from them, but will rather give them what I may have, for this is the best plan.

Considering that this land is so great and of such good climate, and considering the danger and inconvenience that the enemy and corsairs may commit in it every day, and that they may possess themselves of those that lie to the North and near to Tierra Nova [Newfoundland and the northeast generally], where they are tyrannically masters, and that they could easily hold them, I am of opinion that the following things should absolutely be done. Your Majesty may disabuse yourself of the idea that it will not be done at the smallest possible cost to Your Majesty, for, if any loss occurs, it will be at my cost. Your Majesty can increase this amount, as much as you may be pleased, which will be expedient for your royal service, and for the increase of your realms.

This harbor is in twenty nine and a half degress; that of the fort of San Matteo which we took, in thirty and a quarter degrees, for the Frenchmen and their pilots were in error, and I have had them take the sun on shore, in order to verify this. From here to Cape Cañaveral is 50 leagues, and there are three rivers and harbors on the way. From there to Havana is a hundred leagues more or less, which can be navigated in barges coasting along the Island of Cañaveral, and of the Martires, crossing from there to Havana which is 25 or 30 leagues and no more. I propose to take two very good pinnaces which I took from the French, with a hundred men, and go along the coast, the barges going along by sea, and making fast to the shore at night. Being inside of Cape Cañaveral, where the sea is like the river with the barges, I shall, by going along the coast, reconnoitre the island of Cañaveral and all the Martires for the best harbor and situation in which to build a fort, which will be stronger with the one at Havana, as the Havana one will be for this, so as to assure ourselves that, at no time the enemy will be able to attack in the 150 leagues there are between here and Havana; either fortify themselves, or lie in wait for convoys or ships from the Indias, since, with the force from Santo Domingo, which is now at Havana, and that of Pedro de las Roclas, I shall have enough to do during the whole of March, when I shall go across in these pinnaces to Havana, to seek these people, after I shall have found a place for this fort. When Pedro de las Roclas shall arrive at Havana he will find his ship there, for I do not propose to take her out of that harbor, and he will find his men, so that he can go to Spain as strong as he was before, for I shall put 150 men there now, as it will be necessary for them to protect themselves from the Indians, who are very warlike, until they shall have gained their good will; and by the beginning of April I shall be back in these forts, whither I can come in seven or eight days, along the shore.

In May it will be best for me to leave these two forts with the best force possible of 300 soldiers to each, to go, in vessels that draw very little water, and most of which I shall have ready here, which will be this galley and the French brigantine and as many of mine as I can, with 500 soldiers and 100 seamen to settle at Santa Elena which is 50

leagues from here, and has, in a space of three leagues, three harbors and rivers, the largest of which has six fathoms of water and the other four, admirable harbors; and the one which we call Santa Elena, being the third place where the French were, is very small; all three can be navigated inland, from one to the other, so that, whoever is master of one of them will be also of all three. There, in the best place, I shall build a fort, and have in it 300 soldiers who will complete it and then go on further to the Bay of St Mary [Bahía de Santa María, Chesapeake Bay], which is in 37 degrees, 130 leagues beyond Santa Elena, (which is the land of the Indians who are in Mexico) and build another fort, leaving in it the other 200 soldiers. This must be the key to all the fortifications in this land since, beyond here, as far as Tierra Nova, there is no place to settle in, because to the north of this harbor, in the country within 80 leagues is a range of mountains and at the foot of them is an arm of the sea which goes up to Tierra Nova and is navigable for 600 leagues. This arm of the sea runs up into Tierra Nova and ends there. Eighty leagues within this land of the Indian is this Bay of St. Mary, in 37 degrees; and within half a league there is another arm of salt water, running east north east, which, it is suspected, goes to the South Sea. The Indians slaughter there many cattle of New Spain, which Francisco Vázquez Coronado found there, and carry their hides in canoes to Tierra Nova, to sell and barter them with the Frenchmen, by means of this arm of the sea, and from this place, for two years, the fishing vessels have taken to Rochelle more than six thousand of these hides, and through this arm of the sea the Frenchmen can go in their ships' boats, from which they fish, to these lands of the Indians, and so they will come to the foot of the mountains 400 leagues from the Mines of San Martín and Nueva Gallicia and in order for them to command these places at their pleasure, they will have to establish their outposts here and gain the Bahama Channel; and afterwards from this point by entering there, to command the mines of New Spain. This key and power it is absolutely necessary that Your Majesty should hold and be master of, and thus you will be lord of Tierra Nova since with our gallies, by this arm of the sea you can refuse consent to any ship to take fish unless they shall pay tribute and recognize this land to be Your

Majesty's, and so you will secure all the Indies. And if this arm of the sea, as is certainly believed, does go to the South Sea, it is near China, which is a very important thing as respects the enlightenment of that region and the trade with Molucca.

As to the 500 Soldiers and 100 seamen which I must have this May in order to go and fortify Santa Elena and this Bay of St. Mary, I have written to Pedro de Castillo that he has my authority to send me, at my cost 300 soldiers, and one year's provisions for them as well as provisions for the 800 persons whom I have here and in Havana, partly soldiers and partly useless people not counting the 300 soldiers who are on Your Majesty's account.

Your Majesty, by the order of Your Council of War and State, provided that I should be furnished with 500 soldiers paid and equipped for the necessary time, and I, fearing delay, which it was important that I should not experience, as it seemed to me that it was impossible to get them together and to fit out the ships to carry them and the provisions, they ordered me to take 200, and as many more as I could; and contrive, as I could, to find the 500, all good men, and at the time of sailing from Cadiz, Francisco Duarte, who was there as Purveyor, was only willing to pay 300 and very low pay too, (being only 4 ducats, to each, for two payments and for his arquebus), with no more to captains, sergeants or ensigns. Moreover, he would not give provisions for the whole year for the 300 soldiers and 100 seamen, as will be seen by his accounts. On the other hand much of this provision and biscuit was lost, being thrown overboard when we experienced the hurricane, so that these stores were not sufficient to last five months, and as so little provision was furnished me in Spain I loaded much more than I was obliged to, and I gave account of it to Your Majesty, praying that Your Majesty would be pleased to pay the 200 soldiers, over and above the 500, and the stores, since Your Majesty had given the order that they should be supplied me, and since I have done it with such despatch and at so little cost, there is no ground or reason that I should not be paid. I do not know what Your Majesty may have ordered in respect to this, but I pray Your Majesty, if you have not commanded that I should be paid, that you will so order and that I be paid forthwith, so that I may provide myself with the things requisite and necessary to

come out right with this enterprise; and that Your Majesty will be pleased to order that these people shall be provided with the provisions necessary for them, over and above what has been issued to them for one year, for we are suffering for want of food, and the labors and dangers that we undergo are great, the fort that we erect here being built by the labor of every man, of whatever rank, of six hours every day, three hours before noon, and three hours after, and if the men do not endure it well, many of us will be sick and die, and moreover will be discouraged, which is a very bad thing; Your Majesty will also order 200 soldiers to be sent out to make up those whom Your Majesty had provided for this enterprise, so that Your Majesty shall not pay more than 500 of those who are here and who are to come, and, as to the 100 seamen who went in the galleon to Hispaniola that she might lie there in some harbor ready for active service with all the provisions on board; for if the bread should be unloaded and exposed to the air, it would all be spoiled, while it would be kept in good condition on board, with much ammunition which we were unable to take out by reason of the enemy. It will be well that these hundred seamen and the Lombard gunners on board be ready for service, so that, if the enemy should seek them, they may defend themselves, and I shall send vessels, so that in the course of January, she may be unloaded.

I shall send orders to pay off the ship and crew from the first of February, so that, after the first of February, Your Majesty can take other vessels there of the same capacity, and these hundred seamen and lombardiers [artillerymen], that they may bring the stores that are to come, with the artillery and ammunition, according to the memorial that goes herewith, which is a convenient and necessary thing. With these 200 soldiers who are to come at Your Majesty's cost, and the 300 who are to come in other ships at my charge I shall carry out my plan for May, at Santa Elena and the Bay of St. Mary, unless the French anticipate me, for it is a thing of the greatest importance.

Your Majesty will certainly find that instead of the 500 men whom I was bound to place here, I have put a thousand, including those whom I have in Havana. I now ask that 300 may be here in the course of April, and it would be well that 200 more should be sent in the month of October, for the settling of the Bay of Juan Ponce, for the river of the fort of San Mateo which we took from the enemy goes 60 leagues inland within this Bay, and by means of this river we shall easily communicate from one sea to the other. The multitude of Indians there are there will be thus sooner brought to the knowledge of our Holy Catholic Faith, for, in this Bay of Juan Ponce, is the province of Apalache an indomitable people, with whom the Spaniards have never been able to effect anything and as this province is level, we can easily pass over as far as New Gallicia, which may be about 300 leagues distant, about as far to Vera Cruz, and about as much farther to Honduras and to Yucatan. From Yucatan this settlement may be provided with maize, of which there is much in great quantity. One hundred and fifty leagues inland, to the north, is the Province of Coza, friendly to us in 38 or 39 degrees, at the foot of the mountains that begin near the mines Zacatecas and San Martín, and that province must be about 150 leagues from these settlements and forts of ours, and from the river of St. Helena, and the country of the Indians. After the year '65 we may go over to settle at Coza and we may build there a fine city, and there will be no more to do but to settle in Florida, and the way to New Spain will be easily kept open for trade and passage, and we shall get the benefit of the many silver mines there are in that land which are the mines of Zacatecas, and even within a few years the silver that will be obtained from those mines and the mountains of San Martín, will come to these harbors and to Santa Elena and the Bay of St. Mary, because, from the mines of San Martín and Zacatecas to the harbor of San Juan de Lua is more than 200 leagues, and the navigation thence is very bad and dangerous, and from here and from Santa Elena to the Bay of St. Mary it is an easy and short voyage to Spain, ordinarily of forty or fifty days, and as for the hundred leagues more of distance by land that there will be from the mines of Zacatecas and St. Martin to these harbors they will prefer to bring it here, on account of the short and safe voyage, rather than to San Juan de Lua. From this Bay of Juan Ponce to where we should settle in the Province of Apalache, there would not be from these forts by land more than fifty leagues where we could not very easily correspond, help, and succor any one of these harbors from another. As to myself, Your Majesty may be assured, moreover, that, besides all that I am bound for, which I can get among my

relatives and friends, I shall expend all I have in this undertaking, that I may be able to go on with it and succeed in it, that the Gospel may be preached to these natives, and that they may come into Your Majesty's allegiance, and to do this I watch and shall watch by day and by night with mind and soul, so that I may best accomplish it.

And, inasmuch as these lands are great, of many good rivers and harbors, and the population of this country is great, such great results cannot be effected with few Spaniards, it is not expedient in any way that it should be done by degrees, but that we should hasten, so that what might be expended in ten years, should be spent in five, for so will Your Majesty be lord of these great provinces, will enlighten the natives thereof, and greatly increase your kingdoms, for there will be great and very excellent gains to be made in this country, for there will be much wine, many sugar plantations, a great number of cattle, since there are extensive pasture grounds, much hemp, tar, pitch and planking, such as Your Majesty has not in all your realms. Many ships can be built here and much salt made. As to grain on these rivers, we have seen none. There must be all kinds of fruits, there is most excellent water and a fine temperature to the country. There will be much rice, and many pearls in the river of St. Helena, where we have news that there are some, and entering further inland into this land, there must be places where much grain can be gathered and much silk made.

For the things that I send to ask for in Spain for these parts, being absolutely necessary for provisions and equipping ships and for clothes and shoes for the men, I must have 3,000 ducats and I have not a single one. Your Majesty will be pleased to command that the pay for the whole month of January for the galleon shall be paid me, as well as that of the hundred men who came in her with the supplies that are due them, because seamen were not willing to come to these parts for such small pay, and I bound myself to Francesco Duarte to bring them, so that I made the best bargain I could with them, and it is certain that they cost me three thousand ducats over and above what Your Majesty pays them, and Your Majesty commanded me to despatch a vessel from Florida with the news of my arrival, which being my own, I required no freight money. I paid the master, pilot and seamen for wages and provisions one thousand ducats, and this I have need of, confiding in Pedro del Castillo, that he will look for it and will engage to provide me with everything that I sent him to seek; for having no children and being a good Christian, he has taken it upon him, as his principal undertaking, to aid me in this enterprise with all his substance, that I may succeed in it, and without his having any other interest in it but that of being my friend and desiring to do me a favor in a time of so great necessity. I supplicate Your Majesty for the love of Our Lord that you will direct that what is due to me be paid with the greatest despatch, and that Your Majesty will order that such stores as are at Your Majesty's charge shall be provided, also the pay of the men as well as the pay to be given to the 200 soldiers, so that all may be here by the end of April, and that in the first part of May, I may go to Santa Elena, and to the Bay of St. Mary which is the outpost and frontier which Your Majesty must hold to be Lord of these parts, for without this is done we have done nothing, and if the French once set foot there, we shall have to spend a great sum of money, and pass a long time before we can get them out again from there, and this business must not be lightly esteemed.

Diego Flores de Valdés, who goes with this despatch and is to come back with this reinforcement, is a gentleman who, for fifteen years has served Your Majesty in all the fleets under my command as a captain of armed ships, and sometimes as my Lieutenant, and he has always served well and with all intelligence, and he has also done the same in this expedition, so that I have taken him as Admiral of the fleet and my Lieutenant, and to this day, Your Majesty has shown him no favor, nor given him any aid toward his expenses, although Ruy Gomez offered it to him in Your Majesty's name, (as also did Eraso, when he made the voyages to Flanders in the vessels that he took out to him as my Lieutenant,) yet nothing was ever given him. He has gone on spending and has sold and mortgaged the larger part of his patrimony that he inherited from his ancestors, with the hope which he always had that Your Majesty will show him some favor. I have done him but little good on account of my necessities, but I have great need of him that he may serve Your Majesty in matters on the sea in these parts, for he well understands how to do it. I pray your Majesty that you will confer an order of knighthood upon him, and grant him some aid toward his expenses. It will all be for Your Majesty's better

service, and, in order that he may go in the fleet on the seas of this coast, he should have all absolute authority both with friends and enemies, in which this Order will aid him much. He carries with him two pilots, that they may come with the ships which shall bring this reinforcement, for he is one of the best sailors in the whole kingdom, and is very fit, so that with him, and with them, everything will be well directed and come to a good issue.

While writing this, on the tenth of this month, news came to me that the fort which we had taken from the Frenchmen had been burned one night, together with everything that had been taken in it and the provisions. I set out to succor it immediately, departing with the men who were there, together with such provisions and ammunition as there was there. Within an hour of this news came another message to me, that Juan Rivao with 200 soldiers was five or six leagues from here at the place where I had done justice to the Frenchmen out of the three ships under his charge that had been lost; and fearing that the Indians who were friendly to them might unite with him and that so he might give me trouble, I immediately went with 150 soldiers to seek him, and the next day at dawn, on the eleventh of this month, I came up to him, there being a river between us which he could not pass, save by swimming. We made on both sides a demonstration of our force with two colors displayed, and with our drums and fifes, and, on assurance of safety, he sent across his Sergeant-major to speak with me, who delivered me a message from Juan Rivao that I should allow his whole force safe passage to their fort. I answered, as I had to the others, that I was his enemy and waged war against them with fire and blood, for that they were Lutherans, and because they had come to plant in these lands of Your Majesty their evil sect, and to instruct the Indians in it; that he might undeceive himself as to his fort, for that we had taken it; that they might surrender their flags and arms to me, and place themselves at my mercy, that I might do with their persons as I should please, and that they could not do or agree otherwise with me. And the sergeant-major having gone back with this message, the same day in the evening, under assurance of safety, Juan Rivao came over to speak with me and to treat with me, of some course more safe for him; but, as I was not willing to accede to it, he said that the next morning he would return with his reply, and so he did, with about 70 companions, many principal men among them, three or four captains, among them Captain Cerceto, who was a long time captain of arquebusiers in Lombardy; Captain Lagrange, who was a captain of land infantry, was already dead. There also came with Juan Rivao among these men, four others, Germans and relatives of the Prince de Porance, great Lutherans. I wished to make sure whether there were any Catholic among them, but found none. I spared the lives of two young gentlemen of about 18 years old, and three others, drummer, fifer and trumpeter, but Juan Rivao and all the others I caused to be put to the knife, understanding this to be necessary for the service of God Our Lord, and of Your Majesty. I hold it our chief good fortune that he is dead, for with him the King of France could do more with 500 ducats, than with any others with 5,000, and he would do more in one year than any other in ten, for he was the most skilful sailor and corsair that was known, very experienced in this navigation of the Indies and of the coast of Florida and so much a friend to England that he had so great reputation in that kingdom that he was nominated as Captain General of all the English fleet against the Catholics of France, in those past years when there was war between France and England. The rest of the people whom Juan Rivao had with him, who may be 70 or 80 persons, fled to the mountains, and refused to surrender unless their lives were spared. These with 20 others, who escaped from the fort and 50 others who were taken by the Indians from the ships that were lost, who may be in all 150 people, less, rather than more, are all the Frenchmen now alive in Florida, separated from each other, fleeing in the mountains, and others captives among the Indians, and because they are Lutherans, and that so wicked a sect shall not remain alive in these parts, I shall do everything on my part, and shall induce the friendly Indians on theirs, so that, within five or six months, no one of them shall remain alive; and of the thousand Frenchmen who had landed, when I arrived in these provinces, and their fleet of twelve sail, but two vessels alone have escaped, in very bad condition, with 40 or 50 persons on board, who, as they go so ill provided and equipped, may never arrive in France, and if they should arrive, would not carry the news of the death and destruction of Juan Rivao and his fleet, and the later that they come to know this in France, the better it will be, for they will be at ease, thinking they have still a good force here, so that now it is more than ever necessary that, with great secrecy and diligence, everything be provided that I have asked, and be here in the course of April, so that, in the coming spring, I shall be master of this coast of Florida, and so Your Majesty will remain Lord of it without opposition or uneasiness; being master of Florida You will secure the Indies and the navigation to it; and I assure Your Majesty that henceforth Florida will make very little cost, but will bring in much money to Your Majesty and will be worth more to Spain than New Spain or even Peru; and it may be said that this land is a suburb of Spain, for in truth, the voyage from there is not above 40 days to come here, and as many more ordinarily, to return to that kingdom.

From the burning of the Fort we suffer very great hunger, and the biscuit that we landed here is spoiling and being used up, and unless we are speedily succored, we shall suffer, and many will pass out of this world from starvation. So, trusting that Your Majesty is assured that I am serving you with all fidelity and love, and that in everything I am dealing and always shall deal truly, I shall say no more, but shall advise Your Majesty, in every way that I can, of all that may occur.

May Our Lord preserve and prosper Your Majesty's Royal Catholic Person, with increase of greater realms and kingdoms, as Christianity requires, and as we, Your Majesty's servants desire.

From this Province of Florida, and the river of San Pelayo and Fort of San Agustín, this fifteenth of October, in the year 1565. Your Majesty's humble servant kisses Your Royal hands.

[signed:] Pedro Menéndez

312. December 5, 1565. Pedro Menéndez de Avilés to Philip II.

Menéndez set off for Cuba early in November in order to make longer-term plans for supplies and the disposition of forces. On his way he discovered a French party entrenched near Cape Cañaveral. He drove them from their fort and induced them to surrender, in this case sparing their lives. He then placed a garrison at a post he named San Antonio on the St. Lucie River, to guard the southeastern part of the peninsula. He received some reinforcements for Florida at Havana and sent their ships chasing French pirates, among whom he believed the younger Ribault (who had in fact gone to France) might well be included. He learned that strong reinforcements were on their way to him. These should, he thought, go directly to Santa Elena and the Bahía de Santa María to which he was sure the next French fleet (which he presumed there would be) would come. He set out some, though not all, of his problems of raising stores for Florida from the uncooperative governor of Cuba—part of whose obstructiveness may have been caused by Menéndez's insistence that he alone (and he requested special powers from the king for this) should be responsible for tracking down French pirates throughout the Caribbean, as well as on the shores of eastern North America.

Navarrete, Colección, XIV (1971), fols. 300–312v.; translated by Henry Ware, "Letters of Pedro Menéndez de Avilés," Massachusetts Historical Society Proceedings, second series, VIII, 440–453.

Royal Catholic Majesty. I wrote to Your Majesty from Florida in October, by the Captain Diego Flores de Valdés, giving a detailed account of all the good success that Our Lord had given me, up to that date, as well in the taking of the Fort of the French Lutherans who were in it, as in the destruction of their fleet and the annihilation and execution of all or the greater part of them; among whom was Juan Rivao who was Viceroy of these Provinces and all the principal captains, no one of them surviving. I also forwarded this despatch to Your Majesty, by way of Santo Domingo; so that I am assured that Your Majesty, by this time will have received that despatch, as the Captain Diego Flores must have arrived.

On the very day after he left these provinces of the Fort of San Agustín, I received information from the Indians, that 70 or 80 Frenchmen were collected together, building a fort at Cape Cañav-eral and a vessel to send to France to ask for succor, and that they had much artillery and ammunition that they had taken out of the flag ship of Juan Rivao that had been lost there, and that, about thirty leagues from the place where they were, is the beginning of the Cape of the Bahama Channel. So I took three light barks for oars and sails, and put a hundred men on board of them, going myself by land with 150, and left the Fort of San Agustín on the 2nd of November, and on All Saints' Day in the morning we came upon them, the barks by sea, and I by land. We were discovered before we attacked them; and the Frenchmen seeing us, were afraid of us, and abandoning the fort, took to flight to the mountain. We put in a place of safety six pieces of artillery that they had and the powder and ammunition with which they were moderately provided, and burned and razed the fort, and also burned the bark which was nearly finished. Seeing that the mountain was so thickly wooded that we could not catch any of them, and that it would not be proper that so wicked a sect should remain in the land, I sent a French trumpeter who had been with Juan Rivao, whom I had brought along with me, into the mountain to tell them to surrender, and give up their arms and that, if they would come to me, I would spare their lives. So they all came, save he whom they had chosen for captain, and three or four others men from Navarre and servants of the Prince of Conde.

Having done this we departed, the boats by sea and I by land, down the Bahama Channel. Having gone 15 leagues we found a harbor, although not a very good one, but which has a fine river of more than fifty leagues in length, so that it is navigable for galliots, brigantines, frigates, and ships drawing one fathom of water; and there we found a principal cacique, who has many people on that river, with whom I made great friendship, giving him many articles of clothing, as well as to his wives and kindred; and, in the eight days I was there, I so gained their good will that they told me they should rejoice to have me remain in their land, which was what I desired and strove to do. So I left a Captain with 200 men and one of the barks, that they should fortify there; also provisions for 15 days, as our need of provisions is very great. With the other 80 men and two barks I went along down the Bahama Channel to seek provisions in Havana, to supply the forts and these people; arriving there in three days. I discovered, on my way, two good harbors, and it is a wonderful thing that we can sail with such facility down the Bahama Channel. I always have held it certain that we could so navigate, for all along the shore, there is water on the back side, inland; this I have formerly seen; and, separated from the land it runs out to the open sea. It is a very great thing to have discovered this navigation and these harbors for the ships from the Indies that sail through the channel, for as they are often damaged in their rigging there, and have no harbor they dismantle their ships taking the money out into barges; others go to the bottom; others still, arriving at Havana all broken to pieces. Now, when any storm strikes them, they can go along the shore, which is very clear and with good bottom, and put into the harbors that I have discovered, or come to this harbor of Matanzas, or to Havana. That is where the French desired to come and settle in the coming spring, on account of their having gallies, (for it is very good for them,) and they have many harbors, as they enter at once on the Martires and the Tortugas, and sailing along their coast, could be masters of Havana and the whole island of Cuba, and there set at liberty all the negroes in all the Indies, for so they thought to become Lords of this land without making war, without labor or cost.

I found at Havana the flag ship of Pedro de las Roclas with 130 men, seamen and land troops, and also Pedro Menéndez Marquéz, my cousin, with three ships that carried a quantity of ammunition, and two hundred men, and I received certain information that many French and English corsairs were going about at Porto Rico and Hispaniola, and at this island of Cuba, to plunder and to trade in negroes and linen goods, bartering them for gold and pearls, sugars and hides; and that many Portuguese ships were doing the same thing. Thinking this to be great damage to Your Majesty's service, and fearing that Jaques Rivao [Jacques Ribault], the eldest son of Juan Rivao, having the two ships from the fleet with which he fled, the day we took the fort, with 70 or 80 men on board, when he had seen all the French who were in the fort put to death, and knowing that his father was then at sea with the greater part of the fleet, went out to seek him at this island of Hispaniola, so as to join him and the other corsairs

who might be there, and tell them what had happened at the fort, and that the French had been put to death, meeting with the corsairs, might be able to make descents on various settlements in these parts, burning and sacking them, and committing cruelties upon the people whom they should find in them, as well as upon the ships and crews of Your Majesty's vessels, which they might take. I fitted up the flag ship and the three pataches, (small vessels) which Pero Menéndez Marqués, my cousin had brought with three hundred and fifty seamen, in these four vessels all good arquebusiers and good men; and to serve Your Majesty at my own cost, I provisioned and supplied them, and sailed out of the port of Havana in the last of November, to find, pursue and chastise them, wherever they might be, and to spend the three months of December, January and February in doing this, and, in the beginning of March, to return the flag ship to Pedro de las Roclas, with all his crew, at Havana, I, with my ships, to go back to Florida to await the succor which I sent to ask from Your Majesty, to carry out the plans of which I wrote for the settlement of Santa Elena and in the Bay of St. Mary, which are essential and necessary, in order that Your Majesty shall be Lord of these provinces in quiet. And the day that I left Havana with this fleet, which, as I have said was in the last part of November, we discovered a sail and I ordered the tenders to give chase to her, but she took to flight up the Bahama Channel, fearing that she must certainly be a corsair, or some prize that they had taken. They could not overhaul her that day, but the next day, in the morning, being at the mouth of the Channel, we saw her quite near us, and she fled towards this port of Matanzas, and we came up with her within the harbor, where her crew abandoned the vessel and fled in the boats to the shore. I sent a crew on board the ship to visit her and they found her to be Your Majesty's despatch ship; so I sent to look up her crew, who, thinking us to be corsairs, had taken to flight. The master of the ship told us that, by Your Majesty's orders, the officers of the Casa de la Contratación had despatched him to Santo Domingo and to Havana with Your Majesty's instructions to the President, the Audiencia and the Governor, that they should get ready immediately beef and fish for eighteen hundred men for nine months, for that so many men were coming to Florida; but gave no letter to me from Your Majesty, or from any private individual of your kingdom. He gave me a letter from the President and Auditors of the Audiencia of Santo Domingo, in which they tell me the same that the master had told me.

Considering that, as Your Majesty sends these troops, it must be for the reason that the King of France is sending some fleet to Florida, it is therefore not expedient that I shall be absent from Florida, although I have left there very excellent captains, very well informed as to what may possibly happen, I abandon the fine plan that I had against the corsairs, and return to Havana with the fleet, where I shall do every thing in my power to send on provisions to Florida for the people there up to March; the men whom I have here I shall detain here till that time, for they have nothing there to eat, and I shall manage, when I go to Florida in the month of March, to take food sufficient to last until supplies shall arrive from your kingdom; but, unless they are succored, or unless God sustains them, one of two things cannot fail to happen, either they will perish with hunger, or will break with the Indians, on account of taking food from them, and in order that neither one nor the other may happen, I shall do everything to the extent of my power, to supply them.

The fleet of Santo Domingo up to this day has not arrived at Havana; but a frigate that went in company with it arrived at Havana a week ago, whose captain says that, in a storm he separated from a store ship that was conveying the men from Santo Domingo, of whom Gonzalo de Peñalosa was captain, that with him came Estéban de las Alas, with four others of my tenders that sailed from Asturias and Biscay; that likewise Pero Menéndez Marqués, who came as Admiral with Estéban de las Alas, had parted company two months before. The captain of the frigate also says that 30 horses that Gonzalo de Peñalosa, was carrying to Florida died on his hands, and were thrown into the sea, the third day after he sailed from Santo Domingo, (except one), so that not one single horse has arrived in Florida from Santo Domingo, Porto Rico or anywhere else. I paid off the crew and the frigate that they should not make cost to Your Majesty, (and so, that all the men who would not go with me to

Florida, might return to Hispaniola, whence they came, and that they should not go to Peru without Your Majesty's license,) as Your Majesty will understand, by the vouchers that go herewith.

As to the armed ship with 50 soldiers and 20 horses which Your Majesty ordered the Governor of Havana to provide, paid and supplied for four months, I did not ask for them, so that I might not make cost for Your Majesty, and because I thought them not necessary at present, the Frenchmen in Florida being dead.

When Estéban de las Alas and Pero Menéndez Marqués were coming on their voyage from your kingdom to Florida, they discovered two sails to the north of the island of Hispaniola, off Porto Rico, and thinking them to be corsairs or prizes, they gave chase to them, when Pero Menéndez took one of them and Estéban de las Alas the other finding, when they came up with them, that they were two Portuguese caravels, and the whole of their crews Portuguese, who, contrary to the orders, regulations and Royal Ordinances of Your Majesty and without registers, had come to trade in these parts. The one which Pero Menéndez took was of small value; but he instituted process against them and took them into Havana as prizes. When I arrived there he gave them up to me with the other caravel and the goods, which were sold at public auction; the money from the proceeds thereof I took and with it bought provisions which I sent in two barks to Florida, one of them a tender of seventy tons, in charge of the Captain Diego de Maya, for the people in the two forts of San Mateo and San Agustín; the other, in command of Gonzalo Gallego, for the two hundred Spaniards whom I left in the channel, this side of Cape Cañaveral, in the harbor of which I have spoken, which I have since named Puerto del Socorro, because, for four days there were 150 soldiers in it with nothing to eat or drink, except palmettos and water and herbs. Diego de Maya, with the three barges and the hundred men whom he carried, arrived with the provisions with which he succored us, so that we gave the place for this reason the name of Puerto del Socorro. With this provision that they carried, there will be enough for all January, though on very short rations. The testimony and the proceedings against the Portuguese accompany this, as well as the prize proceedings. The Portuguese

I take in the barges, at the oar, until Your Majesty shall otherwise command, although certainly they show no such courtesy to the Castilians whom they take in Mina, or Molucca, lands of Your Majesty, which they hold in pledge, for all of Your Majesty's vassals whom they take, they sew up in sails and throw overboard alive. As to the other caravel which Estevan de las Alas took, I do not know what became of it in the storm, nor even of him, nor whether they are dead or alive, for nothing appears of him or of either of these ships. Our Lord may have been pleased to bring them into port in safety. I am told that his caravel had on board four thousand or more hides, and nothing else, for the two caravels had sent on shore, by some of their crews, in barges, what money they had, and these could not be captured. They also tell me that this prize which Estevan de las Alas took will be worth near six thousand ducats, more or less. If he has not lost it, I shall receive it and order it to be sold, and from the proceeds supply the people whom I have in Florida.

At the time the Purveyor Francisco Duarte despatched me from Cadiz, I could not take on board all the provisions which he gave me for the 300 soldiers and 100 seamen whom Your Majesty paid to go to Florida, because I had laden in the galleon some provisions, and he caused them to be laden on board a large caravel of 120 tons which I chartered; and inasmuch as her crew was nearly dead from the heat, I put on board of her 80 soldiers, and Francesco Duarte made the master of the galleon give him a bill of lading for the provision which he loaded on the caravel, as Your Majesty paid the freight on the galleon; and, in order not to have any difficulty with him, I acquiesced, as I saw clearly that the supplies for 400 men could not be carried in the galleon. When I left the Canary Islands, this caravel was separated from me, came into port at Santo Domingo and left Santo Domingo in company with another shallop of mine and a brigantine, and off the Cape of Tiburon they met four French corsairs, and took a part of the crew on board the brigantine, and the rest fled in the boat, for the caravel carried no guns. There remained on board the caravel about 40 persons, most of whom were sick, and the corsairs took her and carried them off. A month after, this caravel was lost, with all her cargo, in a storm near the port of Matanzas; the crew escaped being twelve Frenchmen and

about 20 very sick men of the 40 whom they captured on board of her, for the other twenty had been thrown overboard, having died. The Governor of Havana had the Frenchmen put on trial and hung them. I lost the provisions of this caravel, which was fully loaded, and was worth about four thousand ducats, in addition to the other three thousand that had been paid to the men and in wages to the master and seamen of the caravel, all the stores that came in her being Your Majesty's, and not mine, I giving from that which was laden in the galleass, at the time Your Majesty ordered me to take it, as much more for the 300 soldiers and 100 seamen, who went to Florida on Your Majesty's account. I pray Your Majesty, that, considering all this and that in order to sail against the corsairs, as I did at my own cost, having paid out, in order to supply myself and equip myself fully to go, as I did, with the 350 men whom I took in my ships more than four thousand ducats, Your Majesty will do me the favor to allow me the proceeds of these two caravels, if the one taken by Estevan de las Alas shall appear, provided they were not worth, with their cargoes, more than I have hereinbefore said; for I need and require it all desperately, in order to supply that part of my force which I have in Florida; for, so doing, Your Majesty will do me a great favor, especially as the greater part of this goes to the men and to the ships, as the greater part of right belongs to them.

For the ship of Pedro de las Roclas which he sent to me from Cabo de San Antonio, he appointed as captain Juan de la Parra, an old soldier who has served Your Majesty many years by sea and by land, who pursuing his voyage towards Havana, was cast by the weather upon Matanzas; and, about the time he was going into the harbor, he saw a caravel lying there, and ordered Antonio Gómez who is Captain of Artillery of the same ship to go and reconnoitre her; who, having gone, found it to be a Portuguese caravel laden with hides, which had also some pearls and gold, having come without a Spanish register to trade in negroes and other merchandise on Terra Firma or the coast of Venezuela, and at the Island of Hispaniola; and he brought her alongside of the captain ship. And the Captain Juan de la Parra, who was captain of the ship and crew, having inspected the prize and her crew, commenced proceedings against her, and was going to Havana with her and with his ship. García Osorio, who was Governor of that island at the time that the Captain's ship and the caravel entered that harbor, sent to take the caravel which was anchored at a distance from the ship, but he who was in charge of her, by command of Captain Juan de la Parra, would not give her up, saying that his Captain had commanded him to remain in her and hold her with all she had on board, and that, without his permission, he should not allow any one to come on board. So, because he made this reply to the *alguazil* who went for the caravel, and would not suffer him to come on board, the Governor sent men from the town, armed, in two boats; to take the caravel, and, in order that the soldiers who were on board guarding her, might not defend her and be killed, the Captain, Juan de la Parra, ordered the men on board not to defend her, but that they should abandon her, and so they did. By the Governor's order, they took the caravel with all there was in her, also him who was in charged to keep her by command of the said Parra, Gonzalo Gallego by name, a pilot well skilled in the navigation of the Indies, and chief pilot of the Captain ship, and, without making any charge, or obtaining any confession from him, nor commencing any process against him, the Governor commanded him to be maimed because he had not given up the caravel to him the first time that he had sent to ask for it, and he, from fear of his Captain, who had placed him there to guard her, could not give her up without his leave. And the said Captain Juan de la Parra showing some resentment at the violence which the Governor had done him in taking the caravel and maiming his pilot, (though he was able to prevent both the one and the other, for he had his ship with one hundred and fifty men, and was captain of them all by command of Pedro de las Roclas, until he should give the ship and the crew over to me,) in his passion at the injury that the Governor had done him, said words at which the Governor took offence, although certainly without reason, for they were entirely without prejudice to his honor; yet he took occasion to give them another meaning, although, even if they were as he would understand them, he would have no cause to hold him for an hour. The Governor therefore came himself to the Captain ship with five, or six men only, with irons and an *alguazil* and told the Captain that he had come to take him prisoner and carry him ashore. And the Captain, answering him that he was not strong enough to do it unless he pleased, but begging him not to do it, and that he should not take him, for that it would be an ill service to Your Majesty, and that the crew of his ship would be scandalized by it, so that, even if he should give himself up a prisoner, they would not consent to it. And the Governor, having sworn by God and by the life of Your Majesty, very many times that he would take him prisoner, and the Captain Parra, seeing his determination, commanded all in the ship to remain quiet, without moving, and making his protest against the Governor, gave himself up prisoner. And immediately the Governor, in the very cabin of the Captain where he was, put him in irons, and took him out of the ship with them, and from there took him prisoner to the prison where it is now going on three months that he has kept him in this manner, changing him from one part to another. When I came to Havana, he carried him to the house of a brother of Juan de Roxas, where he keeps him in irons and with a chain that passes into the wall, with the doors and windows stopped up, having put in guard over him this brother of Juan de Roxas, who is named Gómez de Roxas, without consenting that anyone shall see him or speak with him nor give evidence concerning him, or present any petition, and without any complaint filed against him; and so, justice is lost for this Captain, and every body in the town says that a notorious wrong is done him. And, by the truth which I shall speak before God our Lord, and to Your Majesty, I have so understood that the charges which it is said that he alleges, are so trivial that they are all contained in this, that he did not dip his colors to the Governor, at Cabe de San Antonio, when he came in another ship, and because he said to him that it would be better to defend his caravel, and that they should not mutilate his pilot, if the whole town should be destroyed, since they did him so great violence without justice, not being his judge. And, as I understand, Juan de la Parra endured these injuries in patience, understanding that he permitted his pilot and himself to be put into prison, when he saw that, in fact, the Governor did it, that he was doing Your Majesty service in suffering it; and that, when I should arrive, the Governor would give him up to me, with such charges as there might be against him; as being a person under my orders, having the largest crew and ship, as Your Majesty had commanded by your Royal orders, after Pedro de las Roclas had left here. When I arrived in Havana, I would not speak to the Governor concerning this business in the first two days, and on the third, desiring to do it by petition and with all courtesy, he, hearing of it sent to tell me by Juan de Yñistrosa, Your Majesty's Treasurer in this Island, that no one should speak to him concerning the Captain Juan de la Parra, for that in no manner should he be spoken with nor seen, nor would he give him up to me. I hearing this, and that they were treating him as no Christian ought to be treated, nor as I am bound that they should treat one on his way to report to me as Captain of a ship and crew to serve Your Majesty in my company in whatever I should command and order him; so with all patience and in courteous terms I asked, as earnestly as I could, of the Governor, that he should permit me to see and speak with him, and that he would give him up to me with the proceedings against him. He would do neither the one nor the other, and on the other hand was offended, that, having sent word to me that I should not speak to him concerning this matter, I should not have complied. And although I very easily and without any trouble could have taken Juan de la Parra out from where he was to his ship so that he could return to duty, inasmuch as there was no complaint nor charge against him, or if there were and the proceedings were given over to me, I might have proceeded against him, according to justice, yet I was unwilling to do it for fear of Your Majesty's displeasure. And by a requisition I prayed the Governor that he would give him up to me, a copy of which, with his reply accompanies this. After Parra heard what was going on, and that I was about to sail against the corsairs and that he was to remain, he shouted like a madman in the prison and darkness where he was, and it is feared he will lose his senses and is publicly stated that the Governor is afraid that when he gets out from there, he will demand justice against him. I did not know Parra and never saw him or spoke to him, but, if he had been taken, even for some treason, and I had given my word, as I did, to the Governor that I would not attempt to free him nor take him from him against his will, and asked him to permit me to see and speak with him, even in the presence of a notary and he would not do it. I

do not know what will be the end of a thing like this, but I am sure that it will end the life of Captain Juan de la Parra, before his complaint can come to Your Majesty's knowledge; for this reason I have thought proper to notify Your Majesty of it, that you may order that he shall be given over to me, with the proceedings, or that he send him bound or free to Your court with the proceedings.

Moreover, the crew of the ship came to me requesting that I should procure that their caravel which had been taken from them, should be restored with what was in it, and I spoke to the Governor to that effect, praying him in all friendship that he would do it, or that he would assist me, or favor me with a portion of the money proceeds of the caravel, in order to supply the people who were in Florida on Your Majesty's account, who were 300 soldiers, and I said that I would give him bonds to repay all that should be given me, so soon as Your Majesty should so order, and I represented my great necessities; and if he would not do this, that he would lend me some money to buy some stores with, and that I would bind myself to pay it, but he would do neither one nor the other. So I made my protest against him, a copy of which, and of his reply accompanies this.

I found myself with very little artillery to go against the corsairs, and the *Capitanía* of Pedro de las Roclas had very few and very small guns, because he carried out to Havana four large guns of Your Majesty for the fort that is building there, so that with these he came very strong, and as he had no great present need of them, and there was much artillery in the town, the brass guns of the two ships which were there, yet he would lend me none of them. So, I drew up a protest against him, a copy of which with his reply accompanies this.

The stores which I was able to pay for at Havana were given me at the same prices at which they are sold to merchant ships coming and going there, without showing me any favor, although the inhabitants desired to do so, but, as the people are, for the most part, poor, they could not although they desired to do so. Other things also the Governor did to me, not treating me with the hospitality and respect to my person which were reasonably due to my office and the confidence that Your Majesty has always shown and still shows to me. And I surely tell the truth to

Your Majesty when I say that I consider it a greater victory that I had the patience to endure and dissimulate under the bad treatment that he gave me, than even the victory that I gained over the Frenchmen in Florida. And as I have every day an absolute necessity to go and come to this Island, and to Hispaniola and to Porto Rico, and also my ships to be provided and equipped with every thing necessary, and to get cattle and beef for Florida, these things cannot be suffered to pass, for, if he does this with me, he will do it so much the more with the Captains and officers of the fleet under my charge, and with the shallops and zabras which may come into port in this island. If I had understood the necessity there is that I should have some authority in these islands, before the agreement I made, I would not have accepted it, unless Your Majesty had given me some right to be supplied and succored from here, so as to do every thing and endure all those dangers and toils with the greater content. As this is expedient for Your Majesty's service I shall do what seems most proper for it, for I say the whole truth to Your Majesty, as I am bound to do, and which every faithful servant should tell to his prince; that, if I had the government of this island, I could do more in Florida in four years than I shall do in ten, and at much less cost to Your Majesty's royal treasury.

Considering that Your Majesty sends me 1800 men to Florida, troops and seamen, I suspect that the King of France or his vassals are about to send out some great fleet; and if this is the case, Your Majesty should understand, unless you are already informed, that, although I may resist them in Florida, as I hope in God that I shall, so that they shall do me little harm in the parts where I may be, yet that they hold many other ports in Florida, to which they may go, very good country, and I cannot prevent them with the force I have, and they may be able to turn back upon some of the fleets from the Indies, for this is their whole design, and then fall upon these islands of Porto Rico, San Domingo and Cuba, and will be able to take and plunder the settlements in them and burn them and commit cruelties upon the inhabitants, if they set themselves to do this, according to what I know of the small force of either of them, and I assure Your Majesty that, unless God shall miraculously defend them, they will succeed in doing this. I have written to the

Governor of Porto Rico that he should keep that town on the lookout, for, although he may think that it is very strong, having a good fortress and plenty of guns, and a round tower with eight very good pieces, which are at the entrance, a hundred arquebusiers would be enough to take the town and sack it, by landing, at the round tower in boats, as they can very easily do, for there is not a single man or soldier in it who sleeps there; thence they can go to the town, which is only a quarter of a league distant, and burn and sack it, without the fort doing them any damage. I have also written to Santo Domingo to the President and Auditors that they should be prepared and should notify all the harbors within their jurisdiction that they also be ready. I shall also tell it to the Governor of this Island, for I fear very much for Havana, being so good a harbor and on account of the preparations they have made, that they may come and take this fort and put it into a condition for defence, and, considering the armament it has, it would be hard to take it back again. I shall exceedingly desire to know if they come, and what force they will bring, and what Your Majesty sends to me, that we may make an end, once for all, with these Frenchmen who come to the Indies in time of peace, and that they shall lose the desire of going there again, for it would be very important to know this, and it might be that Our Lord would be pleased to give me victory over them; and in order that I may certainly know it, I despatch this tender express to Your Majesty that you may be pleased to advise me concerning the whole matter.

As to the fleet and succor that is coming to me for Florida, after they have passed the Canary Islands, they have no occasion to go to any one of these islands, but can go straight to Florida in 29 and a half or 30 degrees, which is where the two forts of San Agustín and San Mateo are, for there is a very good pilot who will know how to bring them there, Domingo Fernandez, who is in the despatch-tender; for so they will make a shorter course and come in less than half the time; but, if they come by Santo Domingo, and the Cape of San Antonio, Your Majesty should understand that the voyage is very long and that they will arrive very late in Florida. I shall have two frigates like gallies, each of 20 oars in a side, that will carry two guns amidships, each of twenty hundred weight, which are very light both for sails and oars, and with these and the fleet that Your Majesty will send me, if it comes in time, I shall put myself into Santa Elena and into the Bay of St. Mary, and shall engage the French fleet, if it comes, so that, neither in Florida nor in the Indies, can they do any damage, neither to the merchant fleets; but, as I tell Your Majesty, it is very necessary that the succor that shall be sent to me shall sail direct for Florida, which is a voyage of forty or fifty days, and to a very healthy place, where the men will not be sick, and even if it should start by the beginning of March, it will arrive in sufficient time; but, if it comes by way of Santo Domingo, besides that many will die there, it cannot arrive in Florida for three or four months, and the French, arriving first, will be able to make themselves strong in Santa Elena, on which they have fixed their eyes, and where I am advised that there is a harbor and river of six fathoms of water at low tide; that the river runs up a hundred leagues inland to the mountains, and that from there to Zacatecas it is not two hundred and fifty leagues. They have called this harbor, being so good, Port Royal.

I have also learned, from a Frenchman whom I took in the last fort, that Jaques de Soria, he who took Havana and burned the fort, was to come out there in the beginning of the spring with a great fleet and afterwards fall upon some merchant fleet. Your Majesty will know this better than I can, for it may be that this man lied to me. I shall have these two frigates launched in the beginning of March, for I shall give the bevels and lines to the owners who are to build them, so that they will be better for these parts than gallies; and as for security that I shall be able to pay for them, and for the wages, I shall deposit jewels and clothes, and shall find friends who will be sureties for the pay, and when they are bought they will not cost above six thousand ducats, fitted out as they should be with their oars and swift rowers and provisions for the first six months and seamen, and there are few ships that can keep up with them without wind and in calm.

If Your Majesty shall send me a commission of Captain General of these parts of the Indies, Terra Firma, and the Ocean Islands, with power to pursue corsairs, and to take ships that come to barter and trade in these parts against Your Majesty's will, and contrary to your royal Provisions and Ordinances, and without registers, I will have the galley slaves which these frigates will need, and with two others to be built like them, Your Majesty holds the Indies and Florida secure, so that no corsair will come to these parts, and if they do come, they will be destroyed, neither will ships come to trade without license; for it is told for certain that what the Portuguese, English and French have carried away and stolen in this year, is worth more than a million; also by trading and bartering with Your Majesty's vassals in these parts, under permits and royal patents with which they were provided, but without having registers; the cost of these four ships will be very small; and this land being thus subject to Your Majesty, you will be pleased to give orders that I shall be repaid the outlay that I shall make in them, and that all that I shall take shall be for myself; and if nothing is given me to reward me in the service of Your Majesty, I have the hope that you will favor me for such signal service by sending me the commission, either perpetual in form or for such time as shall be Your Majesty's pleasure. I shall have two of these vessels ready in March, and in March of the next year, I shall have the other two, which shall be four in all. I only ask that Your Majesty will grant me licenses for a thousand slaves, that I may sell them, in order to buy slaves for these vessels, for my wish is in everything to serve Your Majesty, with fidelity and truth as is due to Your Royal service and to my profession as a mariner. I inform Your Majesty of all this, for it seems to me due to Your Royal service, that you may provide everything that you may think fit.

I have ordered this tender to touch at Hispaniola and deliver a letter of mine at Puerta de Plata, or Monte Christo, or wherever else they may land on the island, that it may be forwarded with all despatch to the Audiencia, in which I write that they shall not prepare any beef, and that, if they have already done so, they shall sell it; for, when the fleet shall arrive there, it will not do for it to take on board a quantity of prepared beef, for it decays in the heat, and the crews will get sick with it, and it makes a bad smell in the ships, and at much less cost I will provide the crews fresh meat while they are cruising, also fresh meat on shore, with the two barks that may come and go, and much better than what they can prepare at San Domingo; and for this Your Majesty shall pay me whatever you may be pleased to allow, and as to fish, as three or four fishing smacks are coming, and as I have two barks engaged in fishing from the smacks, I can give any quantity of very good and fresh fish to all the men, better than can be got from St. Domingo or any other place, for that will spoil, just like the beef, and give out a bad smell that cannot be endured; so I write to the Audiencia not to get ready any fish; and I tell the same thing to the Governor of Havana, not to get ready any beef or any fish. And if Your Majesty shall be pleased to pay me, through the Governor, the proceeds of the caravel, I shall be able to provide everything that may be necessary here, and will render good and true account.

I promised Diego de Miranda, who is one of the principal gentlemen of the Asturia, the eldest son of an eldest son, the heir of his house, to appoint him principal Notary of Florida, and Secretary of the Government, and gave him his commission accordingly, for he has served Your Majesty many years in the fleets under my command, and is a man worthy of all confidence, and who assisted me in my undertaking to bring a quantity of men into Florida, I pray Your Majesty to show him this favor, for it is very necessary.

I also promised Estévan de las Alas, and Pero Menéndez Marquéz, and Hernando de Miranda the offices of Auditor, Purveyor and Treasurer, for all three are persons of trust, and all among the principal men who have served Your Majesty many years in my company, all having married noble women, and who, through their desire of these offices, and their attachment to myself, may bring out their wives and families, and for their sakes other married people will come out, which will make a great beginning in the settling these Provinces of Florida with a noble race. I pray Your Majesty to look favorably on this, and do me the favor to grant these commissions. I agreed to give to the crew of this tender for wages and provisions, for carrying my letter to Hispaniola and this one to Your Majesty, one thousand ducats, for it being December, in winter time and dangerous, I could not make any better bargain with the pilot and master. I pray Your Majesty to direct that the amount be given to Pedro del Castillo, prefect of Cadiz, that he may pay them. And if Your Majesty will reply to me you will be able to do it immediately, for this vessel is to return at once to Florida with some ammunition

that I have sent for, and a thousand half gallon bottles, a thousand pair of sandals, and some matters of fish hooks and trinkets for barter with the Indians, for these are very necessary.

At the time I made my agreement with Your Majesty I was still to furnish six shallops of 50 tons each; these should have been of one hundred tons, but, by error, it was set down 50, and that Your Majesty may understand that all these shallops are of one hundred and twenty tons each, more or less, you will direct it to be examined in Your Majesty's pay books for they are all measured in this manner, and are of these contents; and, as I saw that the agreement said 50 tons, which is small so that they are dangerous for the voyage from this Kingdom to Florida, and the provisions that they can carry are hardly sufficient for the crew that sail them for the outward and return voyage, beside that they cannot carry any guns to go against the corsairs, except very small and insufficient ones. I pray Your Majesty to cause the pay books to be examined for the contents of these shallops, and finding that they are of a hundred and twenty tons, more or less, as it will appear, that you will order your certificate to be given me setting forth that they are of this tonnage, in order that I may sell the little ones, and take them of this tonnage, for with them to come and go in, I can do great damage to the corsairs, and supply provisions and cattle to Florida with great facility.

May Our Lord protect and prosper Your Majesty's Royal Catholic Person with increase of greater kingdoms and realms as we, Your Majesty's servants desire, and Christendom needs. Amen. From Matanzas, on the 5th of December 1565. Your Majesty's humble servant kisses your Royal hands.

[signed:] Pedro Menéndez.

313. December 12, 1565. Pedro Menéndez de Avilés to Philip II.

Although he was still involved in supply problems in Cuba, Menéndez was especially concerned to keep in view the need to guard against French attempts to enter the Bahía de Santa María (Chesapeake Bay) and so make their way to the Pacific. He considered that on his way back to Florida he himself should reconnoiter the bay, so that he could give instructions on where the Spanish reinforcements should deploy themselves.

Navarrete, Colección, XIV (1971), fols. 312v.–317v., newly translated.

Catholic Royal Majesty: On the fifth of this month I sent to Your Majesty a packet boat from the port of Matanzas: with this I sent a long letter concerning everything that had happened to me up till now in the provinces of La Florida, and what seemed to me to be the most convenient arrangements for the service of Your Majesty concerning this enterprise. As the patache was leaving Matanzas at the start of this voyage, with the other two ships of the Navy it was taking for defence against pirates (my nephew, Pedro Menéndez Márquez, was taking them in his charge: he was going to La Yaguana to find out news about Estéban de las Alas, and to load provisions for La Florida, since they are cheaper there than here, and I think that the President and Oidores of Santo Domingo will lend me the money to buy it, for the Governor of this island was not willing to do that) they saw a sail by the Bahama Channel; thinking it was a pirate, they went after it: it ran into Matanzas, where they came back to find out who it was, and they discovered it was the caravel loaded with hides that Estéban de las Alas had captured from the Portuguese; it told them how the transport ship that they had been preparing in Santo Domingo had been lost, and that Estéban de las Alas was coming there with this caravel and a shallop of mine with men and provisions that had come from Asturias and Vizcaya; all the men and the bronze artillery of Your Majesty escaped, but all the equipment and provisions were lost; none of it survived: and that also a *zabra* of mine had been lost, all of whose crew were saved as well; and that as Estéban de las Alas found he had not enough provisions for so many men, he and Gonzalo de Peñalosa, who was coming as Captain of those men from Santo Domingo, decided to land the men there, where the ships were lost, which was at the north of this island, a hundred and fifty leagues from here and twenty-five or thirty from Bayamo: and that they had decided to go with the

men by land to Bayamo or to Puerto del Príncipe, to find something to eat: and that they had put on the caravel the men that were unfit from the hulk (*urca*) and those that had been injured in the escape, which would be about 40 people: and that the sloop was staying and loading the artillery which had been saved, while its launch was moving the men from the small island where the transport ship had gone down to Tierra Firme. As soon as Pedro Menéndez Márquez had been told this and had found out in detail what had happened, he came with all speed from Matanzas to Havana to tell me it, bringing with him the Master of the Caravel himself, who was there; it seemed to me probable that when Captain Peñalosa arrived at Bayamo or Santiago de Cuba, he was wanting to provide more provisions for these men at the expense of Your Majesty, and to look for a ship to bring the men to this port, and that this would cost much and cause delays, and remembering that Your Majesty had ordered me to expel the French from La Florida and then discharge these men from service, and since the French have been expelled I was afraid that Your Majesty would hold it against me if I did not discharge them, I sent at once a message that they should be discharged, as Your Majesty will see from the copy of that order which accompanies this letter; and I wrote to Estéban de las Alas who is coming with the men in his charge in the company of Captain Peñalosa who is bringing the men from Santo Domingo, saying that once Captain Peñalosa had dismissed the men, as I had sent the instructions for him to do, that any of those men who should wish to go with me to La Florida he should take in and lodge and keep in his company with the other men he is commanding, and that with both groups together he should stay where he is, in Bayamo or Puerto del Príncipe, giving them food at my expense, since provisions are half as expensive as they are here (or even a third the price), and I sent him credit so that they could give the men all they might need: for Juan de Ynistrosa, Your Majesty's treasurer on this island, has been favorable to me in this matter and in any other matter that he can, to aid my needs and my men, since he realizes he is serving Your Majesty in this. I beg Your Majesty to write to him acknowledging the service. And I said in the letter to Esteban de las Alas that when it was necessary I would send ships for him and his men

THE SPANISH CONQUEST OF FLORIDA, 1565

to take them to La Florida, since now in winter time they have no food over there and there is no need for them to go yet. And I wrote to Captain Peñalosa that for those of the discharged men who did not want to come into service with me in La Florida, he should give the order for them to return to Hispaniola, since staying in this island they would go on to Peru and other parts of the Indies without the permission of Your Majesty; and that if pirates should come to Hispaniola this summer, it is as well that these men should be on that island to defend it; and I made both these arrangements because it seemed to me to be most convenient this way for the service of Your Majesty, and saving money for the Royal Treasury.

The Master of this caravel said that Esteban de las Alas had sold two thousand hides from it in La Yaguana in order to get provisions for his men, and that the rest are coming in the caravel: many of them are wet and in bad condition, since the caravel is taking in a great deal of water as a result of the storm they had. And because of the great necessity I am in, and in order to give food to the men I have here, and keep them content, and help with provisions the men who are in La Florida, and be able myself to pay some of the debts I have contracted here, I have tried to sell these hides, and the caravel: not seeing either the hides or the ship here, they did not want to do business: one Francisco de Reynoso came to an agreement—he was in my company at the service of Your Majesty, and I owed him the sum of two thousand ducats—and he bought the caravel and the two thousand five hundred hides it had for four thousand ducats, and of these he has to pay a thousand to the sailors that are going in this caravel, so that they can take them for pay and food, and he gave me the other thousand ducats there and then: and thus the favour which in this I have begged Your Majesty to grant concerning this caravel and the hides, which could be worth six thousand ducats, comes altogether to the value of five thousand, that is, the three thousand that I have been given here, and the two thousand for the two thousand hides that Esteban de las Alas sold from this caravel in La Yaguana: and as for the other thousand ducats that Your Majesty was going to have to pay for the hire of the Patache that was going with the news, Your Majesty does not have to pay any of this: for of the

four thousand ducats for which the caravel and hides have been bought, a thousand are going to the men who are bringing this message for their pay and food, for since it is December and winter weather despite giving them that I am sending them against their will. And I have decided that Pedro Menéndez Marquéz should leave at once for Matanzas (I am quickly repairing the caravel at the expense of its owner), and that he should take the message which I had given for Your Majesty to the patache I was sending, and that without stopping at Hispaniola or anywhere else he should go straight to Your Kingdoms, and that wherever he should land he should go and give Your Majesty this letter and the one which I was sending with the patache. And so that he should explain to Your Majesty in detail how very important it is that the Fleet which is to come here from there with 1800 sailors and soldiers should not go to Dominica, nor to Santo Domingo, nor to this island, because if they do they will arrive very late at La Florida, and the French will have arrived first and will land at their ease at the Point of Santa Elena, where there is a port which is said to be best there is in the whole of La Florida, and has a river which goes a hundred leagues inland to the mountain ranges [sierras], and from those to Zacatecas must be about 250 leagues (from what I understand it cannot be 300); or else they will go to the Bay of Santa María which is 100 leagues north of Santa Elena, where the Indian Velasco is from who is in New Spain, and from there eighty leagues inland are the mountains, and behind them there is an arm of the sea which canoes can sail, and it comes to Tierra Nova, which is about 500 leagues' journey, and it finishes there in an anchorage which there is behind the sierra, which is 80 leagues inland from the Bay of Santa María as I said: and next to that anchorage, a quarter or half a league away, there is another arm of the sea which goes in the direction of China, and comes out in the Southern Sea, and this is absolutely certain, although nobody has ever gone this way to the Southern Sea, but they have gone 500 leagues by sea in the direction West North West, starting at 42 degrees north and going as far as 48 degrees, and they were 500 leagues from Mexico from North to South, and thus consequently they were not a hundred leagues from the South Sea, or from the land of China itself. And these are purposes which the

French will be able to pursue at their ease if we do not get in first: and they are of tremendous value to them, both in prestige and profit, and all I have done at Your Majesty's service in La Florida is little in comparison with what the French will be able to do if they go there in the service of their King. And if so far they have not fortified themselves there, it has been because they were going into the Indies, and had their frontier on the Bahama Channel, where they had their fort, in order to control the warships and fleets that should sail that way, and once having made that secure they aim to settle at Santa Elena and the Bay of Santa María, which they have thoroughly reconnoitred, and to fortify themselves on the strip of land which there is a quarter or half a league behind the sierras which are to the north of the Bay of Santa María, as I have said, in order to control that arm of the sea which goes to Tierra Nova, and that which goes to the Southern Sea in the direction of China, and to benefit from the mines they might find in the sierra, and even to go without difficulty that way to the mines of San Martín and Zacatecas, and their journey will be much shorter and easier than ours is now, since from France to Tierra Nova, where that arm of the sea begins to go into the area of the mines, is a journey of 20 or 25 days, and from there they could go in small boats up that arm of the sea, to near the sierras, where they could profit from the mines, and much more expensive are the coined silver that is taken from Zacatecas to the port of San Juan de Lua; and Your Majesty should be in no doubt that the French have reconnoitred this, and that if they do not do it next summer they will the one after, and that once they establish themselves there they will be difficult to dislodge, for they will be very easily supported at little cost by Tierra Nova, where they are so in control and so many ships and men stay every year.

If the Fleet and the men that Your Majesty should send me come straight to La Florida, they might arrive in time for me to anticipate the enemy and be the first to settle each place, and taking as I shall the two frigates, very suitable and quick by oar and sail, since each has 40 oars, as I have said, and if Your Majesty gives me the favour of the thousand slave licences I have asked for, then I trust in God to be able to damage the French fleet. And if Your Majesty has news that it is coming, please tell the Governors in these

parts and the Generals of the Fleets to go very carefully, if the French fleet does arrive, even if it achieves nothing in La Florida, if it can in the towns of the Indies it will try with considerable cruelty to do harm and damage to the people and their possessions, and also in the ships and fleets that are sailing. I have wanted to give Your Majesty a detailed account of all this and send Pedro Menéndez Marquéz, my nephew, with this message, so that if necessary he can explain it to you in greater detail with the navigation chart in his hands, and so that Your Majesty should decide in each matter what is best for Your Royal Service, for in whatever concerns me I shall carry it out faithfully, carefully and diligently, as I should, and as Your Majesty entrusts it to me.

I beg Your Majesty to do me the favour of sending Pedro Menéndez Marquéz away with all speed, as he is carrying an order of mine to Pedro del Castillo that he should send him back at once in a light patache or caravel, and load in it a thousand casks of a certain size [botas de azumbre], and two thousand rope shoes for the men who go exploring, and some trinkets for the Indians, and tools for working the land, and saddles and straps for horses, and some farm workers and their wives, and come with all this to Havana here, so that from here it can be shared out among the three forts I have and in the fort I intend to make this February and March in the Bay of Juan Ponce, which will be fifty leagues from the others by land, and I shall be able to provide and provision myself with many things from Campeche and New Spain, and from there then there are no more than 50 leagues to the three forts so I can supply them with many things, and thus soon they will spread out and deal one with another. And if I leave these supplies and men to work the land with them, with clerics to expound the doctrine to the Spaniards and the natives, then I shall be able to go to Santa Elena and the Bay of Santa María to do what is necessary there, and to leave the best supplies that I can so that the land already gained and discovered is not lost. So it would be best if Your Majesty could order that Pedro Menéndez be sent off at once, to whom I shall leave orders and instructions in this Port that he should share out whatever he brings to the people that come here according to the state of the land and the need of the towns. And from the Bay of Santa María I shall go by land to the forts of San

Agustín and San Mateo, since it is no more than fifty leagues, and I shall go exploring that way and opening it out, always trying to win the goodwill of the Indians, and I shall take for this purpose 150 men and twenty horses, and I shall leave a hundred other men in the settlement I shall found on the Bay of Santa María; and by the middle of April at the latest I shall be, with the help of our Lord, in the forts of San Mateo and San Agustín, waiting for the help which I sent asking for from Your Majesty with Captain Diego Flores de Valdés, and as much as Your Majesty is pleased to send, so that when it has come I shall leave those two forts with the best supplies and organization that I can and go to the Point of Santa Elena and the Bay of Santa María to fortify myself there and wait for the enemy if they come.

I sent word to Francisco Osorio, Governor of this island, as soon as I had decided to send the patache to Your Majesty in Your Kingdoms, and send Pedro Menéndez Marquéz with the message, so that if he wanted to write to Your Majesty or other people in those kingdoms he could do so, and told him the message would be carried swift and sure. He replied that he did not wish to send a letter on the ship I was sending, for he wanted to send the caravel which came from those kingdoms with the instructions of Your Majesty that on Hispaniola and on this island, nine months supply of meat and fish should be prepared for the 1800 sailors and soldiers that Your Majesty ordered to be assembled. And when I caught up with this caravel in Matanzas it seemed to me a sufficiently fast ship by sail and oars for the exploration of La Florida and its rivers, and I spoke to the pilot, the Master and the sailors on it asking, would they like to come with me to La Florida in the summer? And they told me they liked the idea, and under this verbal arrangement they did not bring the message which they were bringing from Your Majesty for the Governor of Matanzas here by land, but brought it by sea. And although I told all this to the Governor, and the imperative need which I had of it, since my *zabra* from Santo Domingo had been lost, which was very quick by oar and sail for finding any ship on the sea, and rivers and anchorages on the coast, and that no ship was more suited to this than this caravel, and that no expense would be incurred to Your Majesty by taking the messages in the ship which I am send-

ing anyway, which is in any case the best ship for this in this winter weather, this caravel being small; despite all this, he has not wanted to do it; and although I could buy it and take it, for the owner was willing, I was afraid he would object, and even though he could not stop me I left it there, although I do need it badly. I am telling Your Majesty so that you should know what is happening in this matter, and how little help and favor I am getting in these matters which are so important to the success of my enterprises; and if Your Majesty does not put this right by writing to him about this, I and my officers continue to suffer, for we have to come here every day, and to all the island, with my ships to provide for and supply ourselves; and since the zeal with which I serve your Majesty is as great as it should be, I have no more to say: may Our Lord watch over and increase the Catholic Royal Person of Your Majesty with the growth of greater Kingdoms and Realms as Christendom needs and we, Your Majesty's servants, desire. From Havana, 12th December 1565. Your Majesty's humble servant, who kisses Your Royal hands,

[signed:] Pedro Menéndez.

[In margin] The next part is written in the hand of King Philip the Second himself.

Decree of the King: It will be as well to write at once to this Governor and to Pedro Menéndez on what he should do with those taken alive, taking them into service in the galleys there if there is one and it seems safe: or sending them to go in the galleys here. And this for those whose lives he spared, since with the others he has done very well in imposing justice [that is in having them killed.].

314. December 16, 1565. Pedro Menéndez de Avilés to Philip II.

Menéndez continued to be obsessed with the idea that the French could push through by way of the Bahía de Santa María (Chesapeake Bay) to the Pacific, and on hearing of Urdaneta's successful return from the Philippines, when he made a landfall in western North America at about 50°, he thought the news of this, when it reached the

French, would lead them to push ahead with plans for further expeditions.

Navarrete, Colección, *XIV (1971), fols. 318–318v., translated by Henry Ware, "Letters of Pedro Menéndez de Avilés,"* Massachusetts Historical Society Proceedings, *second series, VIII, 460.*

Royal Catholic Majesty.

At this moment a particular friend of mine has arrived from Campeachy, a man of character and veracity, and he tells me as a certain fact, that Pedro de las Roclas arrived at Puebla de los Angeles in the month of October last; and that, one month before, of the four ships of Your Majesty's fleet that went to China two had returned to the port of la Navidad, whence they sailed, and that their return voyage was of seventy days' sailing; that they carried a great quantity of gold dust; it is said that they certainly had a million; and that the crews of the *capitania* and of the other ships had built a fort on an island near China, and that they had planted guns on it and put in a garrison and they say that it is the richest land that, up to this day had been discovered; and that, in order to return to the port of la Navidad, whence they took their departure, they made their course to the north as far as 50 degrees, back of Florida. I have thought fit to advise Your Majesty of this, because I hold it to be very certain news; and also to warn Your Majesty that, if there is intelligence that the French are arming for these parts, there may be some danger to the fleet of New Spain, which will bring much money and have but a small force, and it will be well that Estevano de las Alas embark here with some armed vessels of the fleet, which can very easily be done, and Estevano de las Alas is a very good man who has served Your Majesty on the seas for many years, and will know how to serve you well, whom all who sail in this trade with the Indians, love, fear and respect; for, although he who came as Admiral of the fleet is a very excellent gentleman, he is young, and has had very little experience at sea, nor any of fighting at sea, and has never sailed, except one other time to New Spain with Pedro de las Roclas his uncle. Finding myself here it seemed to me well to notify Your Majesty of this, that you may make such provision as you may see fit.

May Our Lord protect and increase Your Majesty's Royal Catholic Person with increase of greater kingdoms and realms as Christianity requires, and as we, Your Majesty's servants desire. From Havana 16th of December, in the year 1565. Your Majesty's humble servant kisses Your Royal hands.

[signed:] Pedro Menéndez.

315. January 30, 1566. Pedro Menéndez de Avilés to Philip II.

Remaining in Havana during January, Menéndez's information about Florida in November and December, 1565 continued to be secondhand. He repeated his earlier story of discovering a French post near Cape Cañaveral and capturing it, and also of establishing the San Antonio garrison in the country of the Ays tribe. He had, subsequently, bad news of this post whose soldiers had scattered in search of food. He himself was anxious to explore the whole western side of the Florida Peninsula as soon as possible. He believed the St. Johns River flowed into the Bay of Juan Ponce [de León], apparently Charlotte Harbor. Nor was news from San Agustín and San Mateo good, since the garrisons there were found by a ship that arrived with some food supplies to be in greater need than the ship could provide. There was a serious danger of mutiny if more supplies were not sent rapidly. Moreover, news also came that Frenchmen who had escaped northward from La Caroline had established themselves with the Guale Indians and might well make for Santa Elena to hold out there until a fresh French fleet came. Menéndez did not think he would be able to send vessels up the coast to deal with the French until later in the spring of 1566. His main complaint was that the governor of Cuba would not give him sufficient supplies with which to keep the Florida garrison fed and in good condition. At the end of 1565 and the beginning of 1566, therefore, Menéndez was still planning ahead for bigger and better explorations and conquests, but he had not yet solved the lesser problem of maintaining a Spanish force in relatively few garrisons on the east coast of the Florida Peninsula.

Navarrete, Colección, XIV (1971), fols. 318v–325v.; translated by Henry Ware, "Letters of Pedro Menéndez de Avilés," Massachusetts Historical Society Proceedings, *second series, VIII (1894), 460–468.*

Royal Catholic Majesty.

By my cousin the Captain Pedro Menéndez Marqués, who sailed from Havana on the 19th of the last month, with a despatch-tender, I wrote to Your Majesty at length and very particularly of the good success which Our Lord had given me in Florida against the French Lutherans who had occupied it; how they were all destroyed and put to death; and how on the 2nd of November, with 250 men, and three barges for oars, I went from the Forts of San Mateo and San Agustín to the Cape Cañaveral, where I was informed that seventy or eighty Frenchmen were building a fort and a bark to send out and ask for succor. I also wrote how, one morning I came upon them with 150 men by land and with the barges by sea; how we were discovered, they being afraid of us, and betaking themselves to the mountains; how we took their fort and what provisions they had, and burned their bark; and how, that this evil Lutheran sect might not remain in the land, I sent a trumpet to the Frenchmen, offering them their lives, if they would surrender and lay down their arms and their colors; how all this was done accordingly; and that, from there I went 15 leagues further down the Bahama Channel, to a very beautiful river, where was one of the principal caciques whose name was Ays, who received us with great friendship, and how, being there, we had no sort of food, nor did this cacique give us any, saying that he had not got it, for that they ate shell fish and fish and the roots of herbs, and that if we went into the fort, we could have nothing to eat there nor where to get it from, even ever so little; so that for our relief I had determined to go down the Bahama Channel, to explore its navigation and harbors, as far as this harbor of Havana, and I did so accordingly, with 70 men in two barges, leaving the rest of the men and the other barge. I also wrote Your Majesty that arriving here I should send back to them the two barges, laden with provisions; also of the small aid and favor that was given me by Garcia Osorio, the Governor of this Island, and of the great necessity

there was that Your Majesty should order this to be remedied henceforth. I also wrote that, this month I should go to explore the Bay of Juan Ponce, in order, if there was any good harbor, to settle it, because the river of San Mateo [the St. James] empties on that coast, or near it, and our people will be easily able to communicate with each other; also to see if it be navigable between the Tortugas and Florida, and if there be any good harbor at the head of the Martires, which is very important for short voyages and safety to the ships and fleets that sail to the Indies. I also sent a duplicate of this letter subsequently to Your Majesty by a despatch caravel sent out to Your Majesty by the Governor of this Island. I trust that Our Lord will have been pleased to bring these ships in safety with these letters that Your Majesty may understand in detail all that has happened; although, only two days after the Captain Pedro Menéndez Marqués sailed, there was a very great storm here. What there is new to advise Your Majesty to-day of is this; that within 15 days after the barge laden with provisions for the Spaniards who remained in the Channel of the settlement of Ays sailed from here, she returned to this port with news that she arrived in safety, and found the soldiers whom I left there, all scattered and divided into little companies without leave of their Captain, for they were perishing with hunger where they were; that the cacique with his people had gone away and got together a number of men in order to make war upon them; and that they had come 20 leagues this way where they had found better land and some food of palmettos and other fruits called icacos, (cocoa plum) and many mulberries and fish, and there they all collected together in a fort which they had thrown up as well as they could in the time, and many peaceful Indians had come to them showing themselves friends, with some display of gold and silver, and they advised me of all this by Captain Juan Velez de Medrano who is there in command of all these men. Two days ago arrived Captain Diego de Amaya, who sailed in the other barge of 70 tons, laden with provisions for the two forts of San Agustín and San Mateo, and he brought me news that he arrived in safety at fort San Agustín and there discharged the stores that were to remain there, of 150 sows with young that he took out, 50 had died, and he landed 80 of them there, and that, within six days he would have departed with the ship and the provisions that he was carrying for Fort San Mateo; but being in December the weather changed so one night that at dawn there was a great storm and very heavy sea, so that he was obliged to attempt the bar of San Mateo and he ran aground in such a manner, although the vessel required but little water, she thumped and was stranded near the land, where all the crew went ashore, and the vessel went to pieces, and a part of the provisions was saved although very little. They say that the men in the forts are well and very resigned; that, in the cold of winter, being ill clothed, more than a hundred persons died, and that they were in a very great necessity of food, and still are; the Commandant and the Captains who were there had agreed that as one of the two brigantines was finished which I had left orders that they should build for me wherewith to explore the coast in the spring, and go to Santa Elena and the Bay of St. Mary. Captain Diego de Amaya should return to inform me of the strait they were in for want of food, shoes and clothing, that I might provide them without delay; and how the ship which was going to them had been lost with part of the provisions; for, when Captain Diego de Amaya left here, I ordered him, after having landed his provisions at the two forts, to proceed, with all despatch to the Island of Porto Rico or Hispaniola to look for the galleon San Pelayo which had on board two thousand quintals of biscuit and much wine, vinegar and other stores; that he should load his ship with all of these and go back to Florida with it. The Commandant and the Captains also wrote me that the two French ships which escaped when we took the fort of San Mateo in which Juan Rivao's eldest son escaped the day that he was in the fort by swimming to one of these ships, had gone five and twenty leagues beyond, towards the north to a very good harbor called Guale, the Indians there being their friends, and that there are, within a space of three or four leagues, forty villages of the Indians of two brothers, one of whom is called Causin, and the other Guale, and these two brothers are great friends of the General Ludunier who was in Florida before the coming of Juan Rivao. The day that we took the fort, he jumped over the wall in his shirt, and fled to the mountain, wounded by a pike, and we never heard any further news of him, save that it was said that the Indians, his enemies, had killed him.

It seemed to me that he reached the shore before the son of Juan Rivao got over the bar, that he took him in and, as he knew of the harbor of Guale and the two caciques were his friends, that he went there with the two ships, and that, in great haste, he threw up a fort, and that he had in it seventy or eighty men; that he had sent one of the ships to France and kept the other there. They must have much artillery and ammunition and stores, for these two ships had not yet discharged what they brought from France, and one of them carried four heavy brass guns on her broadside. If they are succored through the friendship that they have with the Indians, having there plenty of food of maize, beans, pumpkins, and much fish and game, it will be a bad thing, and it will be afterwards very hard to eject them, having so good a harbor. Some Frenchmen whom I have here assure me, that when I arrived in Florida, Juan Rivao was about to send there a Captain with 200 men to settle that harbor, which he had very well surveyed, and the Indians desired him to do so, and that this spring with the people who were to come from France, he intended to settle in Santa Elena, which is admirably good, for these Frenchmen say it is the best harbor that they have discovered in Florida and that they would also this spring have settled in the Bay of St. Mary. Even if I had men enough, I could not go to Guale, where these Frenchmen are, before the end of March, or the beginning of April, for this coast is stormy, and we must go along the coast with great care to make the harbor; but I have resolved with the help of Our Lord, to go within eight days to the Bay of Juan Ponce, and to explore the entire coast from Philippina and the bays of San Jusepe as far as the Martires, and between the Tortugas and Florida, to see if there is any navigable channel for the fleets from New Spain for, if there is, they can sail much more easily from New Spain to Havana; and if I find any good port on that coast and Bay of Juan Ponce, I shall settle there and fortify, for the river of San Mateo [the St. James] empties on that coast, or cannot be above 15 or 20 leagues from it and by land the forts of San Mateo and San Agustín are not above 50 leagues distant and they can easily communicate with each other, and bring the Indians into friendship with us, and the priests can instruct them with less risk. And by that coast and Bay of Juan Ponce I shall be able to get supplies easily, from New Spain and Campeachy, and from this Island of Cuba, and from that harbor I shall be able to supply the forts of San Mateo and San Agustín, and reinforce them whenever it may be necessary, and when my galleons are going to New Spain, they can land men and provisions there without going out of their course and the same when they are returning from New Spain to Spain; and thence they can settle, with the people who may come from Spain, the river bank of San Pelayo that goes toward the fort of San Mateo, which they say is inhabited by Indians and has plenty of food. These two forts of San Mateo and San Agustín, and in case of finding a harbor in the Bay of Juan Ponce, the one which I settle there together with the shore of San Pelayo being near each other, will be under the command of a Captain and there will also be an Alcayde in each fort, and this office I propose to confide to Estevano de las Alas, being a gentleman and a good Christian and of good deportment, while I shall go to the coast of Philippina, as far as the Martires and Tortugas, until the middle of March, exploring it by land and sea, in order to settle in the best harbor and land location that I shall find, for I have four brigantines and two gallies, very sufficient for that purpose, either for oars or sails, and two very good tenders for the accommodation of the troops and to carry provisions for them, I having been engaged all this time in equipping and careening them. I shall leave Estevano de las Alas the best supply possible, with 100 men, in the settlement that I shall make on the coast and at the Bay of Juan Ponce, so that the men who may come to me from Havana in my tenders may be all taken there, so as to be divided between the two forts of San Mateo and San Agustín and the place where he shall be; and if priests come, they will have plenty to occupy themselves with. From Havana to the place where I shall leave him they can easily come in two days more, especially if I shall discover a navigable channel between the Tortugas and Florida, for the prevailing wind there is northeast, and this is favorable both for going and returning. From the middle of March onward, leaving to Estevano de las Alas one of the brigantines, so that he may go and come to Havana for provisions for his men, I shall go directly to where the Captain Juan Velez de Medrano is, and take him off with what men he may have for the Captain Diego de Amaya, who came

from there, reported to me that many of them are dead from hunger, and that the Indians who have risen against them and are very warlike and treacherous, have killed others; and I shall take these men with me to the forts of San Agustín and San Mateo, where, in each fort I shall leave a Captain with 150 soldiers, and then, with the largest force I can get together, which shall be, if possible, not less than three hundred men, for this is little enough, I shall go to Guale, where Ludunier and Juan Rivao's son are, and endeavor to take their fort and expel them from the land before they can be succored from France; and, if Our Lord gives me the victory, I shall leave there a captain with a hundred soldiers, and go on to St. Elena with the other one hundred and fifty; and if meanwhile, the reinforcements of Your Majesty shall arrive at this port of Havana I shall leave my order here with the Treasurer, Juan de Yñistrosa, (and also leave one of my servants) that they shall immediately succor Estevano de las Alas with two or three hundred men and provisions for them; and that, with the rest they shall go to the forts of San Agustín and San Mateo, and I shall leave a pilot to take them there, that he may leave them men and provisions as I have ordered, and with the rest and the whole fleet they shall pass on to Guale, for I shall leave pilots to take them there; so that, if the French fleet comes, it shall find us in a state to defend ourselves and that we may hold the forts we have taken which they had explored. And if they shall proceed to the Islands, with the intent of committing robbery and cruelties, or shall attempt to lie in wait for any fleet from New Spain, I may be able to spy them and give such favors as I may be able, on the one side or the other; but if the French should come before Your Majesty shall reinforce me, we shall all be in great trouble and danger. I shall do all that is possible for a man, and I shall do it to the end, and I am certain that, much and well as I desire to serve Your Majesty and to give you these Provinces of Florida cleared so that the Holy Gospel may be preached in them, and the natives brought to Your Majesty's allegiance, so that neither the French nor any other nation shall have any part in them, what is possible for me does not equal my zeal and desire; but Your Majesty may be certain that all I have and all I can get from relatives and friends, I shall devote and expend in this undertaking, and as so great sums are needed to support the one and the other, if Your Majesty should do it at your cost, you would incur very great expense, and in order that I may support the one and the other, it will be well that Your Majesty should pay out from your treasury to assist me, for in no other way can I obtain credit to incur such great expenses as I do, which are all absolutely necessary in order to expel the enemy from the land, and to prevent them from returning into it.

The Governor of this Island as I have written Your Majesty, has not helped me with a single real, although I had two orders from Your Majesty that he should give me an armed ship, with fifty armed men, provisions for four months, that this should cost above twenty thousand ducats; and although now he sees my strait, and the need I have of provisions to take with me, to supply the forts, and to take to Guale to eject the French, and to Santa Elena, and the great scarcity there is of them in this place, and the amount that I have expended for the troops that I had and still have here, and the large sum that the two vessels cost me which I sent with provisions to Florida; that Your Majesty has three hundred men at your charge in Florida, that they have nothing to eat and are perishing with hunger, and that he is bound to supply them, yet he has not found means to aid me with one single real, nor a load of cassavi, nor an arroba of beef, nor any thing worth a single maravedis. Even if he had no money of Your Majesty's, for this purpose, it is enough that he has fourteen or fifteen thousand ducats from the caravel that he took in my name and with them or a portion of them, he might assist me, since I bound myself to repay it, whenever Your Majesty shall so order. He also obstructs and hinders me, publicly and in secret, as much as he can, giving opportunity to my men to mutiny and desert, and that not a man who leaves me shall return; also the physician and surgeon whom I was to carry have left me eight days ago, as soon as they knew the voyage I was going, and they are in a house here and he knows it, yet gives no orders to search for and take them, though knowing that I cannot go on my voyage without them. Evidence of all these things accompanies this, that Your Majesty may be satisfied of the truth of what has occurred. I suffer all, and shall suffer, as I have written Your Majesty, understanding that this is expedient for Your Majesty's service; but if in future Your Majesty does not remedy this, it will be impossible to do what should be done for Your Majesty's service in the exploration of Florida, except with great danger, cost and delay, none of which ought to be incurred or endured.

More than forty men of the company of the *Capitania* of Pedro de las Roclas, (may he be in Heaven) have deserted, in order not to go to Florida, and are waiting until I shall have departed to return to the town, for the Governor says that he has need of them to guard the place. I shall take about eighty persons from the ship; these will be with Estevano de las Alas until the fleet from New Spain shall arrive at this port, and will then immediately return here, as I do not want to take a single man or gun from this ship, for it seems to me that it will be necessary for the safety of the fleet.

I conversed with Padre Fray Andrés de Urdaneta, who has arrived here from China, concerning the strait which it is certainly supposed there is in Florida, going in the direction of China, concerning which he has had a full account for many years, and the way in which we must proceed to learn this secret is that which I have communicated to Your Majesty in a memorial some years ago, for thus it can be done most speedily, best, at the least cost, and the truth of that secret will be best known and quickest, and being a matter of such importance to the service of God Our Lord and to the increase of Your Majesty's kingdom and Royal treasury, I shall contrive in every possible way to be this coming winter in Your Majesty's kingdom. If I can, I shall send Captain [ ] with the Indian of the Bay of St. Mary, in order that with his own eyes he may see this arm of the sea, so that Your Majesty may make such provisions in relation thereto, as shall be expedient to Your Majesty's service, and I shall make report of the things that I may have discovered and seen on the coast and in the land of Florida, and of the necessity there will be to people them and to support them, without Your Majesty expending upon this anything out of your Royal treasury, except, it may be some small amount, during the first two or three years, although it will be proper that my going shall be kept very secret, that it may not come to the knowledge of the enemy on account of the danger to which my person would be exposed from them, for I shall leave the land of Florida, and the forts and settlements that remain in very good condition, and the winter so defends that coast that they will be very secure from enemies.

It will be well that Your Majesty should make an order so that my tenders and small vessels which I am to bring, according to the compact may if necessary, carry that part of the clothing which they were to take to Florida to New Spain and Campeachy, so that they may obtain thence the provisions and necessary things that we require for Florida.

I wrote to Your Majesty how the fleet of Santo Domingo had been lost on this island, one hundred and fifty leagues from here, near Baracoa and how Estevano de las Alas had saved all the men in the vessel that he took for his flag-ship from Asturias and Biscay; and as Your Majesty had commanded me that when the French were driven out of Florida I should discharge the troops for Santo Domingo and send them to that Island, I, seeing that the French were dead, sent it there to be paid off, where it was lost near Hispaniola. This I did to obey what Your Majesty had commanded me in this matter, and so, that more easily and at less cost they could return to Santo Domingo. This errand of mine went speedily to Gonzalo de Peñalosa who came in command of these men, and he considered them as discharged, but made a contract with a greater part of the men to come to this port of Havana; others went to Santiago de Cuba and to Bayamo, in order to cross over to the New Kingdom, Peru, Honduras and New Spain, and all those who came here came with the intention of going on to Honduras & New Spain. I spoke with Peñalosa and all these soldiers, stating to them that Your Majesty would be greatly displeased, if those who did not go with me to Florida should not go back to Santo Domingo, but I perceived that none of them would go to Florida with me, though I would willingly receive them all, as well as all the other men, but it appeared to them a very laborious expedition and fifteen days ago a vessel left here for Campeachy, which the Governor visited, but would not permit me visit, and after eight days, the weather being unfavorable, she returned; and she had on board 35 of these Santo Domingo soldiers and some of those of my command, and proposed to sail again in two days, it being fine weather. Seeing such irregularities and ill service

of Your Majesty, and that I could not remedy it, I issued a proclamation, a copy of which goes herewith, at which the Governor and Peñalosa and his soldiers were much offended.

The Commandant and Sergeant Major write me from Florida that the trouble is insupportable that they have with the greater part of the men there, on account of their desertion from the country and speaking ill of it, and discouraging those who are not there, in order that they may be able to go over to the Indies, for many of them came with this intent; and unless Your Majesty shall take sufficient measures in all the courts of the Indies, so that they may take within their districts, or even out of them if they can, all the men who shall have come to Florida, and left there without my leave, and send them prisoners to me in Florida, so that they shall serve perpetually at the oar, and so that those who come from Spain may not deceive themselves but understand that they are to remain here; and that the Indies may not be filled up with knaves, and that I and my officers shall not have mutinies, neither with the people who shall reside in Florida, I fear that I shall have no power to prevent it.

I showed to the Padre Fr. Andres de Urdaneta samples of the gold and silver that there is in Florida; and I am told that the Captains and soldiers who are there have got by barter a quantity of above a thousand ducats, and it is said there is among them a quantity of common gold.

May Our Lord protect and prosper the Royal Catholic person of Your Majesty with increase of greater kingdoms and realms as Christianity requires, and as we Your Majesty's servants desire. From Havana, January 30th 1566. Your Majesty's humble servant kisses your Royal hands.

[signed:] Pedro Menéndez.

316. 1565. Gonzalo Solís de Merás's account of Pedro Menéndez de Avilés's attack on the French fort in Florida.

Gonzalo Solís de Merás's account of the Spanish intervention is a classical one. He was present at the events he describes. He was the brother-in-law of the adelantado. *He was apparently also official recorder to the expedition. The only (somewhat defective) manuscript of his "Memorial" was published for the first time by E. Ruidíaz y Caravia, La Florida, 2 vols. (Madrid, 1893) and occupied the whole of volume I. It was translated and edited by Jeanette T. Connor, Pedro Menéndez de Avilés. Memorial by Gonzalo Solís de Merás (Deland, Fla., 1923; reprinted Gainesville, Fla., 1964), and here reprinted.*

The early part of the memoir gives a biography of Menéndez until 1565, from his birth at Monte de Rey, Pravia, near Avilés in Asturias, through his career in the royal service, chiefly as the organizer of the fleets, Flota and Galeones, which sailed each year to the Spanish Indies and joined to return under convoy to Europe. His imperious manner and his disregard of formal regulations made him many enemies among the officials at Seville and in the Indies. His breach of the regulations of the Casa de Contratación at Seville brought him a fine of 1,000 ducats, but this did not reduce Philip II's respect for his ruthless ability. The extracts given here are from the Connor translation, pp. 64–137, and cover his appointment as adelantado, *his expedition, and his conquest of French Florida, with the execution of almost all its defenders.*

MEMORIAL
Written by Doctor Gonzalo Solís de Merás of all the voyages and deeds of the Adelantado Pedro Menéndez de Avilés his brother-in-law and of the conquest of Florida and the justice he worked on Juan Ribao and other frenchmen

6.

Other events and exploits, as singular as they appear incredible, proved Pedro Menéndez to be the foremost man of his time; but applause, as general as it was sincere, was not sufficient to free him from thrusts of envy; since having been ordered in the year 1561, to return to the Indies with the fleet, he arrived in Spain laden with riches and rivals, who gave cause for the imprisonment which will now be treated of; having accomplished more on this occasion than on the others.

The said Pedro Menéndez went to present him-self before the Casa de Contratación of the city of Seville, before the judges thereof, who commanded them to give bail [to appear] at the trial and sentence, and although they knew... guaranteed, they would not take it... two persons among the most wealthy... and when they finished taking the... imprisoned in Las Atarazanas and... that city, with two *alguaciles* ... each one and each *alguacil* earned... every day; and the day following they impeached them... there were five *informaciones* against Pedro Menéndez... most of them, whence resulted... the whole accusation, made by Licentiate Banegas, the Fiscal of that Casa de la Contratación, without holding any commission from the judges therefor, and he made... concealment and made the charges and... followed and accused the said Pedro Menéndez and his brother, Bartolomé Menéndez, and [when this was] seen by the lawyers of... Pedro Menéndez, who was Licentiate Martín Alonso, a great... friend, and he had been many years a censor for the Casa de la Contratación, and drew a salary from his Majesty therefor, and was in the habit of remaining in the place of some of them as a judge of that Casa de la Contratación, when they absented themselves; and he could not plead in any lawsuit of that Casa without the permission of the judges, and if he did so, he lost the salary and office he held therein: he asked permission of the judges to plead in [that trial]: they would not give it to him, as he and Pedro Menéndez were great friends; and as it was understood that he was... he chose to lose the salary he received... de la Contratación, and defend him... lawyer and that of Bartolomé Menéndez, his brother, and so... them with the accusation, he put in an answer in the suit... and that of Pedro Menéndez: he said he gave... amended the testimonies in the five summary *informaciones* which had been made against Pedro Menéndez... and he demanded the sentence: as it appeared to the officials that by this means they [Menéndez and his brother] would be getting out of the... with their case, the Fiscal asked for a *termino ultramarino* in order to prove the things of which he held him accused: this was granted him: it was requested on behalf of Pedro Menéndez that in the meantime he be released on bail: they would not do this, and so he remained a captive in that prison 20 months, and Bartolomé Menéndez, his brother, 25; [and] although on behalf of both, all possible efforts were made with the Contratación to have them tried, they could not get the time shortened, on account of the delay there was in their case so as to lengthen their prison term, until [the coming of] the 1st and 2d cédulas from his Majesty [to the effect] that they should be sentenced. Since their cases had been finished many days previous, and the charges reported to his Majesty could not be proved against them, they sent their cases and persons to his Majesty and the Señores of his Royal Council of the Indies, and [decided] that they [Pedro and Bartolomé] should give six thousand ducats [and] should go to present themselves before that Court with an *alguacil* and two guardsmen for security: they complied with the sentence: they gave the bail: they asked for the proceedings: they would not give them the originals: they ordered that copies be made: two months went by during this, without [the copies] being given to them: when they had been given them, and they asked that the *alguacil* and the two guardsmen be appointed to take them to Court, they set new guards over them, saying that the Fiscal in the service of the Indies had appealed from that sentence, and likewise he of the Casa de la Contratación.

There was much wonder and murmuring at this among lawyers and persons of importance, on seeing that at the end of so many prison [terms] and annoyances and accusations as had been imposed on Pedro Menéndez and his brother, and the many *informaciones* that had been taken against them in the kingdom and out of it (for in the suit against Pedro Menéndez alone, there were three *informaciones* against him, taken in the kingdom and out of it); that when he had been such a famous Captain-General for so many years, in positions of such trust; and that no particular person at any time, nor then, had asked or demanded anything of him and his brother, save only Licentiate Banegas, the Fiscal of that Contratación of Seville; that at the end of so many prosperous occurrences and voyages which Our Lord had granted him in the service of his Majesty, and when he was expecting that his Majesty would bestow on him a notable reward, they should behold him a prisoner, accused by his Fiscal, and [serving] such a long prison term; see him come out with such a trifling sentence and such a small guard for him and his brother; and

see that because the judges at Seville cannot try a case in a higher court of claims (for it must of necessity come before the Council [of the Indies] in whatever form it may be, either by appeal or by a trial which they provide), the Fiscal of the Royal Council of the Indies had likewise appealed from that sentence: [therefore] the Adelantado was advised by persons learned in the law that it was proper for him to break prison, leaving therein his brother, Bartolomé Menéndez, and travel by post and go to his Majesty with great secrecy, which he did; and entering the palace, [his Majesty] saw him coming through a hall, at nine o'clock in the morning, and he sent him a page of the bed-chamber to tell him to come up to speak to him; and because the said General had been warned that, as he had not been cleared of the accusations which there were against him, he would transgress the law if he spoke to the King before speaking to the members of the Royal Council of the Indies, he sent to tell his Majesty that owning to this, he dare not kiss his hands, nor go up at his summons, for fear the Señores of the Council of the Indies would order him to be punished: he spoke with the Señores of the Council: they commanded him to be put into prison, and time went by and his case was heard: he was tried in the primary and secondary court of claims, without any other proceedings being instituted in the case against him, or in that against his brother, than those which had been taken in Seville, by the same judges who had competence in jurisdiction; and they and the Fiscal were prosecuting them and conducting the case and they were to sentence them; and they had written to his Majesty that [Pedro and Bartolomé Menéndez] had transgressed the law in many serious and shocking things, and they [the judges] must be willing to find them guilty so that everything might be made true; and the said Pedro Menéndez was condemned to pay one thousand ducats and his brother Bartolomé Menéndez, 200, because of the guilt resulting from the lawsuit aforesaid, without knowing on what charges; his Majesty, on account of them, having spent for his Royal Exchequer more than 2,000 ducats, in sending to have *informaciones* taken in the kingdom and out of it, in order to find evidence against them, because his Fiscal wanted to find them guilty.

His Majesty regretted that sentence, since he sent to summon him; and as he was a servant of his, he granted him the mercy of reducing that penalty by one half, and he commanded him to return to serve as General in that *Carrera* [of the Indies], together with his brothers and kinsmen, as of yore, saying he would thereby hold himself to be well served; would reward him for having previously served him well, and would vindicate him openly for the insult which had been offered him, for it was well understood throughout his whole kingdom that he had been accused falsely. Pedro Menéndez replied to him with all humility, kissing his hands for the grace and favor he did him in telling him that he was satisfied with his services and considered him so good a captain; and for the conviction [his Majesty] had that he had been accused falsely and that the judges had been prejudiced against him. He aspired to no further favor from his Majesty than this, which was as much as he could desire: the satisfaction that his services were acceptable to his Majesty, and that he served him with all love and fidelity; [but] he was in great affliction, because having but one only son, who was a gentleman of his Majesty's household, he had disappeared while coming as the General of a fleet and armada from New Spain, in a storm which came upon him off an island near Florida they call Bermuda; it was in the natural order of things either that the ship had sunk with all on board, or that they had escaped to that island or to Florida; and on account of his imprisonment he had been unable to go in search of them, in order if they were there, to save them and restore them to life; because there came on that ship besides his son, many of his kinsmen, friends, followers and soldiers, all of whom had been serving his Majesty under him for a long time; all of whom he had left with [his son] in New Spain, and loved like children; he intended from the contributions he obtained from relatives and friends, to equip two pataches at once and go to that island and the coast of Florida, sailing close to the shore, and landing at some points, in order to ask the Indians by signs if there were bearded men in that country, or in any island near by, since none of the Indians have beards; and until he could start on that undertaking, it seemed to him that he was not satisfying his conscience, nor the love he had for that only son, because he had no other; or for the kinsmen and friends who were with him; [he said] that when he had made that voyage he would go to his home, wife and chil-

dren, whatever the result might be, for in eighteen years he had only been there . . . times, because he had been occupied in his Majesty's service; during which period he had attended, as he was in duty bound, to serving him; and that even though it were in great poverty, he wanted to end his days at home in the service of God.

His Majesty had pity and compassion on him; he told him that he would help him in the one and the other [purpose], and to come to speak to him the following day, and the said Pedro Menéndez did so. His Majesty told him that he was sorry for his hardships and troubles; that he wished to aid him in the voyage he wanted to make in search of his son, provided that after he had finished his search, he would navigate along the whole coast of Florida, in order to discover the inlets, harbors and shoals that were there, so as to record them with exactness and set them down on marine charts; because, on account of this not having been done, many ships had been lost which went to and from the Indies, with much treasure and many people on board; and many armadas the Emperor, his father, of glorious memory, and his Majesty [himself] had equipped for the conquest and settlement of that land of Florida.

Pedro Menéndez answered that would to God his Majesty understood that which he was saying as fully as was fitting for the service of God and his own, since that was one of the necessary things which he must provide and remedy in his kingdom, especially at a time when so many Lutheran heretics were springing up in Flanders, Germany, France, England and Scotland, all of them lands near to Florida, which is such a large country with such a good altitude and climate for all kinds of products that it must perforce contain many good things; and [since] it was entirely peopled by savages, without faith and law, unenlightened by the law of Our Lord Jesus Christ, his Majesty was in duty bound by the powers which the Holy Pontiffs of Rome had given long ago to the Kings of Castile for the conquest and settlement of that land, to try to implant the Holy Gospel therein; and he [Menéndez] would take that enterprise under his charge with greater zeal than any for the many armadas, or any office which his Majesty might entrust to him in his kingdoms. His Majesty answered him that he would take much pleasure in committing that undertaking to his care, and in making a contract with him in order that he might do it, [granting] everything within reason; and so his Majesty made a contract with the said Pedro Menéndez, leaving in his charge the conquest and settlement of that land, with [everything pertaining to] the journey; and after having collected his cédulas and decrees, [Menéndez] departed for Asturias and Biscay, to assemble his fleet.

7.

Pedro Menéndez feared that his Majesty might have thought ill of him because of what his ministers had said of him, as they believed the tale-bearers who had spoken ill of the Adelantado; and he [believed] that he had fallen in his [Majesty's] disfavor, who might not have as good an opinion of him as was just; he desired to regain his reputation, which he had obtained through such hardships and dangers, at the cost of his property, and the loss and death of his son, brothers, kinsmen and friends; and when he saw the captains and men of noble birth who had followed him and served his Majesty in his company, poor and in need, without being able to help them, because he was so likewise, nothing he might undertake appeared difficult, especially that [conquest] of Florida, which was so much for the service of God Our Lord and of his Majesty, and for the general welfare of his kingdoms; wherefore he had thought that if the King's reward should fail him, that of God Our Lord could not, nor His aid, which was what he needed, and was the particular interest he was trying for therein; and he dispatched from there three messengers to different parts, writing to his friends and to Francisco de Reinoso, a military man of his Majesty, so that they might bring him as many men as they could; and he told Francisco de Eraso that his Majesty would be very ill served by the delay in his going to Florida; that it did not appear fitting to him to be detained for those ships, supplies and men because he did not know where he could find the ships; that he had a galleon of one thousand tons, the best thing there was on the sea, very fast and well armed, ready for war; that the merchants of Seville were giving him twenty-five thousand ducats' worth of freight so that she might go laden to Nombre de Dios, and that he was already loading her; that he was willing to lose that interest and would collect as many men as he could; that notice should be sent to the officials of Seville to take and prepare her to carry on board as many people as she could hold, and that any dispatch his Majesty was to give him in Valladolid, could be sent to him in Seville: this appeared very good to Francisco de Eraso, who enjoined him so to do, and to make his voyage with speed. The Adelantado managed so well by way of Cadiz and Biscay, that on St. Peter's Day he set out from Cadiz with that galleon *San Pelayo* and ten other sail; and five from Asturias and Biscay, and 2,150 soldiers and sailors on board thereof, as has been said; and of all these his Majesty paid for 300 soldiers and one ship; all the rest was at the expense of the Adelantado, who sought all the aid he could from kinsmen and friends, who helped him very much, knowing that that enterprise was greatly for the service of God Our Lord and his Majesty; and Pedro del Castillo, a citizen and *regidor* of Cadiz, a great friend of the Adelantado, distinguished himself in this more than all [of them], in helping him from his own means and those of his friends, for he alone lent him twenty thousand ducats; the Adelantado realizing the great service he was doing his Majesty in this, in order to go straight to Florida, as he did, to destroy the enemy before they could fortify themselves and gain the good-will of the caciques and Indians of that land, as has been said.

8.

Having seen that for that journey to Florida his Majesty was giving him decrees, and sufficient assurance that in the Indies they would furnish him with 200 horses, 400 soldiers paid for 4 months, artillery and 3 armed ships, munitions and provisions and all the things he should ask for and have need of, to drive out the French Lutherans who were in Florida; it appeared to him that by departing from Cadiz by June, '65, as it had to be then, and going through the islands of the Indies collecting that infantry and those horses and armed ships, he would be much delayed, and could not go to Florida until the spring of the year '66; and that by then, as has been said before now, the French who were in Florida would have so fortified themselves through having received much succor in men, artillery, arms, munitions and supplies, that when the Adelantado arrived there by March, '66, he could not bring about the same results as he could if he were to go directly from Cadiz to Florida, where the Frenchmen were, before they could have been succored; or in case they had been, before they could have fortified themselves and won the good-will of the caciques; for this was the greatest fear the Adelantado had, because if he should have the native Indians of Florida as enemies, as well as the French who would train them to fight, the forces the Adelantado brought with him would not be sufficient to gain a footing in that country, or to drive the Lutherans out of it. The Adelantado told this fact to his Majesty in Santa María de Nieva in April, '65, and in La Mejorada; and he said it to the Señores of the Royal Council of State and War, who were with him; afterwards he came to say so in Madrid, where the Court was, to the President of the Royal Council of Castile and the Señores of the Royal Council of the Indies, in order that they might give him two galleys and two galliots [then] in charge of Don Alvaro de Bazán, [and] with his *zabras* and pataches he might push on to Florida before the French could be succored; and if they had been, he would land in another harbor, the nearest to theirs he could find; he could do this, as the ships he took drew but little water; and there he would fortify himself, trying to do the enemy all the harm he could, and to gain the good-will of the caciques; and in the spring, with the horses that should come to him from the Indies, he would get control of the country and the [Frenchmen's] harbor, because they had their fort two leagues inland up the river; so that they could not be succored nor the Indians treat with them; and that in this manner war could be made on them in all good order and activity, and they could soon be driven out of the land of Florida, in order that they should not implant therein their evil Lutheran sect.

Because his Majesty had been advised that the powerful Turk was marching on Malta, that the galleys he had to oppose him were few, and that therefore he could not give them, although the reason the Adelantado gave seemed a very good one to him; and all the other Señores aforesaid with whom he communicated, said likewise; his Majesty on the following day in La Mejorada provided through his Council of State and War, that they should give the Adelantado 500 men, paid and equipped, with 4 armed ships, all at the expense of his Majesty; so that with the 500 men and 10 shallops and *zabras* the Adelantado was

taking at his expense, in accordance with the *asiento* he had made with his Majesty concerning the conquest and settlement of Florida, he should go to the islands of Puerto Rico, Hispaniola and Cuba, to assemble the horses, infantry and ships.

The Adelantado named very important persons as officials to the Royal Exchequer, and among them Hernando de Miranda as Factor; whereof he gave an account to the King, who approved the selection; for one cannot go to conquer and settle new lands without taking them [the officials], and their appointment belongs to the General.

On the 5th of May Menéndez wrote, by order of the King, that Francisco de Eraso must raise more people, and the same day the proper order was given by the officials of the Casa de la Contratación, whereby the Royal Atarazanas were opened and Pedro Menéndez was given artillery, munitions of war and food supplies, and although his Majesty ordered that 500 men be given him, this was not carried out; for the King's account there were given only 299 soldiers, who received the pay apportioned to 200 men; 95 sailors with the chief pilot, and everything else that he held necessary; as the same order had allowed him to dispose of a larger equipment than that [called for] by his obligation.

9.

Juan de San Vicente arrived in Seville from Italy with a comrade of his, called Francisco Pérez; they were both natives of Medina del Campo: they brought letters from Luis de Quintanilla, a great friend of the Adelantado, wherein he assured him that San Vicente was a very good soldier [and] asked that he honor and favor him in whatever way he could, for he [San Vicente] had a brother in Italy who was a captain serving with great credit; and as this was the first thing his friend begged of him, and he believed that the bravery of the protégé would be equal to that of his brother, of whom the Adelantado had heard much, he made him a captain, and his comrade an ensign.

He carried to that conquest 2,646 persons in 34 vessels, among them being 4 very large ones, provided with much more than had been stipulated. Before sailing out of the Bay of Cadiz he wished to take the muster-roll of the people who had embarked there; but Francisco Duarte, the Factor (without an order from the King, because he did not show any to the Adelantado, although he asked him for it), wanted to interfere with this, saying it was his right, and he insisted so much that [the Adelantado,] in order not to waste in quarrels on land, the auspicious weather at sea for his navigation, consented to the Factor's demands, although he had no jurisdiction; [but] he represented to the King that in accordance with the patent and instructions he carried, the officials of the Casa de la Contratación of Seville could not interfere in anything without a special royal cédula; and that when he was in San Lucar with the armada of protection for the Indies, about to set sail, wishing to take the muster-roll of the soldiers and sailors, and aid them before the royal officials in compliance with his instructions, Francisco Duarte, the Factor, had requested him to join with him and the other officials, but when he asked him for the order he could not produce it; and that as the wind was favorable and in order that the royal service should not suffer, [the Adelantado,] holding it for certain that his Majesty would reprimand that infraction and would command it to be remedied for the future, had joined him at his house, where the roll was taken; and he supplicated his Majesty to order the officials referred to, not to intrude themselves in anything concerning that fleet, nor in the visitation thereof, without a special royal cédula, since he would permit [the visitation] when it should be for the royal service: "because," he added, "the people of the said armada would show the greatest discontent if the officials of the Casa de la Contratación were to be their judges; and for this same reason I fear that the armada may disband if the men should know that they have any other judges than the Council of the Indies."

The muster-roll was called, and the fleet was composed of one galleon, chartered for his Majesty's account, of 996 tons; and 10 ships wherein were going 995 sailors and soldiers, 4 secular priests with licenses to receive confession, and 117 tradesmen: locksmiths, millers, silversmiths, tanners, sheepshearers and others, with all the artillery necessary for building forts and defending oneself. All the people were going at the expense of the Adelantado, except 299 soldiers and 95 sailors, with the chief pilot.

[There was] the galleon *San Pelayo*, which was the flagship, with the Adelantado on board and 317 soldiers, 299 thereof for the King's account;

[and] 4 cannon, with the rest of the artillery and provisions bought by Pedro del Castillo, a citizen and *regidor* of Cadiz; [also] the shallop *Magdalena*, of 75 tons; the shallops *San Miguel* and *San Andrés*, of 100 tons, Gonzalo Bayón, shipmaster; and *La Concepción*, of 70 tons, carrying 96 men; the galley called *Victoria*, with 17 benches; the brigantine *La Esperanza*, with 11 benches; the caravel *San Antonio*, of 150 tons, carrying 114 soldiers; the caravel *La Concepción*, laden with supplies, which only went as far as the Canaries; the caravel of shipmaster Juan Ginete; the caravel *Nuestra Señora de las Virtudes*, Hernando Rodriguez, shipmaster, a citizen of Cadiz; the vessel *Espíritu Santo*, of 55 tons, Alonso Menéndez Marqués, shipmaster; the vessel *Nuestra Señora del Rosario*, Pedro Suarez Carvayo, shipmaster; and 5 others, the names whereof have been lost, making in all 19, for the others were being equipped in Asturias and Biscay.

And [the fleet] having set sail from the Bay of Cadiz on the 29th of June, as the warnings and notices against the Huguenots had deferred the departure, such a severe storm arose that it was driven back to land, to the great grief of the Adelantado at the delay: he gathered more people in Cadiz, and the weather growing clear, he set out another time and arrived safely at the Canaries, where he resumed taking the roll of the men he carried, a thing he had been unable to do in Cadiz because Francisco Duarte, the Factor, absented himself; and he found he had 1,504 persons, not beggars and of the rabble, to beat whom, says Jacobo Le Moine, 50 Frenchmen were sufficient; but among them were some of the principal gentlemen of Asturias, Galicia and Biscay, whom a thousand Frenchmen would not dare to face.

Two days after he had departed, Captain Luna with 90 men arrived in the Bay of Cadiz, and requested Francisco Duarte, the Factor, to give him a ship wherewith to go over to Florida: Francisco Duarte declined, and sent him to Pedro del Castillo, who freighted a caravel for him, with supplies and everything needful, and 67 persons embarked, not counting the sailors.

At the same time that the Adelantado was preparing in Andalusia all that he thought proper for the service of his Majesty and the renown of so great a general [as himself], Estébano de las Alas, his lieutenant, embarked in the port of Avilés, 257 persons, sailors and soldiers, in three ships laden with arms and munitions for the same conquest; and there set sail from the harobr of Gijón, on the 25th of May, in charge of Pedro Menéndez Marqués, a nephew of the Adelantado and the Admiral of that fleet (who was also Accountant for his Majesty in Florida), two vessels with supplies, munitions, arms and accoutrements, with 78 persons. Among the people who embarked in Asturias were 11 friars of San Francisco, ordained priests, and one lay-brother; one friar of Mercy, one priest and 8 [members] of the Society of Jesus, and most of them did not arrive because of the tempests. From Santander and other parts of Biscay many ships set out in the same enterprise, laden with supplies and munitions; in such wise that on this voyage, the zeal of the Adelantado exceeding his obligation, he carried so many persons that he had no need of the 500 negroes, nor did he take out the royal license therefor; besides, the rumor of the [contemplated] destruction of the heretics who had settled in the lands of the King induced the people to embark, so that if he had had the inclination he could have taken over as many as he wished. He conducted 2,646 persons, among them 26 married citizens with their families, the Adelantado spending in 14 months nearly one million ducats, as the whole armada was at his expense, except one vessel and 299 soldiers for the King's account: a thing surely incredible, if the expense were not authenticated by valid documents, and more so because the salaries were then so low, for to the highest officials were given 6 ducats a month; to the sailors, 4; to the ship-boys, 1,000 maravedis; to the cabin-boys, 2 ducats; to the pilot, 24; to the artillerymen, 5; to the other shipmasters, 9; to the captains, 40; to the ensigns, 15; to the sergeants, 8; to the corporals, fifers and drummers, 6; to the quartermasters and pikemen, 3; to the arquebusiers and halberdiers, 4 ducats a month; to the corporals' aids, 4 ducats, and to the soldiers, 2.

He carried with him royal cédulas to the effect that in the Indies he should be given what he asked for, but they were not carried out.

Having set sail from the Canaries, within a short time a fierce tempest arose, and the flagship with a patache broke away from the armada, without being seen any more; and the next day a shallop turned back to land, for she was leaking badly and could not be succored. The course of the other ships that went in charge of Estébano de las Alas was not known; only five vessels sailed together; and on the 20th of July so great a hurricane came upon them that it was necessary to lighten them and throw overboard the best part of the cargo. Luis de Cabrera says that they arrived at the island of Hispaniola, and on the 9th of August at San Juan de Puerto Rico, where were already waiting the flagship and patache which had been separated from them in the storm: there the Adelantado took on 43 men who had been enrolled in advance, as he had taken on at Hispaniola the provisions he needed: and knowing that Juan Ribao was ahead, and had captured a dispatch boat on her way to the islands, he determined to follow him, although the Adelantado had with him less than one third of his men and his fleet, not knowing whether the others had been lost in the storm, and whether the ships from Asturias and Biscay would arrive. Seeing that the people who were with him were persons of much reliance and bravery, despite [the fact] that many of the soldiers were not trained, he summoned all the captains to a council, and told them that he had not taken that expedition under his charge through vanity or [personal] interest, but for the honor of God, Who already appeared to be manifesting His mercies, since to show His hand visibly, He had permitted that the powerful fleet which sailed from Teneriffe should arrive near Florida so impaired in order that the success of whatever famous action could be achieved should be attributed to Him. [He said] that trusting in the Divine Will, he held it to be very proper that they should set sail thence for Florida, without waiting for or seeking further aid; for if they succeeded in finding the place where the Lutherans were settled he considered victory to be beyond a doubt, as the French would be taken unawares, and the more so if succor had not reached them; whereas if they should wait for the whole armada at the Windward Islands, there would follow the difficulty of their arrival being made known, and of the enemy having the opportunity so to fortify themselves as to become invincible; which fears would vanish by going in search of them promptly. In case they should find them fortified and with ample aid, and should not be able to land near by because of recognizing some great danger, they would turn back their prows toward Hispaniola and Cuba, where they could discuss what had to be done, while being reinforced by the men, supplies and munitions that would be arriving; although he held it for certain that such valiant and honorable gentlemen as had assembled there, were equal to attempting more arduous feats; and in this undertaking they could lose nothing, for if they had to return to the said ports, they would have gained much honor, and learned the way to attack the enemy with the other [troops]. He begged them to give their opinions, for he would follow the most suitable and reasonable.

The camp master, Don Pedro de Valdés, his son-in-law, said that what the Adelantado proposed appeared good to him, and that the more the voyage was delayed, the more this would weaken resolution. Others followed him; but Captain Juan de San Vicente and some who had the intention of remaining in Hispaniola to go to Peru or New Spain, and desert that undertaking, replied that it would be best to wait and know the fate of the armada and the strength of the enemy, in order to proportion thereto the preparations which had to be made to obtain the greatest renown in an enterprise of such importance; whereupon they began to quarrel one with another, but came to an agreement that the opinion of the Adelantado should be followed; who [was] very joyful at this decision, because he had always believed that the successful outcome of that expedition depended on swiftness; he thanked them and had the vessels overhauled with great care.

10.

That day in the afternoon, the Adelantado commanded that all the ships' arms should be delivered to the captains, so that they should distribute them among their soldiers, who were to keep them clean and ready, and that each soldier should shoot three rounds every day until they reached Florida, in order to lose fear of the arquebuses and be trained, as they were raw recruits for the most part. They were to shoot one round with bullets in a space arranged within the said galleon, prizes being awarded to the soldiers in the companies who shot best, and to their captains so that they should take great care to make them skilful; and with that exercise, which was done each day, they daily repeated the Christian doctrine and the litanies, saying prayers and making supplications to God Our Lord, and beseeching Him to grant them victory in everything. They sailed until August 28th, St. Augustine's Day, on which they sighted the land of Florida; all of them kneeling, saying the *Te Deum Laudamus*, they praised Our Lord, all the people repeating their prayers, entreating Our Lord to give them victory in all things.

And because they knew not in what part the Lutherans had fortified themselves, they sailed for four days along the coast, very much distressed, and in great suspense, not knowing whether the French were north or south of where the said Adelantado was going with his armada, sailing by day and anchoring at night; and one morning he saw Indians on the coast: he sent his camp master to land with 20 arquebusiers: he did not wish to land more men so that the Indians might not be frightened and flee. When the camp master disembarked among the Indians with the 20 soldiers, they came with their bows and arrows, and as our men went toward them, they retreated toward the woods: the Christians fearing that if they followed them there might be an ambuscade of many men, and they would run a risk; and that if they did not seek information from them to learn in what part the Lutherans were, it would be a bad state of things; for as the coast and sandbanks were not known either to the said Adelantado or to his pilots, if some storm should come up they were in danger of losing themselves with the fleet; to remedy this, the camp master ordered a soldier who had committed a crime, to lay down his arms and go to the Indians with certain little things as presents, and the soldier did so: the Indians awaited him, received him well and were reassured: then the camp master arrived and spoke with them, and through signs they told him that the French were about 20 leagues from there, to the north. The Indians asked whether the General of the armada was on board the ships, or among them: they were told that he was on the ships: they answered that they desired greatly to see him and know him: [the Spaniards] wanted to take them to the ships, but they would not go: they said that they were afraid and would await him there on land. And so the camp master returned to the flagship with his 20 soldiers, where was the said Adelantado, and he related to him everything that had taken place with the Indians and that they were awaiting him on shore; and because of the desire he had to see them, and to satisfy himself [of the truth] of what the Indians said by signs, that the French were 20 leagues from there toward the north; he went to land with 2 boats and 50 arquebusiers, and as soon as the Indians saw him land, leaving their bows and arrows, they came to the said Adelantado, [and] began to sing and to make gestures with their hands raised toward heaven, in manner of adoration, so that it was a wonderful thing to see. The Adelantado gave them many things and sweets to eat, which he had in one of the boats: they reiterated what they had said, that the French were 20 leagues from there; the Adelantado left them very happy and embarked on his ships and went sailing along the coast with his armada, and discovered 8 leagues from there a good harbor, with a good beach, to which he gave the name of St. Augustine, because that was the first land he discovered in Florida, and he did so on the very day of St. Augustine. On the following day, three hours after noontime, as he was proceeding along the coast, he discovered four large galleons at anchor. As it appeared to him that that was the harbor where the French were, that succor had come to them and that those galleons belonged to their armada, he entered into council with his captains and told them that as he held it for certain that the French armada had come and that their fort could not be taken, nor their armed harbor, [the captains] should say to him what it seemed to them ought to be done. Different opinions were given, but most of the captains decided that the said Adelantado should return to Santo Domingo with the five ships he had, and that there he should gather most of the ships of his fleet which had become separated in the storm, and 6 others he expected from Biscay and Asturias, for he had left orders at the Canaries that they should go to Puerto Rico. He would likewise collect two armed ships and the horses, infantry and supplies that his Majesty had ordered to be given him in that island of Santo Domingo and that of Cuba; and so with everything being gathered together, he could go to Havana, and in the coming month of March he would return to Florida with large forces to accomplish whatever good result he could; [but] the said Adelantado was afraid that if he acted on that opinion he would run the risk of defeat, because his presence

with his 5 ships was already revealed to the French fleet. There was no wind and the sun gave promise of fair weather, but on account of the storm they had had 4 of the ships had remained without foremasts and lacked others which had been broken, so that the French armada could pursue his, especially as he had notice that they had vessels with oars; and he answered the captains that the Frenchmen could not reasonably expect him so soon on that coast; they would have their infantry on land and be unloading the supplies, as those vessels, being large, could not enter the harbor laden; and it seemed to him that they [the Spaniards] should go to fight with them, for if they captured them, the French would not have an armada sufficient to go out in search of him on the seas; and that they could return to the port of St. Augustine, which was twelve leagues from there, and disembark in that harbor and fortify themselves, and send the ships to Hispaniola to give tidings to the armada he was in need of; and that the infantry, horses and supplies his Majesty had ordered to be given him, should all come together in March to that port of St. Augustine, and once they had arrived there, they could go against the enemy by land and sea, capturing their harbor, because they had their fort . . . leagues inland, on the river bank. In this way succor could not come to them from France; [the Spaniards] with the horses would be masters of the country, so that they [the French] could not have dealings or intercourse with the Indians, and they [the Spaniards] could wage war on the French within a brief time, without danger to the said Adelantado's fleet, nor to himself, nor to his men: this was to be done when they had reconnoitred the fort of the French, and [felt] that they were so strong that they could run the danger of giving them the assault and conquering the fort with their arms. Owing to these reasons which the said Adelantado gave, all the captains approved this opinion and advice, and before coming to a decision they prayed to Our Lord, beseeching Him to favor them in everything and grant them victory over their enemies; and when the prayer was ended, the said Adelantado told them that he had determined to attack the French armada, which they all approved. Then he ordered the captains to go to their ships and gave them instructions as to what they had to do, and he gave orders to the Admiral of the fleet as to what point he was to support and what position he was to take, with two vessels he indicated to him and the one whereon he was, which made three in all; the other ship, a patache, the Adelantado commanded not to leave the side of his flagship. And so, sailing along with fair weather, they were about 3 leagues from the French armada, which was anchored off its harbor and consisted of 4 large galleons, when the wind died down, and there was much thunder and lightning and a heavy shower, which lasted until 9 o'clock at night, and then the sky became very serene and clear, and the wind shifted toward land. As it appeared to the Adelantado that it would be almost midnight when he arrived near the enemy, and that it would not be safe to grapple with the ships because of the danger from the incendiary missiles which the enemy is wont to carry; that they could better avail themselves thereof by night than by day; and if the vessels of both fleets should burn, the enemy could escape in the boats and skiffs they had at the poop; a thing they could easily do, as the land was theirs; and they would come off victorious and the said Adelantado would be defeated; he decided to anchor in front of their bows, in such manner that when the cables were let loose after the anchors had caught, the sterns of the ships of the said Adelantado would overlap the prows of the enemy's ships, and at dawn the next morning, by loosening the cables they could board the enemy, who could not be aided by their vessels which were within the harbor; as the bar was a long one, those ships could not come out by night; and at dawn it would be low tide, so that they would have to wait until it was high, and that would be at midday. And so [the Adelantado] commanded his captains to come on board his flagship, and told them his decision, which they all approved as being very good; and when they arrived near the French armada at about half past 11 at night, [the French] began to fire artillery pieces therefrom, and the balls passed through the masts and rigging of the said Adelantado's vessels without harming anything whatever; he did not permit that any artillery should be fired from his ships; on the contrary, he ordered that on all the ships and on his own all the soldiers should clear the decks so that they should not be injured, for since they were to anchor and not to board the enemy, it was not safe that they should remain on deck with the artillery; and with great courage

and coolness, unmindful of the guns [the enemy] were firing, he passed by the French flagship, for the four ships were all together; and he paid no attention to them. They had flags and pennants, and on the mainmast of the flagship were hoisted a flag and a royal stanard: and on the Admiral's galleon, at the top of the foremast, was the Admiral's flag. When the said Adelantado had anchored with his 5 vessels turned with their prows toward the shore, he had the cables loosened, and the poop of his flagship was between the prows of the enemy's flagship and Admiral's galley, and their prows reached his vessels like long pikes; and then he had the trumpets sounded hailing the enemy, and they answered him hailing him with theirs; and presently when these salutes were ended, the said Adelantado spoke to them with much courtesy, saying: "Señores, whence comes that armada?" One only replied that it came from France. He asked them again: "What is it doing here?" They said to him: "We are bringing infantry, artillery and supplies for a fort which the King of France has in this country, and for others which he is to build." Said the Adelantado to them: "Are you Catholics or Lutherans, and who is your General?" They answered that they were all Lutherans of the new religion, and that their General was Juan Ribao; and [they wanted to know] who they were, who was he who asked this, and whose armada that was; why it had come to that country and who was the General thereof.

The Adelantado replied to them: "He who asks this of you is called Pedro Menéndez, this armada belongs to the King of Spain and I am the General thereof; and I come to hang and behead all the Lutherans I may find on this sea and in this land; and thus do I bring instructions from my King, which I shall fulfil at dawn when I shall board your ships; and if I should find any Catholic, I will give him good treatment."

Many together answered many shameless and insulting words against the King our Master, calling him by his name, and against the said Adelantado, saying: "Let that be for the King, Don Felipe, and this for Pedro Menéndez, and if thou beest a brave man, as they say, come and wait not until tomorrow." The Adelantado, on hearing such unseemly words to the detriment of his King, ordered the cables to be loosened to board the enemy, and as the sailors did this unwillingly, he leaped down from the bridge to hasten them. The cable was wound round the capstan; it could not be loosened so quickly: when the enemy saw this, and heard sounded the Adelantado's command, they feared him, cut the cables, unfurled the sails and fled.

The said Adelantado did the same with his ships, and pursued them in such manner that when he was in the midst of them, he followed [in the flagship] with a patache, the two [galleons] which took the direction of the north, and his Admiral pursued, with the three ships, the other two which turned to the south. By the patache the said Adelantado sent a message to his Admiral that by dawn he was to return off the harbor, and that he would do likewise, to see if they could capture it; and that if not, they would go to land at the port of St. Augustine, as had been agreed; for in case no ship of the said Frenchmen should be taken (because theirs outsailed those of the said Adelantado, which lacked some of the masts owing to the storm they had had), 3 or 4 days would pass before the enemy could come together again, wherein the said Adelantado would either capture their harbor, or disembark in the port of St. Augustine; as the other French vessels in the harbor would not dare to come out with the four [galleons] not appearing; and if they should come out, there was no reason to fear them. And thus it happened that the said Adelantado chased the two French galleons northward for about 5 or 6 leagues, until dawn, and his Admiral went as many after the other two which sailed to the south; and the said Adelantado, with his 5 ships, lay off the harbor of the French at 10 o'clock the next morning, and trying to enter it, he saw two infantry flags at the end of the bar, artillery began to fire and there were 5 vessels anchored within. As it seemed to the said Adelantado that he ran the risk of failure if he tried to capture the habor from them, and that meantime the 4 ships which had fled might unite with the 5 which were within, and that [then] he could escape neither by land nor by sea; he decided, without losing time, to put his flagship under full said and order the others to do likewise, and he went to the harbor of St. Augustine, where he arrived on the eve of Our Lady of September; and as soon as he reached there he landed about three hundred soldiers, and sent 2 captains with them, who were to reconnoitre at daybreak the next morning the lay of the land and the places which seemed to them

strongest [for defence], in order that they might dig a trench quickly while it was being seen where they could build a fort, so that the next day when the said Adelantado should land, they could show him what they had observed, and decide what would be most proper to do about it.

And on the following day, the day of Our Lady of September, the said Adelantado landed near noon, when he found many Indians awaiting him there, as they had had tidings of him from the other Indians with whom he had spoken four days before: he had a solemn mass said in honor of Our Lady, and when that was ended, he took possession of the country in the name of his Majesty; he received the solemn oath of the officials of his Majesty's Royal Exchequer, the camp master and the captains, that they would all serve his Majesty with entire loyalty and fidelity, and this being done, the said Adelantado had the Indians fed and dined himself. On finishing, he went immediately to see the locations which appeared to the captains he had sent, suitable for the trench; and leaving the site marked out, he returned to the ships, having first held a council and decided that within three days everything possible should be unloaded from the vessels, and that then, two of them should be sent to Hispaniola, for as they were large they could not enter the harbor, and if the French armada came, it would capture them. The diligence the Adelantado showed in unloading those ships to send them away, so that the enemy should not take them from him, as it seemed to him that on the fourth day the French armada would come upon him—was such that all who were there were astounded; for although the ships were anchored more than a league and a half away from the landing place, in two days and a half he took ashore the people, the artillery, the munitions and a large part of the supplies; and without waiting for the third day, one night at midnight, fearing that the French fleet would be upon him at dawn, he made them set sail for Hispaniola without trying to unload more of the provisions. He placed about 150 soldiers he had with him on board a shallop of about 100 *toneles*, and he himself got into a large boat which he carried with him astern of his flagship when he chased the French fleet; and in order the better to flee, he cut it loose, and went to anchor off the bar with that boat and the shallop, in two fathoms of water. At dawn the French armada was near there, a quarter of a league away, where the said Adelantado had been at midnight [and] whence he had sent the vessels to Hispaniola, and a ship and three shallops of the enemy came on, and because of the extreme low tide and the sea's not being very calm, it was dangerous to cross the bar. When the said Adelantado saw the enemy upon them so that they could not escape, they all prayed to God Our Lord and his precious Mother to save them from that danger; and as the Lutherans were already beside him, he cut the cable with which his boat and the shallop were anchored, and entered over the sand-bars at great risk, and Our Lord was pleased to bring him safely within the bar. The enemy feared the entrance and waited until the tide should be high. At that time the ships which the said Adelantado had sent to Hispaniola must have been about five or six leagues from them, and so they saved themselves from that peril without being discovered; and about two hours from the time the enemy were waiting for the tide to be high, God Our Lord performed a miracle; for the weather being fair and clear, suddenly the sea rose very high, and a strong and contrary north wind came up, which made the return to their fort and harbor difficult for the French. This became known to the Adelantado, who was already on land with his people, having a mass said to the Holy Ghost which he wished everyone to hear, supplicating him to enlighten him and set him on the right path in a decision he wanted to make; and when the mass was over, he entered into council with his captains, the first council he had held in the land of Florida, and none of them knew why they were summoned; and being assembled, he said to them:

"Gentlemen and Brothers: We are shouldering a very hard task, very full of trials and dangers, and if this were only for the King our Master, I should not be surprised if some of us should become tired and make some show of the weakness of cowards, in not being able to undergo so many hardships as confront us; but since this burden we are carrying is the enterprise of God Our Lord and of our King, that agent among us who should show weakness and not encourage the officers and soldiers in their duty, should hold himself as accursed, for this is of much importance to us; and so, Gentlemen, I beg of you as a mercy, as earnestly as I can, [to consider] that since in this matter we serve God and our King, the

guerdon of heaven cannot fail us; and let us not be dismayed by the scarcity of the supplies we have, or by our being left isolated in this land: I beg of you as a favor that we may all take courage and make efforts to bear our sufferings with patience."

They all answered very well, each and all together offering to do their uttermost.

Then the Adelantado said to them, having thanked them for their favorable reply:

"Gentlemen, I feel impelled to tell you of a very good opportunity which presents itself to my soul and reason, for we must not lose it, and it behooves us to take advantage of it and not allow it to pass by, and it is that I consider (and this is common sense), that as the French armada fled from me four days ago and now comes in search of me, they must have strengthened themselves with part of the men they had as a garrison in their fort, and these must be from among the best [men] and captains: the wind is too contrary for them to return to their harbor and fort, and to all appearance it will last so for many days; and since these are Lutherans, and this we knew before departing from Spain through the proclamations which Juan Ribao, their General, issued in France when on the point of sailing; [to the effect] that under penalty of death no one should embark who was not of the new religion, and under the same penalty, no one should take books along which were not of that faith; and since likewise they themselves certified this to us, when our fleet lay at anchor with theirs outside their harbor, for they said there was no Catholic among them, and when I wished to punish them, they set sail and fled; for this reason the war we have with them, and theirs with us, cannot be carried on save with fire and blood, as they, who are Lutherans, seek us, who are Catholics, to prevent our implanting the Holy Gospel in these provinces; and we seek them because they are Lutherans, in order that they shall not implant their evil and detestable sect in this land, nor teach their belief to the Indians; [and] it seems to me that we must take 500 men, two thirds of them arquebusiers, the other third pikemen, and rations for 8 days in our knapsacks, without any porters, carrying our arms on our backs; and that you ten captains, each with your banner and officers, with the number of 50 men to each captain, should go [with me] to reconnoitre the country and the fort where the

Lutherans are, and the way to them; for although we know not the way, with our compass I shall know how to guide you, within two leagues right or left of the right direction; and wherever we find woods, we shall open a path with the hatchets so as to pass and know how to return; for I am taking a Frenchman with me who has been more than a year in that fort; he says he is acquainted with the country for two leagues around and can take us to the fort; and if we see that we are not discovered, it may be that a quarter of an hour before dawn, we can capture their fort by setting up twenty ladders which we shall make when we are near there, and risking the loss of 50 soldiers; and if we should find that we are discovered, since we are certain that the woods are less than a quarter of a league away, by planting our ten banners along the edge of the woods as if on [our] quarters, it will appear to them that we have a number of more than two thousand men; and we can send them a trumpeter telling them that they must give up the fort to us and depart from that land, and that they will be given ships and supplies wherewith they may go to France; but that if they will not, we shall put them to the sword, every one; and if they do not [surrender], we shall have gained much in reconnoitring the country and the fort, and they will be afraid of us in such manner that it will be a reason why they will leave us here in security, this winter until next March, when we shall have forces enough to go and seek them, by sea as well as by land."

There was much discussion on this speech which the Adelantado made, as it appeared to some that the journey should not be made, and to others that it ought to be: it was decided that it should be made: the Adelantado ordered there and then that by the third day at dawn they should all hear mass, and when that was done they should start immediately; he commanded the camp master, who was called Don Pedro Menéndez de Valdés and was betrothed to his elder daughter, and Gonzalo de Villarroel, captain and sergeant major, to arrange at once for the selection of the men who were to go, and [said] that they should be given a sufficient amount of powder, wicks and lead so that they might make small shot and bullets; and he provided that Captain Bartolomé Menéndez, brother of the said Adelantado, should be in charge of the soldiers who were to remain there, with artillery, arms, ammunition

and supplies; and that Diego Florez de Valdés, who was Admiral of the armada, should remain as captain of the artillery and General of the three ships which were left there from the fleet, having them under his charge [and keeping] them and the sailors thereof, in readiness; and when they had come out of his junta with this agreed upon, it became public news at once throughout the camp, and [the men] began to make and provide those things which the Adelantado had ordered, whereat the whole camp showed great contentment.

On the morning of the following day, the Adelantado was informed that some captains were complaining at the decision he had taken to go in search of the Frenchmen's fort, and they said this so publicly and justified it in such a manner, that it was clearly seen that the soldiers were becoming faint-hearted who, the day before, showed great satisfaction over the agreement. Some of the captains decided among themselves, especially Juan de San Vicente, Francisco de Recalde and Diego de Maya, that when the Adelantado had finished dining, they would tell him as friends of his, on behalf of most of the captains and people who were there, that he must change his mind so that in no wise would he go to the fort of the Frenchmen: the Adelantado was notified thereof, and he commanded a very good meal to be prepared and told them to tell the captains to come and dine with him, likewise other gentlemen among the soldiers of the expedition, and most of the ensigns; and when they had finished dining, he said to them:

"Gentlemen and Brothers: After we had landed, we captains came together in council, which was done with great secrecy, and we only who were there and no others, knew the words which passed between us there: and as I now understand that all the soldiers and women who are here know them, and are having stubborn arguments among themselves as to which of us spoke rightly or wrongly, in such wise that there is murmuring against our plan and it would be temerity to carry out what has been agreed upon; it appears to me a very bad thing, worthy of great rebuke and chastisement; [but] although I know who are the most to blame for this, and they are here, I do not wish to punish anyone, nor to do more than ask you, Gentlemen, as a favor, that hereafter each of you shall remedy this by observing great secrecy in the matters that may be treated of in our councils, since in wars where there is no secrecy nor diligence, success is seldom attained, and he who shall commit a sin against this, even a slight one, will be punished as though it were a mortal sin; for it can be well understood that if a captain is faint-hearted and fears this expedition for his soldiers, the 50 soldiers who have to go with him will fear for him and his ensign, and not for themselves; but if the soldiers go about cheerfully, polishing their arms and preparing their knapsacks for their rations, it is clear that because they are hopeful, and desirous of undertaking the journey, their captains and officers encourage them." [The Adelantado added] that if it still appeared to them that he ought to change his mind, they should tell him so; [but that] he would punish the captain who, once out of the council, should speak against what had been decided, by taking his company away from him and not admitting him to councils.

All replied that what his lordship said was very good, but to some it appeared that he ought to change his mind; to others it appeared the contrary, that the agreement and decision that had been reached in this, should be carried out: and so the Adelantado told the captains that each of them was to send the knapsacks to the keeper of supplies, and a person to receive the rations, so that by dawn of the following day they could hear mass and set out as had been agreed; and he ordered that each should go and attend to what he had to do, and so they went away.

The next day at daybreak they sounded reveille with trumpets, fifes and drums; the bells chimed and all thronged to mass; and having heard it, they departed hopefully, all setting out marching in order.

The Adelantado took 20 soldiers, all Biscayans and Asturians, with their hatchets; a Biscayan captain with them who was called Martín Ochoa, and 2 Indians who had come there, brothers, who seemed to be angels that God was sending; these told them by signs that they had been in the fort of the French 6 days before; and he went ahead, marching as far in front as he could, marking the path, blazing the trees with the hatchets, so that the men should not lose it and should know it on their return, [and] leaving the camp master and sergeant major to follow in good order; and whenever it seemed best to the Adelantado to call

a halt in a suitable place where there was water, he did so; he waited until they were all assembled and gave them orders to rest, and would then depart at once, opening the way and marking it, as has been said, and he would again call a halt in the place that seemed best to him to pass the night. [Marching] in this order, on the fourth day at sunset he went to reconnoitre the land around the fort, half a league therefrom, where he stopped; and as it was a wet and stormy night, and in order not to be discovered it seemed to him expedient to draw nearer into a pine grove, he approached to less than a quarter of a league from the fort, where he decided to spend that night in a very bad and swampy place; and on account of the bad night he turned back to look for the rearguard so that they should succeed in finding the way. It was after 10 when they finished arriving, and as during those 4 days there had been much rain, they had crossed many marshes, and had carried their arms and knapsacks with food, on their backs, the soldiers arrived very tired and weak; and because the showers that night were so heavy, there was no way to keep the powder and wicks from being all wet, and the little biscuit they had in their knapsacks, and no one wore anything on his body that was not soaked with water: at this point the Adelantado feared greatly to take counsel with the captains, either as to going back or going forward to the fort of the Frenchmen, because some were beginning to be insolent, and his officers were saying abusive words against him so audibly that he heard many of them, especially those of an ensign of Captain San Vicente, who placed himself near the Adelantado and said loudly, so that he might hear him:

"[See] how we have been sold by that Asturian *corito*, who knows no more about land warfare than an ass! If my advice had been followed on the first day we set forth from St. Augustine to make this journey, he would have been given the reward he must now take."

Then the Adelantado feared the more and pretended he did not hear him.

Captain San Vicente, whose ensign this man was, said at the time of departure from St. Augustine that his leg and stomach pained him, so he remained there; and there was much grumbling at his staying behind, and at the insulting words of his ensign, because it came out that when some of those who remained, reproved Captain San

Vicente for not having gone with the Adelantado, he replied:

I swear to God that I am expecting the news that all our soldiers have been killed, so that we who remain here may embark on these three ships and go to the Indies, for it is not reasonable that we should all die like beasts."

The Adelantado, about two hours before daylight, sent four soldiers who were near him, servants of his, to go running among the men and call to the camp master, the sergeant major and the captains to come and join him, and they did so; and when they were all assembled, he said to them:

"Gentlemen: Although I am a great sinner, I have all this night entreated Our Lord and his precious Mother to show us favor and put us on the right path in what we must do, and I believe, Gentlemen, that you have done the same. Let us discuss what is best for us to do considering the straits we are in, without food or ammunition, and with the soldiers very tired, bewildered and disheartened."

Some answered him [asking] what was the use of discussing any other arrangement than that they should retreat as soon as day dawned, and return to St. Augustine, eating palmettos [on the way], and [saying] that it seemed foolhardiness to treat of anything else.

The Adelantado approved of this and said to them: "Gentlemen, for the love of God hear this my plan, and be not displeased because I tell it to you, as I am not doing so to make you act on what I say. You shall do what you wish and what appears best to you, for up to now you have always followed my advice and counsel, and now that I see myself in this great danger, I wish to follow yours."

They answered that his lordship should speak, for they were desirous of hearing him and giving their opinion.

Then he said to them: "Gentlemen, are you confident that the forest is very near the fort?"

They replied that they were.

He said to them: "Then it appears to me that we ought to go and try our fortune, as has been agreed; for even if we cannot capture the fort, we must not fear the thought that if we should send them the trumpeter they will sally out to look for us at the edge of the woods, where we shall have halted in our quarters and set up our flags; and for this we shall have little need of powder or fuses, because even if we are discovered retreating in the morning, the enemy will not take courage, and will hold us as cowards and men of little worth, and this will mean as much to them as victory."

Some captains replied, especially the camp master and sergeant major, that the argument appeared to them good, and that the decision agreed upon for the undertaking should be carried out to the end, and after a discussion with those who thought differently, all agreed that so it should be done.

Then the Adelantado ordered that all should kneel and say their prayers to Our Lord, entreating him to give them victory against their enemies in that enterprise they were attempting and the danger they were to encounter; and they made this prayer at once, with as much fervor as if their enemies were before them, wishing to give battle. When it was ended, after indicating the captains who were to go in the vanguard and the rearguard, and the points and manner in which each was to attack the fort; and charging each of them for the love of God to encourage his soldiers; he gave the order to march, he himself going ahead, taking with him the Frenchman whom they had as guide, with his hands bound behind him by a rope, the end whereof was held by the Adelantado himself. It was about an hour before daybreak, and they lost the way before a quarter of it had passed, on account of the great darkness and the great tempest of wind and rain, and the path's being very narow, in such wise that some thought they were going forward when they were going back. As the Adelantado realized this and it seemed to him that the rear-guard might march away from the vanguard, he sent an order along the line that they should halt, and that until daylight none of them should stir from where they were, for fear they should become separated from one another; as many of them did, in a swamp where the water reached above the knees, and the Adelantado was one of them. When daylight had come the Frenchman recognized the path along which to guide them, and the Adelantado set out on the march and sent orders with all speed from mouth to mouth that all must follow him, under penalty of death, for it appeared to him that that was no time to take counsel as to what he had to do, as the captains were quite a distance apart; and when they had arrived at a little rise in the ground, the Frenchman told him that behind there, below, was the fort; that the water from the river washed against it, and that it was about 3 arquebuse shots from there.

The Adelantado gave the Frenchman over to Francisco de Castañeda, the captain of his guard, who never left his side; and bending forward very quickly he went to the top of the hill, discovered the river and saw some houses, but he could not see the fort, although it was near them. Returning where he had left the captain of the guard, with the Frenchman beside him, he found the camp master, who had arrived, and Captain Martín Ochoa, and he said to them:

"Brothers, I want to go down to that plain with 5 or 6 soldiers, to the point where there are some houses, to see if I can find the sentinels, so that they can give us information concerning the fortress of those [people] and the [number of] men they have; because as it is already daylight and the sun has risen, we cannot attack without powder unless we reconnoitre the fort." Then the camp master told his lordship to remain [where he was]; that that business was his; and he took with him only Captain Martín Ochoa, not wishing to take any other person, so as not to be discovered; and on arriving near the houses they saw the fort, and as they were returning with the news, they found two paths. They did not take the one whereby they had come, and after walking a little along [the other] they met with a fallen tree: then the camp master said that they were lost, and as Captain Martín Ochoa was behind at the time they had turned back, he was [now] ahead; it seems that they were seen by the sentinel, who thought that they were Frenchmen: he came to see who they were, and met them, and as he did not know them, he stopped, saying: "Who goes there?"

Martín Ochoa answered: "A Frenchman."

And as it appeared to the sentinel that they were French, he came nearer, and Martín Ochoa did likewise; and when the Frenchman [found that he] did not know him, he stopped, and Captain Martín Ochoa closed with him, and with his sword in its scabbard gave him a slash across the face, although he did not wound him very much, as the Frenchman warded it off with his sword. They grasped their swords, and the camp master arrived, who already had his unsheathed, with a buckler in his hand; and as he made a lunge at him, the Frenchman fell backwards to avoid it, and at this he began to shout.

The camp master placed the point of his sword on his breast, telling him to be silent, otherwise he would kill him, and the Frenchman became so. They raised him and took him bound to the Adelantado, asking about the fort and the people who were there. At the shouts that Frenchman gave, it seemed to the Adelantado that they were killing the camp master and Captain Martín Ochoa; and his men and several captains with their flags, being already assembled hear him, especially the sergeant major, Francisco de Recalde, Diego de Maya and Andrés López Patiño, the Adelantado cried in a loud voice:

"Santiago! At them! God is helping! Victory! The French are killed! The camp master is inside the fort and has captured it!"

And then all began to run forward in disorder along the path, but the Adelantado remained motionless, always repeating this, without ceasing. The soldiers held it for certain that many had gone with the camp master and that the fort was won: they felt great joy and satisfaction, in such wise that he who could run fastest was considered the most valiant, and there were no cripples, nor maimed, nor cowards; and as they presently reached the place where the camp master and Martín Ochoa were coming along with the Frenchman, Martín Ochoa ran ahead without orders to ask the reward from the Adelantado, for telling him that they were bringing the sentinel as a prisoner. The camp master, fearing that they might be discovered, ran the Frenchman through with his sword, who passed away; and leaving him dead, he took the lead [of the Spaniards], saying: "Brothers, do as I do, for God is with us"; and then he encountered two Frenchmen in their shirts and slew one of them: Captain Andrés López Patiño, who came back of him, slew the other: they passed on running, and when they arrived near the fort, the postern of the principal gate was opened at the shouts raised by the people outside the fort, when they saw them [the two Frenchmen] killed; the camp master closed in on the postern, slew the man who opened it and stole in, and after him those who could enter the soonest: some of the Frenchmen in the houses came out in their shirts and others who were clothed, to find out what was happening: these were killed at once, and others took to flight and threw themselves down from the walls of the fort. 2 flags were presently brought in: one belonged to the sergeant major, which was raised on a *caballero* by his ensign, who was called Rodrigo Troche, of Tordesillas; the other belonged to Diego de Maya, and it was set up on another *caballero* by his ensign, Cristóbal de Herrera, a mountaineer: there was some quarrelling between these 2 ensigns as to who had been first: this could not be ascertained. The trumpeters entered at the same time as those two flags and they placed themselves on those *caballeros* near the flags, sounding victory; whereat all the French became terrified; and all our men came running through the gate, which was opened wide to them, and went through the quarters of the French without leaving one alive.

The Adelantado, where he stood when half of the soldiers had gone by him, told Francisco de Castañeda, the captain of his guard, to whom he had delivered the Frenchman with his hands bound behind him, to remain where he was, crying out victory, until the rear-guard should arrive; because it behooved him [the Adelantado] to overtake those ahead and be in the midst of that danger; and he did so, running with the utmost speed. He arrived at the fort where our soldiers were killing the Frenchmen: then he said in a loud voice, running from one point to another: "Under penalty of death, let no one wound or kill any woman, or boys under 15 years." And so this was done, for 70 of those persons escaped: the rest all died, except about 50 or 60, who threw themselves down from the walls of the fort and took refuge in the woods.

The Adelantado then went out of the fort to some houses which were near the ramparts, where Captain Castañeda arrived with the Frenchman, who pointed out a large house to the Adelantado, and said they called it the grange; and it was full of articles for barter, cloths, linens and munitions.

The Adelantado left there 6 men as a guard, so that no one should center; [he did this] so that everything therein should belong to the camp in general, in order to use and distribute it among those most in need. He went to the river bank, where there were 3 ships, very well armed, with their prows moored to the fort; and calling a trumpeter, he made him sound a peace call, using a white cloth as a flag [of truce], and saying that they should land in their boats: the Frenchmen

replied that they would not, but the Adelantado assured them on his word that they could come: [still] they would not: he hastened to the fort and had 4 pieces of bronze artillery set up to send the ships to the bottom, and went about looking for powder. He found 2 barrels half full, which held about a hundredweight of powder, and about 20 balls, in a gunner's house which a Frenchwoman showed him, wherewith they loaded the pieces; but before firing, again he asked them to land in their boats. They answered, from the ship to which the Adelantado was speaking, that they would send the boat so that someone could go back therein to speak with them, and tell what we wanted: the Adelantado ordered that it should come, and in order that they might believe what he should say to them, he took the Frenchman he kept bound and released him, and told him to go to those ships and tell the principal commander thereof to select from all three the vessel they wanted; [take] the women and children who had been saved and the supplies that might be necessary, and go to France with the aid of God, without carrying any artillery or munitions, for he would give them a passport and safe-conduct so that they should not receive ill-treatment at whatever place they might arrive, and should be allowed to go to France in safety; but if they did not do this, he would send them to the bottom and order that all of them should be killed and hanged, without leaving one alive.

The boat came to shore, and the Frenchman went therein with that message, and by then the Adelantado had ordered the sergeant major to distribute among the soldiers a barrel of very good powder for arquebuses, which was in the house of that gunner, with the cannon powder.

The Frenchman returned to the Adelantado with the reply, and said that the principal commander of those ships was Jaques Ribao, eldest son of Juan Ribao, who, he said, was Viceroy and Captain-General of that country for the King of France; and that he had come by his King's order, in company with his father, to bring people, artillery and supplies to that fort with those vessels, wherein he had committed no crime; rather had he, as a loyal vassal, done what he was bound to do; and that if the Adelantado meant to wage war, he would wage war against the Adelantado.

Then the Adelantado commanded aim to be taken with the best piece of bronze artillery, against one of the best ships, which appeared to him to be on her first voyage, and was anchored where she could conveniently be hit, for the other two were not. Captain Diego de Maya did this, and fired the cannon, as it appeared to the Adelantado that he would take aim better than any other. He hit the ship at the water line in such a manner that they were sinking, and they could not resort to the pumps because they would have had to stay in the open above deck, and could have been killed by the artillery. When the Frenchmen who were on the vessel saw that they were lost, they lowered themselves into the boat on one side thereof, and the 2 boats from the other two ships came to that vessel, and carried all the people from her to the two ships: she sank, and then the other two cut the cables, and they went down stream with the strong current there was, and anchored at a place where the artillery could not do them much harm, especially as the Adelantado did not dare to waste the powder, since up to then they had not been able to find more in the fort. And during all that time, the wind and rain from heaven were such as to be a thing of wonder; and as the soldiers were joyful over the victory and the booty, they did not retire and rest themselves after the hardships and the bad night they had had. The Adelantado, for the good of all, had them quartered in the many houses there were outside the fort, 20 men in each, and a whole outfit of shirts and clothes given to them, as there was a quantity thereof in the grange; likewise good rations of bread, wine, lard and bacon, whereof there was [also] a quantity; and at about midday he undressed and went to bed, where they gave him food, and he ordered all the captains to come to him by 4 o'clock in the afternoon, as he wished to enter into council with them, and they did so; whereupon the Adelantado, having risen and dressed, said to all of them assembled, while his eyes filled with tears:

"Gentlemen and Brothers: God does these things miraculously, in behalf of His cause: let us know how to praise and serve Him for such a great mercy as He has done us; and now, more than ever, is the time for us to commend ourselves to Him in prayer, and provide all things so that we can defend this place against the French armada when it returns to it. Let us likewise insure the safety of our people, artillery, arms, munitions and supplies we left at St. Augustine; and for this purpose let a muster-roll of the people who are here be called immediately, for it appears to me that many are missing from the 500 men who set out from St. Augustine, as we must see which are to remain here and which are to return; for it behooves me to return the day after tomorrow with those who must go back, because it is needful that St. Augustine be well protected; so that while we shall be defending this [fort] against the French if they come with their armada, they cannot set foot in this country [by] going to disembark in St. Augustine, which has a better harbor."

And he made Captain Gonzalo de Villarroel, who was the sergeant major, *alcaide* of that fort and governor of that district; who had worked very hard and with much system and care, and who appeared to him a very good and trustworthy soldier for the office; and it was delivered to him and he took the accustomed oath, and [the Adelantado] gave the fort the name of San Mateo because the day he captured it was St. Mathhew's Day. He commanded that from that day forward he [the sergeant major] should hold and defend it in the name of his Majesty with 300 soldiers whom he would leave him for the guarding thereof; and he ordered the camp master to go at once and make the list of all the people there; of those who were to remain and those who were to return with the Adelantado; he did so, taking the sergeant major with him. In that council the Adelantado had first appointed Rodrigo Montes as the keeper of supplies in that fort, and [directed] that all the provisions there were should be delivered to him; likewise that on the following day they should bring him a memorandum of what had been delivered, so that he might leave instructions as to the manner in which rations were to be given out. The Adelantado decreed in that council that the two coats-of-arms which were over the principal gate of that fort, [those] of the King of France and the Admiral, should be immediately taken off; but when they went to remove them, a soldier had already pulled them down and demolished them; and he ordered that an escutcheon be made at once with the royal arms of Spain. [those] of the King Don Felipe our Master, with a cross of the angels above the crown; which was painted very well by some Flemings who were soldiers there, and placed where the others had been.

On the morning of the following day, the Adelantado, having heard mass, had 2 crosses raised in the places that seemed best to him; he marked out the site for a church, where a wooden chapel was to be erected immediately, so that mass might be said every day; for the French had there a large quantity of sawed lumber for a galley they were building; and giving Gonzalo de Villarroel, the *alcaide* and governor of that fort and district, a memorandum of the supplies which had been found, the Adelantado instructed him as to how he was to use them and give out the rations. They brought him the list of the persons there: there were found to be less than 400, because some of the others who completed the 500 had given out on the journey from exhaustion; and the rest, owing to cowardice and the danger ahead which was described to them, returned to St. Augustine saying they had lost their way; as was found out later. The Adelantado ordered that 300 soldiers should remain, and 100 go with him, with Captains Andrés López Patiño, Juan Vélez de Medrano and... de Alvarado; these captains and soldiers said that they were in no condition to walk, especially as it had rained very hard, so that it was impossible to cross the marshes, rivers and brooks there were on the way; and although the Adelantado made great efforts to have them go, he saw it was not possible because of the many reasons they had against it, their lack of desire to set out, and their being very tired from the journey's hardships. Then he went through the soldiers' quarters, and among those least tired, and best known to him, he found 35 who were willing to follow him, with the captain of his guard, and he notified them that they were to start on the next morning. The Adelantado ordered that the camp master should set out at once (it was about 9 o'clock in the morning), with 50 soldiers, for a place one league from there in a straight line, where the French ships were anchored; as they had weighed anchor that morning and gone down [the river], and it seemed likely to the Adelantado that the 50 or 60 Frenchmen who had thrown themselves down from the ramparts when their fort was captured, would hasten through the woods to the right of the ships, to call the ships' boats to take them on board. The camp master scattered the soldiers through the wood: they met about 20 Frenchmen, who fled, and not being able to overtake them, they fired upon them with the arquebuses, and killed them; of the others, about 30 had embarked, among them Captain Ludunice, the *alcaide* of the fort, who had escaped by throwing himself from the ramparts with the rest: the

other ten had sought refuge with the caciques; the Adelantado ransomed them later and sent them to France, and they told how Ludunice, with the 30, had embarked on those ships. And when the camp master, Captain Martín Ochoa, and Diego de Maya, with the men they had taken [with them], had returned by nightfall of that day, the Adelantado commanded all the captains to be called to a council, and told them that his departure for St. Augustine was set for the following morning, whence he would immediately send 2 vessels of the 3 he had left there, well armed and with good artillery, in order that they should capture those 2 French ships before they went out of the harbor, as they had but few soldiers on board, according to what the Spaniards had understood from the French who were at the fort; and if the French vessels should have sailed away, they would set in the fort, in the places where it would be the most necessary, the artillery which their own two ships would bring, so as to be more strongly fortified when the French should come; for the Adelantado always feared that when the French armada returned, with the Indians friendly to them, they would want to capture that place and avenge themselves. [He told them also] that one of his vessels, would take those French-women and children to the island of Santo Domingo, and that he would write to the Audiencia so that they should send them to Seville, and thence they should go to France; and he would give instructions to the masters of those 2 ships to take on supplies from the galleon *San Pelayo*, which the Adelantado had sent to that island of Santo Domingo. And on the morning of the following day, the Adelantado, having heard mass, departed with Francisco de Castañeda, the captain of his guard, and the 35 soldiers he had picked out; and he commanded that the camp master and the other captains should remain in that fort until he should order them to do something else, and that the 3 captains, Alvarado, Medrano and Patiño, with the remainder of the one hundred men, should start for St. Augustine as soon as they were fit to march, without losing time; and they did so within 8 days.

11.

The sufferings and dangers which the Adelantado and those who returned with him from San Mateo, encountered on that day he left, and on the second and third day, until they arrived at St. Augustine, were so great as to be beyond belief, except to those who saw them; because on that day he set out from San Mateo, when they had gone about 2 leagues [and] it was about 2 o'clock in the afternoon, they entered a wood through which they had previously passed, and having gone therein half a league, they found much water; and thinking they would get out of it quickly, they proceeded over half a league farther, finding more and more water, in such manner that they could not go forward; and when they went back the streams were more swollen, and there was more water in the woods. They lost their way in such wise that they knew not whether they were going forward or back: [the Adelantado] wished to search for a place where they could halt and build a fire by which to rest during that night: none could he find: he wanted to climb the trees: they were so high and straight that it was not possible there he felt himself entirely lost, and his companions were discouraged, not knowing what remedy could meet the situation. He made a soldier, the most agile he could find, climb a very high tree to discover any dry or level spot; this soldier said, when he had reached the top, that all he could see was water, and that there was no dry or level land: the Adelantado ordered him to look and see if there were any indication as to which way the sun was moving: he said there was none: he ordered him to remain there until later: God willed that the weather cleared a little, and the soldier saw where the sun was setting, and pointed out the place.

The Adelantado recognized the direction in which he had to emerge from the woods, as there was no undergrowth and the trees were far apart. By cutting down some pines for the places where there was a great depth of water, he came out by a deep and narrow river, which he had crossed with the men when he went from St. Augustine to San Mateo, although not at that point. He had the trees which were at the river's edge cut down at the foot with 5 hatchets the soldiers carried, in such a way that they fell across to the other side of the river; and they passed over with much peril, and in so doing, two soldiers miraculously escaped drowning. He ordered the man who had climbed the tree, to go up another one, and he discovered dry land in a place by which they had passed

before; and they reached the path and went to take up their quarters in a spot where they made great fires and dried their clothing, for it was all soaked with water; and toward daybreak it began to rain very hard, and as it was already light, they set out. It took them 3 days to arrive in St. Augustine, for owing to the victory Our Lord had given them, they did not feel the journey, nor the hardships thereof, in the desire they had to give this good news to their comrades: one league before reaching St. Augustine, that soldier [who had climbed the tree] begged the Adelantado as a favor to allow him to go ahead to announce the welcome tidings; the Adelantado granted this to him. The people who had remained there held them for lost, because of the bad weather they had had and the news given them by those who had returned, as they knew that they had no kind of food, powder nor wicks; but when the good news came, 4 priests who were there immediately set out, holding the cross aloft, and followed by all the sea and land forces, the women and children, in a procession, singing the *Te Deum Laudamus;* they received the Adelantado with great pleasure and rejoicing, everyone laughing and weeping for joy, praising God for so great a victory; and so they escorted the Adelantado in triumph to the intrenchment and settlement of St. Augustine, where he related to them in detail the very great mercy which Our Lord had shown them through his victory. He presently ordered the two armed ships to be made ready; and within 2 days, being about to depart with them for San Mateo, there came tidings that the 2 French ships had already left the bar; so he sent one of his vessels with artillery, powder and ammunition in order that they should be in the fort, and everything be in a good state of defence; and he occupied himself in fortifying [St. Augustine] as well as he could, to await the French armada if it should come there. The following day some Indians arrived, who told them by signs that 4 leagues away there were many Christians who could not pass an arm of the sea, even though it was narrow, which is a river inside a bar, that they were compelled of necessity to cross in order to reach St. Augustine.

Then the Adelantado took with him 40 soldiers that afternoon, and after midnight he came near that arm of the sea, where he halted. In the morning, leaving his soldiers in ambush, from the top of a tree he discovered what was going on: he saw many people and two flags on the other side of the river, and the said Adelantado, to prevent them from crossing, approached close enough for them to count his men, so that they might think that there were many [behind]. When they [saw they] were discovered, one man presently swam across: he was a Frenchman, and said that the people there were all French; that they had been shipwrecked in a storm and had all escaped.

The Adelantado asked him what Frenchmen they were.

He said there were 200 persons, captains and soldiers of Juan Ribao, Viceroy and Captain-General of that land for the King of France.

The Adelantado asked if they were Catholics or Lutherans. He said that they were all Lutherans of the new religion; although the Adelantado already knew this, for they had said this when he met their armada, and the women and children whose lives he had spared when he captured the fort, had told him so; and he had found within the fort 6 coffers full of books bound and gilt-edged, all concerning the new religion; [he knew] also that they did not say mass, and that their Lutheran faith was preached to them every afternoon; he had ordered those books to be burned, not leaving one.

The Adelantado asked him why he had come. He said that their captain had sent him to see what people they were.

The Adelantado asked him if he wished to return.

He replied that he did, but that he wanted to know who they were.

This man spoke very clearly, for he was a Gascon, from San Juan de Luz.

Then the Adelantado told him that he should tell his captain that he [the Adelantado] was the Viceroy and Captain-General of that land for the King, Don Felipe; that he was called Pedro Menéndez; that he was there with some soldiers to find out who they were, as they [the Spaniards] had had news the day before that they were there and were arriving at that hour.

The Frenchman went with that message, and returned presently, begging that safe-conduct be given to his captain and to 4 other gentlemen who wished to come to see [the Adelantado], and that a boat be loaned him which the Adelantado kept there, which had then come down the river with supplies. He told the Frenchman to say to his captain that he could come over in safety, under the pledge of his word; and he sent for them at once with the boat, and they came immediately.

The Adelantado, with about 10 persons, received him very well, and he commanded the others to keep back a little among some bushes, in order that they might all be seen, in such wise that the French might think that there were more men.

One of these Frenchmen said that he was the captain of those people, and that they had been wrecked in a storm, with 4 galleons and several shallops belonging to the King of France, which had foundered within 20 leagues of one another; that they were the men belonging to one of those ships, and they desired that the Adelantado should favor them by lending them the boat with which to cross that arm of the sea, and another 4 leagues from there, which was that of St. Augustine, as they wished to go to a fort they had 20 leagues from there: this was the fort that the Adelantado had taken from them.

The Adelantado asked them if they were Catholics or Lutherans.

The captain said that they were all of the new religion.

Then the Adelantado said to them:

"Gentlemen, your fort has been captured, and the people therein killed, except the women and the boys under 15 years; and in order that you may know for certain that this is so, there are many things [from there] among some of the soldiers who are here; there are also 2 Frenchmen whom I brought with me because they said they were Catholics: be seated here and dine and I will send you the 2 Frenchmen and the things that those soldiers have taken from the fort, that you may satisfy yourselves.

The Adelantado did this, ordering food to be given them, and he sent them the 2 Frenchmen and many things that the soldiers had taken in the fort, so that they might see them; and he withdrew to eat with his men; and an hour from then, seeing that the Frenchmen had dined, he went over to them and asked them if they believed what he had told them.

They said they did, and begged him as a mercy to give them ships and supplies wherewith they could go to France.

The Adelantado replied that he would willingly do so, if they were Catholics and if he had the ships therefor, but that he did not have them as he had sent two to San Mateo with the artillery; and that they were to take the Frenchwomen and children to Santo Domingo, and seek supplies; the other was to go to Spain with dispatches to his Majesty concerning what had happened to them in those parts.

The French captain answered that he might grant them all their lives, and they would remain with him until there should be ships for France, since they were not at war, and the Kings of Spain and France were brothers and friends.

The Adelantado replied that that was the truth, and that he would aid Catholics and friends, understanding that he served both Kings thereby; but that as they belonged to the new religion he held them to be enemies, and would wage against them a war of fire and blood, and carry it on with all possible cruelty against those he should find in that land and on that sea, where he was Viceroy and Captain-General for his King; and that he came to implant the Holy Gospel in that land, in order that the Indians might be enlightened and come to the knowledge of the holy Catholic faith of Jesus Christ, Our Lord, as it is preached in the Roman church; that if they wanted to give up their flags and arms to him and place themselves at his mercy, they could do so, in order that he might do with them what God should direct him; or that they could do what they wished, for any other truce or friendship they must not form with him; and although the French captain replied, nothing else could be obtained from the Adelantado. And so the French captain went to his men in the boat wherein he had come, saying that he was going to tell them what was occurring, and to decide what they must do, and that within 2 hours he would return with the answer.

The Adelantado told him that they should do what appeared best to them, and that he would wait.

When 2 hours had gone by, that same French captain returned with the same gentlemen, and told the Adelantado that there were many noblemen over yonder, who would give him 50 thousand ducats as ransom in exchange for his granting them all their lives.

The Adelantado replied to him that although he was a poor soldier, he did not wish to give such a sign of weakness as to appear covetous to them;

that when it was his duty to be liberal and merciful, it must be without any interested motive.

The French captain persisted in this: the Adelantado undeceived him, [saying] that if the earth were to join with the sky, he should do no more than what he had told him; and so the French captain returned to where his men were, telling the Adelantado that he would return at once with what had been agreed upon; and he came back within half an hour, bringing the flags in the boat, and about 60 arquebuses, 20 pistols, a quantity of swords and bucklers, and some helmets and breastplates; and he came to where the Adelantado was and said that all those Frenchmen gave themselves up to his mercy, and he surrendered the flags and arms. Then the Adelantado ordered 20 soldiers to enter the boat to bring the Frenchmen over, ten at a time: the river was narrow and easy to cross; and he instructed Diego Florez de Valdés, the Admiral of the fleet, to receive the flags and arms, and go in the boat to bring the Frenchmen across; [he ordered] that the soldiers should not give them ill treatment; and the Adelantado withdrew from the shore a distance of about two arquebuse shots; behind a sand dune, among some bushes, where the men in the approaching boat, who were bringing the French, could not see him: then he said to the French captain and the other 8 Frenchmen who were with him:

"Gentlemen, I have but few soldiers, and they are not very experienced; and you are many, and if you are not bound, it would be an easy thing for you to avenge yourselves on us for the death of your people whom we killed when we took the fort; and so it is necessary that you march with your hands tied behind you, to a place 4 leagues from here where I have my camp."

The Frenchmen replied that so it should be done; and with the ropes from the soldiers' fuses they fastened their hands behind them very securely; and the ten who came over [each time] in the boat could not see those whose hands were being tied behind them, until they met them, because it was expedient so to do in order that the Frenchmen who had not crossed the river, might not understand what was happening and be warned; and thus 208 Frenchmen were bound, of whom the Adelantado asked if there were any Catholics among them who might wish to confess: eight of them said that they were Catholics: these he took away from there and placed them in the boat to be sent up the river to St. Augustine: the others replied that they were of the new religion, and held themselves to be very good Christians; that that was their faith, and no other.

The Adelantado commanded that they should march, after having first given them food and drink when they arrived in tens, before they were bound; this was done before the next ten came; and he told one of his captains, who is called . . . that he was to march with them in the vanguard, and that at a cross-bow shot's distance from there he would find a line which he [the Adelantado] would draw with a *jineta* he carried in his hand; [that place] was a sandy stretch over which they had to march to the Fort of St. Augustine; that there he was to kill them all, and he ordered the captain who came with the rear-guard to do likewise; and so was it done, and they were all left there dead; and that night he returned to St. Augustine toward dawn, because the sun had already set when those men died.

12.

On the day following that on which the Adelantado had arrived in St. Augustine, the same Indians came as before, and said that many more Christians were on the other side of the river than there were previously. The Adelantado realized that this must be the party of Juan Ribao, General of the Lutherans on land and sea, whom they called the Viceroy of that country for the King of France, and he set forth at once with 150 soldiers, [marching] well in order, and at midnight he arrived and quartered himself where he had been the first time. At dawn he came near the river, and scattered his men, and as the daylight grew stronger he saw many people on the other side of the river, two arquebuse shots away, and a raft made to take them across to the point where the Adelantado was. Presently the Frenchmen, when they saw the Adelantado and his men, sounded an alarm and unfurled a royal standard and two field banners, playing their fifes and beating their drums in very good order; and they offered battle to the Adelantado, who had commanded his men to sit down to breakfast, and make no demonstration of anger whatever. He himself walked along the shore with his Admiral and two other captains, paying no attention to the anger and battle

stir of the Frenchmen, in such manner that they stopped running, and in battle array as they were, they halted, stopped playing the fifes and drums, and, sounding a bugle, they raised a white cloth in token of peace.

The Adelantado called at once to another bugler he had with him, a very good one, and drew from his pocket a small cloth, and began to wave it as a signal of peace.

A Frenchman got on the raft, and asked in a loud voice that we should go across to them.

A reply was sent to them by order of the Adelantado, that if they wished anything they should come to where he was, since they had the raft and they called to him: he who was on the raft answered that it was a poor one whereon to cross, because of the strong current; [he asked] that they send him a canoe which was there, belonging to some Indians.

The Adelantado told him that he should swim across for it, under the pledge of his word: then a French sailor came over, but the Adelantado would not consent that he should speak: he ordered him to take the canoe and go to tell his captain that if he wanted anything of the Adelantado, he should send to tell him, since it was the French captain who had called to the Adelantado. That sailor returned presently with a gentleman who said he was the sergeant major of Juan Ribao, Viceroy and Captain-General of that country for the King of France, and that Juan Ribao sent him to say that he had been shipwrecked with a fleet in a storm at sea, and that he had with him there about 350 Frenchmen; that it was his purpose to go to a fort he had 20 leagues from there; that he wished the Adelantado to do him the favor of lending him boats wherein to cross that river, and another there was 4 leagues from there, and that he desired to know if they were Spaniards and who their captain was.

The Adelantado replied that they were Spaniards, and that their captain was he with whom the sergeant was speaking, who was called Pedro Menéndez; that he should tell his General that the Adelantado had taken the fort which Juan Ribao said he had 20 leagues from there, and had slain the Frenchmen therein, and others who had come from the shipwrecked fleet, because they had ill conducted themselves; and they walked to the place where the French lay dead, and he showed them to him, [telling him to inform his General] that he had no reason left for wishing to cross the river to his fort.

The sergeant, with great composure, without showing any sign of grief at what the Adelantado said to him, asked him if he would do him the kindness to send one of his gentlemen to tell that to his General, so that they might negotiate regarding their safe-conduct because his General was very tired, and he wished that the Adelantado would go to see him in a boat he had there; and the Adelantado answered him thus:

"Brother, go with God's blessing and give the reply which has been given you; and if your General should wish to come to speak with me, I give him my word that he can come and return safely, with about 5 or 6 companions whom he may bring with him from those of his council, so that he may follow the advice which suits him best." And so that gentleman left with that message.

Within half an hour he returned to accept the safe-conduct that the Adelantado had given, and to ask for the boat, which the Adelantado would not give him, sending him to say that they might take it from him; that Juan Ribao could come across in the canoe, which was safe, since the river was narrow; and thus that gentleman again went back, and presently came Juan Ribao, whom the Adelantado received very well, with 8 other gentlemen who came with him, all of very fine address and appearance, holding positions of authority, and he had a collation served to them from a certain barrel of preserves, and gave them some drink; and he said that he would give them food if they wished it.

Juan Ribao answered with much humility, rendering thanks for the kind of reception given him; and said that in order to cheer their spirits, which were sad because of the news of their comrades' death, they wished to breakfast with the preserves and wine, and that for the time being they wanted no other food; and thus they did.

Juan Ribao said that those comrades of his who lay dead there, and he saw them near by, might have been deceived [concerning the capture of the fort], and that he did not wish to be: then [the Adelantado] commanded that each one of the soldiers who were there should come with whatever he had from the fort, and the things Juan Ribao saw were so many that he held it for certain

that was the truth; although he had already heard that news, and could not believe it, because among the French was a barber whom the Adelantado had ordered killed with the rest, who had remained for dead among the others, for at the first knife-thrust given him he let himself fall, pretending he was dead; and when Juan Ribao had arrived there the barber had swum over to him, and he [the barber] held it for certain that the Adelantado had deceived them in saying that the fort was captured when it was not, and so had Juan Ribao up to that time.

The Adelantado said that in order that they should believe it fully and satisfy themselves thereof, Juan Ribao should speak apart with two Frenchmen who were there, and he did so; and then he came toward the Adelantado, and told him that he was certain that all he had told him was the truth, and that what was happening to him might happen to the Adelantado; that since their Kings were brothers and such great friends, the Adelantado should treat him like a friend, giving him ships and supplies wherewith he could go to France.

The Adelantado replied to him as he had to the first Frenchmen upon whom he had worked justice, and Juan Ribao in discussion with him was unable to obtain anything else: then Juan Ribao said to him that he wished to report to his men, for there were many noblemen among them, and he would return or send an answer as to what he should decide to do: within 3 hours Juan Ribao came back in the canoe and said that there were different opinions among his men, as some wished to place themselves at the Adelantado's mercy, and others did not.

The Adelantado replied that he cared nothing whether they all came, or came in part, or did not come, any of them; they should do what seemed best to them, since they were free to do so.

Juan Ribao told the Adelantado that half of them were willing to place themselves at his mercy, and would pay as ransom more than one hundred thousand ducats; and the other half could pay more, as there were among them wealthy persons of large income who intended to settle in that land.

The Adelantado answered: "It would grieve me deeply to lose such a good ransom and booty, for I have dire need of that help to aid me in the conquest and colonizing of this country; it is my duty, in the name of my King, to spread therein the Holy Gospel."

Juan Ribao used much cunning here, to see if it might be of use to him, because it seemed to him that the Adelantado, on account of greed for the money that they could give him, would not kill Juan Ribao or those who entrusted themselves to his clemency; it appeared to him that the Adelantado's not killing them, through an agreement that Juan Ribao would make with him, would be worth more to him than 200 thousand ducats; and he told the Adelantado that he would return to his people with the answer; that because it was late he begged him to have the kindness to remain there until the day following, when he would come with the decision that might be agreed upon.

The Adelantado replied that he would wait, and told him to rejoin his men as the sun was already setting; and in the morning Juan Ribao returned in the canoe and delivered to the Adelantado two royal standards, one of the King of France, the other of the Admiral; two field banners; a gilt sword and dagger, a very fine gilt helmet, a buckler, a pistol, a seal he had with him, which the Admiral of France had given him to stamp all the edicts he should issue and titles he might give. He said to the Adelantado that about 150 persons of the 350 with him, were willing to come and place themselves at the Adelantado's mercy; that the others had departed that night, and that the boat should go over for those who wished to come, and for their arms.

The Adelantado immediately directed that Captain Diego Flórez de Valdés, the Admiral of his armada, should have them brought over as he had the others, ten at a time; and taking Juan Ribao behind the sand dune, between the bushes, where he had taken the others, he had his hands and those of all the rest, tied behind their backs, as was done to the previous ones, telling them that they had to march 4 leagues on land, and by night, so that he could not allow them to go unbound; and when they were all tied, he asked them if they were Catholics or Lutherans, and if there were any who wished to confess.

Juan Ribao answered that he and all those who were there were of the new religion, and he began to sing the psalm, *Domine memento mei;* and when it was finished he said that from earth they came, and unto earth must they return; that twenty years more or less were of little account;

that the Adelantado was to do with them as he wished. And the Adelantado, giving the order that they should march, as he had to the others, in the same order and to the same line in the sand, commanded that the same be done to all of them as to the others: he only spared the fifers, drummers, trumpeters, and 4 more who said that they were Catholics, in all 16 persons: all the others were put to the knife.

13.

That night the Adelantado went to St. Augustine, where some persons considered him cruel, and others, that he had acted as a very good captain should. It was thought that even if they had been Catholics, and he had not worked justice upon them, both Spaniards and Frenchmen would have died of hunger on account of the Adelantado's scarcity of provisions; and the French, because they were more numerous, would have killed us, as Fort San Mateo, which the Adelantado had captured from them, burned down with much property and many supplies within eight days after it was taken. The fire started in a house wherein lived Captain Francisco de Recalde, for a servant had set it on fire by sticking a lighted candle on a post, and the candle had fallen; suspicion was aroused thereby because there was much discord between Captain Villarroel, the sergeant major, and Francisco de Recalde; and some soldiers were beginning to say that since there were no supplies and the fort had been captured, they ought to demolish it . . . [and go] to the Indies in the 2 ships which the Adelantado had sent them from St. Augustine with the artillery. Some of the captains did not dare to declare themselves, because the camp master and Villarroel, the most important persons among the soldiers, were the Adelantado's friends, and they had some kinsmen and servants there. At that time it was not known at San Mateo that the Adelantado had won victories over Juan Ribao and his men, and had killed them; and it was found out from the Frenchwomen and youths who were spared when the fort was taken, that Juan Ribao and his captains, at the time they embarked with the fleet, had consumed two barrels of wine, some of them giving mocking toasts to the Spaniards, saying: "I drink to the head of Pedro Menéndez and the men who are with him"; and other insults, such as: "Spanish Marranos, we shall punish them by hanging them from the yard-arms of their own ships and ours, so that they shall not come another time to look for us in this our land." [This was done] in such a manner that it appeared to many people of noble birth who were with Juan Ribao, that those words and insults uttered against the Spaniards were in very bad taste.

And within 20 days after the French were put to the knife, Indians came to the Adelantado and told him by signs that at 8 days' marching from there, toward the south, within the Bahama Channel, there were many men who were brethren of those whom the Adelantado had ordered killed, who were building a fort and a ship. The Adelantado suspected at once that the Frenchmen who withdrew might be fortifying themselves and building a vessel with the timber, artillery, supplies and munitions from the French armada which was wrecked, in order to send to France to ask for succor; and he immediately dispatched ten soldiers from St. Augustine to San Mateo, giving notice of everything and of how he wished to go [after the French], so that enough men should come to him from those who were there, to make up 150, counting the 35 he had brought from there when he captured the fort and returned to St. Augustine; and the camp master sent them at once, with Captains Juan Vélez de Medrano and Andrés López Patiño, and they arrived at St. Augustine on the 23d of October. The Adelantado having heard mass on the morning of the 26th, set out with 300 men and 3 boats which carried the arms and supplies by sea; and the boats went no faster than the men marched on land, for wherever they passed the night the boats anchored, as the whole coast was sandy and clear.

Before the Adelantado's departure from St. Augustine, he appointed a *junta* and government in the name of his Majesty, and the *junta* and captains together formed a *cabildo*. It was set down in the books of the *cabildo* that the proper daily rations should be given from the supplies that remained, and the same with the supplies which should come: he left the fort traced out and the work of erecting it equally divided among squads of men, and they were to work at the fortifications each day 3 hours in the morning and 3 in the afternoon. He left as *alcaide* and governor, Captain Bartolomé Menéndez, his brother, who had always filled those offices, and still does:

he provided that all criminal sentences should be imposed by the *cabildo*, because the captains themselves were the *regidores;* that all appeals should be heard before the camp master, on whom he conferred sufficient authority to be his Lieutenant-General, as his Majesty had given him power in due form to appoint to that dignity whomsoever he wished, whenever he should be absent. He sent the same orders and instructions to Gonzalo de Villarroel at San Mateo, so that he should observe the aforesaid; and before departing from St. Augustine, he dispatched Diego Flórez de Valdés, the Admiral of the armada, to his Majesty by the ship which was there, giving him an account of what had taken place up to that time. All the government officials of St. Augustine, and the men and women who were there, begged the Adelantado as a favor that he should not return to that port with the soldiers unless he brought food, as the fewer who remained there, the longer the supplies they had would last.

The Adelantado took with him in the 3 boats, provisions to last the 300 men for 40 days, and the ration of one day lasted for two; and he promised the people that he would try to do in everything what was for the general good, even though he might undergo dangers and hardships. [He told them] that he trusted that the kindness and mercy of God would help him in all ways, so that he might succeed in so good and holy an undertaking; and thus he bade them farewell, while many of them wept, because he was much beloved, feared and respected by all.

And by making good marches, he arrived on All Saints' Day, at dawn, at the fort the Frenchmen were building, for some Indians were guiding him, as he marched by land with the soldiers, while the 3 boats went by sea under the charge of Captain Diego de Maya; and as they were seen from the fort, the Frenchmen within it fled to the woods, not one remaining, and the Adelantado sent them a trumpeter assuring them that their lives would be safe [and telling them] that they should return and he would give them the same treatment he gave the Spaniards: about 150 came to the Adelantado, but the captain thereof, with 20 others, sent him word that he would rather be eaten by the Indians than surrender to Spaniards.

The Adelantado received these people very well and gave them very good treatment: he set fire to the fort, which was of wood, and destroyed it; and he burned the ship which was being built, and buried the artillery, as the boats could not carry it because they were small. Later in the afternoon of that day, he marched southward along the beach, and the 3 boats cruised in search of a harbor and river which were 15 leagues from there, where were some pueblos of Indians, for the Adelantado wanted to see if he could leave his men quartered there with some cacique, and if he could go by the Bahama Channel to the island of Cuba in search of supplies; and on the third day, the 4th of November of the said year '65, they arrived at that port which is called Ays, because the cacique who lived there was thus named. He was a very good Indian, who received the Adelantado very well; neither he nor his people left their homes; rather did he await the Adelantado with all the people of the pueblo, which was a demonstration of confidence which gave much pleasure to the Adelantado, for up to then the inhabitants of all the Indian villages where he had arrived, had fled to the woods, leaving the houses deserted.

The Adelantado did not allow any damage to be done in their homes, or to the furniture therein; rather did he leave, in return for hospitality received in the houses of the caciques, some gifts of mirrors, knives, scissors and bells, things which they prize greatly. He remained there 4 days, during which he went down a river to see some places the cacique told him were good to settle; and without going out to sea, he reached a small harbor which was about 15 leagues from there, inside the Bahama Channel. As the land did not satisfy him, he returned; and as he had but little food, and the Indians of that land had none either, unless it were fish, cocoa-plums and palmettos, it was agreed and requested by all the people who were there—who saw the danger of their all dying of hunger—that his lordship the Adelantado should leave with two of the boats for the island of Cuba, although it was the middle of November, a dangerous time to sail in the Bahama Channel, which is very stormy, and although the boats were very small; in order to send supplies to them and to the people at St. Augustine and San Mateo.

The Adelantado did so, taking with him 50 persons, counting sailors and soldiers, and 20 of the Frenchmen from Canaveral, for he had taken them all with him; and this was the reason that the provisions for 40 days which he had brought from St. Augustine, gave out sooner, for the same rations were given to the French as to the Spaniards, and in the distribution of the rations no preference was shown even to the Adelantado. They consisted of half a pound of biscuit each day for each soldier—though they should have been a pound and a half—without wine, or any kind of food save the palmettos and cocoa-plums they gathered in the fields: there in Ays there was a soldier who sold 4 pounds of biscuit at 25 reals each, and who ate so many palmetto berries and other kinds of fruit which had a pleasant taste, that one day at nightfall he was well, and at midnight he died.

The fact that the Adelantado made this journey on foot was something that everybody admired; for he had no horse; and on the third day there were 50 soldiers whom he had left in the rearguard, who did not arrive, owing to the many so exhausted they could not walk. Two of the strongest who came there, each of them between 25 and 30 years of age, who had been among the first to enter the Fort of San Mateo when it was captured from the French, and marched in the vanguard with the Adelantado, felt ashamed at seeing how he was marching; and in order not to leave him they forced themselves beyond reason, and as they walked along, one of them said to the other: "Comrade, I want to sit down a little while, for I am very tired." Without the Adelantado's noticing it these two remained where they were, and in a quarter of an hour, without rising from where he was, the one who had spoken gave up his soul to God. The other forced himself to keep up with the Adelantado, but one night he disappeared and they never saw him more. All the men marched along the sea-shore from 2 o'clock after midnight until sunrise, and then they halted, and the soldiers scattered in the savannas to eat palmettos and cocoa-plums, some of which they gathered to take with them: they remained there for two hours and marched [again] until 10 or 12 o'clock of the day: then they rested until 2 hours after midday, and marched once more until the sun went down; there was no day during which they did not march from 8 leagues upward, a thing which everyone marvelled at because of the difficulty of advancing over those sandy stretches and because of the lack of food.

Cacique Ays was much grieved at the Adelantado's departing from there, and he and his children wept, for during those days that the Adelantado remained there he made him many presents and gave him many things for barter, and did likewise to his principal Indian men and women; and the Adelantado, fearing that the soldiers and the Indians would break out in war against one another, wherein his men ran the danger of being slain because they lacked food and did not know the country and were so thin and feeble, arranged before his starting for Havana to leave them in a place 3 leagues from there, which the Indians said was very good, as there were palmettos, cocoa-plums and fish, for it was on the river; and in two days he conveyed the men there in the boats. He greatly feared his departure, one reason being that it appeared to him that the soldiers were becoming emaciated and discouraged; another, because no ship had ever been seen to reach the island of Cuba through the Bahama Channel, although many had attempted it, as the current always runs very strongly toward the north, while the Adelantado had to sail southward to the island of Cuba, and he had the current against him, which struck the ships' prows; and if it had not been for the relief of these people and those left behind in St. Augustine and San Mateo, he would have preferred to send someone else in the two boats, and remain with the other and with his men, rather than to subject himself to that risk, which was great. The soldiers desired his depar-ture because of the hope they had of obtaining supplies if he went in person, and so he decided to depart from that port of Ays on . . . of November, with 50 soldiers and sailors and 20 Frenchmen, leaving Captain Juan Vélez de Medrano in charge of those people, to whom and to all those who remained with him, the Adelantado made a speech, strengthening and consoling them and asking them to pray for him every day, as he was exposing himself for them to one of the greatest dangers ever encountered by man; and to suppli-cate God Our Lord and his precious Mother to give him a safe voyage; and while all were kneel-ing, singing the litanies and praying, the Adelan-tado set out. He had such a favorable wind that although there were one hundred leagues from there to Havana, and contrary currents, he made the journey in 2 days, a thing to marvel at, because all the pilots who sail in the Indies were of opinion that with galleys provided with oars, it was not possible to go against that current. He sailed along the whole coast and country of Florida, and upon crossing to the island of Cuba, he met with choppy seas and a great storm from

the north, and high seas ran from poop to prow: through one whole night that this gale lasted he steered, not trusting the helm to any of his sailors: there were among the 20 Frenchmen he had with him, the chief pilot of Juan Ribao and another who seemed to him a very efficient mariner. The Adelantado asked him if he were a good helmsman: he replied that he was: the Adelantado gave him the helm toward morning, and that Frenchman steered very well; and thus, until they arrived at Havana, the Adelantado and the Frenchman steered.

The boat in which the Adelantado was, carried no compass, because on departing from Ays he had it taken from its place, and they found it broken.

Captain Diego de Maya said that the boat wherein he was, outsailed the Adelantado's and carried a compass, and as the Adelantado's was broken, he should trim his sails and not go far from land, and be careful not to become separated from him [Diego de Maya]; and on the second night, when the storm was almost over and day was approaching, the Adelantado lost sight of the other boat and passed beyond the harbor of Havana, thinking he had not yet arrived there.

At about 10 in the morning, he recognized the port of Bahíahonda, which is 15 leagues farther than Havana, and saw a small vessel enter it: he went after her and reached her: in her were some Indians from Havana who were going hunting. They gave the Adelantado much meat and cas-sava, which is the bread of that land, and palmet-tos; and the Indians told him that Pedro Menén-dez Marqués, his nephew, had reached Havana with part of the fleet from Biscay and the As-turias, which during a storm had become sepa-rated from General Estébano de las Alas; and that all the people were very sad, as they did not know what had happened to the Adelantado, who, they feared, had perished at sea in a tempest, or had been destroyed by the enemy; as they could not suspect or believe that he would dare to go to Florida with so few ships, nor did the thought cross their minds that he was there.

The Adelantado landed with his men in that harbor of Bahíahonda, and all of them kneeling, gave many thanks to Our Lord for the kindnesses he had done them in carrying them through to safety. He called the Frenchmen and told them to behold the power and goodness of God, and that if they were Lutherans, they should repent and become Catholics; that he would give them good treatment, no matter what their faith was, and give them liberty to go in the first ships to Spain, and thence to France; that he said that to them because he desired to save them.

There were some of them who, weeping, began to strike their breasts; and praising Our Lord and begging him for mercy, they said that they had been wicked Christians and Lutherans, and now they had repented; and that henceforth they wished to renounce their evil sect and become Catholics, making confession and receiving the Communion, and to cherish and observe that which is required by the Holy Mother Church.

The Adelantado regaled and strengthened them, telling them that they should rejoice and not be grieved at their sufferings; that he would take care of them as though they were his brothers; and this he did for those men, as he did for all the others whose lives he spared, each one according to his rank: he invited the nobleman to sit at table with him, supplying him with clothing; and the sailors sat with his pilots and sailors, and the soldiers, with his captains and soldiers.

That night the Adelantado departed from that port of Bahíahonda to return to Havana, but as the wind was contrary and very strong—for it drove him out to sea, farther than he wished, in the direction of Florida—he did not arrive in Havana until the following night, at midnight. Diego de Maya had arrived two days before; he feared that the Adelantado was lost, and everyone held this for certain, for as the storm had been so great and he had no compass, they thought that in the hurricane the boat had been ripped open and had sunk; and according to report, great was the sorrow felt for him by the people of Havana and by his armada. On the day after he arrived there, when he entered the harbor rowing, as the wind was blowing from land, the sentinel on watch to guard the harbor called out and asked who came on board the boat that was entering: they replied, the Adelantado Pedro Menéndez: the sentinel answered, saying: "Blessed be Our Lord, that the Señor Pedro Menéndez is alive"; and [he asked] that they wait a little, while he went to tell Governor García Osorio, so that they should not be fired upon from the fortress.

The Adelantado himself said to the sentinel, who was very near:

"My brother, go with God and I will wait"; and so he waited long enough for the sentinel to be able to go and return; and as he saw that he delayed, he ordered his boat to enter; and within a short time it became known in the harbor that this was the Adelantado, and the ships therein began to discharge the pieces of artillery, for there was anchored the armada from Biscay and the Asturias, under the charge of his nephew, Pedro Menéndez Marqués; and they began to give many indications of pleasure and to fire many rounds in sign of rejoicing.

The Adelantado saw these demonstrations, and that there were illuminations, with a flag, and that they beat a drum and sounded a fife, with great acclamations; and as it appeared to him that they were awaiting him, in order to land he went directly to the quay, without going on any of his ships or being detained on board of them. The Governor was there, but when he saw the Adelantado arrive he went away, with the greater part of the people he had with him: only Juan de Ynistrosa remained, with a few *regidores* of the pueblo; he was the Treasurer of his Majesty on that island, and he took the Adelantado to his house and entertained him very well, likewise all those who came with him.

The Governor sent to call on the Adelantado: this act, the little satisfaction and the lack of pleasure shown by the Governor at the Adelantado's arrival in safety, and at the artillery's being fired, surprised everyone; for whenever the Adelantado had seen his soldiers discontented, his refrain to console them had been:

"Make an effort, my brothers, for García Osorio, the Governor of the Island of Cuba, will send us a sufficient supply of food for all of us who are in Florida; for so was I promised in Seville, and his Majesty has charged and commanded him to do this."

And the next day in the morning the Adelantado heard mass, and as he was going out [of church] the Governor entered; they spoke to each other, and all noticed the great abruptness with which the Governor spoke to the Adelantado, for it was as though he had never known him; and so they took leave of each other.

After the Adelantado had dined, he went to see the Governor and told him the great necessity in which the people of Florida found themselves. He showed him the decrees whereby he was commanded to give one armed ship, 40 soldiers and 20 horses, with pay for 4 months, and all the help and favor that he might ask or need of him for the conquest and settlement of Florida; and he showed him how 500 men were in Florida for his Majesty's account, who were without supplies and would all perish of hunger if they were not succored; [he said] that he did not want the armed ship, nor the horses nor soldiers, for all of it would cost more than twenty thousand ducats; that with three or four thousand he might give him, he could relieve until spring those soldiers who were in Florida for his Majesty's account.

The Governor replied that he did not want to give them. The Adelantado asked that they might be loaned him, and [said] that he would guarantee them and give a bondsman for them.

The Governor replied that he did not have them.

The Adelantado said that [the Governor could help him] from the ten or twelve thousand ducats he held from a Portuguese caravel which Captain Juan de la Parra had taken [while commanding] the flagship of the Fleet of New Spain, which vessel and soldiers and sailors were under orders to the Adelantado, and that money belonged to the Adelantado and to the ship's people, as being the persons who had captured the caravel with what she contained, because she went about trading in the Indies, against the statutes and decrees of his Majesty and without being registered.

The Governor answered that he would not give those to him either, because he said that they did not belong to him.

The Adelantado begged that he lend him on endorsed security the four thousand ducats from those [ten or twelve thousand; and] that if his Majesty commanded him to return them, he would.

The Governor did not want to do this. He held prisoner Juan de la Parra, the captain of that flagship: the Adelantado told him to deliver him to him, with the record of his offence.

The Governor said that although he was his [the Adelantado's] soldier, it was he, as Governor of the country, who should punish him, and the other soldiers of the Adelantado who might do unlawful things in his district.

The Adelantado replied to him:

"Sir, may this reception that your Honor gives me in your district be for the love of God: I am determined to arm myself with patience to go through all these things your Honor makes me endure, for I believe that in doing this God gives me a greater victory than that I won over Juan Ribao and the other Lutherans who were in Florida, and that I am rendering his Majesty a great service"; and he doffed his hat to him and went out through the door, without awaiting the Governor's reply. And the Adelantado immediately ordered a proclamation to be issued that all the soldiers and sailors who were there from Biscay and the Asturias, and those of the flagship of the Fleet of New Spain, should assemble on the ships during the whole of that day; that he wanted to take the muster-roll of the men he had, in order to employ them in the service of his Majesty.

And the next day in the morning, they heard mass at break of day and went on board the vessels, and the Adelantado made a list of 550 men, and he summoned the captains and pilots to the flagship; he went into council with them, and when they were together, he said to them:

"Gentlemen and Brothers: We find news here that there are many French and English corsairs going about, robbing the subjects of his Majesty. As we are at peace, they deserve to be punished; and it is held for certain, and several of you, Gentlemen, who arrive from there, say that among these corsairs there are two English and three French vessels, which carry on board more than half a million of plunder, and purchase money for negroes and merchandise; and that they are wintering off that island of Santo Domingo, at the northern end, so as to go to France in the spring. Since I have here four very good sailing vessels and this flagship, all well armed, with a large quantity of good munitions; and there are 550 soldiers and sailors on board, all very good men; it appears to me that within ten days we shall be able to collect our stores of water, wood and meat (for we have most of the supplies on board, as the ships brought them from the Asturias and Biscay); grease the vessels and make them ready, and then go out to sea at the first opportunity and go in search of those corsairs, wherein we shall be rendering great service to God Our Lord and his Majesty in punishing those Lutheran corsairs and this will be for the general good of all the Indies, and we shall be able to profit very much thereby; and to send to our comrades in Florida, as soon as we reach [the corsairs], 2 or 3 ships of supplies. In the spring we shall take our vessels to Florida, laden with food and cattle, in order to make explorations and discoveries inland: and we shall have freed ourselves from the danger which it seems to me some of us are running, of being ruined by this Governor, and of losing patience, as I tell you for my part, Gentlemen, that although it be in December and navigation through the Bahama Channel is dangerous, I would rather sail through there and on the ocean than remain in this town; because even though I may know how to conduct myself with the Governor, I fear that some of you may not, and the blame for whatever might happen would be placed on me, for seeing the danger and not forestalling it: I beg of you as a favor, Gentlemen, to advise me as to whether I must take this decision."

They all approved and held it to be good, and showed great satisfaction thereat.

And the Adelantado at once ordered the captains and pilots there to prepare to be able to set sail within twelve days; and he caused to be summoned the masters and boatswains, officers and stewards of all the ships, and told them his decision, and he ordered and charged them all to have a care to place their vessels in readiness, and they offered to do so, showing great pleasure and satisfaction at the voyage, and the sailors, shipboys and cabinboys of the armada did likewise; and the Adelantado, in the presence of all, named as Admiral thereof his nephew, Pedro Menéndez Marqués.

And at the time appointed, which was within twelve days, the ships were ready to set sail. The Adelantado went on board and sent a requisition to the Governor, to deliver to him Captain Juan de la Parra: he would not do so.

During those 15 days there were many dangerous matters of discussion between the Adelantado and the Governor: many observed the patience of the Adelantado, who sailed on his voyage in the beginning of December, and on the third day after setting out from the port of Havana, he sighted a sail: he chased her, thinking she was a corsair, until she reached Matanzas, a harbor of the island of Cuba, where he found on coming up to her that there was no one on board, because the crew had gone to the woods. He ordered Pedro Menéndez Marqués, his nephew, the Admiral of that armada, to go on board, so that with a few sailors he might guard well all that she carried, and bring her to anchor near the flagship whereon was the Adelantado, for he wished to cast anchor in that harbor, as he did: and they heard voices in the woods, for the armada had anchored near there; the Adelantado sent a boat to land, to see what was the matter: some Portuguese ran there, and when they understood that the armada was Spanish and that the Adelantado was the General thereof, they rejoiced greatly and called their comrades. They got into the boat and were brought to the flagship, before the Adelantado, and they told him with great pleasure that they had come from Spain on that caravel, by command of his Majesty, with dispatches for him, which they gave him, whereby his Majesty advised him how in France a large armada was being prepared to come over to attack him in Florida; and in order that the Adelantado might defend Florida and succor the places and islands of Puerto Rico, Hispaniola and Cuba, his Majesty was sending him one thousand, five hundred soldiers, with a large quantity of supplies and 17 ships; and telling him to take the measures which might appear necessary to him, on sea as well as on land, to injure that armada if it should attack him or his territories.

Then the Adelantado summoned his captains to a council, and having shown them the letter, he said:

"Gentlemen and Brothers: It seems to me that in all things, and especially in war, new events bring new ideas; and it is my feeling that I must not remove myself from Havana, because they write to me that these reinforcements will arrive here during March. Let us return there, and I shall send one or two of these ships to Campeche, to be laden with maize for Florida; another I shall send to Puerto de Plata, so that she may be laden with meat and cassava; and another I shall have laden in Havana, as soon as I can, and although I have no money I will sell or pawn some of the artillery, or these munitions I carry, even if the price be below their value; and the gold chains and jewels there may be among us; and we shall amuse ourselves the best way we can, trying not to have a break with the Governor, no matter what may happen; because now that I have been given this dispatch, I should deserve to be punished by his Majesty for any misfortune that might occur if I were to go with this armada to make war on corsairs, and the reinforcements should come to Havana from another direction, and the French fleet should go to Florida."

They all approved the Adelantado's decision, and held it to be wise and of good counsel; and so they departed for Havana the following day, with all the armada; and when they had arrived the Adelantado sent the ships as he had agreed; and sent his nephew, Pedro Menéndez Marqués, to Spain in a patache, to inform his Majesty of what had occurred up to then.

317. 1565. Bartolomé Barrientos on Pedro Menéndez de Avilés's successful attack on the French colony.

Barrientos, who had not been to Florida, compiled a little later than Solís de Méras another work on Pedro Menéndez de Avilés, "Vida y hechos de Pedro Menéndez de Avilés ... largamente se tratan las conquistas y poblaciones de la provincia de la Florida." It was first published by Genaro García, ed., Dos antiquos relaciones de la Florida (Mexico City, 1902), pp. 1–49. It was translated by Anthony Kerrigan, Pedro Menéndez de Avilés, Founder of Florida, written by Bartolomé Barrientos (Gainesville, Fla., 1965), together with a facsimile of the 1902 edition. Extracts from the translation, from pp. 21–26, 37–39, 44–45, 59–60, 66–70, are given here.

Barrientos prefaced his account of the attack on the French colony by an account of the earlier services of Pedro Menéndez de Avilés to the crown.

His Majesty now commanded Menéndez to serve him in the Indies trade as before, in company with his brothers and members of his family. By this, the King said he would consider himself well served and would reward Menéndez for past services. And, added the King, he and everyone else in his kingdom was fully aware that Menéndez had been unjustly accused.

Very humbly, Menéndez kissed the hands of the King in appreciation of the grace extended him by His Majesty's expression of satisfaction with his services and in gratitude for the King's having understood the nature of the charges.

Menéndez then spoke to the King of the loss of his son. The latter was a gentleman of His Majesty's household who had disappeared off the island Bermuda, near Florida, while serving as general of the fleet and armada of New Spain. Menéndez said that natural reason impelled him, while paternal love demanded that he go in search of his son—not only so that his boy might be restored to life but also that the lives of the kindred, friends, and soldiers who had long served the King and were now lost along with the son might be saved. Menéndez told His Majesty that he would like to sail along the Florida coast with two *pataches* to see if he could find the castaways. If he did find them he would then return to his own family and wife, whom he had seen only a very few times in the course of the last eighteen years of active service to the Crown. He would have accomplished his aim before, he added, had he not been in prison.

The King replied he would aid Menéndez in his project, provided he would coast the Florida littoral (once his search was over), explore the estuaries, harbors, and bays, and set down their exact locations on his sea-charts. Many ships had been lost in the conquest of Florida precisely because this investigation had not been carried out.

Menéndez acknowledged the importance of the enterprise, and the desirability of settling a land so rich and temperate, especially now that the Lutherans threatened to occupy it—for their presence would endanger the whole fabric of trade and navigation to the Indies. Thereupon the King promised Menéndez the rights to the conquest, administration, and settlement of that country. Accepting the charge, Menéndez made his departure for Asturias, there to organize the armada for the conquest of Florida.

6.

Before beginning a narrative of the deeds of Pedro Menéndez from the time he was named Adelantado of Florida by His Majesty, it is first necessary to describe that vast country. It was called by its present name either because it was first discovered by Christians on Easter Sunday [*pascua florida*] or because of its fresh greenery and trees. Florida has a promontory which extends a hundred leagues into the sea and narrows to a cape called Head of the Martyrs. This cape lies in twenty-five degrees of latitude. Twenty-five leagues directly south lies the island of Cuba and its port of Havana. On the east is the Land of Cod and Newfoundland; to the west, New Spain; to the north, China and Tartary. The area, which is settled and boasts coastal forts built by the Adelantado, runs from the land of Cacique Carlos, over towards New Spain, to the head of the Martyrs, and from there to San Felipe, north of Santa Elena. It is a distance of nine hundred leagues from the Head of the Martyrs to Cape Catoche in the province of Yucatán, which is west of Duba. The two promontories of Florida and Yucatán form the Gulf of Mexico, or Gulf of Florida. A great current pours without ebb between Cuba and Yucatán into this gulf, to emerge between Cuba and Florida. This is one of the reasons that ships going to the Indies cannot go back as they have come, for the current is constant and there is no wind blowing along the route of entrance, so that the mariners go north to search for one. Thus it is a matter of great moment in the preservation of the Indies, and for its trade and commerce, that Florida remain Spanish and be strongly guarded, and that no nation other than the Spanish control it. The Spanish nation should be careful that the administrators of Florida be men intensely devoted to the Crown and concerned with maintaining loyalty in the forts, fortresses, outposts, and towns under their jurisdiction. Measuring around the Florida coasts, which extend from the port of Pánuco, a port in New Spain, to Newfoundland, the distance is about thirteen hundred leagues. Florida borders New Spain and is part of the mainland. At the time of this writing it has still not been determined either by exploration or calculation whether or not Florida joins Tartary, Muscovy, and China in the north.

Many large islands, and keys (which are small islands), lie along the Florida coastline. Good harbors abound. With the same meticulous and careful attention he has ever devoted to the royal service, Pedro Menéndez has discovered, within a three hundred league distance, four harbors boasting a depth of four fathoms or more at full tide. In addition, he found ten other harbors with two and a half to three fathoms depth. Menéndez personally inspected and examined each one of them. He sailed into them with five or six brigantines and as many pilots. The entrances were sounded three times and marked. This activity will prove a great boon. For, when Pánfilo de Narváez went to Florida, one of the reasons that he and all his men and armada were lost was that they found no port in which to anchor the ships. They entered only bays or arms of the sea.

Along this three hundred leagues of coastline are numerous caciques and Indians. These natives Menéndez treated so considerately, politely, and humanely that they rejoiced at being Christian vassals of the King and friends of the Adelantado. Within this area Menéndez has established three forts and four settlements, all of them on harbors. These ports will contribute to making this territorial enterprise lasting and strong. The explorer who does not search out a port and establish a settlement, once he has found an unknown country, will not succeed in the conquest.

Most of the coastline and beach is made unsteady and treacherous by an endless number of rivers flowing into the sea; the tide rises inland for fifteen leagues (and up to twenty-four leagues, as along the San Mateo). The land is flat, so that the sea washes across it and leaves a sandy deposit; even inland, therefore, canoes and boats are used. The coast itself is turned into islands surrounded by swamplands. Even horses cannot ford them, and are swallowed up. The coastal islands are covered with trees, however, and abound in game. Around them there is an abundance of shellfish, fish, flounder, and oysters. Some of these islands are inhabited by Indians. Although the land is all flat, far inland there are some mountain ranges. Everywhere are extensive woods, undergrowth and trees. Some of the trees are marvelously tall; among them are walnut, laurel, liquidamber, savine, wild olive, live oak, oak, pine, and plum. There are also wild vineyards, cereals, and palmettos like those of Andalucía. Mulberry trees, suitable for silk-making, are plentiful. Large lakes are numerous, and many of them are deep. Maize fields are on every hand.

Game, too, is infinite in number. For instance,

deer, hares, rabbits, bears, lions, and other wild beasts were seen by Alvaro Núñez Cabeza de Vaca and others of Pánfilo de Narváez' soldiers. Among the animals seen was one which carries its young in a stomach pouch. The young are kept there as long as they are small. If people appear while the animals are out hunting food, the mother gathers all her offspring into the pouch before she flees. Much of the country is cold, with extensive pasturage very suitable for livestock. Geese abound, as do ducks, muscovies, flycatchers, night herons, herons, partridges, falcons, peregrines, sparrow hawks, merlins, and other diverse birds.

The Florida natives are large of body. They are great archers, slender, very strong, and swift. The bows they carry are eighty-eight to ninety-six inches long. At two hundred paces they can shoot with such accuracy and in such certainty that they never merely wound their prey—as was demonstrated by those Indians the Adelantado brought to Spain in 1567.

There is an abundance of pastel plant and pearls. Because pine groves are numerous a quantity of tar and pitch is available. The wood necessary to build houses, ships, and boats, for which we now send to Germany, is abundant. The trees are so immense that they would more than suffice for the above-mentioned construction, and they exceed the German wood in quality. This timber could be easily and cheaply transported to Spain.

7.

Having penetrated Florida from the direction of New Spain, Francisco Vásquez Coronado tells of the many rich provinces found in the region he entered, where the produce of the earth was abundant. Thus, there were found beans, maize, squash, and, what is more remarkable, many of the same fruits as in Spain, such as walnuts, chestnuts, filberts, plums, and countless grapes. Very significant traces of silver and gold were found, also quantities of copper wrought like Milan leaf.

Hernando de Soto, who entered the country along the River of the Holy Spirit, was met in the province of Cofitachiqui by a local *cacica*, or female cacique. She came out to greet him in a litter borne on the shoulders of her Indians. As she came up to De Soto she took a pearl necklace from around her neck and threw it to him. She then supplied his men with food, clothing, blankets, exquisite marten furs, deer and cow skins very handsomely tanned, and, for the horses, feather blankets. All this is mentioned here so that one may know what the land produces.

In one of the *cacica's* temples, where her ancestors lay embalmed, great heaps of pearls, both perfect and misshapen, were piled. Many of these pearls were perforated, as the Indians pierced them in order to make strings of them. The province of Coza, apart from being fertile, temperate, and well situated, is so highly populated in one four-league beach that both sides of the Coza River are thick with houses.

In addition to numerous other fruits, muscatel grapes abound, and they are as good as the Spanish variety. Extensive oak groves yield an abundance of acorns. Enclosed gardens are to be found in Coza and other provinces as well. Throughout Florida mulberry trees are common. In Cofitachiqui mulberry groves are so thick that it is necessary to cut them down in order to make plantings. From the mulberries the Indians make raisins, which are good to eat. In Cibola province there are flat-roofed houses like those of Andalucía; their walls are made of clay and stone. The houses near the mountains are many-storied and have stoves like those of Flanders. The wide plains are covered with cows and bulls, although the cattle are not as fully developed as they are in Spain, while the cows [i.e. bison] grow wool instead of hair. Flax is abundant and grows wild, expecially where the cattle roam. Many of these things were seen by Francisco Vásquez Coronado, who explored the region at the order of the Viceroy of New Spain, Don Luis Velasco.

Strings of coral beads, which the Indians say are brought from the South Seas (beyond Florida), have also been found in this land. There are turquoises, and emeralds—the emeralds being common near the mountains. Full-flowing rivers are numerous; their water is fresh and clear and filled with such fish as skate, trout, ray trout, sturgeon, flounder, prawns, and others, all fat and delicious. Oysters and shellfish are plentiful, as are the larger variety of oysters from which pearls are extracted. As there are numberless pine groves, the Indians make bread from pine kernels. Although the pine cones are no bigger than eggs, the kernels themselves are sizable.

While still green, the Indians grind them and shape them into pellets, which they keep to eat later as we do bread. Whales are killed along the Florida coast. The Indians eat the meat and a quantity of fine ambergris is collected.

Throughout Florida the natives wear their hair long; they never cut it unless their cacique, or some other important personage, dies. In the land governed by Cacique Don Luis, north of Santa Elena, the Indians give evidence of good intelligence and are not as rustic or savage as the others. Thus they can boast of established customs. In conformity with their idea of justice, they punish liars, although in reality all Indians are liars, and they abominate thieves.

If Florida were cultivated in the Spanish manner, it could produce wheat, wine-grapes, sugar, and all kinds of produce. The country as a whole has a good climate, and is salubrious.

Unicorns have been seen in this land. Ambergris, which the Indians value highly because they are susceptible to the influence of odor, has been collected on the coast. Wild olive trees are widely scattered and very numerous; their fruit grows quite large, with a good seed. Thus it is reasonable to hope that once the land is cultivated, olive oil will be plentiful.

13.

After the officers unanimously came around to his way of thinking, the Adelantado felt as if he had already gained a victory over the Lutherans. He ordered celebrations throughout the fleet. Drums were sounded and fifes played; banners, standards, and fleet pennants were run up over all the ships. As the royal standard was raised, an appropriate salute boomed out. All the harquebuses and cannon fired at once. A double ration was issued to every man that day. Everyone was vastly pleased and the demonstration of pleasure was universal. The Adelantado's determination was lauded and that of every man pledged.

In the afternoon, the Adelantado arranged for the weapons to be handed out to the lieutenants so they could distribute them to the men, who were to clean and ready them. Provision was made for each soldier to fire a piece three times each day until arrival in Florida, that they might thus lose their fear of the harquebuses and gain experience. Most of the men were raw recruits. Menéndez had them conduct target practice aboard his own galleon, while the men on the other ships did the same. He also watched them carefully, to see that they conducted themselves like good Christians.

On August 28, St. Augustine's Day, they sighted the land of Florida. Thanks were given to God for His mercy in allowing them to arrive safely within sight of this country, and they prayed He might grant them victory in the remainder of their enterprise. Instead of landing at once, they ran along the coast for four days, in search of the Lutheran emplacements; not knowing whether the French were established north or south, the party grew very morose in the quest. At the Adelantado's orders, they sailed by day and anchored at night.

One day they sighted some Indians on the beach. The Adelantado ordered twenty harquebusiers under command of the campmaster to go ashore. He did not want to land a larger number lest the Indians take flight. Even so, the closer the soldiers drew near to them, the farther towards the woods withdrew the Indians, with their bows and arrows. To avoid a possible ambush, the Spaniards halted. Still, they did not want to leave without having made enquiries— for they knew nothing of the coast and its shoals, and they ran the risk of being shipwrecked should a storm come up. The Adelantado therefore sent an unarmed soldier ashore bearing some trinkets. The Indians waited for him to come up, received him peaceably, and were placated. The campmaster then approaching, he asked them by signs where the Lutherans were. In sign language they replied that the French were twenty leagues north. Then in their turn the Indians asked for the leader of the Spanish. When it was explained to them that he was with the fleet, they asked to see him. The Adelantado was therefore called upon, and he came ashore with fifty harquebusiers.

Once they saw the Adelantado ashore, the Indians laid down their bows and arrows. Raising their voices in song, they drew around him, lifting their hands toward the sky. The Adelantado made them numerous presents, and gave them sweets to eat. The Indians repeated the information they had given the campmaster. Both sides parted in a friendly fashion, and the Spaniards re-embarked.

For eight leagues they sailed along the coast. Then they discovered a fine natural harbor with a good river. This site the Adelantado named St. Augustine, for the reason that it was the first place he had discovered in the land of Florida, which in turn had first been sighted on St. Augustine's Day. This harbor of St. Augustine is north of the cape known as the Head of the Martyrs, which Florida thrusts into the Bahama Channel. Fort San Mateo is twelve leagues distant, the Fort Santa Elena is sixty-two. Further north is the Bay of Santa Maria [Pensacola Bay]. St. Augustine is in latitude twenty-nine degrees.

As the Spanish sailed along the coast, the day following the discovery of St. Augustine, at three in the afternoon, they sighted four large galleons anchored close to the harbor of San Mateo. This Menéndez was convinced was the Lutheran port, that their reinforcement had arrived, and the galleons must belong to the reinforcing fleet. He therefore summoned his captains into council. He saw no reason to doubt, he told them, that the Lutheran fleet had arrived. There was no possibility of being able to take the enemy harbor or seize their fort. He requested his captains' view of the matter.

The captains reached the conclusion that they should put back to Santo Domingo, and there assemble the remaining ships of the fleet (which the storm had scattered), as well as the ten vessels of the Biscay-Asturias armada which, in accordance with the orders left for them in the Canaries, should now be waiting in Puerto Rico. The Adelantado could add the two ships His Majesty had ordered put at his disposal in those islands, and the horses, infantry, and supplies likewise requisitioned. With all this armament he might proceed to Havana. Then, in the following March, he might set out for Florida, supremely powerful and assured of victory.

This plan seemed sensible and sound, but the profound intelligence and imagination of Menéndez saw further into the future. Should the suggested plan be carried out, all might be lost. For the Lutheran squadron had already sighted them, the wind was calm, and the sun gave indications of good weather; four vessels of the Spanish fleet had been left without main topmasts by the storm through which they had come, and even some of the smaller masts had been split. In this situation the Lutheran fleet could easily overtake them, especially since (as he understood) they had brought oar-driven ships in their fleet. Then, too, he added, it was reasonable to assume that the Lutherans would not have been expecting him along that coast. They must have put their infantry ashore, and must now be engaged in unloading supplies. Since the four galleons were large, they would be unable to enter the harbor still loaded. In his opinion, the Spaniards should give battle now. If they could take the French galleons, the Lutherans would not then have enough strength to chase them out to sea. Once the galleons were taken, the Spaniards could proceed to the port of St. Augustine twelve leagues away, build fortifications, and send to the islands for the rest of the armada.

In this way they could carry the war to the French on land and at sea. They could capture their harbor—for the French fort was on a riverbank two leagues inland. Thus, too, they would cut off all support from the Lutherans of France. The Spanish cavalry would dominate the country and prevent the French from carrying on any intercourse or having any dealings with the Indians. By this vigorous action the war would be brought to a quick conclusion, without risking the fleet or the lives of the men. Cut off by land and by sea, the Lutherans must yield. For in truth their fort was so constructed and fortified that it could neither be attacked nor taken by force of arms.

All his officers approved the Adelantado's views and his resolution. He set about making the necessary preparations to attack the Lutheran fleet....

16.

That same day, the eve of Our Lady's Day in September, the Adelantado reached port. As soon as he had landed he sent out three hundred soldiers to reconnoiter and find the most suitable place to dig trenches for protection during the interval in which the location of the fort was decided. At about midday on the following day he went ashore to meet a numerous concourse of Indians who were awaiting him. They had heard of his arrival from the first natives who had seen and spoken with him.

The Adelantado took formal possession of the country for His Majesty after hearing a solemn High Mass to Our Lady. He administered a solemn oath to the officials of the royal treasury, the campmaster, and the captains, in which they swore to serve our Catholic King with the complete fidelity and loyalty due such a lord. Then he inspected the site chosen for the entrenchments.

Within three days he had directed the unloading of everything in the ships. The two largest he had to send to Hispaniola, because they could not enter the harbor owing to their size and would be taken by the Lutherans if they remained outside. He had seen to the unloading of the ships in the fastest possible time in anticipation of what later actually came to pass. So quickly was the work done that, at the end of two days and a half, despite the vessels being anchored a league and a half from the point of disembarkation, all the artillery, men, munitions, and a large part of the provision had been landed.

That midnight he sent off the two ships going to Hispaniola, under the command of Captain Julio del Busto and Sancho de la Bimera, shipmaster. These vessels carried twenty-five Lutherans, who had been denounced to the Adelantado by the Holy Inquisition at Seville. After making an investigation, he had ordered the men held as prisoners, and was now sending them to Santo Domingo or Puerto Rico, to be sent back to Seville. They managed, however, to kill the captain and the shipmaster, as well as the other Catholics on board. They set sail for their home then, but were wrecked on the coast of Denmark in a violent storm, after having passed within sight of Spain, France, and Flanders. Thus did they finally leave the Adelantado's galliass, which was one of the two ships sent to Hispaniola, and was of one thousand tons burden. . . .

Menéndez had remained behind to put the finishing touches to the fort. Leaving his brother Bartolomé in command, he now set out with twenty men to find the Florez' party. Forces joined at midnight. Lieutenant de Cornas returned and reported having sighted campfires and a great force of people. The French, he said, were apparently about a league beyond their side of the river. Menéndez ordered the advance resumed, and sometime after midnight they reached the estuary, where they halted. The following morning, having concealed his men in the thickets, the Adelantado climbed a tree and from there spied the multitude of people moving about on the opposite shore. He could see the flags of two companies of troops. When later he came closer, however, the people proved too numerous to count. He approached within view of the

enemy—so that from his aggressive attitude and unconcern they might gather he had a numerous force with him. As soon as the French saw him, one of the Lutherans swam across to our side.

Menéndez had dressed himself in a French outfit and wore a cape, while in his hand he carried the short, gilt-pointed, tasseled lance of a Spanish captain. He stood alone with his Frenchman near the riverbank, a short distance from his men. The Adelantado's Frenchman recognized the Lutheran who was swimming across. Turning to Menéndez he said: "Would you please spare the life of the man coming to us, for my sake, for he is my wife's brother and a Catholic." Coming to shore, the swimmer did not know the Adelantado and pretended not to know his own brother-in-law, until the latter told him not to be frightened, for he was not going to die. The swimmer fell at the Adelantado's feet, and there declared that all the people on the opposite bank were French; they had been lost in the storm, and, their ships driven ashore, had been castaway. They were six hundred in number, plus twenty captains. All served under Jean Ribaut, viceroy and captain in that land for the King of France. This was the stock claim made by these heretics to lend authority to their evil designs; but they spoke falsely, for in these days the King of France was an ally and close kin to our most formidable King Philip, who was married to the renowned and Catholic Elizabeth, our Queen. All of their party, he said, were Lutherans of the New Religion; thus did they designate their diabolically perverse and heretical sect. The Adelantado queried why had he been sent across the river. To see what people were on the opposite shore, he answered. Did he want to return, he was asked. He did not, he said, he wished to remain with the Adelantado. The swimmer spoke Spanish quite well, for he was a Gascon from Saint-Jean-de-Luz. He was told to return, and take this message: The speaker was Adelantado and captain general of this land; his name was Pedro Menéndez; and he was present with some number of his soldiers to reconnoiter the other party. . . .

Menéndez directed Admiral Diego Florez de Valdéz to bring the French across as they had the first contingent, in groups of ten. Ribaut was led into the bushes, behind the same sand dune where the others had been taken. The same command as before was issued and, excepting Ribaut, they were all ordered bound. The Adelantado once more explained how they must proceed four leagues farther, and how they could not be allowed to go unbound. Once they were tied, he asked them if they were Catholics or Lutherans, and if there was anyone who wished to confess himself. They were, each of them, of the New Religion, said Captain Ribaut. From earth had they come, and to earth they must return. Twenty years, one way or another, was of small moment in the general sum. The Adelantado might do with them as he would.

Menéndez now ordered them marched off as before. At the same line where the others had fallen, he ordered this group cut down. The fifers, drummers, and trumpeters alone were spared, in addition to four men who said they were Catholics—in all, sixteen people. The rest were knifed to death. As regards Ribaut, Menéndez had ordered Captain Juan de San Vicente and Gonzalo de Solís de Merás to take him away, after having privately commanded them to kill him. Ribaut had been wearing a felt hat and Captain San Vicente now asked him for it. When it was handed him he said: "You know that captains must obey their generals and carry out their orders, and so we must tie your hands." His hands bound, Ribaut was marched ahead for a little distance. Captain San Vicente then thrust a knife in his belly, and Gonzalo de Solís ran him through the heart with a pike; then they cut off his head.

Among those killed in this group was Captain Esparza de Artiaga, one of the leading gentlemen of Navarre, who had been sent as a prisoner to the Court by the Duke of Albuquerque, when the latter was Viceroy at Navarre. He had been subsequently released and allowed to go to France, and had now come with Jean Ribaut. Also put to the knife was Captain Cossette [Corceto], a soldier famous on land and sea and a mortal enemy of the Spaniards. Many French nobles perished, including M. de Jaueni's nephew by the same name, Captain Langrage, Captain Sainte-Marie, and many other brave captains and gentlemen.

When the justice deserved by these men had been meted out, the Adelantado sent his force under command of two captains in pursuit of those Lutherans who had refused to surrender. This party crossed the river and then traversed the beach. They did not know where the French had gone, but some Indians told them they had taken refuge in a near-by woods. The Spanish thereupon fired the thicket. They searched all they could, but no one was found; the French had drawn farther away. Night was approaching, and provisions had not been brought up; our men, therefore, returned to camp.

25.

Thus was justice meted out to those Lutheran tyrants who aspired to seize what was not theirs and to establish sovereignty where they had neither right nor reason to be. Thus it was that Our Lord, the Supreme Judge, confronted them with a strict, just, and incorruptible judge, to make them pay for their doubly nefarious crime of heresy and tyranny. It was already late when this so justly deserved punishment was administered. Night was falling, but the Adelantado ordered the return march, for he knew the danger to which his headquarters and men were exposed in the absence of their chief. The fort was reached some little time after midnight.

There, as it is man's nature to judge the deeds of others rather than to take action, the Adelantado's heroic conduct in putting the Lutherans to the knife was deprecated and misunderstood by some, and he was thought cruel. His partisans thought he had done well, and argued he had acted as a good captain should. No one considered the fact that food stocks were low even for the Spaniards themselves, let alone for so many additional men, and that they would all have died of hunger, whether they were Catholics or not. This reason alone justified the action. Nor was any consideration given the fact that the French numbered six hundred soldiers, all well equipped, while the Spaniards were few in number. They would daily have been a source of alarm to the Spaniards, for it could be anticipated that the French would be devising some treachery to revenge the fall of their fort and the deaths of their comrades at San Mateo, so that those who had vanquished the French might now die at their hands. Also forgotten was the military proverb: "Of the enemy, the least possible number." And that other proverb: "A dead man tells no tales."

These Lutherans were enemies of our Holy Catholic Faith. They had already subverted and agitated the once flourishing, powerful, and

Christian kingdom of France, having taken arms against its King and its law. Had not the Adelantado treated them as they deserved, strong grounds would have existed for a protest from the King of France, who could have complained to our King Philip on the Adelantado's not having availed himself of the opportunity to punish the lost souls of that evil sect (who in his own kingdom sought his death). To have sent them back to France would have been even less to his liking, for since they were all Lutherans, the number of his enemies at home would have thereby been increased. Safely ensconced in France, they would have continued to plan a return with greater numbers of supporters and ships, in order to gain revenge. Thus would Florida find itself in a state of ceaseless turmoil and agitation. Then, too, had he not killed them, it would have been said that he refrained, not from mercy, but in order to collect the ransom agreed upon. Had he spared their lives only to have some of our own men lose theirs as the price of sustaining the French, and as a consequence be forced to abandon the country, our Catholic King would have had more than enough grounds for censuring him severely and punishing him for not having foreseen such a development. The fact that food stocks were low was self-evident at the time. For the fort at San Mateo had burned with the loss of all its stores, so that their needs there had to be supplied from St. Augustine. Had the Adelantado wanted to send them back to their own country, he had neither the necessary ships nor stores.

In addition to all these reasons, which should be more than sufficient, Menéndez would have violated his orders from the King had he not killed them—for it was to do precisely this that His Majesty sent him to Florida, to drive them from the land and strike them down as damned men who attempt, against the law of God and man, to take what is not theirs. The Adelantado learned, furthermore, from the Lutheran youths he captured, that when the French fleet set out to attack the Spaniards, Ribaut and his men had drunk a toast to the Adelantado's head and another to the lives of his followers; they had drunk two pipes of wine, and had jeered at the Spaniards, calling them convert Jews and Moors. They would, they had said, hang them all from the yardarms of their ships. It was God's judgment that within twenty days the drinkers themselves should lose their heads—at the hands, moreover, of the very people they cursed.

On his part, Menéndez acted like a good inquisitor, for when he asked them if they were Catholics or Lutherans, they dared publicly proclaim themselves Lutherans, without fear of God or human shame. This conduct he rewarded by the death their insolence deserved. In his method of meting out death he proved merciful, moreover, since he nobly and honorably put them to the sword, when by every right he could have burnt them alive. He was censured, however, for inhumanely condemning so many souls to hell forever, while had he waited they might have been saved. The Adelantado, on the other hand, had convinced himself that they were in league with the Devil, for when brought face to face with death they still proclaimed themselves Lutherans. In all their dealings during their lives they had never drawn back or shown fear, and so they were very likely to continue on their wicked course. Through their talk and evil influence they might well have sown discord among the Spanish themselves and polluted their pure Christianity.

For my part, I hold and firmly believe that he killed them by divine inspiration, rather than from any dictate of human understanding, for he did not want his people to be smeared and blackened by handling pitch. In this spirit did His Majesty approve his action, as he afterwards wrote so soon as he learned of the encounter, in the following formal sentences, which are extracted from the letter signed by his royal hand:

"We have been most gratified to learn of the success you have scored in your undertaking. We have in memory the loyalty, love, and diligence with which you have served us, and the labors and dangers in which you have placed youself, so that we may grant you favor. We are sure that in the future you will carry on in the manner we have come to expect from one of your character and virtue. As concerns the justice you meted out to the Lutheran corsairs who attempted to occupy and fortify Florida in order to sow the seeds of their wicked sect and from there extend their campaign of depredations and damage against the service of God and ourselves, we believe you were fully justified and acted with entire prudence. We feel we have been well served by your action."

The Adelantado had at once written His Majesty about his good fortune, giving an account of developments and Captain Diego Florez had carried the letters. In these reports Menéndez explained that the fort at San Mateo had burned; he had not waited for the fleet out of Spain which had been scattered by the storm; he had not yet embarked the people His Majesty had assigned him from the islands; the contingent under Risa had not yet appeared; and he was in need of men and supplies.

Chapter Thirty-six
The Diplomatic Context of
the Franco-Spanish Conflict in America

THIS EPISODE, lasting from 1562 to 1569, was a continuation of the earlier involvement of France in Brazil during the years 1555–1559, and represented the attempt by France to obtain a foothold for herself somewhere in the more promising regions of the New World, since Canada had proved so unpromising in the 1540s. The French attempt failed primarily because it was not thought to be a sufficiently important one on which to challenge Spain to a new war (peace only having been achieved in 1559 after a long struggle). Spain had made it clear that she regarded French intervention in Florida as a hostile act. The other aspect is that the Florida intervention, as the Brazilian one before, was primarily the work of the Huguenots. During the years 1562 to 1565, the Florida venture was the responsibility of Gaspard de Coligny, Admiral of France, although Charles IX lent his (limited) authority to it by allowing Coligny to issue commissions in his name to the leaders of the Florida expeditions. The real ruler of France was the Queen Mother, Catherine de Médicis, whose son was the young king of France and whose daughter was the wife of Philip II. Catherine was willing to involve France in Florida so long as she could throw the odium it aroused in Spain onto the shoulders of Coligny. At the same time she was usually (until 1572) able to tolerate his retention of power over French maritime and colonial activities. Raimonde de Beccarie de Pavie, Baron de Fourquevaux, French ambassador in Spain, did his best to defend French activity in Florida. The French intervention in Florida brought Spanish recriminations in 1565 and French responses that the voyagers had gone indeed to New France, not New Spain. In 1565 both sides were aware of the nature and extent of the clash which was building up in Florida waters and let it take its course. Philip expected Menéndez to win. Catherine and Coligny alike hoped that a French victory might give them cause to press for the further extension of French claims. But to Catherine the whole affair was secondary. The actual achievement of Menéndez in destroying the French colony was known in France long before Spain made her official protest in March, 1566. Although Catherine deplored the killing of Frenchmen out of hand and retained her claim that the land of Florida was French not Spanish, she did not make a major diplomatic issue of the matter. She allowed Spain to get away with no more than a formal protest at her actions.

No attempt has been made here to give a full selection of the diplomatic exchanges, but merely to provide a few illustrations of the sort of documents that were being exchanged. The episode attracted Parkman who gave a full account of it in his *Pioneers of France in the New World*. Paul Gaffarel, *La Floride française* (Paris, 1875), provided a good account from the French side, and printed many of the documents. *Lettres de Catherine de Médicis*, edited by Hector de la Ferrière-Percy, II (Paris, 1885), especially pp. 337–341, and *Dépêches de M. de Fourquevaux*, edited by Célestin Douais, 3 vols. (Paris, 1896–1904), contain almost all the French materials; some additional items of substantial value will be found in the André de

Coppet Collection, Department of Manuscripts, Princeton University (though many are already in print). Henry Folmer, *Franco-Spanish Rivalry in North America, 1524–1763* (Glendale, Calif., 1932), is useful, as are the appropriate sections in Charles de la Roncière, *Histoire de la marine française*, 2nd edition, IV (Paris, 1923), especially pp. 63–65, and Charles-André Julien, *Les voyages de découverte et les premiers établissements* (Paris, 1948). It appears as only a minor episode in most Spanish treatments of their New World enterprises in the sixteenth century.

318. November, 1565. Philip II complains to Charles IX about the activities of his French subjects in Florida.

Through his ambassador Francisco de Alava, Philip II delivered a formal written protest, as well as a verbal one, as soon as he knew that the French Florida colony had been destroyed by Pedro Menéndez de Avilés (even though he concealed this knowledge). The original has not been located. It was published from a copy in Bibliothèque Nationale (B.N.), Fonds français 10751, fols. 57–61, in Célestin Douais, ed., Lettres de Charles IX à M. de Fourquevaux (Paris, 1897), p. 3; there is another copy in the André de Coppet Collection, Princeton University Library. Spanish, translated.

Complaint of the Ambassador of the Catholic King, presented to the Most Christian King about what happened in Florida.

His Majesty has been informed that some subjects of his brother the Most Christian King went to Florida to take over that province which was discovered and taken so many years ago by His Majesty, and ordered an expedition to be sent to punish them as pirates criminals and destroyers of the public peace; having made this provision, he would have thought no more of it, but the brotherhood he has with the Most Christian King, and the clarity and sincerity with which he has to proceed with him and with her [Catherine de Médicis] this friendship in every matter makes him unwilling to keep quiet about what has happened there, so that they should know about it and have the necessary order given to hold back those who are in Florida from this enterprise, and issue a prohibition with the necessary firmness that no more of their subjects should go to those areas; for it does not seem right that his brother the Most Christian King should be here, and in such a relation of love trust and brotherhood, while his subjects should go there and stir up trouble one against the other.

319. November 28, 1565. Charles IX delivers a written reply on Florida to the Spanish ambassador.

In November, 1565 King Charles IX gave a formal interview to Francisco de Alava, the Spanish ambassador, who delivered a verbal protest at French actions in Florida, handing the king Philip II's formal protest (318). The king, besides replying verbally, handed to him a formal response to Philip II's protest. In writing on November 28 to M. de Fourquevaux, his ambassador in Spain, Charles reported the protest and its reply and went on to say that "when all is said, I do not see much point in my attempting to frustrate a thing where my subjects have for long planted my arms and possess without interference." He did not yet know that the French colony had been destroyed.

The "Résponse" was copied and sent with Charles IX's letter to Fourquevaux on November 28, 1565. It was printed by Paul Gaffarel, La Floride française (Paris, 1875), p. 413, and (from the original in the Chateau de Fourquevaux) by Célestin Douais, ed., Lettres de Charles IX à M. de Fourquevaux (Paris, 1897), p. 3.

Reply of the King concerning the Florida question.

The King does not intend that his subjects should encroach in any way or in any place whatever, upon the lands possessed and conquered by his good brother the Catholic King of the Spains. But all the same it would not be reasonable if his Catholic Majesty should wish to prevent, curb and coerce [coarcter] the freedom of his Majesty's subjects to sail the seas to such an extent that they could not undertake navigation and settling in other places, even in that which was discovered, almost a hundred years ago, by the latter's subjects, and which has ever since that time (as testimony and in remembrance of its discovery by the French) been known as the Land and Coast of the Bretons. But if his Catholic Majesty thinks that the French should intend to undertake there, whether by land or by sea, anything which might be prejudicial to the subjects and lands of his Catholic Majesty, the King of France will be ever ready to listen to any permissible methods by which the necessary order and security may be achieved there. And if the latter's subjects should forget themselves and do anything to jeopardize the peace treaty, he will have them so severely punished, it will be well known that his sole desire and intention is to live perpetually in the mutual sincerity and fraternal friendship which until now have been preserved and maintained between these two Majesties.

320. January 20, 1566. Letter by Catherine de Médicis, the Queen Mother, to M. de Fourquevaux about Spanish pressure over the presence of French subjects in Florida.

Although unofficially news of the French disaster in Florida had long before reached France and the details were well known at court, official news from Spanish sources had not yet arrived when this letter was written. In it the Queen Mother expresses her strong resentment at the threatening pressure which was being applied at the French Court on behalf of Philip II by his ambassador Francisco de Alava. She is, of course, telling a diplomatic lie when she says that her son, King Charles IX, was in no way responsible

for the Florida ventures, since both René de Laudonnière and Jean Ribault had gone to Florida with commissions under his name, issued by the Admiral of France, Coligny, with his knowledge.

Printed from the copy in B.N., Paris, Fonds français 10751, fols. 162–167, in Hector de la Ferrière-Percy, ed., Lettres de Catherine de Médicis, II (Paris, 1885), 337–41. The original letter is in the André de Coppet Collection, Princeton University Library. French, translated.

Monsieur de Fourquevaux,

In my last dispatch I undertook to inform you later of what I should learn from the Spanish ambassador on the occasion of the gentleman you recently sent here bringing his dispatch. I had expected the gentleman sooner, but I can tell you that, since his indisposition has prevented his coming to see me for two days, he has not been to an audience and has not said a single word about the conversation that passed between my son-in-law the King of Spain, the Duke of Alva, the Prince of Eboli and yourself concerning the marriages, which are mentioned in the memorandum you gave to the gentleman. Nor has he touched upon anything that might lead one to believe he has received any written communication on the subject. I, for my own part, have given nothing away either, and will wait until time and opportunity shed more light on the subject. In all this there is scarcely anything which has distressed me apart from the fact that you have shown your hand to such an extent without there being the slightest need for it. But I wrote enough about all that in my last dispatch.

What the ambassador said was that his master wishes to know whether my son the King ordered those who went to Florida to undertake the venture and to engage in trade over there, and whether he accepts responsibility for them, especially as it would be against our mutual friendship and the excellent peace that exists between us. My reply was that he and his master the King have had ample opportunity of judging from our actions how much we have always desired the preservation of this peace and friendship; and we do desire it most particularly, being of the opinion that it is mutually useful to both of us, for our individual well-being and for the universal good of

Christendom. This should really make the ambassador believe that, if some of our subjects have entered a land belonging to his master the King and have undertaken any venture there, it has not been done with the knowledge or at the behest of my son the King or myself. As regards trade, we have always considered it free between subjects of friendly powers, and held the view that the sea is closed to no man who goes and trades in good faith. I well knew that some of our people had gone to a land called the Land of the Bretons, discovered long ago by subjects of this crown; in so doing they had no thought of undertaking anything prejudicial to this peace and friendship. Nor did we think they had in any way erred, since it is a land we consider our own. But if they had done wrong and touched anything belonging to the King of Spain, I said that they would have been reprimanded long since and ordered to do something about it, and then to leave with the assurance that my son the King would make them realise how much they had offended him. Such have always been our intentions in these matters. I said also that if our subjects were on our own land, we believed his master the King would not wish to molest them or to prevent their trading. If his people were willing not to interfere with ours, so he would find we would reciprocate.

The ambassador showed himself little satisfied with all these reasons, although they are just and true, and came to tell me that his master could not tolerate such behaviour without resenting it. He added some words that I took for threats. I told him that as the mother of these two kings, it was likely I would be extremely distressed, should any occasion arise to spoil that friendship which I wish with everything in my power to preserve between them. It seemed to me he ought to be satisfied with the truth which I was giving him and to be convinced of the sincerity of our actions in this and every other circumstance, where neither he nor his master would find anything exceptionable. I told him also he should remember that the kings of France are not accustomed to let themselves be threatened; that my son might be very young, but was for all that so conscious of his status, that it was always more difficult to restrain than to goad him and that before long he would be taking offense at the least provocation. In my opinion his master would gain nothing by this. I was disposed to believe that the threat did not come from his master.

This reply, that of a mother who knows her son well and who would not on any account wish him to be less courageous and honourable that his predecessors, brought the ambassador back to milder words. He said that what he was doing was a result of his desire to see the affection between us going from strength to strength; that his master had no less an opinion of our goodwill towards him, than we ought to have of his goodwill towards us. But he said that he had heard others were speaking about the Florida incident in different terms. So it was that in the end he was satisfied with our reasons, and afterwards came on to the topic of various depradations made on the subjects of his master the King, which are special cases and for which he was now seeking justice. I assured him it would be done so well that I ask none better for our subjects when they have interests over there. I wish that those responsible for such misdeeds were equally loyal observers of the laws, and of the goodwill which my son the King and I bear towards this land, as is necessary. The fact remains that you can make assurances everywhere that I will always be ready to punish those found guilty so severely that their example will bring law and order over there, which is what I desire. Moulins, the 20th day of January, 1566.

[signed:] Caterine

321. February 18, 1566. M. de Fourquevaux gives Charles IX details of the Spanish victory in Florida.

M. de Fourquevaux had, before this letter was written, learnt in general terms of the French defeat and the Spanish victory in Florida. In this letter he gives the first circumstantial details that had reached Spain. The man who told it had come on Jacques Ribault's ship, which had arrived some time before at La Rochelle, and so his father's fate and that of the colony had long spread through France. This man Perrico, who told the tale, was a Basque whose basic allegiance was to Spain and so it was, ironically, from a survivor of La Caroline that Fourquevaux was able to get the first story.

Dépêches de M. de Fourquevaux, edited by Célestin Douais, 3 vols. (Paris, 1896–1904), I, 57, translated.

Sire, I wrote to Your Majesty on 11th of this month about a fellow from Biscay called Perrico, who having arrived at La Rochelle with Jean Ribbault's son, came bursting with news of Florida to tell his story to the Catholic King. He says he married the sister of an Indian chief twenty leagues away from the French fort; he speaks the Indian language better than Spanish or even his native tongue. For this reason the Spanish King is sending him back over there as ambassador, in order to win over his brother-in-law and other native kings to hostility against the French. He is taking them clothing, swords, daggers, knives, chisels, axes and other similar things as presents from His Majesty, and he is under instruction to penetrate as deeply as possible into the country.

Definite news of Florida came by a cousin of Pedro Menéndez who arrived last Saturday. He has described how Pedro Menéndez, advancing with his naval force to attack the French in the harbor, experienced a nocturnal storm which scattered all the ships, leaving him alone with just one large galley. Fearing that if he waited for daybreak he would be sighted and followed by four French ships that were in the harbor, he put out to sea. Then at first light he retired into an estuary on the coast of Florida ten miles from the French fort, so that he could hide while waiting for his force to reassemble, which it did. Thereupon, Sire, Captain Jean Ribbault, who had sighted the naval force, intending to go out and fight the Spanish, borrowed men from the fort leaving behind only a handful. He guessed that because of the storm a part of their force would have taken shelter in the estuary, and so he made his way towards it. A further storm arose, however, so violent that the four French ships capsized, the men escaping to the shore and assembling in two troops a few leagues apart from one another.

Pedro Menéndez in the meantime had disembarked four hundred soldiers who crossed the swamps up to their armpits in water because of the heavy rains and arrived at the fort in five days. They easily captured it, for only a very few soldiers had remained there; they were all killed apart from four or five who escaped, the captain being one; the women and children were spared. After that, Sire, hearing of the shipwreck, they set off to find one of the troops of Frenchmen, perhaps two hundred of them unarmed and dying

of hunger. A small stream between the two sides halted the Spanish, so that the French had an opportunity to use all the arguments they, as soldiers, could think of in an attempt to soften the hearts of their enemies. The Spanish, nonetheless, rejecting this plea for mercy, killed them all. They then proceeded as far as the place where captain Jean Ribbault was, on the other side of a small river [illegible] about four hundred men as naked and starving as the first troop had been. Ribbault when he saw the Spanish approaching, sent a sergeant in a little boat to request that they be treated well, as befitted subjects and soldiers of the King of France, the friend and brother-in-law of their lord the King of Spain. The Spanish refused and shouted to the French that they could kill each other if they wished, for they were destined to die without mercy. Thereupon forty or fifty of the French troop fled to the mountains and no news has been heard of them since. Ribbault, notwithstanding his protestations that it was Your Majesty who had sent him out there, had his head cut off; all his companions were massacred apart from one drummer, one fife-player and one carpenter.

Menéndez continued with the fortification of the fort and the conquest and exploration of the country. Presumably the army now being sent over there by the Catholic King will do the same. The man who brought this news is called Florez and was received with great delight. In fact the court here rejoiced even more than if it had been news of a victory against the Turks. They have said also, and are still saying that Florida brings them in more than Malta. As a reward for Menéndez's massacre of your unfortunate subjects, Florida is to be made a marquisate and he is to be created its marquis.

The marquis of Falces is going as viceroy to New Spain and I hear that the fleets which are supposed to be going not only to Peru but also to New Spain and to Florida will be sailing in convoy from Seville.

322. March 2, 1566. Philip II to Guzmán de Silva, his ambassador in England, on Florida.

Before his ambassador in France had formally protested about the French colony in Florida and admitted it had been destroyed, Philip II sent the views he wished to convey to Queen Elizabeth I to his ambassador in London. These were to the effect that Coligny alone appeared to be responsible for the French being in Florida but that he had written to protest their presence to the French Crown.

Entry Book of Letters, Diego de Guzmán de Silva Papers, Pierpont Morgan Library, New York, translated. Published (with permission) for the first time.

A matter has arisen here which you should be informed of: we received information that a number of French pirates had gone to occupy the Province of Florida, which was discovered many years ago and taken into possession in the name of the Crown: since it is a place which, as you must know, anyone who wished to disrupt the trade to the Indies could use to disrupt ours to such an extent that trade could hardly be carried on at all, we made this known to the King of France, and the Queen His Mother: they replied to us several times that these Frenchmen had not gone there, nor would any others of their subjects ever go to our lands at their orders and instruction, so we sent Pero Menéndez de Avilés with ships and men to throw them out of there: which they did, as effectively as you will see from an account which is being sent to you with this letter, so that you should know how all this has ended, and you may inform Her Highness the Queen of England of this, and anyone else you wish: but do not give a copy of it to anyone, for that is most convenient. And since, in addition to what is included in this account, from certain documents discovered in Florida, and from the confessions of some of those who were captured alive, as far as we have managed to find out so far it looks as though it was the Admiral of France who had made that expedition and who had ordered the Frenchmen who were there to go and occupy the place where they had fortified themselves, with the intention of going on further to occupy others of our ports and settlements, to the damage and harm of the voyages of our subjects: so we have sent a letter of complaint to the Queen Mother and the King her son, saying that as I had told them would happen from the start I had sent someone to punish these pirates as justly as they deserved, who were aiming to disrupt the public peace, and give a bad

name to the good friendship and brotherhood that exists between us, for which very same reason and cause, since it had been this Admiral who had arranged what had been attempted against us in those parts, we could not omit to ask them with urgency that they should order him to be punished as exemplarily as his insolence and the extreme nature of the case requires: and that if any subject of mine, whatever his rank, should dare to do anything against them, I would punish him with such a severe example that it would prevent anyone else from daring to try such a venture again. In this matter I have instructed Don Francés de Álava to make to these Christian Kings most forceful and pressing representations over the punishment of this Admiral, and that if they do that they will be doing what they ought and what is most suitable of all for them to do, for it is so widely and well known that he is the poison of that kingdom, and the source and organizer of all the plots that are hatched and carried out there.

We shall see how they receive that in France, and I will order that you be informed of whatever reply I may get from there.

Madrid, 2nd March 1566.

I, the King.
G. Pérez.

[Addressed.] To Diego de Guzmán de Silva of His Majesty's Council and His Embassy in England.

323. March 17, 1566. Catherine de Médicis to M. de Fourquevaux protesting about the Spanish massacre.

The Spanish ambassador delivered his official protest at the intrusion of the French and his explanation of the harsh treatment of them by Pedro Menéndez de Avilés, by which time Catherine knew details of the massacre from other sources. She brushed aside the complaint that these men were Huguenots and maintained they were Frenchmen operating on soil long discovered and claimed by France. Her dignified protest however did not contain any threat of reprisals since she was, ultimately, willing to give way to Spain and not make this a cause over which France could fight.

Printed from B.N., Fonds Français 10751, fol. *199 ff., in* Lettres de Catherine de Médicis, *edited by Hector de la Ferrière-Percy, II (Paris, 1885), 358–62; the original is in the André de Coppet Collection, Princeton University Library, translated.*

Monsieur de Fourquevaux,

Before the Spanish ambassador had sent his courier, your first missive arrived, as mentioned in our other dispatch. By this dispatch of yours I have been informed in great detail of this wretched massacre in Florida, of the Duke of Alva's conversation with you on the subject, and of your reply to him, which was excellent, pertinent and just what such a cruel and inhuman business requires. Until yesterday I had preferred not to make any fuss and not to admit that I knew anything about it, but yesterday the Spanish ambassador, after requesting an audience with my son the King, and with me, presented himself. After speaking of various other matters, he told us he had been commanded by his master, my son-in-law, to notify us that a captain had arrived in Spain with the following news.

In Florida Pedro Menéndez came across some Frenchmen under the patronage of his Excellency the Admiral, who had provided them with letters of support. The Frenchmen had among their number several ministers, who were disseminating the new religion, and Menéndez had chastised them, as, so he maintains, his master the King of Spain had ordered. He freely admitted that it had been done a little more severely and cruelly than his master would have wished, but, he said, he could do no less than attack them as though they were pirates and men who had come to encroach upon that which belonged to his King. In spite of this admission, his master the King, so he said, was demanding justice of the Admiral.

My son the King, who was still in bed quite weak as a result of his illness, from which by the grace of God he is now completely recovered, wanted me to answer the ambassador. My reply was that I already knew about the massacre from a man who had returned from Florida; that, as the common mother, I could not but feel an unbelievable heartache at the news that subjects of my son the King had been so foully slaughtered, when princes are so friendly, so allied and so related as

are these two kings, when we have been accustomed to see such a goodly state of peace between them and such dutiful feelings of friendship. I replied that until now I had not wanted to speak of the massacre to my son the King because of his illness; that I was beside myself when I thought about it; that I could not believe that his master the King would not make reparation and see justice done. For, I continued, there was not any point in hushing it all up on the avowal of the Admiral that it was a storm in a teacup, since it was unlikely that the Admiral had allowed so many people to leave this kingdom except with the authority [*sous le sceu (= sceau?) du Roy mon fils*] of my son the King, who is of the opinion that trade and shipping are free everywhere to his subjects. I told him that this land where the incident occurred is not the King of Spain's, but was discovered so long ago by our subjects that it still bears their name, as you have already made quite plain to the King and his ministers. Even if our subjects had entered lands of his master the King and done things inappropriate between friends, the Spanish ought to have been satisfied with taking them prisoner and then handing them over to my son the King for punishment, if they had done wrong, without treating them as they have done. I could not believe, I added, that the King of Spain would not give us satisfaction. It seemed one was trying to bridle my son the King, to imprison him within the confines of this kingdom, to clip his wings, something which he could not tolerate, nor would he be advised to do so. This sort of approach was providing my son the king with a very good reason for changing his policy and for looking after his affairs by different methods, which he will well know how to do, God willing. Nor did he lack the means, so I was hoping that he would not care a jot for his neighbors, nor respect them more than they respected him. My son's kingdom, thanks be to God, was in a goodly state of peace, and he himself better obeyed than ever, from which the conclusion could easily be drawn that it would not be at all difficult for him to make it known and felt to those wishing him ill that he had no lesser means of self-protection than those kings who had preceded him.

The ambassador was constantly trying to put the blame on the Admiral. He said there were ministers of religion there, which was most displeasing to his master, but I replied that we had not made enquiries about the kind of people going on the voyage, and that if one could make wishes, mine would be that all the Huguenots were in that land, where his master the King cannot with truth pretend he has interests, since the land is ours, as we claim. The Spanish were making it obvious to us that they were scarcely in favour of peace in this kingdom, since they wished to deprive us of every means of achieving it. In any case it was not their business to punish our subjects; we were not arguing about whether our subjects there professed the new religion or not, but about the murder that the Spanish had committed, for which it was extremely reasonable that his master should see justice done, as we were demanding.

At this point it seemed to me that the ambassador was lost for a reply, and he set himself to bolster up his complaints. He spoke to us about Corsica, whither according to him several ships are in the habit of sailing from Provence laden with victuals, arms and men; the Genoese were complaining about them. I satisfied him very well on this point and he agreed it was a case of the usual lies. He spoke also of some galleys which, he said, we were arming at Marseille. This I confessed to be the truth, the purpose being to protect our coasts which are infested with innumerable corsairs, attracted by his quarrel with us, whom we have with great distress tolerated out of respect for him. When all is said and done, he has assembled a host of complaints to lend credence to the one about Florida, where there is just as little foundation.

He left the audience with the certain knowledge that we were extremely displeased with him; nor is he under the impression that we will forget it. I wanted to write to you about all this at length on behalf of my son the King, imploring and commanding you to make his Majesty the Catholic King understand it, and to beg him very affectionately in the name of duty and reason to make reparation and see justice done, as such a momentous outrage demands, thereby providing worthy proof of the friendship and peace that exist between us. Let his Majesty also consider the wrong he would be doing us by not affording us satisfaction; my son the King is expecting it and I for my part wish it too. For I will never be at ease nor perfectly content until I see his Catholic Majesty matching the sincerity of our affections and our actions with regard to him; I would be very annoyed to think they had been abused. I

would be unbelievably sorry, if all the trouble, care and means, by which I have sought to nurture these two princes and their crowns in a state of perpetual peace, should prove of no avail; if instead of the good which I hoped to see come from it, the King my son should one day reproach me that while he was relying on me to conduct his affairs, I allowed such damage to be done to his reputation.

I implore you that in your next dispatch you will enlighten me and assure me that the ambassador has not forgotten anything in passing on all I have said to him about the harm being inflicted on the well-being of this kingdom, which is what I seek. For, to speak frankly, I believe that the Huguenots in Florida could not have wished for better news, for by it they know that the friendship we expect from Spain is illusory, seeing that our subjects are treated thus. I hope God will not let it go unpunished.

I wish you to make all this quite clear to my daughter the Queen, in support of the letter I am writing to her, and you will show her this letter, if she wishes to see it.

I have after all looked at what you write about the marriages, which have been somewhat driven from my mind. My son the King is quite young enough to wait for something better, and he is such a great prince that it is not possible he should ever lack the opportunity of choosing from the whole of Christendom, whatever obstacle is thought up, as I know and understand is done. Praying that God will take care of you, Monsieur de Fourquevaux. Written at Moulins, 17th day of March, 1566.

[signed:] Caterine

I cannot help myself telling you further that other parties are offering themselves for my son the King; they are among the greatest in Christendom. The worst fear I have is that it will in the end be necessary, because of the wrong done to him, for him to take a bride not of our religion; we will only resort to this in desperation.

324. [1566–1567]. Statement on behalf of Pedro Menéndez de Avilés on the reasons for his actions in Florida.

The most satisfaction the French Court could obtain from Spain was a statement that Philip II induced Pedro de Menéndez de Avilés to make, possibly as late as Menéndez's return to Spain in July, 1567. The French were, in his view, pirates whom he could execute at will. Further, he had no supplies or prisons for such numbers. His only solution was to kill them, which he did.

The original has not been located. Copy, André de Coppet Collection, Princeton University Library. Spanish, translated; apparently published (with permission) for the first time.

The reasons that the Governor Pero Menéndez de Avilés had for not being able to do anything other than what he did in Florida.

The said Governor, Pero Menéndez de Avilés, was carrying in his Orders the general section which is usually given in all Orders to the captains that are sent against pirates, that is, that if he finds any he may hang and execute them without leaving any. He arrived at Florida with a third of his fleet, because, in view of the need for speedy action, he did not want to wait for the rest. He was there with two hundred and fifty men: the French soldiers he held outside the fort would be as many as his own men, or more. If he wanted to keep them with him, he had no way of guarding against the chance that at any minute they might rise up and cut the throats of his men and himself: all the more so since Pero Menéndez had to leave there and go to other places where he had been sent and he needed to go. If he took them with him, being, as he was, fewer in numbers than them, that would be placing himself at their mercy: as for giving them ships to leave in, he did not have them, nor the provisions for them even if he had had them: and if it is possible to judge the future on the basis of what happens in the present, it was quite obvious that such a large number of soldiers would do, for a few of those that Pero Menéndez imprisoned in his own ship took possession of it, killed the Spaniards on guard, and, under strong winds, eventually landed up in Denmark. And to leave them on land, while leaving so few Spaniards in the fort as he was going to have to do, would have meant handing the fort over to them, and its people with it. As for leaving them on land, saying that they had no arms and so could do no harm, it is clear that from the people who actually lived in that country they could get arms to help them, to overwhelm and barricade the Spaniards in the fort, and starve them out. So all the things he could have done with them—i.e., as said, taking them with him, or giving them ships, or leaving them as prisoners of the men in the fort, or leaving them on land and forgetting about them—had obvious drawbacks, none less than the possibility that Pero Menéndez could lose his men, and the fort, and the object of his mission, and it can be clearly seen that for these reasons he had no option to do other than he did. From which it can be easily seen that what he did was as a precautionary measure against the possibilities mentioned rather than as punishment, although the punishment was very well deserved; and this cannot and ought not be attributed or ascribed to cruelty (if one fully appreciates the position Pero Menéndez was in) any more than it could be ascribed to cruelty if, mindful of the proper defence of the state, his King and his men, and himself, he had had them executed.

IX

Spanish Florida I

The creation of Spanish Florida was a military necessity. Pedro Menéndez de Avilés might suffer at times from delusions of grandeur which led Narváez, Hernando de Soto, and Luna to disaster, but his main objective was to settle Spanish garrisons in the Southeast, so that France or England might never again threaten the Spanish Caribbean and the fleets which sailed from there. The experiments of the period 1565 to 1574 that Menéndez made were of considerable interest and involved the first serious attempt to transfer Spanish concepts of urban settlement to North America, but they were peripheral to the creation and maintenance of a military presence and their failure did not basically alter the overriding official military objective of Philip II's government. At the same time they provide the first clear evidence we have of the practical problems of attempted colonial settlement on a substantial scale. Their interest is, therefore, much wider than the creation of military presence alone. Much of the resistance of European populations to adapt themselves to living conditions in North America, later to be exhibited by the English and French, were first to be experienced by the Spaniards in the early years of the Florida experiment.

Chapter Thirty-seven
The Creation of Spanish Florida,
1566–1574

THE HISTORY of Spanish Florida is one of the most persistent, significant, and revealing European initiatives in North America in the early phase of colonial settlement. It was built on the experiences and failures of the period from 1513 to 1561 which have already been chronicled, although it had behind it an enormous wealth of experience in empire-building. It started as an act of aggression against France that was seen from the Spanish point of view as merely the defense of a legitimate sphere of Spanish enterprise against illegitimate interlopers. It was begun with high hopes by a very able Spanish commander who expected to make of Florida much more than a mere holding garrison on the fringes of the Spanish land and maritime empire—which is how the governing authorities in both Mexico and Spain saw it—indeed a great and varied colony.

The eastern shore of the Florida Peninsula, which was the crucial area so far as defense of the fleets and the succoring of ships, sailors, and cargoes was concerned, was only one small item in the great domain that Pedro Menéndez de Avilés hoped to create. During the years in which Florida remained in his charge, from 1565 to 1574, he set his sights on control of the whole of the Gulf Coast, from Pánuco around to Florida, on the quelling of Indian resistance (long experienced by Spanish invaders) on the west coast of Florida, and on the exploration and eventual occupation of much of the east coast, perhaps as far as the Baccalaos (Newfoundland). He was concerned to explore the interior behind the Florida-Georgia-South Carolina coastland, which had been penetrated by Soto and which had bemused and misled Luna. He had a special interest in the Bahía de Santa María, the Bay of St. Mary (Chesapeake Bay), which he had entered and partly explored in 1561 (even though we lack details of what precisely he did there). An imperial vision that stretched from Mexico to Newfoundland was a proud one, even if, also, it was to be one that was quite beyond Menéndez's ability to encompass. In the end the exploring impetus that he provided was to be greater than the consolidation he attempted, and much greater still than what he was able in the end to achieve. In one sense his career in Florida is the climax of the application of the spirit of the *conquistadores* to North America—Oñate may be compared with him but is a much lesser figure. The wide vision, the immense energy, the failure to adapt to reality, all are reflected in him as they had been in Ponce de León, Narváez, Soto, Luna, and the rest. But, unlike his predecessors, he did not fail utterly and left a monument to himself, if not that which he would have wished, in Florida. Partly this was because of his own indomitable spirit: intolerant, cruel at times, but always resourceful. Ultimately it was due to something more mundane, the determination of the Viceroy in Mexico and of the Council of the Indies in Spain to keep Florida as a going concern, even if only for the lesser and narrower purpose of being a guardship for the fleets on their homeward track from the western Indies.

Menéndez de Avilés tried to do a great many things at once. When we consider that he concentrated his attention on Florida mainly into two years 1565–1567, his achievement was remarkable. After hunting down and slaughtering the last Frenchman (except for two or three bandsmen), he had to build up an administration from scratch. He filled most of the useful and superfluous offices alike with his own relatives, but some of them turned out to be useful assistants. He had to attempt to spread garrisons throughout the area—he aimed first to ring the peninsula east and west—and to fill in around the garrisons with civilians who would form the nucleus of a Spanish population. Finally, he had to come to terms with or destroy the native population. This latter activity employed his soldiers rather too fully for his liking, nor indeed was it always successful since the Indians often defeated and sometimes even ate his men; it also involved him in complex diplomacy in languages imperfectly understood. On the positive side, he began the long and only ultimately successful attempt to introduce Christianity to the Indians, both for the good of their souls and for the comfort of their Spanish neighbors. In his former objective he began well. At San Agustín (it seems best to keep the purely Spanish form rather than the American Saint Augustine, for the post-1763 city) he hoped as *adelantado* to lay out a great *encomienda*, an estate comprising many Indian villages whose inhabitants would supply labor and taxes in kind, an area cultivated by Spanish farmers brought from his native Asturias, and also plantations around his own major household worked by imported Negro slaves. But Avilés' Florida was never like this. To illustrate his attempted achievements and his failures would take a volume in itself, and even then we would be without some essential knowledge, since many documents of the early years are missing. His garrison-colony-mission stations, set up rapidly in 1565 and 1566, were quickly overrun by the Indians—especially those on the west where the Calusa were formidable foes—or they were starved out when essential supplies did not come, or they were deserted by their settlers when they could not make a living on the spot and they left for San Agustín or, if they could make it, Cuba. They might even be recalled by formal orders from San Agustín when the continuance of a post was seen to be useless. The major effort was put into San Agustín, although neither Indian tributaries, Spanish settlers, nor laboring Negro slaves created much impact on Anastasia Island (where San Agustín first was located) or on the facing mainland. Garrisons were maintained, and a small nucleus grew around the necessary offices of the administration and the ecclesiastical buildings essential to any Spanish settlement. San Mateo, too, and two small blockhouses at the mouth of the St. Johns River were maintained as symbols of victory over the French, but as a garrison group only. More importance was attached to Santa Elena, since this could act as a genuine outpost against a return of the French and could provide a springboard for further advances to the Carolina Outer Banks (formally annexed in 1566) or Chesapeake Bay (where a mission post was established in 1570). But Santa Elena was to be a Spanish colony as well as a garrison. Asturian farmers, given some livestock on onerous terms by Menéndez de Avilés, were installed, first it seems on the mainland and, then, after Indian attacks, huddled against the fort on the limited arable land of Parris Island. The garrison found means to survive, even if usually by plundering the neighboring Cusabo Indians, but the settlers found life very difficult, even intolerable. Some died; some drifted away on each supply ship that put in. They were reinforced from Spain itself in 1572 by the *adelantado* and again shortly before his death in 1574, but no roots were ever established.

One key to the great difficulty Spain had in establishing the Florida colony lay in finance. Philip II was willing to pay most of the costs of eliminating the French and to continue some payment in order to help to get the settlement under way. But at an early stage, after 1566, the crown only kept up payment for the limited garrison that was on the official establishment—150 men—except in an emergency. The *situado*, which was their pay, came from Mexico in cash, but it was seldom on time and never enough, nor was it intended to be, for the colony as a whole. Pedro Menéndez de Avilés was expected to pour his personal fortune into Florida. He did so during the first two years and continued to dole out large sums from time to time almost until his death. But he was supposed to make revenue and profits out of the colony by what he could grow there and sell elsewhere. This he never succeeded in doing. Some corn was grown for domestic use, and gradually gardens and even orchards were built up round the houses. Anastasia Island proved infertile, and it was repeatedly claimed that the mainland was not much better. The superior ground was occupied by Indian villages. These could and were made to supply a tax in corn, which was of some assistance. The men were employed for porterage, when they could be rounded up for this purpose. They did not make—nor were ever to make—reliable field labor. The Negro slaves were too few to create plantations for which the accessible land was in any case unsuitable, so they were either sent back to Havana or became household slaves only for members of the garrison. To begin with, the latter were mainly single men. Later, as farming settlers failed to establish themselves, soldiers were encouraged to send for wives, and so army families came to make up the bulk of the civilian population, such as it was, of San Agustín. The few high officials who decided to make their home in Florida also had households in San Agustín. The Negro slaves were distributed among these. But the great *hacienda* of Menéndez de Avilés himself never took shape so far as can be ascertained, although some fields were cultivated for his use. If there were married soldiers at San Mateo, they lived inside the fort compound not in a village outside. At Santa Elena successive handfuls of farmers' and of soldiers' families kept up some sort of tiny colony outside the fort perimeter. The missionaries, Dominicans and Jesuits alike, were, in the early years, totally unsuccessful, being both unintelligible and so alien in their outlook that the Indians took no notice whatever of them. Ultimately, except for one or two the Indians thought worth killing, they retreated for good. The rhythm of change in the early years was rapid—a great effort early in the year; then decline the following year; then, sometimes, disaster; then when supplies came, new efforts on a less ambitious scale; decline again and perhaps some examples of success. Then, again, a process of gradual attrition began. Gradually the scale of movement became slower. After 1567, when Menéndez de Avilés's prime task was serving the king in command of treasure fleets rather than in running Florida for himself, except for brief though effective visits, the scale of activity settled down to concentration on maintaining the three centers, San Agustín, San Mateo, and Santa Elena, with only occasional new initiatives that demanded investment of men and effort.

But exploration there was. This is more easily illustrated in documentary form than the complex ebb and flow of more routine activity. Menéndez learned much about the west coast of the Florida Peninsula, but the more he learned, the less he liked the Indians; his recommended program, and that of his successors, was mass murder or transportation, but the Calusa survived these threats though they didn't escape occasional raids. A similar program was projected for the tribes of the southern tip of the peninsula. A very promising initiative under the two soldiers, Pardo and Boyano, for a short time gave the colony some depth (331–334). They penetrated, by way of the Savannah River Valley, into the Piedmont and thence, over the Appalachians, into the Tennessee Valley. From Santa Elena, briefly, a chain of posts was

established as far as Soto's (and Luna's) Coosa. Great things were hoped of this expedition, even
a land link to Mexico. But the forces were too small and were not supported. After two seasons
they passed into a limbo from which they never emerged. The attempt to repenetrate the
interior was not resumed for some thirty years. In 1566, too, Menéndez de Avilés stretched out,
as he hoped, toward the Chesapeake, but the reconnaissance expedition he sent could not find
an entry. Making its way south, a landing was made and the Carolina Outer Banks, as they are
known to us, were formally annexed to the crown of Spain (335–340). But there was no attempt
to follow discovery by exploration, nor did the total absence of Indians on whichever part of the
Banks this was, invite further intervention. The final episode is distinctive, namely an attempt
to repeat the experiment made by Father Cáncer in 1549 to establish an independent mission,
entirely outside the zone of Spanish influence, and without assistance from Spanish officials or
soldiers. The Jesuit mission on the Chesapeake in 1570 had results as tragic, or more so, than
that of 1549; all were killed except one boy. A rescue mission found him and so the story
emerged. The outcome was a voyage led by the *adelantado* himself, for revenge and slaughter
(343–344). All these initiatives provide excellent coverage for the period. Historically, they
were abortive.

The final organization of the treasure and trading fleets to and from the Caribbean emerged in
the early 1560s. Menéndez de Avilés had much to do with its successful operation, especially in
seeing that the combined fleet passed safely through the Florida Strait on its homeward way
before the hurricane season started in August. The Florida colony was one keystone on the
homeward route, but so well were the fleets run in the early years and so fortunate were they
also that, after the initial hurricane that interfered with the Spanish invasion of 1565 and
played a major part in the defeat of the French, the Florida garrison had little to do for some
years in the way of rescue operations, though this was not true of later years. But the very
presence of the colony gave confidence to the captains, and the existence of lookout towers near
San Agustín and later elsewhere provided an aid and rescue service that was no less valuable for
not always being continually in active use.

The possibility of a French return remained. Garrisons, especially that at Santa Elena, north
of which the French had had contacts with the Indians, were constantly on the alert, and rumors
of French activity were common. Nonetheless, the French attack, when it came in 1568, during
the absence of the *adelantado*, took the garrisons by surprise. With the aid of the local Indians
(whom the Spaniards believed they had subdued) Dominique de Gourgues was able to wipe out
most the garrison of San Mateo and its attendant blockhouses, except for a certain number who
escaped to San Agustín. This was purely an act of savage revenge, not an attempt to retake
Florida, although, indeed, Gourgues could have taken and destroyed San Agustín with little
difficulty (345–346). Thereafter, in 1569, there was a new wave of building, garrisoning, and
alertness, but soon, again, some loss of vigilance and retreat. Once more, late in 1571, there was
a further alarm. Three English ships under William Winter reconnoitered San Agustín and
fired a few shots at the fort, though they did little harm and sailed away. Menéndez de Avilés,
shipwrecked himself at this time, well to the south in the peninsula, made a forced march back
to the *presidio* where he was able to restore morale and obtain some aid to guard against further
interventions, which did not come (347–348).

Menéndez de Avilés died in Spain on September 17, 1574, when he was undertaking a final
task for his king, namely the equipping of a fleet (which never sailed) that was intended to drive

the Dutch Sea Beggars from the seas. From 1574 Florida was to be governed for many years by his relatives, principally by his nephew Pedro Menéndez Marqués, who for nearly twenty years was to be the strongest influence on Florida, although he was not continuously in charge there and frequently had to sacrifice Florida's interests for those of Philip II in other spheres. Yet the heroic period was over. The years after 1574, although still providing dramatic episodes, were mainly the history of a garrison striving to maintain itself, but not really emerging as a colonial society even comparable with one of the minor Spanish coastal provinces in Central or South America.

325. 1566–1567. Gonzalo Solís de Merás on the achievements of Menéndez de Avilés in Florida.

The "Memorial" of Gonzalo Solís de Merás gives the clearest continuous account of the achievements of the adelantado *during a period of nearly two years when he was able to give his full attention to Florida.*

Continued from (315), Gonzalo Solís de Merás, Pedro Menéndez de Avilés *(1923), pp. 138–245, in Jeanette T. Connor's translation.*

14.

And at the beginning of the following year, '66, Estébano de las Alas arrived; he was the General of the Armada of Biscay and the Asturias, and a storm had separated him from Pedro Menéndez Marqués, the Admiral thereof, and he had been in Yaguana. Great was the joy and satisfaction which the Adelantado felt at his arrival, for he brought 2 vessels and 200 men; and the Adelantado immediately ordered that during that month those 2 ships should be equipped, likewise the 2 he had brought from Florida, a new brigantine which Diego de Maya brought from Florida when he had gone there with supplies, a French patache which the Adelantado bought in Havana, and a new shallop; and he had all those 7 ships calked, greased and placed in readiness, and on the 10th of February, with 500 soldiers and sailors on board, he sailed for Florida to discover if there were deep water and good navigation between [the islands of] Las Tortugas and Los Mártires, because it was very necessary to know this for the

Fleets of New Spain and Tierra Firme, and other vessels which might sail in those parts. Finding the navigation very good, he went forward along the coast of Florida, in search of some men and women who, it was said, had been captives for twenty years, in the power of a cacique they call Carlos; and each year he killed some of those people, making a sacrifice of them to the devil; and they all went about naked, having become savages like the very Indians; and the Adelantado, pitying those slaves, wished to undertake that expedition, and go from there to the provinces of Santa Elena, 50 leagues to the north of the Fort of San Mateo which was won from the Lutherans, because the Indians had told the soldiers in that fort that in the harbor of Guale there were some Frenchmen newly arrived.

And having had many masses said to San Antón, that he might intercede with Our Lord so that he could find the harbor where those Christians were, and the Christians themselves; he met them within 8 days of his departure from Havana. It was in this manner: he left his flagship to Estébano de las Alas, making him his lieutenant and General of those vessels, and embarked with 30 men, soldiers and sailors, in a brigantine which did not draw more than half a fathom of water; and he ordered Captain Diego de Maya, who went as the Admiral of the ships, to go with him on board another brigantine drawing very little water, on which he was with 30 persons, the two brigantines sailing together along the coast, while most of the vessels proceeded out at sea, for the coast was low. On the 3d day, owing to dark and cloudy weather, the Adelantado with the two brigantines became separated from his 5 ships;

and on the 4th day, as they sailed along near shore, a canoe put out to Captain Diego de Maya's brigantine, half a league ahead, and one man came therein, and when he arrived near her, he spoke, saying:

"Spaniards, Brothers, Christians, be welcome! We have been expecting you for 8 days, for God and Holy Mary told us that you were coming, and the Christian men and women who are here alive, have ordered me to come and await you here with this canoe, to give you a letter which I bring you."

Captain Diego de Maya and those who were with him in the brigantine, felt great joy and satisfaction at seeing that they had discovered what the Adelantado was in search of, and so much desired, and they received that man on board, who came naked and painted, turned into an Indian, with a belt around his loins.

The captain embraced him and asked him for the letter.

The man drew a cross from under the deerskin belt he wore, and gave it to the captain, telling him that that was the letter which the Spaniards and Christians who were captives there sent to him; and that they entreated him, for the sake of the death that Our Lord had received on that cross in order to save us, not to pass by without entering the harbor, and endeavoring to rescue them from their cacique and take them to a land of Christians.

At that moment the Adelantado arrived with his brigantine, and this man came before him, where he heard more in detail from this Christian all that had happened, and about the character of the country and the condition of the Indians; and all, on their knees, worshipped the cross, rendering thanks to Our Lord.

The Adelantado entered the harbor and anchored near the shore, for they could jump from the brigantine to land without wetting their shoes. The pueblo, where were a few Spanish women and other Christians, was about half a league from there, and two other Christian men and women were at a distance inland; for more than 200 Spaniards from ships of the Indies, lost off the country of that cacique 20 years before, had all been brought to him by his subjects, and his father and he had killed them during their feasts and dances, sacrificing them to the devil.

The Adelantado did not dare reveal to that Christian that he thought of taking away the Christian men and women who were there, because it appeared to him that he knew little, and that whatever he told him, he might repeat to the cacique: so he only told him to say to the cacique that he was bringing him many things for him and his wives, and that he should come to see him. The cacique, hearing of the small number of men the Adelantado had with him, came the next day in the morning with about 300 Indian archers, near the brigantines, down to the shore; while the prow of one touched the stern of the other, and the artillery in them was placed on the landside, with much hail-shot ready for whatever might offer itself; and the Adelantado had a platform set up, that the cacique might sit thereon, and he did so, with his principal Indians around him. The Adelantado disembarked from the brigantines, with 30 arquebusiers with their fuses lighted, and seated himself near him, the cacique and his principal men paying much homage to him.

The Adelantado gave him a shirt, a pair of silk breeches, a doublet and a hat, and other things for his wives: he looked very well, because he was very much of a gentleman, and was about 25 years old; the Adelantado also made gifts to his principal Indians, and gave them biscuit and honey, which they ate very willingly.

The cacique bestowed on the Adelantado a bar of silver worth about 200 ducats, and asked him to give him more things, and more to eat.

The Adelantado told him that he had not food enough for so many people; that he should come aboard the brigantines with his principal men, and that [there] he would feed them and give them many things for their wives and themselves. Prompted by covetousness, the cacique did this, and took with him about 20 Indians.

The Adelantado commanded, with great secrecy and diligence, that there should be a soldier near each Indian, and 66 [others] near them, and if they should want to throw themselves overboard, not to allow them to do so; and he ordered that the cables should be loosened wherewith the brigantines were fastened to the land, and went out to sea. The Indians were a little disturbed, but they were told by the interpreter that they must not be frightened, for the brigantines had withdrawn from land to prevent more Indians from entering them; as they were small, more people in them might upset them.

The cacique and the Indians believed him, and

they were given food and many things, and [then] the cacique wished to go.

The Adelantado told him that the King of Spain, his Master, had sent him for the Christian men and women whom he [the cacique] held prisoners, and that if he did not bring them to him, he would order him to be killed; that he prayed him to give them up, and would bestow on him many things in exchange for them and would be his great friend and brother.

The cacique said that he was satisfied and would go for them.

The Adelantado told him that if he went, his [the Adelantado's] men would kill him because he was allowed to go; that he entreated him to send some Indians for them.

The cacique did so because of fear, and within an hour they brought 5 women and 3 Christian men, to whom the Adelantado ordered some shirts and chemises to be given at once; and from some English woolen cloth he carried with him, he ordered 4 or 5 tailors who came there to make clothes for them, and the same for the Christian men; they wept for joy, so that it was a wonderful thing to see. The Adelantado consoled the women and gave them many presents, and they said that they felt great sorrow on account of the children that they were leaving there.

The Adelantado bestowed many things on the cacique and his men, and sent him away very well pleased, the cacique telling him that within 3 months he would have there for him 2 other Christian men and one Christian woman, who were some distance inland; and that he prayed him to come the next morning, before he should depart for his village, in order that his wives might see him. The Adelantado answered that he would do so. In the morning the cacique sent many canoes for him: [and] the Adelantado being suspicious at his departure, that Christian with the cross who had gone out to sea in the canoe, and who had returned with the cacique to visit his wives on behalf of the Adelantado, to take them a present, arrived in a canoe and told the Adelantado that he must not go to the village because they had planned to kill him; and the Indians in the canoes, who knew of the treachery, suspected that that Christian was revealing it, and fled. The Adelantado, in order that the cacique and the Indians might think that he did not know of it, hoisted the anchors of the brigantines and rowed

to a point near the village, where he dropped anchor, and there, with 2 bugles sounding, and flags displayed, he signalled that the canoes should come for him, because the brigantines could not go farther; and as no canoe would come the Adelantado sailed out of the harbor to search for his 5 ships, and as they did not appear, the Christians told him that 50 leagues farther from there was a very good harbor, where there were 3 other Christian captives in the power of the Indians. It seemed to the Adelantado that his vessels might have gone there; he felt a desire to ransom those 3 Christians, and he went there, and found neither the ships nor the Christians; but on returning he discovered the 5 vessels anchored off that harbor of Carlos, and that Estébano de las Alas had gone to the village with one hundred soldiers. When the Indians saw so many ships and people, and went to reconnoitre them in the canoes, they were afraid, and gave a good reception to Estébano de las Alas: the soldiers there got more than 2,000 ducats' worth of gold and silver from the Indians, in exchange for baubles.

The Adelantado resolved to send the Christian to Carlos, that he might give him to understand that the Adelantado knew nothing of the treachery planned to kill him. Carlos believed him, and prompted by the greed he felt that he might be given other things, and the wish to take the Adelantado for a friend, he came to see him with 5 or 6 Indians, no more, and told him that he wanted to take him for his elder brother, to do all that he should command him to do, and that he wanted to give him for a wife a sister he had, older than he, whom he loved very much, in order that the Adelantado might bring her to a land of Christians, and if he should send her back, that when she returned, he would go likewise and become a Christian, with all his Indians; that it appeared better to him than being an Indian; and that he prayed him to come for her, and to see his wives and village.

The Adelantado said that he would go the next day, and he made him many presents and sent him home. The captains and soldiers would have wished that the Adelantado had not let that cacique go, because they said he had a great deal of money, and that he would give it all to him to be set free. The Adelantado would not do this, because it seemed to him that owing to the confidence the cacique had in him, it would be an act of knavery, and that [if he did so] the Indians would never become Christians.

All the captains, soldiers and sailors who were there were surprised at the reply the Adelantado gave them, for they knew how much he had spent in that enterprise, and the little assistance his Majesty had given him; that he was in debt in Spain, likewise his relatives and friends; that he was also in Havana, and had sent to borrow money in New Spain; and we held him to be a man of poor judgment, who with little trouble might have drawn one hundred thousand ducats from that cacique; for even though he did not have them, his Indians and his friends among the caciques would have, in whose possession was some gold and silver from wrecked ships, and they did not know their value nor what the thing was; through them he might have freed himself from his obligations, also those who were in debt for the love of him; and they would have found themselves more strengthened and encouraged for such a good and holy conquest as that was, in order to try, as he was trying, according to the great inclination which we all saw he had, to establish the Holy Gospel in that land; for the Indians did not know what gold or silver was, and for a playing card, which was an ace of diamonds, one of them gave a soldier a piece of gold worth 70 ducats; and for a pair of scissors, half a bar of silver worth 100 ducats. All the soldiers who had first arrived with Estébano de las Alas, and those who came with the Adelantado in the two brigantines, obtained by barter on that one occasion about 3,500 ducats' worth altogether, which made them very pleased and joyful, and they began to gamble, holding the money of little account: the Adelantado did not take away from them anything of what each one had acquired, nor did he himself obtain anything by barter, so that the Indians should not think that he came in search of gold. And the day following that on which Cacique Carlos departed from the brigantines, the Adelantado went to dine with him, taking 200 arquebusiers with him and a flag, 2 fifers and drummers, 3 trumpeters, one harp, one violin and one psaltery, and a very small dwarf, a great singer and dancer, whom he brought with him. The cacique's house was about two arquebuse shots from where he landed, and 2,000 men might gather therein without being very crowded: the Adelantado's people marched in order to that

house and he did not allow them to enter it, but stationed them outside, ready for any emergency, with their fuses lighted.

He entered the cacique's house alone, with about 20 gentlemen, and stood where there were some large windows, through which he could see his men: the cacique was in a large room, alone on a [raised] seat with a great show of authority, and with an Indian woman also seated, a little apart from him, on an elevation half an *estado* from the ground; and there were about 500 principal Indian men and 500 Indian women: the men were near him, and the women near her, below them.

When the Adelantado mounted to that place, the cacique yielded his seat to him, and drew quite a distance apart.

The Adelantado placed him near him, and then the cacique rose, and went toward the Adelantado to take his hands, according to their custom; going through a certain ceremony which is like kissing the King's hand here; no greater mark of deference can be given among them, and it is that which Indian vassals are in the habit of giving to their caciques: then came the Indian woman, and did likewise; and then all the principal Indian men and women who were there; and more than 500 Indian girls, from 10 to about 15 years, who were seated outside the window, began to sing, and other Indians danced and whirled: then the principal Indian men and women who were near the cacique sang, and they said, according to what was afterward found out, that this was the greatest demonstration of rejoicing, for a ceremony of allegiance, that that cacique or any other of that country, could give the Adelantado, because the brothers of the cacique danced, and his uncles and aunts; for there were some who danced among those principal Indian women, who were 90 or 100 years old: they all showed themselves to be very pleased and joyful.

After the cacique's principal Indians had finished dancing and singing, the Indian women who were outside, at no time left off doing so, until the Adelantado departed, and they sang with much order: they were seated in groups of 100, and 50 of them would sing a little and stop, then another 50 would sing. The cacique asked the Adelantado, after his principal Indians had danced, whether he wished that they should bring the food for him and his Christians.

The Adelantado told him that it was too soon;

and he carried with him many written words in the Indian language, which were very polite and friendly, in order that he might speak to Carlos's principal wife and to his sister; and thinking that she who was there was the principal wife of the cacique, he said to her in her own language the words he intended to say to her: the cacique and the Indians were surprised: they thought that the paper spoke, and what was written thereon; and the cacique thought that the Adelantado believed that that woman was his principal wife, and he told him through the interpreter they had there to understand each other, who was one of the Christian captives, that that woman was not his wife, but his sister; the one whom he had given the Adelantado for a wife.

Then the Adelantado rose and took her by the hand, and seated her next to him, between him and the cacique, and through what he carried written, he said many things to her in her language, reading from the paper; whereat they rejoiced, and all the Indian men and women who were there. This Indian woman was about 35 years old, not at all beautiful, although very grave, so much so that as time went on we were all surprised at this, because it seemed as though they had trained her from birth to know how to keep silence.

The Adelantado begged the cacique to bring his principal wife there, which he did: she was 20 years old, very comely and beautiful, with very good features: she had very fine hands and eyes, and looked from one side to another with much gravity and all modesty: she had a very good figure, for even among the many Indian women who were there seen to be handsome, not one was as handsome as that one: her eyebrows were very well marked, and she wore at her throat a very beautiful collar of pearls and stones and a necklace of gold beads: she was naked like the other, the cacique's sister, with only a covering in front.

The Adelantado took her by the hand, and seated her between the Indian woman and the cacique, and in her language he spoke many words to her, which he carried written on the paper, whereat she rejoiced greatly; and especially because, the Adelantado having been told that she was very beautiful, he carried written words in her own language in order to tell her that; whereat she showed herself not to be displeased, and she blushed very prettily, looking

modestly at her husband. The cacique showed that he regretted having brought his wife, and ordered her to depart, thinking that they wanted to take her from him: [but] the Adelantado told him through the interpreter not to send her away, and asked that she might dine there with him, because he had many things to give her; and presently he had the gifts brought, and he had the sister of the cacique clothed in one chemise and his wife in another, and he bestowed green gowns on them, one for each, wherein the cacique's wife looked very lovely. He gave them beads, scissors, knives, bells and mirrors, wherewith they were much pleased, especially at the mirrors, when they looked at themselves therein; and the Indian men and women who were there, laughed greatly at this; and he gave the cacique another garment, besides that he had already given him, and other trifles for barter, two hatchets and two *machetes;* and likewise made gifts to the principal Indian men and women who were there, without their making any kind of return to the Adelantado for this, or his asking for any. He ordered the food to be brought, which consisted of many kinds of very good fish, roasted and boiled; and oysters, raw, boiled and roasted, without anything else. The Adelantado had had landed one hundredweight of very good biscuit, one bottle of wine and one of honey, and divided them among all those principal Indians; and through the interpreter he commanded them to bring bowls, to give them some of that honey: he gave them some sweetmeats and quince preserves, and the Adelantado ate from a plate of his own, the cacique's sister from another, and the cacique and his wife from another, but on a table and tablecloths, and with napkins which the Adelantado had had brought: they well understood that our food was better than theirs.

When the repast was being carried in, the Spaniards blew the trumpets which were outside, and while the Adelantado was eating, they played the instruments very well and the dwarf danced: 4 or 6 gentlemen who were there, who had very good voices, began to sing in excellent order, for the Adelantado was very fond of music and always tried to take with him the best he could; when the Indians heard it they were strangely pleased. The cacique told the young girls to stop singing, for they knew little and the Christians knew much: their music ceased: the cacique prayed that until the Adelantado should depart, his men should always keep on singing and playing the instruments: the Adelantado commanded that it be so. They finished [eating] and the table was removed: then he said he wished to go.

The cacique told him that he should go and rest in a room which was there, with his sister, since he had given her to him for his wife, and that if he did not do this the cacique's Indians would be scandalized, saying that the Adelantado was laughing at them, and at her and held her to be of little account; and there were in the pueblo more than 4,000 Indian men and women.

The Adelantado showed a little perturbation, and said to him through the interpreter that Christian men could not sleep with women who were not Christians.

The cacique replied to him that his sister and he and his people were Christians already since he had taken him for his elder brother.

The Adelantado answered him that before they became Christians they would have to know and believe many things; and he told them who God was, and His wisdom, power and goodness, and that all creatures who are born on earth must worship Him alone, and do that which He commands; that we Christians who do so, go to heaven when we die here on earth, and that there we live forever without dying and we see our wives, children, brothers and friends, and we are always joyful, singing and laughing; and that they, because they do not know this, do not serve nor worship God, but serve a very warlike and deceitful cacique, who is called the devil; and that when they die they go to him, and are forever weeping, because sometimes they are very cold, and other times they are very hot, and nothing satisfies them. He gave other very effective reasons, and Carlos replied that as he had observed from the customs of the Spaniards, their music and their food, that their religion was better than his, he wanted to adopt it; and that he had given him his sister, and was giving her to him again, that he might take her away; wherefore the Adelantado was compelled to take her to the harbor with some Indian men and women to accompany her; and after consulting on the matter with his captains, he pointed out to them that it seemed to him there might come a break with the Indians [if he did not], and that would not do because of the Adelantado's plans, for since he had left Spain everything showed that his particu-

lar interest was that the Indians should turn Christians; and the captains answered him that it was fitting that much attention should be paid to her and the Indian men and women who were with her, and that that night there should be much music and rejoicing, and they should baptize her and give her a name; and the Adelantado should sleep with her, for this would be a great beginning to their trusting him and the other Christians; that all those Indians and the caciques, their neighbors, would [then] become Christians, and that in no manner was it advisable to do anything else.

The Adelantado showed much... to try some other expedient, but as none could be found, it was decided that thus it should be done.

Then the Christian women who were there bathed and clothed her, and she appeared much better than before, when she was naked; and the captains praised her intentionally as being very beautiful and dignified: they gave her the name of Doña Antonia, and that of San Antón to the harbor, on account of the prayers the Adelantado had made to Señor San Antón in order that he might meet with those Christian men and women whom he started out to seek. The supper, the music and the merriment took place on land, in some tents the Adelantado had had set up, near his ships, [and lasted] until two o'clock in the morning. The Adelantado had her seated next to him, and said many things to her through the interpreter which pleased her, and she answered so discreetly and in so few words, that we all of us marvelled at her. Her Indian women and the Christian women danced with the soldiers, and when that was ended, they conducted her to rest on a bed which the Adelantado ordered to be made, and he followed her; and in the morning she arose very joyful and the Christian women who spoke to her said that she was very much pleased; she at once sent 2 Indian men and 2 Indian women to her brother in a canoe which was there, and he came to see her, and the Adelantado received him very well, and told him that he desired that he should have a large cross erected near his house, and that every day in the morning the men, women and children should go to kiss it and worship it, and take it for their greatest idol; he told him the reason for this, and that he should give up the other idols he had.

The cacique said that he would do so, but that

he could not give up his idols so soon; [he would wait] until his sister should return, and the Indians who were going with her, and they would tell them what they ought to do.

This cacique was called Carlos because his father was so called, and his father gave himself that name, because the Christian captives he had, told him that the Emperor Charles was the greatest King of the Christians.

The cross was made and the Adelantado had it set up there, and with much music and great devotion he knelt before it and kissed it, and all the Spaniards who were there did likewise: then the Indian woman, Doña Antonia, did so, and most of the men and women she had with her: then Carlos and his Indians kissed and worshipped it. This Carlos had a captain, a very good Indian, who was married to a sister of Carlos and Doña Antonia, and the cacique had married the captain's sister; and the Indians apparently, according to what the Christians said, feared that captain more than the cacique. He told his cacique that he must be the captain of that cross, in order that all of them should do what the Adelantado commanded, [that is,] to go and kiss and worship it in the morning; and so the Adelantado delivered it to him and with great reverence he carried it on his shoulders to the canoes; and then the Adelantado proceeded to embark, taking with him Doña Antonia, 3 Indian men, 4 Indian women and 7 Christian men and women who had been prisoners, because 2 of the women had already gone back to the Indians, from the longing they had for the children that they were leaving behind. He gave orders to Estébano de las Alas to sail for Havana with that Indian woman and her people, and to deliver her to Treasurer Juan de Ynistrosa, who was the lieutenant for the Adelantado in that island for the matters pertaining to Florida; and he wrote to him to give orders that she and those who went with her should be taught the Catholic faith, and given all good treatment, and be made Christians when the time came; that within 3 or 4 months he would return to Havana, to take her back to her country; and that he [Ynistrosa] was to give as many supplies as he could, in cattle and poultry, to Estébano de las Alas, and then dispatch him with the 5 vessels he was commanding, to the Fort of St. Augustine, where the Adelantado would expect him to go against the French, who, it was said, were in Guale and Santa Elena; for he himself was going with 2 brigantines, to discover all that coast near Los Mártires, to see if he found any good harbor in the Bahama Channel, and to try to promote friendship with the caciques and pueblos he ran across; and thus they departed with a prosperous wind: Estébano de las Alas with 5 vessels, for Havana, and the Adelantado with 2 brigantines, along Los Mártires to St. Augustine.

15.

And 8 days after he left the port of San Antón, which is where Cacique Carlos lives, he entered a harbor he found in the Bahama Channel; and setting out the next day, he sighted a vessel, went to reconnoitre her, and saw that she was a caravel which they had sent from Havana to Campeche to be laden with maize. He reached her, went on board and found more than 130 persons, and the whole ship laden with maize, and [their narrative] was in this manner: That Fray... de Toral, Bishop of Yucatan, and Don Luis de Céspedes, Governor of that island [sic], had loaded that caravel with maize and chickens, honey, sandals and other things, on receiving letters from the Adelantado and at his request; and when she was returning to Florida she put in at Havana; and Juan de Ynistrosa, as lieutenant of the Adelantado for matters pertaining to Florida, dispatched her at once and ordered that she should go to the country of Ays and the harbor of Santa Lucia, where Captain Juan Vélez de Medrano had remained, when the Adelantado left him there with the 13 Spaniards and Frenchmen and went with the 2 boats to Havana to seek supplies. The Adelantado had already succored him with the cargo of a patache; [he had said that the caravel] should leave them a certain amount of *fanegas* of maize, chickens and meat, and should go on to St. Augustine with the rest; and the master of the caravel in order to do so, wished to unload the maize when he arrived at Santa Lucia; whereupon the soldiers seized the master and prepared to make off with the caravel, and because Captain Juan Vélez de Medrano wished to prevent this, they tried to kill, but wounded... de Ayala, his ensign, who was likewise preventing their making off with the caravel; and they had all embarked on board of her and were on their way to Havana, and had already sailed more than 15 leagues.

The Adelantado placed some of his gentlemen on board of her, and he went on to St. Augustine, where he entered with her on the 20th of March, '66. He found the camp master very ill, and without supplies; there had been very great mutinies there, and in the Fort of San Mateo; and there was so much connivance between certain captains and most of the soldiers, that as neither the camp master, who was in St. Augustine, nor Gonzalo de Villarroel, in whose charge was the Fort of San Mateo, could stop this, they overlooked some things which were unwisely provided and ordered; and Captain Diego de Maya having arrived at the end of December with a vessel of 80 *toneles* laden with cassava, meat and cattle, although all together it was but little, and having left part of it at the Fort of St. Augustine, he went with the rest to San Mateo, and at the entrance of the bar, the ship and supplies were lost [and] the crew escaped. The Adelantado was notified at once, and in the beginning of February he sent them a frigate of 70 *toneles* laden with maize, wine, oil, cloth, canvas, some ship tackle, rigging and oakum, all this having a value of more than six thousand ducats: from one merchant alone he bought four thousand ducats' worth of those materials and supplies, on credit for one year; and when the frigate arrived at St. Augustine, the soldiers mutinied one night, before she was unloaded; seized the camp master, the magistrates and the *regimiento* that were there, and the keeper of supplies; spiked the artillery, and appointed a sergeant major and an *electo* to govern them; for they [sergeant majors] were respected and obeyed. They remained 6 days in this manner, at the end of which they embarked on the frigate with 130 men; and because she could not hold all the mutineers, the sergeant major they had appointed, went about indicating those who were to go on board, who had to be [taken] from those who had been the most rebellious and treacherous to his Majesty in that rebellion. That sergeant took with him to guard his person 12 arquebusiers and 6 halberdiers; and while he was on the point of going on board with those men who were guarding him, the camp master succeeded in freeing himself, and he unbound 8 others, soldiers and officials of his Majesty's *regimiento;* and without being heard they took their arquebuses and went and set upon the mutineers: they deserted the boat, and the camp master took her:

when they saw they were lost, they surrendered and gave up their arms to him: he had them put into custody: he impeached them; there was a disturbance among some men, friends of those whom they held prisoners there who had not been able to find room on board the frigate; and the camp master having had their confessions taken, caused the sergeant to be hanged during the night, before daybreak. Pity was felt for the *electo* whom he had likewise made prisoner, because he was foolish, and had accepted that office very much against his will: therefore in the morning the camp master released him and the others whom he held in custody, giving them a reprimand; and in order that the frigate might not be able to set sail, he armed a patache he had there, to go and attack her; this having been done, he took on board the patache with him the soldiers in whom he had the most trust, and began to fire at the frigate so as to sink her; the rebels cut the cable which held her at anchor, hoisted the sails and fled: the camp master returned to the fort, disarmed the patache and put his men under orders and discipline, as before.

The Adelantado felt great sympathy for the camp master, on seeing him so weak from the shock he had had at finding the soldiers wanting in respect to him: it was the 20th of March when the Adelantado arrived there: Bartolomé Menéndez likewise, who was governor and *alcaide* of that fort and district, and the brother of the Adelantado, was in bed, very ill; when the mutiny broke out, he had been away with some soldiers, seeking maize from the Indian enemies; if he had been there at the time, they would have killed him, for he was disliked. Everyone was sad and distressed, and it was a great pity, but with the coming of the Adelantado they were cheered at once, and the sick became well, for the caravel brought much maize and honey, many chickens and sandals; and the same day Estébano de las Alas entered the harbor, returning from Havana, where he had left Doña Antonia and the other Indians; for he, also, brought supplies, meat and cattle, and great was the satisfaction, merriment and rejoicing of them all.

16.

At the time this meeting took place in St. Augustine, there was also one at San Mateo, for it was found out that there was a preconcerted arrangement and an exchange of letters going on from one fort to another between some captains, officers and soldiers, who ordered that the camp master be asked with all insistence that a vessel in the manner of a galley, which the French had left on the stocks at San Mateo, should be finished, and that a patache which was in St. Augustine should be prepared; [the mutineers would then carry off] the first supply ship that might arrive, and would leave the country with the 3 vessels, seizing the soldiers and captains who should want to go, so that it might be thought they were taking them away by force; and if any captain remained of those in the mutiny, it seemed to them that he would be compelled to depart when any other ship came, because with so few people they could not defend themselves from the Indians if they should be enemies. In this manner his Majesty would keep them in service for remaining there at the time of the mutiny, and during the departure from the country afterward, so that all of them would not perish; and all secrecy was to be observed in carrying this out, for they were afraid of the camp master, and of not being able to bend to their wills the governors and *alcaides* of the forts, who were Bartolomé Menéndez, the brother of the Adelantado, in St. Augustine, and Gonzalo de Villarroel in San Mateo; but the camp master, although he realized that making ready the ships was wrong, did not dare to do anything else, because the men were already stirred up: he therefore told them that they themselves must prepare the letter to be sent to San Mateo; that he would sign it; and so it was done: he wrote another, [however], to Gonzalo de Villarroel, and he had it sewed in the back of the messenger's coat, so that they should not find it; and therein he told Villarroel that he must hinder the completion of that vessel as much as he could, because he had not been able to do otherwise than give the letter the men demanded, as they were in a disturbed state of mind; and that if the soldiers at San Mateo should want to rise in rebellion, he must deal with them as best he could, and according to circumstances, and in such manner that they would not kill him. These mutineers began five days after the Adelantado departed from St. Augustine, to go to Cape Canaveral to search for the Frenchmen who had fortified themselves there, as has been said; for he left St. Augustine for the Cape on the 26th of October, '65; and from the 1st of November there were letters written from one fort to the other, wherein they began to seek an excuse to leave the country, there being no reason or foundation for this beyond its appearing to them that they had no tidings of any gold or silver in that land, and most of them held as impossible the victory which God Our Lord had given the Adelantado over the Lutherans. From Santo Domingo and the island of Cuba they could pass on to Peru and New Spain, which were rich and fertile lands, and that was the principal object they had had in setting out from Spain; and as they had not stopped at those islands, and God gave the victory against the Lutherans, in casting them out of the country, and those Spaniards did not want to be conquerors and colonizers there, it seemed to them that this was a good opportunity to say that they were leaving it on account of lack of food, but this they should have settled at the beginning—for the Adelantado had taken away the 300 men for the second fort, whom he afterward left with Captain Juan Vélez de Medrano; and the sailors who manned the vessels he sent for provisions, and the dispatch boat he sent to Spain; they had enough until the end of March, with the great quantity of very good fish, large oysters, *cangrejos* and palmettos, and a quantity of oil which the Adelantado had landed; and before the Adelantado captured the enemy's fort, he had arranged that a pound of biscuit should be given as a ration, which was very good in a [campaign for] conquest; and meat, at times; dried peas, at others, cooked in oil and vinegar; fish, at others. And in the name of all, Juan de San Vicente replied to him. He was a soldier of Medina del Campo, who arrived in Seville at the time the Adelantado wanted to sail for Florida; he came from Italy because of some quarrel he had had there, and brought a letter of introduction to the Adelantado from Luis de Quintanilla, wherein he told him that San Vicente was a very good soldier, and it appeared to him that he might show as much spirit and valor as Captain San Vicente, his brother; he begged the Adelantado to honor and favor him whenever it might be possible. The Adelantado was a great friend of Luis de Quintanilla, and this was the first thing he had asked of him: he had heard that Captain San Vicente, in Italy, the brother of this soldier, was a good captain: it appeared to him that this man might also make a good one, so he appointed him a captain; and he appointed as his ensign a comrade of his called Fernando Pérez, who came with him; he was likewise from Medina del Campo, and they had been together in Italy.

And that captain and his ensign said to the Adelantado: "A ration of one pound of biscuit to each soldier, is little."

And although the Adelantado demonstrated with sufficient reasons that it was enough, and that considering the need and the circumstances, more biscuit ought not to be given out, San Vicente insisted, and some of his soldiers came up to say that one pound per ration could not be endured; on this account the Adelantado decided to make it a pound and a quarter, and he remained very suspicious of that captain and his ensign.

And after the capture of the Frenchmen's fort, which burned down with the supplies, there yet remained more than one hundred casks of flour: many of the soldiers increased their eating, without system, and not wanting their rations made smaller. By the middle of February the supply gave out, and they would have wished this to happen much sooner, as was afterward seen; then a frigate of 70 *toneles* arrived, laden with provisions, and they mutinied and went off on board of her; then other supply ships arrived, which the Adelantado brought from St. Augustine, and the men at San Mateo, who had risen in mutiny, had not yet departed: he informed them at once of the sufficient amount of supplies which he was bringing, and that there were tidings of Frenchmen coming upon them; [he said] that he forgave them the disturbance, and if he had been with them he would have left the country before then, so as not to perish from hunger; that he did not consider them at fault for having mutinied to depart from the country, when they had no food; but now that there was enough, it would be great treason against his Majesty to abandon the two forts he had in that land; especially because, if there remained a few Christians only, the Indians would immediately become enemies, and there were some Frenchmen among them who would train them to make war on those who might remain in the forts, for in order to serve his Majesty and be loyal vassals to him, some of the soldiers would not want to abandon them. They received that message, which the Adelantado sent by a notary public. He notified them on behalf of his Majesty, that under penalty of being considered as traitors, they should return to the fort, observe that order and comply therewith: they replied that they did not know how to cultivate or plough, and that land was not good for anything else; that they wanted to go to the Indies to live like Christians, and not remain to live like beasts in Florida.

On that vessel there were over one hundred and twenty soldiers who had risen in mutiny: 35 of them, who were gentlemen, answered that they wished to return to the fort, to serve their King and obey their General; that they wanted to be landed, as they were about two leagues from the fort: the rest said they did not wish to be: those 35 replied, saying that the others risked trouble for themselves in deserting, for in whatever land of Christians they might come to, they would have to tell the authorities about the mutiny, and how they had departed from the country leaving the fort abandoned, and within it only the *alcaide*, Gonzalo de Villarroel; his ensign, Rodrigo Troche; Don Hernando de Gamboa; Rodrigo Montes, a first cousin of the camp master, and four of his relatives; Martín Ochoa, his ensign and sergeant, with other friends; and Captain Francisco de Recalde and a servant of his; 21 persons in all.

Francisco de Recalde's ensign and sergeant, who were the chief heads of the mutiny, had done much harm to the Indians and killed several, especially three principal ones, causing the rest to go to war, although up to then they had been so friendly with Saturiba and his vassals, that many of them intended to come and settle near the fort. The rebels knew that if they landed the 35 [gentlemen], as they asked to be, the Indians would kill them; and in order that this might happen the more quickly, the mutineers stripped them of their clothes, and robbing them of whatever they had, took them on shore in a boat; and as they began to walk toward the fort, the Indians sallied forth very fiercely and with their arrows killed them all.

Gonzalo de Villarroel was ignorant of all the aforesaid, and as he was short of men, he sent Rodrigo Troche, his ensign, with one soldier, to ask succor at St. Augustine thinking the trail was very safe, as it had been up to then; but they had scarcely left the fort when the Indians met them, calling them: "Christians, brothers and friends." The two did not conceal themselves from them, and they were taken unawares, and carried prisoners to Saturiba, who knew Rodrigo well. He commanded at once that his breast be split open and his heart taken out, and that the same be done to the other man, in order to terrify the rest with these cruelties, and make them leave the country as the mutineers had done.

The Adelantado was then in St. Augustine, preparing to go on his voyage to Guale and the province of Santa Elena, having already picked out 300 soldiers with their captains, and among them Juan de San Vicente; and before dispatching to Havana the two pataches of Juan de Llerena and Diego de Miranda, he placed a caravel in readiness to bring supplies and munitions from Santo Domingo; but as he knew the boldness of the mutineers, and that his pity and tolerance had made them worse, he ordered a vessel to be made ready to go and fight them: at the time of embarking, Juan de San Vicente came and asked permission to leave on the caravel with his ensign.

The Adelantado refused to grant it, to avoid the bad example, telling him that the proper thing was to drive the French out of Guale and fortify themselves [there], for it was a good land; this he could not do with less than 300 men; and it was necessary to send 100 to Gonzalo de Villarroel, and to leave another 100 in St. Augustine with the camp master; that as soon as the reinforcements he expected from Spain arrived he would give him permission to go. The captain answered that he and his ensign were in ill health and insisted on its being given him.

The Adelantado ordered them to draw up a petition, and they presented it without delay, more than 100 soldiers presenting others, each signed by 12 or 15 of them. The Adelantado, on seeing the disturbance, denied all the petitions; but as he feared that a greater mutiny might break out in that fort if he absented himself in Santa Elena, and that the lives of the camp master and the other officials might be in danger, he notified Captain San Vicente and others that leaving the country did not befit the royal service, and that during his absence in Santa Elena, they must not stir up rebellions or mutinies, but each one must attend to his duty; that when soldiers arrived from Spain, he would give leave to depart to all who asked for it; that if they wanted to name men to go to Santo Domingo in the caravel, thence to sail for Spain for their private affairs, they should do so at once; but that if, after those had left, the rest intended to mutiny, deserting the forts, they should tell him so; that it was less harmful to leave the forts deserted than in the care of such wicked men. They must understand, [however,] that they were to go as prisoners to Seville, under the orders of the royal officials of the Casa de la Contratación; and if they did not wish to go through that disgrace, but remained in the fort like good soldiers, he would thank them very much; but if they created any riot, they would be condemned to death, their property would be confiscated, and they would be declared traitors.

They replied that if permission were granted them, it should be as his lordship wished; and [the Adelantado] seeing that his efforts were of no use, and would only result in the ruin of the others; and [believing] that the caravel would only have room for 50 or 60 men, gave them leave to embark; but they accommodated themselves in such wise that more than 100 went on board. The pilot was given orders to take them to Puerto Rico and return to St. Augustine with supplies: the penalties already mentioned were intimated to those on board, to which they agreed; but they had hardly left land when they rose in mutiny on the caravel and compelled the pilot to set sail for Havana, whence they thought they would obtain better opportunities to go to New Spain, Peru, Honduras or Campeche. A contrary wind arose, and not wishing to land in Puerto Rico, they made their way to Santo Domingo and Puerto de Plata, having first drawn up a statement that they came by permission, each one swearing falsely for the others.

The pilot informed Francisco de Ceballos, who was governing there, of the truth of the matter; but he took no notice thereof; on the contrary, he, the authorities and the rest of the residents received the mutineers very well, although they knew that they had royal cédulas in that town and in other parts of the Indies, to the effect that they were to arrest all the soldiers coming from Florida, and send them back there; but the judges and governors would not comply with them as they appeared to them very rigorous; and if they arrested anyone, they immediately freed him, allowing him to go to Peru or New Spain, as did several of these conspirators; but most of them died without going any farther, for there came in the caravel many more than she could carry: they were very crowded, the heat was intense, the voyage usually took 10 or 12 days and they were over thirty in making it, and the food and water gave out; it was a miracle that any remained alive.

The Adelantado was advised of all this, and that the other 120 soldiers who had risen in St. Augustine, and sailed in the frigate laden with supplies, had arrived there, and been shown much honor and courtesy: he gave notice to the Royal Audiencia of that island, that since those soldiers were not sent back to him in Florida, in accordance with his Majesty's cédula, they should be sent to Spain, for his Majesty would be very ill served by their going farther into the Indies. Most of them passed over to those parts to which they wished to go; and others presented themselves before the Audiencia, saying that they had served very well, were not in fault and should be set free; especially Captain San Vicente and his ensign; a thing which caused surprise, and was a very bad example for the larger number of soldiers who remained in Florida in his Majesty's service; for his Majesty through his royal decrees, which were presented before that Audiencia, did not command that the cases pertaining to Florida should be tried, but did expressly stipulate that any person setting out therefrom without license from the Adelantado, should be taken back, well guarded, as a prisoner; and although these decrees were presented before, and made known to, all the judicial authorities throughout the Indies, out of 500 soldiers who left Florida as mutineers, and 500 others who started for that country and remained in the Indies (the whole thousand of whom the Adelantado brought from Spain at his expense, even giving them passage and ship-stores), they have not, up to this day, sent ten of them back to him in Florida. The Adelantado informed his Majesty of everything, so that he might dispatch his decrees all through the Indies, that the deserters might be sent as prisoners to these kingdoms, and that there should not be so many malcontents in those parts. In order to justify their weakness, most of them, wherever they went, and those who returned to these kingdoms, spoke ill publicly of the country and the Adelantado's enterprise; of his officials, relatives and friends who remained there, and the hunger, hardship and dangers that might come to pass; and this was the reason that many persons [changed their minds], who at the beginning, when the Adelantado sailed, had wanted to go and settle there; and because of these tales the deserters told, and the letters written by Captain San Vicente, Fernando Pérez, his ensign, and others who had shown weakness—letters as prejudicial to the Adelantado as to his agents and officers, in speaking ill of the country against all reason and truth—not a man was found willing to go and live, settle and conquer there. These letters and tidings gained so much credit throughout all Spain and the Indies, that it was said that many condemned the Adelantado for persisting in wanting to settle that land; to such an extent that it was said that several of his Majesty's ministers held him to be in fault; and they did not take note that all those who said these things had only gone along the sea-shore, through swamps and sandy stretches, guarding the forts and making war against the Lutherans; and that there was not one of them who had gone one league inland in Florida.

17.

Because, as has been said, Captain Juan de San Vicente and his ensign had departed from the Fort of St. Augustine with the hundred and odd persons in the caravel, to go to Puerto de Plata, the Adelantado changed his mind, for instead of taking 300 men to Guale and Santa Elena, he left 150 in the two forts of St. Augustine and San Mateo, with the people who were already there, and sailed with the other 150 in two brigantines and a ship of 100 *toneles*, directly to Guale, and on the way he stopped at San Mateo, left the men and provisions and visited that fort: his arrival greatly rejoiced Gonzalo de Villarroel and those who were with him: in St. Augustine and San Mateo Captain Francisco de Recalde was being held much to blame for the mutinies that occurred; and the general investigation which was made among those who were inculpated resulted against him more than anyone else.

The Adelantado did not wish to punish anyone: he sent the report of the proceedings to his Majesty, and Francisco de Recalde as a prisoner to the Casa de Contratación of Seville: the report arrived, [and] it was found that Recalde's offence had been taken out of it; and when he reached Seville, he did not present himself at this court. On seeing that he was not blamed in the report, he begged favors of his Majesty, who delayed granting them until the arrival of the Adelantado in Spain.

It was held for certain that the Adelantado would order Captain Francisco de Recalde to be punished because of his offence which [had] appeared in the report, and because in his coffer certain letters were found from a priest of Seville, called Licentiate Rueda, who had been at the Fort of St. Augustine, and one of the chiefs of the mutineers, and who, owing to the statement he made before the authorities of the city of Santo Domingo, taking other mutinous soldiers as witnesses, now serves as *cura* in that city, and they show him much courtesy.

The Adelantado, leaving the two forts of St. Augustine and San Mateo protected as well as he could, consistently with the [little] time and supplies he had, left San Mateo for Guale at the beginning of April of the said year '66. Having sailed for 3 days, he discovered a harbor; he got into the 2 brigantines with about 50 persons, leaving Estébano de las Alas with the other 100 in the vessel of 100 *toneles*: the Adelantado went to reconnoitre a harbor he saw at a distance and disembarked there, near the pueblo, about a quarter of a league therefrom: many Indian archers came running, and one Christian among them, likewise naked, with his bows and arrows; he spoke in Spanish and said: "What people are you [and] whence come you, brothers?" The Adelantado replied: "We are Spaniards," and asked him: "Brother, who are you and what are you doing here?"

The man answered: "I am a Frenchman, although I was born and reared in Cordova: about 15 years ago I escaped from the Castle of Triana, where they held me prisoner, and fled to France: there, in Abra de Gracia, I married: since then I have always journeyed on the sea. I was 6 years in Brazil, learning the language of the Indians there in a harbor of that country. Captain Villagañon was there, who was Captain-General of that country, and he went to France to ask for succor, and a Portuguese armada arrived there, and captured the fort he had. Some died and others remained alive: I escaped to the Indies, for I know the language very well: afterward a French vessel came there and aboard of her I returned to France: then the Admiral of France got a fleet together: he sent me therein as an interpreter to this land, and Juan Ribao came as Viceroy of all Florida; he was the General of the armada: I came with him, and I am here as interpreter."

Then the Adelantado asked him the name of that country and the cacique thereof.

He said that it was called Florida; that the lord of that land, and the village which appeared near by, was called Guale; and that he sent him to find out what people these were, in order that if they should be Spaniards, the Indians should not let them disembark, for that cacique and his people were friends of the French. The Adelantado said to him: "We do no harm to the Indians; on the contrary, we do them good; and we do not want to go to their land against their will; come hither, brother, for it grieves me to see you go about in this manner." And he gave him a new shirt, a pair of breeches, a hat and some food; and said that if the Indians wished to eat, they were to come there.

The interpreter called the Indians, and presently they came: they sat on the sand, and were given biscuit, which they ate very willingly, and some dried figs: there were about 40 Indians. The Adelantado made them all some gifts, whereat they took much satisfaction, and they praised the Adelantado by signs, asking him to come to their home.

The Adelantado asked the interpreter what they were saying; he replied that they were delighted with the Adelantado, and were requesting him to come to their pueblo to see their cacique.

The Adelantado told the interpreter to tell them that so he wanted to do; and he immediately took with him 30 arquebusiers and 4 halberdiers, and landed, leaving the 16 men to guard the brigantines; and the Indians had no fear. As he walked to the village the Adelantado spoke with the interpreter, and inquired of him who had left him there. He said that 6 months before, Juan Ribao had been shipwrecked with part of his armada, while he was going in search of General Pedro Menéndez, who came to that land to make the Indians Christians; and Juan Ribao, and the captains and men who were with him, belonged to the new religion; and all the Frenchmen who came in that armada, and the Admiral of France, wanted all the Indians to become Lutherans of the new religion, like themselves, and bring them to submission so that they might render obedience to the King of France, and [the French might] keep galleys there, to capture the fleets and vessels that passed on their way from the Indies. The armada was wrecked in a storm and the men escaped: its General sent a boat with a son-in-law of his, 2 other captains and 12 sailors, and the interpreter among them, so that they might go to a fort they had, to ask that 2 or 3 vessels be sent for the men, for these ships were in the harbor near the fort; and entering the harbor where the fort was, the friendly Indians told them that other Christians like themselves had captured their houses and property and the fort, and had slain the men who were therein. Presently a Frenchman ran down to the shore, who had escaped to the Indians, and he related all that had passed; and then the people in the boat decided to go to Santa Elena, because the Indians there were their friends, and they [the French] knew the country and the language, as 6 years before they had built a fort there [which they had for] 3 or 4 years, and because the captain did not wish to go to France, his soldiers killed him, built a ship, and sailed in her to England. A servant of this dead captain fled to the woods among the Indians, and remained with them, so that they should not slay him, [thinking] that he would tell in France what had happened: the Indians married him to a daughter of the cacique.

That interpreter also told the Adelantado the state of affairs in Guale; that its cacique was at war with Orista and held 2 of his principal Indians as prisoners, whom he would shortly put to death, as he did the other enemies he captured; and that there was little food in the land, as there had been no rain for 8 months. Many other things the Frenchman said, until they arrived at the pueblo. The cacique, already an elderly man, came forth to receive them peacefully, with two of his sons and some of the principal Indians. The Adelantado went through the same ceremonies with him as he had with the rest, and the cacique rejoiced greatly at seeing him, because the Frenchman easily persuaded him that the Adelantado and his men were good people who did no harm to the Indians, but much good. They spoke on some matters, wherein the French interpreter served well; and among other things, the cacique asked the Adelantado how it was that he was at war with the other Christians and killed them, when they were all from one land. He replied to him that they were false Christians and his enemies, being rebels against God, the church and their King, who was a true Christian; that others as wicked as they, wanted him [their King] to be a false Christian, by force of arms, and that if the King of Spain, the Adelantado's master, had not helped him to chastise them, they would have wrested the kingdom from him, to bestow it on one of their false sect; that those whom the Adelantado had slain, deserved a death more cruel, because they had come there, fleeing from their country, to deceive the caciques and their Indians, as they had deceived the good Christians, in order that the devil might carry them off. They were so fiendish and pernicious that no one could have any dealings with them, until they were silenced by being put to death; that was the reason for making war upon them, until such a wicked and pestilential sect was destroyed. But the Adelantado did not think that the cacique had reason for the cruel war he was making on Orista, since they were all of one same country, and the wrongs which had been done were hardly worth the whipping of one subject. Guillermo the interpreter explained all the aforesaid very clearly to the cacique, and the cacique answered the Adelantado that he wanted to be a true Christian, not a false one, like the other Christians who had been there. The Adelantado told him the power and goodness of God, and all that he told the other caciques; and that he should order his people to come and hear the chants which the youths recited; that that was the Christian doctrine; and to come and kiss the cross; and afterward they would tell him what those chants meant. He said he would do so; and the Adelantado had a large cross set up there; and all of them having gathered and sung the litanies, kneeling, they went to kiss and worship the cross: the cacique and all the Indian men and women did likewise. The Adelantado prayed the interpreter, since he was born in Spain, to turn to Catholicism and the faith of Jesus Christ, [saying] he would cherish him greatly and give him many things; and if he wished to go back to France, he would send him to Spain, because he could make his way to France from there; but if he wished to remain where he was, he could do that: he replied that there he wanted to be and remain, and that he wanted to become a Christian and a Catholic, and that he would work to the end that the Indians might become so.

The Adelantado thanked him very much, and told him that next day in the morning they should discuss with that cacique a peace between him and the Cacique of Santa Elena, and that he [the interpreter] should be the good mediator for that purpose, so that they would not kill those two principal Indians of Orista. He promised him to do what he could in the matter; and the next day in the morning, the cacique and all the Indian men, women, boys and girls, when they saw that the Christian doctrine was being repeated, hastened there and knelt: after which, the soldiers went to worship and kiss the cross, kneeling, and the cacique and all the Indians did the same: then the Adelantado took the cacique by the hand, led him to his house and requested that he would have his principal Indians summoned, as he wished to speak to them; and thus about 10 or 12 came.

The Adelantado said through the interpreter that he had learned that they were at war with the Indians of Santa Elena; that he begged them to be friends; that he would go to treat of peace, and they should give him the two Indians they held as prisoners in order to take them with him; and if the Cacique of Santa Elena did not want to be their friend, he would bring them back. Guale spoke with his Indians, and replied that he could not consent, because Orista would take the Indians from him, and would not want to be his friend.

It had not rained for 8 months in the country, and their corn fields and farming lands were dry, whereat they were all sad, on account of the little food they had. The Adelantado told them that God was angry with Guale, because he was at war with Orista and two other caciques, and because he slew the men he captured, and this was the reason God would not give him water; that he would leave him 2 Christians as hostages for the 2 Indians, and that if he did not make peace with Orista and bring Guale back the 2 Indians, he could kill those 2 Christians.

Cacique Guale spoke a while with his men, and replied that he was satisfied, and the Adelantado told him that next day he must depart. All the Indians, big and little, showed great pleasure at [the prospect of] that peace the Adelantado wished to conclude, for the Indians of Santa Elena were more powerful than they, and slew many Indians of that Cacique Guale. The Adelantado presently went to breakfast with his soldiers, and took with him the cacique and 2 sons he had, very good fellows, and went 2 leagues from there, to see the island and the lay of the land.

The cacique, being old, turned back after going half a league: the Adelantado found the land very good and fit for raising grain and grapes. When he returned to the village, the cacique asked him to show him the 2 Christians who were to remain with him: he did so at once, because in his own mind he had already picked them out: the two soldiers were silent, without answering anything, appearing very sad: the cacique said that he did not want those two Christians: that he was to take the two he wanted: the Adelantado said that he was satisfied, and the cacique should choose them immediately: he pointed out a nephew of the Adelantado, called Alonso Menéndez Marqués, and Vasco Zabal, the ensign of the royal standard, for he saw that they sat at the Adelantado's table, and it was thought likewise that the interpeter might have told him that those 2 were among the most important men.

The Adelantado said that he was glad that those should remain; that they were both his captains, among those he loved the most, and he would leave each of them a Christian to wait on him, and the youths who were to teach the Christian doctrine.

The cacique showed himself very joyful at this, and went to embrace and thank them in his manner, in order to do them honor. They became very sad, saying that it was not right to remain with those savages.

The Adelantado replied that he would willingly stay; that they had nothing to fear; that he prayed them earnestly to try through that interpreter to make them understand what bestial lives they led, and how good it was to be Christians: then he told the cacique to treat his Christians well, and if he did them harm, the Adelantado would order that he and all his people should have their heads cut off; because he would make peace and bring principal Indians from Santa Elena to conclude it, and would return as soon as he could.

The cacique was frightened, and if the Adelantado had urged him, he would willingly have given to him the Christians with the Indians, on condition that the Adelantado should leave his country; for the Indians stood in great fear of the Adelantado; they had already had tidings of the victories he had won over the French Lutherans, for in that land, news of the things that happen travels fast from cacique to cacique: he replied to the Adelantado that he would treat his people well, and that neither he nor his men would kill them, if the cacique of heaven did not do so. Thus the Adelantado departed for Santa Elena the next day, in the morning, leaving those 6 Christians there as hostages and teachers of the Indians: he embarked in his brigantines, went out to sea at midday, discovered a vessel, went toward her, recognized her as being his, at anchor: he boarded her: very great was the pleasure of Estébano de las Alas and his men on meeting the Adelantado, for they had feared much that he was lost; it was 4 days since he had left them to reconnoitre the harbor, which should have been a delay of 2 or 3 hours only, and that night was stormy. They sounded the trumpets for joy and discharged the artillery: the two Indians whom the Adelantado was taking to Santa Elena, and a principal one from Guale, who went along to be present at the peace negotiations, were much frightened at the noise, saying it gave them much pain in the head and heart; that the Spaniards should sound the trumpets, that was a good thing; but not to fire any more.

The Adelantado commanded it should be so, and told Guillermo, the interpreter, to talk to the Indians, since he understood them, and gladden and cheer them as much as he could; and he charged all the soldiers to treat them very well.

The Adelantado ordered the ship to hoist anchor, and sailed for Santa Elena with her and the 2 brigantines: then he related to Estébano de las Alas, and most of the men, what had happened to him, whereat they were all pleased, although they regretted greatly that Alonso Menéndez Marqués had remained behind, as he was much beloved by all. They arrived at Santa Elena the next day in the afternoon, for the 3 Indians they boought knew the harbor very well: they entered it at the place to which the Indians guided them, for they were skilful pilots, being accustomed to going there fishing in their canoes. Having entered the harbor and gone a league up the river, the Indians ordered that the large vessel should anchor, as she could not go farther, and they should embark in the brigantines and go to the village: the Adelantado did this, and embarked in the brigantines, and took with him Estébano de las Alas and about one hundred persons. He arrived at the pueblo of the Indians, which was 2 leagues from there, and found it burned, and [the inhabitants] beginning to build a few houses again. A few Indians appeared, much disturbed, with their bows and arrows and ready for war: the two

Indians the Adelantado had with him, told him that those others thought that he and his men were some of the false Christians, who had captured them in the war, while helping Guale; that they would land and tell them we were very good, and enemies of those people, and the reason we came. The Adelantado let them go, and within half an hour he landed with all his people, leaving 10 in each brigantine to guard it; and the Indians immediately came to the Adelantado without bows and arrows, with great humility and making great demonstrations of respect, and many ran off, some by one trail, others by another: this was to notify the pueblo, the caciques and captains, that they should come to see the Adelantado: then they built a great fire, and brought a quantity of shell-fish, and the Adelantado and his men took supper. Many Indians came running, all of them to speak with and pay their respects to the Adelantado, for the love and joy these Indians showed him was something to see. That night came three caciques, subjects of Orista, and told him that he should go to a village one league distant from there, as Orista and others of his captains and caciques would come there to eat: next day the Adelantado did this: Orista came and 2 other caciques and captains: great was the delight of all on seeing Guillermo, the interpreter, to whom Orista had given a daughter of his for wife, at the time he first came there. The Adelantado ordered him to tell Orista to gather his principal Indians, because he wished to speak to them: this was done: the Adelantado commanded Guillermo, who was the interpreter, to tell them (the 3 Indians being present whom the Adelantado had brought with him) all that had passed in Guale concerning the making of peace. Orista said that he would reply presently, and he spoke with his Indians more than half an hour, discussing the subject, without their wanting Guillermo to be there, so that he should not understand what they were treating of; and then they called the interpreter, to whom they talked a very long time, and afterward the interpreter told the Adelantado, on behalf of Orista, that it would please him much to make peace, as the Adelantado ordered him to do; and he would be even more pleased to become a true Christian, with his people, as those of Guale wanted to be, for those people were not to be better than they; that his Indians, whom the Adelantado had brought from Guale, had told them who God was and how good it was to be Christians; that they wished very much to have the Adelantado live in that land and to take him for an elder brother, in order to do what he should command them; and that they would hold the false Christians as enemies, since they were those of the Adelantado. He replied to them, showing there was great joy in his heart, that he loved them much, but did not think he could live in that land, because it was bad, and his own was better; and that if Orista's Indians killed his Christians, and if they did any harm, the Adelantado would at once kill him who did it, because the Christians he brought would not hurt the Indians; that he would like to live there solely in order that they might learn to become Christians, so that when they died they might go to heaven. He told them the power and goodness of God, and all that he told the other caciques, that they might become Christians: they showed great satisfaction at hearing him, and repeated that they wished to become Christians, praying him to leave them someone to teach them: they begged for this with so much earnestness, that the Adelantado offered to leave a man; but [said] that if Orista or his people killed him, he would return to make war on them, and cut off the heads of all of them.

Then came many Indian women, carrying maize, fish boiled and roasted, oysters and many acorns; and the Adelantado ordered biscuit, honey and wine to be brought, and divided it among the Indians, who drank the wine well, but ate the biscuit dipped in honey-water, better, because they are very fond of sweets. When the meal was over, during which there was great merriment and rejoicing, they seated the Adelantado in the seat of the cacique, and with various ceremonies Orista came to him and took his hands: afterward the rest of the caciques and Indians did the same: the mother and the relatives of the two slaves he had brought from Guale, caressed him very much and wept for joy: then they began to sing and dance, the caciques and several principal Indians remaining with the Adelantado, and the festivities and demonstrations lasted until about midnight, when they withdrew. The next day, the Indians issued many proclamations in the village, in order that no one should do any harm to the Christians, and the Adelantado said to the cacique that he was going in search of a good site where he could make a

settlement for his Spaniards, for it was not right that they should live among the Indians, and quarrel afterward. The cacique told him of one, near the place where the vessel was anchored, and he embarked, without any suspicion whatever, with his wife and 12 Indians, in the Adelantado's brigantines; and they all went very gaily together as far as the spot where they were to land. There the Adelantado gave the Indians their midday meal, and the Spaniards landed to go to Orista's village, where they were very well entertained that night. Next morning the cacique took the Adelantado to a very large house, and seated him in his seat, going through the same ceremony with him as he had in the previous pueblo, and ordering the same proclamations to be made. They spent the following day in reconnoitring the site to begin the settlement, and it appeared to all of them very good and pleasant; and without losing time, the Adelantado, Estébano de las Alas and other captains marked out the fort, and its erection was committed to the charge of Antonio Gómez, whom he had taken with 50 soldiers, and others who were sailors, from the ship of the fleet which was in Havana, so that up to the end of May they could be with him in Florida; and they served him very well.

18.

A fort was built of stakes, earth and fascines, and the Adelantado called it San Felipe. He named Estébano de las Alas as governor of it and of that land and left him 110 men: then he sent the vessel with 20 on board to Santo Domingo, to be laden with supplies so that the fort might be provisioned, for he had little to leave there. He likewise dispatched a brigantine to St. Augustine and San Mateo, to give news of everything.

He sent some Indians inland to tell the caciques that very good Christians were there; that they did no evil or harm to the natives, but much good, giving them presents; and that Orista and others had taken him for their elder brother, to defend them from their enemies, whereat all the Indians were very much pleased and desired to be Christians; that if those others wished to do the same and to see him, he was waiting for them to give them some of the things he had brought. Within 15 days, the time he tarried there, many caciques came to visit him, and he paid them many attentions, so that they took him for their elder brother, to command them at his will: they told him they wanted to be Christians and he should give them a cross, and some of his men, to teach them in their country.

The Adelantado did so, giving to each cacique 1 or 2 Christians, and tools for erecting a cross in each village, admonishing them that every day, morning and evening, they should repeat the Christian doctrine and worship the Holy Cross, in order that the Indians might learn it and imitate them. To all the caciques he gave presents, and a hatchet to each one, with which they were very much delighted, and they gave him well tanned deerskins and some pearls, of which there are many in that country, although they are of little value because they are burned.

Taking his leave of Cacique Orista, who was very joyful at having Spaniards [left with him], the Adelantado set out for Guale, taking 20 soldiers, 2 of Orista's principal Indians to negotiate the peace, and Guillermo the interpreter. In Santa Elena remained Estébano de las Alas, and the men who were with him, who were pleased because there appeared to be a very good beginning of turning the Indians into Christians, which, next to driving the Lutherans out of the land, was all that they desired; but they had great fear of lack of food, for they had very little remaining; and much work to do in finishing their fort, for each day they expected French Lutherans, who had had tidings of the Adelantado's successes against them, on sea as well as on land, in destroying them and eradicating them from that country, so that they should not teach their evil faith to the Indians. To avenge the injuries they had received from the Adelantado and his men, and return to settle in that land, they were getting together a great armada; but hearing that the Adelantado was awaiting them, they did not dare go in search of him, and went to the island of Madeira, which belongs to the King of Portugal, and took it and sacked and robbed it, and returned to France. Even if the Indians had been willing to give food to Estébano de las Alas and his men, they had none, for it had not rained for many months. The Adelantado arrived in Guale, with 20 persons, on May 8th: Guillermo landed first: he told the cacique about the peace that had been concluded, and to Alonso Menéndez [Marqués] and Vasco Zabal and the other 4 Christians who had remained with him, he told all that had happened to

them, whereat they were much pleased. The Adelantado disembarked: he was very well received by Guale and all his Indians: then Orista's two Indians told Guale their errand to Guale, while he had his principal Indians gathered round him, whereat he showed much satisfaction, he and all his people, big and little; but he regretted that the Adelantado had started a friendship with those of Santa Elena, and that those caciques had taken him for an elder brother; and presently he said to the Adelantado through the interpreter that he was glad about the peace, and that he wanted to take him for his elder brother, to do what he should command him; that they wanted to be true Christians, not false ones, like the French who had been there; and that the Adelantado should leave him people to live in his land, since he had done so for Orista.

The Adelantado told him that he had none, but would soon send him some.

The cacique replied that he should leave those who were already there, as they were good men, to teach them to be Christians, and that afterward he could send him more.

The Adelantado said that he would answer him next day in the morning.

Then the cacique told the Adelantado that since he was already a Christian, and had made peace with Orista in order not to anger God, he should beseech Him to give him water for his maize fields and other cultivated lands, as it had not rained for 9 months.

The Adelantado told him that God was very angry with him, because He had ordered him to do many things and he had not done them, and on this account He would not give the cacique water, although he besought Him to do so.

The cacique turned away very sadly and went to his house: the youths who had been left to teach the natives the doctrine, hearing of this, went to the cacique with the interpreter and told him not to be sad; that they would supplicate God that it might rain.

The cacique gave them many *gamuzas*, which are dressed deerskins, and some maize and fish, all of which they took, and went off with them.

When the Adelantado heard this, he ordered that they should give up everything, and be stripped to be whipped. The cacique heard this, and came to the Adelantado very sadly, saying that he was deceiving him, since he would not ask the cacique of heaven for water, and wanted to whip the boys because they had asked Him for it; he begged that they might not be whipped, and no longer wished that they should pray God for water; he said he was content that it should rain when God willed.

The Adelantado said to the cacique that those youths were rogues; that they tricked him and told him those falsehoods in order that he should give them the food and deerskins, and that God was angry with them because they were rogues. He ordered that the boys should not be whipped, and said that if the cacique wished to be a true Christian, God would sooner give water to him than to the Adelantado, or to the youths who told him falsehoods in many things.

The cacique replied sorrowfully that he had been a true Christian since the very first day; and he went directly to the cross which was near there, and knelt before it and kissed it, and turned to the Adelantado and said to him through the interpreter: "Behold, how I am a true Christian."

This occurred at about 2 o'clock in the afternoon: not half an hour had gone by when there came thunder and lightning, and it began to rain very hard, and a bolt struck and splintered into many pieces a tree near the village: all the Indian men and women ran to it to take the broken branches and bring them to their houses, to keep them: then they all went with the cacique to the Adelantado's house, some of them weeping, some throwing themselves at his feet, and others taking his hands, imploring him to leave Christians there.

19.

Alonso Menéndez [Marqués], the Adelantado's nephew, and Vasco Zabal had told him that the French interpreter who was there was a Lutheran and a great Sodomite; that when the Adelantado had departed thence for Santa Elena, he went to the Indians [telling them] they should kill them; and that through Guillermo he could inform himself of what was happening in this [matter], so that he [Guillermo] could speak with 2 Indians with whom he [the interpreter] was living, one of whom they said was the cacique's eldest son.

The Adelantado made inquiries with great secrecy; and learning that it was the truth, and that they saw him [the interpreter] spit on the cross many times before the Indians, scoffing at the Christians, he spoke with Alonso Menéndez [Marqués], his nephew, and with Vasco Zabal, the ensign of the royal standard, who knew this and had seen it, and told them that it was not well to leave that cacique and his people disconsolate, since they wanted to become Christians, and that it would please him greatly if they would remain there, as before.

Vasco Zabal replied that he would sooner the Adelantado had him beheaded, than be left there.

Alonso Menéndez [Marqués] said that he would much regret staying, but since his lordship ordered it, he would do so, on condition that that Frenchman should be killed, or the Adelantado would take him with him; for otherwise nothing could be accomplished, and the Indians would slay him and those who remained with him; that the son of the cacique had more authority than his father, and liked that interpreter very much; that if they [the Spaniards] killed the interpreter [openly], the Indians would be angered and again break out in war. This reasoning appeared very good to the Adelantado, and because he trusted Guillermo, and held him to be a Catholic, he called him: he told him to tell that interpreter that he should go with him to Santa Elena, for they can go there in a canoe in 2 or 3 days, by a river, without putting out to sea; that Estébano de las Alas, who was a very good captain and liberal, would make him many presents; and that he would bring back a gift to his cacique, for the Cacique of Santa Elena had sent word to him to send for it. The interpreter was pleased at this, and without knowing that the Adelantado knew it, he came to beg him to give him a letter for Estébano de las Alas so that he might know him, and to give him a hatchet, because he wished to set out to get the present which the Cacique of Santa Elena was to send to his Cacique Guale. The Adelantado told him to give him paper and ink, that he would write the letter at once; and so he did, writing one very favorable to the interpreter, and giving it to him.

Then Cacique Guale dispatched that interpreter in a canoe, with 2 of his Indians, that they might go and return immediately. The son of the cacique showed much sorrow because the interpreter was going, and prayed him, weeping, to return at once. The Adelantado sent a soldier with a letter to Estébano de las Alas in order that he might have that interpreter killed with great secrecy, as he was a Sodomite and a Lutheran;

and if he returned alive, the Indians of Guale who desired to be Christians, would not as quickly become so; that he might greatly entertain the two Guale Indians who went with the interpreter; that Orista should do likewise, giving them a handsome present, sending another to Guale, and offering him his friendship; and that Estébano de las Alas should feign great regret because the interpreter did not appear, [saying] that as he was a false Christian, he must be hiding in the woods so as not to return to Guale, and so that if some ship should come from his country, he might go back on board of her. And therefore Estébano de las Alas had him garroted with great secrecy, and the two Indians returned to Guale; and the Adelantado had already departed for San Mateo and St. Augustine, leaving in Guale his nephew, Alonso Menéndez [Marqués], and the 4 Christians who were with him: he took away Vasco Zabal.

That rain which fell in Guale lasted 24 hours, and extended over the whole island, which may be 4 or 5 leagues in length.

20.

The Adelantado started for San Mateo in the brigantine, sailing along the waterway between the islands and the coast, without going out to sea. Indians in canoes came out to meet him, saying: "Spain, friends, brothers, we want to be Christians"; because these Indians had heard what had passed in Santa Elena and Guale, and how it had rained in this latter island.

The Adelantado would land and make them some gifts, and had many small crosses erected, one for each village; and he proceeded in this way until May 15th, when he arrived at San Mateo, where he found the men of that fort well, but in great need of supplies, and all the Indians on the war path. He learned that twice at night they had shot arrows at the sentinels at St. Augustine, and had killed two soldiers and set fire to the pow-derhouse, the roof whereof was thatched with palmetto leaves; in this way the fort was burned; and at night they shot their fire arrows at the magazine, and thus the fire started, and because there was a breeze it spread in such a manner that it was not possible to control it, and the powder and munitions, cloth and linen, flags and stan-dards, those of the Adelantado as well as those won from the Lutherans, were all burned without anything escaping. [He also heard] that the camp

master and all the others were in the greatest difficulties through lack of provisions, and the peril from the Indians, who went about in ambush in small groups so that, when any Christian came forth in search of palmettos or shell-fish, they shot their arrows at him. As these Florida Indians are agile, and feel certain they cannot be over-taken, they are very bold in coming near the Christians, and at other times lying in wait for them; and when the Christians retire, they are in much danger from the Indians, for they shoot their arrows with such force that they pass through the soldiers' clothing and coats of mail, and the Indians are very quick in shooting. Once a soldier has discharged an arquebuse, he cannot reload it before the Indian, on account of his fleetness, comes up with him and fires 4 or 5 arrows at him; and while he is putting in the powder to prime it, the Indian withdraws through the woods and high grass (for that is very good land), and watches for the instant when the pow-der takes fire; then he stoops, and as he is naked, he crawls along through the grass, and when the arquebuse is fired, he rises in a different spot from where he was when the soldier sought to take aim at him; and they are so dexterous in this, that it is a thing for admiration. They fight in skirmishes: they jump over the bushes like deer: the Spaniards are far from being as swift as they are; and if the Christians follow them, and the Indians are afraid, they go to places where there are rivers or swamps, for there are many near the sea-coast, as they swim like fish, lifting with one hand their bows and arrows above the water, so as not to wet them; and once on the other side, they begin to shout to the Christians and laugh at them; and when the Christians retire, they turn back to cross the river and follow them until they reach the fort, sallying forth from among the thickets and shooting arrows at the Christians, for when they see an opportunity they do not miss it. On this account very unsuccessful war can be waged against them, unless one goes to their villages in search of them, to cut down the plant-ings and burn the houses and take the canoes and destroy the fishways, which is all the property they have, so that they must leave the land, or keep their word with the Christians so that the caciques and Indians may make friends with them, [the Christians] giving them good treat-ment when they go to the Forts of St. Augustine and San Mateo; [but] if they are not given food, clothes, iron hatchets and articles for barter, they go away very angry; they declare war, killing the Christians they find. They are very treacherous Indians, and in this manner, by treason under cover of friendship, the Indians have slain more than 100 soldiers at these 2 Forts of St. Augustine and San Mateo, where the French lived: these are the most treacherous.

The Adelantado was much disturbed at the burning of the powderhouse and fort, supplies and munitions, and at the great need and danger wherein were the camp master and his brother Bartolomé Menéndez, and all the other people.

He hastened to St. Augustine, bringing some men, munitions and provisions, from the little there was in San Mateo: he took with him Gonzalo de Villarroel, who was very ill as a result of past hardships, to send him to Havana to be cured: he left Vasco Zabal, the ensign of the royal standard, in his place.

He arrived in St. Augustine on the 18th of May: great was the happiness of those who were there: they wept for joy at the mercy Our Lord was granting them in succoring them at such a time with the arrival of the Adelantado, who related to them the pleasant events which had occurred in Guale and Santa Elena, and the good beginning that had been made so that the Indians might become Christians, whereat they all greatly rejoiced: he ordered the supplies and munitions he brought to be unloaded, and the rations to be given them.

He entered into counsel with the camp master and captains. It was resolved that they should move from there and erect a fort at the entrance of the bar, where now stands the Fort of St. Augustine, because there the Indians could not do them so much harm; and that they should place the artillery in it, because from there they could defend themselves better against any vessels of enemies, which might want to enter the harbor; and when that had been done, if the supplies did not arrive within 15 days, the Adelantado should go in search of them in three brigantines he had there, for of the ships he sent in charge of other persons, none had ever returned. This decision was made public: it gave great satisfaction to all, although it caused them much concern that the Adelantado should leave them, as they heard that the camp master had to go to San Mateo and stay

there during Villarroel's absence, for so the soldiers who remained there had requested, and the Adelantado had promised it to them.

Thereupon that day and the following were spent at the bar: they began to mark out their fort and build it with the greatest diligence, and they worked from 3 in the morning, before day, until 9, and from 2 in the afternoon until 6: they divided the men into 4 squads and the work into 4 parts, and threw the dice to see what part of it fell to each squad. So great was the order, in building this fort in a short time, for fear the Indians should fall upon them, that it was a pleasure to see it: about 170 persons worked at the fort: in 10 days it was in a reasonable state of defence, and the artillery in position. No ship arrived with supplies: they ran the risk of all perishing from hunger: so it was agreed unanimously that the Adelantado should sail at once for Havana with the 3 brigantines, and take back the 100 persons, most of whom came from the flagship of the Fleet of New Spain, and the Adelantado was obligated to take them to Havana during May; and as there remained but 70 rations, not more, [the settlers] could sustain themselves a few days until some vessel arrived. And so the Adelantado embarked with the hundred men in the 3 brigantines, at the beginning of June; and the day he departed, he met with one of his own ships, of 60 *toneles*, laden with provisions, under the command of Francisco Cepero; and aboard of her came Captain Diego de Maya, very ill. If the Adelantado had not met with them at that moment, they would have run on the shoals; and the vessel was already in a place where, if she had not cast anchor, she would have been lost, for they believed that they were entering over the bar, and it was high tide, and they were in 2 fathoms of water, and at low tide there was none left. The sea ran high, and when the ship loosened her cable, she struck, and the Adelantado boarded her and so exerted himself that he brought them to safety: otherwise everything would have been lost, and all those who came in her would have been drowned. He wrote to the camp master that he should divide those supplies between the forts, and go at once to San Mateo, and not leave that fort until the Adelantado's return, which would be immediately, in the shortest time; that they should load with maize a brigantine that remained to them in the harbor, and send her to Estébano de las Alas, and this was done; and when that ship had been unloaded he was to sink her in order that 20 more men she brought should stay in the fort (for they were very good people), and that the soldiers might not mutiny, not having a vessel with which to leave the country: and so the camp master did it.

It was great good fortune that the Adelantado should have met with that ship, because otherwise, all those who remained in the fort would have perished of hunger.

And the Adelantado set sail at once and arrived in Havana with the two brigantines, within 8 days; the other could not turn her bow, for the wind and the sea were very high and she put in to the island of Santo Domingo.

The Fleet of New Spain had arrived in Havana 2 days before, with Licentiate Valderrama, of the Royal Council of the Indies, on board; he had been sent as *visitador* of New Spain by order of his Majesty, and having accomplished his mission, was now returning to Spain.

When the Adelantado landed in Havana he went to church with his soldiers in order to say prayers, and before entering his inn he went to call on Valderrama, as it appeared to him that by finding him there he could quickly succor the forts with men and supplies, for more than 300 soldiers had fled there from Florida. Valderrama lodged in the Governor's house, and thus he and the Adelantado spoke to each other standing, not sitting, saluting and embracing each other very courteously. The Adelantado told him that he considered it very good fortune to find him there, as he had to go back within 4 or 5 days; that he begged him as a favor to name him an hour so that he could talk with him and give him a detailed account of matters pertaining to Florida, of the great need in which those forts were left, and that his Majesty kept 500 men there at his own expense; and although he [the Adelantado] had brought plenty of supplies for the Governor of that island, the Governor had not aided him with anything.

Valderrama replied that every time the Adelantado might desire that they should meet, he would be delighted thereat.

And the following day the Adelantado found out when Valderrama was going to church, and he went likewise; and mass being over, he told him that he was in debt in that country, on account of the supplies he had bought for Florida, and that

for 8 months he had been providing for the soldiers his Majesty kept there, who were left in extreme need of food and peril from the Indians; that those of the region where were the Forts of St. Augustine and San Mateo were all on the war path, there were few soldiers in the forts, and most of them were ill and misused and very discontented, owing to the great hardships and dangers they had had and were having every day; that there had been mutinies and double-dealing among some of the captains, wherefore more than 400 soldiers had gone from those 2 forts; that there were more than 500 in that island of Cuba, not only of those who had set out from the forts as rebels, but also of those who came from Spain to Florida, who because of a storm had become separated from the Adelantado, had landed on that island and had remained there, without desiring to go to Florida; that although he had many times had recourse to the Governor so that he might succor him with some supplies for his Majesty's account, and order that those men be gathered and delivered to him, the Governor had been unwilling to do this; that since he [Valderrama] was there in order to inform his Majesty of everything, he begged him to make a report; and in order that the Adelantado might return soon, to succor him with 2 or 3 thousand ducats of those his Majesty carried in that armada; that if his Majesty were not pleased thereat, he would pledge himself to return them, and that Valderrama should enjoin on the Governor that of the soldiers [recruited] for Florida who were going about that town and island, he should give the Adelantado 200 to fortify the 2 forts of San Mateo and St. Augustine. He related to him what had happened in Guale and Santa Elena; how the Indians of that land were all his friends and wished to become Christians, and how he had built a fort and left Estébano de las Alas therein, with 110 soldiers, and the title of Governor of that district; [he said] that he wanted to depart the next day in the morning for the country of Cacique Carlos, and take back to him his sister who was then in Havana, because the principal Indian men and women she had brought with her had died, and she had but two left, and if she and they were to die, he would think that the Adelantado had had them killed; and that cacique was the ruler over much land, Los Mártires and the Bahama Channel, where the vessels of the Indies run the greatest danger in [the course of] that navigation; that it was very important to have him for a friend and try to make him and his Indians turn Christians, and that he would return within 10 or 12 days, in which time the 200 soldiers could be assembled there, and the supplies he would have to take.

Valderrama answered him drily that he could not give the money; that as for the soldiers, he would speak to the Governor and recommend to him [to give them]; and that he held no commission to make the report the Adelantado told him he should make concerning the Governor's ill treatment of him in order that he might assure his Majesty of the truth.

Those of us who were present saw the Adelantado change color from grief, and he said to Valderrama:

"Señor, during the time until I return from Carlos, your Honor will realize how you can serve his Majesty in this, and will do me the favor which is called for; because it is in your Honor's hands to do that which I beg, in order that Florida may not be lost, that the souls and natives thereof may be saved, and his Majesty's purpose be furthered, which is to prevent the Lutherans from setting foot in that land, and to endeavor to implant the Gospel therein."

Valderrama did not reply to him, and presently the Adelantado very sorrowfully took leave and went to his inn. He told Juan de Ynistrosa, the Treasurer of that island, and his lieutenant for matters pertaining to Florida, the little help he had received from Valderrama, and everything which had passed with him: and Juan de Ynistrosa consoled him greatly, saying:

"Señor, I have done all I could for your lordship with my means and my person, and now I shall try to do it with those of my friends. Let not your lordship be discouraged: go tomorrow to Carlos, as you have decided, and I will send to look for some maize, meat and cassava that you must take for the men's food; and meantime I will solicit Licentiate Valderrama, for since he is of his Majesty's Council, and sees how essential it is to give this aid, wherein his Majesty will hold himself to be very well served, I consider it as certain that he will do this."

The Adelantado thanked him, and charged him so to do.

Ynistrosa told him likewise that the Indian woman, Doña Antonia, the sister of Carlos, was very discreet, and of such grave demeanor that she astonished those of the town; that she and a maidservant of hers, of whom she was very fond, had learned in a few days with great facility all the things pertaining to prayers and the Christian doctrine, so that she might be baptized, and therefore she had been already; that she had been very sad, because of the absence of his lordship, and the deaths of her Indian men and women, but that since they had told her that his lordship had come, great was her delight and pleasure, and she wept for joy; that it was needful to entertain her and make much of her; that as he wished to take her away, it was fitting that she should go saying much good of them, for he and the people of Havana had shown her great consideration in entertaining her and making her contented.

The Adelantado said to him that the day previous, when they had disembarked, he had sent to call upon her, and that that day he would go to see her, and would do so when he had finished dining, and so he did; sending her first some of the food he was eating and certain chemises and clothing which he charged the Treasurer to buy for him, that the Indian woman might be pleased and see that he was bringing something; and he took with him when he went to see her, many persons of agreeable manners who accompanied her, and the music, for the Adelantado never went without it. He found the Indian woman sad, and although the Adelantado made her many gifts, she would not be comforted: he prayed her many times through the interpreter to tell him why she was sad: she told him that she wished that God might kill her, because when they landed the Adelantado had not sent for her to take her to his house, to eat and sleep with him.

As the Adelantado knew her to be such an important woman, of such good understanding and knew that she was not lacking in sense, he said to her that when the Christians who wore that cross—for the Adelantado is a Knight of the Order of Santiago—landed from an expedition against their enemies, they could not sleep with their wives until 8 days had passed, and that he wished that these had gone by, because he loved her much.

The Indian woman half laughed and half cried, and said that if she could believe he was telling the truth she would be happy.

The Adelantado begged that she would become so, for he was telling her truth; and she said, beginning to count on her fingers, that 2 days were passed already, and she named the remaining 6; that when those were passed, she would go to his house. The Adelantado told her to do so, and he rose, and she embraced him with great rejoicing, and took his hands, and ordered the instruments to be played, because those she had not seen in that land and they appeared very good to her: the Adelantado remained there more than an hour cheering her.

A *regidor* of that town, called Alonso de Rojas, had charge of this Indian woman: his wife is a person of standing, who was godmother to this Indian when she was baptized, and loved her very much and taught her, and she related to the Adelantado many instances of her good understanding, wherein the Adelantado took much satisfaction. And he asked the Indian woman if she had any desire to go to her country: she said yes, and a very great one: the Adelantado asked her if she wished that they should go the next day: she said yes, and that she entreated him very much that they might go: the Adelantado told her that they would do so, and he took leave of her and went to his inn, which was near there.

It happened that night that midnight being passed, and the Adelantado being asleep in his room, with a lighted candle, that Indian woman said to a woman who was her friend, whom she loved greatly, one of those whom the Adelantado had brought from Florida, whom Carlos, her brother, held as a slave; that she was to go with her to the house of the Adelantado, because he had ordered her to go there. The woman believed this and went with her, and with the Indian woman her maidservant, and she [the Christian woman] knocked at the door of the Adelantado's inn: they opened to see who it was: they recognized her: she said that the Adelantado had ordered her to go there with the Indian woman, and the youth who opened the door, thinking she spoke the truth, let them in and took them to the Adelantado's room, where there was a lighted candle; and the Indian woman took it in her hand, and looked to see if any woman were in bed with the Adelantado, and afterward she looked around the bed, and underneath it.

The Adelantado awoke, although he was very weary and exhausted, and when he saw her with the candle in her hand, he was disturbed, and he spoke across to the woman who came with her, and said:

"What is this, sister?"

Doña Antonia seated herself at the head of the bed with the candle, to see what the Adelantado was saying: the woman replied to the Adelantado that Doña Antonia had told her that his lordship had ordered that she be brought to him at that hour, and that she, believing this, had done so.

The Adelantado, with a gay and amused countenance, laughing greatly at this, told her to tell Doña Antonia that he would be very glad if the 8 days were passed, so that she might lie there beside him.

Doña Antonia said to him through the interpreter that she prayed him to let her lie in a corner of the bed, and that she would not come near him; in order that her brother Carlos might know that they had slept together, for in any other manner he would think that the Adelantado was laughing at her, and he would refuse to become a friend in truth of the Christians, or to become a Christian like herself, whereat she would be greatly grieved.

The Adelantado called a servant of his and told him to draw some things from a chest: they were 3 chemises, and mirrors and necklaces of glass beads for each of them; articles for barter which the Adelantado had had collected that day to take to her brother, Carlos; and she said to the Christian woman who came with her that she had intended, if the Adelantado had not awakened, to put out the candle and lie down beside him; and with this they went away satisfied.

Immediately after in the morning, the Adelantado went to embark, and took the Indian woman with him, and her maidservant, and 2 of the Christian women who had been captives: he started in a patache and a little shallop, with about 30 soldiers and sailors: he set sail with a prosperous wind: he arrived at the pueblo of Carlos on the third day: he anchored at the entrance of the harbor because as he brought few men, he did not dare go up to the town: then the Indian woman told the Adelantado that he should land with her and go to the pueblo.

The Adelantado said to her that in no manner could he do this, as it was necessary that he should go at once in search of Christians, so that they could live there, and teach her brother and the Indians of that country to become Christians, if they wished to be; that he promised to build her then a house in that country, in which she should live, in the pueblo of the Christians; and that the relatives of the Indian men and women who had died in Havana, would believe that the Adelantado had killed them, and would want to do harm to him and his soldiers; wherefore war with her brother might break out, and this he would greatly regret, because he liked him very much, for the love of her, and held him to be his brother; and that he wished to return at once. The Indian woman answered him that she was very sorrowful because the Adelantado did not disembark and remain a few days on land, until the 8 days were over, in order that he might sleep with her; but that she likewise feared that the Indians might feel warlike and might do him some harm; that she prayed him to come back as soon as he could, and bring Christians so that they might live there, and turn her brother and the other Indians into Christians.

Then there came many canoes, and Doña Antonia sent to tell her brother that she was there and that he should come for her: it was something to see the joy of the Indians at the sight of her, and others wept in grief for the Indian men and women who had gone away with her and died. Within 2 hours [came Carlos], with as many as 12 canoes, and two of them fastened one to the other, with decks covered with awnings of hoops and matting; and first he and the captain, his brother-in-law, got into the patache with the Adelantado, [then] 6 other principal Indians: it was something to see how Doña Antonia and her brother received each other, and the ceremonies they performed. The Adelantado ordered them to bring food and to play the instruments, and to give some maize and cassava to the Indians in the canoes, likewise some knives and scissors, mirrors and bells; and having finished dining, he made a present to Carlos for his wife, and gave another to the captain for him and his wife, who was the sister of Doña Antonia; and he gave to the principal Indians who were there, and to Doña Antonia some things which he had brought for her. The Adelantado asked Carlos if he wanted to become a Christian and cut his hair, and if he would like to go to a

land of Christians as he had promised him; and that he should bring him the Christians he had said he would give him when he [the Adelantado] should return there.

Carlos replied that they must allow him to speak apart with his captain, and that then he would give him the answer; and so they spoke aside for more than a quarter of an hour, and they said to the Adelantado that for those 9 months Carlos could in no manner go to a land of Christians, nor could he turn Christian at that time so that his Indians would not rise against him and slay him; that when that time had passed, the Adelantado might return; and he justified [himself] with sufficient reasons.

The Adelantado entrusted Doña Antonia to him and went back to Havana, where he found that some meat and cassava had been bought through the efforts of Juan de Ynistrosa; but he did not find any men, nor other things that he needed; wherefore he was compelled to have recourse to Don Cristóbal de Eraso and Don Bernardino de Córdoba, who were there and who had come from Tierra Firme and New Spain. He represented to them his dire necessity, and that he desired to return to Florida with some supplies which he did not have, nor had he the money to buy them; he thought that when they understood the straits he was in, they would speak to the Governor or to Valderrama; that from each of the more than 30 ships in the fleets and the armada, they could give him one hundredweight of biscuit and one jar of wine; and that with some maize and cassava he begged from his friends in Havana, from each one his share as charity, he could return to Florida with 50 or 60 sailors and soldiers he had there.

They succored him with nothing. The Adelantado, seeing this, and [remembering] how few people he had left in the forts, took a frigate, a brigantine and a little shallop, and put on board about 65 persons, 5 of whom were delivered to him by the Governor; and on a gold-embroidered suit and garments and other things, he obtained 500 ducats, with which he bought maize, meat and cassava. He sailed from Havana on the 1st of July, in company with the Fleets of New Spain and Tierra Firme, that were going to Spain, and immediately after that day he separated from them. He arrived in Florida, at Fort San Mateo, within 8 days, where he found a vessel anchored off the bar: he went to reconnoitre her: he learned that she had come from Spain with provisions. The men on board of her said that in the harbor of St. Augustine there were 14 other ships, and in that of Santa Elena 2 more, and they all came laden with supplies, and brought 1,500 infantry to succor those forts and the Indies, because there was news that French Lutherans were getting together a great fleet to come to those parts.

21.

The satisfaction the Adelantado and his people received from this was very great, for he came back much aggrieved at the little favor and help he had found in Havana, though so many servants of the King were there, in such prominent positions, and all gentlemen of high standing, who had given him no succor, alms nor charity; it was especially wrong since he knew the sufficient provisions and cédulas of his Majesty, to the effect that from his Royal Exchequer García Osorio, Governor of that island, should give him what he asked him for and might need. The Adelantado crossed the bar of San Mateo: he went to the fort: he found Captain Aguirre, who had come from Spain as a soldier, because of the absence of Juan de Oruña, who was going as colonel of these men and had remained in San Lucar by order of his Majesty, to whom it appeared that he was not needed in Florida, on account of the good captains the Adelantado had with him; and the day they arrived in St. Augustine, Sancho de Arciniega, who came as the General of that armada and relief expedition, gave the colonel's company, of 250 soldiers, to this Aguirre, that he might go to the assistance of Fort San Mateo, because the camp master had come at once from San Mateo to St. Augustine, as soon as he knew that reinforcements had arrived, leaving that fort in charge of Vasco Zabal. The Adelantado found Vasco Zabal with the Adelantado's own soldiers, inside the fort, and Aguirre quartered outside, and differences between them, because Vasco Zabal requested that this Captain Aguirre should place himself inside the fort with the soldiers, and he said he would do so, but it was for him to place the sentinels and give the password: Vasco Zabal said that the care and defence of the fort were his duty, and he would

not consent to his demands. The Adelantado ordered that Captain Aguirre should put 50 soldiers in the fort every night, and that Vasco Zabal should place the sentinels and give the password; and leaving them very much in accord, he departed for St. Augustine. On the way he met the camp master, sailing in a brigantine, who was coming to San Mateo to adjust the disagreement between Captain Aguirre and Vasco Zabal: the Adelantado was extremely pleased to see him. The camp master related to him the miseries, hardships and perils they had suffered before the arrival of the reinforcements, and how the Indians, near Fort San Mateo, had treacherously killed Captain Martín Ochoa and other soldiers; and how in that of St. Augustine they had killed in the same manner Captain Diego de Hevia, a relative of the Adelantado; and as they had no food, they were forced to go out in search of large oysters, crawfish, and palmettos: it was necessary that most of the men of the fort should go for this together; otherwise he who went alone did not return. The Adelantado was very sorrowful at the death of these two captains, for he loved them very much, and Martín Ochoa had greatly distinguished himself at the capture of the fort, and during all the rest of his service he had been very faithful; in such wise that those who mutinied had wanted to kill him many times, because he upheld with great spirit his Majesty's service, condemning the weakness they showed.

The Indians had likewise treacherously slain with their arrows 5 other soldiers and an interpreter among them; they were much beloved of the Adelantado, had been among the first to enter when the fort was captured, and had assisted through hardships and dangers, obeying the Governor in everything, without wanting to desert the fort and go off with the mutineers: one of them was Don Hernando de Gamboa, a natural son of Don Prudencio de Bendaña; another, Juan de Valdés, a first cousin of the camp master: another was Juan Menéndez, a second cousin of the Adelantado. He felt this very much, but when he saw how much the camp master must be grieving, he concealed his sorrow and said: "In such undertakings these deaths, hardships and perils cannot be avoided: may God forgive them, for I certainly feel this deeply."

Then the camp master told him in detail about

the reinforcements which had arrived, and the names of the captains, and how badly they had behaved to him; for when they arrived and landed, they quartered themselves around the fort; and the first two nights when the camp master arrived, he had the sentinels stationed at the points where they should be, and gave them the password. They were satisfied that the camp master, with the powers the Adelantado had given him, was his lieutenant; but afterward the captains heard that the powderhouse and the Fort of St. Augustine where they were at first had burned with everything therein, all the supplies and papers, and among them the commission that the camp master had from the Adelantado; [so] they agreed to place the sentinels themselves, and give their password, and wanted to name a camp master and sergeant major. To some this appeared right, to others, wrong, and there was some discord among them; but in effect, they went ahead with this action. The camp master was surprised at this change, for never had they said one word to him, nor asked him for his commission, before or after: he sent to tell them that they should all meet, as he wished to speak to them, and when they had done so, he said to them:

"Gentlemen, the Adelantado has left me in these provinces as his lieutenant, by the authority which he holds for this purpose from his Majesty, and he gave me sufficient powers therefor. Those papers have been burned, but the notary before whom they were executed is here, and all have knowledge of them, and respect and obey me as the Adelantado's lieutenant. Your Honors can obtain information on this from the captains and soldiers who are in the province, for they are here, and they are Bartolomé Menéndez, regular Captain to his Majesty, brother of the Adelantado, *alcaide* of this Fort of St. Augustine and governor of the district; and Gonzalo de Villarroel, *alcaide* and governor of the Fort of San Mateo and its district; the other is Estébano de las Alas, *alcaide* and governor of the Fort of San Felipe and its district, which is in Santa Elena; they are all three persons of reputation, noblemen and very good soldiers, from whom your Honors can satisfy yourselves of this; and it being as I have said, his Majesty will be served by your obeying me while I am in office; and let us

give orders that all suitable measures be taken, as befits his Majesty's service, sending men and supplies to Santa Elena, to Estébano de las Alas, who is in great need, and fortifying ourselves, for if the enemy come upon us, and it is said they are coming and are strong, we are not [prepared] as soldiers should be."

[The camp master went on to say] that Sancho de Arciniega, who was General of the armada, and whom they all held to be the head, replied to him that he could not deliver the men before the Adelantado returned, because it had been so decided between him and the captains he brought with him; and that they said his lordship was drowned, because when he set out from St. Augustine for Havana in search of supplies, with the three brigantines, one of them could not turn her prow and put in to Hispaniola; there were two days of strong winds and heavy seas, wherefore they held him for lost, and were thus determined to be the heads themselves, and name the officials who were necessary, and remain in that land until they could notify his Majesty. The camp master had answered Sancho de Arciniega that he regretted deeply to hear such things, because he knew his Majesty would not be pleased therewith, and his royal service would cease in those provinces; and that since they were determined so to act, he and the *alcaides* of the forts, with the soldiers therein, would hold them in the name of his Majesty, as they were holding them, and would defend them to the death against friend and foe; while Arciniega and his men would be quartered in the fields, accomplishing nothing, wasting the royal funds and supplies; and that if this enterprise were to continue, they must be good friends: they replied to the camp master that so it should be done, and they would maintain that friendship; and he had put up with those things as he saw he could not do otherwise, and it was for the benefit of his Majesty's service to overlook them. In that manner had they been governing themselves, without working at the fortifications or doing anything else, for 12 days; since that armada and relief expedition had entered the harbor. The Adelantado thanked the camp master very much for the wisdom with which he had conducted himself, and said that he had acted like a very good captain, because in conquests and settlements of new lands it is needful for those in power to overlook such insubordination at times, when they can do nothing else; and that that was the true way to serve his Majesty and do what was proper. The Adelantado arrived that day in St. Augustine: he was very well received by all.

General Sancho de Arciniega was on board his ship, and as it was late, did not come on land.

The next day in the morning, when the Adelantado had heard mass, he sent to request the captains to come to the fort, because he wanted to talk to them, and enter into council with them: this was done, and Sancho de Arciniega came, who was General of the armada and the forces in that relief expedition and carried a cédula from his Majesty to the effect that he should deliver everything to the Adelantado, and do that which he ordered and commanded. He brought with him Captain Juan de Ubila, Admiral of the fleet: the Adelantado received him very well, because Sancho de Arciniega had been a great friend of his for many years.

General Sancho de Arciniega gave into his hands his Majesty's dispatches, the armada and the men. When the Adelantado had read the dispatches he acknowledged the receipt thereof, and said to the General that he had brought with him some bad advisers, since he had not gone through that formality on the day of his arrival, with the camp master as the Adelantado's lieutenant in those provinces, by commission from his Majesty; and that the Adelantado could hardly be in all parts of Florida at once, as it was such a large country; that if Arciniega were as familiar with the affairs of war on land as with the same at sea, he would not have believed his advisers, nor allowed himself to be deceived by them; that the Adelantado did not lay as much blame on him as on some captains who, because they wanted to govern and follow their private interest, did not advise him what was fitting for him or for his Majesty's service; but that as this was past, and remedied by his arrival, he did not intend to speak any more about it, and begged of them as a favor to consider him as a brother and friend, and to advise him in all the things wherein it appeared to them that his Majesty would best be served; and that at the proper time he would entreat his Majesty to reward him who had served him well: and he added other remarks whereat, without passing over the wrong they had done, nor acquiescing in it, he left them very much satisfied.

They all replied that they would do as he wished, and received great gratification from the good words the Adelantado had spoken to them.

Then the Adelantado went to visit all the women who had come in that armada, of whom there were 14, to whom he had sent an order to assemble in one house, and he congratulated them on their arrival, and they were much pleased at the Adelantado's visit and the favor he did them. He spoke with the priests who were with these people, of whom there were 5: he recommended to them to attend with a Christian spirit to the duties of their charge: he gave them the vicar whom they were to obey, who was Chaplain Mendoza, of Xerez on the Frontier; a very good religious and soldier, who had come from Spain with the Adelantado, and he had made him vicar of that fort and that of San Mateo; and so they replied they would do it, and pledged obedience to the vicar. The Adelantado went—with all the captains who accompanied him for this, and with the advice and concurrence of them all, giving and taking [opinions] about it in order to decide the better—to mark out the site, place and space where they were to fortify themselves, which was in the same spot that the Adelantado had fortified; but because the sea was eating away the fort, they retired further inland, taking a *caballero* from the fort that had been made, for the one that was to be begun. He divided the men into squads and companies, and the work likewise: they cast the dice, so that chance might decide at which part each one was to work, and it was settled in this manner, to the satisfaction of all, so that next day in the morning each captain, man and squad understood which part of the fort had fallen to their share.

Next morning, at dawn, they rang the bells, which was the signal for all to rise; [and] they beat the drums, mustering their men, who all came hastening to work so that it was a pleasure to see them.

22.

On the third day, when the Adelantado saw that the task was progressing as it should, he summoned the captains to a council, and told them that it would be well to discuss where his Majesty's reinforcements were to be stationed; and after arguing about it, it was agreed that half of the 1,500 soldiers should remain in those parts, in the 3 forts of St. Augustine, San Mateo and San Felipe; that the Adelantado should go with the rest, and 6 vessels, one frigate and one patache, with their crews—about one thousand men altogether—to cruise about the islands of Puerto Rico, Santo Domingo and Cuba, in order to chastise the corsairs who might be there, and to fortify those places; and that the other ships should take their departure shortly and go to Spain under the command of Sancho de Arciniega and Juan de Ubila, who, as has been said, had come as General and Admiral of that relief expedition. In the meantime the 6 ships which the Adelantado was to take from the armada, the frigate and the patache, were being unloaded and outfitted. He wanted to go to visit the Fort of San Mateo and leave therein Gonzalo de Villarroel, who was in St. Augustine and had returned from Havana, with all the people under his charge; thence he wished to pass on to Guale and Santa Elena, to visit the Fort of San Felipe and put it in a state of thorough defence, because 2 vessels had sailed for there, the flagship and 2 other large ones, with 300 soldiers and Captain Juan Pardo in charge of them, and it was not known that they had arrived, nor the state of things in those parts.

With the concurrence and advice of all the captains, he named Captain Juan de Zorita to succor Puerto Rico; Captain Rodrigo Troche, who was one of the first who had gone to Florida with the Adelantado, to succor Santo Domingo; and Ensign Baltasar de Barreda to succor Havana; and he departed for San Mateo, where he left Gonzalo de Villarroel in that fort, with Captain Aguirre's company and the rest of the veteran soldiers who were there.

With one hundred soldiers and some sailors, in 3 brigantines, he ascended the River of San Mateo for more than 50 leagues; up to that time he had not done so. His object was to make friends with the caciques and discover the secret as to whether that river went toward the coast of New Spain.

The day after he left San Mateo, having ascended that river 20 leagues, he disembarked, and with a guide he had brought with him he walked 5 leagues through the good level lands of a cacique they called Hotina. When he was one

league from his pueblo he sent him 6 soldiers with this guide, who was an interpreter; and on arriving there they gave him a present which the Adelantado sent him, and told him that the Adelantado was coming to see him because he held him to be his friend. He received the 6 soldiers very well and replied to them that he stood in fear of the Adelantado, and that if he wished to come to his village he should bring not more than 20 men, and should pray to God as he had done for Cacique Guale, that it might rain on his maize fields, which were dry.

The Adelantado was following close behind the 6 soldiers, and when the answer came back to him, he was about one quarter of a league from the village. He halted, and ordered 80 of the soldiers to remain there, and went on with 20, laughing at what the cacique asked about the rain; and when he arrived in the pueblo it began to rain very hard, and it was more than 6 months since it had done so. He reached the cacique's house, and did not find him: he told 5 or 6 Indians who were there to go in search of him, and to say that he had come with the 20 men and the rain. One of the Indians went, and returned with the answer, saying that the cacique was hidden in the forest, and sent him word that he was in great fear of a man who had such power with God; that he was to depart with God, since he was His friend. The Adelantado regretted this, for he much desired to see this cacique, as it was said that he had a very good understanding and was very powerful on that river bank of San Mateo; and he sent him back a message that he prayed him greatly to come to see him, and not to be afraid, since he had not more than 20 men with him, and the cacique had more than one thousand Indians, all with their bows and arrows. Hotina replied that if the Adelantado was helped by his cacique, who was God, he had many men in those 20 soldiers; that he prayed him to be gone, and from that time he was taking him for his elder brother and he was his friend, as long as the cacique was in his land and the Adelantado in his; and that he did not want to fight with the Adelantado or his men, but his Indians did, and that he caused him much anxiety because he did not go.

The Adelantado sent to tell him that he would go to please him, but that he was not afraid of him or his men; that he would sail up the River of San

Mateo; that the cacique was to notify those of his villages through which the Adelantado would have to pass, that the men and women were to remain therein and not be afraid, and that if they fled, the Adelantado would make war on them, burning their villages and canoes and fishways. And so the Adelantado returned to where the 80 soldiers had halted, and taking them with him, he reached the brigantines at nightfall: his march was a thing they all marvelled at, for it was one o'clock in the morning when he left the brigantines to go and find Hotina, and he was there two hours, and it was still day when he returned; 10 leagues are a long way, although many thought it was 12. That night was very bad for it rained very hard and they could not embark, and as they camped in a wet field they all had a hard time.

The next day in the morning the Adelantado sent the largest brigantine with 50 men back to San Mateo, and he went on his way up the river with the other 50, the 2 brigantines and some supplies; for as he had provisions for 10 or 12 days [only], if all the men had gone with him the quantity could not have lasted and he could not have discovered the secret of that river.

He was very well received in the pueblos he found along the river banks, for they said that their Cacique Hotina had sent to command them to do so.

The Adelantado tried hard to carry with him some guide, to learn the secret of the river by means of presents he gave the Indians and the kindness he showed them, but no one wanted to go with him. He sailed up quite as far as the French had gone, having with him two who had guided them: the tide rose and fell for a distance of full 40 leagues, a thing which much astonished the Adelantado. He ascended that river about 50 leagues, two leagues farther than the French had gone, as far as [the domains of] a cacique they called Macoya, a friend of Saturiba who was a powerful cacique of the coast and country where are the Forts of San Mateo and St. Augustine; this Macoya retired with his Indians, leaving the pueblo deserted.

The Adelantado landed, entered the houses, allowed no damage to be done, and then turned back and withdrew: he sent the interpreter to see if any Indian appeared: they came to meet him, for they knew him: they were much pleased at seeing this interpreter. He said that the Chris-

tians and their captain were there, and that they should send to tell their Cacique Macoya to come to the village with his men, and have no fear: some Indians went in search of him to tell him this; others came back to their houses and brought the Adelantado much fish: he made them some gifts and received them very well, and prayed them to go and summon the cacique, because he wished to give him many things he brought for him and his wives. They went, and these and the first who had gone, returned and told the Adelantado that their cacique held him in great fear and would not come, and that he and his Indians were his friends, because they knew that he did no harm to any cacique; but that he was to return without going farther up the river, for the cacique's Indians were angry because he had come to their land without their permission.

The Adelantado sent him word that he wished to pass up the river, to see some Christians; that he prayed him to give him 2 or 3 Indians as pilots.

The cacique replied that he would not.

The Adelantado commanded the oars to be used, and began to go up the river, rowing about a league: it was already late: he saw many excited Indians with bows and arrows, and on arriving at a narrow pass, he found the river barred with a row of stakes: he broke through and went farther on: the river became no wider than two pikes' lengths, and very deep: there he encountered a very swift current against him, for up to then there had been none whatever, except the rising and ebbing of the tide: the Adelantado feared that the Indians might shoot at the rowers.

2 or 3 Indians came down to the river bank and told him on behalf of Cacique Macoya that he must not go farther and must turn back; if he did not, they would begin to make war upon him.

The Adelantado answered them that he did not come to harm them, and they could make war when they wished; that he was obliged to go up that river, and as it was night, he wanted to stay there until morning, and he did so. The guide and interpreter the Adelantado brought with him had been a slave of a cacique of Ays whom they called Perucho, who lived 20 leagues up the river and knew this Macoya; he told the Adelantado that he ought to return, for there were many and very warlike Indians in that land, and that they told him that the river became very narrow from there inland for more than 30 leagues, until it emptied into a large lagoon they call Maymi, which they say has a circuit of more than 30 leagues, and which gathers into itself many streams from the hill range; and that [a branch of] this lagoon discharged itself in the country of Cacique Carlos, which is on the coast of New Spain, and that another branch drained the land of Tequesta, which is at Los Mártires.

The Adelantado desired greatly to discover this secret, because of the friendship he had established with Carlos and because he wanted to know if that river were navigable, for that would be a very advantageous thing for the conquest and settlement of Florida; but on the other hand, he feared that if the canoes of warlike Indians came out in that narrow pass while he was within the barrier of stakes, he might be harmed by them; especially as it had been raining hard, and the soldiers' powder and fuses were damp. He retired one league back with his two brigantines, and next morning decided to return; and on the way, 7 or 8 leagues down the river, he landed at a pueblo where some Indians were waiting for him: he gave them presents and told them to summon their cacique, who came, and whom they call Calabay. He said to him through the interpreter that Macoya had sent to tell him not to pass up that river, and that his soldiers had been much angered against Macoya and wanted to land and burn his village and the canoes, and destroy his fishways; and to prevent their doing it, he was returning.

Calabay replied that he wanted to be his friend and take him for an elder brother, to do what he should command him; that he prayed him to give him a cross, and 6 other Christians, as he had to Guale; that he and his Indians wanted to be Christians; that he would show that river, as far as the lagoon of Maymi, to the 6 Christians who might remain with him, because the Indians did not fear a few Christians, but did fear many, and that he would do them no harm.

The Adelantado was afraid of this cacique, because, being a vassal of Hotina, he might rise against the Adelantado, and he was a great friend of Cacique Saturiba; but as there were only 12 leagues by land from there to St. Augustine, he decided to leave him the men and give him the cross, and told him that if anyone killed them he would come and make war on him, in such wise that he would burn the houses and canoes and

destroy the fishways, and cut off his head and those of his men, women and children, for the Adelantado was a friend of his true friends and an enemy of his enemies. The cacique said that he was satisfied, and immediately there were many soldiers who begged that they might be left there.

The Adelantado left those who appeared to him the most willing and the best fitted to teach the Indians the doctrine: he gave this cacique a present for himself and another for Macoya, and prayed him that he should send Macoya three of those Christians, who should live with him and teach him and his Indians.

Calabay said that he would do this, and so it was done, for he sent Macoya the present and the Christians: Macoya would not receive them but took the present. He sent to tell the Adelantado that he was his friend and held him to be his elder brother, which is all the obedience the caciques of Florida can give; but that if he came to his country he would hold him to be his enemy.

When Saturiba heard that Calabay had Christians, he sent two of his sons and other Indians to slay them. Calabay would not allow this: Saturiba sent to tell him to kill them, or send them to him, and if he did not, he would hold him for an enemy.

Calabay, fearing Saturiba, sent them to San Mateo. When the Adelantado was on his way back to San Mateo, all the people, big and little, in 3 or 4 villages of Hotina by which he had previously passed, awaited him with much rejoicing; he made them some gifts and had the instruments played, whereat they were all delighted: they were sorrowful because he was going so soon. He arrived at the place where he disembarked when he went overland to see Hotina: he sent word to him that as he had gone to see him in his pueblo, Hotina should come there to see the Adelantado, and that if he did not do this, he would consider him as his enemy. Hotina feared to anger the Adelantado, and he had heard of the great friendliness the Adelantado had shown in those of Hotina's villages where he had stopped, in all of which they liked him very much; so he came to see the Adelantado, with 300 warriors, and at a quarter of a league from the brigantines he halted, and sent to tell the Adelantado to come there with 20 Christians. He did this, bringing with him 20 skilful arquebusiers, marching in very good order. When he arrived near Hotina, the cacique was frightened, and sent to tell the Adelantado to come to him with 2 persons, no more; and at a distance of about half an arquebuse shot, the Adelantado halted with the 20 soldiers, and with two only, and the interpreter, he went to Hotina, who was surrounded with his 300 bowmen, seated on the ground. Hotina showed much humility, rendering the Adelantado the greatest homage which is customary among them; and then came his principal men one by one, doing likewise, and all the other Indians who were there did that.

The Adelantado clothed Hotina in a shirt, for he was naked, with only a belt round his loins, and so were all his Indians; and he clothed him in a pair of breeches and a doublet of green silk, and put a hat on his head. That Indian was much of a gentleman in face and figure, about 25 years old and very discreet: he told the Adelantado that he took him for his elder brother, to do what he might command him; that he should leave him a cross, as he had to Guale, and Christians to teach the doctrine to him and his people; and a trumpeter, since he was in truth his brother.

The Adelantado did so, for he left him the cross and 6 Christians, and the trumpeter among them; he gave him some presents for his wife, and made gifts to the principal Indians who were there: they parted very good friends. The Adelantado embarked and reached San Mateo within 12 days from the day he had set out: he found the whole fort in very good condition, and Gonzalo de Villarroel pleased with the men, although some of them, without his order, had gone two leagues from there to rob certain houses of Saturiba: the Indians came out upon them, and out of 12 arquebusiers who went, 8 were killed, and 4 returned to the fort within three days, very badly wounded, having hidden in the forest. The Adelantado remained there two days: he departed for Santa Elena: he dispatched notice to his Majesty that the reinforcements had arrived and [told him of] the state of those affairs. He sent a captain with 30 soldiers and 2 Dominican friars to the Bay of Santa María, in 37°, with an Indian who was the brother of the cacique of that country, and who had been 6 years with the Adelantado: he was very crafty, a good Christian with very good understanding, called Don Luis de Velasco; so that with his assistance they might settle in that land and try to make the Indians Christians.

The friars were from Peru and New Spain, a very fertile country [sic]: they had suffered hunger, hardships and dangers in Florida. As it appeared to them that they could no longer endure such a difficult life, they secretly drew some of the soldiers into a conspiracy, for there was no need of much effort to accomplish this, and won over the pilot; and being in accord, and taking testimony to the effect that on account of a storm they had been unable to go to the Bay of Santa María, they went to Seville, defaming the country and speaking ill of the King and the Adelantado, because they wanted to conquer and settle it.

The Adelantado arrived at Santa Elena: he found Estébano de las Alas in his fort with the first soldiers sent there, and Juan Pardo quartered outside, building houses to lodge the men, because he had brought an order from General Sancho de Arciniega that one night he should give out the password, and the next night Estébano de las Alas should do so, and therefore Pardo showed Las Alas the order he carried.

Estébano de las Alas said to Juan Pardo that he was much pleased at his arrival, and that he had orders from the Adelantado Pedro Menéndez, his Captain-General, to guard and defend that fort in the name of his Majesty; that it was his duty to place the sentinels and give the password, and nobody else's; and that on this condition Pardo could lodge himself in the fort with all his men, or with the part of them he wished; or camp in the fields; whichever appeared best to him.

Juan Pardo was a good soldier, zealous in the service of his Majesty: it seemed to him that Estébano de las Alas was in the right, and Sancho de Arciniega was not; and that he on arriving in Florida, was obliged to obey and comply with the commands of the Adelantado, and not those of others: he pledged obedience to Estébano de las Alas for the defence of the fort, giving him a squad of soldiers for the sentinels' guard, and [saying that], if it were necessary, he would assist with the rest; and he quartered himself in the fields, and they all began to work to place the fort in a good state of defence.

Great was the joy and gladness which all received on the arrival of the Adelantado. He heard that the Indians were very friendly, and that Estébano de las Alas was in great need of men and supplies when Captain Juan Pardo arrived with 300 soldiers and 2 vessels laden with provisions; because one month before, the Adelantado having sent a boat of supplies, the day after she arrived the soldiers mutinied and went off in her before unloading anything, leaving Estébano de las Alas a prisoner, with his officers who came with him from Havana, and about 60 men; and in the Bahama Channel they ran into a storm which compelled them to put into a harbor of Florida, at the beginning of Los Mártires. They found a pueblo, the cacique whereof the Indians called Tequesta, who was a near relative of Cacique Carlos and the Indian woman, Doña Antonia, for 2 Christians who had been captives there many years, and who came to meet them in a canoe, told them this; and that those Indians used to kill all the Christians from the ships that were wrecked, but that now they loved them very much because they knew that the most important man among them had a relative of theirs for a wife, a sister of Carlos; that they should have no fear; that the cacique sent to find out from them if they were some of those Christians, and they said they were; and that near there, in a village on the coast, were many more of those Christians, and that was the truth; for of the soldiers who had mutinied at San Mateo, about 20 landed there, when they were on their way to Havana: a very strong wind had come up, the vessel spread her sails, leaving them in that country, and the Indians treated them very well, sharing with them what they had, for love of the Indian woman, Doña Antonia. Likewise, about 20 of Estébano de las Alas's soldiers had deserted him and gone inland: he had about 25 in the fort when Juan Pardo arrived, and no food other than that which the Indians sent him.

After Captain Juan Pardo's arrival he had hanged 2 soldiers for mutiny: he held 3 others prisoners: 6 had deserted. The men were half uneasy, as it appeared to them that there was discord between him and Estébano de las Alas when there was not, but much harmony, and no less than what is told.

The Adelantado entered into council: he decided on the way that they should proceed: he remained there 8 days, during which the caciques his friends came to see him, and prayed him to wait there a month, because many caciques from inland wanted to come to see him, to take him for their elder brother: he could not do this, owing to the need there was of his returning shortly to St. Augustine, to dispose of the reinforcements in the

manner his Majesty might direct. He released the 3 soldiers whom Juan Pardo held prisoners, giving them a reprimand, and spoke to all of them, encouraging and entreating them to remain steadfast in the service of his Majesty's provinces, because he wanted to take the reinforcements with him, as he did; the camp master for his lieutenant and Admiral of the armada; and he gave orders to Juan Pardo to go inland, toward New Spain, with 150 soldiers, to visit the caciques who wanted to come to see the Adelantado; and with all possible friendliness, in what appeared to him the most convenient place for the safety of his soldiers, he was to fortify himself, and see that the Indians became Christians.

And so the Adelantado departed from Santa Elena at the end of August, having confirmed the peace with the caciques, and charging Estébano de las Alas to preserve it.

23.

He arrived in Guale in 2 days; he found the Indians very sad at the death of Alonso Menéndez Marqués, the Adelantado's nephew, whom they greatly loved, and who was the head of the Christians who were there.

Many caciques of that district came there with the desire of seeing the Adelantado: he stopped there 8 days, during which 14 of 15 of them came: they begged him for crosses and Christians, to teach them to be Christians: the Adelantado agreed to leave there one captain with 30 soldiers, most of them important men, who requested that they might be left there, because it seemed to them that [thus] they could best serve God and the King.

The Adelantado set forth: he arrived in San Mateo in another 2 days, where he found all the people well: he took Gonzalo de Villarroel with him to St. Augustine, where he found that many soldiers wanted to mutiny and leave the country. The camp master had hanged 3 of them: he held others prisoners, also Captain Pedro de Rodabán, who was one of the captains whom his Majesty had sent with that relief party. He had acted with disrespect toward the camp master, and was accused of being the leader who had given the order and the occasion for them to mutiny; but although the Adelantado found cause to work justice upon them, he spoke with the camp master and told him that, since they did not know those captains and soldiers, and as many of them had been disobedient, it was necessary to overlook things and do what they could, not what they would; that for the sake of peace it was proper that the Adelantado should rebuke this captain, then free him, leaving the charge against him as it was: this seemed right to the camp master, and so it was done.

The Adelantado was very joyfully received by all the captains, soldiers and sailors who were there: he sent the ships to Spain: he started with the armada to pursue corsairs and bring succor to the islands of Puerto Rico, Hispaniola and Cuba, as had been resolved. He sailed on the 20th of October, although he had been ready to set out at the end of September and could not do so owing to contrary winds. In order to take the corsairs by surprise, he arrived on the 5th of November, with half the armada, at Mona Island, and the camp master, with the other half, at San German, because those are the places to which the corsairs and robbers are accustomed to go, but they found none.

24.

These were the captains of the 6 vessels of the armada: the Adelantado, who was the General of his ship; the camp master, who was the captain and admiral of his; Juan Vélez de Medrano, of another; Ensign Cristóbal de Herrera, of another; at the time he was ensign to Captain Diego de Maya, he was the first to plant the flag on the Fort of San Mateo when it was captured from the French; Captain Pedro de Rodabán, of another; Baltasar de Barreda, of another; García Martínez de Cos [was captain] of the frigate, and Rodrigo Montes, of the brigantine; he was the first cousin of the camp master and was likewise one of the first to enter the fort.

As soon as the camp master with his vessels anchored at San German, he received tidings from the people on land how a dispatch boat was at Guadinilla, 15 leagues thence: the crew whereof foresaid that on the 25th of September of that year '66, 27 armed ships had departed from France; that they had separated into 3 divisions, and the first had captured the island of Madeira on the 6th of October; that they knew not where the other 2 parts of the armada might be, and that the whole of it was bringing 6,000 soldiers and sailors.

The camp master at once sent Hernando de Miranda, his Majesty's Factor in Florida, to inform himself and learn particularly about this; he went to Guadinilla and spoke with the master and the pilot of the patache, who were his friends, and who told him the same thing. They gave a written statement of what had occurred in this, signed by a *regidor* of La Palma, who was in the island of Madeira when the French captured it, and they remained there 17 days; and on the ships came some Portuguese whom that *regidor* knew, who related to him all that was happening. On the third day Hernando de Miranda returned to San German and gave a report of everything to the camp master, who, because it appeared to him that the Adelantado should know these things (so that his fleet could assemble and a decision be taken as to what he ought to do), sent him the intelligence to Mona Island, 20 leagues from there, where he was with 3 ships. When the Adelantado had received the dispatch, he sent the fleet to San German, with orders to the camp master to careen and grease the vessels and put them in very good condition, and he went to Santo Domingo, 50 leagues from there: he was very well received by the Audiencia of that city, for 2 days before they had had news of the French armada and they feared greatly that it might come there. The Adelantado went to the Audiencia, where the President and *oidores* were assembled: he showed them the cédula he held from his Majesty in order to raise assistance: he told them that he brought one thousand soldiers and sailors, all very good men, pilots and sailors, for he had taken for that purpose the seamen he had in Florida, who were very good; and that he came with the determination to chase and entrap all the corsairs there might be in those parts, in order to punish them, so that in times of peace they should not go about perpetrating such extortions and thefts from, and injuries to the subjects of his Majesty; but that owing to the tidings he had that the French armada was coming to those parts, he begged them as a favor to give him their advice thereon; and the Audiencia, after discussing the matter, summed it up by telling him that the advice they gave was that he should fortify that city and fortress, that of Puerto Rico, that of Havana and other neighboring ports, as his Majesty ordered him to do, and should then return speedily to Florida.

Much did the Adelantado regret that advice, because he desired to encounter one of those three divisions of the French armada, and other corsairs who went about separately in those parts, who had become very wealthy from the plunder they had collected; but it appeared to him that his Majesty ordered him by his cédula to do what the Audiencia counselled, and so he determined to do it. He requested them to keep themselves free that afternoon and the next day, in order to see the best method to be followed for the fortifying of that city and fortress, and to examine and understand the points where the enemy might land, so as to station sentinels; and in order likewise that the wheels and gun carriages of the artillery might be replaced because those they had were decayed, so as to set them up and make them ready at the points where they were most needed; which was all done with great diligence and care.

The Adelantado left Captain Rodrigo Troche in that city, with 150 soldiers, two thirds of them arquebusiers and one third, pikemen: he left Captain Antonio Gómez as captain of artillery, for he was very skilled in this and a great man for handling powder, and within 6 days the Adelantado went back to San German. He arrived in 3 days, [and] he sent Captain Cristóbal de Herrera on his hooker, with supplies, munitions and twenty hundred weight of powder for cannon and arquebuses, for the defence of the fortress and the city.

There were in that city 10 vessels laden with hides and sugar for Spain: the Audiencia made that hooker the flagship and Cristóbal de Herrera the General, as he was a good soldier on land and sea, and with all of them he arrived in Seville in safety.

As soon as the Adelantado reached San German, he found the ships quite prepared for war: he entered into council with the camp master and the captains: he told them the decision he had taken on the advice of the President and *oidores* of the Royal Audiencia of Santo Domingo, and that he had to abide by and fulfil it. He immediately dispatched Captain Juan de Zorita, with his armed ship, and 100 arquebusiers and 4 artillery pieces on board, with a supply of powder; and the Adelantado went by land from San German to [San Juan of] Puerto Rico, where he was very well received by the Governor and citizens, as they were in great fear that the French armada might arrive. He told them what his Majesty had com-

manded him: he showed the cédula to the Governor and the *regimiento*, and [said] that 100 soldiers, 4 pieces of artillery and munitions would soon be there on an armed ship, because he had just left them in San German about to be dispatched: he visited the fortress and the entrance to the harbor, where orders were given to fortify a tower there, by another and better plan which he had; and he visited other places which were dangerous because the enemy could disembark there. With the advice and concurrence of the governor and the *alcaide* of the fortress, Juan Ponce de Leon, and of other *regidores*, he decided on the manner in which they were to fortify and defend themselves, in case the French armada, or a division thereof, should come there. Most of the residents had fled to the woods, with their wives, children and property, being afraid that the French armada would arrive: the Governor could not bring them to the pueblo, [but] with the arrival of the Adelantado they all came and organized public rejoicings and processions, supplicating Our Lord to give them victory against their enemies, because all the citizens were determined that if the enemy came there, they would sooner die than surrender.

On the fourth day the Adelantado departed for San German, and on the third day after he arrived there, he set sail for Puerto de Plata, where with the advice, help and accord of the *regimiento* and judicial officials of Puerto de Plata, and the citizens thereof, he designed a fortified tower and went on to Monte Cristo, La Yaguana and Puerto Real, to offer soldiers; but under different pretexts, they would not receive them; for which state of doubt they suffered in the ravages that the French armada made among them. The Adelantado had gone to all 3 of these towns, and they would not receive soldiers. In those days 2 vessels came upon Santiago de Cuba: the Adelantado had left there 50 arquebusiers;—... de Godoy, a good soldier, as captain thereof; and 4 pieces of bronze artillery, with their powder and munitions; this prevented any landing. Those ships went to Cabo de Cruz and Manzanilla, a port of Bayan: they seized 5 very rich vessels, with much money and many hides. The Adelantado reinforced Havana with 6 pieces of artillery and 200 soldiers, and Baltasar de Barreda as the captain thereof, as had previously been agreed and provided; he took that succor to Havana on the . . . of January, a thing which appeared done by enchantment, that in such a few days the Adelantado should have distributed so much succor, where navigation was so difficult, for on October 20th he had departed from Florida, and had been in San German, Mona Island, Santo Domingo and Puerto Rico. He sailed to Puerto de Plata with the armada he had left: having given that succor, he sent the camp master by the old channel, with the 3 vessels, to reinforce Havana; on the way he met with a very great storm from the north, and was many times on the point of being lost. The Adelantado, with the other ship, went to Monte Cristo, Puerto Real and La Yaguana, and offered them soldiers to defend them against the corsairs, and they did not want them: [he sailed] to Santiago de Cuba, Cabo de Cruz and Macaca, a port of Bayan: there he left the ship loading with supplies for Havana, bound thence to Florida, and went on board a *zabra;* and sailing between rocks and shoals, he arrived at a harbor south of Havana, called . . . ; went by land to Havana and arrived on the . . . of . . . ; he made this journey by land and sea, from Bayamo to Havana, in 8 days; a thing whereat people marvelled, for it is a journey of at least one month. Great was the joy of the camp master and the captains, the sailors and soldiers, on beholding the Adelantado: he at once gave orders to fortify that place and harbor, as his Majesty had commanded him: he collected all the munitions on board one of the 3 ships that were there: he sent the other two to Spain: and leaving there Captain Baltasar de Barreda with the 200 soldiers, for the defence of the fortress and harbor, as his Majesty ordered him by his royal cédula to succor that place with the [number of] men he thought best, he dispatched the camp master to Florida with the munitions which were left over, and the supplies brought by the vessel the Adelantado had left in Macaca, being laden with supplies from Bayan, and he likewise sent away that ship which was at his Majesty's expense, as well as the others. He also sent off at once the vessel of Puerto Rico and the hooker that arrived in Santo Domingo, in order to spare expense to his Majesty; for if his Majesty had had to meet the cost of that armada, without the men and supplies, counting only the cost of arming and the other things which ships of the armada need, more than twenty thousand ducats would have been spent for his Majesty's

account, and in the Indies, more than forty thousand; and the Adelantado did not spend one ducat, because with the officers he had in Florida (whom he had brought with him at his expense), and other things, he did it all with a part of the vessels, men and supplies that had gone to the relief of Florida and the islands, and with 150 other sailors, pilots and men he had; the frigate and brigantine belonged to the Adelantado, and the crews thereof, with no cost to his Majesty whatever. And the Adelantado gave orders to the camp master when he sailed for Florida, which was on . . . , that being arrived in St. Augustine and having visited that fort and the Fort of San Mateo, he was to go up the River of San Mateo with 150 men, and 3 of the Adelantado's own brigantines which he kept in Florida for explorations, until he arrived in the district of Cacique Macoya, the point the Adelantado had reached when he turned back. The same day the camp master sailed, the Adelantado departed from Havana for the country of Cacique Carlos, with 6 pataches and brigantines, and he told the camp master that he would try to learn if there were a river in [the land of] Carlos which extended to [the land of] Macoya, and that he would explore that coast.

25.

Previous to the Adelantado's leaving Florida in order to obtain succor, he had decided to dispatch Francisco de Reinoso, a very good soldier of his Majesty, to Cacique Carlos with 30 soldiers and send him to the cousin of Carlos who was his heir, who was given the name of Don Pedro when he was baptized and [it was given likewise] to a servant of his. It appeared to the Adelantado that this Indian, the heir of Carlos, had a very good understanding and was a great friend of his, and he did not wish the Indians to kill Reinoso; and Don Pedro showed signs of becoming a good Christian, and the Adelantado was trying to marry him to the Indian woman, Doña Antonia, since they were to be the heirs of the possessions of Carlos, and would try to make the Indians become Christians. He appointed Francisco de Reinoso as captain of those 30 soldiers, and gave him instructions to build a blockhouse in Carlos's pueblo, and all of them to endeavor with great devoutness to worship the cross mornings and evenings, repeating the Christian doctrine so that the Indians should do the same, and working to indoctrinate them as well as they could; and through their friendship with the Indians they were to try to find out if a river which was 2 leagues from there, went to empty into the Lagoon of Maymi, and what the distance was in leagues; for the Adelantado already knew how many leagues there were from that lagoon to Macoya, and that there was a passageway; and within 3 or 4 months he would go to Carlos with a sufficient number of ships, to see if he could travel by that river to San Mateo and St. Augustine, which was what the Adelantado much desired, because of the great service he knew he would be doing his Majesty, the traders in the Indies and the general good of those who went to conquer and settle in Florida; and he gave Francisco de Reinoso a present for Carlos, another for his wife and another for the Indian woman, Doña Antonia.

And when Francisco de Reinoso in the brigantine had reached Carlos with his 30 soldiers, Don Pedro, the Indian, Carlos's heir, and the other Indian, they landed the two Indians in order that they might speak with Carlos and Doña Antonia, and great was the satisfaction the Indians received on seeing them; and presently Carlos came to the patache, offering his friendship to Captain Francisco de Reinoso and his soldiers, [and saying] that since the Adelantado was his elder brother, and sent to order him to receive them and give them good treatment, he must do so, and that neither he nor his Indians would do him any harm: so they landed with great contentment and rejoicing, and he took them to his pueblo. Francisco de Reinoso gave him the present he brought, with a letter, and the interpreter made clear to him what the Adelantado said therein, which was to enjoin on him earnestly that the Christians should be well treated by him and his Indians; and Carlos promised Captain Reinoso to do so, and he had a house built for him wherein [the Spaniards] gathered; and near it they erected a cross, which they went to worship mornings and evenings, repeating their Christian doctrine; and all the Indian men and women came to it with great devoutness.

He sailed for Havana in the brigantine with 5 or 6 sailors, as the Adelantado had ordered: he took with him Doña Antonia, the Indian woman, with 5 or 6 principal Indians, as the Adelantado had so commanded for the safety of Captain Francisco de Reinoso and the 30 soldiers with him, because he had very little confidence in Carlos, for when he had had dealings with him he saw him give many signs of being a traitor.

When the Indian woman arrived in Havana on the brigantine, within 6 days of her sailing from Carlos, Alonso de Rojas, a *regidor* of that town, came at once to the shore, and took Doña Antonia and her Indians to his house, as he had done before; and his wife, who was the godmother of Doña Antonia, received her very well, entertaining her greatly and giving her good treatment; and soon the brigantine and the patache were laden with livestock and some supplies, and went with them to Carlos.

Captain Francisco de Reinoso wrote of the hardships and dangers they lived through, and that 2 or 3 times Carlos had wanted to kill them treacherously, and that he sent to tell his sister, Doña Antonia, and the other Indians that he had a very great desire to see them and they should return at once, so that when he had them with him he could slay Francisco de Reinoso and the soldiers who were with him, for that cacique and his father were very bloodthirsty to kill Christians. Those men and women whom the Adelantado had found prisoners there, said that in 20 years the father and son had slain more than 200 Christians, sacrificing them to the devil, and holding their feasts and dances on those occasions; and that they were all people from shipwrecked vessels of the *Carrera* of the Indies, because even though they were lost 100 leagues from there, they were brought to him, as he was the cacique of much of the sea-coast near Los Mártires and the Bahama Channel, which is where the ships which go from the Indies to Spain run the greatest danger; wherefore the Adelantado was making great efforts to settle that coast, and bring the caciques and Indians into friendly relations with him.

And so [the Adelantado sailed for Carlos] with the 6 brigantines he obtained in Havana with 150 men, on the day that the camp master departed for St. Augustine, on the vessel laden with supplies and munitions which had been taken from the surplus of the armada; this was on . . . ; and the Adelantado had given him orders to go up the River of San Mateo as far as Macoya, for he was on his way to learn if he could go to Macoya from the direction of Carlos, in order to go from there to St. Augustine and San Mateo; he took

Doña Antonia with him, and the Indian men and women she had with her, and he arrived in 2 ordinary days, with a prosperous wind.

He had with him Father Rogel, of the Society of Jesus, a very great and learned religious, and Father Francisco [de Villarreal], of the same Society; likewise some principal Indians of Tequesta, which was where the ship, coming from San Mateo with the men who had mutinied, left the 20 soldiers; and when a brigantine which the Adelantado was sending from Florida to Havana for supplies succeeded in getting through [the channel] and arrived off that harbor, it struck a contrary wind, and entered therein, and found all the Christians among those rebels who had remained there very well. They told them the good treatment given them by the cacique and his Indians, because the Adelantado had Doña Antonia for a wife, and that 5 or 6 of them had gone inland; and the men of the brigantine took about 15 of those soldiers and the cacique sent a brother of his on that brigantine, 3 Indian men and 3 Indian women, to tell the Adelantado that he and his Indians wished to become Christians and he should come to see him, because he wanted to take him for his elder brother, to do what he commanded him. There was a great war between that cacique and Carlos, and the reason was that Cacique Tequesta used to be subject to Carlos, and when Carlos learned that he had those Christians, he sent for them and Tequesta would not give them to him, and afterward he sent to have them killed treacherously: Tequesta heard this, defended them and slew two of his own Indians who went about trying to kill the Christians.

And the Adelantado was taking with him this third time those messengers of Tequesta, as well as Doña Antonia, all of them together, in order to treat of peace and friendship between Carlos and Tequesta; and when the Adelantado entered the harbor belonging to Carlos 2 days after he left Havana, as has been said, he was seen by Captain Francisco de Reinoso and his soldiers, and by Cacique Carlos and his men. They hastened to him at once with the canoes and brigantines: the Adelantado landed: he was very well received by the Christians and Indians: he had a house built for Doña Antonia near the Christians' house, and a chapel where Father Rogel said mass. He preached to the soldiers the next day, for they had sore need of being taught, and because of the good

example he gave them they begged the Adelantado that he might be left with them, for otherwise they would soon be savages like the Indians themselves; and the reason was that the Indian women loved them greatly, to such an extent that if the Adelantado had not arrived there, Carlos and his Indians—even though they should lose Doña Antonia, the sister of Carlos, and the six Indian men and women she had with her—were determined to kill Francisco de Reinoso and all the Christians who were with him, although because of the warning the Indian women gave the Christians, that Carlos and his Indians wanted to slay them, they lived with great caution.

Francisco de Reinoso reported formally to the Adelantado on the habits and customs of Carlos and his Indians, and on the many occasions when they had wanted to slay them; [he said] that great was the devoutness they showed before the cross, although Carlos was very troublesome and laughed at our ceremonies. The Adelantado greatly pleased Carlos and all his men: he took him twice to dine with him, and his wife, and his principal men and women.

The Adelantado learned that the passage he was seeking was not to be found there, but that 50 leagues farther on, in a pueblo they call Tocobaga, he would find a waterway.

The cacique of that land was a great enemy of Carlos and made much war on him.

Carlos had asked the Adelantado and Francisco de Reinoso to go with him and his men to make war on Tocobaga.

Francisco de Reinoso said to Carlos that he could not do this without orders from the Adelantado, because if he did, the Adelantado would command that his head be cut off.

And the Adelantado replied to Carlos that the King of Spain, his Master, had not sent him to that land to make war on the Indian caciques, but that if they were quarrelling he would try to make them friends, and ask them if they wanted to become Christians; he would teach the doctrine to those who did, for it showed the manner of becoming so, in order that when they died on this earth, they might go to God in heaven, who is the Lord of all the earth; that therefore he wanted to be a friend of Tocobaga, and would go to treat of peace with him.

Carlos regretted very much that the Adelantado would not go to make war on Tocobaga, but told him that he wished to go with him in his brigantines to Tocobaga, with about 20 of his principal Indians, and that there the Adelantado could discuss peace.

The Adelantado was pleased at this, and at once discussed the peace and friendship between Carlos and Cacique Tequesta, with Carlos, Tequesta's brother whom the Adelantado had there, 2 other Indian men and 3 Indian women: they were settled very satisfactorily: the Adelantado left a very friendly feeling confirmed between the Indians and soldiers: and until he should return from Tocobaga he left there Tequesta's Indians with the Christians, and the two fathers of the Society of Jesus.

Father Rogel was making haste to learn with a vocabulary the language of Carlos and Tocobaga, to begin to preach to the Indians.

Father Francisco was learning the language of Tequesta, because the Adelantado intended, on his return from Tocobaga, to leave Father Rogel at Carlos and take Father Francisco to Tequesta.

Within 3 days after he reached Carlos, he sailed with all 6 brigantines in the direction of Tocobaga: he took Carlos with him and 20 of his principal Indians: he arrived at the harbor the 2d day, at night. The cacique lived 20 leagues inland, and one could sail up close to the side of his house by a channel of salt water: an Indian of those who came with Carlos, steered in such a manner toward the north, although it was at night and there was no moon, that with a propsperous wind, the Adelantado arrived one hour before daybreak near the house of Tocobaga, without being discovered, and he ordered the brigantines to anchor with great secrecy.

Carlos prayed the Adelantado to let them land, burn the pueblo and kill the Indians.

The Adelantado would not do so, telling him that [if he did], the King of Spain, his Master, would order his head to be cut off, because neither Tocobaga nor his Indians had ever done him harm; but that if they had, he would do what Carlos said. Carlos remained very sad at this, and he asked the Adelantado to land him and his Indians, [saying] that he would go and set fire to the cacique's house, and would swim back to the brigantines.

The Adelantado told him not to do so, nor would he consent to it, since Carlos came with him to treat of peace and friendship: Carlos was much angered thereat, and wept in his spite.

The Adelantado consoled him the best he could, and said that he would try to make a very honorable peace between Carlos and Tocobaga, who should give up to Carlos 10 or 12 of his Indian men and women whom he held as captives. Carlos was greatly cheered at this, because there was among them a sister of his and of Doña Antonia, and he said to the Adelantado that with that he was satisfied. The Adelantado commanded that a small shallop with 8 rowers, and a Christian of those who had been captives in Carlos—who knew Tocobaga's language—should go up to the cacique's house; and he ordered that once near there he should tell him in a loud voice, in his language, to have no fear; that all the men brought by the ships that were there were his friends, Christians in truth; and when he had done so, the Indians awakened, and saw the ships close to the houses, and started to flee, with their wives and children.

The cacique remained quiet, with 5 or 6 Indians and one wife; and the day having come he sent a Christian he had to the Adelantado, to tell him that he thanked him greatly for not having killed either him or his people, or burned his village; that that Christian he sent him was the only one he had; that his people had fled, and he had remained in the house of his gods, his house of prayer; that he would sooner die than forsake them; that if the Adelantado wanted him to go to his ships, he would do so, and if the Adelantado wanted to land, to give him life or death, he could do that, for he was awaiting him.

The Adelantado was much pleased with the message and with the Christian who brought it, who was a Portuguese from Tavila, which is in the Algarve. He said that he had been a prisoner there 6 years; that they were in a bark laden with maize and chickens, honey and woolen blankets, bound from Campeche to New Spain, that a storm had cast them ashore there and that the Indians killed them all within one hour; that he had hidden in the woods so they could not find him, and had gone about for a month, concealed therein, eating palmettos, acorns and some shell-fish; that some Indian fishermen saw him by chance, seized him and brought him to this cacique, and that he had been serving them by carrying wood and water and cooking for them; that from the day he had been shipwrecked until now, he supplicated God each day to free him from captivity, and that he had been expecting Christians for eight days, for every night of the 8 days he had dreamed that Christians were coming there to live, whereat he was very glad. He told the Adelantado of matters concerning that land, although he knew very little, never having gone more than 20 leagues out of that pueblo; and the Adelantado would not say to that Christian that Carlos had come there, nor that Tocobaga should come to the ship, for love of Carlos: he sent him to say that he would land and go to speak with Tocobaga, who should have no fear; and he enjoined on the Christian that he must encourage him, that the Adelantado would do him no harm, and that Tocobaga was to send and tell his Indian men and women to return to the village: and so the Christian went with that answer, and the Adelantado landed at 8 o'clock in the morning. He spoke with the cacique who received him very well and seated him near him, in the highest and most prominent place: the cacique had with him 6 Indian men and one Indian woman. He told the Adelantado through the interpreter that he had not thought the Christians were so good; that well did he realize they could slay him and his people, and burn his idols and his village; that he had known for a long time that Christians went about in that country, who had sent to tell the caciques, his friends, that they must give them maize, and if they did not, they would kill them, and because they gave them none, the Christians slew many; that he had great fear of them, and afterward there came other Christians who killed the first; and that it was said the caciques and Indians greatly loved these last Christians, and [he wished to know] which they were.

The Adelantado replied to him that he and his men were some of the last Christians, who had come to slay those first ones who came to make slaves of the Indians and caciques; that those were false Christians, wherefore he would kill them; that he and his men were Christians in truth, and had not come to slay or enslave the Indians, or seize their maize, but only went about asking them if they wished to be Christians, teaching them how to become so, and to make them friends and brothers; that he came not to wage war, or to slay any cacique or Indian save those who wanted to harm him, or kill some

Christian; and that if Tocobaga and his men wanted to become Christians, he would rejoice thereat.

The cacique was much pleased at what the Adelantado told him, and he rose: he and his 6 Indians rendered the Adelantado great homage very humbly, and kissed his hands, and then they sat down again. Then the Adelantado said to the cacique that he was a friend of Carlos and kept Christians in his land, and that was no reason why he should be an enemy to Tocobaga; that he had Carlos with him on board the brigantines, had brought him to treat of peace and friendship with him, and he should return to him the 12 persons whom he held as prisoners; and that if he and his Indians were willing to become Christians, the Adelantado would be greatly gratified thereat and would leave him Christians there as he had in Carlos, in order that they might defend them from their enemies and teach them to be Christians.

He replied that he had far from there his principal men and the caciques, his friends and subjects, and that he could not answer the Adelantado without their coming and his speaking with them; that the Adelantado should wait 3 or 4 days, and he would send to summon them.

The Adelantado said that he would be glad [to do it], and so the cacique sent to summon his principal Indians and the caciques, and he prayed the Adelantado to order his soldiers not to go near the house of his gods, whom that cacique held in great veneration.

That night the Adelantado and his men went back to sleep on the brigantines, and the next day in the morning Cacique Tocobaga came to see him. He and Carlos spoke together and had several arguments: Carlos wanted to disembark with Tocobaga and his Indians, but because the Adelantado considered Carlos very treacherous he hesitated to take the risk, thinking that Carlos might speak ill of him and his Christians to Tocobaga, and the 2 caciques might agree so that Carlos would kill the Christians that he had in his country, and Tocobaga, those he might leave with him. On the other hand, the Adelantado dared not anger Carlos, and therefore he allowed him to land, but with 2 interpreters who should always go about with him so that he could not speak ill of the Christians to the cacique and his Indians.

In those 3 days came more than 1,500 Indians,

with their bows and arrows, all men of very good appearance.

When the Adelantado saw so many people, he told the cacique that his soldiers were joyful because they thought that the cacique's Indians wanted to be warlike and fight them; that he had better keep the principal men with him, to treat of peace, and send back the others. The cacique did this.

On the fourth day, 29 caciques having assembled, with about 100 principal Indians whom they kept with them, the cacique sent word to the Adelantado to come and treat of peace; and so he went, taking Carlos with him; and when they were assembled, the Adelantado being seated in the most prominent place, Tocobaga said to him that he had told those caciques and Indians who were there, all that the Adelantado had said, and that if he said those things in truth, all would be glad to take him for an elder brother and turn Christians; and make peace with Carlos, and give him his people; but that if Carlos should again make war upon him, the Adelantado was to help him, and if he should break the peace with Carlos, the Adelantado should help Carlos; because he wanted to make peace with the true Christians, not the false ones; and [he asked] that the Adelantado should leave him a captain with 30 Christians, to teach him and his caciques to be Christians. Everything was done in this manner, peace being made with Carlos, and his people returned to him; and the Adelantado left 30 soldiers there, under the charge of Captain García Martínez de Cos, who remained sorely against his will; and the Adelantado left him because he was displeased with him owing to a certain disobedient act of his, but likewise because he was a good Christian and had a good understanding; and Tocobaga told the Adelantado that he could not go to Macoya with so few men, for the Indians on the way were numerous and warlike.

Immediately after he departed thence with his brigantines, within 4 days of his arrival, and within 8 he sailed back to the village of Carlos; and on the way he perceived that Carlos's rage and vexation were very great, on account of the warm friendship the Adelantado had formed with Tocobaga, and he tried very hard to conciliate him, but could not. A sailor passed in front of Carlos and happened to let the end of a rope fall on his head, and he, thinking the sailor had done it on purpose, gave him a great blow in the face and grappled with him to throw him overboard: the Adelantado ran up and wrested him from him: the sailor was one of the best they had there. This was greatly resented, and the Adelantado resented it much more, but as he had brought him on his brigantine, and had taken him from his country, it appeared to him that he was bound to take him back there; for otherwise it was understood that he would command him to be hanged because of that blow, and because also he had heard from the interpreters that Carlos was threatening the Adelantado and his Christians, and that he would give orders that none should escape him.

The Adelantado left him in his pueblo: he caused the Christians to fortify themselves better than they had been: he left them certain culverins, and soldiers in addition to those who were there, so as to make a complement of 50; likewise Father Rogel, of the Society of Jesus, to teach the Indians. He departed with Father Francisco, Father Rogel's companion, and with the Indians of Tequesta, to take them to their cacique and tell him of the peace which had been concluded between him and Carlos. The Adelantado left Doña Antonia there with the Christians: he had no good opinion of her; she was much on the side of her brother Carlos, and very sad on account of the peace he had made with Tocobaga: she spoke very resentful words to the Adelantado because they had not burned and killed Tocobaga and his Indians, and burned the pueblo and the house of his idols; and [she said] that the Adelantado had two hearts, one for himself, and the other for Tocobaga, and that for herself and her brother he had none.

The Adelantado satisfied her as best he could, took leave of her, and went to embark to go to Tequesta; and when the ships were on the point of sailing, to take back the Indians he had there, confirm the peace and go thence to the Forts of St. Augustine and San Mateo, he saw a vessel enter the harbor, whereat he was astonished, not knowing what she might be; and when she had anchored, he recognized her as a patache of his which he had left in the harbor of St. Augustine when he set forth with the armada against the corsairs. She had been sent to Havana from the Forts of St. Augustine, San Mateo and San Felipe, to give notice to the Adelantado that he must send supplies; and when that brigantine had reached Havana, Treasurer Juan de Ynistrosa, the lieutenant of the Adelantado for the affairs of Florida in that town and island, sent her on with advices to the Adelantado, and she likewise brought letters from all the *regidores* of Havana. The situation was that when the Adelantado sailed from Havana on that last voyage, at the very time he wanted to leave, a captain called Pedro de Rodabán, one of those his Majesty had sent to the Adelantado with reinforcements, had risen in rebellion and escaped to the woods with the flag, with the design of passing over to New Spain, which was then in a disturbed state.

The Adelantado feared his going: he delayed several days, thinking he could seize him, and he instituted proceedings against him, summoning him to appear by proclamation, sentencing him as a rebel and notifying Governor García Osorio of the sentence, so that if that captain could be captured, they should send him to Spain, to his Majesty, with the papers in the case; and [his friends] wrote him by that brigantine that the day after the Adelantado left that town of Havana, Captain Rodabán was walking openly about that town, and accompanied the Governor, and dined with him, with many of the rebel soldiers who had fled from Florida; and that within 6 days after the Adelantado departed, the Governor had sent for Captain Baltasar de Barreda, whom the Adelantado had left in that town with 200 soldiers, for the defence of the fortress and the harbor thereof, as his Majesty ordered him. The captain went and found the Governor in the company of his Majesty's officials of that island, and the *regidores* of the town; and the Governor made the captain sit near him, and ordered his ensign and other gentlemen who came with him, to go out; and he told the captain that he wished to see the instructions he held from his Majesty for the defence of that fortress and harbor.

The captain said that the Adelantado had sent them to him originally by a notary, as his Majesty commanded him, but that he had with him there a certified copy thereof, with the order the Adelantado had left with him; and he put his hand in his pocket and drew it forth, and gave it to the Governor, who said that if it were not the original he did not wish to see it.

The captain replied that the notary who had signed it was one of those present there.

The Governor would not take it, and directed a notary who was present to order the town crier to make a proclamation that under penalty of death, all the soldiers of Captain Baltasar de Barreda's company were to keep to their barracks, and none should come out without his order and permission.

Captain Barreda was surprised thereat, and remained silent, answering nothing; and after a little he saluted the Governor, saying to him and most of those who were there that he kissed their hands, and he rose to go.

The Governor rose and laid hold of him, saying: "Prisoner of the King." Two *alguaciles* with 7 or 8 *porquerones* immediately came forward and seized the captain, but as they could not make him relinquish his sword which he held, they went circling round. His ensign who was outside—a good soldier, a gentleman from Trujillo, called . . .—heard the nose: he entered, and seeing how badly they were treating his captain, he grasped his sword and attacked like a lion those who were hemming in the captain: they left him and retreated into an apartment, and the Governor with them: they locked the door inside.

The captain and the ensign went out of the house: they found many soldiers coming, much disturbed: the captain ordered them to retire to the guard-house under penalty of death; and Captain Rodabán controlled many of Captain Baltasar de Barreda's soldiers, having caused them to mutiny; and he had gathered many others of the rebels, and it was said that they were in the Governor's house, so that Captain Baltasar de Barreda being seized, his flag and company should be delivered to Captain Rodabán. The Adelantado received certified testimony of all this by that brigantine, and a letter which all the *regidores* had written to him, beseeching him to come at once to Havana and remedy these things, because otherwise great evil might befall.

When the Adelantado had seen those dispatches, he sent the Indians to Tequesta and he went to Havana, and arrived within 3 days: Captain Rodabán at once absented himself in the woods.

He investigated what was happening, and was compelled to delay there a month, so as to see whether he could capture that Captain Rodabán, who had taken to the woods with 15 or 20 arquebusiers. He used spies and artifice so that he caught him, and brought him to justice: he sentenced Rodabán to be beheaded; he wanted this carried out: but many flocked to the Adelantado, requesting him to grant him an appeal, and advising that he should do it, in order the better to justify the case to his Majesty. The Adelantado granted it; and leaving matters there in as much security as he could, he sailed for Florida with some supplies obtained from other vessels which he had sent to Campeche to be laden with maize; he went to Tequesta, where he was very well received by that cacique and those Indians: he made great peace with them: they took him for their elder brother: he left there 30 soldiers, and ... as their captain; and left them a saw, and some carpenters to build a blockhouse. He erected a cross with great devoutness: the Indians worshipped it: he left there Father Francisco, of the Society of Jesus: he remained 4 days in that pueblo: great was his satisfaction at seeing that every morning and evening all the Indian men and women, big and little, hastened to the cross to worship it and kiss it with great devotion. The cacique gave the Adelantado a brother of his and two principal Indians, one of whom was the captain of one of Carlos's villages, in order that he might carry them to Spain; and the Adelantado sailed with them, in good weather. The third day he arrived in San Mateo, where he found Gonzalo de Villarroel and his men, all very well; that Saturiba was mustering a great number of warriors, and that some caciques and Indians, his subjects, had killed all his [de Villarroel's] cattle. He held prisoners, in chains, Cacique Emoloa, a son of his, two others, heirs of two caciques; two other principal Indians of Saturiba, for there were 16 Indians in all, whom he held in prison, in chains; and the Adelantado learned how the camp master, with 3 brigantines, had sailed up that River of San Mateo for 50 leagues, as far as Macoya; and because he found a great number of Indians, and the river was narrow and both banks densely wooded, he had turned back, as he had no news of the Adelantado, who had told him that he himself would have to go inland from the side where Carlos lived. And although the Indians in Tocobaga had told the Adelantado, when he went there with the brigantines and left the Christians, that there was a river in those parts which went on to Macoya, he had but few men to go there, and there were many Indians, very warlike all of them, who were enemies of Tocobaga; [but he had

said] that when the Adelantado came another time, he and his warriors would go with him.

In agreement with Gonzalo de Villarroel, the Adelantado decided the second day after his arrival at San Mateo, to set free one Indian of those that Villarroel held prisoners in chains, and he sent him to Saturiba to tell him that the next day in the morning he should be at the point of the bar, which is two leagues from there, because the Adelantado wanted to go to St. Augustine and desired to see and speak with him, for the Adelantado had never seen this cacique and desired greatly to talk with him, and they said that the cacique liked the Adelantado very much, but stood in great fear of him.

Saturiba, who was 2 leagues from the Fort of San Mateo, received the message: he replied to the Adelantado that he would go to the bar, as he ordered him to do, and he prayed him to bring the Indians with him, because he wanted to see them.

The next day in the morning the Adelantado departed from the fort, leaving the soldiers as much cheered as he could, entreating and encouraging them to be steadfast in the service of his Majesty, because he had to sail at once for Spain, as all prayed him to do in order that his Majesty might succor them with pay and supplies, in order to clothe themselves, for they now went about little less naked than Indians. He took with him Gonzalo de Villarroel: they found Saturiba at the bar, quite a distance from the shore, and many Indians with him: the Adelantado brought there with him Emoloa and 6 other principal Indians: the Adelantado set one free and sent him to tell Saturiba to come down there to the shore, under the pledge of his word.

Saturiba replied that the Adelantado was to land Emoloa and the Indians he brought with him, because he wanted to speak to them first.

The Adelantado did so, but kept on them the chains which they had on their feet, and placed them in front of a brigantine, holding 20 arquebusiers in readiness and two demi-culverins with small shot, in order to be able to kill any Indians who might want to carry them off on their backs.

Saturiba would not come to speak to Emoloa: he sent two of his principal Indians, who spoke with him: these came and went between Saturiba and Emoloa for a space of more than two hours: it was found at the end that their parleying was for the purpose of freeing the Indians and inducing the Adelantado to land, so that they might shoot arrows at him and the soldiers he had with him, for the Indians Saturiba held in ambush were many; the Adelantado obtained knowledge of the plot from a soldier, a friend of Emoloa, who was entrusted with the task of feeding him and his Indians, and understood their language, although they did not know it. The Adelantado took back on board his brigantines Emoloa and the other Indian prisoners he had landed: he sent to tell Saturiba that he had always desired to be his friend, and desired it then also, and that it caused him great regret that he did not wish to be his: that from then on Saturiba should consider the Adelantado as his enemy, and to avenge the Christians he had treacherously killed, the Adelantado would command that his head be cut off, or that he be driven out of his country.

The cacique sent him many insulting messages, saying that although he had told the Adelantado's captains many times that he was his friend, he did not say it with a willing heart, because he held all Christians as enemies; and that the Adelantado and his soldiers were hens and cowards; that they ought to land and fight with him and his Indians.

26.

The Adelantado left him, without desiring to answer him: he crossed the bar and went to St. Augustine, where he found the camp master and the other captains all well, although the soldiers of that fort were very discontented on account of the ill treatment they were receiving from Captain Miguel Enríquez, one of the captains his Majesty had sent with the reinforcements, and the great disobedience and lack of respect which he had shown by reason of the Adelantado's absence, to his governor and *alcaide* of the fort, whom they honored and from whom they asked the password; for among other things which showed his insubordination was his changing, against the Governor's will, the sentinels whom the Adelantado had ordered to be kept: and likewise against the Governor's will, his commanding soldiers to bear arms who had been deprived of that privilege because of crimes they had committed, and his appointing them as sentinels. When the Governor wanted to strike a soldier for disrespect, the captain, sword in hand, rushed to take him away; and within 8 days as the captain could not punish any soldier of his in a criminal way because the Governor was there, he maimed two of them without bringing formal charges against them; clubbed an *alguacil*; and perpetrated other misdeeds, ugly and serious all of them, in opposition to his Governor whom he had obeyed as such. The Adelantado brought legal proceedings against him: he expressed his anger, impeaching [the captain] and receiving his answer: he refrained from working justice upon him because the Governor was Captain Bartolomé Menéndez, his brother.

The Adelantado gave this captain's company to Francisco Muñoz, and to his sergeant and officers: he delivered the captain's person, with the record of the case, to his Majesty and the Señores of the Royal Council of the Indies.

The Adelantado appointed Estébano de las Alas, who was there, his lieutenant of those provinces, as he had done before: he discussed in council the manner of war which was to be waged against Saturiba, and it was agreed upon; he left instructions concerning this, and before his departure he made an attack at 4 points, and went in person with 70 soldiers, to the place where Saturiba was understood to be. In order not to be heard, he marched ten leagues that night, until dawn: neither he nor the others could find Saturiba: about 30 Indians were killed: the Indians slew one sailor and 2 soldiers, and wounded 2 others, but not one of the men with the Adelantado was either hurt or wounded.

They retired to the Fort of St. Augustine: he spoke to the captains and soldiers who remained there, encouraging them and begging them to be very firm in the service of his Majesty. He embarked in a brigantine for Santa Elena, where is the Fort of San Felipe, and the camp master [went] in a frigate: the Adelantado took with him as prisoners the two captains, Miguel Enríquez and Pedro de Rodabán, to take them to Spain, and 3 principal Indians, one of them a son of Emoloa; and he freed Emoloa and all the other Indians, telling them that he would treat well the 3 whom he was taking to Spain, with the other 3 from Tequesta, and would bring them back; and that if Saturiba made war on the Christians, and Emoloa and his Indians, and the other principal Indians whom the Adelantado was setting free helped him [Saturiba], he would cut off the heads of those 3 he took with him; and with a prosperous wind, he arrived on the third day at Santa Elena and the Fort of San Felipe, where he found Captain Juan Pardo very well and all the soldiers much pleased with the fair country they had seen when they went inland about 150 leagues, and they had left a fort erected at the foot of the sierra, in the land of Cacique Joada. The Adelantado had received advices from his Majesty that a large armada of Lutheran corsairs had sailed from France bound for those parts as they said, and he should be thoroughly prepared for war; wherefore the Adelantado had sent orders to Captain Juan Pardo that leaving some soldiers in that inland fort, to take care of the Indians and friendly caciques and teach them the doctrine, he should come at once to the coast and place himself in the Fort of San Felipe, so that if a French armada arrived there, they could defend the fort.

27.

Captain Juan Pardo told the Adelantado of the great friendship the caciques and Indians of the inland country had shown him, and of the desire they had to be Christians like the Adelantado and take him for an elder brother, to do that which he should command them; that the caciques of the coast and their Indians of that province were just as friendly, and that all desired greatly to behold him and turn Christian.

The Adelantado would have liked well to tarry there a month, to confirm the friendship with these caciques and Indians; but the supplies he was leaving in the forts were very few and the rations the soldiers ate were very short; it was 10 months since he had written to his Majesty that he would soon be in Spain, and he had received intelligence that Flanders was in rebellion against his Majesty and that his Majesty was going there; and so, for the relief of the soldiers who were in Florida under his charge, as well as of those who were in the islands of Puerto Rico, Hispaniola and Cuba—that they might be succored and paid, for they suffered from great need of food and clothes—and in order that he might give a detailed acount to his Majesty of the state of things in Florida and in all the islands and Indies, and of the robberies the corsairs were committing, for if a remedy were not found, so much would be lost; likewise [to suggest to his Majesty] how he could better conditions, and maintain the forts of Florida at much less cost to his Royal Exchequer;

and to be able to serve him in the campaign of Flanders; he embarked in the frigate, which was of about 20 *toneles*, made to order and very swift with both oars and sails. The brigantine he had brought from St. Augustine with that frigate was not strong enough, and she was laden with 50 hundredweight of biscuit and sent to St. Augustine and San Mateo, for as some of the soldiers of Fort San Felipe had gone inland, this biscuit had been saved.

28.

The Adelantado took with him in the frigate the camp master and Francisco de Castañeda, Captain of the Adelantado's guard; Captain Juan Vélez de Medrano, to whom the Adelantado had given leave to return to Spain because of his lack of health; Francisco de Cepero, Diego de Miranda, Alonso and Juan de Valdés, ... de Ayala, the ensign of Captain Medrano; ... de Salcedo, Juan de Aguiniga, Aº. de Cabra, Licentiate ..., who was a priest; Captain Blas de Melro and other gentlemen, to the number of 25, all of them with their arquebuses and their good firearms; persons who were in the habit of accompanying the Adelantado and eating at his table, most of them; and there were 5 others who were sailors; for the rest of those soldiers were sailors as well, and understood navigation; [there were likewise] 6 Indians, and the 2 captains the Adelantado held prisoners, Pedro de Rodabán and Miguel Enríquez, 38 men in all. The Adelantado had such a prosperous wind, and the frigate was so fast, that in 17 days he sighted the islands of the Azores, having averaged 72 leagues a day, as will be seen on the chart of the voyage. When he saw the islands in such a short time he was greatly pleased, for that demonstrated the great swiftness of his frigate: he entered the harbor of Terceira Island: he had tidings that his Majesty was on his way to embark at Corunna, to go to Flanders, and it appeared to him that if he followed that course he might overtake him before his departure from Corunna, and that he could flee by means of his oars and sails from the corsairs with large seagoing vessels he might encounter thereabouts; while if he took the course to Cape Saint Vincent of Seville, and ran across any Moorish *fustas*, they might overtake him by rowing. He had some contrary land winds until he reached Corunna, and arrived off that harbor on

Saint Peter's Day: near it, about 3 leagues away, he encountered two French vessels and an English one which pursued him: he ran from them and on the second day entered the harbor of Vivero, 20 leagues from Corunna, where he learned that his Majesty was at Court, that he had not left yet for Corunna. From Vivero he sent the two captive captains, Rodabán and Miguel Enríquez, and placed them in charge of Ensign Ayala, so that in custody and under good guard he might deliver them to the court prison and hand over the record of the case to the Royal Council of the Indies.

He wrote to his Majesty of his arrival in that harbor and that he would shortly go to kiss his hands; and the day following his arrival there, he left at noon for Avilés, 28 leagues from Vivero, where were his wife and his home: he had such a prosperous wind that in that same day he sailed 25 leagues and entered a bay they call Artedo, where were anchored 10 ships, which, when they saw that frigate of a new type, and so plentifully equipped with oars that she seemed like a Turkish craft of the seas of the Levant, were afraid of her, and the crews deserted their vessels and started to flee to land in the ships' boats; and one of the vessels, which was laden with iron, ran aground in the sand; her hull was torn open, so that if the Adelantado were a corsair, he could not make away with her. He anchored with his frigate in the midst of those ships: there was not a man or a boat on board of them: he was very anxious at this, since one of them was stranded: he made great efforts, ordering a sailor of the frigate to call to some boat to come alongside. She carried 3 small pieces of bronze artillery, and two of the 5 sailors were very good buglers: the Adelantado, to avoid any disturbance, would not let them play their instruments or fire any artillery. The men on the frigate went to rest, since it was already 10 o'clock at night, and no boat had come to reconnoitre the frigate: at midnight a boat arrived, well equipped with oars, and from a distance its men called to the men on the frigate, inquiring what vessel theirs was and where she came from: they answered them from the frigate that she belonged to the Adelantado Pedro Menéndez, who came from Florida, and asked them to come on board: the men in the boat feared to do so, thinking they were being deceived, for many of the sailors thereabouts knew the Adelantado well, and they said that they were afraid they were being de-

ceived; that if the Adelantado would speak to them, they would certainly know him.

The Adelantado, who was listening, said to them: "My brothers, do me the favor of going to that vessel which is aground, going to pieces, and tell her crew that I am the Adelantado Pedro Menéndez and that I come from Florida, so that they may try to save their ship; and tell the same to the men of those other vessels, for it appears to me that they have fled to the woods, and left their vessels yonder to shift for themselves; and this done, return here, for I should like to speak to you." They were to tell the masters of the other ships to come in their boats and board the frigate. They replied from the boat that his lordship was welcome, and they would go and do what he commanded them; and they did so at once. Those men in the boat were detained until dawn, giving notice to the crews who had fled from the vessels, and helping to save that ship laden with iron; and at daybreak they all came in their boats and boarded the frigate, where the Adelantado had a streamer of crimson damask unfurled as a standard, and a field banner, and he ordered the bugles to be sounded and the 3 artillery pieces to be fired: the boatmen were alarmed, thinking he was a corsair, and turned and fled: the only boat to remain was that which had first spoken the Adelantado, the men whereof had recognized him.

There were 5 Portuguese caravels, laden with salt; 3 others were fishing vessels, and the other two were laden, the one with iron and the other with lumber.

That boat turned back at once to reassure the rest, and they came on board the frigate to speak with the Adelantado: all were very glad to see him and marvelled ... sailed such a distance in so small a vessel; and certain it is that this is one of the ... things which up to this day have been seen on the sea.

29.

The Adelantado set sail, and within 2 hours he entered his town, where they already knew he was coming, because a man in the boat which was sent to land, to give notice who he was, went by land that night to ask the reward for good news from the Adelantado's wife and kindred.

The rejoicing of his wife, relatives and neighbors was such, at his arrival in that town, that it cannot be described; for besides the fact that the Adelantado and his kindred are among the important persons of that district, he is so well beloved and well thought of by all, that many dropped on their knees, with their hands raised to heaven, praising Our Lord who had brought him safely home, and gazing at the frigate, at which they marvelled, seeing such a small vessel with so many banners and pennants, and the arquebuses and pieces of bronze artillery, which the men fired; and the sounding bugles, and strange, ragged-looking soldiers; it was as if a spell had been cast over all the beholders, as they stared at one another. The Adelantado went directly to the church, to render thanks to Our Lord and his blessed Mother for the mercy he had shown him in thus bringing him safely through the voyage: he was accompanied as far as his house by the inhabitants of the pueblo, and then he was received by his wife and daughters, and his sisters and nieces who were with them, awaiting the Adelantado, as may well be supposed. The Adelantado had been 18 years in the service of his Majesty, in the capacity of Captain-General of the armadas of the coasts of Biscay, the Asturias and Flanders, and of the *Carrera* of the Indies, during which time he had been at his home but 4 times and in them . . . [the Adelantado] was received very favorably by his Majesty, who considered that the expedition had been a great service and [said] that he would reward him. The Adelantado related at length the destruction of Ribao and the other heretics, and that within 300 leagues of coast he had discovered 4 harbors, the shallowest having at least 4 fathoms at high tide, and 20 others of two fathoms and a half, all of which he had entered and reconnoitred in person with 4 or 5 brigantines, exploring them, taking soundings and marking the entrances; that he had established peace and friendship with the caciques within those 300 leagues, except Saturiba, who would not have it; that he had made 7 settlements, 3 forts and 4 pueblos; and he gave an account of the fortifications of St. Augustine, San Mateo, San Felipe; of 5 other blockhouses he left, with soldiers and munitions, in Ays, Tequesta, Carlos, Tocobaga and of that which Juan Pardo erected inland.

The King was much pleased to see the Indians, and he and the members of the Council were so satisfied that they asked the Adelantado to put in writing what presented itself to his mind about the matters concerning the Indies, and particularly Florida, which he did; they asked him for a memorandum of many things in order to provide them, which he gave.

Among the things he said was this: many captains and soldiers among the Florida mutineers had made reports wherever they arrived, before the Governor of Havana and other courts of justice, some taking oaths in favor of the others [to the effect] that they had served very well, and more signally than those who remained there [in Florida] in the service of his Majesty, [who were] those who had distinguished themselves in his royal service, in the capture of the forts from the Lutherans as well as in sharing the hardships, famines and dangers, and wars with the Indians, which occurred in that country. Through these reports which the mutineers made, so favorable to themselves, they felt so confident that they all, captains as well as soldiers, spread them all over the Indies and Spain, in order to vindicate their weakness at the time they had mutinied, and had taken prisoners the camp master, the officials of justice and the *regimiento*, spiked the guns and seized their supplies, leaving them without any; and the Indians being friendly, had killed three of the principal ones, that the caciques and Indians of that land might unite, as they did, and kill the camp master and the soldiers, who remained in the forts without any food; because in this manner those [Spaniards] who remained in Florida would perish, and his Majesty reward the mutineers liberally, in return for their report.

Wherever these rebels were, they spoke ill of the Adelantado and all those who remained with him, and this they based on many lies and falsehoods, giving the best reasons they could, in order to be believed.

Some begged his Majesty to grant them favors for their services, which his Majesty postponed doing until the arrival of the Adelantado; and as he reported on several of these matters, they absented themselves.

The Adelantado saw that some of the members of the Royal Council of the Indies had become convinced to his detriment, that what these mutineers said was the truth. Several others of his Majesty's ministers, who were close to his royal person, held the belief that the Adelantado, in some things, went beyond what was reasonable; and it appeared to them that the Adelantado had undertaken that expedition and enterprise more for his particular interest than for the service of God Our Lord and of his Majesty; which was quite the reverse, as was seen and known; and he had been the same all the time he had served his Majesty, as is notorious through his experience of 18 years during which he was Captain-General, fulfilling such important duties with large armadas; a position of such trust, honor and profit, that if he had so desired, he could have become very rich; but without being reckless, or making heavy expenditures, he had two very good galleons and thirty thousand ducats in money before being general of his Majesty's armada; and since then he had made prosperous ventures and voyages with many galleons, vessels, armed ships, *zabras* and pataches of his own, wherewith he has won great renown in the short and successful voyages he has undertaken; and he has held his profits very much at the service of his Majesty and without prejudice to his office, in which he has made more than two hundred thousand ducats. All this he has spent, like a good captain, for things needful in the service of his Majesty, that the affairs in his charge might come to a successful issue, for neither his Majesty nor his ministers would provide them; and in carrying very good captains and soldiers, people of standing and trust, both sailors and soldiers, in all the fleets under his command, to whom he gave many inducements, as neither his Majesty nor his ministers would do so. And because he never called on his Majesty for more pay and perquisites than were due him for the time he actually served, and this was less than was given to other generals; and the voyage once ended, his Majesty dismissed him; and until another offered itself, there remained under his care the captains, officials, and noblemen who followed him and served his Majesty in his company, whom he maintained like... [MS ends.]

326. 1566–1567. Some episodes on Pedro Menéndez de Avilés by Bartolomé Barrientos.

Bartolomé Barrientos's "Vida y hechos de Pero Menéndez de Avilés," translated in Anthony Kerrigan, Pedro Menéndez de Avilés, Founder of Florida, written by Bartolomé Barrientos (Gainesville, Fla., 1965), extracts from pp. 82–85, 90–92, 94–98, 103–104, 134–136, 138–142 (continued from 316).

30.

Menéndez sailed into Carlos Bay and anchored close inshore, so that they could jump ashore from one of the brigantines without getting their feet wet. The village of Cacique Carlos was about half a league from the landing place. The Indian chief had given himself this name because the Christians had told him that the greatest lord in Christendom, of whom they were subjects, was thus called. Cacique Carlos' territory lies in the area between the Florida Keys, or rather at the Head of the Keys, and the Bay of Juan Ponce which is west of the Head of the Keys. Nine Christians were then in his power: five women and four men. Two other men and one woman had gone inland. A total of two hundred Christians had been lost on this coast inside the Bahama Channel and along the Keys, which is the route between the Indies and Spain. All had been sacrificed by Cacique Carlos and his father to their idols, except for the small number now remaining. Devising a way to rescue these Christians, the Adelantado began by telling the Spanish messenger to take word to the cacique that the Spaniards were bringing him and his wives many presents, and that he was also conveying a message from the Catholic and most powerful King of Spain, who wished to be his friend.

When the cacique learned how few men the Adelantado had with him, he came up with three hundred archers. Menéndez thereupon had the two brigantines brought close inshore, the bow of one hard upon the bow of the other. Culverins and other artillery, heavily loaded with shot, were emplaced on the landward side, to deal with any eventuality. Menéndez had a carpet taken ashore and laid on the sand, upon which the cacique sat with his chiefs around him. The Adelantado landed in the midst of thirty harquebusiers with lighted slow matches. He went and sat beside the cacique, and Carlos and his chiefs paid him great homage. The cacique knelt, the palms of his hands turned up so that the Adelantado might place upon them the palms of his own hands. This act is the supreme tribute paid by these natives to their leaders—as we kiss the hands of the King. Carlos and all his Indians were naked, carrying their bows and arrows, their private parts bound in deerskin. The Adelantado dressed the cacique in a shirt, a jacket, a pair of silk breeches, and a taffeta hat. He gave him other small presents for himself and for all his wives, of which the cacique had a great number. Carlos was about twenty-five years old, very tall and comely; clothed he looked quite a gentleman. The Indian chiefs were all given numerous presents and clothes; biscuit, honey, and wine were brought for all of them, which they enjoyed very much. Carlos then gave Menéndez a bar of silver, which must have been worth about two hundred ducats, a number of small pieces of gold, and other valuables. He asked Menéndez for more food and wine. The Adelantado answered that he did not have enough provision for such a concourse. If the cacique and his chiefs would come aboard the brigantine, he said, they would be served some very delicious food and would be given some to take to their wives. Covetous of the promised delicacies, Carlos went aboard one of the brigantines with twenty of his Indians. Very quickly and quietly the Adelantado directed that a soldier should remain close to each Indian and hold the savage by the hair should he attempt to jump into the sea. The cables were ordered slacked, and the vessels stood from the shore. The Indians were thrown into a panic. But in their own tongue, through the interpreter, the Adelantado told them to be calm, since the ships were putting to sea only to prevent greater numbers of visitors from coming aboard the small vessels and sinking them under their weight. The Indians believed him, and were given more food and presents, especially beads and hawkbells. When the cacique wished to depart, the Adelantado told him that the Catholic King of Spain had sent him on a mission of peace and friendship; he petitioned him, therefore, to hand over whatever captive Christians he had in his power. Should this request not be carried out, the cacique would be killed. If he complied and gave them up, he would be given numerous presents, would be accepted by the Adelantado as an ally and a brother, and would be supported by the invincible Spaniards against any caciques who were his enemies. Keeping a good countenance,

the cacique answered that he appreciated the offer of so powerful a prince and would in all things carry out the Adelantado's wishes insofar as possible; he would be happy enough to give up the Christians, and would go to fetch them. The Adelantado thanked him for his answer, but added that, if he allowed the cacique to go off by himself, Menéndez' own men would kill him for letting Carlos go, because they were brothers to the captives; he thus must send after them. Within the hour the Indians went and brought back five women and three Christian men. The captives were immediately clothed, and their happiness moved them to tears. Their joy was mixed, however, because they grieved over the children they left among the Indians. Cacique Carlos was given a great quantity of clothes, axes, and knives, as were all the other Indians who had come aboard with him. Carlos promised that within two months he would hand over two more men and another woman captive who were at present further inland. He begged Menéndez to visit him in his village the next morning, before he sailed, so that his wives might see him. This the Adelantado promised to do. But, when in the morning a great fleet of canoes came to take him, Menéndez became suspicious.

At this time the Christian who had put out to sea bearing the Cross arrived. He had accompanied the cacique to take the wives a present from the Adelantado. This Christian warned Menéndez not to go to the Indian village, for the savages wanted to kill him. Their plan was as follows: they were to appear without bows and arrows, bearing only palm fronds and singing as if in joyous celebration, but when they reached the Christians, each Indian was to lift a Spaniard to his shoulders as if in token of honor; then, when they all reached a wood situated between the village and waterfront, where a large number of savages would be lying in ambush, each Indian would hold tight the hands of his Spaniard while the others killed him. At this juncture Carlos and a great horde of Indians arrived on the scene. They were all singing and giving large demonstrations of joy. Carlos announced that he had brought such a sizable party in order to carry the Spanish on their backs, a token of esteem they deserved by virtue of their high merit. He himself wished to bear the Adelantado. His chiefs would be glad to bear the Spanish captains and other leaders. The rest of the concourse would accompany the party by way of demonstration, just as they had when welcoming other Christians who had passed that way—for they were all servants of God.

Menéndez replied by thanking him for his great courtesy. But, he added, whoever they were who had let themselves be carried about in the manner described were false Christians. The Spanish would admit of no such honor. The Indians might as well leave, therefore, for the Adelantado wished to proceed to the village with a few of his own men, otherwise unaccompanied. The savages now realized that the Christian messenger had revealed their plans, and they sped away in their canoes. Still pretending that he knew nothing, Menéndez had the brigantines brought close to the village. When they had come as close as they could, he directed two trumpets to be sounded and the banners unfurled, while he signaled the canoes to come for him. The Indians would not approach, for Carlos was afraid that his plot was uncovered.

The Adelantado then sailed out of the harbor to assemble his five ships. He could not immediately find these vessels, however. Meanwhile the Christians told him that fifty leagues away there was another good harbor where three additional Spaniards were held captives. Suspecting that his missing ships had proceeded to that very harbor with a desire to trade and anxious to save the other prisoners, Menéndez proceeded to the port mentioned. He found neither ships nor captives, and returned to Carlos Bay. Here he found his five ships at anchor. Estéban de las Alas had gone on to the village with a hundred soldiers, and the Indians, overawed by so many ships and men, had given him a good reception. . . .

33.

Eight days after setting out from Port San Antonio, as the harbor of the land of Cacique Carlos was called, Menéndez discovered a harbor within the Bahama Channel. On leaving it later he encountered the caravel he had sent from Havana to Campeche to load maize. Aboard her was Gonzalo de Solís de Merás and more than one hundred and thirty other persons. She was fully loaded with maize, honey, chickens, and other fowl and provision which the bishop of Yucatán, Don Antonio de Toral, and the governor of that territory,

Don Luis de Céspedes, had put aboard her in response to the Adelantado's letters of entreaty.

En route back to Florida this caravel had put in at Havana, where Juan de Hinestrosa had sent her with orders to proceed to the land of Ays and the harbor of Santa Lucía, where Juan Vélez de Medrano had remained with the three hundred French and Spaniards at the time the Adelantado had gone to Havana with the other vessels in search of food. This group had already been brought the necessary supplies by a *patache*, which had then taken the rest of its cargo to St. Augustine. This was unknown to Hinestrosa, and he had therefore sent the caravel to relieve the party at Santa Lucía. When the caravel reached this port, the soldiers seized the shipmaster and took possession of his vessel. Captain Juan Vélez de Medrano and his lieutenant, Gabriel de Ayala [*graviel de añana*], a native of Salinas de Ayala, were both wounded when they attempted to stop the mutineers.

The rebels set sail and headed for Havana. They had already sailed about fifteen leagues, when the Adelantado came upon them. Aboard the caravel were the ensign and soldiers who had fled from Havana with the royal flag. They had been imprisoned at Merida, Yucatán, when Gonzalo do Solís was on his way to Mexico. The Adelantado went aboard the caravel with some of his gentlemen, and the ship was headed back to St. Augustine.

At the port of Ays, where the Adelantado had left Juan Vélez de Medrano and his soldiers, many of those who remained were unwilling to endure hunger and discomfort in the interval required for Menéndez to send supplies from Havana. These men now marched out of Ays. When Captain Medrano and his lieutenant Ayala went out to bring them back, they found many of the party dead and others drowned as a result of their attempt to cross the local rivers. Twenty-three leagues beyond Ays the Spaniards found a harbor, which they named Santa Lucia because they discovered it on that Saint's Day. It was to this port that the Adelantado sent supplies from Havana. A settlement was established there, and although the Indians pretended to be friendly, they actually plotted to kill the colonists, for they saw how weak they were from hunger. The savages were also aware that the party possessed no harquebuses—fatigue had caused them to abandon these weapons along the way. One day five hundred Indians descended on our men and killed fifteen soldiers. The savages' manner of fighting allowed them to escape unscathed from the harquebuses, for during the time one soldier fired a shot, an Indian loosed twenty arrows.

When Lieutenant Gabriel de Ayala saw that our tactics were wholly unsuccessful, he sallied out with thirty soldiers armed with swords only. In this fashion were the savages driven back; although every day they continued to approach the camp with the intention of doing damage. During the next eight days the Spaniards built a fort, in which they set up their defense. As their answer to this, the Indians attacked one morning a thousand strong. Discharging their arrows without cessation, they fought for four hours during which time six thousand arrows fell inside the fort. Many of our men were wounded, including the captain and his lieutenant. Eight soldiers were killed. Provisions on the Spanish side were so low during these almost daily encounters with the Indians, that no more than a single pound of maize was issued to ten soldiers. When this supply was gone, a palmetto was sold for one ducat, a snake for four, and a rat cost eight *reales*; excessive prices since there was very little money. The soldiers began to fall from hunger; in the end only thirty men were left to bear arms. The bones of animals and fish dead for years were barbecued over the fire and then picked, as were swords, belts, and shoes. Lieutenant Ayala, saddened by the suffering of his soldiers, decided to go to Havana in search of relief. He and Mendoza, the vicar, took a small boat, without a seaman or any practiced navigator. On putting out to sea they were blown back to their starting point. Six days later the above-mentioned caravel arrived with supplies....

34.

Estéban de las Alas, who had gone to Havana to escort Doña Antonia and the other Indians, arrived at St. Augustine the same day as the Adelantado. He was bringing general supplies, meat, and cattle, much to the satisfaction of everyone.

The men at Fort San Mateo had mutinied simultaneously with those at St. Augustine, a coincidence which seemed unusual. But on investigating the causes for this uprising, it was found that it had occurred not so much from the scarcity of food, as from the fact that they realized this country contained neither the gold nor the silver of Mexico and Peru, whither they desired to go. Thus, the mutineers had hurried to complete a ship already on the way, in the intention of seizing the first store of supplies which might chance their way and then leaving.

The campmaster, who was at St. Augustine, wrote Gonzalo de Villaroel at San Mateo advising him to delay the completion of the ship. He also suggested that he present as good a face as possible to his men to avoid being killed, for it was the campmaster's information that the entire garrison there was ready to revolt.

The mutineers carried out their plans. As soon as the frigate loaded with supplies appeared, they seized her. One hundred and twenty soldiers, among them thirty-five gentlemen, went aboard the newly constructed and readied ship. They had not yet set out when Menéndez arrived at St. Augustine. He immediately sent word informing them that he was bringing supplies, and would grant a general amnesty to all rebels without prejudice for he felt their conduct was attributable to lack of food. Had he himself been on the scene, he wrote he too would have abandoned the country to avoid dying of hunger. Now that he brought the necessary provision, however, they would be committing treason toward His Majesty if they abandoned their post. Since the remaining Christians were few in number, the enemy Indians, with the help of some Lutherans, would war upon them and capture the fort. When the Adelantado's message was received, the thirty-five gentlemen immediately abandoned the frigate, very much to the disapproval of the other mutineers. They went ashore in a boat and started for the fort. Only the warder, Gonzalo de Villaroel, Don Hernando de Camboa, Rodrigo Montes—first cousin to the campmaster—four other relatives of the campmaster's, Captain Martín Ochoa with his lieutenant and his sergeant, and Captain Francisco de Recalde and a man-servant, a total of twenty-five men, were left inside the fort.

The mutineers had killed three Indians, two of them chiefs, and thus caused the savages to break the treaty of friendship which they had maintained up to that time. The natives were aroused at these murders, and so they shot and killed the gentlemen while they were on their way to join the garrison.

Gonzalo de Villaroel, who remained at Fort San Mateo with twenty-five men, was unaware that the Indians had gone on the warpath. He sent Rodrigo Troche, his lieutenant, with a dispatch addressed to the campmaster explaining that he was left with but a few men. On the way to St. Augustine, Troche was met by some Indians. He and a companion were seized and brought before Saturiba. The cacique, who knew the two Spaniards very well, had their hearts cut out and their bodies shot full of arrows.

As soon as Menéndez knew that the mutineers' vessel was sailing, he determined to go in its pursuit and punish the rebels. When he was on the point of departure he was approached by Captain Juan de San Vicente, and the latter's lieutenant, Francisco Pérez. They asked permission to set out in a caravel the Adelantado was sending to Hispaniola to load supplies. Menéndez answered that, in the first place, the time was ripe for a Spanish force consisting of four ships and three hundred men to sail for Guale and Santa Elena and drive out the Lutherans who were said to be there. Furthermore, the Indians were presently in turmoil and it was necessary to reinforce Gonzalo de Villaroel and the one hundred men with him at San Mateo, while a hundred men must be left at St. Augustine under the campmaster. Should San Vicente now undertake to leave, the rest of the men would want to do likewise, and the Spanish force would consequently be left in a decimated condition, with the expectation of facing a new Lutheran force which was about to descend on them from France, as His Majesty had warned. Despite all these considerations and additional reasons for his not going, Menéndez was unable to put an end to the importunities of San Vicente and the clamor of some one hundred other men who wanted to set sail in the caravel. The Adelantado therefore directed that this group be taken to Puerto Rico, where the vessel would load supplies for a return trip to Florida. But as soon as they put to sea, this mutinous party forced the pilot to head for Havana, whence they could proceed more quickly to Peru, Mexico, Honduras, and Campeche. But the ship encountered a contrary wind, and they were driven to Puerto de Plata, on the island of Hispaniola. They

arrived there weak and ill, by reason of their scanty food stocks and the close-packed quarters in which they suffered intense heat for more than thirty days of voyaging, over a course which normally requires ten or twelve days.

The one hundred and twenty soldiers who had seized the supply frigate at St. Augustine landed at the same port. From Puerto de Plata they went to different places. Those who came to Spain spread ill reports concerning the land of Florida and of the Menéndez attempt to conquer it. As a result the Adelantado later had difficulty finding any settlers. Menéndez was also blamed for persevering in his plans. The calumniators, however, had not been inland for as much as a league, but had stayed along the coast, which is composed of sand and swamp.

35.

After losing so many of his soldiers, Menéndez changed his plans. Of the three hundred men whom he had meant to take to Guale and Santa Elena he now left a hundred and fifty at the two forts of St. Augustine and San Mateo. The other hundred and fifty he put aboard two brigantines and a hundred-ton ship. He delivered the requisite men and food to San Mateo, where he visited the fort, but did not punish the mutineers. He stocked the fort as well as time and circumstances would allow. At the beginning of April, 1566, he sailed again, and within three days discovered a harbor. Leaving Estéban de las Alas a hundred soldiers, in the other ship, he put fifty men aboard the two brigantines, then entered this harbor with them and reconnoitered it. Here he disembarked a quarter-league from the local village. Numerous Indian archers approached, and among them was a naked Christian who also carried arrows and a bow. He asked the Spaniards who they were and where they were bound. When Menéndez heard him speak Spanish, he queried him and learned that he was a Frenchman, although born in Córdova. Fifteen years previously he had escaped from the Castle of Triana [a "gypsy" suburb of Seville, across the Guadalquiver River], where he had been held prisoner. He had fled to France, and had married there; but he had fallen into disgrace again and gone to sea. He had spent six years in Brazil and there had learned the language of the Indians, going from there back to France. Eventually he had come to Florida with Captain Jean Ribaut, as an interpreter. The language he now spoke was the Florida language. He said that the lord of this land and of the nearby village was called Guale, who had sent him to question the landing party. If they were not Lutherans, but Spaniards, they were not to be allowed to disembark.

To this the Adelantado replied: "We do not harm Indians. On the contrary, we deal with them with every possible favor. Against their will we would not care to visit their land or even to disembark." He next asked the Frenchman to come closer, and gave him a new shirt, a pair of breeches, and something to eat. The same treatment was accorded the forty-odd Indians who had come with him. Sitting there in the sand, they were all served biscuit and dried figs. Gifts were given all around. Then, by means of signs, the Indians invited the Adelantado to their village. Accompanied by thirty harquebusiers and four crossbowmen, he landed. Sixteen soldiers were placed as guard around the brigantines.

En route to the village Menéndez asked the Frenchman how he had come to stay with the natives. The interpreter answered that six months had gone by since Jean Ribaut had been lost with all his fleet while seeking out General Pedro Menéndez. Fifteen Lutherans had come ashore at this point. After they had been there for five months, living in a dwelling of their own construction, they had built a boat. Fifteen days ago, the others had set sail for Newfoundland, intending to continue to France in one of the ships which came there to fish. Menéndez was next told that caciques of Guale and of Santa Elena were bitter enemies and waged relentless war upon each other. The cacique of Guale had made use of the fifteen Frenchmen who had been there against the other cacique, although the French had served with great reluctance because Orista, the Santa Elena cacique, was a friend of the French. The Guale Indians had taken the boat belonging to the French and after a voyage of four days had captured a canoe bearing four Orista Indians, two of them kin to the cacique. On their way back to Guale, two of the prisoners had jumped overboard and swum back to Santa Elena. There they told the cacique of how the Christians who had been in his land six years

before had seized them and their boat. Cacique Orista had then sent to threaten the Lutherans, with the result that within two days the Guale chiefs had planned to kill them.

Menéndez was well received at the village, and was lodged in the house where the Lutherans formerly lived. As was his custom, he immediately directed three youths in his party to recite the Christian Doctrine in front of the Cross which he always had his men erect wherever they lodged. When this ceremony was performed the soldier would come up and kiss the Cross. With the Adelantado's men was a French Catholic called William, who had been brought from Florida in a frigate which Diego de Mazariegos, governor of Cuba, had sent to the Florida coast to investigate the possible presence of any Lutherans there. Menéndez had brought William along because he had previously been assigned to learn the language, and the governor, acting on orders from the King, had attached him to this expedition. This interpreter had learned that the other interpreter at Guale was a Lutheran, and the Adelantado, apprised of the fact, and after some discourse with this man, found that it was indeed so, Menéndez told the Lutheran that he and his men had come to this land to make Christians of the Indians, and if the Spaniards should learn that he was a Lutheran they would kill him. He must assure everyone that he was a Catholic and tell the cacique that the Lutherans who had been there were false Christians, while the present party were true Christians, servants of God who were on their way to kill the warring and false Lutherans. Should the cacique decide to be a Christian, the Adelantado would defend him against his enemies.

Badly frightened, the Lutheran interpreter accurately repeated all these statements to the cacique and all the chiefs. Present at this time was the Adelantado's own interpreter, William, the Frenchman, who knew the language of Guale, which he had learned in Santa Elena, only eighteen or twenty leagues away....

37.

The next day the party set out to inspect the proposed site for the fort. They found it good and pleasant. It was located on an island four leagues long, and boasted a very fine harbor, which extended a league inland from the bar, and could be strategically fortified. Whenever vessels entered, they could be sighted from the fort. Plans were drawn up with the cooperation of Estéban de las Alas and the other captains present. Captain Antonio Gómez was entrusted with the speedy construction of the fortification.

This Captain Gómez had been detached at Havana from duty aboard the flagship of the New Spain fleet. He had been wintering in the Cuban port and had reported for duty with the Adelantado, along with fifty soldiers and seamen, for service in Florida until May. This group carried out their tour of duty in Florida enterprise wholly satisfactorily.

The Spanish force of one hundred and fifty men was now divided into squads. Some carted lumber, others brush. Some drove stakes, others dug trenches. Within fifteen days, the Spaniards and their Indian helpers had put the place in a fair state of defense. Six bronze cannon were then emplaced, and Estéban de las Alas was named warder of the fort and governor of the district. One hundred and six men were assigned to him. . . .

49.

Menéndez had now decided to return to Spain and report to His Majesty on the progress of the conquest of Florida. He also planned to take the necessary steps looking toward the completion of his expeditionary project. Before setting out he issued the orders he thought requisite governing the conduct of his captains during his absence in Spain. Captain Andrada he directed to await the relief shipment due in Florida, and then to proceed, with one hundred of the men in his company to Polican, an island close to the Matanzas River, some five leagues south of St. Augustine in the direction of New Spain, and there build a blockhouse. In the interval of construction, Captain Hernando Muñoz and his lieutenant with fifty of their men were to stand guard. A second blockhouse was to be erected alongside the first, and here soldiers were to be stationed constantly so as to watch the movements of any ships at sea. The blockhouses were to be built on high ground for maximum effect, and were to keep in communication with St. Augustine. The entire island was to be kept free of Indians, since the natives, subjects of Saturiba, are enemies of the Spaniards; such a

policy would also safeguard the Spanish cattle. The order would be enforced by letting dogs loose on the island, so that whenever a native was found he would be hounded to death. This measure would guarantee that the Indians would stay away and would prevent their crossing at night to kill the cattle. The dogs were to be kept tied up during the daylight hours, and let loose at night. They were to be trained to hunt down Indians. Still another blockhouse, similar to the one at Polican, was to be erected in Soloy, the district of Cacique Soloy, by Francisco Muñoz with about the same number of men as was assigned to Polican. Construction of this last-mentioned post was to be undertaken by the end of July, 1567. Three leagues outside of San Mateo, in the village of Saturiba which the Adelantado had visited, Gonzalo de Villaroel was to build yet another blockhouse and there station some soldiers. Other outposts were planned on a height overlooking the residence of Cacique Alimacani, and at old St. Augustine. All these blockhouses were to be built in the designated places to overawe the unfriendly Indians who had never desired alliance with the Christians. Communication between one fort and another would be assured, and Saturiba would be forced to move to another region and leave our people in peace.

Menéndez ordered the tracking down and slaying of Cacique Tacurun. For although the Adelantado had done his people favors, and though the Spaniards had never harmed them but had, on the contrary, been their friends, this cacique was responsible for the slaying of the Jesuit Father Martínez, and of a number of his companions. He had also slain Captain Pedro de Larando and ten of his soldiers in the cacique's own house after having in apparent friendship hailed the Spanish party at the seashore, invited them to his dwelling, and received them amicably. Here he slew them as they innocently slept. A Guale cacique had also met his death at the order of Tacurun, because he had shown friendship for the Adelantado. Another blockhouse was ordered built in Guale, to be garrisoned with fifty soldiers. All these outposts were to be under the jurisdiction of the governors of San Mateo and St. Augustine: those at Guale, Alimacani, Tacatacuru, and Saturiba subject to San Mateo, and the outposts and garrisons at Soloy, and St. Augustine, Polican, and Matanzas subject to any and all orders from the warder and governor of the fort at St. Augustine. All Spaniards in the area between the island lying just north of the Isle of Whales and Santa Elena, those north of Santa Elena, and all individuals who traveled inland as far as the mountains, were to render obedience and carry out the orders of the warder and governor of Fort San Felipe, who had his headquarters at Santa Elena at the beginning of September, 1566, with a hundred and twenty harquebusiers and according to the orders, thus to prevent them from making any observations which would allow surprise assault. Menéndez warned all soldiers against committing any aggression upon the Indians; on the contrary, they were to treat them kindly, and give them presents. Captain Juan Pardo had been sent inland from the fort of Santa Elena at the beginning of September, 1566, with a hundred and twenty harquebusiers and crossbowmen. Their assignment was to march as far as Zacatecas, and the mines of San Martín, in New Spain, some eighty leagues from Mexico City, making friends wherever possible with any caciques and Indians they chanced to meet. As soon as word was received concerning the oncoming Lutheran fleet, Menéndez summoned Captain Pardo back to the coast.

50.

The dispatches and letter from His Majesty had fully warned the Adelantado of the departure from France of the large Lutheran fleet of corsairs bound for the Spanish New World, and Menéndez had been directed to be on a war footing. For this reason, although much against his inclination, he had been forced to order Captain Juan Pardo's expedition to turn back. He was enjoined, nevertheless, to establish a fort in the interior for the protection of allied Indians and their caciques, and so that they might be taught the Catholic religion. Pardo was ordered to the coast, and specifically to Fort San Felipe, which he was directed to defend in case of a Lutheran attack. Captain Pardo reported to the Adelantado concerning the fine reception and friendly attitude he had encountered among the Indians of the interior; the friendships he had established; the desire of the natives to become Christians in imitation of the Spaniards, to adopt King Philip, and the Adelantado as the King's chief representative, as their Elder Brother and lord whose

commands they would obey. According to Pardo, all the caciques along the seacoast were animated with the same spirit and desire. They were very desirous of seeing and meeting the Adelantado and of becoming Christians, especially since the greatest cacique of them all, King Philip of Spain, was a Christian. . . .

51.

Menéndez set out from the harbor of Santa Elena on his return to Spain May 18, 1567. His voyage was so skillfully and quickly managed that he reached the island of Terceira, one of the Azores, on June 15, after only eighteen actual sailing days at sea. He was greatly pleased to make a landfall on the Azores in such a short time. At Terceira he was told that His Majesty was on his way to La Coruña to sail for Flanders. Menéndez therefore shaped a course for that port, and on the Feast of St. Peter lay off the harbor mouth. As he was on the point of entering, however, he was set upon by two French vessels and an English ship, which gave chase. He eluded them, and on the second day made port at Vivero, twenty leagues from La Coruña, and there he learned that the King was still at court. He sent Lieutenant Ayala to the Supreme Court of Indies with the proceedings in the case of the two captains, whom Ayala was to hand over for incarceration in the court prison. To His Majesty Menéndez now addressed himself, and in a letter announced his arrival in Spain and his expectation of kissing the King's hands. Meanwhile, he proceeded to Avilés, where his wife and household were established, at a distance of some twenty-eight leagues from Vivero. The most unusual aspect of this voyage, and one most universally admired, was the hitherto unheard-of speed of Menéndez' voyage over such a perilous and immense stretch of ocean in a vessel so tiny.

Arrived at Avilés, the Adelantado first repaired to the church, where he thanked Almighty God for His favors. Thence he went to his own house, accompanied en route by his kinsmen, his friends, and his neighbors—for apart from being one of the ranking men of his land, he is generally loved by the people of his native town. In fully eighteen years Menéndez had not been home more than four times, and then he had stayed a total of only twenty days. This time he remained eighteen days. The campmaster was from a place only four leagues from Avilés, and he now went to visit his parents. The Adelantado went on to Madrid shortly to kiss the King's hands. He arrived there on July 20 in company with six naked Indians carrying their bows and arrows after the Florida manner. To His Majesty he reported on the state of affairs in Florida, and described the need of the soldiers for supplies. He described the damage done by corsairs along the Indies trade route and on the islands, and the danger attending the transport of treasure by the fleets. The King made provision to relieve the suffering soldiers, and directed Menéndez to furnish a list of recommendations on the best ways to overcome the corsairs (who plundered the Kings' subjects, notwithstanding the prevailing peace) and restrain their depredations. Menéndez was also to hold himself in readiness to accompany the King on the voyage to Flanders. The relief for the Florida garrisons was to be conveyed by one of the Adelantado's own captains. Menéndez replied to the King by saying that he would pray God to help him in one and the other endeavor so that he might better succeed in serving His Majesty; and then he approached to kiss the King's hands.

The campmaster, who was only twenty-four years old, received the King's commendation and thanks for having served with distinction in the Florida enterprise, where he comported himself ably, and for having been before that a soldier in Italy. He likewise commended and thanked the other captains and gentlemen whom the Adelantado had brought with him to court. The Royal Council of Indies was ordered by the King to assemble in session to hear a report from the Adelantado, particularly in regard to Florida affairs. His Majesty also asked Menéndez for his written recommendations so that they might be carried out.

At this time the King and the Council of Indies were disabused of certain falsehoods which mutinous soldiers from the forts had circulated, and they were correctly informed as to the mutinies in the forts. A rumor had spread that the Adelantado had undertaken the Florida enterprise for personal gain and not for the service of Our Lord or His Majesty—when the opposite was the truth; for when the Adelantado was a general in His Majesty's fleet he owned two very good galleons and was worth thirty thousand ducats.

Later, following his success, he had acquired many armed vessels, galleons, *zabras*, and *pataches*, and with these he had earned a large income. All the profit he gained in the service of the King, which amounted to over two hundred thousand ducats, was without prejudice to his official capacity. All this money he spent in the King's service, in order to insure the success of all his undertakings; he employed first-rate captains and soldiers, offering them special inducements at his own expense. That his disinterest was a true one is illustrated by the fact that on the Feast of St. Peter he set out from Cádiz on the Florida enterprise with a thousand-ton galleon of his own, the finest ship afloat at the time, very trim and very well gunned, and with ten other ships. From Asturias and Biscay he brought five other vessels, with two thousand one hundred and fifty men aboard maintained at his own expense; while His Majesty provided only three hundred soldiers and one ship at the royal expense. When his own funds were not sufficient to meet the cost of this large outlay, he did not hesitate about becoming indebted to his relatives and friends; and he was still in debt when he returned to Spain in 1567 from this enterprise (as can be adduced from our history). After his present visit to the court, it has become clearly understood that he has ably and loyally served Our Lord and the King in this Florida enterprise, and the importance of his service to His Majesty and to Christianity is now realized.

In this year of 1567, so well strengthened and ready for action are the forts he established, and the caciques have been rendered of such a friendly disposition, that even though the Lutherans might assemble a monstrously large fleet, they can never hope to carry out an attack on the Florida coast. At this moment, as I finish writing this chapter in the closing days of December, the Adelantado is in Seville fitting out two ships scheduled to sail for the relief of Florida.

52.

On his arrival in Spain, Menéndez presented to the King the following report detailing his actions in Florida and embodying his recommendations for the safeguarding of that land:

The Adelantado Pedro Menéndez skirted the coast of Florida on three or four occasions, sailing in frigates or brigantines, for a distance of more than three hundred leagues. All harbors, shoals, rocks, inlets, and prevailing currents have been investigated along this three hundred-league stretch. This area boasts three forts, and comprises four provinces. About one hundred and fifty soldiers are distributed through the territory teaching the Indians the Christian Doctrine, and upholding the peace and amity established with the natives; meanwhile, they are learning the language.

All the caciques in the interior of this territory have proclaimed themselves allies of the Adelantado and vassals of the King. Most of them have done away with their idols, and now worship the Cross; excepting those caciques who inhabit the area thirty to forty leagues around the former Lutheran fort. These are on the warpath and try to let no Christian escape with his life. In this region it is impossible to march from one fort to the other with less than fifty harquebusiers.

Some one hundred and fifty leagues inland, at the foot of the sierra and on the road to Zacatecas, another fort has been established in order to further the conversion of the Indians and induce them to pay obedience to the King. Thus, the Indians there are friendly, venerate the Cross, and are learning the Christian Doctrine. From as far away as one hundred leagues beyond this fort in the direction of Zacatecas, caciques have come to pledge their allegiance to His Majesty before the captain in charge of the fort. They very earnestly asked to be accepted as Christians.

Stationed throughout Florida, in the villages and in the forts, are one thousand two hundred soldiers, not counting another one hundred and fifty seamen aboard the twelve frigates and brigantines employed in exploration and supply operations for the forts. Throughout all this region, work parties put ashore can find a plentiful supply of wood for making ships' masts (which are not be found in Spain, where they must be imported from France). There is also an abundant supply of tar for vessels (another resouce unavailable in Spain, which imports it from Germany). Pine and oak planks could be easily procured (and in Spain these are usually shipped to Cádiz in hookers from Germany to be used in ship and house construction). Hemp, to be made into rigging for ships, is probably procurable (while at home this comes from France, Flanders, or Germany).

By reason of the extensive and fine forests, a fleet of ships might be built easily and at little expense. Dried fish for export to Spain is readily available in Florida, and we would thereby avoid handing out money to other nations for this product. Fresh-water rivers are numerous in Florida, as well as extensive meadow lands for the grazing of cattle and sheep; so that hides, wool, dried beef, and bacon could be produced for the Spanish market, for there is abundant supply of acorns in the oak forests.

Large, fine pearls are numerous. In the interior low-grade gold of eight or nine carats is found. As regards copper, people who know say that its presence is the best sign of gold. Veins of ore suitable for making iron of high quality have been located in quantity. Sumach trees are numerous. The terrain is healthful and the weather good.

The King considered himself ably served and now well informed as regards Florida affairs and the proper way to safeguard this territory and the other islands and harbors of the Indies. And so in Madrid, on September 15, 1567, His Majesty granted the Adelantado Pedro Menéndez the title of captain general of all the West. He was given twelve armed ships fitted with galleys, two thousand infantrymen, and two hundred thousand ducats as part of the cost, to protect the Indies trade route from corsairs. Because in his opinion it seemed *important* that the island of Cuba be under the Adelantado's command the better to assure the Florida enterprise, the King also made Menéndez governor of that island. This history ends at the end of December, in 1567.

327. October 15, 1566. Pedro Menéndez de Avilés to a Jesuit.

Menéndez was clearly worried about the lack of missionary activity. He earlier reported the killing by the Indians of their first Jesuit victim, Father Pedro Martínez, and urged his friend in the Cadiz House of the Order to attempt to get misionaries of a high caliber sent to Florida, so as to start the task of conversion of Indians to

Catholic Christianity as rapidly and effectively as possible. There is more than one sign of disillusionment in his letter.

E. Ruidíaz y Caravia, La Florida, *2 vols. (Madrid, 1893), II, 54–160, translated. The opening paragraph is Ruidíaz's summary of its contents.*

Florida, 15th October 1566. Pero Menéndez writes to a Jesuit friend of his who lives in Cádiz, giving him the news that he has received the help sent by the King, and expressing his regret that no men of religion of the Company of Jesus had come. He describes the habits and customs of the natives of those lands, and says that many of them wish to embrace the Catholic religion. He recounts the killing of Father Martínez by the Indians, which happened one league from the fort of San Mateo. He details the arrangements made so that all the men of religion that the Company should send should arrive without difficulty in those lands, etc.:

"From letters of Pedro del Castillo I have understood the great favour in which I am held in all those kingdoms, in the Order of the Company of Jesus: and by means of their prayers, Our Lord has shown me many favours, and does so every day, giving me victory and success in every enterprise which I and the Spaniards with me have undertaken since arriving in these provinces. And although we have suffered very great hunger, hardship and dangers, and there have been some who could not endure it, and have fainted through weakness, others of us, including myself, despite being a greater sinner than all the rest, were sure that we were suffering for the sake of Our Lord, and I was certain that his reward would come to me, and never felt the sufferings, and continued as fit, healthy, well and content as I have ever been: even at the time of greatest need, when the Indians used to come two or three times every week, and kill two or three of our men and wound others, and we had nothing to eat, and those of us in the one fort did not know, two months ago, whether those in the other fort were dead or alive. On the day before St Peter's

day—the very same day that I had set out from Spain with the Fleet for this land—there appeared at the entrance to this Port of San Agustín seventeen ships: they all came in safely, and they were bringing one thousand five hundred soldiers and five hundred sailors, and much artillery and ammunition, and were all loaded with provisions: which gave us all great comfort and delight, and those who were in this fort went round welcoming each other, weeping with pleasure, their hands and eyes lifted to the Heavens, praising our Lord.

At this time I was not at this fort. I came within eight days, and when I came I saw how much help and sustenance His Majesty King Don Felipe was sending us, and that Our Lord had brought them safely.

On one hand I was delighted to see how well Our Lord the King helped us, and on the other I felt upset and thwarted to see that nobody of the Company was coming, nor even a learned man of religion; for in view of the many chiefs we have as friends, and the good understanding and sense of the natives of these provinces, and the great desire they have to be Christians and know the Law of Jesus Christ, six such men of religion will do more in a month than many thousands of us laymen will achieve in many years: for we needed them to explain the doctrine to ourselves. It is just a waste of time in a place like this to think of establishing the Holy Gospels here with soldiers alone. Your Honour should be sure that, unless I am much mistaken, the Word of Our Lord will spread in these areas. For most of the ceremonies of these people involve worshipping the sun and the moon, and they use dead game animals as idols, and other animals too: and each year they have three or four festivals for their devotions, in which they worship the sun, and go for three days without eating, without drinking and without sleeping, which is their fasting. And those who are weak and cannot endure this is considered bad Indians, and are thus despised by the noble people; and the one who comes best through these hardships is considered the most valiant, and he is shown the greatest respect.

They are people of great strength, fast and good swimmers; they are often fighting among themselves, and no chief is known to be powerful among them. I have not wanted to undertake friendship with any chief for the sake of making war on his enemy, even if he is my enemy too, for I am telling them that Our Lord is in Heaven and He is Chief of all the chiefs of the earth and of all creation, and that he is angry with them for making war and killing each other like wild beasts. And thus some of them have let me make peace between them, and have taken down their idols, and have asked me to give them crosses to worship at: I have already given them them, and they worship them, and I have given them some boys and soldiers to teach them Christian Doctrine.

They ask me to make them Christian as we are, and I have told them that I am waiting for Your Honours, so you can make wordlists, and quickly learn their language, and then tell them how they are to be Christians, and enlighten them that if they are not they are serving and having as their Lord the most evil creature of the world, which is the devil, who is deceiving them, and that if they are Christian, they will be enlightened and serve Our Lord, who is Chief of Heaven and earth; and then, being happy and content, they will be our true brothers, and we will give them whatever we may have.

And as I had told them that in this help that was coming were coming these men of religion, who would soon talk to them and teach them to be Christians, and then they did not come, they took me for a liar, and some of them have taken umbrage, saying I was having them on, and the chiefs who are my enemies are laughing at them and at me.

It has done a great deal of damage that there have not come any of Your Honours nor other learned men of religion to explain the doctrine to these people; for as they are highly treacherous and unreliable, if with time and firm foundations the peace I have made with them is not strengthened, to open the door to the Holy Gospels being preached, and to what the men of Religion have to say making sure of the chiefs, then we will be too late and achieve nothing, if they think we are deceiving them. May Our Lord encourage that good Company of Jesus to send to these parts up to six Companions, and may they be such, because they will be bound to achieve very much.

On the 14th September 1566, with an onshore wind, there arrived near this Port of San Agustín, about two leagues off, a ship: and it looked to me as if it did not recognize the Port, so I sent out a fully-equipped launch with many oars to bring it in: and the sea was strong, and the tide contrary, so it could not go out, and within two days a storm came on us; and fifteen days later a boat was found in the river of the Fort of San Mateo, anchored near the sea, with six Flemings inside, and no kind of food: two of them were mortally wounded by arrows; and there was also one Spaniard.

They said that one day earlier, a league from there, Indians who are enemies had killed Father Martínez, of the Company, and three other men; and that the boat which had passed by here was the transport boat in which he was coming, and that it had not recognized the port: and that fifteen days earlier the Pilot of the transport boat had dropped them in the boat on land, to try and find out where they were: and as the storm blew up they could not go back to the transport boat: and that all these days they had met many Indians who said they were my friends and brothers, who had welcomed and entertained them very well: and this misfortune happened to them one league from the fort of San Mateo: and that Father Martínez was bringing all the messages of the Holy Father, and those he was also carrying, all were lost. May Our Lord be blessed for everything. And since His Divine Majesty permits and wishes it, let us give him infinite thanks for everything: for we who are here are so little deserving that Our Lord has wished to give us this blow, that he has removed from our company the great benefit of Father Martínez, of whom we had such great need, both the Spaniards in this land and the natives.

I believe that the transport ship was not in danger, and it will have arrived at the Island of Puerto Rico, Santo Domingo or Cuba. I am sending a boat, and in it a servant of mine, to go these islands: and wherever this transport ship is going, he is to tell its pilot to go to Havana: and that the two Fathers of the Company that are going in it, he should bring them with him and look after them: and they will be occupied until the end of February, until winter has gone, in making wordlists and learning the language of the land of Carlos, a chief who is very friendly. And there is there in Havana someone who knows the language very well: and at the beginning of March they will go to that chief in two days, for it is very good sailing, and then through well-settled land, without getting on board again, to these forts: for most of the towns they have to come through are friendly to us, they have crosses which I have given them, and boys and soldiers to teach them the doctrine.

We have not gone inland, because we are fortifying ourselves along the coast, and trying to make friends with the chiefs there, to have our rear safe, and so we have not seen large populations, although there are many Indians and boys. It is said that there are lots of people inland, and there are great stories of the Salt River which goes to China. So the men of religion who come here had better be of sufficient quality, or else it would be better for them not to come. And as Your Honour understands it better than I will be able to write it, this is enough for the Company to provide in this what is needed. I will be in those kingdoms for all May at the latest, and it could be many days earlier: and it would be best for me not to spend a day of July in these kingdoms, so that I can come to this coast in good weather, and bring the people who may be coming with me in greater safety: because at that time the weather and sailing is good for coming to these provinces.

And those of the Company and other men of religion that might want to come, I will bring them and serve them and look after them as if they were the King himself; and in these parts, as long as I live I shall order that they be respected as Ministers of Our Lord, in the certainty that if any man of religion should not deserve that, his companions will make him deserve it: and if ever they cannot, they will send him to those kingdoms; for in this new land it is best that there should be all this. And it is a way of best serving Our Lord God, because all good doctrine and example has to come from the man of religion, and so he has to be respected and honoured. To all those gentlemen of the Company with you, I kiss their hands many times: and may I have the reward from Our Lord for the many favours they do me in asking Our Lord to help and favour me in everything. And thus I beseech them as much as I can to continue it. And if Your Honour takes this letter in Cádiz to Pedro del Castillo, I kiss his hands, and he should take this letter as his own.

May Our Lord keep and increase the very magnificent person and estate of Your Honour, as I wish. From Florida, from this fort of San Augustín, 15th October 1566. The servant of Your Honour,

[signed:] Pedro Menéndez.

SPANIARDS AND INDIANS IN FLORIDA
ABOUT 1566

A DOCUMENT that gives in note form particulars of which Spaniards were in Florida shortly after the conquest and also annotates some Florida Indian customs is of some special interest. The details of the Spanish establishment (329) seem to belong to the period shortly after the burning down of the old fort taken from the French and the buildings of the new fort of San Mateo—when the garrison was quartered at Tacatacuru a little to the north of the mouth of the St. Johns River.

The details of Indian customs (328) stress human sacrifice and funeral customs but also give a brief note on Indian whale fishing. The author is unknown.

A.G.I., Seville, Indiferente General 1530 (145/7/9), typescript, copy in Division of Manuscripts Library of Congress, translated.

328. 1566. Customs of the Indians of Florida.

Memorial. Where the Indians are in Florida.

Firstly the Indians of the same country of Carlos have the custom that each time a son of the chieftain [casique] dies, they sacrifice the sons and daughters which kept company with him.

After the death of the son of the chief the second sacrifice that takes place is when the chief or the chief's wife [casica] dies, and they sacrifice his or her servants. And this is the second sacrifice.

The third sacrifice is that every year they kill a Christian captive to give him to the Idol, whom they worship, to eat;—whom they worship and they say of it that their Idol eats human eyes. They hold a memorial ceremony each year over the head, which is a custom with them.

And the fourth sacrifice is that after the spring come certain enchanters [hichiseros] before the Demon, wearing certain horns on the head and howling like wolves.

And they have many other different idols that make noises like mountain animals. And they are their idols. And there are these idols which never cease night or day for four months and run with such fury into such bestiality that cannot be told.

Memorial of the Indians and the Indian ceremonies of Tacobaga.

When one the principal chiefs dies they take him to pieces and place them [to boil?] in large jars. And after two days when the flesh is detached from the bones,—they take the bones and put one together with the other until they assemble the man as he was. And they put it [the skeleton] in a house which they hold for a temple. While they are completing the restoration [of the bones] they fast for four days. And at the end of four days they bring all the people of the village together and go out with him in a procession and enter it [the skeleton] with much reverence.——And they say that all those who go in the procession gain indulgences.

The Indians of Tegesta which is another province from Los Martires to El Cañaberal.

And whenever a head chief dies they dislocate and remove the principal bones and the lesser bones they inter with the body. And in the chief's house they place a great box and in this box they instal the principal bones. And there the village also comes to worship, and they take these bones for Gods.

And in the summer all the canoes [canoas] go to sea. And amongst all these Indians there goes one particular Indian with three spikes [harpoons?] in his girdle and he launches a shot at the neck and when the whale goes to sound he puts a spike into one of its nostrils, and so it stifles itself. It does not miscarry for it [a rope?] goes under her and so kills her, and they pull her out. After they run her aground on the sand the first thing they do is to break open the head and draw out two bones she has set into her brain [casco]. And these two bones they put with the deceased and worship them there.

[Endorsed:] Chiefs and customs of the Indians of Florida.

329. 1566. Establishment of Florida about the beginning of 1566.

In the country of Carlos Captain Reynoso with 40.

In Sant Agustín Estevano de las Alas and Bartolomé Melendez with 700 [=300?].

Sant Mateo is discharged and has passed to Tacatacaru where the artillery was transferred. Vasco Cavali is there with 200 men.

In Sancta Elena Pero Meléndez Marqués 500 with 48 married persons.

Pedro Menéndez [a relative of the Adelantado].

Captain Reynoso, governor of the provinces of Carlos and the fort of Sant Anton which is more than 50 leagues [=140 miles or more?] from Sant Mateo from north to south.

Florencio de Esquinal.

Captain Juan Pardo.

Hernando de Miranda.
Salzedo, native of Madrid.
Don Antonio who was page to the archbishop.
Captain Antonio de Prado.
Escalante.

There are there:
Estevan de las Alas, lieutenant general
Captain Pedro Menéndez Marqués, discoverer of the coast, and governor and warden of Sancta Elena
Bartolomé Menéndez, warden and governor of Sancto Agustín.
Vasco Çaval, captain and governor of Catacoru
Diego García de Sierra, governor of Guale
And the *alcaldes* and *regidores* in all five territories, and, I say, in the two which are Sancta Elena and Sancto Agustín.

330. 1566. Gonzalo de Peñalosa reports to the *Audiencia* of Santo Domingo on the problems of reinforcing Pedro Menéndez de Avilés in Florida.

Navarrete, Colección, *XIV (1971), fols. 327–328; E. Ruidíaz y Caravia, La Florida, 2 vols. (1893), pp. 473–476, translated. The heading is that of Ruidíaz.*

An account of the voyage which Captain Gonzalo de Peñalosa made to Florida in 1566 to assist General Pedro Menéndez de Avilés, commissioned by the President and Administration of the Royal Audiencia and Chancellery of Santo Domingo.

"Most Powerful Lord. - I, Goncalo de Peñalosa, your Captain, report: that I was instructed by Yourselves to give an account of the fleet which went under my command to the assistance of General Pero Menéndez: what happened is as follows. On Friday the twenty-eighth of September I left this port of Santo Domingo, and on the second of October in the anchorage of La Beata a sail appeared, and since it was to windward it went without our finding out anything about it. Four days after this, continuing our voyage, I arrived at Cape Tiburón, where there is a river called Doña María: in this anchorage appeared two sails, and the frigate went after them. One of them was a boat belonging to one Martín de la Yaguana: it was being taken by a French patache, which abandoned it at sea without leaving anyone or anything on board, and the frigate took it at midnight. The following day, by the anchorage of La Yaguana, again we saw another sail: it seemed to be the French patache: the frigate went after it and caught it. It found in it eight Frenchmen, who said that they had been lost in a large storm, that they were with a large ship in the anchorage of La Tortuga. In the evening five ships approached the transport ship in which I was going and made us put in for that night, thinking they were French, in a port which was near there, called Puerto Paraíso.

Next morning, as we were setting sail to continue our voyage, and in search of the frigate, we found that the same five ships were waiting for us at sea: and since it looked as though we would be unable to go far enough to stop them overtaking us, we went towards them and they fled. We managed to catch up, with a Portuguese caravel which they were taking, and from them we discovered that the ships were those which Estevan de las Alas was taking from the Governor Pero Menéndez to the assistance of Florida. We were so short of water, and they of all supplies, that even if the weather had offered us the opportunity, which it did not, of not going into La Yaguana, this shortage made it necessary for us to put in there. I found the frigate in the port with the French patache. I was in this port for fifteen days, in which time Estevan de las Alas and I took in the provisions that were necessary. At this time I heard the news that there were two Portuguese caravels in a port called Goabo, three leagues from La Yaguana. I investigated and sent the frigate off to them: it found them at sea, followed them for all one night and a day: one of them escaped, it captured the other and brought it back to my command: there were in it three negros, 500 hides, more or less; I sold the hides and the caravel and took the negros with me. I will give an account of who to, how and for how much, should You send for it from me.

At the end of the fifteen days, I left to follow Pero Menéndez, as instructed by Yourselves, by the old channel; in it the transport ship was lost with the weather that God sent. It was in the anchorage which they call Cayo Romano. I was there for fifteen days waiting for weather to go out in the remaining ships of Estevan de las Alas and the French patache, where I had gone with the men, provisions, artillery and ammunition that could be saved. Since the provisions were running out, and God was not giving the weather for us to leave there, I decided with Estevan de las Alas and the other nobles who were there that we should leave to look on dry land. We put this into effect, leaving together the ships and the people that stayed on them. Two hundred of us set out, with which, within ten or twelve days, we went to [   ]; we were there for eight days, then we went to embark twelve leagues from there at a port which is called Puerto Higuey, to go to Havana; here none of the men which Estevan de las Alas took out with him remained with him: up to forty deserted from me, useless people. We arrived at La Sabana, which they call Vasco Porcallo, where I found an order from Pero Menéndez, in which he was dismissing the men, because Florida was won in this town. About eight or ten men were left of those I took: I went to Havana with the men that were left, where I found the men that I had left on the ships. Once I had arrived, I gave the letters and the account which You instructed me to give to Pero Menéndez. He was very pleased: I wanted to return at once in the frigate and patache which had belonged to the French; I could not, because he took both off me, saying that God and Yourselves had need of them, for they were fitted out in the way most convenient for that coast and for taking provisions to the soldiers who were dying of hunger in Florida. With the frigate he took two bronze artillery pieces; your Governor of Havana, Garci Osorio, took another off me, although this was not my wish. I stayed waiting in Havana for two months, not having ship nor provisions. At the end of those two months Pero Menéndez set off for Florida, and he sold me a caravel which I had brought here. I had to careen it, since it was letting in water fit to sink. This took twenty days, at the end of which I left Havana, although your Governor and the people did not want me to, for the great fear they had of the French. I left them forty soldiers, good men, to serve You in that force until help can come to them from Spain. I had a hundred soldiers when I embarked: I came

to Puerto Rico, where five or six stayed, and was there for eight days while I took on food: I came here, where I am very ready to serve You and gladly give an account of whatever I may be asked.—Captain Gonzalo de Peñalosa."

331. Captain Juan Pardo's account of his expeditions into the interior in 1565 and 1566.

Pedro Menéndez de Avilés (whose geographical concepts were mainly erroneous) instructed Juan Pardo to march inland with his sergeant Boyano so as to sketch out a route to Zacatecas (in northern Mexico) and to lay the foundations for Christian missions as they proceeded. The exploration inland from Santa Elena brought the explorers in successive missions from Santa Elena to the Appalachians, across them, down the Tennessee Valley, and over the watershed into the territory of the Upper Creeks at Coosa (where Soto's and Luna's men had already been).

Successive accounts need to be read together with some care. An attempt to disentangle the story will be found in D. B. Quinn, North America from First Discovery to Early Settlements *(1977), pp. 271-274.*

A.G.I., Seville, Patronato 1/1/1/19; printed in E. Ruidíaz y Caravia, La Florida, *2 vols. (Madrid, 1893), II, 465-473, translated.*

An Account of the Exploration and Conquest which Captain Juan Pardo was Commissioned to undertake in 1565 by Pero Menéndez de Avilés in the interior of Florida: written by Juan Pardo himself.

"I left the Port of San Lucas on Easter Saturday 1565 in the division of Sancho de Archiniega with eighteen seagoing ships: in them I took my company of two hundred and fifty soldiers. Within three months, on the day before St. Peter's Day, seventeen of our ships arrived at San Agustín; for one lost the way, but turned up later. As I said, all the infantry landed at San Agustín; we did not find the Governor Pero Menéndez there. The Commander of San Mateo, with the

Captains and General Sancho de Archiniega, came: he said that San Mateo needed to be garrisoned at once, so it was, and the Colonel's company was sent; also that another company should be sent to Santa Elena, so they sent me with two ships, the flagship and the ship of Zebieta. When we had been there for a few days Governor Pero Menéndez de Avilés arrived: he reviewed my company, finding two hundred and forty eight soldiers in it. After that he ordered me to advance next St. Andrew's Day inland, to make it known to the Indians how they were living in error and to bring them under His Holiness and His Majesty. So, when St. Andrew's Day came, I set off with one hundred and twenty five soldiers. In this account I will not mention the first forty leagues, for the land is all marshy, and there are few Indians and some of those had come to Santa Elena, and I had already talked to them on behalf of His Majesty and His Holiness, and so on my expeditions.... We came to where there is a big river. I sent for the Indians, for the chiefs were there, and I gave them the talk on behalf of God and His Majesty, as instructed, and they replied that they were ready to obey His Holiness and His Majesty. From there I set off for Canos: after the first day I halted in the open country for there was no town, and the next day I arrived at Canos, where I found a large number of chiefs and Indians, and I gave them the usual talk on behalf of God and His Majesty, and they were quite content and obedient in the service of God and His Majesty. It has a full river and the land is very good. From there I left for Tagaya, where I assembled the Indians and chiefs, and gave them the same talk, and they similarly were brought under the power of His Holiness and His Majesty.

The next day I went to Tagaya el Chico, and similarly assembled the Indians and the chief, and gave them the same talk, and they were brought under the power of His Holiness and His Majesty. The next day I left and went to a place whose name I cannot remember, and gave the same talk, and they were brought under the power of His Holiness and His Majesty. From there I went to Ysa, which is a large tribal area, where I found many chiefs and a large number of Indians, and I gave them the usual talk, and they were brought under the power of His Holiness and His Majesty. I left there the next day and went to a settlement of the same Ysa, and assembled the Indians and

gave them the same talk, and they were brought under the power of His Holiness and His Majesty. All this is very good land, with a full river. Next day I left and slept in open country, for there was no town; next day I left and went to Juada, where I found a large number of Indians and chiefs, and gave them the usual talk, and all were brought under the power of His Holiness and His Majesty. I was here for fifteen days, because they asked me for Christians to explain the doctrine to them: and I made a fort, where Boyano, my sergeant stayed, and some soldiers, with their provisions of gunpowder, rope, bullets and corn to eat. After those fifteen days, I set off Northwards, and stopped for the night in the country, for there was no town, next to a full river that passes through Juada: all this land is very good. Next day I went down river and similarly stopped for the night in open country, in very good land. Next day I left and went to Quihanaqui, and assembled the chief and the Indians (he has a lot) and gave them the usual talk, and they were brought under the power of His Holiness and His Majesty; I was here for four days: it has very pleasant fertile river banks and the full river passes through it. And at the end of this time I left and went to another tribal district whose name I do not remember, and I assembled the Indians and the chief, and I gave them the usual talk, and they were brought under the power of His Holiness and His Majesty. I was here for two days: it is very good land and the full river passes through it. Next day I left and stopped in open country, for there was not a town, and next day I arrived at Guatari: here I found more than thirty chiefs and a large number of Indians, and I gave them the usual talk, and they were brought under the power of His Holiness and His Majesty. I was here for more or less fifteen or sixteen days; here these chiefs asked me to leave them people to explain the doctrine to them, so I left them the chaplain of my company and four soldiers; because a letter reached me there from Estevan de Las Alas, telling me to go to Santa Helena; for thus I would be serving His Majesty, since there was news of the French. Next day I left and went to a piece of open country, where I stayed the night: next day I went to Guatariatiqui, where I gave the usual talk, and they were brought under the power of His Holiness and His Majesty. Next day I left and stayed in the country, for there was no town: all this land is very good. Next day I arrived at Racuchilli, where I found a number of Indians and chiefs, and I gave them the usual talk: it is very good land. Next day I left and went to a tribal area whose name I cannot remember, and gave the usual talk, and they were brought under the power of His Holiness and His Majesty: it is very good land. Next day I left on the same road I had taken before, which goes to Tagaya Chiquito, and again I gave them the usual talk, and again they confirmed themselves in it. Next day I came to Tagaya, and similarly again they confirmed themselves in their previous acquiescence. Next day I came to Cajuos, where I was for two days, and I gave them the usual talk, and they confirmed themselves again. And from there I went to Guiomae in two days, where I gave them the usual talk again, and they confirmed themselves in their previous acquiescence. I have already said that I will not give a full account of the forty leagues from here, since the land is marshy and has been under the power of Santa Elena, that we were in every day. This is what happened in the first expedition.

Governor Pero Menéndez de Avilés arrived at the city of Santa Elena in 1566, where he ordered me to undertake the expedition again: I was to leave on the first of September of that year, and wherever they asked me for some Christians to explain the doctrine to the Indians, I was to give them: and so I left on the first of September. I have already said that I shall give no account of those forty leagues, the land being as it is. And so after my days' marching I arrived at Guiomae, where I found a very good reception, and a house made for His Majesty, which I had ordered them to make when I first passed through. I was there for two days: then I left and arrived in another two days at Canos, where I found a large number of Indians and chiefs, and I spoke to them again on behalf of His Holiness and His Majesty, and they replied that they were ready, and under the power of His Holiness and His Majesty. I left here and went to Tagaya, and gave them the same talk, and they replied that they were ready as they had promised the first time. Next day I arrived at Tagaya Chico, and gave the same talk, and they replied that they were ready as the first time. From there I went to a tribal area whose name I do not remember, and I gave the same talk, and they said they were ready as the first time. From

there I went to Racuchi and assembled the Indians and chiefs, and gave them the same talk, and they said that they were ready as the first time. Next day I left and stopped in open country. Next day I left and went to Quatariaatiqui, where I found a number of Indians and female (¿?) chiefs, where I gave them the usual talk, and they said that they were ready as the first time. From there I went to a tribal area whose name I do not remember, and I gave them the usual talk, and they replied that they were ready as the first time, to be under the power of His Holiness and His Majesty. Next day I left and went to Quirotoqui, and I assembled all the Indians and chiefs, and gave them the usual talk, and they replied that they were, as the first time, under the power of His Holiness and His Majesty. Next day I went to open country: and all this land I have been talking of is very good. Next day I came to another piece of open country, and that is very good land. Next day I arrived at Juada, where I found that Sergeant Boyano had left the fort where I had left him and the soldiers, and that the Indians had surrounded him. At this news I gave the usual talk to Juada and its Indians, and they replied that they were ready to comply as the first time, under the power of His Holiness and His Majesty. So I left at once and crossed the sierra in four days of open country, arriving at Tocalques: this is a very good town, and its houses are of wood, and there there was a large number of Indians and chiefs, and I gave them the talk on behalf of His Holiness and His Majesty, and they replied that they were willing to be Christian and to have His Majesty as their Lord. Next day I left and slept in open country. Next day I left and arrived at Canche, where the land is very good; it has an important river, and very large fertile river banks, and there I found a large number of Indians and chiefs, and I gave them the usual talk on behalf of His Holiness and His Majesty, and they replied that they were willing to be Christian and to have His Majesty as their Lord. I was here for four days, for I gathered that the Indians who used to consider themselves as enemies were now friendly, gathering that I was coming. Next day I left and went to a piece of open ground, and the next day the same. Next day I arrived at Tanasqui, where there is a full river, and the town is surrounded in one part by a wall, with turrets and parapets, where I assembled all the Indians and gave them the usual talk, and they replied that they were ready to do what His Holiness and His Majesty required; this land is very good, and I think there are metals of gold and silver. Next day I left and arrived at Chihaque (also known as Lameco), where I found Sergeant Boyano and the soldiers. There they told me how the Indians had driven me out, so I assembled all the Indians and chiefs and gave them the talk on behalf of His Holiness and His Majesty, and they were brought under the power of His Holiness and His Majesty, as everywhere else. I stayed here for ten or twelve days, to let people rest; here I found out from friendly Indians that six or seven thousand Indians were waiting for me in a pass, where were Carrosa and Chisca and Costeheycoza; and despite all this, I decided to continue my journey, and I set off towards Zacatecas and the mines of San Martín. I went three days through open country, and after the three days I arrived at a town whose name I do not remember, and I assembled the chiefs and Indians and gave them the usual talk, and they replied to me that they were ready to do what His Holiness and His Majesty ordered, and that they were willing to be Christian; this land is very good, and I think there are metals in it of gold and silver.

Next day I left and arrived at Satapo, where I found a large number of Indians, and there I was not well received, in the same way as I had been until there, for the chief refused: so I called a meeting, to tell them what they had to do on behalf of God and His Majesty, and few of them turned up, although there were many of them, and made no reply at all, but rather laughed, and there were many of them that understood us; and that night the native interpreters came to me and said that they were not going to go on with me, because they knew that there was a large number of Indians waiting for me to massacre me and my soldiers; also an Indian came to me from the town itself and told me that if I gave him a knife he would tell me something of great importance to me, so I gave it him and he told me how the Indians of Chisca and Carrosa and Costeheycoza were waiting for us a day away; that there were a hundred and more chiefs, and part of them were in dispute with the Indians of Zacatecas. In view of this I assembled my officers and we went into a council, and we concluded that even if we were to break the enemy, we could not make any real gain on account of the food supplies, which they were giving us themselves, so we decided to recommend it to God and turn round; in four days we returned to Lameco (also called Chiaha). All this land, as I have said, is very good. Here in Lameco all of us agreed to make a fort, so that if it was to His Majesty's advantage to continue the expedition this place should remain a permanent gain; everyone was agreed on this, as I said. So a corporal and thirty soldiers stayed there, with provisions and ammunition. At the end of fifteen days when this had been done, I left and arrived at Cauchi, coming all the way through open country, where the chief asked for some Christians to explain the doctrine to them; and all were agreed to leave him twelve soldiers and a corporal there in a fortification which was made in eight days, leaving them gunpowder and ammunition. From there I returned to Tocae in two days, where I spoke again to the same chiefs and Indians, and all agreed that they were obedient to His Holiness and His Majesty. I was there for two days and then left for Juada, crossing the land in four days; here I found a large gathering of Indians, and gave them the usual talk, and they said that they were ready to do what they had promised: I left there my Lieutenant Alberto Escudero with thirty soldiers, so that he could keep in control with the fort that had been made in this place, so that from there he could back up the other soldiers who were left on that side of the sierra. After spending ten days in Juada, as I said, I left for Guatari and was four days getting there: here I found the Indians and chiefs gathered, and I gave them the usual talk, and they replied that they were ready to do what His Holiness and His Majesty required, and they asked me to leave them Christians; So I made a fort and left there seventeen soldiers and a corporal; at this time I stayed there in Guatari sixteen or seventeen days, more or less. Seeing that the time was running out which the Governor Pero Menéndez de Avilés had given me, I set off on the marches back to Santa Elena. This land, as I said, Guatari, is one of the best lands in the world, and since I gave an account on my first expedition from Guatari to Santa Elena, I will not give it again here for reasons of space.

[signed:] Juan Pardo.

332. July 11, 1567. A report by Francisco Martinez, a soldier who accompanied Juan Pardo on his journey into the interior.

The report was sent to García Osorio, governor of Cuba, and the copy was made by the scrivener, Bartolomé de Morales, at Havana on October 6, 1567.
A.G.I., Seville, Patronato 1/1/1/19; printed in E. Ruidíaz y Caravia, La Florida, 2 vols. (Madrid, 1893), pp. 477–480, translated.

This is a copy, well and faithfully taken from a simple copy which was taken of a book and memorial of the Conquest and the Land of the Provinces of Florida, which the Illustrious Señor García Osorio, Governor and Captain General of this island for His Majesty, gave to me, the scribe written below, which was taken from a book and memorial which Francisco Martínez showed Your Honour, a soldier of the conquest of that Florida, which deals with the entry into and conquest of that land and new discoveries in it, whose content is as follows:

"From the city of Santa Elena left Captain Juan Pardo on the first of November 1566, to go inland to discover and conquer the land from here to Mexico. So he came to a tribal area called Juada, where he made a fort and left his sergeant with thirty soldiers, for there was so much snow on the sierra that he could not advance, and the Captain returned with the rest of his men to this point of Santa Elena, where the land is that had been seen up till then; it is good for bread and wine and any kind of livestock that might be put on it, for it is flat land with many pleasant rivers, and good groves of trees, such as walnuts and black mulberries and white mulberries and medlars (?) and chestnuts, balsam and many other kinds of tree groves. It is similarly a land of much game, both deer and hares, rabbits, chickens, bears and lions.

Thirty days after arriving at this point of Santa Elena, a letter arrived for the Captain from his Sergeant, in which he said that he had been at war with a chief called Chisca, who is an enemy of the Spanish, and that they had killed more than a thousand Indians and burnt fifty huts, and that they had done this with fifteen soldiers, and of those only two emerged with wounds, and they were not dangerous. And in the same letter he said that if Señor Estevan de las Alas and the Señor Captain ordered him to, he would go ahead and see what happened: so the Captain replied that he should leave ten soldiers in the fort at Juada and a corporal with them, and that with the others he should find out what he could; and while this letter was arriving, a chief from the sierra sent a threat to the Sergeant, saying that he was going to come and eat them all and a dog that belonged to the sergeant. In view of this he decided that it would be better for him to go and seek them out than for them to come and seek him out, so he left the fort of San Juan with twenty soldiers and walked for four days through the sierra; one morning he came upon the enemy, and found them so well fortified that he was surprised, because they were surrounded by a very high wooden wall with a little door with transverse bars. The sergeant saw that there was no way of getting in except through the door, so they made a coordinated charge under the shelter of their long shields and entered with considerable danger, for they wounded the sergeant in the mouth and nine other soldiers in assorted places, although none of the wounds was dangerous: eventually they captured the fort, and the Indians retired to the huts they had inside, of which they are below ground, from where they came out to skirmish with the Spanish: killing many Indians they reached the doors of these huts and set fire to them and burnt them all, so that 1500 Indians were killed and burnt; it was there that the letter arrived for the sergeant from the Captain, in which he gave the orders I mentioned above, that he should leave ten soldiers in the fort of San Juan and go with the rest of his men to find out what more he could. Taking the road to a large tribal area which is at that end of the sierra, which is called Chiaha, he came to one of its towns, after walking for four days, which he found excellently surrounded with a wall standing out with its turrets strong in a group: this town was between two full rivers and had more than 3000 Indian warriors inside, for there was no—one else, no women or children, who received them very well and gave them good food to eat.

Next day they set off through this area already

mentioned and walked for twelve days, always through towns of this tribal area, where they gave them all they needed and Indians to carry their baggage: they came to the town where the main chief was, who received them very well and gave them Indians so that he could make a fort there and wait for the Captain, because this chief said he wanted to be a friend of the Captain and do what he should order him to. So the sergeant made the fort, where he waited for the Captain, who is going to leave this fort in the middle of August. To this fort of Santa Helena have come very many chiefs and Indians from inland, each of them bringing the best he has, which is deer, leather and meat: a great number of Indians went out four and six leagues to receive the Captain, and they ran, carrying him in a chair, until they reached the town, and there they brought him all the provisions that were needed for his company, of corn, deer, hens and fish, and the Indian who did not reach the chair in which the Captain was going felt ashamed: some came dancing, others jumping, much painted in several colours: and the land is very good, both the one we are in and the others further ahead, for we have tried sowing wheat and barley and it grows as well as in Spain: also other seeds, radishes, turnips, melons, ten-kilo pumpkins, and any seed grows very well.

The fort which the Captain made in Juada is a hundred and twenty leagues from this point of Santa Helena, and from there to where the Sergeant is is a hundred and forty leagues: so that the conquered land extends for two hundred and sixty leagues. And all that is written here has been seen by the witnesses whose signatures are here, and is true.

Made in Santa Helena on 11th July 1567. - Alonso García - Pedro de Hermossa - Pedro Gutiérrez Pacheco - Pedro de Olivares.

This copy I, the scrivener written below, got out, corrected and checked with the simple copy, under the instructions of the said Señor Governor, To whom I gave it and handed it in the town of Havana in this island of Cuba on the 6th October 1567; I gave it him signed with my name and my notarial sign, the witnesses being Alonso de Reyna and Bernaldino de Mata. And so hereunto I placed my sign. In witness to the truth - Bartolomé de Morales, Public and Registry Scrivener of His Majesty.

333. November 30, 1567. News of Juan Pardo reaches France.

Le Prêtre, usher of the Privy Chamber of Charles IX, reports news that had come from Spain. The details of the Pardo expeditions are vague and imprecise, but they show that the expeditions were of some international interest. The geographical views are pale reflections of those of Pedro Menéndez de Avilés, some of whose activities in connection with his Florida enterprise are also reported.

Dépêches de M. de Fourquevaux, *edited by Célestin Douais, 3 vols. (Paris, 1896–1904), I, 304-305, translated.*

Captain Juan Pardo governor of the cape of Santa Helena in Florida has written that he has sent thirty of his soldiers on a brig up the Santa Helena river for about a hundred leagues. Some of them landed on the north bank and journeyed across land for thirty leagues away from the river. At the foot of the mountains they came across an open village with stone houses and a little castle with a tower also of stone. The inhabitants are peaceful and seem good people. They are clad in cotton shirts and the skins of various animals. They cultivate maize and other grains. There are cattle, though they are small. The soil is fertile and they have trees bearing various kinds of fruit which are good to eat. There are gold and silver mines. The soldiers were told that some days' journey further on there was a population of bearded men, but they could not make out whether this was French or Spanish, and were not permitted to go on any further. The Indians willingly gave them food and enough provisions for the return to their brig, and so they returned to the fort.

The opinion of these explorers is that the river leads to Canada and that there is a passage through to the South Sea and to China. I hear that Pedro Menéndez too maintains the truth of this. With this in view he has built in Biscay twelve ships in the manner of *reberges*, the smallest being of two hundred tons. They will be ready by next April when Menéndez is counting on going back to Florida with the intention of working miracles, as I have already written in other memoranda.

At the fort in Florida called St Mathieu [San Mateo], which Menéndez seized from the French, there are two hundred men. At Fort St Augustin [San Agustín], the harbor where he landed, there are two hundred, and at Fort Ste Hélène [Santa Elena] there are only sixty. All these men would constitute but a poor defense, since they and their forts are more or less worthless, so I have been told. It is true that they have artillery. Menéndez has gone to Seville to fit out three ships and lade them with flour, wine and other victuals to send to the forts which are almost without.

334. January 23, 1569. Account by Juan de la Vandera of the places reached by Juan Pardo in his expeditions in 1566 and 1567.

Vandera gives the most specific account we have of the places visited by the Pardo-Boyano expeditions of 1566 and 1567. It would appear to be based on a journal of the expedition of 1567. It is mainly concerned with the quality of the various locations. The account was not written down until several years later, though it is almost certainly not based solely on memory. It demonstrated the continuance of the illusion that the Alabama River Valley would give easy access to Mexico.

Printed by T. Buckingham Smith, Colección de varios documentos para la historia de la Florida, I (London, 1857), 155 ff., and E. Ruidíaz y Caravia, La Florida, 2 vols. (Madrid, 1893), pp. 481-486, translated. The heading is from Ruidíaz.

An account written by Juan de la Vandera of the places, and of what land is each place of those of the Provinces of Florida, where Captain Juan Pardo, at the order of Pero Menéndez de Avilés, went inland to discover a way to New Spain, from the point of Santa Elena in these provinces, in the years 1566 and 1567: which all goes as follows:

"First he left Santa Elena with his company, for this purpose, and the day he left he went to sleep at a place called Uscamacu; here is an island surrounded by rivers, sandy soil, of very good clay for cooking-pots and tiles and other necessary things; there are in this land good stretches of land for maize, and many vinestocks.

From Uscamacu he went straight to another place called Ahoya, where he halted and slept. This Ahoya is an island: some parts of it bounded by rivers, and the rest as firm soil, reasonable for maize, and many vinestocks, with many shoots.

From Ahoya he went straight to another place called Ahoyabe, a small town subject to Ahoya, and of the same land as Ahoya.

From Ahoyabe he went straight to another place called Cozao, which is quite a large capital, and has a lot of good land like the others mentioned, and many stretches of stony soil where can be cultivated maize, wheat, barley, vines, all kinds of fruit and vegetables, because there are rivers and fresh water streams and reasonable land for everything.

From Cozao he went straight to another small place, which belongs to a delegate of Cozao itself: the land of this place is good but small.

From this place he went straight to another called El Enfrenado; the land is poor, although there are many patches of very good land, like the others mentioned.

From El Enfrenado he went straight to another place called Guiomaez, which is forty leagues distant from the point of Santa Elena; the route he took is rather difficult, but it is land where can be cultivated as much as in Cozao, or even more: there are some large deep marshes, but that is because of the great flatness of the land.

From Guiomaez he went straight to Canos, which the Indians call Canosi, and by another name Cofetazque; within the bounds of this land there are three or four reasonable rivers, one of them very full, or even two; there are some small marshes which anyone, even a child, can cross on foot; there are in this stretch steep valleys, with many stones and rocks, and shallow ones; it is reddish soil, very good indeed, much better than all those mentioned.

Canos is land through which passes one of the two full rivers, nearby, and other streams: it has very large and very good fertile banks, and here, and from here on, much maize is harvested, and there are a lot of thick grapes, very good, and also bad, thick and thin, and of many other kinds; in sum, it is a place where a major town can be sited. It is fifty leagues from Santa Elena, and some twenty leagues from the sea; it can be reached along the river mentioned, through the land, and one can go much further along the same river, as well as along the other one that goes near Guiomaez.

From Canos he went straight to another place called Tagaya, very good land, no marshes, flat land, with few trees, dark and reddish, very good with a lot of good water, springs and streams.

From Tagaya he went straight to another place called Gueza, which is land just the same as the last, abundant, good.

From Gueza he went straight to another place called Aracuchi, which is also very good land.

From Aracuchi he went straight to another place called Otariyatiqui, which is the tribal head for much land beyond; land very abundant, good: from this Otari to another place called Guatary it is about fifteen or sixteen leagues, to the right, further south than this other place. Here there have been, and still are, two women chiefs, and of no little consequence, compared with the other chiefs, for in their dress they are served by pages and ladies. It is rich land: in every place there are very good houses and earthen huts, round, very big and very good: it is mountain land, and good flat arable land. We saw this place and stayed there for twenty days on the way back; next to this place there runs a very full river, which goes on to Sauapa and Usi, where it becomes salt water, by the sea, sixty leagues from Santa Elena. From Santa Elena to this Guatary there are eighty leagues, and up this river can come any boat, so they say, more than twenty.

From Otariyatiqui he went straight to another place called Quinahaqui, where there passes another very full river: it is very good land.

From the last mentioned place, twelve leagues away to the left, there is another place called Issa, which has very attractive banks and the whole land very pleasant, many rivers and springs. In the territory of this place Issa, we found three mines of very good crystal: these are provisionally registered, as if later advantage would be taken of them. We saw and gathered all this on our return journey to Santa Elena.

From Quinahaqui he went straight to another place called Aguaquiri, which is perfect land, good and fertile.

From Aguaquiri he went straight to another place called Joara, which is near the mountains, and is where Juan Pardo reached on his first journey, and his sergeant stayed. I can say that it is as beautiful land as there is in the best of all Spain, for every kind of thing that men might wish to grow there. It is a hundred leagues from Santa Elena.

From Joara he went into the mountains, straight to another place called Tocar: it took us three days to go through them. In these mountains there are many grapes, many chestnuts, many walnuts, many other fruits: it is better than the Sierra Morena, because there are there many fertile plains and the land is not at all rough. It is very good land in Tocar, where large cultivations of any kind can be undertaken.

From Tocar he went straight to another place called Cauchi, with excellent land: from here on the land reminded me of Andalucía, because it is all very rich land.

From Cauchi he went straight to Tanasqui: it took us three days to get there, through unpopulated land: the land is so rich that I don't know how to praise it enough.

From Tanasqui he went straight to another place called Solameco, or by another name, Chiaha: it is very rich wide land, a large place, near very beautiful rivers: there are all around this place, one league, two leagues, three leagues away, and more, and less, many small places, all surrounded by rivers. There are some wonderful areas, a lot of very good grapes, many medlar trees: truly it is a land for angels.

From Solameco he went straight westward to a place called Chalahume; it took us three days to get there through unpopulated land, and there we found rougher mountains than the ones mentioned before. In these strongholds we were passing through it is very rich agreeable fresh land: climbing up one of these ridges we found traces of metal, and we asked the mineral men, who swore it was of silver: we arrived at Chalahume, which has as good a site on the land as can be compared with Córdoba city, very large good fertile plains: there we found grapes as good as there are in Spain: I can say that it is land which seems to have been cultivated by Spaniards, it is so good.

From Chalahume he went straight to another place, two leagues away, called Satapo, from where we returned: it is a reasonable town, of good houses and much maize and wild fruit; the land rich and very pleasant; and all these places and those before, sited near very attractive rivers.

From Satapo we were to go straight to Cosaque, I believe, according to what I found out from Indians and from a soldier who went there from this company, and returned and gave an account of what he saw: it is five or six days journey to Cossa, very sparsely populated land, for there are no more than three small places: the first, two days journey from Satapo, called Tasqui: in these two days journey there is good land and three large rivers: and a little further on, another place called Tasquiqui, and another day's journey further on from there another ruined town called Olitifar, all good flat land, and another two days' journey further on from there, through unpopulated land, is a small place, and further on from this another, about a league away. Cossa is a big town, the largest there is beyond Santa Elena, and we went that way till we reached it: it must have some hundred and fifty citizens, judging from the size of the town: it is a place richer than any of the others mentioned: there are usually a large number of Indians there: it is sited on low land, at the foot of a ridge: there are around it, at half a league, quarter a league, and a league away very many large places: it is very abundant land: it is to the south, or slightly east of south. From Cossa we were to go straight to Trascaluza, which is the end of the populated part of Florida. There are seven days' journey from Cossa to Trascaluza, and in all those I think there are two or three places: the rest is all unpopulated. Trascaluza is said to be to the south; and from here to the land of New Spain some people say there are nine days' journey, others eleven, others thirteen, but the consensus nine: all unpopulated, and in the middle of the whole way there is one place of four or five houses: and after that, following the same direction, the first settlement there is belongs to New Spain, so they say. I beg Our Lord to provide as will best serve him, Amen.

Dated at the Point of Santa Elena, 23 January 1569,

[signed:] Juan de la Vandera.

Chapter Thirty-eight
The Spanish Annexation of the Carolina Outer Banks in 1566

SINCE HIS EXPLORATION of Chesapeake Bay (Bahía de Santa María) in 1561, Pedro Menéndez de Avilés had been determined to return there because he believed that it, or one of its associated channels, led to Tierra Nueva (the Northeast, including Newfoundland, Labrador, and perhaps the Maritimes), and from there to a passage in temperate latitudes to the Pacific Ocean. In 1561 he determined to send back to the bay the hispaniolized Algonkian Indian Don Luis, captured by him in 1561. He was to be accompanied by a party of Dominican friars, under the leadership of Fray Pablo de San Pedro, and by a small force of soldiers. They were to establish both a military outpost and a mission, but the emphasis was to be on missionary work, so that Spanish influence and authority could later be extended to the area.

Menéndez drew up instructions for the expedition at San Mateo on August 1, 1566, appointing Pedro de Coronas to command the expedition, and naming several associates, while Fray Pablo de San Pedro was to be responsible for relations with the Indians and the setting up of the mission. The soldiers were to be subject to his guidance (335). A list of persons to take part was drawn up, including a number of Portuguese. Domingo Fernández, the pilot (who is apparently the same as Baltasar Fernández of Tenerife on the list) and Sebastián Prieto, of São Miguel, were both from the Azores so that it may be that Azorean Portuguese were believed to know already something of this coastline (336). They made a landfall at 37° 30′ N. on August 14 (337), were unable to enter a river there (Chesapeake Bay?), and ran southward to 36°. Don Luis contended that this was still within the authority of his tribe which extended from 36° to 39° N. (338). They took possession of this land on August 25, 1566, as the Río de San Bartolomé (339). The ship *La Trinidad* sailed directly back to Spain, reaching Cadiz on October, 1566. Nothing, so far as we know, was done to follow up this discovery.

The documents were located and translated (and the episode for the first time elucidated) by Louis-André Vigneras, "A Spanish Discovery of North Carolina in 1566," *North Carolina Historical Review*, XLVI (1969), 398–415. Documents (335–339) are extracted from the Register of Diego de Camargo, notary to the expedition (which has not yet been published in full), in A.G.I., Seville, Patronato 257, N. 3, R. 4, and (340) from A.G.I., Seville, Indiferente General 2004, fol. 420.

335. August 1, 1566. Instructions from Pedro Menéndez de Avilés for the expedition under Pedro de Coronas to go to the Bahía de Santa María.

I Pedro Menéndez de Avilés, His Majesty's governor, captain general and commander of the land and coast of the provinces of Florida, say that it befits the service of God Our Lord and of His Majesty that I send Don Luis, Indian, to his country, which according to him is between the 36th and 39th degree along the shore, and all the people of that territory are his friends and the vassals of his three brothers.

[It is fitting] that I also send with him two friars and from 12 to 15 soldiers, whom the said Don Luis says that he will treat as companions and friends, and all the Indians in those parts will become Christians.

Therefore it is right that I send a captain who will command christianity. And since you are highly qualified, you Pedro de Coronas, Asturian, who have served in these provinces as ensign [alférez], in the company of Captain Troche, and because you have served His Majesty long and well, and were one of the first to enter Fort San Mateo when it was taken from the French Lutherans, who held it in order to spread their evil doctrine in these parts and teach it to the natives, and because before that you had served for many years in my company, in the armadas of which I was captain general, for all these reasons, in the name of His Majesty and by the power vested in me, I appoint you captain in those parts of the said soldiers and of the others whom I may send there, and as such it is my wish that they heed and obey you and carry out your orders as if they were my own.

And because you, Pedro de Salazar, are highly qualified, and because you have served His Majesty faithfully and well in these provinces, I appoint you ensign [alférez]; and for the same reasons I appoint you, Diego de Camargo, notary public, secretary of the expedition and recorder of the acts and resolutions agreed upon, and to you both I give full power to exercise your offices.

And to you, Pedro de Coronas, Asturian, I give power to appoint and remove in the said offices, if it should appear to you that it befits His Majesty's service, the men who are going with you, and later to appoint as mayors, local administrators, and to other suitable offices, any of the men who take part or will take part in that expedition, according to their rank and service. And under the pain of being denounced as traitors and sentenced to death, I order all persons, whatever their estate, rank, preeminence and dignity, to acknowledge you as their captain, and to comply with and carry out whatever order, written or oral, which you may give without exceeding your authority.

And whereas Padre Fray Pablo de San Pedro, born in Jerez de la Frontera, who professes the faith in the Order of Santo Domingo and is a spirited and virtuous man, goes on the said expedition with a companion, to attract the Indians to the service of God, that they may become Christian; and because it is fitting that the soldiers who are now going and those who may be sent later live in calm and peace of mind, maintain friendship with the Indians and set them a good example; and because Padre Fray Pablo should be in charge of all things, spiritual and temporal, and should be all the more loved, feared and respected, and because God and His Majesty will be better served if he is superior to you the said captain and to the said soldiers, and if all matters are provided for and settled with his consent, counsel and opinion, and in no other way, and likewise if all cases to be appealed, civil and criminal, come before him, that he may pass upon them as the superior authority.

By the present I order that it be so provided until I or Padre Fray Pablo's superior decide otherwise, and under the penalties included here, I order all to obey, heed, honor and respect the said Padre Fray Pablo as they would my own person and even more if possible. He accepted the said office with the permission of his Superior, Fray Martín de Niebla, who was present; and a copy of this title is given, signed and certified, to the said Padre Fray Pablo and the said Pedro de Coronas, and another copy is included in the register of the expedition, so that those who go now or may go later be informed of the government of those territories and know whom they should obey.

Dated in the Provinces of Florida, in Fort San Mateo, the First of August 1566.

[signed:] Pedro Menéndez.

336. August, 1566. The complement of the ship *La Trinidad* in the expedition to the Bahía de Santa María.

List of the persons who, in the service of God Our Lord and of His Majesty, by order of commander [*adelantado*] Pedro Menéndez, go from Fort Santo Agustín in Florida, to the land which is in the 36th degree and beyond, called Bay of Santa María and Land of Santiago.

Fray Pablo de San Pedro, governor, son of Gil García and Ana García who reside in Villalva de Guete

Fray Juan de Acuña, son of Mastre Juan Pepín and Esperanza Rodríguez de Acuña, born in Granada

Captain Pedro de Coronas, son of Suero de Coronas and Teresa Pérez de Cangas, who reside in the district of Tineo, in Asturias

Alférez Pedro de Salazar, son of Pedro de Salazar and Francisca de Morales, who reside in the town of Palomares, in the Mancha de Aragón

Diego de Camargo, notary public and recorder of deeds and secretary of the said expedition, son of Sancho de Camargo and doña Leonor de la Serna, who reside in Granada

Lázaro de Ripalta, son of Pablo de Salamanca and Juana Gómez, who reside in Toledo

Antonio Morales de Carrasquilla, son of Juan Ruíz de Carrasquilla and Marí Díaz, who reside in Ronda

Lázaro de Vitoria, son of Periche de Vitoria and Ysabel Mozárabe who reside in Toledo

Antonio Osorio, son of Martín López Osorio and María Brizeño, who reside in El Corral de Almager

Juan Ramírez de Alfaro, son of Juan Ramírez Rabadán and Catalina de Alfaro, who reside in Triana

Pedro de la Paz, son of Pedro de Quesada and Leonor de la Paz, who reside in Granada

Garcí[a] Martín de Zarzuela, son of Francisco Martín and Leonor García, who reside in El Almendralejo, in the Maestrazgo de Santiago

Francisco Cardoso, son of Francisco Cardoso and Ysabel Rodríguez, who reside in Segura de León

Alonso Meleno, son of Pedro Meleno and Beatriz Fernández de Mella who reside in Toro

Antonio Pereira, son of Blas Pereira and Ana Carneira, who reside in Oporto in Portugal

Sebastián Prieto, son of Alonso Preto and María Hernandez, who reside in the Isle of Saõ Miguel

Antonio López, son of Vicente López and Inés del Aguila, who reside in the city of Avila

Juan de Baños, son of Juan de Baños and Catalina de Lara, who reside in Zaragoza

Pedro de Arnao, son of Juan de Arnao and Lucia Maestra, who reside in Guete

Baltasar Fernández, son of Antonio Hernández and Catalina Domínguez, who reside in Tenerife

337. August 14, 1566. *La Trinidad* makes a landfall at 37° 30′ N.

On the 14th of August of the said year 1566, sailing along the coast of the said provinces of Florida, the pilot Domingo Fernández anchored at the mouth of a river at the latitude of 37° 30′, which according to Don Luis was in his territory. As they were taking out the boat to sound the bottom of the river, a contrary wind arose which forced them to weigh anchor with all speed and put out to sea. The contrary wind, very strong, lasted four full days. Of all this, I the said secretary [*escrivano*] give testimony.

[signed:] Diego de Camargo.

338. August 24, 1566. Driven from the entry to Chesapeake Bay, they enter a river at 36° N.

The location of the "river" was clearly that of an entry through the Carolina Outer Banks into the Sounds behind. As no Indians were seen, and as the main entry into the country, Albemarle Sound, was, twenty years later, found to be thickly inhabited, the entry may have been one then open through the Banks into Pamlico Sound, just north of modern Cape Hatteras. The only evidence is that the latitude determination of the mouth of Chesapeake Bay was 30 minutes too high, and that the same range of error would bring the landing point to 35°30' N. which could point to this solution. There is no certain evidence on where precisely the place was.

The contrary wind which arose at the mouth of the river in 37° 30 having subsided, the pilot Domingo Fernández steered toward the land and cast anchor at the mouth of a river on the said coast in 36°, on the 24th of August of the said year, and since the Indian Don Luis claimed that his territory extended from the 36th to the 39th degree along the coast, the said pilot Domingo Fernández took the ship inside the river. To all this I bear witness and give testimony whereof, as the said Domingo Fernández requested.

[signed:] Diego de Camargo.

339. August 25, 1566. Possession is taken of the land and of the Río de San Bartolomé for the crown of Spain.

And having thus entered the river, Fray Pablo de San Pedro, governor, Captain Pedro de Coronas and all the soldiers made their way to the shore in the boat. And I, the said *escrivano*, was called there by Captain Pedro de Coronas, who requested me to bear witness to all that I would see and hear, and to all that would take place in my presence. And in my presence, the said captain declared that, since he had been appointed captain by the most illustrious señor Pedro Menéndez de Avilés, governor and captain general for His Majesty of the land and coast of the provinces of Florida, and had received instructions and title for it, he nevertheless wished to further enhance His Majesty's service and authority, and seize and take possession of the said land and harbor, he requested that I record in the register of the expedition the said declaration of ownership and give him a transcription of the original as evidence. The said captain then walked through the land, cut branches, made a

cross and planted it on the beach, and declared that he gave to the river the name San Bartolomé, because it was discovered on the day of the Blessed Apostle San Bartolomé. All this Captain Pedro de Coronas said that he was doing and did as evidence of ownership, for the governor general and in the name of King Felipe [Philip], our rightful king and lord, and for the acquisition of what belongs to Him, he was doing and did all that was within his authority. And he requested me, the said *escrivano*, to bear testimony.

All this I certify that it happened in my presence. Dated the 25th day of the said month and year.

[signed:] Diego de Camargo.

340. October 23, 1566. Antonio de Abalia informs the Council of the Indies of the return of *La Trinidad* to Spain.

In this bay has entered a vessel called *La Trinidad*, which comes from the provinces of Florida, and according to what I understood from those who came on it, it seems that the governor Pedro Menéndez de Avilés dispatched that ship and Captain Pedro de Coronas, Asturian, from San Mateo, with orders to go with the Indian Don Luis, two Dominicans and fifteen soldiers, along the coast as far north as the 39th parallel, because he had been informed that Don Luis had his home there and was cacique [chief]. They sailed from San Mateo on the 2nd of August of the present year. Because of a hurricane which lasted 3 or 4 days, they turned back from that coast and came here, as Your Majesty will see more fully through the declaration of the said captain, through the instructions and title which the governor gave him, and through some acts and discussions which deal with their turning back and coming to this country. The original will be sent with this letter. The pilot is going to the Court with dispatches he brings from the said governor. Fray Pablo de San Pedro and Fray Juan de Acuña are also going there and are taking with them the Indian Don Luis. God keep the sacred royal person of Your

Majesty and increase your kingdoms and dominions.

Cádiz, 23ᵈ day of October 1566.

Your Majesty's humble servant,
    [signed:] Antonio de Abalia.

[Notation in the Council of Indies:] Seen and no need to answer.

341. August, 1568. Plea by Pedro Menéndez de Avilés for the dispatch of his colonists to Florida.

From 1565 to 1573 Menéndez was concerned to install farmer-colonists in Florida. He recruited successive batches of them from Asturias and brought or sent them to Florida. The story of their successive failures at both Santa Elena and San Agustín is an important part of the history of the colony. However, he was handicapped also in Spain. In 1568 he was in controversy with Antonio de Abalia, chief official at Cadiz in charge of the despatching of the fleets to the Indies, about the lack of transport for 200 farmers and officials who were held up there. As part of his ammunition against the bureaucracy, he sent the following letter to the king and forwarded a copy to the official concerned at Cadiz.

A.G.I., Indiferente General, Armadas y Flotas: expedientes de individuos que servieron en las armadas y flotas, 1529 to 1572, Indiferente General 2673 (153/1/18), copy in Division of Manuscripts, Library of Congress, translated.

Royal Catholic Majesty:

The Adelantado Pedro Menéndez de Avilés, Governor and Captain General of the Provinces of Florida, says that about eight months ago he arranged with about two hundred married farm-workers that they should go with their wives and children to settle in and cultivate the provinces of Florida: and with another hundred unmarried farm-workers and skilled carpenters and sawyers and stonemasons and pump-workers and other craftsmen, all of them pure-blooded natives of these kingdoms: and he has had them all gather in the city of Cádiz so that from there they can go in the boats which, according to the agreement which Your Majesty ordered to be drawn up with him, are permitted to go to Florida: and since he has four of these boats in the Canary Islands, for the purpose of taking these workers, he had some caravels fitted out so that they could go in them from this city of Càdiz to the Canary Islands; and for more than a month and a half now more than a hundred married farm-workers, with their wives and children, making four hundred people in all, and another hundred unmarried farm-workers and others have been in this city of Cádiz, and more are joining them every day: for more than three months he has had a boat fitted out to go to Florida with as many farm-workers as it could take, and a caravel to take to the Canaries those workers that could go in it, to embark there on these vessels, having first been checked and authorized by Your Majesty's Official Judge who lives there; and he asked Antonio de Abalia, Your Majesty's Official Judge in this city of Cádiz, for this authorization for these workers, in accordance with the agreement which Your Majesty ordered to be drawn up with the Adelantado, and the Cedula in which this agreement was ordered to be observed: but this Antonio de Abalia was not willing to authorize them, saying that the period of three years was now past, in which the Adelantado was supposed to convey these farm and other workers: and he sent asking for advice on this matter from Your Majesty, and in a letter which Your Majesty ordered to be written to him, dated the seventeenth of this month, he was instructed to authorize the departure of these people and stick to the agreement and the Cedulas that were issued to promote it; notwithstanding the fact that this period of three years is over; and although this letter was delivered to him, and he has been asked and requested to authorize these people who are to go in this boat to Florida, and not to obstruct those who are to go to the Canaries to embark there on the boats that are waiting to take them to Florida, he has not been prepared to do so and still will not do so; all this is confirmed in the testimony presented with this letter: and it is great harm to the service of Your Majesty and damage to the settlement of Florida, for all the value and use of it is based on their going there farm and other workers to cultivate the land and build houses and settle; and it is causing great harm to the Adelantado, because this Antonio de

Abalia, as well as preventing him from settling Florida, is causing him great cost and expense on these farm and other workers, and on the ships and their sailors, and is making him miss the best time for these ships to be sailing with the workers to Florida: and Your Majesty should not allow this to happen, rather Antonio de Abalia ought to be showing every favour and help to this expedition, as he has been ordered to by Your Majesty, instead of preventing it: so he asks and begs Your Majesty to issue a Royal Cedula that Antonio de Abalia straightaway and without delay should send off this boat, with provisions and workers for Florida, and that he should also permit the other farm-workers and others to go to the Canary Islands, so that there their departure can be authorized by Your Majesty's Official Judge that lives there, and they can be put on board the boats that the Adelantado has there fitted out for them to go in to Florida; for all this is to the greater service of Your Majesty and the general good of the Provinces of Florida.

Chapter Thirty-nine
The Jesuit Mission on Chesapeake Bay, 1570–1571

MEMBERS OF THE DOMINICAN and Jesuit Orders had been active, if not successful, in missionary work in Florida since 1565. In 1568 Pedro Menéndez de Avilés sent out fourteen members of the Jesuit Order, under a vice-provincial, Juan Baptista de Segura, being shortly afterwards fortified by a letter from Pope Pius V urging him to forward missionary work for the glory of the Faith. Segura had little success and left Florida for a time, but by 1569 he was back and had missionaries working in, and both north and south of, Santa Elena, with singularly little effect on the Indians. In collaboration with Menéndez, Segura planned to revive the mission on the Bahía de Santa María, which the Dominicans had failed to plant in 1566. Don Luis, more like a Spaniard than ever it seemed, would lead the missionaries to his tribal area on Chesapeake Bay where they would need no soldiers to guard them. Fathers Segura and Quirós, with five ancillary members of the Order, a boy from the Santa Elena colony, Alonso de Olmos, and Don Luis, made up the party that entered Chesapeake Bay and landed on September 10, 1570. On the advice of Don Luis they sailed some way up a large river and then landed; their goods were taken up a subsidiary stream and then portaged to another great river on the side of which a mission was established. Father Félix Zubillaga (*La Florida. La misión Jesuítica (1560–1572) y la colonización Española* [Rome, 1941]) argued that they landed on the bank of the York River and set up their mission on the bank of the Rappahannock: Fathers Lewis and Loomie, with much circumstantial detail, argued for a landing on the James River, a passage up College Creek, a portage to Chiskiak, and a mission on the York (C. M. Lewis and A. J. Loomie, *The Spanish Jesuit mission in Virginia, 1570–1572* [Chapel Hill, 1953]).

The history of the mission was short and tragic. Don Luis soon returned to his tribe, and the latter left the mission severely alone. On February 4, 1571, three members of the mission, Segura, Quirós, and another, when attempting to acquire food by barter, were set on and killed, the mission then being attacked and all its members killed, except for the boy Alonso de Olmos. A supply ship in 1571 was attacked and took some prisoners from whom it was learnt that something tragic had happened to the mission. The following year, 1572, Pedro Menéndez de Avilés paid his last visit to Florida, recolonizing Santa Elena and reviving the Florida colony. On his return voyage he entered Chesapeake Bay to find or avenge the missionaries. Indians came to trade without suspicion, but were set upon and made prisoner; they included the ruling chief, uncle of Don Luis. Through an Indian taken in 1571, they learnt of the survival of Alonso de Olmos and managed to rescue him, while they tried and executed a number of Indians on his testimony for their part in the killings.

Félix Zubillaga edited all the Latin and Spanish documents in *Monumenta antiquae Floridae (1566–1572)* (Rome, 1956) and Fathers Lewis and Loomie, *Spanish Jesuit Mission*, edited and translated those which are crucial to the understanding of the mission. From these have been selected (342) September 12, 1570. Fathers Luis de Quirós and Juan Baptista de Segura to Juan de Hinistrosa (Yñystrosa), T. Buckingham Smith MS, New York Public Library, II, Lewis and Loomie, pp. 89–92; (343) August 28, 1572. Father Juan Rogel to Father Francisco Borgia. Jesuit Archives of the Province of Toledo, A.T. 1157 (2), fols. 496–497, Lewis and Loomie, pp. 107–112; (344) March 1, 1600. Relation of Father Juan de la Carrera to Father Bartolomé Perez, Jesuit Archives, Rome, Histor. Soc. 177, ff. 153–161, extracts in Lewis and Loomie, pp. 131–139.

342. September 12, 1570. Luis de Quirós and Juan Baptista de Segura to Juan de Hinistrosa.

[a] Illustrious Lord,

The grace of the Holy Spirit be always in your soul, Amen. Since Father Vice-Provincial [Segura] has no opportunity to write to you, because of his concern over despatching the pilot in haste to your land, he has asked me to forward to you in his name an account of our journey up till now.

After having been delayed in arriving here much more than we had expected by those adversities which you understand are usual in the discovery of new regions, and by the discomforts of the weather, as the pilot will narrate to you more at length, we arrived here and unloaded our cargo yesterday, which was the tenth day of September. We departed as you know on the fifth of August from Santa Elena. We find the land of Don Luis in quite another condition than expected, not because he was at fault in his description of it, but because Our Lord has chastised it with six years of famine and death, which has brought it about that there is much less population than usual. Since many have died and many also have moved to other regions to ease their hunger, there remain but few of the tribe, whose leaders say that they wish to die where their fathers have died, although they have no maize, and have not found wild fruit, which they are accustomed to eat. Neither roots nor anything else can be had, save for a small amount obtained with great labor from the soil, which is very parched. So the Indians have nothing else to offer to us and to those who came on the ship but good will, and certainly these

Indians have shown that in a kindly manner. They seemed to think that Don Luis had risen from the dead and come down from heaven, and since all who remained are his relatives, they are greatly consoled in him. They have recovered their courage and hope that God may seek to favor them, saying that they want to be like Don Luis, begging us to remain in this land with them. The chief has kept a brother of Don Luis, a boy of three years, who lies seriously ill, 6 or 8 leagues from here and now seems certain to die. He has requested that someone go and baptize him, for which reason it seemed good to Father Vice-Provincial to send last night one of Ours to baptize the boy so close to death.

Thus we have felt the good will which this tribe is showing. On the other hand, as I have said, they are so famished, that all believe they will perish of hunger and cold this winter. For only with great difficulty can they find roots by which they usually sustain themselves, and the great snows found in this land do not allow them to hunt for them. Seeing then the good will that this tribe has shown, great hope is had of its conversion and of the service of Our Lord and His Majesty and of an entrance into the mountains and to China, etc. Therefore, it has seemed best to Father to risk remaining despite such scanty stores, because on our trip we have consumed two of the four barrels of biscuit and the small amount of flour which was given us for the journey. We had to help the entire ship with some supplies, as we were ill-provisioned for the journey.

I am convinced that there will be no lack of opportunity to exercise patience, and to succeed we must suffer much. But it has seemed good to expose ourselves to that risk and this especially so, since in your kindess you might be able to send us a generous quantity of corn to sustain us and to let all this tribe take some for sowing. As it touches the service of Our Lord and His Majesty, it would be best that you see to it that we are supplied with all speed possible. If it cannot be done in the winter, it is imperative that some provisions arrive some time during March or at the beginning of April so that we can give seeds to the tribe for planting. At this time the planting is done here, and thus many of the tribes will come here after being scattered over the region in search of food and there will be a good opportunity for the Holy Gospel. The chief has sought this very thing especially. As to information about the land that touches the route along which the pilot must be directed, he himself will give it. It is not convenient to enter by the river we did, for we did not have as good information from the Indians as was necessary about the place we should have entered. And so, today, the pilot has gone overland 2 good leagues away to see a river, which he will enter when with good fortune he comes again to help us and visit us. Through this region he can go by water up to the place where we plan to make our encampment. To reach this spot, it is 2 good leagues by land and 2 others or more by water, so that the goods, which we have unloaded in this uninhabited place reached by the river where we now are, must be carried by the Indians on their shoulders for these 2 leagues and then embarked in canoes, which is sufficiently laborious.

From some Indians whom we met farther down this river we have some information about the region farther inland. Three or four days' journey from there lie the mountains. For two of these days one travels on a river. After crossing the mountains by another day's journey or two, one can see another sea. If any new information can be had with more certainty and clarity, we will get it. Furthermore, in making this trip a good shallop is a necessity, since with the famine and death this tribe does not have the canoes in which the trip could be made. The pilot has managed his voyage very well and has toiled in every possible way and has brought all the provisions that we took at Santa Elena. Moreover seeing our need of getting these provisions overland, he has helped us by giving us a large earthern wine jug, sacks for transporting the flour, and a chisel he brought along. He has also given us half his supply of tar to patch up one of the leaking canoes that the Indians have. With the great need of provisions for the entire crew, it has been thought necessary that they leave today, and we will remain here in this lonely region amid the trials mentioned above. So there has not been opportunity to get more information or to write further. May God Our Lord grant you prosperity in all your undertakings in His holy service as you desire.

From this port on the 12th of September, 1570.

By order of Father Vice-Provincial.

Your chaplain
[signed:] Quirós.

[b] My Lord, Since I could not do more, I ordered Father Quirós to give a long account to you of everything. I am writing to His Majesty about the conditions which I find in this region for spreading the Holy Gospel, and about the grave necessity in which we remain in the course of accomplishing our mission. I believe there is no need to return, but I must entreat you anew to send us with all speed a shipload of grain, but no other trifles, since you easily see the great importance of this being done at once. It is for the help and protection of the entire tribe, and for the service of God Our Lord and His Majesty. I am also writing to His Majesty that you will send on to His Majesty detailed information of the route to Axacam as far as it is known. In no way does it seem best to me to send you any Indian boy, as the pilot will explain, and for other reasons too. May Our Lord protect you unto a long life and favor you in His love and grace.

[signed:] J. Baptista de Segura.

Above I had forgotten to write to you that from the time it is understood that the frigate is to come with the help requested, one or two Indians will be sent with a letter to the mouth of the arm of the sea, along which any ship coming must sail. Thus, when they see the ship, they will make a large smoke signal by day and a fire at night. Furthermore the people there will have a sealed letter of yours and they will not return it until they receive another like it, which is to be a sign that those who come are friendly and are the ones who bring the message. Take heed of this sign or inform whoever comes about it. Our letter will carry information about the way which must be followed in entering and will serve as a guide. May Our Lord be with you, Amen.

Don Luis has turned out well as was hoped, he

is most obedient to the wishes of Father and shows deep respect for him, as also to the rest of us here, and he commends himself to you and to all your friends.

By a bit of blundering (I don't know who on the ship did it) someone made some sort of a poor trade in food. I see now the misfortune which followed, in that while up till now the Indians whom we met on the way would give to us from their poverty, now they are reluctant when they see they receive no trinkets for their ears of corn. They have brought the ears of corn and other foods and asked that they be given something when they handed them over. They say that they have done that with the others. Since Father had forbidden that they be given something, so that they would not be accustomed to receiving it and then afterwards not want to bargain with us, the Indians took the food away with them.

Thus it seemed good to Father that he should tell this to you since we must live in this land mainly with what the Indians give us. Take care that whoever comes here in no wise barters with the Indians, if need be under threat of severe punishments, and if they should bring something to barter, orders will be given that Don Luis force them to give in return something equal to whatever was bartered, and that they may not deal with the Indians except in the way judged fitting here.

Christ Our Lord be with everyone, Amen.

[signed:] Quirós.

343. August 28, 1572. Juan Rogel to Father Francisco Borgia.

Our Most Reverend Father in Christ,

At the end of last June, I wrote to Your Paternity from Havana, telling how, under an order of holy obedience, I made ready to make this journey in search of Ours who had come to these parts. Although I had written from there that at the end of the trip I had to go to the Isles of the Azores, because the Governor Pedro Menéndez was obliged to take the ship, in which I had come here, for the trip to Spain; nevertheless, when he reached San Agustín, he changed his plans. He decided to make this trip in person at the head of his fleet, and on completing the trip, to give me a ship in which I might go back to the island of Cuba. Thus, on July 30, we left San Agustín for this purpose, and after staying at Santa Elena for five days, we arrived at the Bay of the Mother of God. With me are Brothers Juan de la Carrera and Francisco de Villareal and the small store of supplies we had on Santa Elena. After this we will all go to Havana to await the order of Father Provincial since Father Sedeño would order me to do that.

Reaching this bay, the Governor immediately ordered us to search for Alonso, the boy who came with Father Baptista. He had not died, according to what we heard from one of the Indians of this region, who was captured by the pilot on his second trip. This Indian has been brought along in chains. Anchoring the fleet in a port of this bay, the Governor sent an armed *fragatilla* with 30 soldiers to a fresh-water stream where Ours disembarked when they came here. This place is 20 leagues from this port. It seemed best to me to take the bound native in my company to be our spokesman. The order of the Governor was to take the uncle of Don Luis, a principal chief of that region, as well as some leading Indians. On taking them, we were to ask them to give us the boy and we would let them go. Everything happened in excellent fashion, for within an hour after our arrival, he took the chief with five of his leaders and eight other Indians.

This was the method of capture. After we had anchored in the middle of the narrow stream, Indians soon appeared on the bank and some entered the boat. To these the Spaniards gave gifts and made some exchanges. When they left the boat very contentedly, others arrived. With a third group came the chief and his leaders; one of them wore as a decoration or trinket a silver paten that Ours had brought. At once the Spaniards seized them and forced them down into the boat, and dressing the ship, passed to the mouth of the stream 3 leagues away by oar. On the way, the soldiers killed some Indians who were trying to shoot arrows at us and had wounded a soldier.

At the mouth of the river, which was very wide, we anchored again an arquebus shot away from the shore. Canoes of Indians came in peace, and they said that the boy was in the hands of a leading chief who lived two days journey from there, near this port. They asked that we give them time to send for him and bring him. This we did, and we gave them trinkets to give the chief who held the boy and we stayed there waiting for him. It seems that as soon as the chief learned of the capture of the others and about the fleet and the imminent death of the Indians, he sought to curry favor with the Governor. For he did not want to let the boy be brought to our ship, but he sent him to this port with two Indians. It is a marvelous thing in how short a time the Governor learned what was happening there from the mouth of the boy.

When the Indians did not bring the boy, we fought off an ambush of many canoes loaded with archers ready to attack the vessel. First there came two large canoes filled with Indians who were so concealed that no one was seen except the two who steered and they pretended they brought us oysters. Before they got aboard the watchman discovered them. We made ready and the others retreated. At my request, the steersmen were not fired upon, for we were still not certain whether it was an ambush or whether they came in peace. When the time was up and the boy did not come we waited for a night and further into midday and finally we set sail with our captives. By way of farewell, the pilot steered the ship towards land with the excuse that he wanted to speak to them, and then he ordered a blast from the arquebuses into the group of Indians who were standing crowded together on the shore. I believe many of them were killed, and this was done without any knowledge of mine until it happened. Then we returned to this port.

Now I will relate to Your Paternity how Ours who were here suffered death, as this boy tells it. After they arrived there, Don Luis abandoned them, since he did not sleep in their hut more than two nights nor stay in the village where the Fathers made their settlement for more than five days. Finally he was living with his brothers a journey of a day and a half away. Father Master Baptista sent a message by a novice Brother on two occasions to the renegade. Don Luis would never come, and Ours stayed there in great distress, for they had no one by whom they could make themselves understood to the Indians. They were without means of support, and no one could buy grain from them. They got along as best they could, going to other villages to barter for

maize with copper and tin, until the beginning of February. The boy says that each day Father Baptista caused prayers to be said for Don Luis, saying that the devil held him in great deception. As he had twice sent for him and he had not come, he decided to send Father Quirós and Brother Gabriel de Solís and Brother Juan Baptista to the village of the chief near where Don Luis was staying. Thus they could take Don Luis along with them and barter for maize on the way back. On the Sunday after the feast of the Purification, Don Luis came to the three Jesuits who were returning with other Indians. He sent an arrow through the heart of Father Quirós and then murdered the rest who had come to speak with him. Immediately Don Luis went on to the village where the Fathers were, and with great quiet and dissimulation, at the head of a large group of Indians, he killed the five who waited there. Don Luis himself was the first to draw blood with one of those hatchets which were brought along for trading with the Indians; then he finished the killing of Father Master Baptista with his axe, and his companions finished off the others. This boy says that when he saw them killing the Fathers and Brothers, he sought to go among the Indians as they inflicted the wounds so that they might kill him too. For it seemed better to him to die with Christians than live alone with Indians. A brother of Don Luis took him by the arm and did not let him go. This happened five or six days after the death of the others. This boy then told Don Luis to bury them since he had killed them, and at least in their burial, he was kind to them.

The boy stayed in the same hut for 15 days. Because of the famine in the land, Don Luis told him that they should go and seek grain. Alonso came in this way with him to the chief where he remained. The chief told the boy to stay and he would treat him well and hold him as a son. This he did. Finally Don Luis distributed the clothes of the Fathers among himself and his two brothers who shared in the murders. The boy took nothing but the relics and beads of Father Baptista which he kept till now and handed over to us. After this Don Luis went away very anxious to get hold of the boy to kill him, so that there would be no one to give details of what happened to Ours, but because of his fear of the chief with whom the boy was staying, he gave up the idea.

When he had learned the truth, the Governor

acted in this fashion. He told the captured chief that he must bring in Don Luis and his two brothers for punishment, and if he did not do this, the Governor would punish all those captured. Since three had been killed in that chief's lands, he could not escape blame for the murders. The chief promised that he would bring them within five days. We are waiting for this time to elapse, and I am not sure whether the Governor will send us on our trip to the island of Cuba before the time is up. He will report to Spain, God willing, whatever action he will have taken. The country remains very frightened from the chastisement the Governor inflicted, for previously they were free to kill any Spaniard who made no resistance. After seeing the opposite of what the Fathers were, they tremble. This chastisement has become famous throughout the land, and if this further one is done, it will be all the more famous.

I have noticed something about this region. There are more people here than in any of the other lands I have seen so far along the coast explored. It seemed to me that the natives are more settled than in other regions I have been and I am confident that should Spaniards settle here, provided they would frighten the natives that threaten harm, we could preach the Holy Gospel more easily than elsewhere. We are keeping this boy with us. He is very fluent in the language and had almost forgotten his Spanish. After he was freed from his captivity, we asked him if he wished to be with us, or go with his father who is also here. He said that he wanted to be with us only. In order to make sure that he retains the language and does not forget it, I am debating whether to bring along with me an Indian boy, who has come along with Alonso, leaving his parents and home to be with him. Thus he might train in the language, unless, meanwhile, Your Paternity or Father Provincial order otherwise.

For my part, I can say to Your Paternity that if it is judged in Our Lord that this enterprise ought to be begun, and if you desire that the task should fall to me, I would consider myself most fortunate. I fear that there will be the same difficulty among these people in making conversions, as has been found in the places where we have been. If there is to be some fruit here, it will have to be by wearing them away like water on a rock. I believe there are fewer inconveniences and difficulties than in regions where I have already stayed.

First, because the country is so cold, there will be no reason for long absences away from their huts in winter. Also it appears to me that there are more tribes and more natives in this region than in others where I have dwelt.

When this boy was with Don Luis, following the death of the others, Don Luis left the vestments and books and everything else locked up in chests. On returning, they took up their share of spoils. He said that a brother of Don Luis is going around clothed in the Mass vestments and altar cloths. The captured chief told me that Don Luis gave the silver chalice to an important chief in the interior. The paten was given to one of those Indians we captured, while the other images were thrown away. Among other things there was a large crucifix in a chest; some Indians told this boy that they do not dare approach that chest since three Indians who wanted to see what was in it, fell down dead on the spot. So they keep it closed and protected. About the books, Alonso said that after pulling off the clasps, the Indians tore them all up and threw them away.

If I should learn any other details, whether those sent out by the Governor bring in Don Luis and his companions, I will write them from Havana to Your Paternity, when, in Our Lord's pleasure, we arrive there.

As I can not think of anything else to write, I close. I commend myself to the holy sacrifices and prayers of Your Paternity and of the Fathers and Brothers of the Company. God Our Lord grant Your Paternity His Holy Spirit for all success in fulfilling His Divine Will.

From the Bay of the Mother of God in Florida, August 28, 1572.

Your Paternity's unworthy son and servant in Our Lord,

[signed:] Juan Rogel.

344. March 1, 1600. Juan de la Carrera to Bartolomé Pérez.

A short time previous to these events, an Indian from Florida arrived in Havana; he called himself Don Luis de Velasco. He was a person of note and had been raised in Mexico by the friars of Saint Dominic and had been baptized there at the instance of the Viceroy Don Luis de Velasco, who was, as I understand it, his godfather and gave him his name. This fellow had been educated at the court of King Philip II and had received many favors from him. Finally the King sent him back to his own country, where he said he was a chief, in the company of some Dominican friars. For some reason or other, he found himself deserted by the friars; so he began to tell his plan to the Admiral, Pedro Menéndez. From what the Indian told him of the grandeurs of his land and the information he already had about the existence of another sea in this region and another navigation route of great importance for the discovery of great kingdoms such as Tartary and others contiguous to it, the Admiral heard the Indian and discussed the matter with Father Baptista [de Segura], who was at that time with the Admiral in Havana, where all this was going on. The two easily came to an agreement, nor was there further discussion. The Father believed that God had granted to him, as to Father Master Francis Xavier, another Paul of Holy Faith and another greater and more important Japan. Longing to spread our holy Catholic Faith, he prepared himself for the trip and had a boat made and equipped with everything necessary for both the sea voyage and that land which was to be stocked with different sorts of animals and birds and many other things. With all this equipment he sailed from Havana in the month of July or August in 1571, by my reckoning. He arrived in good weather at the point of Santa Elena in Florida, where I was staying at the time, and there we all had a meeting.

Since we treated one another with great love and familiarity, he confided to me all the plans and designs and hopes for this journey. These were all clearly praiseworthy, for they came from a holy, sincere Christian heart, and I gave him high praise. But I pointed out the difficulty in the execution of the plan, saying that the Indian did not satisfy me, and judging from what he had told me, I saw that he was a liar. I begged and entreated him to examine the plan more thoroughly, to talk it over with the Fathers present and to decide what was best in conformity with their advice. The idea of a superior wanting to go to

such remote and distant lands relying on an Indian, leaving everything behind, without a guard of soldiers or any people other than his own [Jesuits], was in my opinion not as good as that of having another Father go and travel light to look around the country and see what there was in the whole notion and learn if the Indian was lying or telling the truth. That is how it looked to me. All the Fathers assembled there reached the same conclusion except Father Quirós, who was to go along, and he had just come from Spain without any experience. In spite of all this he [Segura] decided to go, according to the arrangements already made, and stay there alone with his companions. This was to prevent anyone from giving a bad example to the Indians. His companions were Father Quirós, Brother Linares, Brother Zavallos, Brother Gabriel Gómez, and three novices, one of whom was named Juan Baptista Méndez, and Gabriel de Solís and Cristóbal Redondo and a boy called Alonso. This mission seemed to him to be more in conformity with the will of Our Lord which he desired to accomplish in everything, and with this resolution he left, firm in his high purpose.

Then his companion, Father Quirós, a man of distinguished learning, came to me with a long list, on which he asked me to give him the best and the larger portion of everything I had in my charge, especially the church goods. When I saw the list I was a little upset and I said to him, "Father, I would gladly give you everything you ask of me, even though I know that it is all going to be lost, were it not for the fact that I know for certain that all this will contribute greatly to the death of everyone going there. Will your Reverence do me the kindness of saying this for me to Father Vice-Provincial [Segura], and after that if he wants me to give you what you ask, well then here it is at your command." He came back with the answer that I should give him everything for which he had asked. I fulfilled his request, but there were also fulfilled the forebodings I expressed. I gave Father Quirós as much as he wanted, and it was the greater part of the best and richest articles that I had in the way of chalices, monstrances, and vestments and other articles besides church furnishings. With these they completed their equipment for their journey.

The novices that he was taking with him came

to say good-bye to me with great tenderness and tears. I was deeply stirred because I loved them kindly as one who had reared them. Now when they told me that they were going to their death, I replied that they should be consoled wherever holy obedience was sending them and that God would be with them and that from Him they would receive the pay and reward of their labors, and that it was a great blessing to die for God and obedience. I felt the same tender sorrow when Father Vice-Provincial and the rest of his companions, whom I was not to see again in this life, departed amidst the tears of all.

They arrived at the country of this Indian Don Luis in August. Its name is Ajacán. They expected through him to do great things in that land, and in all the other lands they hoped to discover, because the Indian was a big chief and a clever talker. Our Fathers and Brothers disembarked in a great and beautiful port, and men who have sailed a great deal and have seen it say it is the best and largest port in the world. So, if I remember rightly, the pilot remarked to me. It is called the Bay of the Mother of God, and in it there are many deep-water ports, each better than the next. I saw this port myself when I went with the Admiral, as I will narrate later. It seemed to me (for as it looked to me and I was given to understand), it was about 3 leagues at the mouth, and in length and breadth it was close to 30. They say that at the end of it the other sea begins. Also there is the very important navigation route, mentioned before, which the Admiral wanted to explore. I understand he would have done this, had he lived long enough. There is a large population on the shores of this port and inland.

After he unloaded all his effects at this beautiful port, Segura decided to remain there without soldiers or guards other than our Fathers and Brothers, and to trust in God's care and protection and the help of His most Holy Mother and of the saints and angels in heaven. He placed himself in the hands of this Indian whom he trusted, for if he was what he ought to be, there would certainly be a rich harvest gathered through him. But it was far to the contrary, for he was very different from what he had seemed to be and what Father Baptista [Segura] had believed about him. The Father bade farewell to all the people in the boat and remained alone with his own men, who carried all the baggage to the village of a brother of

Don Luis. This was very fatiguing labor because of the distance from the port and the poor footpaths and swamps that abounded in the whole region.

Then this wretched native saw himself the master of the Father and his sons and all their supplies. There was no one to fear because he was among his brothers and relatives and friends and many leagues away from the sea. They had no one on land to help them, and aid by water would have been difficult. At the beginning, I understand, he did not show at once his criminal intent, and the Fathers built their poor little hut and chapel and began to treat with him the office of preaching the gospel for which they had come. But this second Judas began to indulge in vices and sins publicly without fear of God or man and then to relinquish their conversation and company. Since he was acting more like a pagan than a Christian in his manners, dress, and habits, he went off and lived with his uncle, a chief, in a country far distant from ours. There he allowed himself free rein in his sins, marrying many women in a pagan way. Neither reasoning nor any other method which Father Baptista tried to release him from his sinful life and draw him back to himself had any effect.

By my reckoning, from the end of August to the Purification of Our Lady these blessed Religious, our Fathers and Brothers, lived in that country in continual fright and alarm, awaiting death each day. It was in the control of this Indian and his kinsmen to take away their lives, when and in what way they wanted without meeting any resistance. Therefore Father Vice-Provincial with several expedients prepared and disposed himself and his companions for a death they held as certain. The first arrangement he made was that all should give themselves to longer and more continual prayer, readying themselves with exhortations and conferences, which he frequently gave them, and with other good spiritual exercises, and he had all of them make a general confession of their past life. Their mortification was great and they must have undergone great austerity even without wanting it, for the supplies they brought ran out, and they were obliged to sustain themselves on the roots and herbs of the countryside, like the Indians who live off the land, for their food usually fails around that time.

The good Father was more despondent over

the tiresome work of his sons than his own, because he was naturally compassionate, pious, and meek and very charitable and when he saw them suffering so much his heart was greatly stirred. It seemed to him that the cure for their misfortunes would be to bring back to friendship that evil and rebellious Indian. So he decided to send Father Quirós and two Brothers to try and succeed. On the way they took some sustenance and some mats which would be some protection against the great cold they endured, because the ground was cold and the house in which they were living was so wretched that its chief covering was palm leaves which served as roof and walls. I know this from experience too, for I have lived many times in similar houses suffering much from the cold, even though the lands were not so cold.

This Father and the Brothers made a cautious trip to the country of Don Luis' uncle, where he was living, as has been narrated. While going along safely with these bundles on their back, lo! the traitor with armed companions suddenly springs out on the path to kill them with bows and arrows. When they saw the sudden attack, Father Quirós turned to Don Luis and asked him what they wanted to do and why they were about to kill them. Then the good Father began to preach to them but the answer was a volley of arrows, and so after wounding them many times they slew Father Quirós and Brother Gabriel de Solís. Brother Baptista Méndez fled to the woods with blood running from his deep wounds. There he hid himself that night and in the morning he was discovered and killed. After that the murderers burned the bodies and stole their clothing and bundles.

Good Father Baptista Segura, who was anxiously awaiting the companions and the successful outcome of their embassy, grieved deeply over their tardiness and feared some mischance and frequently said so to his companions with great sorrow of his heart and soul. Before dawn of the morning of the same day, as I understand, of Our Lady of Candlemas, when he was praying as usual with all his sons, Segura heard someone calling at the door, and all around the house a great noisy crowd of people with their captain and leader, Don Luis. They told the Fathers to give them all the axes and machetes used to cut wood, because they were going into the forests for it. The good Father, oblivious of the evil the Indians were plot-

ting against him, and innocent of their evil intention, said that they would give everything to them, and two of the house would go along to the forest and carry their bundles of wood to warm themselves. The traitor Don Luis, seeing himself in control of the weapons, with which, as he looked at it, they could defend themselves, used the following stratagem.

The Indian archers approached the house from the back, so that if anyone came out he would be killed at once. Don Luis, dressed in the clothing which he had stolen from Father Quirós on the path when he killed him, went inside with some picked followers, keeping the axes and machetes he already had. He assigned his warriors each to a different man, so that all were killed at the same time, without being able to help one another. The wretched and perverse Don Luis attacked Father Baptista first to pay him back for the many kindnesses shown him, and when the Father saw him come in and recognized him he thought he came in for a very different purpose. They say that he spoke joyfully at his sight: "You are very welcome, Don Luis!" Certainly before he got any further the Indian replied with his axe and gave him many blows on the head, the arms, the legs, and his whole body, which lay gravely wounded and maltreated. While the captain was dealing with the Father, the other murderers were occupying themselves similarly with the rest, like wolves among gentle sheep who were doing evil to no one but good to all. They went into the kitchen where they found a Brother named Cristóbal Redondo, who was in soul and body, disposition and speech, more of an angel than a man. When that meek lamb saw himself attacked by those wolves and was wounded by them he raised his voice saying: "Help me, my Fathers, they are going to kill me." But by this time it was useless to look for help, for they were all dead; not one of those who were in the house remained. As to the two who had gone out into the woods, they split the head of one, Brother Zaballos, an old Brother of great virtue, and he lay there dead. They did not touch the boy who had gone with him saying that they did not want to kill him but only the Fathers. When he saw them dead and so badly wounded he asked them in deep sorrow of soul to kill him too. He preferred to die with them rather than live without them among infidels and barbarians. Despite this they spared him. Then he asked the murderers to bury their bodies all naked and cut to pieces by the hands of those enemies of our holy Faith. The Fathers had longed and tried in every way to bring them to the knowledge of their Creator and Lord. As the boy recalls, the wicked Indian who fostered this crime, though evil and hardened in his errors and sins, was so touched at seeing them dead that he wept copiously and called them martyrs. They dug a long ditch and there they buried them each one separately with their crosses in their hands, first Father Baptista and the rest in order.

Then they turned to stealing whatever they found in the house, leaving nothing that had been brought there except a box in which there was a devotional crucifix surrounded by other pious objects. For when they irreverently opened the box, three Indians fell dead at once; the rest were very frightened and did not dare touch it. They profaned the holy vessels dedicated to the divine service and drank from the chalices and hung the patens around their necks and dressed themselves in the sacred vestments.

It pleased Our Lord that this boy who was called Alonso de Olmos should remain alive in order that from his mouth as from an eye-witness we should learn all these things. Then after all this they wanted to kill him too; so he fled to the territory of a chief who was an enemy of these murderers and defended him with his own hands and kept him in his own custody until we took him from his protection when the Admiral went in person to administer punishment for the massacre and we went with him. Later I will tell how this was.

To resume the thread of our story again, after the departure of the Father and his companions to Ajacán, we remained, as already mentioned, at the port of Santa Elena in Florida, and then all embarked for Havana according to his instructions. There we received letters from the same Father brought back on the boat which had carried them up. A soldier in their service gave them to us. From his report as well as the letters, we saw the great peril in which all our Fathers and Brothers were placed, and so we took steps that a relief ship be dispatched with all speed to bring reinforcements, provisions, and a good stock of supplies. But for all the haste with which we acted, it was God's will that they be already dead.

The Father had given definite signals to the pilot so that when the ship should reach port they would see certain things that the Father wanted, and if they did not find those signals, it was an indication that they were dead. Since the pilot went and did not find the signals, he suspected some foul play, and refused to set foot on land but made for the sea; no matter how many gestures the people on land made calling them in, the pilot, like a prudent man, always refused to land. When they saw this they determined to attack them in numbers with their canoes and capture the ship. These canoes are their ships; and so there was a sharp fight on both sides. The guns that they had on board were not as useful to them as a great pile of rocks which they were carrying for ballast. When they saw so great number of rocks falling on them (a thing they had never seen, for there are no rocks in that region and they do not know what they are), the natives retired with damage and the loss of two captured Indian chiefs. With these the Spaniards returned, not knowing for certain if the Fathers were dead or alive, nor could they get anything out of the Indians.

This news put us all in a state of great perplexity and anxiety. Now we lived for a long period in deep fear and trembling unable to know anything certain about them. With greater probability we took it as more certain that they had killed our beloved superior and our Fathers and Brothers and in my particular pain and anxiety, I spoke to Father Juan Rogel, who was the superior when Father Sedeño was in Florida with the Admiral Pedro Menéndez. I expressed my sad feelings in these words: "I am deeply afflicted by the memory of Father Vice-Provincial and his companions our brothers, not knowing if they are dead or alive. It occurs to me as a good idea to rid ourselves of this doubt by having some one of us go and find out for certain and bring a good supply of provisions for the journey." He said that he himself saw that already, but did not know what to do or what means to take. I said that if it were agreeable to him I would undertake the task of going up and risking the endangering my life for the welfare of our Fathers and Brothers. This the Father regarded highly and thanking me he ordered me to take charge of the mission. I did this with all possible energy. In a short time I equipped myself with all necessary items: a ship, a pilot and sailors, supplies, clothing and miscellaneous items and everything necessary. Besides this boat of ours, two others were prepared with a large and capable crew, and these three ships sailed together from the port of Havana for Florida, where the Admiral was with his household and Father Antonio Sedeño with Brother Villareal. . . .

We embarked on that [second relief] ship [from Santa Elena] and sailed amid fierce storms and no less dangers to our lives, but the Lord delivered us from every threat and brought us to Ajacán safely in August, 1572. After the Admiral had given out instructions about his own affairs, he divided all the people and soldiers among the three ships. We made landfall in the Bay of the Mother of God, and in this port we found a very beautiful vineyard, as well laid out and ordered as the vineyards of Spain. It was located on sandy soil and the vines were laden with fair white grapes, large and ripe. These the Lord had prepared there for us and we gave Him many thanks. Also within the vineyard there was a great number of plum, cherry, and persimmon trees like those in Spain. We ate from the laden branches and took some away for our journey; it was a great windfall and we glorified the Lord for it.

The Admiral sent out a well protected ship, carrying many soldiers and the pilot who had brought Ours there, to reconnoiter the land inside the bay. In the country of Don Luis' uncle he captured the chief and several of his men who were found guilty and brought them before the Admiral. The captain killed many in their country, and took the paten from an Indian who was wearing it around his neck and the chasuble from another who was walking about in it. We also got hold of the boy who was a companion of Ours; he was in the custody of the other chief. We learned from him all about the way things happened, and this has been related here.

When the chief stood in the presence of the Admiral and saw Father Rogel and Brother Villareal and me dressed like those whom they had slain, he was thunderstruck and thought we had risen from the dead. The Admiral told him to bring him Don Luis in three days; if not, they would all be killed. And so he sent back one of the Indian prisoners. Since he did not come back at the appointed time, he hanged them all from the yardarms of the ship. Previously Father Rogel had baptized the chief and his men.

When the Admiral had accomplished this, as has been related, he started on his way for Spain in search of his fleets, which he found before reaching Spain near Islas Terceras. Then we returned to the island of Cuba and our house in Havana.

Chapter Forty
Attacks on Spanish Florida

THE FRENCH REPRISAL ON SAN MATEO BY DOMINIQUE DE GOURGUES

THE LONG DIPLOMATIC exchange between the French and Spanish crowns offered no redress or even apology to the French, who had suffered a blow to their pride as well as to their country's interest in 1565. The privateers who gained their living from the robbing of Spanish ships in the Caribbean and in European waters eventually determined to undertake their revenge themselves. Dominique de Gourgues, himself a Catholic, undertook to lead an expedition with three ships against the Spaniards in Florida. He carried out, between August, 1567 and the early months of 1568, a routine voyage through the Caribbean taking prizes and then, on the way home invaded Florida in March. He landed at Tacatacuru north of the St. Johns River and was soon joined by Saturiwa, and with Indian help made short work of the two blockhouses which guarded the approaches to San Mateo. Then, with his Indian allies, he overran San Mateo, the greater part of the garrison attempting to take to the woods and being, according to Gourgues's account, rapidly cut down. No mercy was shown on the field and a number of men were reserved for judicial hanging at each blockhouse and the fort. According to Gourgues himself, a legend was affixed to the scaffolds, "Je ne fay cecy comme à Espagnols, ny comme à marranes, mais comme à traistres, voleurs & meurdriers." On his return to France on June 6, 1568, Gourgues was feted, and in spite of strong Spanish protests, Catherine de Médicis refused to hand him over to the Spaniards.

A pamphlet on the affair *Histoire memorable de Dominique de Gourgues de la reprinse de l'isle de la Floride, faict par François* (1568), was promptly printed without place of publication or name of printer. Gourgues wrote his own longer version, which was not published at the time. A copy was available to Lancelot Voisin, Sieur de Popelinière, *Les trois mondes* (1582). It was partly from his report and partly from the published pamphlet that Martin Basanier put together the section on "The fourth voyage," which he (or he and Richard Hakluyt) added to Laudonnière's *Histoire notable*, before publishing it in Paris in 1586. This duly appeared in Hakluyt's translation *The notable history* (1587) and *Principal navigations*, III (1600), 357–361 (IX [1904], 100–111), from which most of it is given here (345). Paul Gaffarel, *La Floride française* (Paris, 1875), pp. 483–515, printed Gourgues's own account in full, and it has been edited in Susanne Lussagnet, *Les Français en Amérique dans la deuxième partie du XVIe siècle*, part II (Paris, 1959), pp. 241–251. The French consistently exaggerate the number of Spaniards killed, indicating that it equalled the number killed by Menéndez in 1565. An account by Esteban de las Alas on May 5, 1568 (346), written when the smoke had cleared, gives consistently smaller figures for the total number of men engaged on the Spanish side, indicates that some escaped from the blockhouse, and appears to imply that all or most of the 120 men who broke out of San Mateo survived, whereas in the French account they all fell victim to the Indians.

345. 1568. The Laudonnière-Gourgues account of the French revenge attack on San Mateo.

The fourth voyage of the Frenchmen into Florida, under the conduct of Captaine Gourgues, in the yeere, 1567.

Captaine Gourgues a Gentleman borne in the Countrey neere unto Bourdeaux incited with a desire of revenge, to repaire the honour of his nation, borowed of his friends and sold part of his owne goods to set forth and furnish three ships of indifferent burthen with all things necessary, having in them an hundred and fiftie souldiers, and fourescore chosen Mariners under Captaine Cazenove his lieutenant, and Francis Bourdelois Master over the Mariners. He set forth the 22 of August 1567. And having endured contrary winds and stormes for a season, at length hee arrived and went on shore in the Isle of Cuba. From thence he passed to the Cape of Saint Antony at the end of the Ile of Cuba, about two hundred leagues distant from Florida, where the captaine disclosed unto them his intention which hitherto he had concealed from them, praying and exhorting them not to leave him being so neere the enemie, so well furnished, and in such a cause: which they all sware unto him, and that with such courage that they would not stay the full Moone to passe the channell of Bahama,[1] but speedily discovered Florida, where the Spanyards saluted them with two Canon shot from their fort, supposing that they had beene of their nation, and Gourgues saluted them againe to entertaine them in this errour, that hee might surprise them at more advantage, yet sailing by them, & making as though he went to some other place until he had sailed out of sight of the place, so that about evening, hee landed 15 leagues from the fort, at the mouth of the River Tacatacouru, which the Frenchmen called Seine, because they thought it to bee like Seine in France. Afterward perceiving the shore to bee covered with Savages with their bowes and arrowes, (besides the signe of peace and amitie which he made them from his ships) he sent his Trumpetter, to assure them, that they were come thither for none other ende but to

renew the amitie and ancient league of the French with them. The Trumpetter did his message so well (by reason he had bene there before under Laudonniere) that he brought backe from king Satourioua, the greatest of all the other kings, a kidde and other meat to refresh us, besides the offer of his friendship and amitie. Afterward they retired dansing in signe of joy, to advertise all the kings Satouriouaes kinsmen to repaire thither the next day to make a league of amitie with the Frenchmen. Whereupon in the meane space our generall went about to sound the chanel of the river to bring in his ships, and the better to traffike and deale with the Savages, of whom the chiefe the next day in the morning presented themselves, namely the great king Satourioua, Tacatacourou, Halmacanir, Athore, Harpaha, Helmacapé, Helicopilé, Molloua, and others his kinsmen and allies, with their accustomed weapons. Then sent they to intreate the French general to come on shore, which he caused his men to do with their swords and harquebusies, which he made them leave behind them, in token of mutuall assurance, leaving his men but their swords only, after that the Savages complaining thereof had left and likewise sent away their weapons at the request of Gourgues. This done Satourioua going to meet him, caused him to sit on his right hand in a seat of wood of lentisque covered with mosse made of purpose like unto his owne. Then two of the eldest of the company pulled up the brambles & other weeds which were before them, and after they had made the place very cleane, they all sate round about them on the ground. Afterward Gourgues being about to speake, Satourioua prevented him, declaring at large unto him the incredible wrongs, and continuall outrages that all the Savages, their wives and children had received of the Spanyards since their comming into the Countrey and massacring of the Frenchmen, with their continuall desire if we would assist them throughly to revenge so shamefull a treason, aswell as their owne particular griefes, for the firme good will they alwayes had borne unto the Frenchmen. Whereupon Gourgues giving them his faith, and making a league betweene them and him with an othe gave them certaine presents of daggers, knives, looking glasses, hatchets, rings, belles, and such other things, trifles unto us, but precious unto these kings: which moreover, seeing his great liberality, demanded eche one a shirt of him to

_____

1. Sidenote: "The channel of Bahama betweene Florida and the Isles of Lucayos."

weare onely on their festivall dayes, and to be buried in at their death. Which things after that they had received, and Satourioua had given in recompense to Captaine Gourgues two chaines of silver graines which hung about his necke, and ech of the kings certaine deere skinnes dressed after their manner, they retired themselves dansing and very jocond, with promise to keep all things secret, and to bring unto the sayd place good companies of their subjects all well armed to be avenged throughly on the Spanyards. In the meane space Gourgues very narrowly examined Peter de Bré borne in Newhaven, which being but a yong stripling escaped out of the fort into the woods while the Spanyards murdered the rest of the French, & was afterward brought up with Satourioua, which at that time bestowed him on our generall, whose advise stoode him in great steade: Whereupon he sent to discover the fort and the estate of the enemies by certaine of his men, being guided by Olotacara Satouriouaes nephew which hee had given him for this purpose and for assurance of Estampes a gentleman of Cominges, and others which he sent to discry the state of the enemies. Moreover he gave him a sonne of his starke naked as all of them are, and his wife which he loved best of all the rest, of eighteene yeeres olde, apparelled with the mosse of trees, which for 3 dayes space were in the ships, untill our men returned from discrying the state of the enemie, and the kings had furnished their preparation at their rendevous. Their marching being concluded, and the Savages rende-vous being appointed them beyond the river Salina-cani, of our men called Somme, they all dranke with great solemnitie their drinke called Cassine, made of the juice of certaine hearbs (as they are wont to do, when they go to any place of danger,) which hath such force, that it taketh from them hunger and thirst for 24 houres, and Gourgues was faine to make as though he drank thereof for company. Afterward they lift up their handes and sware all that they would never forsake him. Olotocara followed him with pike in hand. Being all met at the river of Sarauahi, not without great trouble, by reason of the raine and places full of water which they must needes passe, which hindred their passage, they were distressed with famine finding nothing by the way to eat, their Bark of provision being not arrived, which was to come unto him from the ships, the oversight and charge whereof he had left unto Burdelois with

the rest of the Mariners. Now he had learned that the Spanyards were foure hundred strong, devided into three forts builded and flanked, and well fortified upon the river of May, the great fort especially begunne by the French, and afterward repaired by them: upon the most dangerous and principall landing place whereof, two leagues lower and neerer towarde the Rivers mouth, they had made two smaller Forts, which were defended, the river passing betweene them, with six score souldiers, good store of artillery and other munition, which they had in the same. From Saracary unto these smal forts was two leagues space, which he found very painful, because of the bad waies and continual raines. Afterward he departed from the river Catacouru with 10, shot, to view the first fort, and to assault it the next day in the morning by the breake of day, which hee could not doe, because of the foule weather, and darknesse of the night. King Helicopile seeing him out of quiet in that he had failed of his purpose there, assured him to guide him a more easie way, though it were farther about. Insomuch as leading him through the woods, he brought him within sight of the fort, where he discerned one quarter which was but begun to bee entrenched. Thus after he had sounded the small river that falleth downe thereby, hee stayed untill ten of the clock in the morning for an ebbe water, that his men might passe over there, unto a place where he had seene a litle grove between the river & the fort (that he might not be seene to passe and set his souldiers in array) causing them to fasten their flasks to their Morions, & to hold up their swords and kalivers in their hands, for feare least the water, which reached up to their girdles, should not wet them: where they found such abundance of great oysters, and shels which were so sharpe, that many had their legs cut with them, and many others lost their shoes. Notwitstanding assoone as they were passed over, with a French courage they prepared themselves to the assault on the sunday eve next after Easter day, in Aprill 1568. Insomuch that Gourgues to employ the ardent heat of this good affection, gave twenty shot to his Lieutenant Cazenove, and ten Mariners laden with pots and balles of wild fire to burne the gate: and then he assaulted the Fort on another side, after he had made a short speech unto his men of the strange treasons which the Spanyards had plaid their companions. But being discried as they came holding downe their heads within two hundred paces from the Fort, the Gunner being upon the terrace of the Fort, after he had cried, Arme, Arme, these be French men, discharged twise upon them a colverine, whereon the Armes of France were graven, which had bin taken from Laudonniere. But as he went about to charge it the third time, Olotocara, which had not learned to keepe his ranke, or rather moved with rage, lept on the platforme, and thrust him through the bodie with his pike and slew him. Whereupon Gourgues advanced forward, and after he had heard Cazenove cry, that the Spaniards which issued out armed at the cry of the alarme, were fled, hee drew to that part, and so hemmed them in betweene him and his Lieutenant, that of threescore there escaped not a man, saving only fifteene reserved unto the same death which they had put the French unto. The Spanyards of the other fort in the meanewhile ceased not to play with their ordinance, which much annoied the assailants: although to answere them they had by this placed and oftentimes pointed the foure pieces found in the first Fort. Whereupon Gourgues being accompanied with fourescore shot went abord the barke which met him there to good purpose to passe into the wood neere unto the Fort, out of which he supposed the Spanyards would issue to save themselves thorow the benefit of the woods in the great fort, which was not past one league distant from ye same. Afterward the Savages not staying for the returne of the bark, lept al into the water holding up their bowes & arrowes in one hand, & swimming with the other, so that the Spaniards seing both ye shores covered with so great a number of men, thought to flee towards the woods: but being charged by the French, and afterward repulsed by the Savages, toward whom they would have retired, they were sooner then they would bereft of their lives. To conclude they al there ended their dayes saving 15 of those which were reserved to be executed for the example of others. Wherupon Captaine Gourgues having caused al that he found in the second fort to be transported unto the first, where he ment to strengthen himselfe to take resolution against the great Fort, the state whereof hee did not understand: in fine a Sergeant of a band one of the prisoners assured him that they might be there very neere 300 wel furnished under a brave Governor, which had fortified there, attending farther succours. Thus having obtained of him the platforme, the height,

the fortification and passages unto it, and having prepared eight good lathers, and raised all the Countrey against the Spanyard, that he neither might have newes, nor succours, nor retract on any side, he determined to march forward. In the meane while the Governour sent a Spanyard disguised like a Savage to spie out the state of the French. And though he were discovered by Olotocara, yet he used all the cunning he could possibly to perswade them that he was one of the second fort, out of which having escaped, and seeing none but savages on every side, he hoped more in ye Frenchmens then their mercy, unto whom he came to yeeld himself disguised like a savage, for feare lest if he should have bin knowen, he should have bin massacred by those Barbarians: but the spie being brought face to face with the sergeant of the band, & convicted to be one of the great fort, was reserved until an other time: after that he had assured Gourgues that the bruit was that he had 2000 Frenchmen with him for feare of whom the 200 and threescore Spaniardes which remained in the great fort, were greatly astonied. Whereupon Gourgues being resolved to set upon them, while they were thus amazed, and leaving his Standard-bearer and a Captaine with fifteene shot to keepe the Fort, and the entry of the River, he caused the Savages to depart by night to lye in ambush within the woods on both sides of the river, then he departed in the Morning, leading the Sergeant and the spy fast bound along with him, to shew him that in deede, which they had only made him understand before in paynting. As they marched Olotocara a resolute Savage which never left the Captaine, said unto him, that he had served him faithfully, and done whatsoever hee had commaunded him, that he was assured to dye in the conflict at the great Fort, wherein neverthelesse he would not faile, though it were to save his life: but he prayed him to give that unto his wife, if hee escaped not, which he had meant to bestow on him, that shee might bury the same with him, that thereby hee might be better welcome unto the village of the soules or spirits departed.[2] To whom Captaine Gourgues answered, after he had commended his faithfull valour, the love toward his wife, and his noble care of immortall honour, that he desired rather to honour him alive then dead,

2. Sidenote: "The cause why the Floridians bury their goods with them."

and that by Gods helpe he would bring him home againe with victorie. After the discoverie of the Fort, the Spanyards were no niggards of their Canon shotte, nor of two double Colverines, which being mounted upon a Bulwarke, commaunded all along the River, which made captaine Gourgues to get to the hill covered with wood, at the foot whereof the Fort beginneth, and the forrest or wood continueth and stretcheth foorth beyond it: so that he had sufficient coverture to approch thereunto without offence. He purposed also to remaine there untill the Morning, wherein hee was resolved to assault the Spaniards by scaling their walles on the side toward the hill, where the Trench seemed not sufficiently flanked for the defence of the courtains, and from whence part of his men might draw them that were besieged, which should shew themselves to defend the rampart while the rest were comming up. But the Governour hastened his unhappy destinie, causing threescore shotte to sallie foorth, which passing through the Trenches, advanced forward to descrye the number and valour of the French, whereof twentie under the conduct of Cazenove, getting betweene the Fort and them which now were issued foorth, cut off their repassage, while Gourgues commanded the rest to charge them in the Front, but not to discharge but neere at hand, and so that they might be sure to hitte them, that afterward with more ease they might cut them in pieces with their swordes. So that turning their backs assoone as they were charged and compassed in by his Lieutenant, they remayned all slaine upon the place.[3] Whereat the rest that were besieged were so astonied, that they knew none other meane to save their lives, but by fleeing into the Wooddes adjoyning, where neverthelesse being incountred againe by the arrowes of the Savages which lay in wayte there for them (whereof one ranne through the target and body of a Spanyard, which therewithall fell downe starke dead) some were constrayned to turne backe, choosing rather to dye by the hand of the French, which pursued them: assuring themselves, that none of them could finde any favour neyther with the one nor the other Nation, whom they had alike and so out of measure cruelly intreated, saving those which were reserved to be an example for the time to come. The Fort when it was taken, was found well provided of all necessaries: namely of five double Colverines, and foure Mynions, with divers other small pieces of all sorts, and eighteene grosse cakes of gunnepowder, all sorts of weapons, which Gourgues caused with speede to be imbarked, saving the powder and other moveables, by reason it was all consumed with fire through the negligence of a Savage, which in seething of his fish, set fire on a traine of powder which was made and hidden by the Spanyardes, to have feasted the French at the first assault, thus blowing up the store house, and the other houses buylt of Pine trees. The rest of the Spaniards being led away prisoners with the others, after that the Generall had shewed them the wrong which they had done without occasion to all the French Nation, were all hanged on the boughes of the same trees,[4] whereon the French hung: of which number five were hanged by one Spaniard, which perceiving himselfe in the like miserable estate, confessed his fault, and the just judgement which God had brought upon him. But in stead of the writing which Pedro Melendes had hanged over them, importing these wordes in Spanish, I doe not this as unto French men, but as unto Lutherans, Gourgues caused to be imprinted with a searing iron in a table of Firrewood, I doe not this as unto Spaniardes, nor as unto Mariners,[5] but as unto Traitors, Robbers, and Murtherers. Afterward considering he had not men inough to keepe his Forts which he had wonne, much lesse to store them, fearing also lest the Spaniard which hath Dominions neere adjoyning should renew his forces, or the Savages should prevaile against the French men, unlesse his Majestie would send thither, hee resolved to raze them. And indeede, after he had assembled, and in the ende perswaded all the Savage kings so to doe, they caused their subjects to runne thither with such affection, that they overthrew all the three Forts flatte even with the ground in one day. This done by Gourgues, that hee might returne to his Shippes which were left in the River of Seyne called Tacatacourou, fifteene leagues distant from thence, he sent Cazenove and the artillery by water: afterward with fourescore harquebusiers, armed with corslets, and matches

3. Sidenote: "The slaughter of the Spaniards of the third Fort."

4. Sidenote: "The writings hanged over the French and Spaniards slaine in Florida."
5. Paul Gaffarel, *La Floride française* (1875), p. 510, shows the word used was *Marennes*, indicating that the Spanish were despicable descendants of Moors and Jews!

light, followed with fortie Mariners bearing pikes, by reason of the small confidence he was to have in so many Savages, he marched by land alwayes in battell ray, finding the wayes covered with Savages, which came to honour him with presents and prayses, as the deliverer of all the countries round about adjoyning. An old woman among the rest sayd unto him, that now she cared not any more to dye, since she had seene the Frenchmen once againe in Florida, and the Spaniards chased out. Briefly being arrived, and finding his ships set in order, and every thing ready to set sayle, hee counselled the kings to continue in the amitie and ancient league which they had made with the king of France, which would defend them against all Nations: which they all promised, shedding teares because of his departure. Olocotara especially: for appeasing of whom he promised them to returne within twelve Moones, (so they count the yeeres) and that his king would send them an army, and store of knives for presents, and all other things necessary. So that after he had taken his leave of them, and assembled his men, he thanked God of all his successe since his setting foorth, and prayed to him for an happy returne. The third of May 1568, all things were made ready, the Rendez-vous appoynted, and the Ankers weighed to set sayle so prosperously, that in seventeene dayes they ranne eleven hundred leagues: continuing which course they arrived at Rochel the sixt of June, the foure and thirtieth day after their departure from the River of May, having lost but a small Pinnesse and eight men in it, with a few gentlemen and others which were slaine in the assaulting of the Forts....

346. May 5, 1569. Account by Esteban de las Alas on the loss of San Mateo.

A.G.I., Seville, transcript in Division of Manuscripts, Library of Congress, translated.

Most Excellent Lord.

I received Your Honour's letter of the ninth of April from the pilot Andrés Pérez, who arrived here on Good Friday morning, and whose coming cheered up our Easter; but what happened in the following week clouded it for us very much. This is what happened, for I wish to recount it from the start, for as the events are so unpleasant it needs rather a long explanation.

The last day of March, a quarter of an hour before dawn, the fort of San Mateo was attacked by about four hundred Indians; they came in on the river side, which was open for part of the way on account of a flood there had been, giving great shouts. They had fierce fighting for a while: Castellón was wounded, who was in command of that fort, from seven or eight arrows: some of the wounds were very dangerous; they wounded three other soldiers, and one of them died. The Indians withdrew, and many traces of blood were found next day in the part where they went. I had news of this, and sent to that fort Captain Francisco Núñez at once, with fifty soldiers, the best there were here, to encourage those men and help them build up that stockade which had fallen, and to report to me on the situation. So with all speed he wrote that it had been done, and that the governor of that fort was now better. And I wrote to him, telling him that when he saw he was well, that he should come back with the men he had taken.

At three o'clock in the afternoon on Good Friday five sailing ships appeared by the estuary of San Agustín: three of them seemed to be quite large, the other two were smaller. They must have been about a league from that fort. I had a shot fired towards them, so that they should realize that there were people and a port here, thinking that they would be ships from Spain; and that if they were enemy ships, that they should also know that there were people here. On hearing the shot they pulled into the shore and went off towards San Mateo.

Next day I sent a ship with 1760 kilos of corn to San Mateo, with news of these ships which had gone by; and here we noticed a number of things that were not as ready for war as they should have been, and we were very vigilant, to see if they would be wanting to take land around here, to defend our way out against them, because I realized that they were privateers since they did not wish to hear from us.

On the morning of Easter Sunday the sergeant from San Mateo arrived at this fort with thirty two people: he had been with thirty men in one of two blockhouses which had been built by the estuary at San Mateo, and he said that at midday on the previous Saturday he had seen from the house where he was (which is on the side of the river of San Mateo nearer this fort) many Indians approaching and another group of armed men, with artillery pieces and armor and arquebuses and four battle flags and their trumpets and drums; these immediately attacked the house that was on the other side, on the island of Alimacani, where thirty other soldiers had been, who panicked so badly that they abandoned the blockhouse; and even those most fit for flight did not get far, for of them all only five escaped. The sergeant was firing from the house that he was in with two artillery pieces that he had there until the ammunition ran out, and since it was unlikely that help could come for them from the fort of San Mateo soon, since the tide was unfavourable, and the weather was blowing strong from the Northeast, he spiked the cannons and came, as I said, to this fort.

In the afternoon of that same Easter Sunday I sent a soldier with a letter for the Captain Francisco Núñez and the governor there, in which I told them to act as was expected of them, for they had such good men with them and a good fort and other things to encourage the men: and if more assistance should be needed, I would help them.

So this same day, at night, I sent two soldiers inland to Utina, to collect half a dozen Indians and come downstream in a canoe, with a letter for the men mentioned above, saying the same as the other one: they were to arrive at the fort at midnight, so that if the fort were surrounded they could go in and out without risk.

The Saturday when the attack was made on this blockhouse on the island of Alimacani, of the five men who escaped by swimming, three reached the house where the sergeant was, and came here with him: and the other two reached the fort of San Mateo at sunset and told them what had happened. At once the soldiers began to get jumpy: let's go, let's go, there are more than five hundred of them and they won't leave any of us alive. Such was the panic that got into them that even the Captain's orders could not prevail: they took ammunition, and all that night they did nothing but grind corn, cook and roast chickens, and pack their kitbags, and at dawn on Easter

Sunday they began to leave the fort. It is said that they took Captain Francisco Núñez and the governor out with them by force; thus they left it all abandoned without spiking the artillery or throwing the ammunition in the river. At the end they were in such a hurry that of the two men that were wounded in the fight they had had with the Indians, one of them they left by the fort and they left the other behind on the way.

After they had left the fort, Captain Francisco Núñez took the rear, and after going about a league he took seven soldiers with him and went back to the fort. And some of the soldiers went back to look for him when they saw that he was staying, and they did not find him nor reach him: and despite all this they pressed on towards this fort, where they arrived on Monday, Easter Monday, just before dusk.

The next day, Tuesday, in the morning, I sent the sergeant of the men from San Mateo with forty-six soldiers in good order, to carry out a quick reconnaissance of the fort at night: I told them that if Captain Francisco Núñez was in it with those few soldiers, they should go in: and if it was occupied by the French, that he should withdraw without risking the men he was taking with him. He arrived the following Wednesday night, realized that there were in the fort Indians and fires and confused noise, so he came back here with his men the following Friday.

This report did not satisfy me, so next day, Saturday, the 1st of May, I sent the Royal Lieutenant, Juan de Bassoçaval, in this frigate and a launch with fifty soldiers, to reconnoiter the houses and the fort, and to go by day, so that he could be sure of what he saw; and if any of the houses or the fort should be standing they were to fortify themselves in it and occupy it until I could send enough assistance. He arrived at midday one league from the estuary of San Mateo, disembarked the men there and went into the forest, to avoid being seen, to approach one of the houses by the estuary: and the frigate and the launch went to anchor by the estuary. He came upon that blockhouse and found no one there, but the blockhouse burnt and four men hung inside. He had their ropes cut and threw them into the sea. He crossed to the other side in the launch, to the other blockhouse of Alimacani, and exactly the same, he found it burnt with another four men hung: and he disposed of them as the others. He went off upstream towards the fort; he found this entirely burnt down, with no artillery nor anything else at all, and in it two more men hung. So with this news he came back the following Sunday.

Then on Monday I sent him out again with forty soldiers four or five leagues from here to see if he could track down some Indian to tell him who these people had been, for I am pretty sure myself that they were privateers and in need of water. And as they are our enemies around Tacatacuru, they must have given them something to win them over and get them to give them water, and at the same time the Indians will have told them that we had a blockhouse just nearby, so they should help them take it. And they came inland through some channels and made that first attack on the blockhouse. And as the Indians must have seen our men leave and abandon the fort, they went inside, since no one was stopping them, and burnt it down and did what I said.

Captain Francisco Núñez, with his seven soldiers, when he separated from the men who were coming here, returned to the fort and stayed there until almost night: he saw some people go by in four canoes and shot at them with an artillery piece, damaging the front one, whereupon the men in the others turned round and headed back whence they had come. He sent three soldiers to the lookout post, and they said that they had seen, beside the river on the fort side, two flags, and had heard drums and seen thirty or forty men, either French or English, they did not know who. Although I cannot believe that in such weather they could have crossed that river, in canoes, in battle armor and carrying pikes, because such a storm was blowing from the Northeast that no one could have stood up to it.

When Captain Francisco Núñez had been told this news, he got them to throw the gunpowder in the river and spike the artillery, and with his seven soldiers he got into a boat he had there, and with the lame soldier that they had left behind there, and he went upstream to the area of Autina. He arrived here tonight.

The way the people in the fort behaved has been one of the most cowardly actions that anyone has ever done; because without even seeing the face of a single enemy they abandoned everything. To tell the truth, of the more than a hundred and twenty that there were in the fort, less than fourteen can be absolved from blame,

and even that is difficult. I do not know what to resort to, I do not know what I will do, for I feel so ill and am lying in bed, after being bled, with a slow fever. Even so I shall note down what I think best at the appropriate time, for it is not right that a matter like this should be left unpunished, either financially or personally.

If there should be a ship going to Spain, let this letter go on it, or a copy of it in any other letter Your Honour should write to the adelantado. I would send at once people to build a fortified blockhouse on the island of Alimacani, and man it with suitable people, if we were not so short of food and all the necessary equipment. When the help comes, which we are hoping can come as soon as possible, I will go and do that and all the other things that need doing which are not being done now, as I say, for shortage of provisions.

I received from the pilot everything which you sent me and I divided it as you instruct in the letter; and for the part that came to me I give you a thousand heartfelt thanks, for I do not know when I can pay you as much as I owe. This letter will serve for both Your Honour and the Captain Pero Menéndez Marqués, for since this is the only sheet of paper I have I cannot write to anyone else. You will give my best wishes to Captain Varreda and all the gentlemen and ladies of your house.

I have detained the boat till now, partly because it was not the weather to leave; and I detained it for three or four days, sending it to San Mateo.

I am entrusting the pilot with anything else that needs to be said here. And eating at three-quarter rations we have enough to eat till exactly the tenth of June. For the love of God do not forget these men. If some corn should come, Your Honour should not fail to send two hundred fanegas, or a hundred, or as much as you can, while we are waiting for that transport ship to come from Campeche, or some help from Spain. May the Lord look after and increase the most magnificent person and household of Your Honour.

Written in the fort of San Agustín, the 5th May 1568. I expect Señor Pero Menéndez Marqués at any moment.

Kisses your hands,

[signed:] Estevan de las Alas.

AN ENGLISH RAID ON SAN AGUSTÍN IN DECEMBER, 1571

SIR WILLIAM WINTER led three ships on a piratical raid into the Caribbean in 1571 about which little or nothing is yet known from English sources. On their return voyage in late December, they crossed the bar opposite San Agustín and commenced an artillery attack on the fort, which appears to have responded vigorously. We do not know whether any attempt to land and take the fort was made. It was defended by Pedro Menéndez de Avilés himself. Earlier, he had been making his way by sea to Havana when his vessel went aground. He got his men ashore and marched them briskly some eighty miles to San Agustín. A few days later the English vessels appeared—without his presence and that of his men, Spanish commentators believed the fort would have fallen.

The sources so far published are translated in Irene A. Wright, ed., *Documents Concerning English Voyages to the Spanish Main, 1569–1580* (London, Hakluyt Society, 1932), pp. 37–39; (347) May 24, 1572. Sancho Pardo Osorio to the Licentiate Ovando, President of the Council of the Indies, from A.G.I., Seville, Patronato 257(2/5/4/12[3–15]), extract; and (348) May 25, 1572. The same to the President and Officials of the Casa de Contratación, from A.G.I., Seville, Contratación 5105 (41/6/5, 40), extract. Both letters were written from Havana.

347. May 24, 1572. Sancho Pardo Osorio to the Licentiate Ovando.

Very Illustrious Sir

The report that the *adelantado* was lost has been so general in the Indies that I presume it will have reached your court, and will have inspired in your lordship no little regret. Therefore I have desired to be the first, though only by a few days, to inform your lordship of the facts.

The *adelantado* left the fort at Saint Augustine on December 20 for this city, with two shallops and a small bark. As he was coasting along the Florida shore he was struck by a storm in which both shallops rode and lost sight of one another. The bark, which was farthest out to sea, did its best and put in here, affirming that the other two vessels would enter next day.

But one shallop was wrecked on the shore of the province of Ais itself. Being by heavy rains prevented from making use of their harquebuses, those on board were killed by the Indians, who spared not one, and burned the shallop.

With his own shallop the *adelantado* struck on Cape Cañaveral. Of planks and other wreckage he built a sort of fort, and with about thirty persons, armed with some wet harquebuses, he faced the Indians and kept them off that day. That night he set out with such skill and fortune that, sometimes fighting the Indians and sometimes giving them of the little he had, he arrived without the loss of a man at San Agustín, a distance of thirty-one leagues.

Whither it seems that God led him by a miracle, that that fort and the people in it should not be lost; for a few days later there appeared off the fort three large English ships, carrying a large number of men. When they attacked, the fort was well defended. Perhaps, had it lacked so valiant a defender, it might have been in danger.

On April 10, having no other news of the *adelantado* than the above, a little frigate left this port, trusting to fortune to find him, as it did. He embarked aboard it and reached this harbour on Holy Friday. He was here fifteen days...

Havana, May 24, 1572.

Very Illustrious Sir Your lordship's servant kisses your lordship's illustrious hands.

[signed:] Sancho Pardo Osorio.

348. May 25, 1572. Sancho Pardo Osorio to the President and Officials of the Casa de Contratación.

Very Illustrious Sir

On the way from the fort at Saint Augustine with two shallops, the *Adelantado* Pedro Menéndez was wrecked on the Florida coast. One went aground in the province of Ais. It is believed that the Indians killed all on board. The other shallop, in which the *adelantado* was, struck on Cape Cañaveral, where, on shore, he fortified himself as best he could and faced the Indians that day. That night he set out for San Agustín, which is thirty-one leagues away, where he arrived, sometimes fighting the Indians and sometimes temporizing.

It seems that miraculously God brought him thither, for a few days later three large ships manned by English arrived off the fort and, had he not been there, would have taken the place and the people in it. They fought them and defended it against them.

On Holy Friday the *adelantado* reached this city. Leaving me with its government, he sailed for La Española. . . .

Havana, May 25, 1572.

Very Illustrious Sirs Your servitor, who kisses your honor's very illustrious hands.

[signed:] Sancho Pardo Osorio.

349. 1571. Sassafras from Florida, a universal remedy.

*Nicolas Bautista Monardes, a Seville doctor, first included his account of sassafras (*Sassafras officinale L.) *in his* Segunda parte del libro de las cosas que se traen de nuestras Indias Occidentales que sirven al uso de medicina *(Seville, 1571), and reprinted it in his* Primeray segunda y tercera partes de la historia medicinal de las cosas que se traen de nuestras Indias Occidentales *(Seville, 1574). It was translated by John Frampton as* Joyfull newes out of the newe founde worlde *(London, 1577, enlarged in 1580 and 1596), edited by Stephen Gaselee, 2 vols. (London, 1925), where*

sassafras occupies pp. 99–120 (extracted below). Sassafras remained one of the chief attractions of the North American coast for Spanish, French, and English until well after 1612.

Of the Tree That is Brought from The Florida, Whiche is Called Sassafras.

From the Florida whiche is the firme Lande of our Occidentall Indias, liyng in xxv. degrees, thei bryng a woodd and roote of a tree that groweth in those partes, of greate vertues, and great excellencies, that thei heale there with greevous and variable deseases.

It maie bee three yeres paste, that I had knowledge of this Tree, and a Frenche manne whiche had been in those partes, shewed me a peece of it, and tolde me merveiles of his vertues, and how many and variable deseases was healed with the water, whiche was made of it. I gave at that tyme no credite to hym, for that in these thynges of Plantes, and Hearbes, whiche is brought from other places, thei saie muche, and knoweth little, unlesse it bee by a man that hath experience of theim, with care and diligence, the Tree and the partes thereof liked me well, and I judged that, which now I dooe finde to bee true, and have seen by experience. He tolde me that the Frenchemen, which had been in the Florida at that tyme, when thei came into those partes, thei had been sicke the moste of theim, of greevous and variable deseases, and that the Indians did shewe them this Tree, and the maner how thei should use it, and so thei did, and thei healed of many evilles, whiche surely it doeth bryng admiration, that one onely remedy should doe so variable, and so marveilous effectes.

After that the Frenche menne were destroied, our Spaniardes did beginne to waxe sicke, as the Frenche menne had dooen, and some whiche did remaine of them, did shewe it to our Spaniardes, and how thei had cured them selves with the water of this marveilous Tree, and the maner whiche thei had in the usyng of it, shewed to theim by the Indians, who used to cure theim selves therewith, when thei were sicke of any grief.

Our Spaniardes did begin to cure theim selves with the water of this Tree, and it did in theim great effectes, that it is almoste incredible: for with the naughtie meates and drinkyng of the rawe waters, and slepyng in the dewes, the moste parte of theim came to fall into continuall Agues, of the whiche many of theim came to opilations, and of the opilations thei came to swell, and when the evil began: imediatly it began to take awaie the luste that thei had to their meate, and then came to theim other accidentes, and deseases, as suche like Fevers are accustomed to bryng: and havyng there no remedie to bee healed, thei did what the Frenche menne had counsailed them, doyng that whiche thei had doen, whiche was in this forme.

Thei tooke up the roots of this Tree, and tooke a peece thereof, suche as it semed to theim beste, thei cutte it small into verie thinne, and little peeces, and cast them into water, at discretion, that whiche thei sawe was needefull, little more or lesse, and thei sodde it the tyme that semed nedefull, for to remaine of a good coulour, and so thei dranke it, in the mornyng fastyng, and in the daie tyme, and at dinner and supper, without kepyng any more waight, or measure, than I have saied, nor more keepyng, nor order then this, and of this thei were healed of so many griefes, and evill deseases. That to heare of them what thei suffred, and how thei were healed, it doeth bryng admiration, and thei whiche were whole dranke it in place of wine, for it doeth preserve them in healthe: as it did appeare verie well by theim, that hath come from thence this yere, for thei came all whole and strong, and with good coulours, the whiche doeth not happen to them that dooeth come from those partes, and from other con-questes, for thei come sicke and swolne, without coullour, and in shorte space the moste of theim dieth: and these soldiours doeth trust so muche in this woodde, that I beyng one daie emongest many of them, informing my self of the thynges of this Tree, the moste parte of them tooke out of their pokettes, a good peece of this woodd, and said: Maister, doe you see here the woodde, that every one of us doth bryng for to heale us with all, if we do fall sicke, as we have been there: and thei began to praise so muche, to confirme the mervel-ous workes of it, with so many examples of them that were there, that surely I gave greate credite unto it, and thei caused me to beleeve all that thereof I had heard, and gave me courage to experimente it, as I have doen, and as we shall see in the mervailes, whiche wee shall treate of it: and

now we come to shewe the discription, and forme of this Tree.

The Tree from whence thei dooe cutte this woodde, whiche thei newlie brought from the Florida, called Sassafras, it is a Tree that com-meth to bee verie greate: there bee of the middle sorte, and lesser sorte, the greater sorte is of the bignesse of a Pine Tree, of a meane height, and well nere to the makyng of it, for he is straight, he dooeth caste out no more but one braunche of bowes, after the maner of a Palme Tree, onely in the highest parte, he casteth out bowes after the maner of a Pine Tree, made clene, makyng of the bowes whiche he doeth caste forthe, a forme of roundnesse: it hath a grosse rinde of a Taunie coulour, and upon it an other thinne rinde, of the coulour of Ashes, and upon the inner parte thereof, the Trees and bowes bee white, and nere like to Taunie, the Tree and bowes are verie light, the rinde beeyng tasted, it hath an excellente sweete smell, and it is somewhat like to the smell of Fenell, with muche sweetnesse of taste, and of pleasaunte smell, so muche that a little quantitie of this woodde beyng in a chamber, dooeth fill the ayre conteined in it, and his rinde hath some sharpenesse of taste, the inner parte hath little smell, the higher part that doeth contain the bowes hath leaves, the whiche bee greene, after the maner of a Figge Tree, with three poinctes, and when thei are little, thei be like to the leaves of a Peare Tree, in onely the shewyng their pointes, thei bee of coullour a sadde Greene, and of a sweete smell, and muche more when thei bee drie. The Indians doeth use to put them beaten or stamped upon bruses, or of any manne beaten with drie blowes, and beeyng drie, thei are used in Medicinable thynges. Thei lose not their leaves, thei are alwaies greene, if any dooe drie and fall, there spryngeth other, it is not knowen that it hath any flower, or fruite.

The rootes of this Tree be grosse, or sclender, conformablie to the greatnesse of the Tree, thei bee light, but not so muche as the bodie of the Tree, and his bowes, but for his greatnesse, he is notable light.

The roote of this Tree is verie superficiall, spreadyng in the upper face of the soile or grounde, and so thei roote theim up easily, and this is a common thyng in the Trees of the Indias, that moste of them hath their rootes of smal depth, and if thei carrie any plantes from Spaine to plant if thei doe not sette them of small depth in the ground, thei give no fruite.

The beste of all the Tree is the roote, and that dooeth woorke the beste effecte, the whiche hath the rinde verie fast to the inner parte, and it is of the coulour Taunie, and muche more of swete smell then all the Tree, and his braunches, the rinde dooeth taste of a more sweete smell, then the Tree, and the water beeyng sodden with the roote, is of greater and better effectes, then of any other parte of the Tree, and it is of a more sweete smell, and thereof the Spaniardes dooeth use it, for that it is of better and greater effectes, and for the aboundaunce that there is of it, it is a Tree that groweth nere unto the Sea, and in temperate places, that hath not muche drouthe, nor moisture, there be Mountaines growyng full of theim, and thei dooe caste a moste sweete smell: and so at the beginning when thei sawe them, thei thought that thei had been Trees of Sinamon, and in parte thei were not deceived, for that the rinde of this Tree hath as swete a smell, as the Sinamon hath, and it dooeth imitate it in coulour and sharpenesse of taste, and pleasaunte smell, and so the water that is made of it, is of moste sweete smell and taste, as the Sinamon is, and doeth the same woorkes and effectes that it doeth.

The Tree groweth in some partes of the Florida, and doeth not grow in others, for that it is in the port of sainct Elen [Santa Elena], and in the porte of saincte Mathewe [San Mateo], and it is not in any other partes, but when the Soldiours did waxe sicke, in places where this Tree was not, either thei carried them to bee healed to the saied places, or thei did sende theim the Trees, or their rootes chiefly, and therewith did heale them. The beste of the Tree is the Roote, and after the Bowes, and after the Tree, and the beste of all is the Rindes. The complexion and temperature of the Tree and of his Bowes is hotte and drie in the seconde degree, the Rinde is somewhat more hotte then the reste, for that it entereth into the thirde degree, of heate and drieth, and this is manifestly seen in the water, and so thei that shall nede of it, must procure to have the Rootes or Bowes, whiche hath the rinde, for that whiche is without it, doeth not take so good effectes.

The name of this Tree as the Indians dooeth name it, is called Pauame, and the Frenche menne doeth call it Sassafras. I knowe not wherefore our Spaniardes doeth call it after the same maner, beyng taught by the Frenche menne, although that some doeth corrupte it, and calleth it Sassafragia, by the name that we have from thence, and thei of these partes doeth call it Sassafras.

The use of the Roote, or of the woodde of this Tree the whiche we have treated of here, is by the waie of Seethyng, and in this forme the Indians did shewe it to the Frenche menne, and thei unto us, and as the Indians hath neither weight nor measure, thei have not kepte in those partes any order in the makyng of the water of this wood, for that thei doe no more in those partes, then to put a pece of woodde, or the roote at their discretion made peeces, in the water as thei dooe thinke beste. And thei doe Seeth it after their maner, without consumyng more quantitie, then when thei dooe see that the Seethyng is sufficiente, so that all thei whiche hath come from those partes, are verie variable in their maner of Seethyng, whiche is no small confusion to them that shall use it: and likewise to the Phisition that shall minister it, that whiche I doe in this I wil saie, I doe looke upon the complexion, and temperature of the sicke persone, that shall take and use this water, as also the maner and qualitie of the desease, and conformablie I doe make the water, and give it to the sicke person, givyng to the Cholericke lesse seethyng, and lesse quantitie of wood, and to the Flegmaticke more seethyng, and more quantitie of woodde, and to the Sanguine meanablie: and so after this sorte to their infirmities, accordyng to the qualities of them, for that if it bee not doen accordyng to this order, thei can not lette to make many errours in the use of this water, and so it is convenient that in the more thei kepe the use of the diet and government which is necessary for the desease whiche thei dooe pretende to cure. Let none thinke that to take this water without order and good consideration, as many doeth, that there shall followe health, rather takyng it without measure and without order, it shall doe unto them muche hurte, whereby it doeth seeme to me, that when this water shall bee ministered, as well in the deseases that it dooeth profite, as any other what soever thei bee, that thei goe to some learned Phisition, that maie dispose in the manner and makyng of the water, and the order whiche thei shall have in takyng of it, for that in the Winter it shall be taken otherwise then in the Summer. And otherwise it must be given to the leane person then to the strong, and in an other maner it muste be taken of the cholericke, then of the flematicke, and one order in the colde Region, and an other order in the hotte. Whereby it is convenient to keepe order, measure, and forme, in the taking of it, for that there goeth no lesse in it then health and life, considering that we see it hath no price in the worlde, and not to let it alone to the judgement, of hym that knoweth it not. . . .

Chapter Forty-one
The Last Years of Pedro Menéndez de Avilés's Control of the Florida Colony

THE ADELANTADO'S last direct contact with his North American lands was when he entered Chesapeake Bay on his way home to Spain in 1572. Then, and in the two years following that were left to him, the Council of the Indies investigated closely the situation in the Florida colony in view of hostile reports that came from there or from officials in Cuba. The most damning of these came from a high but anonymous official in Havana. He based what he had to say on reports from Florida and not on personal knowledge, but he alleged that both San Agustín and Santa Elena were useless both as forts and as colonies, that they were being mismanaged by Menéndez and by members of his family who were left in office there, and that the soldiers were being exploited by not being given their full pay (though they could buy themselves out of the colony and their *plazas* would then become dead-pays, payments to notional men whose money went into the officials' pockets). He urged that the whole colony should be moved to western Florida, which was much more fertile and accessible, and be put under the management of the governor at Havana (350).

Menéndez had his own remedies for some of the problems of Florida. One was to kill and enslave all the Indians of the Florida cays and those as far north as the Bay of Tocobaga. He reported to this effect shortly after his return in 1572 (351). He returned to this subject with more detailed plans for disposing of the Indians (which was necessary, he said, to keep the colony alive) either in 1573 or early in 1574 (352). The Council of the Indies opened its examination of the situation early in 1573, and on February 4, 1573, examined, for example, a returned settler from Santa Elena, Martín Diez, whose report (353) on Santa Elena and, incidentally, on San Agustín, was a very gloomy one. This was only one of many such examinations, and they were gone over systematically by the Council of the Indies in July, 1574. No decisions had been made at the time of Menéndez's death, but it is clear that his stewardship and even the continuance of the colony were seriously in doubt.

350. [*Circa* 1572]. A critical report on Florida from an official in Cuba.

Pedro Menéndez de Avilés was continually in controversy with officials in Cuba. In 1565–1566 he complained about the governor of Cuba, García Osorio de Sandoval (1565–1567), and interfered so much with the business and military arrangements of that island that the governor resigned. After a short interval Menéndez himself succeeded as governor of Cuba in 1567, but governed by deputies with whom he was also frequently on bad terms. The second of these, Juan de Yñestrosa (Hinistrosa elsewhere), was a strong-

minded man, who might possibly have written this report in 1570, but it is more likely to be the work of Sancho Pardo Osorio, who had to deal with Menéndez during the last years he held office in 1572–1573. It is possible it was written for the information of the incoming governor Gabriel Montalvo (1573–1577), as well as for the authorities in Spain. It is a valuable corrective to those who praised Menéndez's work, although it is possible that it plays down too much what he had achieved. It certainly represents strongly the Havana views of Florida affairs. See Irene A. Wright, The Early History of Cuba *(Havana, 1916), 273–290.*

Navarrete, Colección, *XIV (1971), fols. 347–356*v., *translated.*

An Account of the Population on the Coast of Florida, and obstacles that were encountered for its fortification and defence.

Although I did not go to Florida, because of the expense and difficulties that arose, I shall here give an account of what happens in those forts from what can be found out and verified in this town of La Havana, without those who might give an account of them being able to speak at length: for concerning the community and the dealings there are here every day, it is well known, and although the poor people who are there very much wanted me to go there, it would not have done them any good, or at least it would not have achieved what they wanted, since I had no authority to help them, or set right their grievances, or see to what needed doing, and so it will be more or less possible to give an account from here of the most important matters, as I would have done from there, gathered from many people who have now come here from there, and from others who have been there and seen what happens and told me, and from what I have myself seen and heard happen here.

Santa Elena.

Santa Elena, where the fort is, is not on the mainland of Florida, but is a small island, one league long and half a league wide, in many places much less wide: the length of it runs from Northwest to Southeast, and it is at 32 and a half degrees: it has a harbor and a sea inlet like a river

going from the harbor to the fort; and from the harbor, where the ships drop anchor, to the fort must be more or less one arquebus' shot in distance, and by the side of this inlet is the fort. From Santa Elena to the mainland there are cays and little islands and sea and inlets, about 10 leagues at most (others say 20); all these cays are low, liable to be under water, useless marshes. This Island of Santa Elena is covered with seawater every full moon, and running water on three-quarters of it, everywhere on half of it, except for the part where the fort is, which is higher: and this half cannot be cultivated, nor can it be of any use, because the sea comes over it and makes it useless. The other third part used to be all forest, and now there are some small derelict wooden cabins, and they indicate that they will be some of them like two, others like three, others like six groups of houses of farmworkers in Castille; these, those who have gone there have destroyed, and cut down the trees in the forest, which was very high and thick with oaks, pines, balsam, walnut trees and laurel (although not native) and brambles, and after clearing and cutting this they have sown corn there. All the area which is open and cleared and able to be sown must be land in which 7 or 8 fanegas of corn can be sown, and no more in all the island. These rocks are destroying the fertility of the land, which gives little produce, and they say that within five or six years it will not be giving any at all, nor will it be possible to sow there, for already they are producing little. In the garden areas of the houses or cabins they sow lettuces, radishes, cabbages and pumpkins. The corn sown is very little, it cannot be much for there is not the land, and a single man with a hoe cannot sow much, and there are many places, particularly with a large number of crows, where the crows pull up and eat the corn as soon as it first grows, and before it grows moles eat the seed, and afterwards, when it ripens, the crows eat it again then too, and thrushes, and squirrels, and foxes, so that they sow and reap with tremendous difficulty, and in all the Island there is nothing else for people to eat except just this little bit of corn, and the land is quite unsuitable for anyone to get anything useful out of it at all, with any amount of trouble and toil, which could help sustain human life. There are no cows there, or pigs, or sheep, or goats, or any other livestock, nor can there be any, nor can they be raised, for there is no place in which they could even be kept alive on anything: for some pigs which someone took there from the island of Cuba went and died of hunger on him, for he could not keep them alive—even until he weighed them and sold them to the people there, despite giving them corn to keep them going, and the bears, and lions, and wolves, and foxes, which there are there, eat them, so that the people are never able to eat meat, and if at all it has to be salted meat brought from the island of Cuba: all they can do is fish in the sea and the inlets there are there and so they normally fish to keep themselves alive, and they have gone many days, even months, without corn or anything else, just with the fish they can catch, and that they have to catch with fishhooks because there are no dragnets, or fishnets, except in the house of the Governor for his own use.

The fort is of beams and planks, made by the soldiers, who always work at cutting, carrying and sawing this timber and beams, for there are no horses or mules, or any other beast of burden, and they work in these duties and labours every day, and do other things for the household of the Governor... and indeed they work more as labourers and peons than as soldiers.

Santo Agustín, what it is.

Santo Agustín, where the fort and the people were first, is a small island, and Santo Agustín, where the fort and the people are now, is another one next to the first one, where the fort used to be first, and this one where the fort is now is almost an island, because it is surrounded by water, although it has in one place an open stretch over which they can go onto the mainland: it is at 29 degrees and a half: it is 3 or 4 leagues long, and its width is very small, it is narrow, up to half a league, and in some places less. Every year the sea covers a large part of this land: it is all wooded with holm-oaks, pines and oaks, and a palm grove which is low, full of roots, and cannot be cultivated except in one part where it is sandy, and here they sow corn, and of this land, most of it belongs to the governor, who makes the soldiers sow for him there.

There are in Santo Agustín 13 married men, settlers, apart from the soldiers, some of whom are married. Each settler will have as much land as a medium sized vegetable garden, which is quite enough for one man alone to dig, with only a hoe, particularly since half of every day is spent in grinding the corn that is to be eaten that day, for it cannot be kept from one day to the next either ground or cooked, and it is a great and continual labour to grind it every day by hand: all that is sown is corn and pumpkins, for other vegetable seeds do not grow well. Each settler sows 12, 15 or even 20 pounds of corn, no more; they say someone once sowed 40 or 50 pounds. They do not sow more because each of them has just got his hoe, and they have to grind the food by hand every day. There is nothing else of which they can make use, and the state of the land is such that there could not be, however much hard work and effort was put into it.

In the small island where the fort was first, which is next to the one where it is now, there are about fifty cows, which are of no use to the settlers or the soldiers, nor are they killed for food except when the Governor occasionally wants one killed for himself. These fifty cows do not increase, and if they do give birth to a calf it dies through lack of food, and from the many large horseflies that there are there, and many mosquitos, and bears, and lions, and the herd has no fresh water to drink except when it rains. There are some 50 pigs, and these too increase very little, and the young ones have been dying and will die through lack of food and fresh water, and they are eaten by bears and lions, and they have been of no use except when the Governor has occasionally had one killed for himself. These have gone and fled and are thin and wander round the wooded area, but they are no use, if there is one it is no good. It is not the land for raising herds; there is no other animal, no sheep, no goats, nothing else that can be eaten, and thus they have to eat only what they can fish. The settlers raise some few hens, not having the corn to feed them or to eat themselves, and these few hens eat shellfish, so they taste of that, and of fish.

The fort is made of planks and thick beams for pillars: it lasts 4 or 5 years, since the wood rots with the dampness of the land, and because the land is salty, and the soldiers repair it, and they work all year in this fort and in the houses for the Governors and other things, and despite all this for many months they get no rations or pay: so they have been wanting to mutiny because of the hunger and lack of clothing that they suffer, but since there is nowhere they can go by land, and they have no boat in which to leave by sea, they have not done so: and when they do give them rations, they do not give them what His Majesty orders, for they are given half a pound of flour, and since they are exhausted from their work and have to grind and cook the food themselves, not having anyone else to do it, they are badly off: and this ground corn or flour, when there is some, they make into pancakes and cook or bake them in the ashes or embers when they are to eat it.

From the harbor where the ships come to where the fort is, there is more or less half a league. From the fort they are unable to defend themselves against any ships that should come, to stop them entering the harbor, nor, once any ships have entered the harbor, can they attack or damage the ships in the harbor.

These two forts, as they are called, or settlements, are not suitable to be settled, nor can people sustain themselves there in any way, for there is not the land, as I said before. On the mainland, inland, they say there is the land, and the cabins, for cultivation, and for raising herds.

These two forts, as they are called, and the people, and the other things there are there, are not enough either to defend or attack if enemy soldiers should come to them.

Fulfilment of the agreement.

As for the fulfilment of the agreement and arrangement which was made with the Adelantado Pedro Menéndez de Avilés, it is obvious from what is said above that he has not complied: for he did not settle in Florida but in a place that can be neither settled nor inhabited, where cattle can neither feed nor raise young, where it is impossible to achieve the purpose of the agreement: he did not settle on the mainland where he was supposed to settle: it could be said that this is not in Florida at all, and, given that, it seems that there is no need to deal with the fulfilment of the other sections of the agreement, and arrangements, to have them fulfilled; nor is there need to order him to comply with them in these two forts or settlements, but on the habitable mainland: for even if the farmworkers went there which he is obliged to send, and the rest, it would be to lose them and everything else: and what was the second most important thing after the settlement, bringing in 500 negro slaves to break the land and cultivate it and make a fort of stone or

earth, he has done nothing at all, and the Adelantado Pedro Menéndez said so himself in reply to a Royal Decree which was communicated to him, and the workers which he did convey there are very disillusioned and upset because he took them to a place where they can neither cultivate nor even feed themselves, so they complain loudly about that.

The complaints and grievances they have.

The people who are there, both soldiers and those few farmworkers, are in the greatest discontent, and like forced labourers and captives: so he who has any money left from what he brought from Spain or from his pay, it is said that they aim to collect it together and ransom themselves, giving it to the Governor who is there at the time, to let them go: and in this way they have given many people leave to go, some of them part colored, others white, and they all buy their way out, although the money is taken from them under the pretext of its being payment for the fleets for having brought them from Spain when they came, when the Adelantado is in fact obliged to bring them at his own expense. This was established in the judicial enquiry which was undertaken here into Pedro Menéndez Márquez, and some others have just now arrived here under the same arrangement. I don't think the Adelantado Pedro Menéndez is to blame for this, but the people he sends there as Governor, because they are changing all the time, and he sends whoever he wants, and they are all his family and relations, and they take accounts from each other and inquire into each other, and they lose no opportunity at all of doing themselves some good and whatever is to their advantage.

They also complain that the rations are not given to them as His Majesty orders, and they say that it will be given to them in money where there is nowhere in the land that they can buy the rations from, and even the money has not been given them for two years now.

Item: they say that they ordered the rations to be given them in money because these Governors are the people that will sell them it, and since they sell it to them at whatever price they like, and all the money which His Majesty spends comes into their hands, and since they are the ones to get the money and the ones to pay it out, they please themselves in this way and keep the lot.

Item: they say and complain that when a boat goes there from this island of Cuba with salted meat and salt, or other things, that they do not allow to go in the boat any salted meat that belongs to anyone else other than themselves, the Adelantado and the Governors, nor any other goods, because they sell it at the price they wish: and here three men from Florida asked me to make them carry some meat and other things like that, because they were not allowed to carry it, nor did the ship's master want to take it, because Pedro Menéndez de Avilés, who has been here, would not permit it.

Item, that the linen clothes and the shoes and the other clothes, since it is in the hands of the Governors that the Adelantado sends, and from the Adelantado himself they sell it at the very excessive price they wish, and the soldiers find themselves without clothes or shoes, and do not receive their pay, nor do they know if they are going to be paid, or when, the soldiers take it at any price, and this is so high that it ought to be put right. What I have seen here and now concerning this is that Pedro Menéndez Márquez brought from the mainland 17 short accounts collected from the officers of His Majesty of the money which His Majesty has allotted for these forts, and he brought a large part of them spent on clothing and goods, up to 100 ducats, and part of it he sold here in his house, and the rest of the money that he brought he kept: he neither took it nor sent it to Florida: he sent a boat with some of the clothing and goods to be shared out among the soldiers, and so it was shared out among them, at excessive prices, as those who have come from there have said, so that he has kept here, and satisfied himself with it, the total amount of money as the clothing which was sent came to: thus in both ways he gets ahead and collects a considerable amount: and all this is lost by the soldiers, who in a free market would get their provisions quite cheaply. This is not all that happened, for there came from San Agustín to this town of La Havana a Pedro Menéndez de Avilés, [a relative of the adelantado], who was there as Governor, to collect from Pedro Menéndez Márquez these 17 accounts which he had brought, and Pedro Menéndez de Avilés has done the same again: without taking any at all to Florida, he has taken the amount of 40 ducats in clothing from Pedro Menéndez Márquez, and a further amount

from other people, and he sent that to Florida and the forts in order to spend all this amount that was collected in the mainland, without a penny going to Florida in money, with a small amount of clothing on which they had spent some of the very money collected, and they sent from here to the Adelantado 110 ducats which they say they owed him for other things of this nature, and provisions, and everything else is run like this in every matter, and the poor people get neither pay nor rations.

Item: as Pedro Menéndez de Avilés took the account here from Pedro Menéndez Márquez, of the 17 accounts which he brought in a galleon from the mainland, and as they are all together and related, he passes him in the accounts a large amount of expenses, and thus he has given him 1,200 ducats for some days which he says he spent in collecting the accounts from the officers on the mainland, having gone and come back being paid by His Majesty as the captain of a galleon or warship which was ordered to become flagship [*Capitana*]. And similarly of the total amount that he collected for the soldiers of this fort of La Havana, the officers of this town give him another portion: and, in all, everything which His Majesty has allotted and spends on those forts, they say that it is well known that it ends up in the hands of 3 or 4 people, and thus although it seems that that is little in relation to the population, which indeed it is, it is a considerable amount of money that His Majesty spends there, with little or no results to show for it, and it would be best for note to be taken of this and that it should be put right and in order, so that His Majesty should not spend so much so fruitlessly.

It looks as if these forts should not be kept going.

These forts called Santa Elena and San Agustín, and the people who are in them, do not seem to be worth supporting by His Majesty at such a cost, nor at any cost: for either the service to His Majesty is that they should be supported in order to increase the Royal Dominions, and spread our Holy Catholic Faith in the Indies, or so as to prevent pirate ships from gathering in those harbors to wait, as they say, to rob merchant ships that pass that way, or to prevent the French coming in to settle there.

If it is to increase the Royal Dominions and our

Holy Faith, there is no need to support the forts, because the Royal Dominions are not increased by settling those two islets or cays: rather they are diminished because of the large amount which is spent uselessly every year from the Royal Treasury and Exchequer without increase nor any useful results at all, nor anything else of benefit to the Royal Exchequer or to any subject: rather there is lost money which those people elsewhere could use productively: nor is our Holy Faith increased because there are no Indians and no-one is taught the doctrine, and religion and devotion is rather being lost among the Christians who are there, because they have been for a long time without a priest, nor a friar, in San Agustín who might say Mass for them and administer the Sacraments, and although friars have now come they are already going, and have gone, some of them, somewhere else.

If it is to stop pirates gathering and resting there to wait for shipping, they should not be supported for this reason either; for even if they came, those forts cannot prevent any Frenchman or pirate doing whatever he wants to do, for from San Agustín to Santa Elena there are 20, or over 20, similar harbors, many of which are large, and the forts and the people in them cannot prevent them from going into any of those and staying there as long as they want, whether the people in the fort find out about them or not: particularly since if a pirate wants to lie in wait for a merchant ship there are many other places to do it, such as Cape St. Vincent on the Spanish coast, where the ships are more certain to pass and they wait for them with less cost and risk, nearer to home than Florida: and they could to it at the Cape of Sant Anton [Cabo de San Antonio, Cuba], and in many other places: and the ships that the French capture are always small ones that go unarmed from place to place in these parts, or are lying dismantled in harbors, so the French are not going to stop going to that coast and those harbors because of the forts and defences in Santa Elena and San Agustín, if that is what they wanted to do.

If it is to stop them settling there, then that is no reason for supporting the forts either, because none of the French pirates, nor those of any other nation, go to the Indies to settle, but to rob at their ease, nor have settlers ever come this way, so there is no need to fear this happening except at the orders of their King, and except if this were to happen at his expense, with his favour, at his orders: and this too is nothing to fear, because even if they were to settle, which is the most difficult thing there is, they could not support them there, for the land is of no assistance and they would have to bring food from France, and everything else, and they are hardly likely to bring out such expensive cargoes for so little result: and thus they had already been in Santa Elena before His Majesty or the Pilot of the Merchant ships of the Indies knew of any harbors on that coast [1562], and they left Santa Elena where they were because of the land was so poor, for they could neither take it nor support it; thus an inscription was found there, when Governor Mazariegos of this island, at the orders of His Majesty [1564], sent men from this town to investigate and sound out those harbors, and find out their depths and state, and it can be clearly seen, since even now, despite all that His Majesty spends on them, and having these islands from which they are supplied so close at hand, they cannot be supported; and even granted that they might be settled and supported, any time that His Majesty wished to drive them out of there, I mean from these two forts of Santa Elena and San Agustín, he is bound to be able to do it easily from this island of Cuba and from that of Santo Domingo: and even when this should become necessary, driving them out of there could be achieved with less expense than His Majesty now spends on them every single year, particularly since the forts and the people there are not enough to prevent them from settling on that coast and land, and not even in the very settlements where they are now, should they come determined to do that.

Item, the French would easily be able to settle in many harbors and areas of this island of Cuba and that of Santo Domingo, and on the mainland and Honduras and New Spain and other places, being large and unpopulated areas, and they do not do this because they see that once they had settled they could easily be driven out of there from the nearest land: and so no expenses are incurred in order to stop them settling in all these areas, because they would be money lost, and they could not be enough: so also there is no need to spend money in order to stop them settling in these two forts or settlements which are of less use: and thus it seems that His Majesty could well save himself the expense which is incurred with them.

The mainland area of Florida can be settled without expense.

Should His Majesty desire Florida to be settled for the purposes and reasons mentioned above and others, it would have to be the mainland of Florida, where there is land to cultivate and produce fruits and those who lived there could support themselves, and not these forts, which are not Florida; settling the mainland, the purpose and intent of His Majesty would be achieved, and settlements would be established, and many rewards, and the Royal Dominions would increase, and our Holy Faith would spread among the Indians, and they would be taught its doctrine, and be subdued peacefully; and the settled community would have large lands, for they say there are such, and herds, and large estates, and would defend them themselves, both from Indians and from pirates, without His Majesty having to bear the cost of soldiers, but instead benefit from the settlements; and thus it would be possible to order the Adelantado Pedro Menéndez to fulfil the agreement and arrangement that was made with him, in Florida mainland, a wide land, as he is obliged to do, and as was the intention of His Majesty and the said agreement and arrangement.

The settlement of the mainland will be done better by His Majesty than by agreement with anyone else.

This settlement of the mainland of Florida, even if an agreement is made with the Adelantado Pedro Menéndez de Avilés, would certainly be settled better if His Majesty ordered a Governor to settle it at his expense, and if another Governor went every four years, rather than by an agreement which is never fulfilled: and it will cost less than the sum total His Majesty gave to the said Adelantado to help settle it, because all those who make these agreements are looking to their own advantage and interest, nothing else, and it is undeniable that they look for and accept them in order to squeeze money out of the settlers, not to pay towards the settlement out of their own pockets, particularly since they are all poor and do not have the money to do it, and have to take from the settlers rather than give to them.

And making the settlement at the expense of the Royal Exchequer, so that the settlement could be very sure and firm and lasting and ever increasing, His Majesty could give or lend to each of 300 farmers for 6 years two slaves, or one, with which to settle the land and break it and cultivate it, and if these had an estate each they would live cheerfully there and not wish to leave, rather they would attract others: and it would not cost much to bring the slaves from Guinea or Santo Tomé, and this, and the slaves, and the whole settlement will not cost as much as His Majesty spends in one year on these forts: and out of this His Majesty would come to have income from the settlements: and it is certainly very advisable that the Governor should go every four years, and not that one should hold it for ever and own it all and the settlers' community, as owner of all the settlement and the settlers: and with this the royal income would grow and the expenses which are now incurred every day would end, along with the suffering of the unfortunate and unhappy men in these forts.

What would best be provided for the forts as they are now.

It seems that it would be a good idea to have an account and stocktaking of what has been spent on these forts of Santa Elena and San Agustín, and of what has been sent to them from Spain since they began, for they have passed through many hands, and of people who are not so well off that money could be got out of them for any deficits there may be: and to take an account of what has been spent from the first day and of the benefit that it has had, and with this the provisions that should best be made from now on could be seen.

Item, that whoever goes there should find out about all this and be given a special memorandum about it: and he should have authority to pass judgements and repair grievances and provide whatever should be needed, having the matter in front of him.

Item, that the Governor of this island of Cuba, because it is nearby, or another suitable person, should take an account and conduct an inquiry every two years, at least, of the Governors named by the Adelantado Pedro Menéndez, who change every day, because it is clear that having as governor people named by him rather than provided by His Majesty causes countless problems in every matter; and to want to say that in order to support those forts, it is as well that he should govern this island and that area together, is a great fraud—indeed, it has been harmful to all concerned, because what can be taken there from this island of Cuba is salted meat, cassava and livestock, and the community here want nothing other than to give and sell it to them, because it is their farm produce, and that is all they live on: and whoever were Governor in this island of Cuba will then provide for it and make them give whatever was needed without trickery.

Item, since the soldiers are not being given their rations, and it is essential that they get them, and not in money. It would be best to send from Spain whatever were necessary for provisions and clothes, and that they should be given it without anyone making a profit on it, as payment on account for their wages or pay.

Item, that since money is brought from New Spain for these forts [the *situado*], that the officers of the Royal Exchequer in Spain should be told to send it in the fleets with either all of it or part of it (depending on the advice they are given) in the form of flour, shoes, coloured cloth of that land, and other things which are cheap in New Spain, and that it should be sent to the officers of this town of La Havana, so that it can be sent on from here, and with this they would be supported without difficulty and would be in better spirits, without being cheated of what His Majesty orders to be given them.

Item, that neither these provisions nor the clothes should come into the hands of the Adelantado, nor any relation nor servant of his, nor any person or officer appointed by him, nor any captain, but that it should come into the hands of someone appointed by His Majesty, and that he should share it out fairly in front of a notary, and give faithful witness of it.

Item, that when it should be necessary to go and pay them, which is always eighteen months and more behind, that this should not be done by the Adelantado Pedro Menéndez, nor an officer or person appointed by him, nor a relation of his, but that there should go with the pay some person or official of this town of La Havana, and that *he* should give the pay to the soldiers, and in addition whoever it was could share out the supplies, and even conduct an enquiry if he went at the right time and was a suitable person.

Item, that the officers of this town of La Havana should send three times a year to the said

forts a boat with salted meat, and cassava, and salt, and other small things, for the soldiers and settlers, and that they should share it out on account for their rations, for this can be done so easily, and they would do this whenver they saw that it was needed and that whatever was due to come from Spain or from New Spain had not turned up.

Item, that whoever should go to give out the pay should have orders to pay out first whatever he was given for the food of the soldiers, or to another person or relation so that they could find someone to provide for and help them with their needs.

Item: the soldiers who leave, who the Governors give leave to go, leave powers with the Governor, Captain or his servants, to collect the pay and rations which are still owing to them, giving them these powers so that they should let them go and grant them leave: thus the order should be given that pay should not be given under such powers to anyone at all, except to the settlers who may have given food or clothing to such soldiers as these; that these should be paid under these powers, but nobody else.

Item: a great deal of profiteering is made in sending to New Spain or the mainland for the allotted money, and they give each other excessive pay and expenses, and those who go to collect it benefit greatly from it, since they take it in kind and despite their money they pay the soldiers in clothing: thus it should be arranged that it is not sent for, and that the officers of the mainland, or New Spain, should send it in the fleets specifically addressed to the officers of His Majesty in this town of La Havana, and that it should be delivered to a presiding magistrate or judge who should have an inventory made of it, and have it sent in the Fleets so that there should be no shortage or carelessness; and from this town could go the Governor, or an officer, or someone else to give out the pay and share out whatever came in clothes, as said above.

Item, that the order should be given that any settler or soldier who wanted to take from the island of Cuba meat, cassava, corn, salt, or anything else, or goods for his house, or to sell, that they should take it in the ships that were going there, and not be prevented, and that the Governor of this island should be entrusted with the task of compelling the masters of the ships of any kind to take it: and that the Governors of the said forts should not put any fixed price or levy on them, and let them be sold freely, because otherwise they are going to put a fixed low price on them so that none of them should want to take it there again and they alone would sell what they bring in at the price they liked; that is what they do now, and it has been seen to be done in this island of Cuba.

Item, that if a settler should want to go to the island of Cuba to buy provisions and other things, that between 4 or 5 of them they could give one person enough to spend or buy provisions, then they should not prevent his going, leaving his wife, house and children as security that he will return with his farm produce and provisions, for this will be some kind of relief for their needs, and they will provide themselves with little things they need.

351. 1572. Pedro Menéndez de Avilés recommends the killing and removal of certain Florida Indian tribes.

In his report on the deaths caused by the Indians of Cabeza de los Martíres, those on the southwest coast of the peninsula and also those along the Bahama Channel (Florida Strait), Menéndez showed that he had become convinced of the hopelessness of controlling the Indians of the southern part of Florida, and considered they should be largely killed off and the remainder taken as slaves to the larger Caribbean islands.
A.G.I., Seville, 2/5/4 (3.20,1), printed in J. T. Connor, ed., Colonial Records of Spanish Florida, 1570–1580, *2 vols. (Deland, Fla., 1925–1930) I, 30–35, where it is translated.*

Royal Caesarian Majesty

The Adelantado, Pedro Menéndez, says that it is seven years since he went upon the conquest and settlement of Florida from these parts, and he has tried and is trying his utmost that the Indians may be taught and very well treated, and no trouble or vexations be caused them, in order that they may listen to the religious, and render obedience to your Majesty, with the more love and willingness; but all the Indians, from the river of Mosquitos, at the beginning of the Bahama Channel, as far as Los Mártires, and returning up to the bay of Tocobaga (although great gifts and demonstrations of friendship have been made them, and many were brought to Havana and taken back to their lands, and gave allegiance to your Majesty)—have broken the peace many times, slaying many Christians, and they have been forgiven. And yet withal this is of no use, nor has it been, for they have been accustomed since the Indies have been discovered to kill all the people from the ships which are, the most of them, lost in this district; and although concerning this I have told the caciques of that land they should not do it, and that if they slew them I would make war upon them, killing them and making slaves of those I captured alive—and they promised me not to do it—they do not keep their word, nor have they wished to comply. I have made peace with them three times, and three times they have broken it, and when they saw they could kill Christians safely, they did it, as it happened after this in Tocobaga, when they treacherously slew twenty soldiers. At Los Mártires, about twenty months ago, they killed eight Spaniards from a boat which was going from Florida to Havana; and in Giga, which is in that same Bahama Channel, when an English corsair had seized a vessel wherein came thirty persons, and they, under a deceptive peace [between English and Indians], were preparing the boat so that it would have more available space, that they might go therein to Havana, the Indians killed them all, except one woman with two little girls, and one little boy, and one man whom they left for dead, and he lived, for afterward I had him removed and taken to Havana. Two other ships, which were going from New Spain to Santo Domingo to take on sugar and hides, were lost by reason of a storm off Cape Cañaveral, at the end of the Bahama Channel; and as the crews were journeying to the fort of San Agustín, thirty leagues thence, the Indians slew most of them, when they had gone half the distance, and they kept others alive to use as slaves, whom I afterward ransomed; others took refuge at the fort of San Agustín. About thirteen months ago, when I sailed from Florida with two frigates to go to Havana, and thence in search of corsairs, I was wrecked at Cape Canaveral because of a storm which came upon me, and the other boat was lost fifteen leagues farther on in the Bahama Channel, in a river they call Ays, because the cacique is so called. Seeing the opportunity, he killed nineteen persons who were on board the frigate, without leaving one, and I, by miracle, reached the fort of San Agustín with seventeen persons I was taking [with me]. Three times the Indians gave the order to attack me, and the way I escaped from them was by ingenuity and arousing fear in them, telling them that behind me many Spaniards were coming who would slay them if they found them; that they should seek safety in the forest. The first year I set out on the conquest, I ransomed from among the Indians thirty-two persons, men and women, who had been slaves of the caciques and Indians for fifteen, eighteen and twenty years. There were some who had been numbered among two hundred and thirty Spaniards, men and women together, from wrecked ships, and each year [the Indians] sacrificed seventeen or eighteen in the feasts they hold, and they used the heads in their balls and ceremonies. They are so bloodthirsty in this because they consider it a great glory and victory for them and that the other caciques of the interior may hold a high opinion of them and they may triumph, saying that they live on the seashore and are the masters of the Christians and hold them as slaves. They follow this custom because they consider it the pious and natural order of things, without observing amity [with us], nor [is there] hope that later on they may observe it in the service of God Our Lord and of your Majesty. It is needful that this should be remedied by permitting that war be made upon them with all rigor, a war of fire and blood, and that those taken alive shall be sold as slaves, removing them from the country and taking them to the neighboring islands, Cuba, Santo Domingo, Puerto Rico. So that in this manner, besides the service rendered to God Our Lord and to your Majesty, this district where war must be made on such people, because it is the most full of danger and where many ships are lost coming from the Indies to these kingdoms, will remain clear and unobstructed. It is very poor land, subject to inundation, and the Indians cannot sustain themselves except on roots and shellfish. And if this be done, no Indian will be living therein, and if any vessel shall be wrecked, the people can easily go in safety to the fort of San Agustín and take refuge there; and this will arouse fear, and be a great example among the friendly Indians, so that they may observe and fulfil the amity they establish; wherefore, etc.

[signed:] Pedro Menéndez.

352. [1573]. Pedro Menéndez de Avilés provides detailed plans for the disposal of the enslaved Florida Indians.

A.G.I., Seville, 2/5/4 (3.20,2), printed in J. T. Connor, ed. Colonial Records of Spanish Florida, *I (125), 78–81, translated there.*

Royal Caesarian Majesty

The Adelantado, Pero Menéndez, says that through the reports he has presented, it will be found that God Our Lord and your Majesty will be well served in giving up as slaves the Indians of the Cabeça de los Mártires and the Bahama Channel, from Ays to Tocobaga, which is in the provinces of Florida; for all of them, since the Indies were discovered, have killed many Christians, under the pledge of peace and friendship they made to the captains-general who have gone there by order of your Majesty. And although, since he has gone about pacifying them, he has exerted his utmost ability with them, fearing God and your Majesty, trying to do all the good he could among them to preserve the friendship they established with him after having rendered obedience to your Majesty, and to pass over without coming to an open breach, many cases of Christians slain by them; and giving them to understand that he did this because he loved them and that if he wished to harm them he could safely do so, whereby they might be killed and made captive; and they knew this to be the truth, without their being able to help it—it was not enough. On the contrary, they have continued in their evil ways, killing Christians under the peace pledge, exulting in victory over the inland caciques, their enemies; telling them that the Spaniards are their slaves, and that for this reason the inland caciques must obey them; these caciques of the coast being infamous people, Sodomites, sacrificers to the devil of many souls, in their ancient ceremonies; wherefore it would greatly serve God Our Lord and your Majesty if these same were dead, or given as slaves. Being informed of all this by the aforesaid reports, your Majesty replies to the last petition presented concerning this matter, on the seventeenth of this [month], that at present there is no occasion for giving up the Indians as slaves; and because the injury from delay may be irreparable, and Our Lord and your Majesty may be very ill-served thereby:

He beseeches your Majesty to be pleased to command that all the reports which he has given on this be examined, and that if expedient, what he has petitioned be decreed; for he knows that Our Lord will be well served thereby. It may appear that he will be better served if such Indians of that said district are not allowed to be sold or given as slaves, except in the islands of Hispaniola, San Juan and Cuba for a period of twelve years, the buyers of them obligating themselves to teach them, and endeavor that they become Christians and be saved; and that before they land they shall be declared before the royal officials of your Majesty's Exchequer, in order that there may be no trickery so that, instead of the Indians of Florida, they might want to make slaves of others who are not from there; and if your Majesty should decree neither the one nor the other, he fears that the Indies of Florida will be depopulated of the Spaniards who are settled there. Because they are the key to all the Indies, as the treasure that comes therefrom must pass through that Bahama Channel; and because even though your Majesty may spend much from your Royal Exchequer, you will not be able to bring them to the point where they now are; besides the risk there is of Lutherans settling there, on account of the many Indian friends they have in those provinces—he entreats your Majesty to order that it all be examined, and, if there be reason, that what he has begged for be decreed; and if not, this is the last he asks, since thereby God Our Lord and your Majesty and the profit of your Royal Exchequer will be so greatly served; and it is for the general good of all the Indies and those who navigate therein. And since he is occupied in your Majesty's service in these parts and the states of Flanders, let it not at any time be held to be his fault and charge if the settlers should depart from that land, because of the notable injuries they receive from the said Indians.

Let all the reports be brought.

[signed:] Secretary Ledesma.

353. February 4, 1573. Martín Diez questioned about his life as a settler in Santa Elena.

A.G.I., Seville, 2/1/1,27, ramo 5, printed in J. T. Connor, ed., Colonial Records of Spanish Florida, I (1925), 82–87, translated there.

In Madrid, on the fourth day of the month of February, in the year one thousand five hundred and seventy-three, the Illustrious Señor Licentiate Gamboa, of the Council of the Indies, caused to appear before him, by order of the Señores of the said Council, a man who calls himself Martin Diez: and before me, Francisco de Valmaseda, notary of the said Council, he took and received from him an oath in due form of law concerning the condition wherein are the affairs of Florida, and the people, arms and munitions thereof: and having been sworn, and being questioned, he declared the following.

On being asked what governors there have been in Florida and the forts thereof, he said that he knew Captain Juan Pardo, Doctor Juan Martinez, Pedro Menéndez the Younger [and] Juan de Junco, and he does not remember any others.

Being asked his name, he said Martin Diez, a farmer, a resident at Fort San Mateo, in the province of Florida, and a native of the town of Meneses.

On being asked how long it is since he went over to Florida, and in whose company, he said that it is about four years since he went to that country as a farmer from Cadiz, whence he went to the Canary Islands, and from there to Florida, with his wife and children; and that he settled at the fort of Santa Elena, where he has lived three years, more or less, occupied in his work as a farmer.

Being asked how many farmers there are, he said that at the said fort of Santa Elena there may be forty-five farmers, more or less, who busy themselves with sowing and cultivating the soil in maize, garden stuff and vegetables; and that at the fort of San Agustín there are six married farmers occupied in the aforesaid; that there are no farmers or soldiers at the fort of San Mateo because it is destroyed and abandoned; that at the fort of Santa Elena there may be twenty-five soldiers, and in San Agustín about as many more; that the soldiers and farmers are for the account of Pedro Menéndez, not his Majesty; that the first year the farmers were given as much as there was in rations, and since then nothing has ever been given them, nor anything of what was promised them, which was all kinds of cattle, twelve females and one male: of that nothing has been given them; and that having promised to settle them in a very good region, as fertile as the plain of Carmona, he [Pedro Menéndez] has kept and is keeping them on the seacoast, which is all sand, and not fruitful: wherefore they have suffered and are suffering extreme hunger and need, and the wife of this deponent died of hunger. Being asked what cattle the said Adelantado had brought into the land, and how he apportioned it, and who wanted it, and under what conditions: he said that he had brought as many as two hundred hogs into Santa Elena, and wished to divide them up among the farmers, on condition that no one, within ten years, was to venture to kill any of the increase of the head of cattle; and that the time having elapsed, the increase the ten years following was to be divided in half between the citizens and the said Adelantado, without the said Adelantado putting in any expense: for which reason neither this witness nor the said farmers were willing to receive anything thereof, because the said division did not suit them, nor was the land adapted for cattle raising. And the said farmers begged the said Adelantado to take the said cattle away from there, because they ate the maize in their maize fields; and in that state did this witness leave the land, and he asked permission of the said Adelantado to return in the galleons, on the pretext that this witness was going to his wife's country in order to take more farmers to Florida. With that excuse he let him come, for in any other way he would not have allowed him to do so.

On being asked how many arms and how much artillery and munitions there are in the said two forts of Santa Elena and San Agustín, he said that in the fort of St. Augustine there were six pieces of bronze artillery, large and small: two of them were mounted on a *caballero*, and the others were on the ground; that there are munitions, the amount of which this witness does not know; that what there is in the fort of Santa Elena this witness knows not, and that there are likewise some arquebuses, but he does not know how many; and that this witness knows that the pay, which is thirty reals each month, was given them lately when the said Adelantado went there, wherewith the said soldiers remained satisfied; but that the said soldiers are very badly treated because of hunger and [lack of] clothes, and that in those forts there was for about two years, as governor and lieutenant of Pedro Menéndez, one Juan de la Vandera. In that time he did the settlers many wrongs, especially in consuming his Majesty's food and supplies, and selling the food in places which he had fixed upon therefor; and for this reason the said settlers endured much hardship and want, and were not given rations or anything to eat; and so great was the barrenness [of the land] that they were driven by hunger to the coast with their wives and children, to eat shellfish and oysters, for it they had not done so, they would have perished from hunger. And every time that the said Juan de la Vandera wanted something for his benefit from the houses of the said settlers, and they did not give it to him, he treated them very badly by word and by deed, and he beat them, and took it from them against their will. And in addition to that, this witness saw that the said Juan de la Vandera, in order to appropriate a married woman, sent her husband to Spain; and without orders from his general he left the fort and built a blockhouse near the houses of the settlement, and took the said woman to the said house. And her husband was in Spain; and after he had kept her a certain time, he cast her out of his house before the husband returned, and went off with a woman neighbor of his; and after the said husband came back, and knew of the case, he led her a very hard life. For these things, and others he does not remember, the said settlers were determined to ask the said Vandera to let them go to Havana: and on being advised thereof, he embarked in a canoe, and went to the fort of Santa Elena, where he made the said settlers prisoners one by one, and two by two, and imprisoned them very wrongfully, trying to sentence them there to take from them what they had in property. This witness knows and saw that the notary, who was called Juan Perez, did not write what the witness said, but what the said Juan de la Vandera ordered him; and so he condemned them in large sums of maravedis which remained in the possession of the said notary and Juan de la Vandera, whereof the said Adelantado likewise will give an account. And that he does not know that the other governors have done any wrong, and that the soldiers from Florida that are here know the aforesaid. And he knows nothing else, according to the oath he took; and because he knows not how to sign, he asked me, the said Valmaseda, to sign for him.

Executed before me,

[signed:] Valmaseda.

354. June 1, 1574. Philip II restricts the grant recently made to Pedro Menéndez de Avilés of land between the Río Pánuco and the Río de las Palmas.

The adelantado's ambitions for his Florida dominion lasted almost to his death. In February, 1573 his rights had, after long argument, been extended to the Río Pánuco. Now, in 1574, the king had second thoughts. The line was retracted to the Río de Palmas, only 24 leagues (less than 60 land miles to the east) but sufficient to show that Philip was not satisfied that the new Florida dominion could be extended all the way around the Gulf to link up with Mexico.

John Carter Brown Library, Reales Cédulas, Codex Sp 8, fols. 141 v.–142 (second foliation), translated.

So that the bounds of the governorship of Florida do not extend further in the direction of New Spain and New Galicia than up to the Río de las Palmas, despite the agreement with the Adelantado Pedro Menéndez that they extend as far as the river of Pánuco.
By the King

Wherefore, by a certain contract and capitulation which on 23 February in the past year of 1573 we ordered to be made with the Adelantado Pedro Menéndez de Avilés for the exploration and settlement of certain lands within boundaries to which we consented to extend the governorship, and the [right to] discover and to settle the provinces of Florida which we have entrusted to him, we enlarged the said limits in the direction of New Spain and New Galicia up to the river of Pánuco, and [wherefore] we are now informed that several disadvantages, doing us ill service, arise from the said governorship of Florida reaching as far as the said River, besides which it has been the understanding that the governorship of New Spain and New Galicia reaches as far as the Río de Palmas which is twenty-four leagues closer to the said provinces of Florida, so that the extent of the said bounds in that direction would fittingly reach only so far as the Río de Palmas, we, having inquired into this and having had it discussed by those of our Council of the Indies, have consented to it, notwithstanding what the said capitulation says, and we require, and it is our will, that the bounds of the governorship and of [the rights to] explore and settle the said provinces of Florida shall not reach in the direction of the said New Spain and New Galicia farther than the said Río de Palmas [modern Setola marina?], and we command the said Adelantado Pedro Menéndez and his lieutenant as governor of the said provinces of Florida not to enter upon, nor to engage themselves to enter upon any settlement or government in the borderland that lies from the said Río de Palmas towards the said New Spain and New Galicia, [and we command, further] that the area shall remain included in the governorship of the said New Spain and that it may be governed, explored and settled by the person who shall hold from us the governorship of the latter and by his representative, since this is what is of service to us; and insofar as this may make [it] necessary, we re- ˙oke and declare null the said capitulation and the other decrees we have given on the above subject, though for the rest they remain in full force and application.

Signed in San Lorenzo el Real [the Escorial] on the first of June in the year one thousand five hundred and seventy-four
[signed:] I the King

By command of His Majesty, Antonio de Erasso.

NOTES ON THE MAPS

69. 1528. World Map in *Libro di Benedetto Bordone* (Venice, 1528).

This is a frivolous map so far as the New World is concerned. Most of North America becomes "terra del laboratore."

70. 1540. Map of the Americas as "The new island," Published at Basel in 1540.

71. *Circa* 1544. Map Showing the Discoveries of Hernando de Soto and Moscoso.

Seville, Archivo General de Indias, Mapas y Planos, Mexico 1.

This map was a valuable record of the discovery of the whole southern part of North America, including the Mississippi, but it proved confusing to later explorers.

72. *Circa* 1575. Manuscript Map of the Caribbean and Florida by Juan López de Velasco.

Providence, R.I., Brown University, John Carter Brown Library.

This is a useful general representation of Florida and is closely associated with the completion of López de Velasco's, *Geografía universal de las Indias (1571–1574)* (Madrid, 1894). The map is damaged and the show through reads "Descripcion de la Audiencia de Espanola."

73. *Circa* 1575. Manuscript Map of the Caribbean and Much of North America by Juan López de Velasco.

Providence, R.I., Brown University, John Carter Brown Library.

The map covers a wider range than the previous plate, showing both the east and west coasts (the latter with the name "California"), and giving a northern boundary for the Audiencia of Mexico. The show through reads "Descripcion de las Indias del Norte."

74. 1554. Jean Bellere's Map of the Americas.

Jean Bellere added this map to Francisco López de Gomara, *Mexico* (Antwerp, 1554), a version of his *Historia de las Indias y conquista de Mexico* (Saragossa, 1552). It represented views (mainly derived from Spanish sources) of the outlines of the American continent current in North Europe at the time.

75. 1555. An Exotic View of North America by Guillaume Le Testu.

Paris, Ministère des Armées, Guillaume Le Testu, "Cosmographie universelle," manuscript atlas, D.I.Z. 14, fol. 53*v*.

This highly stylized representation of the coast from Florida to Labrador contains many exotic scenes of the supposed occupants, human and animal, of North America.

76. 1562. Diego Gutierrez's Printed Map of the Americas, the Northern Section.

London, British Library, Map Library.

This gives much detail and illustrates very well the standard Spanish profile of eastern North America. Apart from an indication of the Gulf of California, it evades a definition of the west coast.

77. 1563. Map from Lázaro Luís Atlas, Showing the Caribbean and Eastern North America, Oriented to the West.

Lisbon, Academia das Cienzias, fol. 7*v*. See Cumming, Skelton and Quinn, *Discovery of North America* (1971), p. 63.

With West at the top; the Indians of Mexico and North America are given elaborate houses, some of the latter however, suggesting the Indian long house.

78. 1561. Outline Chart of the North Atlantic by Richard Eden.

The chart from Richard Eden, *Art of navigation* (London, 1561), translated from Martin Cortes, *Breve compendio de la spera y de la arte de navegar* (Seville, 1551).

It illustrates the nature of English knowledge of the North American coastline at this period.

79. 1562. Nicolas Barré's map of the French Florida Expedition of 1562. Oriented to the West.

Madrid, Museo Naval, Colección Navarrete, XIV, fol. 459.

This is an almost contemporary Spanish copy of a French map. It was first identified by W. P. Cumming, "The Parreus map (1562) of French Florida," *Imago Mundi*, XVII (1963), 27–40, and throws valuable light on the voyages of Jean Ribault in that year.

80. 1562. Engraving, after Jacques Le Moyne de Morgues, of the First French Reconnaissance of the St. Johns River.

Theodor de Bry, *America*, part ii (Frankfurt-am-Main, 1591), plate 2; see the reproduction with notes in Paul Hulton, *The Work of Jacques Le Moyne de Morgues* (London, 1977).

Before his death in 1588, Jacques Le Moyne de Morgues provided Theodor de Bry with many drawings of French activity in Florida between 1562 and 1565. He clearly had some maps and sketches at his disposal, but how far particular drawings, especially after embellishment by the engraver, are from the original scene is a matter for speculation. This river was to be the site of the French fort, La Caroline, occupied from 1564 to 1565, and taken by the Spanish in 1565.

81. 1562. Engraving, after Jacques Le Moyne de Morgues, of the First French Reconnaissance of the Satilla River.

Theodor de Bry, *America*, part ii (Frankfurt-am-Main, 1591), plate 3; see the reproduction with notes in Paul Hulton, *The Work of Jacques Le Moyne de Morgues* (London, 1977).

82. 1565. Map of French Florida, 1562–1565, by Jacques Le Moyne de Morgues.

This was compiled between his return from Florida in 1565 and his death in London in 1588. It was engraved for Theodor de Bry, *America*, part ii (Frankfurt-am-Main, 1591).

83. 1612. Marc Lescarbot's Map of French Florida, 1562–1565.

Marc Lescarbot, *Histoire de la Nouvelle France*, 2nd edition, Paris, 1612.

This gives an amusing, if inaccurate, picture of the French presence in Florida, 1562–1565. It presents an extraordinary picture of the St. Johns River, developed from mistakes in the Le Moyne map published in 1591, but possibly relying also on independent contemporary sources.

84. 1567. Map of Eastern North America by Alonso de Santa Cruz.

Madrid, Archivo Histórico Nacional.

The result of a lifetime of experience in the cartography of North America, the map shows how Santa Cruz, some twenty years after his "Islario," accepted the pulling southward of Gomes's discoveries which would now appear to begin at 38° North and so assimilate with what is named by other cartographers (not by him) as Punta de Arenas (which began as Gomes's name for Monomoy Point and gradually moved south to occupy the place of Cape Henry). See Cumming, Skelton and Quinn, *Discovery of North America* (1971), p. 173.

85. 1570. World Map by Jehan Cossin, Suggesting Exploration in the Hudson River-Long Island Region before 1570.

World Map by Jehan Cossin, 1570. Paris, Bibliothèque Nationale, Cartes no. 17784.

The not otherwise remarkable outline of eastern North America appears to record some exploration which revealed the mouth of the Hudson River and possibly Long Island. If this is not a quirk of the cartographer, we may assume that some French privateer, homebound from the Caribbean, put in there to trade with the Indians, get wood and water, and that he recorded it on paper. Nothing has so far been found to confirm this presumed discovery. See Cumming, Skelton and Quinn, *Discovery of North America* (1971), p. 274.

86. 1570. Map of the Americas by Abraham Ortelius.

The famous atlas by Abraham Ortelius, *Theatrum orbis terrarum* (Antwerp, 1570) contained this well-known map of the Americas. For eastern North America, its information is very similar to that on the 1569 Mercator World Map, though it does not feature mountains in the interior. The map does not indicate whether or not a Northwest Passage was thought to exist. There is some further extension of North America to the west than in earlier maps and also considerable distortion of South America. In later years it was to be revised in various respects in successive "Additamenta" to the atlas.

87. The American Portion of the World Map in Ortelius, *Theatrum Orbis Terrarum*.

This varies in detail from the map in the previous plate.

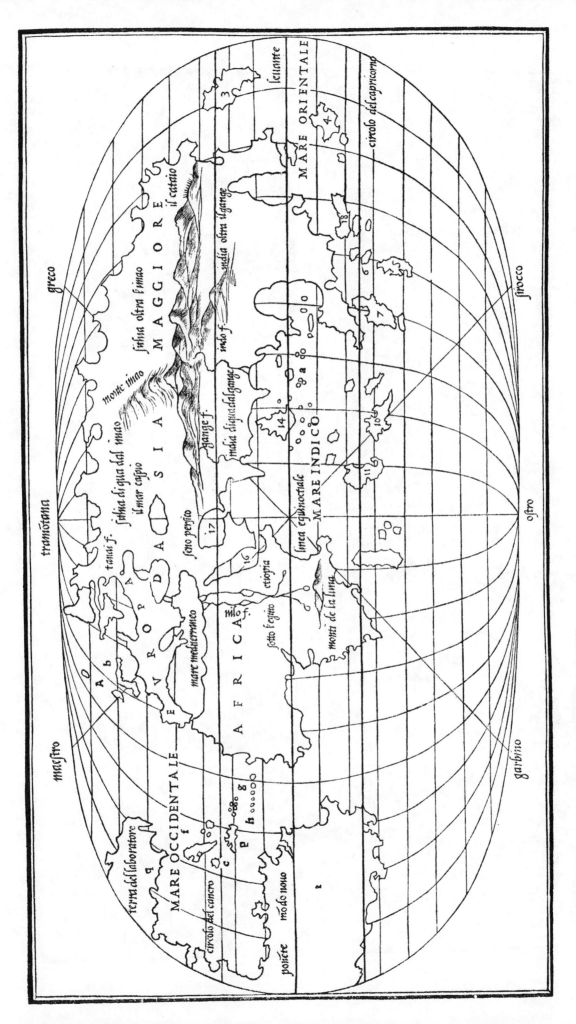

69. 1528. World Map in *Libro di Benedetto Bordone* (Venice, 1528).

Tauola dell' isole nuoue, le quali son nominate occidentali, & indiane per diuersi rispetti.

Cathay
Quinsay
INDIA superior

Hibernia
Hispania
AFRICAN pars

Sinus Atlanticus

Exteriores
Medera
Fortunatæ inf.
Inf. Hesperidum
S. Iacobi

Cortise
Oceanus occidentalis
FRANCISCA
C. Britonum

Terra florida
Panuco Inf. Torcuari
Chamaho
Zipangri
Archipelagus 7448 insularũ

CVBA
Iucatanus
S. Paulo
Cozumela
Baragua
Iamica
Artilla
Dominica

PARIA sabundat auro & margaritas

Caribali

7. insulæ Mar. guerrari

Nouus orbis
Insula Atlantica quam uo/ cant Brasilŭ & Americam.

Cadgan

Die Nüw Welt

Regio Gigantum

Fretum Magaliani

Mare pacificum

Inf. infortu natæ

Inf. p. domum

Calenfuan

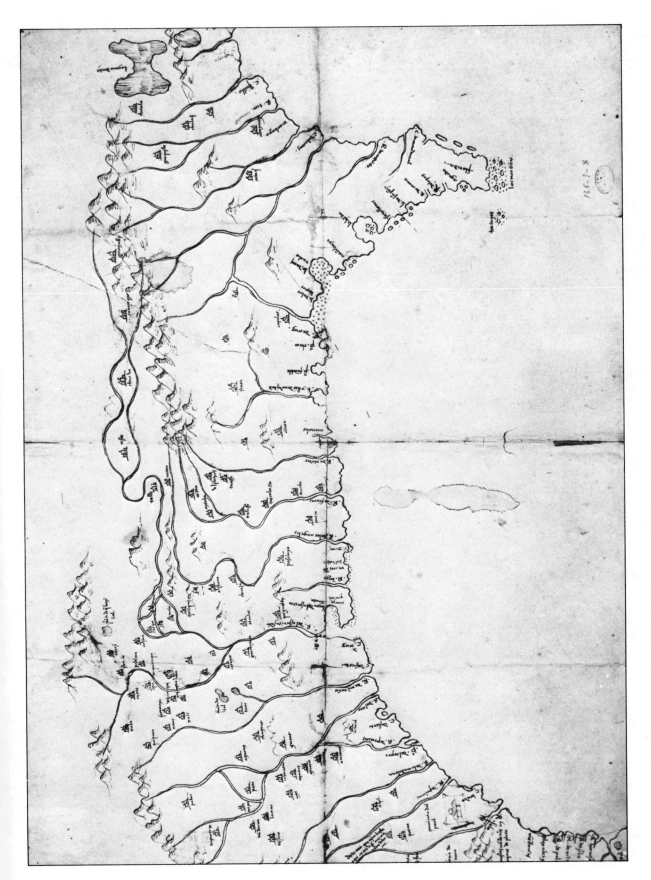

71. *Circa* 1544. Map Showing the Discoveries of Hernando de Soto and Moscoso.

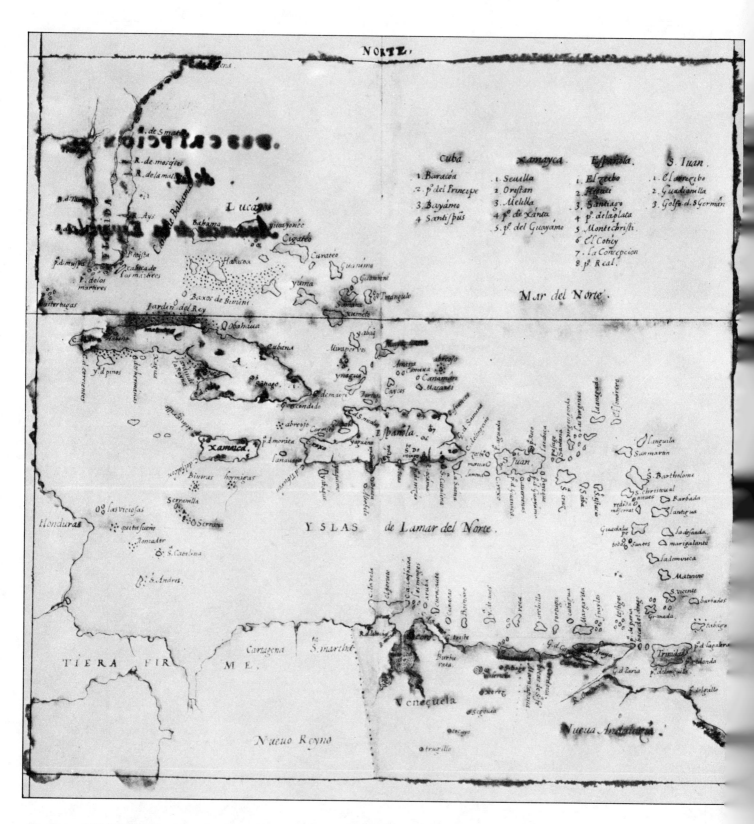

72. *Circa* 1550. Manuscript Map of the Caribbean and Florida by Juan López de Velasco.

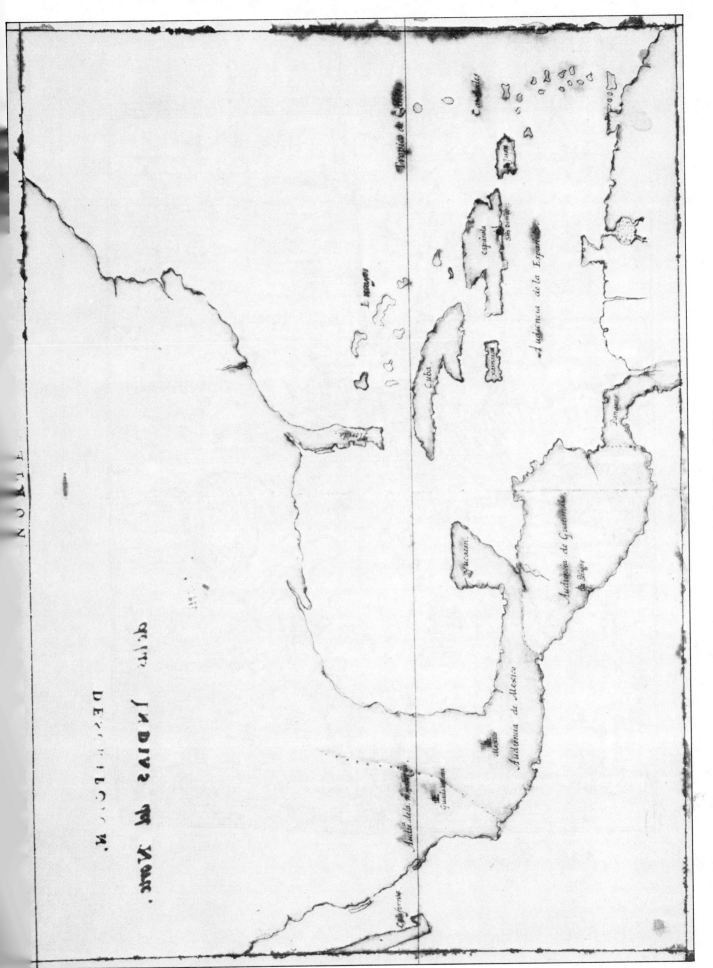

73. *Circa* 1550. Manuscript Map of the Caribbean and Much of North America by Juan López de Velasco.

74. 1554. Jean Bellere's Map of the Americas.

75. 1555. An Exotic View of North America by Guillaume Le Testu.

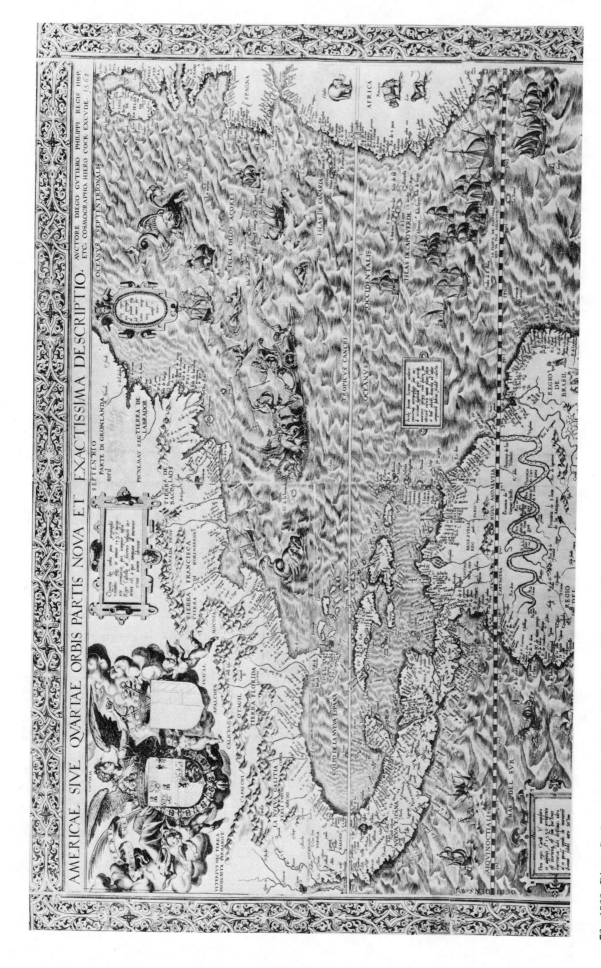

76. 1562. Diego Gutierrez's Printed Map of the Americas, the Northern Section.

77. 1563. Map from Lázaro Luís Atlas, Showing the Caribbean and Eastern North America, Oriented to the West.

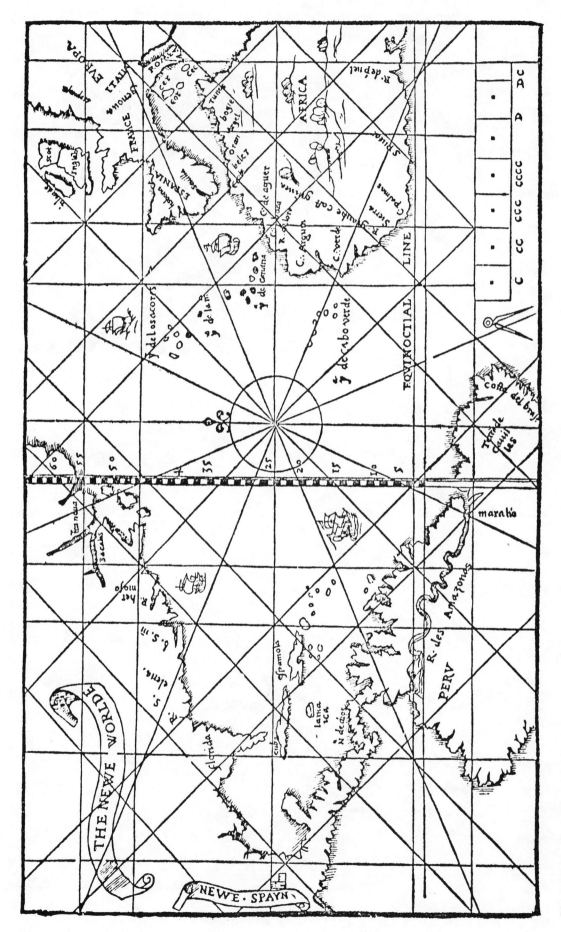

78. 1561. Outline Chart of the North Atlantic by Richard Eden.

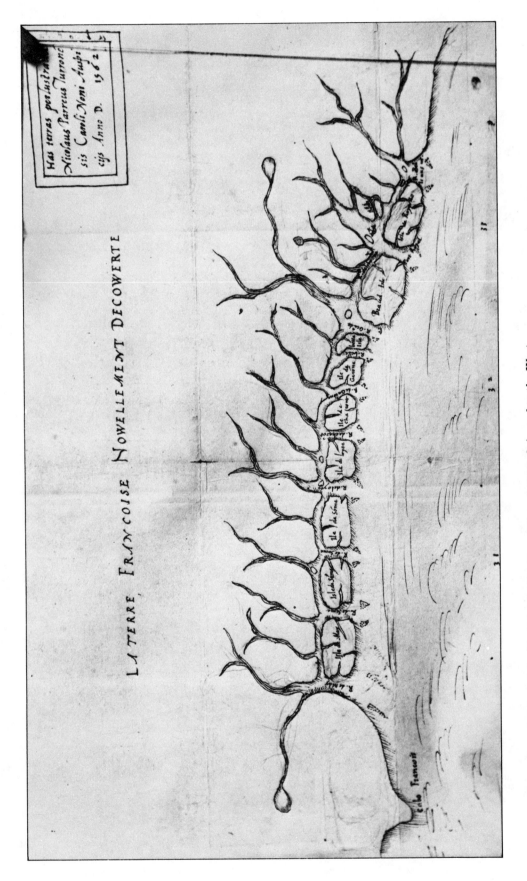

79. 1562. Nicolas Barré's Map of the French Florida Expedition of 1562. Oriented to the West.

F. Mai[

80. 1562. Engraving, after Jacques Le Moyne de Morgues, of the First French Reconnaissance of the St. Johns River.

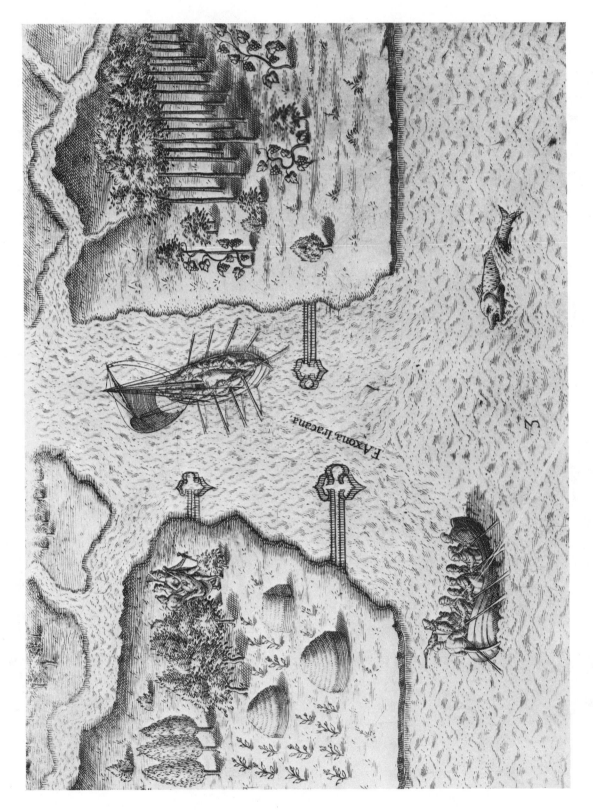

FAXona Iracana.

81. 1562. Engraving, after Jacques Le Moyne de Morgues, of the First French Reconnaissance of the Satilla River.

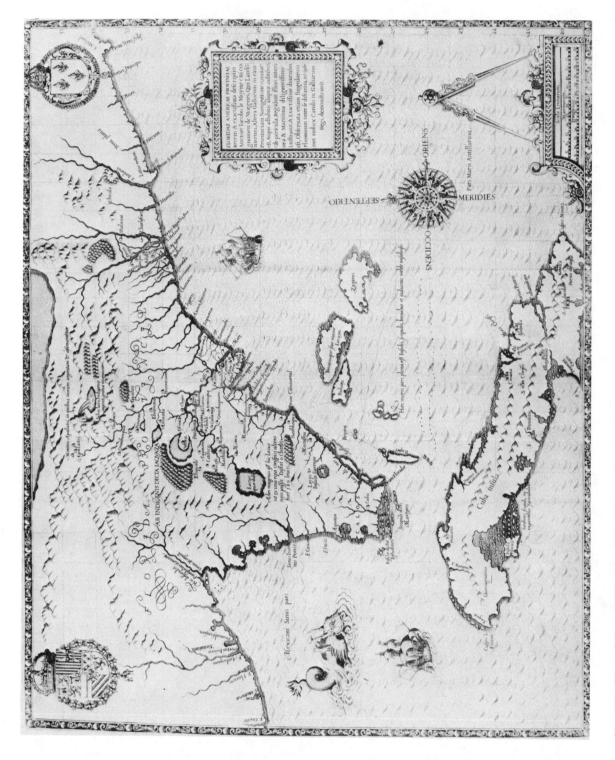

82. 1565. Map of French Florida, 1562–1565, by Jacques Le Moyne de Morgues.

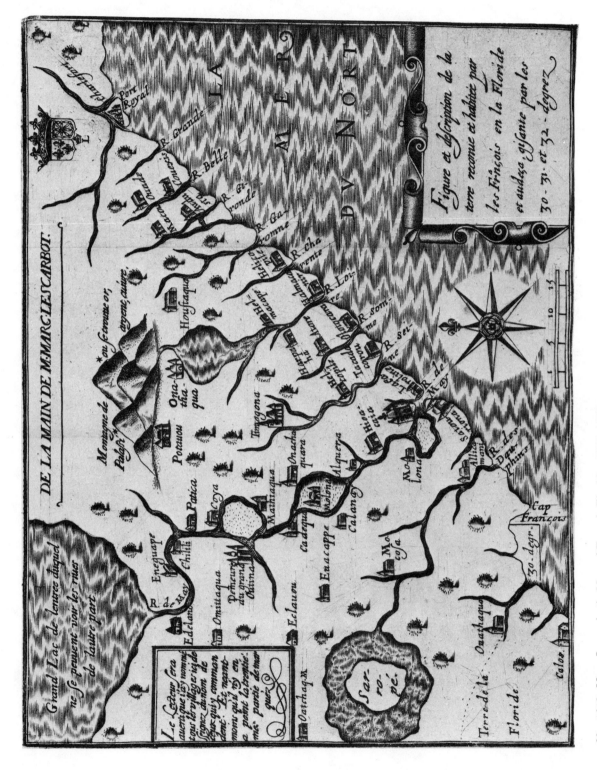

83. 1612. Marc Lescarbot's Map of French Florida, 1562-1565.

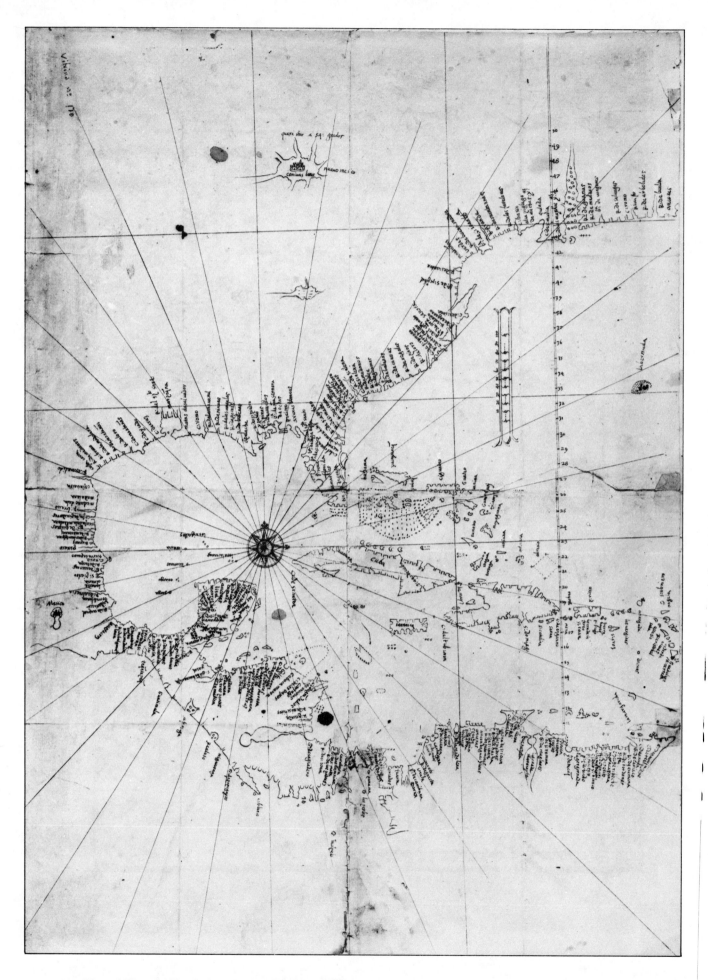

1567. Map of Eastern North America by Alonso de Santa Cruz.

85. 1570. World Map by Jehan Cossin, Suggesting Exploration in the Hudson River Long Island Region before 1570.

86. 1570. Map of the Americas by Abraham Ortelius.

87. The American Portion of the World Map in Ortelius, *Theatrum Orbis Terrarum.*